AF655636

McGraw Hill edge® COURSEWARE

McGraw Hill Edge Courseware is a versatile learning and assessment solution, that uses credible content and innovative pedagogies to make the readers' exam preparation journey holistic and adaptive to changing examination trends. By blending the strengths of authoritative McGraw Hill books with cutting-edge digital resources and latest updates, this Courseware offers a dynamic content solution for exam aspirants. It provides the students a thorough understanding of the subject matter, enhances learning and retention, and shares deep insights about their performance, ultimately boosting their confidence. This Courseware is at the forefront of innovation; revolutionizing learning to guide learners on their path to success!

Unlock Your Potential with McGraw Hill Edge Courseware

Conceptual Videos
To transform abstract ideas into engaging visual storytelling!

Study Aids
To simplify learning with visual summaries, mind maps, flash cards, infographics etc.

Knowledge Enrichment Content
To craft your path to success with exclusive reading materials

Previous Years' Questions
To practise from an extensive collection of PYQs with detailed explanations

Mock Tests
To simulate real exam conditions and boost confidence

Performance Analytics
To optimise exam preparation with data-driven insights

Live Interactive Sessions
To gain valuable insights from the author through interactive sessions

eBook Access
To conveniently access study materials anytime, anywhere

Note: These features are indicative and may vary by product.

What do you get with **Courseware on Indian Economy 2026–2027?**

This Courseware is a ***comprehensive and exam-focused learning resource*** meticulously crafted for UPSC aspirants preparing for ***Prelims, Mains, and the Interview*** stage. Here's what you can expect:

- **Author-Guided Conceptual Clarity:** Gain expert insights through 45+ chapter-wise explanatory videos that highlights the significance of each Chapter and break down complex concepts for quick understanding and long retention.
- **PYQs:** Access ***2011–2025 UPSC questions (Prelims: 1400+ and Mains: 80+)***
- **Practice Questions:** ***Practice 300+ objective sample questions and 150+ Subjective questions*** to enhance your exam readiness.
- **Sample Model Answers:** Each chapter include one sample main model answer to enhance exam readiness and writing skills.
- **In-Depth Coverage:** Detailed insights into economic theories, policies, reforms, and contemporary issues to strengthen your conceptual foundation.
- **Exam Essentials:** Carefully curated key topics that hold ***high relevance for the UPSC exam*** have been strategically highlighted and tagged as ***EXAM ESSENTIALS*** in each chapter ***to help you prioritise critical areas for focused preparation.***
- **Latest Updates & Insights:** Stay ahead with the latest Economic Survey, Union Budget, key government schemes, policy changes, and economic developments.

SCAN NOW

Scan this QR code to know all about this Courseware

APPEAL

COUNTER THE COUNTERFEIT & BUILD A STRONG FOUNDATION FOR SUCCESS

Books are our best friends, is the adage we have grown up with. However, the pirates of piracy are continuously forging 'our best friends'. Our books and their supplementary online resources are copyrighted, and we don't lend any right-to-copy. Piracy is synonymous to stealing books.

Knowledge comes real, let's not encourage its counterfeit. Therefore, we appeal all our readers to discourage pirated books and **choose authentic ones.**

HOW TO IDENTIFY THE PIRATED BOOKS?

1 TRANSPARENCY CODE ON THE BOOK

Scan with the Transparency app XXXXXXXX

Congratulations! The book you have purchased is protected by Transparency. Transparency by Amazon is a unit-level product serialization service that verifies a unit's authenticity and enables you to view rich information about the product you purchased. Please look for the Transparency logo and code on the book back cover (Transparency barcode is a square code that can be found next to the "T" symbol). You can scan the barcode with the Transparency app to verify the book's authenticity. Simply download the Transparency app from the App Store or Google Play. Scan the barcode with the app. The app will display a green checkmark when the book has been verified as authentic.

2 COVER AND SPINE

- Look and feel (new or used book)
- Blurred images on the cover
- Hologram pasted on front
- Defective spine (wrinkles) or air pocket at its bottom
- Unclear ISBN/bar codes
- Missing/non-operational Unique Coupon Code for exclusive access to McGraw Hill Edge

3 TEXT/PRINTING/BINDING

- Uneven inking of pages
- Poor quality or blurred photographs/images/charts
- Substandard paper quality and opacity
- Misaligned pages
- Missing pages
- Inferior binding quality

You can further watch this video on How to identify a pirated book

For more information about identifying piracy, visit https://www.mheducation.co.in/piracy

To report a pirated book, send 'Hi' on WhatsApp code given on the back cover or write to us at support.india@mheducation.com.

Reported pirated books are examined to combat their piracy.

Let's fight the Pirates of Piracy and resolve to go for original!

18e

2026–27

Courseware on

INDIAN ECONOMY

For UPSC and State Civil Services Examinations

Ramesh Singh

Director, *EcoMadeEasy*

New Delhi

McGraw Hill Education (India) Private Limited

Published by McGraw Hill Education (India) Private Limited
Registered Office: Anjana Complex No: 5/90 A, Butt Road, St. Thomas Mount, Chennai – 600016

Courseware on Indian Economy, 18e

Copyright © 2026, by McGraw Hill Education (India) Private Limited. All rights reserved.

First reprint 2026

This book is protected under copyright law. Any unauthorized copying, reproduction, distribution, adaptation, conversion, transmission, storage or use of this publication or any part or extract of it, through any means or any medium, including electronic, mechanical, photocopied, recorded, or otherwise, whether for any direct/indirect commercial gain or not, and without the prior written consent of the publisher, is explicitly prohibited and will result in severe legal consequences. Such restrictions apply to social media channels/groups, YouTube videos, audiobooks, AI applications, and any other means of copying, reproducing, distributing, adapting, converting, transmitting, storing the content of this book, using current or future technologies.

This edition can be exported from India only by the publisher,
McGraw Hill Education (India) Private Limited.

Print Edition:
ISBN-13: 978-93-6444-657-0
ISBN-10: 93-6444-657-7

E-Book Edition:
ISBN-13: 978-93-6444-404-0
ISBN-10: 93-6444-404-3

02 03 04 05 06 MAG 30 29 28 27 26

Information contained in this work has been obtained by McGraw Hill Education, from sources believed to be reliable. However, neither McGraw Hill Education nor its authors guarantee the accuracy or completeness of any information published herein, and neither McGraw Hill Education nor its authors shall be responsible for any errors, omissions, or damages arising out of use of this information. This work is published with the understanding that McGraw Hill Education and its authors are supplying information but are not attempting to render engineering or other professional services. If such services are required, the assistance of an appropriate professional should be sought.

Typeset at DCG Data-Core Systems (India) Pvt. Ltd., DG-4, Sec-2, Kolkata - 700 091 and Printed and bound in India at Magic International Pvt. Ltd., Plot No. 26E, Sector-31 (INDUSTRIAL), Site-IV, Greater Noida - 201306

Cover Design: Yaman

Cover images and media used in this publication are sourced under license from Adobe Stock

Visit us at: www.mheducation.co.in

Write to us at: support.india@mheducation.com

CIN: U80302TN2010PTC111532

Toll Free Number: 1800 103 5875

In the loving memories of my parents

P.N. Singh

&

R.N. Devi Singh

About the Author

Ramesh Singh is an alumnus of *Delhi School of Economics* and an education consultant with three decades of experience in guiding the aspirants of various Civil Services and other competitive exams. He is a prolific writer and has authored several books both in English and Hindi for McGraw Hill, including *Indian Economy* (available in Marathi too), *Bhartiya Arthavyavastha, Contemporary Essays, Objective Indian Economy and Social Development,* and *1000 Plus Questions on General Science.* He is also a popular columnist of the Publication Division journals, the *Yojana* and *Kurukshetra.*

A teacher par excellence, he is endowed with an exceptional quality of simplifying the most difficult concepts of economics in an easy-to-understand style, making economics easy for even those who have no background in it. He is the founding-director of the institution *EcoMadeEasy,* which offers courses in economics for a diverse range of exams. He lives in Delhi and keeps himself busy in diverse academic and social activities.

Preface to the Eighteenth Edition

It feels really good in presenting the ***18th Edition 2026-27*** of the **Indian Economy**. So far the affection shown for the book by readers has been a humbling experience for me, however, with every new edition comes the bigger responsibility of meeting the evolving standards of *Union Public Service Commission* (UPSC) and sustaining the *best-seller* position year after year and these have been very taxing and challenging tasks for me. In this process, I have been trying to beat my own efforts of past.

As per the *Economic Survey 2025-26*, the global economic environment remains uncertain, shaped by geopolitical tensions, trade disruptions, and divergent growth and inflation outcomes across major economies. Against this backdrop, the Indian economy has maintained strong growth momentum in 2025-26 largely driven by domestic demand. The ongoing war between US-Israel and Iran has exacerbated the global energy economy in a very hard way creating inflation risks for India.

The *Union Budget 2026-27* remains hopeful for the year (but cautions about the elevated global uncertainties), supported by macroeconomic stability and ongoing reform efforts, the economy appears well-positioned to sustain growth in the near term alongside evolving external conditions.

The *latest edition* of the book has been designed and restructured to help the civil services aspirants prepare the social and economic development of India in an exam-focused way with following special features:

Special features of the book

- It aims to cover all those concepts and theories which are required to help the reader develop a 'fundamental' and 'application-based' (one of the three reasons due to which the syllabus was changed by the UPSC last time) understanding of economics along with its subtle linkages to real policy issues and the areas of governance, polity, diplomacy, ethics, technology etc. in an *inter-disciplinary* manner– so that economics become easy for even those who have 'no background' in it.
- All of the chapters have been added with **sample objective and subjective questions** at the end besides **previous years' questions (PYQs)** of the preliminary and main exams from **2021 to 2025** (for **pre-2020 PYQs** scan the QR code and **login to McGraw Hill Edge**).

  These questions have been added given as per their closest connections to the chapters–readers will need understanding beyond the concerned chapters to solve them.
- **Sample Model Questions/Answers** have been added for the *Main Examination* at the end of every chapter with the hope that they guide the readers to create/develop the right answers *(Remember that your writing ability makes a huge difference!)*.
- The **first** chapter aims to present a simplified and application-based insight into *Economics* to 'lessen the fear' of readers, especially, those who have no background in the discipline.
- The book aims to provide ***basic to advance*** level 'understanding' in an ***'easy-to-understand'*** style following an interdisciplinary approach–fully updated with the ***latest economic developments***.
- Sectoral areas such as *Agriculture, Industry* and *Services* have been **fully updated** with the latest developments.
- The segments on *inflation* and *price management, banking, insurance, external sector,* and *human development* etc. have all been **fully revamped and updated** as per the changed times.

- *Taxation* and *Budgeting*– the very core of policy making– have been presented in an **exam-oriented, updated, and simplified style**.
- Thoroughly **revised and updated with all the latest and major official sources** such as *Economic Survey* ***2025-26****; Union Budget* ***2026-27****; Indian Economy: A Review;* and major reports of the *NITI Aayog* and the relevant central ministries.
- *Glossary* being among the **most useful segments of the book**, has been added with new items and made exam-oriented by simplifying the core 'concepts' and 'terms' in an objective and comprehensive style.
- *Exam Essentials* **and** *Word Bank* **are some special features of the book which aim to attract readers' attention to exam-focused areas of importance.**

With all sense of responsibility, hereby, I present this book to the readers with the wish that it serves their needs of the exams taking place in 2026 and 2027 in a better way.

Constructive suggestions from the readers are always welcome.

Wishing all the very best to the readers in their endeavours!

Ramesh Singh
www.rameshsingh.online
dr.rmsh@gmail.com

www.facebook.com/IndianEconomyMHE

Preface to the First Edition

I felt my first serious inclination towards writing when my first article was published in the journal *Mainstream* way back in 1988 while pursuing my post graduation studies at the Delhi School of Economics. My interaction with the students inside and outside the classroom in 1990-91, when India faced a serious financial crisis, made me realise that there was an immediate need of a book on Indian Economy, which could educate the students about the various aspects and challenges of the Indian economy in a simple and lucid manner. It took nearly two decades to fulfil this dream of mine.

The book has been designed to cater to the requirements of the General Studies paper for various Civil Services Examinations (Union as well as the States), and the optional Economics. It would also be useful for graduate and postgraduate courses in Economics of various universities. Adequate and required notes and references have been given after consulting and referring to an array of sources. I have taken care of both the objective and the subjective aspects based on my classroom experience of interacting with the students.

I am grateful to Prof. Majid Husain for the inspiration and motivation I got from him to complete this work. I have especially learnt the art and importance of work, punctuality and honesty in a very practical way from him.

Thanks are also due to Mr. Rajesh Kumar Baghel, Mr. Rakesh Kumar, Md. Ishtiaq, and Mr Vikash. I am indebted to my wife, Mrs Ila Singh, for her full support and my two little daughters, Medha and Smiti, for providing the sparkle in an otherwise monotonous work.

Finally, my special thanks to the team from McGraw-Hill, who took great pains to finalise the project and complete it in a record time with all the possible expertise. I welcome from the readers constructive advice and comments, which could guide me in further revision of this book.

www.facebook.com/IndianEconomyMHE

Ramesh Singh

www.rameshsingh.org
dr.rmsh@gmail.com

How to use the Book?

- **THE FIRST THING:** You don't need to be an economist to score high marks in the civil services exams! Rather, you simply need to develop the knack/sense of economics and its applications in everyday life, particularly in the arena of policy making! And doing this is very much possible for every aware reader!
- Economics can't be understood in parts (i.e., one chapter at a time)– the reason, every chapter of the book is connected to every other chapter.
- Economics being a very dynamic discipline, to acquire the ability to solve questions, especially the objective questions, one does not need only an overall understanding of economics, Indian Economy, and current economic events but the ability to integrate and apply them too.
- First go through the 'NOTE FOR THE READER' and watch the 'Introductory Videos' of the chapters before reading them and take benefit of the videos on concepts too– simply scan the QR Code given at the top right corner of the Chapter page and Login to McGraw Hill Edge
- The 'sample' questions given at the end of the chapters will require understanding of many other chapters. Thus, readers are advised to first refer all chapters thoroughly together with the *footnotes* and *Glossary* before sitting to solve them.
- Writing answer is a different ball game–having knowledge or understanding is not enough! One needs enough 'writing practice' to acquire the right ability to create/develop quality answers.

WARNING*

Be careful to determine that your sources and data are reliable. The internet and other electronic media are easy to use and equally easy to abuse. The web is the closest thing in economics to a free lunch. Remember the adage, "You only get what you pay for."

* P. A. Samuelson and W. D. Nordhaus, *Economics* (New Delhi: McGraw Hill Education, 2020), p. xlvii.

About the Civil Services Examination

The Civil Services Examination comprises two successive stages:

(i) Civil Services (Preliminary) Examination (Objective Type) for the selection of candidates for Main Examination; and

(ii) Civil Services (Main) Examination (Written and Interview) for the selection of candidates for the various services and posts.

Scheme and subjects for the Preliminary and Main Examination.

A. PRELIMINARY EXAMINATION

The Examination shall comprise two compulsory Papers of 200 marks each.

Note:

(i) Both the question papers will be of the objective type (multiple choice questions).

(ii) The question papers will be set both in Hindi and English. However, questions relating to English Language Comprehension skills of Class X level will be tested through passages from English language only without providing Hindi translation thereof in the question paper.

B. MAIN EXAMINATION

The written examination will consist of the following papers:

Qualifying Papers

Paper A: (One of the Indian Language to be selected by the candidate from the Languages included in the Eighth Schedule to the Constitution). **300 Marks**

Paper B: English **300 Marks**

The papers on Indian Languages and English (Paper A and Paper B) will be of Matriculation or equivalent standard and will be of qualifying nature. The marks obtained in these papers will not be counted for ranking.

Papers to be counted for merit

Paper I: Essay **250 Marks**

Paper II: General Studies-I **250 Marks**
(Indian Heritage and Culture, History and Geography of the World and Society)

Paper III: General Studies-II **250 Marks**
(Governance, Constitution, Polity, Social Justice and International relations)

Paper IV: General Studies-III (Technology, Economic Development, Bio-diversity, Environment, Security and Disaster Management) **250 Marks**

Paper V: General Studies-IV (Ethics, Integrity and Aptitude) **250 Marks**

Paper VI: Optional Subject - Paper 1 **250 Marks**

Paper VII: Optional Subject - Paper 2 **250 Marks**

Sub Total (Written test) **1750 Marks**

Personality Test **275 Marks**

Grand Total **2025 Marks**

Candidates may choose any one of the optional subjects from amongst the list of subjects given below:

List of Optional Subjects for Main Examination

(i) Agriculture
(ii) Animal Husbandry and Veterinary Science
(iii) Anthropology
(iv) Botany
(v) Chemistry
(vi) Civil Engineering
(vii) Commerce and Accountancy
(viii) Economics
(ix) Electrical Engineering
(x) Geography
(xi) Geology
(xii) History
(xiii) Law
(xiv) Management
(xv) Mathematics
(xvi) Mechanical Engineering
(xvii) Medical Science
(xviii) Philosophy
(xix) Physics
(xx) Political Science and International Relations
(xxi) Psychology
(xxii) Public Administration
(xxiii) Sociology
(xxiv) Statistics
(xxv) Zoology
(xxvi) Literature of any one of the following:
Assamese, Bengali, Bodo, Dogri, Gujarati, Hindi, Kannada, Kashmiri, Konkani, Maithili, Malayalam, Manipuri, Marathi, Nepali, Oriya, Punjabi, Sanskrit, Santhali, Sindhi, Tamil, Telugu, Urdu and English.

Contents

CHAPTER 1

An Introduction to Economics

> Economics is the study of how goods and services are produced, distributed and consumed. As resources are always in short supply, the British economist Lionel Robbins in 1935 described the discipline as 'the science of scarcity'.
>
> **- David Orrel and Borin Van Loon**
> *Introducing Economics: A Graphic Guide*
> (London: Faber & Faber, 2011), p. 3.

To watch the Author's videos on the significance of the Chapter, scan the QR Code given here

Exam Essentials...

- Laws of Demand
- Stages of Growth
- Animal Spirit
- Factors of Production
- Three Problems of Economic Systems
- Post-Washington Consensus

Note to the Reader...

Economics is a concepts-based discipline. This is why students need to develop a *working understanding* of the fundamentals of economics to handle the questions asked in various examinations.

This chapter tries to simplify economics and its operations for the reader, especially for those who do not have a background in the subject. Readers should use the book's *Glossary* along with it to take maximum benefit from it.

In This Chapter...

MORE THAN A DISMAL SCIENCE

Economics has been called a 'dismal science', precisely a depressing and poor science[1]. Other than this, the discipline has also been criticised for being a kind of riddle for common people to comprehend. It has also been called a 'failed science' (more so after its failure to predict the US *sub-prime mortgage crisis* of 2008). Still, nobody can deny the invaluable role played by economics in making this world a better place.

Understanding economics and its nuances has always been a challenge, especially for those who do not have a background in it. It does not mean that those with a background (university-educated) in economics are very comfortable - many of such people face an altogether different sort of problem - they *understand* less economics than they *know*! Missing the applicatory dimension of economics is a general problem among such people. Today, emphasis being on the *applications of economics* (especially in the competitive exams), 'knowing' economics is not enough; rather, one is required to have the ability to apply economics in everyday life - and this is only possible if one 'understands' it!

Making economics easier for both categories of readers has been one of the prime aims of this book. However, this has not been an easy task for two reasons - firstly, keeping the soul of concepts intact while simplifying them; and secondly, educating the reader about the contemporary economic issues. Developing a book on Indian economy would have been an easier task had simplifying economics not been among the aims. This is why, along with the analyses of economic issues, there flows an undercurrent of economic theory throughout the book. For this, it will be *wiser* on the part of the reader to keep in touch with the footnotes and glossary to feel and comprehend the subject matter in a desired way.

[1] T. Carlyle, the Scottish historian, coined this term (in his work *Occasional Discourse on the Negro Question,* 1849) while making a point against the emancipation of the Negro slaves (as per his belief, it will leave slaves worse off due to the economic principle of demand and supply). Later on, his belief was also addressed to the 'depressing' (dismal) proposition of T.R. Malthus (in his work *An Essay on the Principle of Population,* 1798) that in future, food supply would not match the rise in population.

DEFINING ECONOMICS

Simply put, 'economics studies economic activities of the human being' (a *working definition*). Humanities are intricately connected as all aim to study the er-disciplinary approach to studying humanities is considered wiser.

What are economic activities? In simple terms, all activities where money is involved can be referred to as economic activities. And wherever money comes into question, there comes the economic motive/gain. Several examples can be taken of it - getting a job, giving a job, buying and selling something, conducting a business and so forth. Things are still a bit complicated! Visiting religious places for prayer is clearly not an economic activity, but what about giving alms to beggars at such religious places or offering money at the places of worship or even, for that matter, religious donations? Can we call them our economic activities? Does it look difficult to say? Here, right from visiting religious places to offer prayer all are non-economic activities!

However, defining economics has not been as easy as it has been presented here - defining every discipline has been a complex and contentious task for that matter. Widely used and quoted definitions of the discipline revolve around the uses of resources and their distribution. Let us feel the technicality involved in a typical definition with the help of two such acclaimed definitions taken as reference:

> *Economics is the study of how societies use scarce resources to produce valuable commodities and distribute them among different people.*[2]
>
> *Economics studies how individuals, firms, governments and other organisations within our society make choices and how these choices determine a society's use of its resources.*[3]
>
> Economics as the study of 'how society uses its scarce resources' is probably the most used definition which is catchy as well as concise[4].

[2] P.A. Samuelson and W.D. Nordhaus, *Economics* (New Delhi: McGraw Hill Education, 2020), p. 4.

[3] J.E. Stiglitz and C.E. Walsh, *Economics* (New York: W.W. Norton & Company, 2006), p. 6.

[4] M. Bishop, *Economics–An A-Z Guide* (London: Economist Profile Books, 2009).

MICRO AND MACRO

After the Great Depression (during the 1930s), the domain of economics was divided into two broad branches - microeconomics and macroeconomics. John Maynard Keynes is considered the *father* of macroeconomics (the branch came into being after the publication of his seminal work, *The General Theory of Employment, Interest and Money*, in 1936).

Simply put, if macroeconomics (macro) is about the forest, microeconomics (micro) is about the trees. While the former deals with the big picture (the forest), the latter deals with the details (the trees that make up the forest). Micro and macro are the *Greek* words which mean 'small' and 'big', respectively.

While micro takes a bottom-up approach to analyse economy, macro takes a top-down approach. Taking an example, while micro tries to understand the choices which consumers make and the income they earn, macro tries to understand the dynamics of inflation and growth. Though they appear to be different, they are actually interdependent and complementary since there are many overlapping issues between them. For example, a rise in inflation (macro effect) will cause a rise in the cost of raw materials, leading to rise in prices which consumers will pay (micro effect).

Micro theory evolved from the theories of how prices are determined; macro, on the other hand, is rooted in empirical observations that existing theory could not explain. While there are no competing schools of thought in micro, macro includes schools such as the New Keynesian or New Classical. Since the late 1980s, however, these divisions have been becoming narrower[5].

Scan this QR Code to watch a author's video lecture that simplifies this topic

Econometrics is the third core area of economics other than the micro and macro. This field seeks to apply statistical and mathematical methods to economic analysis. The sophisticated analyses of micro and macro sub-fields would not have been possible without the major advances made in econometrics over the past century or so.

Laws of Demand

1st Law As per it, when price rises people create lower demand.

2nd Law As per it, demand is more responsive to price in the long-run than in short-run (because consumption does not change drastically with price changes).

3rd Law Consumption of higher-grade products increases when a fixed cost is 'added' (due to tax, transportation, etc.) on two substitutes. This is because the 'added' per-unit amount decreases the relative price of the higher-grade product. For example, it is harder to find 'good' apples in the prime apple-growing region of a country.

Source: Armen A. Alchian and Wiliam R. Allen, *Exchange & Production: Competition, Coordination & Control*, Wadsworth Pub. Co., Belmont, California, USA, 1983.

WHAT IS AN ECONOMY?

Economy is economics in action. It is a still-frame picture of economic activities. A country, a company and a family all have their own economies. It is popularly used in the case of countries - Indian economy, the US economy, the Japanese economy and so forth. While the principles and theories of economics remain the same, economies (of countries) show diversities given the socio-economic diversities countries have.

Sectors and Types of Economies

Economic activities in a country/economy are broadly divided into three main sectors[6] and derive their types by the dominant form of economies they operate.

Primary Sector This sector includes those economic activities which take place while exploiting natural resources, such as mining, agricultural activities and oil exploration. When the agriculture sector (one of the sub-sectors of the primary sector) contributes to half of the national income and livelihood of a country, it is referred to as an *agrarian economy*.

[5] O. Blanchard, G. Dell'Ariccia and P. Mauro, 'Rethinking Macroeconomic Policy', *International Monetary Fund, SPN/10/03*, 12 February 2010.

[6] M.P. Todaro and S.C. Smith, *Economic Development*, 8th ed. (New Delhi: Pearson Education, 2003), p. 440.

Secondary Sector It contains all of the economic activities under which the raw materials extracted out of the primary sector are processed (also called the industrial sector). One of its sub-sectors, manufacturing, proved to be the largest employer across the western developed economies (which made them emerge as the world's most industrialised economies). When the secondary sector brings in half of the national income and employment of a country, it is referred to as an *industrial economy*.

Tertiary Sector All of the economic activities where services are produced fall under this sector, such as education, health care, banking and communication. When this sector contributes half of the national income and livelihood of a country, it is referred to as a *service economy*. Later on, experts created two more sectors of economy - quaternary and quinary. They are, however, sub-sectors of the tertiary sector.

Stages of Growth

Looking at the growth pattern and process of the developed countries, a theory about it was proposed by W.W. Rostow[7] in 1960 according to which economies grow following *five linear stages* through the three main sectors, i.e., agriculture, industry and services. However, several countries did show exceptions to this standard pattern – India and many other Southeast Asian countries such as Indonesia, Philippines, Thailand and Vietnam fall under this category. These countries moved from the stage of an agrarian economy to service economy without much healthier expansion of their industrial sector.

India saw a transition from the dominance of the agriculture sector to services sector by the late 1990s when the contribution of services in its national income crossed the 50 per cent mark.

Quaternary Sector Also known as the 'knowledge' sector, the activities related to education, and research and development come under it. The sector plays the most important role in defining the quality of human resources an economy has.

[7] Walt. W. Rostow, *The Stages of Economic Growth: A Non-communist Manifesto* (London: Cambridge University Press, 1960), pp. 1-5.

Quinary Sector All activities where top decisions are made fall under it. The highest level of decision-makers in government (inclusive of their bureaucracy) and the private corporate sector falls under it. The number of people involved in this sector is very low; rather, they are considered the 'brain' behind socio-economic performance of an economy.

ECONOMIC SYSTEMS

Human life depends on the use (consumption) of certain things (goods and services), some of which, up to a level, are also essential (such as food, water, shelter, clothing) for survival. How to enable people to have these things (which are called goods and services in economics) was the *formost challenge* for humanity[8]. This challenge has two dimensions to it - firstly, these things need to be created (produced); and secondly, they should reach (distributed/supplied to) to those in need.

For production, one needs to set up productive assets for which money needs to be spent (known as investment). But 'who' will invest and 'why'? In the process of taking on this challenge, there evolved different types of economic systems (i.e., different ways of *organising an economy)*. We can prepare a long list of economic systems, however, three of them are considered the major ones - a brief overview of which is presented in the following sections.

Market Economy

This is considered the first formal economic system emerging out of the traditional economic system. Its origin is traced back to the work (*An Inquiry into the Nature and Causes of the Wealth of Nations, 1776*) of the Scottish philosopher-economist Adam Smith (1723-90). His main ideas can be summed up, in a simplified way, as follows:

- It is self-interest which motivates individuals/ firms to carry out economic activities out of which society gets goods and services. It means the products that a society gets are unintended social benefits of someone's self-interested actions. Adam Smith called this motivating factor the *invisible*

[8] Enhancing the well-being (life satisfaction) of mankind has been the second major challenge for economics - the efforts in this direction led to the evolution of the ideas of growth, development, human development and finally happiness (which will be discussed in the next chapter, i.e., Chapter 3).

hand (often called the 'animal spirit'). This way, questions like 'who' will invest in productive assets and 'why' seem to get answered.

Animal Spirit

The 'animal spirit' which worked as the invisible force behind this economic system has been defined by J.M. Keynes as the 'confidence' or the 'naive optimism' of entrepreneurs under the spell of which they set aside the chances of loss and think of profit only (as a healthy person puts aside the chances of death).

But from where does this animal spirit come has been a mystery– can it be created from outside or is it an innate thing some are born with are yet to be fully answered!

- To attain higher prosperity, there should be increasing *division of labour* (specialisation of labour force by breaking down large jobs into smaller components). Specialisation brings in speed, precision and quality in the labour force.
- For an invisible hand to operate properly, a suitable environment (i.e., market) determined by the forces of demand and supply (called the market forces) is required. Decisions such as what to produce, how much to produce and at what price to sell (i.e., supply) all depend on these forces.
- Such an economic system needs to be regulated by *competition* prevailing in the market.
- For efficient operation of the economic activities, the government should follow a policy of *laissez faire* (French word which means 'leave it alone', which is generally translated by economists as 'non-interference'). The lesser interference by the government, better the economic performance. Here, non-interference by the government means different things such as the government playing no or least econo mic role (producing none of the goods and services), no economic regulation and no taxes imposed.

Adam Smith himself called such an economic system 'the system of natural liberty'. Rather, these ideas were the drivers of two major economic systems - 'capitalism' and 'free market economy'. Though they are based on the same economic environments (demand and supply), there are subtle differences between them.

Factors of Production

In the process of production (i.e., output), we need to employ various items (i.e., inputs). These inputs are called factors of production in economics. They are generally classified into three broad categories:

1. Land (simply put, this is all the natural resources used in the production process such as—air, land, water, minerals, fuels, etc.).

2. Labour (this is *labour force* put in action to produce things).

3. Capital (also called *capital goods* which are used to produce other things such as machines, tools, infrastructure, hardware, software, etc.).

Some experts consider **entrepreneurship** as the *fourth* factor of production. Entrepreneurship is the ability of a person to organise/run a business and take risks and rewards that come with it.

Points to Ponder

As human labour is being replaced by robot labour, do you think in coming times the difference between labour and capital will get blurred? Such a transition, however, gives the producing company/firm much autonomy/control over the production process. Will it decrease the number of buyers and their income?

While capitalism is focused on the creation of 'wealth' and ownership of productive assets, free market economy is focused on 'exchange' of wealth (through production and supply of goods and services).

In a capitalist system there might be some government regulations, but private owners can have monopoly on the market and thus prevent competition. However, a free-market economy is solely based on market forces (demand and supply), and there is little or no government regulation. That is why in a free market economy, free competition is possible without any intervention from outside forces.

Such an economic system was *first* tested in the United States in 1777 from where capitalism spread across to the whole of Euro-America (Northern America and Western Europe). These economies enjoyed high prosperity and operated well till they were hit by the Great Depression[9] in 1929. By that time great capital was amassed by few (the multi- and transnational companies), while the majority remained poor – widening inequality in the process over time. Taxes were imposed, but they were very few in number and at very low rates with the state playing a negligible welfare role.

Cons of This System Supported by democratic rights and freedoms, this system provided a conducive environment for individual success, innovation and business activities. Though it looks smoothly operating for over one and a half centuries (with subtle changes), it had its own set of limitations which can be summarised precisely in the following way:

- There was almost no tool to look after those who had lower purchasing power (i.e., the poor).
- Negligible to total absence of welfare actions from the state.
- Widening economic inequality even after launching distributive measures such as progressive taxation (in which the richer are taxed with higher rates).

The existing set of policy approaches could not help these economies to recover out of the Depression. It was in wake of this crisis that we see the rise of a new branch of economics – the macroeconomics – proposed by the British economist John Maynard Keynes (1883–1949) in his seminal work *The General Theory of Employment, Interest and Money, 1936*. Together with analysing the causes which might have caused this crisis, Keynes suggested a new set of policy approaches to help economic recovery. In simple terms, Keynes suggested these economies include certain traits from the other economic system (non-market economy) to correct the crisis faced by them. After including the Keynesian advice, these economies recovered out of the Depression and, in this process (practically), the *mixed economic system* evolved.

[9] Depression is a stage in an economic system which shows certain sticky traits such as excessively lower aggregate demand, abnormally lower rate of inflation with higher rates of unemployment and/or lower rates of employment, leading to locking down of production centres. A detailed and objective analysis is presented about Depression and Recession, among others, in Chapter 7.

Non-Market Economy

Rooted (basically) in the ideas of Karl Marx (1818–83), it had two variants – *socialist* and *communist*. While in the socialist model (ex- USSR, 1917–89) the state had ownership control of only natural resources, in the communist model (China, 1949–85) the state had ownership control over labour as well. It was also known by other names such as *state economy, command economy* and *centrally planned economy*. Basically, this system evolved in 'reaction' to the market economy and was based on the following main beliefs:

- Resources of a country should be used for the well-being of all.
- Resources are best used once they are under the ownership of society/community (socialism/communism). Thus, all economic roles will be played by the state only.
- No property rights were given to individuals guided by the belief that it promotes exploitation of the labourers (i.e., proletariat) and helps a small minority (i.e., bourgeoisie) to get richer over time, resulting in increasing economic inequality.
- Absence of market (i.e., inter-play of demand and supply was totally absent).
- No idea of competition (i.e., total state monopoly in economic sphere).
- People to play an economic role (employed in the state-owned enterprises) *according to their ability* and in return to get all the facilities from the state *as per their needs*.
- The decisions such as what to produce, how much to produce and how to supply them to people were taken by the state itself.

This system was first tested by the Bolsheviks in the ex-USSR (in 1919) from where it spread across the whole of eastern Europe (the so-called socialist bloc countries) of the time, finally resulting in its purest form in communist China (in 1949) – emergence of the socialist and communist models of the non-market economy.

Cons of This System Even after being fully committed to the 'well-being of masses' and absence of poverty (theoretically speaking), this system had its own limitations which can be summarised briefly in the following way:

- Though the aim was to serve all, there was no idea of creating capital or wealth, which created a scarcity of investible capital in the future.

- State used to prioritise the uses of resources, thus the best or optimum uses of resources (driven by market forces) were denied, leading to their misallocation and wastage.
- In the absence of property rights there was no motivation to work hard and tap the animalistic spirit of the people (as no money was paid to them), leading to virtual absence of innovation (i.e., research and development) and a process of internal decay.
- Being non-democratic political systems, things such as *liberty* and *freedom* were totally absent. Aimed at avoiding exploitation of the labourers at the hands of capitalists, the state itself emerged as the sole agent of exploitation - critics called this 'state capitalism'.

A process of internal decay was being faced by these economies since the early 1970s caused by the in-built shortcomings they faced. It was way back in the mid-1950s that the Polish philosopher Oskar Lange[10] had advised these economies to embrace 'market socialism', which was outrightly rejected by both the Soviet Bloc and China. At last, by the mid-1980s, state economies moved to modify their economic systems by including certain traits of the market economy:

- Ex-USSR, by the late 1980s, announced the twin policies of *Perestroika* (restructuring) and *Glasnost* (openness), switching over to a mixed economy with fundamental traits of a market economy. Similar changes were adopted by the existing East European socialist economies and the CIS (Confederation of Independent States).
- China, by the mid-1980s, announced its *Open Door Policy* embracing mixed economy with fundamental traits of the market economy. Rather, China had started preparations for this change by mid-1970 itself, but they were not explicit in nature.

In a way, the two major and contrasting economic systems of the time had completed the full circle and moved closer to borrowing traits from each other - the evolution of the mixed economy (where we find the mixture of traits of both economic systems). This event has been also phrased as the *end of ideology* - as the ideological divide between these economic systems looked bridged now, eventually ending the long-drawn *Cold War* which originated from this ideological difference.[11]

Mixed Economy

In practice, the mixed economic system was already present (by the late 1930s) once the market economies adopted certain policy changes (borrowing from the non-market economy) to recover out of the Depression. But the first country to announce adopting this system was France (in 1944–45, with the announcement to adopt national planning). The system was further strengthened once the non-market economies started modifying themselves by the mid-1980s. It was with few reports of the World Bank that helped the world agree on the best model of the economic system:

- The World Bank accepted the need of 'state intervention' in the economy (i.e., the market economy) which used to be an ardent advocate of the free market economy. But the time and nature of the intervention cannot be universal.[12]
- The World Bank further concluded that neither of the economic systems (market and non-market) is free from flaws, and even a novice of economics can agree that the best economic system can be a mixture of both. But the state and market mix in any country has to be decided by its socio-economic needs of the time as there cannot be a fixed model of mixed economy.[13]

The *chief characteristics* of the mixed economy may be summarised in the following way:

- Both state and private sector to have economic roles.
- The private sector to play those roles where an invisible hand (the motive of profit) can work properly. Production and supply of the 'private goods' (the goods and services which people use by purchasing them from their own income) is the best example in this case. But the state is not prohibited from playing this role.

---

[10] Oskar Lange (1904-65) praised the state economy for many of its good traits but advised for inclusion of the good traits of the market economy, naming the new model as 'market socialism' [J.K. Galbraith, *A History of Economics* (London: Penguin Books, 1991), pp. 188-89].

[11] F. Fukuyama, *The End of History and the Last Man* (New York: Free Press, 1992).

[12] World Bank, *The East Asian Miracle: Economic Growth and Public Policy*, World Bank Policy Research Report (New York: Oxford University Press, 1993).

[13] World Bank, *World Development Report 1999/2000: Entering the 21st Century* (New York: Oxford University Press, 1999).

- Those roles which the private sector will not be motivated to play (due to absence of any profit element) should be better taken care of by the state. Supply of the 'public goods' (the goods and services which are consumed by all without making any direct payments from their individual income) is the best example in this case. But the private sector is free to play this role as well.
- The economic roles played by either the state or private sector may not remain fixed for a period of time and may be modified as per need.
- Regulation (such as rules, competition and taxation) of the economic system to be taken care of by the state.

It means that a mixed economic system is not a *finality* which the market or non-market economic systems used to be, but, rather, continuous change is its main feature - capable of modifying as per the socio-economic needs of the hour. This way, the long-drawn debate about the possible *role of the state*[14] in an economy was also decided.

Three Problems of Economic Systems

Every economic system/organisation has faced three 'fundamental' problems since humanity is there, namely ***what*** to produce, ***how*** to produce, and ***for whom*** to produce.[15]

Today, in most countries, these decisions depend on market—producers produce the things which give them the highest profits (the *what*) by using the least costly process (the *how*) which the consumers (the *whom*) can pay for.

DISTRIBUTION SYSTEMS

Along with the three economic systems, three distribution systems also evolved. While the capitalist economy distributed the goods and services through the market (people buying according to their needs from the market at a price decided on market principles), the state economy distributed them without any aid of the market (the state directly supplied them to the people without any payment). In the case of a mixed economy, the distribution system was a hybrid of the former two models of distribution - state and market both being used (certain goods and services people used to buy from the market, while certain others were supplied by the state either free or at subsidised prices).

Though we see a kind of consensus emerging in favour of the mixed economic system, the future had much in store. Over time, it came under the influence of several ideologies, some of which also left an enduring impact on world economies. The major ones are briefly explained in the following sections.

WASHINGTON CONSENSUS

It is a set of reform policy packages which were suggested by the International Monetary Fund (IMF), the World Bank (WB) and the US Department of the Treasury (i.e., the US finance ministry) towards the developing countries facing an economic crisis. Since all of these institutions were based in Washington, the policy prescription was called the Washington Consensus by the US economist John Williamson[16]. The 10-point reform policy prescriptions are as given below:

1. Fiscal discipline
2. A redirection of public expenditure priorities towards fields offering both high economic returns and the potential to improve income distribution, such as primary health care, primary education and infrastructure
3. Tax reform (to lower marginal rates and broaden the tax base)
4. Interest rate liberalisation
5. Competitive exchange rate
6. Trade liberalisation
7. Liberalisation of FDI inflows

[14] J.E. Stiglitz, *The Role of State in Economic Development*, the keynote address at the Annual World Bank Conference on Development Economics, New York, 1996.

[15] P.A. Samuelson and W.D. Nordhaus, Economics (New Delhi: McGraw Hill Education, 2020), pp. 8-11.

[16] J. Williamson, 'What Washington Means by Policy Reform', in *Latin American Adjustment: How Much Has Happened?* Chapter 2, J. Williamson, ed. (Washington, DC: Institute for International Economics, 1990); J. Williamson, *What Should the Bank Think About the Washington Consensus*, Background Paper, (Washington DC: World Bank's World Development Report 2000, July 1999).

8. Privatisation
9. Deregulation (in the sense of abolishing barriers to entry and exit)
10. Secure property rights

However, later the term became synonymous with *neo-liberalism* (in Latin America), *market fundamentalism* (as George Soros stated in 1998) and even *globalisation* across the world. It has often been used to describe an extreme and dogmatic commitment to the belief that **markets can handle everything**.

But the reality has been different - the *set of polices* was already being recommended by the IMF and the WB together with the US Treasury, especially during the period of the 1980s and early 1990s.[17] The prescription was originally intended to address the real problems occurring in Latin America at the time, and its use later to handle a wide array of other situations has been criticised even by original proponents of the policies. The term 'Washington Consensus' has often been mentioned as being somewhat unfortunate, especially by its creator. John Williamson[19] stated that "audiences the world over seem to believe that this signifies a set of neo-liberal policies that have been imposed on hapless countries by the Washington-based international financial institutions and have led them to crisis and misery - there are people who cannot utter the term without foaming at the mouth." He further adds that many people feel that it gives the impression that the points outlined represent a set of rules imposed on developing nations by the United States. Instead, Williamson always felt that the prescription represented a consensus precisely because it was so universal. Many proponents of the plan do not feel that it represents the hardline *neo-liberal* agenda that anti-free-trade activists say it does. They, instead, present it as a relatively conservative assessment of what policies can help bring to a country for economic stability.

Post Washington Consensus

Over time, faith in the Washington Consensus has eroded. The experts have cited the Southeast Asian currency crisis of 1996–97, the US sub-prime crisis of 2007 (followed by the Great Recession in the western world) among its major failures in particular, and its inability to address the development concerns of the developing world in general. This erosion of faith in the Washington Consensus gave rise to the *post-Washington Consensus Consensus* which suggests to adopt the following[18] major ideas:

- A state-market balance in the economy (in place of dominance of market) as well as intervention of state if a situation demands; and
- Success should not be measured only by GDP, but by socio-economic inclusion, distribution, and environmental sustainability.

But the policy prescription led to processes which are known as liberalisation, privatisation and globalisation, thus cutting down the role of the state in the economy - more so in the nations which received developmental funding from the WB or went to the IMF in times of the Balance of Payment crises (as in the case of India which commenced its reform process in 1991 under the 'conditions' of the IMF). It was as if Adam Smith's prescription of 'free market' (liberalism) had taken its rebirth (in *neo-liberalism*).

By the early 2010s, global faith in the Washington Consensus started declining– and world governments started realising the limitations of 'market' in taking care of their economic ills. And in place, we see a rising faith in the *role of state in the economy* across the world (i.e., the rise of *development state*). This new view is getting even more strengthened due to increasing geoeconomic fragmentation today in the wake of the supply chain disruption caused by the COVID-19 pandemic, Russia-Ukraine conflict and tensions in the Middle East.

---

[17] J.E. Stiglitz, Initiative for Policy Dialogue, Paper presented at the Conference from the Washington Consensus towards a New Global Governance, Barcelona, September 2004. The conference was sponsored by the Ford Foundation, the MacArthur Foundation, and the Mott Foundation.

[18] Joseph E. Stiglitz, "Is there a Post Washington Consensus Consensus?", in Narcís Serra, and Joseph E. Stiglitz (eds), *The Washington Consensus Reconsidered: Towards a New Global Governance*, Initiative for Policy Dialogue (London: Oxford Academic, Online edition, 1 May 2008), pp. 41-56; and Stephen R. Hurt, 'Washington Consensus,' *Encyclopaedia Britannica*, 28 May 2020.

[19] J. Williamson, *Did the Washington Consensus Fail?* (Washington, DC: Institute for International Economics, 2002).

BEIJING CONSENSUS

Economic rise of China since the mid-1980s needs no introduction. Whether this rise was led by any conscious development model has been an issue of scholarly debate. Finally, the idea of the Beijing Consensus[20] was forwarded by Joshua Cooper Remo in 2004.

Also known as the Chinese model of economic development, this refers to the policies which were followed by Deng Xiaoping since 1976 (the year Mao Zedong died). Later on, this model was seen as an *alternative* to the Washington Consensus (i.e., an anti-Washington Consensus view) for the developing countries. Over time, experts interpreted this model in different ways, rather believing it to be based[21] on three main pillars:

1. Constant experimentation and innovation
2. Peaceful distributive growth with gradual reforms
3. Self-determination and inclusion of selective foreign ideas

The model received higher attention in the wake of the great recession hitting the western economies (when China still remained dynamic), with experts portraying it as China's alternative to the liberal market approach of the Washington Consensus.[22] Whether the developing countries should embrace the Chinese Model has been a contentious issue. Experts believe that the things which worked for China may not work for others looking at the heterogeneity of Chinese performance.[23] Again, in the wake of the rise of China, wherein experts almost declared the 'death of market' and 'rise of state-led growth', such hurried conclusions might rather be misplaced because China's best economic performance came when the market was a dominant force.[24]

Until 2010 we found rising interest in this model across the developing world, but once the Chinese growth took a downturn in recent times, experts have advised double caution in blindly following this model. Some experts believe that the rising protectionism across the world (especially the United States, the United Kingdom and other countries) has been caused by an inclination towards this model.

SANTIAGO CONSENSUS

This is yet another alternative to the Washington Consensus. It was put forward by the then World Bank Group President James D. Wolfensohn[25] (in Santiago) for the developing countries. The core idea of this model is *inclusion*, which should not only be economic but social too. This way, this is a socio-economic development model and is bound to have its local characteristics (we find similar 'social overtones' in the case of the Beijing Consensus too).

In addition to financial resources, the WB proposed to harness the incredible power of the information technologies and new spirit of openness and partnership (under the spell of rising globalisation) to make knowledge of global best practice in development accessible to all. The WB started building an internal architecture of a 'knowledge bank' for this purpose.

This proposal from the World Bank inspired the world governments to focus more on aspects of inclusive socio-economic growth. We see this happening in India too, with the Government launching the *third generation of economic reforms* in 2002 (which was aimed at making the fruits of reforms become inclusive in nature).

CAPITALISM AS A TOOL OF GROWTH PROMOTION

Capitalism as an economic system failed in the wake of the Great Depression (1929) and was purposefully modified into the mixed economy. But we find countries coming under the spells of capitalism in the near future as well. Two such clear spells can be cited - the *first* under the influence of the Washington Consensus (post-1985) and the *second* after the official acceptance to globalisation (*via* the

[20] J.C. Ramo, *The Beijing Consensus* (London: Foreign Policy Centre, May 2004).

[21] Z. Weiwei, 'The Allure of Chinese Model', *International Herald Tribune*, 2 November 2006.

[22] 'Beware the Beijing Model', *The Economist*, London, 26 May 2009.

[23] J. Williamson, *Is the Beijing Consensus Now Dominant* (Washington, DC: Asia Policy, 26 January 2012).

[24] Y. Huang, *Rethinking the Beijing Consensus* (Washington, DC: Asia Policy, 7 January 2011).

[25] J.D. Wolfensohn, *The Santiago Consensus: From Vision to Reality*, Speech of the President of the World Bank Group, Santiago, Chile, 19 April 1998.

World Trade Organisation (WTO), post 1995). Experts believe that the ensuing Great Recession (after the US subprime crisis of 2007) among the developed countries was largely caused by the extreme capitalistic inclinations (neo-liberal policies) found among them. This way, the world has witnessed the devastating effects of capitalism twice by now.

Over time, a kind of agreement has emerged across the world that though capitalism is not an ideal (or sustainable) type of economic system, such policies can be quite helpful in promoting the causes of growth. This is why today we find countries across the world maintaining a capitalistic policy orientation (i.e., *pro-business* policies) under the overall design of a mixed economy - one set of policies (capitalistic) aiming towards higher growth while the other aiming at effective welfare. Such a clear policy shift has been seen in India as well - it was in the wake of the criticism to the *Union Budget 2015-16* (of being *pro-rich* or *pro-corporate)* that the erstwhile finance minister categorically clarified that the Budget was trying to be pro-corporate as well as pro-poor. Basically, over time, experts started treating capitalism less as an economic system and more as a tool for promoting growth and income.

PREVIOUS YEARS' QUESTIONS

Prelims

1. With reference to the sectors of the Indian economy, consider the following pairs: (2024)

Economic Activity	Sector
Storage of agricultural produce	Secondary
Dairy farm	Primary
Mineral exploration	Tertiary
Weaving cloth	Secondary

How many of the pairs given above are correctly matched?

(a) Only one **(b)** Only two
(c) Only three **(d)** All four

2. With reference to physical capital in Indian economy, consider the following pairs: (2024)

Items	Category
Farmer's plough	Working capital
Computer	Fixed capital
Yarn used by the weaver	Fixed capital
Petrol	Working capital

How many of the above pairs are correctly matched?

(a) Only one **(b)** Only two
(c) Only three **(d)** All four

3. Consider the investments in the following assets: (2023)

(i) Brand recognition
(ii) Inventory
(iii) Intellectual property
(iv) Mailing list of clients

How many of the above are considered intangible investments?

(a) Only one **(b)** Only two
(c) Only three **(d)** All four

4. Which of the following activities constitute a real sector in the economy? (2022)

(i) Farmers harvesting their crops
(ii) Textile mills converting raw cotton into fabrics
(iii) A commercial bank lending money to a trading company.
(iv) A corporate body issuing Rupee Denominated Bonds overseas.

Select the correct answer using the code given below:

(a) (i) and (ii) only
(b) (ii), (iii) and (iv) only
(c) (i), (iii) and (iv) only
(d) (i), (ii), (iii) and (iv)

5. Consider the following statements: (2021)

Other things remaining unchanged, market demand for a good might increase if

(i) price of its substitute increases
(ii) price of its complement increases

(iii) the good is an inferior good and income of the consumers increases

(iv) its price falls

Which of the above statements are correct?

(a) (i) and (iv) only

(b) (ii), (iii) and (iv)

(c) (i), (iii) and (iv)

(d) (i), (ii) and (iii)

Answer: 1. (b) 2. (b) 3. (c) 4. (a) 5. (a)

Explanation

1. (b) Except the 'dairy farm' and 'weaving cloth' rest are matched with the wrong sectors. Mineral exploration is a primary sector activity while storage of anything, a tertiary (i.e., service) sector activity.

2. (b) This question revolves around the idea of capital which is required to create productive assets, namely 'fixed' and 'working' capitals. While fixed capital is a one time expenditure it is used time and again and depreciates on annual basis (such as tractor, plough, pump set, etc. in case of a farmer), the working capital is used in one go (such as seeds, diesel to run pump set, pesticides, etc. all raw material needed for farming in case of a farmer). From this point of view only two pairs (i.e., 2 and 4) are correctly matched.

3. (c) Companies make investments in various **Tangible and Intangible** assets. Some of the tangible assets include equipment, buildings, inventory, etc. On the other hand, intangible assets include Brand recognition, Intellectual property, customer lists, etc.

The companies make investments in marketing, leading to Brand recognition. This can enable them to make more profits. Inventory comprises goods that are yet to be sold and hence become tangible investments. Intellectual property such as Patents, Copyrights etc. may not have physical substance but bring long-term value to the company. Hence, they are considered intangible assets.

Mailing list of clients enables the companies to capitalise on marketing strategies and better market their products. Hence, they can be considered intangible assets.

4. (a) All enterprises (excluding financial firms such as banks, financial institutions, etc.) doing all the productive activities of an economy come under the real sector.

5. (a) When green vegetables get costlier, people shift to potatoes (the substitute). An increase in the price of complements will decrease its demand, while with a rise in income, people buy less of the inferior goods (such as wheat flour, potatoes, etc.). When the price of the good falls, its demand goes up.

Mains

1. Is inclusive growth possible under market economy? State the significance of financial inclusion in achieving economic growth in India. (2023)

SAMPLE OBJECTIVE QUESTIONS

1. How many of the following statement (s) is/are correct? Use the code given below to select your answer:

(i) The Beijing Consensus is an anti-Washington Consensus proposition.

(ii) While the Santiago and Beijing Consensuses have local overtones, the Washington Consensus has a global overtone.

(iii) India's third generation economic reforms were inspired from the Beijing Consensus.

Code:

(a) Only one **(b)** Only two

(c) All three **(d)** None of these

2. How many of the following is/are considered synonymous with the Washington Consensus?

(i) Globalisation
(ii) Neo-liberalism
(iii) Market fundamentalism

Code:
(a) Only one (b) Only two
(c) All three (d) None of these

3. Consider the following statements related to post-Washington Consensus Consensus:
(i) It was released by the World Bank in the wake of the sub-prime crisis of the USA by the early 2010s.
(ii) It favours state-market balance in the economy.
(iii) It emphasises socio-economic inclusion besides national income as the measure of development.

How many of the above statements are correct?
(a) Only one (b) Only two
(c) All three (d) None of these

4. Consider the following statements related to the model of mixed economy:
(i) Mixed economies of the world have become more protectionist in the wake of the COVID-19 pandemic and geopolitical tensions.
(ii) India has become more liberal mixed economy and avoids protectionism today.
(iii) Today, India favours de-globalisation.

How many of the above statements are correct?
(a) Only one
(b) Only two
(c) All three
(d) None of these

5. Consider the following statements related to capitalism:
(i) Its name was given by Adam Smith.
(ii) It was based on the idea of natural liberty.
(iii) Market economy is a reformed version of it.

How many of the above statements are correct?
(a) Only one
(b) Only two
(c) All three
(d) None of these

6. Which of the following is incorrect about the non-market economies?
(a) All of them believed in state control of resources.
(b) They were advised to adopt market principles by 1950s itself.
(c) Today, most of them are following market-based system of economy.
(d) Most of them have become mixed market economies today.

7. Consider the following statements related to Washington Consensus:
(i) It is a set of rules which promotes capitalism, as per the World Bank.
(ii) Santiago Consensus of the World Bank was a kind of modification in it.
(iii) Beijing Consensus presents an alternative to it.

How many of the above statements are correct?
(a) Only one
(b) Only two
(c) All three
(d) None of these

8. Which of the following describes 'Animal Spirit' in the best way?
(a) J.M. Keynes visualised it as the confidence of human beings.
(b) It is the brut materialistic desire to grab more.
(c) Under its spell, entrepreneurs achieve less than their potential.
(d) None of the above.

9. Consider the following statements related to distribution systems:
(i) Capitalism had market-based model of it.
(ii) Non-market economies had only public distribution.
(iii) India's public distribution system for food is one of its examples.

How many of the above statements are correct?
(a) Only one
(b) Only two
(c) All three
(d) None of these

10. Consider the following statements about economic systems and their policies:
    (i) Pro-business economic policies are necessarily anti-poor.
    (ii) Polices favourable to the poor are not liked by the corporate houses.
    (iii) The idea of public welfare originated out of the failure of capitalism.
    (iv) Welfare capitalism was basically a capitalism oriented towards welfare.

    How many of the above statements are correct?
    (a) Only one
    (b) Only two
    (c) Only three
    (d) All four

Answers: 1. (b) 2. (c) 3. (b) 4. (b) 5. (b) 6. (a) 7. (b) 8. (a) 9. (c) 10. (b)

SAMPLE SUBJECTIVE QUESTIONS

1. Is it possible to promote inclusive growth through capitalism? Give your suggestions to orient capitalism towards inclusive growth and welfare.
2. What do you mean by pro-corporate and pro-poor policy stance of the Government? Give suitable illustrations from the government of India's policies of recent times.
3. 'Today, capitalism is used more as a tool of growth promotion rather than an economic system.' Substantiate your views with the help of suitable examples.
4. Has India become a service economy? Discuss the views and counter-views related to the proposition.
5. "Market economy, in reality, is a reformed and democratic form of capitalism." Explain with suitable examples.

SAMPLE MODEL ANSWER

1. **'Today, capitalism is more taken as a tool of growth promotion rather than an economic system.' Elucidate.**

Ans. Capitalism as an economic system is considered a failed economic system in the wake of the Great Depression (1929); afterwards, it was modified into the mixed economy. But this system influenced the majority of the countries in coming times–two such clear spells can be cited in this regard:

1. The first under the influence of the Washington Consensus (post-1985)
2. The second is after the official acceptance of globalisation (via the WTO, post-1995).

Experts believe that the ensuing Great Recession (after the US sub-prime crisis of 2007) among the developed countries was largely caused by the extreme capitalistic inclinations (neo-liberal policies) found among them.

Thus, we can say that by now the world has witnessed the negative effects of capitalism twice. Over time, a kind of agreement emerged across the world as per which, though capitalism is not an ideal (or sustainable) type of economic system, such policies can be helpful in promoting the cause of growth. This is why today, we find countries across the world having capitalistic policy orientation (i.e., pro-business policies) under the overall design of a mixed economy having the following two sets of policies:

- one set of policies (capitalistic) aiming at higher growth, and
- the other aiming at effective welfare.

Such a clear policy shift has been seen in India too, where the Government has been following a pro-corporate and pro-poor policy stance (since 2014–15). Basically, over time, experts seem to take capitalism less as an economic system and more as a tool for promoting growth.

CHAPTER 2

National Income

> The welfare of a nation can scarcely be inferred from a measurement of national income.
>
> **–Simon Kuznets**
> *National Income, 1929-1932*, 73rd US Congress, 2nd Session, Senate document no. 124, p. 7

To watch the Author's videos on the significance of the Chapter, scan the QR Code given here

Exam Essentials...

- PPP
- Potential GDP
- Background of National Income in India
- National Income Estimates for 2024-25
- National Income estimates for 2025-26
- New Series 2022-23 Estimates

Note to the Reader...

In objective examinations, a number of questions are asked about national income. In the written exams, candidates need to use it indirectly. This chapter aims to simplify this area in a simple and exam-oriented manner.

In This Chapter...

INTRODUCTION

Measuring progress has been a major riddle for experts. Income as an indicator of progress was tried by many before the idea of the gross domestic product (GDP) was put forward by the US economist Simon Kuznets[1] in 1934. The method tries to calculate (account) a country's income at domestic and national levels - in gross and net forms - having four clear concepts - GDP, NDP, GNP and NNP. A brief and objective overview is presented below.

GROSS DOMESTIC PRODUCT (GDP)

GDP is the value of all *final* goods and services produced within the boundary of a nation during a one-year period. For India, this calendar year is from 1 April to 31 March.

It is also calculated by adding national private consumption, gross investment, government spending and trade balance (exports minus imports). The use of the exports minus imports factor removes expenditures on imports not produced in the nation, and adds expenditures of goods and services produced which are exported, but not sold within the country.

It will be better to understand the terms used in the concept, *'gross'*, which means the same thing in economics and commerce as 'total' means in mathematics; *'domestic'* means all economic activities carried out within the boundary of a nation/country and by its own capital; *'product'* is used to define 'goods and services' together; and *'final'* means the stage of a product after which there is no known chance of value addition to it.

The different uses of the concept of GDP are as given below:

1. Per annum percentage change in it is the 'growth rate' of an economy. For example, if a country has a GDP of 107 which is ₹7 higher than the last year, it has a growth rate of 7 per cent. When we use the term 'a growing' economy, it means that the economy is adding up its income, i.e., in quantitative terms.
2. It is a 'quantitative' concept and its volume/size indicates the 'internal' strength of the economy. But it does not say anything about the 'qualitative' aspects of the goods and services produced.
3. This is a very commonly used indicator to compare the economies of the world. The International Monetary Fund (IMF) ranks world economies according to their sizes (i.e., their GDPs). Earlier, the ranking was done at the prevailing rate of exchange in the US dollars but later on, it began at purchasing power parity (PPP) too when the new idea got introduced in 1990 by the IMF. As per the latest[2] data of the IMF, the size of India's economy is *fifth largest* at the prevailing exchange rate of rupee in US dollars, and *third largest* at PPP in the world (China and the USA being the largest and the second largest economies).

Word Bank

PPP

Purchasing power parity (PPP) is a method of calculating the correct/real value of a currency which may be different from the market exchange rate of the currency. Using this method economies may be studied comparatively in a common currency. This is a very popular method handy for the IMF and WB (introduced by them in 1990) in studying the living standards of people in different economies.

[1] S. Kuznets, an economist at the US National Bureau of Economic Research (NBER), presented the National Income 1929-32 Report to the US Congress in which he used the concept of GDP to capture the value of the total income generated in the country. The concept was used by the US government as a tool to understand and measure the recovery process of the economy out of the Great Depression of 1929. The US Presidents Herbert Clark Hoover (tenure 1929-33) and F. Roosevelt (tenure 1933-45) used the concept vigorously. The idea was adopted as a standard tool to account for national income by the WB and IMF right since they started their operation in 1944-45. Importance of this contribution can be guessed by the fact that Kuznets was awarded the Nobel Prize for Economics (in 1971) for this single contribution. Attempts to calculate national income were made earlier too, but this was the first empirical attempt towards it. He is popularly called as the father of the ideas of the GDP (Gross Domestic Product) and national income.

[2] *World Economic Outlook* (Washington, DC: IMF, October 2024).

The concept of the PPP was developed by the great European conservative economist, Gustav Cassel (1866–1944), belonging to Sweden. This concept works on the assumption that markets work on the *law of one price*, i.e., identical goods and services (*in quantity* as well as *quality*) must have the same price in different markets when measured in a common currency. If this is not the case, it means that the purchasing power of the two currencies is different.

Let us look at an example. Suppose sugar is selling $1 in US and ₹20 in India a kilo, then the PPP-based exchange rate of rupee will be $1 = ₹20. This is the way how *The Economist* of London has prepared its 'Big Mac Index' (comparing the Mc Donald's Big Mac burger prices in different economies).

In theory, the value of currencies in terms of their market exchange rate should converge with their value in terms of the PPP in the long run. But that might not happen due to many factors like the fluctuations in inflation; level of money supply; follow-up to the exchange rate regimes (fixed, floating, etc.), and other.

For the calculation of the PPP, a comparable basket of goods and services is selected (a very difficult task) of the identical qualities and quantities. The other difficulty in computing PPP arises out of the flaw in the 'one price theory', i.e., due to transportation cost, local taxes, level of production, etc. The prices of goods and services cannot be the same in different markets (This is correct in theory only, not possible in practice.)

NET DOMESTIC PRODUCT (NDP)

NDP is the GDP calculated after adjusting the weight of the value of 'depreciation'. This is, basically, *net form* of the GDP, i.e., GDP minus the total value of the 'wear and tear' (depreciation) that happened in the assets while the goods and services were being produced. All assets (except human beings) go for depreciation in the process of their uses, which means there is 'wear and tear'. The governments of the economies decide and announce the rates by which assets depreciate (carried out in India by the Ministry of Commerce and Industry) and a list is published, which is used by different sections of the economy to determine the real levels of depreciation in different assets. For example, a residential house in India has a rate of 1 per cent per annum depreciation and an electric fan has 10 per cent per annum, which is calculated in terms of the asset's price. This is one way how depreciation is used in economics. The other way it is used is in the external sector while the domestic currency floats freely as against foreign currencies. If the value of the domestic currency falls following market mechanism in comparison to a foreign currency, it is a situation of 'depreciation' in the domestic currency, calculated in terms of loss in the value of the domestic currency.

Thus,

NDP = GDP - Depreciation.

This way, NDP of an economy has to be always lower than its GDP for the same year, since there is no way to cut the depreciation to zero. But mankind has developed several techniques and tools such as 'ball-bearing' and 'lubricants', among others, to cut the loss due to depreciation.

The **different uses** of the concept of NDP are as given below:

1. For domestic use only: This was used to understand the historical situation of the loss due to depreciation to the economy. It was also used to understand and analyse the sectoral situation of depreciation in industry and trade in comparative periods.

Potential GDP

It represents the maximum sustainable level of production (i.e., optimum) an economy can have. This is determined by the economy's capacity to produce which depends on the available factors of production (i.e., inputs) and its technological efficiency—potential GDP varies as these variables change.

Scan this QR Code to watch a author's video lecture that simplifies this topic

2. To show the achievements of the economy in the area of research and development, which have tried cutting the levels of depreciation in a historical time period.

However, NDP is not used in comparative economics, i.e., to compare the economies of the world. Why is this so? This is due to different rates of depreciation which is set by the different economies of the world. Rates of depreciation may be based on logic (as it is in the case of houses in India - the cement, bricks, sand and iron rods which are used to build houses in India can sustain it for the coming 100 years, thus the rate of depreciation is fixed at 1 per cent per annum). But it may not be based on logic all the time; for example, up until February 2000, the rate of depreciation for heavy vehicles (vehicles with six wheels and above) was 20 per cent, while it was raised to 40 per cent afterwards to boost the sales of heavy vehicles in the country. There was no logic in doubling the rate. Basically, depreciation and its rates are also used by modern governments as a tool of economic policymaking, which is the third way how depreciation is used in economics.

GROSS NATIONAL PRODUCT (GNP)

GNP is the GDP of a country added with its 'income from abroad'. Here, the trans-boundary economic activities of an economy are also taken into account. The items which are counted in the segment 'Income from Abroad' are as follows:

1. **Private Remittances:** This is the net outcome of the money which inflows and outflows on account of the 'private transfers' by Indian nationals working outside of India (to India) and the foreign nationals working in India (to their home countries). On this front India has always been a gainer - until the early 1990s from the Gulf region (which decreased afterwards in the wake of the heavy country - bound movements of Indians working there due to the Gulf War) and afterwards from the United States and other European nations. As per the World Bank, India received an estimated $129.1 billion in remittances in 2024, which was the highest ever for any country in a single year.[3]

2. **Interest on External Loans:** The net outcome on the front of the interest payments, i.e., balance of inflow (on the money lent out by the economy) and outflow (on the money borrowed by the economy) of external interests. In India's case it has always been negative as the economy has been a 'net borrower' from the world economies.

3. **External Grants:** It means the net outcome of the external grants, i.e., the balance of such grants which flow to and from India. Today, India offers more of such grants than it receives. India receives grants (grants or loan-grant mix) from a few countries as well as UN bodies (such as the UNDP) and offers several developmental and humanitarian grants to foreign nations. In the wake of globalisation, grant outflows from India have increased as its economic diplomacy aims at playing a bigger role at the international level.

Ultimately, the balance of all the three components of the 'Income from Abroad' segment may turn out

Background of National Income in India

Data related to national income are vital for formulating polices and planning — taking step in this direction the Government set up the National Income Committee (NIC) in 1949 — with P.C. Mahalanobis as its Chairman (and D.R. Gadgil and V.K.R.V. Rao as members) — it got advices from Simon Kuznets, J.R.N. Stone, and J.B.D. Derksen. The Committee prepared the first set of official estimates of national income (NNP) for 1948–49 to 1950–51 at current and constant (1948–49) prices — and laid the foundations for estimating national income in the country. The NIC adopted the same methodology which was devised by V.K.R.V. Rao for his estimate for British India for the period 1931–32.[4]

India shifted to the new System of National Accounts (SNA) in 2015 which was recommended by the UNO in 2008 (till now it was based on the method recommended by the UNO in 1993) — the base year for the new method of India is 2011–12 (which is supposed to 2021–22 in 2025–26).

[3] Migration and Development Brief (Washington DC: World Bank, USA, December 2024).

[4] K.L. Krishna, 'National Income' in *The Oxford Companion to Economics in India,* vol. II, Kaushik Basu and A. Maertens, eds. (New Delhi: Oxford University Press, India, 2012), pp. 488-491.

to be positive or negative. In India's case it has always been negative (due to heavy outflows on account of trade deficits and interest payments on foreign loans). It means the 'Income from Abroad' is subtracted from India's GDP to calculate its GNP.

The normal formula is

> 'GNP = GDP + Income from Abroad'. But it becomes GNP = GDP + (− Income from Abroad), i.e., GDP − Income from Abroad, in the case of India. This means that India's GNP is always lower than its GDP.

The **different uses** of the concept, GNP are as given below:

1. It is a more exhaustive concept of national income than the GDP as it indicates the *'quantitative'* as well as the *'qualitative'* aspects of the economy, i.e., the *'internal'* as well as the *'external'* strength of the economy.
2. It enables us to learn several facts about the production behaviour and pattern of an economy, such as how much the outside world is dependent on its product and how much it depends on the world for the same (numerically shown by the size and net flow of its 'balance of trade'); what is the standard of its human resource in international parlance (shown by the size and the net flow of its 'private remittances') and what position it holds regarding financial support from and to the world economies (shown by the net flow of 'interests' on external lending/borrowing).

NET NATIONAL PRODUCT (NNP)

NNP of an economy is the GNP after deducting the loss due to 'depreciation'. The formula to derive it may be written as:

> NNP = GNP - Depreciation

or,

> NNP = GDP + Income from Abroad − Depreciation.

The **different uses** of the concept of NNP are as given below:

1. This is the **'National Income' (NI)** of an economy. Though the GDP, NDP and GNP all are 'national incomes', they are not written beginning with capital letters 'N' and 'I'.
2. This is the *purest form* of the income of a nation.
3. When we divide NNP by the total population of a nation, we get the 'per capita income' (PCI) of that nation, i.e., 'income per head per year'. A very basic point should be noted here that this is the point where the rates of depreciation followed by different nations make a difference. The higher the rates of depreciation, the lower the PCI of the nation (whatever be the reason for it logically or artificially as in the case of depreciation being used as a tool of policymaking). Though economies are free to fix any rate of depreciation for different assets, the rates fixed by them make a difference when the NI of the nations is compared by the international financial institutions such as the IMF, WB and ADB.

The 'base year', together with the 'methodology' for calculating the national accounts, was revised by the Central Statistics Office (CSO) in January 2015, which is explained in the following sections.

Points to Ponder

- To avoid double counting, the GNP does not include intermediate goods and services (since they are already incorporated in the value of final goods and services).
- All the four national income data sets can be derived for any time period; however, they are annual concepts.
- By dividing them with the population we get the per capita income of the country. However, when we use the term NI (National Income, with initials in capital letters), we mean the NNP only. Similarly, per capita income of a country, called PCI, is NNP divided by its population.

COST AND PRICE OF NATIONAL INCOME

While calculating national income the issues related to 'cost' and 'price' also need to be decided. Basically, there are two sets of costs and prices, and an economy needs to choose at which of the two costs and two prices it will calculate its national income. Let us understand[5] its relevance:

[5] The information on issues such as 'cost', 'price', 'taxes' and 'subsidies' are based on the different discussion papers released by the Central Statistical Organisation (GoI) from time to time.

1. **Cost:** Income of an economy, i.e., value of its total produced goods and services, may be calculated at either the 'factor cost' or the 'market cost'. What is the difference between them? Basically, 'factor cost' is the 'input cost' the producer has to incur in the process of producing something (such as cost of capital, i.e., interest on loans, raw materials, labour, rent and power). This is also termed as the *'factory price'* or 'production cost/price'. This is nothing but the 'price' of the commodity from the producer's side. While the 'market cost' is derived after adding the indirect taxes to the factor cost of the product, it means the cost at which the goods reach the market, i.e., showrooms.

   India officially used to calculate its national income at *factor cost* (though the data at *market cost* were also released which were used for other purposes by the governments, commerce and industry). Since January 2015, the CSO has switched over to calculating it at *market price* (i.e., *market cost*). The market price is calculated by adding the *product taxes* (generally taken as the *indirect taxes* of the centre and the states) to the factor cost.

   This way India switched over to popular international practice. Once the GST has been implemented, it became easier for India to calculate its national income at market price.

2. **Price:** Income can be derived at two prices, constant and current. The difference in the constant and current prices is only that of the *impact of inflation*. Inflation is considered standstill at a year of the past (this year of the past is also known as the 'base year') in the case of the constant price, while in the current price, present-day inflation is added. Current price is, basically, the maximum retail price (MRP) which we see printed on the goods sold in the market.

REVISED METHOD OF NATIONAL INCOME ACCOUNTS

The Central Statistics Office (CSO), in January 2015 released the **new** and **revised** data of National Accounts effecting two changes:

1. The *base year* was revised from 2004-05 to 2011-12. This was carried out in accordance with the recommendation of the National Statistical Commission (NSC), which had advised to revise the base year of all economic indices every 5 years.
2. This time, the *methodology* of calculating the National Accounts has also been revised in line with the requirements of the System of National Accounts (SNA), 2008, an internationally accepted standard.

The **major changes** incorporated in this revision are as given below:

1. **Headline Growth Rate** will now be measured by the *GDP at constant market prices,* which will henceforth be referred to as 'GDP' (as is the practice internationally). Earlier, growth was measured in terms of growth rate in *GDP at factor cost and at constant prices.*
2. Sector-wise estimates of the Gross Value Added (GVA)[6] will now be given at basic prices[7] instead of factor cost. The relationship between GVA at factor cost, GVA at basic prices and GDP (at market prices) is given below:

GVA at basic prices = CE + OS/MI + CFC + production taxes less production subsidies

GVA at factor cost = GVA at basic prices – production taxes + production subsidies

GDP = GVA at basic prices + product taxes – product subsidies

[where, **CE**: compensation of employees; **OS**: operating surplus; **MI**: mixed income; and **CFC**: consumption of fixed capital (i.e., depreciation)].

[6] GVA, which measures the difference in value between the final goods and the cost of ingredients used in its production, widens the scope of capturing more economic activity than the earlier 'factor cost' approach - a sum of the total cost of all factors used to produce goods or service, net of taxes and subsidies.

[7] The basic price is the amount receivable by the producer from the purchaser for a unit of goods or service produced as output minus any tax payable (such as sales tax or VAT the buyer pays), plus any subsidy receivable, on that unit as a consequence of its production or sale; it excludes any transport charges invoiced separately by the producer. In other words, the basic price is what the seller collects for the sale, as opposed to what the buyer pays.

Production taxes or **production subsidies** are paid or received with relation to production and are independent of the volume of actual production. Some examples of **production taxes** are *land revenues, stamps and registration fees* and *tax on profession.* Some **production subsidies** are subsidies to railways, input subsidies to farmers, subsidies to village and small industries, and administrative subsidies to corporations or cooperatives. **Product taxes** or **subsidies** are paid or received on per unit of the product. Some examples of product taxes are excise tax, sales tax, service tax and import and export duties. **Product subsidies** include food, petroleum and fertiliser subsidies, interest subsidies given to farmers and households, through banks and subsidies for providing insurance to households at lower rates.

3. Comprehensive coverage of the *corporate sector* both in manufacturing and services by incorporation of annual accounts of companies as filed with the Ministry of Corporate Affairs (MCA) under their e-governance initiative, MCA21. Use of MCA21 database for manufacturing companies has helped in accounting for activities other than manufacturing undertaken by these companies.
4. Comprehensive coverage of the *financial sector* by inclusion of information from the accounts of stock brokers, stock exchanges, asset management companies, mutual funds and pension funds and the regulatory bodies including the Securities and Exchange Board of India (SEBI), Pension Fund Regulatory and Development Authority (PFRDA) and Insurance Regulatory and Development Authority (IRDA).
5. Improved coverage of activities of *local bodies* and *autonomous institutions,* covering around 60 per cent of the grants/transfers provided to these institutions.

COMPARING GVA AND GDP

Economic growth is estimated using two main methods - demand side and supply side. Under *supply side,* the value added by the various sectors in the economy (i.e., agriculture, industry and services) is added up to derive the GVA. This way, it captures the income generated by all economic actors across the country.

Under the *demand side,* GDP is arrived at by adding all expenditures carried out in the economy. Broadly speaking, there are four sources of expenditures in an economy - namely, private consumption (individuals and households), government, business enterprises and net exports (exports minus imports). It includes all the taxes received and all subsidies disbursed by the government. Thus, GDP is equal to GVA added with the net taxes (taxes minus subsidies).

While GDP is a good measure in comparative studies (comparing economies), GVA is a better measure to compare different sectors *within* the economy. GVA is more important when looking at *quarterly* growth data because quarterly GDP is arrived at by apportioning the observed GVA data into different spender categories.

FIXED-BASE AND CHAIN-BASE METHODS

The Government is at present exploring the idea of shifting to the *chain-base* method for calculating the GDP from the *fixed-base* (year) method. In the new method GDP estimates are compared with those of the previous year instead of a fixed base year which is revised every 5 years.

In a fixed-base method, the weights assigned (in the index) to various economic activities (i.e., the goods and services produced) stay unchanged even if the economy changes structurally. Besides, this method does not factor in relative changes in prices and impact on demand. While in a chain-base method, weights assigned to economic activities change annually and, thus, capture structural changes more quickly. The current gig economy India is argued to reflect in the current GDP statistics of India, for instance. The new method will have several *advantages* over the existing one:

- It will capture structural changes in the economy faster by allowing new activity and items to be added every year. Current GDP estimates are based on data for 2011-12 (the base year) and are due for revision. New items and firms involved in the production process will be captured more quickly rather than a gap of 5 years (which practically takes 7-8 years to reflect).
- Comparing India's growth datasets with other countries will get easier and better as this is the

best international practice[8] today. In a globalising world economy, investment and trade decisions depend heavily on such comparative datasets.

- It is believed to bring more authenticity and transparency in the datasets related to India's national income. [9]

National Income Estimates for 2025–26

As per the National Statistics Office (NSO), the major features[9] related to India's national incomes accounts for the financial year 2025–26, are as given below:

- **Real GDP** (or GDP at Constant Prices) is estimated to be ₹201.90 lakh crore, registering a growth rate of 7.4 per cent.
- **Nominal GDP** (or GDP at Current Prices) is estimated to be ₹357.14 lakh crore in the FY 2025–26, against ₹330.68 lakh crore, showing a growth rate of 8.0 per cent.
- **Real GVA** (at Constant Prices) is estimated to be ₹184.50 lakh crore in the FY 2025–26, registering a growth rate of 7.3 per cent.
- **Nominal GVA** (at Current Prices) is estimated to be ₹323.48 lakh crore, showing a growth rate of 7.7 per cent.
- **Per Capita Income** (at Constant Prices) is estimated to be ₹1,21,968, registering a growth rate of 6.3 per cent.
- **Per Capita Income** (at Current Prices) is estimated to be ₹2,19,575, showing a growth of 6.9 per cent.

NEW SERIES 2022-23 NATIONAL ACCOUNTS

The MoSPI (Ministry of Statistics and Programme Implementation) on February 27, 2026 released the New Series of National Accounts. The exercise involves incorporation of several methodological and statistical upgrades (based on the reports of various sub-committees) aimed at making India's national account datasets (like GDP and GVA) more accurate and granular. Major changes effected in this regard are summarised below:

Base year: The base year has been revised to 2022-23 (from 2011-12)– the revision was delayed due to various reasons, one being the COVID-19 pandemic.

Methodology upgrades: The major methodological changes effected are as given below:

- 'Activity-wise' share for a company has been used to calculate the value added in each business activity in case of the non-financial private corporate sector. In the older series (i.e., 2011-12 as the base year), the entire GVA of such companies were allocated to the sector while they operated across the sector.
- The General Government (i.e., Centre plus States) now include the value of 'housing services' provided by the governments to their employees.
- It captures the value addition by the autonomous institutions and local bodies.
- 'Double-deflator' (in place of 'single deflator') method has been used to capture price movements in a better way– an international best practice.

Households' contribution: It uses the Annual Survey of Unincorporated Sector Enterprises (ASUSE) and Periodic Labour Force Survey (PLFS) on an annual basis (instead of extrapolating data in the older series). Thus, the contribution of the sector will get estimated every year.

Private final consumption expenditure (PFCE): The PFCE is basically all consumption spending done by the people, which is now being measured in a more granular manner through the enhanced use of Household Consumer Expenditure Surveys (HCESs) and direct estimation based on production and other data sources.

New data sources: Several new data sources have been used, namely:

- GST data was so far being used in the quarterly accounts (of GDP and GVA), and only for some sectors in the annual data.
- GST data have been used to estimate the regional output of private corporations and will also be used to more accurately determine the contribution of the value added by private companies to the GDP of the country.

[8] The United States of America shifted to the chain-base or chain-weighted index in 1996 and other developed countries followed – in most of the cases it produced better outcomes.

[9] *First Advance Estimates,* National Statistical Office (New Delhi: Ministry of Statistics and Programme Implementation, GoI, 07 January 2026).

The GST data will also be used to identify active private companies to improve the accuracy of estimating the value added by non-reporting companies.

- UPI transactions have been used to capture the informal and other sectors like gig workers, digital economy, etc. of the economy.

Better Data from States, Banks & Informal Sector

- Data from the Statistical Table Related to Banks in India (STRBI) of the Reserve Bank of India have been used to estimate the activity of banks.
- The earlier proxy-based approach to estimate the activity of private Non-Banking Financial Companies (NBFCs) has been replaced with their financial data from the Ministry of Corporate Affairs.
- The ASUSE data has been used more effectively to capture aspects (that were earlier not being included accurately), such as the activity of insurance agents, and the gross fixed capital formation of the unincorporated sector.
- In the agriculture sector, it incorporates updated methodologies and data sources based on studies done by the Inland Grassland and Fodder Research Institute, Central Marine Fisheries Research Institute, Central Inland Fisheries Research Institute, and the Agricultural Development and Rural Transformation Centre.

New Series 2022–23 Estimates

The national income estimates, as per the new series are as given below:

Real GDP (or GDP at Constant Prices) is estimated at ₹322.58 lakh crore for 2025–26 (against the First Revised Estimate of ₹299.89 lakh crore in 2024–25). The ***growth rate*** in Real GDP during 2025–26 is estimated at 7.6 per cent (as compared to 7.1 per cent in 2024–25).

Nominal GDP (or GDP at Current Prices) is estimated at ₹345.47 lakh crore in 2025–26 (against ₹318.07 lakh crore in 2024–25), showing a growth rate of 8.6 per cent.

Real GVA is estimated at ₹294.40 lakh crore in the year 2025–26 (against ₹273.36 lakh crore in 2024–25), registering a growth rate of 7.7 per cent as compared to 7.3 per cent in 2024–25.

Nominal GVA is estimated at ₹313.61 lakh crore during in 2025–26 (against ₹288.54 lakh crore in 2024–25), showing a growth rate of 8.7 per cent.

GDP (Gross Domestic Product) for the base year 2022–23 is estimated as ₹261.18 lakh crore. *Real GDP* (or GDP at constant prices) for the years 2023–24 and 2024–25 stands at ₹280.01 lakh crore and ₹299.89 lakh crore, respectively, showing a growth of 7.2 per cent during 2023–24, and 7.1 per cent during 2024–25.

Nominal GDP (or GDP at current prices) for the years 2023–24 and 2024–25 stands at ₹289.84 lakh crore and ₹318.07 lakh crore, respectively, exhibiting a growth of 11.0 per cent during 2023–24, and 9.7 per cent during 2024–25.

GVA (Gross Value Added) The *nominal GVA* at basic prices has increased by 9.6 per cent during 2024–25 compared to growth of 10.7 per cent during 2023–24. *Real GVA* (or GVA at constant prices), increased by 7.3 per cent in 2024–25, compared to 7.2 per cent in 2023–24.

PCI (Per Capita Income) at current prices for the years 2022–23, 2023–24 and 2024–25 is estimated at ₹1,59,557, ₹1,76,465, and ₹1,92,774, respectively.

GNDI (Gross National Disposable Income) at current prices is estimated at ₹324.52 lakh crore for 2024–25, while the estimate for the year 2023–24 stands at ₹294.55 lakh crore, showing a growth of 10.2 per cent for year 2024–25 as compared to growth of 10.9 per cent in 2023–24.

Savings Gross Saving during 2024–25 is estimated at ₹111.13 lakh crore against ₹95.17 lakh crore during 2023–24. The major share in Gross Saving during 2024–25 is 62.1 per cent in Household sector and 28.9 per cent in non-financial corporations.

GCF (Gross Capital Formation) at current prices is estimated at ₹109.25 lakh crore for 2024–25 as compared to ₹100.00 lakh crore during 2023–24. The rate of GCF to GDP is 34.3 per cent during 2024–25 as against 34.5 per cent in the 2023–24. The rate at constant prices was 34.9 per cent in 2023–24 and 34.6 per cent in 2024–25.

PFCE (Private Final Consumption Expenditure) at current prices is estimated at ₹179.71 lakh crore for the year 2024–25 as against ₹163.77 lakh crore in 2023–24. In relation to GDP, the PFCE to GDP ratio at current prices is 56.5 per cent for both

2023–24 and 2024–25. At constant prices, the PFCE is estimated at ₹157.85 lakh crore and ₹167.00 lakh crore, respectively for the years 2023–24 and 2024–25. The corresponding PFCE to GDP ratio for the years 2023-24 and 2024–25 are 56.4 per cent and 55.7 per cent respectively.

PCPFCE (Per Capita Private Final Consumption Expenditure) at current prices, for the years 2022–23, 2023–24 and 2024–25 is estimated at ₹1,07,910, ₹1,17,356, and ₹1,27,627 respectively.

GFCE (Government Final Consumption Expenditure) at current prices is estimated at ₹33.95 lakh crore for the year 2024–25 as against ₹30.74 lakh crore during 2023–24. At constant prices the estimates of GFCE for the years 2023–24 and 2024–25 stand at ₹29.08 lakh crore and ₹30.96 lakh crore respectively.

WAY FORWARD

The *Economic Survey 2025–26* has summarised[10] the economic prospects and concerns for the upcoming year **2026–27** in the following ways:

1. Fiscal 2025–26 was an unusually challenging on the *external front* — which saw imposition of high penal tariffs from the USA (which was declared void by the US Supreme Court; however, this could not reduce uncertainties) creating stress for manufacturers, exporters, and affected business confidence. [The government responded by using this crisis as an opportunity to push through key measures such as — GST rationalisation, faster deregulation, and further simplification of compliance requirements across sectors. The fiscal 2026–27 is therefore expected to be a year of adjustment, however, external environment remains uncertain, which will shape the overall outlook for the year.]
2. At the global level, growth is expected to remain modest, commodity price broadly stable, inflation trending downward, with monetary policy expected to be more accommodative/supportive of growth. However, certain key risks persist:
   - **(i)** If the AI boom fails to deliver the anticipated productivity gains, it could trigger a correction in overly optimistic asset valuations, with the potential for broader financial contagion;
   - **(ii)** Trade conflicts may hit investment and further weaken the global growth outlook. Thus, downside risks to global growth remain prominent.
3. For India, these global conditions translate into — external uncertainties, tariff induced disruptions to trade, export, and investment sentiment. Ongoing trade negotiations with the United States are expected to conclude during the year, which could help reduce uncertainty on the external front. The forthcoming rebasing of the CPI series in the coming year will also have implications for inflation assessment and warrant careful interpretation of price dynamics.

Taking these considerations together, the Survey projects real GDP growth in 2026–27 in the range of **6.8 to 7.2** per cent. The outlook, therefore, is one of steady growth amid global uncertainty, requiring caution, but not pessimism.

[10] *Economic Survey 2025-26* (New Delhi: Ministry of Finance, GoI, 31 January 2026), pp. 30-35.

PREVIOUS YEARS' QUESTIONS

Mains

1. Explain the difference between computing methodology of India's Gross Domestic Product (GDP) before the year 2015 and after the year 2015. (2021)
2. Do you agree that the Indian economy has recently experienced V-shaped recovery? Give reasons in support of your answer. (2021)
3. Define potential GDP and explain its determinants. What are the factors that have been inhibiting India from realising its potential GDP? (2020)

SAMPLE OBJECTIVE QUESTIONS

1. How many of the following statement(s) is/are correct about the revised method of the national income accounting? Select your answer by using the code given below:
   - (i) GVA at factor cost includes no taxes and excludes no subsidies.
   - (ii) GDP at market cost includes all taxes and excludes all subsidies.
   - (iii) GVA at basic prices added with net taxes is equal to GDP.

   Code:
   (a) Only one (b) Only two
   (c) All three (d) None of these

2. How many of the following statement(s) is/are correct about economic systems? Select your answer by using the code given below:
   - (i) Mixed economies are generally inclined towards state economy.
   - (ii) India's national income has always been higher at current prices and lower at constant prices; however, it may be other way round.
   - (iii) A pro-corporate government is not much careful about welfare.
   - (iv) While the private sector does not produce public goods, governments do not produce private goods in the country.

   Code:
   (a) Only one (b) Only two
   (c) Only three (d) All four

3. Consider the following statements related to the accrual-based accounting which was in news recently:
   - (i) Under it, transactions are counted as they happen.
   - (ii) In this system, income is counted when cash is really received.
   - (iii) This method has been adopted in India's new method of national income accounting.

   How many of the above statement(s) is/are correct?
   (a) Only one (b) Only two
   (c) All three (d) None of these

4. Consider the following statements about capital consumption:
   - (i) Lubricants help reduce it.
   - (ii) Its higher levels help firms earn higher profits.
   - (iii) In national accounts it is called as consumption of fixed capital.

   How many of the above statement(s) is/are correct?
   (a) Only one (b) Only two
   (c) All three (d) None of these

5. Which of the following is the correct equation for India's NNP at market prices?
   - (a) Total GVA at basic prices + Production taxes (less Production subsidies)
   - (b) CE + MI + CFC + Product taxes + Production taxes (less Product and Production subsidies)
   - (c) Total GVA at basic prices + Product and Production taxes (less all subsidies)
   - (d) CE + MI + CFC + Product taxes (less Product subsidies)

6. Consider the statements about the interest rate growth rate differential (IRGD) of the country:
   - (i) India's IRGD has remained negative not due to higher growth rate but lower interest rate.
   - (ii) Over the last two and half decades India had a negative IRGD.
   - (iii) Higher growth with lower interest rate keeps the IRGD positive

   How many of the above statement(s) is/are correct?
   (a) Only one (b) Only two
   (c) All three (d) None of these

7. Consider the following statements related to the national income accounts of the country:
   - (i) Total gross value added (GVA) will always remain lower than the gross domestic product (GDP).

(ii) The GDP of the country is the total GVA added with net taxes

(iii) Higher taxes boost the GVA but is not sustainable in the long run.

How many of the above statement(s) is/are correct?

(a) Only one (b) Only two
(c) All three (d) None of these

8. Consider the following statements related to the ideas of cost and price in the national accounts of the country:

(i) Market cost is factory price added with all of the indirect taxes.

(ii) Ex-factory price and market cost are the same things.

(iii) Market cost and maximum retail price are the same things.

How many of the above statement(s) is/are correct?

(a) Only one (b) Only two
(c) All three (d) None of these

9. Select the correct statement about the purchasing power parity (PPP).

(a) It is a way of determining exchange value for different currencies in the US dollar term according to their relative strengths in their own economies.

(b) It developed as a reaction to resistance to World Bank's idea of poverty.

(c) India's national income at it had been sometimes higher than that of the prevalent exchange rate of the Indian Rupee.

(d) None of the above.

10. The National Income of a country in a given year is equal to:

(a) money value of final products produced.

(b) sum of total consumption and investment.

(c) total value of goods and services produced by the nationals.

(d) net value of total products produced by the nationals as well as foreigners.

Answers: 1. (c) 2. (d) 3. (a) 4. (c) 5. (b) 6. (a) 7. (b) 8. (b) 9. (a) 10. (a)

SAMPLE SUBJECTIVE QUESTIONS

1. Discuss the recent changes introduced by the government in the area of national income accounting and the expected benefits from it.

2. Briefly examine the benefits of shifting from fixed base to chain base method of accounting the national income in the country.

3. Compare the ideas of the gross value added (GVA) and gross domestic product (GDP) in measurement of the national income and growth rate of an economy.

4. 'The idea of the per capita income is of only academic importance similar to the World Bank's idea of poverty line.' Elaborate.

SAMPLE MODEL ANSWER

1. Briefly examine the recent revision in the base year for the national accounts and summarise the benefits expected to accrue out of it.

Ans. The Ministry of Statistics and Programme Implementation (MoSPI), Government of India, released a major update on *27 February 2026*, in which the base year of the national accounts has been revised from 2011-12 to 2022-23. As per the ministry, the reasons and purposes of the revision are as given below:

(i) *Reflecting the structural shifts in the economy*

- The older base year (2011-12) had become outdated over time, which failed to capture new shifts in the economy since then, such as the digital economy, e-commerce, the UPI, and the gig economy.
- The revision includes emerging industries such as renewable energy and advanced manufacturing.
- It aims to capture the changed household consumption patterns and their shift from the older to newer basket of items.

2. *Delayed revision and selection of a normal year*

- India's base year revision was due since 2017-18; however, due to reasons like demonetisation, the introduction of the GST, and lastly the COVID-19 pandemic, it got much delayed.
- The year 2022-23 has been selected as the benchmark year (i.e., base year) as the period from 2019 to 2021 saw an artificial rebound effect in the economy (due to several concessions and stimulus from the Government).

3. *Methodological upgrades*

- The new series integrates modern databases like GST filings, e-Vahan (vehicle registrations), and the public financial management system (PFMS).
- India has moved to double deflation from single deflation (aligned with the international best practice) for the manufacturing sector. Under it, input and output prices are adjusted separately, aligned with the real inflation rates, which will significantly improve the accuracy of the 'real' GDP estimates.
- It aims to capture the contribution of the *informal sector* by using surveys like the Annual Survey of Unincorporated Sector Enterprises (ASUSE), which was based on decade-old proxies.

4. *International best practices*

- The revision has aligned India's national accounts to the best international practice as advised by the UNO (thus, it addresses the concern raised by the IMF, which had flagged India's previous national accounts data with a 'C' grade due to the outdated base year and reliance on single deflation).
- India has committed to revise the base year every 5-10 years, aligned with international best practices, which will help make comparisons with other economies credible and comparable.

CHAPTER 3

Growth, Development and Happiness

> Happiness is a result of creating strong social foundations, for which it is time to build 'social trust' and 'healthy lives', not guns and walls.
>
> *World Happiness Report 2017*, SDSN, (New York: UNO, 2017).

To watch the Author's videos on the significance of the Chapter, scan the QR Code given here

Exam Essentials...

- Economic Man
- Economic Development
- What is Happiness?
- Happiness Economics

Note to the Reader...

Economics has been used by humanity to improve the well-being of mankind. In the process of doing so, the debate has revolved around development. To the extent the term 'development' is concerned, it has been defined in highly diverse and nuanced ways by the experts. The term is still in the process of evolution. This chapter tries to simplify the idea of development for the readers.

In This Chapter...

- Introduction
- Progress
- Economic Growth
- Economic Development
- Happiness
- Re-imagining the Idea of Happiness
- Insights into Human Behaviour
- Nudge and Public Policy

INTRODUCTION

Like seers and philosophers, economists were also party to mankind's quest for a better tomorrow. We have been a witness to a number of notions arising from the economics literature in this area - starting with a very humble and layman's term such as 'progress' to technical terms such as 'growth', 'development' and 'human development'. With greater dependence on the idea of the 'economic man', the world created immense wealth in the post-war decades. It was in the 1980s that social scientists started finer studies in the area of mankind's actions, finally challenging the very idea of the 'economic man' ('rational man'), thus starting mankind's urge to introspect the lives of humanity on planet Earth. Meanwhile, humanity was faced with the unique riddle of climate change. Now, courtesy of the United Nations Organization (UNO), the world has the World Happiness Report.

Economic Man

Economic man (or homo economicus in Latin where 'man' stands for mankind) is an idea which is used in economics to understand human action/behaviour. As per it:

- man is a *rational being,*
- man is *narrowly self-interested*, and
- man's actions are based on the *cost-benefit analysis*.

Brief origin: The term was first used by *J.S. Mill* (1806–73) in his paper of 1836 (*On the Definition of Political Economy, and the Method of Investigation Proper to It*). However, the origin of the idea is traced from the 18th century thinkers *Adam Smith* (1723–90) and *David Ricardo* (1772–1823) who considered man as a 'rational and self-interested' economic agent (they believed in the idea of 'animal spirit') and even *Aristotle* (384–322 BC) who talks about man's 'self-interested tendencies' in his work *Politics*.

The idea was strengthened later on mainly by philosophers like Leon Walrus (1834–1910), Vilfredo Pareto (1848–1923), and Lionel Robbins (1898–1984). Pareto is credited with cementing the idea in the worldview of the time. The other contemporary ideas (like pragmatism, existentialism, materialism, etc.) strengthened it.

However, there has been disagreement too. The critics (i.e., behavioural economists), on the basis of empirical studies, say that man's actions can be very irrational. For rational actions, the actors need all information which is not available all the time and even if they are available, actors may not comprehend them—one commonly cited example is the irrational consumer behaviour (they do not change their brands even if they are offered better products at better prices!).

Some major critics of past have been Thorstein Veblen (1857–1929), J.M. Keynes (1883–1946), Herbert Simon (1916–2001) and the Austrian school, while Francis Fukuyama, T. Hashimoto, M.D. Hauser, A.S. Guha and B. Guha are the contemporary critics.

PROGRESS

Progress is a general term frequently used by experts to denote betterment or improvement in anything. In economics, the term was used for a long time to show the positive movement in the lives of people and in an economy. It had both quantitative and qualitative aspects to it. After a point of time, some economists started using all the three terms - progress, growth and development - interchangeably to mean almost the same thing. But it was only during the 1960s, 1970s and 1980s that a clear meaning of these terms really evolved.[1] The term 'progress' became a general term with no specific meaning in economics or denoting both growth and development. But growth and development were allotted their clear-cut meanings.

ECONOMIC GROWTH

'Growth', a term arising from the life sciences, in economics means economic growth. Economic growth is an increase in economic variables over a period of time. The term can be used in an individual case or in the case of an economy or for the whole world. The most important aspect of growth is its *quantifiability*, i.e., one can measure it in absolute terms.[2] All the units of measurement may be applied, depending upon the

[1] Based on the analyses in M.P. Todaro and S.C. Smith, *Economic Development*, 8th ed. (New Delhi: Pearson Education, 2004), pp. 9-11.

[2] As the IMF and the WB considered this yardstick of development as quoted in G.M. Meier and J.E. Rauch, *Leading Issues in Economic Development* (New Delhi: Oxford University Press, 2006), pp. 12-14.

economic variable, where growth is being studied. We have a few examples:

1. An economy might have been able to see growth in food production during a decade which could be measured in tonnes.
2. The growth of a road network in an economy might be measured for a decade or any period in miles or kilometres.
3. Similarly, the value of the total production of an economy might be measured in currency terms, which means the economy is growing.
4. Per capita income of an economy might be measured in monetary terms over a period.
5. We may say that *economic growth is a quantitative progress.*

To calculate the *growth rate* of an economic variable, the difference between the period concerned is converted into percentage form. For example, if a dairy farm owner produced 100 litres of milk last month and 105 litres in the following month, his dairy has a growth rate of 5 per cent over a period of two months. Similarly, we may calculate the growth rate of an economy for any given successive period. Growth rate is an *annual concept* which may be used otherwise with the clear reference to the period for which it is used.

Though growth is a value-neutral term, i.e., it might be positive or negative for an economy for a specific period, we generally use it in the positive sense. If economists say an economy is growing, it means the economy is having a positive growth, otherwise they use the term 'negative growth'.

Economic growth is a widely used term in economics which is useful in not only national level economic analyses and policymaking but also highly useful in the study of comparative economics. International level financial and commercial institutions go for policymaking and future financial planning on the basis of the growth rate data available for the economies of the world.

Measuring Development

Although economists were able to articulate the differences between growth and development (Mahbub ul Haq, a leading Pakistani economist had done it by the early 1970s), it took some more time when the right method of measuring development could be developed. It was an established fact that the goal of progress goes beyond the mere 'increase in income'. International bodies such as the UNO, IMF and WB were concerned about the development of the comparatively underdeveloped regions of the world. But any attempt in this direction was only possible once there was a tool to know and measure the level of development in an economy and the determinants which could be considered as the traits of development. The idea of developing a formula/ method to measure the development was basically facing two kinds of difficulties:

1. At one level it was difficult to define what constitutes development. Factors which could show development might be many, such as levels of income/consumption, quality of consumption, health care, nutrition, safe

Economic Development

For a comparatively longer period of time after the birth of economics, economists remained focused on aspects of expanding the quantity of production and income of a country's economy. The main issue economists discussed was how to increase the quantity of production and income of a country or a nation-state. It was believed that once an economy is able to increase its production, its income will also increase and there will be an automatic betterment (quality increase) in the lives of the people of the economy. There was no conscious discussion over the issue of quality expansion in the lives of the people. Economic growth was considered as a cause and effect for the betterment of the lives of the people. This was the reason why economists, till the 1950s, failed to distinguish between growth and development, though they knew the difference between these terms.

It was during the 1960s and in the later decades that economists came across many countries where the growth was comparatively higher, but the quality of life was comparatively low. The time had come to define economic development differently from what the world meant by economic growth. For economists, development indicates the quality of life in the economy, which might be seen in accordance with the availability of many variables such as:

- The level of nutrition
- The expansion and reach of healthcare facilities – hospitals, medicines, safe drinking water, vaccination, sanitation, and so forth
- The level of education
- Other variables on which the quality of life depends

Here, one basic thing that must be kept in mind is if the masses are to be guaranteed with a basic minimum level of quality-enhancing inputs (above-mentioned variables such as food, health and education) in their life, a minimum level of income has to be guaranteed for them. Income is generated from productive activities. It means that before assuring development we need to assure growth. Higher economic development requires higher economic growth. But it does not mean that a higher economic growth automatically brings in higher economic development – a confusion the early economists failed to clarify. We may cite an example here to understand the confusion: two families having the same level of income, but spending differing amounts of money on developmental aspects. One might be giving little attention to health, education and going for saving, and the other might not be saving but taking possible care of the issues of health and education. Here, the latter necessarily will have higher development in comparison to the former. Thus, we may have some diverse cases of growth and development:

- Higher growth and higher development
- Higher growth but lower development
- Lower growth but higher development

The above-mentioned combinations, though comparative in nature, make one thing clear that just as for higher income and growth we need conscious efforts, and the same is true about economic development and higher economic development.

Without a conscious public policy, development has not been possible anywhere in the world. Similarly, we can say that without growth, there cannot be development either.

The first such instance of growth without development, which the economists saw, was in the Gulf countries. In these economies, though they had far higher levels of income and growth, the levels of development were not of comparable levels. Here started the branch of economics which came to be known as *development economics*. After the arrival of the World Bank (WB) and International Monetary Fund (IMF), conscious economic policies were framed and prescribed for the growth and development of less developed economies.

We can say that economic development is a quantitative as well as qualitative progress in an economy.[3] It means, when we use the term 'growth', we mean quantitative progress and when we use the term 'development', we mean quantitative as well as qualitative progress. If economic growth is suitably used for development, it comes back to accelerate the growth and ultimately greater population is brought under the arena of development. Similarly, high growth with low development and ill-cared development finally results in fall in growth. Thus, there is a circular relationship between growth and development. This circular relationship broke down when the Great Depression occurred. Once the concept of the *welfare state* was established, development became a matter of high concern for the governments of the world, policymakers and economists alike. A whole new branch of economics, 'welfare economics', has its origin in the concept of welfare state and the immediacy of development.

drinking water, literacy and education, social security, peaceful community life, availability of social prestige, entertainment and pollution-free environment. It has been a really difficult task to achieve consensus among the experts on these determinants of development.

2. At the second level it looked highly difficult to quantify a concept as development constitutes quantitative as well as qualitative aspects. It is easy to compare qualitative aspects such as beauty and taste, but we do not have any measuring scale to measure them.

Human Development Index

The dilemma of measuring the developmental level of economies was solved once the United Nations Development Programme (UNDP) published its first Human Development Report (HDR) in 1990. The report had a Human Development Index (HDI) which was the first attempt to define and measure the level of development of economies. The 'index' was a product of a select team of leading scholars, development

[3] World Bank, *World Development Report 1991* (New York, NY: Oxford University Press, 1991), p. 4.

practitioners and members of the HDR office of the UNDP. The first such team which developed the HDI was led by **Mahbub ul Haq** and **Inge Kaul**. The term 'human development' is a corollary of 'development' in the index.

The HDR measures development by combining three indicators - *health, education* and *standard of living* - converted into a composite HDI. The creation of a single statistic in HDI was a real breakthrough which was to serve as a frame of reference for both 'social' and 'economic' development. The HDI sets a minimum and a maximum for each dimension, called *goalposts*, and then shows where each country stands in relation to these goalposts, expressed as a value between 0 and 1 (i.e., the index is prepared on the *scale of one*). The *three* indicators[4] used to develop the composite index are as given below:

The **Education** component of the HDI is now (since HDR-2010) measured by two other indicators:

1. **Mean of years of schooling (for adults aged 25 years):** This is estimated based on educational attainment data from censuses and surveys available in the UNESCO Institute for Statistics database and *Barro and Lee* (2010) methodology.
2. **Expected years of schooling (for children of school entering age):** These estimates are based on enrolment by age at all levels of education and population of official school age for each level of education. Expected years of schooling are capped at 18 years.

These indicators are normalised using a minimum value of zero, and maximum values are set to the actual observed maximum value of mean years of schooling from the countries in the time series, 1980-2012, that is 13.3 years estimated for the United States in 2010. The *education index* is the arithmetic mean of these two indices.

The **health** component is measured by the *life expectancy* at birth component of the HDI, and is calculated using a minimum value of 20 years and maximum value of 83.57 years. This is the observed maximum value of the indicators from the countries in the time series, 1980-2012. Thus, the longevity component for a country where life expectancy at birth is 55 years would be 0.551.

The **standard of living** component is measured by *GNI* (Gross National Income/Product) per capita at 'Purchasing Power Parity in US Dollars' (PPP $) instead of GDP per capita (PPP $) of past. The *goalpost* taken for minimum income is $100 (PPP) and the maximum is US $87,478 (PPP), estimated for Qatar in 2012. The HDI uses the logarithm of income, to reflect the diminishing importance of income with increasing GNI.

The scores for the three HDI dimension indices are then aggregated into a composite index using geometric mean. The HDI facilitates instructive comparisons of the experiences within and between different countries.

The UNDP ranked[5] the economies in accordance with their achievements on the above given three parameters on the scale of one (i.e., 0.000-1.000). As per their achievements, the countries are today classified into the following *four categories* (till 2022 there were only three such broad groups) with differing ranges of their points on the index:

1. Very High Human Development Countries: 0.800 or greater points on the index.
2. High Human Development Countries: 0.700-0.799 points on the index.
3. Medium Human Development Countries: 0.550-0.699 points on the index.
4. Low Human Development Countries: below 0.550 points on the index.

The ***latest*** Human Development Report is covered in ***Chapter 21*** of the book.

The Debate Continues

Though the UNDP commissioned team had evolved a consensus as to what constitutes development, academicians and experts around the world have been debating this issue. By 1995, economies around the world had officially accepted the concept of human development propounded by the UNDP. Basically, the UNDP designed HDR was used by the WB since the 1990s to quantify the developmental efforts of the member countries and cheap developmental funds were allocated in accordance. Naturally, the member countries started emphasising on the parameters of income, education and life expectancy

[4] United Nations Development Programme (UNDP), *Human Development Report, 2013* and *Human Development Report, 2010* (New York, NY: UNDP, 2013 and 2010).

[5] Todaro and Smith, *Economic Development*, p. 58.

in their policymaking, and in this way the idea of HDI got obligatory or voluntary acceptance around the world.

For many years, experts and scholars came up with their own versions of defining development. They gave unequal weightage to the determinants defining development, as well as selected some completely different parameters which could also denote development in a more suitable way. Since quality is a matter of value judgement and a normative concept, there was scope for this representation. Most of such attempts were not prescriptions for an alternative development index, but they were basically trying to show the incompleteness of the HDI, *via* intellectual satires. One such attempt was made by economists and scholars of the London School of Economics in 1999, which concluded that Bangladesh was the most developed country in the world with the United States, Norway and Sweden getting the lowest ranks in the index.

Basically, it is very much possible to come out with such an index. As for example, we may say that peace of mind is a necessary element of development and betterment in human life which depends heavily on the fact as to how much sleep we get every day. House theft and burglary are major determinants of a good night's sleep which in turn depends on the fact as how assured we go to sleep in our homes at night from burglars and thieves. It means we may try to know a good sleep by the data of thefts and burglaries in homes. Since minor house thefts and burglaries are underreported in police stations, the surveyor supposedly tried to know such cases with data as to how many 'locks' were sold in a country in a particular year. In this way a country where people hardly have anything to be stolen or no risk of being burgled might be considered having the best sleep at night, and thus the best peace of mind, and that is why this will be the most developed country.

Basically, the HDI could be considered as one possible way of measuring development which was evolved by the group of experts concerned with the maximum degree of consensus. But the index which calculates the development of economies on certain parameters might be overlooking many other important factors, which affect the development of an economy and standard of living. As per experts, such other determinants affecting our living conditions might be:

- cultural aspects of the economy,
- outlook towards aesthetics and purity of the environment,
- aspects related to the rule and administration in the economy,
- people's idea of happiness and prestige,
- ethical dimension of human life.

Introspecting Development

Deeper introspection about the real meaning of development started only after the WB and the IMF came into being. As experts were studying the development process of the developing world, they were also surveying the performance reports of the developed world. As the western world came to be regarded as developed, having top 20 ranks on the HDI, social scientists started evaluating the conditions of life in these economies. Most of such studies concluded that life in the developed world is anything but happy. Crime, corruption, burglaries, extortion, drug trafficking, flesh trade, rape, homicide, moral degradation, sexual perversion and so forth - all kinds of the so-called vices were thriving in the developed world. It means development had failed to deliver them happiness, peace of mind, a general well-being and a feeling of being in good state. Scholars started questioning the very efforts being made for development around the world. Most of them have suggested a need of redefining development which could deliver happiness to humankind.

Why has development not delivered happiness to the developed world? The answer to this question does not lie in any one objective fact, but touches so many areas of human life. First, whenever economists from the outset talked about progress, they meant overall happiness of human life. Social scientists somehow have been using terms such as progress, growth, development, well-being and welfare as synonyms of 'happiness'. Happiness is a normative concept as well as a state of mind. Therefore, its idea might vary from one economy to the other.[6]

[6] There were diverse opinions about the real meaning of 'development' - since the mid-1940s up to almost the whole 1950s it meant 5-7 per cent growth rate in an economy, even by the IMF and WB. By the late 1960s new views of development started emerging. A. Lewis had seen development in the sense of *human freedom* in 1963 itself when he concluded that 'the advantage of economic growth is not that wealth increases happiness, but that it increases the range of human choice'. For him development means a freedom from 'servitude' - humankind could be free to have choices to lead a life full of material goods or in spiritual

Second, in the period in which development was defined, it was considered that with the supply of some selected material resources for humans, their life can be improved. These resources were pinpointed as better level of income, proper level of nutrition, healthcare facilities, and proper levels of literacy and education.

Happiness is a broader thing than development. The so-called 'development' for which the world has been striving hard for the last many decades is capable of delivering material happiness to mankind. Happiness has its non-material side too. It means, while the world has been trying to maximise its prospects of development, i.e., material happiness, it could not attend the non-material part of happiness. The non-material part of our life is rooted in ethics, religion, spiritualism and cultural values. As development or human development was defined on material terms, it could only deliver us material happiness which is visibly available in the developed world. Due to partial definition of development, the developed world has been able to achieve development, i.e., happiness, but only of the material kind. For the non-material part of happiness, we need to redefine our 'ideas' of development.

Somehow a very small kingdom had been able to define development in its own way, which included material as well as non-material aspects of life and named it the Gross National Happiness (GNH). This country is Bhutan.

Gross National Happiness

Bhutan, a small Himalayan kingdom and an economic non-entity, developed a new concept of assessing development in the early 1970s - the Gross National Happiness (GNH). Without rejecting the idea of human development propounded by the UNDP, the kingdom has been officially following the targets set by the GNH. Bhutan has been following the GNH since 1972 which has the following parameters to attain happiness/development:

- Higher real per capita income
- Good governance
- Environmental protection
- Cultural promotion (i.e., inculcation of *ethical* and *spiritual* values in life without which, it says, progress may become a curse rather than a blessing)

At the level of real per capita income, the GNH and the HDI are the same. Though the HDI is silent on the issue of 'good governance', today it should be considered as being promoted around the world once the WB came with its report on it in 1996 and enforced it upon the member states. On the issue of protecting environment, though the HDI did not say

---

contemplation [W. Arthur Lewis, *The Theory of Economic Growth* (London: Allen & Unwin, 1963), p. 420].

For D. Seers 'development' meant more employment and equality besides a falling poverty ('The Meaning of Development', a paper presented at the 11th World Conference of the Society for International Development, New Delhi, 1969, p. 3). Dudley Seers was later supported by many other economists such as D. Goulet [*The Cruel Choice: A New Concept in the Theory of Development* (New York, NY: Atheneum, 1971), p. 23], R. Brinkman (1995), P. Jegadish Gandhi (1996) and many others.

The International Labour Organization (ILO) had also articulated by the mid-1970s that economic development must be able to deliver the economic ability that people can meet their basic needs (the concept of 'sustenance') besides the elimination of absolute poverty, creating more employment and lessening income inequalities [*Employment, Growth and Basic Needs* (Geneva: ILO), 1976]. A. Sen articulated a similar view *via* his ideas of 'capabilities' and 'entitlements' ('Development: Which Way Now?', *Economic Journal* 93, December 1983, pp. 754-57).

By 1994, the United Nations looked at including the element of 'capabilities' in its idea of development when it concluded that 'human beings are born with certain potential capabilities and the purpose of development is to create an environment in which all people can expand their capabilities in present times and in future. Wealth is important for human life. But to concentrate exclusively on it is wrong for two reasons. First, accumulating wealth is not necessary for the fulfillment of some important human choices.... Second, human choices extend far beyond economic well-being.' [UNDP, *Human Development Report 1994* (New York, NY: Oxford University Press, 1994), pp. 13-15].

The World Bank by 1991 had also changed its views about development and had concluded that for improving the *quality of life* we should include education, health, nutrition, less poverty, cleaner environment, equality, greater freedom and richer cultural life as the goals of development.

A. Sen, a leading thinker on the meaning of development, attracted attention for articulating human goals of development. He opined that enhancing the lives and the freedoms we enjoy should be the concerns of development known as the 'capabilities' approach to development (see his *Commodities and Capabilities*, North Holland, Amsterdam, 1985 and *Development as Freedom*, Alfred Knopf, New York, NY, 1999).

anything directly, the WB and the UNO had already accepted the immediacy of sustainable development by then (in 1987), and by the early 1990s there was a separate UN Convention on the matter (follow-up on this convention has been really low till date, which is a different issue altogether).

It means the basic difference between the GNH and the HDI looks at the level of assimilating the ethical and spiritual aspects into our (UNDP's) idea of development.

An impartial analysis sufficiently suggests that material achievements are unable to deliver us happiness devoid of some ethics at its base. And ethics is rooted in the religious and spiritual texts. But the new world is guided by its own scientific and secular interpretation of life, and the world has always been suspicious about recognising the spiritual factor in human life. Rather, the western idea of secularism was defined after rejecting the very existence of anything like God and also rejecting the whole traditional hypothesis of spiritualism as instances of ignorance and orthodoxy. And there should not be any doubt in accepting it that the western ideology in the name of development has, ultimately, dominated the modern world and its way of life. The idea of development which was followed by a large part of the world has been cent per cent 'this-worldly'. And anybody can assess today what kind of happiness the world has been able to achieve in the end.

An important study by a senior economist from the UNDP on the Bhutanese development experience under the GNH vindicated the idea of 'gross happiness' which development must result in. As per the study, the period 1984-98 had been spectacular in terms of development with life expectancy increasing by a whopping 19 years, gross school enrolment reaching 72 per cent and literacy touching 47.5 per cent (from just 17 per cent).[7]

After the terror attack on the World Trade Centre in the United States, the whole world has gone through a psychic metamorphosis, and at the very least, the euphoria of development from this world to that world has been shaken from its very base. The world, which is in the process of globalisation, has started introspecting whether multicultural co-existence is possible. The HDR of 2004 was titled as *Cultural Liberty in Today's Diverse World.* We may conclude that mankind is passing through a phase of serious introspection and transition where the dominant view in the world may metamorphose into redefining the very idea of development by including ethical values and spiritualism as important parts. But till now the proponents of development look a bit shy in believing and accepting whole-heartedly that there exists a non-material part of life too, which needs to be realised to make our development result in happiness.

[7] S. Priesner, a senior economist with the UNDP, conducted the study for the John Hopkins University, USA, in 2005.

HAPPINESS

The word 'happiness' is quite complex and is not used lightly. Happiness is an aspiration of every human being, and can also be a measure of social progress. Yet, are the citizens of different countries happy? If they are not, what, if anything, can be done about it? Its proper measurement must begin with the meaning of the word 'happiness'. As per the World Happiness Report (WHR) 2013, the problem, of course, is that happiness is used in at least **two** ways:

1. As an emotion ['Were you happy yesterday?'] and
2. As an evaluation ['Are you happy with your life as a whole?'].

If individuals were to routinely mix up their responses to these very different questions, then measures of happiness might tell us very little. Changes in reported happiness used to track social progress would perhaps reflect little more than transient changes in emotion. Or impoverished persons who express happiness in terms of emotion might inadvertently diminish society's will to fight poverty. Fortunately, respondents to the happiness surveys do not tend to make such confusing mistakes. Both the WHRs of 2012 and 2013 did show that the respondents of the surveys clearly recognise the difference between *happiness as an emotion* and *happiness in the sense of life satisfaction.* The responses of individuals to these different questions are highly distinct. A very poor person might report himself to be happy emotionally at a specific time, while also reporting a much lower sense of happiness with life as a whole; and indeed, people living in extreme poverty do express low levels of happiness with life as a whole. Such answers should spur our societies to work harder to end extreme poverty.

The *WHR* is based on the primary measures of subjective well-being,[8] life evaluations,[9] life satisfaction[10] and happiness with life as a whole.[11] Thus, happiness appears twice, once as an emotional report and once as part of a life evaluation, giving considerable evidence about the nature and causes of happiness in both its major senses.

The Background

In July 2011 the UN General Assembly passed a historic resolution.[12] It invited member countries to measure the happiness of their people and to use this to help guide their public policies. This was followed in April 2012 by the **first** UN high-level meeting on happiness and well-being, chaired by the Prime Minister of Bhutan. At the same time the **first** *World Happiness Report* was published,[13] followed by, some months later the OECD Guidelines setting an international standard for the measurement of well-being.[14]

RE-IMAGINING THE IDEA OF HAPPINESS

Search for a 'happier' life has been the ultimate aim of not only saints, seers and philosophers, but of economists too. The whole gamut of economic literature on progress, growth and development is ultimately aimed at bringing more 'happiness' into the lives of human beings. Over time, diverse ideological currents impressed upon humanity to take a variety of 'meanings' out of the highly subjective term 'happiness' and finally, humanity is where it is today.

There was also a time when many scholars and world leaders raised the ultimate question, 'are we happier today'? And in the wake of this increased 'scrutiny' around the world, there came the UN resolution of 2011 which invited member countries to measure the

What is Happiness?

The World Happiness Report of the UNO captures/defines happiness in terms of the following *six variables:*

1. GDP per capita (at purchasing power parity)
2. Social support (someone to count on)
3. Healthy life expectancy at birth
4. Freedom to make life choices
5. Generosity
6. Perception of corruption

   Other than the six data sets mentioned above, citizens' opinions (through surveys) are also taken on the following *three subjective* indicators:

   (i) *Life evaluations:* Citizens situate their lives on a ladder from 0 at the bottom to 10 at the top (representing the worst and the best possible life, respectively).

   (ii) *Positive emotions:* Citizens' feeling of 'happiness, laughter and enjoyment' (on the day and the day before the survey).

   (iii) *Negative emotions:* Citizens' experience of 'worry, sadness, and anger' (on the day and the day before the survey).

Officially, the happiness report aims to serve two purposes—firstly, to measure global happiness and secondly, as a guide to public policy of the member nations.

---

[8] Guidelines on *Measuring Subjective Well-being,* OECD, Paris, 2013.

[9] Used in the *World Values Survey, the European Social Survey* and many other national and international surveys. It is the core 'life evaluation' question recommended by the OECD (2013), and used since the first *World Happiness Report.*

[10] The *Gallup World Poll (GWP)* includes the 'life satisfaction' question on a 0 to 10 scale on an experimental basis, giving a sufficiently large sample to show that when used with consistent samples the two questions provide mutually supportive information on the size and relative importance of the correlates.

[11] The *European Social Survey* contains questions about 'happiness with life as a whole' and about life satisfaction, both on the same 0 to 10 numerical scale. The responses provide the scientific base to support the WHR findings that answers to the two questions give consistent (and mutually supportive) information about the correlates of a good life.

[12] UN General Assembly, *Happiness: Towards a Holistic Approach to Development* (United Nations, 19 July 2011).

[13] J.F. Helliwell, R. Layard, and J. Sachs (eds.), *World Happiness Report 2012* (New York, NY: Earth Institute, 2012).

[14] *OECD Guidelines on Measuring Subjective Well-being* (Paris: Organisation for Economic Co-operation and Development, 2013).

happiness of their people and to use this to help guide their public policies. The *WHR 2012* itself provides a very interesting and eye-opening enquiry into the state of human happiness in the world. To understand the 'shift' which is expected to take place among policymakers around the world in the coming years, it will be better to ***lift some ideas*** from the **first** WHR:[15]

1. This is an age of stark contradictions. While on the one hand the world enjoys technologies of unimaginable sophistication, on the other hand, at least one billion people are living without enough to eat. The world economy is propelled to soaring new heights of productivity through ongoing technological and organisational advances, yet it is relentlessly destroying the natural environment in the process. Countries achieve great progress in economic development as conventionally measured, yet along the way countries succumb to new crises of obesity, smoking, diabetes, depression and other ills of modern life. These contradictions would not come as a shock to the greatest sages of humanity, including **Aristotle** and the **Buddha** who taught humanity, time and again, that material gain alone will not fulfil our deepest needs. Material life must be harnessed to meet these human needs, most importantly to promote the end of suffering, social justice and the attainment of happiness.
2. The *WHR 2012* took key examples from the United States - the world's economic superpower - which has achieved striking economic and technological progress over the past half century without gains in the self-reported happiness of the citizenry with the following serious 'concerns' of today:
   (i) uncertainties and anxieties are high,
   (ii) social and economic inequalities have widened considerably,
   (iii) social trust is in decline and
   (iv) confidence in government is at an all-time low.

   Perhaps for these reasons, life satisfaction in the United States has remained nearly constant during the decades of rising Gross National Product (GNP) per capita.
3. The realities of poverty, anxiety, environmental degradation and unhappiness in the midst of great plenty should not be regarded as mere curiosities. They require our urgent attention, and especially so at this juncture in human history. For we have entered a new phase of the world, termed the *Anthropocene*[16] by the world's Earth System scientists. The Anthropocene will necessarily reshape our societies. If we continue mindlessly along the current economic trajectory, we risk undermining the Earth's life support systems - food supplies, clean water and stable climate - necessary for human health and even survival in some places. In years or decades, conditions of life may become dire in several fragile regions of the world. We are already experiencing deterioration of life support systems in the dry lands of the Horn of Africa and parts of Central Asia.

   On the other hand, if we act wisely, we can protect the Earth while raising the quality of life broadly around the world. We can do this by adopting *lifestyles* and *technologies* that improve **happiness** (or life satisfaction) and reduce human damage to the environment. Sustainable Development is the term given to the combination of human well-being, social inclusion and environmental sustainability. There is no doubt in concluding that the 'quest for happiness' is intimately linked to the 'quest for sustainable development'.
4. In an impoverished society, the urge for material gain typically makes a lot of sense. Higher household income (or higher per capita GNP) generally signifies an improvement in the life conditions of the poor. The poor suffer from dire deprivations of various kinds: lack of adequate food supplies, remunerative jobs, access to health care, safe homes, safe water and sanitation, and educational opportunities. As incomes rise from very low levels, human

---

[15] J.F. Helliwell, R. Layard, and J. Sachs (eds.), *World Happiness Report 2012* (New York, NY: Earth Institute, 2012).

[16] Anthropocene is a newly invented term that combines two Greek words: 'anthropo' for human and 'cene' for new, as in a new geological epoch. Anthropocene is the new epoch in which humanity, through its technological prowess and population of 8 billion, has become the major driver of changes of Earth's physical systems, including the climate, carbon cycle, water cycle, nitrogen cycle and biodiversity.

well-being improves. Not surprisingly, the poor report a rising satisfaction with their lives as their meager incomes increase.

On the opposite end of the income spectrum, for most individuals in the high-income world, the basic deprivations have been vanquished. There is enough food, shelter, basic amenities (such as clean water and sanitation) and clothing to meet their daily needs. In fact, there is a huge surfeit of amenities above basic needs. Poor people would swap with rich people in a heartbeat. Yet all is not well. *The conditions of affluence have created their own set of traps*.

Most importantly, the lifestyles of the rich imperil the survival of the poor. Human-induced climate change is already hitting the poorest regions and claiming lives and livelihoods. It is telling that in much of the rich world, affluent populations are so separated from the poor that there is little recognition, practical or moral, of the adverse spillovers (or 'externalities') from their own behaviour.

5. **Affluence** has also created its own set of afflictions and addictions (problems) - obesity, adult-onset of diabetes, tobacco-related illnesses, eating disorders such as anorexia and bulimia, psychosocial disorders, and addictions to shopping, TV and gambling, are all examples of disorders of development. So too is the loss of community, the decline of social trust and the rising anxiety levels associated with the vagaries of the modern globalised economy, including the threats of unemployment or episodes of illness not covered by health insurance in the United States (and many other countries).

6. Higher average incomes do not necessarily improve average well-being, the United States being a clear case in point, as noted famously by Professor Richard Easterlin[17] - where GNP per capita has risen by a factor of three since 1960, while measures of average happiness have remained essentially unchanged over the half-century. The increased US output has caused massive environmental damages, notably through greenhouse gas concentrations and human-induced climate change, without doing much at all to raise the well-being even of Americans. Thus, we do not have a trade-off between short-run gains to well-being versus long-run costs to the environment; we have a pure loss to the environment without offsetting short-term gains.

   The ***paradox*** that Easterlin noted in the United States was that at any particular time richer individuals are happier than poorer ones, but over time the society did not become happier as it became richer. This is due to four reasons:

   (i) Individuals compare themselves to others. They are happier when they are higher on the social (or income) ladder. Yet when everybody rises together, relative status remains unchanged.

   (ii) The gains have not been evenly shared, but have gone disproportionately to those at the top of the income and education distribution.

   (iii) The other societal factors - insecurity, loss of social trust, declining confidence in government - have counteracted any benefits felt from higher incomes.

   (iv) Individuals may experience an initial jump in happiness when their income rises, but then at least partly return to earlier levels as they *adapt* to their new higher income.

7. These phenomena put a clear limit on the extent to which rich countries can become happier through the simple device of *economic growth*. In fact, there are still other general reasons to doubt the formula of ever rising GNP per person as the route to happiness. While higher income may raise happiness to some extent, the *quest* for higher income may actually reduce one's happiness. In other words, it may be nice to have more money, but not so nice to crave for it. **Psychologists** have found repeatedly that individuals who put a high premium on higher incomes generally are less happy and more vulnerable to other psychological ills than

[17] Among the foremost contributors to the *Happiness Economics*, Easterlin is particularly known for his 1974 article 'Does Economic Growth Improve the Human Lot? Some Empirical Evidence' (his ideas today known as the *Easterlin Paradox* was proposed by him in this article). Here he concluded that contrary to expectation, happiness at a national level does not increase with wealth once basic needs are fulfilled.

Word Bank

Easterlin Paradox

Easterlin Paradox is named after the economist Richard Easterlin (1926–2024) who is generally considered as the father of happiness economics. He summed up (in his essay of 1974) that 'in short-run (till basic needs are not fulfilled) happiness varies with income but in the long-run (once the basic needs have been met) that does not happen.' His findings were based on empirical data collected from the lives of the US citizens. Many experts criticised the idea supported by empirical evidences many of which were counted by Easterlin himself.

Scan this QR Code to watch a author's video lecture that simplifies this topic

We find such a paradox confirmed in the case of the USA by the first World Happiness Report 2012 (which has a special chapter on the country). As per the report, in the *last five decades while the country has achieved striking economic progress, self-reported happiness saw no gains*. It further highlights some serious concerns about the lives of the US citizens—high anxieties and uncertainties, widening socio-economic inequality, declining social trust and all-time low confidence in the government (perhaps for these reasons, life satisfaction in the United States has remained nearly constant during the decades of rising per capita Gross National Product, according to it).

individuals who do not crave higher incomes. Aristotle and the Buddha advised humanity to follow a middle path between asceticism on the one side and craving material goods on the other.

8. Another problem is the creation of new material '**wants**' through the incessant advertising of products using powerful imagery and other means of persuasion. Since the imagery is ubiquitous on all of our digital devices, the stream of advertising is more relentless than ever before. Advertising is now a business of around US $500 billion per year. Its goal is to overcome satiety by creating wants and longings where none previously existed. Advertisers and marketers do this in part by preying on psychological weaknesses and unconscious urges. Cigarettes, caffeine, sugar and trans-fats all cause cravings if not outright addictions. Fashions are sold through increasingly explicit sexual imagery. Product lines are generally sold by associating the products with high social status rather than with real needs.

9. The thought of becoming happier by becoming richer is challenged by the law of *diminishing marginal utility of income*[18] - after a certain point, the gains are very small. This means that poor people benefit far more than rich people from an added dollar of income. This is a good reason why tax-and-transfer systems among high-income OECD countries on balance take in net revenues from high-income households and make net transfers to low-income households. Put in another way, the inequality of household income is systematically lower with net of taxes and transfers than before taxes and transfers.[19]

10. The western economist's logic of ever higher GNP is built on a vision of humanity completely at variance with the wisdom of the sages, the research of psychologists and the practices of advertisers. Economists assume that individuals are '**rational decision-makers**' who know what they want and how to get it, or to get as close to it as possible, given their budget. Individuals care largely about themselves and derive pleasure mainly through their consumption. The individual's preferences as consumers are a given or change in ways actually anticipated in advance by the individuals themselves. Some economists even say that drug addicts have acted 'rationally',

[18] Suppose that a poor household at ₹1,000 income requires an extra ₹100 to raise its life satisfaction level (or happiness) by one notch. A rich household at ₹1,000,000 income (one thousand times as much as the poor household) would need one thousand times more money, or 100,000, to raise its well-being by the same one notch. Gains in income have to be of equal proportions to household income to have the same benefit in units of life satisfaction.

[19] On an average across the OECD countries, cash transfers and income taxes reduce inequality by one-third. Poverty is around 60 per cent lower than it would be without taxes and benefits. Even among the working-age population, government redistribution reduces poverty by about 50 per cent *(OECD, 2008)*.

consciously trading off the early benefits of drug use with the later high toll of addiction.

11. We understand that we need a very different model of humanity, one in which we experienced complicated interplay of emotions and rational thought, unconscious and conscious decision-making, **fast** and **slow** thinking. Many of our decisions are led by emotions and instincts, and only later rationalised by conscious thought. Our decisions are easily 'primed' by associations, imagery, social context and advertising. We are inconsistent or 'irrational' in sequential choices, failing to meet basic standards of rational consistency. And we are largely unaware of our own mental apparatus, so we easily fall into *traps* and *mistakes*. Addicts do not anticipate their future pain; we spend now and suffer the consequences of bankruptcy later; we break our diets now because we aren't thinking clearly about the consequences. We also understand (again!) that we are **social animals** through and through. We learn through imitation, and gain our happiness through meeting *social norms* and having a sense of *belonging to the community*.

12. Human beings feel the pain of others, and react viscerally when others are sad or injured. We even have a set of 'mirror neurons' that enable us to feel things from the point of view of others. All of this gives us a remarkable capacity to cooperate even with strangers, and even when there is little chance of reward or reciprocity, and to punish 'non-cooperators', even when imposing punishment on others is costly or puts us at risk.

Of course, there are limits to such cooperation and fellow feeling. We also cheat, bluff, deceive, break our word and kill members of an out-group. We engage in identity politics, acting as cruel to outsiders as we are loving to our own group. All these lessons of human nature matter more than ever, more even than when the Buddha taught humanity about the illusions of transient pleasures, and the Greeks warned us against the tempting siren songs that could pull us off our life's course. For today we have more choices than ever before. In the ancient world, the choice facing most of humanity most of the time was little – to work hard to secure enough to eat, and even then to face the risk of famine and death from bad weather or bad luck.

13. Today, we face a set of real choices. Should the world pursue GNP to the point of environmental ruin, even when incremental gains in GNP are not increasing much (or at all) the happiness of affluent societies? Should we crave for higher personal income at the cost of the community and social trust? Should our governments spend even a tiny fraction of the $500 billion spent on advertising each year to help individuals and families to understand better their own motivations, wants and needs as consumers? Should we consider some parts of our society to be 'off bounds' to the profit motive so that we can foster the **spirit of cooperation, trust** and **community**? An analyst[20] of Finland's school system, for example, writes that Finland's excellence (ranking near the top of international comparisons in student performance) has been achieved by fostering a spirit of community and equality in the schools. This is in **sharp contrast** to the education reform strategy at work in the United States, where the emphasis is to put on *testing, measurement* and *teacher pay* according to student test performance.

INSIGHTS INTO HUMAN BEHAVIOUR

The WB in its report (*World Development Report 2015: Mind, Society, and Behaviour*) said that development policies become more effective when combined with insights into human behaviour. It further adds that policy decisions informed by **behavioural economics** can deliver impressive improvements in promoting development and well-being in society. It provides some examples from **India** in the areas of healthcare and education:

- Open defecation dropped 11 per cent from very high levels after a Community-Led Total Sanitation (CLTS) programme was combined in some chosen villages with the standard approach of subsidies for toilet construction and information on the transmission of diseases.
- The likelihood of default on loans became three times less with a simple change in the periodicity of meetings between microfinance clients and their repayment groups to weekly rather than monthly.
- Research showed that boys from backward classes were just as good at solving puzzles as boys from the

[20] 20 P. Sahlberg, 'Education Policies for Raising Student Learning: The Finnish Approach', *Journal of Education Policy* 22 (2) (March 2007), pp. 147–71.

upper castes when caste identity was not revealed. However, in mixed-caste groups, revealing the boys' castes before puzzle-solving sessions created a significant 'caste gap' in achievement with the boys from backward classes under-performing by 23 per cent (making caste salient to the test takers invoked identities, which in turn affected performance, as per the report).

The *Report* has recommended that the presence of a stereotype can contribute to measured ability differences, which in turn reinforce the stereotype and serve as a basis for exclusion, in a vicious cycle - finding ways to break this cycle could increase the well-being of marginalised individuals enormously.

Social Norms, Culture and Development

Economic development is not only dependent on fiscal policy, monetary policy and taxation, but is also rooted in human psychology, sociology, culture and norms. In economics, there has been a bit of resistance in emphasising other aspects of development because it is thought of giving ground to the neighbouring disciplines.[21] The *WDR* of 2015 focuses on the behavioural and social foundations of development, and has been very well received.

Government documents (generally, hard-nosed), usually, make no mention of the role of social norms and culture in promoting development and economic efficiency. However, there is now a growing body of literature that demonstrates how certain social norms and cultural practices are vital ingredients for economic efficiency and growth. Groups and societies that are known to be honest and trustworthy tend to do better than societies that do not have this reputation. There have been broad cross-country studies and also laboratory experiments that illustrate this. More generally, what is being argued is that a nation's success depends of course on its resources, human capital and economic policies, for instance fiscal and monetary policies, but also on the cultural and social norms that permeate the society. Societies that are endowed with personal integrity and trustworthiness have the natural advantage, in that no third party is required to enforce contracts. For outsiders the mere knowledge that a particular society is trustworthy is reason to do more business and trade with it. One reason why these 'social' causes of development do not get enough recognition in the literature on economic policy is that the science of *how* these economics-friendly social qualities are acquired is not yet fully understood. Fortunately, the new discipline of **behavioural economics** is beginning to give us some insights into the formation of customs and behaviour:[22]

- It is, for instance, known that buildings and office spaces which are cleaner and aesthetically better maintained result in individuals being more honest and desisting corrupt activity. It is almost as if we have a mental inclination not to defile a good ambience through acts of corruption.
- New York City's notorious high crime was controlled, among other things, by cleaning up the city and removing graffiti from the walls. New York's police department took a decision to deter vandalism and graffiti that scar public spaces. This act of making the cityscape more aesthetic somehow made potential criminals less prone to crime.
- One sees casual evidence of this in the behaviour of Delhites using the metro. It has been widely noted that people behave better when they travel on Delhi's well-maintained metro (postponing their bad behaviour to when they come up to the surface again, some would add).

All this is in keeping with the influential *broken windows* theory in sociology, which maintains that, if we control low-level, anti-social behaviour and take small steps to improve the environment, this will have a natural deterrent effect on larger criminal behaviour and acts of corruption. Also, the sheer recognition and awareness that some collective qualities of citizens, such as honesty and trustworthiness, enable the entire society to do well, prompts individuals to adopt those qualities and overcome the ubiquitous free-rider problem.

There is a growing literature[23] in economics arguing that **pro-social behaviour**, which includes *altruism* and *trustworthiness*, is innate to human beings and, moreover, forms an essential ingredient for the efficient functioning of economies. In other words, human beings have a natural ability to forego personal gains for the sake of other people or because that is what is required because of a promise the person had made. This trait may well have evolutionary roots, but

[21] K. Basu, Chief Economist, World Bank, *Livemint*, New Delhi, February 3, 2015.

[22] *Economic Survey 2009-10* (New Delhi: Ministry of Finance, GoI), pp. 34-5.

[23] Over half a dozen contemporary works have been cited as references by the Ministry of Finance, *Economic Survey 2010-11*, GoI, New Delhi, p. 40.

its existence is now well demonstrated in laboratory tests by recent studies.

Values and Economics

There is research[24] in psychology and evolutionary biology which shows that **morality**, **altruism** and other regarding **values** are an innate part of the human mind, even though the social setting in which a person live can nurture or stunt these traits. However, the recognition that these human and moral qualities can have a large impact on economic development came relatively late to economics. Hence, the literature on this is relatively recent and brief. In fact, recent research shows that having a few 'good' human beings in society can give rise to dynamics through which we end up with an overall better society. There is also evidence that social norms and habits that at first sight seem ingrained in a society can change over short periods of time. By this argument it is possible for a country to nurture and develop the kinds of social norms that enable a more vibrant economy.

In talking about a nation's economic progress, all attention, including both praise and criticism, is usually focused on the government. It is, however, important to recognise that much also depends on civil society, the firms, the farmers and ordinary citizens. The social norms and collective beliefs that shape the behaviour of these agents play an important role in how a nation performs.

Honesty, punctuality, the propensity to keep promises, the attitude towards corruption are matters shaped in great part by norms and social beliefs and the behaviour patterns can become habitual. Moreover, in a democracy like India, what can be done by the government depends in great measure on how ordinary people think and what people believe in. That is what electoral politics is all about. An important reason why this got so little attention in the past is because so much of traditional economics was written as if these noneconomic facets of life did not matter. But we now know that a market economy cannot function if people are totally self-serving. While self-interest is a major driver of economic growth, it is important to recognise that honesty, integrity and trustworthiness constitute the cement that binds society. At times economists treated these social norms, preferences and customs as unalterable. If that were so, there would not be much point in analysing their effect. But we do know that these qualities in people can change. Honesty and integrity can be nurtured and aversion to corruption can be shored up.

NUDGE AND PUBLIC POLICY

Behavioural economics provides insights to **nudge**[25] people towards desirable behaviour. By now, nudge has been successfully used in India as an instrument

> **Happiness Economics**
>
> Happiness economics or economics of happiness is a new branch of economics which studies the quantitative and qualitative aspects of human life and tries to capture happiness (i.e., life satisfaction, quality of life, and well-being). It tries to study human well-being with the help of subjective measures (such as self-reported happiness, positive/negative emotions, etc.) more than objective measures (such as income, profit, wealth, etc.). This branch of economics is considered to bring economics closer to other social sciences such as sociology, psychology and physical sciences.
>
> Its origin is traced from the 'utilitarian approach' of the British philosopher *Jeremy Bentham* (1748–1832). To study happiness, economists normally use the term 'utility' of consuming something on total derived satisfaction. Richard Easterlin (1926–) is normally considered the *father* of happiness economics (first economist to study happiness through data).

---

[24] Several seminal literatures have been quoted by the *Economic Survey 2011-12*, Ministry of Finance, GoI, New Delhi, p. 44:

- **(i)** F. Fukuyama, *Trust: The Social Virtues and the Creation of Prosperity* (New York: NY, Free Press, 1996).
- **(ii)** A.S. Guha and B. Guha, 'The Persistence of Goodness', *Journal of Institutional and Theoretical Economics*, 2012.
- **(iii)** M.D. Hauser, *Moral Minds* (New York, NY: Harper Collins, 2012).
- **(iv)** T. Hashimoto, 'Japanese Clocks and the History of Punctuality in Modern Japan', *East Asian Science, Technology, and Society 2*, 2008.

[25] Nudge literally means to prod (someone) gently with one's elbow in order to attract attention. It is a concept of behavioural science which proposes *positive reinforcement* and *indirect suggestions* as ways to influence the behaviour of individuals or groups. Nudging contrasts with other ways to achieve compliance, such as education, legislation or enforcement – it is different from giving incentives or penalising. The concept of nudge was popularised by Richard Thaler and C.R. Sunstein in the book *Nudge:*

of public policy (in the *Swachh Bharat Mission* (SBM) and *Beti Bachao Beti Padhao* (BBBP) campaigns) and it can be further used to aim even higher goals[26] such as:

1. from BBBP to BADLAV (*Beti Aapki Dhan Lakshmi Aur Vijay Lakshmi*),
2. from *Swachh Bharat* to *Sundar Bharat*,
3. from 'Give it up'(for the LPG subsidy) to 'Think about the Subsidy' and
4. from tax evasion to tax compliance.

Nudges can be used in policymaking with effective outcomes by taking the following three policy actions:

1. People's behaviour is influenced by social and religious norms. Thus, beneficial norms can be used as positive influencers (friends and neighbours as role models) to modify people's behaviour.
2. As people have an inclination to go for 'default' option in their actions, changing the default can be a very effective policy.
3. Policy of reminders and repeated reinforcements help sustained change in behaviour as people find it difficult to sustain good habits.

Common people fail to connect to policy actions of the governments. For an effective use of nudges in public policy, it is essential to relate economics to common person[27] using something that he or she encounters every day, for example, *a plate of food*.

Improving Decisions about Health, Wealth, and Happiness, Yale University Press, New Haven, CT, 2008. Thaler was awarded Nobel Memorial Prize for Economic Science in 2017 in recognition to his contributions to Behavioural Economics.

[26] *Economic Survey 2018-19*, vol. 1, pp. 30-56, Ministry of Finance, GoI, New Delhi.

[27] *Thalinomics: The Economics of a Plate of Food in India*, Economic Survey 2019-20, vol. 1 (New Delhi: Ministry of Finance, GoI), pp. 260-85.

SAMPLE OBJECTIVE QUESTIONS

1. As per the recent World Happiness Reports, how many of the following dilute(s) the negative effects of crime, violence, corruption, inequality and poverty on human happiness? Select the correct code:

(i) Welfare schemes
(ii) Family warmth
(iii) Supportive social relationships

Code:

(a) Only (i) **(b)** Only (ii)
(c) All three **(d)** None of these

2. Which of the following is/are correct about India's idea of inclusive growth? Select the correct code from the choices given below:

(i) It is an economic as well as social concept.
(ii) It must include women and minorities.
(iii) The idea evolved under the influence of the World Bank.
(iv) Poverty alleviation is its integral part.

Code:

(a) Only (i) **(b)** Only (ii)
(c) Only (iii) **(d)** All four

3. As per behavioural economics, which of the following has/have been found to be correct in the case of human beings and society? Select your answer by using the code given below:

(i) Men are born selfish.
(ii) Men are born selfless and cooperative.
(iii) Social trust and healthy lives are the foundations of happiness.
(iv) Man's behaviour cannot be always rational.

Code:

(a) Only (i) **(b)** Only (ii)
(c) Only (iii) **(d)** All four

4. How many of the following statements(s) is/are correct about development economics? Select your answer by using the following code:

(i) Today, human capital is considered as tangible wealth.

(ii) Market-led resource allocation gave an edge due to which the market economies developed better than the non-market ones.

(iii) Genes have been found to play no role in human happiness.

(iv) Mental illness is the biggest single reason for misery in rich countries.

Code:

(a) Only (i) (b) Only (ii)
(c) Only (iii) (d) All four

5. Which of the following is/are correct about the concept 'invisible hand'? Select the answer using the code given below:

(i) This is the intrinsic human motivation to work for gains.

(ii) It cannot work in the absence of market forces.

(iii) It is also known as 'animal spirit'.

How many of the above statement(s) is/are correct?

(a) Only (i) (b) Only (ii)
(c) All three (d) None of these

6. Consider the following statements related to the economics of development:

(i) There were times when a certain level of per capita income was considered the trait of development.

(ii) Human development gives equal weightage to income, education and longevity.

(iii) Longevity finds a nuanced place in the United Nations' idea of happiness.

How many of the above statement(s) is/are correct?

(a) Only (i) (b) Only (ii)
(c) All three (d) None of these

7. Consider the following statements related to the UN's idea of happiness and its influence on India's economic policies:

(i) Idea of happiness is inspired by behavioural economics.

(ii) India has officially criticised the idea of happiness for having Western bias.

(iii) Transformative reforms in India are inspired by behavioural economics.

How many of the above statement(s) is/are correct?

(a) Only (i) (b) Only (ii)
(c) All three (d) None of these

8. Consider the following statements about economic policies:

(i) Distributive growth leads to social development.

(ii) Transfer payment is a time-tested tool of socio-economic welfare.

(iii) Inclusion of masses in growth is a marker of inclusive development.

How many of the above statement(s) is/are correct?

(a) Only (i) (b) Only (ii)
(c) All three (d) None of these

9. Consider the following statements related to the World Happiness Report 2024:

(i) Positive association between age and life satisfaction exists only in high-income nations.

(ii) Older women in India reported higher life satisfaction than older men.

(iii) Caste status plays a role in the life satisfaction of older people similar to the caste system.

How many of the above statements are correct?

(a) Only (i) (b) Only (ii)
(c) All three (d) None of these

10. How many of the following statement(s) is/are correct about the idea of development today? Use the code given below to select your answer:

(i) Development is all about making human life happier.

(ii) Happiness depends more on non-economic variables.

(iii) Income has been found to play a negligible role in human happiness.

(a) Only (i) (b) Only (ii)
(c) All three (d) None of these

Answers: 1. (b) 2. (d) 3. (c) 4. (b) 5. (c) 6. (c) 7. (b) 8. (c) 9. (a) 10. (b)

SAMPLE SUBJECTIVE QUESTIONS

1. 'Post-war period has seen a paradigm shift in human understanding of development.' Elucidate.
2. 'Happiness is a result of creating strong social foundations.' Explain.
3. 'Public policies need restructuring for promotion of holistic development.' Elucidate.
4. 'Over-emphasis on gross domestic product has increased human misery.' Analyse with the help of suitable illustrations.
5. Write a note on India's idea of inclusive growth and discuss the policy steps taken by the government to promote it.
6. Do you think India has used nudges in making more effective developmental policies? Explain with the help of suitable illustrations.

SAMPLE MODEL ANSWER

1. **'Use of nudge in making public policy can be highly effective in India.' Explain with the help of suitable illustrations.**

Ans. Behavioural economics provides insights into 'nudge' (which literally means to prod someone gently with one's elbow to attract attention) people towards desirable behaviour. By now, nudge has been successfully used in India as an instrument of public policy (in the Swachh Bharat Mission (SBM) and Beti Bachao Beti Padhao (BBBP) campaigns), and it can be further used to aim even higher goals such as:

- from BBBP to BADLAV (Beti Aapki Dhan Lakshmi Aur Vijay Lakshmi),
- from Swachh Bharat to Sundar Bharat,
- from 'Give it up' (for the LPG subsidy) to 'Think about the Subsidy', and
- from tax evasion to tax compliance.

Nudges can be used in policymaking with effective outcomes by taking the following three policy actions:

1. People's behaviour is influenced by social and religious norms. Thus, beneficial norms can be used as positive influencers (friends and neighbours as role models) to modify people's behaviour.
2. As people are inclined to go for the 'default' option in their actions, changing the default can be a very effective policy.
3. A policy of reminders and repeated reinforcements helps sustain change in behaviour, as people find it difficult to sustain good habits.

Common people fail to connect to policy actions of the governments. For an effective use of nudges in public policy, it is essential to relate economics to the common person using something that they encounter every day, for example, a 'plate of food' (as the Economic Survey 2019-20 did show).

CHAPTER 4

Evolution of the Indian Economy

After 1757, when the East India Company took over the governance of Bengal, the British relationship with India became exploitative, as exports to Britain and opium exports to China were financed out of the tax revenue from Bengal. There is not much evidence of significant transfer of European technology to Asia. To understand why, it is useful to scrutinise the experience of China and India, as they accounted for three-quarters of the Asian population and GDP in 1500 AD.

- A. Maddison

Growth and Interaction in the World Economy: The Roots of Modernity
(Washington, DC: The AEI Press, 2005), p. 60.

To watch the Author's videos on the significance of the Chapter, scan the QR Code given here

Exam Essentials...

- Trickle-down Theory
- Spillover Effect
- Multiplier Effect

Note to the Reader...

For better understanding of the Indian economics/ economy, readers are advised to read this chapter as the 'prequel' to the Chapter 10 of the book. While Chapter 4 deals with the 'foundational' economic policies, Chapter 10 deals with the 'non-foundational' ones – reading them in this order makes better sense in understanding the evolutionary way as how economic policies in India have evolved over the time. Direct questions in the civil services exams may be rarely asked from this chapter but the knowledge gained here should be considered by the readers as the "undercurrent" which will help them to crack the nuances and riddles of the contemporary developmental challenges of India.

In This Chapter...

THE BACKGROUND

The economic profile of India was in complete distress at the time of independence. Being a typical case of colonial economy, India was serving a purpose of development not for itself but for a foreign land - the United Kingdom. Both agriculture and industry were having structural distortions while the state was playing not even a marginal role. During the half century before India became independent, the world was having accelerated development and expansion in its agriculture and industry on the shoulders of the active role being played by the states, with the same was happening in United Kingdom itself.[1]

There was not only the unilateral transfer of investible capital to Britain by the colonial state (the 'drain of wealth'), but the unequal exchange was, day by day, crippling India's commerce, trade and the thriving handloom industry too. The colonial state practised policies which were great impediments in the process of development in the country. Throughout the colonial rule, the economic vision of the state was to increase India's capacity to export primary products, and increase the purchase/import of the British manufactured goods and raise revenues to meet the drain of capital as well as meet the revenue requirements of imperial defence.[2]

The social sector was a neglected area for the British rulers which had a negative impact on the production and productivity of the economy. India remained a continent of illiterate peasants under the British rule. At the time of independence, India's literacy was only 17 per cent with 32.5 years of life expectancy at birth.[3]

Industrialisation of India was also neglected by the colonisers - the infrastructure was not built to industrialise India but to exploit its raw materials. Indian capitalists who did emerge were highly dependent on British commercial capital, and many sectors of the industry were dominated by British firms, for example, shipping, banking, insurance, coal, plantation crops and jute.[4]

The pre-independence period was altogether a period of near stagnation, showing almost no change in the structure of production or in the levels of productivity - the aggregate real output during the first half of the 20th century estimated at less than 2 per cent a year or less.[5]

The overall economic performance of India under the British rule was very low. According to economic statistician Angus Maddison, there was no per capita growth in India from 1600 to 1870 - per capita growth was a meagre 0.2 per cent from 1870 to 1947, compared with 1 per cent in the United Kingdom.[6] The per capita incomes of ₹18 for 1899 and ₹39.5 for 1895, in current prices convey the true story of the abject poverty Indian masses were faced with.[7] The repeated famines and disease epidemics during the second half of the nineteenth century and the first half of the twentieth century show the greatest socio-economic irresponsibility and neglect of the British government in India on one hand and the wretchedness of the masses on the other.[8]

Both the political leaders and the industrialists were very much aware and conscious about the economic inheritance once India became independent. Somehow,

---

[1] B. Chandra, M. Mukherjee, and A. Mukherjee, *India After Independence* (New Delhi: Penguin Books, p. 341).

[2] B. Chandra, 'The Colonial Legacy', in *The Indian Economy: Problems and Prospects,* B. Jalan, ed. (New Delhi: Penguin Books, 2004), revised edition, p. 5.

[3] B.R. Tomlinson, *The Economy of Modern India 1860-1970* (Cambridge: Cambridge University Press, 1993), p. 7.

[4] A. Maddison, *The World Economy: A Millennial Perspective* (Paris: OECD, 2001), p. 116.

[5] A. Vaidyanathan, 'The Indian Economy Since Independence (1947-90)', in *The Cambridge Economic History of India,* vol. II, D. Kumar, ed. (Cambridge: Cambridge University Press, 2005), expanded edition, p. 947.

[6] Angus Maddison, *The World Economy: A Millennial Perspective* (Paris: OECD, 2001), p. 116.

[7] The respective data of Digby and Atkinson have been quoted by S. Sarkar, *Modern India 1885-1947* (New Delhi: Macmillan, 1983), p. 42.

[8] Recounted vividly by M. Davis in his *Late Victorian Holocaust: El-Nino Famines and the Making of the Third World* (London; New York, NY: Verso, 2001), p. 162, where he links the monsoon failures in India to El Nino - Southern Oscillation (ENSO) climate fluctuations in the western Pacific. The monsoon failure leading to drought and hunger one year and then to a severe malaria epidemic the next when the rains reappeared and a burst of mosquito abundance afflicted a weakened population.

these dominant lot of people who were going to lay down the foundation stones of the independent Indian economy almost had a consensual[9] view, even before independence, on many major strategic issues:

1. State/governments should be given a direct responsibility for development.
2. An ambitious and vital role to be assigned to the public sector.
3. Necessity for the development of heavy industries.
4. Discouragement to foreign investment.
5. The need for economic planning.

Once India became independent, it was a real challenge for the government of the time to go for a systematic organisation of the economy.

This was a task filled with challenges and hurdles as the economy had hardly anything optimistic. The need for delivering growth and development was in huge demand in the face of political leadership as the country was riding on the promises and vibes of nationalist fervour. It was not a simple task.

Now the decisions which were to be taken by the political leadership of the time were going to shape the very future of India. Many important and strategic decisions were taken only by 1956 which has shaped Indian economic journey till date - undoubtedly they heavily dominated the pre-reform period, but the post-reform period is also not completely free of its impact. To understand the nature and scope of the Indian economy in current times, it is not only useful but also essential to go through the facts, reasons and delicacies which made the economy evolve and unfold the way it did. A brief overview follows.

PRIME MOVING FORCE: AGRICULTURE VS. INDUSTRY

A topical issue of the debate regarding India has been the choice for the sector which will lead the process of development. The government of the time opted for the industry to be India's prime moving force (PMF) of the economy. Whether India should have gone for agriculture as its PMF for better prospects of development is a highly debatable issue even today among experts.

Every economy has to aim for development through the exploitation of its natural and human resources. There are priorities of objectives set by the economy which should be realised in a proper time frame. The availability and non-availability of resources (natural as well as human) are not the only issues which make an economy decide whether to opt for agriculture or industry as its PMF. There are other socio-political compulsions and objectives which play a major role in such decision-making.

The political leadership selected industry as the leading force of the economy after independence - this was already decided by the dominant group of nationalist leaders way back in the mid-1930s when they felt the need for economic planning in India before setting up the National Planning Committee in 1938. Given the available resource base, it seems an illogical decision as India lacked all those pre-requisites which could suggest the declaration of industry as its PMF:

1. Almost no presence of infrastructure sector, i.e., power, transportation and communication.
2. Negligible presence of the infrastructure industries, i.e., iron and steel, cement, coal, crude oil, oil refining and electricity.
3. Lack of investible capital - either by the government or the private sector.
4. Absence of required technology to support the process of industrialisation and no research and development.
5. Lack of skilled manpower.
6. Absence of entrepreneurship among the people.
7. Absence of a market for industrial goods.
8. Many other socio-psychological factors which acted as negative forces for the proper industrialisation of the economy.

The obvious choice for India would have been the agriculture sector as the PMF of the economy because of the following two reasons:

1. The country had the natural resource of fertile land which was fit for cultivation.
2. Human capital did not require any kind of higher training.

[9] B. Chandra et al., *India's Struggle for Independence*, op. cit, p. 15.

By only organising its land ownership, irrigation and other inputs to agriculture, India could have gone for better prospects of development. Once there were no crises of food, shelter and basic healthcare to the masses, one goal of development could have been realised - a general welfare of the people. Once the masses were able to achieve a level of purchasing capacity, India could have gone for the expansion of industries. India was capable of generating as much surplus income for its masses as was required by the emerging industries for market success. The People's Republic of China did the same in 1949 - taking a realistic evaluation of its resources, it declared agriculture as its PMF for the economy. The surplus generated out of agriculture was suitably invested to develop the prerequisites for industrialisation, and the country went for it in the 1970s.

The emergence of industrial China was so vibrant that its impact was felt in the so-called highly developed and industrialised economies of the world - the industrial homework of China catapulted it into a giant.

Was the political leadership of independent India not able to analyse the realities as we did above and conclude that agriculture should have been the moving force of the economy in place of industry? Is it possible that Pandit Nehru in command could have missed the rational analysis of the Indian realities, a giant among the Asian visionaries of the time (Mao was still to emerge on the international scene)? How could India have not opted for agriculture as its PMF whose leadership had fought the nationalist movement on the Gandhian fervour of villages, agriculture and rural development? Even if Gandhi was not in the government, there were many devout Gandhians in it, and no one should doubt that the main internal force which vibrated throughout the governmental decisions were nothing but 'Gandhian Socialism'. There were many decisions which were taken under the influence of the main political force of the times, and still some very vital ones were influenced by the visionary hunches of the political leadership, mainly being J.L. Nehru. This is why the economic thinking of independent India is considered and said to be nurtured by Nehruvian Economics even today. If we go through the major literatures on the Indian economic history, views of the critiques of the time and the contemporary experts, we may be able to realise the answer as to why India went for industry as its PMF in place of an obvious and logical choice of agriculture (we should not be content with knowing that even today this is a highly debatable issue among experts):

1. Looking at the resources available, agriculture would have been the obvious choice as the PMF of the economy (i.e., cultivable land and human power). But as Indian agriculture was using traditional tools and technology, its modernisation as well as future mechanisation (later to some extent) would have been blocked due to the lack of indigenous industrial support. If India would have gone for import, this would have required enough foreign reserves and a natural dependence on foreign countries. Secondly, the agricultural machines and tools available for imports were not suitable for India's farm sector as they were developed by the exporting countries as per their requirements. By choosing industry as the PMF, India opted to industrialise the economy as well as modernise the traditional mode of farming.
2. The dominant ideology around the world as well as in the World Bank (WB) and the International Monetary Fund (IMF) was in favour of industrialisation as a means to faster growth, which could be translated into faster development. These international bodies were supporting the member countries from every point of view to industrialise. The same was the case with the developed economies. It was possible not only to industrialise faster on these supports of the organisations but also hope for emerging as an industrial exporter in the future. The same kind of support was not offered to an economy that opted for agriculture as the PMF. Basically, going for the agriculture sector was considered a symbol of 'backwardness' at that time. The political leadership wanted to carry India ahead, and not in the backward direction. It was only in the 1990s that the world and the WB/IMF changed its opinion regarding the agriculture sector. After the 1990s, emphasis on this sector by an economy was no more considered a sign of backwardness.
3. The Second World War has proved the supremacy of defence power. For defence, a country needs the support of not only science and technology but also an industrial base. India also required a powerful defence base for itself as a deterrent force. By opting for

industries as the PMF of the economy, India tried to solve many challenges simultaneously - first, industry will drive faster growth; second, agriculture will be modernised in no time; and third, the economy will be able to develop its own defence against external threats. Since the economy had also opted for scientific and technological preparedness, its achievements were to sustain the pace of modernisation.

4. Even before independence, there was a socio-economic consensus among social scientists along with the nationalist leaders that India needed a boost towards social change as the country lagged behind in the areas of modernisation. A break from the traditional and outmoded way of life and cultivation of a scientific outlook was a must for the country. Such feelings also made the political leadership of the time go in favour of wholehearted industrialisation.
5. By the time India achieved her independence, the might of industrialisation was already proven, and there were no doubts regarding its efficacy.

Given above are some of the important reasons that worked to make Indian political leadership go in favour of industry as the economy's PMF. Probably, the resource related and temperamental realities of India were marginalised in the hope and wish of a future industrialised and developed India. It is yet impossible to conclude whether the economy has completely failed to do so or not. Experts have divided opinions on this issue.

The last decade of the 20th century (i.e., the decade of the 1990s) saw major changes taking place in the world economic idea about the agriculture sector. It was no more a symbol of backwardness for an economy that emphasised on the agriculture sector as the engine of growth and development. China had proved to the world how agriculture could be made the PMF of an economy and generate internal as well as external strength to emerge as an industrial economy. In the wake of the ongoing reform process, India was introspecting almost all economic policies it followed since independence. It was time for the agriculture sector to have the prime attention. A major shift[10] took place in the Indian economic thinking when the government announced in 2002 that from then onwards, in place of industry, **agriculture will be the PMF** of the economy. This was a policy shift of historic importance which was announced by the highest economic think tank of the country - the Planning Commission - as the economy commenced the Tenth Plan (2002-07).

As per the Planning Commission,[11] such a policy shift will solve three major challenges faced by the economy:

1. Economy will be able to achieve food security with an increase in agricultural production. Besides, the agricultural surplus will generate exports in the globalising world economy benefiting out of the World Trade Organisation regime.
2. The challenge of poverty alleviation will be solved to a great extent as the emphasis will make agriculture a higher income-generating occupation and induce growth in the rural economy by generating more gainful employment.
3. The situation of India as an example of 'market failure' will cease.[12]

Though the world's perception regarding agriculture had changed by the mid-1990s, India recognised the sector as the PMF of the economy a bit late, i.e., by 2002. Now, there is a consensus among experts and

[10] The Government of India had shown such an intention in two regular union budgets (i.e., the fiscals 2000-01 and 2001-02) but had not announced the shift officially.

[11] Planning Commission, *Tenth Five Year Plan (2002-07)* (New Delhi: Government of India, 2002).

[12] It has been argued by economists' time and again that India is a typical example of 'market failure'. Market failure is a situation when there are goods and services in an economy and its requirement too, but due to lack of purchasing power, the requirements of the people are not translated into demand. Whatever industrial goods and services India had been able to produce, they had stagnated or stunted sales in the market as the largest section of the consumers earned their livelihood from the agriculture sector, which is unable to create a purchasing power to the levels required by the market. As agricultural activities will become more gainful and profitable, the masses depending on it will have the level of purchasing capacity to purchase the industrial goods and services from the market. Thus, the Indian market won't fail. The view has been articulated by A. Sen and J. Dreze in their monograph titled *India: Economic Development and Social Opportunity* (United Nations University, 1996).

policymakers regarding the role of agriculture in the Indian economy. Agriculture and allied activities remained the major source of livelihood for about 46 per cent of the Indian population with about 16 per cent contribution in the GDP.[13]

Once India started the process of economic reforms, it began thriving in the industrial sector - as the economy received its structure through the successive industrial policies, it seems a common undertaking. To the extent the agriculture sector is concerned, reforms were initiated a bit late - by the early 2000s. Three *major reasons* may be cited for this delay:

1. Agriculture being always open for the private sector, it was now difficult to go for further privatisation for encouraging investments. The need was for 'corporate' and 'contract' farming under the leadership of the *corporate world.*
2. Lack of awareness about the contours of the economic reforms among the farm community.
3. The heavy dependency of population on agriculture for livelihood could not permit the government to opt for the right kind of agricultural reforms at the right time - first, the industrial sector (*via* manufacturing) needed expansion to lessen the population dependency on the agriculture sector.

Any one sector in which the governments at the centre and states have been facing the biggest hurdles has been the farm sector. The major reform needs and the hurdles being faced may be summed up as follows:

1. A *national agri-market* is the need of the hour, but there is a lack of a political will among the majority of states to put in place the right kind of Agricultural Produce Market Committee.
2. The need for promoting *corporate investment* in the farm sector is hurdled by the lack of an effective and transparent land acquisition law.
3. *Labour reforms* need fine-tuning to promote industrial farming, which is impeded due to a long tradition of complex labour laws of the country.
4. *Farm mechanisation* is hindered by the lack of investment in industries.
5. *Research and development* needs huge investment from the private sector, but there is a lack of a conducive atmosphere for it.
6. Right kind of *downstream and upstream requirements,* together with a proper kind of *supply chain management,* is absent in the area of agri-goods.
7. Expansion of the right kind of *commodity trading* in agri-commodities.
8. Strengthening the farm sector to face the competition posed by the agricultural sector of the developed world, with regard to subsidies and prices, in the wake of the globalising world economy.
9. Making farming *remunerative* to check farm crisis of contemporary times.

Experts believe that for taking the right policy steps in the sector, a high degree of federal maturity in the country is needed. Increased awareness among farmers, together with the right government support to prevent farm distress, will serve the purpose in a great way.

PLANNED AND MIXED ECONOMY

Independent India was declared to be a planned and a mixed economy. India needed national planning, which was decided by the political leadership almost a decade before Independence.[14] India was not only facing regional disparities at the level of resources, but inter-regional disparities were also prevalent for centuries. Mass poverty could only be remedied once the government started the process of economic planning. Economic planning was thus considered an established tool of doing away with such disparities.

Basically, it was the abject poverty of the masses which made the government opt for planning so that it could play an active role in the allocation of resources and mobilise them for equitable growth and development. Though India was constitutionally declared a federation of states, in the process of planning, the authority of regulation, directing and

[13] *Economic Survey 2024-25* (N. Delhi: Ministry of Finance, GoI, January 2025), p. 245.

[14] National Planning Committee (New Delhi: GoI, 1949).

undertaking economic activities became more and more centralised in the Union government.[15]

India's decision for a planned economy was also moulded by some contemporary experiences in the world.[16] *Firstly*, the Great Depression of 1929 and the reconstruction challenges after the Second World War had made experts to conclude in favour of a state intervention in the economy (opposite to the contemporary idea of 'non-interference' as proposed by Adam Smith). *Secondly*, it was the same time that the command economies (i.e., state economies) of the Soviet Union and the East European countries started making news about their faster economic growth. In the 1950s and 1960s, the dominant view among policymakers around the world was in favour of an active role of the state in the economy. *Thirdly*, a dominant role for the state in the economy to neutralise market failure situations (as happened during the period of the Great Depression when demand fell to the lowest levels) was gaining ground around the world. For many newly independent developing nations, economic planning was therefore an obvious choice. Economic planning was considered to help states to mobilise resources to realise the prioritised objectives in a well-defined time frame.

Once the political leadership had decided in favour of a planned economy for India and a major role for the state in the economy, they needed to clarify the organisational nature of the economy - whether it was to be a state economy or a mixed economy - because planning was not possible in a free market economy (i.e., capitalistic economy). The idea of planning in India was inspired from the Soviet Planning, which was a command economy and did not suit the requirements of democratic India, which was till now a privately owned economy.[17] The dominant force behind planning in India, at least after independence, was Nehru himself who had strong socialist leanings. He thought it was important to define the role of the state in the economy, which was going to be at times similar to the state in the Soviet Union and at times completely dissimilar to it. Though there was an example of a capitalistic democratic system going for planning, France by that time (1947), it had little experience to offer the Indian policymakers (France had gone for a mixed economy by 1944-45). With the basic urge to accelerate the process of economic growth, the planners went on to define the respective roles of the state and the market, in the very first plan. The following lines look refreshingly ahead of the times and are crystal-clear about the scope of the government's role in the economy *vis-à-vis* the private sector.

Trickle-Down Theory

This is an idea of supply-side economics according to which *tax reliefs given on income and wealth (for corporations and wealthy people) ultimately trickle down to everyone*. Governments have normally followed such policies conjoined with market deregulation (less regulation of market). The trickle-down effect is believed to occur through the interplay of 'spillover effect' (used in the sense that corporations and wealthy people earning more will, in turn, spend more, which will benefit the economy at large through 'multiplier effect' (investment and spending benefit the whole economy).

The US humourist and social commentator William Rogers (1879–1935) is credited with coining this term. Trickle-down economics was first tried as a remedy to the Great Depression of 1929 in the USA (by the Hoover administration)—followed by its most ardent supporter Ronald Reagon and recently Donald Trump. Most of the world governments (including India—J.L. Nehru had praised it in one of his writings of 1933) came under its influence by 1950s.

The idea has been criticized on various counts. Firstly, it is not clear as how much of the tax reliefs offered by governments reach to how many people and in how much time. Secondly, the empirical data from the USA show otherwise (rise in inequality). By early 2010s the idea was canceled out by the IMF/WB.

[15] B. Jalan, *India's Economic Policy* (New Delhi: Penguin Books, 1993), p. 2.

[16] C. Rangarajan, *Perspectives on Indian Economy* (New Delhi: UBS3D, 2004), p. 96.

[17] R. Mohan, 'Industrial Policy and Control', in *The Indian Economy: Problems and Prospects*, B. Jalan, ed., op. cit, p. 101.

Spillover Effect

It is an effect of an event of one economy on another economy/ economies (used in macroeconomics). For example, fall in India's exports to the USA if the latter sees an economic slowdown. Under it, unconnected events can also have such effects (such as earthquakes, stock market crash, pandemic, etc.).

Scan this QR Code to watch a author's video lecture that simplifies this topic

The term is also used (in microeconomics) to mean the effect of one event on some other events in the same economy. For example, rise in incomes of the richer people leaves similar effects on the people who are dependent on the former (such as employees of companies getting more bonuses/ other benefits once the companies' earnings increase).

'This brings us to the problem of the techniques of planning. A possible approach to the problem is, as mentioned earlier, through a more or less complete nationalisation of the means of production and extensive system of government controls on the allocation of resources and on the distribution of the national product. Judged purely as a technique of planning, this may appear a promising line of action. But, viewed against the background of the objectives outlined above, and in the light of practical considerations, such an expansion of the public sector is, at the present stage, neither necessary nor desirable. Planning in a democratic set-up implies the minimum use of compulsion or coercion for bringing about a realignment of productive forces. The resources available to the public sector have, at this stage, to be utilised for investment along new lines rather than in acquisition of existing productive capacity. Public ownership of the means of production may be necessary in certain cases; public regulation and control in certain others. The private sector has, however, to continue to play an important part in production as well as in distribution. Planning under recent conditions thus means, in practice, an economy guided and directed by the state and operated partly through direct state action and partly through private initiative and effort'.[18]

The above-quoted lines are imaginatively ahead of the times. It will be suitable to note here that as the 1950s and 1960s made the world experts favour state intervention in the economy, the *East Asian Miracle*[19] of the coming three decades was going to define the very limits of such an intervention. The East Asian economies were able to sustain a high growth rate over three decades and had revived again the discussions regarding the respective roles of the state and the market as well as the nature of the state's role in the economy. The kind of conclusions drawn were very similar to the view presented in India's First Plan itself which was presented by the WB in 1993.

The real nature of the Indian brand of mixed economy, though beautifully outlined in 1951 itself, went through a process of detailed evolution in the 1950s.[20] By the end of the 1950s, the concept of the mixed economy was almost buried and rose from hibernation only by the mid-1980s and finally early in the 1990s, in the wake of the process of economic reforms.

Multiplier Effect

This is an economic term which refers to change (increase or decrease) in incomes of people as a result of expenditures, investment or withdrawal of capital, tax breaks/cuts or imposition of new taxes or increase in rates of the existing taxes. For example—rise in government expenditures increases the income of people, offerings of subsidies enhance beneficiaries' per capita income, etc.

Normally used in proportional sense, it may be used in non-proportional sense too.

We see the government modifying the process of planning and functions of the Planning Commission in the wake of the reform process - an attempt to redefine the roles of government and private sector in

[18] Planning Commission, *The First Five Year Plan: A Draft Outline* (New Delhi: GoI, 1951).

[19] World Bank, *The East Asian Miracle* (Washington, DC: World Bank, 1993).

[20] We see the process of evolution specially in the industrial policies, India pursued since 1948 to 1956.

the economy. In a sense, India was increasingly getting more dependent on the latter for the promotion of growth and development.

By the early 2015, we saw some major changes taking place in the area of planning in India. The Government replaced the existing body, *Planning Commission,* with the *NITI Aayog* (a new economic 'Think Tank') with the aim of 'overhauling' the very process and method of planning in the country. This move is believed to originate out of India's experiences of development planning spanning over six decades. Co-operative federalism, bottom-up approach, holistic and inclusive development with the need of an Indian model of development are some of the hallmarks of the new design. The move is also seen in the light of the changed needs of the economy.

Atmanirbharta Push

Even though self-reliance had been one of the six major objectives of planning, a renewed push for it has been announced by the government in the wake of the *COVID-19* pandemic. In 2020-21, the Government launched the *Atmanirbhar Bharat Abhiyan (Self-Reliant India Campaign)* to support this cause. The government aims at attaining self-reliance with the help of the *five pillars* of the *Abhiyan,* namely Economy, Infrastructure, System, Vibrant Demography and Demand. This is for the *first time* that clear pillars have been defined by the Government in this regard.

Some critics have shown their reservations regarding the *Abhiyan* and have called it similar to the Make in India, a scheme of the past. However, some experts have seen it in the backdrop of the limits of a global supply chain (caused by the recent pandemic and similar possibilities in future) - India's urge to redesign its economic space, relationship with the environment and economic diplomacy.

EMPHASIS ON THE PUBLIC SECTOR

The state was to be given an active and dominant role in the economy - it was very much decided by the time India became independent. There were no doubts about it in the minds of the people who formed the dominant political force at the time. Naturally, there was going to be a giant structure of government-controlled enterprises known as public sector undertakings (PSUs). Criticism aside, there was, at that time, a strong logic behind the glorification of PSUs. Some of the reasons for heavy investments in the PSUs were purely natural while others were consequential in nature. There were certain highly commendable objectives set for them, where some other goals would go on to serve the very soul of the mixed economy. We must go for an impartial and rational analysis of the matter, in the midst of all the criticisms of PSUs and the contemporary moves of privatising them, to understand their roles in the Indian economy. We may understand the reasons behind the ambitious expansion of the PSUs in the face of the following major requirements:

1. **Infrastructural Needs** Every economy, whether it is agrarian, industrial or post-industrial, needs suitable levels of infrastructure such as power, transportation and communication. Without their healthy presence and expansion, no economy can grow and develop.

   On the eve of independence, India had almost no presence of these three basic requirements. There was just a beginning in the area of railways, and post and telegraph. Power was restricted to selective homes of the government and princely states. [It means, even if India had opted for agriculture as its PMF, it had to develop the infrastructure sector.]

   These sectors require too much capital investment as well as heavy engineering and technological support for their development. Expansion of the infrastructure sector was considered not possible by the private sector of the time as they could not possibly manage the following components:

   (i) heavy investment (in domestic as well as foreign currencies),
   (ii) technology,
   (iii) skilled manpower, and
   (iv) entrepreneurship.

   Even if these inputs were available to the private sector, it was not feasible for them as there was no market for such infrastructure. These infrastructures were essential for the economy, but they needed to be either subsidised or almost free supply as the masses lacked the market-determined purchasing capacity. Under these typical conditions, it was only the government which could have shouldered the responsibility. The government could have managed not only the inputs required for the development of the sector but also the Supply and distribution of them to disadvantaged areas and consumers for proper growth of the economy. There were no alternatives, which is why the infrastructure sector in India has such a dominant state presence that many areas have obvious government monopolies - as in power, railways, aviation, telecommunication and so forth.

2. **Industrial Needs** India had opted for the industrial sector as its PMF, as we saw earlier. Now there were some areas of industries which the government had to invest in, due to several compulsive reasons. For industrialisation to take place, the presence of certain industries is essential (these industries have been called in the country by different names - *basic industries, infrastructure industries, core industries, core sector*). To the initial group of six industries, in 2013 two new industries (Natural Gas and Fertilisers) were added. The combined weight of these eight industries in the new series of the Index of Industrial Production (IIP) is 40.27 per cent. These industries are as follows (their percentage weights in IIP are given in brackets)[21]:

   (i) Refinery products (11.29)
   (ii) Electricity (7.99)
   (iii) Steel (7.22)
   (iv) Coal (4.16)
   (v) Crude Oil (3.62)
   (vi) Natural Gas (2.77)
   (vii) Cement (2.16)
   (viii) Fertilisers (1.06)

   Similar to the infrastructure sector, these basic industries also require high level of capital, technology, skilled manpower and articulation in entrepreneurship which was again considered not feasible for the private sector of the time to manage. Even if the private sector supplied goods from the 'basic industries', they might not be able to sell their products in the market due to the lower purchasing power of the consumers. Perhaps, that is why again the responsibility of developing the basic industries was taken up by the government.

   Out of the six basic industries, the cement industry had some strength in the private sector, while in the iron and steel industry a lone private company was present. The coal industry was controlled by the private sector and crude oil and refining was just a beginning by then. The level of demands of an industrialising India was never to be met by the existing strength of the basic industries. Neither the required level of expansion in them was possible by the existing number of private players. With no choice left, the government decided to play a main role in industrialising the country. In many of them we, as a result, see a natural monopoly for the PSUs, again.

3. **Employment Generation** The PSUs were also seen as an important part of the employment generation strategy. A government in a democratic set-up cannot think only economics, but it has to realise the socio-political dimensions of the nation too. The country was faced with the serious problem of poverty, and the workforce was increasing at a fast rate. Providing employment opportunities to underprivileged people is a time-tested tool of poverty alleviation. The PSUs were thought to create enough jobs for the employable workforce of the economy.

   There was also felt an immediacy for a social change in the country. The poverty of a greater section of the country was somehow connected to the age-old caste system which propitiated the stronghold of the upper castes on the ownership of land, which was the only means of income and livelihood for almost over 80 per cent of the population. Along with the ambitious policy of land reforms, the government decided to provide reservations to the weaker sections of the society in government jobs. The upcoming PSUs were supposed to put such jobs at the disposal of the government which could have been distributed along the decided reservation policy - such reservations were considered an economic tool for social change.

[21] The revised *Index of Industrial Production (IIP)* was released by the Central Statistics Office (CSO) on 12 May 2017. Aimed at capturing the structural changes in the economy and improving the quality of representation, the revision includes many things such as shifting the base year to 2011-12 from 2004-05 and changes in the basket of commodities and their weights.

In the highly capital-intensive sectors in which the government companies were going to enter, managing investible funds to set them up was not going to be an easy task. The government did manage the funds with sources such as taxation, internal and external borrowing and even taking a last refuge in the printing of fresh currencies. The government went on to justify the high taxation and heavy public indebtedness in supplying employment to the Indian employable population.

The PSUs were considered by the government as the focus of the 'trickle-down effect'. The government did everything to set up and run the PSUs as the benefits were supposed to percolate to the masses, finally reinforcing growth and development in the country. Employment in the PSUs was seen as the effort of the trickle-down theory, simply put. At a point of time, Nehru even referred to the PSUs as being the 'temples of modern India'. The government went on to commit a job to every household *via* the PSUs - without calculating the dimensions of the future labour force in the country and the required resources to create jobs at such a high scale. But the government went on creating new PSUs without analysing the fiscal repercussions - moreover believing them to be the real engine of equitable growth. The employment generation responsibility of the PSUs was extended to such an extent by the government that most of them had an over-supply of labour force which started draining its profits on account of salaries, wages, pensions and provident funds (the latter two had late financial impact).

4. **Profit and Development of the Social Sector** The investment to be made by the government in PSUs was in the nature of asset creation, and these entities were to be involved in production activities. It was natural for the government to gain control over the profits and dividends accruing from them. The goods and services the PSUs produced and sold provided disposable income to the government. The government had a conscious policy of spending the income generated by the PSUs. They were to be used in the supply of the 'social goods' or what is called the 'public goods'. And thus, India was to have a developed social sector. By social goods the government meant the universal supply of certain goods and services to the citizen. This included education, healthcare, nutrition, drinking water and social security in India. It means that the PSUs were also visioned as the revenue generators for the development of the social sector. Due to many reasons the PSUs would not be able to generate as much profit as was required for the healthy development of the social sector. This eventually hampered the availability of public goods in the country. In place of giving profits back to the government, a large number of the PSUs started incurring huge losses and required budgetary support regularly.

5. **Rise of the Private Sector** As the PSUs took the responsibility of supplying the infrastructure and the basic industries to the economy, a base for the rise of private sector industries was slowly established. With the rise of private sector industries in the country, the process of industrialisation was thought to be completed. Out of the many roles the PSUs were supposed to play, this was the most far-sighted. How and why government's approach to the PSUs changed during the period of economic reforms, we will understand in *Chapter 10* of the book which is dedicated to *Industry and Infrastructure*. Here we have analysed why the government of India after Independence opted for such an ambitious plan of expansion of the public sector.

Besides, the PSUs were aimed at many other connected areas of developmental concerns, such as self-sufficiency in production, balanced regional development, spread of small and ancillary industries, low and stable prices, and long-term equilibrium in balance of payment. Over time the PSUs have played a critical role in promoting the growth and development of the country.[22]

By the mid-1980s, there emerged a kind of consensus across the world (including the IMF and WB) regarding the inefficiency and under-performance of the PSUs (in the wake of the idea of the Washington Consensus which is said to

[22] S. Bose and S. Kumar, 'Public-Sector Enterprises', in *The New Oxford Companion to Economics in India*, Vol. II, K. Basu and A. Maertens, eds. (New Delhi: Oxford University Press, 2012), pp. 578-83.

promote 'neo-liberal' economic policies across the world). In the wake of it, there commenced a process of privatisation and disinvestment of the PSUs among the majority of the economies in the world - India being no exception to it. By the late 1990s, new studies proved that under-performance and inefficiency could be present in the private sector companies too. By the late first decade of the new millennium (in the wake of the US *subprime crisis* of 2007-08), a new consensus emerged among the international organisations that state/government need not exit the economy, and a kind of slowdown towards privatisation moves of the PSUs across the world (the world, in a sense, is pushing the 'pause' button on neo-liberalism) is under process.

India pursued a less ambitious disinvestment policy from 2003-04 to 2015-16 (the government has decided to own controlling shares among the divested PSUs). Since the 2016-17 financial year, the government had decided to restart the process of 'strategic disinvestment' (in which the ownership of the PSUs may also be transferred to the private sector). Such a policy of disinvestment was launched by the government in 2000 (which was paused by the government in 2003-04). The government has also decided in favour of selling increased shares of the PSUs to the foreign institutions, at par with the domestic financial institutions. Such policy moves[23] of recent times should be seen in the light of certain important contemporary realities - need of promoting investment in the economy; need of the government to quit undesirable areas of economic activities and expanding in the areas of need and where private sector will not enter (welfare actions) and revenue generation by stake sale, monetisation of their assets and enhanced profit from the PSUs (by selling majority stakes in the PSUs, on the one hand, the government will de-burden itself from the owner's responsibility, while, on the other its share of revenue from the divested PSUs will increase as the new owner will run the enterprise on market principles).

[23] We find such policy advices coming from the *Economic Survey* in the past including *Economic Survey 2022-23, 2021-22, 2020-21* and *2019-20*. Further, the governments have been increasingly acting upon such policy advice (examples may be taken from the *Union Budgets spanning between 2015-16 to 2025-26*.).

SAMPLE OBJECTIVE QUESTIONS

1. How many of the following statements is/are correct about the economic condition of India on the eve of Independence? Select your answer with the help of the codes given below:

(i) The government aimed at making India exporters of primary and secondary articles.

(ii) Unequal exchange rate helped India get cheap foreign loans.

(iii) Infrastructural initiatives of the first half of the 20th century worked as a foundation for the future.

Code:

(a) Only one **(b)** Only two

(c) All three **(d)** None of these

2. Consider the following statements about India's economy during the British rule – and select your answer with the help of the codes given below:

(i) Its per capita income increased by around 3 per cent in the second half of the1890s.

(ii) Occupational structure shifted in favour of the power loom industry.

(iii) India was a major exporting country on the eve of Independence.

Code:

(a) Only one **(b)** Only two

(c) All three **(d)** None of these

3. Which of the following statement(s) is/are correct about India's economy at the time of independence? Select your answer with the help of the codes given below:

(i) Its life expectancy at birth was meagre 42 years.

(ii) Due to increased attention given to education, literacy had improved to 27 per cent.

(iii) Banks of Indian origin had around one-fourth share in the banking industry.

Code:

(a) Only one **(b)** Only two

(c) All three **(d)** None of these

4. Which of the following statement(s) is/are correct about India's economy during the first half of the 20th century? Select your answer with the help of the codes given below:

(i) The indigenous handicraft industry was damaged by a biased tariff policy followed by the British government.

(ii) India was flooded with cheap imports from the United Kingdom.

(iii) Frequent shortages of goods produced in the country were a hallmark of the period.

Code:

(a) Only one **(b)** Only two

(c) All three **(d)** None of these

5. Consider the following statements related to India's decision about its economic system after independence:

(i) Capitalism was cancelled out as it went against the aspirations of socialistic goals.

(ii) The dominant view of the business class of independent India was in favour of capitalism.

(iii) Economic liberalism was against the basic features of the Constitution.

How many of the above statement(s) is/are correct?

(a) Only one **(b)** Only two

(c) All three **(d)** None of these

6. Consider the statements related to the pre-reforms period of the country's economy:

(i) Sub-optimal multiplier effect was mainly due to the misallocation of investible capital.

(ii) Expansion of the public sector was modelled on the trickle-down theory.

(iii) Agriculture sector had higher potential of spillover effect than industry.

How many of the above statement(s) is/are correct?

(a) Only one **(b)** Only two

(c) All three **(d)** None of these

7. Consider the following statements related to the prime moving force of India's economy:

(i) As the largest employer agriculture should have been its natural choice.

(ii) Movement from industry to agriculture shows a smooth economic transition.

(iii) At present this role is being played by the services.

How many of the above statement(s) is/are correct?

(a) Only one **(b)** Only two

(c) All three **(d)** None of these

8. Consider the following statements related to the economy of the country:

(i) Economic planning remains a foundational economic policy even today.

(ii) Over-emphasis on industry has been the reason for agrarian crisis of today.

(iii) Structural reforms in industry were more successful than in agri sector.

How many of the above statement(s) is/are correct?

(a) Only one **(b)** Only two

(c) All three **(d)** None of these

9. Which of the following is correct about the country's economy of today?

(a) Over dependence on services sector is hampering agri development.

(b) Under-development of vocational education is the main reason for unemployment.

(c) Sector agriculture has higher returns on investment than industry.

(d) Socio-economic dividends from demographic shift depend more on attitudinal shifts.

10. Consider the following statements related to the pre-independence economy of the country:

(i) The colonial government gave step-brotherly treatment to agriculture sector.

(ii) India had an emerging capitalist class which was not dependent on foreign firms.

(iii) Public sector companies dominated the economic space.

How many of the above statements are correct?

(a) Only one **(b)** Only two

(c) All three **(d)** None of these

Answers: 1. (d) 2. (a) 3. (d) 4. (a) 5. (a) 6. (b) 7. (d) 8. (b) 9. (b) 10. (d)

SAMPLE SUBJECTIVE QUESTIONS

1. Briefly discuss the difficulties faced by the emerging industrial and business classes during the first half of the 20th century during the colonial rule.

2. 'India's over-dependence on the public sector enterprises did more harm than help to the economy.' Explain.

3. Do you think that India's faith in the idea of trickle-down effect helped her alleviate poverty during four decades after independence? Give illustrations to substantiate your points.

4. 'India's decision to go with mixed economy after Independence is considered ahead of time.' Elucidate.

5. Why were the public sector undertakings called the temples of modern India? Analyse with suitable examples.

6. 'Liberal economic policies would have served India better after independence.' Examine in the backdrop of the contemporary global economic order.

SAMPLE MODEL ANSWER

1. Briefly explain about the reasons due to which the Government shifted from industry to agriculture as the prime moving force of the economy. Give suitable examples.

Ans. After Independence, the industrial sector was opted for by India as the prime moving force of the economy. There were valid reasons for such a policy option. But in 2002, the Government shifted from industry to agriculture as the prime moving force of the economy. This shift did not take place overnight; rather, we find changing official perception in this regard due to the experience and the changed priorities of the times. Major reasons cited by the Government for this shift were:

- Such a policy shift will help strengthen the livelihood of the largest chunk of the population, the farm community;
- The goal of food security will get easier as a result;
- It will help the country enhance farm income through value addition by promoting the food processing industry; and

- Creating a higher number of employment opportunities in the sector will help rural development and lessen the urban settlements, which were becoming overcrowded due to mass rural-urban migration, etc.

To boost this policy-shift, the Government had already effected major policy changes (in 2000), such as– agriculture being declared as an industry, contract and corporate farming being allowed, suitable reforms in labour laws being promised/started, etc.

This was a major shift in policy, and to realise its benefits, the governments need to cooperate and coordinate with a long-term vision and commitment–experts believe that the policy think tank Niti Aayog will help the economy in this regard.

CHAPTER 5

Economic Planning

> The idea of planning and a planned society is accepted now in varying degrees by almost everyone. But planning by itself has little meaning and need not necessarily lead to good results. Everything depends on the objectives of the plan and on the controlling authority, as well as, of course, the government behind it.
>
> - **Jawaharlal Nehru**
>
> *The Discovery of India*, 6th Impression (1st Edition 1946, Oxford, London), New Delhi, 1994, p. 501.

To watch the Author's videos on the significance of the Chapter, scan the QR Code given here

Exam Essentials...

- From Practice To Theory
- Atmanirbharta Push

Note to the Reader...

This chapter deals with the economics and theories of planning - it should be seen as the "prequel" to Chapter 6 which follows the next. Planning being a highly applied and analytical area conceptual clarity is essential which this chapter aims to provide.

In This Chapter...

INTRODUCTION

Today, most of the world economies are planned, and the world has seen major experimental breakthroughs in the area of economic planning by now. India has been a planned economy right since its independence and continues to be so under the policy think tank NITI Aayog. This chapter intends to introduce the reader to the major ***Whats, Hows*** and ***Whys*** of the 'concept of economic planning' - picking real examples from major planned economies of the world including India. Besides being a theoretical foundation, it aims to provide a theoretical anchor to ***Planning in India*** (Chapter 6).

DEFINITION

A number of definitions have been forwarded by different economists from time to time since the term 'planning' entered the domain of economics. To make us develop a clear understanding of planning, we need to see only a few of them which will enable us to draw a working definition that fits contemporary times.

A large number of economists and experts have agreed that perhaps the best definition is given by H.D. Dickinson, according to whom economic planning is 'the making of major economic decisions - what and how much is to be produced and to whom it is to be allocated by the conscious decision of a determinate authority, on the basis of a comprehensive survey of the economic system as a whole'.

It was the National Planning Committee, set up in 1938 by the Indian National Congress, which, for the first time, tried to define planning (in 1940, though, its final report was published in 1949) in India. It could be considered the broadest possible definition of planning: 'planning, under a democratic system, may be defined as the technical coordination, by disinterested experts of consumption, production, investment, trade, and income distribution, in accordance with social objectives set by bodies representative of the nation. Such planning is not only to be considered from the point of view of economics, and raising of the standard of living, but must include cultural and spiritual values, and the human side of life'.[1]

By the late 1930s, there was an almost political consensus that independent India will be a planned economy. As India commenced economic planning by the early 1950s, the Planning Commission of India also went on to define planning. According to the Planning Commission, 'planning involves the acceptance of a clearly defined system of objectives in terms of which to frame overall policies. It also involves the formation of a strategy for promoting the realisation of ends defined. Planning is essentially an attempt at working out a rational solution to problems, an attempt to coordinate means and ends; it is thus different from the traditional hit-and-miss methods by which reforms and reconstruction are often undertaken'.[2]

[1] S.R. Maheshwari, *A Dictionary of Public Administration* (New Delhi: Orient Longman, 2002), p. 371.

[2] Planning Commission, *First Five Year Plan (1951-56)* (New Delhi: Government of India, 1991), p. 7.

In the post-war period, a large number of the newly independent countries were attracted towards planning. Many new forces of change kept refining the very idea of planning due to the compulsive necessities of industrialisation or the issue of sustainability of the development process. But to carry forward our discussion, we need a working as well as a contemporary definition of planning. We may define it as *a process of realising well-defined goals by optimum utilisation of the available resources.*[3] While carrying out economic planning the government sets developmental objectives and attempts to deliberately coordinate the economic decision-making over a longer period to influence, direct and, in some cases, even control the level and growth of a nation's main economic variables (i.e., income, consumption, employment, saving, investment, exports and imports).[4]

An economic plan is simply a set of specific economic targets to be achieved in a given period of time with a stated strategy. Economic plans may be either

From Practice to Theory

Planning was first applied by policy makers in some countries after which its theories and types evolved! Since planning was a way to pursue development it will vary from one to another country - in practice getting influenced by socio-economic realities. This is why at the level of theory we may see many similarities in planning processes of two countries, but at level of practice very few similarities are found - it is kind of *as many countries as many kinds of planning*. But still, for academic purposes, countries are clubbed in one or the other category of planning.

Since planning is a process of "optimum utilisation of resources to achieve a goal", in practice, it can be tried in all possible areas where there is a need of systematic development. For example it can be as simple as time planning and as complex as *family planning, city/country planning*, etc.

[3] After the emergence of the concept of Sustainable Development (1987), experts across the world started using the term 'optimum' in place of the hitherto used term 'maximum'.

[4] M.P. Todaro, *Development Planning: Models and Methods* (Nairobi: Oxford University Press, 1971).

comprehensive or partial. A ***comprehensive plan*** sets targets to cover all major aspects of the economy, while a ***partial plan*** may go for setting such targets for a part of the economy (i.e., agriculture, industry and public sector). Taken broadly, the planning process itself can be described as an exercise in which a government first chooses social objectives, then sets various targets (i.e., economic targets) and finally organises a framework for implementing, coordinating and monitoring the development plan.[5]

One very important thing which should be clear to all is that the idea of planning first emerged in its applied form and after studying and surveying the experiences of different countries which followed it, experts started theorising about planning. Thus, in the case of planning, the direction has been from practice to theory. This is why the form and the nature of planning kept changing from country to country and from time to time. As we will see in the following pages, the types of planning itself evolved through time as different countries experimented with it.

As per our working definition, we may observe the following things about planning:

1. **Planning is a Process:** It means planning is a process of doing something. Until we have some goals and objectives left regarding our lives, the process might continue. With the changing nature of our needs, the nature and scope of the planning process might undergo several changes. Planning is not an end in itself. As processes accelerate and decelerate, change direction and course, so also does planning.
2. **Planning Must have well-defined Goals:** After the Second World War, several countries opted for development planning. As these nations faced enormous socio-economic hurdles, they first set some goals and objectives and then started their process of realising them *via* planning. In due course of time, there emerged a consensus that planning must have some goals and those goals should be well defined (not vaguely defined) - so that the government's discretionary intervention in the economic organisation could be democratically transparent and justified. Even in the non-democratic nations (i.e., erstwhile USSR, Poland and China), the goals of planning were clearly defined.[6]
3. **Optimum Utilisation of the Available Resources:** Here we see two welcoming concepts. *First* is the way of utilising the resources. Till the idea of sustainability emerged (1987), experts tried to 'maximise' resource exploitation. But once experts around the world introspected the untenability of such a method of resource utilisation, the sustainable approach was included into planning, and herein entered the idea of utilising resources at its 'possible best', so that environmental degradation could be at its minimum and the future generations could also be able to continue with their progress. *Second* is the idea of the natural resources which are available. Resources (i.e., natural as well as human) could be of indigenous origin or exogenous. Most of the countries carrying out planning tried to utilise their indigenous resources, yet some tried to tap into the exogenous resources too, taking leverage of their diplomatic acumen. For example, the first country opting for national planning, i.e., the Soviet Union, leveraged resources available in the East European countries. India also used exogenous resources for its development planning wherever it was necessary and possible to tap.[7]

By the 1950s, planning had emerged as a method or tool of utilising resources to achieve any kind of goals for policy makers, around the world:

1. Trying to achieve a particular size of family for different countries came to be known as ***family planning***.
2. The process of providing suitable physical and social infrastructure for the erstwhile or the upcoming urban areas came to be known as ***town/urban planning***.
3. A country trying to optimise the use of its revenues for different categories of expenditures came to be known as ***financial planning***.

[5] United Nations Department of Economic Affairs, *Measures for Economic Development of Underdeveloped Countries* (New York, NY: UNO, DEA, 1951), p. 63.

[6] The Gosplan, *First Five Year Plan (1928-33)* (USSR, 1928).

[7] Many of the PSUs in the 1950s and the early 1960s were not only set up with natural resources (capital as well as machines) from the USSR and Germany but even human resources were also tapped from there for a few years.

Financial planning is more popularly known as ***budgeting***. All budgets, be it of the government or the private sector, are nothing but exercise in financial planning.

4. Similarly, at the macro and micro levels, there might be any number of planning processes - agricultural planning, industrial planning, irrigation planning, road planning, house planning, etc.

Simply put, the art of achieving any kind of goal with the use of the resources we have is the process of planning. We may cite a very general example - students of a class are able to join the class at the right time coming from different places of their stay. How they are able to do so? All of them must be planning their time in such a way that they are able to join the class at the same time though their places of residence are not at an equal distance from the class. All might be having their own ways of time planning - some might be having bed tea, some might not, some might be having breakfast at their place, yet others might think to take their breakfast in the college canteen, and so forth.

It means that even if we are not consciously planning or have not announced it, we are always planning our days. The same is true in the case of countries. Many countries announced that they will be planned economies, yet some others did not opt for any such policy announcements. The Soviet Union, Poland, China, France and India are examples of the former category, while the United States, Canada and Mexico fall into the latter category.[8] But here we are concerned with the conscious process of planning. There will be some methods, tools and types of planning emerging through time as different countries will start their processes of planning.

ORIGIN AND EXPANSION OF PLANNING

Planning is a method of achieving faster economic progress. It has been tried by different countries at different times and at different levels. We may see them as follows:

1. **Regional Planning:** It was at the regional level that planning was used as a part of development policy by any country for the *first time*. United States started the first regional planning after the Tennessee Valley Authority (TVA) was set up in 1916 - for a large-scale rehabilitation in south-eastern United States covering parts of seven states. With the primary aim of flood control, soil conservation and providing electricity, the TVA/the regional plan was also involved in many related activities such as industrial development, forestry, wildlife conservation, town planning, construction of road and rail, encouraging sound agricultural practices and malaria control in the defined region.[9] The US experience of regional planning became such a success in realising its well-defined goals that it emerged as a role model and an object of inspiration for many countries around the world in the coming decades - the Damodar Valley Corporation (DVC) in India (1948), the Volta River Project in Ghana (1966) and so forth.

2. **National Planning:** The official experiment in the area of national planning is rooted in the Bolshevik Revolution of Russia (1917) - the Soviet Union. Dissatisfied with the pace of industrialisation, it was in 1928 that Joseph Stalin announced its policy of central planning for the Soviet Union. The collectivisation of agriculture and forced-draft industrialisation were other radical new policy initiatives announced by Stalin besides economic planning in 1928.[10] The Soviet Union went for its first five-year plan for the period 1928-33, and the world was to have its *first* experience of *national planning*. The famous Soviet slogan 'great leap forward' was initiated for rapid industrialisation through the introduction of economic planning at the national level. The nature and scope of Soviet planning (called ***the Gosplan***) will have its direct or indirect bearings on all those countries which opted for economic planning, be it state or capitalist or mixed economies. India was to have a direct influence of Soviet planning on its planning process. In the first Soviet Plan, heavy industries were favoured over light industry, and consumer goods were the residual sector after all the other priorities had been met. We see the

[8] Though the United States was the first to opt for planning, at the regional level (Tennessee Valley Authority, 1916) it never announced its intention for national planning.

[9] G.C. Leong and G.C. Morgan, *Human and Economic Geography* (Oxford: Oxford University Press, 1982), p. 145.

[10] A. Nove, *An Economic History of the USSR*, 3rd ed. (Baltimore, MD: Penguin Books, 1990), p. 139.

same emphasis in the Indian planning process.[11] The Soviet model of economic planning spread to the East European countries, especially after the Second World War and found its purest form of such planning in the People's Republic of China (1949). During the early 1940s, the concept of national planning was borrowed by France, and the world saw national planning being initiated by a hitherto capitalist economy as well as by a non-centralised political system (i.e., democratic system). France started economic planning at the national level after announcing itself as a mixed economy.

TYPES OF PLANNING

After the first national planning was started by the Soviet Union, many more countries followed it, but with variations in their methods and practices. Though there are many variants of planning, the most important one is on the basis of the type of economic organisation (i.e., state economy, mixed economy). During the course of evolution, planning, based upon the type of economic system prevalent in the country, has been classified into two types.

1. **Imperative Planning:** The planning process followed by the state economies (i.e., the socialist or communist) is known as the imperative planning. This is also called ***directive*** or ***target planning***. Such planning had two main variants. In the socialist system, all economic decisions were centralised in the hands of the state with collective ownership of resources (except labour). In the communist system (i.e., China of the past) all resources were to be owned and utilised by the state (including labour). Thus, communist China was the purest example of such planning. In the case of the Soviet Union a little bit of 'market' did exist - even after the collectivisation of agriculture was enacted by Stalin in 1928 only 94 per cent of Soviet peasants could be included in the process.[12] Basic features of such planning are as follows:
   - **(i)** *Numerical (i.e. quantitative) targets* of growth and development are set by the plan. As, for example, five lakh tonnes of steel, two lakh tonnes of cement, 10,000 km of national highways, 5,000 primary schools and so forth will be produced/ built in the coming 5 or 6 years.
   - **(ii)** As the *state* controls the ownership rights over the resources, it is very much possible to realise the above-cited planned targets.
   - **(iii)** Almost *no role for the market,* no price mechanism with all economic decisions to be taken in the centralised way by the state/government.
   - **(iv)** No private participation in the economy, only the state plays the economic role.

The ***Command Economies*** followed this kind of planning. That is why such economies are also known as the ***Centrally Planned Economies*** - the USSR, Poland, Hungary, Austria, Romania and finally China. Basically, it was the migration of some of the great economists from the Soviet Bloc countries to Britain and the United States that a proper study and discussion started on the very nature and purpose of planning in the command economies. Many of these economists went back to their countries of origin after the Second World War to serve and, in some measure, suffer the revolution there.[13] It was their articulate and contemporary economic thinking which formed the basis for the idea of a mixed economy in the post-war world. One among them was Oskar Lange, the famous Polish economist, who, after returning home to serve as the Chairman of the Polish State Economic Council (as India had the Planning Commission), suggested and coined the

[11] R. Mohan, 'Industrial Policy and Controls', in *The Indian Economy: Problems and Prospects*, B. Jalan, ed. (New Delhi: Penguin Books, 2004), p. 101. Also see B. Chandra et al., *India After Independence* (New Delhi: Penguin Books, 2000), pp. 341-42, as well as A. Vaidyanathan, 'The Indian Economy Since Independence (1947-70)', in *The Cambridge Economic History of India*, vol. II, D. Kumar, ed. (Cambridge: Cambridge University Press, 1983), pp. 949-50.

[12] P.A. Samuelson and W.D. Nordhaus, *Economics* (New York, NY: McGraw-Hill Companies, 2005), p. 591.

[13] From Poland two great economists Oskar Lange (1904-65) and Michal Kalecki (1899-1970); from Hungary, William J. Fellner (1905-83), Nicholas Kaldor (1908-86), Thomas Balogh (1905-85) and Eric Roll (1907-95); from post-war Austria Ludwig von Mises (1880-1973), Friedrich A. von Hayek (1899-1992), Fritz Machlup (1902-83), Gottfried Haberler (1900-96) and Joseph A. Schumpeter (1883-1950) [J.K. Galbraith, *A History of Economics* (London: Penguin Books, 1987), pp. 187-90].

concept of *market socialism* in the 1950s. His ideas of market socialism were cancelled by not only Poland but also by other state economies of the time.[14]

The peak of this type of planning was reached in China after the Cultural Revolution (1966-69), which led to an economic slowdown in the country, which had adopted a Soviet-style central planning system after 1949. Under Deng Xiaoping (1977-97), China decentralised a great deal of economic power with its announcement of the open-door policy in 1985 to save the economy. The Chinese ***open-door policy*** was an initiative in the direction of 'market socialism' under the communist political design (a popular student demand for political reform in favour of democracy was ruthlessly repressed in Tiananmen Square in 1989). Similarly, the Soviet Union under the leadership of Mikhail Gorbachev began a process of political and economic reforms, called ***prestroika*** (i.e., restructuring) and ***glasnost*** (i.e., openness) in 1985 to save the failed economic experiments in the state economy. Other East European economies followed similar economic reforms from 1989 onwards. Thus, the whole world of the state economies had moved towards market economy by the late 1980s. Since then, none of the countries have followed imperative planning.

2. **Indicative Planning:** In the following two decades after the soviet planning commenced, the idea of planning received attention from the democratic world. A time came when some such economies started national planning. As they were neither state economies nor communist/socialist political systems, the nature of their planning was different from the command economies. Such planning has been termed indicative planning by economists and experts. The identifying features of indicative planning may be summed up as follows:
   - **(i)** Every economy following the indicative planning was mixed economies.
   - **(ii)** Unlike a centrally planned economy (countries following imperative planning), indicative planning works through the market (price system) rather than replaces it.[15]
   - **(iii)** Side-by-side setting of numerical/ quantitative targets (similar to the practice in the imperative planning), a set of economic policies of indicative nature is also announced by the economies to realise the plan targets.
   - **(iv)** The indicative nature of economic policies, which are announced in such planning, basically encourage or discourage the private sector in its process of economic decision-making.

After converting to mixed economy by the mid-1940s, France commenced its first six-year plan in 1947, which received popularity as the ***Monnet Plan*** (he was the first chairman of the General Planning Commission and the then Cabinet Minister for planning in France).[16] Later, the Monnet Plan became synonymous to indicative planning. This plan is also sometimes described as the *basic sector planning* as the government had selected eight basic industries as the core of development in which the nature of planning was almost *imperative*, i.e., under state monopoly (these sectors were owned by the private sector till 1944 when France opted for their nationalisation).[17] Other economic activities were open for private participation wherein an indicative type of policy planning was essential. France as well as Japan has followed indicative planning with great success. It was in 1965 that the United Kingdom commenced such a planning with the National Plan and abandoned it in 1966 after being overtaken by events (a balance of payment crisis resulting in a deflationary package

[14] It was blasphemous to preach in favour of market in the socialist world at that time - being not put behind bars was a great mercy on him. Oskar Lange towards the end of his life told Paul M. Sweezy, the most noted American Marxist scholar, that during this period he did not retire for the night without speculating as to whether he might be arrested before the dawn (J.K. Galbraith, *A History of Economics*, p. 189).

[15] *Collins Internet-linked Dictionary of Economics*, Glasgow, 2006.

[16] G.A. Steiner, *Government's Role in Economic Life* (New York, NY: McGraw-Hill, 1953), p. 152.

[17] India had a French influence on its development planning when it followed almost state monopoly in the six infrastructure industries also known as the *core* or the *basic* industries, i.e., cement, iron and steel, coal, crude oil, oil refinery and electricity.

of measures). Since then, the United Kingdom never opted for planning.[18]

Though the ***first use of*** economic planning as an instrument of economic progress was carried out by the United States (with the Tennessee Valley Authority in 1916 at the regional level), it never opted for a *formal* national planning. In the 1940s, some economists had suggested in favour of the use of national planning. We may have a reflex of indicative planning in the United States if we look at the *Presidential Reports* which come after regular intervals. These reports are just 'benchmarks' in the area of resource utilisation and governmental announcements of its objectives - basically trying to motivate the private sector towards the area of public objectives. The indicative planning which is practised by mixed economies, growth targets can only be achieved once the public and the private enterprises worked in tandem. This is why, besides the plan targets, the governments need to announce some set of indicative policies to encourage and motivate the private sector to accelerate their economic activities in the desired direction.

After the Second World War, almost all of the newly independent countries adopted the route of planned development. Though they followed an overall model of the indicative planning, many of them had a serious inclination towards imperative planning. As in the case of India, the heavy bias towards imperative planning could only be reformed once the process of economic reforms was started in 1991.

Today, as there are mostly only mixed economies around the world, any country's development planning has to be only of the indicative type. After the revival of the role and the need of market in promoting growth and development *via* the Washington Consensus (1985), the World Trade Organisation (1995) and the Santiago/ New Consensus (1998) only indicative planning has remained possible with the state playing only a marginal role in the economy, especially in the areas of social importance (i.e., nutrition, healthcare, drinking water, education and social security).

[18] Though the planning agencies, the National Economic Development Council (NEDC) and the Economic Development Committees (EDCs) continued functioning, it was in 1992 that the NEDC was abolished (*Collins Dictionary of Economics*, 2006).

Some Other Types

There are still many **other types** of planning depending upon the point of view we are looking at. For example, from the territorial point of view, planning could be ***regional*** or ***national***. From the political point of view, planning could be ***central***, ***state*** or ***local***. Similarly, from the participatory point of view, planning has been categorised into ***centralised*** and ***decentralised***. Again, from the temporal point of view, planning could be ***long-term*** or ***short-term*** (in a relative sense). Similarly, planning can be ***sectoral*** and ***spatial*** too. While sectoral planning emphasises the specific sector in the economy (i.e., agriculture, industry or the services), in the spatial planning development is seen in the spatial framework (which aims at influencing the distribution of people and activities in spaces).

One **major classification** of planning, which has been in news for the past few years, is carried out on the basis of the 'value system' of the society - ***systems*** and ***normative*** planning. The systems approach to planning is largely *value-neutral* and remains fully focussed on the economic aspects of development. Socio-cultural variables are not given much importance in it, and it quite mechanically targets the planned goals. This emerged as the most favoured type of planning across the world as it was very much in harmony with the idea of secularism, equality and other democratic ideals of modern time. The most important part of this approach was its neutrality to the social diversities. Such an approach to planning suited India quite perfectly as it had very high socio-cultural diversities. The normative approach of planning is *value based.* This process of planning remains in conformity to the value system of the target population - having quite a diversified approach to development. This approach of planning was largely avoided by the world and never tried at the macro level till the first decade of the twenty-first century. With the rising acceptance to the *behavioural economics,* we find normative approach gaining ground across the world. It received faster recognition among the experts and policymakers

Scan this QR Code to watch a author's video lecture that simplifies this topic after two major international events - firstly, it was the publication of the first *World Happiness Report (2012),* and secondly, the *World Development Report 2015 (World Bank),* with the latter highlighting the importance and impact of including behavioural dimensions of people in formulating public policies.

The Case of India

The *Economic Survey 2010-11* is the first document of the Government of India which advocates the need for a ***normative approach*** to planning in India. It is believed that until a programme/scheme run by the governments is not able to connect with the customs, traditions and ethos of the population, their acceptability will not be of the desired level among the target population. Establishing an empathic relationship between the programmes/schemes and target population is now considered an important aspect of planning and policymaking. Such a change in the thinking is based on the experiences of India and other countries of the world.

In January 2015, the Government of India replaced the erstwhile body, Planning Commission, by the *NITI Aayog* (a policy *think tank*). If we look into the functions and guiding principles of the new body, we become aware of the fact that India has officially moved towards ***normative planning*** - the new body has to follow a *development model* which is 'all round, all pervasive, all-inclusive and holistic'. In this process, the NITI Aayog has been further asked to enable the country to draw on the vitality and energy of the bedrock of our *ethos, culture* and *sustenance.*

In recent times we see the Government employing nudges[19] to modify people's behaviour to take desired socio-economic outcome aimed at development - i.e., using behavioural insights to frame economic policies. All such policy actions are the examples of normative planning.

Atmanirbharta Push

The ***Atmanirbharta*** (self-reliance) push of the Government is a ***value-laden idea*** with local overtones (such as 'vocal for local' blurring the lines between nationalism and protectionism) and, thus, is guided by ***normative insights*** – be it aimed at emerging as a 'pharmacy of the world' or exploring the possibilities of an alternative to the global supply chain.[20]

[19] *Economic Survey 2018-19*, vol. 1 (New Delhi: Ministry of Finance, GoI), pp. 30-56; *Economic Survey 2019-20*, vol. 1 (New Delhi: Ministry of Finance, GoI), pp. 260-85.

[20] *Economic Survey 2020-21*, vol. 2 (New Delhi: Ministry of Finance, GoI), pp. 97-9.

SAMPLE OBJECTIVE QUESTIONS

1. Consider the following statements related to 'economic planning':

(i) Short-term plans are normally for a period of one year.

(ii) Short-term plans are suitable from the point of 'scenario' planning.

(iii) 'Vision' planning is normally absent in the short-term plans.

Which of the statements given above are correct?

(a) (i) and (ii) only **(b)** (ii) and (iii) only

(c) (i) and (iii) only **(d)** (i), (ii) and (iii) all

2. Consider the following statements related to 'target planning':

(i) Such planning has been highly successful among the mixed economies.

(ii) It originated in the state economy by the early 20th century.

(iii) It has been relatively successful in India.

Which of the statements given above are incorrect?

(a) (i) and (ii) only **(b)** (ii) and (iii) only

(c) (i) and (iii) only **(d)** (i), (ii) and (iii) all

3. Consider the following statements related to 'economic planning':
   - **(i)** Maximum utilisation of resources is one of its chief features.
   - **(ii)** It cannot be carried on as per the 'value system' of the target region.
   - **(iii)** Its 'systems' approach is easier than that of the 'normative' approach.

   Which of the statements given above are incorrect?
   - **(a)** (i) and (ii) only
   - **(b)** (ii) and (iii) only
   - **(c)** (i) and (iii) only
   - **(d)** (i), (ii) and (iii) all

4. Select the correct statement(s) related to the 'approach' of economic planning using the code given below:
   - **(i)** Targeting economic goals are easier through 'systems' approach.
   - **(ii)** Realisation of the economic goals set by planning depends on social realities too.
   - **(iii)** Its 'normative' approach is much nuanced than that of the 'systems' approach.
   - **(iv)** India has used more of the normative approach than the systems.

   Code:
   - **(a)** (i) and (ii) only
   - **(b)** (i), (ii) and (iii) only
   - **(c)** (ii) and (iv) only
   - **(d)** (i), (iii) and (iv) only

5. Consider the following statements about 'decentralised' planning:
   - **(i)** It is carried out by all levels of the government in a country.
   - **(ii)** Lower levels of the governments may not be given financial autonomy under it.
   - **(iii)** It originated in the Ex-USSR.
   - **(iv)** People's Republic of China officially follows such a planning.

   Which of the statements given above are correct?
   - **(a)** (i) and (ii) only
   - **(b)** (ii), (iii) and (iv) only
   - **(c)** (iii) and (iv) only
   - **(d)** (i), (ii) and (iv) only

6. Consider the following statements related to the types of economic planning:
   - **(i)** Indicative planning emerged in the USA.
   - **(ii)** Every indicative plan has the elements of the target planning.
   - **(iii)** India shifted from target to indicative planning during the economic reforms process.
   - **(iv)** Before economic reforms India was largely following target planning.

   Which of the statements given above are correct?
   - **(a)** (i) and (ii) only
   - **(b)** (ii), (iii) and (iv) only
   - **(c)** (iii) and (iv) only
   - **(d)** (i), (ii) and (iv) only

7. Consider the following statements about development planning:
   - **(i)** It traces its origin in the capitalist economic system.
   - **(ii)** It was adopted at the national level by the USA for the first time.
   - **(iii)** Imperative plans of the world have been more performance-oriented than that of the indicative ones.
   - **(iv)** Regional disparities call for the regional planning.

   Which of the statements given above are correct?
   - **(a)** (i) and (ii) only
   - **(b)** (i), (iii) and (iv) only
   - **(c)** (iii) and (iv) only
   - **(d)** (i), (ii) and (iv) only

8. Consider the following statements about the process of economic planning:
   - **(i)** Before its theories came into being, many countries had already adopted it.
   - **(ii)** It was practiced in India in pre-Independence period too.
   - **(iii)** Officially, India adopted its model of planning more from France than the Ex-USSR less.

   Which of the statements given above are correct?

(a) (i) and (ii) only
(b) (ii) and (iii) only
(c) (i) and (iii) only
(d) (i), (ii) and (iii) all

9. Which of the following is incorrect about the process of economic planning?
(a) It has been more popular at national level than that of at the regional level.
(b) Regional planning is senior in origin than the national planning.
(c) China and India both follow indicative planning.
(d) National Planning in the USA has always been indicative in nature.

10. Consider the following statements related to the process of development planning:
(i) Planning process of mixed economies were more influenced by the Polish philosopher Oskar Lange than the French administrator Jean Monnet.
(ii) Mixed imperative planning is synonymous with the Monnet Planning.
(iii) Oskar Lange was involved with development planning of India.

Which of the statements given above are correct?
(a) (i) and (ii) only
(b) (ii) only
(c) (ii) and (iii) only
(d) (iii) only

Answers: 1. (c) 2. (c) 3. (a) 4. (b) 5. (d) 6. (a) 7. (b) 8. (a) 9. (d) 10. (d)

SAMPLE SUBJECTIVE QUESTIONS

1. 'Nations with high poverty levels find it difficult to follow sustainable economic planning.' Explain.
2. Why does the optimum utilisation of the resources is considered as a good practice in the area of development planning? Give suitable examples from India to support your view.
3. 'Economic objectives of planned development are better realised if the behavioural dimension of the society is aligned with it.' Elaborate.
4. 'The history of economic planning is the history of the evolution of mixed economy.' Elaborate.
5. Briefly examine the reasons due to which normative approach of planning is considered superior than the systems approach. To support your views cite suitable examples from India.

SAMPLE MODEL ANSWER

1. **'Planning in coming times will become more indicative'– explain this announcement of the Government while launching the process of economic reforms in 1991.**

Ans. While launching the measures of the economic reforms process in 1991, the Government announced that the nature of planning will become more indicative in the coming times. Such an announcement can be understood in the following ways:

➤ Economic planning of the mixed market economies has been indicative in nature. In indicative planning, planned development has both the government and the private sector as the stakeholders (unlike the 'target planning' in which this is the sole responsibility of the government). India being a mixed economy, its planning has been indicative in nature right since independence.

- As the process of economic reforms in 1991 invoked for higher private involvement in development, the nature of the mixed economy of India was headed for privatisation and liberalisation.
- To make development planning successful, the Government needed to chalk out more liberal and indicative policies, which could encourage the private sector to play an enhanced economic role in the country. Globalisation was yet another attraction of the reform process for the private sector.

As the role of the private sector has been enhanced in the country, the nature of planning in India has become more indicative, which can be seen across the economy, such as in energy, transportation, electricity, telecommunication, defence, space, education, health, etc. This is why the Government made such an announcement while launching the process of reforms in 1991.

CHAPTER 6

Planning in India

> NITI Aayog will work on a development model– rooted in our wisdom of civilisational history and ethos, i.e., Bharatiyata– which is all round, all pervasive, all inclusive, and holistic.*
>
> *NITI Aayog (New Delhi: Government of India, February 8, 2015), p. 16.

To watch the Author's videos on the significance of the Chapter, scan the QR Code given here

Exam Essentials...

- Damodar Valley Corporation (DVC)
- Some Area-wise Reports
- NDC vs GC
- The Five-Year Plans
- Conceptual Timeline of Indian Planning
- Development Monitoring and Evaluation Office
- Specialised Wings in the NITI Aayog
- Concluding Remarks

Note to the Reader...

India is a 'planned economy' right since independence, and its history of development has been the history of planning. The roots of planning go back to the 1930s when Meghnad Saha advised making rivers the unit of economic planning in the country. Even after the replacement of the economic think tank the Planning Commission by the Niti Aayog, India remains a planned economy. This shows the 'significance' of this chapter.

In This Chapter...

INTRODUCTION

It was the Soviet Union which explored and adopted *national planning* for the first time in the world. After a prolonged period of debate and discussion, the First Soviet Plan commenced in 1928 for a period of five years. But the rest of the world was not fully aware of the *modus operandi* of development planning till the 1930s. It was the exodus[1] of the east European economists to Britain and the United States in the 1920s and 1930s that made the world aware as to what economic/national planning was all about. The entire colonial world and the democracies of the time were fascinated by the idea of planning as an instrument of economic progress. The nationalist leaders with a socialistic inclination of the erstwhile British colonies were more influenced by the idea of economic planning. The whole decade of the 1930s is the period in the Indian history when we see nationalists, capitalists, socialists, democrats and academicians advocating for the need of economic planning in India at one point or the other.[2]

Independent India was thus destined to be a planned economy. The economic history of India is nothing but the history of planning.[3] Even if the so-called economic reforms started in 1991-92, all the humble suggestions regarding the contours of reforms were very much outlined by the Planning Commission (PC) by then.[4] Once the reforms commenced, the think tank started outlining the major future direction for further plans.[5] Going through the history of planning in India is a highly educational trip in itself - for though the PC has been a political body, it never hesitated in pointing out good economics time and again. Let us therefore find out about the unfolding of the planning process in India.

[1] J. K. Galbraith, *A History of Economics* (London: Penguin Books, 199), p. 187.

[2] B. Chandra, 'The Colonial Legacy', in *The Indian Economy: Problems and Prospects*, B. Jalan, ed. (New Delhi: Penguin Books, 2004).

[3] A. Sengupta, 'The Planning Regime Since 1951', in *Looking Back: India in the Twentieth Century*, N. N. Vohra and S. Bhattacharya, eds. (New Delhi: National Book Trust, 2001), p. 121.

[4] Planning Commission, *Seventh Five Year Plan (1985-90)* (New Delhi: Government of India), 1985.

[5] Planning Commission, *The 8th, 9th, 10th and 11th Plans*, (New Delhi: Government of India).

BACKGROUND

By the decade of the 1930s, the idea of planning had already entered the domain of intellectual and political discussion in India. Many fresh proposals suggesting immediacy of planning in India were put forward, though the erstwhile British government remained almost immune to them. But these humble proposals of planning served their purpose once India became independent and decided to adopt a planned economy.

The Visvesvaraya Plan

The credit of proposing the first blueprint of Indian planning is given to the popular civil engineer and the ex-Dewan of the Mysore state, M. Visvesvaraya. In his book *The Planned Economy of India*, published in 1934, he outlined the broad contours of his plan proposal.[6] His ideas of state planning were an exercise in democratic capitalism (similar to the United States) with emphasis on industrialisation - a shift of labour from agricultural to industries, targeting to double the national income in one decade. Though there was no follow-up by the British government on this plan, it aroused an urge for national planning among the educated citizens of the country.

The FICCI Proposal

In 1934, a serious need for national planning was recommended by the Federation of Indian Chambers of Commerce and Industry (FICCI), the leading organisation of Indian capitalists. Its president N. R. Sarkar proclaimed that the days of undiluted *laissez faire* were gone forever, and for a backward country like India, a comprehensive plan for economic development covering the whole gamut of economic activities was a necessity. Voicing the views of the capitalist class, he further called for a high-powered National Planning Commission to coordinate the whole process of planning so that the country could make a structural break with the past and achieve its full growth potential.[7]

By the late nineteenth century, the economic thinking of the nationalists (such as M. G. Ranade and Dadabhai Naroji) was in favour of a dominant role of

[6] S. Sarkar, *Modern India: 1855-1947* (New Delhi: Macmillan, 1983), pp. 360-61.

[7] B. Chandra, et al., *India After Independence, 1947-2000* (New Delhi: Penguin Books, 2000), p. 341.

the state in the economy and doubted the prudence of the 'market mechanism'. This thinking was further reinforced by the Keynesian ideas in the wake of the Great Depression, the *New Deal* in the United States and the Soviet experiment in national planning. Thus, the Indian capitalist class were also influenced by these events which were voiced in the FICCI articulation for planning.

The Congress Plan

Though the Gandhians and some of the business and propertied representatives were opposed to commit the party to centralised state planning (including Mahatma Gandhi),[8] it was on the initiative[9] of the INC president Subhash C. Bose that the National Planning Committee (NPC) was set up in October 1938 under the chairmanship of J. L. Nehru to work out concrete programmes for development encompassing all major areas of the economy. Basically, the NPC was set up in a conference of the Ministers of Industries of the Congress-ruled states (though other states were also invited to participate) where M. Visvesvaraya, J. R. D. Tata, G. D. Birla and Lala Sri Ram and many others including academicians, technocrats, provincial civil servants, trade unionists, socialists and communists were also invited. The 15-member NPC with 29 sub-committees and a total of 350 members produced 29 volumes of recommendations.[10] The work of the committee was interrupted when the Second World War broke out, and in the wake of the Quit India Movement many of its members including the chairman were arrested, and between 1940 and 1945 the Committee had only a nominal existence. Though the final report of the NPC could only be published in 1949, many developments related to planning took place during the Interim Government up to 1946.

'A series of valuable reports were published which brought together the constructive thinking done by the committee and the sub-committees and the materials collected in the course of their work. The importance of the NPC lies not so much in these reports as in the wide interest it created throughout the country for coordinated planning as the only means of bringing about a rapid increase in the standards of living and its emphasis on the need for bringing fundamental changes in the social and economic structure'.[11]

Some of the important developments after the NPC was set up which prepared a foundation for coordinated planning in independent India are given below:

1. **Post-War Reconstruction Committee:** Early in June 1941, the Government of India (GoI) formed (on popular demand) a Post-War Reconstruction Committee which was to consider various plans for the reconstruction of the economy.
2. **Consultative Committee of Economists:** A consultative committee of economists under the chairmanship of Ramaswamy Mudaliar was set up in 1941 as a 'think tank' to advise the four post-war reconstruction committees for executing a national plan for the country.

   Though the committee suggested many plans for different areas of the economy, they had negligible practical significance as these suggestions were imbued with academic biases.
3. **Planning and Development Department:** After all possible delays, it was in 1944 that the government created a Planning and Development Department under a separate member of the Viceroy's Executive Council for organising and coordinating economic planning in the country. Ardeshir Dalal (the Controller of the Bombay Plan) was appointed as one of its acting members. More than 20 panels of experts were set up. The central departments and the governments of the provinces and Indian states were invited to prepare detailed plans for industrialisation.[12] This department was abolished in 1946.
4. **Advisory Planning Board:** In October 1946, the GoI appointed a committee called the Advisory Planning Board[13] to review the planning

[8] A. Vaidyanathan, 'The Indian Economy Since Independence (1947-70)', in *The Cambridge Economic History of India*, vol. II, D. Kumar, ed. (Cambridge: Cambridge University Press, 1983), p. 949.

[9] S. Sarkar, *Modern India*, op. cit. p. 360.

[10] Publications Division, *The Gazetteer of India*, vol. 3 (New Delhi: Government of India, 1975), p. 2.

[11] Ibid., pp. 2-3.

[12] There was a popular view in favour of rapid industrialisation among the important nationalists, economists and the business class of that time.

[13] The Board was set up by the interim government formed in 1946.

that had already been carried out by the British government, the work of the NPC and other plans and proposals for planning and to make recommendations regarding the future machinery of planning as well as in regard to objectives and priorities. The Board strongly recommended the creation of 'a single, compact authoritative organisation ... responsible directly to the Cabinet ... which should devote its attention continuously to the whole field of development'.[14] This was an emphatic advice for the creation of a National Planning Commission, similar to FICCI's view of 1934, which will have autonomy and authoritative say on the process of development planning, working in tandem with the Union Cabinet and also influencing the developmental decisions of the states. This happened in 1950 with the setting up of the PC.

The Board, in its Report of January 1947, emphatically expressed the opinion that the 'proper development of large-scale industries can only take place if political units, whether in the provinces or states, agree to work in accordance with a common plan'.[15] This suggestion worked as a great influence on the planning process of independent India as it always tried to provide a unifying nature to development planning. But this process also induced a serious tendency of centralisation in Indian planning to which a number of states were to pose objections and straining the centre-state relations, time and again.[16] However, the political leadership, right from the 1920s, was very conscious of the need for decentralised planning in the country.[17]

The Bombay Plan

The Bombay Plan was the popular title of 'A Plan of Economic Development for India', which was prepared by a cross section of India's leading capitalists. The eight capitalists involved in this plan were Purshotamdas Thakurdas, J. R. D. Tata, G. D. Birla, Lala Sri Ram, Kasturbhai Lalbhai, A. D. Shroff, Ardeshir Dalal and John Mathai.[18] The Plan was published in 1944-45. Out of these eight industrialists, Purshotamdas Thakurdas was one among the 15 members of the NPC (1938);[19] J. R. D. Tata, G. D. Birla and Lala Sri Ram were members of the sub-committees (29 in total) of the NPC.[20]

The popular sentiments regarding the need of planning and crisscross of memberships between the NPC and the Bombay Plan club made possible some clear-cut agreements between these two major plans, which ultimately went to mold the very shape of the Indian economy after Independence. We may have a look at some of the very important agreements:[21]

1. A basic agreement on the issue of the ***agrarian restructuring*** - abolition of all intermediaries (i.e., zamindari abolition), minimum wages, guarantee of minimum or fair prices for agricultural products, cooperatives, credit and marketing supports.
2. Agreement on ***rapid industrialisation*** for which both the plans agreed upon an emphasis on heavy capital goods and basic industries (the Bombay Plan had allocated 35 per cent of its total plan outlay on basic industries).
3. Taking clues from the Soviet Planning, the NPC and the Bombay Plan both were in favour of a simultaneous ***development of the essential consumer goods*** industries, but as a low-key affair.
4. Both the plans agreed upon the importance of promoting the ***medium-scale***, ***small-scale*** and ***cottage industries*** as they could provide greater employment and required lesser capital and lower order of plants and machineries.
5. Both the plans wanted the ***state to play an active role*** in the economy through planning, controlling and overseeing the different areas of the economy, i.e., trade, industry and banking,

[14] D. Kumar (ed.), *The Cambridge Economic History of India*, vol. II (University of Cambridge, Cambridge, England, 1983), p. 950.

[15] K. Datta, *An Advanced History of India*, 4th ed. (New Delhi: Macmillan, 2006), pp. 955-56.

[16] S. N. Jha and P. C. Mathur (eds.), *Decentralisation and Local Politics* (New Delhi: Sage Publications, 2002), pp. 28-30.

[17] A. H. Hanson, *The Process of Planning: A Study of India's Five-Year Plans, 1950-1964* (London: Oxford University Press, 1966), pp. 152-55.

[18] B. Chandra, 'The Colonial Legacy', op. cit. p. 23.

[19] P. Chatterjee, 'Development Planning and the Indian Planning', in *State and Politics in India*, P. Chatterjee, ed. (New Delhi: Oxford University Press, 1997), p. 273.

[20] R. Mohan, 'Industrial Policy and Controls', in *Indian Economy: Problems and Prospects*, B. Jalan, ed. (New Delhi: Penguin Books, 1994).

[21] B. Chandra, 'The Colonial Legacy', op. cit. pp. 23-31.

through state ownership (public sector) or through direct and extensive control over them.

6. Large-scale measures for ***social welfare*** were favoured by both the plans, which suggested to be based on issues such as right to work and full employment, the guarantee of a minimum wage, greater state expenditure on housing, water and sanitation, free education, social insurance to cover unemployment and sickness and provision of utility services such as electricity and transportation at a low cost through state subsidies.
7. Both the plans agreed upon a planning which could do away with gross ***inequalities*** through measures such as progressive taxation and prevention of concentration of wealth. Inequality was considered undesirable as it tended to restrict the domestic market.

Damodar Valley Corporation (DVC)

India's DVC (a joint project of the Government of India, the then Bihar and West Bengal), launched in 1948 (suggested by the Technical Committee in 1944), was modeled on the Tennessee Valley Authority (TVA) of the USA. Like the latter, the DVC too had similar primary objectives (flood control, soil conservation, providing electricity) and associated objectives (industrial development, forestry, wildlife conservation, town planning, construction of road and rail, encouraging sound agricultural practices and malaria control).

All of the river-based projects in India are modeled on the DVC.

Sources: G. C. Leong and G. C. Morgan, *Human and Economic Geography* (Oxford: Oxford University Press, 1982), p. 145; and *First (1951–56) and Second (1956–61) Five Year Plans*, Planning Commission, GoI, N. Delhi.

The Gandhian Plan

Espousing the spirit of the Gandhian economic thinking, Sriman Narayan Agarwal formulated the Gandhian Plan in 1944. The plan laid more emphasis on agriculture. Even if he referred to industrialisation, it was to the level of promoting cottage and village-level industries, unlike the NPC and the Bombay Plan which played a leading role in the heavy and large industries. The plan articulated a 'decentralised economic structure' for India with 'self-contained villages'.

It needs to be noted here that the Gandhians did not agree with the views of the NPC or the Bombay Plan, particularly on issues such as centralised planning, dominant role of the state in the economy and the emphasis on industrialisation.[22] For Gandhi, the machinery, commercialisation and centralised state power were the curses of modern civilisation thrust upon the Indian people by European colonialism. It was industrialism itself, Gandhi argued, rather than the inability to industrialise, which was the root cause of Indian poverty. This was until the 1940s that the Congress supported the above-given view of Gandhi to mobilise a mass movement against the colonial rule. But it was in the NPC that the Congress tried to articulate a different view on these issues, almost taking a break from Gandhi's ideas. The very first session of the NPC was brought to an impasse by J. C. Kumarappa (the lone Gandhian on the 15-member NPC) by questioning the authority of the NPC to discuss plans for industrialisation. He said on the occasion that the national priority as adopted by the Congress was to restrict and eliminate modern industrialism. The impasse was normalised after Nehru intervened and declared that most members of the NPC felt that large-scale industry ought to be promoted as long as it did not 'come into conflict with the cottage industries'.[23] This was a long-drawn ideological impasse which made it necessary to articulate the Gandhian view of planning *via* this plan.

The People's Plan

In 1945, yet another plan was formulated by the radical humanist leader M. N. Roy, Chairman of the Post-War Reconstruction Committee of the Indian Trade Union. The plan was based on Marxist socialism and advocated the need of providing the people with the 'basic necessities of life'.[24] Agricultural and industrial sectors both were equally highlighted by the plan. Many economists have attributed the

[22] D. Kumar, *The Cambridge Economic History of India*, op. cit. p. 949.

[23] P. Chatterjee, 'Development Planning and the Indian Planning', op. cit. p. 275.

[24] S. K. Ray, *Indian Economy* (New Delhi: Prentice Hall, 1987), p. 369.

socialist leanings of Indian planning to this plan. The common minimum programmes of the United Front Government of the mid-1990s (twentieth century) and that of the United Progressive Alliance of 2004 may also be thought to have been inspired from the same plan. 'Economic reforms with the human face', the slogan with which the economic reforms started in the early 1990s also has the resonance of the People's Plan.

The Sarvodaya Plan

After the reports of the NPC were published and the government was set to go for the Five-Year Plans, a lone blueprint for the planned development of India was formulated by the famous socialist leader Jayaprakash Narayan - the Sarvodaya Plan was published in January 1950. The plan drew its major inspirations from the Gandhian techniques of constructive works by the community and trusteeship as well as the Sarvodaya concept of Acharya Vinoba Bhave, the eminent Gandhian constructive worker. Major ideas of the plan were highly similar to the Gandhian Plan such as emphasis on agriculture, agri-based small and cottage industries, self-reliance and almost no dependence on foreign capital and technology, land reforms, self-dependent villages and decentralised participatory form of planning and economic progress, to name the major ones.[25] Some of the acceptable ideas of the plan received their due importance when the GoI promoted the Five-Year Plans.

By the early 1960s, Jayaprakash Narayan had become highly critical of the Indian planning process, especially of its increasing centralising nature and dilution of people's participation in it. Basically, the very idea of democratic decentralisation was disliked by the established power structure, namely the MLAs/MPs, the bureaucracy and the state-level politicians.[26] This led the Jayaprakash Narayan Committee (1961) to decide against the centralising nature of Indian planning. The Committee pointed out that after having accepted Panchayati Raj as the agency responsible for planning and execution of plans, there is 'no longer any valid reason for continuing the individual allocations subject wise even to serve as a guide'.[27]

[25] A. H. Hanson, *The Process of Planning*, op. cit. p. 175.

[26] G. Mathew, *Power to the People*, in *50 Years of Indian Republic*, M. K. Santhanam, ed. (New Delhi: Publications Division, Government of India, 200), p. 32.

[27] L. C. Jain, et al., *Grass without Roots* (New Delhi: Sage Publications, 1985).

Disregarding the humble advice of the Committee, central schemes such as Small Farmers Development Agency (SFDA), Drought-Prone Area Programme (DPAP), Intensive Tribal Development Programme (ITDP) and Intensive Agricultural District Programme (IADP) were introduced by the government and were put totally outside the purview of the Panchayats.

It was only after the 73rd and 74th Amendments to the Constitution (1992) that the role of local bodies and their importance in the process of planned development was accepted and the views of Jayaprakash got vindicated.

Some Area-wise Reports

The idea for the need of planned development of India became more popular by the 1940s. It was under this pressure that the GoI started making some planned actions in this direction. In the 1940s, we see several area-specific reports being published:[28]

1. Gadgil Report on Rural Credit
2. Kheragat Report on Agricultural Development
3. Krishnamachari Report on Agricultural Prices
4. Saraiya Report on Cooperatives
5. A series of reports on Irrigation (ground water, canal etc.)

All these reports, though prepared with great care and due scholarship, found that the government had hardly any zeal to implement the plans on their findings. But independent India was greatly benefited when the planning started covering all these areas of concern.

There is no doubt in drawing the conclusion that prior to independence there was, thus, a significant measure of agreement in India between the GoI under the Secretary of State, the Indian National Congress, prominent industrialists and others on the following principles:[29]

1. There should be central planning, where the state should play an active part, for social and economic development to bring about a rapid rise in the standard of living.

[28] A. H. Hanson, *The Process of Planning*, op. cit. p. 180.

[29] Publications Division, *The Gazetteer of India*, op. cit., p. 5.

2. There should be controls and licensing in order, among other things, to direct investments into the desired channels and ensure equitable distribution.
3. While there should be balanced development in all sectors of the economy, the establishment of basic industries was especially important. In this, state-owned and state-managed enterprises have an important role to play. There were, however, differences of approach with regard to the specific fields to be allocated to the public and private sectors.

It is highly interesting and important to note that all the above agreements and opinions were reached through an evolutionary manner in the last two decades before independence in the deliberations and exercises regarding the need for economic planning in the country.

'The plans prepared by the GoI, the Bombay Plan and other above-discussed plans (except the NPC and the Sarvodaya Plan) suffered from serious limitations. When they were prepared, it was known that transfer of power was to take place quite soon, but the exact form of the future government was not known, and the plans consisted largely of proposals of experts, which were not effectively coordinated. They had no social philosophy behind them. With the advent of independence, they became inadequate, though the thinking that had taken place on planning generally and its techniques proved useful for the future'.[30]

MAJOR OBJECTIVES OF PLANNING

Planning for India was an instrument to realise the aspirations and dreams of the future. We know that the foundations of future India were not laid in one day. The cherished dream about future India had evolved through a long-drawn process of the entire period of the freedom struggle. These aspirations and goals received their proper place and due importance in the reports of the NPC, in the deliberations of the Constituent Assembly, and finally in the Constitution of India. From the margins of the ripening nationalist movement, as well as taking cues from the Soviet and the French styles of planning, the NPC articulated the objectives of planning in India. The process of planning in India tried to include all the aspirations of the nationalist movement as well as of the future generations. But this will be a highly general comment upon the objectives of planning in India. We need to delve into the specific and objective goals of planning in India to further our discussions. Some of the historic deliberations regarding planning will serve our purpose:

1. Reviewing the entire situation, in the light of the social philosophy evolved over the decades, the Constituent Assembly came to the conclusion that to guide this 'revolution of rising expectations' into constructive channels, India should make determined efforts through carefully planned large-scale social and economic development and the application of modern scientific and technological improvements, to bring about a rapid and appreciable rise in the standard of living of the people, with the maximum measure of social justice attainable. On the whole it was a call for India to become a welfare state.[31] This important deliberation does not only call for the necessity of planning for the country, but it also outlines the broader objectives of planning.
2. There are three important features included in the constitutional provisions, which pertain to the objectives of planning in the country:[32]
   - **(i)** 'Economic and social planning' is a concurrent subject. Also, while framing the Union, State and Concurrent Lists, allocating subjects and other provisions, the Constitution vests power in the Union to ensure coordinated development in essential fields of activity, while preserving the initiative and authority of the states in the spheres allotted to them.
   - **(ii)** The Constitution includes provisions for promoting cooperation on a voluntary basis between the Union and the states and among states and groups of states in investigation of matters of common interest, in legislative procedures and in administration, thus avoiding the rigidities inherent in Federal Constitutions (Articles 249, 252, 257, 258, 258-A, and 312). In other words, the objective is co-operative federalism.

[30] Ibid., p. 5.

[31] Ibid.

[32] Ibid., pp. 7-10.

(iii) The Constitution also sets out in broad terms the pattern of the welfare state envisaged and the fundamental principles on which it should rest.

These are the major cornerstones of planning and its objectives enshrined in the Constitution that will breed enough Union-State tussle in coming decades and make it compulsive for the government to resort to 'reforms with a human face' rhetoric. We can see the methodology of planning, taking a U-turn in the era of the economic reforms since the early 1990s.

3. The government resolution announcing the setting up of the PC (March 1950) started with a reference to the constitutional provisions bearing on the socio-economic objectives of the Constitution. The Fundamental Rights and the Directive Principles of the Constitution assure every citizen, among other things, adequate means of livelihood, opportunities for employment and a socio-economic order based on justice and equality. Thus, the basic objectives[33] of planning were already given in the provisions of the Constitution of India. These were emphatically stated in the First Five-Year Plan (1951-56) itself, in the following words:

'The urge to economic and social change under present conditions comes from the facts of poverty and of inequalities in income, wealth and opportunity. The elimination of poverty cannot obviously, be achieved merely by redistributing existing wealth. Nor can a programme aiming only at raising production remove existing inequalities. These two have to be considered together...'.

4. The above objectives of planning were time and again emphasised in one form or the other. As the Second Five-Year Plan (1956-61) stated:

'The Plan has to carry forward the process initiated in the First Plan period. It must provide for a larger increase in production, in investment and in employment. Simultaneously, it must accelerate the institutional changes needed to make the economy more dynamic and more progressive in terms no less of social than of economic ends.'

5. The same objectives were repeated by the Sixth Five-Year Plan (1980-85) in the following terms:

'The basic task of economic planning in India is to bring about a structural transformation of the economy so as to achieve a high and sustained rate of growth, a progressive improvement in the standard of living of the masses leading to eradication of poverty and unemployment and providing a material base for a self-reliant economy.'

6. It will be highly needful to enquire about the objectives of planning in the era of the economic reforms initiated in the fiscal 1991-92 as this new economic policy (NEP) made the experts and economists to conclude many questionable things about the objectives of planning in the country:

(i) The need to shift dependence from wage to self-employment.

(ii) The state is rolling back and the economy is becoming pro-private, and sector-wise the social purpose of the planning will be lacking.

(iii) The objectives of planning nearly outlined hitherto have been blurred.

(iv) The promotion of foreign investment will induce the economy into the perils of neo-imperialism.

But all the above-given doubts were cleared by the forthcoming plans in straightforward terms. We may quote from the following plans:

- 'For the future economic development, the economy will be more dependent upon private participation and the nature of planning will become more indicative with the major objectives of planning remaining the same'. This was announced by the government while launching the economic reforms (23 July 1991) and commencing the Eighth Five-Year Plan (1992-97). 'There was no change in the basic objectives of planning even though there was change in instruments of policy' - this was announced by the government while announcing the NEP (1991).
- While the Ninth Plan (1997-2002) was being launched, it was announced that 'The goals of planning in India, which were set by Panditji have not changed. The Ninth Plan does not attempt to reinvent the wheel. At the same time, the goals and targets this Plan attempts to achieve are based on the lessons of experience including the Eighth Plan. They address today's problems and challenges

[33] Ibid.

and try to prepare the nation for tomorrow as well'.[34]

Finally, a broad consensus appears evolving through the process of planning and crystallising on the six major objectives of planning[35] in India which are as follows:

1. **Economic Growth:** Sustained increase in the levels of production in the economy is among the foremost objectives of planning in India, which continues till date and will be so in future, without any iota of doubt in it.
2. **Poverty Alleviation:** Poverty alleviation was the most important issue which polarised the members of the NPC as well as the Constituent Assembly that a highly emphatic decision in favour of a planned economy evolved even before independence. In this direction several programmes have been launched by the central governments till now, one of them is still in operation which is even supported by an Act of the Parliament (i.e., the Mahatma Gandhi National Rural Employment Guarantee Act, 2005).
3. **Employment Generation:** Providing employment to the poor has been the best tool of economics to alleviate poverty. Thus, this objective of planning in India comes naturally once it commits itself to alleviate poverty. Employment generation in India has been, therefore, part and parcel of the objective of poverty alleviation in India. General programmes and schemes have been launched by the governments from time to time in this direction, some based on the wage employments, and others based on self-employment.
4. **Controlling Economic Inequality:** There were visible economic inequalities in India at the inter-personal as well as at the intra-personal levels. Economic planning as a tool of checking all kinds of economic disparities and inequalities was an accepted idea by the time India started planning.[36] To fulfil this objective of planning the governments have enacted highly innovative economic policies, at times even inviting a tussle with regard to the Fundamental Rights enshrined in the Constitution. Though Indian planning has socioeconomic objectives to fulfil, only economic planning was made a part of the planning process (technically speaking) and social planning (better called social engineering) was left to the political process. That is why reservation in government jobs and admissions in premier academic institutions, land reforms, and promoting inter-caste marriages do not fall under the purview of the PC.
5. **Self-Reliance:** During the 1930s and 1940s, there was an ardent desire among the nationalists, capitalists and NPC for making the economy self-reliant in all economic spheres. Self-reliance was defined not as autarchy, but as an effort to strike against a subordinate position in the world economy. As Jawaharlal Nehru asserted, self-reliance 'does not exclude international trade, which should be encouraged but with a view to avoid economic imperialism'.[37] India still strives for self-reliance in every field of the economy, as well as serving the realities of higher interdependence in the globalising world post-World Trade Organisation (WTO).

   In the wake of unprecedented disruptions brought by the **COVID-19** pandemic, the Government has given a renewed push towards self-reliance by announcing the ***Atmanirbhar Bharat Abhiyan*** (Self- Reliant India Campaign) in May 2020. The *Abhiyan,* which is based on five pillars, namely economy, infrastructure, system, demography and demand, has been visualised by the experts as India's alternative to rising global protectionism. This is for the *first time* that India has given clear specifications for attaining self-reliance. How India coordinates its new brand of self-reliance with globalisation (which India supports vigorously) only coming times can say!
6. **Modernisation:** Modernising the traditional economy was set as a foremost objective of

[34] Deputy Chairman, Planning Commission, May 1999. It is interesting to note here that the composition of the polity in the Centre was dominated by the BJP, while the view of Deputy Chairman, Planning Commission K. C. Pant (an old congress man), was continuity in the basic ideas and objectives of planning being maintained.

[35] Publications Division, *India* (New Delhi: Government of India, various years).

[36] Duly discussed by the NPC as well as the Constituent Assembly.

[37] *National Planning Committee Report;* Also, Nehru in *The Discovery of India.*

planning. Specially the agriculture sector of the economy needed an immediate inclusion of modern methods and techniques of farming, dairying, and so on. Similarly, in education too, India needed to opt for inclusion of a modern education system.

India did not miss the chance of accepting the importance of modern science and technology. As the economy had selected industry as its prime moving force (PMF), it was essential to adopt the changing dimensions of science and technology.

The major objectives of planning in India are not only broad but open-ended. That is why it hardly needed any change and modification with changing times. It means, after the completion of one plan, the objectives for the new plan are automatically set. Coming to the composition of the objectives, we may confidently conclude that all the aspirations of the Preamble,[38] the Directive Principles of the State Policy,[39] the Fundamental Duties and the Fundamental Rights have received their due place and weightage. All the aspirations of the nationalists and the freedom fighters resonate with the very soul of the Indian planning system.

The above-given objectives of planning were abolished with the PC. Under the new body - NITI Aayog - *holistic and federal* objectives of planning have been set by the GoI (they have been discussed under the heading, NITI Aayog at the end of this chapter).

PLANNING COMMISSION

Once the NPC published its Report (1949), there was a firm inclusion of the need for 'Economic and Social Planning'[40] in the Constitution, the stage was set for the formal launch of planning in the country. Though the economy was run on the principles of planning very much after independence itself,[41] it was in a piecemeal manner only. For formal planning to begin, for the whole economy at the national level, there was a need for a permanent expert body which could take over the responsibility of the whole gamut of planning, i.e., plan formation, resource aspects, implementation and review - as planning is a technical[42] matter. Thus, in March 1950[43] the PC was set up by the government by a Cabinet Resolution (without resorting to legislation). Important details regarding the composition, legal status and so on of the PC were as under:

1. An ***extra-constitutional*** (i.e., non-constitutional) and ***non-statutory*** body (though planning originates from the Constitution there is no reference to the PC in it).
2. An ***advisory body*** to the GoI on an array of issues of economic development.
3. A 'think tank' on economic development with the Prime Minister as its *ex officio* Chairman and with the provision of a Deputy Chairman to be appointed by the former.[44] The main function of the Deputy Chairman was to ***coordinate*** the work of the Commission.[45]
4. Had an open provision for the number of its membership (as many area experts are required by the particular proposed period of planning) other than six Union Cabinet Ministers as its ***ex officio members***[46] and a Member Secretary.

[38] The Preamble was declared by the Supreme Court as an *integral part of the Constitution* and any amendments amounting to a change in its meaning and spirit amounted to the violation of the 'basic structure' of the Constitution (*Keshvanand Bharti* case (1973) and *S. R. Bommai* case (1994)). This further magnified the objectives and role of 'planning' in India.

[39] As the different Articles of the Directive Principles were interpreted as being complementary parts of the Fundamental Rights, their enforcement became obligatory for the government in coming times, still broadening the objectives of planning in the country.

[40] Distribution of Legislative Power, List-III, Entry 20.

[41] Though formal planning commenced in the fiscal period 1951-52, planning had already commenced with the Industrial Policy Resolution, 1948. More so, the Prime Minister of India who headed the NPC had already taken a firm decision that India would be a planned economy by August 1937 (Congress Working Committee, Wardha). Thus, the economy takes its first wink in the planned era!

[42] A. W. Evans, 'Economic and Planning', in *Studies in Social Science and Planning*, J. Forbes, ed. (Edinburgh: Scottish Academy Press, 972), p. 121.

[43] I Publications Division, *The Gazetteer of India*, op. cit., p. 10.
II S. R. Maheshwari (Indian Administration, New Delhi: Orient Longman, 2002), p. 121.
III 'The Indian Economy Since Independence', p. 949.

[44] The post of Deputy Chairman was later given a cabinet rank in the Union Council of Ministers.

[45] Publications Division, *Gazetteer of India*, p. 11.

[46] Publications Division, *India 2008* (New Delhi: Ministry of Information and Broadcasting, Government of India, 2009), p. 676.

The Minister of Planning is already an *ex officio* member of the PC.[47]

5. An ***autonomous body*** entitled to form its own views on important issues and place them before the governments. It worked closely with the Union and State cabinets and had full knowledge of their policies.
6. It was invariably ***consulted*** on changes proposed in social and economic policies. To ensure free and full exchange of ideas, the PC had established a ***convention*** that it will not give publicity to differences of views between the Commission and the Union and State governments.
7. ***Linked*** with the Union Cabinet at the secretariat level, the PC was part of the Cabinet organisation and the 'demand for grants' for it was included in the budget demand for the Cabinet Secretariat.
8. Seated at the 'Yojana Bhavan', the Commission had a staff of secretaries and advisers and also a research organisation.[48]
9. The PC was a ***technical body*** with experts and professionals coming from an array of specific areas as per the need of planning of the concerned period (see footnote 42).
10. The Commission had ***executive powers***.[49]

Functions of the Planning Commission

Though the PC was set up with a definite purpose of planning, nobody knew that it would extend its functions over the entire spectrum of administration in the country. It was described as the 'Economic Cabinet of the country as a whole' even encroaching upon the constitutional body like the Finance Commission[50] and not being accountable to the Parliament.[51] Through time it built up a heavy bureaucratic organisation[52] which led even Nehru to observe - 'The Commission which was a small body of serious thinkers has turned into a government department complete with a crowd of secretaries, directors and of course a big building'.[53]

Though the functions of the PC were extended to include timely changes in the planning needs (in the reforms era), its functions were announced by the same government order which did set up the PC. The order[54] says:

'The Planning Commission will:

1. Make an assessment of the material, capital and human resources of the country, including technical personnel, and investigate the possibilities of augmenting such of those resources as are found to be deficient in relation to the nation's requirements;
2. Formulate a plan for the most effective and balanced utilisation of the country's resources;
3. On a determination of priorities, define the stages in which the plan should be carried out and propose the allocation of resources for the due completion of each stage;
4. Indicate the factors which are tending to retard economic development, and determine the conditions which, in view of the current social and political situation, should be established for the successful execution of the plan;

[47] There was a provision of only *three* Cabinet Ministers as its *ex officio* members, namely the Finance, Human Resource Development and Defence up to July 2004 when the United Progressive Alliance Government increased it to include the other *three* Cabinet Ministers, *viz.* the Railways, Agriculture and Information Technology. It has been only once in the history of the PC that it had *six* Cabinet Ministers as its *ex officio* members, i.e., in the final years of the Rajiv Gandhi regime (*The Economic Times*, 16 July 2004, New Delhi edition).

[48] Publications Division, *Gazetteer of India*, op. cit., p. 11.

[49] Prima facie a body should have been either constitutional or statutory to wield the executive powers, but as number of Cabinet Ministers as well as the PM himself were directly involved with the PC, it used to wield executive powers for all practical purposes.

[50] Rajamannar was the Chairman of the Fourth Finance Commission. See *Report of the Fourth Finance Commission* (New Delhi: Ministry of Finance, GoI, 1965), pp. 88-90.

[51] By the 1950s it was a general criticism of the PC which looked highly logical. But through the entire period of planning the Government never did think to convert the PC into a constitutional body. Practically enough, the Union Cabinet and the whole Government is accountable to the Parliament for the functions of the PC as it has complete mandate and support of the governments of the time.

[52] P. H. Appleby, *Public Administration in India: Report of A Survey* (Ford Foundation, 1953), p. 22.

[53] As quoted in D. D. Basu, *An Introduction to the Constitution of India* (New Delhi: Wadhwa & Company, 1999), p. 330.

[54] Publication Division, *The Gazetteer of India*, op. cit., pp. 10-11.

5. Determine the nature of the machinery which will be necessary for securing the successful implementation of each stage of the plan in all its aspects;
6. Appraise from time to time the progress achieved in the execution of each stage of the Plan and recommend the adjustments of policy and measures that such appraisal may show to be necessary; and
7. Make such interim or ancillary recommendations as appear to be appropriate either for facilitating the discharge of the duties assigned to it; or on a consideration of the prevailing economic conditions, current policies, measures and development programmes; or on an examination of such specific problems as may be referred to it for advice by Central or State governments'.

With the commencement of the Tenth Plan (2002-07), the government handed over ***two new functions*** to the PC in 2002, namely:

1. To monitor the plan implementation with special reference to the process of 'economic reforms' with the help of the steering committees.

   It should be noted here that once the process of economic reforms was initiated in the country (early 1990s), there was a diminishing role proposed for the state in the economy in some areas and increased role for the state in some other areas. The re-definition of the state's role in the economy (though it was the contemporary thinking worldwide) made most of the experts and the business community to conclude that there will be no role for planning in the economy. The NEP of 1991-92 was a *prima facie* proposal for the expansion of the market economy in the country. But it was not the case altogether. Planning had not become irrelevant though it needed to search for a new orientation. And it was highly essential that the process of planning keeps its relevance to the bigger and the broader process of economic reforms. This new function of the PC must particularly be seen in this light.
2. To monitor the progress of various central ministries, it should be noted here that for the first time, the PC went to set the 'monitorable targets' for 10 areas indicating development. The central ministries have been linked to these monitorable targets. The timely performances of the Ministries are now monitored by the PC as per its new function.

With the inclusion of the above-mentioned two functions in the existing functions (which were already very broad), the PC had emerged as a real 'super cabinet'. Since it was basically the Deputy Chairman who officiated the general meetings of the Commission, he had a high-level say[55] in articulating the direction and the nature of the economic policies. Through the first new function it articulated the future dimensions of the economic reforms and through the second new function, it influenced the works of the various ministries - ultimately it seems as if the PC had been able to emerge as the real think tank of development in the country.[56]

The PC had also been able to influence the economic policies of the states since 2002 in a great way. Though the PC did not make the state plans,[57] it was able to influence the overall economic policies of the states. It had been possible due to the setting of 'monitorable targets' for states for the same development indicators/areas as was set for the centre.[58] The states were liable for being monitored by the PC concerning their performances regarding these monitorable targets. This way the central government had started having its say over the state governments *via* the new functions of the PC.

We may conclude that the PC had been able to unify not only the various economic policies of the centre but also those of the states with the help of these two new functions. Earlier, there had always been a lack of

[55] It is not without reason that the Government decided to call in Montek Singh Ahluwalia, an economist of international repute, to officiate as the Deputy Chairman of the PC. Every idea and opinion of Mr. Ahluwalia was understood by the coalition partners of the UPA Government as a thing the government is necessarily going to implement in future. One can imagine the increased role of the office of the PC. There is always a hue and cry every time the Deputy Chairman articulates an idea or opinion. Though the PC is chaired by the PM, it seems that the Deputy Chairman has started availing enough autonomy to speak his mind.

[56] Ibid.

[57] As per the original mandate, the PC was supposed to formulate the state plans also. By 1960s, with the decision to follow the multi-level planning (MLP) in the country the states started having their own state planning boards (SPBs).

[58] In setting these targets the concerned states were consulted by the Planning Commission.

congruence among the policies of the various central ministries and the ideas articulated by the PC.

An Epitaph to the Planning Commission

On 1 January 2015, the government formally abolished the PC by replacing it with the newly created body – the NITI Aayog. With this ended an era in the economic history of independent India. Whether it was better to revive the PC or abolish it has been a matter of much debate among the discipline experts, politicians and the media. The debate, at times, had emotional tones, too. But the government has its own wisdom behind the action (a detailed discussion on it has been included in this chapter titled as the '**NITI Aayog**').

As an 'epitaph' to the PC (may be an 'ode'), it will be quite relevant to have an eye on the report of the Independent Evaluation Office (IEO) on the former which was submitted to the Prime Minister Office by late June 2014. According to it, the PC was created in response to the unique challenges faced by a nascent democracy and a fledgling economy – it conceived a 'top-down approach' to planning that envisaged a dynamic Central government building up the economic and social order of weak states. The report called the PC in its current form and function a hindrance and not a help to India's development. It further added that it is not easy to reform such a large *ossified body* and it would be better to replace it with a new body that is needed to assist states in ideas, to provide long-term thinking and to help cross-cutting reforms. Some of the ***major*** recommendations of IEO on the PC are as follows:

1. The PC be scrapped and replaced with the *Reform and Solutions Commission* (RSC), which should be staffed with experts with domain knowledge and kept free from any ministerial administrative structure. The new body should have full-time representation of major trade and industry organisations, civil society representatives and academics, so as to capture their concerns and benefit from their expertise in formulating a long-term strategy.
2. The RSC will perform ***three*** main functions:
   - **(i)** Serve as a solutions exchange and repository of ideas that have been successful in different aspects of development in various states and districts, and in other parts of the world;
   - **(ii)** Provide ideas for integrated systems reform; and
   - **(iii)** Identify new and emerging challenges and provide solutions to preempt them.
3. The current functions of the PC be taken over by other bodies, 'which are better designed to perform those functions'.
4. Since the state governments have better information about local requirements and resources than the central government and central institutions, they should be allowed to identify priorities and implement reforms at the state level, independent of mandatory *diktats* from the central institutions.
5. The task of long-term economic thinking and coordination can be performed by a new body established to act solely as a 'think tank' within the government.
6. The Finance Commission be made a *permanent body* responsible for the allocation of centrally collected revenue to the states and the finance ministry be tasked with the division of funds among the various central ministries.

The recommendations of the IEO (a brainchild of the PC itself) on the PC were quite surprising, even shocking to few. Whether the new body replacing the PC will be a betterment over the latter and will be able to carve out its desired aims is a matter to be evaluated and analysed in future. Meanwhile, we can visibly find some of the recommendations of the IEO resonating in the newly created body, the NITI Aayog, the replacement for the PC.

NOTE: While a detailed literature has been included on the 'NITI Aayog' in this chapter, the literature on the PC has been left unchanged for ease of understanding and comparative purpose.

NATIONAL DEVELOPMENT COUNCIL

The National Development Council (NDC) was set up on August 6, 1952 by a Resolution[59] issued from the Cabinet Secretariat. The First Plan recommended its formation with a very concise and suitable observation:

'In a country of the size of India where the states have under the constitution full autonomy within their own sphere of duties, it is necessary to have a forum

[59] Cabinet Secretariat, ***Resolution No. 62/CF/50*** (06.08.1952) Government of India, New Delhi.

such as a National Development Council at which, from time to time, the Prime Minister of India and the Chief Ministers of the states can review the working of the plan and of its various aspects'.[60]

There were some strong reasons why the NDC was set up, which may be seen as follows:

1. The Central Plans were to be launched in the states and the UTs with the participation of the state-level personnel. The PC was not provided with its own implementation staff (though the PC was given the responsibility of plan implementation) for this purpose. Therefore, the consent and co-operation of these federal units was a must.
2. Economic planning as a concept had its origin in the centralised system (i.e., Soviet Union). For India, to democratise/decentralise the very process of planning was not a lesser task/ challenge than promoting development itself. Indian planning is rightly said to be a process of trial and error in striking a balance between liberty and progress, central control and private initiative and national planning with local authority.[61]

   The setting up of the NDC can be considered as a step towards decentralised planning.
3. In the constitutional design of the federal rigidities, it was necessary to provide the whole planning process a unified outlook. The NDC serves the purpose of diluting the autonomous and rigid federal units of the Union of India.[62]

The NDC initially comprised of the Prime Minister of India (*de facto* Chairman), the Chief Ministers of all the states and the members of the PC (replaced by the NITI Aayog since January 2015). In the first meeting of the NDC held on 8-9 November 1952, Jawaharlal Nehru stated that the NDC is 'essentially a forum for intimate cooperation between the State Governments and the Central Government for all the tasks of national development'. In the *words* of Nehru, setting up of the NDC may be regarded as one of the most significant steps taken for promoting understanding and consultation between the Union and the State Governments on planning and common economic policies.

Considering the recommendations of the Administrative Reforms Commission, the NDC was reconstituted, and its functions redefined by a Cabinet Resolution on 7 October 1967. The reconstituted NDC comprised of the Prime Minister, all Union Cabinet Ministers, Chief Ministers of all States and Union Territories and the Members of the PC. Delhi Administration was represented in the Council by the Lt. Governor and the Chief Executive Councilor, and the remaining Union Territories by their respective administrators. Other Union Ministers and State Ministers may also be invited to participate in the deliberations of the Council. In the reconstituted Council, the Secretary of the PC acts as Secretary to the NDC, and the PC was expected to furnish such administrative or other assistance for the work of the Council as may be needed. The basic nature, origin and legal status of the Council are similar to the PC. The **revised functions**[63] of the NDC are:

1. To consider the proposals formulated for Plans at all important stages and accept them;
2. To review the working of the Plans from time to time;
3. To consider the important questions of social and economic policy affecting national development; and
4. To recommend measures for the achievement of the aims and targets set out in the national plan, including measures to secure the ***active participation*** and *cooperation* of the people, improve the *efficiency* of the administrative services, ensure the fullest development of the less advanced *regions and backward sections* of the community and through sacrifices borne equally by all citizens, build up resources for national development.[64]

Though the First Plan of India was launched before the arrival of the NDC, the body had many meetings

[60] Planning Commission, *First Five-Year Plan: A Draft Outline* (New Delhi: Government of India, 1957), p. 253.

[61] Publications Divisions, *The Gazetteer of India*, p. 10.

[62] The Advisory Planning Board (1946) set up by the Interim Government had suggested for such a consultative body with the representatives from the provinces, the princely states and some other interests to advise the Planning Commission for the success of planning in India.

[63] Other than the ***Cabinet Resolution***, it is also quoted in The ***Gazetteer of India*** (Publications Division, *The Gazetteer of India*, p. 15).

[64] The *italicised* words highlight the level of the Government's consciousness about the concerned issues of decentralised planning, regional and individual inequalities to which the planning was to be especially attentive.

before the terminal year of the plan, and useful deliberations (almost all) after due consideration were included by the government into the planning process. But after the death of Jawaharlal Nehru - the greatest champion of democratic decentralisation in the country[65] - the NDC had become a small gathering of only those who had the same vested interests with only the Congress CMs participating in its meetings. The CMs belonging to other political parties usually did not come to its meetings; the government hardly gave any importance to their advice. A phase of tussle between the Centre and the states started worsening from here onward with a degradation in principles of the **co-operative federalism**, with every five-year plan which followed. It was only by the mid-1990s that we see the revival of the lost glory of NDC as well as that of the spirit of decentralised planning. This has been possible due to three major reasons:

1. In the era of economic reforms, with greater dependence on the private capital made it necessary to allow states greater autonomy in economic matters. Once the WTO regime started, it became an economic compulsion.
2. The enactment of the 73rd and the 74th Constitutional Amendments had made local-level planning a constitutional compulsion.
3. And lastly it was the compulsion of coalition politics in the formation of the Union Government which made the Centre to favour the states.

As per the major experts on the issue of decentralised planning, the last of the above-given three reasons has played the most important role. By 2002, in the area of development planning we find an enhanced level of federal maturity, and we see the last three five-year plans (Tenth, Eleventh and Twelfth) adopted by a consensual support of the NDC members.

NDC had its last meeting (57th) in December 2012, and since the new policy think tank NITI Aayog was set up it has not been assigned any work. It is believed that in coming times it will be either abolished or merged with the NITI.

NDC vs GC

At the level of composition the NDC and Governing Council (GC) of the NITI Aayog look quite similar; however, they have nuanced and subtle differences. Fostering ***federal cooperation*** is the core objective for both, but the way it was/is done was/is better in the case of the GC (in the case of the NDC, states' dissent had no value while in the case of the GC, developmental decisions are taken through majority view of its members[66]). The opinion of the GC is necessary for the desired functioning of the NITI as the former is an integral part of the latter. This way the GC seems to be a better body in comparison to the NDC. This rationale is doubly vetted by the Government's belief that the NITI is the 'State's best friend at the Centre' (the 3rd function of the NITI).

Scan this QR Code to watch a author's video lecture that simplifies this topic

CENTRAL PLANNING

The Plans which are formulated by the Central Government and financed by it for the implementation at the national level are known as Central Plans. Over the years, the centre has launched three such plans, and the governments have maintained continuity in their implementation. The three central plans are the following:

1. Five-Year Plans (FYPs),
2. Twenty-Point Programme (TPP), and
3. Member of Parliament Local Area Development Scheme (MPLADS).

A brief description of these plans, as per the Plan Reviews of the Planning Commission and NITI Aayog (for the 12th Plan only) are given below:

[65] G. Mathew, undoubtedly among the legendary commentators on the Panchayati Raj/democratic decentralisation, calls Nehru as 'its most eminent champion at the national level'. Similarly, the reputed historians B. Chandra and others call Nehru as 'the greatest champion of planned economic development'. For Nehru the process of planning in the country was to be democratic about which seems very clear, as his writings support.

[66] It works as a forum for fostering cooperative and competitive federalism, as per Arvind Subramanian, the former Chief Economic Advisor to the Government of India in his book *Of Counsel–The Challenges of the Modi-Jaitley Economy* (Gurugram: Penguin Random House, India, 2018), p. 192.

1. The Five-Year Plans

This is the most important among the central plans and is being continuously implemented one after the other since planning commenced in India. As planning has been a purely political exercise in India, the five-year plans of the country have seen many unstable and critical moments till date. Several new developments related to planning also took place during the years. Given below is a concise summary of the plans as we see their different periods of implementation:

First Plan (1951–56) The plan had the following main features:

- It was based on the famous **Harrod-Domar Model** (the model emphasises on the dual character of capital in an economy— capital at the one hand boosts demand which, on the other hand, boosts supply— ultimately leading to enhanced national income).
- Economist ***K. N. Raj*** was its main architect (at a tender age of 26 years, he helped in drafting of this plan).
- Some popular programmes such as the CDP (Community Development Programme) and National Programme for Family Planning were launched in 1952.
- It was focused on Agriculture (in the wake of large-scale imports of foodgrains), Irrigation [the famous river valley projects such as Bhakra Nangal, Damodar Valley, Hirakud, etc. were launched— the DVC (Damodar Valley Corporation which was cleared in 1945 became the role model for all upcoming river-based irrigation projects].
- The food aid programme of India, the **PL 480** was signed by India with the USA in 1954.
- Price stability, rural development, power and transport were other major areas of emphasis.
- About 44.6 per cent of plan allocation went in favour of the public sector undertakings (PSUs)— beginning of the ***glorification*** of the PSUs started which will be called the **temples of modern India**.
- Growth rate was 2.1 per cent; however, it realised a growth rate of 3.6 per cent.

Second Plan (1956–61) This plan was aimed at boosting growth which laid emphasis on rapid industrialisation with a focus on heavy industries and capital goods.[67] The major features of the plan were as given below:

- This was based on the popular **Nehru-Mahalanobis** strategy which is also called the famous ***Sector Model*** (it was focused on two sectors— consumer goods and capital goods).
- Investment in the heavy industries was emphasised— being a long-term strategy, this continued till the Fifth Plan (1974–79).
- Industry saw huge investment— rapid industrialisation, self-reliance, and heavy industries which were in focus (these ideas are said to be borrowed from the ex-USSR).
- Emphasis was given on imports (to attract further investment), development of townships putting the PSUs in centre (inspired from the idea of the ***Growth Pole*** of regional planning which was successfully experimented in France. However, no such official acceptance is found), and import substitution.
- The plan shifted its focus from agriculture to industry— the beginning of industry as the Prime Moving Force (PMF) of the economy.
- Growth rate target was of 4.5 per cent; however, it realised only 4.27 per cent growth.

Third Plan (1961–65) The plan specifically incorporated the development of agriculture[68] as one of the objectives of planning in India besides, for the first times, considering the aim of balanced, regional development. Major features of the plan were as summarised below:

- It was based on development models of ***John Sandy*** and ***Sukhamoy Chakraborty*** and also called Gadgil Plan (as ***D. R. Gadgil*** was the Vice-Chairman of the Planning Commission at the time).

[67] S. Chakravarti, *Development Planning: The Indian Experience* (New York: Oxford University Press, 1989), pp. 9-11.

[68] C. Rangarajan, *Indian Economy: Essays on Money and Finance* (New Delhi: UPSBD, 1998), p. 272.

- The aim was to make India a 'self-reliant' and 'self-generating' economy (based on the supply of basic materials and services from the public sector undertakings and led by the private sector. However, due to the absence of a conducive atmosphere, expected investment could not be attracted from the private players)— such an emphasis originated from the thinking that the economy was in the 'take off' stage of growth and expansion.
- The focus remained on heavy industries and foodgrain production— however, a few union budgets priority allocations were to the agriculture sector (which was aimed at supporting exports and industry).
- Growth rate target was of 5.6 per cent; however, the realised growth was of 2.84 per cent only.

A series of misfortunes awaited this plan – two wars, one with China in 1961–62 and the other with Pakistan in 1965–66 along the Gujarat border, coupled with a severe drought-led famine in the same period (1965–66). Due to heavy drain and diversion of funds, this plan utterly failed to meet its targets.

Three Annual Plans (1966–69) These were launched as three consecutive Annual Plans. Though the Fourth Plan was ready for implementation in 1966, the weak financial situation as well as the low morale after being defeated by China, the government decided to go for an Annual Plan for the period 1966–67. Due to the same reasons the government opted for another two such plans in the forthcoming years. The broader objectives of these Annual Plans were within the design of the Fourth Plan which would have been implemented for the period 1966–71 had the financial conditions not worsened by then. Major features of the plan were as summarised below:

- The most important contribution of this plan was the launch of the *New Agricultural Strategy (NAS)* in 1965–66 (which is popularly known as the **Green Revolution (GR)** in the country).Modern techniques of farming began under the GR which included inputs like— high yielding variety (HYV) seeds; chemical fertilisers, insecticides, pesticides, herbicides; irrigation.
- Some economists as well as the opposition in the Parliament called this period as a discontinuity in the planning process, as the plans were supposed to be for a period of five years. They named it a period of **'Plan Holiday'**, i.e., the planning was on a holiday.[69]

Fourth Plan (1969–74) The plan had the following main features:

- It was based on the **Gadgil strategy** with special focus on the ideas of growth with stability and progress towards self-reliance—by putting focus on 'agriculture' sector.
- The plan saw record agricultural productions in its first two years. However, the momentum got lost in the rest of the plan period (droughts and the Indo-Pak War of 1971–72 led the economy to capital diversions creating financial crunch for the plan).
- Growth rate target was of 5.7 per cent; however, the realised growth was of 3.3 per cent only.

The 'politicisation' of planning started from this plan, which adopted a serious 'populist' design in the coming plans. Frequent double-digit inflations, unreigned increase in the fiscal deficits, subsidy-induced higher non-plan expenditures and the first move in the direction of 'nationalisation' and greater control and regulation of the economy were some of the salient features of this plan, which continued unchanged till the early 1990s. The search for political stability at the centre converted planning into a tool of real politics with greater 'centralisation' ensuing plan after plan.

Fifth Plan (1974–79) The plan had the following main features:

- It had its focus on poverty alleviation and self-reliance.[70] The popular rhetoric of poverty alleviation was sensationalised by the government to the extent of launching a fresh plan, i.e., the Twenty-Point Programme (1975), with a marginal importance being given to the objective of 'growth with stability' (one of the major objectives of the Fourth Plan). The planning process became more politicised.
- The havocs of hyper-inflation led the government to hand over a new function to the Reserve Bank of India (RBI) to stabilise the inflation (the function which the RBI carries forward even today).
- A judicious price wage policy was started to check the menace of inflation on the wage earners.

[69] It should be noted here that as per the official version of the Government of India, the planning has been a *continuous process* in the country, and there is no term like 'Plan Holiday' in its official documents. The term was given by the critics and popularised by the contemporary media.

[70] Experts believe this Plan to be somewhat based on the ideas of D. P. Dhar, the Minister for Planning at that time.

- This plan saw an increase in the socio-economic and regional disparities despite the many institutional, financial and other measures which were initiated by the government to attend to them.
- The nationalisation policy continued. There was an overall decay in the quality of 'governance'.
- A nexus of the 'criminal-politician-bureaucrat' seems to emerge for the first time to hijack the political system.[71]
- Growth rate target was of 4.4 per cent; however, the realised growth was a bit better at 4.8 per cent.

The plan period was badly disturbed by the draconian emergency and a change of the government at the centre. The Janata Party came to power with a thumping victory in 1977. As the government of the time had then complete say in the central planning in India, how could the new government continue with the Fifth Plan of the previous government which had still more than one year to reach its completion. The dramatic events related to Indian planning may be seen objectively as given below:

1. The Janata Government did cut short the Fifth Plan by a year ahead of its terminal year, i.e., by the fiscal 1977–78, in place of the decided 1978–79.
2. A fresh plan, the Sixth Plan for the period 1978–83, was launched by the new government which called it the **'Rolling Plan'**.[72]
3. In 1980, there was again a change of government at the Centre with the return of the Congress who abandoned the Sixth Plan of the Janata Government in the year 1980 itself.
4. The new government launched a fresh new **Sixth Plan** for the period 1980–85. But by that time, two financial years of the Janata Government's Sixth Plan had already been completed. These two years of the plan were adjusted by the Congress Government in a highly interesting way:
   - **(i)** The first year, i.e., 1978–79, was added to the Fifth Plan which was cut short by the Janata Government to four years. And thus, the Fifth Plan officially became of 5 years again (1974–79).
   - **(ii)** Now what to do with the second year, i.e., 1979–80. The Congress Government announced this year to be a year of one Annual Plan.

This Annual Plan (1979–80) may be considered the lone independent remnant of the 'Rolling Plan' of the Janata Government.

The Sixth Plan (1978–83) which could not become an official plan of India laid emphasis on some of the highly new economic ideas and ideals with almost a complete no to foreign investment; new thrust on price control; rejuvenation of the Public Distribution System (PDS); emphasis on small-scale and cottage industries; new lease of life to Panchayati Raj Institutions (PRIs) (i.e., the second phase of the revival of the PRIs); agriculture and the subject of rural development getting their due; etc., being the major ones.

Sixth Plan (1980–85) The major features of the plan were as summarised below:

- The plan was launched with the slogan of *Garibi Hatao* (alleviate poverty).[73] Already, a programme (the TPP) was tested and tried by the same government in the Fifth Plan which tried to improve the standard of living of the poor masses with a 'direct approach' (the idea of poverty alleviation, but such a slogan of *Garibi Hatao* was not given to the programme). The plan placed emphasis on socio-economic infrastructure in the rural areas;

[71] N. N. Vohra Committee Report, Government of India, New Delhi, 1993.

[72] It should be noted here that there is nothing like the 'Rolling Plan' in the official documents of planning in India. Basically, the origin of the concept of the 'Rolling Plan' goes back to the period when India went for the Annual Plans (1966-69) for the first time and the critics noted it as a *discontinuity* in the planning process, calling it a period of the 'plan holiday'. The basic trait of the 'Rolling Plan' was its *continuity*, while the Congress commenced its sixth Plan (1980-85) the idea of the 'Rolling Plan' was cancelled, as for the new Government the element of 'rolling' (continuity) was already in the Indian Planning - India was following the approach of the 'perspective planning'. A separate Division of Perspective Planning was already functioning in the *Yojana Bhavan* since the mid-1970s. The two elements which make any plan a 'perspective plan' are, firstly, the 'continuity' and secondly, 'evaluation-based' planning. For the Congress Government, logically, the planning in India was not only 'rolling' but more than that it was evaluation-based, too.

[73] Some experts see this plan as a symbol of the planning being converted to a complete politics - with utter populism entering into the planning process of India. The circle of the politicisation of planning was completed with this plan.

eliminating rural poverty and regional disparities (through the IRDP); commencing 'target group' approach[74] together with launching a number of national level programmes and schemes aimed at specific concerns and areas of development ('target group' approach).[75]

- Growth rate target was of 5.2 per cent; however, the realised growth was a bit better at 5.66 per cent.

Seventh Plan (1985–90) The Plan had the following main features:

- It emphasised on rapid foodgrain production, increased employment creation and productivity in general. The basic tenets of planning, i.e., ***growth, modernisation, self-reliance*** and ***social justice*** remained as the guiding principles.[76]
- The *Jawahar Rojgar Yojana* (JRY) was launched in 1989 with the motive to create wage employment for the rural poor. Some of the already existing programmes, such as the IRDP, CADP, DPAP and the DDP, were reoriented.
- Growth rate target was of 5.0 per cent; however, the realised growth was much better at 6.1 per cent.

Till date, the government has been evaluating the achievements of all the developmental programmes, courtesy of the youngest PM of India. Somehow, democracy and development got connected with a major change in the thinking of the political elite, which decided to go in for democratic decentralisation to promote development. It laid strong foundations for itself as the constitutional amendments – the 73rd and 74th were possible by the early 1990s.

Though the economy had better growth rates throughout the 1980s, especially in the latter half, yet it was at the cost of bitter fiscal imbalances. By the end of the plan, India had a highly unfavourable balance of payments situation. The economy failed to the heavy foreign loans on which the governmental expenditures depended on during the period.[77] The plan was not laid with a strong financial strategy, which put the economy into a crisis of unsustainable balance of payments and fiscal deficits.[78] India basically tried to attend its growth prospects by commercial and other external borrowings on hard terms, which the economy failed to sustain. In the process of liberalisation, an expansion of internal demand for the home market was permitted without generating equitable levels of exports, and ultimately Indian imports were financed by the costly external borrowings. Such an 'inward looking' fiscal policy proved to be a mistake when the external aid environment for the economy was deteriorating.[79]

Two Annual Plans (1990–92) The Eighth Plan (whose term would have been 1990–95) could not take off due to the 'fast-changing political situation at the Centre'.[80] The pathbreaking and restructuring-oriented suggestions of the Eighth Plan, the sweeping economic reforms ensuing around the world, as well as the fiscal imbalances of the late 1980s were the other important reasons for the delay in the launch of the Eighth Plan. The new government, which assumed power at the centre in June 1991, decided to commence the Eighth Plan for the period 1992–97 and that the fiscals 1990–91 and 1991–92 should be treated as two separate Annual Plans. The two consecutive Annual Plans (1990–92) were formulated within the framework of the approach to the Eighth Plan (1990–95) with the basic thrust on maximisation of employment and social transformation.

Eighth Plan (1992–97) The Eighth Plan was launched in a typically new economic environment. The economic reforms were already started (in July 1991) with the initiation of the structural adjustment and macro-stabilisation policies necessitated by the worsening balance of payments, higher fiscal deficit and unsustainable rate of inflation.

---

[74] 'Target group' approach of planning is selecting a group of people where a particular problem is and attacking the problem directly. The TPP was the first such programme in India.

[75] Publications Division, *India 1980-1983* (New Delhi: Government of India).

[76] Planning Commission, *Seventh Five Year Plan (1980-85)* (New Delhi: Government of India, 1980).

[77] Similar financial strategy to promote growth and development had led the Soviet Union to economic collapse *via* the balance of payment crisis during Gorbachev's regime by 1991, as is pointed out by J. Sachs in *The End of Poverty* ((London: Penguin Books, 2005), pp. 131-4).

[78] C. Rangarajan, Indian Economy, p. 274.

[79] Bimal Jalan in B. Jalan (ed.), 1992, pp. 190-1, op. cit.

[80] This is the official version for the delay (Publications Division, *India 2007* (New Delhi: Government of India, 2007), p. 680.

This was the ***first plan*** which went on for an introspection of the macro-economic policies which the country had been pursuing for many decades. The major concerns and pathbreaking suggestions[81] which this plan articulated may be summarised as follows:

1. An immediate re-definition of the state's role in the economy was suggested;
2. 'Market-based' development advised in areas which could afford it, i.e., a greater role for the private sector in the economy;[82]
3. More investment in the infrastructure sector, especially in the laggard states as the ongoing emphasis on greater private sector investment could not be attracted towards these states;
4. Rising non-plan expenditure and fiscal deficits need to be checked;
5. Subsidies need restructuring and refocusing;
6. Planning immediately needs to be 'decentralised';
7. Special emphasis on 'co-operative federalism' suggested; and
8. Greater focus on 'agriculture' and other 'rural activities' was suggested for which the plan cited empirical evidence as they encourage the economy to achieve enhanced standard of living for its people and to promote the cause of balanced growth – a shift in the mindset of planning.

As the economy moved towards liberalisation, criticism came from every quarter against the move. The process of planning was also criticised on the following counts:

1. As economy moves towards the market economy, the planning becomes 'irrelevant';
2. When the state is 'rolling back', planning makes no sense;
3. The planning process should be 'restructured' in the era of liberalisation; and
4. There should be increased thrust on the 'social sector' (i.e., education, healthcare etc.)

Ninth Plan (1997–02) The Ninth Plan was launched when there was an all-round 'slowdown' in the economy led by the South East Asian Financial Crisis (1996–97). Though the liberalisation process was still criticised, the economy was very much out of the fiscal imbroglio of the early 1990s. With a general nature of 'indicative planning', the plan not only did target an ambitious high growth rate (6.5 per cent, however, the realised growth was of 5.35 per cent only) but also tried to direct itself towards time-bound 'social' objectives. There was an emphasis on the seven identified Basic Minimum Services (BMS) with Additional Central Assistance (ACA) for these services with a view to obtaining complete coverage of the population in a time-bound manner. The BMS[83] included the following:

1. Safe drinking water;
2. Primary health service;
3. Universalisation of primary education;
4. Public housing assistance to the shelter-less poor families;
5. Nutritional support to children;
6. Connectivity of all villages and habitations; and
7. Streamlining of the PDS.

---

[81] It should be noted here that the kind of economic reforms, India started in 1991-92 were *almost suggested* exactly by the Eighth Plan. The suggestions were based on India's own experience and the experiences of the world economies after the Second World War. The Sixth and the Seventh Plans had suggested almost on the similar lines which made the governments of the time opt for the so-called 'liberalisation' moves in the mid-1980s.

[82] C. Rangarajan, *Indian Economy*, op. cit. pp. 275-6.

[83] Publications Division, *India 2007*, pp. 682-3.

The issue of fiscal consolidation became a top priority of the governments for the first time, which had its focus on the following[84] related issues:

1. Sharp reduction in the revenue deficit of the government, including centre, states and the PSUs through a combination of improved revenue collections and control of in-essential expenditures;
2. Cutting down subsidies, collection of user charges on economic services (i.e., electricity, transportation etc.), interest, wages, pension, PF, etc;
3. Decentralisation of planning and implementation through greater reliance on states and the PRIs.

Tenth Plan (2002–07) The plan commenced with the objectives of greater participation of the NDC in their formulation. The plan was able to achieve a growth rate of 7.6 per cent against the target of 8 per cent. Some highly important steps were taken during the plan, which undoubtedly point out a change in the planning policy mindset of the government, major ones being:[85]

1. Doubling per capita income in 10 years;
2. Accepting that the higher growth rates are not the only objective – it should be translated into improving the quality of life of the people;
3. For the first time the plan went to set the 'monitorable targets' for eleven select indicators of development for the Centre as well as for the states;
4. 'Governance' was considered a factor of development;
5. States' role in planning to be increased with the greater involvement of the PRIs;
6. Policy and institutional reforms in each sector, i.e., reforms in the PSUs, legal reforms, administrative reforms, labour reforms, etc;
7. Agriculture sector declared as the PMF of the economy;
8. Increased emphasis on the social sector (i.e., education, health etc.); and
9. Relevance between the processes of economic reforms and planning emphasised; etc.

Eleventh Plan (2007–12) The plan targeted a growth rate of 10 per cent and emphasises the idea of ***'inclusive growth'***. The growth target was further revised to 9 per cent; however, the realised growth rate remained at 8 per cent only. In the approach paper, the PC shows its concerns regarding realising the growth targets on account of the compulsions towards the Fiscal Responsibility and Budget Management (FRBM) Act. In recent times, some aberrations in the economy have started to increase the government's concerns in meeting the plan target of 10 per cent growth. The major concerns are as follows:

1. A higher inflation (above 6 per cent) led to the tightening of the credit policy forcing lower investment in the economy (which will lower production);
2. A stronger rupee is making export earnings shrink fast;
3. Costlier foodgrains and other primary articles playing havoc for the poor masses; and
4. Costlier oil prices becoming a burden for the national exchequer, etc.

Not only the government but the Confederation of Indian Industry (CII) as well as the World Bank expressed doubts in the Eleventh Plan realising the ambitious 10 per cent growth.[86]

Twelfth Plan (2012–17) The 'Draft Approach Paper' of this plan was prepared by the Planning Commission after widest consultation till date – recognising the fact that citizens are now better informed and also keen to engage. Over 950 civil society organisations across the country provided inputs; business associations, including those representing small enterprises have been consulted; modern electronic and 'social media' (Google Hangout) were

[84] *Economic Survey* (1998-200) (New Delhi: Ministry of Finance, GoI, Various Years); Publications Division, *India 2007,* p. 683.

[85] Planning Commission, *Tenth Five year Plan (2002-07)* (New Delhi: Government of India).

[86] *World Development Report-2003,* (New York: World Bank), p. 31.

used to enable citizens to give suggestions. All state governments, as well as local representative institutions and unions, have been consulted through five regional consultations. Though the Approach Paper for the plan was approved by the NDC by mid-2011, the Plan Document was finalised much later after the launch of the plan (like the Tenth and Eleventh Plans).

The Draft Approach Paper lays down the major targets of the plan, the key challenges in meeting them and the broad approach that must be followed to achieve the stated objectives which are summed up as follows:

1. Growth rate of 9 per cent is targeted for the plan. However, in view of the uncertainties in the global economy and the challenges in the domestic economy, the Approach Paper indicates that it could be achieved only if some **difficult decisions** are taken.
2. It emphasises the need to intensify efforts to have 4 per cent average growth in the **agriculture** sector during the plan period; with foodgrains growing at about 2 per cent per year and non-food grains (notably, horticulture, livestock, dairying, poultry and fisheries) growing at 5 to 6 per cent.
3. The higher growth in agriculture would not only provide broad-based income benefits to the rural population but also help restrain **inflationary pressure**, which could arise if high levels of growth are attempted without corresponding growth in domestic food production capabilities.
4. It proposes that the major **flagship programmes** which were instrumental for promoting inclusiveness in the Eleventh Plan should continue in the Twelfth Plan – there is a need to focus on issues of implementation and governance to improve their effectiveness.
5. The plan indicates that the **energy** needs of rapid growth will pose a major challenge since these requirements have to be met in an environment where domestic energy prices are constrained, and world energy prices are high and likely to rise further.
6. For the GDP to grow at 9 per cent, commercial energy supplies will have to grow at a rate between 6.5 and 7 per cent per year. Since India's domestic energy supplies are limited, dependence upon imports will increase. Import dependence in the case of petroleum has always been high and is projected to be **80** per cent in the Twelfth Plan.
7. Even in the case of **coal**, import dependence is projected to increase as the growth of thermal generation will require coal supplies, which cannot be fully met from domestic mines.
8. It suggests the need to take steps to reduce energy intensity of production processes, increase domestic energy supply as quickly as possible and ensure rational energy pricing that will help achieve both objectives, *viz.* reduced energy intensity of production process and enhance domestic energy supply, even though it may seem difficult to attempt.
9. It draws attention to evolving a holistic **water** management policy aiming at more efficient conservation of water and also in water use efficiency, particularly in the field of agriculture.
10. It argues that a new legislation for **land acquisition** is necessary, which strikes an appropriate balance between the need for fair compensation to those whose land is acquired and whose livelihood is disrupted, and the need to ensure that land acquisition does not become an impossible impediment to meeting our needs for infrastructure development, industrial expansion and urbanisation.
11. It maintains that **health**, **education** and **skill development** will continue to be the focus areas in the Twelfth Plan, and that there is a need to ensure adequate resources to these sectors – ***universal healthcare*** proposed by it, emphatically. Simultaneously, it also points to the need to ensure maximum efficiency in terms of outcomes for the resources allocated to these sectors. The need to harness ***private investment*** in these sectors has also been emphasised by the approach.
12. It takes cognizance of the fact that achieving 9 per cent growth will require large **investments** in infrastructure sector development – notes greater momentum to public investment and Public–Private Partnerships (PPPs) in infrastructure sector needs to be imparted so that present infrastructure shortages can be addressed early.
13. It has emphasised the importance of the process of **fiscal correction**. However, the paper cautions that fiscal consolidation would imply that total resources available for the plan in the short run will be limited.

Resource limitations imply the need to prioritise carefully and that some ***priority areas***, for example, health, education and infrastructure, will have to be funded more than others.

14. It also emphasises the need for focusing more on **efficient use** of available resources in view of the resource constraints.

The **appraisal document** for the Twelfth Plan, prepared by the NITI Aayog, estimated a growth rate of maximum 7.75 per cent (the plan had a revised growth rate target of 8.2 per cent; however, the realised growth rate remained 6.9 per cent only, as per the final appraisal of the NITI Aayog). Taking clues from the plans the document made a strong case for clear tax policies and focus on manufacturing sector.

2. Twenty-Point Programme

The Twenty Point Programme (TPP) is the second Central Plan which was launched in July 1975. The programme was conceived for coordinated and intensive monitoring of a number of schemes implemented by the Central and the State governments. The basic ***objective*** was of improving the quality of life of the people, especially of those living below the poverty line. Under this, a thrust was given to schemes relating to poverty alleviation, employment generation in rural areas, housing, education, family welfare and health, protection of environment and many other schemes having a bearing on the quality of life in rural areas.

The programme was restructured in 1982 and 1986. The programme, known as the '***TPP-86***', has 119 items grouped into 20 points which are related to the improvement in the quality of life in rural areas. Among the total items, 54 are monitored on the evaluation-based criteria, 65 against pre-set physical targets and rest of the 20 important items on a monthly basis. The targets are fixed by the Ministries at the Centre in consultation with the states and the UTs. The allocation for the programme is done under the various Five-Year Plans.

The 'TPP-86' was restructured and named 'TPP-2006' keeping in view the challenges of the 21st century with particular reference to the process of economic reforms. This was in harmony with the National Common Minimum Programme (NCMP) of the UPA Government.

This was the first programme which had a 'direct attack' approach on rural poverty. The forthcoming five-year plan (i.e., the Sixth Plan, 1980-85), launched with the slogan '*Garibi Hatao*', was based on the experiences of the TPP - a right mix of economics and real politic. Over the years, the programme has been implemented uninterrupted by all political parties which came to power at the Centre.

By mid-2015, the Ministry of Statistics and Programme Implementation (MoSPI), which monitors the programme, in a report to the Prime Minister's Office, had advised to wrap it up as it has outlived its utility. While the PMO decided to 'restructure' it on the recommendations of the Inter-Ministerial Group, which is presently working on it. It should be noted that the Government has restructured the existing 50 Centrally Sponsored Schemes (CSSs) into 30 under the active participation of the GC of the NITI Aayog.

3. MPLADS

The Member of Parliament Local Area Development Scheme (MPLADS) is the last of the Central Plans and latest to have been launched. The scheme was launched on 23 December 1993, with only ₹5 lakhs given to each MPs which was increased to ₹1 crore in the year 1994-95 when the MPs did put a demand to increase the sum to ₹5 crore in 1997-98, finally the government enhanced it to ₹2 crores since 1998-99. In April 2011 the corpus was enhanced to ₹5 crore while announcing the new guidelines for the scheme.

Basically, in the early 1990s there came a demand from the MPs cutting across party lines for such a scheme so that the fruits of development could directly reach the masses *via* their representatives.

The government of the time decided to go in for such a scheme and the MPLADS arrived.

Under this scheme the Members of Parliament[87] recommend some works (i.e., creation of fixed community assets, based on locally felt developmental needs) to the concerned District Magistrate. The scheme

[87] For development works the MP, Lower House (the Lok Sabha) may select one or more districts of their constituency; the MP, Upper House (the Rajya Sabha) may select any one or more districts from their constituency (i.e., a state or a UT); and the nominated MPs may select any one or more districts from their constituency (i.e., the whole country).

is governed by a set of guidelines, which have been comprehensively revised and issued in November 2005. Its performance has improved due to pro-active policy initiatives, focus monitoring and review.[88]

In recent years, many criticisms of the scheme came to the public notice, which concerned either misappropriation of the funds or non-use of the funds, especially from the backward states. The people's representative at the PRI level have been demanding scrapping of the scheme as it infringes the idea of decentralised planning. In its place, they want the funds to be given to the local bodies directly for the same kind of works specified by the MPLADS.[89]

Objective (Basic Principle): To enable the MPs to recommend works of developmental nature with emphasis on 'creation of durable community assets based on the locally felt needs' (which will be accessible to all sections of society).

Revised Guidelines-2023 of the MoSPI (Ministry of Statistics and Programme Implementation) aims to broaden its scope, simplify/check ambiguities, ease implementation, enhance efficiency and effectiveness, besides bringing it in line with the changing development needs of the community. The ***major facts*** related to the new guidelines are as follows:

Permissible works:

- Community buildings, recreational facilities, sports and parks.
- Public conveniences, safety and security.
- Education, public health, drinking water and sanitation.
- Irrigation, drainage and flood control systems, animal husbandry, dairy and fisheries, agriculture and farmer welfare.
- Energy supply and distribution systems, railways, roads, bridges and pathways.
- Environment, wild animals, forest and other natural resources.
- Giving prosthetics, wheel chairs, tricycles (manual or motorised), electric scooters, hearing aids and other such device to differently abled persons.
- Repair and/or renovation works of immovable assets (upto ₹50 lakh per year only).

Non-permissible works:

- Construction of residential buildings for governments, commercial/private assets or individual/family benefits (except for differently abled persons), and pooling with CSR (Corporate Social Responsibility).
- Grants, loans, contribution to any relief fund (of centre, state/UTs).
- Acquisition of land.
- Reimbursement of work.
- Works of religious nature or inside religious premises, construction of *swagat dwars* (i.e., welcome gates).
- Works in unauthorised colony.
- Operation/maintenance and recurring expenditure of any kind.
- Naming of assets after any person, living or dead.

Providing access to persons with disabilities: It is mandatory that all movable/immovable assets are friendly to persons with disabilities.

Special provision for SCs and STs: At least 15 per cent and 7.5 per cent of the funds to be spent for the areas inhabited by SCs and STs, respectively. [In case the constituency of a Lok Sabha Member has insufficient STs population, the fund to be utilised in areas predominantly inhabited by SCs].

As per the new guidelines, entire process of fund to operate through the 'web portal' (which will facilitate real-time monitoring, greater transparency, accountability, and improved efficiency and effectiveness).

MULTI-LEVEL PLANNING

It was by the late 1950s and early 1960s that the states demanded the right to plan at the state level. By the mid-1960s, the states were given the power to plan by the Centre, advising them that they should promote planning at the lower levels of the administrative strata, too, i.e., at the district-level planning - *via* the municipalities and corporations in the urban areas and *via* block level through *panchayats* and the tribal boards. By the early 1980s, India was a country of multi-level planning (MLP) with the structure and strata of planning as follows:

---

[88] As the Government reports in Publications Division, *India 2007*, pp. 711-12.

[89] We may especially quote the '21 Point Memorandum' handed over by the *All-India Panchayat Adhyaksha Sammelan*, mid-2002, New Delhi to the President and the Central Government of the time.

First Strata: Centre-Level Planning

At this level three types of Central Plans had evolved over the years - the Five-Year Plans, the Twenty-Point Programme and the MPLADS.

Second Strata: State-Level Planning

By the 1960s, the states were planning at the state level with their respective planning bodies, the state Planning Boards with the respective CMs being their *de facto* Chairman. The plans of the states were for a term of five years and parallel to the concerned Five-Year Plans of the Centre.

Third Strata: District-Level Planning

By the late 1960s all the districts of the states were having their own plans with their respective District Planning Boards (DPBs)[90] with the respective District Magistrate being the *de facto* Chairman. The district-level plans are implemented now *via* municipalities or corporations in the urban areas and the *panchayats via* the blocks in the rural areas.

Fourth Strata: Block-Level Planning

As a part of the district-level planning the block-level planning was developed which had the DPBs as their nodal body. Below the blocks, India developed the planning at the local level, too.

Fifth Strata: Local-Level Planning

By the early 1980s, plans were being implemented at the local level via the blocks and had the DPBs as the nodal agency. Due to socio-economic differentiations among the population, local-level planning in India developed with its three variants,[91] namely:

1. Village-Level Planning
2. Hill Area Planning
3. Tribal Area Planning

Basically, the MLP was started to promote the process of decentralised planning in the country. It was the Indian version of democratic planning which ultimately sought to guarantee the people's participation in the process of planning. But it failed to do so due to many reasons. The reasons have been discussed below:

1. It could not promote people's participation in the formation of the various plans. The basic idea of the MLP model was that once the local-level plans are handed over to the blocks, the blocks will make their plans, and once the blocks hand over their plans to the districts, the district-level plans will be formulated. Similarly, the state plans and finally the Five-Year Plan if the Centre will formulate one. By doing so, every idea of planning will have the representation of everybody in the country at the time of plan formation - a special kind of plan empathy would have developed out of this process. But this was not the reality. Every stratum made their own plans - lacking the empathy factor.
2. Only central plans were implemented as the states lacked the required level of finance to support the plans. They ultimately had to be satisfied by implementing the Central Plans which failed to include the states' empathy.
3. As the local bodies in India did not have any constitutional mandate, they just played the complementary roles to the state planning process. As they had no financial independence, their plans, even if they were formulated, remained only on paper.
4. The MLP, thus, failed to include the people's participation in planning, greatly betraying the local aspirations.[92]

But at the very least the failure of the MLP enabled the government to think afresh in the direction of decentralised planning, leading to the enactment of the two important Constitutional Amendments - the 73rd and 74th.

WAY TO DECENTRALISED PLANNING

Economic planning was basically an element of the centralised kind of political system (i.e., the socialist

[90] After the implementation of the 74th Constitutional Amendments they have become the District Planning Committees (DPCs).

[91] While people in some areas have socio-cultural similarities (as in the hill areas with no tribal population and the people living in the plains, i.e., villages) they lack economic similarities. Similarly, while people living in the tribal areas and the hill areas have economic similarities, they lack socio-cultural similarities. That is why all these three habitations had three sets of planning patterns.

[92] G. V. K. Rao Committee (CAARD), 1985; L. M. Singhvi Committee (CCPPRI), 1986 and Sarkaria Commission, 1988 all discussed this inter-connection (Suresh Mishra, *Legislative Status of Panchayat Raj in India* (New Delhi: Indian Institute of Public Administration, 1997)).

and the communist). When India decided in favour of a planned economy, it was to face double challenges:

1. The first challenge was to realise the objectives of planning in a time-bound frame and
2. Making economic planning a suitable instrument of development in the democratic set up - to democratise and decentralise the process of planning itself.

The government tried to decentralise the planning process by setting up the NDC and promoting the MLP, but without being able to achieve the desired results. By the late 1980s, a direct link was established[93] between development and democracy. And it was established that the above-given challenges were basically complementary - without solving the second challenge (i.e., decentralisation) the first challenge (i.e., development) cannot be solved. Finally, once the PRIs were given the constitutional status, first-time planning became a constitutional exercise at any level, i.e., at the *panchayat* level.

Though the planning at the central and the state levels are still extra-constitutional activities, it has become constitutional at the level of local bodies. Kerala has shown some pathbreaking good works *via* local body planning.[94] But still there are many hurdles to be solved before the local bodies are really able to plan for their proper development. These hurdles as per the experts are as follows:

1. The financial status of the PRIs is still not stabilised.
2. Which taxes the PRIs can impose are still not clear.
3. The state assemblies have been procrastinating in delegating timely and needful powers to the PRIs.
4. Low level of awareness among the local people regarding their Right to Information and the right functioning of the PRIs.
5. Use of money and muscle power in the PRI elections in some states.

[93] Governments' failure in including the local aspirations in the process of planned development has been considered by major experts as the foremost reason behind the success of the regional political parties, which has led to the governments of the 'compromises', i.e., coalition governments, at the Centre and in the states *via* the 'hung Parliaments' and the 'hung assemblies', respectively.

[94] J. George, "Panchayats and Participatory Planning in Kerala," *The Indian Journal of Public Administration* XLIII, no. 1 (January-March 1997).

By mid-2002, there took place an *All India Panchayat Adhyaksha Sammelan* in New Delhi. At the end of the conference, the *Panchayat Adhyakshas* handed over a '21 Point Memorandum' to the government which specially dealt with the financial status of the PRIs. In July 2002, while the then PM was addressing the annual meet of the District Rural Development Agency (DRDA), he announced that the PRIs will be given 'financial autonomy' very soon. He further added that once there is a political consensus, the government might go in for further constitutional amendment. Unfortunately, the same coalition (i.e., the NDA) did not come to power in the forthcoming general elections. But the UPA Government did not look less serious on the issue of participatory development. By mid- 2006, the PC wrote letters to every Chief Minister of each state that before the Eleventh Plan commences it wants that all the PRIs are duly delegated their functional powers of planning from the concerned states. Otherwise, the funds kept for local development would not flow to the states. This shows the seriousness of the Central Government.

Meanwhile, the Central Government is aimed at **redrawing** the contours of decentralised planning in the country. The new development 'think tank' - *NITI Aayog* - has a completely new orientation towards decentralised planning:

1. The body has to design the development policies keeping in mind the needs of *nation, states* and the *PRIs*. This will be one of its kind - a fully 'integrated' planning process.
2. It has to use the *'bottom-up'* approach unlike the one-size-fits-all ('top-down') approach of the past.
3. To the extent the finalisation of plans and required funds are concerned, all stakeholders will be able to have their say (through the GC which is composed of the CMs of states and the chiefs of UTs).
4. Promoting the idea of *Team India* which will be working on a common 'National Agenda'.
5. It has to promote the idea of *cooperative federalism*, which is in itself a highly decentralised style of promoting development planning.

By early 2015, we saw a change in the Central Government's outlook towards the fund requirements by the states, *viz*:

1. States now get *42 per cent* share in the pool of taxes of the Centre (recommendation of the Fourteenth Finance Commission accepted).

2. States are getting *liberal funding* (loan plus grants) from the Centre to implement the State Plans.
3. One of the aims behind implementing the proposed GST is to enhance the internal financial capacity of the states as the new tax will increase the gross tax collections of the states.
4. States are now free to opt for higher *market borrowings* without any permission from the Centre (but such a move has to come from the Centre). The UDAY (Ujwal Discom Assurance Yojana), launched in 2015–16 is one of such approvals of the Central Government under which states are allowed to issue 'UDAY Bonds' up to 75 per cent of the dues of the electricity distribution companies (Discoms) of the states (by mid-2016, the total discom debt in the country amounted to ₹4.3 lakh crore).

THE PLANNING COMMISSION AND THE FINANCE COMMISSION

Federal political systems provide independent financial control to the central as well as the state governments so that they are able to perform their exclusive functions.[95] For the same objective, the Constitution of India has made elaborate provisions,[96] i.e., setting up of a Finance Commission to recommend to the President certain measures relating to the distribution of financial resources between the Union and the states. But the powers given to the Finance Commission by the Parliament limited its functions to the extent of finding revenue gaps of the states, besides recommending for the grants-in-aid to the states from the Centre. The Finance Commission cannot determine the capital-related issues of the states (though the Constitution does not classify between the capital or revenue related roles of the Commission while determining the Centre's assistance to the states).

In the meantime, to promote the process of planning, an extra-constitutional body, i.e., the PC, was set up even before the First Finance Commission was set up. The PC played a very vital role in the process of determining Central Assistance (CA) to the states as all development plans, programmes and projects are within its purview.

[95] As *K. C. Wheare* writes about the classical federal constitutions in the *Federal government* (New Delhi: Oxford University Press, 1956), p. 97.

[96] Articles 270, 273, 275 and 280 of the *Constitution of India.*

All grants or loans given by the Centre to the states for developmental works were practically dependent on the recommendations of the PC. And that is why the role of the PC was said to 'confine'[97] the role of the Finance Commission, i.e., a non-constitutional body eclipsing a constitutional body. P. J. Rajamannar who headed the Finance Commission (1966–69) suggested to clearly define the relative scope and functions of the two commissions by amending the Constitution, and the PC was advised to be made a statutory body independent of the government. But no such follow-ups came from the successive governments at the Centre. But one thing was important, most of the finance commissions recommended for higher shares in the central taxes (i.e., the income tax and the central excise) and grants-in-aid.

Since the 1990s, certain events made the Central Government change its mindset regarding the role of the states in the process of development. Major events may be counted as follows:

1. The process of economic reforms started in 1991–92 required active economic participation from the states.
2. The constitutional requirement of 'participatory planning' mandated by the 73rd and 74th Constitutional Amendments was enacted in 1993.
3. The arrival of coalition era at the Centre when over a dozen political parties, having regional affiliations, came together to form the government.
4. The recommendations of the Tenth Finance Commission followed by a Constitutional Amendment making Alternative Method of Devolution a law in 1995.
5. Various new needs of the time, such as tax reforms, agricultural development, industrial expansion etc.

The year 2002 could be considered a watershed in the area of promoting the states' need for financial resources in promoting their developmental requirements. In July 2002, while the government was setting up the Twelfth Finance Commission (2005–10) the then Minister of Finance announced that in future the PC will be *playing more or less a role of collaborator to the Finance Commission.* In the same announcement, the government made one member of the PC, a member of the Finance Commission

[97] *Report of the Fourth Finance Commission,* (Ministry of Finance, GoI, New Delhi), p. 88.

too (a symbol of physical and ideological connection between the two bodies).[98] It was as if the government had accepted the suggestions of the Fourth Finance Commission to a great extent. Though the critics took it as an infringement of a constitutional body by a non-constitutional one, the government clarified by calling it a symbol for promoting the contemporary needs of the economy and fiscal federalism.

Another milestone was created in the enactment of the FRBM Act in 2003, which empowers the state governments to opt for market borrowings to fulfil their plan expenditure without prior permission from the Central Government (provided they have enacted their respective Fiscal Responsibility Acts).[99] This has boosted the participatory planning in the country by guaranteeing greater autonomous plan participation from the states.

If we look at the tax reforms process, we see a general tendency of enabling the states to collect more and more taxes, the Value Added Tax (VAT) being a glaring example by which almost all states have been able to increase their gross tax revenue receipts. Implementation of the GST has further strengthened states' fiscal capacity.

In January 2015, the NITI Aayog replaced the PC, thus the comparison between the latter and the Finance Commission no more exists, but it will always have its ***academic importance*** in the area of development planning in the country. Such experiences of the past will function as directives for the policy makers in the future.

Meanwhile, the new body, the NITI Aayog, is totally different in its approach towards fund allocations (unlike the PC, it does not allocate funds to states) to the states to promote the cause of development planning. Basically, the states now sit in the NITI itself, in a very strong position. The NITI Aayog has been termed by the Central Government as the *best friend of states in the Centre.*

A CRITICAL EVALUATION

Planning has been subject to a number of criticisms since its inception in the country. With the passage of time, not only the number of criticisms increased, but more importantly the shortcomings of planning were pointed out. Although after considerable delay, the governments took note of the shortcomings besides taking some major steps. The criticisms stand even today, but with one difference that the government is not only conscious of them but also trying to do away with them. We may now briefly discuss the major criticisms of planning in India as well as the follow-ups from the government to do away with them as:

1. Lack of 'Perspective' in Planning

According to experts, if a nation is opting for economic planning, it must have a 'perspective' element in it. To have perspective in planning, two basic elements need to be fulfilled, namely:

1. Planning should be evaluation-based, and
2. 'Long-term' goals should be followed up besides the 'short-term' goals.

In the Indian context, the succeeding plans have been always commenced without the full evaluation of the preceding plan. This was mainly due to the following reasons:

1. Lack of a nodal body responsible for data collection at the national level;
2. The federal nature of the polity made data collection a delayed process, also due to higher dependence on the states; and
3. Speedier data delivery was not possible.

After the recommendations of the National Statistical Commission (chaired by C. Rangarajan), 2000, the government discussed to set up a nodal body for data collection at the pan-India level, cutting across federal hurdles. Computerisation is already being carried out for speedier data delivery. For the time being the plans were launched on the basis of projected data (provisional, latest etc.), which are almost near the real data. But once the above-discussed arrangements are in place, Indian planning will be based on evaluation, undoubtedly. In the meantime, the 'Quarterly Review' and the 'Performance Budgeting'

---

[98] In the 10th Plan, Som Pal was that common member in both the Commissions (who resigned from the PC once the UPA-I came to power). But this arrangement has been followed by the government in all new Commissions since then - with B. K. Chaturvedi and Prof. Abhijit Sen (Members, PC) being the *Additional Members* of the *13th* and *14th Finance Commissions*.

[99] This should be considered a great fiscal freedom to the states (which even the Constitution could not foresee) and also making them behave with more responsibility in fiscal matters. More than 20 states have passed their Fiscal Responsibility Acts (FRAs) by now and are borrowing from the market for their planned needs.

of the Union Budgets have brought in the evaluation element to a greater degree.

The First Plan had set long-term goals (for the coming 20 years) besides the short-term goals (for five years). But over time, diminishing confidence in mobilising required resources, and political uncertainties at the Centre made it a convention to set only short-term targets of planning. This shortcoming seems to be done away with after the commencement of the Tenth Plan. The plan did not opt for setting long-term goals only but even did set monitorable targets for the Eleventh Plan.

It should be noted here that the government had been conscious about the need for perspective planning as a separate division with the same name, which had been functioning in the *Yojana Bhavan* since the mid 1970s.

2. Failure in Promoting a Balanced Growth and Development

Indian planning is blamed for failing the objective of a regionally balanced growth and development. Though the Second Plan itself had noticed this fact, the measures taken were not sufficient or were short-sighted. Economic planning at the national level has proved to be a highly effective tool for promoting balanced growth. But in the Indian case it turned out to be the opposite.

To take care of the issue of balanced growth, the planning process has been using the right tools, i.e., allocating plan funds on a sectoral (primary, secondary and federal reasons) basis. But due to political reasons, enough discrepancies cropped up in the method of allocating funds to the states. At the theoretical level, the governments knew the remedies, but at the practical levels politics dominated the planning process. Democratic immaturity and politicisation of the planning process is to be blamed for this.

Now things have changed for the better. The government is following a two-pronged strategy to achieve the objective of a balanced growth and development in the country:

1. Backward regions today are prioritised in directing the Central Government investment (very much the same since the 1950s), but a new beginning in the 'differential development strategy' has been made by the Centre with the Tenth Plan. Under this strategy, the developmental constraints of different states are to be tackled with a differentiation in the strategy. The more disadvantaged states receive more funds and assistance from the Centre for their planned development, cutting across the political party lines (it is seen today as a symbol of political maturity on the issue of economic development, at least).
2. There is also a complementary strategy of the planning to address the matter of regional imbalance in the country. After the country started the process of economic reforms, the nature of planning was to incline more and more towards indicative planning. The economy was to be more and more dependent on private sector investment for its future development. And the private sector will be, naturally, more interested in investing in the regions, which have better infrastructure support. Since the developed regions have better infrastructure they will attract the highest level of private investment, which will again accelerate the process of imbalanced growth. To tackle this problem, the Centre is promoting the states with lower infrastructure so that they can overcome the disadvantage. The process is slower, but at least the government is addressing the issue, which is not less satisfying and there is no criticism to this strategy. Still balanced growth and development is going to be a great challenge for planning in India.

3. Highly Centralised Nature of Planning

Decentralising the process of planning has been a major goal of the governments since the 1950s. But after Nehru, with every plan we see greater tendency of centralisation in the planning process. Setting up of the NDC and promoting the MLP did not serve much purpose in this direction. It has been among the criticised areas of planning in India as the NPC as well as the First Plan itself had called for 'democratic planning' in the country.

By the mid-1980s, the mindset of the Centre went for a change and the need for decentralised planning received proper attention. Finally, by the early 1990s, two constitutional amendments (i.e., the 73rd and the 74th) promoted the cause of decentralised planning by delegating constitutional powers to plan to the local bodies. With this, a new era of planning began, but still the planning of local bodies is in a nascent stage due to lack of proper financial provisions for them. Once the financial provisions for local bodies have evolved to the adequate level or the local bodies are given financial autonomy, the process of decentralised planning will surely receive a new direction and meaning, experts believe.

In the meantime, the Tenth Plan emphasised a greater role for the states in the planning process. The plan started a concerted effort to include the states' participation in the national planning process. The Centre is today more concerned about the developmental constraints of the states and is trying to adequately support the state plans to the extent possible. In return, the Centre wants greater and transparent fiscal compliance from the states. This approach continued during the Eleventh Plan and so has been committed for the Twelfth Plan, too. After some time, we may hope that this criticism of Indian planning will lose its ground.

It is high time now that the planning process of the nation tries including mass participation. The ***Economic Survey 2011-12*** rightly devotes a section to delve into contracts and how the civil society and citizens play a key role in fostering economic growth. *Honesty, punctuality, the propensity to keep promises, the attitude towards corruption are matters shaped in great part by norms and social beliefs and the behaviour patterns can become habitual. Moreover, in a democracy like India, what can be done by government depends in great measure on how ordinary people think and what people believe in,* it says. The Survey further adds that the civil society has been campaigning to put in place new institutions, such as the Lokpal Act, to ensure the quality of service and bring about transparency through steps such as auction of natural resources while the government has either been slow or resisted several changes.[100]

4. Lopsided Employment Strategy

Planning in India has been tilted heavily in favour of 'capital intensive' industries, especially from the Second Plan onwards. Such industries in the public sector could not generate enough employment. In place of it, India should have opted for 'labour-intensive' industries. In the era of economic reforms, the attitude changed, and the planning process began promoting the agriculture sector with an emphasis on agri-industries and agro-exports to create more gainful and quality employment opportunities. The earlier emphasis on 'wage-employment' has shifted towards 'self-employment' to do away with the lopsided employment strategy of the past.

5. Excessive Emphasis on PSUs

Indian planning emphasised on PSUs for the right reasons, but in the wrong way and for a considerably longer period of time. State monopolies in certain areas continued over such a long period in losses that there came a demand- supply gap in the major goods and services produced by the PSUs. Though very conducive policy changes were affected after the country started the reform processes, the hangover of the past is still looming large. Several reforms in the PSUs as well as a more liberal approach towards the private sector with market reforms are needed to phase out the discrepancies created by the over-emphasis on PSUs.

6. Agriculture Overshadowed by the Industry

Promoting the cause of faster industrialisation over time became so dear to the planning process that the agriculture sector became greatly overshadowed. Though the plans were highlighting or prioritising agriculture, the industrial sector and the PSUs were glorified in such a way that time and resources both were scarce for the agriculture sector. Such a policy always created a situation of food insecurity (even today) for the country and the masses who depended upon agriculture for their livelihood and income (still being 46.1 per cent)[101] could never increase their purchasing power to a level that the economy could reverse the situation of 'market failure'. In India, even today, industrial growth is heavily dependent on agricultural growth.

The Tenth Plan recognises agriculture as the 'core element' of development. This was a welcome ideological change in the strategy of planning. Now the industries can sustain themselves, but the laggard agriculture sector needs some special care and promotion from the government, so that the masses who earn their livelihood from agriculture can benefit from the WTO-promoted globalisation. The agriculture

[100] Ministry of Finance, *Economic Survey 2011-12* (New Delhi: Government of India, 2012), p. 30.

[101] Ministry of Finance, *Economic Survey* 2024-25 (New Delhi: Government of India, 2025), p. 245.

sector is in urgent need of attention, otherwise, the process of globalisation is going to be ineffective in benefitting the masses.

7. Faulty Industrial Location Policy

There are time-tested theories of 'industrial location' considering the nearness of raw materials, market, cheaper labour, better transportation and communication, and so on. But the plans always prioritised setting up of new industrial units (i.e., the PSUs) in the backward regions of the country, which falsify the theories of industrial location. Due to this the government needed to develop all industrial infrastructure besides setting up the PSUs. As the PSUs require a skilled labour force, the regions failed to gain any employment from the PSUs too. The government still continues with the same policy of setting up industries, but now the new PSUs are hardly set up in traditional areas.

8. Wrong Financial Strategy

Mobilising resources to support the highly capital-intensive plans (due to the PSUs) has always been a challenge for the government. To support the plans, no stones were left unturned, namely opting for a highly complex and liberal tax structure, nationalising the banks, and so on. Ultimately, tax evasion, the menace of the parallel economy and lesser and lesser capital for the private sector were some of the fallouts. Expansion of subsidies, salaries and the interest burden every year provided an upward push to the non-plan expenditure leading to scarcity of funds to support the plan expenditure (i.e., the developmental expenses).

In the era of reforms, the government has started paying attention to the financial strategy of supporting the plans in the right way. Besides tax reforms, the financial reforms, as well as fiscal consolidation have been given proper care in recent years.

9. Politicisation of the Planning Process

In a democratic political system, almost every issue of socio-political importance is influenced by politics. It is more correct in the case of less matured democracies. The same stands true for the process of planning in our country. Greater politicisation of the planning process culminated in such a design that at times economic planning served the opposite purpose. For example, we know that planning is a tool for promoting regionally balanced growth, but in India in the process of serving vested political interests of the Centre, it resulted into promoting an imbalanced growth.

In recent years, the government has tried to address the major criticism of planning in India. More such constructive steps with better results are expected in future. More aware and better-informed citizens will lead to better planning in future.

There has been a general anger among the sections of society regarding coalition politics, scams and so on, in recent years. The ***Economic Survey 2014-15*** rightly *blames coalition politics* and the *federal structure* for tardy decision-making in several areas - from oil subsidy to tax reforms, FDI in retail and free movement of foodgrains. Almost everyone outside the government blamed it for *policy paralysis*. The Survey notes it as an area of concern. The Survey notes that ***politicians*** and ***policy makers*** can set the ball rolling by acting as ***role models***, but it also cites the poor record on enforcement of contract to argue that people's attitudes need to change. *In these everyday situations (such as hiring a cab or a painter) it is cumbersome to bring in the state and the law courts. Here the main guarantor has to be people's personal integrity and trustworthiness,* it says. The statement comes from a government that has been battling a spate of *corruption scandals* - ranging from those in the telecom sector to Commonwealth Games and criticism over poor governance standards and inability to push through critical decisions.[102]

The ***Economic Survey 2012-13*** suggested a new objective for the PC - the global economic and financial crisis has not only exposed the vulnerability of almost all the countries over the globe to external shocks but also brings lessons for the ***planning process***, *viz.* countries need to have inbuilt social safety nets for facing such eventualities, which affect the weak and vulnerable the most, and wipe out the fruits of growth for years. India with its focus on inclusive development and timely interventions had, however, been able to weather the crisis better than many other countries.[103]

[102] *Economic Survey 2011-12* (New Delhi: Ministry of Finance, GoI), p. 30.

[103] *Economic Survey 2012-13* (New Delhi: Ministry of Finance, GoI), p. 269.

Conceptual Timeline of Indian Planning

India's planning process has evolved conceptually over time, adopting new elements and adapting to the new situations in the following ways:

- Both regional (1948) and national (1951) plans were launched—finally merged in 1961.
- From single-level to multi-level planning (between 1951 and 1982).
- From long-term to short-term planning (between 1969 and 2002) and finally long-term (2002 onwards).
- From centralised to decentralised planning (process began in 1952 when the National Development Council was set up culminating in the multi-level planning by 1982).
- From systems to normative planning (however, some traits of normative planning can be found by early 2000s itself, it became prominent under the NITI Aayog after 2015. We find normative pitches in most of the recent calls by the Government such as 'vocal for local' and 'Atmanirbhar Bharat'. It was the Economic Survey 2010–11 which advised to adopt normative policy approach).
- From sectoral to spatial to sectoral-spatial planning (sectoral emphasis was high in the Second and Third plans).

INCLUSIVE GROWTH

Inclusive growth is a growth process which yields broad-based benefits and ensures equality of opportunity for all (*UNDP* and the *Eleventh Plan*). Fundamentally, the ideas of growth and development already include the element of 'inclusiveness' in them, but at times, due to certain reasons, the processes might occur in a non-inclusive manner.

It was in 2000-01 that the GoI came to think clearly about 'inclusiveness' in the economy, while reviewing the performance of the economic reforms. It was found that the reform process enabled economy towards faster and higher 'wealth creation', but all could not be part of it. Only the people with resources (physical or human) were able to receive benefits from the reforming economy. It was assessed that the fruits of reforms could not percolate to the ***disadvantaged*** and ***marginalised*** sections of the society. It means the growth process during reforms was not able to include a big segment of the Indian population. In this backdrop, we see the government adopting a conscious policy towards 'inclusive growth'. Even before reforms commenced in the country, this element was lacking. But during reforms it became more glaring due to the higher pace of growth which the economy attained during this period. Though the government started attending to this issue since 2000-01 itself, it was given real attention in the *Eleventh Plan* (2007-12), where we see a clear policy evolving towards the idea of inclusive growth in the country - 'including the disadvantaged and marginalised sections of the society, especially the SCs, STs, OBCs, minorities and women' in the processes of growth and development. By the *Twelfth Plan* (2012-17), the focus increased when we see the issue of inclusiveness entering into the very slogan of the Plan - 'Faster, Sustainable and More Inclusive Growth'. During the course of time, we see the government evolving a clear *short-term* and *long-term* policy towards the cause of inclusive growth.

Short-Term Policy

This policy is aimed at supplying those goods and services to the disadvantaged and marginalised sections of society which are bare minimum and are essential in nature. Several Central Sector Schemes and CSSs are run by the governments for this purpose. This policy touches the following areas:

1. Food and nutrition (*Annapurna, Antodaya*, Mid-Day Meal, and the last being National Food Security Act, etc.);
2. Healthcare and sanitation (National Health Mission, Total Sanitation Campaign, ASHA, Mission Indradhanush, and the last being *Swachh Bharat Abhiyan*, etc.);
3. Housing (*Indira Aawas Yojana*, Rajiv Aawas Yojana, etc);
4. Drinking water (National Rural Drinking Water Programme, etc);
5. Education (*Sarva Shiksha Abhiyan, Rashtriya Madhyamik Shiksha Abhiyan*, Model School Scheme, etc).

The short-term policy has two drawbacks - *Firstly*, the schemes in it are subsidy-based, which incurred heavy drain on the national exchequer (it means it will not be fiscally sustainable in the long run). *Secondly*, the schemes failed to make the target population self-dependent. This is why the government has also evolved a long-term policy in this regard.

Long-Term Policy

This policy is aimed at bringing in self-dependence in the target population and contains in itself the sustainability element, too. The attempts by the governments may be classified as given below:

1. All the schemes which aim at poverty alleviation and employment generation;
2. All the programmes which promote education at any level;
3. Vocationalisation of education (one such old idea has been the Industrial Training Institutes); and
4. Skill Development (a recent idea).

In recent times, we see increased emphasis on imparting the right 'skill' among the population. Towards this, the government decided in 2008-09 to launch a skill development programme in the country through the National Skill Development Corporation (a joint venture not-for-profit company under the Ministry of Finance). There is an overall target of skilling/upskilling people, mainly by fostering private sector initiatives in skill development programmes and providing funding. The new government at the Centre has also given the same call in the *Skill India*.

This way, we can see an initiative of foolproof policy towards inclusive growth getting evolved by the GoI which is sustainable, too. The PC (*Eleventh Plan*) says that inclusive growth can only be ensured if there is a degree of empowerment that creates a true feeling of participation necessary in a democratic polity. Empowerment of disadvantaged and hitherto marginalised groups is therefore an essential part of any vision of inclusive growth. India's democratic polity, with the establishment of the third layer of democracy at the PRIs level, provides opportunities for empowerment and participation of all groups with reservations for SCs, STs and women. These institutions should be made more effective through greater delegation of power and responsibility.

The strategy for inclusive growth in the *Eleventh* and *Twelfth Plans* is not just a conventional strategy for growth to which some elements aimed at inclusion have been added. On the contrary, it is a strategy which aims at achieving a particular type of growth process, which will meet the objectives of *inclusiveness* and *sustainability*. A key feature of the inclusive growth strategy is that growth of 'GDP should not be treated as an end in itself, but only as a means to an end'. This is best carried out by adopting *monitorable targets*, which would reflect the multi-dimensional **economic** and **social** objectives of inclusive growth. Furthermore, to ensure efficient and timely implementation of the accompanying projects and programmes, these targets need to be disaggregated at the level of the states which implement many of the programmes.

RESOURCE MOBILISATION

Resource mobilisation is a broad term which includes raising and directing the resources (physical and human) of the economy to realise the desired socio-economic objectives. It involves all the economic policies activated by the governments - we can perceive it to be the very essence and the end result of the 'fiscal policies' of both the Centre and the states.

For the Indian economy to move on the path of desired growth and development, the GoI needs to take care of the issue of resource mobilisation for various agents in the economy, namely

1. GoI,
2. State governments,
3. Private sector, and
4. General public

In India, the responsibility of mobilising resources for the *planned* development of the country was given to the PC. The Commission used to take care of the fund requirements of the centre and the state governments. Practically, it was the PC which has to put in place the means by which the required funds for the *planned targets* of the economy were mobilised. These plan targets are set by the GoI through the PC itself. The plan targets set by the states are also duly taken care of the PC in due course of this process. Though the effective responsibilities to mobilise resources ultimately rests with the Ministry of Finance in which the various departments and divisions of the ministry play their diverse and highly focussed roles.

1. **GoI:** To the extent GoI is concerned it needs funds to realise two categories of the **planned targets**, namely:

(i) *Infrastructural targets* (which chiefly include power, transportation and communication; in coming years so many other sectors became attached with it, for example, technology parks, urban infrastructure, etc.); and

(ii) *Social sector targets* (which include education, health, social security, etc. - known as the Human Development related targets since 2010-11). These funds are mobilised through the *Plan Finance-II Division* of the Ministry of Finance.

2. **State Governments:** Other than the fund requirements of the GoI, the states also need funds for their developmental requirements (similar to the GoI) - they get the funds mobilised through three sources: *firstly*, through their own sources of income and market borrowings (after the recommendations of the 13th Finance Commission states are allowed to finance 25 per cent of their Plan Expenditure through market borrowing for which they do not need any permission from the GoI, provided they have effected their Fiscal Responsibility Acts); *secondly*, through the loans they get from the GoI on the advice of the PC (Ministry of Finance, GoI, shows these expenditures in the *Plan Finance-I Division*); and *thirdly*, through the GoI Central Sector Schemes, CSSs and Additional Central Allocations (this includes the fund transfer to the states under 'Special Category States').

3. **Private Sector:** Other than the government, a large amount of fund is required by the private sector to meet their short-term (working capital) and long-term (capital market) requirements. The GoI needs to take care of this issue also - the financial system is managed in such a way that other than the government the private sector is also able to mobilise resources for its various requirements. This becomes even more important in a mixed economy, which is reforming and favours increased participation in the economy from the private sector.

   This needs focused reform in the financial system as it was structured to channelise more funds and resources towards government needs before the reforms commenced. The main idea here is to prevent the governments from 'crowding out' the funds and let it flow smoothly towards the private sector - the process of reforms in the financial sector, tax structure, fiscal policies of the Centre and states and so on come under it.

4. **General Public:** Other than the government and the private sector, common people of an economy also need funds for their *general spending* and *investment*. The government needs to put in place such a fiscal policy which enables them (too) to have their access to funds. The savings common people opt for is used as investment provided, they are able to save. Other than saving, people must get incentive and enough funds which they might directly invest in the primary or secondary security markets or in financial instruments (shares, bonds, mutual funds, pension funds, insurance, etc.). Common people are the main drivers of 'demand' in an economy. In the periods of reforms, the government sets *twin targets* - at the one hand promoting private sector so that 'supply' can be optimised in the economy (through *structural reforms*) and at the other it tries to create adequate 'demand' in the economy (by the process of *macroeconomic stabilisation*).

The government used different 'means' to mobilise resources since Independence, in order to realise the desired and required kind of developmental goals. A part of resources is mobilised for investment purposes (i.e., the creation of productive assets) for which different *investment models* have been tried by now.

INVESTMENT MODELS

Investment is a process of putting money in productive activities to earn income. It can be carried out *directly* (in different activities in the primary, secondary or tertiary sectors) or *indirectly* (as in financial securities, such as shares, debentures, bonds, mutual funds, etc.). In the case of India, 'Investment Models' are the *means and tools* by which the GoI has tried to mobilise required funds (resources) to promote the different goals of planned development. Since India started the planning process (1951), we see differing ***models*** being tried by the governments to mobilise resources - it has been a kind of 'evolutionary' process. We may understand them in the following ***phases***:

Phase-I (1951–69)

This was the phase of 'state-led' development in which we see the GoI utilising every internal and external means to mobilise required resources. The main areas of resource allocations were for infrastructure and social sector. The famous Mahalanobis Plan was implemented during this period. In this period, we see the whole financial system, tax system and fiscal policy of the country getting regulated to drive in maximum funds for the government to meet its planning related financial responsibilities.

This phase was marred by visible mismatches between the need and availability of investible fund - there always prevailed a lag between the requirement of funds and their mobilisation.

Thus, investment targets of the government got derailed many times (war with China and a brief war with Pakistan also eroded and diverted the resource allocation mechanism). But overall, the government was able to start the process of industrialisation almost from nothing by mobilising heavy funds in favour of the infrastructure sector and infrastructure industries (the core sector) - education, health care also received funds but in a subdued manner as the GoI remained greatly preoccupied with the 'glorification of the public sector'. This was the age when the GoI used to consider the PSUs as the 'temples of modern India'.

Phase-II (1970–73)

With the enactment of the Industrial Policy of 1970, we see GoI deciding in favour of including 'private capital' in the process of planned development - but not in a big and open way. The idea of 'Joint Sector' comes under which a combination of partners - Centre, state and private sector - could enter the industrial sector. This was carried out to enable the private sector come up in areas which were open for them, but due to certain technical and financial reasons they were not able to take part. In due course of time the government did quit such ventures and such industrial settlements came under complete private control.

This is for the first time we see the government inclining on private funding for planned development, but we do not see any private entry in the GoI's monopoly areas of industrial activities (which takes place only after the reform process begins in 1991).

Phase-III (1974–90)

With the enactment of the FERA in 1974 we see the government, for the first time, proposing to take the help of 'foreign capital' in the process of planned development - but not *via* cash foreign investment - only through the 'technology transfer' route up to only 26 per cent of the total project value proposed by the private sector. Basically, under the FERA the government tightened the flow of foreign currency inflow into the Indian private sector, which started hampering the technological upgradation process and initiation of the state-of-the-art technologies from the world - the technology transfer route was put in place to fill this gap. It means that even if the GoI tried to include foreign investment in the developmental process its entry remained restricted in two ways:

1. It was not either 'direct' (as we see FDI during the reform process) or 'indirect' (as the PIS), but *via* technology transfer.
2. Foreign entities could enter only those industrial areas which were open for the Indian private sector (under Schedule B of the Industrial Policy Resolution, 1956). The 'monopoly' industries under the GoI (some of the most attractive industries for the private sector) remained closed for entry.

It also means that India failed to articulate an *investment model* which could tap the better elements of the foreign capital - state-of-the-art technologies, better work culture and most importantly, scarce investible capital. Experts believe it as a missed opportunity for India. By 1965-66, South East Asian economies like Malaysia, Indonesia, Thailand and South Korea had opened up their economies for both forms of foreign investments - direct as well as indirect - and the governments there 'decontrolled' the industrial sectors, which were earlier fully under government controls (it should be noted here that these economies had started exactly the same way as India had started after independence). This gave those economies a chance to tap not only scarce investible fund into their economies, but the state-of-the-art technologies from the world and world-class work culture and entrepreneurship, too. Soon these economies came to be known as the Asian Tigers.

The period after 1985 saw dynamism in the area of resource mobilisation - two consecutive PCs suggested for opening up of the economy and inclusion of the Indian and foreign private capital in industrial areas which were hitherto reserved for the government. It suggested that the GoI withdraw from areas where the private sector was capable and fit to function (for example, infrastructure sector) and concentrate on areas where the private sector would not be interested to operate (for example, the social sector). In a sense, during this time, we see an ideological shift in the government towards providing an 'active' or 'central' role to the private sector in the process of economic development. This was an advice for a completely different kind of *investment model.* But due to lack of political will, the governments of the time could not opt for the same. Though, we find the government opting for a kind of limited degree of economic reforms through the Industrial Policies of 1985 and 1986 (this should not be taken as the Economic Reforms in India which officially started only in 1991).

As a **summary** of the investment models up to 1990, we can highlight the following points:

1. Government remains the main investor in the economy, and experts believe that India created undue delay in putting in place an *investment model* by which the potential of the private sector could be channelised into the process of developmental investment.
2. Emphasis on the public sector continued together with nationalisation drives also by the late 1960s and early 1980s (the PSUs, to a large extent, were privatised by the South East Asian economies by now, making these socially oriented and loss-making units to catapult into hubs of profit and real drivers of growth and development).
3. Tax system was structured to raise maximum tax revenue (which led to tax evasion and excessive tax burdens on the citizens).
4. GoI continued cutting its non-plan expenditures so that resources could be allocated for the purpose of planned development (which led to expenditure cuts even in essential areas such as education, health care, etc.).
5. Excessive government dependence on the financial system continued 'crowding out' funds, and as a result, the private sector could not mobilise suitable levels of funds for their requirements.
6. Technological upgradation and initiation of new technologies into the economy was hampered due to non-availability of foreign currency to the private sector (GoI, by late 1970, started facing the difficulty of paying its external liabilities, which were mainly created due to the expansion of the PSUs).
7. Main sources of fund in this model were government tax revenue, internal borrowings, external borrowings and the freshly printed currencies.

There always prevailed a lag between the requirement of funds and their mobilisation resulting into government investment targets getting derailed most of the time. In the meanwhile, the biggest crisis was building up in the areas of infrastructure shortcomings. By the early 1960s itself the Indian private sector was eager to enter this sector so that adequate levels of infrastructure could be developed. But due to several reasons we see the GoI monopolies in many of these sectors even today.

Phase-IV (1991 onward)

Due to prolonged follow-up of weak fundamentals of economics and immediately after Gulf War I, India headed for a severe balance-of-payment crisis by the late 1980s, which made India go to the IMF for financial help. It comes up but at some 'conditions' - the design of the 'conditions' made India to go for a 'restructuring' of the economy under the process of economic reforms commencing in 1991.

Reform era shifted India towards including the 'private sector' (domestic as well as foreign) for the future development of the economy - and here proceeds a different *investment model.* Main elements of this investment model are as given below:

1. The hitherto monopoly sectors of the industry were opened up for private investment - barring Nuclear Research, Nuclear power and Railways (the latter two areas are partially opened) - in all of them direct foreign investments have also been allowed (between 26 and 100 per cent). We see the 'investment model' for the *infrastructure sector* shifting from 'government-led' to 'private-led'.
2. In coming times, the GoI articulated the idea of the PPP model of investment for this sector, to provide confidence and space to the private sector to enter the sectors (as the private sector was not interested to participate due to some inter-related problems in the sector, for example lack of 'market reforms'). By the Tenth Plan we see the private sector putting in around

21 per cent of funds required for the infrastructure projects in the PPP mode which increased up to 32 per cent by the Eleventh Plan. Based on the past two plans, the PC projected that private sector will put in around 50 per cent (48 per cent, to be precise) of the funds required for infrastructure development during the Twelfth Plan (which could not be achieved due to several internal and external reasons till 2015). Here, one point should not be missed that in future the infrastructure sector is to be fully handled by the private sector - as per the idea of the reform process.

3. In 2002, the government articulated the idea of PPP through the Tenth Plan (2002- 07). The idea has its use at the local level where the resources are to be mobilised for the creation of physical and social infrastructure. It was launched in watershed management successfully. Gujarat had shown a highly successful model of this investment in its '*Pani Panchayat*'.
4. To support the private sector to mobilise their share of fund in the infrastructure PPP, the government set up the Infrastructure Development Fund, which also has provision for Viability Gap Funding (VGF).
5. Inside the general idea of PPP, the government has also put in place some other options of investment models, such as BOT (Build-Operate-Transfer); BOO (Build-Own-Operate); BOOT (Build-Own-Operate-Transfer); BLT (Build-Lease-Transfer); BOLT (Build Operate-Lease-Transfer); DBFO (Design-Build-Finance-Operate); DBOT (Design-Build-Operate-Transfer); DCMF (Design-Construct-Manage-Finance); etc.
6. In the area of mobilising resources for the expansion of the **Social Sector**, we see an increased focus coming from the government. But the government still is of the view that there is an inadequacy of funds for the proper and timely development of the sector. Thus, by 2012, the GoI proposed plans to include the participation of the private sector in the sector, mainly education and health care through the PPP mode, which is still to be formally launched. Meanwhile, the provision regarding corporate social responsibility (CSR) *via* the Companies Act, 2013, some additional funds have started flowing to the fund-starved social sector. By early 2015, the government has asked the PSUs to flow their part of the CSR expenditures to the GoI for the newly launched sanitation drive, the *Swachch Bharat Abhiyan.*
7. So that the *corporate sector* can mobilise enough resources for its investment needs in the economy, the governments started to restructure the whole gamut of the tax structure, financial structure and its fiscal policy. Now, as the economy will depend more on private participation for its developmental requirements, the government avoids crowding out the fund from the economy - a process of fiscal consolidation starts in. An increased emphasis comes on the fronts of 'targeting' the subsidies, their better delivery, pension reforms, and so on so that the government could de-burden the financial system from its fund requirements and enough finance flows in the system for the private sector.
8. To take care of the spending and investment requirements of the *general public* the government is committed to put in place a cheap interest rate regime, the right kind of financial environment, a stable inflation and exchange rate besides other instruments. Bringing in 'inclusiveness' in the growth process is now the declared policy stance of the government.
9. Once the new government came to power by mid-2014, we find a renewed synergy in creating a conducive environment for the private sector so that the economy could be able to attract enough investible fund to further the process of development. The government looks committed to the cause of improving the *ease of doing business* in the country. Aimed towards this we find the government busy putting in place the 'right' kind of land acquisition law, labour law, companies' law, tax laws, digitalisation of government processes, etc.

Overall, the current investment model of the economy is **private-led**, and for this the GoI proposes to put in place the right kind of financial system, legal framework, labour laws, etc. The main idea of this model is to 'unshackle' the hidden potential of the private sector. To the extent the role of the government is concerned, it will be limited to being a regulator with an increased tone of a 'facilitator' and a caretaker of the well-being of the disadvantaged and marginalised sections of the society, so that the face of the economic reform remains 'humane'. In wake of the financial crisis in the western economies, the challenge of mobilising resources has become tougher, and it will be good that the government is able to devise out a working investment model.

CENTRAL SECTOR SCHEMES AND CENTRALLY SPONSORED SCHEMES

The exercise of planned development in India has evolved two types of schemes over the time, *viz.* **Central Sector Scheme** and **Centrally Sponsored Scheme (CSSs)**. The names are derived from the pattern of funding and the modality for implementation.

The ***Central Sector Schemes*** are 100 per cent funded by the Union Government with states functioning as implementing agencies. These schemes are mainly formulated on subjects from the *Union List*. In addition, the Central ministries also implement some schemes directly in the states/UTs, which too are called Central Sector Schemes, but resources under these schemes are not generally transferred to states.

As per the **Union Budget 2016-17**, the existing 1,500 such schemes were restructured into 300 by the GoI to prevent overlapping of expenditure and help in better monitoring and evaluation (M&E).

Under the ***CSSs*** a certain percentage of the funding is borne by the centre and the states in fixed ratios, and the implementation is carried out by the state governments. CSSs are formulated on the items from the *State List* to encourage states to prioritise in areas that require more attention. Funds are routed either through the Consolidated Fund of the states and or are transferred directly to state/district level autonomous bodies/implementing agencies. As per the *Baijal Committee Report* (1987), CSSs have been defined as the schemes which are funded directly by Central ministries/departments and implemented by the states or their agencies, irrespective of their pattern of financing, unless they fall under the Centre's sphere of responsibility, i.e., the Union List.

Conceptually, both CSSs and ACA have been passed by the Central Government to the state governments. The difference between the two has arisen because of the *historical evolution* and the way these are being budgeted and controlled, and release of funds takes place. In case of CSSs, the budgets are allocated under concerned ministries themselves which look after the entire process of the release of funds.

Central Plan Assistance

Financial assistance provided by the GoI to support a state's Five-Year Plans is called Central Plan Assistance (CPA) or Central Assistance (CA), which primarily comprises the following:

1. **Normal Central Assistance (NCA):** The distribution of the NCA is formula-based (Gadgil-Mukherjee Formula) and is untied. Gadgil Formula of determining the CA to the State is being adopted from the Fourth Plan and revised subsequently - allocation was made by the PC.
2. **Additional Central Assistance (ACA):** This is provided for implementation of externally aided projects (EAPs), for which presently there is no ceiling. Unlike the NCA, this is scheme-based. The details of such schemes are given in Statement 16 of the Expenditure Budget Vol. I. There can be one-time ACA and advance ACA. **One-time ACA** was assistance given by the PC to particular states for undertaking important state-specific programmes and schemes. These were one-time assistance and thus not recurring. These assistances are discretionary in nature. **Advance ACA** are advances given to *Special Category States* in times of financial stress and recoverable in 10 years.
3. **Special Central Assistance (SCA):** This is provided for special projects and programmes, e.g. Western Ghats Development Programme, Border Areas Development Programme, etc. (in exceptional situations ACA may also be provided). This special plan assistance is given only to *Special Category States* to bridge the gap between their planning needs and resources. In other words, SPAs are ACA for the special category states.

CPA is provided, as per the scheme of financing applicable for specific purposes, approved by the PC (now, the NITI does not approve it but rather only advises). It is released in the form of *grants* and/or *loans* in varying combinations, as per terms and conditions defined by the Ministry of Finance, Department of Expenditure. CA in the form of ACA is provided also for various CSSs, *viz.* Accelerated Irrigation Benefits Programme, *Rashtriya Krishi Vikas Yojana* and so on, and SCA is extended to states and UTs as additive to the Special Component Plan (renamed Scheduled Castes Sub Plan) and Tribal Sub Plan. Funds provided to the states under MPLADS, i.e., ₹5 crore per annum per MP also count as CA.

CSSs Restructured

For the Twelfth Plan period (2012-17) the existing 137 CSSs were restructured into 66 schemes, including the 17 *flagship programmes*. The government had set up an expert Committee (Chaired by B. K. Chaturvedi, member of the erstwhile PC) for the purpose which submitted its report by late-2011.

The *14th FC* recommended that sector-specific transfers from the Union to the states/UTs should be confined to sectors such as education, health, drinking water and sanitation. However, in view of the preponderance of CSSs being interventions in key sectors of national importance, the GoI kept **50** of the **66** ongoing CSSs in the *Union Budget 2015-16*. The balance was in the process of being either taken into the Central Sector or reformulated as new Umbrella Schemes or were transferred to the states. The CSSs funds are released as CA to state plans which are routed through the states' budgets (new method as per the *Union Budget 2014-15*). This provides greater autonomy, authority and responsibility to the states in implementation of the schemes.

In **March 2015**, to rationalise the CSSs, a sub-group of Chief Ministers was set up in pursuance of the decision taken by the *GC* of the NITI Aayog. As per the *guiding principles* of the sub-group, the Union and the States/UTs were supposed to work as 'Team India' to realise the *Vision 2022* while celebrating the 75th year of Independence. The Vision set the following broad objectives:

1. Providing basic amenities to all citizens in an equitable and just manner for ensuring a life with self-respect and dignity, and
2. Providing appropriate opportunities to every citizen to realise their potential.

Accordingly, the existing 50 CSSs were rationalised and restructured into 28 *umbrella* schemes[104] (in normal circumstances number not to exceed 30) by the Union Budget 2016-17. This will avoid overlapping of expenditure, provide visibility and impact. The **major features** of the restructuring are as given below:

1. The CSSs have been divided into *Core* and *Optional* schemes.
2. The new expenditure sharing pattern for the *Core Schemes* is - for 8 North Eastern (NE) states and 3 Himalayan states 90:10; for other States 60:40 (Centre: States) and for UTs 100 per cent to be borne by the Centre.
3. For *Optional Schemes* the expenditure sharing pattern is - for 8 NE and 3 Himalayan states 80:20; for other states 50:50 (Centre: States) and for the UTs 100 per cent to be borne by the Centre.
4. Amongst the Core Schemes, those for social protection and social inclusion should form the *Core of the Core* and be the first charge on available funds for the National Development Agenda.
5. Funds for *Optional Schemes* would be allocated to the states by the Ministry of Finance as a **lump sum**, and states would be *free* to choose which Optional Schemes they wish to implement. In such schemes, states have been given the *flexibility* of *portability* of funds to any other CSSs.
6. Henceforth, the CSSs will come up only in key identified sectors which comprise the *National Development Agenda* (to be decided by the NITI Aayog, in coordination with its GC).
7. NITI Aayog to have concurrent jurisdiction in *monitoring* of the schemes in the states and Central ministries.
8. Third-party *evaluation* by NITI Aayog.

[104] The process of restructuring basically limited to rationalisation (better called 'rearrangement') of the existing schemes into umbrella schemes. But these umbrellas are large enough and include close to 200 schemes. For example, one Core Scheme *Green Revolution* (implemented by the Department of Agriculture, Cooperation and Farmers' Welfare) contains *17 schemes* under its umbrella which are *Rashtriya Krishi Vikas Yojana*; National Food Security Mission; Agriculture Marketing Information; Integrated Scheme on Agricultural Cooperation; Integrated Scheme on Agriculture Census and Statistics; National Agri-Tech Infrastructure; National Mission on Horticulture; National Mission on Oil Seed and Oil Palm; National Project on Agro-Forestry; National Project on Organic Farming; National Project on Soil Health and Fertility; Organic Value Chain Development for North East Region; *Paramparagat Krishi Vikas Yojana*; Rain-fed Area Development and Climate Change and Sub-Missions on Agriculture Extension; Agriculture Mechanisation; Plant Protection; and Plant Quarantine and Seed and Planting Material. [Source: B. Debroy, Chairman, Economic Advisory Council to the PM, *Indian Express*, Delhi, September 12, 2019].

In 2019-20, the CSSs were broadly classified under two categories, *Core of the Core Schemes* and *Core Schemes* (funding pattern remaining unchanged). The list of the 30 schemes[105] is given below.

Core of the Core Schemes

1. National Social Assistance Programme
2. Mahatma Gandhi National Rural Employment Guarantee Programme
3. Umbrella Scheme for Development of Schedule Castes
4. Umbrella Programme for Development of Scheduled Tribes
5. Umbrella Programme for Development of Minorities
6. Umbrella Programme for Development of Other Vulnerable Groups

Core Schemes

1. Green Revolution
2. White Revolution
3. Blue Revolution
4. *Pradhan Mantri Krishi Sinchai Yojana*
5. *Pradhan Mantri Gram Sadak Yojana*
6. *Pradhan Mantri Awas Yojana* (PMAY)
7. Jal Jeevan Mission (JJM)
8. Swachh Bharat Mission (Urban)
9. Swachh Bharat Mission (Gramin)
10. National Health Mission (NHM)
11. National Education Mission (NEM)
12. National Programme of Mid-Day Meal in Schools
13. Umbrella ICDS
14. Mission for Protection and Empowerment for Women (Mission Shakti).
15. National Rural Livelihood Mission (NRLM) - *Aajeevika*
16. Jobs and Skill Development
17. Environment, Forestry and Wildlife
18. Urban Rejuvenation Mission: AMRUT and Smart Cities Mission
19. Modernisation of Police Forces
20. Infrastructure Facilities for Judiciary
21. *Rashtriya Gram Swaraj Abhiyan* (RGSA)
22. *Pradhan Mantri Jan Arogya Yojana* (PM-JAY) - *Ayushman Bharat*
23. Border Area Development Programme (BADP)
24. Shyama Prasad Mukherjee Rurban Mission (SPMRM)

At present the schemes are under the process of evaluation before they can be streamlined as per the recommendations of the Fifteenth Finance Commission (FFC). The Commission has recommended *measurable and performance-based incentives* related to the schemes for states (the Terms of Reference given to the Commission include 'achievements in implementation of flagship schemes of GoI, disaster-resilient infrastructure, sustainable development goals, and quality of expenditure'). Thus, the schemes are headed for further restructuring.

INDEPENDENT EVALUATION OFFICE

An Independent Evaluation Office (IEO) was created by the GoI in February 2014, at an arm's length from the government with the objective of strengthening public accountability of some of the important social sector programmes, which account huge resource mobilisation such as the flagship programmes. Conceived on the lines of IEO of the IMF,[106] the body was created on the basis of international experiences, in cooperation with the *World Bank* and the British *DFID* (Department for International Development) - it was modelled on the lines of Mexico's National Council for the Evaluation of Social Development Policy.

The IEO was an independent office attached to the PC under a Governing Board chaired by the Deputy Chairman of the PC. The IEO was funded by the PC and had, as its head, a full-time Director General in the rank and status of Member of the PC/Union Minister

[105] *Union Budget 2020-21*, (New Delhi: Ministry of Finance, GoI). [Before the last revision in the classification, last two (i.e., the BADP and SPMRM) were implemented as the *Optional Schemes*].

[106] An Independent Evaluation Office (IEO) has been functioning in the International Monetary Fund (IMF) since 2001, which conducts independent and objective *evaluations* of Fund's policies and activities. Under its Terms of Reference, it is fully independent from the Management of the IMF and operates at arm's length from the Board of Executive Directors with the following *three* missions: (i) Enhancing the learning culture within the Fund, (ii) Strengthening the Fund's external credibility and (iii) Supporting institutional governance and oversight [Source: *Independent E-valuation Office* (Washington DC: IMF, 2014)].

of State. The DG had a tenure of 3 years extendable to 5 years. Its staff was selected by the DG without any interference and to have its independent budget.

It was felt that the government programmes can benefit enormously from concurrent independent evaluation. Presently, concurrent evaluation was carried out by the concerned ministries as an ongoing parallel process. Expert evaluation of programmes that have been in operation was carried out by the Programme Evaluation Organisation (PEO) of the PC - the IEO was expected to strengthen this evaluation process. **Main aims** of the office were as follows:

1. To help improve the effectiveness of government policies and programmes by assessing their impact and outcomes.
2. To set guidelines and methodology for all evaluations carried out by various departments and agencies and encourage a culture of openness and learning in government systems.
3. To connect India to the best international evaluated evidence in development practice and knowledge to learn from others' successes and mistakes.

Main features about the functioning of the office may be summed up as given below:

1. It will conduct independent evaluations of plan programmes - especially flagship programmes - and assess their effectiveness, relevance and impact. Besides, it has the freedom to conduct independent evaluations on any programme which has access to public funding or implicit or explicit guarantees from the government.
2. The work programme of the IEO will be prepared through an open process of consultations, including feedback from **civil society** and will be made public.
3. The IEO will prepare the *Terms of Reference* for all independent evaluations, which will be conducted by selected institutes and researchers, selected on a competitive basis.
4. The IEO will provide guidance to any agency or department of the government to improve the quality of its self-evaluation and monitoring system. Such support is intended to bring all evaluations under a common internationally accepted methodology, help achieve better development outcomes and encourage a *culture of learning* in the government.
5. Besides making available on its website and other public avenues, its reports will be submitted to the Parliament and the Prime Minister's Office.
6. It will also make internationally available findings from independently and professionally evaluated Indian programmes in the spirit of South-South learning and cooperation.
7. The IEO will **represent** India as its independent evaluation authority at international forums on development and effectiveness and will endeavour to improve India's evaluation systems in line with international best practices.

The IEO handed over its first report to the Government in September 2014 and in the following week, the DG of the IEO was relieved from his services. Later on, the IEO was *merged* into the newly constituted (September 2015) M&E body, the Development Monitoring and Evaluation Office (DMEO). The functions and the special features of the IEO still reflect in the new body.

PROGRAMME EVALUATION ORGANISATION

The Programme Evaluation Organisation (PEO) was established in October 1952, as an independent organisation, under the general guidance and direction of the PC with a specific task of evaluating the community development programmes and other Intensive Area Development Schemes. The evaluation set up was further strengthened by the development of methods and techniques of evaluation in the First Plan and setting up of evaluation machineries in the States during the Third (1961-66) and Fourth (1969-74) Plans. Gradually, with the extension of the programmes/schemes in a variety of sectors, *viz.* agricultural cooperation, rural industries, fisheries, health, family welfare, rural development, rural electrification, public distribution, tribal development, and social forestry, the evaluation work undertaken by the PEO was extended to other important CSSs.

The broad **functions** of the PEO included undertaking evaluation of selected programmes/schemes under implementation, as per the requirement of the various Divisions of the PC, Central Ministries and Departments of the GoI. The evaluation studies were designed to ***assess***:

1. the performance,
2. the process of implementation,

3. the effectiveness of the delivery systems, and
4. the impact of programmes.

The **objectives** of the PEO were:

1. Objective assessment of process and impact of the development programmes,
2. Identifying the areas of success and failures at different stages of administration and execution, and analysis of reasons for success or failure,
3. Examining extension methods and people's reactions thereto and deriving lessons for future improvement in the formulation and implementation of the new programmes/ schemes.

The PEO was *merged* into the newly constituted (September 2015) M&E body, the DMEO. The functions and the special features of the PEO very well reflect in the new body.

Development Monitoring and Evaluation Office

The Development Monitoring and Evaluation Office (DMEO) was constituted by *merging* the erstwhile Program Evaluation Office (PEO) and the IEO in September 2015. As an attached office under the NITI Aayog, it aims at fulfilling M&E mandate (i.e., function) of the Aayog. It is entrusted with building an M&E ecosystem in the country with the following functions:

1. Monitoring progress and efficacy of policies/ programmes, taking initiatives to help improvements including necessary midcourse corrections.
2. Evaluating implementation of programmes and identification of needed resources to strengthen success and scope of delivery.

As a part of NITI Aayog, DMEO has advisory powers across the Ministries and Departments of the Union Government and is *one of few* institutions within the government to provide a cross- and inter-ministerial perspective. It has mandate of technical advisory to States also. For M&E the 'output-outcome framework' (as prescribed by the Union Budget 2019–20) has been evolved[107]. This framework has *measurable indicators* for the objectives (i.e., 'outcome') for all of the CSSs and central sector schemes. Sectoral reviews are carried out by the office on the basis of the outcomes achieved by the schemes.

All of the functions and special features of the erstwhile bodies, the IEO and PEO, are still with the DMEO added with several new and dynamic features to serve the changed developmental needs of the country on the path of transformation.

[107] To know more about the Output-Outcome Framework, see *Chapter 19*.

NITI AAYOG

By mid-2014, India did show quite a strong mandate and a very stable government came at the Centre. We find the new government showing a renewed vigor and zeal in several areas. One such area has been its attempts at 'redefining' the federal polity of the country for the purpose of promoting growth and development. We see a pronounced policy shift in the direction of 'empowering and keeping state in front' by giving them more[108] financial space and responsibilities. Keeping its promises in the direction, the government abolished the PC and replaced it with a new body - the NITI Aayog. The acronym **NITI** stands for **National Institution for Transforming India**. We see the government aspiring for the emergence of the 'Team India' in the new body. It will be premature to be conclusive on this shift from 'Planning to NITI' (as the government calls). Even an academic comparison between the old and the new bodies will also not serve enough purpose as it needs some time when the outcome of the change will be available. Judgements on this shift will be only good once it is carried out after some period. In the meantime, India remains a planned economy.

[108] Such a stance in the process of planning we find in the document of the 10th Plan (2002-07) for the first time when the government of the time (the NDA-led) made the call: 'if states are developed, the nation is developed'. We find a pronounced shift towards 'decentralised planning' (the Plan was nicknamed as the 'People's Plan'). The new idea of 'monitorable targets' also commenced in this plan giving states more say and accountability in the process of planned development (these targets were continued within the forthcoming plans). Several other steps were also taken in this plan aimed at bringing the states in the mainstream of the developmental process, *viz.* by giving them an increased role and accountability.

The discussion given here is mainly based on the documents and releases which came out from the GoI before and after the **NITI Aayog** was set up (January 1, 2015). In these documents, the government has not only provided the reasons as why does India need to go in for a new 'policy think tank' but also charts out a very encouraging and non-traditional role/function for the new body. An attempt has been made to closely follow the 'government line' of thinking so that the 'spirit' of it is not lost.

Transforming India

The government aims at 'transforming the development agenda of India' with the help of the NITI Aayog and has given a slogan, 'from planning to NITI'. As per the Government, India had undergone for a paradigm shift over the past six decades - politically, economically, socially, technologically as well as demographically. The role of the government in national development has seen a parallel evolution. Keeping with these changing times, the government decided to set up the **NITI Aayog** as a means to better serve the needs and aspirations of the people of India. The government thinks the new institution will function as a catalyst to the developmental process - nurturing an overall enabling environment, through a *holistic approach* to development going beyond the limited sphere of the public sector and the GoI, which will be built on the foundations of:

1. An empowered role of states as equal partners in national development; operationalising the principle of *Cooperative Federalism.*
2. A knowledge hub of internal as well as external resources, serving as a repository of good governance best practices, and a *Think Tank* offering domain knowledge as well as strategic expertise to all levels of the government.
3. A collaborative platform facilitating *Implementation;* by monitoring progress, plugging gaps and bringing together the various ministries at the Centre and in states, in the *joint pursuit* of developmental goals.

Changing Contours of India

The government agrees that the PC has served India well. However, India had changed dramatically over the past six decades at *multiple levels* and across *varied scales.* These transformational forces have changed the very contours of India, highlighted by the government document in six areas:

1. **Demographic Shift:** India's population has increased over three-fold to reach 121 crores. This includes an addition of over 30 crore people to Urban India. As well as an increase of 55 crore youth (below the age of 35), which is more than one and a half times the total population of the country then. With increasing levels of development, literacy and communication, the aspirations of the people have soared, moving from *scarcity and survival* to *safety and surplus.* Today, we are looking at a completely different India, and the country's governance systems need to be transformed to keep up with the changing nation.
2. **Economic Shift:** India's economy has undergone a paradigm shift. It has expanded by over a hundred times, going from a GDP of ₹10,000 crore to ₹100 lakh crore at current prices, to emerge as one of the world's largest economics. Agriculture's share in the GDP has seen a dramatic drop, from more than 50 per cent to less than 15 per cent. The plan size of ₹43 lakh crore of the Twelfth Plan dwarfs the plan size of ₹2,400 crore of the First Plan. Priorities, strategies and structures dating back to the time of the birth of the PC must thus be *revisited.* To align with this shift and sheer scale, India needs to *overhaul* the very *nature* of the planning processes, the government says.
3. **Shift in the Private Sector:** The nature of the Indian economy, and the role of the government in it, has undergone a paradigm shift. Driven by an increasingly open and liberalised structure, India's private sector has matured into a vibrant and dynamic force. The sector is not operating just at the international cutting edge but also at a global scale and reach. This changed economic landscape requires a new *administrative paradigm* in which the role of the government must evolve from simply allocating resources in a command-and-control ecosystem, to a far more nuanced one of directing, calibrating, supporting and regulating a *market ecosystem.* National development must be seen beyond the limited sphere of the 'Public Sector'. Government must, thus, transition from being a 'provider of first and last resort' and 'major player' in the economy, to being a 'catalyst' nurturing an 'enabling environment', where the entrepreneurial spirits of all, from small self-employed entrepreneurs to large

corporations, can flourish. This, importantly, frees up the government to focus its precious resources on public *welfare* domains such as essential entitlements of food, nutrition, health, education and livelihood of vulnerable and marginalised groups of society.

4. **Forces of Globalisation:** In recent decades, the world at large has also evolved. We live today in a 'global village', connected by modem transport, communications and media, and networked international markets and institutions. In this milieu, India's economic actions 'contribute' to the global dynamics, while our economy also gets influenced by the happenings from afar. The framework of *policy making* together with the *functioning of governments* need to incorporate the realities of our continuing integration with the global economic system.
5. **Role of the States:** Indian states have evolved from being mere appendages of the Centre, to being the actual drivers of national development. The development of states must thus become the national goal, as the nation's progress lies in the progress of states. As a consequence, the *one-size-fits-all approach,* often inherent in centralised planning, is no longer practical or efficient. States need to be heard and given the flexibility required for effective implementation. The government quotes Dr. B. R. Ambedkar to bring the point home: 'it is unreasonable to centralise powers where central control and uniformity is not clearly essential or is impracticable'. Thus, while emanating from global experiences and national synergy, India's strategies need to be calibrated and customised to *local needs* and opportunities.
6. **Technology Paradigm:** Technology advancements and information access have unleashed the creative energy of India. They have integrated our varied regions and ecosystems in an interlinked national economy and society, opening up newer avenues of coordination and cooperation. Technology is also playing a substantial role in enhancing transparency as well as efficiency, holding the government more accountable. Thus, India needs to make it central to systems of policy and governance.

Change Must Come

The above-given changes have been recognised by the experts for years now. With changing contours of the economy, the institutions guiding the economy should also change. The government quotes several such *instances* when appropriate changes were advised in the PC by the experts, committees, even the PC, among others:

1. The ***Eight Plan*** (1992-97) document (the very first after the reform process commenced in 1991) categorically stated that, as the role of the government was reviewed and restructured, the role and functions of the PC too needed to be rethought. The PC also needed to be reformed to keep up with changing trends, relieving itself of the old practices and beliefs, which had lost relevance, and adopting new ones based on past experiences of India as well as other nations. Specifically, the PC needed to be in tune with the process of economic reforms.
2. The ***Standing Committee on Finance*** of the 15th Lok Sabha observed in its 35th Report on Demand for Grants (2011-12) that the 'PC has to come to grips with the emerging social realities to re-invent itself to make itself more relevant and effective for aligning the planning process with economic reforms and its consequences, particularly for the poor'. This was the need of making the planning process relevant to the process of economic reforms.
3. The former Prime Minister, Dr. Manmohan Singh, in his farewell address to the PC (April 2014), also urged reflection on 'what the role of the PC needs to be in this new world. Are we still using tools and approaches which were designed for a different era? What additional roles should the PC play and what capacities does it need to build to ensure that it continues to be relevant to the growth process?' This observation has quite high relevance, as Dr. Singh is himself a 'noted' economist.

Taking the cues for a change, the government quotes Mahatma Gandhi before opting for the change: 'Constant development is the law of life, and a man who always tries to maintain his dogmas in order to appear consistent drives himself into a false position'. The government adds further, keeping true to this principle our institutions of governance and policy must evolve with the changing dynamics of the new India, while remaining true to the founding principles of the Constitution of India, and rooted in our *Bharatiyata* or wisdom of our *civilisational history* and *ethos.* It was, in every sense, a kind of pledge to devise

India's own means, methods, tools and approaches to promote development.

For the government, the NITI Aayog is to be the *institution* to give life to these aspirations (discussed above). The Aayog was formed based on extensive consultation across a spectrum of stakeholders, including *inter alia* state governments, relevant institutions, domain experts and the people at large.

Functions of NITI Aayog

With the process of maturity and deepening in Indian nationhood, the country has embraced a greater measure of pluralism and decentralisation. This necessitates a *paradigm shift* in the Central government's approaches to the governments in the state, as well as at the local levels. The *state governments* and the *local bodies* must be made equal partners in the development process through the following changes:

1. Understanding and supporting their developmental needs and aspirations, and
2. Incorporating varied local realities into national policies and programmes with the required flexibility.

This way the new body, NITI Aayog, is designed to live up to the principle of 'Team India' with its following **officially demarcated functions**:

1. **Cooperative and Competitive Federalism:** It will be the 'primary platform' for operationalising cooperative federalism, enabling states to have active participation in the formulation of national policy, as well as achieving time-bound implementation of quantitative and qualitative targets through the combined authority of the Prime Minister and the Chief Ministers. This will be by means of systematic and structured interactions between the Union and state governments, to better understand developmental issues, as well as forge a consensus on strategies and implementation mechanisms. The above would mark the replacement of the *one-way* flow of policy from centre to state, with a genuine and continuing *Centre-State partnership.* The Aayog is supposed to further this cooperation with the enhanced vibrancy of *Competitive Federalism*; the Centre competing with the states and *vice versa*, and the states competing with each other, in the joint pursuit of national development.
2. **Shared National Agenda:** It will 'evolve' a shared vision of national development priorities and strategies, with the active involvement of the states. This will provide the framework 'national agenda' for the Prime Minister and Chief Ministers to implement.
3. **State's Best Friend at the Centre:** It will support states in addressing their own challenges, as well as building on strengths and comparative advantages. This will be through various means, such as *coordinating* with ministries, championing their ideas at the Centre, providing 'consultancy' support and 'building capacity'.
4. **Decentralised Planning:** The new body is to 'restructure' the planning process into a 'bottom-up model', empowering states and guiding them to further empower local governments in developing mechanisms to formulate credible plans at the village level, which are progressively aggregated up the higher levels of the government. The maturing of India's governmental institutions has enabled increasing the specialisation of their functions. There is, thus, a need to separate as well as energise the distinct 'strategy' element of governance from the usual 'process' and 'implementation' element. As a dedicated 'Think Tank' of the government, NITI Aayog will carry out this 'directional' role, strategically charting the future of the nation. It will provide specialised inputs - strategic, functional and technical - to the Prime Minister and the government (Centre as well as the state), on matters critical to the fulfilment of the national development agenda. It means the new body is to function like a 'think tank'.
5. **Vision and Scenario Planning:** To 'design' medium- and long-term strategic frameworks of the big-picture vision of India's future - across schemes, sectors, regions and time; factoring in all possible alternative assumptions and counterfactuals. These would be the 'drivers of the national reforms agenda', especially focused on identifying critical gaps and harnessing untapped potentialities. The same would need to be intrinsically dynamic with their progress and efficacy constantly monitored for necessary mid-course recalibration; and the overall environment (domestic and global) continuously scanned for incorporating evolving trends and

addressing emerging challenges. This would mean a fundamental transition from merely planning for where the nation's money goes, to planning where we want the nation to go. And given its unique position as the aggregator and integrator of all developmental initiatives of the GoI and the states, the new body would be ideally suited for the same.

6. **Domain Strategies:** To 'build' a repository of specialised domain expertise, both sectoral and cross-sectoral; to assist ministries of the Central and state governments in their respective development planning, as well as problem-solving needs. This will especially enable the imbibing of good governance best practices, both national as well as international, especially with regards to structural reforms in the country.
7. **Sounding Board:** To be an 'in-house sounding board' whetting and refining government positions, through objective criticisms and comprehensive counterviews in the economy.
8. **Network of Expertise:** To 'mainstream' external ideas and expertise into government policies and programmes through a collaborative community of national and international experts, practitioners and other partners. This would entail being the government's link to the outside world, roping in academia (universities, think tanks and research institutions), private sector expertise and the people at large, for close involvement in the policy making process. To bring the point home, the document quotes the Rigveda - 'let us welcome noble thoughts flowing in from all directions'.
9. **Knowledge and Innovation Hub:** The body to be an 'accumulator' as well as 'disseminator' of research and best practices on good governance, through a state-of-the-art Resource Centre which identifies, analyses, shares and facilitates replication of the same. The document further adds that an increasingly mature Indian population has steadily increased the focus on, and demand for, actual delivery and results. To keep up with such enhanced aspirations, the new body will have the mandate to go beyond mere planning and strategising, to facilitating *implementation* of the development agenda as well. This would involve making implementation central to the planning process, through an emphasis on tangible outcomes, realistic targets, strict timelines and robust M&E - a transition from the isolated conceptualisation of merely 'planning', to 'planning for implementation'. It will also act as a 'catalyst' to the government machinery at large - filling gaps, enhancing capabilities and de-clogging bottlenecks, as and where required.
10. **Harmonisation:** To 'facilitate harmonisation' of actions across different layers of the government, especially when involving cross-cutting and overlapping issues across multiple sectors through communication, coordination, collaboration and convergence among all stakeholders. The emphasis will be on bringing all together on an integrated and holistic approach to development.
11. **Conflict Resolution:** To provide a 'platform' for mutual resolution of intersectoral, inter-departmental, inter-state as well as centre-state issues; facilitating consensus acceptable and beneficial to all, to bring about clarity and speed in execution.
12. **Coordinating Interface with the World:** It will be the 'nodal point' for strategically harnessing global expertise and resources in India's developmental process - coming in from across nations, multi-lateral institutions and other international organisations.
13. **Internal Consultancy:** It will offer an internal 'consultancy' function to Central and State governments on policy and programme design-providing frameworks adhering to basic design principles such as decentralisation, flexibility and a focus on results. This would include specialised skills such as structuring and executing PPPs.
14. **Capacity Building:** To enable 'capacity building' and 'technology upgradation' across governments, benchmarking with latest global trends and providing managerial and technical know-how.
15. **Monitoring and Evaluation:** It will 'monitor' the implementation of policies and programmes, and 'evaluate' their impact; through rigorous tracking of performance metrics and comprehensive programme evaluations. This will not only help identify weaknesses and bottlenecks for necessary course correction, but also enable data-driven policy making; encouraging greater efficiency as well as effectiveness.

The Guiding Principle

The government document has categorically pointed out the very 'purpose' of the new body - in the process of carrying out its functions, the Aayog will be guided by an overall vision of development which is inclusive, equitable and sustainable. The institution is to follow a strategy of empowerment built on human dignity and national self-respect - the document quoted Swami Vivekananda to emphasise this: 'to encourage everyone in his struggle to live up to his own highest idea'. The new body is supposed to follow a development model which is ***all round, all pervasive, all-inclusive*** and ***holistic***.

Antyodaya To prioritise service and upliftment of the poor, marginalised and downtrodden, (the document quotes the idea of '*Antodaya*' as articulated by Pandit Deendayal Upadhyay). Development is incomplete and meaningless if it does not reach the farthest individual. 'Nothing is more dreadfully painful than poverty' (the centuries-old sage-poet Thiruvalluvar has been quoted).

Inclusion To empower vulnerable and marginalised sections, redressing identity-based inequalities of all kinds - gender, region, religion, caste or class - the document quoted from Sankar Dev, 'to see every being as equivalent to one's own soul is the supreme means (of attaining deliverance)'. Weaker sections must be enabled to be masters of their own fate, having equal influence over the choices the nation makes.

Village To integrate our villages into the development process, to draw on the vitality and energy of the bedrock of our *ethos, culture* and *sustenance*.

Demographic Dividend To harness our greatest asset, the people of India, by focussing on their development, through *education* and *skilling*, and their *empowerment*, through productive livelihood opportunities.

People's Participation To transform the developmental process into a *people-driven* one, making an awakened and participative citizenry- the driver of good governance. This includes our extended Indian family of the non-resident Indian community spread across the world, whose significant geo-economic and geo-political strength must be harnessed.

Governance To nurture an open, transparent, accountable, proactive and purposeful style of governance, transitioning focus from *Outlay to Output to Outcome*.

Sustainability Maintain sustainability at the core of our planning and developmental process, building on our ancient tradition of respect for the environment.

Structure of the NITI

The Aayog will be a lean organisation, modelled as a network of expertise, focusing on functionality, flexibility and domain knowledge, with the following 'structure' and 'mechanism':

1. **Chairman:** the Prime Minister of India (*de facto*).
2. **Governing Council:** comprises the PM; Vice Chairman of NITI Aayog; CMs of states and UTs (with legislature); Lt Governors of other UTs; Ex-Officio Members, Full-Time Members and Special Invitees of NITI Aayog.
3. **Regional Councils:** will be formed to address specific issues and contingencies impacting more than one state or region. Strategy and planning in the Aayog will be anchored from state-level; with regional councils convened by the Prime Minister for identified priority domains, put under the joint leadership of related sub-groups of states (grouped around commonalities which could be geographic, economic, social or otherwise) and central ministries. The regional councils will have the following features:
   - **(i)** Will have specified tenures, with the mandate to evolve strategy and oversee implementation.
   - **(ii)** Will be jointly headed by one of the group Chief Ministers (on a rotational basis or otherwise) and a corresponding Central Minister.
   - **(iii)** Will include the sectoral central ministers and secretaries concerned, as well as state ministers and secretaries.
   - **(iv)** Will be linked with corresponding domain experts and academic institutions.
   - **(v)** Will have a dedicated support cell in the Aayog's secretariat.
4. **Special Invitees:** It will have experts, specialists and practitioners with relevant domain knowledge as special invitees nominated by the Prime Minister.
5. **Full-time Organisational Framework:** In addition to PM as its Chairman, it will comprise the following personnel:
   - **(i)** Vice-Chairperson: to be appointed by the PM.

(ii) Members: all as full-time.

(iii) Part-time Members: maximum of 2, from leading universities, research organisations and other relevant institutions in an *ex officio* capacity. Part-time members will be on a rotational basis.

(iv) *Ex Officio* Members: maximum of 4 members of the Union Council of Ministers to be nominated by the PM.

(v) Chief Executive Officer: to be appointed by the PM for a fixed tenure, in the rank of Secretary to the GoI.

(vi) Secretariat: as deemed necessary.

Specialised Wings in the NITI Aayog

The Aayog will house a number of specialised 'Wings', as per the government document:

1. **Research Wing:** It will develop in-house sectoral expertise as a dedicated think tank of top-notch domain experts, specialists and scholars.
2. **Consultancy Wing:** It will provide a marketplace of whetted panels of expertise and funding, for Central and state governments to tap into; matching their requirements with solution providers, public and private, national and international. By playing matchmaker instead of providing the entire service itself, NITI Aayog will be able to focus its resources on priority matters, providing guidance and an overall quality check to the rest.
3. **Team India Wing:** It will comprise representatives from every state and ministry and will serve as a permanent platform for national collaboration. Each representative in this Wing will:
   - **(i)** Ensure every state/ministry has a continuous voice and stake in the Aayog.
   - **(ii)** Establish a direct communication channel between the state/ministry and the Aayog for all development related matters, as the dedicated liaison interface.

A national 'Hub-Spoke' institutional model will be developed, with each state and ministry encouraged to build dedicated *mirror institutions,* serving as the interface of interaction. These institutions, in turn, will nurture their own networks of expertise at the state and ministry level. NITI Aayog will function in close cooperation, consultation and coordination with the ministries of the Central government and state governments. While it will make recommendations to the Central and state governments, the responsibility for taking and implementing decisions will rest with them.

Vehicle of Good Governance

The Aayog will seek to facilitate and empower the critical requirement of good governance, which is people-centric, participative, collaborative, transparent and policy-driven. It will provide critical directional and strategic input to the development process, focusing on deliverables and outcomes. This, along with being as incubator and disseminator of fresh thought and ideas for development, will be the core mission of NITI Aayog. The document, at the end, quotes from Chanakya to emphasise the importance and need of good governance - 'good governance is at the root of a nation's wealth, comfort and happiness'.

If we look into the state of governance in the country, we find that it has improved a lot at the level of the Central government but at the state level the situation is still not good.[109] As the lives of citizens depend more on the supplies from the state governments the poor state of governance hits their lives in a big way. The Central government's push in favour of good governance has been practically crippled by the inability or unwillingness of the state governments in this regard. It means that the state of governance cannot be improved much till there is an effective co-operation among the governments of the country. Once a very willing beginning has been started under the NITI Aayog ('co-operative federalism' being one of the three foundations on which it is imagined to be built) in this direction it is believed that the quality of governance should improve in the coming years.

We find an intentional attempt by the Government to intertwine the aspect of good governance in the very idea of the NITI Aayog. Not only the word governance

[109] This was explained in detail by the Tenth Five Year Plan (2002-07) citing the example of the *Mid-Day Meal Scheme* run by the Government of India.

but the *established traits of governance*[110] find clear mentions at several places:

1. In the *Foundations* the NITI Aayog is built on (a collaborative platform facilitating implementation);
2. In the *Guiding Principles* (Participation, Inclusion, Governance and *Antodaya*);
3. In its structural composition (GC as a tool to promote participatory federation); and finally,
4. In its *Functions* (co-operative and competitive federalism, best friend of states at the Centre, decentralised planning, harmonisation, conflict resolution, internal consultancy, capacity building, M&E are effective in improving governance).

It means that the very idea of NITI Aayog is very sensitive to the need of good governance in the country, and as the institution succeeds in playing its desired role as governance improves in the country. These are the reasons due to which we see the Government visualising it as the 'vehicle of good governance'.

Concluding Remarks

The idea of NITI Aayog does not only look innovative in its approach but quite contemporary too – imaginatively forging into the emerging idea and the need of including 'happiness' (as the World Happiness Report has suggested) in the policy making framework.

It gives a call for inclusion of *ethos* and *cultural elements* of India in the development model, delicately linking the issue of growth and development to the 'behavioural' dimensions of the people of India (rightly in sync with the proposition of the World Bank in its *World Development Report 2015).* We find several such shining 'stars' in the newly set up body, which will be surely analysed and discussed again and again by analysts, experts, scholars. At the end, we can wisely conclude that the erstwhile PC was aimed at serving some purposes which was suitable for the old time, while the current times require us to carry on the legacy to a new level where we can build India, which can combine and integrate the energy and potential of all who belong to the nation being all open to the world (agreeing categorically to the idea of globalisation).

MAJOR DOCUMENTS OF THE NITI

Aimed at following the idea of *vision and scenario planning,* the NITI Aayog has been working on three documents, namely the Fifteen-Year Vision, Seven-Year Strategy and Three-Year Action Agenda – while the last two have already been published, work on the first one is still in progress. A brief introduction of these two documents has been given below:

Three-Year Action Agenda

Increasingly liberalised economy and the changed global economic dynamism needed new 'tools' and 'approaches' to promote development process (the five-year plans were not vibrant enough to these changed realities). An outcome of extensive consultations between the governments and various stakeholders (including economists, scientists, journalists, NGOs, industry associations and experts from education, health, culture and other areas), the Draft Three-Year Action Agenda (2017-18 to 2019-20) contains 7 parts and 24 chapters.[111] The action agenda is *actionable* as well as *aspirational* which touches several areas of importance such as the following:

1. It proposes reduction of the fiscal deficit to 3 per cent of the GDP and the revenue deficit to 0.9 per cent of the GDP by 2019-20.
2. Doubling farmers' incomes by 2022 together with an emphasis on job creation in industry and services.
3. Generous floor space index (FPI), flexible conversion rules etc. advised for urban areas.
4. Encouraging development outcomes in the North-Eastern Region; Coastal Areas and Islands;

[110] As per the UNO/IMF (Report on Good Governance, 1996), *good governance is the process of decision-making and their implementation which is consensus-oriented, participatory, based on Rule of Law, transparent, accountable, responsive, equitable and inclusive.*

[111] *Draft Three-Year Action Agenda (2017-18 to 2019-20)* (New Delhi: NITI Aayog, PMO, 23 April 2017).

North Himalayan states; and Desert and Drought prone states to take care of regional issues.

5. Emphasis on Transport and Digital Connectivity.
6. Under energy section it aims at consumer-friendly measures, reducing the cross subsidy in the power sector and reforming coal sector by setting up a regulator.
7. Under science and technology emphasis is on developing PPP and creation of a National Science, Technology and Innovation Foundation (to identify national issues) and streamlining of the patent regime.
8. To promote *governance,* shrinking role of the government in undesirable areas.
9. Tackling tax evasion, expanding the tax base and simplifying the tax system and strengthening public procurement.
10. Undertaking judicial system reforms (use of ICT and cutting workload) and police reforms at state level to promote the cause of rule of law.
11. Shift from input-based to outcome-based (with arrangement of 'ranking') in education and skill development.
12. Focus on public health through significantly increasing government expenditure on it.
13. Building an inclusive society.
14. Adopting sustainable practices, tackling city air pollution, policy towards protecting trees sustainable use of water resources.

Seven-Year Strategy Framework

Titled as the *Strategy for New India @75,* it defines clear developmental objectives seeking to make development a '*Jan Andolan*' (mass movement) aimed at making India a $3.0 trillion economy by 2022-23.[112] It is a detailed exposition across 41 crucial areas (covered in the same number of chapters) that recognises the progress already made, identifies binding constraints and suggests the way forward for achieving the objectives. The 41 areas have been discussed in four sections - *Drivers, Infrastructure, Inclusion* and *Governance:*

Drivers focuses on the engines of economic performance with chapters on growth and employment, doubling of farmers' incomes; upgrading the science, technology and innovation ecosystem; and promoting sunrise sectors such as fintech and tourism.

Infrastructure deals with the physical foundations of growth which are crucial to enhancing the competitiveness of Indian business as also ensuring the citizens' ease of living.

Inclusion deals with the urgent task of investing in the capabilities of all of India's citizens. The three themes in this section revolve around the dimensions of health, education and mainstreaming of traditionally marginalised sections of the population.

Governance delves deep into how the governance structures can be streamlined and processes optimised to achieve better developmental outcomes.

The recommendations of the NITI Aayog in the document are practical and detailed to facilitate time-bound implementation - by 2022, New India will provide a solid foundation for clean, inclusive, sustained and sustainable growth for the next three decades.[113]

Vision Document on Health

In December 2020, a sectoral 'vision document' was released by the NITI Aayog. Titled as the *Vision 2035: Public Health Surveillance in India,* it envisages the following four major visions for the sector in a time frame of next 15 years:

- Making public health system more responsive and predictive to enhance preparedness for action at all levels.
- Developing a citizen-friendly public health surveillance system, ensuring privacy, enabled with client feedback mechanism.
- Improving data-sharing mechanism between Centre and states (health data considered as the building blocks for the purpose, with the motto 'Information for Action').
- Providing regional and global leadership in managing events that constitute a public health emergency of international concern.

As a continuation of the work on strengthening of health systems, it pushes in favour of integrating the three-tiered public health system into *Ayushman Bharat.*

[112] *Strategy for New India @75,* (New Delhi: NITI Aayog, PMO, 19 December 2018).

[113] R. Kumar, Vice Chairman, NITI Aayog concludes in the last paragraph of the Preface to the document *Strategy for New India@75.*

It also spells out the need for expanded referral networks and enhanced laboratory capacity.

The COVID-19 pandemic has provided us with an opportunity to revisit (re)emerging diseases due to increased interaction between human-animal-environment. Early identification of this interference is essential to break the chain of transmissions and create a resilient surveillance system. This vision document is a step in that direction.

NITI PERFORMS

Some experts and most of the political parties (in the opposition benches) were quite skeptical about the very idea of the NITI Aayog. Naturally enough, this skepticism was more due to abrupt disconnect being affected by the Government under which the economic think tank PC was abolished which was as old as the very existence of Independent India itself. The prevailing breach of trust and lack of cooperation between the Central and State governments were among the major reasons for the indifference shown to the NITI by the experts, the political analysts and the political parties. Though it will be too early to pass a judgement on its performance still *some major examples* can be cited in this regard:

1. Probably, the first major work by the think tank was its smooth deliberations with the states in restructuring the existing 66 CSSs into 30 giving them more impact, visibility and flexibility.
2. The spirit of 'cooperative federalism' has been greatly strengthened through the NITI Aayog. It has been able to lessen the situation of breach of financial trust between the Centre and states. Implementation of the indirect tax reform GST has been greatly enabled by the NITI Aayog.[114]
3. To promote cleanliness and several other variables of human development and ease of doing business the think tank has launched several indices and started ranking the states - ultimately enhancing the spirit of competition among the governments.
4. It has been able to educate and make states aware about the importance of promoting economic reforms in the country.
5. It is through this platform that the states have been encouraged to go for the UDAY Scheme aimed at financial turnaround of the state electricity boards or the DISCOMs. This is an 'optional' scheme, but due to increased awareness among the states regarding the importance and the need of the factor market reforms most of the states have opted for it.[115]
6. State governments positively taking part in the NITI Initiative to Yield Aspirational Targets and Actionable Means (Niyatam) under which their administrative, developmental and legal structure are aimed to be streamlined.
7. NITI Aayog's advice of 'land pooling' has been well received by the states which have smoothened the issue of land acquisition for different purposes in the country.
8. By now the NITI Aayog has come up with several reports on a variety of sectors to enhance the process of development in the country taking states as an integral partner which range from sports to irrigation to education, health etc.
9. Budgetary and extra-budgetary financial allocations to states from the Centre have also become quite smooth unlike the past when states used to always complain against the PC in this regard.
10. As NITI Aayog monitors and collects developmental data on real-time basis (unlike the PC with almost 2 years of data lag) the element of accountability has improved which has enhanced the quality of governance.

This way, we find NITI emerging into a better think tank than the erstwhile PC in fostering the spirit of federal cooperation. Besides, in the process of transforming the development agenda of India, it has introduced new tools in this regard based on highly objective methods of M&E.

[114] The policy think tank functioned as 'a forum for fostering cooperative and competitive federalism', as per A. Subramanian, the Former Chief Economic Advisor to the Government of India [*Of Counsel–The Challenges of the Modi-Jaitley Economy*, (Gurugram: Penguin Random House India, 2018), p. 193].

[115] The policy think tank functioned as 'a forum for fostering cooperative and competitive federalism', as per A. Subramanian, the Former Chief Economic Advisor to the Government of India [*Of Counsel–The Challenges of the Modi-Jaitley Economy*, (Gurugram: Penguin Random House India, 2018), p. 192].

WAY FORWARD

The COVID-19 pandemic has been rightly called 'once in a century global crisis' by the Economic Survey 2020-21 much in agreement with the international economic organisations - economic damages of which are still being counted across the world. Meanwhile, India looks going beyond the pandemic in a quite imaginative way. To convert the pandemic into an opportunity the GoI called for a 'Self-reliance Campaign' (i.e., the ***Atmanirbhar Bharat Abhiyan***) by early 2020-21. The campaign, which is still in the process of evolution, includes a diverse range of policy steps put forward in the form of incentives (Production-Linked Incentives for industries) and structural reforms (from labour laws to agricultural marketing to PSUs and banking sectors) aimed at making India a US$ 5 trillion economy by 2026-27 and a developed economy by 2047.

India's push for self-reliance has been seen by experts and government documents in the following ways:

- Checking India's 'increasing' dependency on the global value chain (in the backdrop of possible future disruptions similar to the COVID-19 pandemic).
- India's urge to check its rising 'trade deficit' with China besides increasing data and privacy vulnerabilities.
- 'Reimagining' the Make in India scheme aimed at 'Assemble in India' and boosting labour-intensive manufacturing sector.
- Developing a 'Pan-India supply chain' which can be integrated to the global value chain to boost exports.
- A changed stance in 'economic diplomacy' aimed at redefining India's place in the emerging global economic order.
- India's version of 'protectionism' with a blend of its strong support for globalisation and multilateralism.
- Emphasis on import substitution and promoting decentralised industrial expansion (districts to be the unit of focus, in line with the advice of the *Economic Survey 2019-20*).
- Promoting 'circular economy' (a proposal of the NITI Aayog) with an eye on India's commitments towards checking climate change. [For details on Circular Economy see ***Chapter 22***.]

Word Bank

Agile Approach

The Agile approach is a well-established method of decision making increasingly used in fields of project management and technology development. This approach is particularly helpful in making policy decisions when the environment is uncertain. Decisions under it respond quickly as per the outcomes of the past decisions – flexibility and adjustments (as per the changing situations) are its chief features. This is different from the conventional method of framing policies in which rigid up-front approach is followed as it is based on advance understanding of the situation (the element of uncertainty not taken into account), as was the case with India's development plans.

Such an approach of decision making was seen being followed by the Government of India, as per the *Economic Survey 2021–22* right since March 2020 (i.e., during the uncertain times of the COVID-19 pandemic). The Government has been using 80 high frequency indicators (HFIs) to assess the policy outcomes under it to frame its policy response.

- The non-conventional method of policy making - the *Agile* approach[116] - used by the Government has worked well in dealing with the economic uncertainties (caused by the pandemic) and helped India 're-align' its interaction with the external economies.

[116] *Economic Survey 2021-22* (New Delhi: Ministry of Finance, GoI, January 2022).

- Government's pledge to transform the economy from 'command and control' to 'plug and play' is aimed at creating a conducive[117] atmosphere for the growth and expansion of businesses and industries – strengthened by a ***pro-corporate*** policy approach rooted deeply in *pro-poor* results.
- Re-initiation of the ***transformative reforms*** (with an emphasis on structural reforms) is set to bring higher growth[118] in coming decades to India in more self-reliant ways once the negative effects of pandemic-led disruptions, geopolitical issues (primarily, the Ukraine crisis) and higher commodity prices fade away.
- Given the geoeconomic fragmentation and increased geopolitical risks (due to Russia-Ukraine conflict and the instability in the Middle East), as per the *Economic Survey 2023-24*, development planning needs to follow a **bottom-up approach** putting emphasis on ***six areas***– (i) increased private participation, (ii) green transition, (iii) boosting the MSMEs, (iv) agriculture as the engine of growth, (v) education conjoined with skilling, and (vi) enhancing state capacity.[119]
- Other than continuing with the structural and next-gen reforms of the last decade, as per the *Economic Survey 2024-25*, policy actions of federal nature (i.e., combined efforts from centre and states) are required in the areas such as– (i) deregulation in the Factor Market Reforms (i.e., laws that affect the use of land, labour and building), (ii) boosting exports (however, global policymaking has increasingly become more 'inward looking' much away from the days of globalisation), (iii) enhancing economic freedom (i.e., citizens' unhindered ability to pursue legitimate and entrepreneurial aspirations), (iv) boosting the MSMEs with requisite capital and technology to become part of formal economy, and (v) tapping the grassroots level economic potential for job creation and economic growth of future.[120]
- As per the *Economic Survey 2025-26*, economic planning in the country needs to synchronise development with climate. Climate action, when embedded in development priorities, can strengthen resilience, enhance competitiveness, and support India's long-term growth trajectory. For this to happen, India needs national and subnational strategies across adaptation, mitigation, climate finance, and regulation. Environmental regulation in India is transitioning from procedural, command-and-control approaches towards risk-based, technology-enabled, and outcome-oriented governance that supports both environmental protection and ease of doing business.[121]

[117] *Economic Survey 2022-23* (New Delhi: Ministry of Finance, GoI, January 2023) and *Economic Survey 2021- 22*, (New Delhi: Ministry of Finance, GoI, January 2022).
[118] *Economic Survey 2022-23* (New Delhi: Ministry of Finance, GoI, January 2023), pp. 24-40.
[119] *Economic Survey 2023-24* (New Delhi: Ministry of Finance, GoI, January 2024), pp. 155-77.
[120] *Economic Survey 2024-25* (New Delhi: Ministry of Finance, GoI, January 2025), pp. 133-61.
[121] *Economic Survey 2025-26* (New Delhi: Ministry of Finance, GoI, January 2026), p. 382.

PREVIOUS YEARS' QUESTIONS

Mains

1. What are the challenges before the Indian economy when the world is moving away from free trade and multilateralism to protectionism and bilateralism? How can these challenges be met? (2025)

SAMPLE OBJECTIVE QUESTIONS

1. Consider the following statements related to investment models of India:
   (i) Engineering procurement construction (EPC) was a public-private partnership (PPP) model which was modified into the current hybrid annuity model (HAM).
   (ii) Hybrid annuity model is used for all of the infrastructure sectors.
   (iii) A highway project based on public-private partnership model can be constructed using the Swiss Challenge method of public procurement.

   Which of the statement(s) given above is/are correct?

   Code:
   (a) Only one (b) Only two
   (c) All three (d) None of these

2. Consider the following statements related to development planning in the country:
   (i) Planning changed from target to indicative.
   (ii) Under NITI, development planning has become more centralised.
   (iii) Like the NITI, the Planning Commission was also given some guiding principles.

   Which of the statement(s) given above is/are correct?

   Code:
   (a) Only one (b) Only two
   (c) All three (d) None of these

3. Consider the following statements related to the policy think tank NITI Aayog:
   (i) It aims to transform the approach of cooperative federalism in the country.
   (ii) It aims to transform the development agenda of India.
   (iii) It aims at transformative development planning.
   (iv) It aims to transform the attitude towards villages.

   Which of the statement(s) given above is/are correct?

   Code:
   (a) Only one (b) Only two
   (c) Only three (d) All four

4. How many of the following statement(s) related to development planning in the country is/are correct today? Select your answer by using the code given below:
   (i) India's normative development process is eroding its secular character.
   (ii) NITI Aayog draws vitality and energy from our ethos, culture and sustenance.
   (iii) The resource mobilisation for planned development aims to crowd in funds for foreign investment.

   Code:
   (a) Only one (b) Only two
   (c) All three (d) None of these

5. Consider the following statements related to planned development in the country:
   (i) NITI Aayog, similar to the erstwhile Planning Commission plays an active role in strategic disinvestment.
   (ii) NITI Aayog functions as the node of the Government's fund allocation.
   (iii) The erstwhile Planning Commission, however, was responsible for resource mobilisation, it played no role in fund allocation.

   How many of the above statement(s) is/are correct?
   (a) Only one (b) Only two
   (c) All three (d) None of these

6. Consider the following statements related to economic planning in India:
   (i) Its planning has also been called Monnet planning.
   (ii) Beginning as an imperative planner the country adopted multi-level planning later on.
   (iii) Role of the market in planning was increasing even before economic reforms started.

How many of the above statement(s) is/are correct?

(a) Only one (b) Only two
(c) All three (d) None of these

7. Consider the following statements related to the NITI Aayog:
   (i) In vision and scenario planning emphasis is more on long-term goals than the medium-term goals.
   (ii) Digital tools have strengthened the element of perspective in planning under the NITI.
   (iii) NITI is allowed to build capacity for playing all advisory functions single-handedly.

How many of the above statement(s) is/are correct?

(a) Only one (b) Only two
(c) All three (d) None of these

8. Consider the following statements related to the 'sounding board' function of the NITI Aayog:
   (i) Under it, the think tank is free to self-criticise.
   (ii) It may counter the voices of criticism on development planning.
   (iii) This empowers it to refine and whet government position on developmental issues in all cases.

How many of the above statement(s) is/are correct?

(a) Only one (b) Only two
(c) All three (d) None of these

9. Consider the following statements related to the current approach to development planning in the country:
   (i) Increased emphasis on ethos and culture has made country's planning more inward-looking.
   (ii) NITI functions as the nodal point for assimilating external ideas into domestic policies.
   (iii) The spirit of cooperative and competitive federalism has increased the instances of tussle between the Centre and States.

How many of the above statement(s) is/are correct?

(a) Only one (b) Only two
(c) All three (d) None of these

10. Consider the statements related to '*Garibi Hatao*' in the country:
   (i) The Twenty Point Programme addressed it at both rural and urban levels.
   (ii) The Fifth Plan was launched with this slogan.
   (iii) MGNAREGS has emerged as the most inclusive plan in this regard.

How many of the above statement(s) is/are correct?

(a) Only one (b) Only two
(c) All three (d) None of these

Answers: 1. (a) 2. (d) 3. (d) 4. (a) 5. (d) 6. (b) 7. (a) 8. (b) 9. (a) 10. (d)

SAMPLE SUBJECTIVE QUESTIONS

1. 'India needs a federal design of development'. Examine the statement in light of the emerging paradigm of planning under the NITI Aayog.
2. How far the NITI looks like a timely modification upon the erstwhile Planning Commission? Examine.
3. 'The new policy think tank is aimed at developing a new paradigm of decentralised planning.' Comment.
4. Briefly examine the Government statement 'transforming the development agenda of the country through the NITI'.
5. 'Government imagines the NITI Aayog to emerge as the vehicle of good governance.' Elucidate.
6. 'NITI Aayog aims to integrate India's civilisational ethos into its holistic development model.' Comment.

SAMPLE MODEL ANSWERS

1. **'NITI Aayog has been imagined as a vehicle of good governance in the country.' Comment.**

Ans. The Government of India has visualised NITI Aayog as the vehicle of good governance. Governance has improved a lot at the Central level, but at the state level, it has not improved much (as was found by the special volume on governance published by the 10th Plan also). As the lives of citizens depend more on the supplies from the state governments, the poor governance at this level hits their lives in a big way.

The Central government's push in favour of good governance has been practically crippled by the inability or unwillingness of the state governments in this regard. It means that the state of governance cannot be improved much until there is effective co-operation among the governments of the country. Once a very willing beginning has been started under the NITI Aayog ('cooperative federalism' being one of the three foundations on which it is imagined to be built) in this direction, it is believed that the quality of governance should improve in the coming years. We find an intentional attempt by the Government to intertwine the aspect of good governance in the very idea of the Niti Aayog. Not only the word 'governance' but also the established traits of governance find clear mentions at several places.

- In the Foundations, the Niti Aayog is supposed to be built on (a collaborative platform facilitating implementation),
- In the Guiding Principles (Participation, Inclusion, Governance and Antodaya); in its structural composition (the Governing Council as a tool to promote participatory federation); and finally,
- In its Functions (co-operative and competitive federalism, best friend of states at the Centre, decentralised planning, harmonisation, conflict resolution, internal consultancy, capacity building, monitoring, and evaluation are effective in improving governance).

This way, the very idea of Niti Aayog looks very sensitive to the need for good governance in the country - as Niti Aayog will play the role desired from it as the state of governance will improve in the country. This is why experts believe the Niti Aayog is the 'vehicle of good governance.'

CHAPTER 7

Economic Reforms

"An important feature of India's reform programme, when compared with reforms underway in many other countries, is that it has emphasised gradualism and evolutionary transition rather than rapid restructuring or 'shock therapy'. This gradualism has often been the subject of unfavourable comment by the more impatient advocates of reform, both inside and outside the country.*"

*Montek S. Ahluwalia, addressing at the Inaugural Session of the Seminar on 'India's Economic Reforms', (London: Merton College, Oxford University, June 1993).

To watch the Author's videos on the significance of the Chapter, scan the QR Code given here

Exam Essentials...

- What is Economic Reform?
- Post-Liberalism
- Reform Measures
- What Comes First–Demand or Supply?
- Fourth Generation Reforms
- Transformational Reforms

Note to the Reader...

After the economic reforms commenced in 1991, they have been the very undercurrent of policymaking in the country. Much actions have taken place under its spell of about three and half decades by now but a kind of confusion remains in the minds of the readers about the measures of reforms. This chapter aims to help out the readers to understand the process and nuances of reforms from "official perspective" so that they can carry forward their preparation in right way.

In This Chapter...

INTRODUCTION

The Government of India launched a broad process of economic reforms in 1991. It was a policy response to India's very weak economic fundamentals and balance of payment crisis of the late 1980s. However, these reforms were also shaped by the evolving global economic thinking. This chapter aims to simplify this process for the readers mostly taking clues from the official documents, besides the experts who have been at the helm of the reform process.

ECONOMIC REFORMS

Popularly, economic reforms denote the process in which a government prescribes the declining role for the state and expanding role for the private sector in an economy. So, let us unravel the reform process based on the author's classroom interactions with students. It is safer to see economic reform, as a policy shift in an economy from one to another or ***alternative development strategies***. Economists attribute the differences in the performance of economies to the differences in the 'strategies' they follow. The different strategies of development evolved through a long period of trial and error by different countries under the influence of different sets of ideologies. But the process has been like an educational trip. To understand the term 'economic reform', and more so to clarify the confusion concerning it in the Indian context, we must see the different 'alternative development strategies' which evolved through time. A brief description of each is given below:

1. **Planning Model:** Till the rise of the Soviet Union, the prevalent development strategy in the Euro-American countries was the capitalist system of economy, which promoted the principles of *laissez faire* and dominant role for private capital in the economy. Once the Soviet Union went for the planning model (later the East European countries and finally China in 1949), most of the developing countries after their independence were influenced by socialism and the governments there took a central role in planned development. As these economies were dominated by foreign colonisers, they worried that opening the economy to foreign investment would lead to a new form of domination - the domination by large multinationals. That is why most of these countries went for 'protectionist' economic policy with ***import substitution*** as one method, side by side. But by the 1970s, the world had convincing proof that the socialist as well as the planned economies[1] was inclined to follow their own kind of development strategies - either because they had very slow and lower growth rates or were stagnating. The experiences of these economies gave rise to a new ideology which came to be known as the ***Washington Consensus***.

2. **Washington Consensus:** By the early 1980s, a new development strategy emerged. Though it was not new, it was like the old idea getting vindicated after failure of a newer idea. After the world recognised the limits of a state-dominated economy, arguments in favour of the market, i.e., the private sector, were promoted emphatically. Many countries shifted their economic policy just to the other extreme arguing for a minimal role of the government in the economy. Governments of the socialist or the planned economies were urged/suggested to privatise and liberalise, to sell off state-owned companies and eliminate government interventions in the economy. These governments were also suggested to take measures which could boost the aggregate demand in the economy (i.e., ***macroeconomic stability measures***). The broad outlines of such a development strategy were regarded as being inspired by the ***Washington Consensus***.[2]

   This consensus is broadly termed the process of 'economic reform' which was followed by almost all the socialist, communist and mixed economies during the 1980s in one form or the other[3] - and the term economic reform received currency around the world. The term was usually seen as a corollary for promoting 'naked capitalism', openness in the economy and an open attitude towards foreign investments. The governments of the developing economies were criticised by the political parties in the opposition and the critics for being soft to the dictates of the IMF and the WB, and becoming a party to promote 'neo-imperialism'.

[1] There were many developing non-socialist countries which also accepted economic planning as their development strategy (France should not be counted among them as it was a developed economy by then). These countries were following the 'mixed economy' model, but their form was closer to the command economies, i.e., the state economy or the socialist economy.

[2] As the strategy was advocated by the IMF, the WB and the US Treasury (i.e., US Ministry of Finance) all located in Washington, it formally came to be known as the Washington Consensus.

[3] Without changing the broad contours of economic policy, the Government in India had also come under the influence of this consensus, followed a great many *liberal* policies (during Rajiv Gandhi's regime) in the 1980s.

But these policies, in many cases, proved to be little better than the previous policies in promoting economic growth over an extended period of time. But somehow a mood in favour of the market economy had gained ground. The United Kingdom under Mrs. Thatcher had gone for politically most vocal privatisation moves without any political debates (the only such example of privatisation moves among the democracies, till date).[4] It should be noted here that after the Great Depression of 1929, a 'strong state intervention' was suggested (by J. M. Keynes) and such a policy did really help the Euro-American countries to mitigate the crisis. The favour for state intervention in the economy was being reversed by the Washington Consensus. But soon this consensus was also to be replaced by another development strategy. A more detailed discussion on the Washington Consensus and post-Washington Consensus is provided in *Chapter 1*.

What is Economic Reform?

Economic reform is an action under which a 'major shift' takes place in economic policies of a country. Academically, such shifts in policies may be done in any direction - towards 'market' or 'state' economies. But in the post-War period such shifts have been always towards market economy.

Under it, the state or mixed economies have inclined more towards market principles and have launched the processes of liberalisation, privatisation and globalisation, leading to structural reforms in the economies.

3. **Mixed Economy:** By the mid-1990s, it had become increasingly clear that neither of the extremes - the Washington Consensus or the state-led planned economy - was the ultimate strategies of development.[5] The success achieved by the East Asian economies, even if we take into account their setback due to the financial crisis of 1997-98, stands out in marked contrast to the experiences of other economies of the time that were following the Washington Consensus.[6] The East Asian economies have not only been able to propel higher growth rates, but they have been greatly successful in reducing poverty and promoting education and health care.

The East Asian economies had promoted a development strategy which had its most distinctive feature as the balance they were able to strike between the role of the state/government and the market/the private sector in their economies. This was really a new kind of mixed economy, which was never permanently inclined towards either state intervention or the free market, but always a balanced mix of the state and the market according to the requirement of the socio-economic situation of the economy. The East Asian countries had pursued market-oriented policies that encouraged development of the private sector - augmenting and governing the market, not replacing it.[7]

Technically speaking, shifting of economic policy of a country from one to the other above-mentioned three 'alternative development strategies' is economic reform. But in the history of world economy, it was inclination of the economies towards the market economy which has been referred to as economic reforms. In the Indian case, economic reform has always been used in this sense. Here, one should note that when India started the programme of economic reforms in the early 1990s, the world view was in favour of privatisation, liberalisation and de-nationalisation, as the main plank of economic reforms. But by the mid-1990s, not only the world view had polarised in favour of a mixed economy, but another change was about to sweep the world economies, i.e., the favour for globalisation sponsored by the World Trade Organisation (WTO). Now, the developing economies (mixed economies with planning as their development strategy) as well as the transition economies (Russia and the whole Eastern Europe, and China) - who were already promoting the market-oriented reform

[4] *Collins Dictionary of Economics*, (Glasgow: Harper Collins, 2006), pp. 417-18.

[5] World Bank, *The East Asian Miracle: Economic Growth and Public Policy*. (Washington, DC: Oxford University Press, 1993).

[6] *Ibid.*

[7] As is concluded by Stiglitz and Walsh, p. 800, *op. cit.*

process - were faced with a dilemma. To prosper and compete in the globalising environment while they needed immediate liberation from their state-dominated mode of economies at one hand, they also needed to strike a balance between the state and the market on the other. Each one of them tried to strike a balance in their own way with mixed results. In India, the governments have not been able to convince the masses that the economy needs reforms, and the attempted reforms will benefit all. In every election since the reforms of 1991, the voters have not supported a pro-reform government. Though the process of economic reforms started in India with the slogan ***reforms with human face***, the slogan has utterly failed to garner the empathy of the masses. We may hope that in coming times the masses will start connecting with the reforms and will be able to deliver a clear message, i.e., reforms are to benefit all.

ECONOMIC REFORMS IN INDIA

On 23 July 1991, India launched a process of economic reforms in response to a fiscal and balance-of-payment (BoP) crisis. The reforms were historic and were going to change the very face and the nature of the economy in the coming times. The reforms and the related programmes are still going on with changing emphasis and dimensions, but they are criticised as being slow ever since the UPA Government came to power in May 2004. Back in the mid- 1980s, the government had taken its first steps to economic reforms. While the reforms of the 1980s witnessed rather limited deregulation and 'partial liberalisation' of only a few aspects of the existing control regime, the reforms started in the early 1990s in the fields of industries, trade, investment and later to include agriculture were much 'wider and deeper'.[8] Though liberal policies were announced by the governments during the reforms of the 1980s itself, with the slogan of 'economic reforms', it was only launched with full conviction in the early 1990s. But the reforms of the 1980s, which were under the influence of the famous ***Washington Consensus*** ideology, had a crippling impact on the economy. The whole Seventh Plan (1985-90) promoted further relaxation of market regulations with heavy external borrowings to increase exports (as the thrust of the policy reform). Though the thrust increased the growth rate led by higher industrial growth (riding on costly imports supported by foreign borrowings, which the industries would not be able to pay back and service), it also led to a substantial increase in foreign indebtedness that played a major role in the BoP crisis of 1991.[9] The crisis was aggravated faster by the First Gulf War (1991) which had two-pronged negative impacts on the foreign exchange (forex) reserves of India. First, the war led the oil prices to go upward forcing India to use its forex reserves in a shorter period; and second, the private remittances from Indians working in the Gulf region fell fast (due to their emergency evacuation). Both the crises were induced by a single cause, i.e., the Gulf War. But the BoP crisis also reflected deeper problems of rising foreign debt, a fiscal deficit of over 8 per cent of the GDP and a hyper-inflation (over 13 per cent) situation.[10]

The minority government of the time had taken a highly bold and controversial step in the form of economic reforms criticised throughout the 1990s by one and all - right from the opposition in the Parliament, to the communist parties, to the industrial houses and to the business houses, media, experts and masses. By now as the benefits of the reforms have accrued to many, the criticism has somewhat calmed down, but still the reform process is considered as 'anti-poor' and 'pro-rich' by at least the masses - the people who decide the political mandate for the country to rule. At least one belief is followed by everybody, i.e., the benefits of reforms are not trickling down to the masses (the ***aam aadami***) at the desirable pace.[11]

The need of the hour is to go for 'distributive growth', though the reform has led the economy to a higher growth path.

Obligatory Reform

Similar reform processes started by some other economies since the 1980s were voluntary decisions

[8] J. D. Sachs, A. Varshney, and N. Bajpai, *India in the Era of Economic Reforms* (New Delhi: Oxford University Press, 1999), p. 1.

[9] J. Barkley Rosser, Jr. and M. V. Rosser, *Comparative Economics in a Transforming World Economy*, 2nd ed. (New Delhi: Prentice Hall of India, 2005), p. 469.

[10] V. Joshi and I. M. D. Little, *India's Economic Reforms, 1991-2001* (Oxford: Clarendon Press, 1996), p. 17.

[11] The feeling has been shared by the governments too. One may refer to the similar open acceptance by India's Minister of Commerce at the Davos Summit of the World Economic Forum (2007). In an interview to the *CNN-IBN* programme, the cabinet minister for Panchayati Raj, and the North-East (Mani Shankar Aiyar) on 20 May 2007 opined that benefits of higher growth are going to the selected 'classes' and not to the 'masses'.

of the countries concerned. But in the case of India, it was an involuntary decision taken by the government of the time in the wake of the BoP crisis. Under the Extended Fund Facility (EFF) programme of the IMF, countries received external currency support from the fund to mitigate their BoP crisis, but such supports have some obligatory conditionalities put on the economy to be fulfilled. There are no set rules of such conditions already available with the IMF, though they are devised and prescribed to the BoP crisis-ridden economy at the time of need. A point needed to be referred here is that the conditionalities put upon India were of the nature which required all the economic measures to be formulated by them. It means that the reforms India carried or is carrying out at present were neither formulated by India nor mandated by the public. Yes, there was a large section of experts inside and outside the government who believed in similar economic measures to guide the economy on the right path. Some of them were arguing the same since the 1970s, while many other experts believed in them since the mid-1980s.[12] But why, after all, was the Rao-Manmohan Government credited to start the reform process in India? It is because they thought it suitable to follow and make it politically possible in India. Imagine, a government proposing to sell the state-owned companies to the private sector or closing them down in a country which has been convinced that these companies will be the 'temples of modern India'. The masses were convinced that the government has bowed down to the diktats of the IMF, the imperialist forces and the multinationals. Even today such feelings are prevalent in several quarters of the economy. The politics of economic reforms damaged India more than the reform has benefitted the country. It would not be an exaggeration if we conclude that economic reforms had no political consensus. Political parties in India are divided on the issue of reforms - the parties, together with the masses, lack the level of political maturity required for the success of the reform programme. It is right, democratic maturity comes to a multi-party-political system, but it takes time. It takes even more time where masses are unaware and ignorant. The emotional issues of religion, caste and so forth play their own roles in such situations.

The IMF conditions put forth for India were as follows:

1. Devaluation of the rupee by 22 per cent (which was affected in two phases and the Indian rupee fell down from ₹21 to ₹27 per US Dollar).
2. Drastic reduction in the peak import tariff from the prevailing level of 130 per cent to 30 per cent (India completed it by 2000-01 itself, and now it is voluntarily cut to the level of 15 per cent).
3. Excise duties (i.e., CENVAT now) to be hiked by 20 per cent to neutralise the revenue shortfalls due to the custom cut (a major tax reform programme was launched to streamline, simplify and modernise the Indian tax structure which is ongoing).
4. All government expenditure to be cut down by 10 per cent, annually (i.e., cutting the cost of running the government which denotes interests, pays, pension, PF and subsidies, etc. - there was pressure on the government to consolidate the fiscal deficit and go for fiscal prudence).

Though India was able to pay back its IMF dues in time, the structural reform of the economy was launched to fulfil the above-mentioned conditions of the IMF. The ultimate goal of the IMF was to help India bring about equilibrium in its BoP situation in the short term and opt for macroeconomic and structural adjustments, so that in future the economy faces no such crisis.

There was enough scope for the critics to criticise India's economic reforms as prescribed and dictated by the IMF. The process of economic reforms in India had to face severe criticism from almost every quarter of the economy concerned, even though the reforms were aimed to boost growth and deliver competitiveness to the economy.[13]

THE LPG

The process of reforms in India will be completed *via.* three other processes, namely liberalisation, privatisation and globalisation, known popularly by their short form, the LPG. These three processes specify the characteristics of the reform process India initiated. Precisely seen, liberalisation shows the ***direction*** of reform, privatisation shows the ***path*** of reform and globalisation shows the ultimate ***goal*** of the reform. However, it would be useful to see the real meanings of these terms and the exact sense in which they are being used worldwide and particularly in India.

[12] The Seventh and the Eight Plans have many such suggestions to give to the governments of the time, especially the latter one which called for the same nature of the reform process, very clearly.

[13] *Economic Survey 1991-92: Part II Sectoral Developments & New Industrial Policy* (New Delhi: Ministry of Finance, GoI, 1991).

Liberalisation

The term 'liberalisation' has its origin in the political ideology 'liberalism', which took its form in the early 19th century (it developed basically in the previous three centuries). The term is sometimes portrayed as a ***meta-ideology*** capable of embracing a broad range of rival values and beliefs. The ideology was the product of the breakdown of feudalism and the growth of a ***market*** or ***capitalist*** society[14] in its place, which became popular in economics *via* the writings of Adam Smith (its founding father in the United States) and was identified as a principle of ***laissez-faire***.[15]

The term 'liberalisation' has the same connotation in economics as its root word 'liberalism'. Pro-market or pro-capitalistic inclination in the economic policies of an economy is the process of liberalisation. We see it taking place in Euro-America in the 1970s and particularly in the 1980s.[16] The most suitable example of this process could be China of the mid-1980s when it announced its ***open door policy***. Though China lacks (even today) some trademark traits of liberalism, as for example, individualism, liberty and democratic system, it was still called a liberalising economy.

We may take an example from the history of the world economy - putting the United States of the early 20th century and the communist China on two poles of the scale - thus representing the best historical examples of the liberal and illiberal economies. With the United States on the south and China on the north, any policy movement towards the south' is 'liberalisation'. The policy movement from the south to the north will be known as 'illiberalisation'.

It means that the process of decreasing traits of a state economy and increasing traits of a market economy is liberalisation. Similarly, the opposite will be the process of illiberalisation. Technically speaking, both the processes will be known as the processes of economic reforms, since 'reform' as a term does not state anything about the 'direction'.

All the economic reforms in the world have been from the 'north to the south' - same goes correct in the case of liberalisation too.

[14] A. Heywood, *Politics* (New York, NY: Palgrave, 2002), p. 43.

[15] R. Nisbet, *Prejudices: A Philosophical Dictionary* (Massachusetts: Harvard University Press, 1982), p. 211.

[16] 'Economics: Making Sense of the Modern Economy', *The Economist*, London, 1999, pp. 225-26.

It means, in the Indian case the term 'liberalisation' is used to show the direction of the economic reforms - with decreasing influence of the state or the planned or the command economy and increasing influence of free market or the capitalistic economy. It is a move towards capitalism. India is attempting to strike its own balance of the 'state-market mix'. It means even if the economic reforms are directed towards a market economy, it can never be branded a blind run to capitalism. Since the economy was more like the state economy in the former years, it has to go for a greater degree of mix of the market. But in the long run, liberalism curtails the powers of the Parliament.[17]

Post-Liberalism

Post-liberalism is a heterogeneous intellectual idea which emerged in reaction to liberalism and neo-liberalism. It criticises modern liberalism for giving autonomy to the individual at the expense of society. It revolves around the following *core principles*:

1. It rejects individuals as autonomous agents and believes that individuals are shaped by family, community, and faith/religion (which is a bit like 'Communitarianism').
2. It suggests the state should not act as a neutral mediator— rather, it should actively promote social well-being (i.e., promoting the cause of 'Common Good').
3. It criticises 'market fundamentalism' (a synonym for *neo-liberalism* as per which the market can cure every economic ill) and suggests state intervention in the economy to protect labour, lessen inequality, and prioritise social stability over growth (its view of 'Economic Reforms').

Scan this QR Code to watch a author's video lecture that simplifies this topic

[17] J. K. Galbraith, *A History of Economics* (London: Penguin Books, 1991), p. 123.

4. It advises the state to 're-capture' cultural and educational institutions from the elitist liberal hegemony (i.e., 'Institutional Capture').

Chief proponents: Alasdair McIntyre (*After Virtue, 1981*), John Gray (*Post-Liberalism, 1993*), Patrick Deneen (*Why Liberalism Failed, 2018*), and Adrian Vermule (*Common Good Constitutionalism, 2022*) are some of the chief proponents of this idea.

Criticisms: This idea has been criticised on several counts—one group criticises it for promoting democratic backsliding and authoritarianism, while another calls it incoherent because on one hand it wishes to preserve liberal fruits (like prosperity), while on the other it wishes to dismantle the structure which produced them.

Privatisation

The decades of the 1980s and 1990s witnessed a 'rolling back' of the state by the governments, especially in the United States and United Kingdom under the inspiration of the New Right priorities and beliefs.[18] The policies through which the 'roll back' of the state was carried out included deregulation, privatisation and introduction of market reforms in public services. Privatisation at that time was used as a process under which the state assets were transferred to the private sector.[19] The root of the term 'privatisation' goes to this period which received much more currency around the world once the East European nations and later the developing democratic nations opted for it. But during the period, several connotations and meanings of the term 'privatisation' have developed. We may see them as follows:

1. Privatisation in its purest sense and lexically means de-nationalisation,[20] i.e., transfer of the state ownership of the assets to the private sector to the tune of 100 per cent. Such bold moves occurred only once anywhere in the world without any political fallouts - in the early 1980s in the United Kingdom under the Thatcher regime. This route of privatisation has been avoided by almost all democratic systems. In the mid-1990s, some West European nations - Italy, Spain and France - besides the United States opted for such moves.[21] India never ventured into any such privatisation move till 2022 when the government privatised Air India.
2. The sense in which privatisation has been used is the process of disinvestment all over the world. This process includes selling of the shares of the state-owned enterprises to the private sector. Disinvestment is denationalisation of less than 100 per cent ownership transfer from the state to the private sector. If an asset has been sold out by the government to the tune of only 49 per cent, the ownership remains with the state though it is considered privatisation. If the sale of shares of the state-owned assets has been to the tune of 51 per cent, the ownership is really transferred to the private sector where even then it is termed 'privatisation'.
3. The third and the last sense in which the term 'privatisation' has been used around the world is very wide. Basically, all the economic policies which directly or indirectly seem to promote the expansion of the private sector or the market (economy) have been termed by experts and the governments as the process of privatisation. We may cite a few examples from India - de-licencing and de-reservation of the industries, even cuts in the subsidies, permission to foreign investment and so forth.[22]

Here we may connect liberalisation to privatisation in India. Liberalisation shows the direction of economic reforms in India, i.e., inclination towards the dominance of the market. But how will it be achieved? Basically, privatisation will be ***the path*** to reform. It means everything which includes promotion of the 'market' will be the path of the reform process in India.

Globalisation

The process of globalisation has always been used in economic terms though it has always taken political and cultural dimensions. Once economic changes occur, they have several socio-political manifestations.[23] Globalisation is generally termed

[18] A. Heywood, *Politics*, *op. cit.*, p. 100.

[19] Stiglitz and Walsh, *Economics*, op. cit. pp. 802-3.

[20] Collins *Dictionary of Economics* (Oxford: Penguin), relevant pages.

[21] Samuelson and Nordhaus, *Economics*, *op. cit.*, p. 199.

[22] New Industrial Policy, 1991 & several documents of GoI since then.

[23] T. Parsons, *The Structure of Social Action* (New York: McGraw Hill, 1937).

'an increase in economic integration among nations'.[24] Even before several nation-states were even birthed into existence, the countries around the world had opted for globalisation, i.e., 'a closer integration of their economies'.[25] This globalisation lasted from 1800 to almost 1930, interrupted by the Great Depression and the two wars which led to retrenchment, and several trade barriers were erected since the early 1930s.[26]

The concept was popularised by the Organisation of Economic Cooperation and Development (OECD) in the mid-1980s again after the wars. In its earlier de-liberalisation, the organisation had defined globalisation in a very narrow and business-like sense - ***any cross-border investment by an OECD company outside its country of origin for its benefit is globalisation***. After this summit of the OECD, proposals for replacing the GATT by the WTO were pushed by the developed economies of the world, better known as the starting of the Uruguay Round of GATT deliberations which ended in Marrakesh (1994) with the birth of the WTO. In the meantime, the OECD had defined (by mid-1980s) globalisation officially as 'a shift from a world of distinct national economies to a global economy in which production is internationalised and financial capital flows freely and instantly between countries'.[27]

The official meaning of globalisation for the WTO is movement of the economies of the world towards ***unrestricted cross border movements of goods and services, capital and the labour force***. It simply means that for the economies who are signatories to the process of globalisation (i.e., signatories to the WTO), for them there will be nothing like foreign or indigenous goods and services, capital and labour, the world becoming a flat and level-playing field emerging in due process of time.[28]

For many political scientists (who are today a very dominant force in the world), globalisation is the emergence of a situation when our lives are increasingly shaped by the events that occur at a great distance from us about which the decisions are not taken by our conscious selves. One section of experts believe that globalisation subordinates the state, while the other section argues that the local, national and global events constantly interact under it without any subordination of one by the other. Rather, globalisation highlights the deepening as well as broadening of the political process in this sense.[29]

India became one of the founding members of the WTO and was obliged to promote the process of globalisation, though its economic reforms started with no such obligations. It is a different thing that India started the process of globalisation right after the reforms in 1991.[30]

Now we may connect the three simultaneous processes - the LPG with which India launched its reform programme. The process of liberalisation shows the movement of the economy towards the market economy, where privatisation is the path/ route through which it will travel to realise its ultimate 'goal', i.e., globalisation.

It should be noted here that the Indian idea of globalisation is deeply and frequently inclined towards the concept of welfare state, which keeps appearing in the day-to-day public policy as an emphatic reference. Whole world, including the IMF, the WB now increasingly recognises the fact that the official goal of globalisation of the world economies would not take place without providing the poor of the world a better standard of living. Even if globalisation is complete without including almost one-fifth of the world's population, i.e., the poor, will it be called development of the world?

Blend of Protectionism Amidst rising protectionism in the world, India also seems to be fine-tuning its stand on globalisation which has become more visible in the wake of the ***COVID-19*** pandemic. In May 2020, the Government gave a very emphatic call for self-reliance by launching the ***Atmanirbhar Baharat Abhiyan*** (Self-Reliant India Campaign) which aims to boost the MSMEs, agriculture, pan-India supply chain, import

[24] Samuelson and Nordhaus, *Economics*, op. cit., p. 32.

[25] Stiglitz and Walsh, *Economics*, op. cit., p. 804.

[26] T. L. Friedman, *The World is Flat* (London: Penguin Books, 2006), 9. Stiglitz and Walsh, *Economics*, op. cit., p. 804.

[27] As quoted in A. Heywood, *Politics*, op. cit., p. 139.

[28] As Friedman shows in his best-seller, *The World is Flat* (London: Penguin Books, 2006) p. 9.

[29] As put by the *Oxford's Dictionary of Politics* (New Delhi: Oxford University Press, 2004), pp. 222-25. A. Heywood, *Politics*, p. 138.

[30] It should be noted here that the whole Euro-America had already started promoting globalisation by the mid-1980s as the WTO deliberations at Uruguay began. The formation of the WTO only gave globalisation an official mandate in 1995, once it started its functions. It means, for India, globalisation was a reality by 1991 itself - one has to move as the dominant forces move.

substitution, discouraging imports, boosting exports through expansion of labour-intensive manufacturing industries besides unshackling the economic potential through effective and speedier reforms - while officially remaining committed to multilateralism (i.e., globalisation).

Reform Measures

The economic reform programme, that India launched, consisted of *two* categories of measures:

1. Macroeconomic Stabilisation Measures: They include all those economic policies which intend to boost the aggregate *demand* in the economy – be it domestic or external. For the enhanced domestic demand, the focus has to be on increasing the purchasing power of the masses, which entails an emphasis on the creation of gainful and quality employment opportunities.

2. Structural Reform Measures: They include all the policy reforms which have been initiated by the government to boost the aggregate *supply* of goods and services in the economy. They naturally entail unshackling the economy so that it may search for its own potential of enhanced productivity. For the purchasing capacity of the people to increase, the economy requires increased income, which comes in from increased levels of production. Income so increased is later distributed among the people whose purchasing power has to be increased – this will take place by properly initiating a suitable set of macroeconomic policies. For the income to get distributed among the target population, it takes time, but the efforts a government initiates to increase the supply, i.e., increasing production, become visible soon. As production is carried out by the producers (i.e., the capitalists), *prima facie* the structural reform measures look 'pro-rich' and 'pro-industrialist' or 'pro-capitalist', known by different names. Ignorant people easily get swayed by the logic that everything that is 'pro-rich' has to be necessarily 'anti-poor'. But it was not the case with the process of economic reforms. Unless the economy is able to achieve higher growth (i.e., income), from where will the purchasing power of the masses be enhanced? And increased income takes time to reach everybody. If the economy lacks political stability, this process takes even more time due to short-term goals set by the unstable and frequently changing governments – the exact case is with India.

GENERATIONS OF ECONOMIC REFORMS

Though there were no such announcements or proposals while India launched its reforms in 1991, in the coming times, many 'generations' of reforms were announced by the governments.[31] A total of ***three*** generations of reforms have been announced till date, while experts have gone on to suggest the ***fourth*** generation as well. We may substantiate the components of the various generations of reforms to properly understand the very characteristics and nature of the reform process in India.

First Generation Reforms (1991–2000)[32]

It was in the year 2000-01 that the government, for the first time, announced the need for the Second Generation of economic reforms, which was launched the same year. The ones which had been initiated by then (i.e., from 1991 to 2000) were referred by the government as the reforms of the First Generation. The broad coordinates of the First Generation of reforms may be seen as follows:

1. **Promotion to Private Sector:** This included various important and liberalising policy decisions, i.e., 'de-reservation' and 'de-licencing' of the industries, abolition of the MRTP limit, abolition of the compulsion of the phased production and conversion of loans into shares and simplifying environmental laws for the establishment of industries.
2. **Public Sector Reforms:** The steps taken to make the public sector undertakings profitable and efficient, their disinvestment (*token*) and their corporatisation were the major parts of it.
3. **External Sector Reforms:** They consisted of policies such as abolishing quantitative restrictions on import, switching to the floating exchange rate, full current account convertibility, reforms in the capital account,

[31] It should be noted here that many economists regard the economic reforms of the mid-1980s as the First-Generation reforms. However, the governments of the time have not stated anything along those lines. It was only in the year 2000-01 that India officially remarked about the generations of reform for the first time.

[32] Based on the *New Industrial Policy, 1991* and several *Economic Surveys* as well as many announcements by the governments.

permission to foreign investment (direct as well as indirect) and promulgation of a liberal Foreign Exchange Management Act (the FEMA replacing the FERA).

4. **Financial Sector Reforms:** Several reform initiatives were taken up in areas such as banking, capital market, insurance and mutual funds.
5. **Tax Reforms:** This consisted of all the policy initiatives directed towards simplifying, broad-basing, modernising and checking evasion.

A major re-direction was ensued by this generation of reforms in the economy - the 'command' type of the economy moved strongly towards a market-driven economy, private sector (domestic as well as foreign) to have greater participation in the future.

Second Generation Reforms (2000–01 onwards)[33]

The government launched the second generation of reforms in 2000-01. Basically, the reforms India launched in the early 1990s did not take place as desired, and a need for another set of reforms was felt by the government, which was initiated with the title of the Second Generation of economic reforms. These reforms were not only deeper and delicate but required a higher political will power from the governments. The major components of the reform are as given below:

1. **Factor Market Reforms:** Considered as the 'backbone' for the success of the reform process in India, it consists of dismantling of the ***Administered Price Mechanism (APM)***. There were many products in the economy whose prices were fixed/regulated by the government, *viz.* petroleum, sugar, fertilisers and drugs. Though a major section of the products under the APM were produced by the private sector, they were not sold on market principles which hindered the profitability of the manufacturers as well as the sellers and ultimately the expansion of the industries concerned, leading to a demand-supply gap. Under market reforms these products were to be brought into the market fold.

   In the petroleum segment now only kerosene oil and LPG remained under the APM, while petrol, diesel (by March 2014) and lubricants were phased out. Similarly, the income-tax paying families do not get sugar from the TPS on subsidies; only urea, among the fertilisers, remains under APM, while many drugs have also been phased out of the mechanism. Opening the petroleum sector for private investment and cutting down the burden of levy on sugar (levy obligation was abolished by mid 2013) are now providing dividends to the economy. But we cannot say that the Factor Market Reforms (FMRs) are complete in India. It is still ongoing. Cutting down subsidies on essential goods is a socio-political question in India. Till market-based purchasing power is not delivered to all of the consumers, it would not be possible to complete the FMRs.
2. **Public Sector Reforms:** The Second Generation of reforms in the public sector involves emphasis on areas such as greater functional autonomy, freer leverage to the capital market, international tie-ups and greenfield ventures and disinvestment[34] (*strategic*).
3. **Reforms in Government and Public Institutions:** This involves all those moves which really go towards converting the role of the government from the 'controller' to the 'facilitator' or the administrative reform, as it may be called.
4. **Legal Sector Reforms:** Though reforms in the legal sector were started in the first generation itself, now it was to be deepened and newer areas were to be included, such as abolishing

[33] Based on the Ministry of Finance, *Economic Survey 2000-01* (New Delhi: Government of India, 2001); and *Union Budget, 2001-02* especially besides other official announcements by the GoI in the coming years.

[34] Basically, 'disinvestment' started in India in its 'token' form, which is selling of government's minority shares in PSUs. Whereas in the Second Generation, the government went for a 'strategic' kind of disinvestment, which basically involved the transfer of ownership of the PSUs from the state to the private sector, with MFIL and BALCO being the first of such disinvestments. Once the UPA Government came to power in May 2004, the latter form of disinvestment was put on hold. We will discuss it in detail in the chapter on *Indian Industry i.e., Chapter 9*.

outdated and contradictory laws, reforms in the Indian Penal Code (IPC) and Code of Criminal Procedure (CrPC), labour laws, company laws and enacting suitable legal provisions for new areas such as cyber law.

What Comes First—Demand or Supply?

To bring in all-round prosperity, countries need to optimise both demand and supply simultaneously and create a situation where demand catches up with supply, which, in turn, catches up with demand. This cyclical arrangement is attempted by countries by synchronising two sets of policies—one based on demand-side economics and the other on supply-side economics.

5. **Reforms in Critical Areas:** The Second Generation reforms also commit to suitable reforms in the infrastructure sector (i.e., power, roads, especially as the telecom sector has been encouraging), agriculture, agricultural extension, education and health care. These areas have been called by the government as ***critical areas.***[35]

These reforms have two segments. The first segment is similar to the FMRs, while the second segment provides a broader dimension to the reforms, *viz.* corporate farming, research and development in the agriculture sector (which was till now basically taken care of by the government and needs active participation of the private sector), irrigation, inclusive education and health care.

Other than the above-mentioned focus of this generation of reforms, some other important areas were also emphasised:

1. **State's Role in the Reform:** For the first time, an important role to the state was designed, in the process of economic reforms. All new steps of the reforms were now to be started by the state with the centre playing a supportive role.

[35] *Economic Survey 2000-01* (New Delhi: Ministry of Finance, GoI).

2. **Fiscal Consolidation:** The area of fiscal consolidation, though it was a major co-ordinate of reform in India since 1991 itself, gets a constitutional commitment and responsibility. The Fiscal Responsibility and Budget Management (FRBM) Act is passed by the Centre and the Fiscal Responsibility Act (FRA) is followed by the states as an era of new commitments to the fiscal prudence starts in the country.
3. **Greater Tax Devolution to the States:** Though there was such a political tendency[36] by the mid-1990s itself, after the Second Generation reforms started, we see a visible change in the central policies favouring greater fiscal leverage to the states. Even the process of tax reforms takes the same dimension. Similarly, the Finance Commissions as well as the Planning Commission start taking greater fiscal care of the states. And for the first time the states had a net revenue surplus collection in the fiscal period 2007-08.[37]
4. **Focusing on the Social Sector:** The social sector (especially health care and education) gets increased attention by the government with manifold increases in the budgetary allocation, as well as show of a greater compliance to the performance of the development programmes.

We see mixed results of the Second Generation reforms though the reforms still continue.

Third Generation Reforms

The announcement of the third generation of reforms was made on the margins of the launching of the Tenth Plan (2002-07). This generation of reforms commits to the cause of a fully functional Panchayati Raj Institution (PRI), so that the benefits

[36] We see it, especially, when the Coalition Government (i.e., the UF Government) goes to amend the Constitution so that the Alternative Method of Devolution (AMD) of the tax suggested by the Tenth Finance Commission becomes a law before the recommendations of the Eleventh Finance Commission. It should be noted that the AMD had increased the gross tax devolution to the states by a hefty 5 per cent.

[37] The Comptroller and Auditor General, *Provisional Report*, May 2007.

of economic reforms, in general, can reach to the grassroots level.

Though the constitutional arrangement for a decentralised developmental process was already affected in the early 1990s, it was in the early 2000s that the government gets convinced of the need of 'inclusive growth and development'. Till the masses are not involved in the process of development, the development will lack the 'inclusion' factor, which was concluded by the government of the time. The Eleventh Plan goes on to ratify the same sentiments (though the political combination at the Centre had changed) and views regarding the need for the Third Generation of reforms in India.

Fourth Generation Reforms

This is a non-official generation of reform (proposed by experts in 2000–01) which envisions an information technology-enabled (IT-enabled) India. According to it, such a policy emphasis will bring in two clear dividends—firstly, being an industry, it will bring in economic gains and secondly, it will synchronise and speed up the other three generations of reforms in the country.

It still remains a non-official generation. Governments' increasing emphasis on Aadhar, JAM number trinity, direct benefit transfer, and digital India establishes its relevance.

THE REFORM APPROACH

The process of economic reforms commenced in the world by the mid-1980s (in Western Europe and Northern America). Once the idea of the Washington Consensus gained ground, we found similar reforms being followed by different countries cutting across the continents. Over time, experts, together with the IMF and WB, started classifying such countries into two categories, *viz.* one which went for the 'Gradualist Approach' and the other which went for the 'Stop-and-Go Approach'.

India's reform process which commenced in 1991 has been termed by experts as gradualist (also called incremental)[38] in nature with traits of occasional reversals, and without any big ideological U-turn coalitions of various political parties at the Centre and different political parties ruling the states lacked a general sense of consensus on reforms. It reflects the compulsions of India's highly pluralist and participative democratic policy-making process.[39] Though such an approach helped the country to avoid socio-political upheavals/instability, it did not allow the desired economic outcome which could have accrued from the reforms. The First Generation of economic reforms could not bring the expected results due to lack of some other set of reforms for which India goes after almost over a decade - the Second Generation of economic reforms. Similarly, the economic benefits (whatever accrued) remained non-inclusive in absence of an active public policy aimed at inclusion (commencing *via* the Third Generation of economic reforms). This created a kind of disillusionment about the prospects of reforms and failed the governments to muster enough public support in favour of reforms.

Unlike India, several other countries (such as Brazil, Argentina and South Africa) went for the stop-and-go kind of reforms. In such reforms, the governments first decide the sectors where reforms are needed - then they pin-point the prerequisites (which will create a conducive atmosphere for reforms to take place), and finally both set of the reforms are activated simultaneously. In their cases, economic results from reforms were on the expected lines. Though these nations took high risks on the socio-political front, in their case, in medium-term itself, the governments were able to mobilise enough public support in favour of reforms (which encouraged the governments to go for further reforms). Such reforms do not look possible in the case of India - this is why the last few volumes of the Economic Survey (2015-16, 2016-17 and 2017-18) advised in favour of an incremental approach to reforms.

---

[38] I. J. Ahluwalia, 'Industry', in *The New Oxford Companion to Economics in India*, vol. 2, K. Basu and A. Maertens, eds. (New Delhi: Oxford University Press, 2012), pp. 371-75.

[39] M. S. Ahluwalia, 'Planning', in *The New Oxford Companion to Economics in India*, vol. 2, K. Basu and A. Maertens, eds. (New Delhi: Oxford University Press, 2012), pp. 530-36.

Transformational Reforms

The Government launched the transformational reforms again in 2014–15. Some of such reforms of recent times, as per the Government (Union Budget 2017–18), are as given below:

1. Inflation targeting and setting up of the Monetary Policy Committee by amending the RBI Act, 1934;
2. Restarting of the 'strategic disinvestment' of the PSUs;
3. Demonetisation of the high denomination currency notes (aimed at checking corruption, black money, tax evasion, fake currency and terrorism);
4. Enactment of the new Benami Law (aimed at checking black money);
5. Bankruptcy Law (aimed at promoting the 'ease of doing business'); and
6. Enactment of the Aadhar Act (aimed at rationalising and weeding out corruption in the present subsidy regime).

The transformational reforms are **special** in this sense that they are aimed at inducing *behavioural changes*[40] in the actions of the targeted group – by far claimed to be quite successful[41] in doing so. For example, almost 87 per cent cases of the debt default during 2016–22 under the Insolvency and Bankruptcy Code (IBC, 2016) were resolved before the commencement of the insolvency process itself – on account of 'behavioural change' among the defaulting debtors.[42]

Though the overall scheme of reforms in India still remains incremental (i.e., gradual) the 'transformational reforms' are the examples of non-gradual (stop-and-go) brand of reforms. Meanwhile, the government had been advised to go for ***large-scale incremental reforms*** in the country.[43] The government was advised[44] to use its strong mandate to opt for *expeditious reforms* in the economy – we find a series of major structural reforms announced[45] since then, all being 'non-gradual' in nature.

The 'Agile' approach[46] of policy making opted by the Government for the uncertain times (caused by the COVID-19 pandemic) in recent times, can also be termed *transformational* in nature. Under this non-conventional policy approach, while, on the one hand, the aim is to provide safety-nets to cushion the hardships faced by the vulnerable sections of society and businesses, on the other the policy response is kept flexible which can be modified as per the evolving situation (based on the high frequency indicators).

The transformative reforms[47] which were initiated by the Government during 1998–2002 are considered India's *first tryst* with non-gradual set of reforms which propelled India's growth 2003 onwards. The re-initiation of the transformative reforms (emphasis on structural reforms) this time round, however, has faced tough times due to pandemic-led supply shocks, geopolitical issues (Ukraine crisis) and spike in commodity prices. Once these obstacles fade away, India is well placed to grow faster in the coming decade.

---

[40] *Interim Budget 2019-20* (New Delhi: Ministry of Finance, GoI).

[41] *World Development Report-2015*, World Bank, New York.

[42] *Economic Survey 2022-23* (New Delhi: Ministry of Finance, GoI), pp. 91-93.

[43] *Economic Survey 2017-18*, vol. 1 (New Delhi: Ministry of Finance, GoI), p. 140.

[44] *Economic Survey 2019-20*, vol. 2 (New Delhi: Ministry of Finance, GoI), pp. 1-4.

[45] *Economic Survey 2019-20*, vol. 2 (New Delhi: Ministry of Finance, GoI), pp. 29-30. Expeditious reforms mean reforms done with *speed* and *efficiency*.

[46] *Economic Survey 2021-22* (New Delhi: Ministry of Finance, GoI, January 2022), pp. 14-24. For detailed knowledge of the Agile approach, please see *Chapter 6* on *Planning in India*.

[47] *Economic Survey 2022-23*, (New Delhi: Ministry of Finance, GoI, January 2023), pp. 24-40.

REFORMS DELIVER

The government today credits the process of economic reforms for enhancing the overall well-being of citizens in the country. A few remarks from the ***Economic Survey 2025-26*** give pleasing insights into it:

- Policy reforms[48] do matter; process reforms arguably matter more. Processes define the interaction between the government and the governed. So, they make all the difference to the success or failure of policy intent and reforms. The signs are very promising. The deregulation and smart regulation initiatives undertaken by states in 2025-26 provide ample grounds for optimism that the state machinery can reinvent itself and its mission, 'shifting from regulation and control to enabling.' Together with the Union Government's economic reforms and other policy initiatives, this signals that the state understands the significance of the challenge and the need to rise to it.

[48] *Economic Survey* 2025-26 (New Delhi: Ministry of Finance, GoI, January 2026), p. xiv.

- Social sector initiatives, supported by targeted welfare schemes, economic reforms[49] and expanded access to essential services, have contributed to a reduction in poverty levels. In June 2025, the World Bank revised the international poverty line from US$ 2.15 to US$ 3.00 per day (PPP, 2021 prices). Based on the revised poverty line, India's poverty rates in 2022-23 are estimated at 5.3 per cent for extreme poverty and 23.9 per cent for lower-middle-income poverty, noting that these estimates are not directly comparable with earlier poverty lines. Key health and education indicators, such as life expectancy, the infant mortality rate (IMR), and the gross enrolment ratio (GER), have shown steady improvement.
- The Government has successfully aligned[50] the process of economic reforms with inclusive development through welfare programmes and enhanced access to services–enhancing the overall human well-being of the citizens.

[49] *Economic Survey* 2025-26 (New Delhi: Ministry of Finance, GoI, January 2026), p. 29.

[50] *Economic Survey* 2025-26 (New Delhi: Ministry of Finance, GoI, January 2026), p. 515.

SAMPLE OBJECTIVE QUESTIONS

1. Consider the following statements related to India's reform process:

(i) Brahminical entrepreneurship has taken back seat.
(ii) Transformative reforms are based on nudges.
(iii) Non-gradual reforms promote neo-liberalism.
(iv) Speedy reforms weaken the cause of social welfare.

Which of the statement(s) given above is/are correct?

Code:
(a) Only one **(b)** Only two
(c) Only three **(d)** All four

2. Consider the following statements related to the economic reform process in the country:

(i) Second-generation reforms were transformational in nature.
(ii) Setting up new public sector enterprises goes against the spirit of reforms.
(iii) Resolution of the non-performing assets of banks presently takes place through transformative process.

Which of the statement(s) given above is/are correct?

Code:
(a) Only one **(b)** Only two
(c) All three **(d)** None of these

3. Consider the following statement(s) related to the official globalisation:

(i) It promotes structural reforms.
(ii) As per the WTO, it has increased inequality in the world.

(iii) Its cultural dimension is today a major concern for India.

Which of the statement(s) given above is/are correct?

Code:

(a) Only one **(b)** Only two
(c) All three **(d)** None of these

4. Consider the following statements related to India's reforms:

(i) They were forced upon by the International Monetary Fund.
(ii) Disinvestment may lead to de-nationalisation today.
(iii) Public expenditure on social welfare has increased during reforms.

Which of the statement(s) given above is/are correct?

Code:

(a) Only one **(b)** Only two
(c) All three **(d)** None of these

5. Consider the following statements related to the process of economic reforms:

(i) The statutory attempt to target inflation in India comes under it.
(ii) Insolvency and Bankruptcy Law of India is part of its second generation.
(iii) The International Monetary Fund is yet to recognise behavioural change as its part.

How many of the above statement(s) is/are correct?

(a) Only one **(b)** Only two
(c) All three **(d)** None of these

6. Consider the following statements related to India's process of reforms:

(i) Incremental reforms have been called 'substantive' too by the Government.
(ii) Incremental structural reforms have been quite successful in the country.
(iii) Non-gradual structural reforms required strong political mandate.

How many of the above statement(s) is/are correct?

(a) Only one **(b)** Only two
(c) All three **(d)** None of these

7. Consider the following statements related to India's third generation of the economic reforms:

(i) They are inspired by the Santiago Consensus.
(ii) It envisions the public-private-people partnership (PPPP) approach to development.
(iii) Local bodies found their first mention in reform process through it.

How many of the above statement(s) is/are correct?

(a) Only one **(b)** Only two
(c) All three **(d)** None of these

8. Consider the following statements related to policy of economic reforms in the country:

(i) Enhancing the fiscal strength of states is one of its major objectives since 1991.
(ii) States' share in central tax pool has increased throughout the reform period.
(iii) The period of reforms has seen more financial autonomy given to the states.

How many of the above statement(s) is/are correct?

(a) Only one **(b)** Only two
(c) All three **(d)** None of these

9. Consider the following statements related to India's process of reforms:

(i) It launched under the shadow of the Washington Consensus.
(ii) It always had a neo-liberal overtones.
(iii) Its pace during the first two decades was slower mainly due to participative decision-making process.

How many of the above statement(s) is/are correct?

(a) Only one **(b)** Only two
(c) All three **(d)** None of these

10. Consider the following statements related to the reform measures of the Government in the country:

(i) Structural measures of reforms deal with the ownership of the assets.
(ii) Macroeconomic stabilisation measures aim at raising purchasing capacity of consumers.

(iii) Decontrolling industries was a structural measure aimed at raising supply.

How many of the above statement(s) is/are correct?

(a) Only one **(b)** Only two
(c) All three **(d)** None of these

Answers: 1. (b) 2. (b) 3. (b) 4. (b) 5. (b) 6. (a) 7. (c) 8. (c) 9. (c) 10. (d)

SAMPLE SUBJECTIVE QUESTIONS

1. How far do you think India's second-generation reforms have been able to achieve its objectives? Give suitable examples to support your views.

2. 'The factor market reforms are considered as the backbone of economic reforms in the country.' Comment.

3. Briefly examine the relationship between third-generation reforms and India's idea of inclusive growth.

4. Do you think that India has shifted from incremental to substantive reforms in the last decade? Give suitable examples to prove your point.

5. What are transformative reforms? Briefly discuss using suitable examples.

6. 'Economic reforms require reform in mindset and attitude of the stakeholders too.' Explain with suitable examples.

SAMPLE MODEL ANSWER

1. Discuss about the transformational reforms initiated by the Government in recent times.

Ans. We have seen a major change in the Government's stance towards the need for reforms - several steps of reforms have been taken which have been termed 'transformational'. These reforms are 'transformational' in the sense that they are aimed at transforming the very outlook on policymaking and are taken from a long-term perspective. We may have a look at the major ones.

- Inflation targeting and setting up the Monetary Policy Committee by amending the RBI Act, 1934.
- Restarting of the 'strategic disinvestment' of the PSUs.
- Demonetisation of the high-denomination currency notes (aimed at checking corruption, black money, tax evasion, fake currency, and terrorism).
- Enactment of the new Benami Law (aimed at checking black money).
- Bankruptcy Law (aimed at promoting the 'ease of doing business').
- Enactment of the Aadhar Act (aimed at rationalising and weeding out corruption in the present subsidy regime).
- Attempts in the direction of influencing the 'behavioural pattern' of the citizens to promote the cause of socio-economic well-being, etc.

The Union Budget 2017-18 clearly termed them 'transformational reforms'. As these reforms are aimed at long-term gains, there might be some political backlash on them. But this is the way economies grow up and get matured. A remark from the latest Economic Survey 2016-17 looks quite correct in this case - economic reforms are not, or not just, about overcoming vested interests; they are increasingly about shared narratives and vision on problems and solutions.

CHAPTER 8

Inflation and Business Cycle

> Fluctuations in the level of economic activity, alternating between periods of depression and boom, led by one prominent factor, i.e., the expectations of the future demand - intertwined with the inflation - have always been a fascinating topic for economists.*
>
> *See Joseph E. Stiglitz and Carl E. Walsh, *Economics*, 4th edition (New York: W. W. Norton, 2005), pp. 494-96; Collins Internet-Linked Dictionary of Economics, (Glasgow, Scotland: Harper Collins, 2006), pp. 48-49.

To watch the Author's videos on the significance of the Chapter, scan the QR Code given here

Exam Essentials...

- Disinflation vs Deflation
- Phillips Curve
- Skewflation
- GDP Deflator
- New WPI in the Offing
- CPI Series 2024
- Shapes of Recovery
- Recession

Note to the Reader...

This chapter deals with Inflation and Business Cycle (which is considered as an extension of the former). For the ease of understanding this chapter has been divided into two Sections.

To the extent inflation is concerned, it is not only considered among the most dynamic segments of economics but in the civil services exam the maximum number of most difficult questions have been asked on it, especially at the preliminary level. Besides, when it is linked to banking (the subject matter of Chapter 13 of the book) it becomes the second most important area from where questions have been asked. Similarly, business cycle has been in news since the sub-prime crisis of 2007-08 and the ongoing great recession in the advanced economies impacting the global economy in many ways.

While reading the chapter the focus should be on understanding the application (and not on cramming) and its inter-linkages to other segments of the economy of India and the world.

In This Chapter...

SECTION-A: INFLATION

INTRODUCTION

In simple terms, inflation is just price rise. It becomes a matter of everyday discussion if the prices of daily or weekly items start rising. Whatever impact it might be having on other areas of economy, inflation might take an ugly turn and lead to a political crisis - at least in the developing economies. India has seen governments thrown out of power in elections due to price rise in daily-use items. This is not the case in the developed economies, but inflation takes its political toll there too. In the developed economies, more aware and informed voters get carried away by the greater impact of higher or lower inflations in the elections.

Disinflation vs Deflation

Two terms, namely 'disinflation' and 'deflation', are used synonymously to mean 'price fall'. However, they are different and are not the exact synonyms! Both bring comfort to consumers. But in the long-run, deflation is harmful for the consumers and economy at large (which may bring slowdown in the economy and may lead to recessions, depression or even the possibility of a bust). For better understanding, we may take an example from India which targets an annual inflation rate of 4 per cent (with a flexibility band of 2 per cent):

- Till inflation is falling from higher levels towards 6 to 4 per cent, it is disinflation.
- Once inflation dips below 4 per cent, we usually not call it disinflation (rather experts start calling it deflation).
- Once inflation dips below 2 per cent, it is clear deflation.

However, prices keep falling during both disinflation and deflation. Away from this complexity, in practice, inflation is used as a neutral term to mean price rise as well as price fall.

DEFINITION

A rise in the general level of prices;[1] a sustained rise in the general level of prices;[2] persistent increases in the general level of prices;[3] an increase in the general level of prices in an economy that is sustained over time;[4] rising prices across the board[5] - is inflation. These are some of the most common academic definitions of inflation. If the price of only few goods has gone up, it is not inflation; it is inflation only if the prices of ***most*** goods have gone up.[6]

Measurement The rate of inflation is measured on the basis of price indices which are of two kinds - Wholesale Price Index (WPI) and Consumer Price Index (CPI). A price index is a measure of the average level of prices, which means that it does not show the exact price rise or fall of a single good. The rate of inflation is the rate of change of general price level which is measured as follows:

Rate of inflation (year x)
$= [(CPI_{x+1} - CPI_x) \div CPI_x] \times 100$

This rate shows up in percentage form, though inflation is also shown in ***numbers***, i.e., ***digits***. A price index is a weighted average of the prices of a number of goods and services. In the index, the total weight is taken as 100 at a particular year of the past (the ***base year***), this, when compared with the current year, shows a rise or fall in the prices of the current year, there is a rise or fall in the '100' in comparison to the base year - and this inflation is measured in digits.

Point-to-Point Inflation is measured ***point-to-point***. It means that the reference dates for the annual

[1] P. A. Samuelson and W. D. Nordhaus, *Economics* (New Delhi: Tata McGraw-Hill, 2006), p. 439.

[2] B. J. McCormick, et al., *Introducing Economics* (London: Penguin Education, 1974), p. 609.

[3] Graham Bannock and R. E. Baxter, *Penguin Dictionary of Economics*, 7th ed. (London: Penguin Books, 2003).

[4] *Collins Internet-Linked Dictionary of Economics* (Glasgow: Harper-Collins Publishers, 2006).

[5] M. Bishop, *Pocket Economist* (London: The Economist, 2007), p. 121.

[6] J. E. Stiglitz and C. E. Walsh, *Economics* (New York: W. W. Norton & Company, 2005), p. 509.

inflation are 1 January to 1 January of two consecutive years (not for 1 January to 31 December of the year concerned). Similarly, the weekly rate of inflation is the change in one week reference being the two consecutive last days of the week (i.e., 5 p.m. of two Fridays in India).

WHY DOES INFLATION OCCUR?

Economists have been giving different explanations throughout the 19th and 20th centuries for the occurrence of inflation - the debate still goes on. But the debate has certainly given us a clearer picture of inflation. We shall see the reasons responsible for inflation in two parts:

1. **Pre-1970s:** Till the rise of the Monetarist School, economists used to agree upon two reasons behind inflation:
   - (i) *Demand-Pull Inflation:* A mismatch between demand and supply pulls up prices. Either the demand increases over the same level of supply, or the supply decreases with the same level of demand and, thus, the situation of demand-pull inflation arises. This was a Keynesian idea. The Keynesian School suggests cuts in spending as the way of tackling excess demand, mainly by increasing taxes and reducing government expenditure.

     In practice, the governments keep tracking the demand-supply matrix to check such inflation. Depending upon the situation, the goods in short supply are imported, interest on loans increased and wages revised.
   - (ii) *Cost-Push Inflation:* An increase in factor input costs (i.e., wages and raw materials) pushes up prices. The price rise which is the result of increase in the production cost is cost-push inflation. The Keynesian school suggested controls on prices and incomes as the direct measures; and *moral suasions* and reduction in monopolistic power of trade unions as indirect measures to check such inflation pressures (basically, cost-push inflations chiefly used to happen due to higher wages demanded by the trade unions during the era).

     Today, the governments of the world use many tools to check such inflations - reducing excise and custom duties on raw materials, wage revisions, etc.
2. **Post-1970s:** After the rise of Monetaristic School of Economics in the early 1970s (monetarism developed in opposition to post-1945 Keynesian idea of demand management), the school provided monetarist explanation for inflation, the so-called 'demand-pull' or the 'cost-push' which is excessive creation of money in the economy.
   - (i) *Demand-Pull Inflation:* For the monetarists, a demand-pull inflation is creation of extra purchasing power for the consumer over the same level of production (which happens due to wage revisions at the micro level and deficit financing at the macro level). This is the typical case of creating extra money (either by printing or public borrowing) without equivalent creation in production/supply, i.e., 'too much money chasing too little output' - the ultimate source of demand-pull inflation.
   - (ii) *Cost-Push Inflation:* Similarly, for the monetarists, 'cost-push' is not a truly independent theory of inflation - it has to be financed by some extra money (which is created by the government *via* wage revision, public borrowing, printing of currency, etc.). A price rise does not get automatically reciprocated by consumers' purchasing. Practically, people must have received some extra purchasing power which is why they start purchasing at higher prices as well. If this had not been the reason, people would have cut down their consumption (i.e., overall demand) to the level of their purchasing capacity and the aggregate demand of goods would have gone down. But this does not happen. It means every cost-push inflation is a result of excessive creation of money - increasing money flow or money supply.

     For the monetarists, a particular level of money supply for a particular level of production is healthy for an economy.

Extra creation of money over the same level of production causes inflation. They suggested proper monetary policy (money supply, interest rates, printing of currencies, public borrowing, etc.) to check situations of inflationary pressure on the economy. Monetarists rejected the Keynesian theory of inflation.

Measures to Check Inflation

Inflation being a socio-economically sensitive issue, governments across the world try several short- and long-term policy steps to check it from becoming uncomfortable. A brief idea about the steps is given below:

(i) ***Demand side measure:*** In this category mainly two types of steps are taken. Firstly, the consumers are appealed to cut back the consumption of the items which show higher inflation (called *austerity*). This step has generally failed across the world because it does not work in the case of essential items (such as wheat, rice, milk, tea, etc.) and as people who have money do not wish to cut down consumption. Secondly, the government may tighten the flow of money in the system (known as *monetary measure*) - central bank making money costlier (by increasing repo rate, increasing CRR, etc., in the case of India).[7] This step also has its own limitations - it is not effective if the items showing inflation are essential ones (such as wheat, rice, onion, potato, etc., because consumers do not borrow money from banks to buy them). But it can be quite effective if the items are building materials (interest on home loan can be increased to cut back the demand of these items).[8]

(ii) ***Supply side measure:*** Aimed at increasing the supply of the items showing inflation, the government may go in for upscaling the production or import of the items. This measure also has its own limitations - production may not be upscaled in the short run and import may not reach the country in time.[9] Rather in medium and long-run terms, production of these items can be upscaled.

(iii) ***Cost side measure:*** Two variety of steps may be taken under it - in the short run cutting taxes can bring in comfort, but in the long run cutting cost of production is the only way out (by scaling up technology).[10]

TYPES OF INFLATION

Depending upon the range of increase and its severity, inflation may be classified into three broad categories.

1. Low Inflation

Such inflation is slow and on predictable[11] lines, which might be called small or gradual.[12] This is a comparative term which puts it opposite to the faster, bigger and unpredictable inflations. Low inflation takes place in a longer period, and the range of increase is usually in 'single digit'. Such inflation has also been called ***creeping inflation***.[13] We may take an example of the monthly inflation rate of a country for six months being 2.3 per cent, 2.6 per cent, 2.7 per cent, 2.9 per cent, 3.1 per cent and 3.4 per cent. Here the range of change is of 1.1 per cent and over a period of six months.

2. Galloping Inflation

This is a ***very high inflation*** running in the range of double digit or triple digit (i.e., 20 per cent,

---

[7] While inflation started moving upward, during 2009-13, the RBI went for upward revisions in the repo rate 17 times in a row with no effective outcome as the items showing inflationary pressure were essential ones–wheat, rice, pulses, milk, eggs, fish, meat, etc. *[Several monetary policy reviews of the RBI between 2009 and 2013].*

[8] During 2004-05 *(Economic Survey 2004-05)*, when building materials did show higher inflation, the RBI opted for upward revision of the interest rate on home loan (actually, by 2002-03 home loan was made extremely cheaper by the Government in order to encourage the housing sector which boosted the demand for building materials in the country).

[9] This was visible once in 1998 (by the time imported onions reached India, the prices had started touching ₹150 per kg rising from ₹10 a kilo) and second during 2004-05 (when import of building materials were lobbied down by the Indian producers and their production could not be scaled up). *[Economic Survey 1997-98 and 2004-05].*

[10] The Governments have been mainly cutting down custom duty, cenvat, VAT under it - several such instances can be cited between 2004 and 2013.

[11] Samuelson and Nordhaus, *Economics*, op. cit., p. 671.

[12] *Collins Dictionary of Economics*, op. cit., p. 251.

[13] Ibid.

100 per cent or 200 per cent in a year).[14] In the 1970s and 1980s, many Latin American countries such as Argentina, Chile and Brazil had such rates of inflation - in the range of 50 to 700 per cent. The Russian economy did show such inflation after the disintegration of the ex-USSR in the late 1980s.

Contemporary journalism has given some other names to this inflation - *hopping inflation, jumping inflation* and *running or runaway inflation*.[15]

3. Hyperinflation

This form of inflation is *large and accelerating*[16] which might have the annual rates in million or even trillion.[17] In such inflation not only the range of increase is very large, but the increase takes place in a very short span of time, where prices shoot up overnight.

The best example of hyperinflation that economists cite is of Germany after the First World War - in the early 1920s. At the end of 1923, prices were 36 billion times higher than two years earlier.[18] This inflation was so severe that paper German currencies (the Deutsche Mark) were more valuable as stove fuel than as actual money.[19] Some recent examples[20] of hyperinflation had been the Bolivian inflation of mid-1985 (24,000 per cent per annum) and the Yugoslavian inflation of 1993 (20 per cent per day). The latest example has been Venezuela which saw an annual inflation of over 53 million per cent by 2019, as per its central bank. The currency of Zimbabwe was declared *worthless* (by *The Economist*) in the wake of rise in annual inflation to 90 billion trillion per cent by 2008.

Such an inflation quickly leads to a complete loss of confidence in the domestic currency and people start opting for other forms of money, as, for example, physical assets, gold and foreign currency (also known as 'inflation proof' assets) and people might switch to barter exchange.[21]

OTHER VARIANTS OF INFLATION

Other than the three broad categories we analysed above, some other variants of inflation are also considered by governments in their policymaking.

1. Bottleneck Inflation

This inflation takes place when the supply falls drastically and the demand remains at the same level. Such situations arise due to supply-side hurdles, hazards or mismanagement which is also known as 'structural inflation'. This could be put in the 'demand-pull inflation' category.

2. Core Inflation

This nomenclature is based on the inclusion or exclusion of the goods and services while calculating inflation. Popular in western economies, core inflation shows price rise in all goods and services excluding ***energy*** and ***food articles***. First used[22] in India in 2000-01, it does not suit our inflation analysis in the right sense because prices here depend more on food articles and energy. Since 2015-16, a new *core-core inflation* is also measured by India which excludes food, fuel and light, transport and communication. A *refined*[23] *core inflation* was also constructed later on by excluding main fuel items, *viz.*, 'petrol for vehicle', 'diesel for vehicle' and 'lubricants and other fuels for vehicles' (which are not included in 'fuel and light' rather come under the sub-group 'transport and communication' of the miscellaneous group) in addition to 'food and beverages' and 'fuel and light' from the headline retail inflation (CPI-C).

---

[14] Samuelson and Nordhaus, *Economics*, op. cit., p. 671.

[15] As popularised by *The Economist, The Wall Street Journal, The Economic Times* (India), etc.

[16] *Collins Dictionary of Economics*, op. cit., p. 251.

[17] Samuelson and Nordhaus, *Economics*, op. cit., p. 671.

[18] T. Sargent, 'The Ends of Four Big Inflations', in *Inflations, Causes and Effects*, R. Hall, ed. (as quoted by Stiglitz and Walsh, *Economics*, p. 513).

[19] Stiglitz and Walsh, *Economics*, op. cit., p. 512.

[20] J. Sachs, *The End of Poverty* (London: Penguin Books, 2005), pp. 92-108.

[21] Hyperinflation erodes the value of money very fast and at a very high scale. We may put it with an example, suppose the annual rate of inflation is 100 per cent, money loses half its value every year. It means that a note of ₹100 will have a value of just ₹3 after five years.

[22] *Economic Survey 2000-01* (New Delhi: Ministry of Finance, GoI, 2001).

[23] *Economic Survey 2021-22* (New Delhi: Ministry of Finance, GoI, 2022), pp. 162-64.

OTHER IMPORTANT TERMS

Inflationary Gap

The excess of total government spending above the national income (i.e., fiscal deficit) is known as inflationary gap. This is intended to increase the production level, which ultimately pushes the prices up due to extra creation of money during the process.

Deflationary Gap

The shortfall in total spending of the government (i.e., fiscal surplus) over the national income creates deflationary gaps in the economy. This is a situation of producing more than the demand, and the economy usually heads for a general slowdown in the level of demand. This is also known as the ***output gap***.

Inflation Tax

Inflation erodes the value of money, and the people who hold currency suffer in this process. As the governments have authority of printing currency and circulating it into the economy (as they do in the case of deficit financing), this act functions as an income to the governments. This is a situation of sustaining government expenditure at the cost of people's income. This looks as if inflation is working as a tax.[24] That is how the term inflation tax is also known as ***seigniorage***. It means inflation is always at the level to which the government may go for deficit financing - level of deficit financing is directly reflected by the rate of inflation.

> **Word Bank**
>
> **Seigniorage**
>
> A method of generating resource by a government through printing of fresh notes/ currency notes. Money printing at higher rate to pay the government expenditures leads to inflation that enables the government to secure extra resources though that is called 'inflation tax' also.

It could also be used by the governments in the form of prices and income policy under which the companies pay inflation tax on the salary increases above the set level prescribed by the government.[25]

Inflation Spiral

An inflationary situation in an economy which results out of a process of wage and price interaction ***when wages press prices up and prices pull wages up***[26] is known as the inflationary spiral. It is also known as the ***wage-price spiral***. This wage-price interaction was seen as a plausible cause of inflation in the year 1935 in the US economy, for the first time.[27]

Inflation Accounting

This concept is popularly used in corporate profit accounting. When a firm calculates its profits after adjusting the effects of current level of inflation, the process is known as inflation accounting. Such profits are the real profit of the firm which could be compared to a historic rate of inflation (inflation of the base year), too.

Inflation Premium

The bonus brought by inflation to the borrowers is known as the inflation premium. The interest banks charge on their lending is known as the ***nominal*** interest rate, which might not be the real cost of borrowing paid by the borrower to the banks. To calculate the real cost a borrower is paying on its loan, the nominal rate of interest is adjusted with the effect of inflation and, thus, the interest rate we get is known as the real interest rate. Real interest is always lower than the nominal interest rate, if the inflation is taking place - the difference is the inflation premium.

Rising inflation premium shows depleting profits of the lending institutions. At times, to neutralise the effects of inflation premium, the lender takes a recourse to increase the nominal rate of interest.[28] This is why lending institutions keep fine-tuning their lending rates according to the changes occurring

24 Stiglitz and Walsh, *Economics*, op. cit., p. 511.

25 *Penguin Dictionary of Economics*, op. cit.

26 Ibid.

27 J. K. Galbraith, *A History of Economics* (London: Penguin Books, 1991), p. 205, pp. 261-310.

28 Patrick Lane, *Economics* (London: The Economist, 1999), p. 210.

in the rate of inflation - this job has become easier since inflation targeting was started by the RBI in February 2015.

Phillips Curve

It is a graphic curve which advocates a relationship between inflation and unemployment in an economy. As per the curve there is a 'trade-off' between inflation and unemployment, i.e., an inverse relationship between them. The curve suggests that lower the inflation, higher the unemployment and higher the inflation, lower the unemployment.[29] During the 1960s, this idea was among the most important theories of the modern economists. This concept is named after the economist who developed it – Alban William Housego Phillips (1914–15). Bill Phillips (popular name) was an electrical engineer from New Zealand and was an economist at the London School of Economics when he propounded the idea. In 'The Relation between Unemployment and the Rate of Change of Money Wage Rates in the United Kingdom, 1861–1951' (published in *Economica* in 1958), he provided empirical evidence to support his ideas.[30]

By the early 1960s, an economic wisdom emerged around the world that by following a certain kind of monetary policy, unemployment could be checked forever and at the cost of a slightly higher inflation, unemployment could be reduced permanently. The central banks of the developed world started framing the required kind of monetary policies mixing the trade-off between inflation and unemployment. The idea became popular among the developing economies too by the late 1960s, though they were a bit confused, as most of them were fighting the menace of higher inflations (double digit) along with high level of unemployment.[31]

By the early 1970s, two American economists, Milton Friedman (Nobel Laureate, 1976) and Edmund Phelps, challenged the idea of the Phillips Curve. According to them the trade-off between inflation and unemployment was only short-term because once people came to expect higher inflation, they started demanding higher wages and, thus, unemployment will rise back to its *natural rate*.[32] They advocated that there was no long-term trade-off between inflation and unemployment. In the long run, monetary policy can influence inflation. They suggested that if monetary policy tried to hold unemployment below its natural rate, inflation will be rising to a higher level, which is also known as the **non-accelerating inflation rate of unemployment (NAIRU)**.[33] The NAIRU is that rate of unemployment which is consistent with a constant rate of inflation. It means at NAIRU, the upward and downward forces on price (inflation) and wage (unemployment) neutralise each other, and there is no tendency of change in the rate of inflation. We may say that the NAIRU is the lowest unemployment rate that an economy can sustain without any upward pressure on inflation rate.

Word Bank

Natural Rate of Unemployment

The unemployment rate that occurs at full employment when the economy is producing at potential output (i.e., GDP), is usually called the natural rate of unemployment.

Reflation

Reflation is a situation often deliberately brought by the government to reduce unemployment and increase demand by going for higher levels of economic growth.[34] Governments opt for higher public expenditures, tax cuts, interest rate cuts, and so on. Fiscal deficit rises, extra money is generally printed at higher level of growth, wages increase and there is almost no improvement in unemployment.

Reflation can also be understood from a different angle - when the economy is crossing through the

29. Stiglitz and Walsh, *Economics*, op. cit., pp. 821-2.
30. *Penguin Dictionary of Economics*, op. cit., pp. 291-8.
31. G. M. Meier and J. E. Ranch, *Leading Issues in Economic Development* (New Delhi: Oxford University Press, 2006), pp. 31-9.
32. Stiglitz and Walsh, *Economics*, op. cit., p. 822.
33. Samuelson and Nordhaus, *Economics*, op. cit., pp. 680-7.
34 *Collins Dictionary of Economics*, op. cit., p. 446.

cycle of recession (low inflation, high unemployment, low demand, etc.) and the government takes some economic policy decisions to revive the economy from recession, certain goods see sudden and temporary increase in their prices, such price rise is also known as reflation.

Stagflation

Stagflation is a situation in an economy when both inflation and unemployment are at higher levels, contrary to conventional belief. Such a situation first arose in the 1970s in the US economy (average unemployment rate above 6 per cent and the average rate of inflation above 7 per cent)[35] and in many Euro-American economies. This took place as a result of oil price increases of 1973 and 1979 and anticipation of higher inflation. The situation of stagflation continued till the early 1980s. Conventional thinking that a trade-off existed between inflation and unemployment (i.e., Phillips Curve) was falsified and several economies switched over to alternative ways of economic policies, such as monetaristic and supply-side economics.

When the economy is passing through a cycle of stagnation (i.e., long period of low aggregate demand in relation to its productive capacity) and the government shuffles with the economic policy, a sudden and temporary price rise is seen in some of the items - such inflation is also known as stagflation. Stagflation is basically a combination of high inflation and low growth.[36]

INFLATION TARGETING

The announcement of an official target range for inflation is known as inflation targeting. It is carried out by the Central Bank in an economy as a part of their monetary policy to realise the objective of a ***stable*** rate of inflation[37] (the Government of India [GoI] asked the RBI to perform this function in the early 1970s).

India commenced inflation targeting 'formally' in *February 2015* when an agreement between the GoI and the RBI was signed related to it - the **Agreement on Monetary Policy Framework**. The agreement provides the aim of inflation targeting in this way - it is essential to have a modern monetary framework to meet the challenge of an increasingly complex economy. The objective of monetary policy is to primarily maintain *price stability*, while keeping in mind the objective of *growth*. The highlights of the agreement are as given below:

- The RBI will aim to bring CPI-C Inflation below **6** per cent by January 2016. The target for financial year 2016-17 and all subsequent years shall be 4 per cent with a band of ± 2 per cent (it means the 'healthy range of inflation' to be 2-6 per cent).
- RBI to publish the Operating Target(s) and establish an Operating Procedure of monetary policy to achieve the target. Any change in the operating target(s) and operating procedure in response to evolving macro-financial conditions shall also be published.
- Every six months, the RBI to publish a document explaining:
    - Source of inflation;
    - Forecasts of inflation for the period between six and eighteen months from the date of the publication of the document; and
- The RBI shall be seen to have failed to meet the target if inflation is:
    - More than 6 per cent for three consecutive quarters for the financial year 2015-16 and all subsequent years.
    - Less than 2 per cent for three consecutive quarters in 2016-17 and all subsequent years.
- If the RBI fails to meet the target, it shall set out in a report to the GoI:
    - the reasons for its failure to achieve the target underset in this agreement;
    - remedial actions proposed to be taken by the RBI; and
    - an estimate of the time period within which the target would be achieved pursuant to timely implementation of proposed remedial actions.
- Any dispute regarding the interpretation or implementation of the agreement to be resolved between the Governor, RBI and the GoI.

It should be noted that the *Urjit Patel Committee* set up by the RBI on monetary policy gave similar advice by early 2014 - the move is seen as a follow-up to this. This way India joined the club of inflation targeting countries such as United States, United Kingdom, European Union,

---

[35] Stiglitz and Walsh, *Economics*, op. cit., p. 478.

[36] C. Rangarajan, *Indian Economy: Essays on Money and Finance* (New Delhi: UBSPD, 1998), p. 58.

[37] Samuelson and Nordhaus, *Economics*, op. cit., p. 723.

Japan, South Korea, China, Indonesia and Brazil. It was New Zealand which opted for inflation targeting in 1989 for the first time in the world.[38]

Two Regimes After the completion of the first regime (i.e., 2016-21) the RBI was given the second regime (i.e., 2021-26) each of a 5-year period. For both of the regimes, the Government gave the same 4 per cent (±2) target range to the Central bank for inflation targeting.

Performance The experience of inflation targeting has been 'satisfactory' in the country. As per the ***Economic Survey 2025-26***, most of the global rating agencies have acknowledged its effectivenees– as per the S & P, *"monetary policy reform to switch to inflation targeting has reaped dividends. Inflationary expectations are better anchored than they were a decade ago. Between 2008 and 2014, India's inflation reached double-digits on numerous occasions. In the past three years, despite volatility in global energy prices and supply-side shocks, CPI growth averaged 5.5 per cent. In recent months, it stayed at the lower bound of the RBI target range of 2-6 per cent. These developments, coupled with a deep domestic capital market, reflect a more stable and supportive environment for monetary settings."*

Skewflation

Economists usually distinguish between inflation and a relative price increase. 'Inflation' refers to a sustained, across-the-board price increase, whereas 'a relative price increase' is a reference to an episodic price rise pertaining to one or a small group of commodities. This leaves a ***third phenomenon***, namely one in which there is a price rise of one or a small group of commodities over a sustained period of time, without a traditional designation. '**Skewflation**' is a relatively new term to describe this third category of price rise.

Scan this QR Code to watch a author's video lecture that simplifies this topic

In India, food prices rose steadily during the last months of 2009 and the early months of 2010, even though the prices of non-food items continued to be relatively stable. As this somewhat unusual phenomenon stubbornly persisted, policymakers conferred on how to bring it to an end. The term 'skewflation' made an appearance in internal documents of the Government of India and then appeared in print in the ***Economic Survey 2009–10***.

The **skewedness** of inflation in India in the early months of 2010 was obvious from the fact that food price inflation crossed the 20 per cent mark in multiple months, whereas WPI inflation never once crossed 11 per cent. It may be pointed out that the skewflation had gradually given way to a lower-grade generalised inflation (with the economy in the middle of 2011 inflating at around 9 per cent with food and non-food price increasing roughly at the same level).

Given that other nations have faced similar problems, the use of this term picked up quickly, with the ***Economist*** magazine (*January 24, 2011*), in an article entitled 'Price Rises in China: Inflated Fears', wondering if China was beginning to suffer from an Indian-style skewflation.

BASE EFFECT[39]

It refers to the impact of the rise in price level (i.e., last year's inflation) in the previous year over the corresponding rise in price levels in the current year (i.e., current inflation). If the price index had risen at a high rate in the corresponding period of the previous year, leading to a high inflation rate, some of the potential rise is already factored in, therefore, a similar absolute increase in the price index in the current year will lead to a relatively lower inflation rate. On the other hand, if the inflation rate was too low in the corresponding period of the previous year, even a relatively smaller rise in the price index will arithmetically give a high rate of current inflation. For example:

[38] New Zealand passed a law to do this with a target of 0 to 2 per cent inflation with a provision that the Governor of the Reserve Bank of New Zealand could be fired if inflation crosses the 2 per cent upper limit–now this target range has been revised to 1 to 3 per cent (Stiglitz and Walsh, *Economics*, op. cit., p. 849).

[39] J. E. Stiglitz and C. E. Walsh, Economics (N. York: W. W. Norton & Company, USA), p. 478.

	Price Index				Inflation		
	2017	2018	2019	2020	2018	2019	2020
Jan	100	120	140	160	20	16.67	14.29

The index has increased by 20 points in all the three years, *viz.* 2018, 2019 and 2020. However, the inflation rate (calculated on 'year-on-year' basis) tends to decline over the three years from 20 per cent in 2018 to 14.29 per cent in 2020. This is because the absolute increase of 20 points in the price index in each year increases the *base year price index* by an equivalent amount, while the absolute increase in price index remains the same. The 'year-on-year' inflation is calculated by the following formula:

> Current Inflation Rate = [(Current Price Index – Last year's Price Index)]/Last year's Price Index] × 100

EFFECTS OF INFLATION

There are multi-dimensional effects of inflation on an economy both at the micro and macro levels. It redistributes income, distorts relative prices, destabilises employment, tax, saving and investment policies, and finally it may bring in recession and depression in an economy. A brief and objective overview of the effects of inflation is given below:

1. **On Creditors and Debtors:** Inflation redistributes wealth from creditors to debtors, i.e., lenders suffer, and borrowers benefit out of inflation. The opposite effect takes place when inflation falls (i.e., deflation).
2. **On Lending:** With the rise in inflation, lending institutions feel the pressure of higher lending. Institutions do not revise the nominal rate of interest as the 'real cost of borrowing' (i.e., nominal rate of interest minus inflation) falls by the same percentage with which inflation rises.
3. **On Aggregate Demand:** Rising inflation indicates rising aggregate demand as well as comparatively lower supply and higher purchasing capacity among the consumers. Usually, higher inflation suggests that producers increase their production level as it is generally considered as an indication of higher demand in the economy.
4. **On Investment:** Investment in the economy is boosted by the inflation (in the short run) because of two reasons:
   - **(i)** Higher inflation indicates higher demand and suggests that entrepreneurs expand their production level and
   - **(ii)** Higher the inflation, lower the cost of loan (as shown above in no. 2)
5. **On Income:** Inflation affects the income of individuals and firms alike. An increase in inflation increases the 'nominal' value of income, while the 'real' value of income remains the same. Increased price levels erode the purchasing power of money in the short run, but in the long run the income levels also increase (making the nominal value of income to go upward). It means, in a given period of time income may go up due to two reasons, *viz.* inflationary situation and increased earning. The concept of 'GDP Deflator' (GDP at current prices divided by GDP at constant prices) gives the idea of 'inflation effect' on income over a given period.

GDP DEFLATOR

This is the ratio of the GDP at current prices to that of the constant prices. It is derived by using the following formula:

> GDP Deflator = GDP at Current Prices/GDP at Constant Prices × 100

This shows the increase in the value of GDP due to increase in inflation in between the period – base year (i.e., the year of constant prices) and the current year. This is why it is used as a measure of inflation (also known as 'implicit price deflator').[39] Though countries use inflation indices to measure inflation, these indices are not able to capture all goods and services produced by them. In the case of India, while services are not included in the WPI, the CPI contains only those goods and services which households purchase for consumption (such as food, clothing, health, education, etc.) and misses several other goods and services (such as intermediate goods, services required by firms, etc.). Since the deflator covers the entire range of goods and services produced in the economy, it is seen as a more comprehensive measure of inflation.

6. **On Saving:** Holding money does not remain an intelligent economic decision (because money loses value with every increase in inflation), which is why people visit banks more frequently and try to hold the least money with themselves and put the maximum with the banks in their savings accounts (to minimise the loss in value of money with interest earned on it, provided the bank is paying a positive interest on the savings account). This is also known as the ***shoe leather cost***[40] of inflation (as it consumes the precious time of the people visiting the bank frequently tagging their shoe). It means that savings rate increases. But this happens as a short-term effect of inflation. In the long run, higher inflation depletes the saving rate in an economy. Just the opposite situation arises when inflation falls or shows falling traits with decreasing saving, in the short run and increasing saving in the long run, respectively.

7. **On Expenditures:** Consumption as well as investment of both of the expenditures rise as inflation rises. Increased prices make our consumption levels fall as goods and services we buy get costlier. We see a tendency among the people to cut their consumption levels aimed at neutralising the impact of price rise - making consumption expenditure fall. The exact opposite occurs once prices head downward.

   On the other hand, inflations make 'investment' expenditure increase as a result of decreased cost of money/finance (inflation brings benefit to borrower - known as 'inflation premium'). In times of price fall just the opposite takes place.

8. **On Tax:** On tax structure of the economy, inflation creates two distortions:

   (i) Taxpayers suffer while paying their direct and indirect taxes. As indirect taxes are imposed *ad valorem* (**on value**), increased prices of goods make taxpayers to pay increased indirect taxes (such as cenvat, VAT, etc., in India).

   Similarly, due to inflation, direct tax (income tax, interest tax, etc.) burden of the taxpayers also increases as taxpayer's gross income moves to the upward ***slabs*** of official tax brackets (but the real value of money does not increase due to inflation; in fact, it falls). This problem is also known as ***bracket creep*** - i.e., ***inflation-induced tax increases***.[41] Some economies (as in the United States and many European countries) have *indexed* their tax provisions to neutralise this distortion on the direct taxpayers.

   (ii) The extent to which tax collections of the government are concerned, inflation increases the nominal value of the gross tax revenue, while real value of the tax collection does not compare with the current pace of inflation as there is a lag (***delay***) in the tax collection in all economies.

   But governments get an advantage on their interest burden, on their borrowings as inflation benefits borrowers. This benefit, however, depends upon the contemporary levels of fiscal deficit and the total national debt.

   In the case of a government incurring high fiscal deficit (increased borrowing, printing currency), inflation functions as a tax, i.e., ***inflation tax*** *via* which the government fulfils its expenditure by cutting down the expenditure and consumption of the people.

9. **On Exchange Rate:** With every inflation the currency of the economy ***depreciates*** (loses its exchange value in front of a foreign currency) provided it follows the flexible currency regime. Though it is a comparative matter, there might be inflationary pressure on the foreign currency against which the exchange rate is compared.

10. **On Export:** With inflation, exportable items of an economy gain competitive prices in the world market. Due to this, the volume of export increases (keep in mind that the value of export decreases here) and thus export income increases in the economy. It means export segment of the economy benefits due to inflation. Importing partners of the economy exert pressure for a stable exchange rate as their imports start increasing and exports start decreasing (see the next point).

11. **On Import:** Inflation gives an economy the advantage of lower imports and import substitution as foreign goods become costlier.

[40] Samuelson and Nordhaus, *Economics*, op. cit., p. 674.

[41] Ibid.

But in the case of compulsory imports (i.e., oil, technology, drugs, etc.), the economy does not get this benefit and loses more foreign currency instead of saving it.

12. **On Trade Balance:** In the case of a developed economy, inflation makes trade balance favourable, while for the developing economies inflation is unfavourable for their balance of trade. This is because of composition of their foreign trade. The benefit to export which inflation brings into a developing economy is usually lower than the loss it incurs due to its compulsory imports which become costlier due to inflation.
13. **On Employment:** Inflation increases employment in the short run, but becomes neutral or even negative in the long run (see the Phillips Curve and the NAIRU in the earlier sections).
14. **On Wages:** Inflation increases the nominal (face) value of wages, while their real value falls. That is why there is a negative impact of inflation on the purchasing power and living standard of wage employees. To neutralise this negative impact the Indian government provides ***dearness allowance*** (DA) to its employees twice a year.
15. **On the Self-employed:** Inflation has a neutralising impact on the self-employed people in the long run. But in the short run they also get affected as the economy as a whole gets affected.
16. **On the Economy:** 16. On Business/Industry: As inflation rises, businesses/industries are able to produce more, earn more and expand more. This happens due to multiple reasons–demand is higher, cost of loan is lower, and inflation brings an additional element of profit.
17. **On Economic Growth:** A rise in inflation raises economic output/growth. However, this rise is nominal only and that is why to measure real rise in output, inflation is deducted from it. The concept of *GDP deflator* is used here to understand the impact of inflation on output/growth over a period of time.
18. **On Fiscal Deficit:** A rise in inflation increases governments' spendings which results in higher fiscal deficits. However, governments enjoy double benefits due to higher inflation–firstly, their cost of borrowing decreases and secondly, they collect more taxes [see *Effects of Inflation* on lenders and tax collections].
19. **On Government:** A rise in inflation brings three benefits to the governments:
    - **(a)** Tax collections increase,
    - **(b)** Interest liabilities decrease (due to favourable inflation premium), and
    - **(c)** Seigniorage (i.e., creating/printing of new money) takes place.
20. **On Economy:** Economic history suggests that only a particular range of inflation (CPI-C of 2 to 6 per cent in the case of India) is good for an economy. Inflation rates beyond the limits of the range create multiple negative cycles for the economy. These negative cycles may be slowdown, stagnation, recession, depression and even bust (which have been discussed under a separate section BUSINESS CYCLE in this chapter).

Experiences of the world economies in the late 1980s show that only a particular level of inflation is healthy for an economy. This specific level of inflation was called the 'range' of inflation and every economy needs to calculate its own range. Inflation beyond both the limits of the range is never healthy for any economy. In the case of India, it is considered 2 to 6 per cent at CPI(C), which is also known as the 'comfort zone' of inflation in India since 2015. Similarly for Australia, New Zealand, the United States, Canada and the European Union, the healthy range today is 1 to 3 per cent. This is why several economies today are engaged in ***inflation targeting***.

INFLATION IN INDIA

Every economy calculates its inflation for efficient financial administration as the multi-dimensional effects of inflation make it necessary. India calculates its inflation on two price indices, i.e., the WPI and the CPI. While the WPI inflation is used at the macro-level policymaking, the CPI inflation is used for micro-level analyses. The inflation at the WPI is the inflation of the economy. Both the indices follow the 'point-to-point' method and may be shown in ***points*** (i.e., digit) as well as in ***percentage*** relative to a particular ***base year***.

WHOLESALE PRICE INDEX (WPI)

The first index number of wholesale prices commenced in India from the week commencing on January 10, 1942. It was having the base week ending August 19, 1939 = 100, which was published by the office of the Economic Adviser to the Government of India (Ministry of Industry).[42] Independent India followed the same series with a greater number of commodities included in the index. Several changes regarding inclusion of commodities, assigning them the logical weights took place in the coming times including revisions in the *base years* for the WPI. The WPI base year has been revised five times till date. The base years are as given below:

1. 1952-53 Base Year (112 Commodities) issued from June 1952.
2. 1961-62 Base Year (139 Commodities) issued from July 1969.
3. 1970-71 Base Year (360 Commodities) issued from January 1977.
4. 1981-82 Base Year (447 Commodities) issued from January 1989.
5. 1993-94 Base Year (435 Commodities) issued from July 1999.
6. 2004-05 Base Year (676 Commodities) released in September 2011.
7. 2011-12 Base Year (697 Commodities) released in May 2017.

Revised WPI

The new series of the WPI was released[43] by the Government with the *revised* base year as 2011-12. The existing base year was 2004-05. The new base year aligns with the base year of other indicators like the Gross Domestic Product (GDP) and Index of Industrial Production (IIP). A Working Group was set up (March 2012) by the Government to advise on the new series of the WPI (headed by Saumitra Chaudhuri, Member, erstwhile Planning Commission). *Key highlights* of the revised series are as given below:

- WPI continues to constitute three major groups - Primary Articles, Fuel and Power, and Manufactured Products. The number of items has been increased from 676 to 697 in all the 199 new items have been added and 146 old items have been dropped.
- It is more representative with increase in number of quotations from 5482 to 8331 - an increase by 2849 quotations (52 per cent).
- The prices used for compilation do not include indirect taxes in order to remove impact of fiscal policy. This is in consonance with international practices and will make the new WPI conceptually closer to Producer Price Index (PPI).
- Item-level aggregates for new WPI have been compiled using Geometric Mean (GM) following international best practice and as is currently used for compilation of the CPI-C.

The major changes in weights, number of items and quotations between WPI 2004-05 and WPI 2011-12 are given in ***Table 8.1***.

- A new Wholesale Food Price Index (WPFI) has been introduced - combining the Food Articles (belonging to the group Primary Articles) and Food Products (belonging to the group Manufactured Products).

  Together with the Consumer Food Price Index (CPFI) released by Central Statistics Office, this would help monitor the price situation of food items better.
- To keep pace with the changing structure of the economy, it is necessary to follow a dynamic review process of the WPI and related aspects of it. That is why the Government has set up (for the first time) a high-level Technical Review Committee (TRC) for this purpose. The committee is headed by the Secretary, Department of Industrial Policy and Promotion (DIPP).

NEW WPI IN THE OFFING

Meanwhile, a *Working Group* (headed by Ramesh Chand, member NITI Aayog) was set up by the government in *mid-2019* to look into various issues related to the WPI, such as revising the current series of 2011–12 to a new base year; reviewing its commodity basket; reviewing the existing system of price collection in particular for manufacturing sector and suggesting changes for improvement; and suggesting a roadmap to switch over to PPI from the existing WPI.

---

42 *Economic Survey 2006-07* (New Delhi: Ministry of Finance, GoI, 2007), p. 85.

43 *Office of Economic Advisor*, Department for Promotion of Industry and Internal Trade (DPIIT), Ministry of Commerce and Industry, GoI, New Delhi, 12 May 2017.

Table 8.1 Major Groups and their Weights

Major Groups	Weight		No. of Items		No. of Quotations	
	2004-05	2011-12	2004-05	2011-12	2004-05	2011-12
All commodities	100.00	100.00	676	697	5482	8331
Primary articles	20.12	22.62	102	117	579	983
Fuel and power	14.91	13.15	19	16	72	442
Manufactured products	64.97	64.23	555	564	4831	6906

Source: *Office of Economic Advisor*, Department for Promotion of Industry and Internal Trade (DPIIT), Ministry of Commerce and Industry, GoI, New Delhi, 12 May 2017.

CONSUMER PRICE INDEX

India has been measuring inflation at the consumer prices besides at the wholesale prices. But in place of a single[44] CPI, India was managing with four differing types of the CPIs due to the socio-economic differentiations found among the consumers (i.e., people's choices of consumption and their purchasing power). Though in 2011-12 the government announced a new set of consumer indices (i.e., CPI-R, CPI-U and CPI-C), datasets for the older CPIs (to be phased out in coming times) are still announced by the National Statistical Office (NSO). A brief review of the older CPIs is given below:

1. **CPI-IW:** The Consumer Price Index for Industrial Worker (CPI-IW) is compiled by the Labour Bureau on a monthly basis which measures changes in the retail prices of a fixed *basket* of goods and services (a total of 463 items) being consumed by an average working-class family. To capture the latest consumption pattern, the base year[45] of the index was revised to 2016 (from 2001) in October 2020. Besides being a guide for policy making, the index is used for fixing/revising wages, regulating the DAs of manual workers and employees of central and state governments (i.e., industrial workers from the existing *seven sectors* such as Factories, Mines, Plantation, Railways, Public Motor Transport Undertakings, Electricity Generating and Distributing Establishments and Ports and Docks).
2. **CPI-UNME:** The Consumer Price Index for the Urban Non-Manual Employees (CPI-UNME) has 1984-85 (first base year was 1958-59) as the base year and 146-365 commodities in the basket for which data are collected at 59 centres in the country - data collection frequency is monthly with two weeks' time lag.[46]

   This price index has limited use, and it is basically used for determining DAs of employees of some foreign companies operating in India (i.e., airlines, communications, banking, insurance, embassies and other financial services). It is also used under the Income Tax Act to determine ***capital gains*** and by the CSO (Central Statistical Organisation) for deflating selected services sector's contribution to the GDP at factor cost and current prices to calculate the corresponding figure at constant prices. Since the publication of the CPI (U) started, the index was discontinued from January 2011.
3. **CPI-AL:** The Consumer Price Index for Agricultural Labourers (CPI-AL) has 1986-87 as its base year with 260 commodities in its basket. The data are collected in 600 villages with a monthly frequency and has three weeks' time lag.

   This index is used for revising minimum wages for agricultural labourers in different states. As the consumption pattern of agricultural labourers has changed since 1986-87 (its base year), the

[44] The economies of the Euro-American region have a single CPI as the majority of consumers show the same consumer behaviour (see J. B. Rosser and M. V. Rosser, *Comparative Economics in a Transforming World Economy* (Cambridge: Prentice Hall, MIT Press, 2004)).

[45] *Economic Survey 2020-21*, vol. 2 (New Delhi: Ministry of Finance, GoI), pp. 166-68.

[46] *Economic Survey 2001-02* (New Delhi: Ministry of Finance, GoI), p. 90.

Labour Bureau proposes to revise the existing base year of this index. For the revision, the consumer expenditure data collected by the NSSO during its 61st NSS Round (2004-05) is proposed to be used.

The governments at the Centre and states remain vigilant regarding the changes in this index as it shows the price impact on the most vulnerable segment of the society; this segment spends almost 75 per cent of its total income on the purchase of food articles. Governments' failure to stabilise the index in the long range can make them politically volatile and be translated into political debacles. That is why the FCI is always kept ready to supply cheaper foodgrains in the situations of any price rise.

4. **CPI-RL:** There is yet another Consumer Price Index for the Rural Labourers (CPI-RL) with 1983 as the base year; data are collected at 600 villages on a monthly frequency with three weeks' time lag, its basket containing 260 commodities.

   The agricultural and rural labourers in India create an overlap, i.e., the same labourers work as the rural labourers once the farm sector has either low or no employment scope. Probably, due to this reason this index was dropped by the government in 2001-02.[47] But after the government change at the Centre, the index was revived again.[48]

Revision in the CPI

In 2011-12, Government announced a new set of the consumer price indices - *CPI-R* for the rural market, *CPI-U* for the urban market, and by combining them a 'national' CPI. The national consumer price index is called *CPI-C* (where 'C' stands for Combined). In order to make them more robust, the CPIs were further revised in **2015** by incorporating the following changes:

1. The base year has been changed from 2010 = 100 to 2012 = 100.
2. The basket of items and their weighing diagrams have been prepared using the Modified Mixed Reference Period (MMRP) data of Consumer Expenditure Survey (CES), 2011-12 of the *68th Round* of National Sample Survey (NSS). This has been carried out to make it consistent with the *international practice* of shorter reference period for most of the food items and longer reference period for the items of infrequent consumption. The weighing diagrams of old series of CPI were based on the Uniform Reference Period (URP) data of CES, 2004-05, of the 61st Round of NSS.

   With this change in the weighing diagrams, the gap between Weight Reference Year and Price Reference Year (Base Year), which was *six years* in the old series, has now been reduced to *six months* only. Due to change in the *consumption pattern* from 2004-05 to 2011-12, the weighing diagrams (share of expenditure to total expenditure) have changed. A comparison of weighing diagrams of the old and revised series is given in ***Table 8.2***.
3. The number of *Groups*, which was five in the old series, has now been increased to six. 'Pan, tobacco and intoxicants', which was a Sub-group under the group 'Food, beverages and tobacco', has now been made as a separate group. Accordingly, the group 'Food, beverages and tobacco' has been changed to 'Food and beverages'.
4. Egg, which was part of the sub-group 'Egg, fish and meat' in the old series, has now been made as a separate sub-group. Accordingly, the earlier sub-group has been modified as 'Meat and fish'.
5. The elementary/item indices are now being computed using Geometric Mean (GM) of the Price Relatives of Current Prices with respect to Base Prices of different markets in consonance with the international practice. In the old series, Arithmetic Mean (AM) was used for that purpose. The advantage of using GM is that it moderates the volatility of the indices as GM is less affected by extreme values.
6. Prices of PDS items under *Antyodaya Anna Yojana* (AAY) have also been included for compilation of indices of PDS items, in addition to Above Poverty Line (APL) and Below Poverty Line (BPL) prices being taken in the old series.
7. Sample size for collection of house rent data for compilation of *House Rent Index*, which was 6,684 rented dwellings in the old series, has now been doubled to 13,368 rented dwellings in the revised series.

[47] *Economic Survey 2001-02* (New Delhi: Ministry of Finance, GoI), p. 91.

[48] *Economic Survey 2006-07* (New Delhi: Ministry of Finance, GoI), p. 90.

Table 8.2 Weighing in Old and Revised Series

Group Description	Old Series of CPI (Weights Computed on the Basis CES 2004-05)			Revised Series of CPI (Weights Computed on the Basis CES 2011-12)		
	Rural	Urban	Combd.	Rural	Urban	Combd.
Food and beverages	56.39	35.81	47.58	54.18	36.29	45.86
Pan, tobacco and intoxicants	2.72	1.34	2.13	3.26	1.36	2.35
Clothing and footwear	5.36	3.91	4.73.	7.36	5.57	6.53
Housing	-	22.54	9.77	-	21.67	10.07
Fuel and light	10.42	8.40	9.49	7.94	5.50	6.84
Miscellaneous	24.91	28.00	26.31	27.26	29.53	28.32
Total	**100.00**	**100.00**	**100.00**	**100.00**	**100.00**	**100.00**

Source: CSO, February 2015. Here, 'Combd.' stands for Combined while '-' stands for 'not available'.

8. Apart from All-India CPIs (Rural, Urban, Combined) for sub-group, group and general index (all-groups), which were released for the old series, all India Item CPIs (Combined) will also be available.

9. The Consumer Food Price Indices (Rural, Urban, Combined) will be compiled as weighted average of the indices of following sub-groups, as practised earlier in the old series (only the weights have been revised).

Table 8.3 All India Weights of different Sub-groups within Consumer Food Price Index

Sub-Group Code	Sub-group Description	Rural	Urban	Combined
(1)	(2)	(3)	(4)	(5)
1.1.01	Cereals and products	26.14	22.24	24.77
1.1.02	Meat and fish	9.26	9.23	9.25
1.1.03	Egg	1.05	1.21	1.10
1.1.04	Milk and products	16.34	17.98	16.92
1.1.05	Oils and fats	8.90	9.49	9.11
1.1.06	Fruits	6.10	9.80	7.40
1.1.07	Vegetables	15.78	14.88	15.46
1.1.08	Pulses and products	6.25	5.84	6.11
1.1.09	Sugar and confectionery	3.61	3.28	3.49
1.1.10	Spices	6.57	6.05	6.39
All Sub-groups of CFPI		100.00	100.00	100.00

Source: CSO, February 2015. Here, CPFI stands for Consumer Food Price Index.

CPI SERIES 2024

The revised CPI Series 2024 was released by the Ministry of Statistics and Programme Implementation (MoSPI) in February 2026. Major changes effected in the new series are as given below:

Structural Changes

Base Year: Shifted to 2024 = 100 (from 2012 = 100) to align the price reference period closely with the weight reference period.

Weight Reference Period: is taken of the *Household Consumption Expenditure Survey (HCES) 2023–24* (the older weight reference was based on the Consumer Expenditure Survey 2011–12).

Expanded Basket: Total items in the index increased from 299 to **358** (goods increased from 259 to 308 while services increased from 40 to **50**).

Global Standard: The latest **COICOP 2018** (Classification of Individual Consumption According to Purpose) framework of the UNO has been adopted (which replaced the COICOP 1999), increasing the number of divisions from 6 groups to **12 divisions**.

New Inclusions: Rural house rent, online media/streaming services (OTT), pen-drives, external hard disks, and value-added dairy products, etc. have been added (while many items such as VCR, DVD players, tape recorders, CDs/cassettes, second-hand clothing, library charges, horse cart fares etc. have been dropped off as they became irrelevant).

Digital Data: It incorporates **e-commerce prices** from 12 large towns and administrative data for rail and air fares.

Weight Change

The new series re-balances the importance of various categories to reduce volatility from food prices:

Food & Beverages: Weight reduced from 45.86 per cent to **36.75** per cent, though it remains the largest component.

Housing & Utilities: Weight increased from 10.07 per cent to **17.67** per cent (now includes water, electricity, and gas).

Other Key Weights: Transport carries 8.8 per cent, health 6.1 per cent, education Services: 3.33 per cent, and Personal Care & Miscellaneous 5.04 per cent.

Latest Inflation Data (January 2026)

The first official data under the new series was as follows:

Headline Retail Inflation at **2.75** per cent (Combined, i.e., CPI-C), with Rural at 2.73 per cent and Urban at 2.77 per cent.

Food Inflation (CFPI) at **2.13** per cent.

Housing Inflation at **2.05** per cent.

Core Inflation at approximately **3.4** per cent (reflecting stable underlying price pressures).

Linking Factor: To maintain historical continuity, MoSPI provided a *linking factor* of 0.5267 (for Combined General Index) to convert 2012-base data to the new 2024-base.

TRENDS IN INFLATION

Inflation has been a highly sensitive issue in India right since Independence, and it has been so during the ongoing reforms process period, too. It has an incessant tendency of resulting into 'double digits', taking politically explosive proportions like governments falling at the Centre and state levels due to price rise of the commodities such as edible oil, onion, potato, etc. In such situations the government in general has been taking recourse to tighter money supply to contain the state-level disturbances due to price rise of the commodities such as edible oil, onion and potato although it has contained inflation, but at the cost of higher growth. Price rise got rooted in India's political psyche in such a way that the government did check frequent famines quickly at the cost of long-term endemic hunger and sustained malnutrition.[49]

Decadal inflation in India looks comparatively normal with reference to many developing economies.[50] But it has sporadic incidences of double-digit tendencies mainly due to supply-side shortfalls caused by droughts (monsoon failures), price rise of crude oil in the international market or fund diversions due to wars (the Chinese war of 1962 and

[49] P. Bardhan agrees to A. Sen ('How is India Doing?', New York Review of Books, December 1982) in: "A Political Economy Perspective on Development," in *Indian Economy Problems and Prospects*, ed. B. Jalan (New Delhi: Penguin Books, 1992), p. 369.

[50] Rosser and Rosser, *Comparative Economics in a Transforming World Economy.*

the Pakistan wars of 1965-66 and 1971). The decadal inflation in India has been as given below:[51]

1. **During the 1950s:** remained at 1.7 per cent.
2. **During the 1960s:** remained at 6.4 per cent.
3. **During the 1970s:** remained at 9.0 per cent.
4. **During the 1980s:** remained at 8.0 per cent.
5. **During the 1990s:** remained at 9.5 per cent (though it reached 0.5 per cent by the fourth quarter of the fiscal 1998-99)
6. **During the 2000s:** Inflation was at lower levels between 2000 and 2008 (from 3 to 5 per cent). But from 2009 onwards it started moving upward with 'stubborn' tendencies.[52] Between 2009 and 2013, the headline inflation remained stuck at uncomfortable levels, primarily due to 'food articles' (*food inflation*) led by protein-rich items (*protein inflation*) in the consequence of shift in dietary habit, income effect (*via* MGNREGA kind of schemes), increased wages, increase in prices of commodities in the global market (especially, food articles), costlier fodder, costlier energy and fuel, etc. By late 2010, India had the phenomenon of *skewflation* with inflation being in the range of 9-10 per cent.
7. **During the 2010s:** From 2010-11 to 2013-14 inflation remained higher - the average inflation at WPI and CPI was 8 per cent and 9.7 per cent, respectively. Food inflation, led by protein items, breached into double digit.[53] Since mid 2014 inflation started moderating - WPI inflation remained in negative (–5.1 per cent by August 2015) and CPI inflation in positive (at 4.9 per cent by the end of December 2016) - showing a ***wedge*** (i.e., difference) of 10 per cent which narrowed down to 0.2 per cent by the end of 2018-19.

During 2019-20, while the WPI did show falling trends and fell down to 1.7 per cent (chiefly caused by supply glut at wholesale level), the CPI-C ended with 4.8 per cent (caused by increased demand at the retail level and supply bottlenecks). The year did show a much higher price rise in urban areas in comparison to the rural counterpart (in relation to almost all items with food being the prime cause).

RECENT TRENDS: As per the Economic Survey 2025-26, over the *past four years*, inflation has followed a clear downward trajectory from the peak global[54] rate of 8.2 per cent in 2022. The inflationary trends have been summarised[55] below:

- **CPI:** The headline retail inflation (i.e., the CPI-C) declined steadily from 6.7 per cent in 2022-23 to **1.7** per cent in 2025-26 (up to December).
- **WPI:** The factory-gate basic price for producers (i.e., the WPI) has consistently been falling from 9.41 per cent in 2022-23 to **0.04** per cent in 2025-26 (up to December).
- **Core Inflation:** The core inflation has been showing a rising trend in recent years, which rose from 3.19 per cent in April 2024 to 4.62 per cent in December 2025.

Inflationary Causes

A close analysis of inflationary trends does not pinpoint any one reason for inflationary pressures in India. However, experts have cited all good and bad reasons behind it which can be seen as given below:

1. **Structural Inflation:** With few exceptional years, India has been facing the typical problem of bottleneck inflation (i.e., ***structural inflation***) which arises out of shortfalls in the supply of goods, a general crisis of a developing economy, rising demand but lack of investible capital to produce the required level of goods.[56] Whenever the government managed to opt for higher growth by managing higher investible capital, it had inflationary pressures on the economy (seen during the 1970s and 1980s, especially) and growth was sacrificed at the altar of lower inflation (which was politically more justified).[57] Thus, the supply-side

[51] Based on Rangarajan, in B. Jalan (ed.) *Indian Economy: Problems and Prospects, op. cit.*, p. 63.

[52] *Economic Survey 2013-14* (New Delhi: Ministry of Finance, GoI, 2014), pp. 75-77.

[53] *Economic Survey 2014-15*, vol. 2 (New Delhi: Ministry of Finance, GoI, 2015), pp. 69-75.

[54] International Monetary Fund, *World Economic Outlook Update-Global Growth: Divergent and Uncertain* (Washington DC: United Sates of America, January 2025).

[55] *Economic Survey 2025-26* (New Delhi: Ministry of Finance, GoI, January 2026), pp. 207-209.

[56] M. Desai, "Development Perspectives," in *India's Economic Reforms and Development*, ed. I. J. Ahluwalia and I. M. D. Little (New Delhi: Oxford University Press, 1998), p. 41.

[57] J. Bimal, *India's Economic Policy* (New Delhi: Penguin Books, 1992), pp. 52-58.

mismatch remained a long-drawn problem in India for higher inflation. After some time even if the government managed higher expenditure, most of it went to the non-developmental areas, which did show low growth with higher inflation - signs of a stagnating economy.

2. **Cost-Push Inflation:** Due to 'inflation tax' the price of goods and services in India has been rising as the government took alternative recourse to increase its revenue receipts.[58]

   We see it taking place due to higher ***import duties*** on raw materials also.[59] The ***non-value-added*** tax (non-VAT) structure of India in the past was also having a cascading effect on the prices of commodities in the country.[60] The government needed higher revenues to finance its planned development, and thus the above-given factors looked inescapable.

3. **Fiscal Policy:** To finance the developmental requirements of the economy, the governments became trapped in the cyclical process of over-money supply. At first it was done by external borrowings, but by the late 1960s onwards (once ***deficit financing*** got acceptance around the world) the government started taking recourse to heavy internal borrowings as well as printing of fresh currency. A major part of the government's internal borrowing till 2005-06 was contributed by the Reserve Bank of India (RBI) which led to price rise.[61] For any government deficit, if the Central Bank (RBI) is purchasing primary issues of the Government securities or creating fresh advances to the government, the combined effect has to be higher inflation, lower savings rates and lower economic growth[62] - the vices of unsound fiscal policy. The higher fiscal deficit tends to bring about higher interest rates as demand for funds rises, excess demand raises expected inflation and expected depreciation of the currency.[63]

   Once the foreign exchange (Forex) reserves started increasing at a faster pace by the early 2000-01 fiscal period, its cost of maintenance has been translated into higher prices, as the RBI purchases the foreign currencies it supplies into equivalent rupees into the economy, which creates extra demand and the prices go up.[64]

The higher revenue deficits (driven by high interest payments, subsidies, salaries and pensions, basically) and fiscal deficits make the government supply more money which pushes the inflation in the upward direction. Once the Fiscal and Budget Management Act came into force in 2003, the scenario improved in the coming times, though the period from 1999 to 2003 did show high growth with low inflation and the lowest interest rates in India.

Healthy Range of Inflation

Higher inflation and higher growth as a trade-off were questioned in the late 1980s by the developed economies as the economic and social costs of higher inflation also needed policy attention - a costly 'trade-off'.[65] In coming times, most of the world economies opted in favour of a stable inflation (i.e., ***inflation targeting***) though the idea has been ***protested***.[66] India also started inflation stabilisation (informed targeting at WPI) by the early 1970s. It was in 1973 that inflation crossed the 20 per cent mark on account of the international oil price rise and the government (the Indira Gandhi Government) devised a severe anti-inflation package which included directly restricting the disposable incomes of the people (this measure

[58] C. Rangarajan, "Development, Inflation and Monetary Policy," in *India's Economic Reforms and Development*, ed. I. J. Ahluwalia and I. M. D. Little (New Delhi: Oxford University Press, 1998), pp. 56-7.

[59] Jalan, *India's Economic Policy*, op.cit. pp. 191-203.

[60] *Chelliah Committee Report*, 1993.

[61] V. M. Dandekar, "Forty Years After Independence," in *Indian Economy: Problems and Prospects*, ed. B. Jalan (New Delhi: Penguin Books, 1992), pp. 81-8.

[62] Y. V. Reddy, *Lectures on Economic and Financial Sector Reforms in India* (New Delhi: Oxford University Press, 2002), pp. 176-77.

[63] A. Goyal, "Puzzles in India Performance: Deficits Without Disaster," in *India Development Report, 2004-05,* ed. K. S. Parikh and R. Radhakrishna (New Delhi: IGIDR and Oxford University Press, 2005), pp. 191-208.

[64] K. Basu, *India Emerging Economy: Performance and Prospects in the 1990's and Beyond* (New Delhi: Oxford University Press, 2004), pp. 89-103.

[65] S. Fisher, "Modern Central Banking," in *The Future of Central Banking: The Tercentenary Symposium of the Bank of England,* ed. F. Capie et al. (Cambridge: Cambridge University Press, 1994) pp. 262-308.

[66] P. Krugman, "Stable Prices and Fast Growth: Just Say No," *Economist* 31 (1996), pp. 15-18.

was used for the *first* time in India[67]). The package had an impact, and by March 1975 the inflation calmed down to 5.7 per cent. This was the time when the RBI was given a new function 'inflation stabilisation' and India entered the era of monetary controls for inflation. And this is when, there started a debate concerning the healthy range of inflation for the Indian economy, i.e., by the mid-1970s. We may have some official and non-official versions of the suitable range of inflation pointed out from time to time:

1. The ***Chakravarty Committee (1985)*** treated 4 per cent inflation as acceptable for the economy in its report on the monetary system. He also added that this level of price rise will facilitate the purpose of attracting investment for the desired level of growth.
2. The ***Government of India*** accepted a range of 4 to 6 per cent inflation as acceptable for the economy citing the world average of 0 to 3 per cent at the time (1997-98).[68]
3. The RBI Governor ***C. Rangarajan*** advocated that inflation rate must come down initially to 6-7 per cent and eventually to 5-6 per cent on an average over the years.[69]
4. The ***Tarapore Committee*** on Capital Account Convertibility recommended an acceptable range of 3 to 5 per cent inflation for the three-year period (1997-98 to 1999-2000).[70]

June 2003 onwards, the government/the RBI maintained a general policy of keeping inflation below 5 per cent mark - at any cost - as if fixing 4 to 5 per cent as the healthy range of inflation for the economy.[71]

The medium-term objective (i.e., target) of the government was to keep inflation in the 4-4.5 per cent range.[72] One thing should be kept in mind that inflation has always been a political matter in the country. Every time the RBI tried to check the rising inflation *via* monetary measures, a majority of experts objected to it by calling it a move to sacrifice growth for lower price levels. A tighter monetary policy decelerates investment and growth, hampers the growth prospects of the middle class in general and the entrepreneurs in particular while the wage earners as well as the poor segment of society feel relieved (at least in the short term).

In February 2015, India formally commenced the process of 'inflation targeting'. Now, the new monthly CPI (C) is taken as the measure of **headline inflation** and is tracked by the RBI to **anchor** its monetary policy, and the healthy annual range for it is between 2 and 6 per cent.

PRODUCER PRICE INDEX

Producer Price Index (PPI) is a better measure of inflation in comparison to both WPI and CPI. The ongoing process of economic reforms has increasingly connected India to the world which makes it necessary to evolve right comparative indicators. Inflation being among the most vital economic indicators in comparative economics due to which the government proposed to switch over from the WPI to PPI in 2003-04.

Special Features The PPI measures price changes from the perspective of the producer, while CPI from the perspective of the consumer and WPI from the perspective of wholesale 'mandis'. In practice, the wholesalers charge higher prices to retailers, in turn retailers charge higher prices to consumers and the price increase is translated into the higher consumer prices - thus the PPI is useful in having an idea of the consumer prices in the future.[73] In PPI, only basic prices are used while taxes, trade margins and transport costs are excluded. This index is considered a better measure of inflation as price changes at primary and intermediate stages can be tracked before it gets built into the finished goods stage.[74] Due to its better use, many economies have switched over to the PPI -

[67] Ahluwalia and Little, *India Economic Reforms and Development*, op. cit., p. 2.

[68] *Economic Survey 1997-98* (New Delhi: Ministry of Finance, GoI, 1998), p. 92.

[69] Rangarajan, *Development, Inflation and Monetary Policy*, op. cit., pp. 61-63.

[70] We may refer to almost all the credit and monetary policies announced by the RBI during this period.

[71] As the RBI put it in its Credit and Monetary Policy Review of July 31, 2007.

[72] It should be noted here that the level of inflation was below 5 per cent till the new Government came to power and the outgoing Government was blamed to freeze the inflation data to a more politically digestible level (i.e., below 5 per cent). The new Government in the process of preparing a producer price index (PPI) has also committed to make the inflation data automated like the share indices.

[73] Stiglitz and Walsh, *Economics*, op. cit., p. 517.

[74] *Economic Survey 2006-07* (New Delhi: Ministry of Finance, GoI), op. cit., p. 92.

the oldest such series is maintained by the Bureau of Labour Statistics (BLS) for the US economy. The index is capable of measuring prices at the wholesaler or the producer stage and is widely used by private business houses in their price targeting.[75]

By *mid-2019*, Government did set up a ***Working Group*** headed by Ramesh Chand, a member of NITI Aayog, with a wide ***term of reference*** which includes the following issues related to the existing WPI:

1. Suggesting a new base year of WPI. (The last revision in its base year to 2011-12 was done in May 2017.)
2. Reviewing the commodity basket of the WPI and decide on the computational methodology to be adopted for monthly WPI/PPI. (Since 2011-12 significant structural changes have taken place in the economy, and it has become necessary to examine the coverage of commodities, weighting diagram and related issues pertaining to the existing WPI.)
3. Reviewing the existing system of *price collection* in particular for manufacturing sector and suggest changes for improvement. (Data collection method for manufacturing sector has been weak and unable to capture the sector in the real sense.)
4. Devising a new PPI and recommend a roadmap to *switch over from WPI to PPI*. (It has been a long-drawn plan of the Governments to switch over from WPI to PPI - the first Working Group on it was set up in 2004-05 under the chairmanship of Prof. Abhijit Sen, member of the erstwhile Planning Commission, which got inputs from the IMF also. In 2014, another Working Group was set up under Prof. B. N. Goldar to devise a PPI after the RBI began considering CPI-C inflation as a better gauge over the WPI inflation.)

HOUSING PRICE INDEX

India's official Housing Price Index (HPI) was launched in July 2007 in Mumbai. Basically, developed by the Indian home loans regulator, the National Housing Bank (NHB) the index is named ***NHB Residex***.

Currently, it is published for 50 cities (being expanded to cover 100 cities) on a quarterly basis with 2017-18 as the base year. Among 50 cities covered are 21 state/UT capitals and 33 Smart cities. NHB is not computing the composite all India HPI as of now.

Meanwhile, the RBI began compiling an HPI in 2007 with a quarterly HPI for Mumbai city (Base 2002-03 = 100). Since then, it has extended its coverage to nine more cities, revised its base to 2010-11 and started publishing a composite All India HPI. RBI's quarterly HPI is based on transactions data received from housing registration authorities in 10 major cities.

With an overall objective of bringing transparency in the Indian real estate market, the index is expected to serve some highly important and timely purposes:

1. Whether a broker is quoting too high a price for houses in the cities.
2. Banks/housing finance bodies will be able to estimate only if the loan applications are realistic for the properties.
3. This will also show the level of non-performing assets in the housing sector.
4. And most importantly it will serve as a realistic price index for the buyers. (At present, a buyer had no means to judge whether a rise in property price was in the offing with the general level of inflation (i.e., at CPI-C) in the country, or has been scaled up disproportionately. Other than quotes from brokers, there are no means at present to evaluate the changes in price in this sector. At present the only index that gave some idea of housing price changes was the CPI (IW) which being a national index did not show ***regional variations***.)

SERVICE PRICE INDEX

The contribution of the tertiary sector in India's GDP has been strengthening for the past 10 years, and today it stands above 60 per cent. The need for a service price index (SPI) in India is warranted by the growing dominance of the sector in the economy.[76] There is no index, so far, to measure the price changes in the services sector. The present inflation (at the WPI) only shows the price movements of the commodity-producing sector, i.e., it includes only the primary and the secondary sectors - the tertiary sector is not represented by it.

[75] Samuelson and Nordhaus, *Economics*, op. cit., p. 441.

[76] *Economic Survey 2006-07* (New Delhi: Ministry of Finance, GoI), p. 94.

The need[77] for such an index was recommended by the working group (under the Chairmanship of Prof. Abhijit Sen, Member, Planning Commission) set up to revise the WPI (1993-94) series which was reiterated by the National Statistical Commission (headed by C. Rangarajan). The Office of the Economic Adviser, Ministry of Commerce and Industry has been making an effort to develop sector-specific SPI for the country with the technical assistance being received under the World Bank Assisted Economic Reforms Projects (WBAERPs).

Starting in 2005-06, the office has put in place *Experimental Service Price Index* for a total of seven services - railways, postal, air, telecom, port, banking and insurance services. Evolving a single and national SPI is still in the process.

[77] 'The number of National Statistical Agencies collecting service producer prices data, though growing, is still small', points out the *OECD-Eurosat, 2005 Inquiry on National Collection of Services Producer Prices Preliminary Report*, giving information on 45 such countries. The report further adds that while some such agencies have focused exclusively on the price of services provided to enterprises, others have approached the subject more broadly through the development of services producer price indices with varying approaches and coverage. As per the report, at present, 30 countries collect services producer prices while preliminary works have started in other countries, particularly the European countries under the auspices of the Eurosat. Other than the developed Euro- American economies some other countries which worked as inspiration for India which have such an index are China, Hong Kong, Czech Republic, Slovak Republic, Poland, Lithuania, Israel and Vietnam.

SECTION-B: BUSINESS CYCLE

INTRODUCTION

The discussion on growth and development has shown their internal interdependence. If the quality of life in an economy is to be enhanced, there is a need of conscious public policy which can spend and invest in areas such as food, nutrition, health, education, shelter and social security. But for such expenditures and investments, the economy needs equitable level of income, too. The income enhancement in any economy takes place *via* increasing the level of production in the economy, i.e., real gross national product (GNP). It means, development requires higher growth, i.e., higher levels of economic activities and do so governments of the world always keep modifying their policies to keep economic activities at higher and the desired levels. But at times governments fail in this objective and that is why we see economies following ***boom*** and ***bust*** cycle (which is especially seen in the case of the capitalist and market economies) repeatedly. The boom-and-bust cycle is a process in which economies see expansion (i.e., higher levels of economic activities) and contraction (i.e., lower levels of economic activities) - which is studied under the business or economic cycle. While during the boom the economy grows, enormous jobs are created and income expands at higher pace, during the bust the economy shrinks, people lose their jobs and income falls in an unprecedented way. The cycle of boom and bust lasts for varying lengths of time, depending upon the confidence among consumers, investors and the quality of government interventions.

In between boom (phase of *upturn* in the economy) and bust (the limit of the phase of *downturn* in the economy when there is a total collapse of the economy which has never happened till date in the case of any economy) there are many intermediate cycles (i.e., phases or stages) of good and bad kinds, such as - growing growth and growth (the good ones); and slowdown, stagnation[78], recession, depression (the bad ones) and possible recovery after any/every bad cycle. A brief and objective discussion is presented below on **four** of the chief cycles:

1. Depression
2. Recovery
3. Boom
4. Recession

[78] A very lively description of the Great Depression has been presented by *Lee Iacocca* in his autobiography. This is known as the Great Depression due to its length and depth– the economies could recover fully out of it only by the mid-1940s (*Stiglitz and Walsh, op. cit., p. 495*).

DEPRESSION

Though depression has visited the world economy only once in 1929, economists have pin-pointed enough number of traits to recognise it. The ***major*** traits of depression could be as given below:

1. an extremely low aggregate demand in the economy causes activities to decelerate;
2. the inflation being comparatively lower;
3. the employment avenues start shrinking forcing unemployment rate to grow fast;
4. to keep the business going, production houses go for ***forced labour cuts*** or ***retrenchment*** (***to cut down production cost and be competitive in the market***) etc.

The economic situations become so chaotic in the phase of depression that governments have almost no control over the economy. The Great Depression of 1929 gave rise to the ideas of ***strong government intervention***[79] in the economy, such as deficit financing, monetary management and so on.

What the governments may do if depression visits the economy? The simple answer the world has been able to find is to repeat the policy measures of 1929. The best way to avoid depression is not to let it visit. This is why every modern economy keeps extra vigil on the major symptoms of its economy so that the prevention measures can be taken in time and depression is avoided.

RECOVERY

An economy tries to come out of the low production phase to survive. The low production phase might be depression, recession or slowdown with the former being the worst and rare, governments take many new fiscal and monetary measures to boost demand and production and ultimately a recovery in an economy is managed. The business cycle of recovery may show the following ***major*** economic traits:

1. an upturn in aggregate (total) demand which has to be accompanied by increase in the level of production;
2. production process expands and new investments become attractive;
3. as demand goes upward, inflation also moves upward making borrowing cheaper for investors;
4. with an upturn in production, new employment avenues are created and unemployment rate starts declining, etc.

With the above symptoms, people's incomes undergo a certain increase which creates new demand and a cycle of demand and production (supply) starts playing hand in hand to recover the economy. To recover an economy, governments usually opt for tax breaks, interest cuts, an increase in salaries of its employees and so on. Assimilation of innovations by the entrepreneurs and search for new frontiers of enterprise do play a very vital role in the process of recovery provided these activities are at first incentives by the governments.

The Euro-American economies recovered out of the Great Depression with the help of the measures cited above. Such recoveries have been seen many times around the world when economies recovered from slowdown or the recessionary phases. The best example of recent times could be cited from India of 1997 to 2002 when the economy suffered severe bouts of slowdown and recession.[80]

Shapes of Recovery

When economies are coming out of the phase of downturn, the recovery (i.e., upturn) may show varied characteristics. When the datasets of recovery are plotted on the horizontal (x-axis) and vertical (y-axis) lines on a coordinate plane, the 'curve' which emerges on the grid graph resembles the shapes of the English alphabets— after which they are named. Some popular shapes of recoveries are ***J, K, L, U, V, W*** and ***Z***. The arms of these letters simply signify the 'pace and duration' of recovery— the steeper the upward bend of the arm, the faster the recoveries. It should be noted that technically even recessions are named after these shapes.

BOOM

A strong upward fluctuation in the economic activities is called boom.[81] As economies try to recover out of

[79] Suggested by J. M. Keynes in his seminal work *The General Theory of Employment, Interest and Money* (New York: Harcourt, 1935).

[80] *Economic Surveys, 1996-97 to 2002-03,* (New Delhi: Ministry of Finance, GoI).

[81] Stiglitz and Walsh, *op. cit.*, p. 945.

the phases of slowdown, recession and depression, at times the measures taken by the governments as well as the private sector might put economic activities as such which the economic systems fail to digest. This is the phase of the ***boom***. The ***major*** economic traits of boom may be listed as given below:

1. an accelerated and prolonged increase in the demand;
2. demand peaks up to such a high level that it exceeds sustainable output/production levels;
3. the economy heats up and a demand-supply lag is visible;
4. the market forces mismatch (*i.e.*, ***demand and supply disequilibrium***) and tend to create a situation where inflation starts going upward;
5. the economy might face structural problems such as shortage of investible capital, lower savings, falling standard of living, creation of a sellers' market.

The phase of recovery is considered good for the economy, and it reaches the stage of boom which is considered better. But the boom has its negative side also. Boom is usually followed by price rise.[82] As a boom is a strong upward fluctuation in an economy, the supply-side pattern of the economy starts lagging behind the pace of the accelerated aggregate demand.[83] But the dilemma of recovery puts every economy on the path to boom - this has been the experience in the developed world during the 1990s, especially in the US economy. The same scenario developed in India after the economy recovered from the recessionary period of 1996-97 by the year 2002-03 when the rate of inflation peaked to almost 8 per cent for a few months. Majority of the experts felt that Indian economy at that time was passing through a phase of boom and we have seen how the government has been facing difficulty in containing inflation around the 5 per cent mark. Even the government accepted that the economy was overheating by mid-2007. *The symptoms of overheating are as follows:*

1. there is a downturn in the aggregate demand or overall decline in the demand;
2. as demand falls, the level of production (output) in the economy also falls;
3. as producers cut down their production levels, new employment opportunities are not created - thus employment growth rate falls;
4. as demand keeps on falling, usually producers start cutting down their labour force to adjust their overhead expenditure and the cost of production (labour cut is not 'forced' here but 'voluntary') - resulting in increase in the unemployment rate;
5. if the government fails to rescue the economy from the phase of recession, the dangerous stage of ***depression*** remains the logical follow-up;
6. the rate of inflation always remains at lower levels - discouraging new investments and lending.

Recession

This is somewhat similar to the phase of 'depression' – we may call it a *mild form* of depression – fatal for economies as this may lead to depression if not handled with care and in time. The financial crises which followed the US 'subprime crisis' in almost the whole Euro-American economies have basically brought in 'severe recessionary' trends there. Major traits of recession, to a great extent, are similar to that of 'depression' [except the point (4) of the Depression, discussed earlier] – may be summed up as follows:

1. there is a general fall in demand as economic activities take a downturn;
2. inflation remains lower or/and shows further signs of falling down;
3. employment rate falls/unemployment rate grows;
4. industries resort to 'price cuts' to sustain their business.

In the financial year 1996–97, the Indian economy was taken up by the cycle of recession – basically due to a general downturn in domestic as well as foreign demands, initiated by the South East Asian Currency Crisis of the mid-1990s.[84] The whole plan of economic reforms in India was derailed, and it was only by the end of 2001–02 that the economy was able to recover. What may a government do to rescue the economy from the phase of recession? The usual remedies are given below:

1. Direct and indirect taxes should be cut down, so that the consumers have higher disposable incomes (income after paying direct tax, i.e., income tax) on the one hand and the goods

82 Samuelson and Nordhaus, *op. cit.*, pp. 680-84.

83 Stiglitz and Walsh, *op. cit.*, pp. 495-796.

84 *Economic Survey, 1996-97,* (New Delhi: Ministry of Finance, GoI).

should become cheaper on the other hand, thus there is hope that the demand might pick up.

2. The burden of direct taxes, especially the income tax, dividend tax, interest tax, is slashed to enhance the disposable income (i.e., ***income after direct tax payment***).
3. Salaries and wages should be revised upward by the government to encourage general spending by the consumers (as the Government of India implemented the recommendations of the fifth pay commission without much deliberation in 1996–97).
4. Indirect taxes such as custom duty, excise duty (cenvat), sales tax, etc. should be cut down so that produced goods reach the market at cheaper prices.
5. The government usually goes on to follow a cheap money supply policy by slashing down interest rates across the board and the lending procedure is also liberalised.
6. Tax breaks are announced for new investments in the productive areas, etc.

All the above-given measures were taken up by the United Front Government in 1996–97 to pull the economy out of the menace of the recession.[85] The forthcoming government took several other such measures by the end of 1998–99 onwards (the NDA Government). Ultimately, the measures taken up by the governments accompanied by a general recovery in the world economy, the Indian economy started recovering from the bout of recession. Many experts had already predicted a possibility of depression with a zero per cent rate of inflation.[86] Although this did not happen.[87]

The World Bank and IMF define recession technically also (which is called ***technical recession***). Any economy seeing fall in its GDP for two consecutive quarters is said to be hit with *technical recession.* Though, to declare global recession the agencies go into data related to employment, demand of oil, etc., it is defined with the help of global economic growth rate also – global growth rate falling below 2.5 per cent is considered technical recession (2.5 per cent is the *threshold* growth rate for technical global recession).

GROWTH RECESSION

An expression coined by economists to describe an economy that is growing at such a slow pace that more jobs are being lost than are being added. The lack of job creation makes it 'feel' as if the economy is in a recession, even though the economy is still advancing. Many economists believe that between 2002 and 2003, the United States' economy was in a phase of growth recession. In fact, at several points over the past 25 years the US economy is said to have experienced a growth recession. That is, in spite of gains in real GDP, job growth was either non-existent or was being destroyed at a faster rate than new jobs were being added.

Experts have revived this term in the wake of the ongoing financial crises in the Euro-American economies since 2008. The situation is better described by the term ***double-dip recession***.

DOUBLE-DIP RECESSION

The concept of 'recession' in the United States and Euro Zone is quite precise and technical - 'two *consecutive quarters of falling* GDP' - is how it is defined in these economies. And the idea of the 'double-dip recession' is an extension of it.

A double-dip recession refers to a recession followed by a short-lived recovery, followed by another recession - the GDP growth sliding back to negative after a quarter or two of positive growth. The causes for such a recession vary but often include a slowdown in the demand for goods and services because of layoffs (forced job cuts) and spending cutbacks done in the previous downturn. A double-dip (which may be even 'triple-dip') is a worst-case scenario - fear/speculation of it moves the economy into a deeper and longer recession and recovery becomes too difficult. As the world saw in the case of the Euro Zone crisis, there was a fear of such a recession by the first quarter of 2013.

[85] *Economic Survey, 1996-97,* (New Delhi: Ministry of Finance, GoI).

[86] It should be noted here that as an impact of recession on the rate of inflation (at WPI) had been falling down throughout the mid-1998-99 fiscal period finally to the level of 0.5 per cent for a fortnight [*Economic Survey, 1998-99,* ((New Delhi: Ministry of Finance, GoI)].

[87] The literature of Economics and the empirical world experiences suggest that the phase of recession has all the symptoms of depression except one. Everything being the same till producers are cutting the labour by force 'involuntarily *(i.e., forced labour cut)* it is the starting of depression - to be competitive in the market every producer starts 'forced labour cuts' - ultimately putting the economy into the grip of a full-grown depression.

Word Bank

Retrocession

The term has got three different meanings in which it is used:

1. The purchase of 'reinsurance' by a 'reinsurance company' (as in the case of India, the GIC going for 'reinsurance' on the 'reinsurance' it has provided to other 'insurance companies' operating in India). This limits the risk that a reinsurance company may face, since it has purchased insurance against an 'event' that might affect a company that it had underwritten (reinsured). If a reinsurance company continues to purchase insurance, it might 'unknowingly' buy back its own risk, which is known as 'spiraling'.
2. The 'voluntary' act of returning ceded property by one to another which may be a result of 'request' to have property returned. But, by definition, it is not the result of a 'forced' transaction. Returning of Hong Kong to China by the UK in 1997 is the best such example of the recent times.
3. The act of 'differentiating' and 'diversifying' assets by consolidating and then dividing them amongst a number of stakeholders – by doing so the risk involved is 'retroceded' (i.e., cut down or minimised). This is, usually, done by the 'hedge funds' in their day-to-day portfolio management.

CONCLUSION

Business cycles are basically fluctuations in the production levels of economies above and below the trend of the equilibrium levels.[88] But why do economies fluctuate? There are many factors which are said to be responsible for it, as per the experts:

1. Economic instability and uncertainty (due to logical or illogical expectations) may discourage investments, thereby reducing growth in the long term.
2. A lack of the creative destruction (i.e., innovation) may put the economy in a slump or slowdown in its overall production.
3. Anti-inflationary government policies (especially when general elections are nearing) may direct the attraction of investors in the economy.
4. Unforeseen disasters may cause economies to fluctuate.

[88] S. Cox, *op. cit.*, p. 58.

PREVIOUS YEARS' QUESTIONS

Prelims

1. Consider the following statements: (2025)

   Statement-I: As regards returns from an investment in a company, generally, bondholders are considered to be relatively at lower risk than stockholders.

   Statement-II: Bondholders are lenders to a company whereas stockholders are its owners.

   Statement-III: For repayment purpose, bondholders are prioritized over stockholders by a company.

   Which one of the following is correct in respect of the above statements?

   (a) Both Statement-II and Statement-III are correct and both of them explain Statement-I

   (b) Both Statement-I and Statement-II are correct and Statement-I explains Statement-II

   (c) Only one of the Statements-II and III is correct and that explains Statement-I

   (d) Neither Statement-II nor Statement-III is correct

2. Consider the following statements: (2025)

(i) India accounts for a very large portion of all equity option contracts traded globally thus exhibiting a great boom.

(ii) India's stock market has grown rapidly in the recent past even overtaking Hong Kong's at some point of time.

(iii) There is no regulatory body either to warn the small investors about the risks of options trading or to act on unregistered financial advisors in this regard.

Which of the statements give above are correct?

(a) (i) and (ii) only
(b) (ii) and (iii) only
(c) (i) and (iii) only
(d) (i), (ii) and (iii)

Answers: 1. (a) 2. (a)

Explanation

1. (a): *Statements I & II are correct* {Limited liability companies raise long-term funds either by issuing bonds or by selling shares. Bond buyers/bondholders (who get fixed interest as income) become lenders to the company, while share buyers (who get part of the company's profit, called 'dividend') become partners in the company}. *Statement-III is correct* (bondholders are given repayment priority over stockholders).

2. (a): *Statement-I is correct* (as per NSE data and BIS reports, India has become a major hub for equity derivatives, especially options– in 2023, more than 80 per cent of global equity index option trades happened on Indian exchanges). *Statement-II is correct* (in January 2024, India's stock market briefly overtook Hong Kong's to become the 4th largest in the world in terms of market capitalisation). *Statement-III is incorrect* (the Securities and Exchange Board of India is the statutory regulatory authority responsible for overseeing the securities market in India).

Mains

1. What are the causes of persistent high food inflation in India? Comment on the effectiveness of the monetary policy of RBI to control this type of inflation. (2024)

SAMPLE OBJECTIVE QUESTIONS

1. Consider the following statements related to imported inflation:

(i) It will occur once India imports from the countries of higher inflation rates.

(ii) It will hit India if it continues exporting to the countries with higher rates of inflation.

(iii) It will not hit India if it does not import from countries with higher rates of inflation.

How many of the above statement(s) is/are correct?

Code:

(a) Only one **(b)** Only two
(c) All three **(d)** None of these

2. Consider the following statements related to inflation:

(i) Seasonality is a cause bottleneck inflation in India.

(ii) Inflation in food, energy and fuel is called core inflation.

(iii) Stagflation is a situation of slower growth with higher inflation and unemployment.

(iv) Core-core inflation is a narrower core inflation in India.

How many of the above statement(s) is/are correct?

Code:

(a) Only one **(b)** Only two
(c) Only three **(d)** All four

3. Consider the following statements related to the effects of inflation on economy:
   (i) During disinflation, prices fall towards the upper limit of the healthy range of inflation.
   (ii) During deflation, prices fall below the lower limit of the healthy range of inflation.
   (iii) A rise in inflation increases nominal income but decreases the value of money.
   (iv) Reflation is an inflation which is intentionally brought by the government.

   How many of the above statement(s) is/are correct?

   Code:
   (a) Only one
   (b) Only two
   (c) Only three
   (d) All four

4. Consider the statements related to effects of inflation:
   (i) A rise in inflation helps governments collect more taxes; however, their fiscal deficits also rise.
   (ii) Government expenditures rise with an increase in inflation but seigniorage helps the government to create more tax revenues.
   (iii) In case of India, exports rise as inflation rises but trade balance gets more negative.
   (iv) When inflation rises, bondholders and lending institutions both suffer.

   How many of the above statement(s) is/are correct?

   Code:
   (a) Only one
   (b) Only two
   (c) Only three
   (d) All four

5. Consider the following statements related to inflation targeting in the country:
   (i) One term of inflation targeting consists of four consecutive financial years.
   (ii) It is a statutory duty of the Reserve Bank of India to target the headline inflation under it.
   (iii) It involves stabilisation of the wholesale price index, too.

   How many of the above statement(s) is/are correct?
   (a) Only one
   (b) Only two
   (c) All three
   (d) None of these

6. Consider the following statements related to the reasons which caused recent 'protein inflation' in the country:
   (i) Shift in dietary habits
   (ii) Food inflation
   (iii) Costlier fodder and poultry products
   (iv) Income effect
   (v) Transfer payments

   How many of the above statement(s) is/are correct?
   (a) Only one
   (b) Only three
   (c) Only four
   (d) All five

7. Consider the following statements related to rupee's exchange rate and inflation in the country:
   (i) Inflation targeting gives increased predictability to rupee's exchange rate fluctuations.
   (ii) Currency futures help hedge risks of exchange rate fluctuations.
   (iii) Reserve Bank of India actively takes part in currency trading to target inflation.

   How many of the above statement(s) is/are correct?
   (a) Only one
   (b) Only two
   (c) All three
   (d) None of these

8. Consider the following statements related to inflation, government budgeting and taxation in the country:
   (i) Higher rates of inflation generally raise budgetary allocations and transfer payments.
   (ii) Government's market borrowings become cheaper due to rise in inflation but at the cost rupee's depreciation.
   (iii) Higher rates of inflation may normally result in higher twin deficits.

   How many of the above statement(s) is/are correct?
   (a) Only one
   (b) Only two
   (c) All three
   (d) None of these

9. Consider the following statements relating to the relationship between inflation and bonds:
   (i) Bond prices fall when rate of inflation rises.
   (ii) Bond yields are directly connected to the levels of government borrowings.
   (iii) Bond holders suffer due to fall in rate of inflation.
   (iv) Government bonds are immune to inflation rate fluctuations.

   How many of the above statement(s) is/are correct?
   (a) Only one (b) Only two
   (c) All three (d) None of these

10. Consider the following statements related to the acts of the Reserve Bank of India (RBI):
   (i) RBI may use sterilised intervention to stabilise the headline inflation.
   (ii) RBI purchases foreign currencies from forex market to check inflation from falling.
   (iii) RBI sells foreign currencies in forex market to check inflation from rising.
   (iv) To check rupee's appreciation RBI may sell its gold reserve in foreign markets.

   How many of the above statement(s) is/are correct?
   (a) Only one
   (b) Only two
   (c) Only three
   (d) All four

Answers: 1. (b) 2. (c) 3. (d) 4. (b) 5. (a) 6. (d) 7. (c) 8. (c) 9. (b) 10. (b)

SAMPLE SUBJECTIVE QUESTIONS

1. Briefly discuss the reasons behind the recent upsurge in the headline inflation in the country and elaborate the policy steps taken by the RBI and Government to check it.
2. Discuss the major external factors behind the inflation pressure seen recently in the country.
3. Write a note on the experience of inflation targeting in the country and suggest measures to improve it.
4. How far do you think forward market can help India in checking the inflation pressures?
5. Why the country has seen persistent protein inflation in recent times? Suggest policy measures to check it.
6. Write a note on the reasons due to which we normally find a wedge between CPI and WPI in the country.

SAMPLE MODEL ANSWER

1. **'India emerged as the only country among the emerging market and developing economies (EMDEs) to manage high growth and low inflation during 2025-26.' Substantiate with the help of suitable examples.**

Ans. While economic growth in most of the emerging market and developing economies (EMDEs) remained below the EMDE average of 4.2 per cent, inflation outcomes varied widely across countries. In Brazil, headline inflation rose steadily to 5.2 per cent in 2025; Russia experienced subdued GDP growth alongside persistently high inflation. In contrast, inflation moderated in several major Southeast Asian economies, including Malaysia, Indonesia, and the Philippines, supported by lower imported commodity costs. Notably, China experienced significant deflation during the year, driven by weak domestic demand, export pressures arising from tariff regimes, and excess capacity in several manufacturing industries, which kept producer prices in negative territory.

Among major EMDEs, India recorded one of the sharpest declines in headline inflation, amounting to about 1.8 percentage points. Importantly, this disinflation occurred alongside robust GDP growth of 8 per cent in the first half of 2025-26 (April-September)–supported by India's strong macroeconomic fundamentals and its ability to sustain growth while effectively managing price pressures (or, in other words, without overheating).

While upgrading India's sovereign rating, global rating agencies have also acknowledged the credibility and effectiveness of India's inflation management. For instance, S&P observed that– monetary policy reform to switch to inflation targeting has reaped dividends. Inflationary expectations are better anchored than they were a decade ago. Between 2008 and 2014, India's inflation reached double digits on numerous occasions. In the past three years, despite volatility in global energy prices and supply-side shocks, CPI growth averaged 5.5 per cent. In recent months, it stayed at the lower bound of the Reserve Bank of India's (RBI) target range of 2-6 per cent. These developments, coupled with a deep domestic capital market, reflect a more stable and supportive environment for monetary settings.

CHAPTER 9

Agriculture and Food Management

India is now faced with a problem of plenty. With supply outpacing demand, India has surpluses in most food categories which reduces food inflation, resulting in stalling of a large channel of income transfer from food consumers (mostly rich) to food producers (mostly poor).*

*See *Agricultural Reforms*, Neelkanth Mishra, *What the Economy Needs Now*, Abhijit Banerjee, Gita Gopinath, Raghuram Rajan and Mihir Sharma, eds. (New Delhi: Juggernaut Books, 2019), pp. 96-103.

To watch the Author's videos on the significance of the Chapter, scan the QR Code given here

Exam Essentials...

- Kharif and Rabi Crops
- Mission on Pulses
- Land Reforms and Green Revolution
- Rising Significance of Livestock Sector
- Irrigation Water Productivity (IWP)
- PM Dhan-Dhanya Krishi Yojana
- Animal Rearing
- Economic Transformation Through Horticulture
- Market Intervention Scheme
- Price Stabilisation Fund
- Irrigation

Note to the Reader...

The segment agriculture should be understood in the context of India's emerging agri challenges and shift in policy emphasis, especially since 2002 when the sector was formally declared as the prime moving force (PMF) of the economy. A laggard sector in the case of economic reforms, readers 'must' try to understand the 'real' challenges due to which it could not be done! Coming to its importance– It is extensively covered in the General Studies Paper III (UPSC Mains), besides several questions are asked from it in preliminary test and the personality test.

In This Chapter...

- Supply Chain Management
- Upstream and Downstream Requirements
- Farm Mechanisation
- Seed Development
- Fertilisers
- Pesticides
- Agri-Credit
- Agriculture Extension Services
- Agri Insurance
- WTO and The Indian Agriculture: Prospects and Challenges
- WTO and Agricultural Subsidies
- NAMA
- National Food Security Act
- Food Processing
- Major Policy Initiatives
- Doubling Farm Income
- Cash Support to Farmers
- Women Farmers
- Climate-Smart Agriculture
- Way Forward

INTRODUCTION

Agriculture remains the most important sector of the Indian economy, whether it be the pre-independence or the post-independence periods. This fact is emphatically proved by the large number of people who depend on it for their livelihood. Before starting any discussion on Indian agriculture, we must look into its *special features:*

1. Today, agriculture and allied activities contribute nearly **20 per cent** of India's national income at current prices (in comparison to 55.4 per cent in 1950-51) but account for **46.1 per cent** of the country's workforce.[1] Given the large share of employment, the sector remains central to promoting *inclusive growth* and ensuring *food security.*
2. While foodgrain production has increased in recent years, higher-value allied sectors, such as livestock, fisheries, and horticulture, are assuming an increasingly important role in enhancing income opportunities and strengthening rural livelihoods– its contribution has shown an increase of over **11-fold** in the last decade (GVA at current prices rising from ₹40 thousand crores in 2011-12 to ₹50 thousand crores in 2023-24).[2]
3. Agriculture is not only the biggest sector of the economy but also the biggest private sector. It is the only profession which still carries no burden of individual income tax.
4. This is the biggest *unorganised sector* of the economy accounting for more than 90 per cent share in the total unorganised labour force (around 94 per cent of the total labour force of the economy, i.e., 39.0 crore are employed in the unorganised sector).[3]
5. In the last few years, India has emerged as the *net exporter* of agricultural products and has the export growth rate of 14 per cent - exports reached an all-time high of US$ 51.1 billion in 2024-25, as per the *Economic Survey 2025-26.*
6. According to the export figures, agriculture is deeply related to industrial growth and the national income in India – 1 per cent increase in the agricultural growth leads to 0.5 per cent increase in industrial output (growth) and 0.7 per cent increase in the national income of India.
7. The industrial sector was selected as the *prime moving force* of the economy in the late 1940s. But due to market failure the sector failed to lead the economy after independence. Without increasing the income of the people who depend on agriculture for their livelihood, the market was not going to support the industries. As a result, the Government of India (GoI) announced agriculture as the prime moving force of the economy in 2002.[4]
8. With 1 per cent increase in the share of agriculture in India's total exports, the money which flows into agriculture is calculated to be ₹8,500 crores.[5]

[1] *Economic Survey 2025-26* (New Delhi: Ministry of Finance, GoI, January 2026), p. 226.

[2] D. S. Negi, P. S. Birthal, P. S. Roy & Hazrana (2021) in "Crop Choices in Indian Agriculture: Role of Market Access and Price Policy," ***Economic Bulletin***, 41(4), 2249-2256 quoted by the *Economic Survey 2025-26* (New Delhi: Ministry of Finance, GoI, January 2026), p. 226.

[3] Labour Bureau, (New Delhi: Ministry of Labour and Employment, GoI, February 2026).

[4] Planning Commission, *Approach Paper to the Tenth Five Year Plan* (New Delhi: Government of India, 2002).

[5] This was the general opinion of the experts throughout the 1990s, but the official document which accepted this

9. Today, around **46** per cent of India's cultivated land is under irrigation[6] and the rest (around 54 per cent) is rain-fed which remains exposed to the monsoonal uncertainties – the reason we still say that farming in India is a *gamble of monsoon.*

10. Foodgrain production of the country is estimated to be **357.73** million tonnes in the agriculture year 2024-25 (an increase of 25.4 million tonnes over the previous agriculture year).[7]

Kharif and Rabi Crops

There are certain special terms used to understand the cropping seasons of India. The agricultural crop year in India is from *July to June*. The Indian cropping season is classified into two main seasons: (1) kharif and (2) rabi based on the monsoon. The kharif cropping season is from *July to October* during the South-West/Summer Monsoon, and the rabi cropping season is from *October to March* (North-East/Returning/Winter Monsoon). The crops grown between March and June are summer crops known as *jayads*.

Pakistan and Bangladesh are two other countries that are using the term 'kharif' and 'rabi' to describe their cropping patterns. The terms 'kharif' and 'rabi' originate from the Arabic language where kharif means *autumn* and rabi means *spring*.

The kharif crops include rice, maize, sorghum, pearl millet/bajra, finger millet/ragi (cereals), arhar (pulses), soyabean, groundnut (oilseeds), and cotton. The rabi crops include wheat, barley, oats (cereals), chickpea/gram (pulses), linseed, and mustard (oilseeds).

FOOD PHILOSOPHY OF INDIA

Indian food philosophy[8] is generally seen divided into three phases with their own objectives and challenges:

The First Phase

This phase continued for the first three decades after independence. The main aim and the struggle of this phase was producing as much foodgrains as required by the Indian population, i.e., achieving *physical access* to food.

The idea of the Green Revolution (GR) at the end of this phase at least gave India the confidence of realising the objective. At the end of the 1980s, India was a self-sufficient country with regard to food.

The Second Phase

Meanwhile India was celebrating its success of the first phase, a new challenge confronted the country – achieving *economic access* to food. The situation continued to worsen, and by the early 2000 there was a paradoxical situation in the country where there was more than three times the buffer stock of food grains in the central pool, but in several states people were dying due to lack of food – a complete mockery of the logic behind maintaining a buffer stock, success of GR and the concept of India being a welfare state.[9] The Supreme Court intervened after a public interest litigation (PIL) was filed by the People's Union for Civil Liberties (PUCL) and a national level Food for Work Programme was launched by the Government to address the problem of hunger deaths (which was later on merged with the Mahatma Gandhi National Rural Employment Guarantee Scheme). Passing its judgement, the Court said that if foodgrains got rotten in godowns or were destroyed in oceans to manage their market prices, the Court will take the governments to task. To protect itself from the ire of the Court, the Centre resorted to export surplus wheat at a very low price (to clear the stocks before they got rotten). In this process India emerged as the *seventh largest* exporter of wheat (2002). Basically, we were exporting the share of wheat which was not consumed by many Indians due to lack of their economic reach to food.

As the inputs of the GR were costlier, its outputs naturally going to be costlier. To fight the situation there should have been a time-bound and target-oriented macro-economic policy support, which could deliver comparative increase in the purchasing capacity of the masses to make food affordable for them. India fared poorly in this aspect.

contention was the *Foreign Tirade Policy 2002-07*, of the Ministry of Commerce. This view continued with the government in all its forthcoming trade policies for about four decades.

[6] *Directorate of Economics and Statistics*, Department of Agriculture & Farmers Welfare, (New Delhi: Ministry of Jal Shakti, Government of India, March 2026).

[7] *Economic Survey 2025-26* (New Delhi: Ministry of Finance, GoI, January 2026), p. 229.

[8] *Indian Council of Agricultural Research (ICAR)*, New Delhi, 1998.

[9] Publication Division, *India 2000* (New Delhi: Government of India, 2001); *Economic Survey 2000-01* (New Delhi: Ministry of Finance, GoI, 2001).

Mission on Pulses

To make the country self-dependent in these essential protein cereals, the *Union Budget 2025–26* announced to launch a 6-year Mission on Pulses with a special focus of the three pulses— **Tur** (red gram/pigeon pea), **Urad** (black gram), and **Masoor** (red lentil).

Under it, the Government has committed 'guaranteed procurement' of these pulses at their minimum support prices from farmers by the central agencies NAFED (National Agricultural Cooperative Marketing Federation of India) and NCCF (National Cooperative Consumers' Federation) for the next four years.

Scarcity of the pulses has been the 'biggest' reason for recurring protein inflation in the country since 2009 as its production has been stagnating between 15–18 MT (million tonnes) over the last five decades. However, special drives of the Government enhanced its production by over 60 per cent during the last decade (2014–24) from 17.1 MT to 27 MT, helping India become *self-sufficient* by the year 2024–25; however, it remained a bit short of the target at only 25.7 MT due to weather and climatic reasons, as per the *Economic Survey 2025–26*.

The crisis was managed by offering higher food subsidies, affecting government exchequer, resulting in the infrastructural shortcomings in the agriculture sector (due to decreased fiscal strength of the Government caused by rising food subsidy bills, year after year). Even after providing higher food subsidies, some people failed to purchase food, and they were left with no option but to die of hunger.

India is still in this phase and trying to solve the crisis through the twin approach - creating maximum number of gainful employments, and cutting the cost of foodgrains (*via* the Second Green Revolution based on biotechnology).

It must be borne in mind that happiness in regard to food self-sufficiency was a fleeting feeling for India. By the mid-1990s, India realised that its foodgrain production was lagging behind its population surge. It meant India was still fighting to achieve physical reach to the required level of food production.

The Third Phase

By the end of the 1980s, global experts started questioning the very system the world was following with the various modes of production. Agricultural activity was one among which had become hugely based on industries (chemical fertilisers, pesticides, tractors, etc.). The developed economies had declared agriculture to be an industry.[10]

It was time to look back and introspect. By the early 1990s, several countries started opting for ecologically friendly methods and techniques of industrial, agricultural and service sector development. The hyped-up GR was declared ecologically untenable, and the world headed for organic farming, green farming, etc.

It meant that achieving physical and economic reach to food was not the only challenge India was facing, but such aims should not be realised at the cost of the precious ecology and biodiversity - a new challenge. India needed a new kind of GR which could deliver the physical, economic as well as *ecological access* to food - the Second Green Revolution, an all-in-one approach towards the agriculture sector.

LAND REFORMS

The official stance and emphasis on land reforms in India have been changing over time in wake of the emerging issues, which may be seen in the following two phases.

Phase-I

This phase commenced just after independence. All economies were agrarian before they were industrialised, with only their periods varying. Once democratic systems developed, the first thing the developed countries of today did was to complete the agrarian reforms in a time-bound way. As land remains the means of livelihood for the larger section of society in an agrarian economy, the successful completion of agrarian reforms benefited the maximum number of people, thereby improving their economic conditions. At the time of independence, India was a typical agrarian economy and had inherited a very inequitable agrarian system. Land reforms was a major plank of independent India, and as part of the agrarian reforms it was made clear by the pledge of the Indian National Congress in 1935. Land reforms in India had three objectives similar to the other economies which opted for it in the past:

1. Removing *institutional discrepancies* of the agrarian structure inherited from the past which obstructed increasing agricultural production, such as the size of agricultural holding, land

[10] *Brundtland Report* on Sustainable Development after the deliberations at the summit '*Our Common future*', 1987.

ownership, land inheritance, tenancy reforms, abolition of intermediaries, introduction of modern institutional factors to agriculture, etc.

2. The other objective of the land reforms in India was related to the issue of *socio-economic inequality* in the country. The high inequality in land ownership not only had its negative economic impact on the economy, but it was badly intertwined with the caste system in India and the allocation of social prestige and status by the society at large.[11] More than 80 per cent of the population from its livelihood inherited the agrarian system which had inequitable ownership of the asset, i.e., land to earn income. The government wanted to opt for a restructuring of land ownership in the economy on logical grounds and with a public welfare approach. This objective of land reforms received enough socio-political attention as it tried to dismantle the age-old agrarian structure in the country. It became such a hot issue that land reforms in India received a 'bad name', synonymous to land grabbing by the government and allotting them to the landless masses.
3. The third objective of land reforms in India was highly contemporary in nature, which did not receive enough socio-political attention – it was the objective of *increasing agricultural production* for solving the inter-related problems of poverty, malnutrition and food insecurity.

To realise the objectives of land reforms, the government adopted three main steps which included several internal sub-steps:

1. **Abolition of Intermediaries:** Under this step, the age-old exploitative land tenure systems of the Zamindari, Mahalwari and Ryotwari were fully abolished.
2. **Tenancy Reforms:** Under this broader step, three inter-related reforms in protecting the land tenants were affected:
   - **(i)** *Regulation of rent* so that a fixed and rational rate of rent could be paid by the sharecroppers to the land owners;
   - **(ii)** *Security of tenure* so that a sharecropper could feel secure about his future income and his economic security; and
   - **(iii)** *Ownership rights to tenants* so that the landless masses (i.e., the tenants, the sharecroppers) could receive the final rights for the land they plough – *land to the tillers.*
3. **Reorganisation of Agriculture:** This step again has many inter-related and highly logical provisions in the direction of rational agrarian reforms:
   - **(i)** *Redistribution of land* among the landless poor masses after promulgating timely *ceiling laws* – the move failed badly with few exceptions, such as West Bengal, Kerala and partially in Andhra Pradesh.
   - **(ii)** *Consolidation of land* could only succeed in the regions of the GR (i.e., Haryana, Punjab and western Uttar Pradesh) and remained marred with many loopholes and corruption.
   - **(iii)** *Cooperative farming,* which has a high socio-economic moral base, was only used by the big farmers to save their lands from the draconian ceiling laws.

The whole attempt of land reforms in India is considered a big failure by a majority of experts. Many consider the issue of land reforms in India as the most complex socio-economic problem of human history.[12] Data regarding the numerical achievements of land reforms have been highly discouraging.[13]

1. Tenancy reforms provided tenants with rights, but only on 4 per cent of the total operated areas in the country (14.4 million hectares of operated area by 11 million tenants by 1992).
2. Redistribution of ownership rights of land took place, but only up to 2 per cent of the total operated area in the country (less than 2 million hectares among the 4.76 million people by 1992).
3. Taken together, the whole process of land reforms could benefit only 6 per cent of the operated area of the country with a negligible socio-economic positive impact.

It was the failure of land reforms which made the government easily attracted towards the new policy of

[11] L. I. Rudolph and S. H. Rudolph, *In Pursuit of Lakshmi: The Political Economy of the Indian State* (Bombay: Orient Longman, 1987), pp. 45-50.

[12] This was the view of the majority of experts around the world by the late 1960s.

[13] P. S. Appu, *Land Reforms in India: A Survey of Policy, Legislation and Implementation* (Mussoorie: Land Reforms Unit, Lal Bahadur Shastri National Academy of Administration, 1995), pp. 232-33.

the GR in the future - land reforms had failed to increase agricultural production, thus the government opted for increasing productivity to reach the same goal, i.e., initiation of new techniques in optimising agriculture.

Reasons for Failure of Land Reforms

Out of the many reasons forwarded by the experts responsible for the failure of the land reforms in India, the following three could be considered the most important ones:

1. Land in India is considered a symbol of social prestige, status and identity unlike the other economies which succeeded in their land reform programmes, where it is seen as just an economic asset for income earning.
2. Lack of political will which was required to affect land reforms and make it a successful programme.
3. Rampant corruption in public life, political hypocrisy and leadership failure in the Indian democratic system.

Land Reforms and Green Revolution

Once the government launched the GR, the issue of land reforms almost became marginalised due to the following reasons:

1. There is an inherent diabolic relationship between the GR and the land reforms as the former suits bigger and more economic land holdings, while the latter intended to fragment the land among a large number of the masses.
2. The land reforms were socially opposed by the land-owning caste lobbies, while there was no such opposition to the GR.
3. The level of legislative attempts taken by the governments regarding the land reforms till date had almost no positive socio-economic impact on the country, while the GR had the most potential of yielding ample foodgrains.
4. The subsidised supplies of foodgrains under PL480 were hampering India from carving out its independent diplomacy, as well as there always remaining a doubt about the regular supplies of wheat.
5. International pressure as well as the suggestions from the World Bank besides the success stories of the GR from the countries where it had increased the yield of wheat.

Phase-II

The second phase of land reforms can be traced in the process of economic reforms. Economic reforms exposed the economy to the new and emerging realities, such as land acquisition and leasing, food-related issues and the agricultural provisions of the World Trade Organization (WTO). We see a shift (*Economic Survey 2012-13*) in the thinking of the GoI towards the issue of land reforms - a clear three step policy looks emerging:

1. Mapping land carefully and assigning conclusive title,
2. Devising a fair but speedy process of land acquisition and
3. Putting in place a transparent and effective land leasing policy.

Land is probably the single most valuable asset in the country today. Not only could greater liquidity for land allow more resources to be redeployed efficiently in agriculture, it could ease the way for land-utilising businesses to be set up. Perhaps, as important, it could allow land to serve as collateral for credit.

The issue of 'inconclusive' land ownership has been a major developmental concern and matter of high litigation in the country. Presently, a scheme[14] the Digital India Land Records Modernisation Programme (DILRMP), is being run as a central sector scheme aimed at moving from *presumptive title* (where registration of a title does not imply the owner's title is legally valid) to *conclusive title* (where it does). Successful

[14] Aimed at achieving a conclusive land ownership titles, the Department of Land Resources, Ministry of Rural Development launched the *National Land Records Modernisation Programme (NLRMP)* in 2008 - by merging the Computerisation of Land Records (CLR) and Strengthening of Revenue Administration and Updating of Land Records (SRA&ULR) schemes of the late 1980s. The NLRMP was to be completed by the end of 2016-17 (the terminal year of the 12th Plan) but remained unfinished due to several reasons (states' apathy being one major reason). In 2014, the programme was revamped as the *Digital India Land Records Modernisation Programme (DILRMP)*. Started as a centrally sponsored scheme (financed by both the centre and state), in 2016-17, the programme evolved into a central sector scheme (fully financed by the centre). Aimed at providing a system of updated and automated land records, the programme has three major components, namely (1) Computerisation of land record, (2) Survey/re-survey and (3) Computerisation of Registration.

completion of the programme is supposed to speed up the process of development in the country together with saving precious time in land-related litigation. However, the programme has been slow and uneven across states - to speed up the process lessons may be taken from some state initiatives[15] such as the Bhoomi Project in Karnataka, the Rajasthan Urban Ceiling Act of 2016 and the use of blockchain technology to prevent property fraud in Andhra Pradesh.

Meanwhile, a new central sector scheme, the *Swamitva*, was launched (for the period 2020-24) by the Government in 2020-21 to provide the *record of rights* to village household owners in rural areas and issue 'Property Cards' (which has been given different names by different states). It will bring in several benefits such as streamlined planning, revenue collection, clarity of property rights, easier borrowings and decrease in property disputes.

Moving onwards, the GoI passed the *Land Acquisition Bill, 2013*. The bill, besides proposing to amend the *Land Acquisition, Rehabilitation and Resettlement Act, 2011* proposed to put in place transparent, effective and speedy laws regarding the need of land reforms related to leasing and acquisition. By 2015, the new government at the Centre proposed a new land bill (*Right to Fair Compensation and Transparency in Land Acquisition, Rehabilitation and Resettlement Bill, 2015*), which aimed at removing the inadequacies of the Land Act of 2013. Faced with extreme opposition by the political parties, experts and media the Bill (which was already enforced through Presidential Ordinance) was repealed by the Government. Later on, the NITI Aayog was asked to look into advising an effective, fair and transparent land acquisition policy for the country (NITI Aayog suggested a *Model Land Leasing Law in 2016*).

Finer points (as per the relevant official documents) related to this PHASE may be summed up in the following way:

1. Leasing seems a better choice in face of farmer's opposition seen in recent times in different states toward attempts at land acquisition. Again, if the country needs to attract investment from the organised private sector (domestic or foreign) land leasing seems a better option than land acquisition.
2. Corporate farming has not taken place in the country in a big scale, especially in the areas of foodgrains production, which India needs to ensure food security and compete in the global grain market, in particular, and the agri-market in general. This has become even more important in the wake of the Right to Food given to a large segment of the population.
3. Giving primacy to 'leasing' will solve several problems:
    - **(i)** It will keep land ownership in the hands of the existing farmers;
    - **(ii)** It will prevent mass landlessness and unemployment among the farmers;
    - **(iii)** Farmers will get a permanent source of income (in the meantime, they might be imparted skills and provide better employment in industries); and
    - **(iv)** It will make land easily available for use of public and private purposes.

Meanwhile, the **Model Land Leasing Law** advised by the NITI Aayog in 2016 has been well received by the states, and some of them have already tried *land pooling* quite successfully, by early 2020. In this context, the example of Andhra Pradesh[16] has been quite successful which does not offer monetary compensation for the land taken today rather offers a developed piece of land in the future city (25 per cent of every fertile acre pooled to be returned as developed area in future city). The pro-active intermediation of state governments in the process of land acquisition seems to be emerging out of troubled times. But the new concern is the *rising cost of land acquisition* - beginning with the financial year 2013-14 it has increased by over 300 per cent till December 2023 - from ₹0.8 crore per hectare to ₹2.95 crore per hectare (as per the platform *Bhoomi Rashi*, Ministry of Road Transport and Highways).

- In the wake of the process of globalisation, if the country intends to bring in benefits to the agriculture sector, it needs to enhance its agriculture production

[15] *Land Market Reforms*, Maitreesh Ghatak in Abhijit Banerjee, Gita Gopinath, Raghuram Rajan and Mihir Sharma edited *What the Economy Needs Now* (New Delhi: Juggernaut Books, 2019), p. 83. It is referenced with *Land Acquisition and Compensation in Singur: What Really Happened?* by Maitreesh Ghatak, Sandip Mitra, Dilip Mukherjee and Anusha Nath, *Economic & Political Weekly* 48, no. 21 (2013).

[16] *Land Market Reforms*, Maitreesh Ghatak in Abhijit Banerjee, Gita Gopinath, Raghuram Rajan and Mihir Sharma edited *What the Economy Needs Now* (New Delhi: Juggernaut Books, 2019), p. 82.

to surplus levels - and for this India needs to garner the investment potential of the private sector. This cannot occur until the country is able to bring out effective land leasing and acquisition policies.

- The recent emphasis on the promotion of the 'manufacturing sector' and 'smart cities' is hugely dependent on a smoother and speedier process of land acquisition. Without expanding the industrial sector to its optimum levels, the agriculture sector can emerge a remunerative profession - the country needs to migrate the extra labour force of the agriculture sector to industry, smoothly.
- The issue of land acquisition is to establish a logical equation with 'environmental issue', in order to make the process of development sustainable (Niti Aayog gives a right call for it).

It should be noted that while the GoI has changed its orientation towards the issue of land reforms, the states in India are still trying to accelerate and continue the process of land reforms of *PHASE I* (but due to enough resistance from the land-owning section in the country, the process does not seem to be happening, politically).

Agriculture Holdings

The 10th *Agriculture Census 2015-16* was released by the Government in October 2018 (the Census[17] is conducted after every 5 years following broad guidelines of decennial World Census of Agriculture evolved by the Food and Agriculture Organisation of the United Nations). As per the report, the average size of land holding is decreasing due to rapid fragmentation caused by high population growth. The *major highlights* of the Census are as given below (all comparisons made in reference to the last and the 9th Census 2010-11):

- The total area under farming fell from 159.6 million hectares (Mha) to 157.14 Mha.
- Small and marginal farmers (owning less than two hectares) account for 86.2 per cent of all farmers in India, but own just 47.3 per cent of the crop area. In comparison, semi-medium and medium land holding farmers (owning between 2 and 10 hectares) account for 13.2 per cent of all farmers, but own 43.6 per cent of crop area.

[17] The *11th Agriculture Census* was launched in July 2022 with a delay of 1 year due to the COVID-19 pandemic and is expected to be completed by 2025-26.

11th Agriculture Census 2021-22

The new census was launched by the Government in July 2022, which is currently in the data processing and validation stage. This census marks a major shift towards digital data collection using smartphones and tablets for faster, more accurate results.

- The proportion of small and marginal farmers grew from 84.9 per cent to 86.2 per cent, while the total number of operational holdings grew from 138 million to 146 million.
- The number of small and marginal farms rose by about 9 million during the period.
- The small and marginal farmers (around 126 million in number) own about 74.4 Mha of land - or an average holding of just 0.6 hectares each - not enough to produce surpluses which can financially sustain their families, explaining the rising distress in Indian agriculture.
- For all farmers put together, the size of average land holding declined from 1.15 hectares to 1.08 hectares.
- The farmers holding 10 hectares and more account for just 0.57 per cent and had a share of 9.04 per cent in the operated area.
- State-wise data from the survey showed that Uttar Pradesh accounted for the largest number of operational holdings or farmers at 23.8 million followed by Bihar (16.4 million) and Maharashtra (14.7 million).
- Among operated or farmed areas, Rajasthan topped the list with 20.9 Mha, followed by Maharashtra (19.9 Mha) and Uttar Pradesh (17.45 Mha).
- The proportion of farms that are operated by women rose from 12.8 per cent to 13.9 per cent, signifying that more women are managing farm operations (the process of feminisation of farm sector is ongoing).

The *Situation Assessment Survey (SAS) Report 2021* (NSO, 77th Round on 'Land and Livestock Holdings of Households and Situation Assessment of Agricultural Households') shows increasing fragmentation of holdings - the average size of household ownership holdings declined from 0.725 hectare in 2003 to 0.592 hectare in 2013 and further to 0.512 hectare in 2019.

Rising Significance of Livestock Sector

IAs per the ***Economic Survey 2021–22***, given the rise in the number of small farmers and increasing importance of the livestock sector, the governments need to increase focus on measures like:

(a) Development of small farm technology,

(b) Boosting non-farm businesses, and

(c) Development of allied activities including animal husbandry, dairying and fisheries.

GREEN REVOLUTION

It is the introduction of new techniques of agriculture, which became popular by the name of Green Revolution (GR) in the early 1960s - at first for *wheat* and by the next decade for *rice,* too. It revolutionised the very traditional idea of food production by giving a boost by more than 250 per cent to the productivity level.[18] The GR was centred around the use of the High Yielding Variety (HYV) of seeds developed by the US agro-scientist Norman Borlaug carrying out research on a British Rockefeller Foundation Scholarship in Mexico by the early 1960s. The new wheat seeds which he developed *in vivo* claimed to increase its productivity by more than 200 per cent. By 1965, the seeds were successfully tested and were being used by farmers in food-deficient countries such as Mexico and Taiwan.

Components of the Green Revolution

The GR was based on the timely and adequate supply of many inputs or components. A brief review on the GR is given below:

1. **HYV Seeds:** These seeds were popularly called the *dwarf* variety of seeds. With the help of repeated mutations, Mr. Borlaug had been able to develop a seed which was raised in its nature of nutrients supplied to the different parts of the wheat plant - against the leaves and stem in favour of the grain. This made the plant dwarf and the grain heavier - resulting in high yield.[19] These seeds were non-photosynthetic, hence non-dependent on sunrays for targeted yields.
2. **Chemical Fertilisers:** The seeds were to increase productivity provided they received sufficient level of nutrients from the land. The level of nutrients they required could not be supplied with the traditional composts because they have low concentration of nutrient content and required bigger area while sowing - it meant it will be shared by more than one seed. That is why high concentration fertilisers were required, which could be provided to the targeted seed only - the only option was chemical fertilisers such as urea (N), phosphate (P) and potash (K).
3. **Irrigation:** For controlled growth of crops and adequate dilution of fertilisers, a controlled means of water supply was required. It made two important compulsions - firstly, the area of such crops should be at least free of flooding; and secondly, artificial water supply should be developed.
4. **Chemical Pesticides and Germicides:** As the new seeds were new and non-acclimatised to local pests, germs and diseases than the established indigenous varieties, use of pesticides and germicides became compulsory for result-oriented and secured yields.
5. **Chemical Herbicides and Weedicides:** To prevent costlier inputs of fertilisers not being consumed by the herbs and the weeds in the farmlands, herbicides and weedicides were used while sowing the HYV seeds.
6. **Credit, Storage, Marketing/Distribution:** For farmers to be capable of using the new and the costlier inputs of the GR, availability of easy and cheaper credit was a must. As the farmlands suitable for this new kind of farming was region- specific (as it was only Haryana, Punjab and western Uttar Pradesh in India) storage of the harvested crops was to be carried out in the region itself till they were distributed throughout the country. Again, the countries

[18] Consultative Group on International Agricultural Research (CGIAR) (Washington DC: World Bank, 1971).

[19] International Maize and Wheat Improvement Centre (CIMMYT), Mexico, 1971.

which opted for the GR were food-deficient and needed the new yield to be distributed throughout the country and a proper chain of marketing, distribution and transport connectivity was necessary. All these types of peripheral infrastructure were developed by the countries opting for the GR with softer loans coming from the World Bank - India being the biggest beneficiary.[20]

Impact of the Green Revolution

The GR had its positive as well as negative socio-economic and ecological impacts on the countries around the world, but we will specially study India here.

1. **Socio-economic Impact:** Food production increased in such a way (wheat in the 1960s and rice by the 1970s) that many countries became self-sufficient (self-sufficiency of food must not be confused with the idea of food security) and some even emerged as food exporting countries. But the discrepancy in farmers' income it brought with itself increased the interpersonal as well as inter-regional disparities or inequalities in India. Rise in the incidence of malaria due to waterlogging, a swing in the balanced cropping patterns in favour of wheat and rice putting pulses, oilseeds, maize, barley on the margins, etc. were negative impacts.
2. **Ecological Impact:** The most devastating negative impact of the GR was ecological. When the issues related with it were raised by the media, scholars, experts and environmentalists, neither the governments nor the masses (the farmers of the GR region were not educated enough to understand the side effects of the inputs of the GR) were convinced. But a time came when the government and other government agencies started conducting studies and surveys focused around ecological and environmental issues. The major ones among them may be glanced at in chronological order:
   - **(i)** *Critical Ecological Crisis:* On the basis of on-field studies,[21] it was found that critical ecological crises in the GR region are developing.
     - **(a)** *Soil fertility being degraded:* Due to the repetitive kind of cropping pattern being followed by the farmers as well as the excessive exploitation of the land, lack of a suitable crop combination and the crop intensity, etc.
     - **(b)** *Water table falling down:* As the new HYV seeds required comparatively very high amount of water for irrigation - 5 tonnes of water needed to produce 1 kg of rice.
     - **(c)** *Environmental degradation:* Excessive and uncontrolled use of chemical fertilisers, pesticides and herbicides has degraded the environment by increasing pollution levels in land, water and air. In India it is more due to *deforestation* and extensive cultivation in ecologically fragile areas. At the same time, there is an excessive pressure of animals on forests - mainly caused by the population of goat and sheep.
   - **(ii)** *Toxic Level in Food Chain:* Toxic level in the food chain of India has increased to such a high level that nothing produced in India is fit for human consumption. Basically, unbridled use of chemical pesticides and weedicides and their industrial production combined together had polluted the land, water and air to such an alarmingly high level that the whole food chain had been a prey of high toxicity.

The studies and reports cited above made the governments understand that the existing farm system was not sustainable in approach. As per agro-scientists, India needed to go for an *evergreen revolution* which is really 'green' in its approach. India needs a tremendous transformation (as the *Economic Survey 2018-19* outlined) from the philosophy of 'GR'-led productivity to 'green method'-led sustainability such as natural farming to eliminate chemical pesticides and promote good agronomic practices that are eco-friendly and less water consuming. This is why we see the

---

[20] Publication Division, India 2002 (New Delhi: Government of India, 2013).

[21] Based on various empirical studies in the 1990s conducted separately by Vandana Shiva, C. H. Hanumantha Rao, ICAR, Planning Commission, etc.

Government emphasising on natural farming and crop diversification aiming to shift the country's farm systems (from wheat, rice and sugarcane) to eco-friendly, less water consuming, climate resistant and nutritious crops (such as the 'nutri cereals') in recent times *(Economic Survey 2021-22)*.

CROPPING PATTERNS

The set and combination of crops which farmers opt for in a particular region, in their farm practices, is the cropping pattern of the region. Multiplicity of cropping systems has been one of the main features of Indian agriculture, and it is attributed to rain-fed agriculture and prevailing socio-economic situations of the farming community.

The cropping pattern in India has undergone significant changes over time. As the cultivated area remains more or less constant, the increased demand for food, because of increase in population and urbanisation, puts agricultural land under stress, resulting in *crop intensification* and *crop substitution* of food crops with commercial crops.

Cropping systems of a region are decided, by and large, by a number of soil and climatic parameters, which determine the overall agro-ecological setting for nourishment and appropriateness of a crop or set of crops for cultivation. Nevertheless, at farmers' level, potential productivity and monetary benefits act as guiding principles, while opting for a particular crop or a cropping system. The decisions to choose crops and cropping systems are further narrowed down under the influence of several other forces related to infrastructure facilities and socio-economic and technological factors, all operating interactively at the micro level. These factors are as follows:

1. **Geographical Factors:** Soil, landforms, precipitation, moisture, altitude, etc.
2. **Socio-cultural Factors:** Food habits, festivals, tradition, etc.
3. **Infrastructure Factors:** Irrigation, transport, storage, trade and marketing, post-harvest handling and processing, etc.
4. **Economic Factors:** Financial resource base, land ownership, size and type of land holding, household needs of food, fodder, fuel, fibre and finance, labour availability, etc.
5. **Technological factors:** Improved varieties of seeds and plants, mechanisation, plant protection, access to information, etc.

Prevalent Cropping Systems

Multiplicity of cropping systems has been one of the main features of Indian agriculture. This may be attributed to the following two major factors:

1. Rain-fed agriculture still accounts for over 92.8 million hectare or 65 per cent of the cropped area. A large diversity of cropping systems exists under rain-fed and dryland areas with an over-riding practice of intercropping, due to greater risks involved in cultivating larger area under a particular crop.
2. Due to prevailing socio-economic situations, such as dependency of a large population on agriculture, small land-holding size, very high population pressure on land resource, etc.

Improving household food security has been an issue of supreme importance to millions of farmers of India, with the following farm holdings:

1. 56.15 million marginal farmers (<1.0 ha)
2. 17.92 million small farmers (1.0-2.0 ha)
3. 13.25 million semi-medium farmers (2.0-4.0 ha).

They together comprise 90 per cent of the 97.15 million operational holdings. An important consequence of this has been that crop production in India remained to be considered, by and large, a *subsistence* rather than *commercial* activity. One of the typical characteristics of subsistence farming is that most of the farmers resort to growing a number of crops on their farm holdings, primarily to fulfil their household needs and follow the practice of rotating a particular crop combination over a period of 3-4 year, interchangeably on different farm fields.

Under the influence of all the above factors, the cropping systems remain dynamic in time and space, making it difficult to precisely determine their spread using conventional methods, over a large territory. However, it has been estimated that more than **250** double cropping systems are followed throughout the country. Based on the rationale of spread of crops in each district in the country, *30 important cropping systems* have been identified - rice-wheat, rice-rice, rice-gram, rice-mustard, rice-groundnut, rice-sorghum, pearl millet-gram, pearl millet-mustard, pearl millet-sorghum, cotton-wheat, cotton-gram, cotton-sorghum, cotton-safflower, cotton-groundnut, maize-wheat, maize-gram, sugarcane-wheat, soybean-wheat, sorghum-sorghum, groundnut-wheat, sorghum-groundnut, groundnut-rice, sorghum-wheat, sorghum-gram, pigeon pea-sorghum, groundnut, sorghum-rice, groundnut-sorghum and soybean-gram.

Changes in the Cropping Patterns

Due to various reasons, the cropping patterns of Indian farmers have undergone changes over time - we can see them in the following three phases.

Pre-Green Revolution Period In this phase we see Indian farmers opting for a cropping system (generally), which was primarily decided by the socio-cultural and economic factors - more or less they were closer to being *sustainable* as they had developed through the long process of trial and error of their forefathers. A combination of crops was seen being grown by farmers across the country with judicious mixture of crops till the GR. This was a period of subsistence farming with high dependency of population for livelihood on it. The nature of the cropping pattern was too rigid to change through incentives.

Green Revolution Period Under the spell of the New Agricultural Strategy (NAS), more popularly known as the GR, from 1965 onwards, we see a *major shift* in the cropping pattern of Indian farmers. The main forces of change were economic, infrastructural and technological in nature. Initiation of HYVs of seeds, financial supports of chemical and other inputs together with the provision of minimum support price (MSP) gave way to a major shift to the farmers' choices of crops. In the GR regions we see a highly repetitive kind of cropping pattern with the 'wheat-rice' having predominance. In coming times, the GoI started announcing MSPs for many other crops, which had its own impact on the farmers' choices of crops in their cropping systems.

This period was primarily guided by the singular objective of attaining self-sufficiency in food, which may lead the nation to attain food security. By the late 1980s, India was able to manage self-sufficiency in foodgrains. We see the emergence of big farmers in the GR regions for whom at least farming did not remain subsistence - *commercial dimension* enters the Indian farm practices, for the first time.

This is the period when the traditional cropping pattern of India became exposed to new inputs of farming and geographical dimensions of crop selection were undermined. Soon (by 1996-97), the government became more aware that the GR farm practices were ecologically damaging and unsustainable. The GoI officially adopted the idea of *sustainable* agriculture by 1997.

Reform Period Another wave of change in the cropping pattern arose with the process of economic reforms commencing in 1991, which brought in new opportunities together with several challenges in the farm sector:

1. The issue of food security continued to pressurise policymakers as foodgrains production was unable to keep pace with the population growth rate. The situation became even more serious with Food Rights (NFSA) given to a large population of the country recently.

Irrigation Water Productivity (IWP)

Irrigation Water Productivity (IWP) is defined as ratio of the crop output to irrigation water applied (kg/m^3), as irrigation being an economic activity farmer incurs expenditure on it. Thus, IWP is a practical indicator to estimate the crop output obtained with respect to the actual irrigation water applied.

2. Globalisation brought in new opportunities of farm exports together with the challenge of cheap production (need for farm mechanisation and commercial farming so that Indian farm products can compete in the global market) in wake of the agricultural provisions of the WTO. It made India think of mobilising huge investments in the sector. India accepts agriculture as an industry (2000) giving the green signal to *corporate* and *contract* farming.
3. Ecologically sustainable farming became the need of the hour due to ensuing danger of climate change and environment-related constraints.
4. The GoI proposed for the Second Green Revolution in 2002 with inclusion of genetically modified foods (GMFs).

Current Scenario Today, the cropping pattern in India is highly skewed towards *water-intensive* crops which are primarily due to incentive structures such as MSP, heavily subsidised electricity, water and fertilisers. The concerns[22] arising out of it together with their remedies are as given below:

- Around 90 per cent of groundwater extracted is used for irrigation (as per the latest *Asian Water Development Outlook 2019* of the Asian Development Bank), and crops such as paddy and sugarcane consume more than 60 per cent of irrigation water.
- A divergence is seen between land productivity and irrigation water productivity in the major sugarcane producing states in the country reflecting the urgent need to focus on irrigation water productivity to raise agricultural productivity. The states like Tamil Nadu, Karnataka, Maharashtra and Andhra Pradesh which have high land productivity tend to have very low irrigation water productivity, reflecting inefficient use of water and the need to re-calibrate the cropping pattern.
- Fertiliser response ratio has been declining over time, indicating declining responsiveness of soil fertility to fertiliser application. There is a need to use optimal dose of fertilisers based on soil health status together with promotion of neem-coated urea, micronutrients, organic fertilisers and water-soluble fertilisers.

Organic and natural farming techniques can improve both water use efficiency and soil fertility. The main aim of natural farming is to eliminate chemical pesticides and promote good agronomic practices that are eco-friendly and less water consuming.

NATURAL FARMING

Natural farming is a chemical-free *alias* traditional farming method. It is considered as agroecology-based diversified farming system which integrates crops, trees and livestock with functional biodiversity. Mainly aimed at the elimination of chemical inputs from farm practices, the good agronomic practices under it help in other ways too - chemical-free farm produce, restoring soil fertility, reducing water use, and making farming sustainable and climate friendly. It is largely based on:

- On-farm biomass recycling,
- Major stress on biomass mulching,
- Use of on-farm cow dung-urine formulations;
- Periodic soil aeration, and
- Exclusion of all synthetic chemical inputs.

22 *Economic Survey 2018-19*, vol. 2 (New Delhi: Ministry of Finance, GoI), p. 177.

It is being promoted as BPKP (Bharatiya Prakritik Krishi Paddhati Programme, 2021) under centrally-sponsored scheme, the PKVY (Paramparagat Krishi Vikas Yojana, 2018) and is aimed at promoting traditional *indigenous practices*. Under the programme, financial assistance of ₹12,200/ha for 3 years is provided for cluster formation, capacity building and continuous handholding by trained personnel, certification and residue analysis.

Under the *revised guidelines*, it promotes various forms of organic farming such as - Homa Farming (called 'revealed science' by its propagators, an entirely spiritual farming dating back to Vedic period under which chanting of Sanskrit mantras and 'angnihotra pooja' is performed at specific time before the holy fire), Cow Farming, Vedic Farming, and Zero Budget Natural Farming (ZBNF). The ZBNF is being promoted under the RKVY (Rashtriya Krishi Vikas Yojana, 2007) too.

The programme has been adopted in the states of Andhra Pradesh, Karnataka, Himachal Pradesh, Gujarat, Uttar Pradesh and Kerala - several studies have reported the effectiveness of this farming (as per the *NITI Aayog*, February 2022). As per the NITI Aayog, around 2.5 million farmers in India were practicing regenerative agriculture by 2021 and in the next 5 years, it is expected to reach 20 lakh hectares - in any form of organic farming, including natural farming (of which 12 lakh hectares are under BPKP). As per the UN body *HLPE* (High Level Panel of Experts on Food Security and Nutrition), it will reduce dependency on purchased inputs and will help to ease smallholder farmers from credits burden.

Giving a big push to natural farming the ***Union Budget 2022-23*** said it to be spread throughout the country - in the first stage to be started on farmers' land within a 5-km wide corridor along the river Ganges. Under it, states will be encouraged to revise the syllabi of agricultural universities 'to meet the needs of natural, zero-budget and organic farming, modern-day agriculture, value addition and management'.

CROP DIVERSIFICATION

Crop diversification (i.e., crop shift) is the process of including alternative/new crops in the cropping systems (patterns) in a region. As per the FAO, in India, it is generally viewed as a shift from traditionally grown less remunerative crops to more remunerative crops. This can be also used as a tool to promote sustainable agriculture, reduction in import dependence and higher incomes for the farmers. The report of the DFI (Doubling Farmers Income) Committee suggests that shifting some area from staple cereals to high value produce can lead to a sizable increase in the returns for farmers and also bring in *water use efficiency* and *sustainability of soil health*. The existing 'cropping pattern' is skewed towards cultivation of sugarcane, paddy and wheat which has led to depletion of fresh ground water resources at an alarming rate in many parts of our country. As per the *Economic Survey 2021-22*, the regions where the crops like paddy, wheat and sugarcane are grown have high to extremely high baseline water stress levels (baseline water stress implies the ratio of total annual water withdrawals to total available annual renewable supply).

PM Dhan-Dhanya Krishi Yojana

The *Union Budget 2025–26* announced to launch this new centrally sponsored scheme. Motivated by the success of the Aspirational Districts Programme, it will cover 100 districts with low productivity, moderate crop intensity and below-average credit parameters. Estimated to help over 1.7 crore farmers, the scheme has the following *five aims*:

- **(i)** Enhancing agricultural productivity,
- **(ii)** Adopting crop diversification and sustainable agriculture practices,
- **(iii)** Augmenting post-harvest storage at the panchayat and block level,
- **(iv)** Improving irrigation facilities, and
- **(v)** Facilitating availability of credit (both long-term and short-term).

In this regard, a centrally-sponsored scheme, the CDP (Crop Diversification Programme) is being implemented since 2013-14 as a sub-scheme of the RKVY (*Rashtriya Krishi Vikas Yojana*, 2007) which aimed at these two objectives:

- **(i)** To shift the original green revolution states (i.e., Punjab, Haryana and Western UP) from *paddy* (a water-guzzling crop) towards alternative crops like pulses, oilseeds, maize, coarse cereals, nutri cereals, cotton and agro forestry - with the objective of tackling the twin problem of depleting water table and declining soil fertility in these states.
- **(ii)** In 2015-16, it was expanded to include tobacco also under which the aim is to shift areas under tobacco farming to alternative crops in tobacco-growing states (such as Andhra Pradesh, Bihar, Gujarat, Karnataka, Maharashtra, Odisha, Tamil Nadu, Telangana, Uttar Pradesh and West Bengal) with effect from 2015-16.

As per the *Economic Survey* of 2022-23 and 2021-22, the price incentives being offered by the Government under the minimum support prices have helped crop diversification in the country.

MILLETS

The UNO declared the year 2023 as the *International Year of Millets (IYM)* which aligns well with several UN Sustainable Development Goals (SDGs). Millets are 'smart food' with high nutritional value and have very high potential to generate livelihood, increase farmers' income and ensure food and nutritional security all over the world.

Looking at the significance of millets, the Government notified them as *Nutri-cereals* (see the entry in the Glossary for information on it) in April 2018. Aimed at providing nutritional support, millets have been already introduced to the National Food Security Mission (NFSM). A sub-mission on the cereals is being implemented since 2018-19 in 212 districts of 14 States. India has more than 500 start-ups working in the millet value chains, while the Indian Institute of Millets Research has incubated 250 start-ups under Rashtriya Krishi Vikas Yojana-Remunerative Approaches for Agriculture and Allied Sectors Rejuvenation (RKVY-RAFTAAR).

As per the *latest official* information, India produced[23] 18.01 million tonnes of millets in 2024-25, which accounted for about **80** per cent of Asia and **41** per cent of the global production (India is the *largest* producer of these cereals). Average yield of millets in India (1239 kg/ha.) is higher than the global average (1229 kg/ha.). In India, millets are primarily a kharif crop mostly grown in rainfed conditions, requiring less water and agricultural inputs than other staple crops.

[23] *Ministry of Agriculture & Farmers Welfare* (New Delhi: Government of India, March 2026).

Animal Rearing

The economics of animal rearing plays a very vital role in the country. The agriculture sector in India is predominantly a mixed crop-livestock (animals, birds and fishes) farming system. Animal rearing has always remained an integral part of it. Animal rearing (which includes rearing of cows, camels, buffaloes, goats, pigs, sheep, etc.), besides directly contributing to the national income and socio-economic development, plays the following **vital functions** in the country:

- Supplements family income and generates gainful employment in the rural sector;
- Particularly helps the landless labourers, small and marginal farmers and women (economic empowerment of women);
- Provides cheap nutritional food;
- Functions as the best insurance against drought, famine and other natural calamities;
- It is more *inclusive* in nature; and
- Promotes the cause of *sustainable* agriculture.

Major Highlights (as per the *Economic Survey 2025–26* and other *official sources*) related to the allied sectors (called livestock sector also) of agriculture, which includes animal rearing, dairying and fisheries, are as given below:

- **Economic Significance:** With a CAGR (compound annual growth rate) of **12.77** per cent in the last 9 years, the livestock sector has contribution of about **30.2** per cent in total agricultural GVA at constant prices and **5.5** per cent in the total GVA of India.
- **Livestock Population and Production:** As per the latest FAOSTAT (Food and Agriculture Organisation Statistics) production data, India is the *3rd largest* producer of egg in the world (a total of 142.77 billion) with a growth rate of 6.1 per cent and per capita availability (pca) of 106 eggs per annum in 2024–25 (which was 62 in 2014–15). Poultry production in India has taken a quantum leap in the last four decades, emerging from use of unscientific farming practices to commercial production systems with state-of-the-art technology.
- **Dairy Sector:** India is the *largest* producer of milk in the world; during 2024–25, the total production was 247.87 MT, and the growth rate was 6.2 per cent. The per capita availability of milk was 471 grams per day in comparison to the global average of 322 grams. Uttar Pradesh, Rajasthan, Madhya Pradesh, Gujarat, and Maharashtra are the leading producer states in decreasing order of their production.
- As per a study of the NDDB (National Dairy Development Board), the demand for milk and milk products in India in 2030 is projected to be 266.5 MT.
- **Fisheries:** India is the *second largest* fish-producing country in the world, accounting for about 8 per cent of the global production – the total production being 19.77 million tonnes and marine product export of 1.55 million tonnes worth US$7.45 billion in 2024–25, showing an increase by more than 140 per cent during 2014–25, as per the *Economic Survey 2025–26*. The sector contributes 1.31 per cent to the GVA and 7.55 per cent to the agricultural GVA. The sector provides livelihood to over 30 million people in the country, especially to the marginalised and vulnerable communities, and has promoted meaningful socio-economic development. To harness the untapped potential of the sector, the Government has taken several policy initiatives in recent times:
  - *Blue Revolution,* a centrally sponsored scheme was launched in 2015–16 for a 5–year period to catalyse the Integrated, Responsible and Holistic Development and Management of the Fisheries Sector, which ended in March 2020.
  - *Fisheries and Aquaculture Infrastructure Development Fund (FIDF),* a dedicated fund for the sector, was established by late 2018 for setting up fisheries projects by entrepreneurs.
  - *Kisan Credit Cards* are being issued to fishers and fish farmers (as per the latest information available, by February 26, a total of 7.72 crore cards were issued till December 2024).

- *Pradhan Mantri Matsya Sampada Yojana (PMMSY)*, a flagship scheme, was launched in May, 2020 as a part of *Atma Nirbhar Bharat* Package by the Government, realising the potential, scope and importance of the sector – with the following aims:
  - Enhancing fish production to 22 million tons by 2024–25 at an average annual growth rate of about 9 per cent.
  - Increasing aquaculture productivity to 5 tons per hectare (existing national average is 3 tons).
  - Doubling export earnings (to ₹1 lakh crores) and generating about 55 lakh jobs.
  - Providing insurance coverage to fishing vessels (to be introduced for the first time).
  - Enhancing domestic fish consumption and attracting investments in the sector from other sources.

Floriculture—A Sunrise Sector

Floriculture industry of India has earned the status of a 'sunrise industry' today with 100 per cent export orientation—helping to emerge as a vital player in the global flower trade. Commercial floriculture (which includes cut-flower production, loose-flower production, dry flowers, cut greens, pot plants, flower seeds, perfumes, and essential oils) has emerged as a very profitable agri activity. The major features of the sector today are as given below:

- It gives much higher returns than many traditional crops:
  - **(i)** Including flowers in rice-based crop sequences that gives higher net returns than other sequences, such as rice-soybean, rice-bell pepper, rice-fodder maize, rice-cowpea and rice-radish.
  - **(ii)** Inter-cropping flowers are more profitable compared to the options of cereals, pulses, vegetables and oilseeds.
- Sophisticated export-oriented floriculture units have been set up across the states of Tamil Nadu, Karnataka, Madhya Pradesh, West Bengal, Uttar Pradesh and Maharashtra.
- Key export destinations are the USA, Netherlands, UAE, UK, Canada, and Malaysia.
- Government's subsidy support and crop loan financing have made it a promising venture for marginal and small landholdings (which constitute more than 96 per cent of the total landholdings and 63 per cent of the area of cultivation under floriculture).
- In 2023–24, approximately 297 thousand hectares were under floriculture which enabled India to earn USD 86.63 million export revenue.

Source: *Economic Survey 2024–25* (New Delhi: Ministry of Finance, GoI, January 2025), pp. 247–248.

- **Pig Rearing Scheme:** This scheme is aimed to assist farmers/landless labourers/co-operatives and the tribals particularly in the North-Eastern states by rearing pigs under stall-fed condition for quality pork production and organised pork marketing in rural areas and semi-urban areas. The *main objectives* of the scheme are as follows:
  - Encouraging commercial rearing by adopting scientific methods and infrastructure creation;
  - Producing and supplying improved germ plasm;
  - Organising stakeholders to popularise scientific practices;
  - Creating supply chain for the meat industry; and
  - Encouraging value addition for better income.
- **Beekeeping:** Beekeeping (apiculture) is being promoted by the Government under the IFS (Integrated Farming System)— in this regard the NBHM (National Beekeeping & Honey Mission) was launched for three years (2020–21 to 2022–23) as a part of the ANB (*Atma Nirbhar Bharat*) scheme. The Mission aims for the overall promotion and development of scientific beekeeping in the country to achieve the goal of ***Sweet Revolution*** which is being implemented through NBB (National Bee Board).

Beekeeping is an agro-based activity which is being undertaken by farmers/landless labourers in rural areas. Beekeeping has been useful in pollination of crops, thereby, increasing the income of the farmers/beekeepers by way of increasing crop yield and providing honey and other high value beehive products such as bee wax, bee pollen, propolis, royal jelly, bee venom, etc. Diversified agro climatic conditions of India provide great potential and opportunities for beekeeping/honey production and export of honey. As per the latest official export data, India's export of honey has increased by about 140 per cent between 2014–15 and 2024–25.

- **Animal Health:** With the improvement in the quality of livestock through launching of extensive cross-breeding programmes, the susceptibility to various diseases, including exotic diseases has increased. In order to reduce morbidity and mortality, efforts are being made by the state/UT governments to provide better health care through polyclinics/veterinary hospitals/dispensaries/first-aid centres including mobile veterinary dispensaries. For the prevention of various diseases, 27 veterinary vaccine production units are working with dominance of the public sector (20 are in the public sector and rest in the private sector). The 'Livestock Health & Disease Control' is being run as a centrally sponsored scheme to assist the attempts of the states and UTs in the area.

Suggestions for further development of the *livestock sector* are as follows:

- Development of progeny-tested semen for artificial insemination.
- Expansion of fodder availability through innovative means.
- Upgradation of facilities of animal health centres and the effective use of disease control systems on the veterinary side.
- In the drylands and mountain ecosystems, livestock contributes anywhere between 50 to 75 per cent of the total household income of the rural population. Support to these massive and highly diverse livestock populations in these regions is lacking.
- Raising the capability of the rural poor to conserve and manage their livestock resources, and enable them to derive sustainable incomes from these resources.
- Decentralisation and convergence of policy support for these options is crucial for diversification of livelihoods in small-holder farming.

Recent Policy Initiatives

With the aim of promoting the livestock sector the Government has taken the following major policy initiatives in recent times:

AHIDF (Animal Husbandry Infrastructure Development Fund) was set up by late 2020 as a part of the Atma Nirbhar Bharat Abhiyan stimulus package with a corpus of ₹15000 crores. The fund will incentivise investments by individual entrepreneurs, private companies including SMEs, farmers producers' organisations (FPOs) to establish the following:

1. dairy processing and value addition infrastructure,
2. meat processing and value addition infrastructure and
3. animal feed plant.

The beneficiaries will be provided 3 per cent interest subvention with a 2–year moratorium for the loan and 6 years repayment period thereafter. A credit guarantee fund (CGF) of ₹750 crores to be managed by NABARD, will also be set up exclusively for the MSMEs. To ease out the application process, SIDBI has put in place an online system for applicants.

NADCP (National Animal Disease Control Programme), a central sector scheme, was launched to control FMD (Foot and Mouth Disease) and Brucellosis. One hundred per cent of the cattle, buffalo, sheep, goats, pigs, and bovine female calves of 4–8 months of age were to be vaccinated under it in the next 5 years (2019–2024).

RKA (Rashtriya Kamdhenu Aayog) was set in 2019–20 to upscale sustainable genetic upgradation, production and productivity of cows. The commission will also look after effective implementation of laws and welfare schemes for cows.

FOOD MANAGEMENT

Managing enough food in the domestic market has been the prime focus of the government since Independence. Meeting the physical target of food together with the challenge of enabling Indians to procure food for their consumption was also there. Over the year, we see the government devising various ways and means to handle the twin challenges. Once the country joined the WTO, a new need was felt for producing surplus and competing with the world, so that the benefits of globalisation could also be reaped by the agriculture sector. This section discusses the challenges to management of food in the country.

Minimum Support Price

Minimum Support Price (MSP) is a form of market intervention by the GoI to insure agricultural producers against any sharp fall in farm prices - a guarantee price to save farmers from distress sale. The MSPs are announced at the beginning of the sowing season for certain crops on the basis of the recommendations of the Commission for Agricultural Costs and Prices (CACP, 1985). The major objectives are to support the farmers from distress sales and to procure foodgrains for public distribution. In case the market price for the commodity falls below the announced minimum price due to bumper production and glut in the market, government agencies purchase the entire quantity offered by the farmers at the announced minimum price.

Commencing with 'wheat' for the 1966-67, currently the MSPs are announced for 23 commodities including seven cereals (paddy, wheat, barley, jowar, bajra, maize and ragi); five pulses (gram, arhar/tur, moong, urad and lentil); eight oilseeds (groundnut, rapeseed/mustard, toria, soyabean, sunflower seed, sesamum, safflower seed and niger seed); copra, raw cotton and raw jute. The MSPs are fixed at *incentive level*, to fulfil the following purposes:

1. to induce more investment by farmers in the farm sector,
2. to motivate farmers to adopt improved crop production technologies and
3. to enhance production and thereby farmers' income.

In the absence of such a guaranteed price, there is a concern that farmers may shift to other crops causing shortage in these commodities. The agricultural price policy in India emerged in the backdrop of *food scarcity* and *price fluctuations* provoked by *drought, floods* and *international prices* for exports and imports.

Economic Transformation Through Horticulture

Horticulture has potential to transform the rural economies of India. The sector is more productive and profitable than traditional agriculture and is emerging as a fast-growing industry. India has emerged as a leading exporter ($417.07 million in 2023–24) of fresh grapes today. Maharashtra (with the highest productivity and over 67 per cent share in the total production), Karnataka, Tamil Nadu, and Mizoram are the key growing states of grapes.

The Nashik story: Export of grapes has significantly improved the livelihoods of the farmers in Nashik. Higher profits from exports has attracted rural youth to grape farming in the region. Farmers here have adopted advanced technologies like real-time monitoring systems to ensure optimal grape quality. The Nashik grape story shows how export-oriented agriculture, technology, and collective efforts can transform a region's socio-economic conditions.

Source: *Economic Survey 2024–25* (New Delhi: Ministry of Finance, GoI, January 2025), p. 249.

Aimed at making farming remunerative the Government announced to fix the **MSP for crops 50 per cent** above their production cost since 2018-19. The new MSP is fixed by the CACP over the *Cost A2+Fl* (where, *Cost A2* includes all paid out costs borne by the farmer on seeds, fertilisers, pesticides, hired labour, leased-in land, fuel, irrigation, etc. and the *Fl* is imputed cost of unpaid family labour). While farm activists demand it to be fixed over the ***Cost C2*** (which is a more comprehensive cost that factors in rentals and interest forgone on owned land and fixed capital assets on top of *Cost **A2+Fl***).

Procurement Prices

In 1966-67, the GoI announced a 'procurement price' for wheat, a bit higher than its MSP (the purpose being security of food procurement for requirement of the PDS). The MSP was announced before sowing, while the procurement price was announced before

Market Intervention Scheme

The Market Intervention Scheme (MIS) is similar to MSP, which is implemented on the request of state governments for procurement of perishable and horticultural commodities in the event of fall in market prices. The scheme is implemented when there is at least 10 per cent increase in production or 10 per cent decrease in the ruling rates over the previous normal year. Proposal of MIS is approved on the specific request of the state/UT governments, if the states/UTs are ready to bear 50 per cent loss (25 per cent in case of North-Eastern states) incurred on its implementation.

harvesting – the purpose was to encourage farmers to sell a bit more and get encouraged to produce more. But this increased price hardly served the purpose as a suitable incentive to farmers. It would have been better had it been announced before sowing and not after harvesting. That is why since the fiscal 1968-69 the government announced only the MSP, which is also considered the effective procurement price.[24]

Issue Price

It refers to the price at which the government allows offtake of foodgrains from the FCI (the price at which the FCI sells its foodgrains). The FCI has been fetching huge losses in the form of food subsidies. The foodgrains procured are transported to the godowns of the FCI located across the country (counted in the buffer stock). From here they head to the sale counters – to the TPDS or Open Market Sale. The transportation, storage, the cost of maintaining the FCI, carriage losses, etc., make the foodgrains costlier (these additional expenses added with the MSP is known as the 'economic cost of foodgrains'). To make the foodgrains affordable to the consumers, the issue prices for foodgrains are set lower than the total cost of procurement and distribution – the gap converts into the 'food subsidy'.

Economic Cost of Foodgrains

The economic cost of foodgrains consists of three components, namely the MSP including central bonus (the price paid to farmers), procurement incidentals and the cost of distribution.

The economic cost of foodgrains has witnessed significant increase in the last few years proportionate to increase in the MSPs (as per the *Economic Survey 2019-20*, an increase of 1 per cent in the MSP leads to a 0.48 per cent increase in the economic cost in case of wheat). In **2025-26**, the estimated economic cost[25] of rice and wheat increased to ₹41.73 and ₹29.00 per kilogram, respectively, from ₹26.16 and ₹19.08 in 2013-14.

High economic cost necessitated a detailed review of the open-ended procurement policy, especially in states that offer high bonus on top of MSP and those that impose high taxes and statutory levies, as well as stocking and distribution policies. In this regard, the government had set up a *High-Level Committee (HLC)* in 2015 (Shanta Kumar as its Chairman) to suggest inter alia *restructuring* or *unbundling* of the FCI with a view to improve its operational efficiency and financial management.

Open Market Sale Scheme

The FCI has been undertaking sale of wheat at pre-determined prices (reserve prices) in the open market from time to time, known as the Open Market Sale Scheme (OMSS). This is aimed at serving the following *objectives:*

1. to enhance market supply of foodgrains;
2. to exercise a moderating influence on open market prices; and
3. to offload surplus stocks.

Under the OMSS (Domestic), the government now adopts a policy of differential prices to encourage sale of older stock first – sticking to the following policy stance:

1. Keeping the reserve price above MSP, but reasonably below the acquisition cost or economic cost of wheat, so that the buyers remain attracted to purchase of wheat from the *mandis* during the harvest season and the market remains competitive.
2. Maintaining that the market price during the lean season does not increase much and inflation remains under check.

---

[24] New Agricultural Strategy, 1965; the CACP, 1967 and Ministry of Agriculture, GoI, New Delhi.

[25] *Food Corporation of India* (New Delhi: Ministry of Agriculture & Farmers Welfare, GoI, February 2026).

Price Stabilisation Fund

The GoI, by late *March 2015*, launched the Price Stabilisation Fund (PSF) as a Central Sector Scheme to support market interventions for price control of perishable agri-horticultural commodities. The cost is to be borne between the centre and the states in equal ratio (in case of the North-Eastern states, the respective share will be 75:25). The scheme will commence with only two crops, viz. onion and potato.

BUFFER STOCK

Buffer stock refers to a 'reserve' of commodity to offset price fluctuations and unforeseen emergencies. Introduced in 1969 (4th Plan, 1969-74), under it, the GoI maintains a buffer stock of selected *foodgrains* (wheat and rice) in the Central Pool for the following:

1. Meeting the prescribed minimum buffer stock norms for food security,
2. Monthly release of foodgrains for supply through Targeted Public Distribution System (TPDS) and Other Welfare Schemes (OWS),
3. Meeting emergency situations arising out of unexpected crop failure, natural disasters, etc. and
4. Price stabilisation or market intervention to augment supply so as to help moderate the open market prices.

Central Pool consists of stocks held by FCI, stocks of the Decentralised Procurement (DCP) Scheme of the participating states and the state government agencies (SGAs). The minimum stocking norms (for two cereals wheat and rice), set by the Government, is to be maintained on *quarterly basis* and revised after every five years - the combined stock limit for wheat and rice, after the last revision of *January 2015* is given below in the table:

Table 9.1 Revised Buffer Stock

As on	Existing Since April, 2005 (in Million Tonnes)	Revised
1 April	21.2	21.04
1 July	31.9	41.12
1 Oct	21.2	30.77
1 Jan	25.0	21.41

In the last revision, its nomenclature[26] was changed to *Foodgrain Stocking Norms* (from the existing 'Buffer Norms and Strategic Reserve').

To control prices of **pulses**, Government decided in October 2015 to create a 1.5 MT of buffer stock of pulses (which was later increased to 2 MT) - to be procured by the FCI, NAFED (National Agricultural Cooperative Marketing Federation of India Limited) and SFAC (Small Farmers Agri-business Consortium).

While four months requirement of foodgrains for issue under TPDS and OWS are earmarked as 'operational stocks', the surplus over that is treated as 'buffer stock' (physically both are merged into one and are not distinguishable). According to the present practice, the Government treats the food stock over and above the minimum norms as 'excess stock' and liquidates them from time to time through exports, open market sales or additional allocations to states.

The present foodgrain procurement policy has been criticised on various counts - excessive dependence on wheat and rice (which is a water-guzzling crop), stockpiling of foodgrains in godowns much above the buffer norms, financial pressure on the governments, export controls on FCI, concerns of rising agricultural subsidies related to the agriculture clause of the WTO being the major ones. To look into the existing foodgrains procurement by the FCI, the Government had set up a *High-Level Committee* in 2015 (Reorienting the Role and Restructuring of FCI, headed by Shanta Kumar) which advised major changes, which are under the Government consideration.

Decentralised Procurement Scheme

The decentralised procurement (DCP) scheme was operationalised by the government in 1997 (together with the Centre and some of the states also procure foodgrains from the farmers, locally). Under this scheme, the designated states procure, store and also issue foodgrains under the TPDS. The difference between the economic cost of the states and the Central Issue Price (CIP) is passed on to the states by the GoI as a subsidy. The decentralised system of procurement helps to cover more farmers under the MSP operations, improves efficiency of the PDS, provides varieties of foodgrains more suited to local taste and reduces the transportation costs of the FCI.[27]

[26] *Economic Survey 2019-20*, vol. 2 (New Delhi: Ministry of Finance, GoI), pp. 211-12.

[27] *Economic Survey 2011-12*, (New Delhi: Ministry of Finance, GoI, 2012).

The GoI urged *all states* to adopt the DCP scheme so that costs of distribution can be saved and outreach of price support mechanism to the farmers in hitherto weaker areas can be improved. To overcome the problem of gaps in the flow of information about procurement operations on day-to-day basis, an *Online Procurement Monitoring System (OPMS)* has been evolved for reporting and monitoring on a daily basis, procurement operations for wheat, paddy and coarse grains in the country.

States offering bonus over and above the MSP announced by the Government had a distortionary effect on the food procurement process of the GoI. Checking procurement and its cost from rising, Government took two steps - firstly, a limit was put on its procurement from the states paying bonus over and above the MSP up to the needs of TPDS and OWS; and secondly, FCI stopped taking part in MSP operations in the case of non- DCP states declaring bonus.

STORAGE

By the end of 2025, the total storage capacity[28] available with FCI and state agencies for storage of foodgrains was **917.83 LMT** (lakh metric tonnes). Some areas of concerns related to India's storage system, outlined by some official documents of recent times are briefed below:

1. The CAP (Cover and Plinth) of 12.42 LMT capacity cannot be treated as scientific storage.
2. Public agencies do not have warehouses for proper storage of even half of the wheat and rice procured by them.
3. In the wake of persistent seasonal inflation in perishables such as fruits and vegetables, there was no effective strategy to control inflation on a sustainable basis.
4. Cold storage capacity for all types of food items is just 40.02 MT (million tonnes), as per the FCI, while the production of only potatoes was estimated to reach around 60 MT in 2025-26.
5. Cold storage facility is available for only 10 per cent of fruits and vegetables produced in India, as per the Government (wastage of these items range from 20 to 40 per cent).

To bridge the gap between the requirement and availability of scientific storage capacity is the immediate need of the hour. For this, it is advisable to promote the policies by which private sector investment can be attracted to it. To augment storage capacity, few recent steps[29] taken by the Government, are as given below:

1. Construction of godowns under the *PEG* (Private Entrepreneurs Guarantee Scheme) being implemented in PPP (Public Private Partnership) mode in 24 states.
2. Construction of *Steel Silos* in PPP mode to modernise storage infrastructure and improve the shelf life of stored foodgrains with a capacity of 100 LMT is being implemented.
3. Online Depot Management System (ODMS), also known as Depot Online System (DOS), being implemented by the FCI to optimise costs and improving functional efficiency. It will automate the entire process of depot operations including receipt of foodgrains at the depot, storage, maintenance activities and issue of foodgrains.

FARM SUBSIDIES

Farm subsidies form an integral part of the government's budget. In the case of developed countries, the agricultural or farm subsidies compose nearly 40 per cent of the total budgetary outlay, while in India's case it is much lower (around 7.8 per cent of the agricultural GDP) and of different nature.

Direct Farm Subsidies These are the kinds of subsidies in which direct cash incentives are paid to the farmers in order to make their products more competitive in the global markets. The developed countries (United States and Europe) spend huge amounts of their annual budgets on the agriculture, farm and fisheries subsidies. Direct farm subsidies are helpful as they provide the right levels of purchasing power to the farmer and can significantly help in raising the standards of living of the rural poor. They also help in checking the misuse of public funds as they help in the proper identification of the beneficiaries.

Indirect Farm Subsidies These are the farm subsidies which are provided in the form of cheaper credit facilities, farm loan waivers, reduction in irrigation and electricity bills, fertilisers, seeds and pesticides subsidy as well as the investments in agricultural

[28] *Food Corporation of India* (New Delhi: Ministry of Agriculture & Farmers Welfare, GoI, February 2026).

[29] *Ministry of Agriculture and Farmers Welfare*, GoI, New Delhi, February 2026.

research, environmental assistance, farmer training, etc. These subsidies are also provided to make farm products more competitive in the global market.

The subsidies provided on the fertilisers as 'input' subsidies are in the form of *indirect* subsidies. But if the government does not incentivise the farmer by an effective cost reduction in prices of the fertilisers, but provides direct cash incentives after the produce, it is known as a *direct* subsidy.

The WTO has put some ceilings on the amount of direct and indirect subsidies being provided by the various developing and developed nations due to the fact that these subsidies *distort the market forces* which have their own implications.

First thoughts are encouraging. A panel headed by Montek Singh Ahluwalia (the then Deputy Chairman, *Planning Commission*) recommended that the power ministry, instead of paying power distribution companies, hand out electricity subsidies **directly** to farmers through a smart card linked to the unique identity number.

India spends about ₹1,60,000 crore every year or roughly 2 per cent of its GDP on subsidies, *all indirectly*. For example, in fertilisers, which accounts for two-thirds of total subsidies, the government fixes a low selling price and compensates the producers by paying the difference between the selling price and the actual production costs (plus a pre-decided profit margin) as subsidy. *Important issues* related to farm subsidies are as given below:

1. The indirect subsidy has been blamed for benefiting big farmers more than the small and medium farmers, for whom the subsidy is intended. This is because the bulk of the subsidised fertilisers is picked up by the rich farmers because the small and marginal farmers account for just 37 per cent of the farm land.
2. Indirect subsidy has also discouraged improvements in production processes since manufacturers have no incentive to increase efficiency. This will also play a big part in bringing down India's overall subsidy bill. For instance, according to industry estimates, the money spent on poor farmers could potentially come down to ₹37,000 crore from the current ₹100,000 crore.
3. Another advantage of cash subsidies is that it will free up the distribution system and allow the people who receive the subsidy to choose where they buy their goods from. The complexity is not so much in the transfer of funds, as it is in the identification of the beneficiaries.

Other Countries The idea of disbursing subsidies directly to the beneficiaries is becoming popular among the development thinkers and policymakers. It's already a part of policy in many parts of the world - predominantly, in Latin America where 16 countries have this practice, and also in other countries such as Jamaica, Philippines, Turkey and Indonesia.

The biggest and most cited of such programmes is Brazil's *Bolsa Familia.* It started in 2001, with a programme aimed at education. It expanded in 2003 to include a range of services such as food and fuel, and now covers 2.6 million families in that country. The government *transfers cash* straight to a family, subject to conditions such as school attendance, nutritional monitoring and pre-natal and post-natal tests. By many measures, the programme is a success. Brazil's poverty levels dropped by 15 percentage points between 2003 and 2009, at least a sixth, thanks to Bolsa Familia (economic growth played a big part, too). Millennium Development Goals initiative, which in 2000 sought to halve poverty by 2015, doesn't even mention cash transfers. But Brazil achieved the goals 10 years ahead of the deadline. And the cost of these transfers has been 0.4 per cent of GDP.

The big question is not whether a direct cash transfer is the perfect solution, but whether it's an improvement over the existing systems. The evidence - its success in other parts of the world - and the poor performance of indirect subsidies so far would suggest so. Looking at it, the GoI has already started a pan-India scheme to disburse all forms of subsidies directly, through the *Direct Benefit Transfer (DBT)* since 2015-16 onwards.

FOOD SECURITY

Food security is a state when all people have physical, social, and economic access to sufficient, safe, and nutritious food that meets their dietary needs and food preferences (World Food Summit, FAO, Rome, 1996). India attained self-sufficiency in food by the late 1980s, though food security still evades the country. The policy actions of the past 10-15 years have shown good results in this regard. The following two global reports on hunger and malnutrition provide the latest insight into the food scenario in the country:

1. The **State of Food Security and Nutrition in the World (SOFI)** 2025 report (published jointly by FAO, IFAD, UNICEF, WFP, and WHO) identifies India as a *primary driver* of global hunger reduction; however, it continues to face severe nutritional challenges. While the absolute number of undernourished people in the country has declined significantly, it still hosts the world's largest undernourished population due to its scale. Key findings of the report about India are as given below:
   - *Undernourishment:* 12 per cent (about 172 million people), which is a reduction from 243 million in 2006 and the 7th highest in Asia.
   - *Child Wasting:* 18.7 per cent (21 million children), which is the highest in the world.
   - *Child Stunting:* 37.75 per cent (about 37.4 million children), which is chronic under-nutrition– 21st highest globally.
   - *Anaemia (women):* 53.7 per cent (aged 15-49), the highest in Asia and 4th highest in the world.
   - *Diet Affordability:* 42.9 per cent cannot afford a healthy diet which costed US$4.07 in 2024 (rising from US$2.77 in 2017) in PPP terms.
   - *Nutritional Paradox:* India's performance on the food front is marked by a ***nutritional paradox***– improving calorific availability alongside persistent acute malnutrition.
   - *Double Burden of Malnutrition:* Today, India is facing a typical challenge of under- and overnourishment (referred to as the ***double burden of malnutrition***– on one hand, while 12 per cent of people are undernourished, on the other, obesity is rising (adult obesity doubled in the last decade, reaching 71.4 million people in 2024; the number of overweight children under five rose by 66 per cent to 4.2 million between 2012 and 2024).
2. The **Global Hunger Index 2025** ranks[30] India 102nd out of 123 countries, with a score of 25.8, categorised as "serious". While this reflects an improvement from a score of 27.3 in 2024 (105th rank), the report underscores that progress towards "Zero Hunger" by 2030 remains off-track (globally). Key findings of the index about India are as given below:
   - *Child Wasting:* 18.7 per cent (2nd highest globally; reflects acute malnutrition).
   - *Child Stunting:* Undernourishment: 32.9 per cent (21st highest globally; reflects chronic under-nutrition).
   - *Undernourishment:* 12.0 per cent (affects 172 million people, which is worse than in 2016).
   - *Child Mortality:* 2.8 per cent (shows significant long-term improvement since 2000).
   - *Food Affordability:* 42.9 per cent of people cannot afford a healthy diet (food price rises have been a major issue– despite record food production and emerging as a global food supplier, India remains a country of 'nutritional paradox').

Two important things need attention regarding India's food security:

1. Around 22 per cent of India's population is BPL and a greater portion (one conservative estimate suggests that 75 per cent of their household income is spent on food).
2. There is a strong correlation between stability in agricultural production and food security. Volatility in agricultural production impacts food supplies and can result in spikes in food prices, which adversely affect the lowest income groups of the population. Therefore, along with provision of food subsidy, stability in agricultural commodity prices is essential for making the poorer sections food secure. It means, in the direction of assuring food security, India needs to tackle mainly two hurdles:
   - **(i) Enhancing its food production:** If food (i.e., foodgrains) is to be supplied to all today India will face deficit of around

[30] The *Global Hunger Index* (published since 2006) is jointly published by the international non-profit agencies Concern Worldwide (Dublin, Ireland) and Welthungerhilfe (Bonn, Germany), to track and measure hunger at the global, regional, and country levels - with the main aim to trigger action towards reducing global hunger. The *Index* is prepared on the basis of four indicators - child mortality, undernourishment, child wasting (weight for age) and child stunting. This time the major focus of the index was on the relation between climate change and hunger together with the impact of extreme weather on food production and food security also. The Index measures countries on a 100-point scale, where a score of **0** (zero) is considered as best performing countries and **100** is the worst.

30 MT of foodgrains. This shows the food insecurity dimension of India.

(ii) **Strengthening supply chain:** Managing the issues such as storage, transportation, proper retailing and integrating the segmented agri-markets into a national agri-market.

Due to high level of undernourishment and volatility in agricultural prices, India has one of the largest numbers of food schemes in the world to ensure food security:

1. There is entitlement feeding programmes such as the Integrated Child Development Scheme (ICDS - covers all children under six, pregnant and lactating mothers).
2. Mid-Day Meal Schemes (MDMS)which was later restructured as the PM-POSHAN.
3. Food subsidy programmes such as the TPDS (through which the National Food Security Act (NFSA) is being implemented).
4. Annapurna (10 kgs of free foodgrain for destitute poor).
5. Employment Programmes such as Mahatma Gandhi National Rural Employment Guarantee Scheme (MGNREGS 100 days of employment at minimum wages) to ensure food security.
6. To address the issue of 'anaemia' and 'micro-nutrient' deficiency and to promote nutrition security in the country, a centrally sponsored pilot scheme on *Fortification of Rice and its Distribution under Public Distribution System* was approved for a period of 3 years beginning in 2019-20. The pilot scheme will focus on 15 districts, preferably one district per state during the initial phase of implementation. *(Economic Survey 2020-21).*
7. With the objective of providing nationwide portability of ration card under the NFSA through the *One Nation One Ration Card* System, a central sector scheme, the IMPDS (Integrated Management of Public Distribution System) was launched in 2020-21. This system will enable the ration card holders to lift their entitled foodgrains from any fair price shop (FPS) of their choice anywhere in the country by using their same/existing ration card. Under this system, equivalent food subsidy is provided through the DBT (Cash Transfer instead of subsidised foodgrains) to the beneficiaries in Chandigarh, Puducherry, Dadar and Nagar Haveli.

Though these food schemes have shown positive results, they are only short-term interventions. India needs to enable the target population with the market-linked purchasing power as the long-term remedy.

PDS AND FOOD SUBSIDY

The Public Distribution System (PDS was changed to Targeted PDS in 1997) strives to ensure food security through timely and affordable distribution of foodgrains to the BPL population as this section cannot afford to pay market prices for their food. This involves procurement of foodgrain at MSP by the Government, building up and maintenance of food stocks, their storage and timely distribution, making foodgrains accessible at reasonable prices to the vulnerable sections of the population.

Food subsidy comprises of: (1) subsidy provided to FCI for procurement and distribution of foodgrains under NFSA, OWS and maintaining their strategic reserve; and (2) subsidy provided to States for undertaking 'decentralised procurement'. The acquisition and distribution costs of foodgrains for the central pool together constitute the economic cost. The difference between the economic cost and the Central Issue Price (CIP is the price at which beneficiaries get the foodgrains) gives the quantum of food subsidy.

There have been certain anomalies in India's food management under the PDS which need immediate attention:

- The percentage distribution of the economic cost of wheat and rice has been rising fast. The pooled cost of foodgrains (*MSP plus the Bonus which are offered by the individual states*) accounts for *two-thirds* of the economic cost of wheat and rice. This has made the economic cost of foodgrains to the Food Corporation of India (FCI) increase over the years.
- Increasing costs of labour, fertilisers, pesticides and other inputs have made production of crops costlier over the time. This forced the government to keep on increasing the MSPs of the crops, too.
- The increase in the food subsidy bill is determined by the rate at which the MSPs for wheat and rice increase and the *economic cost* of handling grains (their procurement, stocking and distribution to the targeted households). This has been the major factor for ballooning food subsidy bill.
- The procurement incidentals of wheat and rice consist of costs related to mandi charges and taxes,

cost of gunny bags, *arhatiya* commission, *mandi* labour, forwarding charges, internal movement, storage charges, interest, administrative charges and others. Out of these costs, *mandi* charges and taxes constitute more than 40 per cent of the total costs.

Rise in Subsidy Food subsidy bills have been rising in recent past due to many reasons. The highest ever food subsidy was offered by the Government during 2020-21 when it reached to *₹5.29 lakh crore* (from ₹1.13 lakh crore in 2014-15), as per the *Economic Survey 2022-23*. To ease the hardships faced by the poor due to the pandemic, the *Pradhan Mantri Garib Kalyan Anna Yojana* (PMGKAY) was launched for the period April to June 2020, which was extended many times upto December 2022. Under the scheme, 5 kg of additional foodgrains per person per month was provided free of cost to NFSA beneficiaries in all the phases. Besides, till December 2022, the NFSA provided, for coverage of up to 75 per cent of the rural and up to 50 per cent of the urban population, highly subsidised food grains at ₹1/2/3 per kg for coarse grains/wheat/rice, respectively, at the rate of 35 kg per family per month to households covered under *Antyodaya Anna Yojana* (AAY) and at the rate of 5 kg per person per month to priority households.

In *January 2023*, the government withdrew the existing PMGKAY and decided to provide ***free*** foodgrains to all beneficiaries of the NFSA (about 81.35 crore) under the NFSA for one year from January 1, 2023 which was extended in December 2024 for the *next five years* (i.e., till December 2028). This scheme will cost the Government around ₹11.8 lakh crore. There have been many reasons[31] for the rising food subsidy:

- The NFSA has wider coverage than the erstwhile TPDS.
- The *Antyodaya* beneficiaries also get foodgrains at the NFSA prices.
- Under NFSA the categorisation of APL and BPL was abolished.
- Coverage under the NFSA was also delinked from the poverty estimates as it was substantially high to ensure that all the vulnerable and needy sections of the society receive its benefit.
- The build-up of the foodgrain stocks much higher than their buffer norms.
- Increase in economic cost and real MSP.
- Decline in sale to the APL households.

While the economic cost has increased, the selling prices (CIP) for NFSA beneficiaries have not been revised from ₹1, ₹2 and ₹3 per kg for coarse cereals, wheat and rice, respectively. These rates were fixed under the Act initially for a period of three years from the date of commencement of the Act (July 2013) and thereafter were to be fixed by the Government from time to time, while not exceeding the MSP. As no revision has been carried out since then it has resulted in widening of the gap between the economic cost and the CIP and increasing food subsidy bills.

While the interests of the vulnerable sections of the population need to be safeguarded, the food subsidy also needs to be rationalised as it distorts market for foodgrains, pulls inflation down and challenges the sustainability of food security in the country.

AGRICULTURE MARKETING

India's agri-market is presently regulated by the Agricultural Produce Market Committee (APMC) Act enacted by the state governments. There are about 2,477 principal regulated agri-markets and 4,843 sub-market yards regulated by the respective APMCs in India. Thus, India has not one, not 29 (number of states), but thousands of agricultural markets. This Act notifies agricultural commodities produced in the region such as cereals, pulses, edible oilseeds, fruits and vegetables and even chicken, goat, sheep, sugar, fish, etc. and provides that first sale in these commodities can be conducted only under the aegis of the APMC through the commission agents licensed by the APMCs set up under the Act.

The typical *amenities* available in or around the APMCs are auction halls, weigh bridges, godowns, shops for retailers, canteens, roads, lights, drinking water, police station, post office, borewells, warehouse, farmers amenity centre, tanks, water treatment plant, soil-testing laboratory, toilet blocks, etc. Various taxes, fees/charges and cess levied on the trades conducted in the *mandis* are also notified under the Act.

As per the official sources (one being the *Economic Survey 2014-15*), the APMCs of the states levy multiples fees of substantial magnitude which are non-transparent and hence work as a source of political power. The functioning of the APMCs has

[31] *Economic Survey 2020-21*, vol. 2 (New Delhi: Ministry of Finance, GoI), pp. 251-52; *Economic Survey 2019-20*, vol. 2 (New Delhi: Ministry of Finance, GoI), pp. 213-14.

always been a matter of debate among experts and policymakers alike - *major* issues being the following:

- They charge a market fee from buyers, and they also charge a licensing fee from the commissioning agents who mediate between buyers and farmers.
- They also charge small licensing fees from a whole range of functionaries (warehousing agents, loading agents, etc.).
- In addition, commissioning agents charge commission fees on transactions between buyers and farmers.
- The levies and other market charges vary widely in the states. Statutory levies/mandi tax, VAT, etc. are major sources of market distortions.
- Such high taxes at the first level of trading have significant cascading effects on commodity prices, as the commodities pass through the supply chain. For rice, these charges can be as high as 14.5 per cent in Andhra Pradesh (excluding the state VAT) and close to 10 per cent in Odisha and Punjab.
- Even the model APMC Act (described below) treats the APMC as an arm of the state, and, the market fee, as the tax levied by the state, rather than fee charged for providing services. This is a crucial provision which acts as a major impediment to creating national common market in agricultural commodities. Removal of this provision will pave the way for creating competition and a national common market for agricultural commodities.
- Moreover, though the market fee is collected just like a tax, the revenue earned by the APMCs does not go to the state exchequer and hence does not require the approval of the state legislature to utilise the funds thus collected. Thus, APMC operations are independent of scrutiny.
- The rate of commission charged by the licensed commission agents is exorbitant because, unlike direct taxes, which are levied on net income, the commission is charged on the entire value of the produce sold. The license fee charged from various market licensed operators is nominal, but the small number of licences granted creates a premium, which is believed to be paid in cash.
- There is a perception that the positions in the market committee (at the state level) and the market board (which supervises the market committee) are occupied by politically influential persons. They enjoy a cosy relationship with the licensed commission agents who wield power by exercising monopoly power within the notified area, at times by forming cartels. The resistance to reforming APMCs is perceived to be emanating from these factors.

Model APMC Act

Since the State APMC Acts created fragment markets for agricultural commodities and curtailed the freedom of farmers to sell their produce other than through the commission agents and other functionaries licensed by the APMCs, the Ministry of Agriculture (GoI) developed a *Model APMC Act, 2003,* and has been pursuing the state governments to modify their respective Acts along its line. The Model APMC Act provides the following new things:

1. Direct sale of farm produce by the farmer to contract farming sponsors;
2. Setting up 'special markets' for 'specified agricultural commodities' - mostly perishables;
3. Permits private persons, farmers and consumers to establish new markets for agricultural produce in any area;
4. A single levy of market fee on the sale of notified agricultural commodities in any market area;
5. Replaces licensing with registrations of market functionaries, which would allow them to operate in one or more different market areas;
6. Establishment of consumers' and farmers' markets to facilitate direct sale of agricultural produce to consumers;
7. Creation of marketing infrastructure from the revenue earned by the APMCs;
8. Provides some freedom to the farmers to sell their produce directly to the contract-sponsors or in the market set up by private individuals, consumers or producers;
9. Increases the competitiveness of the market of agri-produce by allowing common registration of market intermediaries.

Though slow-paced, a majority of states did reform their APMCs in reference to the Model Act with differentiated success - the Karnataka Model being an ideal example. The Government working closely with the states has taken several *recent initiatives* in the direction of freeing up the agri-market in the country:

1. A comprehensive advisory issued to the states to go beyond the provisions of the Model Act and declare the entire state a *single market*

with one licence valid across the entire state and removing all restrictions on movement of agricultural produce within the state.

2. The NAM (National Agriculture Market) through an Agri-Tech Infrastructure Fund (ATIF) was established by the GoI in July 2015 which will provide a common *e-market platform* of regulated wholesale markets in states/UTs (those states/UTs that are desirous to join the platform).
3. On the request of the central government, a number of state governments have exempted the marketing of fruits and vegetables from the purview of the APMC Act.
4. For augmenting infrastructure facilities, the *Union Budget 2021-22* allowed the APMCs to get funds from the Agriculture Infrastructure Fund (AIF).

MODEL CONTRACT FARMING ACT

The Model Agriculture Produce and Livestock Contract Farming and Services (Promotion and Facilitation) Act, 2018, was enacted in May 2018. Salient *features* of the Act are as given below:

- Contract farming to be outside the ambit of APMC Act.
- Farmers have been considered weaker in case of contract farming.
- Other than contract farming, it covers all 'services contracts' related to pre-production, production and post-production (it means the whole value chain is covered).
- Contracted produce covered under crop and livestock insurance.
- No permanent structure can be developed on farmers' land or premises.
- No right, title of interest of the land shall vest in the sponsor (i.e., the contact farmer).
- If farmers authorise, FPOs (Farmer Producer Organisations), FPCs (Farmer Producer Companies) can be contract farmers.
- The entire pre-agreed quantity of agri-produce to be bought by the contact farmer.
- The RARC (Registering and Agreement Recording Committee) or an officer to be appointed for online registration of the contract agreement (at district, block and taluka levels).
- A CFFG (Contract Farming Facilitation Group) to be set up to promote contract farming (at village and panchayat levels).
- To settle disputes an accessible and simple mechanism to be set at lowest level possible.
- In structure, the Act is facilitative and promotional rather than being regulatory.

The Act is supposed to enhance India's agricultural production together with securing a remunerative income for the farmers - by integrating farmers with bulk buyers, agro-industries. Though an informal contract farming was present in the country for commercial crops (such as cotton, sugarcane, tobacco, tea, coffee, rubber and dairy), it was absent in case of other agri-products. Such an initiative from the Government was long due since contract farming was allowed by the Government in 2000.

AGRI-REFORMS CALLED BACK

Unlike several other developed and developing nations who chose to use cash transfers and big fiscal stimulus to tide over the economic hardships caused by the COVID-19 pandemic, the response from the Government of India has been a bit different *(Economic Survey 2020-21)*. Following two-pronged strategy - while on one hand the Government tried to cushion the economic hardships faced by the vulnerable sections of society and business, on the other a big thrust was given on structural reforms in several sectors *(Economic Survey 2021-22)*. In the agriculture sector, the Government launched a major push towards self-reliance by announcing the *Atmanirbhar Bharat Abhiyan* in May 2020. The campaign includes following three *historic policy decisions* (June 2020) towards agricultural reforms:

1. **Essential Commodities Act amended:** The Act of 1955 has been amended to help both farmers and consumers while bringing in price stability - by creating competitive market environment and preventing wastage of agri-produce that happens due to lack of storage facilities. While India has become *surplus* in most agri-commodities, farmers have been unable to get better prices due to lack of investment in cold storage, warehouses, processing and export as the entrepreneurial spirit gets dampened due to hanging sword of the Act. Farmers suffer huge losses when there are bumper harvests,

especially of perishable commodities. With adequate processing facilities, much of this wastage can be reduced. The following benefits are expected from this reform move:

- Commodities such as cereals, pulses, oilseeds, edible oils, onion and potatoes when *removed* from list of essential commodities will remove fears of private investors of excessive regulatory interference in their business operations.
- The *freedom* to produce, hold, move, distribute and supply will lead to harnessing of economies of scale and attract private sector and foreign direct investment into agriculture sector.
- It will help drive up investment in cold storages and modernisation of food supply chain.
- In situations such as war, famine, extraordinary price rise and natural calamity, such agricultural foodstuff can be regulated. However, the installed capacity of a value chain participant and the export demand of an exporter will remain *exempted* from such stock limit imposition so as to ensure that investments in agriculture are not discouraged.

2. **Barrier-free Trade:** To promote barrier-free trade of farm produce the *Farming Produce Trade and Commerce (Promotion and Facilitation) Act, 2020*, has been passed. Farmers in India today suffer from various restrictions in marketing their produce. There are restrictions for farmers in selling agri-produce outside the notified APMCs (Agricultural Produce Marketing Committees) market yards. The farmers are also restricted to sell the produce only to registered licensees of the state governments. Furthermore, barriers exist in free flow of agriculture produce between various states owing to the prevalence of various APMC legislations enacted by the states. This historic step in unlocking the vastly regulated agriculture markets in the country is expected to bring in the following benefits to the agriculture sector:

- It will create an ecosystem where the farmers and traders will enjoy freedom of choice of sale and purchase of agri-produce.
- It will also promote barrier-free *inter-state* and *intra-state* trade and commerce outside the physical premises of markets notified under state APMC legislations.
- It will open more choices for the farmer, reduce marketing costs for the farmers and help them in getting better prices.
- It will also help farmers of regions with *surplus produce* to get better prices and consumers of regions with shortages and lower prices.
- For ensuring a seamless trade an 'electronic transaction platform' is to be set up.
- Farmers not to be charged any cess or levy for sale of their produce under it.
- A separate dispute resolution mechanism to be set up for the farmers.

The move is aimed at creating additional trading opportunities outside the APMC market yards to help farmers get remunerative prices by inducing additional competition, paving the way for creating *One India, One Agriculture Market.*

3. **Freedom to Engage with Buyers:** To empower farmers to engage with all possible buyers, the Government has passed the *Farmers (Empowerment and Protection) Agreement on Price Assurance and Farm Services Act, 2020.* Indian Agriculture is characterised by fragmentation due to small holdings and has certain weaknesses such as weather dependence, production uncertainties and market unpredictability. This makes agriculture risky and inefficient in respect of both input and output management. The ordinance is expected to bring in the following benefits to the farm sector:

- It will empower farmers to engage with processors, wholesalers, aggregators, large retailers, exporters etc. on a level playing field without any fear of exploitation.
- It will transfer the *risk* of market unpredictability from the farmer to the sponsor and also enable the farmer to access modern technology and better inputs.
- It will reduce cost of marketing and improve income of farmers.
- Farmers will engage in *direct marketing,* thereby eliminating intermediaries resulting in full realisation of price.
- Farmers have been provided adequate protection - sale, lease or mortgage of farmers' land is totally prohibited and farmers' land is also protected against any recovery.
- Provision for effective dispute resolution mechanism with clear redressal time lines.

This Act will act as a catalyst to attract private sector investment for building supply chains for farm produce to *global markets* and enable farmers to get access to technology and advice for high value agriculture.

Postscript The new farm laws were criticised by the farm leaders and the political parties in opposition alike and the country saw a prolonged farm protest (mainly participated by the farmers from Haryana, Punjab and the western Uttar Pradesh). However, the Supreme Court had already put an indefinite stay over the implementation of these laws by early January 2021 (setting up a committee to resolve the impasse between the centre and the protesting farmers' unions), it was in November 2021 that the government announced to withdraw the three farm laws.

AGRI COMMODITY TRADING

Agri commodity trading is aimed at stabilising prices by market-based *price discovery*. Prices of agri-goods in India are set or influenced by the MSPs and the wholesale prices (controlled by the wholesalers). These prices are not error-free as they are not market-based. In this context, agri-commodity market explores market-oriented price determination which brings in multiple *benefits* to the economy in general and farm community in particular:

1. Stable prices benefit sellers (farmers and traders) as well as buyers (traders and food processing industry);
2. Price volatilities due to seasonal variations are minimised;
3. Stock variations due to export and import are also taken care of; and
4. A market-based *price discovery* gives right signal to all stakeholders.

Historical Background During the pre- Independence era, India had a flourishing market for commodities such as cotton, edible oils, etc. In 1952, futures' trading in most commodities was banned due to shortages of essential commodities, which resulted from wars and natural calamities. The ban was lifted in 2002, and several national and regional exchanges were set up (under the regulatory control of the SEBI) for trading commodities:

1. **National Commodity and Derivatives Exchange (NCDEX)** - the largest agri-commodity exchange where agri-commodities account for around 99.9 per cent of its turnover (rest of the 0.1 per cent is the share of bullion).
2. **National Multi-Commodity Exchange (NMCE)** - almost the entire turnover is in agri-commodities (around 99 per cent).
3. **Multi Commodity Exchange (MCX)** - agri-commodities account for around 3 per cent of its total trading turnover.
4. **Indian Commodity Exchange (ICEX)** - around 2 per cent of its turnover comes from the agri-commodities.

Presently, agri-commodities account for around 12 per cent of India's commodity trading while rest non-agri goods account for 88 per cent (such as metal, crude etc.). By *February 2026* (as per SEBI), **113** commodities were notified for future trading in the country which included 17 cereals and pulses (such as wheat, rice, maize, bajra, jowar, ragi, tur, urad, moong, masoor, yellow peas etc.); 12 oilseeds, oilcakes and edible oils (such as sunflower, safflower, soy complex, sesamum, linseed, coconut, castor complex etc.); 13 spices (such as turmeric, cardamom, ginger, cloves, pepper, jeera etc.); 4 fibres (art silk yarn, cotton complex, jute and all jute products, mesta, staple fibre yarn); 2 sweeteners (gur and sugar); 4 plantation crops (cocoa, coffee, rubber and tea); 1 dry fruit (almond) and 13 'Other' goods (such as egg, mentha oil, isabgol, beetlenut, camphor, *onion* and *potato* etc.). Majority of them are today actively traded on the commodity exchanges rather at times, but trading is also prohibited in case of many of them by the SEBI in wake of extra speculation and volatility.

Agri-commodity trading is undergoing a transformation as the *three* biggest bottlenecks - storage, logistics and financing (which used to plague it, resulting in huge harvest and postharvest losses) - finally being eliminated with a synergistic combination of technology, physical infrastructure and stronger regulation. Looking ahead, it appears that the Indian agri-commodities segment is headed for better days. (See *Chapter 15* for more details on Commodity Trading).

SUPPLY CHAIN MANAGEMENT

A *supply chain* is a network of facilities and distribution options that performs the functions of procurement of materials, transformation of these materials into intermediate and finished products and the distribution of these finished products to customers. Supply chains exist in both services, and manufacturing organisations, although the complexity of the chain may vary greatly from industry to industry and firm to firm.

Traditionally, marketing, distribution, planning, manufacturing and the purchasing organisations along the supply chain operated independently. These organisations have their own objectives and these are often conflicting. Marketing objectives of high customer service and maximum sales conflict with manufacturing and distribution goals. Many manufacturing operations are designed to maximise output and lower costs with little consideration for the impact on inventory levels and distribution capabilities. Purchasing contracts are often negotiated with very little information beyond historical buying patterns. The result of these factors is that there is not a single, integrated plan for the organisation - there were as many plans as businesses. Clearly, there is a need for a mechanism through which these different functions could be integrated. Supply chain management is a strategy through which such an integration can be achieved.

Scan this QR Code to watch a author's video lecture that simplifies this topic

Supply chain management is typically viewed to lie between fully vertically integrated firms, where the entire material flow is owned by a *single firm,* and those where each channel member operates independently. Therefore, coordination between the various players in the chain is key in its effective management. Supply chain management can be compared to a well-balanced and well-practiced 'relay team' - such a team is more competitive when each player knows how to be positioned for the hand-off. The relationships are the strongest between players who directly pass the baton, but the entire team needs to make a coordinated effort to win the race.

Supply chain management, hence, is the active management of supply chain activities to maximise customer value and achieve a sustainable competitive advantage. It represents a conscious effort by the supply chain firms to develop and run supply chains in the most effective and efficient ways possible. Supply chain activities cover everything, such as the following:

1. Product development,
2. Sourcing,
3. Production,
4. Logistics and
5. Information systems (for proper coordination).

The organisations that make up the supply chain are 'linked' together through *physical* flows and *information* flows. Physical flows involve the transformation, movement and storage of goods and materials. They are the most visible piece of the supply chain. But just as important are information flows - information flows allow the various supply chain partners to coordinate their long-term plans, and to control the day-to-day flow of goods and material up and down the supply chain.

UPSTREAM AND DOWNSTREAM REQUIREMENTS

'Upstream' and 'downstream' are business terms applicable to the production processes that exist within several industries. Upstream, downstream and midstream make up the stages of the production process for different industries.

Upstream The upstream stage of the production process involves searching for and extracting raw materials - it does not do anything with the material itself, such as processing the materials.

In upstream, firms simply find and extract the raw material. Thus, any industry that relies on the extraction of raw materials commonly has an *upstream stage* in its production process. In a more general sense, upstream can also refer to any part of the production process relating to the extraction stages.

Downstream The downstream stage in the production process involves processing the materials collected during the upstream stage into a finished product. It further includes the actual sale. End users will vary depending on the finished product. Regardless of the industry involved, the downstream process has direct contact with customers through the finished product.

Midstream Several points in between the two points (the place where raw is extracted and till it reaches the final consumer as finished product) are taken as the midstream. It depends on the reference point as how many or which stage is considered as the midstream by an industry.

Whether an activity is upstream or downstream depends on the point of analysis in a supply chain. A manufacturer considers suppliers as upstream and customers as downstream. Within a manufacturer, control over activities in the supply chain is subject to a company's management. Even so, a manufacturing activity that occurs prior to another is considered an upstream activity. Control over activities outside the company is subject to inter-company negotiations, cooperation and technology.

Industries, to have a smooth and uninterrupted functioning, depend heavily on the upstream and downstream requirements. In the case of *India,* we find several bottlenecks in both the processes:

1. In the case of the private sector, the downstream process seems better. But it is not so. Up to the level of 'wholesale' it is somewhat organised, but the retail trading is quite fragmented. India's *retail business* remains least organised. Organised retail is yet to evolve in the country, thus, the levels of uncertainties, potential of market access, monitoring and regulation of retail market are too weak.
2. Upstream processes are also not up to the mark. From the stage where the wholesale comes into picture, things look better. But outsourcing the raw from the local producers is an uphill task in the country. Due to this the upstream segment of the economy has remained too weak and fragmented.
3. The industrial and manufactured sectors have been managing their upstream and downstream requirements, but their heavy dependence on the unorganised sector is a challenging issue in front of India.
4. In the case of agricultural products, the situation is even worse. Agri-markets of regulations by the APMCs did not allow India to establish a common and single market. This has hampered not only the growth and business prospects, but it has also crippled the agricultural sector in a very serious way. It has taken the heaviest toll on the agriculture sector which still remains a non-remunerative profession.
5. As India is to compete in the global market, it immediately needs to strengthen its upstream and downstream process. For this, India is advised to pick the best practices from around the world and integrate itself with the developed world with the better ways and the state-of-the-art tools and means.

FDI in Upstream, Downstream and Supply Chain Management

This segment of India has seen least organised development, even in the reforms period. Due to lack of proper 'market reforms' in the area of agricultural products (as APMCs of different states have failed to develop) which hampered so many aspects of it - storage, grading, packaging, etc. It is believed that this field needs huge investments from the corporate sector. The corporate sector has not been much attracted to this sector. Main factors for the unwillingness among the private sector to put in their money in it are scarcity of capital, logistics, experience and non-conducive policy framework in the agriculture market. This is the reason why the GoI has allowed more freedom to FDI in retail chain development. It is expected that the willing foreign firms will not only bring in the needed fund to the sector, but along with them India will obtain international experience and best practices.

To compete in the globalising world markets and to gain economic benefits out of globalisation, India needs the following features in its supply chain management:

1. An organised retail sectors
2. Proper levels of logistics
3. Fully updated data of raw materials, production, cropping pattern, etc.
4. International class packaging, care towards phytosanitary aspects

It is felt that the above-cited features will be easier to manage for the top global players as they have fund, experience and a willingness to expand their businesses in the growing regions of the world.

It is believed that the Model Contract Farming Act of 2018 will bring in a new synergy in the supply chain management of agri-goods in the country as it aims to free up the agri-product market for agri-exporters, food processing industries and the bulk buyers - given the opportunity, the Government expects higher investments (especially FDI) in the sector from the private players. It will help the growth and expansion of agri-commodity futures also which have been also opened for the foreign portfolio investment.[32]

[32] Greater possibilities in the areas of wholesale and retail will create greater incentives for the private sector to put more money not only into agri-supply chain but they will get more integrated with the *agri-commodity contract market* too.

Irrigation

The Planning Commission[33] classified irrigation projects/schemes in India on the following lines:

1. **Major Irrigation Schemes** – those with cultivable command areas (CCAs) of more than 10,000 hectares.
2. **Medium Irrigation Schemes** – those with CCAs between 2,000 and 10,000 hectares.
3. **Minor Irrigation Schemes** – those with CCAs up to 2,000 hectares. Expansion of irrigation facilities, along with consolidation of the existing systems, has been the main part of the strategy for increasing production of foodgrains.

There is **need** to expand the acreage under irrigation along with adoption of appropriate technologies for efficient utilisation of water through suitable pricing to raise agricultural productivity in India. This could be done through (1) Adoption of irrigation technologies which improve efficiency in the use of water is imperative in a scenario where flood irrigation has resulted in wastage of water and (2) Focus on efficient irrigation technologies is important with increasing water shortages owing to climate change and indiscriminate wastage of water in agriculture and other uses.

Having *more crop per drop* through efficient irrigation technologies should be the motto to improve productivity in agriculture which can ensure food and water security in the future.

Irrigation Potential and Use

As per the latest[34] available information, against a total agricultural land of 180.88 million hectares, the cultivated land in the country was 153.88 million hectares, out of which net 71.55 million hectares are irrigated (around 46 per cent of the cultivated/cropped land). It means around 54 per cent of cultivated land in the country remains rain-fed. Out of the net irrigated area, about 40 per cent is irrigated through canal systems and 60 per cent is irrigated through groundwater. The overall irrigation efficiency of the major and medium irrigation projects is estimated to be around 38 per cent. The efficiency of *surface* irrigation system can be improved from about 35–40 per cent to around 50–60 per cent and that of *groundwater* from about 65–70 per cent to 72–75 per cent. An important challenge facing the irrigation sector in India is the growing gap between Irrigation Potential Created (IPC) and Irrigation Potential Utilised (IPU), and uneven distribution of water over the length of the canal system – caused mainly by the following factors:

- lack of proper operation and maintenance,
- incomplete distribution system,
- non-completion of command area development,
- changes in cropping pattern and
- diversion of irrigated land for other purposes.

Water being a state subject, the central government's role is limited to being catalytic, providing technical support and, in some cases, partial financial assistance to run schemes in the sector. A centrally sponsored scheme (CSS), the *Pradhan Mantri Krishi Sinchayee Yojana* (PMKSY), was launched in 2015–16 (extended till 2025–26) with an ***aim*** to enhance physical access of water on farm and expand cultivable area under assured irrigation, improve on-farm water use efficiency, introduce sustainable water conservation practices, etc.

PMKSY is an ***umbrella scheme***, *inter alia* consisting of *two* major components (implemented by Department of Water Resources, River Development & Ganga Rejuvenation), namely, Accelerated Irrigation Benefit Programme (AIBP), and *Har Khet Ko Pani* (HKKP). HKKP, in turn, consists of four sub-components, being Command Area Development & Water Management (CAD&WM), Surface Minor Irrigation (SMI), Repair, Renovation and Restoration (RRR) of Water Bodies, and Ground Water (GW) Development component. In addition, PMKSY has Watershed

[33] *Planning Commission* (New Delhi: GoI, 1961).

[34] *Directorate of Economics and Statistics,* Department of Agriculture & Farmers Welfare, (New Delhi: Ministry of Jal Shakti, GoI, February 2024).

Development (WD) component being implemented by Department of Land Resources. Further, during the years 2015–22, Per Drop More Crop (PDMC) component was being implemented by Department of Agriculture and Farmers Welfare under PMKSY, which has now been taken up under Rashtriya Krishi Vikas Yojana (RKVY).

Irrigation Efficiency

Agricultural productivity can be boosted in a big way by enhancing irrigation efficiency in the use of irrigation systems. Over time, the conventional systems of irrigation have become non-viable in many parts of India[35] due to the following:

- increasing shortages of water,
- wastage of water through over irrigation and
- concerns of salination of soil.

Economically and technically efficient irrigation technologies like *drip* and *sprinkler* irrigation can improve water use efficiency and reduce costs of production by reducing labour costs and power consumption. With this technology, additional area can be irrigated with the same amount of water compared to conventional method of irrigation. In addition, water deficient, cultivable waste land and undulating land areas can be brought under cultivation due to ease of irrigation. There is also good scope for using this technology in closely spaced crops such as rice, wheat, onion, potato etc. Farm income has seen a substantial gain[36] caused by multiple benefits which accrue out of this technology:

- Saving of irrigation water from 20 to 48 per cent;
- Energy saving from 10 to 17 per cent;
- Saving of labour cost from 30 to 40 per cent;
- Saving of fertilisers from 11 to 19 per cent; and
- Increase in crop production from 20 to 38 per cent.

Water Productivity

Water productivity in India is very low. The overall irrigation efficiency of the major and medium irrigation projects in India is estimated at around 38 per cent. As per the *NITI Aayog*, efficiency of the *surface irrigation* system can be improved from about 35–40 per cent to around 60 per cent and that of *groundwater* from about 65–70 per cent to 75 per cent. Water productivity needs to be enhanced by the following methods:

- tapping, harvesting and recycling water,
- efficient on-farm water management practices,
- micro irrigation,
- use of wastewater and
- resource conservation technologies.

In order to promote judicious use of water ensuring *more crop per drop* of water in agriculture for drought proofing, the GoI recently launched the PMKSY aiming at providing water to every field of agriculture.

Government Promotion: To promote the cause of enhancing *water productivity* and *irrigation efficiency*, the Government has taken the following steps in the direction:

- *Pradhan Mantri Krishi Sinchayee Yojana* (PMKSY) was launched in 2015–16 with the motto of *Har Khet Ko Paani* for providing end-to-end solutions in irrigation supply chain (i.e., water sources, distribution network and farm level applications).

[35] NITI Aayog, *Task Force on Agriculture*, 2015, as quoted Ministry of Finance, *Economic Survey 2015-16*, vol. 2, p. 104.

[36] *Economic Survey 2019-20*, vol. 2 (New Delhi: Ministry of Finance, GoI), pp. 198-99.

- Per Drop More Crop component of PMKSY (PMKSY-PDMC) was launched in 2015–16 aimed at water use efficiency at farm level.
- Micro Irrigation Fund (MIF) has been created with NABARD (with a corpus of ₹5000 crore) to facilitate the States in mobilising the resources for expanding coverage of micro irrigation.

FARM MECHANISATION

India needs to introduce better equipment for each farming operation in order to reduce drudgery, to improve efficiency by saving on time and labour, improve productivity, minimise wastage and reduce labour costs for each operation. Agricultural mechanisation in case of India is increasingly needed as follows:

- Due to shortage of labour for agricultural operations owing to rural-urban migration, shift from agriculture to services and rise in demand for labour in non-farm activities, there is need to use labour for agricultural operations judiciously, which makes a strong case for mechanisation of farming.
- Indian agriculture has a high proportion of female workforce in both the cultivation and processing stages of farming. Therefore, ergonomically designed tools and equipment for reducing drudgery, enhancing safety and comfort and also to suit the needs of women workers would help in better adoption of technologies in agriculture.
- An effective use of agricultural machinery helps in timely farm operations for *quick* rotation of crops on the same land (necessary in wake of shrinking land). By raising a second crop or multi-crops from the same land, there is improvement in the cropping intensity and making agricultural land commercially more viable (NABARD, 2018).

Though farm mechanisation has improved in the recent times, which stands at 45 per cent, it is much lower in comparison to the United States (95 per cent), Brazil (75 per cent) and China (57 per cent). There are intra-national disparities also visible with northern India having higher mechanisation compared to other regions. As per the *Ministry of Commerce and Industry*, farm mechanisation, measured by the sales of tractor and power tillers in the country had compounded annual growth rate (CAGR) of about 9 per cent and 8 per cent during 2024-25, respectively.

Important reasons for lower agricultural mechanisation in the country, as per a study (NABARD, 2018) are - economies of operation due to small holdings, access to power, credit cost and procedures, uninsured markets and low awareness. In recent times (since 2014-15 onwards), the Government has taken several *new steps* to promote[37] farm mechanisation in the country:

- Under the Sub-Mission on Agricultural Mechanisation (SMAM), launched in 2014-15, assistance is provided to State governments to impart training/ demonstration, provide assistance to farmers for procurement of agricultural machineries and for setting up of Custom Hiring Centre.
- The latest agricultural machineries such as laser leveller, happy seeders, combine harvesters and power weeders are being promoted.
- Under the new Central Sector Scheme on Promotion of Agricultural Mechanisation for *in situ* Management of Crop Residue in the States of Punjab, Haryana, Uttar Pradesh and NCT of Delhi (2018-19 to 2019-20), the agricultural machines and equipment for *in situ* crop residue management (aimed at fighting the *stubble burning* in the region) are provided with 50 per cent subsidy to the individual farmers and 80 per cent subsidy for establishment of Custom Hiring Centres (CHC). A multilingual mobile app called FARMS (Farm Machinery Solutions) was developed to help farmers get rented farm machinery and implements through CHC in the area.
- Realising the linear relationship between availability of farm power and farm yield, farm power availability is to be enhanced from 2.02 kW per ha to 4.0 kW per ha by 2030 (to cope with increasing demand for foodgrains).

Though combined sales of tractors and power tillers (which are often used as an indicator of farm mechanisation) touched 9.96 lakh in 2023-24 (from

[37] *Economic Survey 2021-22* (New Delhi: Ministry of Finance, GoI), p. 254 and *Economic Survey 2019-20*, vol. 2, (New Delhi: Ministry of Finance, GoI), pp. 196-98. The Survey has quoted the latest study of 2018 by NABARD in this regard.

6.26 lakh in 2015-16), as per the official sources. As per the *Economic Survey 2022-23*, the increasing fragmentation of farm holdings (with the average size of household ownership holdings declining from 1.23 ha in 2005-06 to 1.10 ha in 2010-11 and further to 1.08 ha in 2015-16) requires machines that are viable and efficient for small farm holdings.

SEED DEVELOPMENT

Seed is the basic input for increasing productivity in agriculture. It is estimated that the quality of seed accounts for 20 to 25 per cent of productivity.[38] Thus, the adoption of quality seeds needs promotion in India. There are multiple challenges to the development and adoption of quality seeds such as:

- Inadequate research inputs for development of new seeds especially,
- Early ripening and resistant (to pest, moisture variations, etc.) varieties,
- High cost of seeds for small and marginal farmers,
- Shortage of quality seeds,
- Decision related to adoption of Genetically Modified Seeds still undecided, and
- Inadequate number of players restricting competition.

The **issues**[39] that require immediate attention are as follows:

- *Affordability:* Open pollinated varieties of seeds can be developed by farmers from their own harvested crops. However, for high-yielding hybrid varieties, the farmer has to depend on the market for each crop which gets very costly for the small and marginal farmers.
- *Availability:* Quality seeds have shortage in supply. While there is a demand for banning non-certified seeds, certification *per se* does not ensure quality seeds. Presence of more players (both public and private) and competition in the market for seeds would improve this situation.
- *Research and development of seeds and seed technology:* The first Green Revolution was driven by indigenously developed HYVs of seeds for paddy and wheat. To initiate another round of the green revolution adequate attention was not given on seed development technologies - this needs to be pursued by involving the private potential in the area.
- *GM crops and seeds:* Concerns about its affordability, environmental and ethical issues, risks to the food chain, disease spread and cross pollination have resulted in their non-introduction.

FERTILISERS

In improving agricultural output, fertiliser is a critical and expensive input. Since the GR (mid-1960s), there has been a sharp increase in the use of fertilisers in India. To facilitate and promote the use of fertilisers, the Government has been providing fertiliser subsidy to farmers. However, the subsidy element has declined speedily even after higher global prices– estimated to decline to **0.43 to 0.44** per cent of the GDP in **2026-27** (i.e., ₹1.71 lakh crore) from 3.8 per cent in 2020-21.[40]

However, the use of fertilisers has not resulted in commensurate growth in agricultural productivity. The declining response ratio or marginal productivity of fertilisers since the 1970s is a pointer to their inefficient use in Indian agriculture. The yield of grain per kilogram use of NPK fertiliser has declined from 13.4 kg grain per ha in 1970 to 4.1 kg grain per ha in irrigated areas by 2025-26.

In the post GR agriculture scenario, there have been **imbalances** in the use of fertilisers such as follows:

1. Excessive dependence on urea owing to low/distorted prices of fertilisers, especially urea and regional imbalance in the use,
2. Neglect/low use of compost, manure and other forms of natural nutrient providers,
3. Discontinuing practices of inter and rotational cropping,
4. Diversion of the subsidised fertilisers to non-agricultural use,
5. Indiscriminate use of fertilisers has not proportionally improved the yield of crops, but has resulted in the depletion of soil fertility and salination of soil in many areas.

---

[38] As per the *DAC&FW (Department of Agriculture, Cooperation & Farmers Welfare)* - as quoted by the *Economic Survey 2015-16*, vol. 2 (New Delhi: Ministry of Finance, GoI), p. 105.

[39] *Economic Survey 2015-16* (New Delhi: Ministry of Finance, GoI), pp. 105-07.

[40] *Union Budget 2026-27* (New Delhi: Ministry of Finance, GoI, February 2026).

Certain ***improvements in fertilisation*** needed in the Indian farm sector may be summed up as follows:

- **Crop-responsive and Balanced Use of Fertilisers:** There is need to facilitate the optimal use of fertilisers depending on the soil health and fertility status. Linking the *soil health card* to provide profile of the soil and fertiliser on the basis of the same profile utilising fertiliser, (even if not subsidised) can improve the yield of crops.
- **Micro Nutrients and Organic Fertilisers:** Indian soils show deficiency of micro nutrients (like boron, zinc, copper and iron) in most parts of the country which limit crop yields and productivity. Fertilisers which supplement micro nutrients can provide an additional yield in cereals in the range of 0.3 to 0.6 tonnes per hectare.[41] This deficiency can be overcome if there by expansion in the use of organic fertiliser. Besides, being cheaper to use organic composting and manure it can help improve and retain soil fertility too. There is great scope for enhancing the use of organic fertilisers as around 67 per cent of Indian soil is characterised by low organic carbon.
- **Nutrient Management:** To maintain soil health and productivity, judicious use of chemical fertilisers, bio-fertilisers and locally available organic manures such as farmyard manure, compost, vermi-compost and green manure based on soil testing is necessary.

  With over 12 crore farm holdings in India, it is a big challenge to provide soil-testing facilities for overcoming the multi-nutrient deficiencies in soils so as to improve agricultural output. Use of information technology and providing soil fertility maps to farmers can go a long way in efficient nutrient management.
- **Regional Disparity in Fertiliser Consumption:** India has wide regional disparities in the consumption of fertilisers. This may be attributed to the availability of irrigation facilities in the high-consuming states (since irrigation is a requirement for proper absorption of fertilisers). It is necessary to reduce the disparities through appropriate soil-testing facilities and other policy measures.

Aimed at *rationalising* fertiliser subsidy, the Government has taken some important steps[42] in recent years:

- All fertiliser subsidies are being disbursed through the DBT system since late 2016-17. Under this system, the subsidies are released to the fertiliser companies on the basis of actual sales made by the retailers to the beneficiaries (identifying them through Aadhaar Card, KCC, Voter Identity card, etc.).
- The New Urea Policy-2015 has been notified with multiple aims - maximising indigenous urea production, promoting energy efficiency, and rationalising subsidy burden.
- In case of P (phosphate) and K (potash) fertilisers, the Government is implementing the Nutrient Based Subsidy (NBS) scheme under which a fixed amount of subsidy is given based on their content (24 grades of P & K fertilisers are today made available to the farmers).
- *Nano fertilisers* (the world's first such urea and phosphatic fertilisers were produced by the Indian Farmers Fertiliser Corporation(IFFCO)) were launched on the government initiative in 2024-25, which is also aimed at efficient use of fertilisers and rationalising the element of subsidies on them. This is undertaken under the *PM-PRANAM* (Prime Minister Programme for Restoration, Awareness Generation, Nourishment and Amelioration of Mother Earth).

PESTICIDES

Due to the presence of weeds, pests, diseases and rodents, the crop yield losses range from 15 to 25 per cent in India. Even though pesticides are essential for improving crop yields, per hectare pesticide use is much lower in India in comparison with other countries. Presently, India uses a low amount of 0.5 kg per ha pesticide compared to 7.0 kg per ha in the United States, 2.5 kg per ha in Europe, 12 kg per ha in Japan and 6.6 kg per ha in Korea. Besides, there are certain concerns regarding pesticides use in the country:

- Use of pesticides without following proper guidelines,
- Use of substandard pesticides, and
- Lack of awareness about pesticide use.

[41] As per the Survey conducted by the *Indian Council of Agricultural Research (ICAR)* - quoted by the *Economic Survey 2015-16*, vol. 2 (New Delhi: Ministry of Finance, GoI), p. 108.

[42] *Economic Survey 2024-25* (New Delhi: Ministry of Finance, GoI), p. 251; and *Economic Survey 2021-22* (New Delhi: Ministry of Finance, GoI), p. 262 and *Economic Survey 2019-20*, vol. 2 (New Delhi: Ministry of Finance, GoI), p. 208.

These practices have given rise to *pesticide residues* being found in food products in India, posing major threats to the environment and human beings. Some **policy steps** which may be suggested in this regard are as follows:

- Farmers need to be educated about the classification of insecticides on the basis of their toxicity and their suitability for aerial application.
- The CIBRC (Central Insecticide Board and Registration Committee) has issued guidelines for the application of pesticides, their dosage, minimum intervals to be maintained and the levels of toxicity. This information needs to be widely disseminated among farmers.
- Greater focus on IPM (Integrated Pest Management) which will encompass a judicious mix of pest control methods by leveraging the cultural, mechanical, biological methods and need-based use of chemical pesticides. It gives preference to the use of bio-pesticides and bio-control agents, too.
- Being environment friendly, non-toxic and cost effective, bio-pesticides need to be promoted among small farmers to improve productivity in agriculture.

AGRI-CREDIT

Agri-credit is an important mediating input for agriculture to improve productivity. Access to institutional credit enables the farmer to enhance productivity by investing in machinery and purchase of variable inputs like fertilisers, quality seeds, and manure and providing funds till the farmer receives payment from sale of produce, which is at times delayed and staggered. Input use by farmers is sensitive to credit flows to the agriculture sector. Some of the concerns regarding agri-credit are as given below:

1. Predominance of *informal sources* of credit: farmers still avail as much as 40 per cent of the funds from informal sources - 26 per cent of the total agricultural credit flow from the local money lenders (highly exploitative lenders).[43] In respect of high interest rates, **DBT** may be considered to replace subvention of interest rates. The intermediation and refinance model to promote agricultural credit needs to be revisited and replaced with DBT that shall subsidise the interest paid by the farmer, instead of subsidising refinance to financial institutions.
2. The ratio of agricultural credit to agricultural GDP has increased from 10 per cent in 1999-2000 to around 48 per cent by 2025-26. However, the share of long-term credit (for more than 5 years) in agriculture or investment credit has declined from 55 per cent in 2006-07 to 29 per cent in 2023-24. The decline in the share of long-term credit in agriculture needs to be arrested and reversed.
3. There is regional disparity in the distribution of agricultural credit. The coverage is very low in the north-eastern and eastern regions of the country.
4. Crop loans being short term (for less than 15 months) in nature are meant to meet the current expenditure till the crop is harvested fail to promote major investments in agriculture. Farm loans up to ₹3 lakh is disbursed at an interest rate of 7 per cent per annum (effective interest rate becomes 4 per cent after 3 per cent interest subvention). The limit of loan was enhanced to ₹5 lakh (through Kisan Credit Card) under the Modified Interest Subvention Scheme by the *Union Budget 2025-26* which continues for **2026-27** too.

Agricultural credit has been enhanced by the Government in recent times– the target for 2025-26 was **₹32.50** crore. The ***Union Budget 2026-27*** has set a *demand-based credit disbursal* for 2026-27, similar to 2025-26 (figures are still to be finalised).

However, the regional distribution of agricultural credit in country has been highly skewed[44] especially in north-eastern, hilly and eastern states. The share of north-eastern States is less than 1 per cent in total agricultural credit disbursement while in case of the southern states it is up to 15 per cent.

AGRICULTURE EXTENSION SERVICES

Another key input to farm sector is 'agriculture extension services (AES)'. These services can improve productivity by providing timely advisory services to farmers to adopt best practices, technology, meet with contingencies, market information etc. The AES

[43] NSSO, 70th Round data quoted by the *Economic Survey 2015-16*, vol. 2 (New Delhi: Ministry of Finance, GoI), p. 110.

[44] *Economic Survey 2019-20*, vol. 2 (New Delhi: Ministry of Finance, GoI), p. 208.

(also called 'rural advisory services') has been defined[45] as 'consisting of all the different activities that provide the information and services needed and demanded by farmers and other factors in rural settings to assist them in developing their own technical, organisational and management skills and practices so as to improve their livelihoods and well-being'.

Though there are multiple agencies in India offering agricultural advisory services, the system is not efficient enough due to the following reasons:[46]

- Lack of functional autonomy,
- Rigid hierarchical structures leading to lack of innovative methods of providing extension services and
- Coordination failures at multiple levels.

For the improvement of the AES in the country the suggested policy steps are as follows:

- Implementing a new scheme or additional outlays in existing schemes.
- Need of 'one-stop shop' that offers both hardware and software solutions to raise the incomes of farmers, especially small and marginal farmers.
- Need of an approach which is 'neutral to input, crop and region'.
- Minimising wastage in inputs as well as produce, till it leaves the farm gate.
- Efforts to enhance post-harvest processing/ value-added activities at the farm.
- Need to share with the farmer, information on weather, in order to improve yield and minimise damage to crops.
- Promoting inter and rotational cropping and efficient utilisation of the inputs.
- Need to shift to demand-driven agricultural advisory services.
- Need of a virtual connect, using IT (mobile and internet) and integration of agricultural extension services.

Over time, the GoI has taken variety of initiatives[47] to strengthen the AES in the country, major ones being:

- *Kisan TV* set up and broadcasting of agri-information by AIR;
- *Agri-Clinic & AgriBusiness* (by agriculture graduates);
- Extension education institutes (EEIs) set up and model training courses for horticulture, animal husbandry, etc. started;
- National Centre for Management of Agricultural Extension (acronym for which is *MANAGE*) set up as an apex institute to train middle and senior level officers of the states/UTs;
- Digital agricultural platform, the *CAPS* (Cyber Agro-Physical Systems) launched to make farming viable, self-sustaining and internationally competitive;
- From 2014-15 to 2024-25, the ICAR has released 2,177 (of the total 2,593) climate-resistant seeds–given the impact of weather and changing climate on agriculture, developing such seeds has become a top priority; and
- Agriculture Education Portal *EKTA* (Ekikrit Krishi Shiksha Takniki Ayaam) launched for integrated online information management with 9 Mobile Apps dedicated to mango, pomegranate, onion, garlic, black pepper, etc.

Increasing R&D spending on agriculture is not only a vital necessity for ensuring food security, but also important from the socio-economic point of view. The *Economic Survey 2021-22* quoted recent research to highlight its importance and comparative advantage - the research shows that every rupee spent on agricultural research and development, yields much better returns (11.2), compared to returns on every rupee spent on fertiliser subsidy (0.88), power subsidy (0.79), education (0.97) or on roads (1.10).

AGRI INSURANCE

The GoI launched a new agricultural insurance scheme in January 2016. The new scheme[48] - *Pradhan Mantri Fasal Bima Yojana* (PMFBY) - has been termed as a *path*

---

[45] *GFRAS (Global Forum for Rural Advisory Services)*, 2010 - quoted by the *Economic Survey 2015-16*, vol. 2 (New Delhi: Ministry of Finance, GoI), p. 111.

[46] NITI Aayog, Task Force on Agriculture, 2015.

[47] *Economic Survey 2024-25* (New Delhi: Ministry of Finance, GoI), p. 251; and *Economic Survey 2019-20*, vol. 2 (New Delhi: Ministry of Finance, GoI), p. 203; *Economic Survey 2021-22* (New Delhi: Ministry of Finance, GoI), p. 254-55.

[48] (New Delhi: Ministry of Finance, GoI, 13 January 2016).

breaking scheme for farmers' welfare. The highlights of this scheme are as given below:

- There will be a uniform premium of only 2 per cent to be paid by farmers for all kharif crops and 1.5 per cent for all rabi crops.
- In case of annual commercial and horticultural crops, the premium to be paid by farmers will be only 5 per cent.
- The premium rates to be paid by farmers are very low and balance premium will be paid by the government to provide full insured amount to the farmers against crop loss on account of natural calamities.
- There is no upper limit on Government subsidy. Even if balance premium is 90 per cent, it will be borne by the Government.
- 25 per cent of the likely claim will be settled directly on farmers account, and there will be one insurance company for the entire state as well as farm level assessment of loss for localised risks and post-harvest loss.
- Earlier, there was a provision of capping the premium rate which resulted in low claims being paid to farmers. This capping was done to limit Government outgo on the premium subsidy. This capping has now been removed and farmers will get claim against full sum insured without any reduction.
- The use of technology will be encouraged to a great extent. Smartphones will be used to capture and upload data of crop cutting to reduce the delays in claim payment to farmers. Remote sensing will be used to reduce the number of crop-cutting experiments.

The scheme replaced the existing NAIS (National Agricultural Insurance Scheme) of 1999 and is being implemented by both private and public sector companies. Though the scheme is voluntary for states, at present, 27 states/UTs are implementing it. The scheme was made more farmer-friendly and flexible after its *revamp* in February 2020 with the following major changes[49]:

- Direct Benefit Transfer (DBT) was introduced in 2017-18 to help farmers receive claims directly in their bank accounts - a deliberate step to weed out ghost/duplicate through Aadhar-based verification.
- National Crop Insurance Portal has been launched to provide interface among all stakeholders.
- Provision of 12 per cent interest rate per annum to be paid by the Insurance Company to farmers for delay in settlement of claims beyond 10 days.
- State Governments to pay 12 per cent interest rate for delay in release of state share of subsidy beyond three months to Insurance Companies.
- Increase in time for change of crop name for insurance from 1 to up to 2 working days.
- Time for intimation of loss due to localised calamities and post-harvest losses has been increased from 48 hours to 72 hours;
- Participation for farmers made voluntary as earlier, the loanee farmers (58 per cent of the total farmers) would compulsorily be brought under this scheme.
- States have been provided flexibility to rationalise the sum insured so that adequate benefits can be availed by farmers.

Aadhar seeding has helped in speedy claim settlement directly into the farmer accounts. Today, the scheme covers over 6 crore farmers every year - even during the COVID-19 lockdown period around 70 lakh farmers benefitted out of it.

WTO AND THE INDIAN AGRICULTURE: PROSPECTS AND CHALLENGES

With the operationalisation of the provisions of the WTO, the process of globalisation commenced in the major parts of the world - the non-member countries, in the coming few years, also started negotiating for entry into the club. There has always been an air of confusion among the members and the non-members of the WTO in assessing the pros and cons of globalisation on the health of their economies. The sector which has created the highest number of deliberations in the WTO as well as views and counterviews has been agriculture - an area of utmost concern for the developed and the developing countries alike. India is no exception to it, but, rather, it has been among the few countries in the world spear-heading the campaign against the biased provisions of the WTO concerning agriculture.

[49] *Economic Survey 2020-21*, vol. 2 (New Delhi: Ministry of Finance, GoI), p. 239.

India was sceptical about the issue even before joining the organisation, but once it became a part of it, it started assessing the situation objectively and moved towards crisis mitigation. Globalisation as such opened unlimited prospects for the economies, but at the same time brought several challenges too. Yes, the challenges were different in nature for the developed and the developing countries. We need to enquire the prospects and the challenges brought by the WTO for Indian agriculture.

Had the agriculture of the leading and politically vocal developing economies not been of subsistence level, the course of the world would have been completely different. It is the biggest hurdle in the process of globalisation and the success of the WTO. Yes, the process of converting the sector into an industry has already started in most of the leading developing economies amidst tough resistance from the farmers, political parties and the NGOs alike.

The Prospects

The oldest and the first document regarding the impact of the implementation of the provisions of the WTO, Uruguay Round (1995-2005) was prepared jointly by the World Bank, the GATT[50] and the OECD[51]. According to the joint document, the WTO provisions were supposed to have the following positive impacts on the world trade:

1. By 2005 there will be an addition of $745 billion in the world merchandise trade.[52]
2. The *GATT Secretariat* provided a full breakup of the above-projected trade increase in the following way:
   (i) The clothing sector to have a share of 60 per cent.
   (ii) The agricultural, forestry and fisheries products to have a share of 20 per cent.
   (iii) The processed food, beverages and drinks to have a share of 19 per cent.

It means that due to the implementation of the WTO provisions, there will be only *one per cent* increase in the trade of all other goods excluding the above-cited sectors. It was a highly inflated view and became a matter of debate around the world. But the areas which were projected to have very high increase in their trade were not mere projections either. Member countries went home and started going for their own studies, estimations and projections - India being no exception. We must see the assessment of India:

1. The products which were projected to have the maximum increase in their trade, India had a traditional great export potential in them. It means the WTO has a great prospect for agriculture in store as maximum goods fell in the agriculture sector. Assuming that India's share in the world exports improves from 0.5 per cent to 1.0 per cent, and India is able to take advantage of the opportunities that are created, the trade gains may conservatively be placed at $2.7 billion extra exports per year. A more generous estimate will range from $3.5 to $7 billion worth extra exports.[53]
2. The NCAER (National Council for Applied Economic Research) survey of the WTO on the Indian economy is cited as the best document in this area. The survey[54] had all important things to say on this issue:
   (i) The exports of agricultural products will be boosted by the WTO accepted regime.
   (ii) Only the foodgrains trade of wheat and rice were projected to be around $270 billion.
   (iii) The survey also pointed out that almost 80-90 per cent of the increased supply of foodgrains to the world is going to originate from only two countries, China and India, as they have the scope for increasing production.

[50] General Agreement on Trade and Tariff (GATT) was a multi-lateral arrangement (not an *organisation* like WTO whose deliberations are binding on the member countries) promoting multi-lateral world trade. Now the GATT has been replaced by the WTO (*since January. 1995*).

[51] *Organisation for Economic Cooperation and Development* (OECD) was set up as a world body of the developed economies from the Euro-American region, which today includes countries from Asia, too (such as Japan and South Korea). The first idea of 'globalisation' was proposed by the OECD in the early 1980s at one of its Annual Meet (at *Brussels*).

[52] Merchandise trade does not include services.

[53] *Economic Survey 1994-95* (New Delhi: Ministry of Finance, GoI, 1995).

[54] *NCAER Survey* headed by its chairman Rakesh Mohan, GoI, 1994.

(iv) But the survey painted a very wretched picture about the preparedness of the Indian agriculture sector to exploit the opportunities. It concluded China to be far better than India in this matter.

(v) It suggested almost every form of preparedness for the agriculture sector (at a glance we may have been on the Second Green Revolution in India - basically the revolution is modelled on the findings and suggestions of the survey).

(vi) Lastly, the survey ended on a high note of caution and concern that if India fails in its preparations to make agriculture come out as a winner in the WTO regime, the economy will emerge as the biggest importer of agricultural products. At the same time, the cheaper agri-imports might devastate Indian agricultural structure and the import-dependence may ruin the prospects of a better life for millions of poor Indians.

(vii) Even if India does not want to tap the opportunities of the globalising world, it has to gear up in the agriculture sector since the world market will hardly be able to fulfil the agri-goods demands of India by 2025. It means it is only India which can meet its own agri-goods demand in the future.

There is no doubt that the WTO has brought probably *the last opportunity* to make our masses achieve better income and standard of living via better income coming from agriculture. But provided we go for the right kind of preparation at the right time. There are enough prospects, undoubtedly.

The Challenges[55]

If the WTO brings high prospects for Indian agriculture, it also brings in some hard-hitting challenges in front of it. These could be seen as individual challenges of the similar economies as well as joint challenges of such economies. The *first* category of challenges pertains to the area of relevant preparations, investment and restructuring of agriculture. And the *second* category of challenges is nothing less than a revision in the very agricultural provisions of the WTO itself (around which today revolves the success and failure of the organisation itself). We may take a look at the challenges before the Indian agriculture:

1. **Self-sufficiency of Food:** Due to inflow of cheaper foodgrains from the world, it would not remain economically viable in India to produce them, and farmers might incline in favour of the profitable agri-products. This will make India heavily dependent upon the world market for its food supplies, marring its achievement of food self-sufficiency.

   This will have serious political and ethical outcomes for India.[56]

2. **Price Stability:** Dependence on the world market for the supply of agricultural products and specially for foodgrains will never be safe for India. As the international market for the products is highly speculative and full of variations (due to natural factors) the price stability will be always in danger - fluctuations hamper the producers and consumers of agri-goods in India. It would be very tough to fight *dumping* of surplus agri-goods from other countries.

3. **Cropping Pattern:** The cropping pattern of agriculture might take a very imbalanced shape, which will be highly detrimental to the ecology at large[57] as the farmers will always be in favour of going for the crops and commodities which have comparative price advantage.

4. **Weaker Sections:** The benefits of globalisation may not be neutral to areas, crops and the

[55] The challenges and their possible remedies discussed in this sub-topic are based on some of the finest and timely debates and articles which appeared in many renowned journals and newspapers between the period 1994 and 2007. For better understanding of the readers only the consensual as well as the less-complex parts have been provided here.

[56] Almost 50 per cent of the Indian population spends 75 per cent of its total income on the purchase of foodgrains - this is why their standard of life and nutrition depends on the indigenously grown food in a great way. Once the self-sufficiency is lost their lives will depend upon the *diplomatic uncertainties* of its regular supply. It will have serious political outcomes for the political scenario of India. Similarly, irregular supply of the foodgrains will create a high ethical dilemma, too.

[57] Farmers might opt for highly repetitive kind of cropping pattern creating problems for soil fertility, water crisis, etc. This will have highly adverse effects on the agriculture insurance companies, too.

people. There will never prevail a certainty as to which area/region or crops or the people are going to benefit from globalisation in which year. At the same time globalisation is a process where profits can be made, but it is a market-based concept. Those who are unable to produce due to lack of capital, investment and entrepreneurship will have no gains from it. They will be net consumers or buyers. Since India has a vast population of the weaker sections (as other third world countries have) this population will neither be able to increase its income nor be able to purchase the agri-foods having no price stability.

It means that the weaker sections of India might miss this chance of growth and development. We need to make the benefits of globalisation reach these people, too. This could be done through a timely and society-oriented public policy which is a big challenge.[58]

5. **WTO Commitments:** There are certain time-bound obligatory commitments of India towards the provisions of the WTO in the area of agriculture, which are highly detrimental to the people and the economy. We may see this challenge from two angles:

 (i) According to the agricultural provisions, the total subsidies forwarded by the government to the sector must not cross 10 per cent of the total agricultural outputs. At the same time, exemptions to farmers are to be withdrawn - hampering the public distribution system badly. India's subsidies are still far below this limit, but commitments pose a threat to the sovereign decision-making.

 (ii) The subsidies (with different names) to agriculture, which are forwarded by the developed countries, are highly detrimental to Indian agriculture and they are very high, too.[59]

None of the above-given challenges are easy to fight. These are not to be fought by India alone, but almost all developing countries are to face it. Once the WTO comes into operation many experts from India and abroad have provided ways to fight these challenges, which may be summed up in the following way:

1. To fight the challenges related to self-sufficiency in food, the price stability and the cropping pattern a judicious mix of suitable kind of agricultural and trade policies will be the need of the hour. To the extent agricultural policy is concerned, India has a limited level of freedom. But the WTO regime does not allow the member countries to impose higher tariff or tariff itself to ward off cheaper agri-goods from entering the economy - this is the main reason behind the above challenges. It means it is essential to modify, change or revise the provisions of the WTO.

   Similarly, the issue of agricultural subsidies (*the boxes*) needs to be equitably defined so that they do not look biased. Here also the provisions of the WTO need revision.

2. To fight out this typical challenge, experts suggested that the *WTO is not God-given.* Its provisions may go in for change if concerted efforts are made by the member countries in this direction. Like-minded nations who face the same kind of crises should come together and opt for a joint effort, from inside the WTO, for the revisions or relaxations in its provisions. Morality related and ethical issues might be used as eye-openers and a handy tool to have the attention of the developed nations and the WTO alike.

Prima facie this suggestion looked to be easier said than done. Post-1995 saw a polarisation of like-minded countries inside the WTO that finally culminated into

[58] The primary examples of corporate and contract farming have given enough hints that economically weaker sections of society have meagre chances of benefitting from the globalisation of agriculture - with major profits going to the corporate houses. Naturally, the governments (centre and states) will need to come up with highly effective policies which could take care of the economic interests of the masses.

The policies may focus on areas such as *health care, education, insurance, housing, social security,* etc. Already the governments have started emphasising the delivery and performance of the *social sector* but in the future, more focused and accountable programmes in the sector will be required.

[59] Some of the developed economies are still forwarding subsidies to the agricultural areas to the tune of 180-220 per cent! Again, the justification for such high subsidies have been provided by defining agriculture subsidies according to their ease - highly blurring and confusing.

failure of the *Seattle Round* of the WTO deliberations. The most powerful country in the world failed to convene a meeting that too in its most distant region (the Alaska) - a moral triumph of the poor over the rich. This incidence while indicating a possible failure of the WTO itself, boosted the morale of the developing countries to opt for stronger groupings and even sub-groupings under the WTO.

After the Doha Round the United States had hinted to forget multilateralism and indicated its intentions towards bilateralism. The European Union had the same intentions, but it did not show it as openly as the United States. The year 2002 came as a watershed period for the WTO when the EU in its new diplomatic move announced to hear the agriculture-related issues of the developing nations. The United States announced the intentions few days after the EU announcement - just few days before the *Cancun Meet* of the WTO. The Hong Kong deliberation of the WTO, though it did not give anything concrete to the developing world, provided enough hope no doubt. The real picture emerges in the next meet for which the different pressure groups had serious deliberations on alternatives of bargaining power.

The second level suggestion to India was in the area of preparedness for the WTO regime. India was required to set new and internationally best standards in the area of production by boosting areas such as research and development, biotechnology, information technology, health and phytosanitary matters. This will make Indian goods and services compete in the international market.[60]

WTO AND AGRICULTURAL SUBSIDIES[61]

The subsidies provided by the government to the agricultural sector (i.e., domestic support) are termed by the WTO as Aggregate Measure of Support (AMS).[62] It is calculated in terms of *product* and *input* subsidies. The WTO argues that the product subsidies such as MSPs and input subsidies (non-product) such as credit, fertilisers, irrigation and power will cut production cost of farming and will provide undue advantage to such countries in their access to the world market - such subsidies are called to cause *distortions* to the world trade. Such subsidies are not permitted in one sense as they have a minimum permissible limit *de minimis* under the provisions which is 5 per cent and 10 per cent of their total agricultural output in the case of developed and developing countries, respectively.

The Boxes

The agricultural subsidies in the WTO terminology have in general been identified by 'boxes' which have been given the colours of the traffic lights - *green* (means permitted), *amber* (means slow down, i.e., to be reduced) and *red* (means forbidden).

In the agriculture sector, as usual, things are more complicated. The WTO provisions on agriculture have nothing like *red box* subsidies, although subsidies exceeding the reduction commitment levels are prohibited in the *amber box*.

The *blue box* subsidies are tied to programmes that limit the level of production. There is also a provision of some exemptions for the developing countries sometimes called the 'S&D box'.[63]

We may see them individually though they are very much connected in their applied form. The objective meaning of each one of them becomes clear, once one has gone through all of them.

Amber Box

All subsidies which are supposed to distort production and trade fall into the amber box, i.e. all agricultural subsidies except those which fall into the blue and green boxes.[64] These include government policies of *minimum support prices* (as MSP in India) for agricultural products or any help directly related to production quantities (as power, fertilisers, pesticides, irrigation, etc.).

Under the WTO provisions, these subsidies are subject to reduction commitment to their minimum level - to 5 per cent and 10 per cent for the developed and the developing countries, respectively, of their total value of agricultural outputs, per annum accordingly.

---

60 Because even the agriculture related provisions are modified the global market will always run after the agri-products which are the best - pricewise, quality wise, etc.

61 A simplified and 'easy-to-understand' analysis done on the basis of the documents of the *Information and Media Relations Division* of the World Trade Organisation Secretariat, Geneva, Switzerland, October, 2007.

62 Defined in *Article 1* and *Annexures 3 & 4*, Agreement on Agriculture (AoA), WTO, 1994.

63 WTO, *Article 6.2*, AoA, 1994.

64 WTO, *Article 6*, AoA, 1994.

It means, the subsidies *directly related* to production promotion above the allowed level (which fall in either the blue or green box) must be reduced by the countries to the prescribed levels.

In the current negotiations, various proposals deal with issues such as deciding the amount by which such subsidies should be reduced further, and whether to set product-specific subsidies or to continue with the present practice of the *aggregate* method.

Blue Box

This is the *amber box with conditions.* The conditions are designed to reduce distortions. Any subsidy that would normally be in the amber box is placed in the blue box if it requires farmers to go for a certain production level.[65] These subsidies are nothing but certain direct payments (i.e., direct set-aside payments) made to farmers by the government in the form of assistance programmes to encourage agriculture, rural development, etc.

At present there are no limits on spending on subsidies in the blue box. In the current negotiations, some countries want to keep blue box as is because they see it as a crucial means of moving away from distorting the amber box subsidies without causing too much hardship. Others want to set limits or reduction commitments on it while some advocate moving these subsidies into the amber box.

Under the agricultural provisions of the WTO, the aggregate measure of support (AMS) given by member countries to the agriculture sector is subject to limit - developing countries can offer non-product specific support (given for fertiliser, irrigation, electricity, etc. in India) upto 10 per cent of their agricultural GDP and product-specific support (such as MSP in case of India) upto 10 per cent the product value. However, India still has some space in case of non-product specific support. It crossed the product-specific limit for the first time in 2020-21. To save itself from violating the WTO provision, India invoked the '**Peace Clause**' (put in place under the MC10, Bali negotiations of WTO ministerial conference, 2013), India is still waiting for a permanent solution from the WTO so that the required amount of public stockholding of foodgrains can be maintained by it to assure food security in the country.

65 WTO, *Article 6*, *Para 5*, AoA, 1994.

Green Box

The agricultural subsidies which cause minimal or no distortions to trade are put under the green box.[66] They must not involve price support.

This box basically includes all forms of government expenses, which are not targeted at a particular product, and all direct income support programmes to farmers, which are not related to current levels of production or prices. This is a *very wide box* and includes all government subsidies such as public storage for food security, pest and disease control, research and extension, and some direct payments to farmers that do not stimulate production such as restructuring of agriculture, environmental protection, regional development, crop and income insurance, etc.

The green box subsidies are allowed without limits provided they comply with the policy-specific criteria.[67] It means, this box is exempt from the calculation under subsidies under the WTO provisions because the subsidies under it are not meant to promote production thus do not distort trade. That is why this box is called *production-neutral box.* But the facts tell a different story.[68]

In the current negotiations, some countries argue that some of the subsidies forwarded under this box (by the developed economies) do seriously distort trade (opposed to the view of minimal distortion as used by Annexure 2) - it is the view of the developing countries. These countries have raised their fingers on the direct payments[69] given by the developed countries to their farmers via programmes such as income insurance and income-safety schemes,[70] environmental protection, etc. Some other countries take the opposite view and argue that the current criteria are adequate, and

66 WTO, *Annexure 2*, AoA, and *Para 1*, AoA, 1994.

67 WTO, *Annexure 2, AoA*, 1994.

68 Basically, a large part of this box is used by the farmers in the United States and the European Union as basic investments in agriculture. India as well as other like-minded countries have this view and want this box to be brought under the AMS, i.e., under the reduction commitments. The United States at the Hong Kong Ministerial meet (December 2005) announced to abolish such subsidies in the next 12 year commencing 2008. The EU also proposed to reduce its 'trade distorting subsidies' by 70 per cent. None of them used the name green box which shows some internal vagueness.

69 WTO, *Para 5, Green Box*, AoA, 1994.

70 WTO, *Para 7, Green Box*, AoA, 1994.

advocate to make it more flexible (so that it could be increased) to take better care of non-trade concerns such as environmental protection and animal welfare.

S&D Box

Other than the above-discussed highly controversial boxes of agricultural subsidies, the WTO provisions have defined yet another box, i.e., the Social and Development Box (S&D Box)[71] allows the developing countries for some subsidies to the agriculture sector under certain conditions. These conditions revolve around *human development issues* such as poverty, minimum social welfare, health support, etc., especially for the segment of population living below the poverty line. Developing countries can forward such subsidies to the extent of less than 5 per cent of their total agricultural output.[72]

Export Subsidies

For export subsidy the WTO has provisions in two categories:

1. Reduction in the total budgetary support on export subsidies and
2. Reduction in the total quantity of exports covered by the subsidy.

Higher reduction commitment for the developed countries and lower for the developing countries are the provisions. But the developed nations forward such an inflated support to their agricultural exports that even after the committed reductions it will be highly price distorting against the agri-exports of the developing countries. It is therefore opposed by the developing countries.

Sanitary and Phytosanitary Measures

The provisions of the WTO allow member countries to set their own health and safety standards provided they are justified on scientific grounds and do not result in arbitrary or unjustified barrier to trade. The provisions encourage use of international standards and also include certain special and differential treatment in favour of developing countries.[73]

Though this provision has realised the scope of unjustified kind of health and phytosanitary measures on the developing countries, the developed nations have been beautifully able to do so by validating their health and related rules on scientific grounds. Such instances have distorted trade in favour of these countries and the developing countries' agriculture has been the real loser. The developing countries accuse such measures as the non-tariff barriers used by the developed nations to block goods from the developing nations.

NAMA

The Non-Agricultural Products Market Access (NAMA) is a part of the WTO provisions which deals with the idea of encouraging market reach to the non-agricultural goods of the member countries.[74] But the encouragement was objected/opposed by the developing countries, especially pointing to the non-tariff barriers enforced by the developed countries. At the Doha Ministerial Conference (November 2001), ministers agreed to start negotiations to further liberalise trade of non-agricultural products. By early 2002, a Negotiating Group on NAMA was created. The members at the meet decided to go for tariff reductions on non-agricultural products adopting the **Swiss Formula**.

One major concern that the members took note was of the small and vulnerable economies for whom a flexibility was committed while going for tariff reductions. For India, market access is not an issue of tariffs alone, but it means elimination of tariff peaks and tariff escalation in the markets of the developed countries. It will also end the abuse of anti-dumping laws and remove non-tariff barriers (NTBs) used to block goods from developing countries.

Swiss Formula: A variety of alternative methods are possible in the process of tariff reductions - some are more common than others. Some are based on *formulas*. But one thing should be kept in mind that whatever formula be agreed upon it does not have value unless it is properly implemented. Even after a formula or combination of formulas has been agreed upon, the final outcome of tariff reductions may depend on the bargaining capacity between countries.

---

71 WTO, *Para 8*, Green Box, AoA, 1994.

72 WTO, *Article 6.2*, AoA, 1994.

73 WTO, *Article 14*, AoA, 1994.

74 As per the provisions of the WTO fishes, fisheries products and forest products don't fall under agriculture and have been classified as the non-agricultural products

The **Swiss Formula**[75] belongs to the classification of formulas known as having harmonising impact. Since such a formula prescribes a higher/steeper cut on higher tariffs and lower cuts on lower tariffs it is seen to harmonise the rates by bringing the final rates becoming closer and bridging the gap.

The formula was proposed by Switzerland in the Tokyo round negotiations of GATT (1973-79). But Switzerland opposes using this method in the current agriculture negotiations - it prefers the **Uruguay Round formula**.

The Uruguay Round (1986-94) negotiations in agriculture produced an agreement for developed countries to cut tariffs on agricultural products by an average of 36 per cent over six years (6 per cent per year) with a minimum tariff cut of 15 per cent on each product for the period. It was a version of *flat rate* method of tariff reductions.

NATIONAL FOOD SECURITY ACT

The National Food Security Act (NFSA) was enacted by the Ministry of Consumer Affairs, Food and Public Distribution by end-December 2013. India's most ambitious and world's largest social welfare programme provides legal right to about 82 crore people for subsidised foodgrains - a historic initiative towards ensuring food and nutritional security. Major highlights of the programme are as given below:

- It will cover up to 75 per cent rural and 50 per cent urban population (around two-thirds of the total population) with uniform entitlement of 5 kg foodgrains per month at highly subsidised prices of ₹3, ₹2 and ₹1 per kg for rice, wheat and coarse grains, respectively. The *poorest of poor* households continue to receive 35 kg foodgrains per household per month under the *Antyodaya Anna Yojana* at the same subsidised prices.
- It provisions for special focus on nutritional support to women and children - *pregnant* women and *lactating* mothers, besides being entitled to nutritious meals as per the prescribed nutritional norms will also receive maternity benefit of at least of ₹6,000. *Children* in the age group of 6 months to 14 years will be entitled to take home ration or hot cooked food as per prescribed nutritional norms.
- Eldest woman of 18 years of age or above will be head of the household for issue of ration card, and if not available, the eldest male member is to be the head of the household.
- For effective implementation, the Act also contains provisions for **reforms** in PDS through *doorstep delivery* of foodgrains, application of information and communication technology (ICT) including end-to-end computerisation, leveraging *Aadhaar* for identification of beneficiaries, diversification of commodities under TPDS, etc.
- The Act provisions state and district-level **redressal mechanism** with designated officers. The states will be allowed to use the existing machinery for District Grievance Redressal Officer (DGRO), State Food Commission, if they so desire, to save expenditure on establishment of new redressal set up. It also provides for **penalty** on public servants or authority, if found guilty of failing to comply with the relief recommended by the DGRO.
- Provisions have also been made for disclosure of records relating to PDS, **social audits** and setting up of Vigilance Committees in order to ensure transparency and accountability.

The NFSA is being implemented (under the existing TPDS) in all States/UTs covering about 80 crore persons. In Chandigarh, Puducherry and urban areas of Dadra & Nagar Haveli, it is being implemented in *cash transfer mode*, under which food subsidy is being transferred into the bank accounts of the beneficiaries who then have a choice to buy foodgrains from open market.

Identification of beneficiaries under it is under two categories - households covered under Antyodaya Anna Yojana (AAY) and Priority Households (within the coverage determined for the State/UT). While the Priority Households are entitled to receive 5 kg foodgrain per person per month, the AAY households (which constitute the poorest of the poor), continue to receive 35 kg of foodgrains per household per month. To ensure adequate availability of wheat and rice and to keep a check on the open market prices, the Government has taken several steps[76] in recent times:

- State Governments, particularly those undertaking Decentralized Procurement (DCP), are being encouraged to maximise procurement of wheat and rice.

[75] WTO, "Formula Approaches to Tariff Negotiations" (Revised), (Geneva, Switzerland, 2007).

[76] *Economic Survey 2019-20*, vol. 2 (New Delhi: Ministry of Finance, GoI), pp. 209-10.

- Strategic reserves of 5 MT of foodgrains over the operational stocks are maintained to be used in extreme situations.
- Sale of wheat and rice is undertaken through OMSS (Domestic) so as to check inflationary trend in prices of foodgrains.
- Commencing PDS reforms such as *One Nation, One Ration Card,* Aadhaar authenticated distribution through *e-POS* machines.

PMGKAY: To lessen the economic hardship caused by the COVID-19 pandemic, the Government launched the Prime Minister Garib Kalyan Anna Yojana (PMGKY) in 2020-21 under which *free supply of foodgrains* (5 kg per person per month) started. After a few extensions given to the scheme, in December 2023, it was scrapped– but the free foodgrain supply was announced to continue for the next 5 years till December 2028 to all 81.35 crore beneficiaries of the NFSA (the estimated expenditure in the 5 years has been estimated at ₹11.8 lakh crore).

FOOD PROCESSING

Indian food processing industry (FPI)[77] has not grown with the pace which we see in the developed countries - there have been certain reasons for it:

- India has a lower urban population (around 30 per cent of the population).
- Whatever urban population India has it does not have the *typical* urban food habits. As majority of it is second or third generation in the urban areas they still continue with the non-urban/rural food habits detrimental to the consumption of the agro-processed items.
- In recent times, there has come enough awareness among the population across the country regarding the chemicals which are used in the agro-processing industries - creating a general tendency to avoid such food articles (much damage has been done to the industry by the 'fast foods', adulteration in food items such as sweets, milk, etc.).
- A wave across the world towards consuming more *which comes on plants* than *what is produced in plants.* A similar wave of 'slow food' has gained popularity across Europe and other parts of the world originating from France.

Moreover, India's agro-processing policy today guided by the following **drivers**:

- As urban population rises and urban food habits evolve, there will be increased demand for processed foods as it occurred across the urbanising developed world. The economy has already started experiencing an informed and increased demand in such food items as 'dietary habits' are in the process of shift (NSSO, 2014).
- External dimension to it was also accepted by the government by the mid-1990s. As per a joint GATT-OECD study, processed food are supposed to account for around 19 per cent of the increased trade after the provisions of the WTO are implemented.
- A very high percentage of food items which have short shelf life get wasted in India. It does not look good for a country which is crippled by the short supply of food and high rate of hunger.

Importance

While increased productivity is an essential component of a vibrant agricultural sector, improved post-harvest handling and processing is essential to ensure value addition, reduction in wastage and to make good quality products reach the markets. Too often, even when the yields are high, producers lose income due to poor postharvest practices.

Aim: Food processing aims to make food more *digestible, nutritious* and *extend the shelf life.* Due to the seasonal variation high levels of wastage or shortages can arise if adequate measures are not taken to preserve and store the food. Food processing covers all the processes that food items go through from the *farm to the consumers' plate.* It includes basic cleaning, grading and packaging as in case of fruits and vegetables and also alteration of the raw material to a stage just before the final preparation. Value addition processes to make 'ready-to-eat' food such as bakery products, instant foods, flavoured and health drinks, etc. are also included in this *definition.*

Food processing *offers* an opportunity for the creation of sustainable livelihoods and economic development for the rural communities. Food processing has come a long way in the last few decades. The ever-changing

[77] The analyses are based on several volumes of *Economic Survey, India* and the relevant documents of the Government of India between the period 2005 and 2015.

lifestyles, food habits and tastes of customers globally have altered the dynamics of the industry. Food processing benefits all sections of society:

- *Farmers* get better returns, higher yield and lower the risks drastically;
- *Consumers* get access to a greater variety, better prices and new products;
- *Economy* gets benefit via creation of new business opportunities, while the workforce gets employment.

With a huge production base, India can easily become one of the leading food suppliers worldwide while at the same time serving the vast growing domestic market of over a billion people. India's large market size with growing incomes and changing lifestyles also creates incredible market opportunities for food producers, food processors, machinery makers, food technologists and service providers in this sector.

Growth in the food processing sector is also expected to open up a lot of opportunities for players having strong linkages in the agri-value chain. Significant investment opportunities are yet to be tapped in the areas of *supply chain management, cold storages, financing, retailing* and *exports.*

Historically, agriculture and FPI have been plagued by factors such as the following:

- Low public investment,
- Poor infrastructure,
- Inadequate credit availability and
- High levels of fragmentation.

Rules and Regulations

Rules and regulations regarding the industry are as given below:

- Most food processing enterprises have been exempted from industrial licensing under the Industries (Development and Regulation) Act, 1951, with the exception of beer and alcoholic drinks, and items reserved for the small-scale sector.
- For foreign investment, automatic approval is given even up to 100 per cent equity for a majority of processed foods.
- For manufacture of items reserved for MSEs, FDI is permissible under automatic route up to 24 per cent.

Economic Importance

Given the tremendous attention by the Government in recent years, the industry has started revealing its expansion. The economic importance[78] of the sector can be gauged by the following statistics:

- During the last 10 years ending in 2024-25, the sector had an average annual growth rate of around 8.5 per cent. It constituted 9 per cent and 11.7 per cent of GVA in Manufacturing and Agriculture sector, respectively, in 2024-25 (at 2011-12 prices).
- According to the latest Annual Survey of Industries for 2022-23, the total number of persons engaged in registered food processing sector was 20.68 lakhs.
- It is one of the largest employers within organised manufacturing, accounting for **12.41** per cent of total employment in the organised sector.
- Unregistered food processing sector supports employment to 53.31 lakh workers as per the NSSO 73rd Round, 2015-16 and constitutes 14.18 per cent of employment in the unregistered manufacturing sector.
- In 2023-24, agri-food exports (which includes processed foods exports too) reached US$ 46.44 billion, constituting roughly 11.7 per cent of India's total exports. Notably, the share of processed food exports within agri-food exports has risen from 14.9 per cent in 2018-19 to **23.4** per cent in 2023-24.

The Government has allowed 100 per cent *FDI in the* sector under the automatic route. However, in case of trading in respect of food products manufactured and/ or produced in India including through e-commerce, 100 per cent FDI is allowed under the Government approval route. The sector has witnessed FDI equity inflow of US$ 7.2 billion during the period April 2014 to September 2024. The FDI equity inflow in FPI sector during 2024-25 (April to September) was US$ 520.23 million in comparison to US$ 480.12 million in the corresponding period last year.

[78] As per the latest information of the Ministry of Finance and Ministry of Corporate Affairs (New Delhi: Government of India, February 2025); *Economic Survey 2024-25* (New Delhi: Ministry of Finance, GoI), p. 267; *Economic Survey 2022-23* (New Delhi: Ministry of Finance, GoI), pp. 255-56; and *Economic Survey 2021-22* (New Delhi: Ministry of Finance, GoI), pp. 255-58.

MAJOR POLICY INITIATIVES

PMKSY The Pradhan Mantri Kisan *SAMPADA* Yojana (PMKSY) was launched as a central sector scheme by the Government in 2016-17 which provides subsidy-based support to create robust modem infrastructure for agriculture and agro-based industries along the entire value-chain. This umbrella scheme consists of the following components:

- Mega Food Parks
- Integrated Cold Chain and Value Addition Infrastructure
- Infrastructure for Agro-processing Clusters
- Creation of Backward and Forward Linkages
- Creation/Expansion of Food Processing and Preservation Capacities
- Operation Greens

Mega Food Parks Scheme (MFPS) The MFPS *aims* to accelerate the growth of the food processing industry in the country by facilitating establishment of strong food processing infrastructure backed by an efficient supply chain. Under this scheme, capital grant of 50 per cent of the project cost is provided in general areas and 75 per cent in difficult and ITDP (Integrated Tribal Development Programme) notified areas (with a ceiling of ₹50 crore). Each Mega Food Park takes about 30-36 months to be completed.

Integrated Cold Chain, Value Addition and Preservation The Scheme for Cold Chain, Value Addition and Preservation Infrastructure was approved in 2008 with an *objective* to provide integrated and complete cold chain, value addition and preservation infrastructure facilities without any break, for perishables from the farm gate to the consumer. The assistance under the scheme includes financial assistance (grant-in-aid) of 50 per cent of the total cost of plant and machinery and technical civil works in general areas and 75 per cent for the North Eastern region and difficult areas (subject to a maximum of ₹10 crore).

Modernisation of Abattoirs The Ministry has approved 10 projects in the first phase which are at various stages of progress. Two projects have been completed. A proposal for up-scaling the scheme is under consideration.

Technology Upgradation Under the Scheme for Technology Upgradation, Establishment, Modernisation of FPIs, financial assistance is provided in the form of 'grants-in-aid' for the setting up of new food processing units as well as technological upgradation and expansion of existing units in the country. The GoI extends financial assistance in the form of grant-in-aid to entrepreneurs at 25 per cent of the cost of Plant & Machinery and Technical Civil Works subject to a maximum of 50 lakhs in general areas or 33.33 per cent subject to a maximum of 75 lakhs in difficult terrains. The Scheme has now been transferred to the states with the launching of the National Mission on Food Processing (NMFP) in the 12th Plan.

Quality Assurance, Codex Standards, R&D and Promotional Activities In the global market today, quality and food safety give a competitive edge which is an important factor for the enterprises producing processed foods and providing services. Apart from domestic standards for food products, processes and management practices, Codex prescribes international standards for safety and quality of food as well as codes of good manufacturing practices, which are accepted worldwide. Further, equal emphasis is required to be accorded to R&D activities for the development of innovative products, cost effective processes and efficient technologies for the food processing sector. The scheme for Food Safety Codex and R&D has been successful in making a dent in this area in the country.

PM-FME The Prime Minister-Formalisation of Micro Food Processing Enterprises (PM-FME) was launched by late 2020-21 (under the Atma Nirbhar Bharat Abhiyan) as a Centrally Sponsored Scheme for the period 2020-25. *One District One Product* (ODOP) approach is to be adopted under it to reap 'benefit of scale' in terms of procurement of inputs, availing common services and marketing of products. States identify 'one food product per district' keeping in view the existing clusters and availability of raw material under it. The scheme also places focus on *waste to wealth* products, minor forest products and *Aspirational Districts* (112 most backward districts of the country have been identified by the Niti Aayog as Aspirational Districts). The existing micro food processing units to obtain the following supports under it:

- Credit-linked capital subsidy (35 per cent of project cost with a maximum of ₹10 lakh) to be given to the units led by individual, FPOs, producer cooperatives and SHGs (Self-Help Groups).

- Credit-linked grant (35 per cent of the project cost) for development of common infrastructure including common processing facility, lab, warehouse, cold storage, packaging and incubation centre through FPOs/SHGs/cooperatives or state-owned agencies or private enterprise for use by micro units in the cluster.
- SHGs to obtain seed capital (₹40,000) for working capital and purchase of small tools.
- 50 per cent grant for branding and marketing.

The scheme has picked popularity very fast and by *April 2021* a total of 35 states/UT had identified hundreds of food products under it.

Operation Greens A central sector scheme, the *Operation Greens* was launched in 2018-19 for integrated development of Tomato, Onion and Potato (TOP) value chain with *five* main objectives - enhancing value realisation for TOP farmers and linking them to market; price stabilisation by targeted interventions; reducing post-harvest losses by creation of farm gate infrastructure, agro-logistics and storage; increasing food processing capacities; and setting up market intelligence network to collect real-time data of demand and supply.

Under *Atmanirbhar Bharat Abhiyan*, the scheme has been extended from TOP crops to 22 perishable crops in long-term, and 41 fruits and vegetables crops in short-term components together with transport subsidy for any fruit and vegetable through the Indian Railways.

Production-Linked Incentive (PLI) Scheme A PLI Scheme was introduced by the Government in *November 2020* in 14 key sectors, including food processing sector, for enhancing India's manufacturing capabilities and improving exports. The food segments identified include ready-to-eat/ready-to-cook marine products, processed fruits and vegetables, mozzarella cheese, and innovative/organic products of SMEs. The scheme also supports branding and marketing abroad.

Institutional Support

A range of institutional support has been put in place by the Government to help the industry grow and attain global class - a brief description is given below:

- **Indian Institute of Crop Processing Technology (IICPT):** The IICPT, formerly known as Paddy Processing Research Centre (PPRC), in Thanjavur, is an autonomous organisation under the administrative control of the MoFPI. It has been in existence for the last three decades. As other commodities such as millets, pulses and oil seeds are gaining importance, it was decided in 2001 to expand the mandate of this institute to also include the above commodities. The institute is now being upgraded to a national-level institute.
- **National Meat and Poultry Processing Board (NMPPB):** The GoI established the NMPPB in 2009. The Board is an autonomous body and was initially funded by the GoI for 2 years and is to be managed by the industry itself. This industry-driven institution has been launched to work as a *National Hub* for addressing all key issues related to the meat and poultry processing sector for its systematic and proper development. The Board serves as a *single window* service provider for producers, manufacturers and exporters of meat and meat products, for promoting the meat industry as a whole.
- **Indian Grape Processing Board:** The GoI, in 2009, gave its approval for the establishment of the Indian Grape Processing Board (IGPB) at Pune, Maharashtra, which is close to the principal grape growing and processing areas in the country. The functions and objectives of the IGPB are as follows:
    - To focus on R&D, extension, quality upgradation, market research, information, domestic and international promotion of *Indian wine*.
    - To foster sustainable development of Indian wine industry.
    - To formulate a vision and action plan for the growth of Indian wine sector including R&D for quality upgradation in new technologies.

  During three years of its existence, the Board has focused on the promotion of *Wines of India* in the domestic as well as international market by participating in important and relevant exhibitions, fairs, consumer awareness and training programmes, undertaking advocacy work with the various state governments/central ministries on various issues related to taxes/levies and promotion aspects. The Board is going to implement a traceability programme 'wine net' for standards and quality in wine sector.

- **National Institute of Food Technology, Entrepreneurship & Management (NIFTEM):** For developing a vibrant food processing sector, India needs not only world-class food technologists to undertake R&D in frontier areas, develop new products, processes, technologies and machineries, set food standards and protocol testing, but also business leaders and managers well versed with the requisite mix of technologies, management and entrepreneurship who can exploit major opportunities in the expanding global food trade.

In the emerging global scenario, there is a need for setting up of an institution of global excellence, which could cater to the needs of the booming food processing sector, various stakeholders such as entrepreneurs, industry, exporters, policymakers, government and other research institutions. NIFTEM was conceived by MoFPI to create an international *Center of Excellence* in the field of Food Sciences & Food Technology. NIFTEM will grow into an apex world-class institute to promote cooperation and networking among existing institutions both within the country and various international bodies. The institute will offer high-quality educational, research and management programme specific to the food industry, provide referral advice on food standards, disseminate knowledge on the food sector and provide business incubation facility. It is situated (2006) at Kundli, Sonipat (Haryana).

DOUBLING FARM INCOME

Remunerative farming is not a precondition for enriching farm community only, but it is considered the biggest incentive to enhance the agricultural output, too. This is why enhancing farm income has emerged among the most immediate policy concerns for the government in recent times. Recently, a shift has been seen in the Government's strategy towards the agriculture sector - from increasing farm output to increasing farm income.

Aimed at *doubling the farmers income by 2022,* the GoI has announced a 'seven-point strategy'. The details of the strategy are as given below:

- Focus on irrigation with bigger budgets aimed at 'per drop, more crop'.
- Provision of quality seeds and nutrients based on soil health.
- Strengthening of warehousing and cold chains to prevent post-harvest crop losses.
- Promotion of value addition through food processing.
- Creation of a national farm market, removing distortions and e-platform.
- Mitigation of risks at affordable cost through suitable kind of farm insurance.
- Promotion of ancillary activities such as poultry, beekeeping and fisheries.

Agri-experts together with the foremost Indian agriculture scientist M.S. Swaminathan have appreciated this initiative of the Government. The challenge of doubling farmers' income within the prescribed time frame is very much possible supported by a good strategy, well-designed programmes, adequate resources and good governance.

CASH SUPPORT TO FARMERS

In the wake of rising farm distress, the GoI announced a Central Sector Scheme (these schemes are fully financed by the Central Government) the *Pradhan Mantri Kisan Samman Nidhi (PM-KISAN)* in 2019-20 (to be implemented from the 2018 kharif season). The scheme provides assured income support of 6,000 per year (in 3 equal instalments of 2,000 each) to the beneficiaries covering all farmers who own land up to 2 hectares. Initially launched for only the small and marginal farm families across the country holding cultivable land up to 2 hectares, its ambit was later expanded (w.e.f. June 2019) to cover all farmer families irrespective of the size of their land holdings. The scheme is expected to benefit over 15 crore farmers, as per the Government.

The Scheme excludes affluent farmers such as Income Taxpayers in the last assessment year, professionals such as Doctors, Engineers, Lawyers, Chartered Accountants, etc. and pensioners drawing at least ₹10,000 per month. Special provisions have been made for the North-Eastern states where land ownership rights are community based, forest dwellers and Jharkhand, which does not have updated land records and restrictions on transfer of land.

Taking cues from the Central Government, some states have also launched income or investment support schemes[79] in recent times which are of two kinds - inclusive or exclusive of the PM-KISAN - as given below:

- **Rythu Bandhu:** Launched from Kharif 2018, this Government of Telangana scheme provides investment support of ₹4,000 per acre per season (for 2 seasons) to all farmers (55 lakh) towards purchase of inputs such as seeds, fertilisers, etc. as initial investment before the crop season. It is estimated to support 55 lakh farmers (*rythus*) in the state. This scheme is independent of the PM-KISAN.
- **KALIA:** The Krushak Assistance for Livelihood and Income Augmentation (KALIA) Scheme was launched in 2018-19 Rabi season onwards by the Odisha government - aimed to accelerate agricultural prosperity and elimination of poverty. Re-named as the CM-KISAN in 2024-25, the scheme is independent of the PM-KISAN and has following components of it:
    - Small and marginal farmers get a financial support of ₹25,000 per farm family over five seasons to purchase inputs such as seeds, fertilisers, pesticides, labour and other investments.
    - Landless agricultural households get a financial assistance of ₹12,500 for agricultural allied activities such as small goat rearing unit, mini-layer unit, duckery units, fishery kits for fisherman, mushroom cultivation and beekeeping, etc.
    - Vulnerable cultivators/landless agricultural labourers get a financial assistance of ₹10,000 per family per year for their sustenance.
    - The scheme also has life and accident insurance covers for the farmers at very nominal premiums.
- **Krishak Bandhu:** The scheme of the West Bengal state launched from Rabi season of 2018-19 gives ₹10,000 per year as income support for two crops to all 75 lakh farmers (including landless farmers also). This scheme is independent of the GoI scheme PM-KISAN.
- **MMKAY:** The Mukhya Mantri Krishi Ashirwad Yojana (MMKAY) of the Jharkhand state gives a grant-in-aid of ₹5,000 per acre per year to the farmers who have arable land up to 5 acres, to reduce their dependence on loans. The cash support is given in two instalments through DBT. The scheme is estimated to benefit over 22 lakh farmers in the state. The state also implements PM-KISAN.
- **Rythu Bharosa:** Launched by the Andhra Pradesh state government in 2019-20 Kharif season, the scheme provides ₹13,500 income support to all farmers owning up to 5 acres of land - ₹6,000 of the PM-KISAN plus ₹7,500 as the state component (as the state also implements PM-KISAN). It is estimated to benefit over 67 lakh farmers in the state.
- **Shift from Loan Waiver to Cash Support:** The instance of states opting for farm income/ investment support schemes[80] over farm loan waiver programmes has been *appreciated* by the Reserve Bank of India. Since 2014-15, a total of 10 states have announced farm loan waiver programmes of ₹2,31,260 lakh crores. In comparison, the total expenditures of states on income/investment support schemes are estimated to be ₹32,861 crores for 2019-20 (up from ₹16,250 crores of 2018-19). To ensure timely payments to farmers and minimising inclusion and exclusion errors, the RBI has suggested the states to take two important steps in this regard:
    - Digitisation of land records and
    - Linking with Aadhar-seeded bank accounts.

WOMEN FARMERS

In the agriculture sector, women play a significant and crucial role. Right from the main crop production to livestock, horticulture, post-harvest operations, agro and social forestry, fisheries and marketing, they are involved at every possible level of farm activity (this was rightly recognised by the National Commission on Women, 2001). For sustainable development of the agriculture and rural economy, the contribution of women to agriculture and food production cannot be ignored.

[79] *Economic Survey 2019-20*, vol. 2 (New Delhi: Ministry of Finance, GoI), pp. 195-96.

[80] *State Finances: A Study of Budgets, Reserve Bank of India*, (New Delhi: 2019).

Globally, there is empirical evidence that women have a decisive role in ensuring 'food security' and 'preserving local agro-biodiversity'. Rural women are responsible for the integrated management and use of diverse natural resources to meet the daily household needs (*Food and Agriculture Organisation, 2011*).

But in this sector India also has a high *gender disparity*. As per the Census 2011, out of the total female main workers, 55 per cent were agricultural labourers and 24 per cent were cultivators. However, only 12.8 per cent of the operational holdings were owned by women. Moreover, there is concentration of operational holdings (25.7 per cent) by women in the marginal and small holdings categories. With growing rural to urban migration by men, there is **feminisation** of the agriculture sector in the country, with increasing number of women in multiple roles - as cultivators, entrepreneurs and labourers.

This requires that women farmers should have enhanced access to resources such as land, water, credit, technology and training which needs critical analysis in the context of India. In addition, the entitlements of women farmers will be the key to improve agriculture productivity. Towards this, the Government has been implementing *various schemes* which help improve the entitlements of women farmers, which will prove to be advantageous in bridging the policy gaps which exist in the sector. The following measures[81] have been taken to ensure mainstreaming of women in the agriculture sector:

- Earmarking at least 30 per cent of the budget allocation for women beneficiaries in all ongoing schemes and programmes.
- Initiating women-centric activities.
- Focus on women SHGs by delivering micro-credit and right information together with involving them in the decision-making bodies.
- Recognising the critical role of women in agriculture, the Ministry of Agriculture and Farmers Welfare has declared 15 October of every year as Women Farmer's Day.

Indian farm sector needs a gender specific policy framework to adjust with the existing and emerging realities in the sector. Such a nuanced policy intervention will not only enhance food security but also promote gender equality, extension services, sustainability and all-round development in the rural areas.

CLIMATE-SMART AGRICULTURE

Climate change can impact the farm sector in different ways - increased variability in temperature, rainfall, extreme weather events like drought and flood. These incidences ultimately hit the farm community in a very negative way. To fight these uncertainties, development of a climate resilient agro-system is the need of the hour.

It is in this backdrop that the new concept of Climate Smart Agriculture (CSA) has emerged.[82] It is an approach that helps to guide actions needed 'to transform and reorient agricultural systems to effectively support development and ensure food security under changing climate'. It aims to provide stakeholders the means to identify agricultural strategies suitable to their local conditions. The CSA aims to tackle *three* main objectives:

1. Sustainably increasing agricultural productivity and incomes;
2. Adapting and building resilience to climate change; and
3. Reducing and/or removing greenhouse gas emissions wherever possible.

Though, this new concept is at a nascent stage in India, the Government has already started taking policy initiatives in this direction.

At present, *climate resilient technologies* are being demonstrated in 446 model villages under KVK (Kisan Vikas Kendra) covering 23 states under National Innovations on Climate Resilient Agriculture (NICRA). In addition, 651 contingency plans have been prepared to manage various weather aberrations such as droughts, floods, cyclones, hailstorms, heat and cold waves.

[81] *Economic Survey 2017-18*, vol. 2 (New Delhi: Ministry of Finance, GoI), pp. 103-04

[82] *Economic Survey 2017-18*, vol. 2 (New Delhi: Ministry of Finance, GoI), pp. 113-14.

WAY FORWARD

The *Economic Survey 2025–26,* in agreement with the previous volumes of it, states that the objective of inclusive development in India cannot be realised without the development of the rural sector which crucially depends on agriculture – it is an *engine of broad-based growth* (says the *Economic Survey 2017–18*). Progress of the sector has a bearing on the fate of the largest low-income group in India, and it will be central to achieving ***Viksit Bharat***, as per the Survey. There is a need for a *paradigm shift* in how we view agriculture from a rural livelihood sector to a modern business enterprise – in this context, both production and post-production needs urgent reforms to enable sustainable and consistent growth. The following suggestions[83] have been provided by the document in this regard:

- *Production and productivity* related – expansion of irrigation, adoption of hybrid and improved seeds, increasing variety replacement ratio and augmentation in seed testing facilities.
- *Post-production* related – arrangement of adequate storage and remunerative markets, integration with nutritional outcomes (by means of food fortification), village-level procurement centres, linkages between production and processing, development of rural markets, option of selling outside the APMC markets, warehouse upgradations, better freight operations by railways, dedicated freight corridors (most of them are being taken up by the Government).
- *Input optimisation* – by all business enterprises (of both knowledge and materials).
- *From producer to entrepreneur* – imparting farmers basic education and training to transform farmers from a producer to an entrepreneur (rural agricultural schools for hands-on training may be explored in this regard).
- *Allied sectors* – looking at animal husbandry, dairying and fisheries becoming a significant source of farm income and employment, measures need to be taken to increase their productivity enhancing their market access.
- *Extension services* – need strengthening to provide farmers knowledge about improved agricultural practices, guidance of their uses and other services.
- *Food subsidy* – While it is difficult to reduce the economic cost of food management in view of rising commitment towards food security, there is a need to consider the revision of CIP (Central Issue Price is the price at which foodgrains are sold by the FCI to the beneficiaries) to reduce the 'bulging food subsidy' bill (which is becoming unmanageably large).
- *Crop diversification* – needed towards oilseeds, pulses and horticulture needs to be given priority by addressing the core issues of irrigation, investment, credit and markets in their cultivation. While the Government has adopted the use of MSP as signal to encourage this, there is also a need for coordinated action from the State Governments to facilitate the shift to high value and less water-consuming crops to enable realisation of the objective of doubling farmers' income in a sustainable way.
- *Research and development (R & D)* – in agriculture and allied sectors can play a major role in realisation of sustainable agriculture practice that efficiently meets the objectives of nutritional security and improvement in farm income – gives better returns compared to the money spent on inputs.
- *Alternative fertilisers* – There is a need to explore options and promote use of alternative fertilisers such as Nano Urea and organic fertiliser which protect the soil, are more productive and contribute to higher nutrient use efficiency.
- *Use of new technology* – Focus should be on the use of new technology including drones and AI-based decision support systems, reduction in the use of chemical fertilisers and use of low-cost organic inputs and supporting start-ups for innovations.

[83] *Economic Survey 2025-26* (New Delhi: Ministry of Finance, GoI, January 2026), pp. 225-253; *Economic Survey 2024-25* (New Delhi: Ministry of Finance, GoI), pp. 245-70; *Economic Survey 2023-24* (New Delhi: Ministry of Finance, GoI), pp. 319-45; *Economic Survey 2022-23* (New Delhi: Ministry of Finance, GoI), pp. 243-58; *Economic Survey 2021-22* (New Delhi: Ministry of Finance, GoI), pp. 263-264; and *Economic Survey 2020-21*, vol. 2 (New Delhi: Ministry of Finance, GoI), pp. 257-58.

PREVIOUS YEARS' QUESTIONS

Prelims

1. Consider the following statements: (2025)

Statement-I: In India, income from allied agricultural activities like poultry farming and wool rearing in rural areas is exempted from any tax.

Statement-II: In India, rural agricultural land is not considered a capital asset under the provisions of the Income Tax Act, 1961.

Which one of the following is correct in respect of the above statements?

(a) Both Statement-I and Statement-II are correct, and Statement-II explains Statement-I
(b) Both Statement-I and Statement-II are correct, but Statement-II does not explain Statement-I
(c) Statement-I is correct, but Statement-II is not correct
(d) Statement-I is not correct, but Statement-II is correct

2. Consider the following statements about turmeric during the year 2022-23: (2025)

(i) India is the largest producer and exporter of turmeric in the world.
(ii) More than 30 varieties of turmeric are grown in India.
(iii) Maharashtra, Telangana, Karnataka and Tamil Nadu are major turmeric-producing States in India.

Which of the statements given above are correct?

(a) (i) and (ii) only (b) (ii) and (iii) only
(c) (i) and (iii) only (d) (i), (ii) and (iii)

3. Consider the following statements about the Rashtriya Gokul Mission: (2025)

(i) It is important for the upliftment of the rural poor, as the majority of low-producing indigenous animals are with small and marginal farmers and landless labourers.
(ii) It was initiated to promote indigenous cattle and buffalo rearing and conservation in a scientific and holistic manner.

Which of the statements given above is/are correct?

(a) (i) only (b) (ii) only
(c) Both (i) and (ii) (d) Neither (i) nor (ii)

4. Consider the following statements: (2024)

(i) India is a member of the International Grains Council.
(ii) A country needs to be a member of the International Grains Council for exporting or importing rice and wheat.

Which of the statements given above is/are correct?

(a) (i) only (b) (ii) only
(c) Both (i) and (ii) (d) Neither (i) nor (ii)

5. Consider the following statements: (2024)

Statement-I: India does not import apples from the United States of America.

Statement-II: In India, the law prohibits the import of genetically modified food without the approval of the competent authority.

Which one of the following is correct in respect of the above statements?

(a) Both Statement-I and Statement-II are correct and Statement-II explains Statement-I
(b) Both Statement-I and Statement-II are correct, but Statement-II does not explain Statement-I
(c) Statement-I is correct, but Statement-II is incorrect
(d) Statement-I is incorrect, but Statement-II is correct

6. With reference to the Digital India Land Records Modernisation Programme, consider the following statements: (2024)

(i) To implement the scheme, the Central Government provides 100 per cent funding.
(ii) Under the Scheme, Cadastral Maps are digitised.
(iii) An initiative has been undertaken to transliterate the Records of Rights from

local language to any of the languages recognised by the Constitution of India.

Which of the statements given above are correct?

(a) (i) and (ii) only (b) (ii) and (iii) only
(c) (i) and (iii) only (d) (i), (ii) and (iii)

7. Which one of the following is the correct description of "100 Million Farmers"? (2024)

(a) It is a platform for accelerating the transition towards food and water systems that are net-zero (carbon), nature-positive and that aims to increase farmer resilience.
(b) It is an international alliance and a network of individuals and farming organisations interested in supporting and strengthening the development of the organic animal husbandry.
(c) It is a digital platform fully integrated with service providers and built on blockchain that lets buyers, sellers and third parties trade fertilisers quickly and securely.
(d) It is a platform with the mission of encouraging the farmers to form Farmer Product Organisations or Agribusiness Consortiums, thus facilitating the access to global open markets to sell their products.

Answers: 1. (d) 2. (d) 3. (c) 4. (a) 5. (d) 6. (d) 7. (a)

Explanation

1. (d): Statement-I is incorrect. Under Section 10(1) of the Income Tax Act, 1961, agricultural income is exempt from tax, which includes income from cultivating and selling agricultural produce, sale of agricultural land, and compensation received from the government for acquisition of agricultural land. Though income from allied agricultural activities (such as dairy farming, poultry, or fisheries) is not treated as agricultural income under the Act and is subject to tax by the central government. Statement-II is correct: as per Section 2(1A) of the Act, rural agricultural land is not classified as a capital asset– thus, any rental income from such land or income earned from growing and selling produce on it is not taxable.

2. (d): **The Government of India in 2023 constituted the National Turmeric Board.** This board is designed to coordinate efforts across various ministries and institutions to enhance production, promote exports, encourage value addition, and improve income for turmeric farmers.

Statement-I is correct (India produces around 75 per cent of the world's turmeric and has a share of around 60 per cent in its exports). Statement-II is correct (diverse soil types and climatic conditions of India enable the cultivation of more than 30 known varieties of turmeric across various states). Statement-III is correct (Maharashtra, Telangana, Karnataka, and Tamil Nadu are consistently among the top turmeric-producing states in India). [The Government constituted the National Turmeric Board in 2023 to coordinate efforts across various ministries and institutions to enhance production, promote exports, encourage value addition, and improve income for turmeric farmers].

3. (c): Statements-I and II are both correct (the scheme was launched in December 2014 under the Department of Animal Husbandry and Dairying, Ministry of Fisheries, Animal Husbandry & Dairying, with aims such as enhancing milk production and productivity of bovines to meet growing demand for milk and making dairying more remunerative to the rural farmers of the country).

5. (d): Statement-I is incorrect as India imports apples from the USA. But Statement-II is correct since India's law prohibits the import of genetically modified foods (GMFs), however, a competent authority may authorise so. In practice, India is yet to officially permit import of such food items.

6. (d): All of 'three' are the correct features of this Central Sector Scheme (which are 100 per cent funded by the Government of India) launched in 2016.

7. (a): The "100 Million Farmers" is a WEF (World Economic Forum) initiative which works as multi-party platform and encourages farmers to adopt climate-smart and regenerative farm practices– aiming to transition to sustainable food systems by 2030.

Mains

1. Explain the factors influencing the decision of the farmers on the selection of high value crops in India. (2025)
2. Elaborate the scope and significance of supply chain management of agricultural commodities in India. (2025)
3. Examine the scope of the food processing industries in India. Elaborate the measures taken by the government in the food processing industries for generating employment opportunities. (2025)
4. What were the factors responsible for the successful implementation of land reforms in some parts of the country? Elaborate. (2024)
5. Explain the role of millets for ensuring health and nutritional security in India. (2024)
6. What are the major challenges faced by Indian irrigation system in recent times? State the measures taken by the government for efficient irrigation management. (2024)
7. Elucidate the importance of buffer stocks for stabilising agricultural prices in India. What are the challenges associated with the storage of buffer stock? Discuss. (2024)
8. Explain the changes in cropping patterns in India in the context of changes in consumption patterns and marketing conditions. (2023)
9. How does e-Technology help farmers in production and marketing of agricultural produce? Explain it. (2023)
10. State the objectives and measures of land reforms in India. Discuss how land ceiling policy on landholding can be considered as an effective reform under economic criteria. (2023)
11. What are the direct and indirect subsidies provided to farm sector in India. Discuss the issues raised by the World Trade Organisation (WTO) in relation to agricultural subsidies. (2023)
12. What is Integrated Farming System ? How is it helpful to small and marginal farmers in India? (2022)
13. Elaborate the scope and significance of the food processing industry in India. (2022)
14. What are the main bottlenecks in upstream and downstream process of marketing of agricultural products in India? (2022)
15. What are the major challenges of Public Distribution System (PDS) in India? How can it be made effective and transparent? (2022)
16. What is Integrated Farming System ? How is it helpful to small and marginal farmers in India. (2022)
17. How and to what extent would micro-irrigation help in solving India's water crisis? (2021)
18. What are the present challenges before crop diversification? How do emerging technologies provide an opportunity for crop diversification? (2021)
19. What are the salient features of the National Food Security Act, 2013? How has the Food Security Bill helped in eliminating hunger and malnutrition in India? (2021)
20. How did land reforms in some parts of the country help to improve the socio-economic conditions of marginal and small farmers? (2021)

SAMPLE OBJECTIVE QUESTIONS

1. Select the correct statement(s) related to the Climate-Smart Agriculture, using the code given below:
   (i) Raising agricultural income
   (ii) Adapting to climate change
   (iii) Reducing greenhouse gas emission

   Code:
   (a) Only one (b) Only two
   (c) All three (d) None of these
2. Select the correct statement(s) related to agricultural subsidies provisioned by the World Trade Organisation, using the code given below:

(i) Subsidies offered by member nations for fertilisers, interest, irrigation, etc. are categorised as product-specific support.

(ii) Member nations are not allowed to announce support prices for agricultural commodities.

(iii) The provision of Peace Clause absolves member nations from offering agricultural subsidies for food security reasons.

Code:

(a) Only one
(b) Only two
(c) All three
(d) None of these

3. Select the correct statement(s) given below related to the market intervention scheme (MIS), using the code given below:

(i) It is implemented in events of over-production or price crashes of agri-commodities.

(ii) Losses are fully borne by the centre in cases of perishable/horticultural items.

(iii) It protects the economic interest of agri-producers more than the agri-consumers.

(iv) Money spent on its implementation is drawn from the price stabilisation fund (PSF) which is reimbursed later on.

Select the correct statements from the above using the code given below:

Code:

(a) Only two
(b) Only three
(c) All four
(d) None of these

4. Consider the latest statements given below related to the agri-sector of the country:

(i) Its share in global imports is higher than that of its share in global exports.

(ii) The last decade saw the second highest increase in the minimum support prices of *moong* (green gram).

(iii) High fragmentation of land holding has made agri-businesses economically non-viable.

Select the correct statement(s) from the above using the code given below:

Code:

(a) Only one **(b)** Only two
(c) All three **(d)** None of these

5. Consider the following statements related to irrigation system of India:

(i) Drip irrigation is technically more efficient method but less economical.

(ii) Sprinkler irrigation reduces labour cost but increases power consumption.

(iii) Drip and sprinkler irrigation is suitable for undulating and water deficient areas.

How many of the above statements are correct?

(a) Only one **(b)** Only two
(c) All three **(d)** None of these

6. Consider the following statements related to farm mechanisation in the country:

(i) As per the NITI Aayog Task Force on Agriculture, farm mechanisation makes farming more productive but less economical as cheaper menial labour is available in abundance.

(ii) As per NABARD, use of machineries makes farming commercially more viable though it a capital intensive measure.

(iii) Increasing shortage of labour is forcing farm mechanisation in the country.

How many of the above statement(s) is/are correct?

(a) Only one **(b)** Only two
(c) All three **(d)** None of these

7. Consider the following statements related to India's farm sector:

(i) Nutri cereals have been included in the public distribution system to improve nutritional security.

(ii) Nutri cereals are sturdy, drought resistant, more nutritious and need less fertilisation too.

(iii) Suitability of nano fertilisers are yet to be verified on the nutri cereals in India.

How many of the above statement(s) is/are correct?

(a) Only one (b) Only two

(c) All three (d) None of these

8. Consider the following statements related to India's farm sector:

(i) The World Trade Organisation prohibits indirect farm subsidies of its members.

(ii) Direct farm subsidies are preferred under the regime of the World Trade Organisation.

(iii) Indirect farm subsidies help fertiliser manufacturers too besides the farmers.

How many of the above statement(s) is/are correct?

(a) Only one (b) Only two

(c) All three (d) None of these

9. Consider the following statements related to the steps towards enhancing farmers' income in the country:

(i) Agri commodity trading is helpful in it but chances of exploitation is always there.

(ii) Allowing 100 per cent foreign direct investment in the agricultural retail will help but chances of stock glut will be there.

(iii) Corporate and contract farming can play positive roles.

How many of the above statement(s) is/are correct?

(a) Only one

(b) Only two

(c) All three

(d) None of these

10. Consider the following statements related to the process of land reforms in the country:

(i) Reorganisation of agriculture sector is no more among its objectives.

(ii) Computerisation of land records is its integral part.

(iii) Land acquisition has emerged as a separate policy outside the domain of this process.

How many of the above statement(s) is/are correct?

(a) Only one (b) Only two

(c) All three (d) None of these

Answers: 1. (c) 2. (d) 3. (d) 4. (d) 5. (a) 6. (b) 7. (b) 8. (a) 9. (a) 10. (a)

SAMPLE SUBJECTIVE QUESTIONS

1. 'A vibrant agri-commodity trading in the country will not only help in boosting farm income but also in inflation management.' Illustrate.

2. Critically examine the significance of crop diversification in special reference to the nutri cereals and government's initiatives regarding it.

3. 'To help farmers tide over financial distress, government should prefer to provide farm income support over farm loan waivers.' Critically examine.

4. 'Enhancing water productivity and irrigation efficiency should be given priority once irrigation capacity expansion looks difficult.' Examine.

5. Why do you think that food subsidies need rationalisation in the country? Give your suggestions in this regard.

6. Briefly discuss about India's challenges in complying to the agricultural provisions of the WTO. Give your suggestions to help government devise a suitable path in this regard.

7. 'Land fragmentation necessitates focus on agri-business and animal husbandry.' Comment.

8. Write a note on the need and challenges related to the climate smart agriculture in the country.

SAMPLE MODEL ANSWER

1. **Write a short note on the Climate Smart Agriculture, its objectives, and Government's policy steps in this regard.**

Ans. Changing climate has emerged as the biggest risk factor for the farm sector. Variabilities in temperature and rainfall, together with extreme weather events like drought and flood, have already started impacting global farm systems–negatively impacting the farm community at the end. The new concept of Climate Smart Agriculture (CSA) has emerged in this backdrop to fight these uncertainties (Economic Survey 2017-18).

The CSA is an approach that helps to guide actions needed 'to transform and reorient agricultural systems to effectively support development and ensure food security under changing climate' (FAO, 2010). It aims to provide stakeholders the means to identify agricultural strategies suitable to their local conditions. The CSA aims to tackle three main objectives:

1. Sustainably increasing agricultural productivity and incomes;
2. Adapting and building resilience to climate change; and
3. Reducing and/or removing greenhouse gas emissions wherever possible.

Though this new concept is at a nascent stage in India, the Government has already started taking policy initiatives in this direction. Climate-resilient technologies are being demonstrated under KVK (Kisan Vikas Kendra), covering over 23 states under National Innovations on Climate Resilient Agriculture (NICRA). In addition, over 651 contingency plans have been prepared to manage various weather aberrations such as droughts, floods, cyclones, hailstorms, heat, and cold waves.

CHAPTER 10

Industry and Infrastructure

> Rapid growth of unskilled-labour-intensive sectors is likely to create many more opportunities for the poor than rapid growth of capital- and skilled-labour-intensive sectors. Such a shift would reinforce rather than impede aggregate growth.*
>
> *See Arvind Panagariya, *India: The Emerging Giant* (New Delhi: Oxford University Press, 2013), pp. 282 and 475.

To watch the Author's videos on the significance of the Chapter, scan the QR Code given here

Exam Essentials...

- Next NIP
- PSEs and PSUs
- Types of Disinvestments
- Disinvestment by States
- Focus on the MSMEs
- FDI Policy Measures
- Opportunistic Foreign Takeover
- India In Global Innovation Index 2024
- TOT Model
- National Infrastructure Pipeline

Note to the Reader...

This chapter offers valuable insights into the evolution of India's 'non-foundational' economic policies, going beyond just the sectors of industry and infrastructure. To gain a well-rounded understanding from a policy perspective, it is best read alongside Chapter 4, which explores 'foundational' economic policies. Together, these chapters serve as a prequel and sequel, providing a comprehensive view of India's economic trajectory.

In This Chapter...

- Introduction
- Review of Industrial Policies up to 1986
- New Industrial Policy, 1991
- Disinvestment
- Comprehensive Management of Public Assets
- Proceeds of Disinvestment
- Performance of CPSEs
- MSME Sector
- Industrial Sectors
- PLI Scheme
- Ease of Doing Business
- Make in India
- Start-Up India
- Industry 4.0
- COVID-19 and Industrial Reforms
- Indian Infrastructure
- Power
- Railways
- Roads
- Civil Aviation
- Telecom
- Digital Infrastructure
- Semiconductor Sector
- Minerals
- PPP Models
- Renewable Energy
- Logistics Sector
- Housing and Urban Infrastructure
- PM Gati Shakti
- Recent Challenges
- Way Forward

INTRODUCTION

Many of the western economies had already written their success stories of industrialisation leading to accelerated growth and development by the time India became an independent economy. Independent India needed to rejuvenate its economy from a completely dilapidated state. The country had many tasks in front of it - the abject mass poverty, shortage of foodgrains, healthcare, etc., calling for immediate attention. The other areas of attention included industry, infrastructure, science and technology, higher education, to name a few. All these areas of development required heavy capital investment as they had been severely neglected by the colonial ruler for the last 150 years or so. Increasing the growth of economy at a faster pace was the urgent need. Looking at the pros and cons of the available options, India decided that the industrial sector should be the 'prime moving force' (PMF) of the economy - the logical choice for faster growth (a fully established idea at that time, the world over). The secondary sector will lead the economy, which was well decided in the 1930s by the dominant political forces among the freedom fighters.

As the government of the time had decided upon an active role for the governments in the economy, naturally, the industrial sector was to have a dominant state role - the expansion of the government-owned companies (i.e., the PSUs) to glorious heights. In many ways the development of the Indian economy has been the development of the government sector. Even though this idea of the state's role in the economy underwent a radical change in the early 1990s with the process of economic reforms, the hangover or the drag of it is still visible on the economy today. The industrial policies which the governments announced from time to time basically molded the very nature and structure of the economy. Any discussion on the Indian economy must start with a survey of the industrial policies of the country. A **brief review** of the various industrial policies of India till date is discussed in the following sections.

REVIEW OF INDUSTRIAL POLICIES UP TO 1986

For a better understanding of the Indian economy, it is advisable to look into the various industrial polices. The official stances keep changing with every upcoming industrial policy. Understanding these policies becomes even more important to understand the finer aspects of the reform process which the country commenced from early 1990s. Here, a brief review of India's industrial policies is presented to serve the purpose.

Industrial Policy Resolution, 1948

Announced on 8 April 1948, this was not only the first industrial policy statement of India, but it also decided the model of the economic system (i.e., the mixed economy). Thus, it included the following:

1. India will be a mixed economy.[1]
2. Some of the important industries were put under the *Central List* such as coal, power, railways, civil aviation, arms and ammunition, defence, etc.
3. Some other industries (usually of medium category) were put under a *State List* such as paper, medicines, textiles, cycles, rickshaws, two-wheelers, etc.
4. Rest of the industries (not covered by either the central or the state lists) were left open for private sector investment - with many of them having the provision of compulsory licencing.
5. There was a 10 year period for review of the policy.

Industrial Policy Resolution, 1956

The government was encouraged by the impact of the industrial policy of 1948, and it was only after eight years that the new and more crystallised policies were announced for the Indian industries. The then new industrial policy of 1956 had the following major provisions:

1. **Reservation of Industries:** A clear-cut classification of industries (also known as the **Reservation of Industries**) was affected with three schedules:
   (i) ***Schedule A:*** This Schedule had 17 industrial areas in which the Centre was given complete monopoly. The industries set up under this provision were known as the Central Public Sector

[1] Here this should be noted that India will be a planned economy was well-decided before this industrial policy which articulated for an *active role* of the state in the economy. The main objective of planning pointed out at this time was *poverty alleviation* by a judicious exploitation of the resources of the country. Only a 'mixed economy' did fit such a wish (*Conference of State Industry Ministers, 1938*).

Undertakings (CPSUs) later gaining popularity as 'PSUs'. Though the number of industries was only 17, the number of PSUs set up by the Government of India (GoI) rose to 254 by 1991. These also included those industrial units which were taken over by the government between 1960 and 1980 under the *nationalisation* drives.[2] These industries belonged to Schedules B and C (other than Schedule A).

(ii) ***Schedule B:*** There were 12 industrial areas put under this Schedule in which the state governments were supposed to take up the initiatives with a more expansive follow-up by the private sector. This schedule also carried the provisions of compulsory licencing. It should be noted here that neither the states nor the private sector had monopolies in these industries unlike Schedule A, which provided monopoly to the Centre.[3]

(iii) ***Schedule C:*** All industrial areas left out of Schedules A and B were put under this in which the private enterprises had the provisions to set up industries. Many of them had the provisions of licencing and had to *necessarily* fit into the framework of the social and economic policy of the state, and were subject to control and regulation in terms of the Industries Development and Regulation (IDR) Act and other relevant legislations.[4]

The above classification of industries had an in-built bias in favour of government owned companies (i.e., the CPSUs) which proceeded according to the ideas of the planning process. Thus, expansion of the public sector became almost a directive principle of economic policy, and the PSUs did expand in the future.[5]

It was this industrial policy wherein the then PM Pandit Jawaharlal Nehru had termed the PSUs the *temples of modern India,* symbolically hinting to their importance.[6] There was a time soon after Independence when the PSUs were regarded as the principal instrument for raising savings and growth in the economy.[7] The rapid expansion of PSUs accounted for more than half of the GDP of the economy by 1988-89.[8]

2. **Provision of Licencing:** One of the most important developments of independent India, the provision of compulsory licencing for industries, was cemented in this policy. All the Schedule B industries and a number of Schedule C industries came under this provision. This provision established the so-called *Licence-Quota-Permit* regime *(raj)* in the economy.[9]
3. **Expansion of the Public Sector:** Expansion of the public sector was pledged for the accelerated industrialisation and growth in the economy - glorification of government companies did start with this policy. The emphasis was on heavy industries.
4. **Regional Disparity:** To tackle the widening regional disparity, the policy committed to set up the upcoming PSUs in the comparatively backward and underdeveloped regions/areas in the economy.[10]

---

[2] The nationalisation of industrial units allowed the government to enter the unreserved areas, which consequently increased its industrial presence. Though the nationalisation was provided a highly rational official reason of *greater public benefit*, the private sector always doubted it and took it as an insecurity and major unseen future hurdle in the expansion of private industries in the country.

[3] The Central government had always the option to set up an industry in any of these 12 industrial areas. This happened in the coming years *via* two methods - first, through *nationalisation*; and second, through the *joint sector.*

[4] Industrial Policy Resolution, 1956 (30 October).

[5] V. M. Dandekar, 'Forty Years After Independence', in *Indian Economy: Problems and Prospects*, B. Jalan, ed. (New Delhi: Penguin Books, 2004), p. 63.

[6] This statement we get in the *Second Five Year Plan (1956-61)*, too.

[7] B. Jalan, *India's Economic Policy* (New Delhi: Penguin Books, 1992), p. 23.

[8] V. M. Dandekar, 'Forty Years After Independence', in *Indian Economy: Problems and Prospects*, B. Jalan, ed. (New Delhi: Penguin Books, 2004), p. 64.

[9] These industries which were set up after procuring '*licences*' from the government had fixed upper limits of their production known as '*quota*' and they needed to procure timely 'permit' (i.e., permission) for the supply of, raw materials - that is why such a name was given to the whole system.

[10] Such a commitment went completely against the 'theory of industrial location'.

5. **Emphasis on Small Industries:** There was emphasis on small industries as well as the khadi and village industries.
6. **Agricultural Sector:** The agricultural sector was pledged as a priority.

Importance

This is considered as the most important industrial policy of India by the experts as it decided not only the industrial expansion but also structured the very nature and scope of the economy till 1991 with minor modifications. All the industrial policies were nothing but minor modifications with the exception of the new industrial policy of 1991 which affected deeper and structural changes wherein India started a wider process of economic reforms.

Industrial Policy Statement, 1969

This was basically a licencing policy which aimed at solving the shortcomings of the licencing policy started by the Industrial Policy of 1956. The experts and industrialists (newcomers) complained that the industrial licencing policy was serving just the opposite purpose for which it was mooted. Inspired by the socialistic ideals and nationalistic feelings the licencing policy had the following reasons:

1. Exploitation of resources for the development of all;
2. Priority of resource exploitation for the industries;
3. Price control of the goods produced by the licenced industries;
4. Checking concentration of economic power;
5. Channelising investment into desired direction (according to the planning process).

In practice, the licencing policy was not serving the above-given purpose properly. A powerful industrial house was always able to procure fresh licences at the cost of a new budding entrepreneur. The price regulation policy *via* licencing was aimed at helping the public by providing cheaper goods, but it indirectly served the private licenced industries ultimately (as central subsidies were given to the private companies from where it was to benefit the poor in the form of cheaper goods). Similarly, the older and well-established industrial houses were capable of creating hurdles for the newer ones with the help of different kinds of trade practices forcing the latter to agree for sell-outs and takeovers. A number of committees were set up by the government to look into the matter and suggest remedies.[11] The committees on industrial licencing policy review not only pointed out several shortcomings of the policy but also accepted the useful role of industrial licencing.[12] Finally, it was in 1969 that the new industrial licencing policy was announced which affected the following major changes in the area:

1. The Monopolistic and Restrictive Trade Practices (MRTP) Act was passed. The Act intended to regulate the trading and commercial practices of the firms and checking monopoly and concentration of economic power.
2. The firms with assets of ₹25 crore or more were put under obligation of taking permission from the GoI before any expansion, greenfield venture and takeover of other firms (as per the MRTP Act). Such firms came to be known as the *MRTP Companies.* The upper limit (known as the *MRTP limit)* for such companies was revised upward to ₹50 crore in 1980 and ₹100 crore in 1985.[13]
3. For the redressal of the prohibited and restricted practices of trade, the government did set up an *MRTP Commission.*

Industrial Policy Statement, 1973

The Industrial Policy Statement of 1973 introduced some new thinking into the economy with major ones being the following:

1. A new classificatory term, i.e., *core industries,* was created. The industries which were of fundamental importance for the development of industries were put in this category, such as iron and steel, cement, coal, crude oil, oil refining and electricity. Later, these industries came to be known as *basic industries and infrastructure industries* in the country.
2. Out of the six core industries defined by the policy, the private sector may apply for licences

[11] There were four specific committees set up on this issue, namely *Swaminathan Committee (1964), Mahalanobis Committee (1964), R. K. Hazari Committee (1967)* and *S. Dutt Committee (1969).* The Administrative Reform Commission (1969) also pointed out the shortcomings of the industrial licencing policy perpetuated since 1956.

[12] *Dutt Committee* (New Delhi: Government of India, 1969).

[13] The upward revision was logical as it was hindering the organic growth of such companies – neither the capacity addition was possible nor an investment for technological upgrading.

for the industries which were not a part of Schedule A of the Industrial Policy, 1956.[14] The private firms eligible to apply for such licences were supposed to have their total assets at ₹20 crore or more.

3. Some industries were put under the *reserved list* in which only the small or medium industries could be set up.[15]
4. The concept of *joint sector* was developed which allowed partnership among the Centre, state and the private sector while setting up some industries. The governments had the discretionary power to exit such ventures in future. Here, the government wanted to promote the private sector with state support.
5. The GoI had been facing the foreign exchange crunch during that time. To regulate foreign exchange, the Foreign Exchange Regulation Act (FERA) was passed in 1973.[16] Experts have called it a *draconian* Act which hampered the growth and modernisation of Indian industries.
6. A limited permission to foreign investment (FI) was given, with the multinational corporations (MNCs) being allowed to set up subsidiaries in the country.[17]

Industrial Policy Statement, 1977

The Industrial Policy Statement of 1977 was chalked out by a different political set-up from the past with a different political fervour - the dominant voice in the government was having an anti-Indira stance with an inclination towards the Gandhian-socialistic views towards the economy.

We see such elements in this policy statement:

1. Foreign investment in the *unnecessary areas* was prohibited (opposite to the IPS of 1973 which promoted FI *via* technology transfer in the areas of lack of capital or technology). In practice, there was a complete 'no' to FI.[18]
2. Emphasis on village industries with a redefinition of the small and cottage industries.
3. Decentralised industrialisation was given attention with the objective of linking the masses to the process of industrialisation. The District Industries Centres (DICs) were set up to promote the expansion of small and cottage industries at a mass scale.
4. Democratic decentralisation was emphasised, and the khadi and village industries were restructured.
5. Serious attention was paid to the level of production and the prices of essential commodities of everyday use.

Industrial Policy Resolution, 1980

The year 1980 saw the return of the same political party at the Centre. The new government revised the Industrial Policy of 1977 with few exceptions:

1. Foreign investment *via* the technology transfer route was allowed again (similar to the provisions of the IPS, 1973).
2. The 'MRTP Limit' was revised upward to ₹50 crore to promote setting of bigger companies.
3. The DICs were continued with.
4. Industrial licencing was simplified.
5. Overall liberal attitude was followed towards the expansion of private industries.

Industrial Policy Resolutions, 1985 and 1986

The industrial policy resolutions announced by the governments in 1985 and 1986 were very similar in

---

14 Out of the six core industries only the cement and iron and steel industries were open for private investment with the rest fully *reserved* for the central public sector investment.

15 This is considered a follow up to such suggestions forwarded by the *Industrial Licensing Policy Inquiry Committee* (S. Dutt, Chairman) (New Delhi: Government of India, 1969).

16 The FERA was executed on 1 January 1974. The private sector in the country always complained against this Act and doubted its official intentions.

17 This limited permission was restricted to the areas where there was a need of foreign capital. Such MNCs entered the Indian economy with the help of a partner from India - the partner being the major one with 74 per cent shares in the subsidiaries set up for by the MNCs. The MNCs invested *via technology transfer route.* Basically, this was an attempt to make up for the loss being incurred by the FERA. This was the period when most of the MNCs had the chances to enter India. Once economic reforms started by 1991, many of them increased their holdings in the Indian subsidiaries with the Indian partner getting the minority shares or a total exit.

18 The permission of operation was withdrawn in the case of the already functioning soft drink MNC the *Coca Cola.* The ongoing process to allow the computer giant *IBM* and automobile major *Chrysler* to enter India was soon called off. These instances played a highly negative role when India invited FDI in the post-1991 reform era.

nature, and the latter tried to promote the initiative of the former. The main highlights of the policies are as follows:

1. Foreign investment was further simplified with more industrial areas being open for their entries. The dominant method of FI remained as in the past, i.e., *technology transfer*, but now the equity holding of the MNCs in the Indian subsidiaries could be up to 49 per cent with the Indian partner holding the remaining 51 per cent shares.
2. The *MRTP Limit* was revised upward to ₹100 crore - promoting the idea of bigger companies.
3. The provision of industrial licencing was simplified. Compulsory licencing now remained for 64 industries only.[19]
4. High level attention was paid on the sunrise industries such as telecommunication, computer, and electronics.
5. Modernisation and the profitability aspects of public sector undertakings (PSUs) were emphasised.
6. Industries based on imported raw materials got a boost.[20]
7. Under the overall regime of FERA, some relaxations concerning the use of foreign exchange was permitted so that essential technology could be assimilated into Indian industries and international standard could be achieved.
8. The agriculture sector was attended with a new scientific approach with many *technology missions* being launched by the government.

These industrial policies were mooted out by the government when the developed world was pushing for the formation of the WTO and a new world economic order looked like a reality. Once the world had become one market, only bigger industrial firms could have managed to cater to such a big market. Side by side sorting out the historical hurdles to industrial expansion perpetuated by the past industrial policies, these new industrial policy resolutions were basically a preparation for the *globalised* future world.

These industrial provisions were attempted at liberalising the economy without any 'slogan' of economic reforms. The government of the time had the mood and willingness of going for the kind of economic reforms which India pursued post-1991, but it lacked the required political support.[21]

The industrial policies conjoined with the overall micro-economic policy followed by the government had one major loophole that it was more dependent on foreign capital with a big part being costlier ones. Once the economy could not meet industrial performance, it became tough for India to service the external borrowings - the external events (the Gulf War, 1990-91) also vitiated the situation. Finally, by the end of the 1980s India was in the grip of a severe balance of payment (BoP) crisis with higher rate of inflation (over 13 per cent) and higher fiscal deficit (over 8 per cent).[22] The deep crisis put the economy in a financial crunch, which made India opt for a new way of economic management in the coming times.

NEW INDUSTRIAL POLICY, 1991

The industrial policies of the past shaped the nature and structure of the Indian economy. The need of the hour was to change the nature and structure of the economy by the early 1990s. The GoI decided to change the very nature of the industrial policy which will automatically lead to change in the nature and scope of the economy. And here came the New Industrial Policy of 1991. With this policy the government kick-started the very process of reform in the economy, which is why the policy is taken *more as a process than a policy.*

Background India was faced with a severe BoP crisis by June 1991. Basically, in the early 1990s, an

[19] A total number of 95 industries had the compulsions of licencing till then. These industries belonged to Schedules B and C of the Industrial Policy Resolution, 1956.

[20] This was similar to the policy being followed by Gorbachev in the USSR with the similar fiscal results - a severe balance of payment (BoP) crisis by the end of the 1980s and the early 1990s [J. Barkley Rosser Jin and Marina V. Rosser, *Comparative Economics in A Transforming World,* (New Delhi: PHI & MIT Press, 2004), pp. 469-75].

[21] The *Seventh Five Year Plan (1985-90)* as well as the *Sixth Five Year Plan (1980-85)* had already suggested the government to re-define the role of the state in the economy and permit the private sector into those areas of industries where the presence of the government was non-essential, etc. But such a radical approach might not be digested by the country as it was like 'rolling back' the state. This is why the government of the time looks not going for full- scale economic reforms or vocal moves of liberalisation.

[22] V. Joshi and I. M. D. Little, *India's Economic Reforms, 1991-2001* (Oxford: Clarendon Press, 1996), p. 17.

inter-connected set of events were becoming unfavourable for the Indian economy:

1. Due to the Gulf War (1990-91), the higher oil prices were quickly[23] depleting India's foreign reserves.
2. Sharp decline in the private remittances from the overseas Indian workers in the wake of the Gulf War[24], specially from the Gulf region.
3. Inflation peaking at nearly 17 per cent.[25]
4. The gross fiscal deficit of the Central Government reaching 8.4 per cent of the GDP.[26]
5. By June 1991, India's foreign exchange had declined to just *two weeks* of import coverage.[27]

India's near miss with a serious BoP crisis was the proximate cause that started India's market liberalisation measures in 1991 followed by a gradualist approach.[28] As the reforms were induced by the crisis of the BoP, the initial phase focused on macroeconomic stabilisation while the reforms of industrial policy, trade and exchange rate policies, FI policy, financial and tax reforms as well as public sector reforms did also follow soon after.

The financial support India received from the International Monetary Fund (IMF) to curb the BoP crisis of 1990-91 include a checklist of conditions to be fulfilled by India. These IMF conditionalities required the Indian economy to opt for a structural re-adjustment. As the nature and scope of the economy were molded by the various industrial policies India did follow till date, any desired change in the economic structure had to be induced with the help of another industrial policy. The new industrial policy announced by the government on 23 July 1991 had initiated a bigger process of economic reforms in the country, motivated towards the structural readjustment naturally obliged to 'fulfill' IMF conditionalities.[29] The major highlights of the policy are as follows:

1. **De-reservation of the Industries:** The industries which were reserved for the Central Government by the IPR, 1956, were cut down to only eight. In coming years many other industries were also opened for private sector investment. At present there are only two industries which are fully or partially reserved for the Central Government:
   - **(i)** Atomic energy and nuclear research and other related activities, i.e., mining, use management, fuel fabrication, export and import, waste management, etc., of radioactive minerals (none of the nuclear powers in the world have allowed entry of private sector players in these activities, thus no such attempts look logical in India, too).
   - **(ii)** Railways (many of the functions related to the railways have been allowed private entry, but still the private sector cannot enter the sector as a full-fledged railway service provider).
2. **De-licencing of the Industries:** The number of industries put under the compulsory provision of licencing (belonging to Schedules B and C as per the IPR, 1956) were cut down to 17 from existing 64. Reforms regarding the area were further followed and presently there are only *four industries*[30] which carry the burden of compulsory licencing:

---

[23] *Economic Survey 1990-91* (New Delhi: Ministry of Finance, GoI, 1991); *Economic Survey 1991-92* (New Delhi: Ministry of Finance, GoI, 1992).

[24] J. D. Sachs, A. Varshney, and N. Bajpai, *India in the Era of Economic Reform* (New Delhi: Oxford University Press, 1999), p. 1.

[25] Department of Economic Affairs, 'Economic Reforms: Two Years After and the Task Ahead', Discussion Paper (New Delhi: Government of India, 1993), p. 6.

[26] Ibid.

[27] B. Jalan, *India's Economic Crisis: The Way Ahead* (New Delhi: Oxford University Press, 1991), pp. 2-12.

[28] Sachs, Varshney, and Bajpai, *India in the Era of Economic Reforms*, op. cit., p. 2.

[29] R. Mohan, 'Industrial Policy and Control's', in *The Indian Economy: Problems and Prospects*, B. Jalan, ed. (New Delhi: Penguin Books, 1992), pp. 92-123.

[30] The policy was liberalised last time in ***2016-17*** *[Industries (Development and Regulation) Amendment Act, 2016]* when the category ***'alcohol and alcoholic drinks'*** was removed from the list and put under two segments - for *potable* (human consumption) and *non-potable* (industrial consumption). While potable part was removed from the central list of licensed industries (in case of which the authority was delegated to states), the non-potable part still remains there. However, it was made a part of another licensed industry the 'hazardous chemicals'. Though the number of industries under compulsory licensing still remains four, major internal reforms were affected by the Government inside a sector. For example, *electronics* is still a licensed sector but many sub-segments of it (such as radio, tape-recorder, VCR players,

(i) Aerospace and defence related electronics
(ii) Gun powder, industrial explosives and detonating fuse
(iii) Hazardous chemicals
(iv) Tobacco, cigarette and related products

3. **Abolition of the MRTP Limit:** The MRTP limit was ₹100 crore so that the mergers, acquisitions and takeovers of the industries could become possible. In 2002, a Competition Act was passed which has replaced the MRTP Act. In place of the MRTP Commission, the Competition Commission has started functioning.

4. **Promotion to Foreign Investment:** Functioning as a typical closed economy, the Indian economy had never shown any good faith towards foreign capital. The new industrial policy was a pathbreaking step in this regard. Not only the draconian FERA was committed to be diluted but also the government went to encourage FI in both its forms - direct and indirect. The direct form of FI was called as the foreign direct investment (FDI) under which the MNCs were allowed to set up their firms in India in the different sectors varying from 26 per cent to 100 per cent ownership with them - *Enron* and *Coke* being the flag-bearers. The FDI started in 1991 itself. The indirect form of FI (i.e., in the assets owned by the Indian firms in equity capital) was called the *portfolio investment scheme* (PIS) in the country, which formally commenced in 1994.[31] Under the PIS the *foreign institutional investors* (FIIs) having good track record are allowed to invest in the Indian security/stock market. The FIIs need to register themselves as a stockbroker with SEBI. It means India had not allowed *individual FI* in the security market yet, only *institutional investment*.[32]

5. **FERA Replaced by FEMA:** The government committed in 1991 itself to replace the draconian FERA with a highly liberal FEMA, which came into effect in the year 2000-01 with a sunset clause of two years.[33]

6. **Location of Industries:** Related provisions were simplified by the policy which was highly cumbersome and had a time-consuming process. Now, the industries were classified into 'polluting' and 'nonpolluting' categories, and a highly simple provision deciding their location was announced:

(i) Non-polluting industries might be set up anywhere.
(ii) Polluting industries to be set up at least 25 km away from the million cities.

Next NIP

At present, the next NIP (New Industrial Policy) is under the consideration of the Government. There is every possibility that the upcoming 'new' policy will be futuristic enough to align with the changes which have occurred in India and the global order since the country announced its NIP in 1991— guided by realism and supported by the dynamics of economic diplomacy.

7. **Compulsion of Phased Production Abolished:** With the compulsion of phased production abolished, now the private firms could go for producing as many goods and models simultaneously.[34] Now the capacity and

---

DVD players, CD, TV, mobile phones, etc.) have been removed from it (but electronics items which are used in aerospace and defence still remain under it).

[31] *Economic Survey, 1994-95* (New Delhi: Ministry of Finance, GoI, 1995).

[32] It becomes very complex and tough to regulate the individual foreign investment in the share market though it is an easier way of attracting foreign exchange. It should be noted that the South-East Asian economies which faced financial crisis in 1996-97 all had allowed individual foreign investment in their share market. As the Indian security market was learning the art of regulation in its nascent phase, the government decided not to allow such foreign investment. The logic was vindicated after the South-East Asian currency crisis when India had almost no shocks [*Economic Survey, 1996-97* (New Delhi: Ministry of Finance, GoI, 1997)].

[33] The delayed action by the government in the foreign exchange liberalisation was due to the delayed comfort the economy felt regarding the availability of foreign exchange.

[34] This was another hurdle which the private sector industries have been complaining about. As the industrial products were completely new to the Indian market and its consumers alike, the government followed this policy with the logic to provide enough time for indigenization of the industrial products i.e., development of awareness about the product and its servicing, maintenance, etc. As for example, the MNC subsidiary Phillips India was allowed to produce a highly simple radio *Commander* and *Jawan* models for comparatively longer periods of time than

capital of industries could be utilised to their optimum level.

8. **Compulsion to Convert Loans into Shares Abolished:** The policy of nationalisation started by the GoI in the late 1960s was based on the sound logic of *greater public benefit* and had its origin in the idea of *welfare state* - it was criticised by the victims and the experts alike. In the early 1970s, the GoI came up with a new idea. The major banks of the country were now fully nationalised (14) and had to mobilise resources for the purpose of planned development of India. The private companies who had borrowed capital from these banks (when the banks were privately owned) now wanted their loans paid back. The government came up with a novel provision for the companies who were unable to repay their loans (most of them were like it) - they could opt to convert their loan amounts into equity shares and hand them over to the banks. The private companies which opted for this route (this was a compulsory option) ultimately became a government-owned company as the banks were owned by the GoI - this was an *indirect* route to nationalize private firms. Such a compulsion which hampered the growth and development of the Indian industries was withdrawn by the government in 1991.[35]

The picture presented by the New Industrial Policy of 1991 was taken by many experts, the opposition in the Parliament and even the public figures as well as the business and industry of the country as a *rolling back* of the state. The glorious role given to the state by the Nehruvian economy seemed completely toppled down. Any one idea the new policy challenged was an emphatic goodbye to the 'control regime' perpetuated till now by the government. There was a coalition of interests of politicians, bureaucrats, multinationals as well as the domestic industrial and business houses whose interests were sheltered and by the control regime.[36] Thus, a memorandum to the government requesting not to dismantle the control regime by the major industrial houses of India as well as arrival of the *Swadeshi Jagaran Manch* were not illogical. But the governments continued with the reform programme at a politically permissible pace, and a time came when the same industrial houses requested the government (2002) to expedite the process of reform. Now the Indian industry and business class has been able to understand the economics of 'openness' and a different kind of the mixed economy. But the process of reforms has still to go miles before its real benefits start reaching the masses and development together with reform could be made a mass movement.

This is why experts have suggested that only assuming that reforms will benefit the masses will not be enough to make it happen politically, but the governments, the administrative agencies and the economists all need to link it positively to *mass welfare* - it might require to create a popular climate and form the political coalitions in favour of the argument that privatisation and accordingly restructured labour laws are basically aimed at creating jobs, better job prospects, alleviating poverty, enriching education and providing healthcare to the masses.[37] In the coming times, the government went from one to another generation of the reforms, setting new targets and trying to make reforms socio-politically possible.

they were allowed to come up with the smaller fashionable radio sets or two-in-ones and three-in-ones. Such provisions hampered their full capacity utilisation as well as achieving the economy of scale had also been tougher. The new industrial policy of 1991 did away with such impediments. By that time, the Indian consumer as well as the market was fully aware of the modern industrial goods.

[35] Combined with nationalisation, this *indirect route* to nationalisation failed to provide the confidence among the entrepreneurs that the industrial units they are intending to set up will be owned by them. This discouraged entrepreneurship in India while taking risk. The abolition of this compulsion was an indirect indication by the government of no more direct or indirect nationalisation in future. This has served the purpose, there is no doubt in it.

[36] This nexus of the interests of the vested groups to the control regime of the economy has been beautifully elaborated by R. Mohan in 'Industrial Policy and Controls', pp. 921-23 op. cit. He also points out that the control system perpetuating the academic and intellectual ideological leanings negated the very need for re-examination of the system. The 'planners' and the 'bureaucrats' were able to preserve their powers *via* the control regime that did everything to maintain the *status quo*, R. Mohan further adds.

[37] First of the series of such suggestions came from Sach, Varshney, and Bajpai, *India in the Era of Economic Reforms*, op. cit., p. 24).

DISINVESTMENT

Government-owned firms, namely the PSUs and public sector enterprises (PSEs), played a foundational role in India's development process. Realising the changed situations, the Government decided to 'redefine' (disinvestment and privatisation) the role for these firms once the reform process began in 1991. By that time, the Government had invested a total of ₹2.4 lakh crores in 244 firms (the journey with 5 firms and a modest investment of ₹29 crores in March, 1951). Rather the process of setting up new Government firms did not stop and by 2019, Government[38] invested with ₹16.41 lakh crores in a total number of 348 such firms.

Scan this QR Code to watch a author's video lecture that simplifies this topic

PSEs and PSUs

The public sector undertakings (PSUs) or public sector enterprise (PSE) refers to a 'government company' in which minimum 51 per cent of the paid-up capital is owned by the government – exclusively or jointly by Centre and State in the case of India (Section 2(45) of the Companies Act, 2013). The term is not intended to mean a 'public company' (i.e., 'Limited' company, where shares are freely transferable and has a shareholder base of more than 200 people), though most of them are today public companies. Central public sector enterprises are classified as *maha-ratnas, navratnas, mini-ratnas,* and *other enterprises,* depending on their performance track record based on guidelines approved by the Government from time to time.

PSUs refer to commercial ventures which charge 'user fees' for the services they provide – the user charges may be market-based or subsidised. Usually, they are fully owned and managed by the Government such as – Railways, Posts, Defence Undertakings, Banks, etc. PSEs, on the other hand, refer to those companies which are registered under the Companies Act, 1951. Predominantly owned by the Government, they are managed by a Board of Directors with Government-appointed Chairmen and Managing Directors together with nominees of Government on board to represent the interests of the Government such as – NTPC, ONGC, SAIL, BHEL, Indian Oil, Coal India, etc.

While the audit of the PSUs is done by the CAG (Comptroller and Auditor General of India), in the case of the PSEs, it is done first by CAs (Chartered Accountants), followed by a supplementary audit done by the CAG.

Disinvestment is the process of 'selling ownership' in a company. Technically, the term may be used in case of any company (i.e., privately owned company), but in practice, it is used only in case of a government-owned company. Disinvestment commenced in the country with three inter-related co-ordinates:

1. As a tool[39] of public sector reforms;
2. As a part of the economic reform process (i.e., as part[40] of the *de-reservation of industries*); and
3. As a tool of resource[41] mobilisation for budgetary needs.

The approach towards public sector reforms in India has been much more cautious than that of the other developing countries. India did not follow the radical

[38] *Economic Survey 2019-20*, vol. 2 (New Delhi: Ministry of Finance, GoI), pp. 221-22.

[39] Publication Division, *India 1991* (New Delhi: Government of India, 1992).

[40] The de-reservation of industries had allowed the private sector to enter the areas hitherto reserved for the Central Government. It means in the coming times in the unreserved areas the PSUs were going to face the international class competitiveness posed by the new private companies. To face up the challenges the existing PSUs needed new kind of technological, managerial and marketing strategies (similar to the private companies). For all such preparations there was a requirement of huge capital. The government thought to partly fund the required capital out of the proceeds of disinvestment of the PSUs. In this way investment should be viewed in India as a way of increasing investment in the divested PSUs (which we see taking place in the cases of BALCO, VSNL, etc.).

[41] Right since 1991 when disinvestment began, governments have been using the disinvestment proceeds to manage fiscal deficits in the budget at least up to 2000-01. From 2000-01 to 2002-03 some of the proceeds went for some social sector reforms or for labour security. After 2003, India established National Investment Fund to which the proceeds of disinvestment automatically flow and is not regarded as a *capital receipt* of the Union Government. This idea of Indian experiment with disinvestment was articulated by Sach, Varshney, and Bajpai, *India in the Era of Economic Reforms*, op. cit. pp. 62-63.

solution to it - under which outright privatisation of commercially viable PSUs is done and the unviable ones are completely closed.[42] There was an emphasis on increasing functional autonomy of public sector organisations to improve their efficiency in the 1980s in India as part of the public sector reforms. Once the process of economic reforms started in the early 1990s, disinvestment became a part of the public sector reforms. The C. Rangarajan Commission on Disinvestment of the Public Sector Enterprises (1991) went on to suggest the government on the issue in a highly commendable and systematic way, taking empirical notes from the experiences of disinvestment around the world. The government started the process of disinvestment in 1991. In 1997, the government did set up a Disinvestment Commission to advise upon the various aspects of the disinvestment process. The financial year 1999-2000 saw a serious attempt by the government to make disinvestment a political process to expedite the process of disinvestment in the country - first a Disinvestment Department and later a full-fledged Ministry of Disinvestment was set up.[43] The new government (UPA) dismantled the Ministry of Disinvestment and today only the Department of Disinvestment is taking care of the matter, working under the Ministry of Finance.

Types of Disinvestments

Since the process of disinvestment was started in India (1991), it's consisted of *two official types.* A brief discussion on them is given below:

1. **Token Disinvestment:** Disinvestment started in India with a high political caution – in a symbolic way known as the *token disinvestment* (presently being called as 'minority stake sale'). The general policy was to sell the shares of the PSUs maximum up to the 49 per cent (i.e., maintaining government ownership of the companies). But in practice, shares were sold to the tune of 5–10 per cent only. This phase of disinvestment though brought some extra funds to the government (which were used to fill up the fiscal deficit considering the proceeds as the 'capital receipts'), and it could not initiate any new element to the PSUs, which could enhance their efficiency. It remained the major criticism of this type of disinvestment, and experts around the world started suggesting the government to go for it in the way that the ownership could be transferred from the government to the private sector. The other hot issue raised by the experts was related to the question of using the *proceeds* of disinvestment.
2. **Strategic Disinvestment:** In order to make disinvestment a process by which efficiency of the PSUs could be enhanced and the government could de-burden itself of the activities in which the private sector has developed better efficiency (so that the government could concentrate on the areas which have no attraction for the private sector such as social sector support for the poor masses), the government initiated the process of strategic disinvestment. The government classifying the PSUs into *strategic* and *non-strategic* announced in March 1999 that it will generally reduce its stake (shareholding) in the *non-strategic* PSEs to 26 per cent or below if necessary and in the *strategic* PSEs (i.e., arms and ammunition; atomic energy and related activities; and railways) it will retain its majority holding.[44] There was a major shift in the disinvestment policy from selling small lots of share in the profit-making PSUs (i.e., token disinvestment) to the strategic sale with change in management control both in profit and loss-making enterprises. The essence of the strategic disinvestment was:
   - **(i)** The minimum shares to be divested will be 51 per cent and
   - **(ii)** The wholesale sale of shares will be carried out with a *strategic partner* having international class experience and expertise in the sector.

[42] As was done by Margaret Thatcher in the UK in the mid-1980s. Her brand of privatisation was driven by the conviction that government control makes PSUs inherently less efficient and privatisation, therefore, improves its economic efficiency and is good for the consumers. However, this idea has been rejected around the world on the empirical bases. *The PSUs could also have comparable economic efficiency even being under full government control.* This was followed by Mrs. Thatcher (1979-90) forcefully in Great Britain conjoined with the supply-side economics as was done by Ronald Reagan (1981-89) in the United States as discussed by P. A. Samuelson and W. D. Nordhaus, *Economics* (New Delhi: Tata McGraw Hill, 2005), p. 703.

[43] A former media expert, A. Shourie remained the minister for the whole term of the NDA government. Some highly accelerated and successful disinvestments were done during this period but not without controversies.

[44] *Concept Classification of the PSEs,* Government of India, 1999.

This form of disinvestment commenced with the Modern Food Industries Ltd. (MFIL). The second PSU was the BALCO which invited every kind of criticism from the opposition political parties, the Government of Chhattisgarh and experts, alike. The other PSUs were CMC Ltd, HTL, IBPL, VSNL, ITDC (13 hotels), Hotel Corporation of India Ltd. (3 hotels), Paradeep Phosphate Ltd (PPL), HZL, IPCL, MUL and Lagan Jute Manufacturing Company Ltd. (LJMC) – a total number of 13 PSEs were part of the *strategic sale or strategic disinvestment* of the PSEs.[45] The new government at the Centre did put this policy of strategic disinvestment on hold practically and came up with a new policy in place.

Disinvestment Policy

India's disinvestment policy[46] has evolved over time since it commenced in 1991. It has two major features – 'ideology' behind the policy and the 'policy' itself. The *ideology* behind the policy is:

1. Public ownership of PSUs to be promoted as they are the wealth of a nation;
2. Government to hold minimum 51 per cent shares in case of 'minority stake sale'; and
3. Up to 50 per cent or more shares might be sold off under 'strategic disinvestment'.

The *policy* of disinvestment followed by the government stood as given below:

1. *Minority Stake Sale* (the policy of November 2009 continues):
   - **(i)** Listed PSUs to be taken first to comply to minimum 25 per cent norm;
   - **(ii)** New PSUs to be listed which have earned net profit in three preceding consecutive years;
   - **(iii)** 'Follow-on' public offers on a case-by-case basis once capital investment is needed; and
   - **(iv)** DIPAM (Department of Investment and Public Asset Management) to identify PSUs and suggest disinvestment in consultation with respective ministries.
2. *Strategic Disinvestment*, i.e., selling 50 per cent or more shares of the PSUs (announced in February 2016):
   - **(i)** To be carried out through consultation among Ministries/Departments and NITI Aayog;
   - **(ii)** NITI Aayog to identify PSUs and advise on its different aspects; and
   - **(iii)** CGD (Core Group of Secretaries on Disinvestment) to consider the recommendations of NITI Aayog to facilitate a decision by the CCEA (Cabinet Committee on Economic Affairs) and to supervise/monitor the implementation process.

Current Policy: In the process of gradual evolution, the disinvestment policy was further tweaked by the Government in the ***Union Budget 2021-22*** with its objectives and features redefined:

Objectives of the Policy

1. Minimising presence of CPSEs including financial institutions (FIs) and creating new investment space for the private sector.
2. Post disinvestment, economic growth of CPSEs and FIs to be through infusion of private capital, technology and best management practices.
3. Disinvestment proceeds to finance various social sector and developmental programmes.

Policy Features

1. Policy covers existing CPSEs, Public Sector Banks and Public Sector Insurance Companies.
2. Various sectors will be classified as strategic and non-strategic sectors.
3. The *strategic sectors* classified are:
   - **(i)** Atomic energy, Space and Defence
   - **(ii)** Transport and Telecommunications
   - **(iii)** Power, Petroleum, Coal and other minerals
   - **(iv)** Banking, Insurance and financial services
4. In *strategic sectors*, there will be a bare minimum presence of PSEs. The remaining CPSEs in the

[45] Publications Division, *India 2003* (New Delhi: Government of India, 2004).

[46] Department of Investment and Public Asset Management (New Delhi: Ministry of Finance, GoI, March 2017).

Disinvestment by States

The Government of India launched a special assistance scheme in 2020–21 under which states are being offered incentive (i.e., 50-year interest free loan for capital expenditures) for privatisation, disinvestment, monetisation and recycling assets of their public sector enterprises (PSEs).

But states have not shown active interest in divesting their public sector enterprises. Experts believe that states' moves of attracting private investment become theoretically weak due to their such an approach to privatisation.

strategic sector will be privatised or merged or subsidiarised with other CPSEs or closed.

5. In *non-strategic sectors,* the CPSEs will be privatised, or shall be closed.

COMPREHENSIVE MANAGEMENT OF PUBLIC ASSETS

Since 2016, disinvestment has become a part of the broader policy known as the *comprehensive management of government investments in the public assets.* Before announcing the current disinvestment policy, the Government changed the name of the existing Department of Disinvestment to the Department of Investment and Public Asset Management (DIPAM) along with its *mandate* from taking care of disinvestment to *Comprehensive management of the Government's investment in the CPSEs.* Under it, the following 'four actions' are to be taken in regard to the CPSEs:

1. Achieving optimum return and accelerating growth.
2. Leveraging assets by capital and financial restructuring.
3. Improving investors' confidence through capital market exposure.
4. Rationalising the decision-making process for efficient management.

The policy considers the CPSEs as an important financial asset and aims to use them for realising a variety of goals such as economic return, investment, growth acceleration, etc. The steps such as monetisation of assets, for debt management and capital expenditures, buyback of shares by the PSUs having huge surplus, merger and acquisition among the PSUs in the same sector and launch of exchange traded funds (ETFs), etc. are being taken under it.

As the private sector keeps exploring all possibilities to employ their investment in the best possible way (and run their firms on 'business line'), the Government also aims at a similar policy in case of public assets. Such a policy shift in the case of the CPSEs, however, has come very late (which was proposed by the late 1980s and was viewed as essential once economic reforms commenced in the country). The policy will not only unshackle the hidden economic potential of the CPSEs but also help in creating a healthy market for growth and expansion of the private sector in particular and economy in general.

National Monetisation Pipeline (NMP) The NMP (announced in the Union Budget 2021-22), developed by the NITI Aayog, aims to lease out public assets to a private sector entity for an upfront or periodic pay-outs. During the period of the lease the private sector entity will operate and maintain the asset and generate returns (through higher operating efficiencies and enhanced user experience). The funds, so received are to be reinvested in new infrastructure projects or deployed for other developmental works. Contracts under it include provision for transfer of asset back to the government at the end of the period (i.e., ownership of assets to remain with government). The asset monetisation plan has been further extended by the *Union Budget 2025-26* for further 5 years with the target of mobilising another ₹10 lakh crore in new projects.

The pipeline includes 'de-risked' and 'brownfield' public assets which have stable profit generation profile to make investment attractive for the private sector. Government estimated to mobilise ₹6 lakh crores over the 4-year period - around 5.4 per cent of the total investment envisaged under the National Infrastructure Pipeline (to which the NMP is co-terminus).

PROCEEDS OF DISINVESTMENT

In the very next year of disinvestment, there started a debate in the country concerning the suitable use of the proceeds of disinvestment (i.e., accruing to the government out of the sale of the shares in the PSUs). The debate has by now evolved to a certain stage panning out basically in three phases:

Phase I This phase could be considered from 1991 to 2000 in which whatever money the governments received out of disinvestment were used for fulfilling the budgetary requirements (better say bridging the gap of fiscal deficit).[47]

Phase II This phase which has a very short span (2000-03) saw two new developments. *First,* the government started a practice of using the proceeds not only for fulfilling the need of fiscal deficit but also used the money for some other good purposes, such as re-investment in the PSEs, pre-payment of public debt and on the social sector. *Second,* by the early 2000-01 a broad consensus emerged on the issue of the proposal by the then Finance Minister.[48] The proposal regarding the use of the proceeds of disinvestment was as given below:

Some portions of the disinvestment proceeds should be used:

1. in the divested PSU itself for upgrading purposes,
2. in the turn-around of the other PSUs,
3. in the public debt repayment/pre-payment,
4. in the social infrastructure (education, healthcare, etc.),
5. in the rehabilitation of the labour force (of the divested PSUs), and
6. in fulfilling the budgetary requirements.

Phase III Two major developments of this phase are as given below:

1. **National Investment Fund:** In January 2005, the GoI decided to constitute a 'National Investment Fund' (NIF)[49] which has the following *salient features:*
   - **(i)** The proceeds from disinvestment will be channelised into the NIF, which is to be maintained outside the Consolidated Fund of India.
   - **(ii)** The corpus of the NIF will be of a permanent nature.
   - **(iii)** The Fund will be professionally managed, to provide sustainable returns without depleting the corpus, by selected Public Sector Mutual Funds *(they are, UTI Asset Management Company Ltd.; SBI Funds Management Company Pvt. Ltd.; LIC Mutual Fund Asset Management Company Ltd.).*
   - **(iv)** 75 per cent of the annual income of the Fund will be used to finance selected social sector schemes, which promote education, health and employment. The residual 25 per cent of the annual income of the Fund will be used to meet the capital investment requirements of profitable and revivable PSUs that yield adequate returns, in order to enlarge their capital base to finance expansion/diversification.

   The income from the NIF investments was utilised on selected social sector schemes, namely the Jawaharlal Nehru National Urban Renewal Mission (JNNURM), Accelerated Irrigation Benefits Programme (AIBP), Rajiv Gandhi Grameen Vidyutikaran Yojana (RGGVY), Accelerated Power Development and Reform Programme, Indira Awas Yojana and National Rural Employment Guarantee Scheme (NREGS).
2. **Restructuring of NIF:** In November 2009, the government approved a change in the policy on utilisation of disinvestment proceeds. In view of the difficult situation caused by the global slowdown of 2008-09 and a severe drought in 2009-10, a *one-time exemption* was accorded to disinvestment proceeds being deposited into NIF - to be operational for the fiscals 2009-12, which was further extended to 2012-13, in view of the persistent difficult condition of the economy. All disinvestment proceeds (*in place of the income accruing out of the investment of the NIF corpus*) obtained during the three-year period were to be used for selected social sector schemes.

Current Policy In January 2013 (which was further revised in February 2013), the government approved *restructuring* of the NIF and decided that the disinvestment proceeds with effect from the fiscal year 2013-14 will be credited to the existing

---

[47] *Various Issues of the Economic Survey* (New Delhi: Ministry of Finance, GoI).

[48] It was proposed by Y. Sinha and thus got popularity as the *'Yashwant Formula'* of using disinvestment proceeds. Being his personal proposal, the Government of the time was not officially bound to it. However, the idea got support inside and outside of the Parliament and looked as having an impact on the government's thinking about the issue.

[49] Ministry of Finance, Disinvestment Policy Announcement, Department of Disinvestment (New Delhi: Government of India, 2005).

Public Account under the head NIF, and they would remain there until withdrawn/invested for the approved purposes as decided by the *Union Budget*. It was decided that the NIF would be utilised for the following purposes:

(i) Subscribing to the shares being issued by the CPSE including PSBs and public sector insurance companies, on *rights basis* so as to ensure 51 per cent government ownership in them.

(ii) *Preferential allotment* of shares of the CPSE to promoters, so that government shareholding does not go down below 51 per cent in all cases where the CPSE is going to raise fresh equity to meet its CAPEX[50] programme.

(iii) *Recapitalisation* of public sector banks and public sector insurance companies.

(iv) Investment by the government in RRBs, IIFCL, NABARD, Exim Bank;

(v) Equity infusion in various metro projects;

(vi) Investment in Bhartiya Nabhikiya Vidyut Nigam Limited (BHAVINI) and Uranium Corporation of India Ltd.;

(vii) Investment in Indian Railways towards capital expenditure.

This way, the policy regarding the use of disinvestment proceeds became *quite flexible* since 2013-14 and gave the Government freedom to spend them as per the socio-economic needs of the hour - for any kind of expenditures (revenue or capital). As per the upcoming ***Union Budgets***, the proceeds will be used to finance various social sector and developmental programmes of the government.

PERFORMANCE OF CPSEs

The Central Public Sector Enterprises (CPSE) policy[51] enunciated by the Government in November 2020 spells a *complete change in paradigm* as compared to its policy of import substitution and self-sufficiency (which became the basis of the Mahalanobis Plan in 1956). However, the inherent inefficiencies leading to low productivity in the PSEs, high-cost structure and strained public finances led the Government to privatise the PSUs after 1991. Thus, began the journey of privatisation and disinvestment in the country. By now, several measures have been taken to reduce their (i.e., the Government) presence in commercial activities - through the stock market route and strategic sale. This 'policy to withdraw' has been a subject of discussion in several *Economic Surveys* (more specifically 2000-01, 2001-02, 2002-03) which reflects Government deliberations on it.

Under the *Atmanirbhar Bharat Mission*, the government has proposed to *rationalise* the participation of the CPSEs in commercial activities with their presence limited only in the 'strategic sectors' - numbers cut down to only *four* - others to be either merged or privatized or brought under holding companies. The enterprises of 'non-strategic sectors' would be privatised. This initiative is expected to bring healthy competition in sectors and will also assist the Government to focus extensively on 'strategic sectors'. So that the retained enterprises are able to meet the expectations of the Government, certain other reforms have also been suggested by the *Economic Survey 2020-21* which are as given below:

1. Revamping their Boards and structure.
2. Enhancing operational autonomy of their Boards coupled with strong norms of corporate governance.
3. Listing on stock exchange for greater transparency.

Besides disinvestment and rationalisation, certain separate steps have also been taken by the Government regarding these enterprises in recent times - revamping of 'performance monitoring system' to make it more objective and forward-looking (based on sectoral indices and benchmarks); timely closure of sick and loss making enterprises; and disposal of their assets being the major ones.

MSME SECTOR

As per the MSMED Act, 2006, the MSME are classified into *manufacturing* and *service* enterprises, and they are defined in terms of investment in plant and machinery. Micro, Small, and Medium Enterprises (MSMEs) form the backbone of India's industrial economy, accounting for approximately **35.4** per cent of manufacturing, around **48.58** per cent of exports,

[50] The Prime Minister's Office has been monitoring the CAPEX (Capital Expenditure) programme and investment plans of selected Central Public Sector Enterprises (CPSEs) since 2012-13. The purpose of this exercise was to enhance investment in the economy, utilising the substantial cash surpluses that are available with some of the CPSEs to drive economic growth.

[51] *Economic Survey 2020-21*, vol. 2, (New Delhi: Ministry of Finance, GoI), pp. 273-75.

and **31.1** per cent of GDP, with over **7.47** crore enterprises employing over **32.82** crore persons; the sector holds its position as the *second-largest employer* after agriculture (globally, MSMEs make up about **90** per cent of businesses and are responsible for over **50** per cent of the total global employment), as per the ***Economic Survey 2025-26***. With India's manufacturing sector positioned for greater global integration, the MSME sector's role is critical in enabling effective supply-chain participation, fostering local value addition, and supporting inclusive regional growth. The sector has huge potential for helping address structural problems such as unemployment, regional imbalances, unequal distribution of national income and wealth. Due to comparatively low capital costs and their forward-backward linkages with other sectors, they are headed to play a crucial role in the success of the Make in India initiative.

Realising the importance of the sector, over time, the government has undertaken a number of schemes for the establishment of new enterprises and development of existing ones such as:

1. PMEGP (Prime Minister's Employment Generation Programme),
2. CGTMSE (Credit Guarantee Trust Fund for Micro and Small Enterprises),
3. CLCSS (Credit Linked Capital Subsidy Scheme) for Technology Upgradation,
4. SFURTI (Scheme of Fund for Regeneration of Traditional Industries), and
5. MSECDP (Micro and Small Enterprises - Cluster Development Programme).

Some of the *major initiatives* undertaken by the government for the promotion and development of the MSMEs have been as given below (upto the *Economic Survey 2024-25*):

1. **UAM (Udyog Aadhar Memorandum):** The UAM scheme was set up, notified in September 2015, to promote ease of doing business. Under it, entrepreneurs just need to file an *online* entrepreneurs' memorandum to get a unique Udyog Aadhaar Number (UAN) - a significant improvement over the earlier complex and cumbersome procedure.
2. **Employment Exchange for Industries:** To facilitate *matchmaking* between prospective job seekers and employers, an employment exchange for industries was set up in June 2015 (in line with Digital India).
3. **Framework for Revival and Rehabilitation of MSMEs:** Under this (May 2015), banks need to constitute a Committee for Distressed MSMEs to prepare a Corrective Action Plan (CAP) for them.
4. **ASPIRE (Promoting Innovation and Rural Entrepreneurs):** Launched in March 2015 with the objective of setting up a *network* of technology and incubation centres to accelerate entrepreneurship and promote start-ups for innovation and entrepreneurship in the rural and agriculture-based industry.
5. **MSE-CDP (Micro and Small Enterprises-Cluster Development Programme)** to develop clusters across the country.
6. **Self-Reliant India (SRI) Fund** set up with a corpus of ₹ 50,000 crore– it has a provision of ₹ 10,000 crore from the government and the rest through private equity/venture capital funds.
7. **MSME Samadhan** and **CHAMPIONS (Creation and Harmonious Application of Modern Processes for Increasing the Output and National Strength)** portals have been set up to address the 'issues' related to the MSMEs.
8. **MSE Facilitation Council (MSEFC)** has been set up to deal with the issues of delayed payments.

Enhancing *ease of doing business* for the sector and their faster growth have been given special attention by the Government in the last few years - with following policy steps[52] taken till *early 2025*:

- Loans up to ₹1 crore to be approved online within 59 minutes;
- Interest subvention of 2 per cent to all Goods and Services Tax (GST) registered firms;
- PSUs to compulsorily procure 25 per cent (up from 20 per cent) with 3 per cent reserved for women entrepreneurs - through the GeM portal;
- 20 Technology Centres (TCs) and 100 Extension Centres (ECs) to be established;

[52] *Economic Survey 2022-23* (New Delhi: Ministry of Finance, GoI, January 2023), pp. 259-91 and *Economic Survey 2019-20*, vol. 2 (New Delhi: Ministry of Finance, GoI), pp. 229-30.

- Government to bear 70 per cent of the cost for establishing Pharma clusters;
- Returns under 8 labour laws and 10 Union regulations to be filed once a year;
- Establishments to be visited by an Inspector will be decided through a computerised random allotment;
- Single consent under air and water pollution laws;
- Returns to be accepted through self-certification and only 10 per cent units to be inspected; and
- For minor violations under the Companies Act, entrepreneurs no longer have to approach the court but can correct them through simple procedures.

COVID-19 Impact In the aftermath of the *COVID-19 pandemic,* the Government was quick to recognise the role of MSMEs in reviving the economy. Under the *Atmanirbhar Bharat Abhiyan* (Self-Reliant India Campaign), several measures were announced by the Government to provide them immediate relief and help grow - the major ones are as given below:

- The distinction between manufacturing and service sector, MSMEs have been abolished and an upward revision in their *definition* has been adopted:
  - *Micro* enterprise investment capital increased to ₹1 crore (from existing ₹25 lakh) and ₹5 crores of turnover (from ₹1 crore).
  - *Small* enterprises investment capital to ₹10 crores of investment (from ₹5 crores) and ₹50 crores of turnover (from ₹2 crores).
  - *Medium* enterprises investment increased to ₹50 crores (from ₹10 crores) of investment and ₹250 crores of turnover (from ₹5 crores).

NOTE: *The Union Budget 2025-26* further enhanced the 'investment' and 'turnover' limits for their classification to 2.5 and 2 times, respectively (the move is aimed at their 'greater formalisation' through–expansion via greater access to fund, adoption of newer technologies, and enhanced competitiveness).

- Collateral-free automatic *loan* of ₹3.0 lakh crore (Government to provide guarantee for the loans) for meeting operational liabilities, buying raw material and restarting businesses.
- Credit Cards with ₹5 lakh limit for Micro Enterprises registered on the Udyam Portal launched by the *Union Budget 2025-26.*
- Approval of 'subordinate debt' to provide equity support to the stressed MSMEs.
- *Fund of Funds* for equity infusion for MSMEs which will also help them get listed in stock exchanges.
- Disallowing global tenders in procurements up to ₹200 crores (to create more opportunities for the MSMEs).
- Clearing of the dues of MSMEs by the Government and PSUs within 45 days.
- A robust ICT (information and communication technology) based system *Champions* launched to help and handhold MSMEs.

Focus on the MSMEs

The sector has been declared by the Government as the ***2nd Engine of Development*** (in the *Union Budget 2025–26*). This is a realisation to the significance of the sector which is the biggest hope for employment generation in the country— this becomes even more important given the long-drawn debate about 'jobless growth' in the country.

INDUSTRIAL SECTORS

Expansion of industrial activities has been among the primary policy concerns of the government. Looking at the critical role played by the sectors such as steel and coal in the economy and scope of employment and export expansion in textile and apparels, we see the Government taking some focused steps in this regard - a brief summary of the recent developments in the areas is given below.

Steel

Steel is one of the critical inputs to industries, urban development and infrastructure development. India is the 2nd largest producer as well as consumer of steel (after China) in the world. However, its per capita total finished steel consumption was around 76.0 kg during 2024-25 as against the global average of 228 kg. Further, the capacity utilisation in crude steel plants continues to be low.

In light of the role this critical input plays in developmental process, the Government announced the NPS-2017 (National Steel Policy-2017) with the vision of expansion in production capacity while being globally competitive. The policy aims at achieving a crude steel capacity of 300 million tonnes (MT) and a finished steel capacity of 230 MT with a per capita consumption of 158 kg by *2030-31*.

The Government took the following initiatives under the *Atmanirbhar Abhiyan* to enhance the domestic production of steel:

- 'Specialty Steel' (4 products) was included for incentives under the Production Linked Incentive (PLI) scheme.
- MSMEs (which are members of Engineering Export Promotion Council) to be supplied steel at 'export parity price' under the duty drawback scheme.
- Domestically produced iron and steel to be given preference in Government procurement (where estimate exceeds ₹25 crores).
- Domestic industry to be protected (against unfair trade practices adopted by other countries) by imposing anti-dumping duty and countervailing duty.

As per the *Economic Survey 2024-25*, the steel sector's performance in the year (April-November) has been robust, with cumulative production and consumption of finished steel at 98 MT and 90 MT.

With the help of the PLI scheme, steel production is estimated to increase by 26 MT. Steel exports are today higher by 20 per cent over the corresponding pre-pandemic levels of 2019-20. In the coming times, the government's thrust towards infrastructure projects, pick-up in construction and real estate activity, and healthy demand from the automobile sector augur well for the demand of steel products. However, export demand may remain subdued due to the global slowdown.

Coal

India is committed to shift to zero emission by 2070, though its dependence on fossil fuels remains high – around 55 per cent of its energy requirements are met by coal. Besides, coal is used as an intermediary by many industries such as iron and steel, cement, paper, brick kilns, etc. Keeping in mind the country's heavy dependence on coal, till early 2025, the government has taken a number of measures[53] to *strike a balance* between energy needs and environment friendliness:

A. Steps towards Clean Coal

By early 2023, about 58,350 hectares (ha) land had been brought under green cover by planting 143 million trees which created estimated carbon sink of 3.1 lakh tonnes of CO_2 equivalent per year. By 2030, the plan is to cover 20,000 ha of additional area by planting 50 million trees.

- Two Coal Bed Methane (CBM) Projects with considerable potential for carbon footprint reduction are in the pipeline.
- Surface coal gasification projects (100 MT of coal) with relatively lesser carbon footprint to be set up by 2030.
- First mile connectivity (transportation of coal from pitheads to dispatch points) projects are in the pipeline.

B. Amendment in Act and Rules and Other Measures

- Mineral Laws (Amendment) Act, 2020, was enacted in March 2020 by bringing several amendments into the Coal Mines (Special Provisions) Act, 2015.
- By early 2022, 28 coal blocks were allocated through auction for coal mining to the *private sector* – and auction process for 88 mines was underway.
- Of the auction of 38 coal mines for commercial mining in June 2020, 19 were successfully auctioned with a success rate of 50 per cent (as compared to 30 per cent in the past).

Self-reliance Different measures have been initiated towards achieving self-reliance in coal production, such as encouraging private participation, FDI under the automatic route, auctioning of coal blocks for commercial production, expansion of existing mines and opening of new mines, greater use of mass production technology in mining, mechanization of loading, development of evacuation infrastructure, and improving system capacity utilisation (from 80 to 90 per cent). The coal industry is expected to grow at 6-7 per cent annually to reach a production level of 1 billion tonnes by 2025-26 and about 1.5 billion tones by 2030.

Pharmaceuticals Industry

The Indian pharmaceuticals industry plays a prominent role in the global pharmaceuticals industry. India's domestic pharmaceutical market is estimated at US$ 41 billion in 2021 and is likely to grow to US$ 65 billion by 2024 and is further expected to reach US$ 130 billion by 2030. India is ranked ***3rd*** worldwide

---

[53] *Economic Survey 2025-26, 2024-25, and 2023-24* (New Delhi: Ministry of Finance, GoI), relevant pages.

in the production of pharma products by volume and ***14th*** by value.

To improve infrastructural facilities of the pharma sector, the government launched the *Strengthening the Pharmaceutical Industry (SPI)* scheme in March 2022 for five years (2021-26) with the following objectives:

(i) It aims to strengthen the existing infrastructure facilities by providing financial assistance to pharma clusters to create common facilities.

(ii) It upgrades the production facilities of MSMEs to meet national and international regulatory standards by providing interest subvention or capital subsidy on their capital loans.

(iii) It also promotes knowledge and awareness about the pharmaceutical and medical devices industry by undertaking studies, building databases and bringing industry leaders, academia and policymakers together to share their knowledge and experience.

Automobile

The automobile sector is a key driver of India's economic growth. In December 2022, India became the 3rd largest automobile market, surpassing Japan and Germany in terms of sales. In 2021, India was the largest manufacturer of two-wheeler and three-wheeler vehicles and the world's fourth-largest manufacturer of passenger cars. The sector's importance is gauged by the fact that it contributes 8.0 per cent to the overall GDP and 49 per cent to the manufacturing GDP while generating direct and indirect employment of about 4.0 crore at the end of 2025.

The automotive industry is expected to play a critical role in the transition towards *green* energy. The domestic electric vehicles (EV) market is expected to grow at a compound annual growth rate (CAGR) of 49 per cent between 2022 and 2030 and is expected to hit one crore unit annual sales by 2030. The EV industry will create 5 crore direct and indirect jobs by 2030. To support and nurture this development, the government has undertaken multiple steps. Despite the upbeat outlook, the automotive industry faces certain challenges:

(i) Higher borrowing costs;

(ii) Tempering (i.e., lower) global demand in near-term; and

(iii) Negative impact of increase in third-party vehicle insurance premiums (it has increased the total insurance cost by about 10-11 per cent, especially for two-wheelers; therefore, the two-wheeler segment is the most affected and witnessed the lowest sales in the last ten years).

Shipbuilding Sector

Shipbuilding is a strategically important industry which plays a crucial role in the areas of energy security, national defence, heavy engineering industry, boosting the demand of industry and services. With its immense direct and indirect linkages with most other leading industries, such as steel, aluminium, electrical machinery and equipment, etc., and its huge dependence on infrastructure and services sectors of the economy, the industry has the potential to strengthen the mission of an 'Atmanirbhar' Bharat. As per various volumes of the *Economic Survey*, its role in growth and development can be observed in the following ways:

- With its links to other ancillary industries (such as steel, engineering equipment, port infrastructure, trade and shipping services), it has the potential to create a collaborative production eco-system. With the development of these ancillary industries, the sector generates opportunities for smaller businesses and strengthens supply chain networks. It is noteworthy that a significant proportion of value addition (around 65 per cent) in the construction of a ship is derived from manufacturers of shipboard materials, equipment, and systems.
- Based on international shipbuilding statistics, if one takes a conservative Marginal Consumption to GDP Ratio (MCGR) of 0.45 for the shipbuilding sector, the investment *multiplier* would be around 1.82. Among manufacturing activities, shipbuilding has one of the highest employment multipliers of 6.48. It is capable of generating mass employment in remote, coastal and rural areas, thereby absorbing the labour migrating from agricultural pursuits to manufacturing facilities established by shipyards and their ancillary industries.
- A study undertaken by the Indian Navy for the construction of warships reveals that around 75 per cent of the total project cost is invested back into the Indian economy - through uses of raw materials, development of equipment and systems installed onboard ships and other manpower services.
- An indigenous shipping and shipbuilding industry can also reduce *freight bills* and *forex outgo*, thereby reducing the current account deficit (CAD).

Textile and Apparels

The textile and apparel industry plays an important role in the overall social and economic development of the country. The industry has high contribution in the economy - 2 per cent of the GDP, 11 per cent of total manufacturing GVA, and direct and indirect employment to about 10.5 crore people. The sector is the *second largest* employment generator in the country (next only to agriculture). Most importantly, a major part of this workforce being women, it plays a vital role in *women empowerment* and in the overall social development of the country.

India is the ***sixth*** largest exporter of textile and apparel products (after China, Germany, Bangladesh, Vietnam, and Italy) and is well known in the global market for many products including cotton yarn, fashion garments, hand-made carpets and has a share of 4 per cent of the global trade in this segment, as per the *Economic Survey 2025-26*. The designing capability of this industry is respected worldwide, which has helped the country to build its image as an industrial powerhouse. The sector is, however, vulnerable to several internal and external economic challenges that affect its overall performance. Besides schemes specific to silk, jute, wool, handloom and handicraft sectors, the Government is implementing the following *major schemes* (upto the *Economic Survey 2024-25*) cutting across sectors to strengthen the industry:

ATUFS The Amended Technology Upgradation Fund Scheme (ATUFS) is a revised version of TUFS (Technology Upgradation Funds, 1999) and has the objective to modernise and upgrade the technology of the textile industry.

SITP The Scheme for Integrated Textiles Park (SITP) is for providing world-class infrastructure facilities - of the 62 sanctioned textile parks, 28 were completed by November 2025.

SAMARTH The Scheme for Capacity Building in Textile Sector (Samarth), a flagship scheme, is a placement-oriented programme targeting skill development of 10 lakh youth (2017-20) in the entire value chain of textiles (excluding Spinning and Weaving) in the organised sector.

MITRA In October 2021, the government notified the PM Mega Integrated Textiles Region and Apparel Park (MITRA) scheme to enhance the competitiveness of the sector under the *Atmanirbhar Bharat* to position India on the global textiles map. A total of 7 such parks are to be set up under the PPP mode (owned by state and central governments). Inspired from 5F's - ***farm to fibre; fibre to factory; factory to fashion; fashion to foreign*** - the scheme is aimed at developing integrated large scale and modern industrial infrastructure facility for entire value-chain for the industry. It is expected to reduce the logistics cost and will help India in attracting investments, and boosting employment generation.

Challenges of the Sector: Despite possessing a complete value chain, as per the *Economic Survey 2025-26* and *Economic Survey 2024-25*, textiles face several challenges[54] today:

- The dominance of MSMEs limits scale and efficiency, while its fragmented nature increases logistical costs.
- India's reliance on cotton, unlike the global shift towards MMF, limits its competitiveness in the worldwide market.
- The sector has attracted limited foreign direct investment, hindering technological advancements and reliance on imported textile machinery.
- A significant skill gap persists, hindering productivity and innovation.

Addressing these challenges is crucial for India to realise its full potential as a global textile powerhouse.

PLI SCHEME

With the objective to boost domestic manufacturing and cut import bills the Government introduced (March 2020) a *production-linked incentive (PLI)* scheme - companies will receive 'incentives' on their incremental sales over the next 5-year period. Till February 2025, ***14 sectors*** were put under the scheme, namely:

(i) Mobile Manufacturing and Specified Electronic Components

(ii) Critical Key Starting materials/Drug Intermediaries and Active Pharmaceutical Ingredients

(iii) Manufacturing of Medical Devices.

[54] *Economic Survey 2025-26* (New Delhi: Ministry of Finance, GoI, January 2026), pp. 309-310; and *Economic Survey 2024-25* (New Delhi: Ministry of Finance, GoI, January 2025), pp. 200-201.

(iv) Advance Chemistry Cell (ACC) Battery
(v) Electronic/Technology Products
(vi) Automobiles and Auto Components
(vii) Pharmaceutical drugs
(viii) Telecom and Networking Products
(ix) Textile Products: MMF segment and technical textiles
(x) Food Products
(xi) High Efficiency Solar PV Modules
(xii) White Goods (ACs and LED)
(xiii) Specialty Steel
(xiv) Drone and Drone Components

These sectors are highly capital-intensive (longer-term Government investments look very difficult into them) which bear benefits over a longer period of time. By offering these sectors incentive, the Government has not only designed a way out to promote investment into them but has also tried making the whole PLI structure compliant to India's commitments to WTO by making it 'non-discriminatory' and 'neutral' with respect to domestic sales and exports.

The Incentives Under the scheme, the incentives (in the forms of sops and bonuses) are to be given as percentage of their production turnover (above a minimum floor value) and investment expenditures (on plant, machinery, equipment, research and development (R&D) and transfer of technology) incurred by the manufacturing companies. However, investments carried out by companies on land and buildings for the project will not be considered for any incentives.

The PLI Scheme across these 14 key specific sectors is poised to make Indian manufacturers globally competitive, attract investment in the areas of core competency and cutting-edge technology, ensure efficiencies, create economies of scale, and make India an integral part of the global value chain. The scheme will benefit the MSME ecosystem in the country. The anchor units built in every sector will require a new supplier base in the entire value chain. Most of these ancillary units will be built in the MSME sector. As per the *Economic Survey 2022-23,* the scheme, which combines well with *Make India 2.0,* can enhance India's annual manufacturing capex (capital expenditure) by 15 to 20 per cent from fiscal 2022-23 to 2025-26.

FDI Policy Measures

Foreign direct investment (FDI) is an important driver of economic growth which helps in sustaining high growth rate, increasing productivity, a major source of non-debt financial resources and employment generation. A favourable policy regime and sound business environment facilitate FDI flows.

The government has taken various reforms to liberalising and simplifying the FDI policy to provide *ease of doing business* climate in the country that will also lead to larger FDI inflows. A number of sectors have been liberalised, including defence, construction, broadcasting, civil aviation, plantation, trading, private sector banking, satellite establishment and operation and credit information companies. By early 2025, the government had taken the following policy steps to promote FDI in the economy:

- 100 per cent FDI allowed under automatic route in *petroleum and natural gas* (in cases where strategic disinvestment of the PSUs has been approved).
- 100 per cent FDI allowed under automatic route in mining and sale of coal.
- 100 per cent FDI permitted in manufacturing of *medical devices;* the *white label ATM* and *railway* infrastructure.
- 100 per cent FDI allowed in marketing of *food products* produced and manufactured in India.
- 100 per cent FDI allowed under automatic route in *telecom sector*.
- 74 per cent FDI allowed in insurance (from existing 49 per cent) in *defence sector* through automatic route seeking new licenses.
- 100 per cent FDI allowed (increased from the existing 74 per cent by the *Union Budget 2025–26*) with clause for the companies to invest total collected premium in India and some other safeguards.
- 100 per cent FDI has been permitted in Intermediaries or Insurance Intermediaries, including insurance brokers, reinsurance brokers, insurance consultants, corporate agents, third-party administrators, surveyors and loss assessors and such other entities as may be notified by the

Insurance Regulatory and Development Authority from time to time.

As per the *Economic Survey 2025–26*, the state of foreign investment inflows did show a mixed[55] trend:

- Gross Foreign Direct Investment **(FDI)** inflows strengthened to **US$ 64.7** billion in 2025–26 (April–November), compared with US$ 55.8 billion in 2024–25 (April–November).
- Net Foreign Portfolio Investment **(FPI)** inflows remained volatile—as of January 2026, FPIs were ***net sellers*** of Indian equities with outflows of ₹16.5 thousand crore. The volatility in portfolio flows underscores the susceptibility of equity and bond markets to global developments. However, the sound economic and corporate fundamentals in India underpin the long-term attractiveness of the Indian equity market for foreign investors.

EASE OF DOING BUSINESS

Doing Business Report, an annual publication (since 2003) of the World Bank Group used to rank the countries of the world on the basis of their 'regulations that enhance business activity and those that constrain it'. In the last report, it used the following 12 parameters[56]; however, in ranking, the last two parameters (in the list below) were not included:

1. Starting a business,
2. Dealing with construction permits,
3. Getting electricity,
4. Registering property,
5. Getting credit,
6. Protecting minority investors,
7. Paying taxes,
8. Trading across borders,
9. Enforcing contracts,
10. Resolving insolvency,
11. Employing workers, and
12. Contracting with governments.

For ranking countries, the report analyses regulation that encourages efficiency and supports freedom to do business - through field surveys and interviews with corporate lawyers and company executives asking the following *three questions* about the government:

1. When do governments change regulation with a view to developing their private sector?
2. What are the characteristics of reformist governments?
3. What are the effects of regulatory change on different aspects of economic or investment activity?

In the *Doing Business 2020* Report India was ranked **63rd** among the 190 countries. This shows a jump of 14 ranks over the preceding report. Though, only two cities, Delhi and Mumbai, are included in the report, it speaks enough about the business regulatory environment in the country. The report recognised India as one of the ten economies that have improved the most (from 142nd in 2014 to 63rd in 2019).

Though India has been able to improve[57] its rank in 7 out of 10 parameters, it needs to work on other indicators as it continued to trail in parameters such as Revoking Insolvency, Registering Property, Paying Taxes and Enforcing Contracts. To get included among the top 30 countries (as the Government has targeted under its Output-Outcome Framework Document), India requires a nuts-and-bolts approach of feedback loops, monitoring and continuous adjustment.

Report Discontinued In September 2021, World Bank Group decided to discontinue the report (after some malpractices were found in preparation). Launched in 2002, the first report was published in 2003 (which covered five indicator sets and 133 economies of the world). Meanwhile, the group is busy in formulating a new approach to assessing the business and investment climate in economies worldwide - under the Business Enabling Environment (BEE) project - which will be published as they become available (as per the World Bank Group, March 2026).

---

[55] *Economic Survey 2025-26* (New Delhi: Ministry of Finance, GoI, January 2026), pp. 174-186 & pp. 127-129.

[56] *Doing Business 2020* (Washington, DC: World Bank, 2020).

[57] *Economics Survey 2020-21*, vol. 2 (New Delhi: Ministry of Finance, GoI), pp. 276-78.

MAKE IN INDIA

Make in India was launched in September 2014 by the GoI to encourage multinational as well as domestic companies to manufacture their products in India. The initiative is set up to boost entrepreneurship, not only in manufacturing but also in relevant infrastructure and *service sectors* as well. **Major features** of the initiative are as given below:

Vision It is to attract both capital and technological investment in India enabling it to become the top global FDI, surpassing even China and the United States.

Objective To focus on job creation and skill enhancement in 25 key sectors of the economy, including automobiles, aviation, biotechnology, defence manufacturing, electrical machinery, food processing, oil and gas, and pharmaceuticals, among others.

Logo The logo, inspired from Ashoka Chakra, is a striding lion made of cogs, symbolizing manufacturing, strength and national pride.

The initiative also aims at imposing *high quality standards* and the dimensions of *sustainability*. Key policies to be followed are: ease of doing business, getting away with archaic laws, 100 Smart Cities, disinvestment of the PSUs, skills and jobs for the youth, etc. Major *challenges* to the initiatives include creating a healthy business environment, removal of unfavourable factors, more focus on Indian's MSMEs, lack of world-class R&D and comparisons with China's 'Made in China' campaign.

Opportunistic Foreign Takeover

To safeguard against opportunistic takeover (which was possible during financial hardships of COVID-19 pandemic) of Indian companies, the Government tweaked the FDI policy in 2020. As per it, all existing and future FDIs in Indian entity, originating from the countries which share land border with India, need prior clearance. The policy related to foreign investment via security market (i.e., the foreign portfolio investment) was left unchanged.

The initiative is based on *four pillars* - new processes; new infrastructure; new sectors; and new mindset. The **major steps** taken by the government in this regard are as summed up below:

1. An interactive portal for dissemination of information and interaction with investors has been created with the objective of generating awareness about the investment opportunities and prospects of the country, to promote India as a preferred investment destination in markets overseas and to increase Indian share of global FDI.
2. *Invest India* set up as the national investment promotion and facilitation *agency*.
3. With the objective of promoting investment in the country, a full-fledged Investment Facilitation Cell has been set up under the Make in India initiative, primarily to support all investment queries as well as to *handhold and liaise* with various agencies on behalf of potential investors.
4. As envisaged by the *National Manufacturing Policy 2011*, 'Make in India' seeks to enable the sector to contribute 25 per cent to the GDP and create 100 million additional jobs by 2022.
5. A number of steps to enhance the skills of workers/the unemployed in India in order to improve their employability.
6. In order to tap the creative potential and boost entrepreneurship in India, the *Startup India* and *Stand-up India* campaign has been announced.
7. An innovation promotion platform called *AIM* (Atal Innovation Mission) and a techno-financial, incubation and facilitation programme called *SETU* (Self-Employment and Talent Utilization) are being implemented to encourage innovation and start-ups in India.
8. For supporting the financial needs of the *small* and *medium* enterprise sector and promote start-ups and entrepreneurship, various steps taken through 'Make in India' include:
   - **(i)** The *India Aspiration Fund* has also been set up under the SIDBI for *venture capital financing* to the MSME sector.
   - **(ii)** SIDBI Make in India Loan for Small Enterprises *(SMILE)* launched to offer quasi-equity and term-based short-term loans to Indian SMEs on liberal terms.
   - **(iii)** A Micro Units Development Refinance Agency *(MUDRA)* Bank set up to

provide development and refinance to commercial banks/NBFCs/cooperative banks for loans given to *micro-units*. MUDRA follows a 'credit-plus approach' by also providing several other services such as financial literacy and addressing skill gaps, information gaps, etc.

In December 2022, the Government launched *'Make in India 2.0'* to further enhance India's integration in the global value chain. Under it, the focus is on 27 sectors, which include 15 manufacturing sectors and 12 service sectors. The sectors have been chosen while keeping in mind the Indian industries' strengths and competitive edge, the need for import substitution, and the potential for export and increased employability. It is further believed that there will be a significant reduction in the trade deficit[58] with domestic production substituting for imports. Sectors under which the PLI scheme has been announced currently constitute around *40 per cent* of the total imports.

START-UP INDIA

The Start-up India scheme was launched by the GoI in January 2016 with a slogan, *Start-up India* and *Stand-up India*. The mission/scheme aims to build a strong ecosystem for nurturing innovation, driving sustainable economic growth and generating large-scale employment opportunities. Apart from the technology sector the start-up movement will extend to a wide array of other sectors including agriculture, manufacturing, healthcare and education; and from existing tier 1 cities will extend to tier 2 and tier 3 cities including semi-urban and rural areas. The proposed *action plan (Economic Survey 2015-16)* for the firms is as given below:

- Creating a compliance regime based on self-certification to reduce the regulatory burden and keep compliance cost low.
- Setting up a Start-up India hub to create a single point of contact for the entire start-up ecosystem and enable knowledge exchange and access to funding.
- Rolling out of a mobile app and portal to serve as the single platform for start-ups to interact with government and regulatory institutions and various stakeholders.
- Relaxed norms of public procurement.
- Legal support and fast-tracking of patent examination at lower costs to promote awareness of IPR (Intellectual Property Rights).
- Faster and easier exit norms.
- Providing funding support through a fund of funds with a corpus of ₹10,000 crore.
- Credit Guarantee Fund to catalyse entrepreneurship.
- Tax exemption on capital gains.
- Income tax exemption (under Section 80-IAC) extended by the *Union Budget 2025-26* for another five years (i.e., the benefit will be available to eligible start-ups incorporated before April 1, 2030).
- Launch of AIM (Atal Innovation Mission) with the SETU (Self-Employment and Talent Utilisation) programme to serve as a platform for promotion of world-class innovation hubs, start-up businesses and other self-employment activities, particularly in technology-driven areas.
- Building innovation centres at national institutes to propel successful innovation through augmentation of incubation and R&D efforts.
- Setting up of 7 new research parks (modelled on the research park at IIT Madras).
- Promoting start-ups in the biotechnology sector.
- Launching of innovation-focused programmes for students to foster a culture of innovation in the field of science and technology.

To encourage the start-ups, the Government has taken several new initiatives in the area:

- Acknowledging the need to reduce the regulatory burden self-certification allowed (under three labour laws and six environment laws).
- Startup India Hub has been developed as a single point of contact for enabling them to exchange knowledge and access fund.
- A *Fund of Funds* for Startups (FFS) with a corpus of ₹10,000 crores have been created which is being managed by SIDBI.
- Several steps have also been taken to promote Industry-Academia Partnership and Incubation. With an aim to foster and facilitate Bio-entrepreneurship, Bioclusters, Bio-Incubators, Technology Transfer Offices (TTOs) and BioConnect,

[58] *Economic Survey 2022-23* (New Delhi: Ministry of Finance, GoI, January 2023), pp. 285-86.

offices are being established in research institutes and universities across India.

- Seed Fund and Equity Funding support is also provided to bio-tech Startups under the initiative.

Capitalising on the digital infrastructure support, India has also emerged as one of the world's most vibrant destinations for start-up ecosystems. Start-ups are being envisioned as the spine of new India, as they encourage the youth to become job creators rather than job seekers.

With the highest FinTech adoption rate of 87 per cent among the public compared to the global average of 64 per cent, India has gained the ***3rd*** place in digital payments only after US and China, signifying that India has an untapped[59] market. These untapped opportunities, along with the favourable ecosystem, create a large growth potential for FinTechs in India. Taking this vision forward, under the government's policy initiative, a world-class FinTech Hub at Gujarat International Finance Tec-City (GIFT)-International Financial Services Centre (IFSC) has been developed.

The year 2024 marked the completion of 8 years of the 'Stand-up India' scheme and the numbers - with more than 1,57,706 recognised start-ups - tell the entire story.[60] Start-ups have moved past the traditional territory of consumer products and services to much larger value-added services such as satellites.

INDUSTRY 4.0

The advent of the fourth industrial revolution or industry 4.0, as it is commonly referred to, has begun. The transformation integrates new technologies such as cloud computing, Internet of Things (IoT), machine learning, and artificial intelligence (AI) into manufacturing processes, leading to efficiencies across the value chain. While the adoption of these technologies in the Indian manufacturing sector is underway, large-scale adoption is yet to happen. However, an enabling environment is rapidly developing. Significant performance of India in enhancing internet penetration and a push towards self-reliance in semiconductor technology - major pillars of the revolution - are policy steps in the right direction aimed at creating hyper-efficient processing technology. Keeping in mind the significance of industry 4.0 and aiming to become a key player in global value chains, the Government has taken well-thought out policy steps[61] in this direction:

- Launching of the SAMARTH (Smart Advanced Manufacturing and Rapid Transformation Hubs) *Udyog Bharat 4.0* under the Ministry of Heavy Industries and Public Enterprises, which aims to encourage technological solutions in manufacturing units through awareness programmes and demonstrations.
- Establishment of the *Centre for Fourth Industrial Revolution* in 2018, which aims to develop the policy frameworks for emerging technologies.

Fostering Innovation The government's efforts towards fostering innovation include incubation, handholding, funding, industry-academia partnership and mentorship. The government has also strengthened its Intellectual Property Right (IPR) regime by modernising the IP office, reducing legal compliances and facilitating IP filing for start-ups, women entrepreneurs, small industries and others. As per the *Economic Survey 2024-25*, this has encouraging results–domestic patent filings had a growth rate of 50 per cent in 2023-24 in comparison to 28 per cent in 2014-15, and patent grants increased by 17-fold since 2014-15.

India In Global Innovation Index 2024

Situation of innovation in India has been summarised by the latest Global Innovation Index 2024 in the following ways:

- Its rank in the Index has improved to 39th (out of 133 countries) in 2024 (from 81st in 2015).
- It ranks 1st among the 38 lower middle-income group economies and 1st among the 10 economies in Central and Southern Asia.
- It holds the 7th position in intangible asset intensity, surpassing the growth rates of many

[59] *Economic Survey 2022-23* (New Delhi: Ministry of Finance, GoI, January 2023), pp. 345-70.

[60] *Department for Promotion of Industry and Internal Trade* (New Delhi: Ministry of Commerce & Industry, GoI, 1 February 2025).

[61] *Economic Survey 2022-23* (New Delhi: Ministry of Finance, GoI, January 2023), pp. 290-91.

high-income economies and matching the intangible investment intensity of Germany and Japan (as a share of GDP).

- It holds 4th position in Science and Technology Cluster Ranking 2024 with 4 cities among the world's top 100 science and technology clusters.

India has been advised by the WIPO to focus on the following aspects to encourage innovation in the country:

i. enhance human capital,

ii. improve access to finance,

iii. reduce regulatory burdens further, and

iv. improve infrastructure.

The annual Global Innovation Index (GII) of the WIPO (World Intellectual Property Organisation) ranks the countries based on innovation performance, comprising around 80 indicators, including measures on the political environment, education, infrastructure and knowledge creation of each economy.

Source: *Economic Survey 2024–25* (New Delhi: Ministry of Finance, GoI, January 2025), p. 204.

COVID-19 AND INDUSTRIAL REFORMS

In the wake of the coronavirus pandemic, India announced a major drive towards self-reliance by launching the ambitious *Atmanirbhar Bharat Abhiyan* in May 2020. Under the campaign, the following industrial reform measures were announced by the Government.

Defence Import of some weapons banned; defence production to be indigenised; provision of a separate budget for defence capital procurement; FDI limit in defence manufacturing under automatic route raised to 74 per cent (from 49 per cent); and Ordnance Factory Board (OFB) to be corporatised and listed on stock market (to improve autonomy, efficiency and accountability).

Space Private participation to be encouraged; creation of a level playing field for private players allowing them to use ISRO facilities and participate in future projects on space travel and planetary exploration; and geo-spatial data policy to be eased to make remote-sensing data available more widely to technology entrepreneurs.

Aviation By 2025-26, six more airports to be auctioned on PPP (private-public partnership) mode; 12 more airports to invite private investment; airspace restrictions eased to make flying more efficient; and MRO (maintenance, repair and operations) tax structure to be rationalised to make India an MRO hub.

Minerals Government monopoly on coal removed and commercial mining introduced (on a revenue sharing basis); private sector to be allowed to bid for coal blocks; and private players to be allowed to undertake exploration activities.

Power Power utilities and distribution companies in Union Territories to be privatised (based on a new tariff policy).

Atomic Research Atomic research reactors to be set up in PPP mode for the production of medical isotopes; facilities to be set up in PPP mode for food preservation using irradiation technology; and TDICs (technology development cum incubation centres) to be set up to link robust start-up ecosystem to nuclear sector.

Social Infrastructure To boost private investment in social infrastructure the viability gap funding (VGF) quantum has been increased to 30 per cent (Centre plus state combined) of the project cost (which used to be 20 per cent as in case of other sectors).

The measures announced the aim at involving greater participation from the private sector. For fulfilling the aims of *self-reliance*, the policy decisions are 'bolder' and 'speedier' in approach, but they seem to be the need of the hour to unshackle the hidden potential of the economy.

INDIAN INFRASTRUCTURE

An Introduction

Infrastructure is the 'lifeline' of an economy as protein is the lifeline of the human body. Whichever sector be the PMF of an economy, i.e., primary, secondary or tertiary, suitable level of infrastructure presence is a prerequisite for growth and development. This is why the GoI has always given priority to the developmental aspects of the sector. But the level of preparedness and performance had been always less than required by the economy. Which sector is called the infrastructure? *Basically, the goods and services usually requiring higher investment considered essential for the proper functioning of an economy is called the infrastructure of an economy.*[62] Such sectors might be as many as required by a particular economy such as power, transportation, communication, water supply, sewerage, housing, urban amenities, etc.

There are three sectors which are considered as the infrastructure universally around the world, namely power, transportation and communication. Since, infrastructure benefits the whole economy, it has been often argued by the economists that the sector should be funded by the government by means of taxation, partly not wholly.

Indian infrastructure sector is clearly overstrained and has suffered from underinvestment in the post-reforms period.[63] Infrastructure bottlenecks are always constraint in achieving a higher growth for the economy. India needs massive investment, both from the public and private sectors, to overcome infrastructure bottlenecks. Investments by the public and private sectors are not alternatives, but complementary to each other as the required investment is very high. Public investment in the sector depends upon the ability to raise resources (capital) in the public sector, and this in turn depends upon the ability to collect the user charges from the consumers. To make this happen following *three* factors are extremely important:

1. Reform of the power sector,
2. Introduction of road user charges (either directly *via* tolls or indirectly *via* a cess on petrol diesel), and
3. Rationalisation of railway fares.

Experts[64] have suggested for expanding public investment in the sector supplemented duly by a vigorous effort of attracting private investment (domestic as well as foreign). Creating a conducive environment to attract private investment in infrastructure should include:

1. Simplification and transparency in the clearance procedures;
2. Unbundling an infrastructure project so that the private sector may opt for only those unbundled segments of the project whose they are able to bear; and
3. Providing credible and independent regulatory framework so that the private players get fair treatment.

Official Ideology

Putting in place the quality and efficient infrastructure services is essential to realise the full potential of the growth impulses surging through the Indian economy. There is now a widespread consensus[65] (clearly accepted by the Planning Commission) that exclusive dependence on the government for the provision of all infrastructure services introduces difficulties concerning adequate scale of investment, technical efficiency, proper enforcement of user charges and competitive market structure. At the same time, complete reliance on private production, particularly without appropriate regulation, is also not likely to produce optimal outcomes.[66] India, while stepping up public investment in infrastructure, has been actively engaged in finding the appropriate policy framework, which gives the private sector adequate confidence and incentives to invest on a massive scale, but simultaneously preserves adequate checks and balances through transparency, competition and regulation.

The approach towards infrastructure has gone through a *transformational change* since the new policy think tank NITI Aayog came into being. The Seven-Year Strategy Framework (titled as 'Strategy for New India @75') document of the NITI has devoted a full section on it (out of its four sections). The document believes that infrastructure is the physical foundations of growth and development which are crucial to enhancing the competitiveness of Indian businesses as also ensuring the citizens' *ease of living*. The sector needs an unprecedented scale of investment, which is why the Government is exploring all possible models of resource mobilisation - the hybrid annuity model (HAM) of the PPP mode is expected to emerge an effective tool in this regard.

62 *Oxford Dictionary of Business* (New Delhi: Oxford University Press, 2004).
63 *India Infrastructure Report 1994* (New Delhi: Government of India, 1994).
64 One of such major suggestion was forwarded by Sachs, Varshney, and Bajpai, *India in the Era of Economic Reforms*, op. cit., p. 79.
65 *Economic Survey, 2006-07* (New Delhi: Ministry of Finance, GoI, 2007).
66 *India Infrastructure Report 2007* (New Delhi: Government of India, 2011).

POWER

Electricity is essential for economic activity and is also required in leisure time. In the last few decades, the power sector has witnessed substantial transformation from both the demand (universal electrification) and supply side (the advent of green energy) - with commendable progress made in the generation and transmission of electricity in India. As per the *Economic Survey 2024-25,* the total installed capacity increased to 456.7 GW by November 2024 with an annual growth rate of 7.2 per cent.

Renewable Energy: As per the *Economic Survey 2024-25,* in the shift towards renewable energy, the power sector has been bolstered primarily by large-scale solar and wind initiatives. By the end of December 2024, the country's total renewable energy installed capacity increased by 15.8 per cent year-on-year, reaching 209.4 GW, up from 180.8 GW in December 2023. Renewable energy now constitutes about 47 per cent of India's total installed capacity, highlighting a growing dependence on cleaner, non-fossil fuel-based energy sources.

State Power Sector Reforms: In 2014, the Government launched the **IPDS** (Integrated Power Development Scheme) to facilitate state utilities (i.e., DISCOMs) to ensure quality and reliable 24 × 7 power supply in the urban areas. By September 2021, distribution strengthening was completed in all of the 546 circles. Further, the country has already accomplished two major landmarks in the arena of rural electrification:

1. 100 per cent village electrification under Deen Dayal Upadhyaya Gram Jyoti Yojana and
2. Universal household electrification under the Saubhagya (the Pradhan Mantri Sahaj Bijli Har Ghar Yojana).

T&D losses have been declining since 2001-02 (32.86 per cent) but are still substantial. As per the latest available data in 2019-20 it was at 20.46 per cent compared to the T&D losses of the peer countries (6 per cent in China, 10 per cent in South Africa, 13 per cent in Russia and 17.5 per cent in Brazil), India's T&D losses are very high (21.5 per cent) against the global average of around 8.5 per cent and South Korea being the best at 3.6 per cent only.

Without improving the performance of the electricity distribution companies (DISCOMs) of the state government efforts towards 100 per cent village electrification, 24 × 7 power supply and clean energy cannot bear fruit. Power outages also adversely affect national priorities such as 'Make in India' and 'Digital India'. In addition, default on bank loans by financially stressed DISCOMs has the potential of seriously impacting the banking sector and the economy at large.

AT&C Losses Due to lack of adequate investment on 'transmission and distribution' (T&D) works, the T&D losses have been consistently on the higher side, and reached to the level of 32.86 per cent in the year 2000-01. The reduction of these losses was essential to bring economic viability to the state utilities (SEBs). As the T&D loss was not able to capture all the losses in the network, concept of *Aggregate Technical and Commercial (AT&C)* loss was introduced. AT&C loss captures technical as well as commercial losses in the network and is a true indicator of total losses in the system.

High technical losses in the system are primarily *due to* inadequate investments over the years for system improvement works, which has resulted in unplanned extensions of the distribution lines, overloading of the system elements such as transformers and conductors, and lack of adequate reactive power support.

The commercial losses are mainly due to:

1. low metering efficiency
2. theft
3. pilferages

This may be eliminated by improving metering efficiency, proper energy accounting and auditing and improved billing and collection efficiency. Fixing of accountability of the personnel/feeder managers may help considerably in reduction of AT&C loss.

Aimed mainly at bringing down the AT&C of the state Discoms, Uday was the 4th scheme sponsored by the Government - the **APRDP** (Accelerated Power Development and Reform Programme) in 2001; Restructured APRDP in 2008; and the IPDS (Integrated Power Development Scheme) in 2014 which subsumed the **R-APRDP**.

For financial and operational turnaround of DISCOMs and to ensure a sustainable permanent solution to the problem, the *UDAY* (Ujjwal DISCOM Assurance Yojana) was launched by the GoI, in November 2015. The scheme also aims to reduce interest burden of the DISCOMs, cost of power and their AT&C (Aggregate Transmission & Technical) losses. Meanwhile, the Government in 2021-22, introduced a revamped, reforms-based and result-linked new *Revamped*

Distribution Sector Scheme (RDSS) for the next five years ending 2025-26. The Scheme seeks to improve the 'operational efficiencies' and 'financial sustainability' of all DISCOMs (excluding Private Sector DISCOMs) by providing conditional financial assistance for strengthening of supply infrastructure. The assistance will be based on meeting pre-qualifying criteria as well as upon achievement of basic minimum benchmarks by the DISCOM evaluated on the basis of agreed evaluation framework tied to financial improvements. Its *objectives* are as given below:

1. Reduction of AT&C losses to pan-India levels of 12-15% by 2024-25.
2. Reduction of ACS-ARR gap to zero by 2024-25.
3. Developing Institutional Capabilities for Modern DISCOMs.
4. Improvement in the quality, reliability, and affordability of power supply to consumers through a financially sustainable and operationally efficient Distribution Sector.

The currently ongoing approved projects under the Schemes of IPDS, DDUGJY (Deen Dayal Upadhyaya Gram Jyoti Yojana) along with PMDP (Prime Minister's Development Program, 2015) for the UTs of J&K and Ladakh has been subsumed in this Scheme.

RAILWAYS

The Indian Railways (IR) can very well be called India's lifeline. It plays a huge role in national integration and regional development. The IR, with over 69,011 route km, is the ***4th*** largest network in the world under single management. Passenger traffic originating in IR was 808.6 crores during pre-COVID-19 period (2019-20), but dipped to 125 crores in 2020-21. It has since recovered to 570 crore in 2023-24 (April-November), which is projected to reach 830 crore in 2024-25 as per the *Economic Survey 2024-25*.

Revenue Generation The IR generated a revenue of ₹1.93 trillion in 2024-25 (April-December) which is about 4 per cent higher than the previous year.

Challenges The IR is faced with a number of challenges, major ones being:

- For speedy capacity creation, IR recognises the importance of enhancing project execution capabilities.
- Considering the enormity of the resources required for plan investment in rail infrastructure, and given the limitation of public resources, efforts are on by IR to generate sufficient *internal surplus*, and
- Tapping innovative methods of financing, to meet these needs.

Focus The focus is on prioritising investments in important areas such as dedicated freight corridors, high speed rail, high capacity rolling stock, last mile rail linkages and port connectivity and attracting private and FDI investments to supplement available resources. Major *initiatives* taken by the GoI are as given below:

- Various measures to improve passenger amenities, infrastructure and services, and initiatives under Make in India, freight initiative, resource mobilisation initiative and green initiatives, etc.
- Mobile application for freight operations - *Parichaalan* - has been introduced.
- IR is installing solar panels on rooftops of coaches for the train lighting system. Solar plants of 50 MW to be set up on the rooftops of IR buildings.
- Diamond Quadrilateral network of High-Speed Rail connecting major metros (Delhi, Mumbai, Kolkata and Chennai) to be set up.
- *Safety* became the highest priority - as a result, the number of train accidents decreased to from 59 in 2018-19 to 55 in 2019-20 (pre-Covid time) and further to 17 in 2024-25.
- Private players allowed to operate in the railways sector through the PPP mode under the ***New India New Railway*** initiative - over 150 pairs of train services identified for the introduction of 151 modern train sets or rakes through private participation.
- The *private entity* shall be responsible for financing, procuring, operating and maintaining the trains and shall have the freedom to decide on the fare to be charged from its passengers.
- *Kisan Rail* service was introduced (in *Union Budget 2020-21*) to provide better market opportunity by transporting perishables and agri-product, including milk, meat and fish.
- ***National Rail Plan*** (NRP) was developed in 2020-21, to develop capacity (both infrastructure and rolling stock) ahead of demand. It aims at developing adequate rail infrastructure by 2030 to cater to the projected traffic requirements up to 2050 - to increase the modal share of rail in freight from the current level of 27 per cent to 45 per cent.

High Speed Train Project The feasibility report of the Japan International Cooperation Agency (JICA) was approved by the GoI in December 2015. A new special purpose vehicle with 50 per cent equity participation from the Ministry of Railways and 50 per cent from the state governments of Maharashtra and Gujarat will be set up to implement the project. *Major features* of the project are as given below:

- Project completion cost is approximately ₹97,636 crores (including price escalation, interest during construction and import duties) - average per km cost of construction works out to be ₹140 crores. To be completed in 7 years.
- Japan's ODA (official development assistance) will be ₹79,165 crores (81 per cent of project cost) for 50 years with 0.1 per cent interest and a 15-year moratorium.
- Total length of the proposed corridor will be 508 km between the Bandra Kurla complex in Mumbai and Sabarmati/Ahmedabad in Gujarat - to cover 12 stations with a maximum design speed of 350 kmph (with a 320 kmph operating speed).

Train 18 India's first engine-less, semi high-speed train (160 kmph), the *Train18* (rechristened *Vande Bharat Express)* was launched in February 2019. The train is equipped with the finest amenities (such as comfortable 180-degree rotational reclining chairs, mobile charging points, diffused lighting and reading lights, GPS passenger information service, CCTV cameras, talkback facility to connect with the driver in case of emergency, sensor-controlled bathroom fitting for differently abled people and modular toilets with bio-discharge vacuum systems).

Designed and built by Integral Coach Factory of Chennai (under the 'Make in India' initiative), it is estimated to cost 40 per cent less than a similar train imported from Europe. Its successor, *Train 20* is also being developed, which will replace the existing long-distance trains of today in the coming years.

Zero Carbon Emission Indian Railways (IR) is a major user of electricity in the country. In 2022-23, it announced its intention to achieve net zero carbon emission by 2030. In this regard, IR has reoriented its energy demand towards greater use of renewable sources. By *November 2024*, plants generating about 168 MW of solar power (both on rooftops and on land) and about 135 MW of wind power have been commissioned by the IR.

ROADS

India runs on the road - be it the passenger or goods movement - road transport is the dominant mode of transportation. The transport sector has a share of 4.6 per cent in the country's GVA of which roughly 67 per cent is contributed by road transport. Today, India has the *2nd* largest road network (around 63.4 lakh kms) in the world after the United States (66.45 lakh km).

Under the proactive policy approach of the Government, road network expanded faster in the last 11 years (2014-24) during which the national highways recorded a compound annual growth rate (CAGR) of 7.5 per cent, followed by rural roads (6.00 per cent) and urban roads (4.25 per cent). As per the *Ministry of Road Transport and Highways*, the pace at which roads have been constructed has grown significantly from 12 km per day in 2014-15 to 37.5 km per day by 2020-21 (with a moderation to 28.64 km per day in 2021-22 due to the pandemic) and rising to 34 km per day by 2024-25 (April-December).

Financing of the NHDP A part of the **fuel cess** imposed on petrol and diesel is allocated to the NHAI for funding the implementation of the NHDP. The NHAI leverages the cess flow to borrow additional funds from the debt market. Till date, such borrowings have been limited to funds raised through 54 EC (capital gains tax exemption) bonds and the short-term overdraft facility. Government has also taken loans for financing projects under the NHDP from the World Bank, Asian Development Bank and Japan Bank for International Cooperation which are passed on to the NHAI partly in the form of grants and partly as loan. The NHAI has also availed a direct loan of US$ 180 million from the ADB for the Surat-Manor Expressway Project.

Special Accelerated Road Development Programme for North-East region (SARDP-NE) aims at improving road connectivity to state capitals, district headquarters and remote places of the north-east region. Development of roads in Left Wing Extremism *(LWE)* - affected areas in the states of Andhra Pradesh, Bihar, Chhattisgarh, Jharkhand, Madhya Pradesh, Maharashtra, Odisha and Uttar Pradesh - is continuing; Prime Minister's Reconstruction Plan *(PMRP)* for Jammu and Kashmir, launched in November 2014.

Pradhan Mantri Gram Sadak Yojana (PMGSY) Launched to provide single all-weather road connectivity to eligible unconnected habitations having population of 500 persons and above in plain areas and 250 persons and above in hill states, tribal (Schedule V) areas, desert (as identified in the Desert Development Programme) areas and LWE-affected districts as identified by the Ministry of Home Affairs. Rural roads have also been identified as one of the *six components* of Bharat Nirman which has the goal of providing all-weather road connectivity to all villages with a population of 1,000 (500 in the case of hilly or tribal areas).

Bharatmala Pariyojana: Launched in 2015-16, this is a new umbrella programme for the highways sector that focuses on optimising efficiency of freight and passenger movement across the country. It *aims* at bridging critical infrastructure gaps through effective interventions such as development of Economic Corridors, Inter Corridors and Feeder Routes, National Corridor Efficiency Improvement, Border and International connectivity roads, Coastal and Port connectivity roads and Green-field expressways. The *objective* of the programme is to achieve optimal resource allocation for a holistic highway development.

CIVIL AVIATION

India has emerged as one of the fastest growing aviation markets in the world. As per the *Ministry of Civil Aviation*, the domestic traffic in India has more than tripled from around 61 million in 2013-14 to around 185.56 million by 2024-25 (April-December), registering a growth of over 17 per cent per annum. Government took various initiatives to boost the aviation sector which included calibrated opening of the domestic sector as the first wave of the pandemic ebbed, introduction of air transport bubbles or air travel arrangements with specific countries, disinvestment of Air India, privatisation and modernisation/expansion of airports, boost to the regional connectivity scheme - the **UDAN** (Ude Desh ka Aam Naagrik), incentivisation of maintenance, repair and overhaul (MROs) operations being the major ones.

Airport infrastructure development continues to be a matter of concern. Upgradation of many airports, including construction of new terminals, upgradation in 37 non-metro airports, for improving air navigation services the Airport Authority of India (AAI) is installing the new ATS automation system. In order to address issues concerning viability of the civil aviation sector, particularly the airline industry, a *Working Group of 2019* gave the following recommendations:

- state governments should rationalise the value added tax (VAT) on aviation turbine fuel (ATF),
- foreign airlines be permitted to invest in domestic airlines undertakings,
- direct import of ATF by airlines for their own consumption be allowed,
- airlines should be asked to prepare their turnaround plans,
- fare structure should be reviewed by airlines to cover the cost of their operations,
- an economic regulatory framework suggested with regard to excessive/predatory pricing.

The sector has great potential owing to growing demand from the middle class, growth in population and tourism, higher disposable incomes, favourable demographics, and greater penetration of aviation infrastructure. This is further supported by the government through schemes such as UDAN, which has considerably enhanced regional connectivity through the opening of airports in India's hinterland.

The government has also accorded 'in-principle' approval for the setting up of 41 greenfield airports across the country. As per the *Union Budget 2025-26*, more than two crore air passengers have availed themselves of the benefit of the UDAN scheme since its inception which government targets to increase to 4 crore in the next 10 years–connecting 120 new regional destinations. The scheme focuses on the connectivity between the Tier-2 and 3 cities in the country and the number of beneficiaries will increase manifold as the connectivity improves between unserved and underserved airports.

TELECOM

The telecom is among the three basic infrastructures of an economy. In case of India, it plays an even bigger role for implementation of the JAM (Jan Dhan-Aadhar Mobile) trinity based social sector schemes and other pro-development initiative of the Government. The sector has been recognised all over the world as a powerful tool for development and poverty reduction. As part of the Digital India Campaign, the Government has laid considerable emphasis on broadband for all.

Efforts are being made to address the digital divide by extending inclusive internet access to every citizen. The sector has grown at a rapid pace in the last few years and as per the *India Brand Equity Foundation (an initiative of the Ministry of Commerce and Industry)*, it stands at a very strong position:

- The total telephone *subscriber base* stood at 1,203.69 million and *Tele-density* of rural subscribers reached 59.59 per cent as of May 2024.
- Total volume of *wireless data* usage increased by more than 10 folds from 4,206 petabytes in 2017-18 to 47,629 petabytes by 2023-24.
- India is one of the *biggest* consumers of data worldwide. As per *TRAI*, average wireless data usage per wireless data subscriber was 19.47 GB per month in December 2023 from 61.66 MB in March 2014.
- India's 5G subscriptions to have 350 million by 2026, accounting for 27 per cent of all mobile subscriptions.

The value of *export of mobile phones* in 2023-24 increased by 42 per cent reaching at US$ 15.6 billion.

Recent Policy Steps Several new policy steps were taken by the Government till February 2023 to bridge the digital divide and enhance the ease of using telecom services across the country. Major ones, as per the government, are as given below:

- Special drive for the saturation of 4G mobile services in uncovered villages (24,680) and villages having only 2G/3G connectivity (6,279).
- For the North-Eastern Region, implementation of the Comprehensive Telecom Development Plan (CTDP) which aims to provide mobile connectivity on 2G in the uncovered villages by installing 2004 towers.
- A separate CTDP launched to connect the islands to the mainland with the help of submarine optical fibre.
- Facilitating faster and easier deployment of telegraph infrastructure to enable speedy 5G rollout (through Indian Telegraph Right of Way Amendment Rules, 2022).
- The National Frequency Allocation Plan 2022 (NFAP) launched to provide a broad regulatory framework, identifying which frequency bands are available for cellular mobile services, Wi-fi, sound and television broadcasting, radio navigation for aircraft and ships, and other wireless communications. It will be useful in aligning spectrum usage with demands from emerging technologies in an efficient manner.

DIGITAL INFRASTRUCTURE

The role of traditional infrastructure is well recognised in socio-economic development. However, in recent years, the role of digital infrastructure has assumed an increased importance. This was especially true during the COVID-19 period when the restrictions on physical interactions and contacts made people search for alternatives. As a result, for *service deliveries* and *remote work*, increased uses of the available digital infrastructure were seen. This made the world realise that in the coming years, the availability and spread of digital infrastructure will contribute significantly to socio-economic development. The ongoing Digital India programme of the Government recognises this very well, which aims to transform India into a digitally empowered society and knowledge economy, and envisions digital infrastructure as a core utility to every citizen. As per the *Economic Survey 2022-23*, the ***focus*** areas of the programme include:

- the availability of high-speed internet as a core utility for delivery of services to citizens,
- unique digital identity,
- enabling citizen participation in digital and financial space,
- shareable private space on a public cloud (citizens can digitally store their documents, certificates, etc. and share them with public agencies or others without the need to physically submit them), and
- a safe and secure cyber-space.

India's digital journey began with the Aadhaar as a medium for service delivery at the doorstep, while the UPI (Unified Payment Interface) strengthened the digital payment infrastructure. With many other initiatives in the area of setting up *digital public infrastructure*, such as - UMANG, Co-WIN, e-RUPI, TReDS (Trade Receivables Discounting System), Account Aggregators, ONDC (Open Network for Digital Commerce), Bhashini (Artificial Intelligence based language translation tool), Web 3.0 based OCEN (Open Credit Enablement Network), etc. - the Government has been able to develop a unique and cogent digital story to tell. The journey is ongoing and there is much untapped potential in India's digital public infrastructure space.

These emerging new technologies have posed new regulatory challenges too - technology and innovation are neither constructive nor destructive; rather, their uses make them so. Besides being committed to keeping pace with the developments in digital landscape, the Government is also trying to put in place an effective and vibrant regulatory framework for them.

SEMICONDUCTOR SECTOR

Everything looked normal with the global supply chains till the inherent weaknesses got exposed in the wake of COVID-19 pandemic. One product from electronics industry, the semiconductor (i.e., chips), remained in spotlight - its shortage crippling the automotive industry globally. Though its supply chain is back to normal, many countries in the world have taken policy initiatives to diversify its supply chain. One of the most notable policies came from the USA in 2022 - which aims to catalyse its chip manufacturing capacity with a government fund support of US$ 280 billion over the next 10 years (71 per cent of the fund to be used on research and development). The country produces 10 per cent of the world's semiconductors but depends heavily on their imports from East Asia.

For attaining self-reliance (Atmanirbharta) and getting part of the global value chain, India, too, announced multiple policy incentives to attract investment for developing a semiconductor manufacturing ecosystem:

- A comprehensive programme (Programme for Development of Semiconductors and Display Manufacturing Ecosystem) with an outlay of ₹76,000 crore (around US$ 10 billion) was approved by the Government in September 2022. Under it, the government will provide financial support for 50 per cent of the capital expenditure to be incurred by the investing firms over the next 6 years. Its component, the Design Linked-Incentive (DLI) scheme, aims to nurture and facilitate semiconductor design by domestic companies with deployment of the intellectual property (IP). As per the *Economic Survey 2022-23*, India possesses 20 per cent of the world's semiconductor design engineers but a minuscule share in the IP.
- The PLI scheme for IT hardware - Scheme for Promotion of Manufacturing of Electronic Components and Semiconductors (SPECS).

By early 2023, many global and domestic players have shown interest in the semiconductor industry of India. India's first chip-making plant is going to come up in Karnataka with a foreign direct investment of ₹22,900 crore from an Israel-based International Semiconductor Consortium (Memorandum of Understanding already signed). Domestic players such as Vedanta and Tata have also indicated similar plans.

MINERALS

Minerals play a vital role in the process of development, and they are slated to play even a greater role in the coming times as economy moves for electric vehicles and the fourth industrial revolution. Though India has huge reserves of important minerals, the country has not been able to realise its mining potential due to several legislative and procedural reasons. To unshackle the hidden potential of the sector, the Government amended (in 2015) the MMDR (Mines and Mineral Development and Regulation) Act, 1957, heralding major structural reforms in the sector:

- The move towards grant of mineral concessions through *auction* as against the earlier method of 'first-come-first-served' brought in transparency and removed discretion in the grant of mineral concessions.
- Establishment of the NMET (National Mineral Exploration Trust) for providing impetus to exploration.
- Uniform lease period of 50 years.
- Dispensing of the requirement of previous approval of the Central Government for grant of mineral concession other than for atomic minerals, coal and lignite.
- Establishing DMF (District Mineral Foundation) for the benefit of people and areas affected by mining.

In *2020-21*, the Government took the following new steps[67] in furthering the reform process:

- The MMDR Act was amended in January 2020 to provide transfer of all valid statutory clearances vested with the old lessee to the new successful bidder up to a period of two years for all brownfield mines (so that there is no disruption in production and supply of raw material in the industry).
- At present after auction of mines, the successful bidder applies for clearances and after obtaining clearances production starts. Generally, getting

[67] *Economic Survey 2020-21*, vol. 2 (New Delhi: Ministry of Finance, GoI), pp. 300-02.

clearances takes a longer time, anywhere around 3 to 4 years and consequently production is delayed. For immediate start of production after auction, the approach adopted in the amended Act is that States need to obtain the clearances before auction - as a result, production will start without any delay (because clearances are already available).

- To boost growth, employment and to bring state-of-the-art technology in the mining sector in general and in exploration in particular, under *Atmanirbhar Bharat Abhiyan,* in 2020-21, the Government announced the following structural reforms:
  - Introduction of a seamless composite exploration-cum-mining-cum-production regime.
  - 500 mining blocks to be offered through an open and transparent auction process.
  - Joint auction of bauxite and coal mineral blocks.
  - Removal of distinction between captive and non-captive mines.
  - Mineral index for different mineral.
  - Rationalisation of stamp duty.
  - Schedule of Charges (SoC) approved (first time) for exploration projects which will be funded from the NMET.
  - So that appropriate and timely policy intervention could be devised, the AIMS (Aluminium Import Monitoring System) and CIMS (Copper Import Monitoring System) to be set up to monitor the import of aluminium and copper.

PPP MODELS

Managing adequate amount of fund for infrastructure development has been always a challenge for India. In the reform era, the government evolved the idea of PPP for the sector aimed at attracting investments from the private sector (domestic as well as foreign). We see an encouraging contribution coming from the private sector in this regard also. But by 2013-14, the PPPs started getting unattractive for the private sector - primarily caused by the in-built flaws in the PPP models together with regulatory reasons - although external reasons have been also present (slowdown in the country's economy due to recession among the western economies).

Various volumes of the *Economic Survey* together with the *Kelkar Committee* on the PPP have discussed about the various flaws in the existing model of the PPP, primarily used for the development of road projects in the country. In this backdrop, a better PPP model was announced by the Government by early 2016 - the *HAM.* A brief review of the major PPP models[68] (few of them are non-PPP models, too) are given below:

1. **BOT-TOLL:** The 'Build-Operate-Transfer-Toll' was one of the earliest models of PPP. Other than sharing the project cost (with the Government) the private bidder was to build, maintain, operate the road and collect toll on the vehicular traffic. The bid was given to the private company offering to share maximum toll revenue to the government. The private party used to cover 'all-risks' related to land acquisition, construction (damage), inflation, cost overruns caused by delays and commercial. The government was responsible for only regulatory clearances.

   Due to inherent drawbacks, this model proved to be unsustainable for the private bidder - undue delay in land acquisition due to litigation, cost over-runs and uncertainties in traffic movement (commercial risk) made the road projects economically unviable.

2. **BOT-Annuity:** This was an improvement over the BOT-TOLL model aimed at reversing the declining interest of the private companies towards road projects by mainly reducing the risk for the private players. Other than sharing the project cost, the private player was to build, maintain and operate the road projects without any responsibility of collecting toll on the traffic. The private players were offered a fixed amount of money annually (called 'annuity') as compensation - the party bidding for the minimum 'annuity' used to get the project. Toll collection was the responsibility of the Government.

   This was different from the previous model (BOT-TOLL) in one sense - private players were not having any commercial risk (traffic) - but they remained very much exposed to other risks (land acquisition delays, inflation, cost over-runs, construction). Even this model, over time proved to be unviable for the private sector due to the leftover risks they were exposed to.

3. **EPC Model:** The PPP model which was seen to be a better way out to promote the infra projects were visibly failing by the year 2010 and Government was unable to attract the

[68] The review is based on various *official documents* published by the Government of India till March 2023.

private players towards the road sector. It was in this backdrop that the Engineering-Procurement-Construction (EPC) Model was announced. In this model, project cost was fully covered by the Government (it means, it was not a PPP model and was like normal contracts given to the bidders) together with majority of the risks - land acquisition, cost over-runs due to delay, inflation and commercial.

The private developers were supposed to design, construct and hand over the road projects to the government - maintenance, operation and toll collection being the government's responsibilities. Contract was given to the private player who offered to construct roads at the lowest cost/price guaranteeing the desired quality levels. It means, the private player in this model was only exposed to the construction-related risks which is a normal risk involved in any contract given by the government to the private party.

EPC Model could have been a temporary way out to develop road projects as it was fully funded by the government - reform era had aimed to attract investment from the private players by evolving a 'business model' for the road sector - need was to develop a new PPP model. In this backdrop we see the government coming up with a new PPP model for the road projects - the HAM.

4. **HAM:** HAM is a mix of EPC and BOT-ANNUITY models. In this model the project cost is shared by the government and the private player in ratio of 40:60, respectively. The private player is responsible to construct and hand over the roads to the government which will collect toll (if wishes) - maintenance remaining the responsibility of the private player till the annuity period. Private player is paid a fixed sum of economic compensation (called 'annuity', similar to the BOT-ANNUITY model of past) by the government for a fixed tenure (normally 15 years, though it is flexible). The private player which demands lowest annuity (in bidding) gets the contract.

   In this model, most of the major risks are covered by the government - land acquisition, clearances, operation, toll collection and commercial - while the risks related to inflation and cost overruns are shared in ratio of the project cost sharing. But the private sector is still exposed to the construction and maintenance risks (delays from the government side in clearances and land acquisition have chances to enhance the degree of risks private players are exposed to). But overall, this is the best PPP model for the time devoid of most of the flaws of past. Private sector has shown good response to this model. By early 2018, this model was notified by the Government for other infra sectors too.

TOT Model

TOT (toll-operate-transfer) model has been evolved by the government for the existing highways (aimed at asset monetisation) and is not a public-private partnership (PPP) model for highway construction. Under it, a private player operates and maintains the highways for a fixed term of 20 years and collects user fee/toll as compensation in accordance with the prescribed fee rates.

5. **Swiss Challenge Model:** The GoI, for the first time, announced the use of this model for redevelopment of railway stations in the country (by late 2015). This is a very flexible method of giving contracts (i.e., public procurement) which can be used in PPP as well as non-PPP projects.

   In this, one bidder is asked by the government to submit the proposal for the project which is put in public domain. Afterwards, several other bidders submit their proposals aimed at improving and beating the original (first) bidder - finally an improved bid is selected (called counter proposal). If the original bidder is not able to match the counter-proposal, the project is awarded to the counter bidder. Government has made it an online method.

   Though the GoI used this model for the first time, this had already been used by several states by now - Karnataka, Andhra Pradesh, Rajasthan, Madhya Pradesh, Bihar, Punjab and Gujarat - for roads and housing projects. In 2009, the Supreme Court approved the method for award of contracts.

6. **PPP Model for Other Sectors:** Though the idea of PPP model was originally evolved for the infrastructure sector, in recent times,

there have been proposals for its uses in other areas too, such as education, healthcare and even agriculture. The model is getting popular support from the ULBs in the country, and it is believed that in the *Smart Cities* scheme it could play a very lucrative role. The **Economic Survey 2016-17** suggested[69] the government to create a new institution as a PPP to compete with and complement existing institutions to procure stock and dispose pulses.

7. **PPPP Model:** Experts have suggested public-private-people partnership (PPPP) model, too, for certain sectors in the country. Though, such a model has been in use since 2000-01 itself in the agriculture sector to promote participatory irrigation development - in the Command Area Development Programme of 1974 (renamed as Command Area Development and Watershed Management Programme in 2004) - in which individual financial contributions come from the farmers (around 15 per cent of the total cost) to develop field channels and drains.

   It is believed that in the area of developing, maintaining and protecting local public assets this model could be highly effective. In future, the local bodies - urban as well as rural - may be using this model to develop social and economic infrastructure.

RENEWABLE ENERGY

India's renewable energy potential has been assessed (in the medium-term) at 8,96,602 MW, which includes the potential from *solar* (7,48,990 MW), *wind* (1,00,000 MW), *small hydro* (20,000 MW) and *biomass* (26,800 MW) power.

Apart from grid power requirement, renewable energy sources are also being used for distributed generation, lighting, pumping and motive power-requirement in remote and inaccessible areas. India is graduating from megawatts to gigawatts in the generation of clean renewable energy. By December 2024, India's total renewable energy installed capacity had reached to 209.4, up from 180.8 GW in December 2023, which shows a growth rate of 15.8 per cent, as per the *Economic Survey 2024-25*. The *major steps* taken by the government in recent times to boost the sector are as given below:

1. *National Offshore Wind Energy Policy 2015* to exploit the vast 7600 km coastline for development of offshore wind energy in the Indian Exclusive Economic Zone (EEZ),
2. Inclusion of renewable energy in the *priority sector* and bank loans up to ₹15 crore limit for purposes such as solar-based power generators, biomass-based power generators, windmills, micro-hydel plants and for nonconventional energy-based public utilities such as street lighting systems, and remote village electrification. For individual households this is up to ₹10 lakh per borrower.
3. Investments in renewable energy are on *automatic route,* i.e., automatic approval for up to 74 per cent *foreign equity participation* in a joint venture and 100 per cent FDI as equity is permissible.
4. In order to facilitate renewable power evacuation and reshaping the grid for future requirements, the Green Energy Corridor (GEC) projects have been initiated, which aims at synchronising electricity produced from renewable sources with conventional power stations in the grid.
5. *National Hydrogen Mission* was launched in 2021-22 aimed at making hydrogen (which has high energy density and versatility) to emerge as the *top clean fuel* for the future. A broad-based research development and demonstration programme on hydrogen energy and fuel is supported by the Government. By April 2023, some of world's biggest 'green hydrogen' projects were in pipeline under few private companies.
6. Aimed at reducing carbon footprint of the farm sector, Pradhan Mantri Kisan Urja Suraksha evam Utthaan Mahabhiyan *(PMKUSUM),* launched in 2019-20, aims to provide energy and water security, de-dieselise the farm sector and generate additional income for farmers by producing solar power.

[69] Basically, the *Economic Survey 2016-17*, vol. 1 (New Delhi: Ministry of Finance, GoI), pp. 156 and 170 has supported the advice of the *Committee on Incentivising Pulses Production Through Minimum Support Price (MSP) and Related Policies* headed by Arvind Subramanian, Chief Economic Adviser (report submitted in September, 2016) - the expert committee was set up by the government on account of the price volatility of pulses seen during 2015-16.

7. *Solar Rooftop:* Grid-connected rooftops systems to come up by 2019-20 under the National Solar Mission (NSM).
8. *Solar Parks:* 35 solar parks and ultra-mega solar power projects with an aggregate capacity of 22,000 MW to be set up in the next five years (from 2015-16 to 2022-23).
9. *Solar Projects under the NSM:* In February 2015, the government announced to set up 15,000 MW of grid-connected solar PV power projects under the NSM by 2018-19.
10. *Solar Pumps:* Target of installing of one lakh solar pumps for irrigation and drinking water by 2016.
11. *Solar Cities:* Approval granted for 56 solar city projects under the Development of Solar Cities Programme.
12. *Surya Mitra:* This scheme was launched in May 2015 for creating 50,000 trained personnel within a period of five years (2015-16 to 2019-20).

NET-ZERO EMISSION The goal of net- zero carbon emission depends on two pillars - transition to clean energy and its storage. In this regard, the World Bank report (titled, *Minerals for Climate Action*) has mentioned that this process will be more mineral intensive. Minerals and metals like copper, aluminum, iron, manganese, nickel etc. are critical for developing clean energy sources like solar PV, wind, nuclear while minerals like lithium and graphite are important for energy storage. As per the *Economic Survey 2021-22*, for this to happen India needs to take the following essential policy actions:

- Shift to clean energy should be speedier (as this will determine the extent and mix of investment in renewable energy sources).
- Need of avoiding the risk of being late-comer - developed countries being the frontrunners of net-zero emission plans, there is a risk of price shoot of minerals in future (due to their inelastic supply).
- For effortless energy transition R&D need encouragement - with a focus on development of the technologies which help recycle, reuse and repurpose the minerals.
- Focus should be laid on building storage for intermittent electricity generation from solar PV and wind farms to ensure on-demand energy supply.

LOGISTICS SECTOR

Logistics is the backbone of supply chain (management of flows of goods from the point of origin to the point of consumption). It includes transportation, inventory management, warehousing, materials handling, packaging and integration of information. Largely 'unorganised', the sector has remained 'unexplored' in India.

Logistics costs in India, as per the *Economic Survey 2022-23,* have been in the range of 14-18 per cent of GDP against the global benchmark of 8 per cent. Key dimensions to be addressed to improve logistics for trade include:

- Ensuring efficiency of the clearance process (i.e., speed, simplicity, and predictability of formalities) by border control agencies, including customs;
- Improving the quality of trade and transport-related infrastructure (e.g., ports, railroads, roads, information technology);
- Easing of arranging competitively priced shipments;
- Enhancing the competence and quality of logistics services (e.g., transport operators, customs brokers);
- Providing for tracking and tracing of consignments; and
- Ensuring timeliness of shipments in reaching destinations.

These aspects have been captured by the World Bank in its Logistics Performance Index (LPI). Better logistics help a country cut the cost of trade and get competitive in world exports market.

National Logistics Policy Aimed at bettering logistics, the Government has already taken many efforts -Ude Desh ka Aam Nagrik (UDAN), Bharatmala, Sagarmala, Parvatmala, National Rail Plan, and through 'process reforms' GST, e-Sanchit, Single Window Interface for Trade (SWIFT), Indian Customs Electronic Data Interchange Gateway (ICEGATE), Turant Customs, and others. However, a need was felt to integrate all these efforts by different government agencies and lay an *overarching interdisciplinary, cross-sectoral, and multi-jurisdictional framework* for the sector. To realise this idea, NLP (National Logistics Policy) was launched in September 2022.

The *vision* of the NLP is "to develop a technologically enabled, integrated, cost-efficient, resilient, sustainable and trusted logistics ecosystem in the country for accelerated and inclusive growth." It is aimed at bringing global standards to warehousing, multimodal digital integration, ease of logistics services, human resources, and skill enhancement. The targets for achieving the vision of the NLP are to:

(i) Reduce the cost of logistics to be comparable to global benchmarks by 2030;

(ii) Improve the LPI ranking - attempt is to be among the top 25 countries by 2030 (India ranks 44th out of 167 countries in the *latest LPI-2018* of the World Bank); and

(iii) Create a data-driven decision support mechanism for an efficient logistics ecosystem.

The Logistics Ease Across Different States (LEADS) index has also been initiated by the Government to take the view of logistics performance at the state level.

HOUSING AND URBAN INFRASTRUCTURE

India is witnessing rapid urbanisation. According to the Census 2011, India's urban population is projected to grow to about 60 crores by 2030 (from 37.7 crores). Urbanisation in India has become an important and irreversible process, and it is an important determinant of economic growth and poverty reduction. Though the cities are engines of growth, a rapid pace of urbanisation poses significant challenges to basic infrastructure services such as water supply, sanitation, solid waste and wastewater management. Some recent steps taken by the Government in this regard are as given below:

- **Deendayal Antyodaya Yojana - National Urban Livelihoods Mission** is being run in all the statutory towns to address the 'social and occupational vulnerabilities' of the urban poor. Under the mission, the urban poor are imparted skill training for self- and wage employment and assisted in setting up of self-employment ventures by providing credit at subsidised rates of interest. The Mission also provides for *shelters* for urban homeless and infrastructure for street vendors.
- **PM Street Vendor's Atmanirbhar Nidhi (PM SVANidhi)** as part of the *Atmanirbhar Bharat Abhiyan* for providing micro-credit facility to the street vendors to restart their businesses post COVID-19 lockdowns. This scheme targets to benefit over 50 lakh street vendors who had been vending on or before March 24, 2020, in urban areas including those from surrounding peri-urban/ rural areas.

Under the Scheme, the vendors can avail a working capital loan of up to ₹10,000, which is repayable in monthly installments in the tenure of one year. On timely/early repayment of the loan, an interest subsidy of 7 per cent per annum will be credited to the bank accounts of beneficiaries through Direct Benefit Transfer on a quarterly basis.

Housing Policy

With an increasingly fluid population, India needs a housing policy which suitably enables horizontal or spatial mobility (i.e., mobility within and between cities) and vertical mobility (i.e., to climb the socio-economic ladder) as opportunities arise. Once the Government is aiming at *Housing for All*, concerns of the twin issues - ***rental*** and ***vacant*** houses - need proper deliberations, which was touched by the *Economic Survey 2017-18* for the first time.

Housing is a key policy priority of the Government today. With an increasingly 'fluid' population the housing policy needs to enable horizontal or spatial mobility (i.e., movement within and between cities) and vertical mobility (to climb socio-economic ladder) as opportunities arise. The **Economic Survey 2017-18** highlighted certain factors in this regard when the country was aiming towards an ambitious scheme - *Housing for All*. Two basic issues related to the sector are rental and vacant houses.

Rental Housing Such housing is important for both horizontal and vertical mobility as it allows people to access suitable housing without actually having to buy it. Across the income spectrum, rental housing is an important foothold into a city for new arrivals, until they purchase their own homes. For rural migrants, in particular, whose financial portfolios may already be tied up in land and livestock, it is access to shelter that is more important than investing in their own houses that is subject to local market risk. Nonetheless, the share of rental housing has actually been declining in Indian cities since Independence from 54 per cent in 1961 to 28 per cent in 2011. Though the country has witnessed a decline in the share of rentals, it is not uniform - it has been sharper in the northern states (excluding the mountain states). Rental is more prevalent in urban areas (31 per cent) than the rural (5 per cent), as per the Census 2011 - with more urbanised states having higher percentages of renting.

Vacant Housing Despite the shortage of housing in urban India (more than 18 million households in 2012), there is also a trend increase in vacant houses (11.1 million in 2011 from 6.5 million of 2001). As per the Census 2011 vacant houses constitute around 12 per cent of the share of the total urban housing stock. The number and share of vacant houses for some major cities include Mumbai with the highest number of total vacant houses (0.48 million), followed by Delhi (0.3 million) and Bengaluru (around 0.3 million). In terms of shares of vacant houses to total residential stock, Gurgaon ranks the highest (26 per cent). The phenomenon of high vacancy rates is not fully understood, but unclear property rights, weak contract enforcement and low rental yields may be important factors. The spatial distribution of the new real estate may also be an issue as the vacancy rates generally increase with distance away from the denser urban cores.

Home ownership is encouraged as part of the socio-economic policy in most parts of the world including India. While there is nothing wrong in encouraging home ownership, it needs to be recognised that the rental market is also an important part of the urban eco-system. Housing needs of India are complex, and policies have been mostly focused on building more homes and on home ownership. In recent decades several factors have constrained this market in the country, such as rent control, unclear property rights and difficulties with contract enforcement. India needs a *holistic housing policy* which is capable of resolving the existing constraints to the sector and the issues of rental and vacant housing.

PMAY-U

The Pradhan Mantri Awas Yojana-Urban (PMAY-U) was launched in June 2015 to provide *pucca houses* with basic amenities to all eligible[70] urban poor by 2022, a part of the 'Housing for All' (Pradhan Mantri Awas Yojana). By early 2023, a validated (by states and UTs) demand of 1.45 crore houses were registered. It is one of the *largest* housing schemes of the world covering the whole of urban India.

Urban habitats and cities are the epicentres of economic growth which contribute over 60 per cent of India's GDP. The construction sector accounts for 8.2 per cent of GDP and employs about 12 per cent of the workforce. Therefore, the investment made under PMAY-(U) not only provides pucca houses to the eligible families to achieve the goal of 'Housing for All' but also triggers *multiplier effect* on the overall economy. The scheme is being implemented through following four verticals:

1. *In Situ Slum Development (ISSR)* works using land as a resource with private participation in which the GoI gives a grant of ₹1 lakh per house.
2. *Credit Linked Subsidy Scheme (CLSS)* provides subsidy to the economically weaker section (EWS) and lower income group (LIG) for new house or incremental housing. The EWS and LIG are defined as a household with up to ₹3 lakh annual income and house sizes up to 30 and 60 square metres, respectively. Both of the beneficiaries get an upfront subsidy at the rate of 6.5 per cent for loans up to ₹6 lakhs.
3. *Affordable Housing in Partnership (AHP)* is being run with the public or private sector including para-statal agencies in which a Central assistance of ₹1.5 lakh per EWS house is given (35 per cent constructed houses are reserved for the EWS category).
4. *Beneficiary Led House Construction/Enhancement (BLC)* is a segment which promotes houses for individuals of the EWS category under which a Central assistance of ₹1.5 lakh per beneficiary is given.

National Infrastructure Pipeline

Government has set a target to achieve the GDP of US$ 5 trillion by 2024–25. To achieve this goal India needs to invest about US$ 1.4 trillion (₹100 lakh crores) during 2020–25 in infrastructure – and to further sustain the growth by 2030 another US$ 4.5 trillion. To enable[71] achieve the target of investment in the sector, the Government launched (in December 2019) the project 'National Infrastructure Pipeline' (NIP). The NIP captures the infrastructure vision of the country for the period 2020–25. This is the *first ever* exercise

[70] *Economic Survey 2019-20*, vol. 2 (New Delhi: Ministry of Finance, GoI), pp. 249-51. Press Release of the Ministry of Finance, 31 December, 2019.

[71] *Economic Survey 2019-20*, vol. 2 (New Delhi: Ministry of Finance, GoI), pp. 232-33. Press Release of the Ministry of Finance, December 31, 2019.

undertaken in the country. Designed on PPP mode this has the following main features:

- The sectoral shares are – on energy (24 per cent), roads (19 per cent), urban infra (16 per cent) and railways (13 per cent).
- Funding will be shared equally by Centre and States (39 per cent each) while 22 per cent is supposed to come from the private sector (Government expects the private participation to increase to 30 per cent by 2025).

Around 42 per cent of the projects under it were supposed to be launched by *early 2020*, while deliberations on the rest of the projects were in the process. The *Task Force* which advised for the launch of the NIP has also recommended for required changes by Centre and States in several key areas such as follows:

1. Developing a robust bond market for infrastructure companies,
2. Speedy resolution of infrastructure disputes,
3. Optimal risk sharing through better and balanced PPP contracts and
4. Sanctity and enforceability of contracts.

The investment target under the NIP looks tough given the past experience of investment carried out in infrastructure, which has been about US$ 1.1 trillion during the whole decade of 2007–18. However, the period in reference is considered the toughest time for infrastructure projects in the country when they faced hurdles such as profit hit with global slowdown, delays in project clearance, delays in land acquisition and lack of funding.

Government hopes that an assemblage of well-prepared projects would be able to attract investment from central and state governments, ULBs, banks and FIs, private equity funds, and private investors, both local and foreign.

PM GATI SHAKTI

The PM Gati Shakti (Prime Minister Gati Shakti - National Master Plan for Multi-modal Connectivity) was launched by the Government in October 2021 for infrastructure sector with the aim of boosting multimodal connectivity and cutting the cost of logistics in the country. This is a *digital platform* that connects 16 ministries (such as roads, railways, shipping, aviation, petroleum and gas, power, telecom, aviation etc.) for ensuring a holistic planning and execution of infrastructure projects. The multi-modal connectivity will provide integrated and seamless connectivity for movement of people, goods and services from one mode of transport to another. It will facilitate the last mile connectivity of infrastructure and also reduce travel time for people. As per studies, logistic cost in India is around 14 per cent of GDP as against about 8 of GDP in developed economies. High logistics costs impact cost structures and make the economy get competitive in the global market. As per the Government, the Gati Shakti is based on the following ***six pillars***:

(i) *Comprehensiveness:* To include all the existing and planned initiatives of various ministries and departments with one centralised portal - with visibility of all activities providing critical data.

(ii) *Prioritisation:* Different departments will be able to prioritise their projects through cross-sectoral interactions.

(iii) *Optimisation:* Facilitation in identification of critical gaps - saving time and cost.

(iv) *Synchronisation:* To help in synchronizing the activities of each department, as well as of different layers of governance, in a holistic manner by ensuring coordination of work between them. [Traditionally, individual ministries and departments often work in silos in the absence of proper coordination in planning and implementation of the project resulting in delays.]

(v) *Analytical:* The entire data to be made available at one place with GIS (geographic information system) based spatial planning and analytical tools having more than 200 layers (of geospatial data), enabling better visibility to the executing agency.

(vi) *Dynamic:* To help visualise, review and monitor the progress of cross-sectoral projects, through the satellite imagery on real time basis.

The Gati Shakti portal would help reduce the human intervention required as ministries will be in constant touch, and projects will be reviewed by the project monitoring group in real time–we may have a look at the Plan through some examples:

- We may see one tunnel being made for roads and another for railways; however, such a platform would allow the ministries to coordinate, and create one large tunnel which may serve both purposes, saving the taxpayer thousands of crores.
- Another similar example has been cited by the director of the BiSAG-N (which has built the portal) in which path to build a railway line was changed slightly following a review of the data available on the portal - saving time and resource for a forest clearance that may have been required otherwise.
- The portal will also highlight all the clearances any new project would need, based on its location - and allow stakeholders to apply for these clearances from the relevant authority directly on the portal. As per the Commerce Ministry, if a railway line is being built, the Ministry of Road Transport may immediately give clearance for an overpass, and the Power Ministry can begin projects to ensure that trains can immediately have access to power on completion of the tracks.

RECENT CHALLENGES

The infrastructure sector has been faced with some long-standing challenges in the country. In the period of reforms, the Government aimed to involve the synergy of the private sector as well. The PPP model was making ground year after year. But due to certain internal and external factors the sector almost got derailed by late 2013-14. As per various Government documents these factors are as given below:

1. **Project delays** which cause high-cost overruns. Though the situation has improved after the new Government took control but the delayed projects were still very high at 419 by February 2025.
2. **Delays in land acquisition.** With the Land Act of 2015 being withdrawn and an effective 'land pooling' policy put in place things have started improving in this regard. Some states have surplus land in the pooling arrangement (such as Andhra Pradesh); however, the cost of land has increased over 3.5 times till February 2025.
3. **Scarcity of funds** due to longer gestation period. With the help of Infrastructure Investment Trusts, 5/25 Refinancing scheme, debt restructuring things improved but not much. Since late 2017-18, the Government has been pursuing an insolvency procedure (under the newly enforced Bankruptcy and Insolvency Act) and things are moving forward.
4. **Weaknesses of the existing PPP models** also took a heavy toll, though it has improved after the new HAM (Hybrid Annuity Model) was launched. The model was put in place for only the road sector but was also notified for other infra sectors by late 2017.
5. **Slowdown** in the economy kick-started by the global financial crisis of 2008 together with a state of 'policy paralysis' prevailing in the domestic economy since 2010 onwards. After the new Government took control, the state of policy paralysis is no longer prevalent, but there are several complex legacy factors which need to be addressed in an effective way. The geo-economic fragmentation after the COVID-19 pandemic and ongoing Russia-Ukraine crisis and the Middle East tensions have taken their tolls on the economic performance.
6. A typical **'twin balance sheet crises'** taking grip over the economy (declared so by the *Economic Survey)* by late 2016-17. Due to this while on one hand the public sector banks are unfit to promote lending (which have been the lead lenders to the sector) hit with high non-performing assets (NPAs), on the other hand big private corporates are not eligible to borrow (due to high losses) and invest in the economy. The situation started improving after the government took certain targeted initiatives such as–enforcement of the Insolvency and Bankruptcy Code (IBC) in 2016; setting up of the National Asset Reconstruction Company Limited (NARCL); and capitalisation of the public sector banks.

WAY FORWARD

To maintain growth momentum in a fast-moving world, India needs to develop its industry and infrastructure. The scope[72] for *Industry 4.0* (4th Industrial Revolution) and *Next Generation* infrastructure is enormous and an opportunity which India cannot afford to miss. Industry 4.0 encompasses automation, whereas next generation infrastructure brings physical infrastructure and technology such as internet of things (IoT) and automation together to maximise the efficiency of physical infrastructure. Together with timely investment, there is a need for suitable policy interventions to enable India to tap the benefits of these emerging ideas. For the upcoming year ***2026–27***, there are many factors[73] which give positive and negative indications for the sector:

(i) On the positive side we can include – easing input cost as international commodity prices have started showing downturn; rising capacity utilisation in manufacturing sector boosted by the PLI scheme; prospects of higher investment by companies as credit growth is rising, and beginning of interest rate cut by the RBI after the headline inflation started cooling by late 2024.

(ii) On the negative side we can include – slowing exports caused by global slowdown; chances of disruptions in supply chain due to international factors (volatility in global commodity prices, increased post-COVID-19 geo-economic fragmentation, geopolitical issues arising from the long-drawn Russia-Ukraine conflict and tensions in the Middle East, increasing protectionism across the world kick-started by the USA by late 2024, etc.); normalcy in China can increase demand of commodity and reverse the recent decline in commodity prices.

In spite of such open questions, industrial output in India should continue to grow steadily based on resilient domestic demand – backed by foreign funds flows (well above pre-pandemic levels), driven by structural reforms, and measures improving the ease of doing business.

---

72 *Economic Survey 2019-20*, vol. 2 (New Delhi: Ministry of Finance, GoI, January 2020), p. 251.

73 *Economic Survey 2025-26* (New Delhi: Ministry of Finance, GoI, January 2026); *Economic Survey 2024-25* (New Delhi: Ministry of Finance, GoI, January 25), pp. 163-218; *Economic Survey 2023-24* (New Delhi: Ministry of Finance, GoI, January 24), pp. 347-373 & pp. 405-445; *The Indian Economy: A Review* (New Delhi: Ministry of Finance, GoI, January 24); *Economic Survey 2022-23* (New Delhi: Ministry of Finance, GoI, January 2023), p. 291.

PREVIOUS YEARS' QUESTIONS

Prelims

1. Consider the following statements: (2025)

(i) India has joined the Minerals Security Partnership as a member.

(ii) India is a resource-rich country in all the 30 critical minerals that it has identified.

(iii) The Parliament in 2023 has amended the Mines and Minerals (Development and Regulation) Act, 1957, empowering the Central Government to exclusively auction mining leases and composite licences for certain critical minerals.

Which of the statements given above are correct?

(a) (i) and (ii) only
(b) (ii) and (iii) only
(c) (i) and (iii) only
(d) (i), (ii), and (iii)

2. Consider the following statements: (2025)

(i) Indian Railways has prepared a national rail plan (NRP) to create a 'future-ready' railway system by 2028.

(ii) The 'Kavach' is an automatic train protection system developed in collaboration with Germany.

(iii) 'Kavach' system consists of RFID tags fitted on the track in the station section.

Which of the statements given above are ***not*** correct?

(a) (i) and (ii) only **(b)** (ii) and (iii) only
(c) (i) and (iii) only **(d)** (i), (ii), and (iii)

3. With reference to India, consider the following pairs: (2025)

Organisation	Union Ministry
(i) The National Automotive Board:	Ministry of Commerce and Industry
(ii) The Coir Board:	Ministry of Heavy Industries
(iii) The National Centre for Trade Information:	Ministry of Micro, Small and Medium Enterprises

How many of the above pairs are correctly matched?

(a) Only (i) **(b)** Only (ii)
(c) All three **(d)** None

4. Consider the following activities: (2025)

(i) Production of crude oil
(ii) Refining, storage and distribution of petroleum
(iii) Marketing and sale of petroleum products
(iv) Production of natural gas

How many of the above activities are regulated by the petroleum and natural gas regulatory board in our country?

(a) Only (i) **(b)** Only (ii)
(c) Only (iii) **(d)** All four

5. Consider the following pairs: (2025)

Country	Resource-rich in
(i) Botswana	Diamond
(ii) Chile	Lithium
(iii) Indonesia	Nickel

In how many of the above rows is the given information correctly matched?

(a) Only (i) **(b)** Only (ii)
(c) All the three **(d)** None

6. Consider the following airports: (2024)

(i) Donyi Polo Airport
(ii) Kushinagar International Airport
(iii) Vijayawada International Airport

In the recent past, which of the above have been constructed as Greenfield projects?

(a) (i) and (ii) only **(b)** (ii) and (iii) only
(c) (i) and (iii) only **(d)** (i), (ii) and (iii)

Answers: 1. (c) 2. (a) 3. (d) 4. (b) 5. (c) 6. (a)

Explanation

1. (c): *Statement-(i) is correct* (the Minerals Security Partnership is a U.S.-led initiative aimed at strengthening and diversifying global 'critical mineral' supply chains. India became its 14th member in June 2023). *Statement-(ii) is incorrect* (India is not resource-rich in many critical minerals). *Statement-(iii) is correct* [in 2023, the Indian Parliament amended the Mines and Minerals (Development and Regulation) Act, 1957, to give the Central Government exclusive powers to auction mining leases and composite licences for 24 critical minerals].

2. (a): Statement-(i) is incorrect The NRP aims to create a 'future-ready' railway system by 2030 and not 2028 (thus, Statement-(i) is incorrect). There is no German collaboration in the development of the Automatic Train Protection (thus, *Statement-(ii)* is incorrect), which uses RFID (Radio Frequency Identification) tags placed on the railway tracks, especially in station sections (thus, *Statement - (iii)* is correct).

3. (d): *Pair (i) is incorrect* (the National Automotive Board functions under the Ministry of Heavy Industries). *Pair (ii) is incorrect* (the Coir Board comes under the Ministry of Micro, Small & Medium Enterprises). *Pair (iii) is incorrect* (the National Centre for Trade Information has been set up by the Ministry of Commerce and Industry).

4. (b): The PNGRB (Petroleum and Natural Gas Regulatory Board) was constituted under the Petroleum and Natural Gas Regulatory Board Act, 2006. Only options (ii) and (iii) are correct (as per the Act, the board has been mandated to regulate the refining, processing, storage, transportation, distribution, marketing and sale of petroleum, petroleum products and natural gas 'excluding' production of crude oil and natural gas).

5. (c): *Pair (i) is correct* (Botswana is one of the world's largest producers of diamonds by value).

Pair (ii) is correct (Chile forms part of the 'Lithium Triangle' along with Argentina and Bolivia, and it has some of the largest lithium reserves in the world, primarily extracted from salt flats). *Pair (iii) is correct* (Indonesia is the world's largest producer of nickel).

6. (a): Except the Vijayawada International Airport rest are greenfield projects.

Mains

1. Discuss the rationale of the Production Linked Incentive (PLI) scheme. What are its achievements? In what ways can the functioning and outcomes of the scheme be improved? (2025)
2. What is the need for expanding the regional air connectivity in India? In this context, discuss the government's UDAN Scheme and its achievements. (2024)
3. Why is Public Private Partnership (PPP) required in infrastructural projects? Examine the role of PPP model in the redevelopment of Railway Stations in India. (2022)
4. Do you think India will meet 50 per cent of its energy needs from renewable energy by 2030? Justify your answer. How will the shift of subsidies from fossil fuels to renewables help achieve the above objective? Explain. (2022)
5. "Investment in infrastructure is essential for more rapid and inclusive economic growth." Discuss in the light of India's experience. (2021)

SAMPLE OBJECTIVE QUESTIONS

1. Consider the following statements related to government's industrial policy:
   - **(i)** Till public sector enterprises remain under governments' control, the process of liberalisation remains incomplete.
   - **(ii)** Automatic route of foreign investment is a structural reform measure.
   - **(iii)** Disinvestment erodes governments' commitment to public welfare.

   Which of the statements given above are correct?

   Code:

   (a) Only one **(b)** Only two
   (c) All three **(d)** None of these
2. Consider the following statements related to the policy of 'comprehensive management of public assets':
   - **(i)** Under it, asset-assessment of the central public enterprises is being pursued on the lines of the private sector.
   - **(ii)** The policy weakens the impact of social welfare and is considered neo-liberal in nature.
   - **(iii)** Governments' expenditures on social welfare have increased since this policy was initiated.

   Which of the statements given above are correct?

   Code:

   (a) Only one
   (b) Only two
   (c) All three
   (d) None of these
3. India's policy regarding inflows of foreign investment has become more liberal over the last decade. Consider the statements given below in this regard:
   - **(i)** 100 per cent foreign direct investment (FDI) is permitted under automatic route in insurance intermediaries.
   - **(ii)** 100 per cent FDI is allowed in marketing of processed foods manufactured in the country.
   - **(iii)** Defence sector is open for 100 per cent FDI under non-automatic route.

Which of the statements given above are correct?

Code:

(a) Only one (b) Only two
(c) All three (d) None of these

4. Consider the statements given below related to the moves of privatisation in the country:

(i) A public sector enterprise may not be disinvested altogether.
(ii) Strategic disinvestment may result in de-nationalisation.
(iii) The recent central de-licensing of alcohol and alcoholic products was a move in this direction.

Which of the statements given above are correct?

Code:

(a) Only one (b) Only two
(c) All three (d) None of these

5. Consider the following statements related to the current government policy for the public sector enterprises (PSEs):

(i) PSEs will have a bare minimum presence in the financial sector.
(ii) The non-strategic PSEs will be either privatised or closed down.
(iii) Some strategic PSEs might be privatised or closed down.

How many of the above statements are correct?

(a) Only one (b) Only two
(c) All three (d) None of these

6. Consider the following statements related to the disinvestment proceeds in the country:

(i) They may be used for financing social sector programmes.
(ii) Government may use them to develop and maintain infrastructure projects.
(iii) The fund may be used for financing revenue deficits.

How many of the above statements are correct?

(a) Only one (b) Only two
(c) All three (d) None of these

7. Consider the following statements related to the current asset monetisation policy of the Government:

(i) The idle or under-used public assets are being sold off to private sector under it.
(ii) This is presently being enforced only for highways.
(iii) Ownership of the public assets under it is transferred to private sector for only a fixed period of time running between 15 to 20 years.

How many of the above statements are correct?

(a) Only one (b) Only two
(c) All three (d) None of these

8. Consider the following statements related to India's index of industrial production (IIP):

(i) Basic sector accounts for over 40 per cent weight in it.
(ii) The combined weight of fertilisers and cement is lower than the crude oil in it.
(iii) Steel carries the third largest weight in core sector.

How many of the above statements are correct?

(a) Only one (b) Only two
(c) All three (d) None of these

9. Consider the following statements related to the micro, small and medium enterprises (MSMEs) sector in the country:

(i) Besides contributing over one third of the GDP, they employ around 10 crore people.
(ii) Business loans offered to them on Government guarantee is a major bad debt concern.
(iii) This sector is the birth place of most of the start-ups.

How many of the above statements are correct?

(a) Only one (b) Only two
(c) All three (d) None of these

10. Consider the following statements related to the power sector of the country:

(i) The aggregate technical and commercial (AT&C) losses occur mainly due to lack of institutional capabilities.
(ii) States are being incentivised to enhance the institutional capabilities of their distribution companies (Discoms).
(iii) Financial turnaround of the state Discoms is main objective of power sector reforms.

How many of the above statements are correct?
(a) Only one
(b) Only two
(c) All three
(d) None of these

Answers: 1. (a) 2. (b) 3. (c) 4. (b) 5. (c) 6. (c) 7. (a) 8. (c) 9. (b) 10. (b)

SAMPLE SUBJECTIVE QUESTIONS

1. 'The New Industrial Policy, 1991 is considered more a process than a policy.' Explain.
2. Examine the rationale behind classification of the public sector enterprises into strategic and non-strategic sectors with reference to the current disinvestment policy.
3. Examine and justify the disinvestment proceeds use policy of the country. Give suitable illustration to support your views.
4. Give your views on the Government policy of the comprehensive management of public assets. Do you think it erodes the idea of public welfare?
5. Write a note on the official ideology related to infrastructure development in the country. Do you think, it is becoming exclusive for those who can pay user charges?
6. 'The Government envisions digital infrastructure as a core utility to every citizen.' Elucidate.

SAMPLE MODEL ANSWER

1. 'New Industrial Policy- 1991 is considered more a process than a policy.' Examine.

Ans. At the first instance, the New Industrial Policy-1991 (NIP) looks like the industrial policies of the past–as it also contains announcements of certain policy changes. But it was new in the sense that it initiated the very process of economic reforms in the country. There are many reasons due to which it is considered more a process than a policy:

- Most of the announcements of the policy were not like 'one-off' changes in the policies but rather the beginning of a process which continues even today–it means this was not a static policy but very dynamic in nature.
- The changes announced in it were to be completed with the help of three simultaneous processes–liberalisation, privatisation, and globalisation–which are still underway.
- Even the reforms which were initiated by this policy were modified with the help of three different generations of reforms in the coming times–which are being fine-tuned today with the help of the transformative reforms.
- The processes of macroeconomic stabilisation and structural reforms initiated by it are still underway.
- Most of the policy announcements of the NIP were embedded with the seeds of reforms. The very design of this policy shows that its success itself depends on the success of the reform process–in a way, the NIP and the reforms reinforce each other.

CHAPTER 11

Services Sector

Developing economies must scale up investment in infrastructure and digitally skilled labour force to minimise job losses in services sector and enjoy the complementarity benefits from artificial intelligence.*

Gen-AI: Artificial Intelligence and the Future of Work, Cazzaniga et al., IMF Staff Discussion Note SDN2024/001 (Washington DC: International Monetary Fund, USA, 2024) quoted by the *Indian Economy: A Review* (New Delhi: Ministry of Finance, GoI), p. 9.

To watch the Author's videos on the significance of the Chapter, scan the QR Code given here

Exam Essentials...

- Services Performance
- Space

Note to the Reader...

This chapter should be read as the bedrock of the long-drawn debate in India as why the agriculture sector has not remained remunerative. Experts have been citing the absence of shift of labour force from the agriculture sector to either the industry or services sector. As artificial intelligence is restructuring the very manufacturing sector via services sector, a new hope is emerging to attract surplus population employed in the agriculture sector to the sectors through requisite kind of skills.

In This Chapter...

- Introduction
- Global Services and India
- Tourism and Hotel Industry
- Real Estate
- IT Services, Telecom and GCC
- Ports and Waterways
- E-Commerce
- Digital Financial Services
- Dematerialisation of Documents
- Manufacturing vs Services
- Way Forward

INTRODUCTION

India's services sector has not only outperformed other sectors of the Indian economy but has also played an important role in India's integration with world trade and capital markets. India's liberalisation of services has been a challenging process in several sub-sectors, but clearly those services where integration through trade and foreign direct investment (FDI) has gone further are also the ones that have exhibited more rapid growth along with positive spill overs on the rest of the economy.

There is, however, a concern[1] about the *sustainability* of a services-led growth process which largely stems from exports of skill-based services. The prevailing view is that for services growth to be sustained, the sector cannot remain dependent on external demand. It must also be driven by internal demand. More broad-based growth within the services is required to ensure balanced, equitable and employment-oriented growth, with backward and forward linkages to the rest of the economy. In this regard further infrastructural and regulatory reforms and FDI liberalisation in services can help diversify the sources of growth within India's services sector and provide the required momentum.

In recent years, there has been a debate in the country regarding the selection of the sector which can lead the growth process in the country. This debate originated from the fact that the services sector contributed over 62 per cent in GDP during the decade 2001-12. But the debate was somewhat solved by the *Economic Survey 2014-15* in favour of the *manufacturing sector.* However, the idea about the services sector has gone for a change in recent times– the sector is boosting growth even in the countries where there is a manufacturing slowdown due to moderation in merchandise trade buoyancy.[2] The increasing ***'servicification'*** of manufacturing, increasing utilisation of services in manufacturing production and post-production value addition has enhanced faith in the sector in propelling growth.[3]

[1] R. Chanda, 'Services-led Growth', in *The New Oxford Companion to Economics in India*, vol. II, eds. K. Basu and A. Maertens (New Delhi: Oxford University Press, 2012), pp. 624-32.

[2] *Economic Survey 2024-25* (New Delhi: Ministry of Finance, GoI, January 2025), p. 243.

[3] S. Pant & D. Chakraborty, *Is service orientation benefitting manufacturing exports from low-middle income countries? Firm-level empirical evidence from WBES data, Working Paper* (New Delhi: Indian Institute of Foreign Trade, Ministry of Commerce and Industry, 2024) quoted by the *Economic Survey 2024-25* (New Delhi: Ministry of Finance, GoI, January 2025), p. 243.

GLOBAL SERVICES AND INDIA

As per the *Economic Survey 2025-26 & 2024-25*, services value added accounts for about 62 per cent of the global GDP (World Bank Indicators), working as the growth engine for middle-income countries like China, Thailand, and India in the last decade. Major highlights[4] of global services and India's position in it by the end of 2024 were as summarised below:

- *Global Services PMI Business Activity Index* rose to a four- month high of 53.8 in December 2024. This signals expansion for the 23rd consecutive month. The growth of new order intakes and employment also strengthened, while business sentiment edged higher. However, global supply chains continue to face significant disruptions due to geo-political uncertainty, i.e., the rise of protectionism, wars, and climate-related challenges which pose a risk to the global services landscape.
- *India's share* in global services exports has been steadily rising for the last two decades which has helped compensate the impact of oscillation in the share of merchandise exports in global merchandise exports to some extent. In *2023*, the United States led global services exports with a dominant 13 per cent share, followed by the United Kingdom with 7.4 per cent, Germany with 5.5 per cent and Ireland, China, and France, each accounting for approximately 5 per cent. India ranks 7th globally, representing a 4.3 per cent share in the global services export.

TOURISM AND HOTEL INDUSTRY

The post-pandemic scenario of global tourism is gradually converging to the pre-pandemic one. As per the *World Tourism Barometer* of the United Nations World Tourism Organisation (November 2024), international tourism showed robust performance in January-September 2025, with international tourist arrivals reaching 71 per cent of the pre-pandemic level. The latest situation of the sector in the country is as given below:

- Its contribution to the GDP of the economy regained the pre-pandemic level of 5 per cent in 2022-23 and created 7.6 crore jobs in the year.

[4] *Economic Survey 2025-26* (New Delhi: Ministry of Finance, GoI, January 2026), pp. 260-267 & *Economic Survey 2024-25* (New Delhi: Ministry of Finance, GoI, January 2025), p. 219-20.

Services Performance

Acknowledged as the *Old War Horse* by the Economic Survey 2024–25, the major features[5] have been as given below:

Scan this QR Code to watch a author's video lecture that simplifies this topic

Contribution in Economy Its contribution in the *Gross Value Added (GVA)* in the economy has been *the steadiest*— which increased from 50.6 per cent in 2013–14 to 55 per cent in 2024–25. Its growth rate has been above 6 per cent in each year in the last decade (except for 2020–21 affected by the COVID-19 pandemic)— the average services growth rate before the pre-pandemic year was 8 per cent which stood at 8.3 per cent between 2022–23 and 2024–25. The sector also provides *employment* to approximately 30 per cent of the workforce. Services also contribute indirectly to the GDP through the 'servicification' of manufacturing (i.e., increasing utilisation of services in manufacturing production and post-production value addition).

HSBC's India Services PMI remained in the expansionary zone for continuous 41 months since August 2021. The index remained above the 60 mark for the first five months of 2024–25. The recent data indicates demand buoyancy continued to drive new business inflows higher, which, in turn, supported output growth and prompted firms to recruit additional workers.

Trade in Services: India remained amongst the top five major countries in terms of growth in services exports in 2024–25 (April–November), which accelerated to 12.8 per cent over 5.7 per cent of the previous year. Computer services and business services exports account for around 70 per cent of the services exports. Services imports during the period grew by 13.9 per cent in 2024–25 in comparison to 2.9 per cent in the previous year.

- India is ranked *10th* out of the top 45 countries in the world in the Medical Tourism Index-2023 (of the Medical Tourism Association). Medical Value Tourism (MVT) was expected to grow to US$ 14 billion by 2023, as per the NITI Aayog - helped by several favourable factors such as the presence of world-class hospitals and skilled medical professionals, superior quality healthcare, lower treatment costs, credibility in alternative systems of medicine, and increased global demand for wellness services like *Yoga* and *meditation.*
- International tourist arrivals (ITAs) in India have rebounded to pre-pandemic level in 2023. The share of India's ITAs in World ITAs stands at 1.45 per cent in 2023.

Aimed at making India an attractive destination for *specialised tourism,* the Government has taken several steps such as - the AYUSH Visa for medial tourists, the launch of the National Strategy for Sustainable Tourism & Responsible Traveller Campaign, the introduction of the *Swadesh Darshan 2.0* scheme, and *Heal in India.* The G20 presidency presented a unique opportunity to promote India as a major tourism destination.

REAL ESTATE

The COVID-19 pandemic brought disruption for every other sector including the real estate too - crippled by project delays, deferment of big-ticket purchases, stagnation of property prices, and scarce funding for developers. Symptoms of recovery were visible by the late 2022, and by December 2024, the sector had performed in the following ways:

- India's real estate market witnessed robust performance under office demand as well as residential sales driven by economic stability and positive market sentiment during 2024-25 (April-December).
- The demand for real estate is increasing not only in tier 1 and tier 2 cities but across the country due to the expansion of metro networks, enhancement to road networks, and improvements in connectivity.

The residential real estate market scaled an 11-year high in sales volume in the first six months of 2024. Housing demand in India is expected to touch 93 million units by 2036.

IT SERVICES, TELECOM AND GCC

Major features related to the performance of the Indian Information Technology enabled Services

[5] *Economic Survey 2024-25* (New Delhi: Ministry of Finance, GoI, January 2025), pp. 221-243.

(ITeS), telecommunication, and Global Capability Centres (GCCs) industries during 2024-25 (April-December) were as given below:

- **ITeS** has a leading position globally and has been a significant contributor to the growth of exports with an estimated revenues of US$ 254 billion, marking a 3.8 per cent year-on-year growth in 2024-25 (excluding e-commerce). Tech exports reached nearly US$ 200 billion, reflecting a growth of 3.3 per cent, while the domestic market is expected to expand by 5.9 per cent, crossing US$ 54 billion in 2024-25.
- **Global Capability Centres (GCCs)** are emerging as *strategic hubs* reshaping the Indian corporate landscape while influencing global business dynamics. The number of GCCs in India has grown from approximately 1430 in 2018-19 to over 1700 in 2024-25, which employ nearly 1.9 million professionals. India has established itself as a prominent player in leveraging its vast talent pool, which accounts for 28 per cent of the global *STEM* (science, technology, engineering, mathematics) workforce and 23 per cent of global software engineering talent.
- **Telecom** sector is expanding with the ***smart phone boom,*** surging data consumption, and the advent of technologies like 5G. India stands as the second largest telecommunications market, with over 1.18 billion telephone subscribers, an overall tele density of 84 per cent, and 941 million broadband users by October, 2024. The country also leads in mobile data consumption per subscriber and offers the world's most affordable data rates. The average monthly wireless data usage per user in 2023-24 grew to 19.3 GB (up from 12.1 GB in 2020-21).

Major reforms initiated by the Government to boost the sectors have been as given below:

(i) Abolition of the 'angel tax' (imposed like an income tax on the investments made in startups),
(ii) Abolition of 2 per cent equalisation levy (see *Chapter 18* on tax for details),
(iii) Reduction in tax deducted at source (TDS) on payment made by e-commerce operators, and
(iv) Relief from GST on data centre exports.

PORTS AND WATERWAYS

The sea has been the source of opportunity and seashores have acted as the gateways to prosperity for India, for ages. The development of ports is crucial for the economy, given that much of the international trade is handled through ports – around 90 per cent by volume and 79.9 per cent by value. Major developments and performance of the sector by December 2024 were as given below:

- The major ports increased their cargo movement to 622 MT upto December 2024, in line with the annual target of 870 MT (up from 819 MT of the previous year).
- To enhance the efficiency of the major ports, the government is focusing on improving port governance, addressing low-capacity utilisation, modernising berths with techno-efficient loading/unloading equipment, and creating new channels for port connectivity.
- For streamlining the major port compliances and for reducing the Turn Around Time (TAT) for vessels, many measures have been taken at these ports towards the digitisation of key EXIM processes.
  (a) Electronic Invoice (e-Invoice),
  (b) Electronic Payment (e-Payment) and Electronic Delivery Order (e-DO) for the physical release of cargo, generation of electronic Bill of Lading (e-BL) and Letter of Credit (LC).
  (c) Radio Frequency Identification Device (RFID) solution implemented to enable seamless movement of traffic across port gates, besides substantial reductions in documentation checks.
  (d) *Portal-Marine* is being developed which will act as a Unified Digital Platform for all maritime stakeholders.

Inland Waterways Inland water transport holds great untapped potential as a means for the transportation of goods and passengers:

- India has a large endowment of rivers, canals, and other waterways - the total navigable length being around 14,850 kilometre.
- The Government has declared 106 new waterways as the National Waterways (NWs), taking their total number to 111.
- As of October 2024, the country has 26 operational waterways of more than 4,800 km. The government is also putting efforts into promoting river cruise tourism on national waterways.

To make inland waterways user-friendly, quicker, cost-effective, seamless with uniform application of rules and regulations, the Government has enforced the new Inland Vessels Act 2021 (which replaced the over 100-year-old Inland Vessels Act, 1917).

E-COMMERCE

The E-Commerce sector grew fastly, witnessing a sharp increase in penetration in the aftermath of the pandemic. Lockdowns and mobility restrictions disrupted consumer behaviour which strengthened online shopping. The major facts related to the sector are as given below:

- As per the *Retail and E-commerce Trends Report 2022* released by Unicommerce and Wazir Advisors, overall e-commerce order volume witnessed a growth of 69.4 per cent in 2021-22, driven mainly by consumers from tier-II and tier-III cities in the last two years.
- The MSMEs who opted for e-commerce and e-procurement, too, were able to increase their revenues and margins, as per a recent study (September 2022) of the IIFT (Indian Institute of Foreign Trade).
- The *GeM* (Government e-Marketplace) also has witnessed tremendous growth catching up with the giants in the sector like Amazon and Flipkart - attaining an annual procurement of ₹2 lakh crore within 2024-25 (a 140 per cent growth over the previous year). The Government took a host of steps to onboard products of Self Help Groups (SHGs), tribal communities, artisans, weavers, and MSMEs (54 per cent of the total business on GeM came through the MSME during 2024-25).
- The recent initiative of the launch of *ONDC* (Open Network for Digital Commerce) is also playing a significant role in democratising digital payments, enabling interoperability, and bringing down transaction costs. *ONDC* provides better market access to sellers and helps bring the country's remotest corners into the e-Commerce framework by empowering them with digitisation.

According to the latest report, *How India Shops Online 2022* (by Bain & Company), the emerging categories such as - fashion, grocery, general merchandise - would support e-commerce growth in India and would capture nearly *two-thirds* of the Indian e-commerce market by 2027. As per the *Global Payments Report* (by Worldpay FIS), India's e-commerce market is projected to post impressive gains and grow at 18 per cent annually through 2025. The Government's push to boost the digital economy, growing internet penetration, rise in smartphone adoption, innovation in mobile technologies, and increased adoption of digital payments further accelerated the adoption and growth of e-commerce.

DIGITAL FINANCIAL SERVICES

Enabled by emerging technologies, digital financial services are accelerating financial inclusion, democratising access, and spurring the personalisation of products. With a strong foundation provided by the *Jan Dhan-Aadhaar-Mobile* (JAM) trinity, UPI, and other regulatory frameworks, the pandemic has aided acceleration in digital adoption and provided a fillip to digital financial services solutions by banks, NBFCs, insurers as well as FinTechs.

However, digital financial solutions accelerated across the world, and India took the lead with the fintech adoption rate of 87 per cent, substantially higher than the global average of 64 per cent.

- In the last few years, the neobanks have expanded with a faster pace, spurred by the need for 'on-demand' and 'easier-to-access' financial solutions by young and increasingly digitally savvy customers (see *Chapter 12* for more).
- The sector has been boosted by the government initiative of the Digital Banking Units (as proposed by the *Union Budget 2022-23*), which aims to take banking solutions to every nook and corner of the country.
- The introduction of CBDC (Central Bank Digital currency) will also significantly boost digital financial services (the currency has already been piloted by RBI in wholesale and retail spaces by late 2022 - see *Chapter 13* for more).

DEMATERIALISATION OF DOCUMENTS

The government initiative to digitalise documents has also played a pivotal role in giving further impetus to digital financial services. Dematerialisation of documents is being visualised as the next wave of digitisation with the launching of the Digital Document Execution (DDE) platform[6] in 2020-21. The core principle of the

[6] The *DDE* was introduced by the National e-Governance Services Limited (NeSL), which is an information utility registered with and regulated by the Insolvency and Bankruptcy Board of India (IBBI) under the IBC, 2016.

platform is to digitise all the steps of the document/agreement execution journey, which include:

- Digital submission of information related to document,
- Flexibility to accommodate document format,
- Consent-based process,
- Digital payment of stamp duty,
- Identity verification using electronic signatures, and
- Secure storage, transmission, and retrieval of document

By eliminating the need for the physical presence of the executants and the manual process, the platform brings in *several benefits,* such as:

- a secure system,
- authorised access,
- lower execution time and cost,
- easy accessibility,
- bulk processing,
- fraud prevention,
- legal robustness, and
- evidentiary value.

While the use of the DDE began for financial documents, the platform shall also enable the digital execution of other documents in coming times. This secure, paperless, hassle-free contracting will have a significant positive impact on the *ease of doing business* in the country.

SPACE

The space programme of India has grown exponentially since its modest beginnings five decades ago, moving from providing simple mapping services in the 1960s to many more uses currently. This includes design and development of a series of launch vehicles and related technologies, satellites and related technologies for earth observation, telecom and broadband, navigation, meteorology and space science, R&D in space sciences, and most recently, planetary exploration. The position[7] of the country's space sector is as given below:

- India spent about US$ 2.0 billion on space programmes in 2022–23. However, India's government space expenditure still lags behind that of the major players in the space sector, such as the ***United States***, which spent about 11 times more than India in the space sector in 2022–23. ***China***, which has become a key player in the space sector in the recent years, also spent about six times more than India in 2022.
- India has launched around 5–7 satellites per year in the recent years with no failures, barring one in 2017. On the other hand, Russia, the United States and China dominate the satellite launching services with 21, 28 and 39 satellites, respectively, in 2022.

There have been *three key areas* of focus for India's space programme, namely:

1. Satellite communication, with INSAT/GSAT system as the backbone to address the needs for telecommunication, broadcasting and satellite-based broadband infrastructure in the country.
2. Earth observation and using space-based information for weather forecasting, disaster management, national resource mapping and governance.
3. Satellite-aided navigation including *GAGAN* and *NavIC*.

In terms of player and applications, the space activity in the world is undergoing tremendous changes. This has been marked by a shift in engagement of space activities – from government agencies pursuing ***national needs*** and space exploration activities to non-governmental (private sector) agencies aggressively pursuing ***commercial needs.*** Space systems are also being actively used for ***national security*** purposes by most countries.

Commercialising Space Sector India's space programme is one of the most well developed in the world and has achieved numerous successes through its state-owned agency, the ISRO (Indian Space Research Organisation) which is responsible for driving the space activities in India. Aimed at

[7] *ISRO* and other official sources; and the *Economic Survey 2020-21*, vol. 2 (New Delhi: Ministry of Finance, GoI), pp. 322-23.

making India a manufacturing hub of space assets, the Government started the process of commercialisation by attracting talent and investment from the private sector in the sector – with the following major steps[8] taken in this direction:

- With the long-term vision of making the country self-reliant and technologically advanced, the Government in June 2020, opened up the space sector enabling the participation of Indian *private sector* in the entire gamut of space activities.
- New Space India Limited (NSIL), a Central Public Sector Enterprise, has been mandated to transfer the technologies emanating out of Indian space programme and enable the Indian industry to scale up a high-technology manufacturing base.
- The Indian National Space Promotion and Authorisation Centre (IN-SPACe) has been set up which shall act as the promotor and regulator of space activities in India by NGPEs (Non-government/private entities). ISRO to share its infrastructure and transfer technology know-how for production and spin-off.
- The Government is committed to provide a predictable, forward-looking, well-defined and enabling regulatory regime for space activities in the country. The first to be updated in this direction were the ***SpaceCom*** (Satellite Communication) and ***SpaceRS*** (Remote Sensing) policies, further liberalising the traditional space sector – thus enabling entrepreneurs/industries to take up end-to-end activities in these domains.
- In February 2021, the Government (DoST) released the new guidelines for the 'creation, acquisition and use of geospatial data, including maps' which aim to build a more permissive regime and open up the industry to collaboration and progress.
- Being critical to mapping activities in India, geospatial data was previously heavily regulated and required licenses to be obtained for the use of such data. Given the increase in freely and publicly available geospatial data and services, the erstwhile restrictions had become redundant and severely hampered technological innovation in the sector, which specifically affected domestic players.
- In August 2021, the Ministry of Civil Aviation (MoCA) notified the liberalised ***Drone Rules*** which replaced the existing Unmanned Aircraft Systems (UAS) Rules of 2021 (which were considered too stringent and restrictive as they involved considerable paperwork, required permissions for every drone flight and very few 'free to fly' green zones were available).

MANUFACTURING vs SERVICES

All the focus being on the manufacturing exports in India has distracted attention from what might be a no less noteworthy development.[9] In the past few years, it is India's exports of services that have changed in the most significant, and perhaps alarming, way. One can see the problem looking at market shares. India's share of world exports of services, after surging in the mid-2000s, has flattened out.

What makes this development puzzling is that in recent years the composition of Indian exports of services is more favourable than that of Indian exports of manufactured goods. More of the former goes to the United States, and more of the latter to Asia. Since Asia has slowed down more rapidly, India's exports of manufacture should have been more affected. Furthermore, in 2015, the rupee has depreciated strongly against the dollar which should have helped India's exports of services.

These developments have longer-term implications. Realising India's medium-term growth potential of 8-10 per cent will require rapid growth of exports. How rapid this should be is suggested by comparing India's export performance in services with China's performance in manufacturing at a comparable stage of the growth surge.

China's global market share in manufacturing exports beginning in 1991 and India's global market share beginning in 2003 were roughly similar. The magnitude of the challenge becomes evident when examining China's trajectory over the last 15 years.

[8] *Economic Survey 2021-22* (New Delhi: Ministry of Finance, GoI), pp. 333-36 and *Economic Survey 2020-21*, vol. 1 (New Delhi: Ministry of Finance, GoI), p. 323.

[9] *Economic Survey 2015-16*, vol. 2 (New Delhi: Ministry of Finance, GoI), pp. 167-68.

To achieve a similar trajectory, India's competitiveness will have to improve so that its services exports, currently about **4.3** per cent (as per the *Economic Survey 2024-25*) of world exports, capture nearly 15 per cent of world market share. That is a sizeable challenge, and recent trends suggest that a major effort at improving competitiveness will be necessary to meet it.

Way Forward

India is an export hub for software services – its IT outsourcing service market is expected to witness 6–8 per cent growth between 2021 and 2025 (with only the home healthcare industry expected to reach US$ 10 billion by 2025). As per the Government, the services sector has large potential, but the same has not been harnessed fully. The following governmental steps[10] are needed for furthering the expansion and growth of the sector:

- The sector needs to develop competitive advantage by adopting newer technologies and required skill sets – with focus on quality, exploring new destinations and services.
- The large pool of skilled manpower, especially in the areas of IT and ITeS, is available at relatively low cost needs to be harnessed.
- Rapidly increasing population of youth looking to migrate from agriculture to other sectors will be a boon to the sector.
- Manpower should be imparted suitable digital and technical skills to benefit from the penetration of Artificial Intelligence (AI) in both manufacturing and services sectors.
- There is an urgent need to review and amend complicated procedures at the grassroots level, regulations and rules that hinder both manufacturing and services.
- Indian missions abroad should start pitching in effectively to explore Indian exports there.

The most successful segment in the services is the IT and allied services, and it flourished on its own capabilities, and without seeking much of the Government's support, which many times comes with the bureaucratic strings and control as well. The Government also has priorities and limitations – it can make focused and policy interventions, help the sector in its nascent stages (i.e., at start-up level), help them grow, check the unfair practices, but can't be seen providing support all the time.[11]

[10] *Economic Survey 2025-26* (New Delhi: Ministry of Finance, GoI, January 2026), pp. 259-291 & *Economic Survey 2024-25* (New Delhi: Ministry of Finance, GoI, January 2025), pp. 219-244 and other *official documents* available till February 2025.

[11] *Economic Survey 2021-22* and other relevant official documents. India Brand Equity Foundation (IBEF), April 2021, Ministry of Commerce and Industry, GoI, New Delhi.

SAMPLE OBJECTIVE QUESTIONS

1. Consider the following statements related to India's services sector:

(i) Its share in total GVA rose by around 7 per cent in the last decade (2013-14 to 2023-24).

(ii) India was the world's second fastest growing market in 2023-24.

(iii) It faces the second highest risk on the jobs due to artificial intelligence (AI) after the manufacturing sector.

How many of the statements given above are correct?

Code:

(a) Only one **(b)** Only two

(c) All three **(d)** None of these

2. Consider the statements given below related to the service industry:

(i) Total public and private spending on the healthcare sector in the country is around 4 per cent.

(ii) Services accounting for over 54 per cent of the gross domestic product, India has emerged as a service economy.

(iii) Services sector today provides employment to around one-third of the labour force.

How many of the statements given above are correct?

Code:

(a) Only one (b) Only two

(c) All three (d) None of these

3. Consider the statements given below related to global trade in services:

(i) The 14th Ministerial Conference of the WTO failed to extend the moratorium on levying customs on digital services.

(ii) Bringing the e-commerce under the preview of the WTO will be highly beneficial for the developing countries.

(iii) India gives preferential treatment to least developing economies (LDCs) in trade of services.

How many of the statements given above are correct?

Code:

(a) Only one (b) Only two

(c) All three (d) None of these

4. Consider the statements given below related to India's services trade:

(i) Services account for around 3 per cent of India's total exports today.

(ii) To achieve trade trajectory like China, India needs to scale up the share of services exports to 15 per cent of the total exports.

(iii) The value of India's services exports in US$ is estimated to be almost double the value of its services imports.

How many of the statements given above are correct?

Code:

(a) Only one (b) Only two

(c) All three (d) None of these

5. Consider the following statements related to the services sector in the country:

(i) The sector is today the largest recipient of foreign direct investment after manufacturing.

(ii) Hospital industry in the country has higher growth rate than that of the healthcare industry.

(iii) Just about 15 per cent of the population lacks telephone connections today.

How many of the above statements are correct?

(a) Only one (b) Only two

(c) All three (d) None of these

6. Consider the following statements related to artificial intelligence (AI) taken from a recent paper of the International Monetary Fund:

(i) Around 40 per cent of the jobs belonging to services sector are exposed to the risk of displacement due to the rise of AI.

(ii) Developing economies must invest in infrastructure to tap AI's potential.

(iii) Digitally skilled manpower will help developing countries harness the benefits of AI.

How many of the above statements are correct?

(a) Only one (b) Only two

(c) All three (d) None of these

7. Consider the following statements related to the manufacturing and services sectors of the country:

(i) Considering the available skill sets, manufacturing sector has a higher potential to generate jobs than the services sector.

(ii) Gig economy of the country is mostly run by the unorganised labour force which does not get any employment related social security benefits.

(iii) Some of the biggest educational services providers in the world are Indian firms.

How many of the above statements are correct?

(a) Only one (b) Only two

(c) All three (d) None of these

8. Consider the following statements related to the space sector of the country:

(i) Entire gamut of space industry has been decontrolled by the Government.

(ii) Private companies in India can now acquire geospatial data from the ISRO.

(iii) The ISRO functions as the promoter and regulator of the private space companies in the country.

How many of the above statements are correct?

(a) Only one **(b)** Only two

(c) All three **(d)** None of these

9. Consider the following statements related to the financial technology (Fintech) sector of the country:

(i) India is today the third largest fintech market in the world after the USA and Japan.

(ii) As per the Bank for International Settlements (BIS), what India achieved in financial inclusion in 5 years, other countries took an average of 40 years.

(iii) India is a leader in global real-time payment transactions.

How many of the above statements are correct?

(a) Only one **(b)** Only two

(c) All three **(d)** None of these

10. Consider the following statements related to the services sector of the country:

(i) The last decade saw a decline in the share of services in the gross value added (GVA).

(ii) Disruptions caused by the COVID-19 pandemic and geopolitical conflicts have been the major reasons for a decline in the services sector.

(iii) The share of services in the GVA is still over 55 per cent.

How many of the above statements are correct?

(a) Only one **(b)** Only two

(c) All three **(d)** None of these

Answers: 1. (a) 2. (a) 3. (a) 4. (b) 5. (b) 6. (c) 7. (b) 8. (a) 9. (a) 10. (d)

SAMPLE SUBJECTIVE QUESTIONS

1. Give your suggestions to boost service economy of the country in special reference to the advent of artificial intelligence.
2. Briefly examine the advantages India enjoys today in the area of services trade and the government initiatives in this regard.
3. 'However, services account for over half of the gross value added of the economy, the employability scope of the sector is yet to be tapped upto optimum level.' Explain with suitable examples.
4. Illustrate the reasons due to which the fintech adoption rate of India has been higher than that of the global average in recent times.

SAMPLE MODEL ANSWER

1. 'What are the challenges due to which the services sector cannot emerge as the primary employment generator even after contributing the highest share of India's gross value added?

Ans. As per the latest final data (of 2024-25), the services sector contributes over 55 per cent to India's gross value added (GVA), but it employs only 29.7 per cent of the total workforce. Promoting it as a primary employment generator faces several structural and systemic challenges, major ones being the following:

1. *The economy has low employment elasticity*
   - Economic growth of the recent years has been output-intensive rather than job-intensive (a state of jobless growth). The sub-sectors like IT-BPM and financial services are capital-intensive but create relatively fewer jobs.
   - During 2011-2021, India's average GDP growth was 5.3 per cent, while employment grew annually by only 0.30 per cent.
   - Growth is often driven by enhanced productivity (via technological advancements) rather than expanding the number of jobs.
2. *Lack of employability*
   - Around 22 per cent of graduates are deemed unemployable (due to skill mismatches)–as per the Economic Survey 2024-25, about 8.25 per cent of graduates are in roles matching their specific qualifications.
   - Only 4.7-5.4 per cent of India's workforce has undergone formal skill training, compared to 80 per cent in Japan and 75 per cent in Germany.
   - Rapid adoption of AI and automation threatens up to 40-50 per cent of existing white-collar roles (as per an IMF paper, 2025), demanding constant reskilling.
3. *Demographic disparities*
   - Over 60 per cent of urban workers are in services, compared to less than 20 per cent in rural areas.
   - Only 10.5 per cent of rural women participate in the services sector (often due to limited mobility and lack of childcare).
   - Just six states generate 40 per cent of India's total services output.
4. *Infrastructure and Regulatory Hurdles*
   - Poor logistics and inadequate digital connectivity in Tier-2 and Tier-3 cities constrain the growth of small service providers (belonging to the MSMEs).
   - Frequent changes in regulations and a lack of a unified Integrated Service Policy (unlike industrial or agricultural policies) create a 'regulatory cholesterol' that hinders scalability of the firms.

CHAPTER 12

Indian Financial Market

> A well-developed financial system should effectively harness domestic savings; facilitate the efficient allocation of domestic and foreign savings to productive investments; allow households and firms to share risk; and support consumption and expenditure smoothening. To meet these goals, the financial system needs a strong banking system as well as a deep equity and bond markets.*
>
> *See E. Prasad, 'Financial Sector Development and Reforms', in *What the Economy Needs Now*, A. Banerjee, G. Gopinath, R. Rajan and Mihir S. Sharma, eds. (New Delhi: Juggernaut Books, 2019), pp. 183–92.

To watch the Author's videos on the significance of the Chapter, scan the QR Code given here

Exam Essentials...

- Weakness of Indian Money Market
- Discount and Finance House of India Limited (DFHI)
- NEDFi
- Project Financing

Note to the Reader...

This chapter provides a foundation to the financial sector/market of the country which includes major financial intermediaries such as banks, insurance, and security market which are the subject matters of the upcoming chapters of the book. Thus, this chapter should be read in sync with its inter-connectedness to the upcoming chapters of the financial sector.

In This Chapter...

INTRODUCTION

The market of an economy where funds are transacted between the fund-surplus and fund-scarce individuals and groups is known as the financial market (*definition*).[1] The basis of transaction is either *interest* or *dividend*. This market might have its organised (institutionalised) as well as non-organised (unregulated/non-institutionalised) segments in an economy.

Financial markets in every economy have two separate segments today: one catering to the requirements of *short-term funds*, and the other to the requirements of *long-term funds*.[2] The short-term financial market is

[1] Based on the discussion in P. A. Samuelson and W. D. Nordhaus, *Economics* (New Delhi: Tata McGraw Hill, 2005), pp. 543–45.

[2] Based on J. E. Stiglitz and C. E. Walsh, *Economics* (New York: W.W. Norton & Company, 2006), pp. 612–14.

known as the **money market**, while the long-term financial market is known as the **capital market**. The money market fulfils the requirements of funds for a period of up to 364 days (*i.e., short-term*),. while the capital market does the same for a period of above 364 days (*i.e., long-term*).[3] A brief discussion on the Indian financial market is given below:

INDIAN MONEY MARKET

Money market is the short-term financial market of an economy. In this market, money is traded between individuals or groups (i.e., financial institutions (FIs), banks, government, companies etc.), who are either *cash-surplus* or *cash-scarce*. Trading is done on a rate known as *discount rate* which is determined by the market and guided by the availability of and demand for the cash in the day-to-day trading.[4] The 'repo rate' of the time (announced by the Reserve Bank of India [RBI]) works as the guiding rate for the current 'discount rate'. Borrowings in this market may or may not be supported by collaterals. In the money market, the *financial assets,* which have quick conversion quality into money and carry minimal transaction cost, are also traded.[5] The money market may be *defined* as a market where short-term lending and borrowing takes place between the cash-surplus and cash-scarce sectors.

The market operates in both 'organised' and 'unorganised' channels in India. Starting from the 'person-to-person' mode and converting into 'telephonic transaction', it has now gone *online* in the age of internet and information technology. The transactions might take place through the intermediaries (known as brokers) or directly between the trading sides.

Need for Money Market Income generation (i.e., growth) is the most essential requirement of any economic system. In the modern industrial economies, creation of productive assets is not an easy task as it requires investible capital of long-term nature. Long-term capital can be raised either through bank loans, corporate bonds, debentures or shares (i.e., from the capital market). But once a productive asset has been created and production starts, there arises the need for another kind of capital, to meet the day-to-day shortfalls of working capital. It means that only setting up of firms does not guarantee production as these firms keep facing *fund mismatches* in the day-to-day production process. Such funds are required only for a short period (days, fortnights or few months) and are needed to meet shortfalls in working capital requirements. This requires creation of a different segment of the financial market which can cater to the short-term requirements of such funds for the enterprises - known as the **money market** or the **working capital market**. The short-term period is defined as up to 364 days.

The crucial role of money market in an economy is proved by the fact that if only a few lakhs or crores of rupees of working capital is not met in time, a firm may default in its payment obligations, start fetching losses or may be forced even to shut down, which has been set up with hundreds and thousands of crore of rupees as investment capital. In case of shut down, the firm might default in its payments, losing its hard-earned credit-worthiness, consequently creating a chain of negative effects in the economic system. This is why it is essential for every economy to organise a strong and vibrant money market which has wider geographic presence.

Money Market in India The organised form of money market in India is just close to four decades old. However, its presence has been there, but restricted to the government only.[6] It was the **Chakravarthy Committee** (1985) which, for the first time, underlined the need of an organised money market in the country[7], and the **Vaghul Committee** (1987) laid the blue print for its development.[8] Today, money market in India is not an integrated unit and has two segments - *Unorganised Money Market and Organised Money Market.*

[3] See *Report on Currency and Finance* (New Delhi: Reserve Bank of India, Government of India, multiple years).

[4] In the capital market, money is traded on interest rate as well as on dividends. Long-term loans are raised on well-defined interest rates, while long-term capital is raised on dividends through the sale of shares.

[5] Such financial assets are known as 'close substitutes for money.'

[6] The only instrument of the money market was the Treasury Bills, which were sold by tender at weekly auctions until 1965. But later these bills were made available throughout the week at discount rates by the Reserve Bank of India.

[7] S. Chakravarthy, *Review of the Working of the Monetary System* (New Delhi: Reserve Bank of India, 1985).

[8] M. Vaghul, *Working Group on Money Market* (New Delhi: Reserve Bank of India, 1987). The committee was set up in 1986, and came to be known as the Vaghul Committee.

1. **Unorganised Money Market:** Before the government started the organised development of the money market in India, its unorganised form had its presence since ancient times - its remnant is still present in the country. Their activities are not regulated like the organised money market, but they are recognised by the government. In recent years, some of them have been included under the regulated organised market (for example, the NBFCs were put under the regulatory control of the RBI in 1997). The unorganised money market in India may be divided into three differing categories:
   - **(i)** ***Unregulated Non-Bank Financial Intermediaries:*** Unregulated Non-Banking Financial Intermediaries are functioning in the form of *chit funds, nidhis* (operate in south India, which lend to only their members) and loan companies. They charge very high interest rates (i.e., 36-48 per cent per annum), and thus are exploitative in nature and have selective reach in the economy.
   - **(ii)** ***Indigenous Bankers:*** Indigenous bankers receive deposits and lend money in the capacity of an individual or a private firm. There are, basically, four such bankers in the country functioning as non-homogenous groups:
     - **(a)** *Gujarati Shroffs:* They operate in Mumbai, Kolkata as well as in industrial, trading and port cities in the region.
     - **(b)** *Multani or Shikarpuri Shroffs:* They operate in Mumbai, Kolkata, Assam tea gardens and North-Eastern India.
     - **(c)** *Marwari Kayas:* They operate mainly in Gujarat with minimal presence in Mumbai and Kolkata.
     - **(d)** *Chettiars:* They are active in Chennai and at the ports of southern India.
   - **(iii)** ***Moneylenders:*** They constitute the most localised form of money market in India and operate in the most exploitative way. They have their two types of lenders:
     - **(a)** The professional moneylenders, who lend their own money as a profession to earn income through interest.
     - **(b)** The non-professional moneylenders, who might be businessmen and lend their money to earn interest income as a subsidiary business.

   Today, India has **eight** organised instruments of the money market which are used by the prescribed firms in the country, but the unorganised money market also operates side by side - there are certain reasons[9] behind this:
   - **(i)** Indian money market is still underdeveloped.
   - **(ii)** Lack of penetration and presence of the instruments of the organised money market.
   - **(iii)** There are many needful customers in the money market who are currently outside the purview of the organised money market.
   - **(iv)** Entry to the organised money market for its customers is still restrictive in nature - not allowing small businessmen.
2. **Organised Money Market:** Since the government started developing the organised money market in India (mid- 1980s), we have seen the arrival of a total of **eight** instruments designed to be used by different entities. A brief description of these instruments follows:
   - **(i)** ***Treasury Bills (TBs):*** This instrument of the money market though present since independence got organised only in 1986. They are used by the Central Government to fulfil short-term liquidity requirement up to a period of 364 days. There developed **five types** of the TBs in due course of time:
     - **(a)** 14-day (Intermediate TBs)
     - **(b)** 14-day (Auctionable TBs)
     - **(c)** 91-day TBs
     - **(d)** 182-day TBs
     - **(e)** 364-day TBs

   Out of the above five variants of TBs, at present only the **91-day TBs**, **182-day TBs** and **364-day TBs** are issued by the government. The other two variants were discontinued in 2001.[10] The TBs are ***zero coupon securities*** and pay no interest. Instead, they are issued

[9] Based on the suggestions of experts belonging to the Indian financial market.

[10] *Economic Survey 2001-02* (New Delhi: Ministry of Finance, Government of India, 2002); *Economic Survey 2009-10* (New Delhi: Ministry of Finance, Government of India, 2010).

at a discount and redeemed at the face value at maturity. For example, a 91-day TB of ₹100 (face value) may be issued at say ₹98.20, i.e., at a discount of say, ₹1.80 and would be redeemed at the face value of ₹100 at maturity.

The TBs, other than providing short-term cushion to the government, also function as short-term investment avenues for banks, financial institutions and individuals, besides functioning as requirements of the CRR and SLR of the banking institutions.

(ii) ***Certificate of Deposit (CD):*** Organised in 1989, the CD was originally used by **banks** to fulfil their funding requirements for a specified period ranging less than 1 year - they are negotiable and tradable in the money market. As per the changes affected in June 2021, banks can issue it for minimum 7 days and maximum 1 year and minimum value of it changed to ₹5 lakh. Later on, RBI allowed more entities to issue it - today, the AIFIs (All India Financial Institutions), Scheduled Commercial Banks (SCBs), Regional Rural Banks (RRBs), and Small Finance Banks all are allowed to issue it. The AIFIs are allowed to issue CD for a period of 1 to 3 years. Individual resident of India is allowed to invest in CD (RBI has removed other categories of investors from its eligibility criteria).

(iii) ***Commercial Paper (CP):*** Organised in 1990, it is an unsecured promissory note and is used by highly-rated corporate borrowers (which should be a listed company with a tangible net worth of not less than ₹4 crores). Later on the All India Financial Institutions (AIFIs), primary dealers (PDs) and satellite dealers (SDs) were also allowed to issue it. It was initiated to fulfil two aims - facilitating short-term fund requirements of the entities and providing an additional instrument to investors. The CP-issuing companies need to obtain a specified credit rating from an agency approved by the RBI (such as CRISIL, ICRA etc). CP can be issued (in denominations of ₹5 lakh and its multiples) for maturities between a minimum of 15 days and a maximum of upto 1 year. Aimed at broadening investor participation, in October 2019, SEBI allowed *listing* of the Commercial Papers.

(iv) ***Commercial Bill (CB):*** Organised in 1990, a CB is issued by the **All India Financial Institutions** (AIFIs), **Non-Banking Finance Companies** (NBFCs), **Scheduled Commercial Banks**, **Merchant Banks, Co-operative Banks** and **Mutual Funds**. It replaced the old Bill Market available since 1952 in the country.

These bills are issued by the seller (drawer) on the buyer (drawee) for the value of goods delivered by him. These bills are of 30 days, 60 days or 90 days maturity. If the seller is in need of funds, he may draw a bill and send it to the buyer - the buyer accepts the bill and promises to make payment on the due date. The seller may also approach his bank to accept the bill - the bank charges a commission for the acceptance of the bill and promises to make the payment if the buyer defaults. Once this process is complete, the seller can sell it in the market. This way a commercial bill becomes a marketable/ tradable instrument.

Weakness of Indian Money Market

India's money market is today counted amongst the best in Asia but with its own weak points:

- Lack of general financial inclusion,
- It serves mainly the governments and regulated public/private financial entities, and
- Shallow penetration as it does not cater to the needs of small entities (i.e., serves only the corporate entities).

Due to these reasons, even after the evolution of eight organised instruments, the older unorganised components of it still operate in the country (as they are the only people to whom unserved go for their short-term needs of funds).

(v) ***Call Money Market (CMM):*** This is basically an **inter-bank** money market where funds are borrowed and lent, generally, for one day - that is why this is also known as **overnight borrowing market** (also called **money at call**). Funds can be borrowed/raised for a maximum period up to 14 days (called **short notice**). Borrowing/lending in this market takes place without any collateral/securities.[11] Rate of interest in this market 'glides' with the 'repo rate' of the time the principle remains, very simple - longer the period, higher the interest rate. Depending upon the availability and demand of fund in this market the real call rate revolves near the current repo rate.

Only scheduled commercial banks and primary dealers (PDs) are allowed to operate in this market as both the borrowers and lenders, while insurance firms, Mutual Funds, IDBI and NABARD are allowed to operate only as lenders.

(vi) ***Money Market Mutual Fund (MF):*** Popularly known as Mutual Funds (MFs), this money market instrument was introduced/organised in 1992 to provide short-term investment opportunity to **individuals**. The initial guidelines for the MF have been liberalised many times. Since March 2000, MFs have been brought under the preview of SEBI besides the RBI. At present, a whole lot of FIs and firms are allowed to set up MFs, *viz.* commercial banks, public and private FIs and private sector companies. By December 2024, the mutual fund companies operating in the country were managing a total asset of 66.9 lakh crores *(Economic Survey 2024-25)*.

(vii) ***Repos and Reverse Repos:*** In the era of economic reforms there developed two new instruments of money market - **repo** and **reverse repo**. Considered the most dynamic instruments of the Indian money market they have emerged the most favoured route to raise short-term funds in India. 'Repo' is basically an acronym of the **rate of repurchase**. The RBI in a span of four years, introduced these instruments - **repo** in December 1992 and **reverse repo** in November 1996.

Repo allows the banks and other FIs to borrow money from the RBI or SBI DFHI (SBI Discount and Finance House of India) for a short-term period (by selling government securities). In **reverse repo**, the banks and FIs purchase government securities from the RBI or SBI DFHI. All government securities are dated and the interests for the repo or reverse repo transactions are announced by the RBI from time to time. The provision of repo and the reverse repo have been able to serve the liquidity evenness in the economy as the banks are able to get the required amount of funds out of it, and they can park surplus idle funds through it. These instruments have emerged as important tools in the management of the monetary and credit policy in recent years.[12]

Accepting the recommendations of the ***Urjit Patel Committee***, the RBI in April 2014 (while announcing the first 'Bi-monthly Credit and Monetary Policy 2014-15') announced the introduction of **term repo** and **term reverse repo**. This is believed to bring in higher stability and better signalling of interest rates across different loan markets in the economy.

(viii) ***Cash Management Bill (CMB):*** The Government of India (GoI), in consultation with the RBI, introduced a new short-term instrument known as Cash Management Bills in 2010 to meet the temporary cash flow mismatches of the government. The CMBs are *non-standard* and *discounted instruments* issued for maturities less than 91 days. The CMBs have the *generic character of TBs* (issued at discount to the face value); are tradable and qualify for *ready forward facility;* and investment in it is considered as an eligible investment in government securities by banks for SLR.

[11] The State Bank of India (operates in this market as lender as it is in a comfortable cash position) lends against government securities, while others lend against the 'deposit receipts' of the borrowing banks. The SBI functions as the 'lender of intermediate resort' (while the RBI functions as the 'lender of last resort').

[12] *Report on Currency and Finance* (New Delhi: Reserve Bank of India, Government of India, 2020-21).

It should be noted here that the existing TBs serve the same purpose, but as they were put under the WMAs (Ways & Means Advances) provisions by the Government in 1997, they did not remain a discretionary route for the government in meeting its short-term requirements of funds at will (see 'Fiscal Consolidation in India', sub-topic in **Chapter 19** for details). The CBM does not come under the provisions of the WMAs.

MUTUAL FUNDS

Of all investment options, Mutual Funds are touted to be the best tool for wealth creation over the long term. They are of several types, and the risk varies with the kind of asset classes these funds invest in. As the name suggests, a mutual fund *is a fund that is created when a large number of investors put in their money, and is managed by professionally qualified persons with experience in investing in different asset classes - shares, bonds, money market instruments like call money, and other assets such as gold and property.* Their names usually provide a good idea about what type of asset class a fund, also called a scheme, will invest in. For example, a **diversified equity fund** will invest in a large number of stocks, while a **gilt fund** will invest in government securities, while a **pharma fund** will mainly invest in stocks of companies from the pharmaceutical and related industries.

MFs, first of all came in the money market (regulated by the RBI), but they have the freedom to operate in the capital market, too. This is why they have provision of dual regulator - the RBI and SEBI. MFs are compulsorily registered with the Securities and Exchange Board of India (SEBI), which also acts as the **first wall of defence** for all investors in these funds. For those who do not understand how MFs operate but are willing to invest, the move by SEBI is seen as a big relief.

Each mutual fund is run by a group of qualified people who form a company, called an *asset management company (AMC),* and the operations of the AMC are under the guidance of another group of people, called *trustees.* Both, the people in the AMC as well as the trustees, have a *fiduciary responsibility,* because these are the people who are entrusted with the task of managing the hard-earned money of people who do not understand much about managing money.

A fund house or a distributor working for the fund house (which could be an individual, a company or even a bank) is qualified to sell MFs. The fund house allots the 'units' of the MF to the investor at a price that is fixed through a process approved by SEBI, which is based on the net asset value (NAV). In simple terms, NAV is the total value of investments in a scheme divided by the total number of units issued to investors in the same scheme. In most mutual fund schemes, NAVs are computed and published on a daily basis. However, when a fund house is launching a scheme for the first time, the units are sold at ₹10 each. There are ***three types*** of schemes offered by MFs:

1. **Open-ended Schemes:** An open-ended fund is one which is usually available from an MF on an ongoing basis, i.e., an investor can buy or sell as and when they intend to at a NAV-based price. As investors buy and sell units of a particular open-ended scheme, the number of units issued also changes every day and so changes the value of the scheme's portfolio. So, the NAV also changes on a daily basis. In India, fund houses can sell any number of units of a particular scheme, but at times fund houses restrict selling additional units of a scheme for some time.
2. **Closed-ended Schemes:** A close-ended fund usually issues units to investors only once, when they launch an offer called *new fund offer (NFO)* in India. Thereafter, these units are listed on the stock exchanges where they are traded on a daily basis. As these units are listed, any investor can buy and sell these units through the exchange. As the name suggests, close-ended schemes are managed by fund houses for a limited number of years, and at the end of the term either money is returned to the investors or the scheme is made open ended. However, there is a word of caution here that usually, units of close-ended funds which are listed on the stock exchanges, trade at a high discount to their NAVs. But as the date for closure of the fund nears, the discount between the NAV and the trading price narrows, and vanishes on the day of closure of the scheme.
3. **Exchange-Traded Funds (ETFs):** ETFs are a mix of open-ended and close-ended schemes. ETFs, like close-ended schemes, are listed and traded on a stock exchange on a daily basis, but

the price is usually very close to its NAV, or the underlying assets, like gold ETFs.

If investments have been made in a well-managed MF, the advantages outweigh disadvantages in the long term, which is 10 years or more. There is a very high probability for investors of making more money than by investing in other risk-free investments such as FDs and public provident fund. Advantages of investing in MFs include the following:

(i) diversification of portfolio,
(ii) good investment management services,
(iii) liquidity,
(iv) strong government-backed regulatory help,
(v) professional service, and
(vi) low cost for all the benefits.

An investor, by investing in a mutual fund scheme that has blue chip stocks in its portfolio, indirectly gets an exposure to these stocks. Compared to this, if the same investor wants to have each of these stocks in his portfolio, the cost of buying and managing the portfolio will be much higher.

MFs invest the investors' money in both the **loan** and **share** markets. Buyers of MF units are given a choice/option as in which of the markets they wish their money to be invested by the fund managers of the MF. This way investors get, for example, the following choices (decided as per the regulatory provisions of the time):

1. *Loan* (100 per cent of the funds will be invested in the loan market),
2. *Share* (100 per cent of the funds will be invested in the share market) and
3. *Balance* (60 per cent of the funds will be invested in the loan market while the remaining 40 per cent in the share market - this provision keeps changing depending upon the health of the share market - clearly announced by the MFs).

By *October 2017*, the SEBI announced to classify the mutual fund schemes into *five broad categories* to cut through the clutter and make it easier for investors to compare plans with similar characteristics - debt, equity, hybrid, solution-oriented (such as retirement and children funds) and other schemes.

Every category is further finely divided, making for a total of *36 different scheme* categories such as Dividend Yield Equity Fund, which would focus on dividend-yielding stocks, or Banking and PSU Debt Fund, which invests a minimum 80 per cent of its corpus in debt paper issued by state-owned firms and lenders. A fund house will be allowed to have only one scheme per category to ensure that there is no duplication.

Discount and Finance House of India Limited (DFHI)

The Discount and Finance House of India Limited[13] (DFHI) was set up in April 1988 by the RBI jointly with the public sector banks (PSBs) and financial investment institutions (i.e., LIC, GIC and UTI). Its establishment was an outcome of the long-drawn need of the following two types:

1. to bring an equilibrium of liquidity in the Indian banking system and
2. to impart liquidity to the instruments of the money market prevalent in the economy.

In 2004, the RBI transferred its total holding in the DFHI to the State Bank of India's arm SBI Gilts Limited. Its new name is SBI DFHI. It functions as the biggest 'primary dealer' in the economy and functions on a commercial basis. It deals in all kinds of instruments in the money market without any upper ceiling. Operating in 'two ways' (as a lender and borrower), its objective is to provide needful liquidity and stability in the financial market of the country.

INDIAN CAPITAL MARKET

The long-term financial market of an economy is known as the 'capital market'. This market makes it possible to raise *long-term money* (capital), i.e., for a period of minimum 365 days and above. Creation of productive assets is not possible without a strong capital market - the market gained more importance once most of the

[13] It was in 1979 that the Chore Committee for the first time recommended for a discount house to level the liquidity imbalances in the banking system. The government became active after the recommendations of the Working Group on the Money Market (i.e., the Vaghul Committee, 1987) and finally established the DFHI in 1988. The Vaghul Committee suggested to set up a discount finance institution which could deal in short-term money market instruments so that liquidity could be provided to these instruments. The Committee also recommended the house to operate on a 'commercial basis', which was accepted by the government while setting up the DFHI.

economies in the world started industrialising. Across the world, banks emerged as the first and the foremost segment of the capital market. In coming times many other segments were added to it, *viz.*, insurance industry, MFs and finally the most attractive and vibrant, the security/stock market. Organised development of capital market together with putting in place the right regulatory framework for it, has always been a tough task for the economies. It is believed today that for strong growth prospects in an economy, presence of a strong and vibrant capital market is essential.

Scan this QR Code to watch a author's video lecture that simplifies this topic

Though the capital market of India is far stronger and better today in comparison to the periods just after independence, the process of emergence has not been easy and smooth. Once India opted 'industry' as its prime moving force, the first challenge was to raise long-term funds for industrial establishments and their expansion. As banks in India were weak, small and geographically unevenly distributed, they were not in a position to play a pivotal role like the one they played in case of the industrialising western economies. This is why the government decided to set up 'financial institutions' which could play the role of banks (till banks gained strength and presence) and carry on the responsibilities of 'project financing'.

Project Financing

After independence, India opted for intensive industrialisation to achieve rapid growth and development. To this end, the main responsibility was given to the public sector undertakings (PSUs). For industrialisation we require capital, technology and labour, all being typically difficult to manage in the case of India. For capital requirement, the government decided to depend upon internal and external sources, and the government decided to set up FIs. Though India owned the banks, due to low saving rate and lower deposits with them, the upcoming industries could not be financed through them. The main borrowers for industrial development were the PSUs. To support the capital requirement of the 'projects' of the public sector industries, the government came up with different types of FIs in the coming years. The industrial financing supported by these FIs was known as 'project financing' in India. An overview of India's capital in present time is given below:

1. **Financial Institutions:** The requirement of project financing made India opt for a number of FIs from time to time, which are generally classified into four categories:[14]

   (i) ***All India Financial Institutions (AIFIs):*** The *AIFIs* are IFCI (1948), ICICI (1955), IDBI (1964), SIDBI (1990) and IIBI (1997). All of them were public sector FIs except ICICI, which was a joint sector venture with initial capital coming from the RBI, some foreign banks and FIs. The public sector FIs were funded by the Government of India.

   By the 1980s, all Indian banks acquired wider capital base, and by the early 1990s when the stock market became popular, it became easier for the corporate world to tap cheaper capital from these segments of the capital market.[15] The era of economic reforms had given the same option to the PSUs to tap new capital. As the AIFIs had more or less fixed rate of interest as compared to the banks which could mobilise cheaper deposits to lend cheaper - the AIFIs seemed to become irrelevant. The AIFIs witnessed a sharp decline in recent years.[16] At this juncture the government decided to convert them into **Development Banks**[17] (suggested by the Narasimhan Committee-I) to be referred to as the All-India Development Banks (AIDBs). In 2000, the government allowed ICICI to opt for a **reverse merger** (when an older enterprise is merged with a newer one) with the ICICI Bank - the first AIDB emerged with no obligation of project financing - such entities in coming times

[14] *Industrial Finance Corporation of India Act, 1948,* (New Delhi: Government of India).

[15] *Economic Survey 2000-01* (New Delhi: Ministry of Finance, Government of India, 2010).

[16] *Economic Survey 2006-07* (New Delhi: Ministry of Finance, Government of India, 2007).

[17] Narasimhan Committee on the Financial System (CFS), 1991 suggested for the conversion of the AIFIs into Development Banks.

will be known as the **universal banks**[18] (allowed to set up as many FIs they wish to, such as insurance, merchant banks, MFs etc.). In a similar move, the IDBI was reverse-merged with the IDBI Bank in 2002, and the second AIDB emerged. But it has still the obligation of carrying its project financing duties.

In 2002, the government proposed to merge IFCI and IIBI with the nationalised bank PNB to create a big Universal Bank. It is believed that PNB was unwilling to opt for this merger as these FIs were running at heavy losses. This move was partly correct as per the recommendations of the Narasimhan Committee-II (to the extent the merger is concerned, following its 3-Tier Banking Structure of India), but partly against it (the committee has advised not to merge weak banks/FIs with either weak or strong banks/FIs).[19] Presently, the government is trying to make the IFCI and IIBI change their business and emerge as profitable entities - they are busy recovering their dues and improving their balance sheet.

New DFI: In the *Union Budget 2021-22*, the Government highlighted the need for a 'professionally managed' development financial institution (DFI) which could act as a provider, enabler and catalyst for infrastructure financing in the economy. As the infrastructure sector needs long-term debt financing, the presence of such an institution was felt since long. Taking steps towards it, the ***NaBFID*** (National Bank for Financing Infrastructure and Development) was set up by the government in the late 2021 which commenced its operations in the financial year 2022-23. It will work as the principal DFIs for infrastructure financing. DFIs are set up for providing long-term finance for such segments of the economy where the risks involved are beyond the acceptable limits of banks and other ordinary financial institutions. Unlike banks, DFIs do not accept deposits from people rather they source funds from the market, government, as well as multi-lateral institutions, and are often supported through government guarantees. The *major features* of the DFI are as given below:

Funding: It has been set up as a corporate body with authorised share capital of ₹1 lakh crores (100 per cent owned by the central government which will be subsequently reduced upto 26 per cent). Its shares may be held by: (i) central government, (ii) multilateral institutions, (iii) sovereign wealth funds, (iv) pension funds, (v) insurers, (vi) financial institutions, (vii) banks, and (viii) any other institution prescribed by the central government.

Functions: It has both *financial* as well as *developmental* functions/objectives. Financial objectives will be to directly or indirectly lend, invest, or attract investments for infrastructure projects located entirely or partly in India. Developmental objectives include facilitating the development of the market for bonds, loans, and derivatives for infrastructure financing.

Source of funds: It may raise fund in the form of loans (both in Indian rupees and foreign currencies) or by issuing bonds and debentures. It may borrow from: (i) central government, (ii) Reserve Bank of India, (iii) scheduled commercial banks, (iii) mutual funds, and (iv) multilateral institutions such as World Bank and Asian Development Bank.

The central government will provide grants worth ₹5,000 crores to it by the end of the first financial year and also guarantee (at a concessional rate of up to 0.1 per cent for costs) its borrowings from multilateral institutions, sovereign wealth funds, and other foreign funds together. Risks related to foreign exchange fluctuations may be reimbursed by the government in part or full, and the bonds,

[18] It was the S.H. Khan Committee on Development Financial Institutions (DFIs), 1998 which forwarded the concept/idea of Universal Banking in India

[19] *Economic Survey 2011-12* (New Delhi: Ministry of Finance, Government of India, 2011), pp. 115-16.

debentures and loans issued by it may be guaranteed by the central government (on the request of the DFI).

NEDFi

North Eastern Development Finance Corporation Ltd (NEDFi) is a 'public financial institution' of the Government with its head office in Guwahati, Assam. Originally set up as a non-banking finance company (NBFC) under Ministry of Finance in 1996, it was shifted to the newly created DoNER (Ministry of Development of North Eastern Region) in 2004. Dedicated to development of entrepreneurship in the North Eastern Region, its *major functions* are:

- Financial support to micro, small, medium and large enterprises for setting up industrial and agri-allied projects;
- Micro-financing;
- Offering 'consultancy and advisory services' to the states, private sectors and other agencies; and
- Functioning as the 'nodal agency' for disbursal of Government incentives to the industries in the region under the NEIIPP (North–East Industrial and Investment Promotion Policy, 2007).

Management: It will be governed by a Board of Directors composed of a chairperson appointed by the central government (in consultation with RBI), a managing director, up to three deputy managing directors, two directors (nominated by the central government), up to three directors elected by shareholders, and a few independent directors. A body constituted by the central government will recommend candidates for the posts of the managing director, deputy managing directors and will appoint independent directors.

Investigation and prosecution: No investigation can be initiated against employees of the DFI without the prior sanction of: (i) the central government in case of the chairperson or other directors, and (ii) the managing director in case of other employees. Courts will also require prior sanction for taking cognizance of offences in matters involving its employees. The institution has also been kept outside the purview of CAG, CVC and CBI.

These steps are aimed at enabling faster decision-making and operational flexibility.

DFIs in private sector: Now, a DFI can be set up in *private sector* also for which a licence needs to be procured from the RBI as these will come under the regulatory purview of the latter.

(ii) ***Specialised Financial Institutions (SFIs)***[20]: Two new FIs were set up by the Central Government in the late 1980s to finance **risk** and **innovation** in the area of industrial expansion; this was India's trial in the area of **venture capital funding**.

(a) *IFCI Venture Capital Funds Ltd (IFCI Venture), 2000:* It was promoted as a Risk Capital Foundation (RCF) in 1975 by IFCI Ltd., a society to provide financial assistance to first generation professionals and technocrat entrepreneurs for setting up their own ventures through soft loans, under the Risk Capital Scheme. In 1988, the RCF was converted into a company - Risk Capital and Technology Finance Corporation Ltd. (RCTC) - when it also introduced the Technology Finance and Development Scheme (TFDS) for financing development and commercialisation of indigenous technology. Besides, under the Risk Capital Scheme, the RCTC started providing financial assistance to entrepreneurs by way of direct equity participation. Based on the IFCI Venture's credentials and strengths, the Unit Trust of India (UTI), entrusted RCTC with the

[20] The write-up is based on information available from SEBI, RBI and different announcements/published reports of the Ministry of Finance, since 1996 onwards.

management of a new venture capital fund named **Venture Capital Unit Scheme (VECAUS-III)** in 1991 with its funds coming from the UTI and IFCI. To reflect the shift in the company's activities, the name of RCTC was changed to IFCI Venture Capital Funds Ltd. (IFCI Venture) in February 2000.

In order to focus on Asset Management Activities, IFCI Venture discontinued Risk Capital and Technology Finance Schemes in 2000-01 and continued managing VECAUS-III. In 2007, as the UTI had ceased to carry out its activities and its assets vested with **Specified Undertaking of the Unit Trust of India (SUUTI)**, the portfolio of VECAUS-III under management of IFCI Venture was transferred to SUUTI.

(b) *Tourism Finance Corporation of India Ltd (TFCI), 1989:* The Government had, on the recommendations of the National Committee on Tourism (*Yunus Committee*) set up under the aegis of the Planning Commission, decided in 1988, to promote a separate All India Financial Institution for providing financial assistance to tourism-related activities/projects. In accordance with the above decision, the IFCI Ltd. along with other all-India financial/ investment institutions (IIs) and some nationalised banks promoted a Public Limited Company under the name of 'Tourism Finance Corporation of India Ltd. (TFCI)' to function as a Specialised All- India Development Financial Institution to cater to the financial needs of the tourism industry.

The TFCI was incorporated as a Public Limited Company in 1989 and became operational with effect from 1989. The TFCI was notified as a Public Financial Institution in January 1990. Its promoter, the IFCI, holds the major share (41.6 per cent) in it, while the rest of the shares are with the 'public' (26 per cent), PSBs, public insurance companies and public mutual fund (i.e., UTI Mutual Fund Ltd.).

(iii) ***Investment Institutions (IIs):*** Three investment institutions also came up in

Project Financing

Project financing is a way of funding *long-term* industrial projects of *huge sizes*, generally of infrastructural nature such as power projects, highways, railways, oil and natural gas, etc. The project financing institutions are known by names like development banks, development finance institution (DFI), etc.

Why such financing is needed when banks are there?

Following are the main reasons due to which a country needs DFI even if it has strong banking industry:

- Banks are not interested in lending of huge sizes (to avoid higher risks);
- Banks are interested in collateral-backed lending (while loans borrowed by infrastructure projects are part backed by collateral and part by the 'cash flow' from the projects - it means banks don't get enough guarantee against default of the borrower);
- Banks generally provide loans for a tenure of up to 15 years which may be extended by another 5 years in special cases (the infrastructure projects loans are needed for even longer tenures which may be of varying periods depending upon the need of the hour).

Public vs Private Financing

Technically, such financing can be made available to both public and private projects - but in India it began with the former only, way back in 1947 - with the launching of the first Government-owned DFI, the Industrial Finance Corporation of India (IFCI). Once the idea of public private partnership (PPP) came up such financing began for privately-owned projects too.

At present, the National Bank for Financing Infrastructure and Development (NaBFID) is the only DFI operating in India which was set by the Government in 2021–22.

the public sector, which are yet another kind of FIs, i.e., the LIC (1956), the UTI (1964) and the GIC (1971).

At present they are no more known as DIIs (Domestic Investment Institutions) or DFIs (Domestic Financial Institutions). The LIC is now the only public sector insurance company in the life segment; the GIC was converted into a public sector re-insurance company in 2000, while the UTI was converted into a mutual fund company in 2002. Now these IIs are no more like they were in the past. The LIC is now called an 'insurance company', part of the Indian Insurance Industry and is the lone public sector in the life insurance segment competing with private life insurance companies. Similarly, the UTI is now part of the Indian Mutual Fund industry and the lone such firm in the public sector competing with other private sector MFs. Similarly, the erstwhile four public sector general insurance companies are part of India's general insurance industry and competing with private companies in the area (they were Holding Companies of the GIC - now these are owned by the GoI directly and GIC only looks after its 're-insurance' business). Today, under this segment, both domestic and foreign institutions (public and private both) are operating, which are broadly known as domestic investment institutions (DIIs) and foreign investment institutions (FIIs).

(iv) ***State Level Finance Institutions (SLFIs):*** In the wake of states' involvement in the industrial development, the central government allowed the states to set up their own FIs (after the states demanded so). In this process two kinds of FIs came up:

(a) *State Finance Corporations (SFCs):* First set up in Punjab (1955) with other states following its example. There are 18 SFCs working presently.

(b) *State Industrial Development Corporations (SIDCs):* A fully dedicated state public sector FI to the cause of industrial development in the concerned states. Such FIs were first set up (1960) in Andhra Pradesh and Bihar.

Almost all of the SFCs and SIDCs are at present running at huge losses. They may be re-structured on the lines of the AIFIs, but there is lack of will from the states and private financiers who are not interested to opt for their takeovers as such.

2. **Banking Industry:** With the passage of time, the industry saw its nationalisation (1969 and 1980) and again opening up for private sector entry (1993-94) to emerge as the most dependable segment of the Indian financial system - in a way its mainstay. By February 2025, there were a total of 137 scheduled commercial banks operating in India - 12 PSBs, 43 RRBs (with over 22 under consideration for amalgamation with their parent PSBs), 22 Indian private sector banks, 11 small banks, 3 payment banks, 3 local area banks, and 46 foreign banks except the scheduled and non-scheduled state co-operative banks - with 74 per cent foreign direct investment (FDI) allowed in the private sector banks (49 per cent under automatic route and above 49 per cent under non-automatic route).[21]

   In the wake of the economic reforms the government has promised speedier expansion of the banking sector. But the entry of new private players in the banking sector has been slow, hampering the growth and expansion of the sector. To promote financial inclusion and create more financing institutions, in 2016, RBI announced the 'on tap' availability (i.e., always available) of bank licences. Till now, RBI used to offer licences to set up new private banks, but it was not a year-round window.

3. **Insurance Industry:** After independence, for the purpose of expanding the industry, one after another, the life and non-life insurance businesses were nationalised by the government (in 1956 and 1970, respectively), and the public sector insurance companies did serve the better purpose in the areas of providing safety net and nation-building. In the wake of the process of economic reforms a restructuring of the sector was started and the industry was opened for domestic and Foreign Private Players (with the FDI limit

---

[21] As per the *Reserve Bank of India*, Mumbai, February 2025.

increased in 2021-22 to of 74 per cent from 26 per cent of 1999 and 100 per cent in 2025-26) and an independent regulator - the Insurance Regulatory and Development Authority of India (IRDAI) being set up in 1999. Since then, many private players have entered the industry. By February 2025, a total of 58 insurance companies were operating in India, of which 24 were in the life segment while 34 were in non-life segment - 1 public sector life insurer (LIC), 4 public sector general insurer, 2 specialised insurers (AICIL and ECGC), 1 public sector re-insurer (GIC Re) and 10 foreign re-insurers.[22]

4. **Security Market:** After the government's attempts to formally organise the security and stock market of India, the segment has seen accelerated expansion. Today, it is counted among the most vibrant share markets of the world and has challenged the monopoly of banks in the capital market of the country.[23] The security market of India is regulated by SEBI. India has also developed a regulated 'forward market', where hundreds of commodities and derivatives are traded on a spot and non-spot basis - regulated by the FMC, which merged into SEBI by late 2015.

FINANCIAL REGULATION

India has a multiple regulatory architecture in the financial sector. The design has developed complexities over time due to: the *number* of regulatory, quasi-regulatory, non-regulatory-but-still-regulating bodies; *overlapping ambiguous* operational design and their influence.[24] A brief overview of the financial regulatory framework is given below.

Regulatory Agencies

India has product-wise regulators - RBI regulates credit products, savings and remittances, SEBI regulates investment products, the Insurance Regulatory and Development Authority (IRDA) regulates insurance products, and the Pension Fund Regulatory and Development Authority (PFRDA) regulates pension products. The Forward Markets Commission (FMC) regulates commodity-based exchange-traded futures (which was merged with the SEBI by late 2015).

Certain entities, primarily engaged in one product (i.e., the insurance companies), also offer other products, making it difficult for product-based regulation (this came to light in the PFRDA-IRDA controversy of the early 2010s). Thus, most regulation turns out to be entity-based. Another example is of *cooperative banks*, which, except in terms of their ownership structure, are very much like other banks - they take deposits and give loans. Still, their regulation is largely left to the Registrar of Cooperatives.

Quasi-regulatory Agencies

Several other government bodies perform quasi-regulatory functions - National Bank for Agriculture and Rural Development (NABARD), Small Industries Development Bank of India (SIDBI) and National Housing Bank (NHB). The NABARD supervises regional rural banks as well as state and district cooperative banks. The NHB regulates housing finance companies, and the SIDBI regulates the state finance corporations (SFCs).

Central Ministries

Certain ministries of the GoI are also involved in policy making in the financial system. The Ministry of Finance (MoF) is most prominently involved, through its representatives on the Boards of SEBI, IRDA and RBI. The MoF and Ministry of Small-Scale Industries have representatives on the SIDBI Board, and the Ministry of Urban Development is represented on the NHB Board. MoF representatives are also on Boards of public sector banks (PSBs) and Development Financial Institutions (DFIs). The Forward Market Commission (FMC), which used to regulate the commodity exchanges and brokers, under the Ministry of Consumer Affairs, shifted to the MoF in 2014 (merged with the SEBI, MoF by September, 2015).

State Governments

Through the Registrar of Cooperatives, who are under the Departments of Agriculture and cooperation, the state governments regulate the cooperative banking institutions in their respective states. The state government has also sometimes claimed a regulatory role in certain other cases. Though it never became an open battle, the Andhra Pradesh government's ordinance directing operations of Micro Finance

---

22 As per the *Insurance Regulatory and Development Authority of India (IARDI)*, (New Delhi: Ministry of Finance, Government of India, February 2025).

23 *Economic Survey 2012-13* (New Delhi: Ministry of Finance, Government of India, 2013), p. 116.

24 Financial Sector Legislative Reforms Commission Report, New Delhi, March 2013.

Institutions (MFIs) - many of them NBFCs registered with and regulated by the RBI - falls into this category.

Such actions by the state government have been matters of contention in the past as well, and some of them also have gone to the courts (the judgement on the court cases to clarify the *RBI vs State Government* issue are up to the Supreme Court).

Special Statutes for Certain Financial Intermediaries

Some key financial services intermediaries such as SBI (and its Associate Banks before their consolidation with SBI in 2017-18), PSP, LIC and GIC are governed by their own statutes. These statutes provide a special status to these institutions *vis-a-vis* the other institutions performing the same functions. Earlier, IFCI, UTI and IDBI also operated under special statutes, but now their special statutes have been repealed.

Establishment of FSDC

A few years ago, an important addition was made to the regulatory architecture - the Financial Sector Development Council (FSDC) was set up which replaced the High-Level Committee on Capital Markets. The council is convened by the MoF and does not have statutory authority - it is structured as a *council of regulators* - with the finance minister as chairman. It has a permanent secretariat.

The council resolves inter-agency disputes; looks after the regulation of financial conglomerates that fall under various regulators' purview; and performs wealth management functions dealing with multiple products.

PREVIOUS YEARS' QUESTIONS

Prelims

1. Consider the following: (2024)
   (i) Exchange-Traded Funds (ETF)
   (ii) Motor vehicles
   (iii) Currency swap

   Which of the above is/are considered financial instruments?
   (a) (i) only **(b)** (ii) and (iii) only
   (c) (i), (ii) and (iii) **(d)** (i) and (iii) only

Answer: 1. (d)

Explanation

1. (d): Except 'motor vehicles' rest of the two are financial instruments. This question is on the greater 'financialisation' happening since 2020-21 in the country, under which more than physical assets people prefer to put their money in financial products (such as shares, mutual funds, debentures, corporate bonds, etc.).

SAMPLE OBJECTIVE QUESTIONS

1. Consider the following statements:
   (i) Without a vibrant money market, only capital market cannot help an economy to grow.
   (ii) A vibrant capital market is more important than the money market in an economy.
   (iii) Security market has emerged as the most attractive and dependable source of long-term funds across the world.

   Which of the above statements are correct?
   Code:
   (a) Only one **(b)** Only two
   (c) All three **(d)** None of these

2. Consider the following statements:
   (i) SBI Discount and Finance House of India covers counter-party risk in money market.
   (ii) Repo is the most preferred money market route to raise short-term funds in the economy.

(iii) Mutual Funds originate in money market, however, operate in capital market too.

Which of the above statements are correct?
Code:

(a) Only one **(b)** Only two
(c) All three **(d)** None of these

3. Consider the following statements:

(i) Commercial Paper was in news recently due to a non-banking financial company.

(ii) Cash Management Bill can be considered as a Treasury Bill with market-driven interest rate.

(iii) All India Financial Institutions can issue for higher periods of loans than that of the banks in the country.

Which of the above statements are correct?
Code:

(a) Only one **(b)** Only two
(c) All three **(d)** None of these

4. Consider the following statements:

(i) Repo operations fall under a category of money market instruments in the country.

(ii) Treasury Bills are issued as zero-coupon bonds.

(iii) Call Money Market operations are unsecured and require no collaterals.

Which of the above statements are correct?
Code:

(a) Only one **(b)** Only two
(c) All three **(d)** None of these

5. Consider the following statements related to the financial market of the country:

(i) The money market has a dual regulator.

(ii) There is an upper ceiling on repo operation for banks.

(iii) Individuals can take part in the money market as investors.

How many of the above statements are correct?

(a) Only one **(b)** Only two
(c) All three **(d)** None of these

6. Consider the following statements related to the capital market of the country:

(i) The Commercial Papers are traded in this market.

(ii) Banks are the most dominant and assured players in this market.

(iii) Currency derivatives are allowed for trading in it.

How many of the above statements are correct?

(a) Only one **(b)** Only two
(c) All three **(d)** None of these

7. Consider the following statements related to financial market regulation in the country:

(i) A unified regulator for the sector is proposed to be set in 2024-25.

(ii) A unified financial regulator of the UK is a role model for India.

(iii) B. N. Srikrishna Committee advised in favour of a unified financial regulator.

How many of the above statements are correct?

(a) Only one **(b)** Only two
(c) All three **(d)** None of these

8. Consider the following statements related to the new development finance institution, the National Bank for Financing Infrastructure and Development (NaBFID):

(i) Set up by the Government it will become the first development finance institution in private sector.

(ii) Mandated to evolve flexible tenures of lending, it can raise funds from external sources too.

(iii) Banks of India might be a source of funds for it.

How many of the above statements are correct?

(a) Only one **(b)** Only two
(c) All three **(d)** None of these

9. Consider the following statements related to the mutual funds in the country:

(i) Mutual fund investments are safer than the investments in share market.

(ii) It operates under more than two regulatory control.

(iii) They are very popular among the investors belonging to the middle class.

(iv) Few schemes of the Government-owned Unit Trust of India offer assured returns too.

How many of the above statements are correct?

(a) Only one **(b)** Only two
(c) Only three **(d)** All four

10. Consider the statements related to financial market regulation in the country:

(i) National Housing Bank operates as a quasi-regulator.

(ii) Few central ministries other than the Ministry of Finance too are involved in it.

(iii) The RBI regulates the State Bank of India like other scheduled commercial banks.

How many of the above statements are correct?

(a) Only one **(b)** Only two
(c) All three **(d)** None of these

Answers: 1. (a) 2. (c) 3. (b) 4. (d) 5. (c) 6. (c) 7. (a) 8. (c) 9. (a) 10. (b)

SAMPLE SUBJECTIVE QUESTIONS

1. 'History of growth has been history of stronger financial market and creative destruction.' Explain with suitable examples.

2. Give your suggestions in favour of making organised money market more vibrant in the country and also describe the Government initiatives towards it which aim to fill the gaps.

3. 'From being a segment of the organised money market, mutual funds have catapulted into a kind of independent industry in the country.' Elucidate with suitable reasons.

4. Briefly examine the advantages and disadvantages of tapping funds from banks and security market. Give suitable examples to support your views.

SAMPLE MODEL ANSWER

1. 'Greater wealth creation, together with increased formalisation of the economy, will lead to greater inclusiveness in the country.' Comment.

Ans. Increasing economic growth is considered the simplest way a country can create wealth. But wealth is created by generating fixed assets also. In a nutshell, generating higher income and creating fixed assets are complementary to each other.

In the modern economy, one time-tested method to create wealth is followed by the formal agencies of growth - namely, the public limited companies, which are also known as the corporate sector. As these firms are joint stock companies owned by many shareholders other than the promoters, the wealth created by them is also shared by many stakeholders, including the common shareholders. Besides, they contribute to the GDP of the country via their production process other than creating jobs. For that matter, even non-public limited firms can also do the same provided they become a formal part of the economy - at least in the eyes of the tax department (i.e., being GST registered, filing income tax returns, etc.).

The other benefit of formal firms is that they need to provide social security benefits to their employees. Such employees, this way, start getting all public benefits, which are offered by either the Centre or the State governments. As the number of formal agencies increases, the number of beneficiaries also expands. This way, it is believed that higher formalisation of the economy leads to a higher degree of inclusive growth in the country.

CHAPTER 13

Banking in India

Banks are perhaps the most important financial intermediaries. In the nineteenth century, banks mainly lent money to firms to help finance their inventories which were held as collateral - in the cases of defaulters, banks seized them. Gradually, banks expanded their lending activities to finance houses and commercial real estates, holding the buildings as collateral. Emergence of information technology has presented special problems to these traditional forms of finance. If the idea does not pan out, the firm may go bankrupt, but there is no collateral - there is little value that the creditor can seize.*

*See J. E. Stiglitz and C. E. Walsh, *Economics*, 4th ed. (New York: W.W. Norton, 2006), p. 205.

To watch the Author's videos on the significance of the Chapter, scan the QR Code given here

Exam Essentials...

- Monetary Policy Stance
- Fractional-Reserve Banking
- Monetary Transmission
- Insolvency vs Bankruptcy
- Capital Adequacy Ratio
- Basel III Compliance in India
- Money Multiplier

Note to the Reader...

It can be considered among the most important chapters for the civil services exams, especially the preliminary test (PT). A number of questions have been asked on it and its relationship with growth, inflation, and budgeting. Similarly, burning issues like monetary policy amidst globalised economy, pressure on rupee's exchange rate (especially against the US dollar), stabilised inflation, etc. are always important for the Main exam.

In This Chapter...

INTRODUCTION

The sense in which we use the term 'banking' today has its origin in the western world. It was introduced in India by the British rulers way back in the seventeenth century.

Since then, a number of changes have taken place in the sector, and today Indian banks are among the finest in the emerging market economics well directed towards becoming global.

NBFCs

Bank is a financial institution engaged primarily in mobilising deposits and forwarding loans. The deposits and loans are highly differentiated in nature. Banks are regulated by the central bank of the country - in the case of India, the RBI (Reserve Bank of India). The other category of financial institution - the ***non-bank*** - is almost similar in its functions with the *main* difference (though, highly simplified) being that it does not allow its depositors to withdraw money from their accounts.

NBFCs (Non-Banking Financial Companies)[1] are fast emerging as an important segment of Indian financial system. It is a *heterogeneous group* of institutions (other than commercial and co-operative banks) performing financial intermediation in a variety of ways, such as accepting deposits, making loans and advances, leasing, hire purchase, etc. They *cannot* have certain activities as their principal business - agricultural, industrial and sale-purchase or construction of immovable property.

They raise funds from the public, directly or indirectly, and lend them to ultimate spenders. They advance loans to the various wholesale and retail traders, small-scale industries (SSIs) and self-employed persons. Thus, they have broadened and diversified the range of products and services offered by a financial sector. Gradually, they are being recognised as *complementary* to the banking sector due to their:

1. customer-oriented services;
2. simplified procedures;
3. attractive rates of return on deposits; and
4. flexibility and timeliness in meeting the credit needs of specified sectors.

[1] RBI update, 11 March, 2016 and the business.gov.in, Government of India, April 2016.

RBI, the regulator of the NBFCs, has given a very wide definition of such companies (kind of a 'umbrella' definition) - a financial institution formed as a company involved in receiving deposits or lending in any manner. Based on their liability structure, they have been classified into two broad categories:

1. Deposit-taking NBFCs (NBFC-D) and
2. Non-deposit-taking NBFCs (NBFC-ND).

It is *mandatory* for an NBFC to get itself registered with the RBI as a *deposit-taking* company. For registration they need to be a *company* (incorporated under the Companies Act, 1956) and should have a minimum NOF (net owned fund)[2] of ₹2 crore.

To *obviate dual* regulation, a certain category of the NBFCs which are regulated by other financial regulators is exempted from the regulatory control of the RBI:

- Venture capital fund, merchant bank, stock broking firms (the SEBI registers and regulates them);
- Insurance company (registered and regulated by the IRDA);
- Housing finance company (regulated by the National Housing Bank);
- Nidhi company (regulated by the Ministry of Corporate Affairs under the Companies Act, 1956);
- Chit fund company (regulated by respective state governments under the Chit Funds Act, 1982).

Some of the ***important regulations*** relating to acceptance of deposits by the NBFCs are as follows:

- Allowed to accept and/or renew public deposits for a minimum period of 12 months and maximum period of 60 months.
- Cannot accept demand deposits (i.e., the saving and current accounts).
- Cannot offer interest rates higher than the ceiling rate prescribed by the RBI.

[2] The term 'NOF' means, net owned funds (*paid-up capital* and *free reserves* minus *accumulated losses, deferred revenue expenditure* and *other intangible assets)* less, (i) investments in shares of subsidiaries/companies in the same group and all other NBFCs; and (ii) the book value of debentures, bonds, outstanding loans and advances, including hire-purchase and lease finance made to, and deposits with, subsidiaries/ companies in the same group, in excess of 10 per cent of the owned funds.

- Cannot offer gifts, incentives or any other additional benefit to the depositors.
- Should have minimum investment grade credit rating.
- Their deposits are not insured.
- The repayment of deposits by the NBFCs is not guaranteed by the RBI.
- Need to maintain Capital Adequacy Ratio (CAR) norm as prescribed by the RBI.

Regulatory Changes For the ease of regulation and providing greater operational flexibility the following changes[3] were made by the RBI in relation of the NBFCs:

- Existing three categories of the NBFCs (asset finance companies, investment companies and loan companies) were merged into a new category - NBFC-Investment and Credit Companies (NBFC-ICCs).
- Now onwards they will be regulated by their activity rather than entity.
- Deposit taking NBFC-ICC will invest up to 20 per cent of its net assets in unquoted shares of another company (which is not a subsidiary or a company in the same group of the NBFC).
- Excluding core investment companies (CICs),[4] the exposures to all of them will be risk weighted as per credit ratings (similar to corporates).

The growing importance of the NBFC sector in the Indian financial system is reflected in the consistent rise of NBFCs' credit as a proportion to GDP as well as in relation to credit extended by SCBs. As per the *Reserve Bank of India*, supported by various policy initiatives, NBFCs could absorb the shocks of the pandemic and were in a strong position by late 2024-25:

- Their asset quality improved with the declining GNPAs (Gross Non-Performing Assets) from the peak of **7.2** per cent recorded in June 2021 to **2.7** per cent in September 2024.
- Against regulatory requirement of between 12 and 15 per cent, their CRAR (Capital-to-Risk-weighted Assets Ratio) was at **26.6** per cent by end-September 2024.
- By September 2024, their lending to various sectors (industry, retail, services, and agriculture) stood at ₹15.75 lakh crore (a decline of 7.8 per cent over the previous year) which is almost equal to the total lending by scheduled commercial banks to them (a decline of around 9 per cent over the previous year).

RESERVE BANK OF INDIA

In the wake of the banking crisis of the early twentieth century, the world felt a need for a central banking body for the first time. Following the global indicator, in India such a body, the RBI,[5] was also set up on 1 April 1935, in accordance with the provisions of the RBI Act, 1934, in Calcutta (shifted to Bombay in 1937). Set up under *private ownership* like a bank, it was designated two extra functions - regulating the banking industry and being the banker of the government. To better serve the purpose, during the mid-1940s, a view emerged across the world in favour of a government-owned central bank - and governments started taking over them. In India too, the RBI was nationalised, in 1949. After nationalisation, it stopped being a 'bank' in a technical sense (as it stopped accepting deposits from the general public). The RBI has been extended quite complex and challenging functions which have been summarised in its *Preamble* as given below:

To regulate the issue of Bank notes and keeping of reserves with a view to securing monetary stability in India and generally to operate the currency and credit system of the country to its advantage; to have a modern monetary policy framework to meet the challenge of an increasingly complex economy, to maintain price stability while keeping in mind the objective of growth.

As per changing needs, the RBI Nationalisation Act of 1949 has been amended several times by the Government and its functions broadened. Its current functions may be summarised objectively in the following way:

[3] Reserve Bank of India, (New Delhi: Ministry of Finance, GoI, 22 February 2019).

[4] CICs are a kind of NBFC (on the basis of their *activity*) which invest in different kinds of securities (shares and debt) - not less than 90 per cent of their net assets. They cannot engage in 'trading' of the instruments they hold. They need to register with the RBI if their asset size is above ₹100 crores and access public funds (through instruments such as Commercial Paper, debentures, inter-corporate deposits and borrowings from banks/financial institutions) - are called *Systemically Important Core Investment Companies (CICs-ND-SI)*.

[5] Based on the RBI Nationalisation Act, 1949 and future amendments, and the RBI website, April, 2020.

1. **Monetary Authority:** It includes formulation, implementation and monitoring of the monetary policy. The broad objective is maintenance of price stability keeping in mind the objective of growth. Today, under price stability it *stabilises* the wholesale price index (WPI) and *targets* the consumer price index (CPI-C).
2. **Currency Authority:** It includes issuing of new currency notes and coins (except the currency and coins of rupee one or its denominations, which are issued by the Ministry of Finance itself) as well as exchanging or destroying ones which are not fit for circulation. This function includes the distribution responsibility of currencies and coins (of those ones too which are issued by the Ministry of Finance). The broad objective is retaining adequate supplies of quality currencies and coins.
3. **Regulator and Supervisor of the Financial System:** It includes prescribing broad parameters of banking operations within which the banking and financial system operates. The broad objective of this function is maintaining public confidence in the system, protecting depositors' interest and providing cost-effective banking services to the public.
4. **Manager of Foreign Exchange:** It includes broad functions such as managing the FEMA (Foreign Exchange Management Act, 1999); keeping the forex (foreign exchange) reserves of the country; stabilising the exchange rate of rupee; and representing the Government of India (GoI) in the International Monetary Fund and World Bank (and other international financial agencies of which India is a member). The objective of this function is facilitating external trade and external payments; and promoting orderly development/maintenance of the foreign exchange market in the country.
5. **Regulator and Supervisor of Payment and Settlement Systems:** It includes functions such as introducing and upgrading safe and efficient modes of payment systems in the country to meet the requirements of the public at large. The objective is maintaining public confidence in payment and settlement system.
6. **Banker of the Governments and Banks (known also as the Related Functions):** It includes three category of functions - firstly, performing the Merchant Banking functions for the central and state governments; secondly, acting as their Bankers; and thirdly, maintaining banking accounts of the SCBs (scheduled commercial banks) - domestic, foreign, public and private - operating in the country. The broad objectives are enabling the governments and banks to mobilise enough liquidity for their functioning under which it lends or manages borrowing plans of the governments and provides short-term and long-term loans to the banks (as *Lender of Last Resort*).

> **Word Bank**
>
> **Merchant Banks**
>
> Merchant banks are a kind of financial institution/company which are involved in providing a variety of financial services in an economy such as underwriting issuance of new shares, credit syndication, mezzanine financing (see this entry in Glossary), portfolio management, managing private placements, corporate advisory services, etc. In India, they are registered and regulated by the Security and Exchange Board of India (SEBI).

7. **Developmental Function:** Unlike most of the central banks in the world, the RBI was also given some developmental functions. Playing this role, it did set up developmental banks such as the IDBI, SIDBI, NABARD, Exim Bank and NHB. Gradually, the ownership of these banks is being transferred from the RBI to the GoI (aimed at enhancing regulatory freedom and professionalism of the central bank and enabling the Government to take care of the dynamic requirements of development in a better way).

The RBI operates today with its 33 regional offices, most of which are situated in state capitals and whose affairs are governed by a central board of directors. The Government constitutes the board by appointing or nominating the directors for a period of four years in the following way:

1. **Official Directors:** Governor and not more than four deputy governors.
2. **Non-Official Directors:** 10 nominated from various fields and two government officials. It

also includes four directors from each of the four local boards of RBI (also known as sub-offices, they are situated at Chennai, Kolkata, Mumbai and New Delhi).

RBI's Subsidiaries There are four fully owned subsidiaries of the RBI, namely the Deposit Insurance and Credit Guarantee Corporation of India (DICGC), Bharatiya Reserve Bank Note Mudran Private Limited (BRBNMPL), Reserve Bank Information Technology Private Limited (ReBIT) and Indian Financial Technology and Allied Services (IFTAS).

New Financial Year Aimed at aligning its financial year with the government's financial year, in February 2020 the RBI decided[6] to shift to April-March as its new financial year from 2020-21 (from its existing financial year July-June). Thus, the RBI will do away with nearly eight decades of practice - it used to follow the January-December financial year before it was changed to July-June in 1940. Such a change was recommended by the *Jalan Committee* (set up by the RBI on the *Economic Capital Framework*, 2019).

RBI's Reserves and Surplus Capital

In 2019-20, a lot of debate was seen on the issue of reserve transfer of the RBI to the Government. To look into the issue, an expert committee on the Economic Capital Framework was set up by the RBI (headed by Bimal Jalan) in 2019, which could advise the manner in which it should share *surplus capital* with the Government. On its advice, the RBI transferred an amount of ₹1.76 lakh crore to the Government and affected *several changes* related[7] to the issue:

- Giving a clearer distinction between the two components of 'economic capital' - realised equity and revaluation balances - the committee recommended that realised equity could be used for meeting all risks/losses as they were primarily built up from retained earnings while revaluation balances could be reckoned only as risk buffers against market risks as they represented unrealised valuation gains and hence were not distributable.
- The revaluation balance of the central bank should not be distributed.
- The entire net income can be transferable to the government only if realised equity is above its requirement. If it is below the lower bound of requirement, risk provisioning will be made to the extent necessary and only the residual net income (if any) will be transferred to the Government.
- On the issue of the RBI's economic capital, the committee reviewed the status, need and justification of the various reserves, risk provisions and risk buffers maintained by the RBI and recommended their continuance.
- On the risk provisioning for market risk, the committee has recommended the adoption of Expected Shortfall (ES) methodology under stressed

Monetary Policy Stance

Considered as the most dynamic and sensitive function of a central bank (i.e., RBI in case of India), this macroeconomic policy is related to monetary matters – chiefly aimed at regulating the size and cost of fund/money in the economic system. From being announced twice a year (before *slack* and *busy* seasons) today the policy is a *bi-monthly* affair announced 6 times in a financial year after the monetary policy committee (MPC) came into being in 2016. Committee-based approach to monetary policy is supposed to add *value* and *transparency* to monetary policy with *statutory* responsibility given to the RBI for targeting inflation (CPI-C) while keeping in mind the objective of growth. The MPC (has to meet four times at the very least every year) has a total of six members nominated by RBI and the Ministry of Finance in equal numbers including the RBI Governor as its Chairman who avails the right of casting vote in case of a tie in decisions. The actual tone of the monetary policy stance of the RBI is set by its first monetary policy of the year announced beginning every financial year – gaining its clues from the annual budget announcements. There are few types of *monetary policy stances* which keep appearing in the media from time to time:

[6] The decision was taken by the Central Board of the RBI on 15 February 2020, and sent to the Government for consideration.

[7] Expert Committee to review the Extant Economic Capital Framework, headed by Dr. Bimal Jalan and the follow-up action of the RBI, 26 August 2019.

1. *Neutral stance* means interest rates may move either way – upward or downward.
2. *Calibrated tightening* means interest rates can only move upward.
3. *Accommodative stance* (also known as *expansionary stance*) means injection of more funds into the financial system. Falling 'headline inflation' inspires the RBI for it, and such a stance is aimed at expansion in lending, investment and growth.
4. *Contractionary stance* means syphoning out of funds from the financial system. Such a stance is generally followed once more than optimum fund is believed to be available in the financial system. At times, it is also aimed at taming inflation in the long term.
5. *Hawkish stance* means the contractionary stance aimed at checking inflation from rising (linked to the statutory goals of inflation targeting the 'headline inflation').

conditions (in place of the extant Stressed-Value at Risk) for measuring the RBI's market risk on which there was growing consensus among central banks as well as commercial banks over the recent years.

- While central banks are seen to be adopting ES at 99 per cent confidence level (CL), the committee has recommended the adoption of a target of ES 99.5 per cent CL keeping in view the macroeconomic stability requirements.
- As per the report, realised equity is also required to cover credit risk and operational risk. This risk provisioning made primarily from 'retained earnings' is cumulatively referred to as the Contingent Risk Buffer (CRB) and has been recommended to be maintained within a range of 5.5 to 6.5 per cent (from the current level of 3 to 4 per cent) of the RBI's balance sheet, comprising 4.5 to 5.5 per cent for monetary and financial stability risks and 1.0 per cent for credit and operational risks.

The committee based its recommendations on the consideration of the role of central banks' financial resilience, cross-country practices, statutory provisions and the impact of the RBI's public policy mandate and operating environment on its balance sheet and the risks involved.

To put in place the desired kind of monetary policy, the RBI uses a range of instruments and tools - a brief description follows:

Cash Reserve Ratio

Banks operating in the country are under regulatory obligation to maintain 'reserve ratios' of two kinds, one of it being the *cash reserve ratio* (the other being 'statutory liquidity ratio', SLR). Under it, all SCBs operating in the country are supposed to maintain a part of their total deposits with the RBI in cash form as the cash reserve ratio (CRR). The RBI could fix[8] it between 3 and 15 per cent of the 'net demand and time liabilities' (NDTL) of the banks. In the wake of the ongoing process of banking reforms, certain changes[9] were affected by the RBI in relation to the ratio since the late 1990s:

1. Aimed at enabling banks to lend more and cut interest rates on loans they offer, in 1999-2000, the RBI started paying banks an interest income on their CRR. The payment of interest was discontinued by late 2007 in the wake of rising prices (to check aggregate demand in the economy).
2. The ratio which used to be generally on the higher side was drastically cut down to 4.5 per cent in 2003 (from a peak of 15 per cent in 1992).
3. A major development came in 2007 when by an amendment (in the RBI Act, 1949), the Government abolished the lower ceiling (called 'floor') on the CRR and gave the RBI greater flexibility in fixing this ratio. It means, it is now possible for the RBI to also fix the CRR below 3 per cent.

[8] As per the RBI Act, 1949, Section 42, sub-section (1). This provision has been amended several times since then. See *Glossary* for more detail on NDTL.

[9] It was a follow-up to the recommendations of the Committee on Financial System, 1991 (Narasimham Committee-I), headed by *M. Narasimham.* The Committee had advised the RBI to pay the banks an interest on CRR so that banks could pass this benefit to borrowers and lending can be promoted to enhance private investment in line with the objective of the ongoing economic reform process.

In February 2020, in a *first of its kind* move, the RBI allowed[10] banks to lend to automobiles; residential housing; and micro, small and medium enterprises (MSMEs), without maintaining the mandatory CRR. The move was aimed at enhancing lending activity to these sectors which have been hit hard with slowdown in recent times. Simply put, the RBI allowed banks to use the CRR money which otherwise would have been deposited by the banks with the RBI. As a result of this exemption given to banks, the RBI will lose a part of its income since the CRR deposits are used by the RBI in its daily business operations.

In **February 2026,** the CRR was **3.0** per cent of the NDTL of the banks - 1 per cent change[11] in it today makes a difference of around ₹2.50 lakh crore on the cash flow in the financial system.

Statutory Liquidity Ratio

Banks operating in the country are under regulatory obligation to maintain 'reserve ratios' of two kinds, one of it being the *SLR* (the other being the 'cash reserve ratio'). Under it, all SCBs operating in the country are supposed to maintain[12] a part of their total deposits (i.e., their NDTL) with themselves in non-cash form (i.e., in 'liquid assets') - the ratio could be fixed by the RBI between 25 and 40 per cent. In practice, banks cannot invest this fund in the liquid assets of their choice rather they are forced to invest in the Government securities (i.e., G-Secs) of various kinds. Banks earn income on this investment as per the configuration of their investments in the G-Secs. In the wake of the ongoing process of banking reforms, certain changes[13] were affected by the RBI in relation to the ratio since the late 1990s:

1. The ratio was drastically cut down to 25 per cent (the floor) in 1997 from the existing level of 32 per cent.
2. By an amendment (in the RBI Act, 1949) made in 2007, the lower ceiling (the floor) of 25 per cent was removed by the Government. This way, the SLR may be fixed by the RBI below 25 per cent also. Since then, the SLR have shown a falling tendency.

In **February 2026**, the SLR was at **18** per cent of the NDTL of the banks. With 1 per cent change in this ratio makes a difference of ₹2.50 lakh crores on banks' lendable capital.

Bank Rate

The interest rate which the RBI charges on its ***long-term*** lending is known as the Bank Rate. The clients who borrow through this route are the central government, state governments, banks, financial institutions, co-operative banks, etc. The rate has direct impact on long-term lending activities of the concerned lending bodies operating in the Indian financial system. The rate was realigned[14] with the MSF (Marginal Standing Facility) by the RBI in February 2012. By **February 2026**, it was at **5.50** per cent.

Repo Rate

The rate of interest the RBI charges from its clients on their ***short-term*** borrowing is the repo rate in India.[15] Basically, this is an abbreviated form of the 'rate of repurchase', and in western economies it is known as the 'rate of discount'.[16]

In practice it is not called an interest rate but considered a discount on the dated government securities, which are deposited by institution to borrow for the short term. When they get their securities released from the RBI, the value of the securities is lost by the amount of the current repo rate. The Call Money Market (CMM) of India (interbank market) operates at this rate, and banks use this route for *overnight* borrowings. This rate has direct relation with the interest rates banks charge on the loans they offer (as it affects the operational

---

[10] *Sixth Bi-monthly Monetary Policy*, RBI, 6 February 2020.

[11] *Maintenance of Cash Reserve Ratio (CRR)*, Press Release, Reserve Bank of India, 6 December 2024.

[12] Based on the RBI Nationalisation Act, 1949, and future amendments; and the RBI website, April, 2020.

[13] These changes were made as a follow-up to the recommendations of the Committee on Financial System, 1991 (Narasimham Committee-I), headed by *M. Narasimham*. The Committee had advised the RBI to stop forcing banks to invest in the G-Secs and allow them to select the liquid assets of their choice for investing this fund. Once banks will earn market-based interest rate on this fund (that will be always higher than the interest they earn from G-Secs) they can lend more loans and cheaper loans which will promote private investment in the economy in line with the broad objective of the economic reform process. The RBI was advised to simply abolish this compulsive investment by banks in the G-Secs for maintaining the SLR.

[14] Through an RBI announcement on 15 February 2012.

[15] RBI Act, 1934, and Banking Regulation Act, 1949.

[16] Stiglitz and Walsh, *Economics*, op. cit., pp. 629-30.

cost of the banks). The rate was **5.25** per cent in **February 2026**.

In October 2013, the RBI introduced ***term repos*** (of different tenors, such as 7/14/28 days) to inject liquidity over a period that is longer than overnight. It has several purposes to serve - stronger money market, stability, and better costing and signalling of the loan products.

> **Fractional-Reserve Banking**
>
> This is a system of banking under which banks keep only a part of the deposits they mobilise as reserve and use the rest of it to offer loans and investment. It is opposite to the 'full-reserve banking' under which total deposits are kept as reserve. The reserve ratios (CRR and SLR) were evolved by the RBI in India under it.
>
> Originating in the late 19th century in Europe, banks in many countries (UK, USA, Canada, Australia, New Zealand, Sweden, Finland and Norway) today, maintain "zero" reserve (rather, in USA, since 2020, banks are paid an interest to maintain it). However, banks with low or no reserve face the risk of **bank run** in the case of mass withdrawal by depositors.
>
> **Bank run** is a situation which occurs when a large number of depositors start withdrawing their money from banks at the same time which leads to banks failure. It was frequent during Great Depression and financial crisis of 2007–08.

Long-term Repo Operation

Aimed at promoting enhanced lending and cutting the cost of short-term funds for the banks, in a first of its kind move; in **February 2020** *(6th Bi-monthly Monetary Policy of 2019-20)*, the RBI announced to offer a long-term repo operation (LTRO) of ₹1.50 lakh crore at a fixed rate (i.e., at the Repo rate). The tenure of the LTRO will be from *one to three* years. This was aimed at ensuring permanent and deeper liquidity in the financial system together with enhancing lending by cutting cost of funds for the banks (enabling them to lend cheaper loans).

Reverse Repo Rate

This is opposite of the repo rate - under it banks park (i.e., deposit) their surplus short-term funds with RBI and enjoy interest over them. This is a collateral-based window of the RBI. Introduced in November 1996, this completed the *Liquidity Adjustment Facility (LAF)* windows of the RBI (the other being the repo rate window) by which short-term funds were regulated by the central bank. In 2022-23, it was converted into *fixed reverse repo rate* and by **February 2026**, it was at **3.35** per cent.

In April 2022, this window of the LAF was replaced by the Standing Deposit Facility (SDF) by the RBI.

Standing Deposit Facility Rate

The Standing Deposit Facility (SDF) was introduced[17] by the monetary policy committee (MPC) in 2022-23 (April 2022). This allows banks to deposit their excess funds with the RBI (similar to the reverse repo window) but without the necessity of collateral in the form of government securities. Being collateral free window, this allows RBI to manage liquidity more effectively. Though this window is available for overnight deposits, the RBI may use it to absorb funds of longer tenors too (with right pricing).

Introduced at a rate of 6.25 per cent, in April 2022, it *replaced the reverse repo rate* as the *new floor* of the Liquidity Adjustment Facility (LAF) corridor. By **February 2026** it was at **5.00** per cent.

Marginal Standing Facility

The MSF[18] is a new scheme announced by the RBI in its Monetary Policy, 2011-12, which came into effect from May 2011. Under this scheme, banks can borrow overnight up to 1 per cent of their net demand and time liabilities (NDTL) from the RBI, at the interest rate 1 per cent (100 basis points) higher than the current repo rate. In an attempt to strengthen the rupee and checking its falling exchange rate, the RBI increased the gap between 'repo' and MSF to 3 per cent (late July 2013). By **February 2026** it was at **5.50** per cent.

---

[17] *Economic Survey 2022-23* (N. Delhi: Ministry of Finance, GoI, January 2023), p. 80.

[18] The write-up is based on the RBI's *Credit & Monetary Policy, 2011-12* (in which the scheme was introduced); and the *European Central Bank*, Frankfurt, Germany and *Federal Reserve System* (also known as the *Federal Reserve*, and informally as the *Fed*) Washington DC, USA.

Other Tools

Other than the above-given instruments, the RBI uses some other important tools to activate the right kind of the credit and monetary policy:

1. **Call Money Market:** The CMM is an important segment of the money market where borrowing and lending of funds take place on overnight basis. Participants in the CMM in India currently include SCBs, excluding regional rural banks (RRBs), cooperative banks (other than land development banks) and insurance. Prudential limits, in respect of both outstanding borrowing and lending transactions in the CMM for each of these entities, are specified by the RBI.

   In recent times, several changes have been introduced by the RBI in this market. By ***April 2016***, banks were allowe to borrow only 1 per cent of their NDTL (net demand and time liabilities, i.e., total deposit of the banks, in layman's term) under overnight facility at repo rate. For the rest of 0.75 per cent of their NDTL, they may use the term *repos* of different tenors. In a sense, since late 2013, the RBI has been discouraging banks to use repo route and switch over to the term repos for their requirements of short-term funds. Promoting stability and signalling better cost of loans are the main objectives of this changed stance.

2. **Open Market Operations (OMOs):** OMOs are conducted by the RBI via the sale/purchase of government securities (G-Sec) to/from the market with the *primary aim* of modulating rupee liquidity conditions in the market. OMOs are an effective quantitative policy tool in the armoury of the RBI, but are constrained by the stock of government securities available with it at a point in time. Other than the institutions, *now individuals* are also allowed to invest in this market (through the ***RBI Retail Direct*** account directly opened with the RBI).

3. **Liquidity Adjustment Facility (LAF):** The LAF is the key element in the monetary policy operating framework of the RBI (introduced in June 2000). On daily basis, the RBI stands ready to lend to or borrow money from the banking system, as per the need of the time, at fixed interest rates (repo and reverse repo rates). Together with moderating the fund mismatches of the banks, LAF operations help the RBI to effectively transmit *interest rate signals* to the market. The recent changes regarding a *cap* on the repo borrowing and provision of the *term repo* have changed the very dynamics of this facility after 2013.

4. **Market Stabilisation Scheme (MSS):** This instrument for monetary management was introduced in 2004. Surplus liquidity of a more enduring nature arising from large capital inflows is absorbed through sale of short-dated government securities and treasury bills. The mobilised cash is held in a separate government account with the Reserve Bank of India. The instrument, thus, has features of both SLR and CRR.

5. **Standing Deposit Facility Scheme (SDFS):** The new scheme was proposed by the *Union Budget 2018-19*. Such a tool was proposed by the RBI in November 2015. The scheme is aimed at helping the RBI to manage liquidity in a better way, especially when the economy is flush with excess fund (as was seen after the demonetisation of the high value currency notes post November 2016). This became the part of monetary policy tools of the RBI since 2022-23 (as an alternative to the erstwhile 'reverse repo' which has changed to a 'fixed rate').

BASE RATE

Base rate is the interest rate below which SCBs will lend no loans to its customers - its means it is like prime lending rate (PLR) and the benchmark prime lending rate (BPLR) of the past and is basically a floor rate of interest. It replaced[19] the existing idea of BPLR on 1 July 2010.

The BPLR system (while the existing system was of PLR), introduced in 2003, fell short of its original objective of *bringing transparency* to lending rates. This was mainly because under this system, banks could lend below BPLR. This resulted in bargaining by the borrower with bank - with ultimately one borrower getting cheaper loans than the other, and blurring the attempts of bringing in transparency in the lending business. For the same reason, it was also difficult to assess the transmission of *policy rates* (i.e., repo rate, reverse repo rate, bank rate) of the Reserve Bank to lending rates of banks. The Base Rate system is **aimed at** enhancing transparency in lending rates of banks and enabling better assessment of transmission of monetary policy.

---

19 *Reserve Bank of India, Announcement,* 5 April 2010 (New Delhi: Government of India).

After its deregulation by the RBI in 2010, banks fix their own base rates. Thus, in practice, base rate shows a differentiation - changing from bank to bank according to differentiation in the operational costs of the banks. Banks were not allowed to lend any loan below their base rates. In **February 2026,** the base rate of the banks was in the range of **8.35-10.00** per cent.

By the *fiscal year 2015-16,* several new initiatives were taken by the RBI in the area of credit and monetary policy management. The *major ones* are as given below:

- Transition to a bi-monthly monetary policy cycle.
- Recognition of the glide path for disinflation (recommendation of the Urjit Patel Committee report implemented). Under it, the CPI (C) is used by the RBI as the 'Headline Inflation' for monetary management.
- A Monetary Policy Framework has been put in place - an agreement in this regard was signed between the GoI and the RBI by late February 2015. Under the framework, the RBI is to 'target inflation' at 4 per cent with a variation of 2 per cent. It means, the 'range of inflation' is to be between 2 and 6 per cent (of the CPI-C).
- Besides the existing repo route, term repos have been introduced for three set of tenors - 7, 14 and 28 days.
- The RBI is progressively reducing banks' access to overnight liquidity (at the fixed repo rate) and encouraging the banks to increase their dependency on the term repos. By March 2016, banks were allowed to borrow only up to 1 per cent of their NDTL from the CMM - 0.25 per cent through repo and the rest of 0.75 per cent through term repo. This aims to improve the transmission of policy impulses across the interest rate spectrum and provide stability to the loan market.
- In 2016-17, individuals were also allowed by the RBI to participate in the government security market (similar to the developed economies like the United States).

MCLR

From the financial year ***2016-17*** (i.e., from 1 April, 2016), banks in the country have shifted to a new methodology to compute their lending currency in circulation rate. The new methodology - ***MCLR*** (Marginal Cost of funds-based Lending Rate) - was articulated by the RBI in December 2015. The *main features* of the MCLR are as follows:

- It will be a tenor-linked internal benchmark, to be reset on an annual basis.
- Actual lending rates will be fixed by adding a spread to the MCLR.
- To be reviewed every month on a preannounced date.
- Existing borrowers will have the option to move to it.
- Banks will continue to review and publish 'base rate' as hitherto.

As per the RBI, 'for monetary transmission to occur, lending rates have to be sensitive to the policy rate'. But this was not occurring by now. During 2015-16, the RBI reduced the policy rate (repo rate) by a total of **1.25** per cent. But in comparison, banks reduced the lending rate by maximum **0.6** per cent. By now, banks have been using either of the following *three methods* to compute their base rate:

1. average cost of funds,
2. marginal cost of funds or
3. blended cost of funds (liabilities).

As per the RBI, the MCLR will bring in the *following* benefits:

- transmission of policy rate into the lending rates of banks to improve;
- computation of the interest rates by banks will become more transparent;
- cost of loan will be fairer to the borrowers as well as the banks; and
- it will help the banks to become more competitive and enhance their long-run value.

This initiative by RBI could not help improve monetary transmission much. By ***February 2026,*** the MCLRs of banks were in the range of **7.70-7.95** per cent.

EBLR

After the initiative of launching, the MCLR (marginal cost of fund-based lending rates) could not help improve monetary transmission much. Finally, RBI introduced (in December 2018) the *external benchmarks-based lending rate* (EBLR) for the banks. Under it, banks were given an option to link their lending rates to one of the following external benchmarks:

1. Repo rate
2. 91-day Treasury Bill yield
3. 182-day Treasury Bill yield

4. Any other benchmark produced by the FBIL (Financial Benchmarks India Private Ltd)[20]

Monetary Transmission

Monetary policy plays a very vital role in the allocation of funds from the financial system. For this, lending rates decided by the banks must be sensitive to the policy rates (i.e., repo, reverse repo, MSF, SDF, and bank rate) announced by the central bank known as 'monetary transmission'. But in recent years (especially, since 2015–16), a healthy monetary transmission has been lacking in the system. After the initiatives like the MCLR (marginal cost of fund-based lending rate) and EBLR (external benchmarks-based lending rate) were taken by the RBI, *monetary transmission* did show mixed results:

Scan this QR Code to watch a author's video lecture that simplifies this topic

- It remained ***weak*** during the entire period[21] between February 2019 and November 2021, during which RBI had cut repo rate by **2.50** per cent. In response, while the EBLR of bank decreased by only **1.25** per cent, the weighted average lending rate (WALR) on fresh and existing loans decreased by only 0.97 and 0.88 per cent, respectively (upto November 2021).
- Healthy monetary transmission was seen during 2025–26 — the RBI went for a cumulative reduction of 1.25 per cent in the repo rate since February 2025, which was effectively *transmitted* to the banking system. The weighted average lending rate (WALR) on fresh Rupee loans declined by 0.59 per cent, while the WALR on outstanding Rupee loans declined by 0.69 per cent between February and November 2025.[22]

It means that the actual lending rates will not remain linked to the internal data of the banks (as the case has been for MCLR) and banks will be forced to link the interest rates of their new loans with an external and market-determined benchmark. After a short delay bank started switching over to the external benchmarks from *October 2019*. Meanwhile, the process has not resulted in a much better monetary transmission.

LIQUIDITY MANAGEMENT FRAMEWORK

A liquidity management framework (LMF) was provisioned by the RBI in 2014 to check volatility in the inter-bank CMM and allow banks to manage their needs of short-term capital. As per the last revision done by the RBI in *February 2020*, the LMF guidelines were as given below:

- The combined repo borrowings of all banks put together in a day cannot be more than 1 per cent of the combined NDTL of the banks (known as the upper ceiling on repo borrowing).
- Individual banks can borrow not more than 1 per cent of their NDTL under repo operation - 0.25 per cent of it as overnight repo and rest of the 0.75 per cent as term repo for 7/14/28 days.
- After exhausting the option of the various repos, banks can borrow up to 1 per cent of their NDTL directly from the RBI for one day (called overnight) under the MSF.
- The long-term repo started by the RBI in February 2020 is an extra window over and above the 1 per cent upper cap on the repo operation.

In a push to bring in more 'stability' and better 'interest rate signalling' in the loan market, the RBI has been trying to inspire banks to think in longer term in their operations. Aimed at making banks follow prudential norms, the *Basel III* norms also has put a clear check on *short-termism* followed by the banking industry.

NATIONALISATION AND DEVELOPMENT OF BANKING IN INDIA

The development of banking industry in India has been intertwined with the story of its nationalisation. Once the RBI was nationalised in 1949 and a central banking was in place, the Government considered the nationalising of selected private banks in the country due to the following ***major*** reasons:

1. As the banks were owned and managed by the private sector the services of the banking were

---

[20] RBI recognises the FBIL as an 'independent benchmark administrator'. The company (set up in December 2014) has been jointly promoted by Fixed Income Money Market and Derivative Association of India (FIMMDA), Foreign Exchange Dealers' Association of India (FEDAI) and Indian Banks' Association (IBA).

[21] *Economic Survey 2021-22* (N. Delhi: Ministry of Finance, GoI, January 2022), pp. 129-30.

[22] *Economic Survey 2025-26* (New Delhi: Ministry of Finance, GoI, January 2026), p. 26.

having a narrow reach, the masses had no access to the banking service;

2. The government needed to direct the resources in such a way that greater public benefit could take place;
3. The planned development of the economy required a certain degree of government control on the capital generated by the economy. Nationalisation of banks in India took place in the following stages.

Emergence of the SBI

The GoI, with the enactment of the *SBI Act, 1955*, ***partially nationalised*** the three Imperial Banks (mainly operating in the three past presidencies with their 466 branches) and named them the State Bank of India, and hence the first PSB emerged in India. The RBI had purchased 92 per cent of the shares in this partial nationalisation.

Satisfied with the experiment, the Government in a related move ***partially nationalised*** eight more private banks (with good regional presence) via the *SBI (Associates) Act, 1959*, and named them as the Associates of the SBI - the RBI had acquired 92 per cent stake in them as well. Later on, the State Bank of Bikaner and Jaipur was created (by merging the State Bank of Jaipur and State Bank of Bikaner, as they used to operate in the same region). Following the banking consolidation process, by 2017-18 the SBI and its Associates were amalgamated into one bank, the SBI.

Emergence of Nationalised Banks

After successful experimentation in the partial nationalisations, the government decided to opt for complete nationalisation. With the help of the *Banking Nationalisation Act, 1969*, the government nationalised a total of 20 private banks:

1. 14 banks with deposits were more than ₹50 crore of nationalised in July 1969, and
2. 6 banks with deposits were more than ₹200 crore of nationalised in April 1980.

After the merger of the loss-making New Bank of India with the Punjab National Bank (PNB) in September 1993, the total number of nationalised banks reduced to 19. Aimed at streamlining their operation and size, the Government started a process of merger and amalgamation of the PSBs in 2020 - after the completion of this process the number of the PSBs reduced to only 12.

After the nationalisation of banks, the Government *stopped* opening of banks in the private sector though some foreign private banks were allowed to operate in the country to provide the external currency loans. After India ushered in the era of the economic reforms, the Government started a comprehensive banking system reform in the fiscal year 1992-93. Three related developments allowed the further expansion of banking industry in the country:

1. In 1993, the SBI was allowed access to the capital market with permission given to sell its share to the tune of 33 per cent through *SBI (Amendment) Act, 1993*.
2. In 1994, the government allowed the nationalised banks to have access to the capital market with a ceiling of 33 per cent sale of shares through the *Banking Companies (Amendment) Act, 1994*.

   Since then, many nationalised banks have tapped the capital market for their capital enhancement - Indian Overseas Bank being first in row. Though such banks could be better called the PSBs (as the GoI holds more than 50 per cent stake in them), they are still known as nationalised banks.
3. In 1994, the Government allowed the opening of private banks in the country. The first private bank of the reform era was the UTI Bank. Since then, a few dozen Indian and foreign private banks have been opened in the country.

CONSOLIDATION OF BANKS

In the backdrop of the recommendations of financial sector reforms (M. Narasimham, 1991 and 1998), we find a broader process of banking consolidation of the PSBs commencing in the country by 1993-94 itself. However, certain confusion remained as how[23] much of the Government ownership in them should be disinvested with. The *broader objective* of banking consolidation is helping the PSBs emerge as significant global players for which the most essential aspect will be broadening[24] of their capital base. In this

[23] As per the *Strategic Disinvestment Statement of 1999*, the Government had decided to cut its holding on them to 26 per cent. The policy was put on hold by the new Government in 2004.

[24] Y. V. Reddy, *Lectures on Economic and Financial Sector Reforms in India* (New Delhi: Oxford University Press, 2002), pp. 137-57.

direction, the following actions have been taken by the Government.

Merger It is aimed at creating bigger and stronger banks besides reducing operational cost and broadening capital base of the banks. Mainly starting with the mergers of the Associates of SBI (all seven such banks merged into one by 2017-18), the biggest such exercise was affected in August 2019 when 10 PSBs were merged into four (their number came down to 12). As per the *Union Budget 2021-22*, in 2021-22, other two to three banks were to be merged.

Disinvestment Both of the routes of disinvestment are to be followed in case of the banks - 'minority' stake sale and 'strategic' (which may also result into privatisation) aimed at infusing fresh capital and managerial professionalism. The Government has clearly announced in the *Union Budget 2021-22* to privatise all 'non-strategic' public sector enterprises (which include some of the PSBs too) while maintaining ownership control in the 'strategic' ones limited to only *four* in number (which will also include few of the PSBs besides some other financial institutions). For more on the 'strategic PSEs' see the topic on disinvestment in *Chapter 10*.

Strategic Partners The Government had decided (in the disinvestment policy announced in October 1999) to sell the majority stakes of the banks to only a 'strategic partner' in case of their privatisation - in whose hands the banks can grow due to their world-class experience (during 1999-2000 this route was used by the Government to privatise the PSEs such as the BALCO, Modern Foods, VSNL etc). Though such a specific stance of strategic disinvestment was not announced by the Government till April 2021, it may be expected any day.

Summary The Government believes that India needs global-sized banks to become a US$ 5 trillion economy by 2024-25. Today, India has only one bank in the top 100 global bank list (i.e., SBI at 55th position), while China and the United States have 18 banks and 12 in the list, respectively.

As per the former *Chief Economic Adviser K. V. Subramanian* (August 2020), India is the fifth largest economy in the world - so, if the Indian banking sector was proportional to the size of its economy, it should have been where South Korea is, which has 6 banks in the global top hundred. He further added that even countries that are a fraction of India's size, for example Finland, Denmark, Belgium, Austria, Norway, have at least one bank in the global top hundred - Sweden and Singapore, which are one-sixth and one-eighth the size of the Indian economy, respectively, have three banks in the list.

REGIONAL RURAL BANKS

The regional rural banks (RRBs) were first set up on 2 October 1975 (only 5 in number), with the aim to take banking services to the doorsteps of the rural masses, especially in the remote areas with no access to banking services, with the intention to fulfil twin duties:

1. To provide credit to the weaker sections of the society at concessional rate of interest who previously depended on private money lending, and
2. To mobilise rural savings and channelise them for supporting productive activities in the rural areas.

The GoI, the concerned state government and the sponsoring nationalised bank contribute the share capital of the RRBs in the proportion of 50, 15 and 35 per cent, respectively. The area of operation of the RRB is limited to notified few districts in a state.

Following the suggestions of the *Kelkar Committee*, the Government stopped opening new RRBs in 1987 - by that time their total number stood at 196. Due to excessive leanings towards social banking and catering to the highly economically weaker sections, these banks started incurring huge losses by the early 1980s. For restructuring and strengthening of the banks, the governments set up two committees - the *Bhandari Committee* (1994-95) and the *Basu Committee* (1995-96). Out of the total, 171 were running in losses in 1998-99 when the Government took some serious decisions:

1. The obligation of concessional loans abolished and the RRBs started charging commercial interest rates on its lending.
2. The target clientele (rural masses, weaker sections) was set free now to lend to anybody.

After the above-given policy changes, the RRBs started coming out of the red/losses. The CFS has recommended to merge them with their managing nationalised or PSBs and finally make them part of the would-be three-tier banking structure of India. By ***February 2026,*** as per the RBI, there were 28 RRBs operating in the country.

CO-OPERATIVE BANKS

Banks in India can be broadly classified under two heads - commercial banks and co-operative banks. While commercial banks (nationalised banks, State Bank group, private sector banks, foreign banks and RRBs) account for an overwhelming share of the banking business, co-operative banks also play an important role. Initially *set up to* supplant indigenous sources of rural credit, particularly money lenders, today they mostly serve the needs of agriculture and allied activities, rural-based industries and to a lesser extent, trade and industry in urban centres. Co-operative banks have a *three-tier structure:*

1. Primary Credit Societies - PCSs (agriculture or urban),
2. District Central Co-Operative Banks - DCCBs, and
3. State Co-Operative Banks - SCBs (at the apex level).

UCBs Primary credit societies (PCSs) in urban areas that meet certain specified criteria can apply to the RBI for a banking license to operate as urban co-operative banks (UCBs). They are registered and governed under the co-operative societies acts of the respective states and are covered by the Banking Regulation Act, 1949 - thus are under dual regulatory control. The *managerial aspects* of these banks - registration, management, administration, recruitment, amalgamation, and liquidation - are controlled by the state governments, while the matters related to *banking* are regulated by the RBI.

Traditionally, the area of operation of the UCBs is confined to metropolitan, urban or semiurban centres and caters to the needs of small borrowers including MSMEs, retail traders, small entrepreneurs, professionals and the salaried class. However, there is no formal restriction as such, and today UCBs can conduct business in the entire district in which they are registered, including rural areas. Well-managed primary UCBs with deposits of over ₹50 crore are also allowed to operate in more than one state subject to certain norms.

As they are covered by the RBI Act, 1934 (2nd Schedule), they have certain rights and obligations - *rights* of obtaining refinance and loans from the RBI and *obligations* such as maintenance of cash reserves, submission of returns to the RBI etc. Presently, there are 29 UCBs.

DCCBs and SCBs As their names suggest, they operate at the district and state levels. One district can have no more than one DCCB with a number of DCCBs reporting to the SCB. They were under supervision of the RBI - later on this function was delegated to the NABARD.

Problems of these Banks

Co-operative banks play a very vital role in India's financial system. But they have also been faced with certain long-drawn problems. They are briefly discussed below:

- Regulation remains the biggest issue as they are under dual regulatory control - the UCBs come under the RBI and the Registrar of Cooperative Societies (RCS) of the respective states, while the DCCBs and SCBs come under the NABARD, the RBI and the RCSs. Given the close links between politicians and co-operatives and the fact that the RCS functions under the state government, in practice this dual (or triple) custody of the co-operative banks has, in practice, led to poor supervision and control. Besides, most co-operative banks are lacking in skill and expertise.
- Recruitments are politicised as are appointments at most levels.
- Income recognition and prudential norms that were introduced for commercial banks in the early 1990s (under the process of banking reforms) are still to be done in this sector.

Co-operative banks have been in the news mostly for fraudulent deals. Due to multiplicity of regulatory control of the federal nature it becomes really difficult to comply these banks to the prudential norms. Meanwhile, the GoI decided (in the ***Union Budget 2017-18***) to bring the co-operative banks into the ambit of the 'core banking' structure. Under the core banking solution (CBS), customers are able to avail banks' services across all of the branches rather the branch where the account is, making them customers of the bank rather than of a branch.

Regulatory Changes In 2020-21, the Government took an effective step (by amending the Banking Regulation Act, 1949) in this direction under which the RBI was given greater *regulatory powers* in case of the UCBs - accordingly, the following changes[25] have come into force:

- The RBI can issue directions relating to the management of UCBs including approval for appointment of Chairman/MD/CEO, removal and remuneration of MD/CEO.
- Board of these banks should have not less than 51 per cent members having special knowledge/ practical experience in specified areas.
- The statutory restriction on grant of director-related loans has been widened and common directorship across banks prohibited.
- The RBI has been vested with powers of approval of the appointment/removal of statutory auditors of UCBs.
- The RBI to specify the guidelines for raising capital by UCBs (by issuing equity, preference, special shares, debentures and bonds).
- The RBI can supersede the Board of Directors of a UCB (in case of a UCB having operations confined to a single State, to be carried out in consultation with the concerned State Government).
- The RBI to sanction voluntary or compulsory amalgamation and to prepare scheme for reconstruction of a UCB with the approval of the Central Government.
- Winding up of a UCB by High Court at the instance of the RBI.
- Priority sector lending (PSL) target for UCBs increased to 75 per cent (from 40 per cent).
- Co-operative banks declared as eligible lending institutions under interest subvention scheme for MSMEs.
- Compulsory reporting of large loans (loans of ₹5 crore and above) given by the UCBs to the CRILC (Central Repository of Information on Large Credits).
- The exposure norms for 'single borrower' and a 'group of borrowers' decreased to 15 and 25 per cent, respectively (from 25 and 40 per cent) for the UCBs.

FINANCIAL SECTOR REFORMS

The process of economic reforms initiated in 1991 had redefined the role of Government in the economy - in future, the economy will be dependent on the greater private participation for its development.[26] Such a changed view to development required an overhauling in the investment structure of the economy. Now the private sector was going to demand high investible capital out of the financial system. Thus, an emergent need was felt to restructure the whole financial system of India.

The three decades after nationalisation had seen a phenomenal expansion in the geographical coverage and financial spread of the banking system in the country. As certain weaknesses were found to have developed in the system during the late 1980s, it was felt that these had to be addressed to enable the financial system to play its role ushering in a more efficient and competitive economy.[27] Accordingly, a ***high level*** Committee on Financial System (CFS) was set up on 14 August 1991, to examine all aspects relating to ***structure, organisation, function*** and ***procedures*** of the financial system - based on its recommendations, a comprehensive reform of the banking system was introduced in the fiscal year 1992-93.

The CFS based its recommendations on certain ***assumptions***[28] which are fundamental to the banking industry. And the suggestions of the committee became logical in light of this assumption, and there was no second opinion about it. The assumption says that ***the resources of the banks come from the general public and are held by the banks in trust that they are to be deployed for maximum benefit of the depositors***. This assumption automatically implied:

1. That even the government had no business to endanger the solvency, health and efficiency of the nationalised banks under the pretext of using banks as resources for ***economic planning, social banking, poverty alleviation*** etc.
2. Besides, the Government had no right to get hold of the funds of the banks at low interest rates and use them for financing its consumption

[25] *Economic Survey 2020-21*, vol. 2 (New Delhi: Ministry of Finance, GoI), pp. 139-40.

[26] Repeated by the Government of India many times, i.e., the *New Industrial Policy 1991; the Union Budget 1992-93; Eighth Five Year Plan (1992-97) Draft Approach*; etc.

[27] Announced by the Government while setting up the M. Narasimham *Committee on Financial System* on 14 August, 1991. See also Publication Division, *India 2011* (New Delhi: Government of India, 2002).

[28] Reserve Bank of India, *Committee on Financial Systems*, 1991.

expenditure (i.e., revenue and fiscal deficits) and thus defraud the depositors.

The recommendations of the CFS (**Narasimham Committee I**) were ***aimed*** at:

1. ensuring a degree of operational ***flexibility***;
2. ***internal autonomy*** for PSBs in their decision-making process; and
3. greater degree of ***professionalism*** in banking operation.

Recommendation of CFS

The CFS recommendation[29] could be summed up under the following five sub-titles:

1. **On Directed Investment:** The RBI was advised not to use the CRR as a principal instrument of monetary and credit control, and in place it should rely on OMOs increasingly. Two proposals were advised regarding the CRR:
   (i) CRR should be progressively reduced from the present high level of 15 per cent to 3 to 5 per cent; and
   (ii) RBI should pay interest on the CRR of banks above the basic minimum at a rate of interest equal to the level of banks' one-year deposit.

Concerning the SLR it was advised to cut it to the minimum level (i.e., 25 per cent) from the present high level of 38.5 per cent in the next five years (it was cut down to 25 per cent in October 1997). The Government was also suggested to progressively move towards market-based borrowing programme so that banks receive economic benefits on their SLR investments.

These suggestions were directed to the goal of making more funds available to the banks, converting idle cash for use, and cutting down the interest rates banks charge on their loans.

2. **On Directed Credit Programme:** Under this sub-title the suggestions revolved around the compulsion of PSL by the banks:
   (i) Directed credit programme should be phased out gradually. As per the committee, agriculture industries and SSIs had already grown to a mature stage and they did not require any special support; two decades of interest subsidy were enough. Therefore, concessional rates of interest could be dispensed with.
   (ii) Directed credit should not be a regular programme - it should be a case of extraordinary support to certain weak sections. Besides, it should be temporary, not a permanent one.
   (iii) Concept of PSL should be redefined to include only the weakest sections of the rural community such as marginal farmers, rural artisans, village and cottage industries, tiny sector, etc.
   (iv) The 'redefined PSL' should have 10 per cent fixed of the aggregate bank credit.
   (v) The composition of the PSL should be reviewed after every three years.
3. **On the Structure of Interest Rates:** The major recommendations on the structure of interest rates are:
   (i) Interest rates to be broadly determined by market forces;
   (ii) All controls of interest rates on deposits and lending to be withdrawn;
   (iii) Concessional rates of interest for PSL of small sizes to be phased out and subsidies on the IRDP loans to be withdrawn;
   (iv) Bank rate to be the anchor rate, and all other interest rates to be closely linked to it; and
   (v) The RBI to be the sole authority to simplify the structure of interest rates.
4. **On Structural Reorganisation of the Bank:** For the structural reorganisation of banks some major suggestions were given:
   (i) Substantial reduction in the number of the PSBs through mergers and acquisitions - to bring about greater efficiency in banking operations;
   (ii) Dual control of RBI and Banking Division (of the Ministry of Finance) should go immediately, and the RBI to be made the primary agency for the regulation of the banking system;
   (iii) The PSBs to be made free and autonomous;
   (iv) The RBI to examine all the guidelines and directions issued to the banking system in the context of the independence and autonomy of the banks;

29 Ibid.

(v) Every PSB to opt for a radical change in work technology and culture, so as to become competitive internally and to be at par with the wide range of innovations taking place abroad; and

(vi) Finally, the appointment of the Chief Executive of Bank (CMD) was suggested not to be on political considerations but on professionalism and integrity. An independent panel of experts was suggested which should recommend and finalise the suitable candidates for this post.

5. **Asset Reconstruction Companies/Fund:** To tackle the menace of the higher non-performing assets (NPAs) of banks and financial institutions, the committee suggested setting up of asset reconstruction companies (ARCs)/ funds (taking cues from the US experience).

The committee directly blamed the GoI and the Ministry of Finance for the sad state of affairs of the PSBs. These banks were used and abused by the GoI, the officials, the bank employees and the trade unions, the report adds. The recommendations were revolutionary in many respects and were opposed by the bank unions and the leftist political parties.

There were some other major suggestions of the committee which made it possible to carry out the following[30] by the Government:

(i) Opening of new private sector banks permitted in 1993;

(ii) Prudential norms relating to income recognition, asset classification and provisioning by banks on the basis of objective criteria laid down by the RBI;

(iii) Introduction of capital adequacy norms (i.e., CAR provisions) with international standard started;

(iv) Simplification in the banking regulation (i.e., via board for financial supervision in 1994), etc.

The recommendations of the CFS became a kind of milestone for the governments of the future to promote financial and banking sector reforms (BSRs). We can see the imprint of the committee's advices even today on most of the actions taken in this direction on the broader framework of the reforms initiated by the Government.

[30] Based on Y. V. Reddy, *Lectures on Economic and Financial Sector Reforms in India, 2002,* op. cit.

BANKING SECTOR REFORMS

The Government commenced a comprehensive reform process in the financial system in 1992-93 after the recommendations of the CFS in 1991. In December 1997, the government did set up another committee on the banking sector reform (BSR) under the chairmanship of M. Narasimham.[31] The objective of the committee is objectively clear by the ***terms of reference*** it was given while being set up:

To review the progress of banking sector reforms to date and chart a programme of financial sector reforms necessary to strengthen India's financial system and make it internationally competitive.

The **Narasimham Committee-II** (popularly called by the GoI) handed over its reports in April 1998, which included the following major suggestions[32]:

1. Need for a stronger banking system for mergers of the PSBs and the financial institutions (AIFIs) was suggested - stronger banks and the DFIs (development financial institutions, i.e., AIFIs) to be merged, while weaker and unviable ones to be closed.
2. A three-tier banking structure was suggested after mergers:
   (i) *Tier-I* to have 2 to 3 banks of international orientation;
   (ii) *Tier-II* to have 8 to 10 banks of national orientation; and
   (iii) *Tier-III* to have large number of local banks.
   The first and second tiers were to take care of the banking needs of the corporate sector in the economy.
3. Higher norms of CRAR were suggested - increased to 10 per cent.
4. Budgetary recapitalisation of the PSBs is not viable and should be abandoned.
5. Legal framework of loan recovery should be strengthened (the government passed the *SARFAESI Act, 2002).*
6. Net NPAs for all banks were suggested to be cut down to below 5 per cent by 2000 and 3 per cent by 2002.

[31] *Economic Survey 1998-99* (New Delhi: Ministry of Finance, Government of India, 1999).

[32] Based on the Report of the *Committee on Banking Sector Reforms,* April 1998 (Chairman: M. Narasimham).

7. Rationalisation of branches and staff of the PSBs was suggested.
8. Licencing to new private banks (domestic as well as foreign) was suggested to continue.
9. Banks' boards should be depoliticised under RBI supervision.
10. Board for Financial Regulation and Supervisions (BFRS) should be set up for the banking, financial and NBFC sectors in India.[33]

The recommendations of the BFR committee were pin-pointed more than the CFS (which was also headed by the same Chairman, M. Narasimham), and they did set a broader outline for the future reforms of the banking industry in the country, especially for the PSBs. We find the Government agreeing with its advice even today on many fronts of banking reforms.

Differential Rate of Interest (DRI)

The DRI is a lending programme launched by the Government in April 1972, which makes it obligatory upon all the PSBs in India to lend 1 per cent of the total lending of the preceding year to ***the poorest among the poor*** at an interest rate of 4 per cent per annum.

Priority Sector Lending

All Indian banks have to follow the compulsory target of priority sector lending (PSL). The priority sector in India at present include agriculture, small and medium enterprises (SMEs), road, water transport, small housing loans (upto ₹35 lakh in metros and ₹25 lakh elsewhere), software industries, start-ups (up to ₹50 crore), agro-processing, small and marginal farmers, artisans, self-help groups (SHGs), distressed urban poor and indebted non-institutional debtors, SCs, STs, minorities (Buddhists, Christians, Muslims, Parsis, Sikhs), healthcare, sanitation, renewable energy, loans to farmers for solar power plants and bio gas plants.[34] The PSL target must be met by the banks operating in India in the following way:

1. **Indian Banks:** need to lend 40 per cent to the priority sector every year (public sector as well as private sector banks, including foreign bank with 20 or more branches) of their total lending. There is also a sub-target - 18 per cent of the total lending must go to agriculture and 10 per cent of the total lending or 25 per cent of the PSL (whichever is higher) must be lent out to the weaker sections. Other areas of the priority sector are to be covered in the remaining amount, i.e., 12 per cent of the total lending.
2. **Foreign Banks:** (having less than 20 branches) have to fulfil only 32 per cent PSL target which has sub-targets for the exports (12 per cent) and small and medium enterprises (10 per cent). It means they need to disburse other areas of the PSL from the remaining 10 per cent of their total lending ***(lesser burden)***.
3. **Regional Rural Banks:** need to lend 75 per cent of their total loans to the priority sector.
4. **Small Finance Banks:** need to lend 60 per cent (reduced from 75 per cent in 2025) of their total loans to the priority sector.
5. **Urban Cooperative Banks:** need to lend 40 per cent of their total loans to the priority sector.

The CFS (1991) had suggested to immediately cut it down to 10 per cent for all banks and completely phase out this policy for the betterment of the banking industry in particular and the economy in general. The committee also suggested to shuffle the sectors covered under the PSL every three years. No such follow-up has been carried out from the government except cutting down the PSL target for the foreign banks from 40 per cent to 32 per cent (remaining same for those which have less than 20 branches). Meanwhile, some new areas have been added to the PSL.

NPAs AND STRESSED ASSETS

The NPAs are the *bad loans* of the banks. The criteria to identify such assets have been changing over time. In order to follow international best practices and to ensure greater transparency, the RBI shifted to the current policy in 2004. Under it, a loan is considered an NPA if it has not been serviced for ***one term*** (i.e., 90 days). This is known as the *'90 day' overdue norm.* For agriculture loans the period is tied with the

[33] An integrated system of regulation and supervision was suggested by the Committee so that soundness of the financial system could be ensured - the concept of a financial *super-regulator* gets vindicated, as opines Y. V. Reddy, in *Lectures on Economic and Financial Sector Reforms in India*, 38, Ibid.

[34] *Priority Sector Lending Guidelines* (New Delhi: RBI, Ministry of Finance, Government of India, 4 September 2020).

period of the concerned crops - ranging from two crop seasons to one-year overdue norm.[35]

Accordingly, the NPAs were classified into three types:

1. **Sub-standard:** remaining NPAs for less than or equal to 12 months;
2. **Doubtful:** remaining NPAs for more than 12 months; and
3. **Loss Assets:** where the loss has been identified by the bank or internal/external auditors or the RBI inspection, but the amount has not been written off.

Current Situation of the NPAs

The scheduled commercial banks (SCBs) in the country have not been able to enhance their profitability but on the back of it their NPAs have also decreased[36] to a multi-decade low:

- The Gross Non-performing Assets **(GNPAs)**, that is NPAs as percentage of gross loans, declined to **2.2** per cent in September 2025 (from the peak of **11.2** per cent in March 2018).
- The Net Non-performing Assets **(NNPAs)**, that is the NPAs as percentage of the total capital, declined to **0.5** per cent in September 2025 (from the peak of **6.0** per cent in March 2018).

Reasons for the upsurge in the NPAs Various reasons (as reported by the Government documents since 2013-14) have been cited for the recent upsurge in the NPAs of the PSBs, the ***major ones*** are being considered as given below[37]:

- Global and domestic macro-economic instabilities due to which a slowdown was seen in the economy diluting the capability of the borrowers to service the loans.
- Delays in project approvals resulting into high-cost overruns. This considerably dented the loan servicing capability of the borrowers.
- Aggressive lending by the banks to high corporate leverage.
- High incidences of *wilful defaults.*
- Cases of loan frauds.
- Instances of corruption in the banking institutions.

Looking at the rising NPAs and stressed assets, the Government commenced a multipronged policy framework to resolve the NPA crisis faced by the public sector banks (PSBs).

Resolution of the NPAs

At one hand, while the RBI tried to check the NPAs from rising by announcing new guidelines for the banks, on the other hand, it took several steps to 'resolve' the problem. By *February 2017* (since 2014-15), the RBI has implemented a number of schemes to facilitate resolution of the NPAs problem of the banks, which are briefly discussed below:

5/25 Refinancing This scheme offered a larger window for revival of stressed assets in the infrastructure sectors and 8 core industries. Under this scheme lenders were allowed to extend the tenure of loans to 25 years with interest rates adjusted every five years, so tenure of the loans matches the long gestation period in the sectors. The scheme thus aimed to improve the credit profile and liquidity position of borrowers, while allowing banks to treat these loans as standard in their balance sheets, reducing provisioning costs against NPAs. However, with amortisation spread out over a longer period, this arrangement also meant that the companies faced a higher interest burden, which they found difficult to repay, forcing banks to extend additional loans (called 'evergreening'). This in turn has aggravated the initial problem.

Asset Reconstruction Companies ARCs were introduced to India under the SARFAESI Act (2002) as specialists to resolve the burden of NPAs. But the ARCs (most are privately owned), finding it difficult to resolve the NPAs they purchased, are today only willing to purchase such loans at low prices. As a result, banks have been unwilling to sell them loans on a large scale. Since (2014) the fee structure of the ARCs was modified (requiring ARCs to pay a greater proportion of the purchase price *upfront* in cash to the banks), purchases of NPAs by them have slowed down further - only about 4 per cent of the total NPAs were sold during 2018-19 and 2019-20.

---

35 Reserve Bank of India, 'Master Circular - Income *Recognition, Asset Classification, Provisioning and Other Related Matters'*, July 2013.

36 *Economic Survey 2025-26* (New Delhi: Ministry of Finance, GoI, January 2026), pp. 91-92.

37 As the then RBI Governor Raghuram Rajan said deposing to the *Parliamentary Accounts Committee* in September 2016 and other official documents.

SDR (Strategic Debt Restructuring) In June 2015, the RBI came up with the SDR scheme to provide an opportunity for banks to convert debt of companies (whose stressed assets were restructured but which could not finally fulfil the conditions attached to such restructuring) to 51 per cent equity and sell them to the highest bidders - ownership change takes place in it. By end-December 2016, only two such sales had materialised, in part because many firms remained financially unviable, since only a small portion of their debt had been converted to equity.

AQR (Asset Quality Review) Resolution of the problem of bad assets requires sound recognition of such assets. Therefore, the RBI emphasised AQR, to verify that banks were assessing loans in line with RBI loan classification rules. Any deviations from such rules were to be rectified by March 2016.

S4A (Scheme for Sustainable Structuring of Stressed Assets) Introduced in June 2016, in it, an independent agency is hired by the banks which decides how much of the stressed debt of a company is 'sustainable'. The rest ('unsustainable') is converted into equity and preference shares. Unlike the SDR arrangement, this involves no change in the ownership of the company.

The various schemes launched by the RBI to resolve the issues of NPAs and stressed assets of the banks could not bring in the desired results due to several reasons and apprehensions. Finally, these schemes were put on hold and the *regime* of insolvency and bankruptcy law commenced by late 2017-18. In this regard, the RBI was vested with the power (via an amendment in the banking regulation act) to direct banks to initiate the corporate insolvency resolution process (CIRP) against defaulting borrowers. A *brief discussion* is given below on the historic insolvency and bankruptcy law and its performance till date.

INSOLVENCY AND BANKRUPTCY

By now several measures were put in place by the Government/RBI to resolve the 'twin balance sheet' (TBS) crisis faced by the economy, but they could not bring out effective results. Finally, we see the Government moving to make the insolvency procedure effective to address the issue. The lenders (banks) and borrowers (private corporate sector) both have been paying a high financial cost of the country's complex and time-consuming process of insolvency and bankruptcy. The new Insolvency and Bankruptcy Code, 2016 (IBC), was amended and enforced by the Government in November 2017. There has been a significant amount of progress in this regard - the entire mechanism for the CIRP has been put in place. A number of rules and regulations have been notified to create the institutions and professionals necessary for the process to work. A large number of cases have entered the insolvency process.

Insolvency vs Bankruptcy

Insolvency is a situation which arises due to the inability of a firm/individual to pay liabilities (of debt, rent, utility bills, suppliers, employee wages, etc.) as assets held are of lesser value than that of the liabilities. *Bankruptcy* is the legal process to declare insolvency by firm/individual (it is conclusion of insolvency). Though a bankrupt would be an insolvent, all insolvency may not lead to bankruptcy.

Insolvency has two options—resolution/recovery or liquidation (i.e., winding up of a corporate body, i.e., a company). *Liquidation* of a company can be initiated by—directors/shareholders/unpaid creditors/regulators. To govern the proceedings of insolvency and bankruptcy, the Insolvency and Bankruptcy Code (IBC), 2016 has been enacted by the Government.

A major factor behind the effectiveness of the new Code has been the *adjudication* by the Judiciary - it prescribes *strict time limits* for various procedures under it. In spite of the large inflow of cases to NCLT benches across India, these benches have been able to admit or reject applications for CIRP admissions with few delays. In addition, appellate courts, including the NCLAT, High Courts and the Supreme Court, have also disposed appeals quickly and decisively. In this process, a rich case law has evolved, reducing future legal uncertainty. In the CIRP, the Committee of Creditors (CoC) invites resolution plans from resolution applicants, and may select one of these plans. The Code originally *does not specify* any restrictions on who these resolution applicants might be though it declares some persons are ineligible to submit resolution plans:

1. an undischarged insolvent;
2. a wilful defaulter;
3. a borrower whose account has been identified as an NPA for over a year and who has not repaid the amount before submitting a plan;
4. a person convicted of an offence punishable with two or more years of imprisonment;
5. a person disqualified as a director under the Companies Act, 2013;
6. a person prohibited from trading in securities;
7. a person who is the promoter or in the management of a company which has indulged in undervalued, preferential or fraudulent transactions;
8. a person who has given guarantee on a liability of the defaulting company undergoing resolution or liquidation, and has not honoured the guarantee;
9. a person who is subject to any of the above disabilities in any jurisdiction outside India or
10. a person who has a connected person disqualified in any manner above.

Performance of the IBC

The performance of the IBC has been quite satisfactory and a kind of learning for the economy. A brief review[38] of it, till *September 2024*, is given below:

Facilitation in 'exit' The Code has facilitated the exit of *distressed firms,* hereby allocating scarce economic resources towards more productive use. Till September 2024, a total of 1068 resolution plans approved under the Code have resulted in creditors realising ₹3.6 lakh crore, which is 161 per cent against liquidation value and 86.1 per cent of the fair value.

Behavioural change The 'deterrent effect' of the Code has affected a far-reaching change in the behaviour of the debtors. The fear of losing control (of management/ownership) has *nudged* thousands of debtors to settle their dues even before the initiation of insolvency proceedings - 28.818 applications (involving underlying default of ₹10.2 lakh crore) were disposed of before their admission into CIRP till March 2024.

Value Realisation Until September 2024, a total of 79 corporate debtors (CDs) amounting to ₹1.4 lakh crore were closed by sale, as against the liquidation value of ₹4678.2 crore (of which liquidators realised ₹3674.1 crore).

Highest Recovery of NPAs The recovery by banks under the Code has been the highest compared to other channels such as Lok Adalats, SARFAESI Act and DRTs (Debt Recovery Tribunals).

Haircut In a public auction-based resolution model (such as the IBC), the extent of the haircut always remains a concern. Since significant value destruction may have already happened in these assets, a comparison of realised value with admitted claims may not be a reasonable indicator of its effectiveness. Further, the rate of recovery depends on a host of factors such as - overall macroeconomic environment, perceived growth prospects of the entity and its sector, and the extent of erosion in the intrinsic value of the entity. As a broad-based recovery gains traction, these factors are likely to turn favourable for financial resolution.

The *haircut* for creditors relative to the fair value of assets in Spetember 2024 was around 14 per cent, while relative to their admitted claims, it was 69 per cent.

WILFUL DEFAULTER

There are many people and entities who borrow money from lending institutions but fail to repay. However, not all of them are called wilful defaulters. As is embedded in the name, a wilful defaulter is one who does not repay a loan or liability, but apart from this there are other things that define a wilful defaulter. According to the RBI, a wilful defaulter is one who:

- is financially capable to repay and yet does not do so;
- or one who diverts the funds for purposes other than what the fund was availed for;
- or with whom funds are not available in the form of assets as funds have been siphoned off;
- or who has sold or disposed the property that was used as a security to obtain the loan.

Diversion of fund includes activities such as using short-term working capital for long-term purposes, acquiring assets for which the loan was not meant for and transferring funds to other entities. *Siphoning of funds* means that funds were used for purposes that

[38] *Economic Survey 2024-25* (N. Delhi: Ministry of Finance, GoI, January 2025), pp. 48-52.

were not related to the borrower and which could affect the financial health of the entity.

However, a lending institution cannot term an entity or an individual a wilful defaulter for a one-off case of default and needs to take into account the repayment track record. The default should be established to be intentional and the defaulter should be informed about the same. The defaulter should also be given a chance to clarify his stand on the issue. Also, the default amount needs to be at least ₹25 lakh to be included in the category of wilful defaults.

If the name of an entity or individual figures in the list of wilful defaulters, the following restrictions are enforced on them:

- Barred from participating in the capital market.
- Barred from availing any further banking facilities and to access financial institutions for five years for the purpose of starting a new venture.
- The lenders can initiate the process of recovery with full vigour and can even initiate criminal proceedings, if required.
- The lending institutions may not allow any person related to the defaulting company to become a board member of any other company as well.

SARFAESI Act, 2002

The GoI finally cracked down on the **wilful defaulters** by passing the *Securitisation and Reconstruction of Financial Assets and Enforcement of Security Interest (SARFAESI) Act, 2002.*

The Act provides far-reaching powers to the banks/FIs concerning NPAs:

1. Banks/FIs having 75 per cent of the dues owed by the borrower can collectively proceed on the following in the event of the account becoming an NPA:
   - **(i)** Issue notice of default to borrowers asking to clear dues within 60 days.
   - **(ii)** On the borrower's failure to repay:
     - **(a)** take possession of security and/or
     - **(b)** take over the management of the borrowing concern and/or
     - **(c)** appoint a person to manage the concern.
   - **(iii)** If the case is already before the BIFR, the proceedings can be stalled if banks/ FIs having 75 per cent share in the dues have taken any steps to recover the dues under the provisions of the ordinance.
2. The banks/FIs can also sell the security to a securitisation or ARC, established under the provisions of the Ordinance. [The ARC is sought to be set up on the lines similar to the United States, few years ago.]

NARCL & IDRCL

Along with the insolvency and bankruptcy law (IBC, 2016), the Government decided to use the 'reconstruction route' to resolve the non-performing assets (NPAs) crisis being faced by the banks, especially the public sector banks. However, this route was put in place by late 1990s itself (on the advice of the Narasimham Committee, 1991). A total of 28 ARCs (asset reconstruction companies) were already operative in the country, due to their smaller capital base they could resolve only low-value NPAs. Finally, in September 2021, the government did set up India's first government-owned ARC named as the NARCL (National Asset Reconstruction Company Limited). *Major facts* related to the ARC and the process related to resolution are as given below:

- The NARCL is supposed to acquire NPAs of the PSBs to the tune of ₹2 lakh crores in phases through 15 per cent cash and 85 per cent in SRs (Security Receipts) guaranteed by the Government of India. Government guarantee will be invoked to cover the shortfall between the amount realised from the underlying assets and the face value of SRs issued for that asset, subject to overall ceiling of ₹30,600 crores (Government guarantee), valid for 5 years. Since there shall be a pool of assets, it is reasonable to expect that realisation in many of them will be more than the acquisition cost.
- The NARCL has been set up as an asset reconstruction company (ARC) under the regulatory control of the RBI, by banks operating in the country – with 51 per cent ownership resting with the PSBs (rest 49 per cent will be owned by private financial institutions). The company is responsible for *aggregating and consolidating* stressed assets of the bank.
- Along with the NARCL the IDRCL (Infrastructure Debt Resolution Company Limited) has also been set up to *manage the assets* undertaken by the NARCL. It will be owned 49 per cent by the public sector banks (PSBs) and public financial institutions and 51 per cent by the private financial institutions

and will work as a service and operational body by engaging market professional and turnaround experts.

It should be noted that the need of setting up such an entity was emphasised by the *Economic Survey 2016-17* for the first time (suggested name was the 'public asset reconstruction agency' i.e., PARA) rather its suggested mandate was bigger (i.e., resolving the 'twin balance sheet' crisis faced by the economy). Though, such a hint was given in the *Union Budget of 2017-18* itself, it took more time to set up such an entity.

Several experts have considered the NARCL as a 'bad bank' but the Government refuted such comparison for which there is a valid reason. Actually, the entity is aimed at turning around the stressed assets with the help of professional experts by using commercial tools. Thus, the company is completely different from similar entities (rightly called 'bad banks') which were set by the South East Asian countries to resolve similar crisis in past (post-1997 financial crises) or by the USA (during the 1980s).

Capital Adequacy Ratio

At first glance, a bank is a business, an industry or a segment of the service sector in any economy. But the failure of a bank may have a far greater damaging impact on an economy than any other kind of business or commercial activity. Basically, modern economies are heavily dependent on banks today than in the past–banks are today called the backbone of economies. Healthy functioning of banks is today essential for the proper functioning of an economy. As credit creation (*i.e., loan disbursals*) of banks is a highly risky business, the depositors' money depends on the banks' quality of lending. More importantly, the whole payment system, public as well as private, depends on banks. A bank's failure has the potential of creating chaos in an economy. This is why governments of the world pay special attention to the regulatory aspects of the banks. Every regulatory provision for banks tries to achieve a simple equation, i.e., *how the banks should maximise their credit creation by minimising the risk and continue functioning permanently.* In the banking business risks are always present and cannot be made 'zero' – as any loan forwarded to any individual or firm (irrespective of their creditworthiness) has the risk of turning out to be a bad debt (*i.e., NPA in India*) – the probability of this being 50 per cent. But banks must function so that economies can function. Finally, the central banks of the world started devising tools to minimise the risks of banking on *one hand* and providing cushions (shock absorbers) to the banks on the *other hand* so that banks do not go bust (i.e., shut down after becoming bankrupt). Providing cushion/shock absorbers to banks has seen three major developments[39]:

1. The provision of keeping a *cash ratio* of total deposits mobilised by the banks (known as the CRR in India);
2. The provision of maintaining some assets of the deposits mobilised by the banks with the banks themselves in *noncash form* (known as the SLR in India); and
3. The provision of the CAR norm.

The CAR norm has been the last provision to emerge in the area of regulating the banks in such a way that they can sustain the probable risks and uncertainties of lending. It was in 1988 that the central banking bodies of the developed economies agreed upon such a provision, the CAR – also known as the **Basel Accord.**[40] The accord was agreed upon at Basel, Switzerland, at a meeting of the Bank for International Settlements (BIS).[41] It was at this time that the **Basel-I** norms of the CAR were agreed upon – a requirement was imposed upon the banks to maintain a certain amount of free capital (***i.e., ratio***) to their ***assets***[42] (i.e., loans and investments by the banks) as a cushion against probable losses in investments and loans. In 1988, this ratio capital was decided to be 8 per cent. It means that if the total investments and loans forwarded by a bank amount to ₹100, the bank needs

[39] Through various legislations, since the *RBI Nationalisation Act, 1949*, and the *Banking Regulation Act, 1949*, were enacted - and further *Amendments* to the Acts, Ministry of Finance, Government of India, New Delhi.

[40] S. Cox (ed.), 'Economics', *The Economist*, 2007, op. cit. p. 75.

[41] The *BIS* is today a central bank for central bankers set up in 1930 in a round tower near Basel railway station in Switzerland as a private company owned by a number of central banks, one commercial bank (Citibank) and some private individuals. Today it functions as a meeting place for the bank regulators of many countries, a multilateral regulatory authority and a *clearing house* for many nations' *reserves* (i.e., foreign exchange).See T. Hindle, 'Pocket Finance' *The Economist*, 2007, pp. 35-36.

[42] Investments made and loans forwarded by banks are known as risky assets.

to maintain a ***free capital***[43] of ₹8 at that particular time. ***The CAR is the percentage of total capital to the total risk–weighted assets*** (see footnote 43).

CAR, a measure of a bank's capital, is expressed as a percentage of a bank's risk weighted credit exposures:

CAR = Total of the Tier-I and Tier-II capitals ^ Risk Weighted Assets

Also known as 'CRAR', this ratio is used to protect depositors and promote the stability and efficiency of financial systems around the world. Two types of capital were measured as per the **Basel II** norms: *Tier-I* capital, which can absorb losses without a bank being required to cease trading, and *Tier-II* capital, which can absorb losses in the event of a winding up and so provides a lesser degree of protection to depositors. The new norms (**Basel III**) have devised a third category of capital, i.e., *Tier-III* capital.

The RBI introduced the ***capital-to-risk weighted assets ratio*** (CRAR) system for the banks operating in India in 1992 in accordance with the standards of the BIS – as part of the financial sector reforms.[44] In the coming years, the Basel norms were extended to term-lending institutions, primary dealers and NBFCs too. Meanwhile, the BIS came up with another set of CAR norms, popularly known as **Basel-II**. The RBI guidelines regarding the CAR norms in India have been as given below:

- **Basel-I** norm of the CAR was to be achieved by the Indian banks by March 1997.
- The CAR norm was raised to 9 per cent with effect from 31 March 2000 (Narasimham Committee-II had recommended to raise it to 10 per cent in 1998).[45]
- Foreign banks as well as Indian banks with foreign presence to follow **Basel-II norms**, w.e.f. 31 March 2008, while other SCBs to follow it no later than 31 March 2009. The Basel-II norm for the CAR is 12 per cent.[46]

Why to Maintain CAR?

The basic question which comes to mind is as to why do the banks need to hold capital in the form of CAR norms? ***Two reasons***[47] have been generally forwarded for the same:

1. Bank capital helps to prevent bank failure, which arises in case the bank cannot satisfy its obligations to pay the depositors and other creditors. The low capital bank has a negative net worth after the loss in its business. In other words, it turns into insolvent capital and, therefore, acts as a cushion to lessen the chance of the bank turning insolvent.
2. The amount of capital affects returns for the owners (equity holders) of the bank.

Basel Accords

The Basel Accords (i.e., Basel I, II and now III) are a set of agreements set by the Basel Committee on Bank Supervision (BCBS), which provides recommendations on banking regulations with regards to capital risk, market risk and operational risk. The purpose of the accords is to ensure that financial institutions have enough capital on account to meet obligations and absorb unexpected losses. They are of paramount importance to the banking world and are presently implemented by over 100 countries across the world. The BIS Accords were the outcome of a long-drawn-out initiative to strive for greater international uniformity in prudential capital standards for banks' credit risk. The objectives of the accords could be summed up[48] as:

1. to strengthen the international banking system;
2. to promote convergence of national capital standards; and
3. to iron out competitive inequalities among banks across countries of the world.

The Basel Capital Adequacy Risk-related Ratio Agreement of 1988 (**i.e., Basel I**) was not a legal document. It was designed to apply to internationally

[43] The capital of a bank was classified into Tier-I and Tier-II. While Tier-I comprises share capital and disclosed reserves, Tier-II includes revaluation reserves, hybrid capital and subordinated debt of a bank. As per the provision, Tier-II capital should not exceed the Tier-I capital. The risk weighting depends upon the type of assets - for example, it is 100 per cent on private sector loans, while only 20 per cent for short-term loans.

[44] The RBI is a member of the Board of the BIS. The financial sector reforms commenced in India in the fiscal 1992-93 after the report submitted by the Narasimham Committee on Financial system (CFS).

[45] *Committee on Banking Sector Reforms* (M Narasimham Committee-II) (New Delhi: Ministry of Finance, Government of India, April 1998).

[46] *Economic Survey 2006-07* (New Delhi: Ministry of Finance, GoI).

[47] D. M. Nachane, P. Ray and S. Ghosh, *India Development Report 2004-05* (New Delhi: Oxford University Press, 2005), p. 171.

[48] Ibid, p. 172.

active banks of member countries of the Basel Committee on Banking Supervision (BCBS) of the BIS at Basel, Switzerland. But the details of its implementation were left to national discretion. This is why Basel I looked G10- centric.[49]

The first Basel Accord, known as **Basel I**, focuses on the capital adequacy of financial institutions. The capital adequacy risk (the risk a financial institution faces due to an unexpected loss) categorises the assets of financial institution into five risk categories (0, 10, 20, 50, 100 per cent). Banks that operate internationally are required to have a risk weight of 8 per cent or less.

The second Basel Accord, known as **Basel II**, is to be fully implemented by 2015. It focuses on three main areas, including minimum capital requirements, supervisory review and market discipline, which are known as the *three pillars*. The focus of this accord is to strengthen international banking requirements as well as to supervise and enforce these requirements.

The third Basel Accord, known as **Basel III**, is a comprehensive set of reform measures aimed to strengthen the regulation, supervision and risk management of the banking sector. These measures aim to[50]:

1. improve the banking sector's ability to absorb shocks arising from financial and economic stress, whatever the source be;
2. improve risk management and governance; and
3. strengthen banks' transparency and disclosures.

The capital of the banks has been classified into ***three tiers*** as given below:

1. **Tier-I Capital:** A term used to describe the capital adequacy of a bank - it can absorb losses without a bank being required to cease trading. This is the **core measure** of a bank's financial strength from a regulator's point of view (this is the *most reliable* form of capital). It consists of the types of financial capital considered the most reliable and liquid, primarily stockholders' equity and disclosed reserves of the bank - equity capital can't be redeemed at the option of the holder and disclosed reserves are the liquid assets available with the bank itself.
2. **Tier-II Capital:** A term used to describe the capital adequacy of a bank - it can absorb losses in the event of a winding up and so provides a lesser degree of protection to depositors. Tier-II capital is secondary bank capital (the *second most reliable* form of capital). This is related to Tier-I Capital. This capital is a measure of a bank's financial strength from a regulator's point of view. It consists of accumulated after-tax surplus of retained earnings, revaluation reserves of fixed assets and long-term holdings of equity securities, general loan-loss reserves, hybrid (debt/equity) capital instruments and subordinated debt and undisclosed reserves.
3. **Tier-III Capital:** A term used to describe the capital adequacy of a bank - considered the *tertiary capital* of the banks which are used to meet/support market risk, commodities risk and foreign currency risk. It includes a variety of debt other than Tier-I and Tier-II capitals. Tier-III capital debts may include a greater number of subordinated issues, undisclosed reserves and general loss reserves compared to Tier-II capital. To qualify as Tier-III capital, assets must be limited to 250 per cent of a bank's Tier-I capital, be unsecured, subordinated[51] and have a minimum maturity of two years.

Disclosed Reserves are the total liquid cash and the SLR assets of the banks that may be used any time. This way they are part of its *core capital* (Tier-I). *Undisclosed Reserves* are the unpublished or hidden reserves of a financial institution that may not appear on publicly available documents such as a balance sheet, but are nonetheless real assets, which are accepted as such by most banking institutions, but cannot be used at will by the bank. That is why they are part of its *secondary capital* (Tier-II).

Basel III Provisions

The Basel III provisions[52] have defined the capital of the banks in a different way. They consider

[49] G-10 comprises Belgium, Canada, France, Germany, Italy, Japan, the Netherlands, Sweden, United Kingdom and United States; later the group incorporated Luxembourg, Switzerland and recently Spain into its fold.

[50] *Bank of International Settlements* (Basel: Switzerland, 15 May 2012).

[51] Subordinated debt ranks below other debts with regard to claims on assets or earnings (also known as a 'junior debt'). In the case of default, such creditors get paid out until after the senior debtholders were paid in full. Thus, such capitals of banks are more risky than unsubordinated debt.

[52] *Reserve Bank of India* (New Delhi: Ministry of Finance, GoI, 5 May 2012).

common equity and retained earnings as the predominant component of capital (as the past), but they restrict inclusion of items such as deferred tax assets, mortgage-servicing rights and investments in financial institutions to no more than 15 per cent of the common equity component. These rules aim to improve the *quantity* and *quality* of the capital.

While the key capital ratio has been raised to 7 per cent of risky assets, according to the new norms, Tier-I capital that includes common equity and perpetual preferred stock will be raised from 2 to 4.5 per cent starting in phases from January 2013 to be completed by January 2015. In addition, banks will have to set aside another 2.5 per cent as a *contingency* for future stress. Banks that fail to meet the buffer would be unable to pay dividends, though they will not be forced to raise cash.

The new norms are based on renewed focus of central bankers on 'macro-prudential stability'. The global financial crisis following the crisis in the US sub-prime market has prompted this change in approach. The previous set of guidelines, popularly known as *Basel II,* focused on 'macro-prudential regulation'. In other words, global regulators are now focusing on financial stability of the system as a whole, rather than micro-regulation of any individual bank.

Basel III Compliance in India

Banks operating in the country have been complying to the Basel norms right since these norms came into being. However, due to various reasons the last dates for compliance have been extended by the RBI many times by now. Meanwhile, a new *draft circular* of 'standardised approach' to Basel III was released by the central bank in October 2021 (open for the comments from the stakeholders by January 2022) which is slated for implementation from April 2023. In order to make the PSBs and RRBs compliant to the *Basel III* norms,[53] the government has been following a recapitalisation programme for them since 2011–12. A *High-Level Committee* on the issue was also set up by the Government which has suggested the idea of 'non-operating holding company' (HoldCo i.e., holding company) under a special Act of Parliament (action is yet to be taken regarding this).

The Governments have been infusing fresh capital into the PSBs since 2012–13 itself to make them comply to the *Basel III norms* through different means – budgetary supports, scheme (i.e., the Indradhanush Scheme of 2015–16) and Recapitalisation Bonds (initiated in 2019–20). As per the ***Economic Survey 2025–26***, the CRAR of the Scheduled Commercial Banks (SCBs) in *September 2025* was at **17.2** per cent (much better than 15.43 per cent in September 2024).

Banks in the West, which are market leaders for the most part, face low growth, an erosion in capital due to sovereign debt exposures and stiffer regulation. They will have to reckon with a permanent decline in their returns on equity thanks to enhanced capital requirements under the new norms. In contrast, Indian banks - and those in other emerging markets such as China and Brazil - are well placed to maintain their returns on capital consequent to Basel III. Financial experts have opined that Basel III is looking at changing the economic landscape in which banking power shifts towards the emerging markets.

STOCK OF MONEY

In every economy it is necessary for the central bank to be aware of the stock (amount/level) of money available in the economy, as only then can it opt for a suitable kind of credit and monetary policy. In other words, credit and monetary policy of an economy is all about changing the level of the money flowing into the economic system. But it can be carried out only when we know the real flow of money. That's why it is necessary to first assess the level of money flowing into the economy.

Following the recommendations of the *Second Working Group on Money Supply (SWG)* in 1977, the RBI has been publishing four *monetary aggregates* (component of money), viz. M_1, M_2, M_3 and M_4 (are basically short terms for Money-1, Money-2, Money-3 and Money-4)

[53] Basel III norms prescribe a minimum regulatory capital of 10.5 per cent for banks by 1 January, 2019 (extended to April 2023). This includes a minimum of 6 per cent *Tier-I* capital, plus a minimum of 2 per cent *Tier-II* capital, and a 2.5 per cent capital conservation buffer. For this buffer, banks are expected to set aside profits made during periods of affluence so that it can be drawn upon during periods of stress.

besides the Reserve Money. These components used to contain money of differing liquidities:

M_1 = Currency and coins with people + Demand deposits of Banks (Current and Saving Accounts) + 'Other' deposits of the RBI.

M_2 = M_1 + Demand deposits of the post offices (i.e., saving schemes' money).

M_3 = M_1 + Time/Term deposits of the Banks (i.e., the money lying in the Recurring Deposits and the Fixed Deposits).

M_4 = M_3 + total deposits of the post offices (both Demand and Term/Time Deposits).

Now the RBI has Started[54] publishing a set of new monetary aggregates following the recommendations of the *Working Group on Money Supply: Analytics and Methodology of Compilation* (Chairman, Dr. Y. V. Reddy) which submitted its report in June 1998. The Working Group recommended compilation of four monetary aggregates on the basis of the balance sheet of the banking sector in conformity with the norms of progressive liquidity: M_0 (monetary base), M_1 (narrow money), M_2 and M_3 (broad money). In addition to the monetary aggregates, the Working Group had recommended compilation of three liquidity aggregates, namely L_1, L_2 and L_3, which include select items of financial liabilities of non-depository financial corporations such as DFIs and NBFCs accepting deposits from the public, apart from post office savings banks. The **New Monetary Aggregates** are as given below:

Reserve Money (M_0) = Currency in circulation + Bankers' Deposits with the RBI + 'Others'[55] deposits with the RBI.

Narrow Money (M_1) = Currency with the Public + Demand Deposits with the Banking System + 'Others' deposits with the RBI.

M_2 = M_1 + Savings Deposits of Post Office Savings Banks.

Broad Money (M_3) = M_1 + Time Deposits with the Banking System.

Broad Money (M_4) = M_3 + All deposits with Post Office Savings Banks (excluding National Savings Certificates).

While the Working Group did not recommend any change in the definition of reserve money and M it proposed a new *intermediate monetary aggregate* to be referred to as **NM_2** comprising currency and residents' short-term bank deposits with contractual maturity up to and including one year, which would stand in between narrow money (which includes only the non-interest-bearing monetary liabilities of the banking sector) and broad money (an all-encompassing measure that includes long-term time deposits). The new broad money aggregate (referred to as **NM_3** for the purpose of clarity) in the Monetary Survey would comprise, in addition to NM_2, long-term deposits of residents as well as call/term borrowings from non-bank sources, which have emerged as an important source of resource mobilisation for banks. The critical *difference* between M_3 and NM_3 is the treatment of non-resident repatriable fixed foreign currency liabilities of the banking system in the money supply compilation.

There are **two basic changes** in the new monetary aggregates. *First*, since the post office bank is not a part of the banking sector, ***postal deposits*** are no longer treated as part of money supply, as was the case in the extant M_2 and M_4. *Second*, the residency criterion was adopted to a limited extent for compilation of monetary aggregates. The Working Group made a recommendation in favour of compilation of monetary aggregates on residency basis. Residency essentially relates to the country in which the holder has a centre of economic interest. Holdings of currency and deposits by the non-residents in the rest of the world sector would be determined by their portfolio choice. However, these transactions form part of balance of payments (BoP). Such holdings of currency and deposits are not strictly related to the domestic demand for monetary assets. It is therefore argued that these transactions should be regarded as external liabilities to be netted from foreign currency assets of the banking system. However, in the context of developing countries such as India, which have a large number of expatriate workers who

[54] The Working Group was set up in December 1997 under the chairmanship of Y. V. Reddy (the then Deputy Governor, RBI) which submitted its report in June 1998.

[55] Others' deposits with the RBI comprise mainly: (i) deposits of quasi-government; other financial institutions including primary dealers, (ii) balances in the accounts of foreign Central Banks and Governments and (iii) accounts of international agencies such as the International Monetary Fund.

remit their savings in the form of deposits, it could be argued that these non-residents have a centre of economic interest in their country of origin. Although in a macro-economic accounting framework all non-resident deposits need to be separated from domestic deposits and treated as capital flows, the underlying economic reality may point otherwise. In the Indian context, it may not be appropriate to exclude all categories of non-resident deposits from domestic monetary aggregates as non-resident rupee deposits are essentially integrated into the domestic financial system. The new monetary aggregates, therefore, exclude only non-resident repatriable foreign currency fixed deposits from deposit liabilities and treat those as external liabilities. Accordingly, from among the various categories of non-resident deposits at present, only Foreign Currency Non-Resident Accounts (Banks) [FCNR(B)] deposits are classified as external liabilities and excluded from the domestic money stock. Since the bulk of the FCNR(B) deposits are held abroad by commercial banks, the monetary impact of changes in such deposits is captured through changes in net foreign exchange assets of the commercial banks. Thus, now the new monetary aggregates NM_2 and NM_3 as well as liquidity aggregates L_1, L_2 and L_3 have been introduced, the components of which are elaborated as follows:

NM_1 = Currency with the Public + Demand Deposits with the Banking System + 'Other' Deposits with the RBI

NM_2 = NM_1 + Short-term Time Deposits of Residents (including the contractual maturity of one year)

NM_3 = NM_2 + Long-term Time Deposits of Residents + Call/Term Funding from Financial Institutions

L_1 = NM_3 + All Deposits with the Post Office Savings Banks (excluding National Savings Certificates)

L_2 = L_1 + Term deposits with Term Lending Institutions and Refinancing Institutions (FIs) + Term Borrowing by FIs + Certificates of Deposit issued by FIs

L_3 = L_2 + Public Deposits of Non-Banking Financial Companies

Data on M_0 are published by the RBI on a *weekly* basis, while those for M_1 and M_3 are available on a *fortnightly* basis. Among liquidity aggregates, data on L_1 and L_2 are published *monthly*, while those for L_3 are disseminated *quarterly*. The working group advised for the quarterly publication of the **Financial Sector Survey** to capture the dynamic linkages between banks and the rest of the organised financial sector.

Money Multiplier

Money multiplier (MM) is measured as the ratio of M_3 and M_0 (i.e., M_3 divided by M_0). It was mostly increasing from the1980s onwards up to 2016–17 but has, however, been declining since then. As per the ***Economic Survey 2025–26***, the MM by December 2025 stood at **6.21** in comparison to 5.70 a year ago. When adjusted for the reverse repo/standing deposit facility (which is analytically akin to bankers' deposits with the central bank), the adjusted MM stood at 6.0. The increase in the MM indicates improved systemic liquidity.

Liquidity of Money As we move from M_1 to M_4 the liquidity (i.e., the quickness by which money is available) of the money goes on decreasing and in the opposite direction, the liquidity increases.

Narrow Money In banking terminology, M_1 is called narrow money as it is highly liquid and banks cannot run their main lending programmes (i.e., long-term lending) with this money.

Broad Money The money component M_3 is called broad money in the banking terminology. With this money (which lies with banks for a known period) banks run their lending programmes.

Money Supply In general discussion we usually use money supply to mean money circulation, money flow in the economy. But in banking and typical monetary management terminology, the level and supply of M_3 is known as money supply. The growth rate of broad money (M_3), i.e., *money supply,* was 10.7 per cent by the end-December 2024, as compared to 10.0 per cent a year ago - with the largest component coming as bank deposits followed by banks' credits to government (through risk-free investments in SLR and G-Sec) and commercial lending by banks.

High Power Money The central banks of all the countries are empowered to issue the currency. The currency issued by the central bank is called 'high power money' because it is generally backed by supporting 'reserves and its value is guaranteed by the government and it is the source of all other forms of money. The currency issued by the central bank in fact is a liability of the central bank and the government. In general, therefore, this liability must be backed by an equal value of assets consisting mainly of gold and foreign exchange reserves. In practice, however, most countries[56] have adopted a 'minimum reserve system'.

Under the *minimum reserve system*, the central bank is required to maintain a certain minimum reserve of gold and foreign securities and is empowered to ***issue currency to any extent***. India adopted this system in October 1956. The RBI was required to hold a reserve worth of only ₹515 crore consisting of foreign securities worth ₹400 crore and gold worth ₹115 crore. In 1957, however, the minimum reserves were further reduced to only gold reserve of ₹115 crore and the rest in the form of rupee securities, mainly due to the scarcity of foreign exchange to meet essential import bill. A gold reserve of ₹115 crore against the currency of ₹40.0 lakh crore in circulation to day (February 2026) makes only 0.0002875 per cent reserve which is of no consequence. This makes the Indian currency system a 'managed paper currency system'. In India, there are two sources of *high power money* supply:

1. RBI and
2. GoI.

The RBI issues currency notes of rupees 2, 5, 10, 20, 50, 100, 500 and 2000 denominations which the RBI calls as the 'Reserve Money'. The RBI issues currency of one-rupee notes and coins including coins of smaller denominations on behalf of the GoI which accounts for around 2 per cent of the total high power money.

Minimum Reserve The RBI is required to maintain a reserve equivalent of ₹200 crore in gold and foreign currency with itself, of which ₹115 crore should be in gold. Against this reserve, the RBI is empowered to issue currency to any extent. This is being followed since 1957 and is known as the Minimum Reserve System (MRS).

[56] In the past, there were two other systems - *the first* belongs to Great Britain in which no reserve was maintained up to a certain limit of currency issued, called 'fiduciary system' and the *second* known as the 'proportional reserve system' in which, generally, 40 per cent reserve was maintained, adopted by France and the United States in 1928 and by India during 1935-56, replaced in October 1956 by a 'minimum reserve system'.

NON-RESIDENT INDIAN DEPOSITS

Foreign Exchange Management (Deposit) Regulations, 2000 permits Non-Resident Indians (NRIs) to have deposit accounts with authorised dealers and with banks authorised by the RBI which include[57]:

- Foreign Currency Non-Resident (Bank) Account [FCNR(B) Account]
- Non-Resident External Account (NRE Account)
- Non-Resident Ordinary Rupee Account (NRO Account)

FCNR(B) accounts can be opened by NRIs and Overseas Corporate Bodies (OCBs) with an authorised dealer. The accounts can be opened in the form of term deposits. Deposits of funds are allowed in Pound Sterling, US Dollar, Japanese Yen and Euro. Rate of interest applicable to these accounts are in accordance with the directives issued by the RBI from time to time.

NRE accounts can be opened by NRIs and OCBs with authorised dealers and with banks authorised by the RBI. These can be in the form of savings, current, recurring or fixed deposit accounts. Deposits are allowed in any permitted currency. Rate of interest applicable to these accounts are in accordance with the directives issued by the RBI from time to time.

NRO accounts can be opened by any person resident outside India with an authorised dealer or an authorised bank for collecting their funds from local bonafide transactions in Indian Rupees. When a resident becomes an NRI, his existing Rupee accounts are designated as NRO. These accounts can be in the form of current, savings, recurring or fixed deposit accounts.

There were two more NRI deposit accounts in operation, viz. *Non-Resident (Non-Repatriable) Rupee Deposit Account* and *Non-Resident (Special) Rupee Account* - an amendment to Foreign Exchange Management (Deposit) Regulations, in 2002, discontinued the acceptance of deposits in these two accounts from April 2002 onwards.

Repatriation of funds in FCNR(B) and NRE accounts is permitted. Hence, deposits in these accounts are

[57] As per the latest update by the *RBI*, April 2023.

included in India's *external debt* outstanding. While the principal of NRO deposits is non-repatriable, current income and interest earning is repatriable. Account holders of NRO accounts are permitted to annually remit an amount up to US$ 1 million out of the balances held in their accounts. Therefore, deposits in NRO accounts too are included in India's *external debt.*

SMALL AND PAYMENT BANKS

The *draft guidelines* for setting up small banks and payment banks were announced by the RBI in July 2014 (the *Union Budget 2014-15* had outlined the need for such banks). The guidelines say that both are 'niche' or 'differentiated' banks with the common objective of furthering *financial inclusion.* The details regarding the provisions to set up such banks and their operational criteria are as given below:

The ***guidelines*** to set up both the banks are the same:

- The minimum capital requirement would be ₹100 crore.
- Promoter contribution would be at least 40 per cent for the first five years. Excess shareholding should be brought down to 40 per cent by the end of the fifth year, to 30 per cent by the end of the 10th year and to 26 per cent in 12 years from the date of commencement of business.
- Foreign shareholding in these banks will be as per current FDI policy.
- Voting rights to be in line with the existing guideline for private banks.
- Entities other than promoters will not be permitted to have shareholding in excess of 10 per cent.
- The bank should comply with the corporate governance guidelines, including 'fit and proper' criteria for directors as issued by the RBI.
- Operations of the bank should be fully networked and technology driven from the beginning.

Small Banks

The purpose of the small banks is to provide a whole suite of basic banking products such as *deposits* and supply of *credit*, but in a *limited area of operation.* The **objective** of the small banks is to increase financial inclusion by provision of savings vehicles to under-served and unserved sections of the population, supply of credit to small farmers, micro and small industries and other unorganised sector entities through high-technology low-cost operations. Other features of the small banks are as follows:

- Resident individuals with 10 years of experience in banking and finance, companies and societies will be eligible as promoters to set up small banks. NFBCs, microfinance institutions (MFIs) and local area banks (LABs) can convert their operations into those of a small bank. Local focus and ability to serve smaller customers will be a key criterion in licensing such banks.
- For the initial three years, prior approval will be required for branch expansion.
- The area of operations would normally be restricted to contiguous districts in a homogenous cluster of states or union territories so that the small bank has a 'local feel' and culture. However, if necessary, it would be allowed to expand its area of operations beyond contiguous districts in one or more states with reasonable geographical proximity.
- The bank shall primarily undertake *basic banking activities* of accepting deposits and lending to small farmers, small businesses, micro and small industries, and unorganised sector entities. It cannot set up subsidiaries to undertake non-banking financial services activities. After the initial stabilisation period of five years, and after a review, the RBI may liberalise the scope of activities for small banks.
- The promoters' other financial and nonfinancial services activities, if any, should be distinctly ring-fenced and not co-mingled with banking business.
- A robust risk management framework is required, and the banks would be subject to all prudential norms and RBI regulations that apply to existing commercial banks, including maintenance of CRR and SLR.
- In view of concentration of area of operations, the small bank would need a diversified portfolio of loans, spread over its area of operations.
- The maximum loan size and investment limit exposure to single/group borrowers/issuers would be restricted to 15 per cent of capital funds.
- Loans and advances of up to ₹25 lakhs, primarily to micro enterprises, should constitute at least 50 per cent of the loan portfolio.
- For the first three years, 25 per cent of branches should be in unbanked rural areas.

By *February 2026*, a total of **12** small banks were operating in the country.

Payments Banks

The **objective** of payments banks is to increase financial inclusion by providing small savings accounts, payment/remittance services to migrant labour, low-income households, small businesses, other unorganised sector entities and other users by enabling high volume-low value transactions in deposits and payments/ remittance services in a secured technology-driven environment.

- Those who can promote payments banks can be non-bank PPIs (Prepaid Payment Instruments), NBFCs, corporates, mobile telephone companies, super market chains, real sector cooperatives companies and public sector entities. Even banks can take equity in payments banks.
- Payments banks can accept demand deposits (only current account and savings accounts). They would initially be restricted to holding a maximum balance of ₹100,000 per customer. Based on performance, the RBI could enhance this limit.
- The banks can offer payments and remittance services, issuance of prepaid payment instruments, internet banking, functioning as business correspondent for other banks.
- Payments banks cannot set up subsidiaries to undertake NBFC business.
- As in the case of small banks, other financial and non-financial services activities of the promoters should be ring-fenced.
- The payments banks would be required to use the word 'payments' in its name to differentiate it from other banks.
- No credit lending is allowed for payments banks.
- The float funds can be parked only in less than one year G-Secs.

By *February 2026*, a total of **6** payments banks were operating in the country.

FINANCIAL INCLUSION

Financial inclusion is an important priority of the government. The objective is to ensure the excluded sections, i.e., weaker sections and low-income groups, access to various financial services such as a basic savings bank account, need-based credit, remittance facility, insurance and pension. The government has recently launched an effective scheme to promote the cause of financial inclusion - the PMJDY.

Pradhan Mantri Jan-Dhan Yojana

To achieve the objective of financial inclusion by extending financial services to the large hitherto unserved population of the country and to unlock its growth potential, the Pradhan Mantri Jan-Dhan Yojana (PMJDY) was launched on 28 August 2014. The Yojana envisages:

- Universal access to banking facilities with at least one basic banking account for every household.
- Financial literacy, access to credit and insurance.
- The beneficiaries will receive a *RuPay* Debit Card having inbuilt accident insurance cover of ₹1 lakh.
- In addition, there is a life insurance cover of ₹30,000 to those who opened their bank accounts for the first time between 15 August 2014 and 26 January 2015 and meet other eligibility conditions of the Yojana.

The Yojana had entered the *Guinness World Records* for opening most bank accounts during the week starting 23 August 2014, as part of the financial campaign.

GOLD INVESTMENT SCHEMES

Two new gold investment schemes were launched by the GoI by November 2015 - the Sovereign Gold Bonds and Gold Monetisation Schemes. The schemes are aimed at twin objectives:

1. Reducing the demand for physical gold; and
2. Shifting a part of the gold imported every year for investment purposes into financial savings.

Brief features of the schemes are as given below:

Sovereign Gold Bonds

These are issued by the RBI on behalf of the Government of India in rupees and denominated in grams of gold and restricted for sale to resident Indian entities only, both in demat and paper form. The minimum and maximum investment limits are 1 and 500 grams of gold per person per fiscal year, respectively. The rate of interest offered on the bond was 2.5 per cent per annum by April 2022, payable on a half-yearly basis. The tenor of the bond is for a period of eight years with exit option from the fifth year onwards. KYC norms are the same as that for gold. Exemption from capital gains tax is also available. Redemption is made in the rupee value equivalent to the price of gold at the time of maturity.

Gold Monetisation Scheme

In this scheme, the BIS (Bureau of Indian Standards) certified CPTCs (Collection, Purity Testing Centres) collect the gold from the customer on behalf of the banks. The minimum quantity of gold (bullion or jewellery) which can be deposited is 30 g, and there is no limit for maximum deposit.

Gold Saving Account can be opened with any designated bank and denomination in grams of gold for a short-term period of 1-3 years, a medium-term period of 5-7 years and a long-term period of 12-15 years - enjoying interest rates varying between 0.50 to 2.5 per cent per annum (as per the latest data of September 2024). The CPTCs transfer the gold to the refiners. The banks will have a tripartite/bipartite legal agreement with refiners and CPTCs.

For the year 2020-21 interest rate is fixed at 2.25 and 2.5 per cent for the medium and long term, respectively. Redemption is made in cash/gold for the short term and in cash for medium- and long-term deposits. The difference between the current borrowing cost for the government and the interest rate paid by the government under the medium-/long-term deposit will be credited to the Gold Reserve Fund.

In ***2019-20***, the RBI liberalised the gold monetisation scheme, allowing charitable institutions, the Centre, states and government entities to deposit the precious metal. Individuals, corporate entities, MFs and exchange traded funds were already allowed to deposit gold under the scheme. The aim of the scheme was to mobilise *idle gold* lying with households and temples into the system, and consequently, reduce imports.

This move will help government agencies to deposit gold confiscated by them. Charitable institutions can now take advantage to deposit their unaccounted gold without disclosing their identity. In the past, several complaints were received by the government about money laundering by charitable trusts (they used to accept money eligible for donation tax benefit and give cash back to the donor). To prevent money laundering, 30 per cent tax has been imposed on charitable trusts for donations received from unidentified persons. It means, now, donors will deposit unaccounted gold and obtain cash after a deduction of 30 per cent from these trusts. But this also allows the unaccounted gold to find its way into the scheme. Some experts believe that money collected by depositors like this could also be used to fund election campaigns.

Under the scheme, a depositor has to give gold to a collection centre, which are also hallmarking centres. These centres issue certificates of purity after melting the gold, which is sent to refineries for converting into bars. Banks issue deposit receipts after collecting purity certificates from the depositors.

MUDRA BANK

As per the GoI, large industries provide employment to only 1.25 crore people in the country, while the *micro units* employ around 12 crore people. There is a need to focus on these 5.75 crore self-employed people (owners of the micro units) who use funds of ₹11 lakh crore, with an average per unit debt of merely ₹17,000. Capital is the key to the small entrepreneurs. These entrepreneurs depend heavily on the local money lenders for their fund requirements.

Looking at the importance of these enterprises, the GoI launched (April 2015) the *Micro Units Development and Refinance Agency Bank (MUDRA Bank)* with the aim of *funding* these *unfunded* non-corporate enterprises. This was launched as the PMMY (Prime Minister Mudra Yojana). Important features of the MUDRA Bank are as given below:

- Under this banking model, the micro units can avail up to ₹10 lakh loan through the refinance route (through the public and private sector banks, NBFCs, MFIs, RRBs, District Banks, etc).
- The products designed under it are categorised into three buckets of finance named *Shishu* (loan up to ₹50,000), *Kishor* (₹50,000 to ₹5 lakh) and *Tarun* (₹5 to ₹10 lakh).
- Though the scheme covers the traders of fruits and vegetables, in general, it does not refinance the agriculture sector.
- There is no fixed interest rate in this scheme. As per the GoI, presently, banks are charging the interest rates between Base Rate plus 1 to 7 per cent per annum. Interest rates on the loans are supposed to vary according to the risk involved in the enterprises seeking loans. There is no general subsidy offered on interest rates except if the loan is linked to some other government scheme.

In the wake of the disruption caused by the *COVID-19 pandemic* several relief measures were announced by the RBI. Loans were restructured and permission given to not declare a loan as NPAs as forbearance will have a negative impact on the loans disbursed under the scheme[58] and the stressed assets under it may rise.

CRYPTO ECOSYSTEM

As per the *Economic Survey 2022-23*, the recent collapse of the crypto exchange FTX, followed by sell-offs in the crypto markets, brought the vulnerabilities of the crypto ecosystem in spotlight. Financial regulators across the world have shown their increasing concerns about these crypto assets (popularly called the cryptocurrencies).

Crypto assets are self-referential instruments and do not strictly pass the test of being a financial asset because it has no intrinsic cashflows attached to them. The regulators in the USA have *disqualified* Bitcoin, Ether, and various other crypto assets as securities. A rare joint statement by the Federal Reserve, Federal Deposit Insurance Corporation (FDIC), and the Office of the Comptroller of the Currency (OCC) on 3rd January 2023 highlighted their concerns about crypto-asset risks to the banking system.

The geographically pervasive nature of the crypto ecosystem necessitates a common approach to the regulation of these volatile instruments. In this context, right now, the global response to cryptos is evolving led by the USA, European Union, Japan, Switzerland, UK, Albania, and Nigeria. (see *Chapter 22* for more on the topic).

CENTRAL BANK DIGITAL CURRENCY

In the last few years, several countries have taken initiatives towards issuing their digital currencies - popularly called the central bank digital currency (CBDC) as they are to be issued by the central banks of the countries. By July 2022, there were 105 countries in the process of exploring CBDC, a number that covers 95 per cent of the global GDP. Many countries have already launched the CBDC, while others were in the pilot stage. The issuance of CBDC in the case of India offers several benefits[59] such as:

- Reduction in operational costs involved in physical cash management,
- Fostering financial inclusion,
- Bringing resilience, efficiency, and innovation in the payments system,
- Boosting innovation in cross-border payments space, and
- Providing public with uses that any private *virtual currencies* can provide, without the associated risks.

Initiative by RBI By now, RBI has run two pilot projects in the area of issuing CBDC - in both wholesale and retail segments:

(i) The pilot for the *Digital Rupee-Wholesale* was launched on 1st November 2022, with the use case being limited to the settlement of secondary market transactions in government securities. Its use is expected to make the inter-bank market more efficient.

(ii) The pilot in the retail segment, known as *Digital Rupee-Retail*, kicked off on 1st December 2022, within a closed user group comprising participating customers and merchants. For full operationalisation of CBDC, RBI is gradually expanding the pilots' scope to include more banks, users, and locations based on feedback received during the pilots.

NEOBANKS

The number of neo-banking platforms and global investments in the neo-banking segment has risen consistently in the country, over the last few years. Neo-banks operate under mainstream finance's umbrella but empower specific services long associated with traditional institutions such as banks, payment providers, etc. Major facts[60] related to these banks are as given below:

- They operate *entirely online* with no physical presence; however, have their offices in the offline world.
- Their growth is spurred by the need for 'on-demand' and 'easier-to-access' financial solutions by a young and increasingly *digitally savvy* population.
- They have eased availability and provided access to financial services to MSMEs and underbanked customers and areas.

[58] Ministry of Finance, GoI, New Delhi, April 2022 and *Economic Survey 2020-21*, vol. 1 (New Delhi: Ministry of Finance, GoI), pp. 200-34.

[59] *Economic Survey 2022-23* (N. Delhi: Ministry of Finance, GoI, January 2023), p. 308.

[60] *Economic Survey 2022-23* (N. Delhi: Ministry of Finance, GoI, January 2023), pp. 307-08.

For the last many years, the government has also been supporting digital banking solutions through many initiatives. To take banking solutions to every nook and corner of the country, the government has also launched the Digital Banking Units (as proposed by the *Union Budget 2022-23*).

WAY FORWARD

Global financial system has faced many disruptions by now and most of them had their impact on India too. For 2026–27 and upcoming years, though the Government[61] looks optimistic. It has shown concerns too:

- As 'headline inflation' (i.e., the CPI-C) has started declining, there is a room for interest cuts by the RBI in coming times. However, inflation still remains a concern.
- High capex (capital expenditure) plan of the Government for 2026–27 will have positive impact on the economy with increased demand for fund in the wake of which the RBI needs to make available suitable amount of liquidity in the system.
- The lending-investment cycle will need continuous monitoring of the risks by the regulators.
- India's strong macroeconomic fundamentals will underpin the return of global capital flows to India once the fog of uncertainty lifts. The financial system will play a key role in realising the objectives of Amrit Kaal.
- Guard against the 'financialisation' (i.e., increased investment in financial assets by investors) is required, given the example of its very adverse consequences in advanced economies.

[61] *Economic Survey 2025-26* (New Delhi: Ministry of Finance, GoI, January 2026), pp. 91-104; *Economic Survey 2024-25* (New Delhi: Ministry of Finance, GoI, January 2025), pp. 76-78; *Economic Survey 2023-24* (New Delhi: Ministry of Finance, GoI, January 2024), pp. 82-83; and *Economic Survey 2022-23* (N. Delhi: Ministry of Finance, GoI, January 2023), pp. 78-116

PREVIOUS YEARS' QUESTIONS

Prelims

1. Which of the following are the sources of income for the Reserve Bank of India? (2025)

(i) Buying and selling Government bonds
(ii) Buying and selling foreign currency
(iii) Pension fund management
(iv) Lending to private companies
(v) Printing and distributing currency notes

Select the correct answer using the code given below.

(a) (i) and (ii) only **(b)** (ii), (iii) and (iv)
(c) (i), (iii), (iv) and (v) **(d)** (i), (ii) and (v)

2. Consider the following statements: (2025)

(i) The Reserve Bank of India mandates all the listed companies in India to submit a Business Responsibility and Sustainability Report (BRSR).
(ii) In India, a company submitting a BRSR makes disclosures in the report that are largely non-financial in nature.

Which of the statements given above is/are correct?

(a) (i) only **(b)** (ii) only
(c) Both (i) and (ii) **(d)** Neither (i) nor (ii)

3. Consider the following statements in respect of RTGS and NEFT: (2025)

(i) In RTGS, the settlement time is instantaneous, while in the case of NEFT, it takes some time to settle payments.
(ii) In RTGS, the customer is charged for inward transactions, while that is not the case for NEFT.
(iii) Operating hours for RTGS are restricted on certain days, while this is not true for NEFT.

Which of the statements given above is/are correct?

(a) (i) only (b) (i) and (ii)
(c) (i) and (iii) (d) (iii) only

4. Consider the following countries: (2025)
   (i) United Arab Emirates
   (ii) France
   (iii) Germany
   (iv) Singapore
   (v) Bangladesh

   How many countries amongst the above are there other than India where international merchant payments are accepted under UPI?

   (a) Only (ii) (b) Only (iii)
   (c) Only (iv) (d) All the five

5. Consider the following statements: (2024)

   Statement-I : Syndicated lending spreads the risk of borrower default across multiple lenders.

   Statement-II : The syndicated loan can be fixed amount/lump sum of funds, but cannot be a credit line.

   Which one of the following is correct in respect of the above statements?

   (a) Both Statement-I and Statement-II are correct and Statement-II explains Statement-I
   (b) Both Statement-I and Statement-II are correct, but Statement-II does not explain Statement-I
   (c) Statement-I is correct, but Statement-II is incorrect
   (d) Statement-I is incorrect, but Statement-II is correct

6. Consider the following statements in respect of the digital rupee: (2024)
   (i) It is a sovereign currency issued by the Reserve Bank of India (RBI) in alignment with its monetary policy.
   (ii) It appears as a liability on the RBI's balance sheet.
   (iii) It is insured against inflation by its very design.
   (iv) It is freely convertible against commercial bank money and cash.

   Which of the statements given above are correct?

   (a) (i) and (ii) only (b) (i) and (iii) only
   (c) (ii) and (iv) only (d) (i), (ii) and (iv)

7. Consider the following statements: (2024)
   (i) In India, Non-Banking Financial Companies can access the Liquidity Adjustment Facility window of the Reserve Bank of India.
   (ii) In India, Foreign Institutional Investors can hold the Government Securities (G-Secs).
   (iii) In India, Stock Exchanges can offer separate trading platforms for debts.

   Which of the statements given above is/are correct?

   (a) (i) and (ii) only (b) (iii) only
   (c) (i), (ii) and (iii) (d) (ii) and (iii) only

8. With reference to the rule/rules imposed by the Reserve Bank of India while treating foreign banks, consider the following statements: (2024)
   (i) There is no minimum capital requirement for wholly owned banking subsidiaries in India.
   (ii) For wholly owned banking subsidiaries in India, at least 50% of the board members should be Indian nationals.

   Which of the statements given above is/are correct?

   (a) (i) only (b) (ii) only
   (c) Both (i) and (ii) (d) Neither (i) nor (ii)

9. With reference to the Indian economy, "Collateral Borrowing and Lending Obligations" are the instruments of: (2024)

   (a) Bond market (b) Forex market
   (c) Money market (d) Stock market

Answers: 1. (d) 2. (b) 3. (a) 4. (b) 5. (c) 6. (d) 7. (d) 8. (b) 9. (c)

Explanation

1. (d): Except for III and IV, all are part of RBI's functions- and through all these activities, RBI earns income.

2. (b): Statement-I is incorrect (SEBI requires the top 1,000 listed companies in India to submit a BRSR). Statement-II is correct (the BRSR is a non-financial reporting framework). The BRSR, a reporting framework, is aimed at improving the disclosure of environmental, social, and governance (ESG) performance by listed companies (which originates from the Voluntary Guidelines on Corporate Social Responsibility of the Ministry of Corporate Affairs, 2009).

3. (a): RTGS (Real Time Gross Settlement) transactions are processed in 'real time' and on a 'gross basis' (which means that the transactions are settled individually as received with virtually 'no waiting' period). National Electronic Funds Transfer (NEFT) operates on a 'Deferred Net Settlement' basis (which means that the transactions are collected and processed in batches at specific intervals; the usual waiting time is half an hour). Both of the services are now available 24 × 7, and inward payments in both are free of charge. Thus, *Statement-I* is correct, while *Statements-II* and *III* are incorrect.

4. (b): As of now, Unified Payments Interface (UPI) is accepted for international merchant payments in the United Arab Emirates (UAE), France, Singapore, Sri Lanka, Mauritius, Bhutan, and Nepal.

5. (c): In case of syndicated loans (which are offered by more than one bank/lender) the risk of default gets divided among all the lenders and are considered better from lender's point of view (thus Statement-I is correct). But syndicated loans can be of a fixed amount as well as a credit line (which keeps flowing over a time period) - thus, Statement-II is incorrect.

6. (d): Digital rupee and non-digital rupee (i.e., paper currencies and coins) are exactly same except their form– and digital currencies can be converted into non-digital currencies also (it means, 1, 2 and 4 are correct). But like normal non-digital rupee, the digital rupee is also not insured against the effects of inflation (i.e., its value rises/falls due to price fluctuations).

7. (d): Liquidity Adjustment Facility (LAF) of the RBI is a window for only the Scheduled Commercial Banks (except the Regional Rural Banks) and the PDs (Primary Dealers) under which these entities borrow/lend short-term loans to/from the RBI. Hence, thehe options 2 and 3 are correct.

8. (b): The RBI has fixed a minimum capital requirement to set up a subsidiary foreign bank in India (thus, the first option is incorrect). As per the RBI, such foreign banks must have minimum half of their board members as Indian nationals (thus second option is correct). Subsidiary banks do not need to get incorporated in India (rather they are incorporated in their countries of origin) but operate as per the banking guidelines of the RBI.

9. (c): The collateral borrowing and lending obligations (CBLOs) are financial activities related to India's money market (where short-term fund is raised). Under it while the borrowers pledge secondary securities (like gold, land, house, etc. as collateral) to the lenders, the lenders provide loans (at a cost called interest).

SAMPLE OBJECTIVE QUESTIONS

1. Consider the following statements about banks' lending activities in the country:
   (i) Collaterals backing loans are called the primary security.
   (ii) The signature of the borrower is the primary security of loans.
   (iii) Secondary security carries more importance than primary security in lending business.
   (iv) Loans cannot be offered backed by only primary security.

Which of the above statements is/are correct?

Code:

(a) Only one (b) Only two
(c) Only three (d) All four

2. Consider the following statements related to banking regulations in the country:
   (i) Monetary policy is anchored to the headline inflation as well as wholesale price index.
   (ii) The RBI has set higher capital adequacy ratio (CAR) for the non-banking financial companies (NBFCs) in comparison to that of the commercial banks.
   (iii) Under its development function, a few development banks are owned by the RBI.

   Which of the above statements is/are correct?

   Code:

   (a) Only one (b) Only two
   (c) All three (d) None of these

3. Consider the following statements related to banking reforms in the country:
   (i) Marginal standing facility rate is overnight window of borrowing for banks over and above the repo window.
   (ii) Long-term repo operation is an extra window for banks over and above the repo operation.
   (iii) Standing deposit facility and the reverse repo windows operate in similar ways but the former does not involve collateral.

   Which of the above statements is/are correct?

   Code:

   (a) Only one (b) Only two
   (c) All three (d) None of the these

4. Consider the following statements about the Basel Accord:
   (i) The Basel IV norms have kickstarted globally.
   (ii) Basel norms III and IV find their origin in the financial crisis of 2007-08.
   (iii) Indian banks are presently complying with the Basel III norms.
   (iv) For now, the regional rural banks (RRBs) in the country do not need to comply with the Basel III norms.

   Which of the above statements is/are correct?

   Code:

   (a) Only two (b) Only three
   (c) All four (d) None of these

5. Consider the following statements related to the act of sterilised intervention by the Reserve Bank of India (RBI):
   (i) It is the simultaneous sale of government securities and purchase of foreign currencies by the RBI.
   (ii) It is the simultaneous sale of foreign currencies and purchase of government securities by the RBI.
   (iii) It aims at inflation targeting and checking the volatility of rupee's exchange rate.

   How many of the above statements are correct?

   (a) Only one (b) Only two
   (c) All three (d) None of these

6. Consider the following statements related to non-banks in the country:
   (i) These shadow banks are not allowed to mobilise deposits from customers.
   (ii) They are eligible entities to set up banks.
   (iii) They offer more flexible and customised loan products than banks to their clients.

   How many of the above statements are correct?

   (a) Only one (b) Only two
   (c) All three (d) None of these

7. Consider the following statements related to compliance with the Basel III banking norms in the country:
   (i) Under it, banks maintain the liquidity coverage ratio (LCR) aimed at short-term resilience to survive acute financial stress.
   (ii) Short-term resilience of banks is measured for a period of one year under it.
   (iii) Enabling banks' to survive acute economic stress is a major objective of these norms.

   How many of the above statements are correct?

   (a) Only one (b) Only two
   (c) All three (d) None of these

8. Consider the following statements related to banking industry in the country:
   (i) Indian oil companies can use the Vostro Accounts of a foreign petroleum exporter to import oil.

(ii) Foreign companies can use their Nostro Accounts to import petroleum products from India.

(iii) The Nostro and Vostro bank accounts can be interchangeably used for both exports and imports.

How many of the above statements are correct?

(a) Only one (b) Only two

(c) All three (d) None of these

9. Consider the following statements related to the regulatory function of the Reserve Bank of India (RBI) in the country:

(i) Banks can offer cheaper loans if the cash reserve ratio (CRR) has been reduced.

(ii) Banks' lending rate are more sensitive to the standing deposit facility rate than the repo rate.

(iii) Monetary transmission is more responsive to repo rate than the bank rate.

How many of the above statements are correct?

(a) Only one (b) Only two

(c) All three (d) None of these

10. Consider the flowing statements related to banking industry:

(i) Banks' loans are a major source of money creation in an economy.

(ii) Credit crunch may create deflationary situation in an economy.

(iii) Higher bad debts and lack of creditworthy borrowers may force banks to cut lending.

How many of the above statements are correct?

(a) Only one (b) Only two

(c) All three (d) None of these

Answers: 1. (a) 2. (a) 3. (c) 4. (b) 5. (c) 6. (b) 7. (b) 8. (c) 9. (b) 10. (c)

SAMPLE SUBJECTIVE QUESTIONS

1. 'Inflation targeting is only possible for the Reserve Bank of India once its non-monetary variables remain favourable.' Explain with recent examples.

2. Briefly examine the performance of the measures taken by the Reserve Bank of India to improve monetary transmission in the banking system. Give recent examples in this regard.

3. Examine the purpose of the capital adequacy norm set for the banks in country. How far the Basel norms help globalise the banking industry of the country?

4. Why Indian banks are not forwarding loans to foreign clients, though the capital convertibility rules allow it? Comment with the help of recent examples.

5. Briefly examine the recent challenges of the Reserve Bank of India in making an effective monetary policy for the economy. Cite relevant examples.

6. Discuss the recent steps taken by the Reserve Bank of India and the Government to resolve the crisis of the non-performing assets of the public sector banks in the country.

SAMPLE MODEL ANSWER

1. "Monetary transmission in 2025-26 has been said to be 'effective' but transitioning into 'wait-and-watch' phase by the Reserve Bank of India." Explain.

Ans. When policy rates announced by the Reserve Bank of India (RBI) are reflected in the lending and deposit rates of the banks, the monetary transmission is called healthy. The state of monetary transmission has been weak throughout February 2019 and 2022-23. But the situation improved a lot in 2025-26. During 2025-26 (February-December), the RBI effected cumulative repo rate cuts of 125 basis points (i.e., 1.25 per cent)–in response, the following transmission trends were seen in the financial sector:

In lending and deposit rates: Following the 125 basis points cut in the repo rate, the weighted average lending rate (WALR) on fresh rupee loans by banks declined by 59 basis points, while the WALR on outstanding rupee loans declined by 69 basis points (between February and November 2025). Similarly, fresh deposit rates declined by 105 basis points during the period. This transmission has been described as 'broad-based' and 'excellent' by the RBI Governor.

Points of friction: Despite cumulative repo rate cuts, transmission in the bond market has been slower compared to previous rate cuts, with less than 10 per cent of the rate cuts visible in bond yields as of February 2026. As per the RBI, this is attributed to hardening G-Sec yields mirroring global trends.

Due to the above-cited reasons, the monetary transmission during 2025-26 has been called effective by the RBI but is transitioning into a 'wait-and-watch' phase.

CHAPTER 14

Insurance in India

Insurance is a kind of gambling in reverse - a major form of risk spreading where one person's risk which would be large is spread around to make it small for a large number of people. In this process it serves two purposes: provides social security net to people and helps in nation building by making available investible capital.*

*See Paul A. Samuelson and William D. Nordhaus, *Economics* (New Delhi: McGraw Hill Education, 2020), pp. 283-284. See LIBNA, 1956 and GIBNA, 1971 of the GoI.

To watch the Author's videos on the significance of the Chapter, scan the QR Code given here

Exam Essentials...

- Functions of Insurance
- Insurance intermediary
- Insurance Penetration and Density
- Adverse Selection
- Moral Hazard

Note to the Reader...

As an integral part of India's financial market, insurance plays as the best hedge against the uncertainties which our lives and assets face. Majority of the Indians are careless about the economic risk to their lives even if they are the sole breadwinners of their families. For example, in the case of life insurance, most of the policies are *savings-linked,* with just a small protection component (it means there are very few 'term insurances' which provide financial security in times of premature deaths)– this is why even after having life insurance cover, most households are exposed to financial risk in the event of premature death of the primary breadwinner. There is a need of 'transformational change' in the behavioural dimension of Indians in this regard.

In This Chapter...

- Definition
- Insurance Industry
- Insurance Reforms
- Reinsurance
- Deposit Insurance and Credit Guarantee Corporation (DICGC)
- Export Credit Guarantee Corporation (ECGC)
- National Export Insurance Account (NEIA)
- New Reform Initiatives
- National Digital Health Mission
- Third-Party Insurance
- New Policy Steps
- Insurance Industry Today
- Way Forward

DEFINITION

In economic terms, anything used to cut down risk is known as insurance. But in familiar terms, insurance is provided by an insurance company which covers a person's life (called life segment) or covers loss of assets or property (called non-life or general segment). The insurance policies are purchased at fixed premiums.

INSURANCE INDUSTRY

Insurance has a deep-rooted history in India. We find its mention in the writings of Manu *(Manusmrithi)*, Yagnavalkya *(Dharmasastra)* and Kautilya *(Arthasastra)*. The writings talk in terms of **pooling of resources** that could be redistributed in times of calamities such as fire, floods, epidemics and famine. This was probably a precursor to modern-day insurance. Ancient Indian history has preserved the earliest traces of insurance in the form of marine trade loans and carriers' contracts. Insurance in India has evolved over time heavily drawing from other countries (England in particular).

Functions of Insurance

Insurance plays three vital functions in modern economies:

(i) Resource mobilisation for investment (helps in nation-building);

(ii) Cutting/hedging financial risk of human life and other assets (a socio-economic function); and

(iii) Providing a safety net (strengthens the idea of welfare state).

The Government "nationalised" the industry in India for the causes cited above. When the industry was decontrolled for the entry of the private sector together with the beginning of de-nationalisation, the functions/objectives of the industry remained the same.

Life Insurance Corporation (LIC) of India

The life insurance business/industry in the country was nationalised by the Government of India (GoI) in 1956 and a fully government-owned company, the Life Insurance Corporation of India (LIC), was set up (at that time 245 Indian and foreign companies were present in the life segment of insurance). Opening of private life insurance companies was prohibited at that time. The LIC was called an investment institution by the government.

Scan this QR Code to watch a author's video lecture that simplifies this topic

The nationalisation was motivated by twin objectives - *first*, to spread the message of life insurance for greater social security; and *second*, to mobilise people's savings (collected as premiums) for nation-building. The LIC had been the biggest investor in the Government's process of planned development purchasing government securities (G-Secs) and equities of the big asset public sector undertakings (PSUs).

General Insurance Corporation (GIC) of India

In 1971, the Government nationalised the private sector companies (107 Indian and foreign companies) prevalent in the general insurance segment and a government company, the General Insurance Corporation of India (GIC), was formed in 1972. The GIC started operation on 1 January 1973, with its four holding companies:

1. National Insurance Company Ltd.
2. New India Assurance Company Ltd.
3. Oriental Fire and Insurance Company Ltd.
4. United India Insurance Company Ltd.

In the era of economic reforms, two major changes took place in this area:

1. In November 2000, the GIC was notified as the Indian Reinsurer[1] (to be known as GIC Re).
2. In March 2002, the GIC was withdrawn from holding company status of the four public sector general insurance companies. Now these four companies are directly owned by the GoI.[2]

Agriculture Insurance Company of India Limited (AICIL)

The public sector insurance company, Agriculture Insurance Company of India Limited (AICIL) was

[1] Publication Division, *India 2002* (New Delhi: Government of India, 2003).

[2] *Economic Survey 2002-03* (New Delhi: Ministry of Finance, Government of India, 2003).

set up by the GoI in December 2002 (commenced its business in April 2003). This is a *dedicated agri-insurance* company and aims 'to serve the needs of farmers better and to move towards a sustainable actuarial regime'.

This company was responsible to look after the National Agriculture Insurance Scheme (NAIS) which was launched in 1999. Since *January 2016*, the company is looking after the newly launched PMFBY (*Prime Minister Fasal Bima Yojana*)[3] which subsumed the existing agri-insurance schemes - the NAIS and the Modified NAIS (of 2010). Before the AICIL could be set up, the agri-insurance responsibility of the Government was looked after by the GIC.

The GIC holds 35 per cent equity of AICIL and NABARD holds 30 per cent while the balance is held equally to the extent of 8.75 per cent by the four public sector non-life insurance companies.

Public Sector Insurance Companies

At present, there are six public sector *insurance companies* in India. Out of it one deals in the life segment (LIC); four are involved in the non-life (general) insurance segment; and one is the dedicated agri-insurer. Other than these companies, there is one *re-insurance company*, the GIC Re (wholly owned by the GoI).

INSURANCE REFORMS

Under the process of economic reforms an Insurance Reforms Committee (IRC) was set up in April 1993 under the chairmanship of the ex- RBI Governor, R. N. Malhotra. The committee handed over its report (January 1994) with the following major suggestions[4]:

1. Decontrolling insurance sector, i.e., allowing Indian as well as foreign private sector insurance companies to enter the sector (the Government did it in 1999 passing the *IRDA Act*).
2. Restructuring the LIC and the GIC and cutting down the Government's holding in them to 50 per cent. By late 2012, the Government started sale of the LIC shares but to PSUs - seen as a welcome move. In 2022-23, the Government diluted its ownership in the LIC by 3.5 per cent through an initial public offer (IPO).
3. Delinking GIC and its four subsidiaries (which was done in 2000).
4. Discarding the system of licensing of surveyors by the Controller of insurance.
5. Restructuring the Tariff Advisory Committee.
6. Setting up a regulatory authority for the insurance industry (the IRDA was set up in 2000).

Insurance Regulatory and Development Authority (IRDA)

The Insurance Regulatory and Development Authority (IRDA) was set up in 2000 (the Act was passed in 1999) with one chairman and five members (two as full-time and three as part-time members) appointed and nominated by the Government. The authority is responsible for the regulation, development and supervision of the Indian insurance industry.

Today, 58 insurance companies are operating in India, of which 24 are in the life segment while 34 in non-life segment - 1 public sector life insurer (LIC), 4 public sector general insurers, 2 specialised insurers (AICIL and ECGC), 1 public sector reinsurer (GIC Re) and 10 foreign re-insurers.

The Government allows 100 per cent foreign direct investment (FDI) in the insurance sector (increased from 74 per cent by the *Union Budget 2025-26*). Permission of 100 per cent FDI in 'insurance intermediaries' was already given in 2019-20.[5]

Insurance intermediary

Insurance intermediary functions between insurance firm (company) and its customers – the entities such as insurance agent, banks, surveyors, third party administrators, etc. being its examples. In 2019–20, the Government of India allowed 100 per cent FDI (foreign direct investment) in this segment, which was always facing requirement of huge capital base and technical expertise.

[3] *Union Budget 2016-17* (New Delhi: Ministry of Finance, Government of India, 2016); and *Economic Survey 2015-16* (New Delhi: Ministry of Finance, Government of India, 2016).

[4] R. N. Malhotra headed the Insurance Reforms Committee, Government of India, New Delhi, January 1994.

[5] *Union Budget 2021-22* and *Annual Report 2018-19 (New Delhi: IRDAI,* Ministry of Finance, GoI).

REINSURANCE

Insurance is a very risky business. While the insurance companies offer insurance to its clients, they themselves get exposed to very high financial risks. Re-insurance business emerged out of this reality. When an insurance company buys insurance cover for its insurance business, a new segment comes into being, i.e., re-insurance.

Experts believe that in the absence of reinsurance, the insurance industry in a country will not grow to the level of the social requirement - as insurance, companies will either not provide insurance cover in several areas or they will charge very high premiums on the policies they offer (to neutralise the risk). Keeping this in mind, the GoI took the initiative to convert the existing public sector general insurer, the GIC, into a reinsurance company (in 2000). Known as the GIC Re, it remains the only reinsurance company in the country till date. Over time, this emerged as a major player in the global reinsurance industry. Reinsurance industry is regulated by the IRDA in the country.

Reinsurance industry had a very low penetration in India. Lack of competition has been cited as a major factor behind it - it had only one player. To promote competition and vibrancy, the IRDA announced (in late 2015) to open up the industry for the entry of foreign companies. By *February 2025*, a total of 10 foreign reinsurance companies were operating in India, which included the top reinsurance companies of the world (the German company *Munich Re* being the largest, the Swiss company *Swiss Re* being the second largest and the German company *Hannover Ruck SE* being the third largest in the world).

DEPOSIT INSURANCE AND CREDIT GUARANTEE CORPORATION (DICGC)

DICGC was set up by merging the Deposit Insurance Corporation (1962) and the Credit Guarantee Corporation (1971) in 1978. While Deposit Insurance had been introduced in India out of concern to protect depositors, ensure financial stability, instil confidence in the banking system and help mobilise deposits, the establishment of the Credit Guarantee Corporation was essentially in the realm of affirmative action to ensure that the credit needs of the hitherto neglected sectors and weaker sections were met. The essential concern was to persuade banks to make credit available to not so creditworthy clients. After the merger, the focus of the DICGC had shifted onto credit guarantees. This owed in part to the fact that most large banks were nationalised. With the financial sector reforms undertaken in the 1990s, credit guarantees have been gradually phased out and the focus of the corporation is veering back to its core function of deposit insurance with the objective of averting panics, reducing systemic risk and ensuring financial stability.

Insurance cover available on bank deposits was increased from the existing ₹1 to ₹5 lakhs by the Government on **1 February 2020**. The move announced in the *Union Budget 2020-21* was believed to come in the wake of the recent crisis related to the Mumbai-based urban cooperative bank, the PMC (Punjab and Maharashtra Cooperative). For deposit insurance, depositors do not pay any premium rather a nominal premium is collected by the DICGC from the banks. The scheme covers all banks operating in India including the private sector, cooperative and even branches of foreign banks in India with certain exemptions such as deposits of foreign governments, deposits of central/state governments and inter-bank deposits.

Background In 2017-18, the Government proposed the *Financial Resolution and Deposit Insurance (FRDI) Bill*, which aimed to reform the existing provisions related to deposit insurance and credit guarantee. The Bill was criticised for the clause which allowed 'writing down of the liabilities of the failed bank'. This clause was inferred by stakeholders as the 'bail-in' clause (when a financial help comes in from within the bank/financial institution). The Joint Parliamentary Committee also had certain apprehensions related to it. The government withdrew the Bill in July 2018 and announced the need of more time to examine the related issues.

Since 1991, the deposit insurance limit has been up to only ₹1 lakh. Many countries revised their deposit insurance limits after the global financial crisis of 2008. The limit was increased up to US$ 2.5 lakh in the United States and US$ 1.15 lakh in the United Kingdom (set around 3-4 times of the per capita income of these economies). Emerging market economies such as Brazil and China have set this limit at 9 times of their per capita income. In case of India, it was still less than its per capita income (which was estimated to be ₹1,11,782 at constant market price, as per the *Economic Survey 2017-18*).

EXPORT CREDIT GUARANTEE CORPORATION (ECGC)

The overseas projects undertaken by the Indian companies face many political and commercial risks in the importing countries. To provide adequate credit insurance cover to such firms, the government has set up the Export Credit Guarantee Corporation of India Ltd. (ECGC) under the Ministry of Commerce and Industry, for medium and long-term exports. But owing to its own limitations, at times it is difficult for the ECGC to cover pure commercial risks in issues such as long repayment period, large value of contracts, and difficult economic and political conditions of the importing country together with the fact that reinsurance cover is generally not available for such projects.[6] Many times such projects seem necessary considering the economic and political relationship of India with the proposed importing country. It means that in the absence of credit insurance cover, the ability of Indian exporters to opt for such export projects is hampered. It should be noted that in many developed economies such projects are covered and underwritten on a government account.[7]

NATIONAL EXPORT INSURANCE ACCOUNT (NEIA)

For facilitating the service of the ECGC (discussed above), the GoI did set up the National Export Insurance Account (NEIA) in March 2006 to promote medium and long-term export by providing credit insurance support in the cases where the ECGC was not able to provide credit cover on its own because of purely commercial reasons[8]:

1. The corpus given to the account was ₹66 crore, raised to ₹246 crore by 2007-08 and was enhanced to ₹2,000 crore in the Eleventh Plan (2007-12).
2. Resources of the NEIA will be the corpus, the premium income, interest income and recovery of all the claims paid.
3. As per the provision, an exposure equal to ten times corpus can be taken by the NEIA.

The NEIA can cover projects which fulfil the following criteria[9]:

1. The project by itself should be commercially viable;
2. The project should be strategically important for India, with regard to the economic and political relationship of India with the importing country; and
3. The exporter should be capable of executing the contract, as evident from his previous track record.

The use and benefits of the NEIA need to be publicised among its beneficiaries. Meanwhile, many export projects pertaining to Indonesia, Vietnam, Iran, Sudan etc. are underway. The NEIA will facilitate potential project exporters to enter the international trade area, as it is expected[10] to be so. In the era of globalisation, it has been praised as a welcome development by the experts and the tradespeople alike.[11]

Insurance Penetration and Density

The growth in the insurance sector is internationally measured based on the standard of insurance penetration. Insurance penetration is defined as the ratio of premium underwritten in a given year to the Gross Domestic Product (GDP). Likewise, insurance density is another well-recognised benchmark and is defined as the ratio of premium underwritten in a given year to total population (measured in US dollars for convenience of comparison). The Indian insurance business has remained under-developed with low levels of insurance penetration and insurance density.

The latest[11] data related to insurance penetration and density in India are as given below:

1. **Insurance Penetration:** India's insurance penetration was **3.7** per cent in 2025 (down from 4.0 per cent in 2023 (much lower from the peak of 5.20 per cent in 2009) – 2.7 per cent for life segment and 1.0 per cent for non-life segment

---

[6] Due to its underwriting constraint, the ECGC is unable to cover such projects on its own.

[7] For example, the United States, France, the United Kingdom and many other Euro-American economies underwrite such medium and long-term projects in the governments' account. The SEIA also covers only medium and long-term export projects.

[8] Announced while setting up the NEIA, Ministry of Commerce and Industry, Government of India, New Delhi, 9 March, 2006.

[9] Ibid.

[10] S. Prabhakaran, Executive Director, ECGC, Mumbai in Survey of Indian Industry 2007, *The Hindu*, p. 84.

[11] *Economic Survey 2025-26* (New Delhi: Ministry of Finance, GoI, January 2026), pp. 139-140.

(i.e., general insurance). Globally, insurance penetration was 7.0 per cent in 2025 (3.0 per cent for the life segment and 4.0 per cent for the non-life segment). In the case of life insurance, most of the policies are savings-linked, with just a small protection component. This is why even after having life insurance cover, most households are exposed to financial risk in the event of premature death of the primary breadwinner.

In 2025, countries like Taiwan, South Africa, the USA, and UK had a higher penetration of 15.3 per cent, 12.5 per cent, 12.2 per cent and 11.6 per cent, respectively (as per the *OECD*, February 2026).

2. **Insurance Density:** India's insurance density was **US$ 97** in 2025 (up from $11.1 in 2001) – US$ 70 for life segment and US$ 25 for non-life segment, much lower than global standards. Globally, insurance density was US$ 875 in 2025 (US$ 390 for the life segment and US$ 485 for the non-life segment). In 2025, countries like the USA, Singapore, and Switzerland had a higher insurance density at US$ 8315, US$ 6810, and US$ 6902, respectively (as per *OECD*, February 2026).

Reasons for Underdevelopment of Insurance

As per the various volumes of the Annual Reports published by the IRDA and other government documents, there have been several reasons responsible for the underdevelopment of the insurance penetration and density in the country:

1. Complex and delayed claim settlement procedures;
2. Vague and incomprehensible rules and regulations of the insurance companies;
3. Lack of education and awareness among the masses;
4. Lower income levels of the population;
5. Socio-cultural factors;
6. Lack of level playing field in the industry; and
7. Less vibrancy in the regulatory framework.

The Insurance Laws (Amendment) Act, 2015 and the recently enacted Amendment Act of 2021 is supposed to have a positive impact on regulatory framework as well as insurance penetration.

Adverse Selection

One among the two kinds of the market failure, often associated with insurance business which means doing business with the people one would have better avoided.

Adverse selection can be a problem when there is an asymmetry in information between the seller and the buyer of an insurance policy – as insurance will not be profitable when buyers have better information about their risk of claiming than does the seller of the insurance policy. In the ideal case, insurance premiums are set in accordance with the risk of a randomly selected person in the insured bracket (such as 40-year-old male smokers) of the population. The other kind of market failure is *moral hazards* which is associated with the insurance sector.

NEW REFORM INITIATIVES

With a view to removing archaic and redundant provisions in the insurance laws, empowering the IRDA to enable more effective regulation and enhancing the foreign equity investment cap in an Indian insurance company with the safeguard of Indian ownership and control, the government has implemented the Insurance Laws (Amendment) Acts of 2015 and 2021.

The Acts paved the way for major reform-related amendments in the Insurance Act, 1938, the General Insurance Business (Nationalisation) Act, 1972 and the Insurance Regulatory and Development Authority Act, 1999. It provides greater powers to the IRDAI by which the insurance regulatory framework is supposed to become more flexible, effective and efficient.

Major changes[12] made (with further policy changes) are as given below:

1. **Promotion of Foreign Investment:** The permissible limit of the FDI in insurance sector was increased to 100 per cent (from the existing 74 per cent) in 2025-26 and allowed foreign ownership and control with safeguards. Greater availability of capital for the

[12] *Union Budget 2025-26; Union Budget 2021-22; Economic Survey 2017-18*; and IRDAI, (New Delhi: Ministry of Finance, GoI).

capital-intensive insurance sector would lead to greater distribution reach to under/unserved areas, more innovative product formulations to meet diverse insurance needs of citizens, efficient service delivery through improved distribution technology and enhanced customer service standards.

2. **Capital Requirement in Government Companies:** The four public sector general insurance companies, presently required as per the General Insurance Business (Nationalisation) Act, 1972 to be 100 per cent government owned, are now allowed to raise capital. This will enable them to have additional capital for the purposes of business expansion in the rural/ social sectors and enhanced competitiveness. The GoI ownership is to be maintained minimum at 51 per cent.
3. **Consumer Welfare:** It will enable the interests of consumers to be better served through provisions like those enabling penalties on intermediaries/insurance companies for misconduct and disallowing multi-level marketing of insurance products in order to curtail the practice of mis-selling:
   - (i) The amended Law has several provisions for levying higher penalties ranging from ₹1 crore to ₹25 crore for various violations including mis-selling and misrepresentation by agents/insurance companies.
   - (ii) With a view to serve the interest of the policy holders better, the period during which a policy can be repudiated on any ground, including mis-statement of facts etc., will be confined to three years from the commencement of the policy and no policy would be called into question on any ground after three years.
   - (iii) The amendments provide for an easier process for payment to the nominee of the policyholder, as the insurer would be discharged of its legal liabilities once the payment is made to the nominee.
   - (iv) It is now obligatory in the law for insurance companies to underwrite third-party motor vehicle insurance as per IRDAI regulations. Rural and social sector obligations for insurers are retained in the amended laws.
4. **Empowerment of IRDAI:** The Act will entrust responsibility of appointing insurance agents to insurers and provides for IRDAI to regulate their eligibility, qualifications and other aspects:
   - (i) It enables agents to work more broadly across companies in various business categories with the safeguard that conflict of interest would not be allowed by the IRDAI through suitable regulations.
   - (ii) The IRDAI is empowered to regulate key aspects of Insurance Company operations in areas such as solvency, investments, expenses and commissions and to formulate regulations for payment of commission and control of management expenses.
   - (iii) It empowers the Authority to regulate the functions, code of conduct, etc., of surveyors and loss assessors. It also expands the scope of insurance intermediaries to include insurance brokers, re-insurance brokers, insurance consultants, corporate agents, third-party administrators, surveyors and loss assessors and such other entities, as may be notified by the authority from time to time.
   - (iv) Furthermore, properties in India can now be insured with a foreign insurer with prior permission of the IRDAI, which was earlier to be carried out with the approval of the Central Government.
5. **Health Insurance:** The Act defines 'health insurance business' as inclusive of travel and personal accident cover and discourages non-serious players by retaining capital requirements for health insurers at the level of ₹100 crore, thereby paving the way for promotion of health insurance as a separate vertical.
6. **Promoting Reinsurance Business in India:** It enables foreign reinsurers to set up *branches* in India and defines 'reinsurance' to mean 'the insurance of part of one insurer's risk by another insurer who accepts the risk for a mutually acceptable premium', and thereby excludes the possibility of 100 per cent ceding of risk to a re-insurer, which could lead to companies acting as front companies for other insurers.
7. **Strengthening of Industry Councils:** The Life Insurance Council and General Insurance

Council have now been made *self-regulating bodies* by empowering them to frame bye-laws for elections, meetings and levy and collect fees, etc., from its members. Inclusion of representatives of *self-help groups* and *insurance cooperative societies* in insurance councils has also been enabled to broadly base the representation on these councils.

8. **Robust Appellate Process:** Appeals against the orders of the IRDAI are to be preferred to Securities Appellate Tribunal (SAT) as the amended law provides for any insurer or insurance intermediary aggrieved by any order made by the IRDAI to prefer an appeal to the SAT.
9. **Capital Market Reforms:** In March 2019, the IRDA announced the redesigned initial public offering (IPO) guidelines for insurance companies which are looking to divest equity through the IPO route. Now insurance companies are allowed to invest up to 10 per cent in additional *tier-I* bonds issued by banks (which are raising capital to comply to Basel III norms).

Thus, the amendments incorporate enhancements in the insurance laws in keeping with the evolving insurance sector scenario and regulatory practices across the *globe*. The amendments will enable the regulator to create an operational framework for greater innovation, competition and transparency, to meet the insurance needs of citizens in a more complete and subscriber-friendly manner. The amendments are expected to enable the sector to achieve its full growth potential and contribute towards the overall growth of the economy and job creation.

Moral Hazard

This is a situation in which someone takes risk knowing that the cost of risk will be borne by someone else – one of the two challenges insurance companies face (the other being 'adverse selection', see the term explained in previous 'Exam Essential' box). This hazard arises when both the parties (Insurance firm and the insured) have incomplete information about each other. Banks also face similar challenges while lending.

In practice, when our houses are not insured, we take more precautions against fire, burglary, etc. but not as much if the houses are insured (due to which the cost of our negligence is borne by the insurance firm)!

NATIONAL DIGITAL HEALTH MISSION

The National Digital Health Mission[13] was launched by the Government in August 2020 (on the 74th Independence Day) aimed at making medical services accessible to all citizens of the country. The mission is slated to maintain the health records of citizens in 'digital' form - which will have the following features:

1. Unique Health ID to be given to citizens;
2. Health Card to be given to citizens;
3. Citizens can share their health data to a third party.

The voluntary healthcare programme aims to integrate doctors, hospitals, pharmacies, insurance companies and make a digital health infrastructure as its *backbone*. The health accounts of citizens will contain details of every test, every disease, the doctors visited, the medicines taken and the diagnosis. The mission is expected to revolutionise the healthcare and related sectors in an unprecedented way besides fulfilling the aim of the universal healthcare (National Health Policy-2017) with diversity of uses:

1. **Healthcare Sector:** The mission will strengthen the healthcare sector in multiple ways - the citizens who need to procure healthcare services from the private or public sector healthcare agencies need to just share their unique health identity number, and their whole medical history will be available to the medical service provider. This will not only speed up the delivery of the health services but also cut down the mistakes and repetition of diagnosis and prescriptions. It will strengthen the healthcare sector by boosting the Government idea of 'tele-consultation' and 'virtual consultation' (announced in *Mission Mode Interventions* in the healthcare sector); synchronisation of the health schemes with the digital health data of the beneficiaries; *synchronising the Aadhaar numbers* of the beneficiaries for cash transfers and boosting the Ayushman Bharat scheme in a big way.
2. **Insurance Industry:** For the insurance industry, the medical history of the insured person is quite important as they are used for the calculation of actuarial and chargeable

[13] Ministry of Health and Family Welfare, August 2020, GoI, New Delhi.

premiums. The insurance industry together with the insured individual both suffer due to absence of authentic medical history of the citizens - insurance companies suffer as they need to settle insurance claims of concealed health issues, while the insured persons bear the burden of higher premium charges than they would have been if medical history were concealed by others (as the company has to recover its losses!).

Naturally, once the authentic medical history will be available to the insurance sector, the premiums of the insurance policies can be planned in a better and rational way. Due to this, the premium for people in good health will fall, while the people who have medical histories need to pay a higher premium. But overall, this will enhance the operational transparency of the insurance sector. Thus, for the insurance industry (especially, the health insurance segment), the mission is expected to be a boon.

3. **Lifestyle Improvement:** When health data of citizens are known, many measures can be taken to improve the lifestyle of the insured citizens (which can also be customised) which will reduce the incidence of diseases and man-hour losses. The insurance regulator (IRDAI) has already allowed insurers to provide such wellness services to customers of health insurance products.

The incidence of lifestyle diseases is rising very fast in the country. We know that such diseases can only be checked by changing the lifestyle of the people. The Government has been placing much emphasis on this aspect in recent times under which themes such as healthy diet, yoga, exercises, walking, cycling to work and so on are being promoted.

THIRD-PARTY INSURANCE

The 'third-party' insurance is provided by non-life insurance companies on vehicles. This insurance covers the risk other than the 'two parties' (i.e. the car and the owner, in case of a car) involved in an insurance policy. The policy does not provide any benefit to the insured; however, it covers the insured's legal liability for death/disability of third-party loss or damage to the third-party property. This insurance is also known as 'act only' cover. In India, it is mandatory (under the Motor Vehicle Amendment Act, 2019) for all new two-wheelers to have a five-year third-party insurance, and cars and commercial vehicles to have a three-year third-party insurance.

The cost of a comprehensive cover is several times that of a stand-alone third-party cover, since damage claims are more frequent than third-party claims. Until now, the premium for motor third-party insurance was calculated on the basis of a schedule of rates provided by the Tariff Advisory Committee, an arm of the IRDAI (the insurance regulator). But the IRDA has done away with the motor tariff. The compensation to the victim is largely decided by the earning capacity of the accident victim.

To make insurance policies of vehicles cheaper, insurance companies have been charging a very low premium for such policies. Due to this, insurance companies have not been settling third-party insurance claims quicker (majority of cases going for litigation). But in recent years, the IRDAI has taken various steps to strengthen this segment of the non-life insurance. By early 2020-21, the IRDAI announced a market-linked increase in the insurance premium for the third-party insurance together with enforcing a stricter regulatory regime for quicker settlement of the third-party claims.

NEW POLICY STEPS

Enhancing insurance penetration and promoting greater social security of the citizens through inclusive insurance have received special attention from the Government in recent times, and several steps have been taken in this direction *(April 2022):*

PMSBY (*Pradhan Mantri Suraksha Bima Yojana*) It offers a renewable one-year accidental-death-cum-disability cover to all subscribing bank account holders in the age group of 18 to 70 years for a premium of ₹12 per annum per subscriber.

The risk coverage available will be ₹2 lakh for accidental death and permanent total disability and ₹1 lakh for permanent partial disability, for a one-year period stretching from 1 June to 31 May.

PMJJBY (*Pradhan Mantri Jeevan Jyoti Bima Yojana*) The scheme offers a renewable 1-year term life cover of ₹2 lakh to all subscribing bank account holders in the age group of 18 to 50 years.

NHPS (National Health Protection Scheme) In September 2018, the Government launched the NHPS under *Ayushman Bharat* to provide coverage of up to ₹5 lakh to more than 50 crore vulnerable families (10 crore families). The scheme is expected to increase penetration of health insurance in India from 34 per cent to 50 per cent.

ANANDA In November 2020, LIC of India launched its ***first*** software application, ANANDA (an acronym for 'Atmanirbhar Agents New Business Digital App') for the on-boarding process with the aid of the agent/broker to get a life insurance policy through *paperless module.* Several other insurance companies are in the process of bringing in such app-based insurance platforms - over 120 digital insurance start-ups (popularly known as InsurTech) are at present operating in the country.

INSURANCE INDUSTRY TODAY

Insurance industry has shown greater dynamism across the world in recent years and this augurs well for India– quoting various global reports, the latest *Economic Survey 2024-25* has outlined[14] the following features for the industry:

Global Prospects As per the *Swiss Re Institute World Insurance Report 2024*, the global insurance market is experiencing a dynamic period of growth and transformation, driven by steady economic expansion, strong labour markets, and rising real incomes. Despite considerable challenges in 2023, including persistently high inflation and geopolitical tensions that constrained the global GDP growth, the insurance sector demonstrated a positive growth rate of 2.8 per cent. The changing macroeconomic environment, climate fluctuations, technological progress, and evolving customer preferences drive transformation in technology, infrastructure, business models, and organisational culture within the insurance industry.

As per the latest *Ernst & Young Report of 2024 (Insurance for All: enhancing insurance coverage across India),* global insurers are actively adopting innovative technologies, expanding their market reach, and prioritising customer-centric approaches to improve efficiency and address emerging demands.

WAY FORWARD

However, several steps have been taken by the Government in recent times to promote and expand the insurance sector, there are still certain older and emerging challenges which have been highlighted[15] by the *Economics Survey 2025–26* in the following ways:

- Evolving customer expectations and emerging risks, such as climate change and geopolitical uncertainty, present significant challenges for insurers. Additionally, increasing life expectancy and a growing elderly population pose underwriting risks related to longevity and highlight the widening pension gap. Non-financial risks have gained importance alongside traditional financial risks.
- The industry must address and manage concerns related to *mis-selling*, delayed claims settlements, AI, cybersecurity, and third-party interactions.
- A clear and quantitative understanding of risk appetite is essential for effective risk management— insurance companies 'must' develop strong capabilities to tackle these emerging risks through rapid innovation while ensuring efficiency and productivity through simplification, standardisation, and digitisation.
- Insurance *penetration* and *density* both being low presents opportunities for insurers to expand their reach. By targeting Tier II and III cities and rural areas where 'awareness' and 'accessibility' are limited, insurers can tap into new customer segments and stimulate growth.

The IRDAI has transitioned towards a principle-based framework that consolidates regulations, reduces compliance burdens, and provides insurers with greater flexibility to innovate. Meanwhile, the *Sabka Bima Sabki Raskha* (Amendment of Insurance Laws, 2025) represents its commitment to digitising the insurance ecosystem and democratising coverage.

[14] *Economic Survey 2024-25* (New Delhi: Ministry of Finance, GoI, January 2025), pp. 62-64.

[15] *Economic Survey 2025-26* (New Delhi: Ministry of Finance, GoI, January 2026), pp. 136-141.

SAMPLE OBJECTIVE QUESTIONS

1. Consider the following statements related to the insurance sector in the country:
   - (i) Insurance penetration declined by around one-fifth during 2009-2019.
   - (ii) Lack of good insurance companies is among the reasons for the underdevelopment of the sector.
   - (iii) Insurance frauds have increased due to the digital insurance apps.

   How many of the above statements are correct?
   (a) Only one (b) Only two
   (c) All three (d) None of these

2. Consider the following statements related to insurance density in the country:
   - (i) It increased by around six times during the last two decades (2001-2021).
   - (ii) It is lower in comparison to the Asian peers due to lower premium pricing by the insurance companies.
   - (iii) Unawareness remains the most important factor for its underdevelopment in general insurance.

   How many of the above statements are correct?
   (a) Only one (b) Only two
   (c) All three (d) None of these

3. Consider the following statements related to the insurance industry in the country:
   - (i) Lack of capital remains a major challenge for public as well as private insurance companies.
   - (ii) Insurance density is per capita premium collected by all insurance companies in a given year.
   - (iii) A rise in insurance penetration may not help insurance density rise too.

   How many of the above statements are correct?
   (a) Only one (b) Only two
   (c) All three (d) None of these

4. Consider the following statements related to health insurance in the country:
   - (i) The COVID-19 pandemic has helped it grow.
   - (ii) India's health insurance penetration is about one-sixth of the global average.
   - (iii) Universal healthcare policy includes compulsory health insurance for the beneficiaries.

   How many of the above statements are correct?
   (a) Only one (b) Only two
   (c) All three (d) None of these

5. Consider the following statements related to insurance companies in the country:
   - (i) They complement government's social security measures.
   - (ii) They are registered as investment institutions by the IRDAI.
   - (iii) Unit linked insurance schemes offered by them are part mutual funds.

   How many of the above statements are correct?
   (a) Only one (b) Only two
   (c) All three (d) None of these

6. Consider the following statements related to insurance penetration:
   - (i) It is a measure of insurance industry in a country.
   - (ii) It is a ratio of the per capita GDP and the number of insurance policies in a country.
   - (iii) It is measured in US dollar for the convenience of comparison.

   How many of the above statements are correct?
   (a) Only one (b) Only two
   (c) All three (d) None of these

7. Consider the following statements related to insurance industry in the country:
   - (i) It faces the issue of adverse selection.
   - (ii) Market failure for it may originate from moral hazards.
   - (iii) Digitalisation of health records will cut the information asymmetry for it.

How many of the above statements are correct?

(a) Only one (b) Only two
(c) All three (d) None of these

8. Consider the following statements related to the situation of insurance activities in the country:
   (i) Deposit insurance is a joint responsibility of the RBI and IRDAI.
   (ii) Export insurance is provided by the EXIM Bank of India in association with the RBI.
   (iii) Export credit insurance operates under the Ministry of Commerce and Industry.

   How many of the above statements are correct?

   (a) Only one (b) Only two
   (c) All three (d) None of these

9. Consider the following statements related to re-insurance business in the country:
   (i) Government owned GIC Re is proposed for divestment in 2024-25.
   (ii) All major reinsurance firms of the world are presently operating in the country.
   (iii) Private sector is not permitted to set up re-insurance company.

   How many of the above statements are correct?

   (a) Only one (b) Only two
   (c) All three (d) None of these

10. Consider the following statements related to insurance companies in India:
   (i) Technically they can be called as hedge funds.
   (ii) They are permitted to offer mutual funds also.
   (iii) Their mutual funds come under the regulatory ambit of the Securities and Exchange Board of India (SEBI).

   How many of the above statements are correct?

   (a) Only one (b) Only two
   (c) All three (d) None of these

Answers: 1. (a) 2. (b) 3. (c) 4. (a) 5. (b) 6. (a) 7. (c) 8. (a) 9. (b) 10. (a)

SAMPLE SUBJECTIVE QUESTIONS

1. Briefly discuss the reasons due to which insurance industry is considered underdeveloped in the country in comparison to, especially, the Asian peers.
2. Examine the role of insurance industry in enhancing socio-economic wellbeing in the country. Cite relevant examples.
3. 'Universal health insurance will be the stepping stone to universal healthcare in the country.' Elucidate with suitable illustrations.
4. 'Digital public health infrastructure will emerge as the backbone of the healthcare sector in coming times.' Examine and cite suitable examples.

SAMPLE MODEL ANSWER

1. **Briefly discuss the recent policy steps taken by the Government/IRDAI to develop and expand insurance sector in the country.**

Ans. The Government of India and the Insurance Regulatory and Development Authority of India (IRDAI) have the following major policy steps to develop and expand the insurance sector in the country:

1. *Transformative policies through Insurance Amendment Laws, 2025 (i.e., Sabka Bima Sabki Raksha Act, 2025)*
   - The limit of FDI in the sector rose from 74 per cent to 100 per cent.
   - 'Composite Licenses' was introduced, enabling a single entity to offer life, health, and general insurance products.
   - The Net Owned Fund requirement for foreign reinsurers to set up branches in India was drastically reduced to ₹1,000 crore (from the existing ₹5,000 crore).
   - The threshold for seeking IRDAI approval for share transfers was increased from 1 per cent to 5 per cent (ease of doing business).
   - Insurance intermediaries to receive one-time, perpetual licences (instead of requiring renewal every three years).
   - The requirement for most directors to be resident Indians was removed (now, only one top leader, such as the CEO, MD, or Chairperson, must be a resident).
2. *Consumer Protection and Market Discipline*
   - IRDAI is empowered to order the 'disgorgement of wrongful gains' from mis-selling.
   - To spread awareness and consumer protection, a dedicated Education and Protection Fund has been established (funded by penalties collected by IRDA).
   - The penalty for violations of insurance laws has been increased from ₹10 million to ₹100 million.
3. *Digital and Operational Initiatives*
   - Online marketplace 'Bima Sugam' has been launched to act as a 'one-stop' shop for policy purchase, claim settlement, and insurance advice.
   - The 'Use and File' framework has been initiated, allowing insurers to launch new products without prior regulatory approval.
   - The 65-year age cap for buying health insurance has been removed.
   - To expand rural insurance, 'Bima Vahak' and 'Bima Vistar' initiatives have been taken through a dedicated female workforce and affordable, befit-based insurance products.

Experts believe that the above-given policy steps will enhance insurance penetration and insurance density in the country, and the Government will be successful in the mission of 'Insurance for All by 2047.'

CHAPTER 15

Security Market in India

Security market is one of the most exciting parts of the modern economies which has made it possible to mobilise enough funds for the creation of the multinational and transnational firms spread across the world today.*

*P. A. Samuelson and W. D. Nordhaus, *Economics* (New Delhi: McGraw Hill Education, 2020), pp. 624-631.

To watch the Author's videos on the significance of the Chapter, scan the QR Code given here

Exam Essentials...

- Market Makers
- Raising Capital in the Primary Market
- Angel Investor
- Hedge Fund
- Gold Exchange Traded Funds
- Financial Stability Development Council
- Financial Action Task Force (FATF)

Note to the Reader...

This chapter deals with the nuances of the security market which consists of instruments like shares, bonds, debentures, mutual funds, pension and provident funds, etc. Being the most glamorous part of the financial markets across the world, every corporate house wishes to raise capital from the security market which helps them divide the financial risks too. However, the security market as a source of investable fund is not as dependable as the banking sector. Besides, the regulators need to guard the risks involved in a very prudent manner.

In This Chapter...

DEFINITION

The segment of a financial market of an economy from long-term capital is raised *via* instruments such as shares, securities, bonds, debentures and mutual funds (MFs) and is known as the security market of that economy.

A security market has components such as a security regulator (SEBI in India), stock exchanges, different share indices, brokers, FIIs, and jobbers. There are different kinds of transactions which take place in a security market such as badla, reverse badla, future trading, insider trading (not allowed), and private placement.

PRIMARY AND SECONDARY MARKETS

Every security market has two complementary markets - primary and secondary. The market in which the instruments of security market are traded (procured) directly between the capital raiser and the instrument purchaser is known as the primary market. As, for example, a share being directly purchased by anybody from the issuer which may be the company itself. The person is known as the primary shareholder. The market where the instruments of security market are traded among the primary instrument holders is known as the *secondary market*. Such transactions need an institutionalised floor for their trading which is made available by the stock exchanges.

STOCK EXCHANGE

It is a physically existing institutionalised set-up where instruments of security stock market (shares, bonds, debentures, securities, etc.) are traded. It serves the following major functions:

1. Makes a floor available to the buyers and sellers of stocks, where liquidity comes to the stocks. It is the single most important institution in the secondary market for securities.
2. Makes available the prices of trading as an important piece of information to the investors.
3. By following institutionalised rules and procedures, it ensures that the participants in the stock market live up to their commitments.
4. Passes updated information to the enlisted companies about their present stockholders (so that they can pass on dividends etc. to them).
5. By publishing its 'Index', it fulfils the purpose of projecting the moods of the stock market.

The world's first stock exchange was established in Antwerp, Belgium (then part of the Netherlands), in 1631, the London Stock Exchange opened in 1773 and then the Philadelphia Stock Exchange (the first in the New World) opened in 1790.[1] The first stock exchange in India, the Bombay Stock Exchange (BSE) known as *The Native Share and Stock Brokers' Association*, was set up in 1870 (under a tree!).[2]

The top five largest stock exchanges (on the basis of market capitalisation) of the world in their decreasing order are the New York Stock Exchange, the NASDAQ, the Tokyo Stock Exchange, the London Stock Exchange and the BSE.[3]

Trading in the stock exchanges takes place *via* the mediators known as the *brokers*, the *jobbers*, the *market makers* (discussed later in this chapter).

As per the latest information,[4] presently, there are a total number of 7 national level stock exchanges operating in India - Bombay Stock Exchange Ltd. (BSE), National Stock Exchange of India Ltd. (NSE), Calcutta Stock Exchange Ltd, Indian Commodity Exchange Ltd, Metropolitan Stock Exchange of India Ltd., Multi Commodity Exchange of India Ltd. and National Commodity & Derivatives Exchange Ltd. A brief account of the 'national level stock exchanges' is given below.

NSE

The National Stock Exchange of India Ltd. (NSE) was set up in 1992 and became operationalised in 1994. The sponsors of the exchange are financial institutions (FIs), including the IDBI, LIC and GIC with the IDBI as its promotor.

It has a 50-share index and a 500-share index known as S&P CNX-50 (Nifty Fifty) and S&P CNX-500, respectively.

The new *Nifty-100 ESG* index was launched by the exchange in 2022-23 to reflect the performance

---

[1] M. Levinson, *Guide to Financial Markets* (London: The Economist, 2006), p. 152.

[2] V. Raghunathan, *Stock Exchanges and Investments* (New Delhi: Tata McGraw Hill, 1994).

[3] M. Levinson, *Guide to Financial Markets*, op. cit., pp. 153-54; *Economic Survey 2005-06* (New Delhi: Ministry of Finance, GoI, 2006).

[4] *Securities and Exchange Board of India (SEBI)* (New Delhi: Ministry of Finance, GoI, April 2022).

of companies within Nifty-100 index based on Environmental, Social and Governance (ESG) risk score.

OTCEI

Though the Over-the-Counter Exchange of India Ltd. (OTCEI) was set up in 1989, it could commence trading only in 1992. India's first fully computerised stock exchange was promoted by the UTI, ICICI, SBI Cap among others, in order to overcome problems such as lack of transparency and delays in settlements prevalent in the older stock exchanges. Another important goal of the exchange was to allow stock market exposure to comparatively smaller companies (with paid-up capital from ₹30 lakh to ₹25 crore). Trading in this exchange takes place *via* market makers and commission is fixed.

ISE

The Interconnected Stock Exchange of India (ISE) is basically a single floor of India's 15 regional stock exchanges (RSEs), set up in 1998. The RSEs were provided increased reach through this. It is a web-based exchange.

BSE

The BSE, earlier an RSE, converted into a national one in 2002. The *biggest* in India, it accounts for almost 75 per cent of total stocks traded in India and is the *fifth* largest in the world (on the basis of market capitalisation).

There are at present four indices connected with the BSE:

1. **Sensex:** The sensitive index (i.e., Sensex) is a 30 stocks index of the BSE which was enlarged to include 50 stocks in 2000 but soon was cut down to the original level. This index represents the Indian stock market.
2. **BSE-200:** This is a 200-stock share index of the BSE (including the 30 stocks of the Sensex) which has its Dollar version too - *the Dollex*.
3. **BSE-500:** In mid-1999, the BSE came up with a 500-stock index representing major industries and many sub-sectors of the economy with information technology getting a significant weightage.
4. **National Index:** An index of 100 stocks being quoted nationwide (Bombay, Delhi, Kolkata, etc.) was developed to give broader/wider representation of the stock market since the Sensex consists of only 30 stocks. The 30 stocks of the Sensex are included in the National Index.

This index is computed by the Statistics Department of the BSE; hence it is called the BSE National Index (BSENI).

Indo Next

A new stock exchange to promote liquidity to the stocks of the small enterprises (SMEs) was launched in 2005 jointly by the BSE and the FISE (Federation of Indian Stock Exchanges, representing 18 RSEs).

It is better known as the *BSE Indo Next*. It was also an effort to rejuvenate the RSEs which were facing falling volumes of trading on their floors. Due to absence of trading at the RSEs, the stocks of the SME have become illiquid. The BSE has transferred all its B1 and B2 groups while the RSEs have transferred their enlisted companies to the exchange. The RSEs will be able to use the BSE online network, the *Webex*.

SME Exchanges: BSE SME and Emerge[5]

SME exchange is a stock exchange dedicated for trading the shares of small and medium-scale enterprises (SMEs) which, otherwise, find it difficult to get listed in the main exchanges. The concept originated from the difficulties faced by SMEs in gaining visibility or attracting sufficient trading volumes when listed along with other stocks in the main exchanges.

To be listed on the SME exchange, the post-issue paid-up capital of the company should not exceed ₹25 crores. This means that the SME exchange is not limited to the small and medium-scale enterprises (which are defined under the 'Micro, Small and Medium Enterprises Development Act, 2006' as enterprises where the investment in plant and machinery does not exceed ₹10 crores). As of now, to get listed in the main boards like the NSE, the minimum paid-up capital required is ₹10 crore and that of the BSE is ₹3 crore. Hence, those companies with paid-up capital between ₹10 crore and ₹25 crore have the option of migrating to the Main Board/ or to the SME exchange. The companies listed on the SME exchange are allowed to migrate to the Main Board as and when they meet the listing requirements of the Main Board. There

[5] This section is based on various sources - the SEBI, NSE, BSE, 'World Federation of Exchanges', select issues of *The Economist* and news reporting of *The HT Live Mint, The Business Line* and *The Economic Times*.

shall be compulsory migration of the SMEs from the SME exchange, in case the post-issue paid-up capital is likely to go beyond the ₹25 crore limit.

World over, trading platforms/exchanges for the shares of SMEs are known by different names such as Alternate Investment Markets or Growth Enterprises Market, SME Board and so on. Some of the known markets for SMEs are the *AIM* (Alternate Investment Market) in the United Kingdom, *TSX Ventures* in Canada, *GEM* (Growth Enterprise's Market) in Hong Kong, *MOTHERS* (Market of the High-Growth and Emerging Stocks) in Japan, *Catalist* in Singapore and *ChiNext*, the latest initiative in China.

Globally, most of these SME exchanges are still at an evolving stage considering the many hurdles they face:

1. Declining prices of listed stocks and their illiquidity.
2. A gradual reduction in new listings and decline in profits of the exchanges etc. (for instance, *AIM* had three predecessors; *CATALIST* succeeded *SESDAQ* with new regulations and listing requirements).
3. In most jurisdictions, the idea of a separate exchange for SMEs has become unviable and hence tends to be platforms of existing exchanges, perhaps cross-subsidised by the main board/exchange.

In India, similarly, after the two previous attempts - ***OTCEI*** (1989) and ***IndoNext*** - the market regulator, SEBI in 2010, permitted setting up of a dedicated stock exchange for SMEs. The existing bourses/stock exchanges in India, BSE and NSE in 2012 launched their separate trading platforms for SMEs naming them the *BSE SME* and *Emerge*, respectively.

Unlike in India, many of these SME exchanges in various countries operate at a global level, due to smallness of the market, allowing for listing by both domestic as well as foreign companies. Though the names suggest that they are set up for SMEs, these exchanges hardly follow the definition of SMEs in their respective jurisdictions. Also, many of them follow a 'Sponsor-supervised' market model, where sponsors or nominated advisors decide if the listing applicant is suitable to be listed or not, i.e., generally no quantitative entry criteria such as track record on profitability or minimum paid-up capital or net worth, and so on are specified to be listed in these exchanges. Instead, they are designed as 'buyers beware' markets for informed investors. The SEBI has also designed the SME exchanges in a similar format with provisions for ***market making*** for the specified securities listed on the SME exchange.

As is the case globally, certain relaxations are also provided to the issuers whose securities are listed on the SME exchange in comparison to the listing requirements in the Main Board (such as in BSE and NSE, in the case of India), which include the following:

1. Publication of financial results on 'half yearly basis', instead of 'quarterly basis', making it available on their websites rather than publishing it.
2. Option of sending a statement containing the salient features of all the documents instead of sending a full Annual Report.
3. No continuous requirement of minimum number of shareholders, though at the time of IPO there needs to be a minimum of 50 investors, etc.
4. The existing eligibility norms such as track record on profits, net worth/net tangible assets conditions, etc. have been fully relaxed for SMEs as is the case globally.
5. However, no compromise has been made to corporate governance norms.

Common Facts about National Stock Exchanges

Before the arrival of national level stock exchanges, India was not having any exchange of national status - there was no Indian stock market, but stock markets showing only regional pictures. Besides, the NSEs did solve some major problems of stock market; we may also call their arrivals as part of the stock market reforms in India. The common features of these exchanges are the following:

1. All are situated in Mumbai;
2. All do screen-based trading (SBT);
3. All have their trading terminals in the major cities of the country;
4. All are web-enabled;
5. All are limited liability companies;
6. The brokers registered here have no say in either the ownership or the management of the exchanges;
7. All are counted among the best and the most technology-equipped stock exchanges in the world.[6]

---

[6] P. Chidambaram while presenting the *Union Budget 2006-07* (New Delhi; Government of India, 2006).

Players in the Stock Exchanges

Broker A broker is a registered member of a stock exchange who buys or sells shares/securities on his client's behalf and charges a commission on the gross value of the deal - such brokers are also known as *commission brokers.*

Brokers who offer services such as investment advice, clients' portfolio planning, credit when a client is buying on margin other than their traditional commission job are known as *full-service brokers.* In India such brokers are just coming up.

Jobber A jobber is a broker's broker or one who specialises in specific securities catering to the need of other brokers - in India they are also known as *Taravaniwallah* (in the BSE).[7] A jobber is located at a particular trading post on the floor of the stock exchange and carries out buying and selling for small price differences, called the *spread.* He has no contact with the investing public.

In the London Stock Exchange, he is called a *market maker,* while in the New York Stock Exchange he is called a *specialist.* The BSE has made it mandatory for every company with a share capital of over ₹3 crore to appoint jobbers or market makers if it seeks enlistment. Such an arrangement enables investors to buy and sell shares on the stock exchange and thus liquidity increases.

Market Makers

Market Makers function as intermediaries in the market, ready to buy and sell securities. They simultaneously quote two-way rates – like a jobber basically with the only difference that they quote two-way rates, for buying and selling at the same time.[8]

On the floor of India's OTCEI, only market makers are allowed to play. In the money market of India, the Discount and Finance House of India (DFHI) is the chief market maker.[9] Since he quotes the selling price while buying a particular share, he makes market for that share, hence such a name.

The NASDAQ of the United States is a market maker's stock exchange where they are connected by the web-enabled trading terminals.

SEBI

The regulator of Indian stock market, it was set up under the *Securities and Exchange Board of India Act, 1992* (as a non-statutory body set on 12 April, 1988, through a government resolution in an effort to give the Indian stock market an organised structure), with its head office in Mumbai. Its initial paid-up capital was ₹50 crore provided by the promoters - the IDBI, the IFCI and the ICICI.

The Board of SEBI comprises nine members including the chairman - one member each from the Ministries of Finance and Law, one member from the RBI and two other members appointed by the central government. It has four full-time members (excluding the chairman).

Main functions/powers of the Board as per the *SEBI Act, 1992* are as follows:

1. Registering and stock exchanges, merchant banks, MFs, underwriters, registrars to the issues, brokers, sub-brokers, transfer agents and others.
2. Levying various fees and other charges (as 1 per cent of the issue amount of every company issuing shares is kept by it as caution money in the concerned stock exchange where the company is enlisted).
3. Promoting investor education.
4. Inspection and audit of stock exchanges and various intermediaries.
5. Performing other concerned functions as may be prescribed from time to time.

COMMODITY TRADING

Commodity trading happens similar to 'stocks' (shares, securities, debentures, bonds) trading in the stock market. However, commodities are actual physical goods such as corn, silver, gold, crude oil, etc. Futures are contracts for commodities that are traded at a futures exchange like the Chicago Board of Trade (CBOT). Futures contracts have expanded beyond

---

7 S. Sundararajan, *Book of Financial Terms* (New Delhi: Tata McGraw Hill, 2004), p. 117.

8 Tim Hindle, op. cit., p. 129.

9 S. Sundararajan, *Book of Financial Terms* (New Delhi: Tata McGraw Hill, 2004), p. 134.

just commodities, now there are futures contracts on financial markets such as foreign currencies, interest rates and so on.

Commodity futures serve a great purpose in any economy. As we see in the case of agricultural commodity, their prices play a key role in determining the fortune of the agriculture and food processing industry in India. These prices undergo a *large degree of fluctuation.* Reasons for price fluctuation are crop failure, bad weather, demand-supply imbalance, etc. This fluctuation, in turn, leads to a 'price risk'. This price risk is largely borne by the farmer and the industries where agricultural commodities are used as raw material. Commodity exchanges are associations that determine and enforce rules and set procedures for trading of commodities. The main objective of the exchange is to protect the participants from adverse movement in prices by facilitating futures trading in commodities.

If the participants *hedge* themselves against this price risk, then they would be able to insulate themselves against the inherent price fluctuations associated with agricultural commodities. One of the methods of doing this would be by using commodity exchanges as a trading platform. Apart from hedging against price risk, a commodity exchange helps in production and procurement planning as one can buy in small lots. Further as the exchange consists of various informed industry participants, *price discovery* is more efficient and discounts the local and global factors.

Let us take a very simple example to understand how trading on commodity exchanges help industry participants. A farmer who is producing wheat can sell 'wheat futures' on a commodity exchange. This will help him lock in a sale price of a specified quantity of wheat at a future date. Hence the farmer would now be able to get an assured price for his produce in future and any decline in the price of wheat would not impact his earnings. On the other hand, a user industry (e.g., a flour mill) could purchase the wheat futures from the exchange. Hence the flour mill would now be able to fix its future purchase cost for a specified quantity of wheat. Therefore, any increase in the price of wheat in future would not impact its cost of production.

By *February 2026,* a total of **113** commodities were notified by the SEBI for trading on the commodity exchange platforms. There are 21 national and regional commodity exchanges in the country - the **6** national exchanges are as follows:

1. National Commodity and Derivatives Exchange (NCDEX)
2. National Multi-Commodity Exchange (NMCE)
3. Multi Commodity Exchange (MCX)
4. Indian Commodity Exchange (ICEX)
5. ACE Derivatives and Commodity Exchange (ACE)
6. Universal Commodity Exchange (UCE).

Improvements in Warehousing The Government has been incentivising private investments in warehousing through various subsidies and tax sops. Under the purview of the Warehousing Development and Regulatory Authority (WDRA), a new breed of storage facilities has come up which are scientifically developed - supported by value-added services, such as weighing, testing, certification and even come equipped with 24 × 7 physical security with a number of them support CCTV-led remote monitoring facilities from a central location.

The most interesting feature of these modern-day warehouses is that they possess an IT backbone, which enables real-time stock updates. As these warehouses undergo regular physical audits, both by internal and external teams, the physical integrity of the stock - both in terms of quality and quantity - can easily be ascertained at any point of time. These state-of-the-art, high-tech warehouses enable the stakeholders to gain finance, using *electronic Negotiable Warehouse Receipts* (e-NWRs).

Regulation and Reform While the FMC (Forward Markets Commission) regulated the commodity markets since 1952, it was perceived as lacking the power to control wild fluctuations in prices and other irregularities. Accordingly, in 2015, the FMC was merged with the SEBI (with reputation of being superior in terms of surveillance, risk-monitoring and enforcement mechanisms, and a more robust regulatory body for the sector). Subsequently, the SEBI has initiated several reforms measures:

- Allowing stock brokers to deal in commodity derivatives (common broking businesses for equities and commodities),
- Permitting the NSE and BSE to commence commodity trading,
- Allowing the FPIs to participate in commodity derivatives contracts traded in stock exchanges subject to certain stipulations,

- Allowing the Category III Alternative Investment Funds (AIFs) to trade in commodity markets.

As per the experts, India's commodity trading market is at the cusp of transformation as multiple changes are taking place in the related areas such as infrastructure, logistics, electronic warehousing, transportation, etc.

SPOT EXCHANGES

In India, spot exchanges refer to electronic trading platforms which facilitate purchase and sale of specified commodities, including agricultural commodities, metals and bullion by providing *spot delivery contracts* in these commodities. Settlement of trade (i.e., transfer of cash and physical delivery of commodities) normally takes 2 working days (i.e., T+2), however, in practice, it takes place 'on the spot' (then and there) at the prevailing price and existing quality.

This market segment functions such as the equity segment in the main stock exchanges. Alternatively, this can be considered as guaranteed direct marketing by sellers of the commodities. Spot exchanges leverage on the latest technology available in the stock exchange framework for the trading of goods. This is an innovative Indian experiment in the trading of goods and is distinct from what is commonly known as 'commodity exchanges' which trade in *futures contracts* in commodities.

Spot exchange has been **defined** by the WDRA (Electronic Warehouse Receipts) Regulations, 2011, as 'a body corporate incorporated under the Companies Act, 1956 and engaged in assisting, regulating or controlling the business of trading in electronic warehouse receipts. However, present-day spot exchange deals not just with warehouse receipts - this is an electronic market where a farmer or a trader can *discover* the prices of commodities on a national level and can buy or sell goods *immediately* (i.e., on the 'spot') to anyone across the country. All contracts on the exchange are *compulsory delivery contracts* - it means that all outstanding positions at the end of the day are marked for delivery, which implies that the seller has to provide delivery and the buyer has to accept the delivery.

The facilities provided by the spot exchange, like a normal stock exchange, include clearing and settlement of trades. Trades are settled on guaranteed basis (i.e., in case of default by any person exchange arranges for the payment of money/good) and the exchange collects various margin payments, to ensure this. The exchange also offers various other services, such as quality certification, warehousing, warehouse receipt financing, etc.

Spot Exchanges in India

At present, there are **four** spot exchanges operating in the country:

1. The National Spot Exchange Ltd. (NSEL), set up in 2008, is a national-level commodity spot exchange promoted by the Financial Technologies India Ltd. (FTIL) and National Agricultural Cooperative Marketing Federation of India Limited (NAFED). After the FTIL was found involved in irregularities, the FMC (Forward Market Commission), by *end-March 2014* asked it to exit the spot exchange.
2. NCDEX Spot Exchange Ltd. (established in October 2006 by the NSE).
3. Reliance Spot Exchange Ltd. (R-Next).
4. Indian Bullion Spot Exchange Ltd. (an online OTC spot exchange).

Advantages of Spot Exchanges

Spot exchange provides various advantages over the traditional way of trading in commodities:

1. Efficient price determination as price is determined by a wider cross section of people from across the country, unlike the traditional 'mandis' where price discovery for commodities used to occur only through local participation.
2. Ensures transparency in price discovery - anonymity ensures convergence of different price perceptions, as the buyer or seller merely expresses their desire to trade without even meeting directly.
3. Ensures participation in large numbers by farmers, traders and processors across the country and eliminates the possibility of cartelisation and other such unhealthy practices prevalent in the commodity markets.
4. It brings in some best practices in commodity trading, such as system of grading for quality, creating network of warehouses with assaying facilities, facilitating trading in relatively smaller quantities, lower transaction cost, etc.
5. Bank finance available against the goods in the warehouse on easier terms improves holding

capacity and can actually incentivise farm production and hence reduce rural poverty.

6. Since the trades are guaranteed (by the exchange), counter-party risk is avoided.

IMPORTANT TERMS OF STOCK MARKET

Short Selling It is a sale of a share which is not owned. This is carried out by someone after borrowing shares from stockbrokers promising to replace them at a future date on the hope (speculation) that the price will fall by then. He fetches profit if the price of the share really drops by the future date of replacement and sustains a loss if the price increased. Recently, short selling has been allowed in India by the SEBI.

Bear and Bull A person who speculates share prices to fall in future and so sells his shares and earns profit is a *bear*. He earns profit out of a falling market. Basically, here he is short selling the shares.

Opposite to bear, bull is a person who speculates share prices to go up in future so either stops selling the select group of shares for that time to be reached (he is basically taking a long position on those shares) or starts purchasing that select group of shares.

Thus, a bear increases the number of shares in a stock market activating a general fall in the index - a bearish market. Opposite to it, a bull creates a scarcity of shares in the stock market activating a general rise in the share prices and the index - a bullish market.

Brokers play as a bear for some stocks and as a bull for some other stocks; while a bear broker is a non-entity, a bull is remembered for long time to come - Harshad Mehta was known as the Great Bull.

Book Building A provision allowed by the SEBI to all Initial Public offers (IPOs) in which individual investors are reserved and allotted shares by the company. But the issuer has to disclose the price (at which shares have been allotted the size of the issue and the number of shares offered to the public).

IPO Initial Public Offer (IPO) is an event of share issuing when a company comes up with its share/ securities issued for the first time.

Price Band A process of public issue where the company gives a price range (known as price band) and it is left upon the share applicants to quote their prices on it - the highest bidders getting the shares. This is a variant of share issue at premium but considered a safer choice.

Scrip Share A share given to the existing shareholders without any charge - also known as *bonus share*.

Sweat Share A share given to the employees of the company without any charge.

Rolling Settlement An important reform measure started in the Indian stock market in mid-2001 under which all commitments of sale and purchase result in payment/delivery at the end of the 'X' days later (where 'X' stands for 5 days. Some shares have X as one, two or three days, too). Today, all shares are covered under this provision.

Badla When the buyers want postponement of the transaction - in the Western world called *Contango*.

Undha Badla When the sellers want postponement of the transaction - also known as the *reverse badla* or *backwardation*.

Futures A trading allowed in shares where a future price is quoted for the shares and the payment and delivery takes place on the pre-determined dates.

Depositories Started in 1996 under which stocks are converted into *paperless form* (dematerialisation of shares shortly known as the 'demat'). At present, two public sector depositaries (Mumbai) are functioning in India set up under the *Depositories Act, 1996*:

1. NSDL (National Securities Depositories Ltd.)
2. CDSL (Central Depositories Services Ltd.)

Spread The difference between the buying and selling prices of a share is called spread. Higher the liquidity of a share, lower its spread and *vice versa*. It is also known as Jobber's *Turn* or *Margin* or *Hair Cut*.

Kerb Dealings The transactions of stocks which take place outside the stock exchanges - unofficial and take place after the normal trading hours.

NSCC The National Securities Clearing Corporation (NSCC), a public sector company set up in 1996, takes the *counter-party risk* of all transactions carried out at the NSE just as an intermediary guarantees all trades.

Demutualisation A process started (2002) by the SEBI under which ownership, management and trading membership was to be segregated from each other. No broker was to be on the Board of Directors or an office-bearer in a stock exchange.

This has been carried out in the case of all stock exchanges except three RSEs in India.

Authorised Capital The limits up to which shares can be issued by a company - also known as the *nominal* or *registered* capital. This is fixed in the Memorandum of Association (MoA) and the Article of Association (AoA) of a company as required by the *Companies Act (Law)*.

Paid-up Capital The part of the authorised capital of a company that has actually been paid by shareholders. A difference may arise because all shares authorised might not be *issued* or issued shares are only partly paid-up.

Subscribed Capital The amount actually paid by the shareholders or committed by them for contribution.

Issued Capital The amount which is sought by a company to be raised by issuing shares which cannot exceed the authorised capital of the company.

ESOP The Employee Stock Ownership Plan (ESOP) enables a foreign company to offer its shares to employees overseas. It was allowed in India (February 2005) provided that the MNC has minimum 51 per cent holding in its Indian company. Earlier permission from the RBI was required for such an option.

SBT Screen Based Trading (SBT) is trading of stock based on the electronic medium, i.e., with the help of computer monitor, internet, etc. The first such trading was introduced in New York in 1972 by the bond broker *Cantor Fitzgerald*. India introduced it in 1989 at the OTCEI. Now it is carried out at all exchanges.

OFCDs Debentures are the debt instruments which may be issued by a listed or non-listed firm to raise funds in a security market. They are of many types, viz. *Redeemable, Non-redeemable, Partially Convertible* and *Fully Convertible*. In case of 'fully convertible debentures' an 'option' (that is why the name OFCDs, i.e., Optionally Fully Convertible Debentures) is given to the debenture holders who may wish to convert their OFCDs into shares (after expiry of the period fixed by the debenture issuing firm - known as 'lock-in' period). But the 'rate' will be decided by the company (e.g., how many shares against how many debentures). For debenture holders the 'option' to convert debenture into shares is profitable and/or safer in either of the following situations:

1. The firm is likely to make high profit (so the shareholder can earn higher dividend) or
2. Firm's share price is likely to rise in the share market (profit can be made by selling shares).

But suppose the firm has a weak balance sheet (going bankrupt), then it is better to keep hold on the debenture rather than converting them into shares because when a company is liquidated (i.e., its assets sold off), the debenture holders get *primacy* over shareholders in payment. It means OFCD is a **tricky** thing and is the only suitable route to invest in the security market for the investors who have some knowledge and understanding of share prices, company performance and so on.

Recently, the OFCDs issued by **Sahara** (an NBFC under regulatory control of the RBI) were in news due to some irregularities - it was a simple case of certain loopholes in the regulation of OFCDs and some violations by Sahara:

1. Actually, an OFCD issue process has to be completed within 10 working days (Sahara continued for over two years).
2. If the OFCD is being issued through the 'Private Placement' route, only 50 individuals/institutions can subscribe to it (Sahara issued it to over 23 million people and raised over ₹24,000 crores).

   Such tricky instruments being issued to novice public was a clear case of financial irregularities.
3. Unlisted companies do not come under the regulatory control of the SEBI. In place they are regulated by the Ministry of Corporate Affairs (both the Sahara firms which issued OFCDs are unlisted). But the SEBI contended that it can regulate even an unlisted firm if it issues OFCDs, as the SEBI Act, 1992 contains the term OFCDs. There was really some regulatory confusion. This is why the government added a 'clause' in the *Companies (Amendment) Act, 2012* which gives the SEBI **undisputed jurisdiction** over any investment scheme involving more than 50 investors whether the company is listed or unlisted. Meanwhile, Sahara has been ordered to return the total capital it raised through OFCDs with an interest of 15 per cent per annum.

Shares 'at Par' and 'at Premium' An ordinary share in India, in general, is said to have a ***par value (face value)*** of ₹10, though some shares issued earlier still carry a par value of ₹100. Par value implies the value at which a share is originally recorded in the balance sheet as 'equity capital' (this is the same as 'ordinary share capital'). SEBI guidelines for *public issues* by new companies established by individual promoters and entrepreneurs require all new companies to offer their shares to the public *at par*, i.e., at ₹10. However, a new company set up by existing companies (and of course existing companies themselves) with a track record of *at least five years* of consistent profitability is allowed to issue shares at a **premium**.

When a company issue shares at a premium, it is able to raise the required amount of capital from the public by issuing a fewer number of shares. For example, while a *new company* promoted by first-time entrepreneurs intending to raise say, ₹1 crore has to offer 10 lakh ordinary shares at ₹10 each (at par), an *existing company* may raise the same amount by offering only 2 lakh shares at ₹50 each (close to the market value of its shares). The latter is said to have issued its share at a *subscription price* of ₹50 (₹10 in the case of the former company), at a premium of ₹40 (being the excess of subscription price over par value). In such a situation in India, the company's books of accounts will show ₹10 towards *share capital account* and ₹40 towards *share premium account*. It means that the higher the premium, the fewer will be the number of shares a company will have to service. For this very reason, following the policy of free pricing of issues in 1993, many companies came out with issues at prices so high that in many cases they were higher than their market prices, leading to under-subscription of such issues. The companies are, however, learning fast about the pitfalls of high pricing of shares, and it is only a matter of time before the issue prices become more realistic.

Raising Capital in the Primary Market

There are three ways in which a company raises capital in the primary market.

Public Issue A public offer is open for all Indian citizens, the most broad-based method of raising capital and the most prestigious, too (the Reliance Industries Ltd. is the biggest company of India in this category).

Rights Issue Raising capital from the existing shareholders of a company, it means it is a preferential kind of issue restricted to a certain category of the public only.

Private Placement Raising capital by selling shares to a select group of investors, usually FIs but may be also to individuals. This is carried out through a process of direct negotiations (completely opposite to the public issue). The advantage of this route is the substantial saving a share issuing company makes on marketing expenses (but the risk of shifting loyalties of the investors in this route is also the highest).

Recent times have seen such capital raising by many companies privately placing their shares to the foreign institutional investors (FIIs) as a route to source foreign exchange in India, and that too quickly.

DERIVATIVES

Derivative is a product whose value is derived from the value of one or more basic variables, called bases (underlying asset, index or reference rate), in a contractual manner.

The underlying asset can be equity, forex, commodity or any other asset. For example, wheat farmers may wish to sell their harvest at a future date to eliminate the risk of a change in prices by that date. Such a transaction is an example of a derivative. The price of this derivative is driven by the spot price of wheat which is the 'underlying' asset.

In the Indian context the *Securities Contracts (Regulation) Act*, 1956 [SC(R)A] **defines derivative** to include the following:

1. A security derived from a debt instrument, share, loan whether secured or unsecured, risk instrument or contract for differences or any other form of security.
2. A contract, which derives its value from the prices, or index of prices, of underlying securities.

Derivatives are securities under the SC(R)A, and hence the trading of derivatives is governed by the regulatory framework under the SC(R)A and are allowed to be traded on the floors of the stock exchanges.

INDIAN DEPOSITORY RECEIPTS

As per the **definition** provided in the *Companies (Issue of Indian Depository Receipts) Rules, 2004*, Indian Depository Receipt (IDR) is an instrument in the form of a depository receipt created by the Indian depository in India against the underlying equity shares of the issuing company. In an IDR, foreign companies would issue shares, to an Indian depository [say the National Security Depository Limited (NSDL)], which would in turn issue depository receipts to investors in India. The actual shares underlying IDRs would be held by an Overseas Custodian, which shall authorise the Indian depository to issue of IDRs.

Just try to understand in a simple way. An IDR is a mechanism that allows investors in India to invest in listed foreign companies, including multinational companies, in Indian rupees. IDRs give the holder the opportunity to hold an interest in equity shares in an overseas company. IDRs are denominated in Indian Rupees and issued by a Domestic Depository in India. They can be listed on any Indian stock exchange. Anybody who can invest in an IPO is/are eligible to invest in IDRs. *In other words, what ADRs/GDRs are for investors abroad with respect to Indian companies, IDRs are for Indian investors with respect to foreign companies.*

FOREIGN FINANCIAL INVESTMENT

India opened its capital market for foreign portfolio investment/foreign institutional investment (FPI/FII) in 1994 - at present, there are 11,743 such firms registered with the SEBI.[10] Today, they are one of the biggest drivers of India's financial markets and have invested around ₹17.76 lakh crore till 2025.[11] Highly developed primary and secondary markets have attracted FIIs/FPIs to the country. Their investments are regulated by the SEBI, while the ceilings on such investments are maintained by the RBI. Almost all *types* are today active in the market - Hedge Funds, Foreign MFs, Sovereign Wealth Funds, Pension Funds, Trusts, Asset Management Companies, Endowments, University Funds, etc. While SEBI regulates these institutional investments, their investment limits are set by the Reserve Bank of India.

Major Regulatory Initiatives The SEBI announced several regulatory changes to encourage safe and higher FPI in the country *till 2025-26*:

- Direct overseas listing of Indian companies allowed.
- The KYC (Know-Your-Client) requirement relaxed.
- Foreign entities allowed to participate in the commodity derivatives.
- NRIs allowed to invest through an FPI route.
- The timeline for public issue of debt securities reduced to 6 days (from 12 days).
- FPIs allowed to invest up to 25 per cent in Category III AIFs.
- FPIs allowed to invest in the Real Estate Investment Trusts (REITs) and Infrastructure Investment Trusts (InvITs).

Today, India is being viewed as a potential opportunity by investors, with the economy having the capacity to grow tremendously. Buoyed by strong support from the Government, FII investments have been strong, even after the disruption caused by the COVID-19 pandemic, and are expected to grow in the coming times.

Classification The FPIs have been classified[12] by the SEBI into three broad categories, namely:

- **Category I:** The Government entities/institutions investing in the Indian security market on behalf of the Central Bank.
- **Category II:** The FIs, MFs, etc. which duly regulated in the countries of their origin.
- **Category III:** The FIs which do not fall under either of the above-given categories.

FPIs in 2024-25 As per the *Economic Survey 2024-25,* the foreign portfolio investment (FPI) flows remained volatile in 2024-25, primarily on account of global geopolitical and monetary policy developments. Net FPI inflows slowed to USD 10.6 billion in the first 9 months of the financial year (from USD 31.7 billion during the same period the previous year). However, the inclusion of India's sovereign government securities (G-secs) of certain tenors in the *JP Morgan EM Bond Index* induced heightened activity within the debt segment of the FPIs.

[10] *Securities and Exchange Board of India* (New Delhi: Ministry of Finance, GoI, February 2026).

[11] *Securities and Exchange Board of India* (New Delhi: Department of Commerce, GoI, February 2026).

[12] *Securities and Exchange Board of India* (New Delhi: Ministry of Finance, GoI, April 2022).

Angel Investor

A new term in India's financial market, introduced in the *Union Budget 2013–14,* which announced that the SEBI will soon prescribe the provisions by which the angel investor can be recognised as *Category I AIF*[13] *venture capital funds.*

An *Angel investor* is an investor who provides financial backing to entrepreneurs for 'starting their business'. Angel investors are usually found among an entrepreneur's family and friends, but they may be also from outside. The capital they provide can be a one-time injection of seed money or ongoing support to carry the company through difficult times – in exchange they may like owning a share in the business or provide capital as loan (in the case of a loan they lend at more favourable terms than other lenders, as they are usually investing in the *person* rather than the viability of the business). Other than investible capital, these investors provide technical advice and also help the 'startup' business with their lucrative contacts.

They are focused on helping the business succeed, rather than reaping a huge profit from their investment. Angel investors are essentially the *exact opposite* of a venture capitalist in their 'intention' (who has high-profit prospects as their prime focus). But in one sense both an *angel investor* and a *venture investor* serve the same purpose for the entrepreneur (who is in dire need of investible capital).

QFI SCHEME

In the Budget 2011-12, the Government, for the first time, permitted qualified foreign investors (QFIs), who meet the KYC norms, to invest directly in Indian MFs. In January 2012, the Government expanded this scheme to allow QFIs to directly invest in Indian equity markets. Taking the scheme forward, as announced in *Budget 2012-13,* QFIs have also been permitted to invest in corporate debt securities and MF debt schemes subject to a total overall ceiling of US$ 1 billion.

In *May 2012,* QFIs were allowed to open individual non-interest-bearing rupee bank accounts with authorised dealer banks in India for receiving funds and making payment for transactions in securities they are eligible to invest in. In *June 2012,* the definition of QFI was expanded to include residents of the member countries of the Gulf Cooperation Council (GCC) and European Commission (EC) as the GCC and EC are members of the Financial Action Task Force (FATF).

The speedier moves in the area of promoting higher foreign investments (FIs) in India should be seen in the light of two broad perspectives:

1. India's rising current account deficit (which crossed an all-time high of 6.7 per cent by *March 2013*) which is creating heavy drain of foreign exchange; and
2. The objective of attracting more FIs while the Western economies are under the spell of recession (cashing in the opportunity).

REGISTERED FOREIGN PORTFOLIO INVESTORS (RFPIs)

In *March 2014,* the RBI simplified FPI norms by putting in place an easier registration process and operating framework with an aim to attract inflows. From now onwards, the portfolio investor registered in accordance with the SEBI guidelines shall be called Registered Foreign Portfolio Investor (RFPI) - the existing portfolio investor class, namely FII and QFI registered with the SEBI shall be subsumed under it. The new guidelines for RFPIs are as given below:

1. They may purchase and sell shares and convertible debentures of Indian companies through a registered broker on recognised stock exchanges in India as well as purchase shares and convertible debentures, which are offered to public in terms of relevant SEBI guidelines.
2. Such investors can acquire shares or convertible debentures in any bid for, or acquisition of, securities in response to an offer for *disinvestment* of shares made by the central government or any state government.

[13] As per the *SEBI (Alternative Investment Funds) Regulations, 2012 (AIF Regulations),* Category I AIF are: those AIFs with 'positive spillover effects' on the economy, for which certain incentives or concessions might be considered by the SEBI or the Government of India or other regulators in India; and which shall include *Venture Capital Funds, SME Funds, Social Venture Funds, Infrastructure Funds* and such other *Alternative Investment Funds (AIFs)* as may be specified.

3. These entities would be eligible to invest in *government securities* and corporate debt, subject to limits specified by the RBI and SEBI from time to time.
4. Such investors would be permitted to trade in all exchange-traded derivative contracts on the stock exchanges, subject to the position limits as specified by SEBI from time to time.
5. The RFPI may offer cash or foreign sovereign securities with AAA rating or corporate bonds or domestic government securities, as collateral to the recognised stock exchanges for their transactions in cash as well as derivative segment of the market.

All investments made by the FIIs/QFIs in accordance with the regulations prior to registration as the RFPI shall continue to be valid and taken into account for computation of aggregate limit.

PARTICIPATORY NOTES

A Participatory Note (PN or P-Note) in the Indian context, in essence, is a *derivative* instrument issued in foreign jurisdictions, by a SEBI registered FII, against Indian securities - the Indian security instrument may be equity, debt, derivatives or even an index. PNs are also known as *Overseas Derivative Instruments, Equity Linked Notes, Capped Return Notes* and *Participating Return Notes,* etc.

The investor in PN does not own the underlying Indian security, which is held by the FII who issues the PN. Thus, the investors in PNs derive the economic benefits of investing in the security without actually holding it. They benefit from fluctuations in the price of the underlying security since the value of the PN is linked with the value of the underlying Indian security. The PN holder also does not enjoy any voting rights in relation to security/shares referenced by the PN.

Reasons for the Popularity of PNs

The reasons why PNs became such a popular route for foreign investors to invest in the Indian security market may be understood through the following points:

1. One of the primary reasons for the emergence of the PN (an 'off-shore derivative instrument', i.e., an ODI) is the restrictions on FIs. For example, a foreign investor intending to make portfolio investments in India was required to seek FII registration for which he is required to meet certain eligibility criteria. Lack of full *Capital Account Convertibility* further enhances the entry barriers from the perspective of a foreign investor. However, since *January 2012*, the Indian Government has taken a decision to give direct access to such prospective 'foreign individual investors' who were hitherto banned to invest in equity of Indian companies.
2. The off-shore derivative market allows investors to gain exposure to the local shares without incurring the time and costs involved in investing directly. In return, the foreign investor pays the PN issuer a certain basis *point(s)* of the value of PNs traded by him as *costs*. For instance, directly investing in the Indian securities markets as an FII, has significant cost and time implications for the foreign investor. Apart from seeking FII registration, he is required to establish a domestic broker relationship, a custodian bank relationship, deal in foreign exchange and bear exchange rate fluctuation risk, pay domestic taxes and/or filing tax return, obtain or maintain an investment identity, etc. These investors would rather look for derivatives alternatives to gain a cost-effective exposure to the relevant market.
3. Besides reducing transactions costs, PNs also provide customised tools to manage risk, lower financing costs and enhance portfolio yields. For instance, PNs can also be designed for longer maturities than are generally available for exchange-traded derivative.
4. PNs also offer an important *hedging tool* to a foreign investor already registered as an FII. For example, an FII may wish to obtain 'long' exposure to a particular Indian security. The FII can hedge the downside exposure to the listed security, already purchased by purchasing a 'cash settled put option'. Although the Indian exchanges offer options contract, these contracts have a maximum life period of three months, beyond which the FII shall have to rollover its positions, i.e., purchase a fresh option contract. Alternatively, it can avail a PN which can be customised to cater to its hedging requirements.
5. Potential investors who would like to take direct Indian exposure in future may make initial investments through the PN route so as to get a flavour of future anticipated returns.

6. Further, trading in ODI/PNs gives an opportunity to offshore entities to have a commission-based business model. This route provides ease to subscribers as it bypasses the direct route which may be resource heavy for them.
7. And *lastly*, it was a highly 'safe and lucrative route' to invest the 'unaccounted', 'even illegal' money into the Indian security market for huge profits (during the booming period). Experts even imagined that it may be allowing the 'black money' of India (stashed away from India through 'hawala' kind of illegal channels and deposited in the tax havens of the world in 'Swiss Bank' kind of FIs) to get invested back in the market. Again, 'terrorist organisations' might have been using this route, too.

PNs are *thus* issued to provide access to a set of foreign investors who intend to reduce their overall costs and the time involved in making investments in India. In other words, the attraction of investing in PNs is primarily one of efficiency (from an infrastructure and time perspective) for which they are willing to forego certain benefits of directly holding the local securities (for example, title and voting rights), whilst also assuming other risks.

Regulation of PNs

PNs are market instruments that are created and traded overseas. Hence, Indian regulators cannot ban the issue of PNs. However, they can be regulated, as the SEBI does – when a PN is traded on an overseas exchange, the regulator in that jurisdiction would be the authority to regulate that trade. PNs have been used by FIIs, since FIIs were permitted to invest in the securities market (1994) – they were not specifically dealt with under the regulations until 2003. According to the *SEBI Regulation, 2004* (and further amended in 2008), with the ***objective*** of tightening regulations in this regard:

1. PNs can be issued only to those entities which are regulated by the relevant regulatory authority in countries of their incorporation and are subject to compliance of KYC norms.
2. Down-stream issuance or transfer of the instruments can also be made only to a regulated entity.
3. Further, the FIIs who issue PNs against underlying Indian securities are required to *report* the issued and outstanding PNs to the SEBI in a prescribed format.
4. In addition, the SEBI can call for any information from FIIs concerning ODIs issued by it.
5. In order to monitor the investment through these instruments, the SEBI on *31 October, 2001*, advised FIIs to submit information regarding issuance of derivative instruments by them, on a monthly basis. These reports require the communication of details such as name and constitution of the subscribers to PNs, their location, nature of Indian underlying securities, etc.
6. FIIs cannot issue PNs to non-resident Indians (NRIs), and those issuing PNs are required to provide an undertaking to the effect.
7. The SEBI has also mandated that QFIs, the recently allowed foreign investor class, shall not issue PNs.

The SEBI in consultation with the Government had decided in *October 2007* to place certain restrictions on the issue of PNs by FIIs and their sub-accounts. This decision was taken with a view to moderate the surge in foreign capital inflows into the country and to address the KYC concerns for PN holders. However, it was found that such restrictions were ineffective. Therefore, the SEBI in October 2008 reviewed its earlier decision and decided to remove these restrictions in the light of the above factors. Rather, more attention is given to effective disclosures. As per a SEBI decision of October 2013, the Category III FIIs are not allowed to issue PNs.

The Concerns Related to PNs

Being derivative instruments and freely tradable, PNs can be easily transferred, creating multiple layers, thereby obfuscating the real beneficial owner. It is in this respect that concerns about the ***identity of ultimate beneficial*** owner and the source of funds arises.

For the reason that such instruments are issued outside of India, these transactions are outside the purview of SEBI's surveillance, and it is the FII which acts as mini-exchange overseas. The actual transactions in the underlying securities are executed by the FIIs only at its discretion, as and when necessary, and there is no one-to-one correspondence between transactions in the underlying instruments and issuance of PNs.

The ex-post reporting requirement enjoined upon the FII in respect of PNs on a monthly basis effectively keeps the transactions in PNs out of the real-time market surveillance mechanism and beyond the enforceability jurisdiction of SEBI.

There are also concerns that some of the money coming into the market *via* PNs could be the ***unaccounted wealth*** camouflaged under the guise of FII investment. However, this has not been proved so far. The SEBI has indeed been successful in taking action against the FIIs who were noncompliant and those who had misreported offshore derivatives [as occurred when the SEBI took action against two FIIs - *Barclays* in December 2009 and *Societe Generale* in January 2010].

At present, PNs are issued by large financial sector conglomerates which not only have a strong presence in the global investment banking arena but also have asset management arms which invest across a number of securities markets globally. These entities are originally incorporated in well-regulated and developed jurisdictions like the United States, United Kingdom and so on. Further, these entities also possess the financial wherewithal to issue PNs, complemented by skilled personnel who are adept at risk management and financial engineering activities.

International Situation

PN-like products are not necessarily used to invest in restricted markets, but also reported to be available in the open developed/advanced economies such as Japan, Hong Kong, Singapore, Australia, the United States and United Kingdom. In response to market manipulation concerns, in December 1999, *Taiwan Securities and Futures Commission* had amended its FII regulations to require periodic disclosure by FIIs of all offshore derivative activities linked to local shares, but this requirement was subsequently removed in June 2000 (as the Ashok Lahiri Committee Report says). *China's Securities Regulatory Commission* requires entities to file reports related to these products with minimal 'reporting requirements that emphasise only on the quota utilised by them'. *Other Asian countries* such as Hong Kong, Singapore and Japan have reported *no restrictions* or requirements on PNs. Malaysia, Indonesia and Philippines which are restricted markets though have no reporting requirements in this regard.

Hedge Fund

This term has emerged from another term ***hedging***, a process by which businesses insulate themselves from the risk of price changes.[14] Hedge funds are mass of investible (free-floating capital) capital which move very swiftly towards the more profitable sectors of an economy.

At present, such funds easily move from the stock market of one economy to the other – away from the low-profit fetching to high-profit fetching ones. As stock markets fall and rise such funds change markets accordingly. By nature, they are temporary. The period for which they continue flowing into an economy there is naturally a boom time. But when they quit for a more attractive economy, the same economy might not be able to manage the accelerated foreign currency outflow, and there are chances of imminent foreign currency crisis.

EXTERNAL COMMERCIAL BORROWINGS (ECB) POLICY

A prospective borrower can access external commercial borrowings (ECBs) under two routes, namely the 'automatic route' and the 'approval route'. ECBs not covered under the automatic route are considered on case-by-case basis by the RBI under the approval route. The High-Level Committee on ECB took a number of decisions to expand by 2011-12 the scope of ECBs which include the following:

1. High net worth individuals (HNIs) who fulfil the criteria prescribed by SEBI can invest in IDFs.
2. IFCs have been included as eligible issuers for FII investment in the corporate bonds long-term infra category.
3. The ECB would be permitted for refinancing of rupee loans of infrastructure projects on the condition that at least 25 per cent of such ECBs shall be used for repayment of the said rupee loan and 75 per cent invested in new projects in the infrastructure sector (but only under the approval route).
4. Refinancing of buyer's/supplier's credit through ECBs for the purchase of capital goods by companies in the infrastructure sector was approved. This would also be permitted only under the approval route.
5. ECBs for interest during construction (IDC) that accumulates on a loan during the project execution phase for companies in the infrastructure sector would be permitted. This would be subject to the condition that the IDC is capitalised and is part of the project cost.

[14] P. A. Samuelson and W. D. Nordhaus, *Economics* (New Delhi: Tata McGraw Hill, 2007), p. 207.

6. Renminbi (RMB) - the Chinese currency - was approved as an ***acceptable currency*** for raising ECBs subject to/limit of US$ 1 billion within the existing ECB ceiling (allowed only through the approval route).
7. The existing ***ECB limits*** under the automatic route were enhanced from US$ 500 million to US$ 750 million for eligible corporates. For borrowers in the *services sector*, the limit has been enhanced from US$ 100 million to US$ 200 million and for *NGOs* engaged in *micro-finance* activities from the existing US$ 5 million to US$ 10 million.

Till **February 2025**, the norms for ECB were further simplified and streamlined by the government - major steps taken in this regard were as given below:

1. Enhancing the limit for refinancing rupee loans through ECB from 25 per cent to 40 per cent for Indian companies in the power sector;
2. Allowing ECB for capital expenditure on the maintenance and operation of toll systems for roads and highways so long as they are a part of the original project subject to certain conditions, and also for low-cost housing projects;
3. Reducing the withholding tax from 20 per cent to 5 per cent for a period of three years (July 2012-June 2015) on interest payments on ECBs;
4. Introducing a new ECB scheme of US$ 10 billion for companies in the manufacturing and infrastructure sectors;
5. Permitting the Small Industries Development Bank (SIDBI) as an eligible borrower for accessing ECB for on-lending to the micro, small and medium enterprises (MSMEs); and
6. Permitting the National Housing Bank (NHB)/ Housing Finance Companies to avail themselves of ECBs for financing prospective owners of low-cost/affordable housing units.
7. In *December 2015*, the RBI announced a *new ECB framework* which was more attuned to the current economic and business environment - from regulatory perspective, now, the ECBs will have three main clear-cut categories:
   (i) Medium-term foreign currency-denominated ECB;
   (ii) Long-term foreign currency-denominated ECB (with minimum average maturity of 10 years); and
   (iii) Indian rupee-denominated ECB.

   The new lenders comprise overseas-regulated FIs, sovereign wealth funds, pension funds, insurance companies, and so on and have an exhaustive list of permissible end-users with only a small negative list for long-term foreign currency-denominated ECB and INR-denominated ECB.
8. In order to facilitate rupee-denominated borrowing from overseas, the Government decided *(December 2015)* to put in place a framework for issuance of rupee-denominated overseas bonds (such bonds have got a popular tag of the ***masala bonds****)*. These bonds will have minimum maturity of 5 years. These bonds cannot be issued for real estate and capital markets sectors. Withholding tax of 5 per cent will be applicable on interest income from these bonds, but the capital gains arising in case of appreciation of the rupee will be exempted from tax.

CREDIT DEFAULT SWAP

Credit Default Swap (CDS) is in operation in India since October 2011, launched in only corporate bonds. The eligible participants are commercial banks, primary dealers, NBFCs, insurance companies and MFs.

The CDS is a credit derivative transaction in which two parties enter into an agreement, whereby one party (called as the 'protection buyer') pays the other party (called as the 'protection seller') periodic payments for the specified life of the agreement. The protection seller makes no payment unless a credit event relating to a pre-determined reference asset occurs. If such an event occurs, it triggers the Protection Seller's settlement obligation, which can be either cash or physical (India follows physical settlement). It means, the *CDS is a credit derivative that can be used to transfer credit risk from the investor exposed to the risk* (called protection buyer) *to an investor willing to take risk* (called protection seller).

It operates like an insurance policy. In an insurance policy, the insurance firm pays the loss amount to the insured party. Similarly, the buyer of the CDS - the bank or institution that has invested in a corporate bond issue - seeks to mitigate the losses it may suffer on account of a default by the bond issuer. Credit default swaps allow one party to 'buy' protection from another party for losses that might be incurred as a result of default by a specified reference instrument (a bond issue in India). The 'buyer' of protection pays a premium to the seller, and the 'seller' of protection agrees to compensate the buyer for losses incurred upon the occurrence of any one of the several specified credit events. Thus, ***CDS offers the buyer a chance to transfer the credit risk of financial assets to the seller without actually transferring ownership of the assets themselves.***

Let us try to understand it by an example. Suppose Punjab National Bank (PNB) invests in ₹150 crore bond issued by TISCO. If PNB wishes to *hedge* losses that may arise from a default of TISCO, then PNB may buy a credit default swap from a financial institute, suppose, Templeton. The PNB will pay fixed periodic payments to Templeton, in exchange for default protection (just like premium of an insurance policy).

The CDS can be *used for different purposes* in a financial system, as follows:

1. Protection buyers can use it to hedge their credit exposure, while protection sellers can use it to participate in credit markets, without actually owning assets.
2. The protection buyer can transfer credit risk on an entity without transferring the underlying instrument, reap regular benefit in terms of lower capital charge, seek reduction of specific concentrations in credit portfolio and go short on credit risk.
3. The protection seller will be able to diversify his portfolio, create exposure to a particular credit, have access to an asset which may not otherwise be available and increase the yield on his portfolio.
4. Banks can use it to transfer risk to other risk-takers and create capital for more lending.
5. Distribute risk widely throughout the system and prevent concentrations of risk.

Some analysts have serious **apprehensions** about CDS. *George Akerlof*, Nobel Prize-winning economist, in 1993, predicted that the next meltdown will be caused by the CDS. In 2003, investment legend *Warren Buffet* called them as 'weapons of mass destruction'. The former US Federal Reserve Chairman *Alan Greenspan,* who betted big on CDS, said after the 'sub-prime' crisis that *CDS are dangerous.* A leading US weekly the *Newsweek* described CDS as 'the monster that ate Wall Street'. Many Indian experts had the opinion that 'CDS will not stabilise the economy rather could lead to destabilisation'.

CDS contracts are dangerous because they can be manipulated for mischief. It's all about the insurable interest which is never there as it is used for *speculation.* A derivative that amounts to an insurance contract with no insurable interest is bad. But do the speculators have insurable interest? No, they don't have any. The US 'sub-prime' crisis was a fallout of such CDS contracts - one defaulting and another claiming the 'protection' finally resulting into the defaulter of the insuring company. Overnight the biggest US insurance giant, AIG, went bankrupt followed up by many banks (over 350 till 2021).

The most damaging aspect of CDS is that the credit risk of one country/region gets exported to another country/region very smoothly and silently. Thus, there is a serious chance of 'contagion effect' suppose there are defaulters there, the incident which occurred during the US 'sub-prime' crisis.

SECURITISATION

This is the process of issuing 'marketable securities' backed by a pool of existing assets such as auto or home loans. After an asset is converted into a marketable security, it is sold to an investor who then receives interest and principal out of the cash flow generated from servicing of the loan. FIs such as NBFCs and microfinance companies convert their loans into marketable securities and sell them to investors. This helps them get liquid cash out of assets that otherwise would be stuck on their balance sheets.

Global experience shows that if the value of the underlying asset falls, then securitised assets lose value as it had happened during the US 'sub-prime crisis' - home loans against which securitised assets were sold to insurance companies and banks lost value, which in turn resulted in a crisis. To prevent such crises, the RBI has taken some precautionary steps in this regard. It has asked companies to hold securities for a certain minimum period:

1. While NBFCs need to keep assets for six months, a minimum retention requirement of 5-10 per cent to ensure that they have a continuing stake in the performance of securitised assets.
2. Micro Finance Institutions (MFIs) need to hold them for three months. Since it was allowed in India by the RBI, it has been in the news - whether the *securitisations trusts* will need to pay tax on it. Meanwhile, the *Government in 2015* cleared the air on the issue. There should not be any additional income tax if the income distributed by the trust is received by a person who is exempted from tax. This is expected to bring back MFs into the securitisation market.

CORPORATE BOND IN INDIA

Economic vibrancy coupled with sophisticated state-of-the-art financial infrastructure has contributed to rapid growth in the equity market in India. In terms of market features and depth, the Indian equity market ranks among the best in the world. In parallel, the government securities market has also evolved over the years and expanded, given the increasing borrowing requirements of the government. In contrast, the corporate bond market has languished both in terms of market participation and structure. The ***Economic Survey 2010-11,*** *for the first time, raised this issue which* cites many reasons for the less-developed bond market in India:

Scan this QR Code to watch a author's video lecture that simplifies this topic

1. Predominance of banks loans;
2. FII's participation is limited;
3. Pensions and insurance companies and household are limited participants because of lack of investor confidence; and
4. Crowding out by government bonds.

The *Survey* concluded[15] that there is now ample empirical research to corroborate Schumpeter's conjecture that financial development facilitates real economic growth. The depth of the financial markets and availability of diverse products should, therefore, not be treated as mere adornment, but as critical ingredients of inclusive growth.

Banks in India accounted for 14.4 per cent of the financing of large firms in 2000-01, which rose further to 25.6 per cent in 2020-21. The *bond market,* on the other hand, has been miniscule in comparison– as percentage of GDP, the corporate bond market is only 18 per cent in India, as opposed to 80 per cent in Korea and 36 per cent in China, as per the *Economic Survey 2024-25.* The thinness of the bond market has been somewhat compensated by foreign borrowing by Indians, which rose sharply over the last decade. Further, India is characterised by a disproportionate amount of secured borrowing. The small size of unsecured borrowing may, at first sight, not seem to be a matter of concern, but it could be a reflection of the weakness of contract enforcement and lack of adequate information. If contracts were quickly enforced and lenders had information on borrowers, they would be more willing to provide unsecured loans. This would extend a nimbleness to the financial markets which they presently lack.

There are ***many reasons*** why bond markets are important for an emerging economy. Prominent among these is the fact that they lead to more efficient entrepreneurship and greater value creation. When an entrepreneur takes a loan or issues bonds, all additional profit over and above the pre-fixed repayment amount accrues to the entrepreneur. So, he or she is better incentivised to take sharper decisions. By having a weak bond market, we may be foregoing this efficiency. And further, this efficiency gap may well mean that there is less lending and hence less investment and entrepreneurship in the economy than is feasible. Further, as India tries to garner 500 billion dollars from the private sector in the Twelfth Plan for investment in the infrastructure sector, having an active bond market would be a valuable avenue for raising money.

There can be many reasons why, despite these advantages, the bond market has not developed adequately. One reason has to do with what economists call 'multiple equilibria'. Consider a situation where the bond market is small. If someone buys bonds and later wishes to sell these off, he anticipates difficulty. Since the bond market is not active, he may not easily be able to sell the bonds and thus he will hold simply because he cannot find a buyer. Hence, this may discourage someone from buying the bonds in the first place. If everybody reasons like this, the bond market remains thin. Hence, the need is for a push that nudges the market to another equilibrium,

---

[15] *Economic Survey 2011-12* (New Delhi: Ministry of Finance, Government of India, 2012), p. 34; quotes many contemporary references to bring the point home.

(a) R. Rajan, and L. Zingales, 'Financial Dependence and Growth', *American Economic Review,* Vol. 88, 1998;

(b) S. Banerji, K. Gangopadhyay, I. Patnaik, and A, Shah, 'New Thinking on Corporate Debt in India', mimeo;

(c) C. K. G. Nair, 'Financial Sector Reforms: Refining the Architecture', in R. Malhotra (ed.), *A Critical Decade: Policies for India's Development* (New Delhi: Oxford University Press, 2012);

(d) T. A. Bhavani, and N. R. Bhanumurthy, *Financial Access in Post-Reform India';*

(e) P. Bolton and X. Freixas, "How can Emerging Market Economies Benefit from a Corporate Bond Market?," in E. Borzenstein, K. Cowan, B. Eichengreen, and U. Panizza (eds), *Bond Markets in Latin America* (Massachusetts: MIT Press, 2008).

where people readily buy bonds because they know that they can easily sell these off, and this becomes a self-fulfilling prophesy and sustains the large bond market.

There is effort currently to try to boost India's debt and bond markets, and success in this can provide another fillip to growth. With the intervention of the ***Patil Committee (2005)*** recommendations, the corporate bond market is slowly evolving. With bank finance drying up for long-term infrastructure projects, in view of asset liability problems faced by the banking system, the need for further development of a deep and vibrant corporate bond market can hardly be over-emphasised. Some major initiatives for further development of corporate bond markets, taken by the Government in recent times, are as given below:

1. Banks are allowed to take limited membership in SEBI-approved stock exchanges for the purpose of undertaking proprietary transactions in the corporate bond markets.
2. To enhance liquidity in the corporate bond markets, the IRDA has permitted insurance companies to participate in the repo market. The IRDA has also permitted insurance companies to become users of *credit default swap* (CDS).
3. The minimum **hair cut** the existing 10 per cent; 12 per cent; 15 per cent to 7.5 per cent; 8.5 per cent; 10 per cent for AAA/ AA+/AA-rated corporate bonds.
4. MFs have been permitted to participate in CDS in corporate debt securities, as users.

Word Bank

Hair Cut

Hair cut is the difference between prices at which a *market maker* can buy and sell a security. The term comes from the fact that market makers can trade at such a *thin spread*. It also means that the percentage by which an asset's market value is reduced for the purpose of calculating capital requirement, margin and collateral. When they are used as collateral, securities will generally be devalued since a cushion is required by the lending parties in case the market value falls.

5. Revised guidelines on CDS for corporate bonds by the RBI provide that in addition to listed corporate bonds, CDS shall also be permitted on *unlisted* but rated corporate bonds even for issues other than infrastructure companies.
6. Users shall be allowed to **unwind**[16] their CDS-bought position with the original protection seller at a mutually agreeable or FIMMDA (Fixed Income Money Market and Derivatives Association of India) price. If no agreement is reached, then unwinding has to be carried out with the original protection seller at FIMMDA price.
7. The CDS shall be permitted on securities with original maturity up to *one year* like CPs, certificates of deposit and non-convertible debentures with original maturity less than one year.

Till *February 2026*, the RBI has taken a number of measures to strengthen the corporate bond market in India. It accepted many of the recommendations of the *Khan Committee* (August 2016) to boost investor participation and market liquidity in the corporate bond market. By early ***March 2025*** the following measures were operationalised by the Reserve Bank of India in this regard:

1. Commercial banks permitted to issue rupee-denominated bonds overseas *(masala bonds)* for their capital requirements and for financing infrastructure and affordable housing.
2. Brokers registered with the Securities and Exchange Board of India (SEBI) and authorised as market makers in corporate bond market permitted to undertake repo/reverse repo contracts in corporate debt securities. This move will make corporate bonds *fungible* and thus boost turnover in the secondary market.

[16] *Unwind* is used to close out a position that has offsetting investments or the correction of an error. Unwind occurs when, for example, a broker mistakenly sells part of a position when an investor wanted to add to it. The broker would have to unwind the transaction by selling the erroneously purchased stock and buying the proper stock. One type of investing that feature unwind trading is *arbitrage in-vesting (as happens in the CDS)*. If, for the sake of illustration, an investor takes a long position in stocks, while at the same time selling puts on the same issue, he will need to unwind those trades at some point. Of course, this entails covering the options and selling the underlying stock. A similar process would be followed by a broker attempting to correct a buying or selling error.

3. Banks allowed to increase the partial credit enhancement they provide for corporate bonds to 50 per cent from 20 per cent. This move will help lower-rated corporates to access the bond market.
4. Permitting primary dealers to act as *market makers* for government bonds, to give further boost to government securities by making them more accessible to retail investors.
5. To ease access to the foreign exchange market for hedging in OTC and exchange-traded currency derivatives, the entities exposed to exchange rate risk allowed to undertake hedge transactions with simplified procedures, up to a limit of US$ 30 million at any given time.
6. Pension and provident fund together with insurance companies have been allowed to invest in the corporate bonds.
7. Corporate bonds rated 'BBB' or equivalent declared as investment grade (as initiated by the *Union Budget 2018-19*) - till now only 'AA' rated corporate bonds were entertained as investment grade.
8. Introduction of an electronic platform for repos operation in corporate bonds.
9. Inclusion of them in the RBI liquidity adjustment facility (LAF).
10. FIIs allowed to invest in the corporate bonds through stock exchanges and primary issuance - overall ceiling of US$ 51 billion (with US$ 25 billion ceiling for G-Secs).

Presently, corporate bonds meet around 35 per cent of the long-term funds of the country's corporate sector. The corporate bond market has been expanding with faster pace as banks have been unwilling to lend to the corporates for the last 7-8 years. As per the latest available data (of the SEBI), the outstanding value of domestic corporate bonds in the country was ₹50.12 lakh crore by September 2024. That was around 15 per cent of the GDP (against 160 per cent of GDP in case of the United States).

To become a developed economy by 2047, India needs to scale up the corporate bond market so that the necessary amount of long-term funds can be mobilised by the corporate sector - they offer an avenue for long-term funding, whereas banks generally prefer short-term lending. Liquidity and stability play a very vital role in bond market. To play these twin roles, the Government proposed to set up a permanent financial institution dedicated to buying and selling (a *backstop* facility) of these debt instruments in *Union Budget 2021-22*. In *February 2023* the country's first such institution was announced to be set up by the SBI Mutual Fund with a corpus of ₹330 billion ($4 billion).

INFLATION-INDEXED BONDS

To protect the returns of investors from the vagaries of inflation, the Reserve Bank of India (RBI) plans to introduce inflation-indexed bonds (IIBs) - it was proposed in the *Union Budget 2013-14*. The Government hopes this will help increase *financial savings instead of buying gold*. In the recent years, the rate of return on debt investments has often been below inflation, which effectively means that inflation was eroding savings. IIBs provide returns that are always in excess of inflation, ensuring that price rise does not erode the value of savings.

In 2013-14, the RBI launched two such bonds - the first one in June 2013 linked with the WPI which had a very weak retail response and second one in *December 2013* linked with the CPI. The latter one is called as **Inflation Indexed National Savings Securities-Cumulative (IINSS-C)** with a 10-year tenure. These are internationally known as *inflation-linked securities* or simply *linkers*. Interest rate on these securities would be linked to final combined consumer price index [CPI (Base: 2010=100)]. Interest rate would comprise two parts: fixed rate (1.5 per cent) and inflation rate, based on a three-month lag to CPI - thus, if a bond is being valued in December, the reference rate will be the CPI of September. The new offering should attract higher attention from savers, especially due to its link to CPI instead of wholesale price index (WPI), which is a less accurate gauge of inflation. The CPI is considered a more accurate gauge of the impact of inflation on consumers because it takes into account increase in the cost of education, food, transportation, housing and medical care; in the WPI, the emphasis is on measuring the prices of traded goods and services.

It was in 1997 that the IIBs were issued for the first time in India - named as the *Capital Indexed Bonds (CIBs)*. But there remains a difference between these two bonds. While the CIBs provided inflation protection only to principals the new product IIBs provides inflation protection to both the components - principal and interest payments.

Gold Exchange Traded Funds

Gold Exchange Traded Funds (ETFs) are *open-ended* MF *schemes* that closely track the price of physical gold. Each unit represents *one gram* of gold having 0.995 purity, and the ETF is listed on stock exchanges. The net asset value of each unit is calculated based on the prices of physical gold prevailing on that day and is designed to provide returns that would closely track the returns from physical gold.

e-Gold

e-Gold is another purchase option, involving investments in units traded on the National Spot Exchange Limited (NSEL). Here, the investor is required to have a demat account with an affiliate of NSEL. e-Gold's brokerage and transaction charges are lower than *gold ETFs* as there are no fund management charges. One can take delivery of gold or sell it in the exchange.

But there is also a *negative point* here from the tax angle – under e-Gold, one has to hold the yellow metal for 36 months to enjoy *long-term capital gain* benefits, and this is taxed at 20 per cent. For ETFs and gold funds, the holding period to be classified as long term is only one year. After a year, ETF and gold funds will suffer 10 per cent tax without indexation and 20 per cent after indexation. For a small investor, gold ETF would appear to be the best option, as it meets his needs without difficulties in terms of creating a separate demat account, tax implications and wealth tax.

CPSE ETF

The Central Public Sector Enterprises Exchange Traded Fund (CPSE ETF) comprising the shares of 10 blue-chip PSUs was listed on the BSE and NSE platforms in April, 2014. The GoI expected to raise a corpus of ₹3,000 crore through the fund while it got over-subscribed to the tune of ₹4,300 crores.

This scheme is conceived by the GoI as a means to *disinvest* a part of its holding in Public Sector Units (PSUs).

ETF is a security that tracks an index, a commodity or a basket of assets such as an index fund, but trades like a stock on an exchange – the CPSE ETF tracks the CPSE Index (of 10 PSUs included in the ETF). CPSE Index has been constructed by including companies that meet the following criteria:

1. Owned 55 per cent or more by the GoI and listed on the NSE;
2. Large PSUs (those having more than ₹1,000 crores as average free float market capitalisation for a six-month period ending June 2013); and
3. With a consistent dividend payment record (at least 4 per cent for 7 years immediately prior to or 7 out of 8/9 years immediately prior to June 2013).

The ten blue-chip PSUs which meet the above criteria and their weightages are: ONGC (26.72 per cent); GAIL (India) (18.48 per cent); Coal India (17.75 per cent); REC (7.16 per cent); Oil India (7.04 per cent); IOC (6.82 per cent); Power Finance Corp. (6.49 per cent); Container Corp. (6.40 per cent); Bharat Electronics (2 per cent) and Engineers India Ltd. (1.13 per cent).

This fund passively tracks the *NIFTY CPSE Total Return Index* and is open for trading on NSE as well as BSE. Till *February 2026*, the Government had offered 7 tranches of the fund. The fund is currently (February 2026) being managed by Nippon AMC.

PENSION SECTOR

Pension has been an integral part of Government jobs in India. Pension serves two important socio-economic objectives:

1. It facilitates the flow of long-term savings for development, i.e., *nation-building;* and
2. Also helps establish a credible and sustainable *social security system* in the country.

The New Pension Scheme, now renamed as National Pension System (NPS), was introduced by the Government on December 22, 2003, and it was made mandatory for Central Government employees (except the armed forces) who join service w.e.f. January 1, 2004. The Scheme was extended to the State Governments, and as of now 28 State Governments have notified the NPS for their employees. The Scheme was extended to all citizens of the country on voluntary basis from May 2009. Although the NPS is perhaps one of the cheapest financial products available in the country, in order to make it affordable for the economically disadvantaged, the Government in September 2010 introduced a lower cost version, known as ***Swavalamban Scheme***, which enables groups of people to join the NPS at a substantially reduced cost. As per the existing scheme under the NPS, *Swavalamban* could be availed either in 'unorganised sector' or in '***NPS Lite***'. NPS Lite is a model specifically designed to bring the NPS within easy reach of the economically disadvantaged sections of the society - it is extremely affordable and viable due to its optimised functionalities, available at reduced charges. Under the *Swavalamban* scheme, the Government provides subsidy to each NPS account holder, and the scheme was extended until 2016-17.

A customised version of the core NPS model, known as the *NPS Corporate Sector Model*, was introduced from December 2011 to enable 'organised sector' entities to move their existing and prospective employees to the NPS under its Corporate Model. All public sector banks have been asked to provide a link on their website to enable individual subscribers to open online NPS accounts.

As per few previous volumes of the *Economic Survey*, the pension reforms in India have generated widespread interest internationally but before universal inclusion of poorer sections of Indian society into the pension network is a reality, the economy needs to solve the following *major challenges*:

1. Lower levels of financial literacy, particularly among workers in the unorganised sector;
2. Non-availability of even moderate surplus;
3. Lukewarm response so far from most of the state/UT governments to a co-contributory *Swavalamban* Scheme; and
4. Lack of awareness, on the supply side, about the NPS and of access points for people to open their accounts individually have been major inhibiting factors.

During 2015-16, the government launched a new pension scheme, the ***APY (Atal Pension Yojana)***. The scheme provides a defined pension, depending on the contribution and its period. The subscribers to it will receive a minimum pension of ₹1000, 2000, 3000, 4000 or 5000 per month, from the age of 60 years, depending on their contributions, which are themselves based on the age of joining the scheme.

The scheme is open to all bank account holders. The central government co-contributes 50 per cent of the total contribution subject to a maximum of ₹1,000 per annum, to each eligible subscriber's account, for a period of five years (from 2015-16 to 2019-20), who joined the APY between 1 June 2015 and 31 March 2016 and who is not a member of any statutory social security scheme and is not an income tax payer.

Rising Significance: As per the *Economic Survey 2025-26*, in India, between 2021 and 2036, the proportion of the old-age population (60+) in the total population is expected to increase from 10.1 per cent to 14.9 per cent. At the same time, the proportion of the working-age population (15-59) is projected to increase marginally from 64.2 per cent to 64.9 per cent during the same period. As today's workers approach retirement, it is essential that they be covered by a stable and secure pension scheme. In this context, the PFRDA has laid the groundwork for a vibrant pension system, offering a range of options for its users and covering a broad population bracket.

Asset Under Management: Today, the NPS architecture caters to a wide range of demographics–central and state government employees, private sector workers, corporate entities, minors under the NPS Vatsalya and individuals from the unorganised sector. By December 2025, there were 211.7 lakh subscribers to NPS and managed assets worth ₹16.1 crore. Over the past decade (2015-25), NPS subscribers have grown with a compound annual growth rate (CAGR) of 9.5 per cent, and the assets under management (AUM) have rapidly increased at a CAGR of 37.3 per cent.

Adequacy and Sustainability: Adequacy and sustainability are becoming key priorities for the pension system as it expands over time. Global benchmarks, such as the *Mercer* CFA Global Pension Index, consistently rank India lower in terms of adequacy and system maturity, reflecting relatively low replacement rates and modest pension assets (around 17 per cent of GDP) compared to OECD peers (at least 80 per cent). Pension assets in India make up around 15-20 per cent of GDP, significantly less than the 60-100 per cent range seen in more advanced pension markets.

Way Forward: The *Economic Survey 2025-26* has outlined the following policy actions[17] for the further development of the pension sector:

- A calibrated expansion of both contributory and non-contributory schemes.

[17] *Economic Survey 2025-26* (New Delhi: Ministry of Finance, GoI, January 2026), pp. 133-136.

- Engagement with state governments, cooperatives, farmer networks, and gig-platform companies can ensure last-mile reach.
- An area for further progress is regulatory coherence (studies highlight the need for better alignment between EPFO, PFRDA, and state-level pension bodies to reduce fragmentation, enhance portability, and streamline governance).
- Strengthening actuarial evaluation frameworks, diversifying long-term investment portfolios, and deepening data-sharing mechanisms across institutions will be essential as longevity increases and old-age dependency continues its structural rise.
- Expanding interoperability across NPS, APY and other schemes will support seamless portability as workers shift sectors or migrate.

Financial Stability Development Council

An apex level body, the FSDC, was set up by the GoI in December 2010. It was in line with the G-20 initiative which came in the wake of the financial crises among the western economies triggered by the 2007–08 'sub-prime' crisis of the United States. The Council has the following *objectives:*

1. To strengthen and institutionalise the mechanism for maintaining financial stability,
2. To enhance inter-regulatory coordination and
3. To promote financial-sector development.

The council is *chaired* by the finance minister and has *heads* of financial-sector regulatory authorities, the Finance Secretary and/or Secretary of the Department of Economic Affairs, Secretary of the Department of Financial Services and the Chief Economic Adviser as members. Without prejudice to the autonomy of regulators, the Council ***monitors*** the following:

1. macro-prudential supervision of the economy, including functioning of large financial conglomerates,
2. inter-regulatory coordination and financial-sector development issues and
3. *financial literacy* and *financial inclusion*.

FINANCIAL SECTOR ASSESSMENT PROGRAMME

The *IMF Board* decided in September 2010 to include 25 *systemically* important economies, including India, under the Financial Stability Assessment Programme (FSAP) for members with systemically important financial sectors. The joint IMF-World Bank Financial Stability Assessment Programme was conducted for India in *January 2013* which assessed Indian financial system in relation to the highest international standards. The **assessment** recognises that the Indian financial system remained *largely stable* on account of a sound regulatory and supervisory regime. However, the assessment identifies *some gaps* in[18] the following:

1. International and domestic supervisory information sharing and co-operation;
2. Consolidated supervision of financial conglomerates; and
3. Some limits on the *de jure* independence of the regulators (RBI and IRDA).

Despite having reservations on few issues, overall, the Indian authorities expect the FSAP exercise to play a *significant role* in shaping India's post-crisis initiatives to strengthen the regulatory and supervisory architecture based on the evolving international consensus as well as careful examination of their relevance in the India-specific context. As a member of the FSB[19],

[18] RBI, 16th January 2013.

[19] The Financial Stability Board (FSB) was established in April 2009 as the successor to the Financial Stability Forum (FSF). The FSF was founded in 1999 by the G-7 for enhancing cooperation among the various national and international supervisory bodies and international financial institutions so as to promote stability in the international financial system. In November 2008, the leaders of the G-20 countries called for a larger membership of the FSF. As announced in the G-20 Leaders' Summit of *April 2009*, the expanded FSF was re-established as the *Financial Stability Board (FSB)* with a broadened mandate to promote financial stability. The FSB is chaired by *Mark Carney*, Governor of the Bank of Canada. Its secretariat is in Basel, Switzerland, and hosted by the Bank for International Settlements.

Its *objective* is to coordinate at the international level the work of national financial authorities and international standard setting bodies and to develop and promote the implementation of effective regulatory, supervisory and other financial sector policies. [*Source*: Financial Stability Board Secretariat, Bank for International Settlements, Basel, Switzerland].

BCBS[20] and IMF, India is actively participating in post-crisis reforms of the international regulatory and supervisory framework under the aegis of the **G-20**. India remains committed to adoption of international standards and best practices, in a phased manner and calibrated to local conditions, wherever necessary, as it is a country characterised by complex and diverse socio-political and economic conditions.

Financial Action Task Force (FATF)

The FATF is an inter-governmental policymaking body that has a ministerial mandate to establish international standards for combating *money laundering* and *terrorist financing*. India joined the FATF as its 34th member in June 2010. At present, the FATF has 40 members comprising 38 countries and two organisations (the European Union and GCC).

REAL ESTATE AND INFRASTRUCTURE INVESTMENT TRUSTS

The SEBI firmed up regulations that will govern REITs, and the Infrastructure Investment Trusts (InvITs).[21] The long-pending proposal of 2008, the trusts have the **objective** of enabling the cash-strapped real estate and infrastructure developers to have easy access to funds. They create a new investment avenue for institutions and high net worth individuals, and eventually ordinary investors.

Real Estate Investment Trusts (REITs)

Major provisions announced by the SEBI for the REITs are as given below:

1. To be close-ended real estate investment schemes that will invest in property with the aim of providing returns to unit holders.
2. The returns will be derived mainly from rental income or capital gains from real estate.
3. Allowed to invest in commercial real estate assets, either directly or through special purpose vehicles (SPVs). In SPVs, an REIT must have a controlling interest of at least 50 per cent of the share capital and will have to hold at least 80 per cent of their assets directly in properties.
4. To raise funds only through an initial offering and units of REITs have to be mandatorily listed on a stock exchange, similar to IPOs and listing for equity shares.
5. Required to have assets worth at least ₹500 crore at the time of an initial offer and the minimum issue size has to be ₹250 crore. The minimum subscription size for units of a REIT on offer will be ₹2 lakh and at least 25 per cent of the units have to be offered to the public.
6. Will be able to raise money through follow-on offers, rights issues or qualified institutional placements and the trading lot for such units will be ₹1 lakh.

According to the norms, although an REIT may raise funds from any type of investors, resident or foreign, initially only wealthy individuals and institutions will be allowed to subscribe to REIT unit offers. The market regulator said an REIT may have up to three sponsors, with each holding at least 5 per cent and collectively holding at least 25 per cent for a period of at least three years from the date of listing. Subsequently, the sponsors' combined holding has to be at least 15 per cent throughout the life of the REIT.

---

[20] The BCBS (Basel Committee on Banking Supervision) provides a forum for regular cooperation on banking supervisory matters. The Committee's members, today, come from 45 nations including India. The present Chairman of the Committee is *Stefan Ingves*, Governor of Sveriges Riksbank. It is located at the Bank for International Settlements (BIS) in Basel, Switzerland.

Its *objective* is to enhance understanding of key supervisory issues and improve the quality of banking supervision worldwide. It seeks to do so by exchanging information on national supervisory issues, approaches and techniques, with a view to promoting common understanding. At times, the Committee uses this common understanding to develop guidelines and supervisory standards in areas where they are considered desirable. In this regard, the Committee is *best known* for its international standards on *Capital Adequacy (i.e., Basel I, Basel II and Basel III, by now)*; the *Core Principles for Effective Banking Supervision*; and the *Concordat* on cross-border banking supervision.

The *Committee* encourages contacts and cooperation among its members and other banking supervisory authorities. It circulates to supervisors throughout the world both published and unpublished papers providing guidance on banking supervisory matters. Contacts have been further strengthened by an *International Conference of Banking Supervisors (ICBS)* which takes place every two years. [*Source*: BIS, Basel, Switzerland].

[21] *Economic Survey 2007-08* (New Delhi: Ministry of Finance, GoI), pp. 229-34.

Similar to the practice in the United States, Australia, Singapore and other nations where REITs are common, the SEBI has decided to allow these trusts to invest primarily in completed revenue-generating properties. To ensure that REITs generate continuous returns, the SEBI proposed at least 80 per cent of the REIT's assets has to be invested in completed and revenue-generating properties. And only up to 20 per cent of assets can be invested in properties that are being developed, mortgage-backed securities, debt of companies in the real estate sector, equity shares of listed companies that derive at least 75 per cent of their income from real estate, government securities or money market instruments. No REIT can invest more than 10 per cent in properties that are under construction.

Infrastructure Investment Trusts (InvITs)

The SEBI also announced the launch of **InvITs** which are *somewhat similar* to REITs. However, an initial offer will not be mandatory for InvITs though listing will be mandatory for both publicly and privately placed InvITs. *Major provisions* are as given below:

1. It can invest in infrastructure projects, either directly or through an SPV. In case of Public-Private Partnership (PPP) projects, such investments will be only through an SPV.
2. While listing, the collective holding of sponsors of an InvIT has to be at least 25 per cent for at least three years.
3. Required to have a holding worth at least ₹500 crore in the underlying assets, and the initial offer size of the InvIT has to be at least ₹250 crore.
4. Any InvIT, which looks to invest at least 80 per cent of its assets in completed and revenue generating infrastructure assets, has to raise funds only through a public issue of units, with a minimum 25 per cent public float and at least 20 investors.
5. The minimum subscription size and trading lot of such a listed InvIT has to be ₹10 lakh and ₹5 lakh, respectively. A publicly offered InvIT may invest the remaining 20 per cent in under-construction infrastructure projects and other permissible investments.

An InvIT that proposes to invest more than 10 per cent of its assets in under-construction infrastructure projects can raise funds only through private placement from qualified institutional buyers with a minimum investment and trading lot of ₹1 crore and from at least five investors, where single holding cannot be more than 25 per cent.

Recent Developments To promote real estate and infrastructure trusts, a friendlier tax regime was put in place by the GoI through successive by February 2025. However, the idea of the trusts could not get much till 2020. Basically, due to subdued market conditions in the sectors, attracting investors - new (greenfield) project or a trust - has remained difficult by now. Majority of the existing projects in the sectors are running into losses with weak balance sheets of their developers, unable to even service their bank loans.

To push the cause of the trusts, in 2019-20, the security market regulator, SEBI, permitted the FPI in the trusts. How much interest the FPIs will show in the trusts will be known only in future; meanwhile, experts believe that real momentum in the sectors can be only expected once the economy comes out of the period of economic slowdown.

ESG INVESTMENT

In the past few years, the world has seen the emergence of a new concept in stock markets - a new set of the environmental, social and governance (ESG) criteria for the listed companies. These criteria precisely have the following meanings[22] embedded in them:

- Environmental criteria look into a company's approach towards the nature (which may include aspects such as energy use, pollution, waste disposal, natural resource conservation, treatment of animals, etc.).
- Social criteria examine a company's relations with employees, suppliers, customers, privacy, data protection and the communities where it operates.
- Governance deals with a company's leadership, executive pay, audits, internal controls and rights of shareholders.

These value-laden criteria are being increasingly (especially, in western countries) screened by the socially conscious investors before making their investment decisions - these criteria help investors find companies with values that match their own. The ESG investing (which is also called *impact investing*) is being taken as sustainable and socially responsible investing which can leave impact not only on our surrounding

[22] Based on several documents of the SEBI, RBI and Ministry of Finance, GoI, New Delhi, April 2021.

but also on the pattern of our investments. Such investments in a sense make investors believe that they are able to avoid and discourage the companies whose practices signal risk factors (as seen in the cases, the 2010 oil spill of BP and 2015 emission scandal of Volkswagen) - share prices of both falling by over 10 per cent as investors' backlash.

As business practices are becoming more conscious of these criteria, investment firms are increasingly tracking their performance. In 2020, financial services companies such as *JPMorgan Chase, Wells Fargo,* and *Goldman Sachs* published their annual reports in which extensive review was given in this regard.

Case with India As per the stock market regulator, the SEBI, the focus on ESG further increased - in line with global trend, investors in India also did show increased interest in ESG investment during 2020-21. In 2021-22 the SEBI announced the ESG Guidelines which were enforced from April 2022.

SOCIAL STOCK EXCHANGE

Social Stock Exchange (SSE) allows the listing of social enterprises (both non-profit and for-profit) on stock exchanges aimed at providing them an additional channel to raise funds. Today, such exchanges are operating in several countries[23] such as the United Kingdom, Canada, Singapore, South Africa, Kenya and Brazil. In India, social enterprises[24] operate in several forms, which can be broadly classified into two categories:

1. *Non-Profit Organisations (NPOs)* which are usually structured as non-governmental organisations (Section 8 Companies, Trusts or Societies).
2. *For-Profit Enterprises (FPEs)* which operate as private limited companies, partnerships or sole proprietorships.

These enterprises depend mainly on philanthropic funds from governments, international donors or companies (chiefly through their corporate social responsibility), and a dearth of funding has always been felt. Given the sustainable development goals of the UNO, India has also been realising the need of inclusive and socially responsible development. In tandem, the corporate sector has begun to adopt a variety of measures to ensure that their activities are not causing harm to society or the environment. Investing has also shifted towards an Environmental Social Governance (ESG) framework.

In this backdrop, it was in the *Union Budget 2019-20* that the Government proposed to set up an SSE under the ambit of the SEBI for social enterprises so that they can raise capital as equity, debt or as units like an MF. Accordingly, on the recommendations of a Working Group (under the Chairmanship of Ishaat Hussain), the SEBI announced (in June 2020) the guidelines (which was in the stage of public feedback by April 2021) for setting up of the SSE in the country. As per the SEBI, the exchange[25] can be housed within the existing stock exchanges (such as BSE and/or NSE), which will help it leverage the existing infrastructure and client relationships of the exchanges to onboard investors, donors and social enterprises (for-profit and non-profit). The SSE will have *two primary* roles:

1. To effectively deploy the fundraising instruments and structures available under the regulatory guidelines towards social enterprises:
   - **(i)** For FPEs: Equity and Social Venture Funds (SVFs).
   - **(ii)** For NPOs: Zero coupon zero principal bonds, SVFs, MFs, various pay-for-success structures, other securities and units that may evolve.
   - **(iii)** For Section 8 Companies: Equity and Debt.
2. To foster overall sector development by creating a capacity building unit which will be responsible for the following:
   - **(i)** Encouraging the setting up of a self-regulatory organization (SRO) that will bring together existing information repositories (IRs), in the immediate term for extending requisite support to the SSE.
   - **(ii)** Implementing the reporting standard for all social enterprises that benefit from the SSE.

[23] Though in the United States we do not find any SSE as such, we find a similar platform called the *Mission Markets* (MM) launched in 2010 which works on 'impact investing' (i.e., environmental, social and governance criteria). But MM do not contain startups as social enterprises, rather the companies which have incorporated social responsibility into their existing for-profit business models.

[24] By April 2021, over 3.1 million non-profit organisations (NPOs) were operating in India which precisely means more than double the number of schools and 250 times the number of government hospitals - one NPO for 400 Indians.

[25] Security and Exchange Board of India, June 2020 and Union Budget 2019-20, Ministry of Finance, GoI, New Delhi.

(iii) Operating the *capacity-building fund* for enhancing reporting capabilities by NPOs (particularly the smaller NPOs). Creating awareness and driving adoption of this fund among NPOs, philanthropists and donors.

(iv) Actively raising awareness and promoting the fundraising instruments/structures available on the SSE among social enterprises and NPOs.

Both these roles are equally important to ensure that the SSE makes a meaningful impact. In order to benefit from the SSE an NPO must commit to reporting in accordance with the minimum standard. In addition, an NPO may choose to register with an IR in order to further signal credibility and legitimacy to investors and funders. As per the working group, this report was the first important phase of a long journey, and more will need to be done in subsequent years so that the market for such kind of funding matures over time.

Markets and socialists have been strange bedfellows and until a few decades prior the world used to consider them mutually exclusive affairs. But this dichotomy seems to be changing - a third dimension is on emergence which includes *social business, impact investing* (i.e., ESG) and now the *SSEs*.

CONCERNS AND OUTLOOK FOR FUTURE

Taking clues from the developments of the past few years, the *Economic Survey 2025-26* has outlined[26] many concerns and prospects which are as given below:

- Equity-based financing has catapulted to popularity, with IPO listings growing six times between 2012-13 and 2023-24 with India being ranked **first** globally in terms of the number of IPO listings in 2023-24.
- Young investors are also driving the equity boom under the age of 30. As a report by the NSE notes, between March 2018 and September 2024, the proportion of young investors surged from 23 per cent to 40 per cent.
- One critical risk to guard against is the dominance of financial markets in shaping policy and macroeconomic outcomes, a phenomenon known as 'financialisation.' The consequences of financialisation are evident in advanced economies, where it has led to unprecedented levels of public and private sector debt– some visible to regulators and some not.
- Economic growth due to higher financialisation becomes overly reliant on rising asset prices to offset leverage, exacerbating inequality and asset market considerations that may overly influence public policies, particularly regulatory ones. A fine balance is required between financial sector development and growth on the one hand and financialisation on the other.
- It means that the country has to chart its path with respect to its context, considering the levels of financial savings in households, its investment needs, and levels of financial literacy. Ensuring that incentives in the sector are consistent with national growth aspirations is a policy imperative.

[26] *Economic Survey 2025-26* (New Delhi: Ministry of Finance, GoI, January 2026), pp. 140-143.

PREVIOUS YEARS' QUESTIONS

Prelims

1. With reference to investments, consider the following: (2025)
   (i) Bonds
   (ii) Hedge Funds
   (iii) Stocks
   (iv) Venture Capital

   How many of the above are treated as Alternative Investment Funds?
   (a) Only (i) (b) Only (ii)
   (c) Only (iii) (d) All the four

2. India is one of the founding members of the International North-South Transport Corridor (INSTC), a multimodal transportation corridor, which will connect (2025)

(a) India to Central Asia to Europe via Iran
(b) India to Central Asia via China
(c) India to Southeast Asia through Bangladesh and Myanmar
(d) India to Europe through Azerbaijan

3. In India, which of the following can trade in Corporate Bonds and Government Securities? (2024)
 (i) Insurance Companies
 (ii) Pension Funds
 (iii) Retail Investors

Select the correct answer using the code given below:
(a) (i) and (ii) only (b) (ii) and (iii) only
(c) (i) and (iii) only (d) (i), (ii) and (iii)

Answers: 1. (b) 2. (a) 3. (d)

Explanation

1. (b): An Alternative Investment Fund (AIF) is a privately pooled fund mobilised from sophisticated domestic or foreign investors (SEBI has regulated it since 2012).
2. (a): The International INSTC is a 7,200-kilometer-long multimodal (including ship, rail, and road routes) transportation network that connects India, Iran, Russia, Central Asia, and Europe which was initiated by India, Iran, and Russia in 2000 and aims to improve trade connectivity by reducing the time and cost of transport.
3. (d): All are the correct customers of the corporate bonds. Corporate bonds are long-term debts raised by the limited liability firms (i.e., a Limited Company) from a variety of clientele in India.

SAMPLE OBJECTIVE QUESTIONS

1. Consider the following statements related to the security market of the country:
 (i) Stock exchanges are permitted to trade in both securities and commodities.
 (ii) Debentures and corporate bonds cannot be issued simultaneously by a company.
 (iii) Debentures may be issued by municipal corporations.

How many of the above statements are correct?
Code:
(a) Only one (b) Only two
(c) All three (d) None of these

2. Consider the following statements related to corporate bonds in the country:
 (i) Bond prices rise as their interests decline.
 (ii) Declining bond yields bleed the banks.
 (iii) Mutual fund companies book more profits once bond prices decline.

How many of the above statements are correct?

Code:
(a) Only one (b) Only two
(c) All three (d) None of these

3. Consider the following statements related to the mutual funds in the country:
 (i) Mutual funds operate in the capacity of a society.
 (ii) Some government-controlled mutual funds offer guaranteed returns to the investors.
 (iii) Some mutual funds mature like time deposits of banks.

How many of the above statements are correct?
Code:
(a) Only one
(b) Only two
(c) All three
(d) None of these

4. Consider the following statements related to the security market of the country:
 (i) Values of derivatives are decided by their underlying assets.
 (ii) Currency and interest derivatives help the RBI in forex management.
 (iii) RBI actively takes part in currency derivative market.

How many of the above statements are correct?

(a) Only one (b) Only two
(c) All three (d) None of these

5. Consider the following statements related to the security market of the country:
   (i) BSE Sensex is comparable to the Dow Jones of the New York Stock Exchange.
   (ii) BSE Sensex consists the scrips of only blue chip listed companies.
   (iii) BSE-50 was abolished soon after its introduction.

How many of the above statements are correct?

(a) Only one (b) Only two
(c) All three (d) None of these

6. Consider the following statements related to the stock exchanges in the country:
   (i) National Stock Exchange is a Government owned platform.
   (ii) On the Over-the-Counter Exchange of India (OTCEI) only market makers can operate.
   (iii) The MSE Exchanges have infused more liquidity element into the shares of the small and medium enterprises.

How many of the above statements are correct?

(a) Only one (b) Only two
(c) All three (d) None of these

7. Consider the following statements related to the participatory notes (P-Notes) in India's security market:
   (i) They provide anonymity to foreign investors in the security market of India.
   (ii) Such instruments are present across most of the security markets in the world.
   (iii) They may be used to launder money.
   (iv) Category III foreign investment institutions (FIIs) are not permitted to issue them as safeguard against malpractices.

How many of the above statements are correct?

(a) Only one (b) Only two
(c) Only three (d) All four

8. Consider the following statements related to foreign investment in the security market of the country:
   (i) Foreign regulated insurance companies can register as foreign portfolio investors.
   (ii) Angel Investment comes under the dual regulatory control of the RBI and SEBI.
   (iii) Venture Capital Funds are registered by the SEBI.

How many of the above statements are correct?

(a) Only one (b) Only two
(c) All three (d) None of these

9. Consider the following statements related to the stock exchange index in the country:
   (i) A rising index indicates the health of the whole economy.
   (ii) Share indexes are driven by speculation too and may not indicate the real health of the concerned companies.
   (iii) Market capitalisation of the Nifty Fifty is larger than that of the BSE-30.

How many of the above statements are correct?

(a) Only one (b) Only two
(c) All three (d) None of these

10. Consider the following statements related to issuing of shares by a limited liability company in the country:
   (i) Public issue is deeper but cumbersome route of raising capital in the primary market.
   (ii) Private placement route to raise capital in primary market is easier but the risk of takeovers always remain there.
   (iii) Secondary market is the safest place to raise long-term capital.

How many of the above statements are correct?

(a) Only one (b) Only two
(c) All three (d) None of these

Answers: 1. (a) 2. (b) 3. (a) 4. (c) 5. (b) 6. (c) 7. (d) 8. (b) 9. (b) 10. (b)

SAMPLE SUBJECTIVE QUESTIONS

1. Examine the role of the corporate bond market in the country and give your suggestions to make it more vibrant.
2. Briefly examine the role played by the participatory notes in the country's security market, the concerns related to them and the regulatory safeguards taken by the SEBI in this regard.
3. Why credit default swaps have been called weapons of mass destruction? Should they be banned in the country? Illustrate with examples.
4. Briefly discuss the main role of the commodity futures and spot trading in the country. Why does the country need to promote them? Give suitable examples to support your views.
5. How can securitisation be disastrous for a financial system? Discuss the safeguards taken in the country by the regulator in this regard.
6. Do you think that inflation-indexed bonds can help in checking imports and smuggling of gold in the country? Elaborate with the help of suitable examples.

SAMPLE MODEL ANSWER

1. **Write a short note on the environmental, social and governance (ESG) criteria of investment and development regarding it in the case of India.**

Ans. In the last few years, a new concept for investing in the listed companies has emerged in some western stock markets - known as the environmental, social and governance (ESG) criteria. The concept, which is also known by its other name, impact investing, explores the following aspects of the company:

1. Environmental criteria investigate its approach towards nature (energy use, pollution, waste disposal, conservation, treatment of animals, etc.).
2. Social criteria examine its relations with employees, suppliers, customers, privacy, data protection, and the communities where it operates.
3. Governance deals with its leadership, executive pay, audits, internal controls, and rights of shareholders.

The value-laden criteria of ESG are being increasingly (especially in western countries) analysed and screened by the 'socially conscious investors' before making their investment decisions. These criteria help investors find companies with values that match their own. Such investments, in a sense, make investors believe that they can avoid and discourage the companies whose practices signal risk factors (as seen in the cases - the 2010 oil spill of BP and the 2015 emission scandal of Volkswagen - share prices of both fell by over 10 per cent as investors' backlash).

As business practices are getting more conscious of these criteria, investment firms are increasingly tracking their performance - since 2020, financial services companies such as J.P. Morgan Chase, Wells Fargo, and Goldman Sachs have started publishing their annual reports in which extensive review was given in this regard.

In India, as per the SEBI, the focus on it has further increased - in line with the global trend, investors in India also did show increased interest in ESG investment during 2020-21. Because of this, the regulator in May 2021 committed to announce relevant ESG guidelines soon. As per the experts, given India's high commitment to the Paris Climate Pact, this becomes even more valid for the country.

CHAPTER 16

External Sector in India

Scale is essential for exports, and the size of exporting firms grows once they get support of conducive factors–land acquisition and labour laws, right skills, infrastructure and logistics.*

**India's Exports*, Gita Gopinath and Amartya Lahiri in *What the Economy Needs Now*, Abhijit Banerjee, Gita Gopinath, Raghuram Rajan and Mihir Sharma, eds. (New Delhi: Juggernaut Books, 2019), pp. 86-93.

To watch the Author's videos on the significance of the Chapter, scan the QR Code given here

Exam Essentials...

- External Debt
- LERMS
- IMF Conditions on India
- Foreign Currency Hedging
- Export Destinations
- Import Sources

Note to the Reader...

This chapter deals with the external face/strength of the Indian economy. Readers should think beyond the simplistic aspects like exports, imports, trade balance, etc. and visualise the changing dynamics of the global landscape– amidst which India needs to carve out an imminent place for herself. Besides, India's aspirations of tapping the 'demographic dividend', eliminations of poverty *via* job creations, becoming a developed economy by 2047 and many other dreams depend on deft handling of her external policies in very strategic and dynamic ways.

In This Chapter...

- Definition
- Forex Reserves
- Fixed Currency Regime
- Floating Currency Regime
- Managed Exchange Rates
- Foreign Exchange Market
- Exchange Rate in India
- Major Terms
- Current Account
- Capital Account
- Balance of Payment
- Convertibility
- Special Economic Zone
- Foreign Investment

- ECB Liberalised
- Trade Facilitation
- Export Promotion Schemes
- Trade Logistics
- India's Trade
- Current Trade Opportunity
- India as Pharmacy of the World
- BIPA and BIT
- RTAs by India
- The Quad
- Deglobalisation and India
- Settlement of Trade in INR
- Way Forward

DEFINITION

All activities of an economy which take place in foreign currency fall in the external sector such as export, import, foreign investment, external debt, current account, capital account, balance of payment (BoP), etc.[1]

FOREX RESERVES

The total foreign currencies (of different countries) an economy possesses at a point of time are its 'foreign currency assets/reserves'.[2] The Forex Reserves (short for 'foreign exchange reserves') of an economy are its 'foreign currency asset' (FCA) added with its *gold reserves*, *SDRs* (Special Drawing Rights) and *Reserve Tranche Position (RTP)* in the International Monetary Fund (IMF).[3] In a sense, the Forex reserves is the upper limit up to which an economy can mobilise foreign currency, if need be.

Scan this QR Code to watch a author's video lecture that simplifies this topic

Major facts related to India's forex reserves and its management, as per the ***Economic Survey 2025-26***, are as given below:

- India's foreign exchange reserves increased to US$ **701.4** billion as of 16 January 2026 (up from US$ 668.34 billion as of the end of March 2025). The increase has come at a time when global interest-rate differentials, capital flows, and commodity prices remain volatile.
- In terms of *adequacy*, the reserves as of 16 January 2026 are sufficient to cover around **11 months** and about **94** per cent of the external debt outstanding at the end of September 2025, providing a comfortable liquidity buffer.
- Foreign Currency Assets (FCA), which form the liquid core of reserves, softened slightly from US$ 567.6 billion at the end of March 2025 to US$ **560.5** billion as of 16 January 2026.
- The gold component of the forex rose sharply to US$ **117.5** billion as of 16 January 2026 (compared with US$ 78.2 billion at the end of March 2025). This increase reflects both valuation gains during a period of elevated global gold prices and a 'continued preference among central banks for diversifying into non-dollar reserve assets' (as per the J.P. Morgan Research). The growing share of gold in reserves aligns with a broader international pattern where many emerging markets have increased gold holdings amid geopolitical uncertainty and shifts in the global interest-rate cycle, as per the Survey.
- The Special Drawing Rights (SDRs) remained stable at US$ **18.7** billion, while India's reserve position in the IMF increased to US$ **4.7** billion.

External Debt

As India started managing its BoP in a more prudent way after the reform period, its external debt position has also improved in a big way. As a standard practice, India's external debt statistics are released by the RBI with a lag of one quarter. As per the *Economic Survey 2025–26*, the latest details related to India's external debt are as given below:

- India's external debt stood at **US$ 746** billion at end-September 2025 (up from US$ 736.3 billion at end-March 2025).
- The external *debt-to-GDP ratio* has remained broadly stable, averaging around **20.2** per cent over the last decade (March 2016–March 2025).

[1] Based on J. E. Stiglitz and C. E. Walsh, *Economics* (New York: W.W. Norton and Company, 2006), pp. 757-58.

[2] Based on P. A. Samuelson and W. D. Nordhaus, *Economics* (New Delhi: Tata McGraw Hill, 2005), p. 604.

[3] Ibid., pp. 605-07.

- Another key factor is that external debt constitutes *less than 5 per cent* of the government of India's total debt, which mitigates the external sector risks.
- Foreign currency risk remains low due to the country's reliance on domestic currency borrowing, with external debt accounting for a small share of liabilities (approximately **2.6** per cent of GDP), largely sourced from multilateral institutions on long-term, concessional terms, thereby insulating public debt from exchange rate and external shocks.

Global external debt: Global external debt continued to rise in the calendar year 2024 amid tight global financial conditions and elevated policy rates. At the end of December 2024, global external debt stood at US$ 104.4 trillion (1.4 per cent higher than the previous year). Advanced Economies (AEs) accounted for 88.1 per cent of the total (US$ 92.0 trillion), while Emerging Market and Developing Economies (EMDEs) recorded a faster expansion, with external debt rising to US$ 12.4 trillion.

India's external debt in a global context: In the global context, India ranked *21st* worldwide and *11th* within the G20 at end-December 2024, with an external debt stock of US$ 718.2 billion (10.7 per cent higher than the previous year). Despite this expansion, India remains modestly leveraged, with an external debt-to-GDP ratio of **18.4** per cent, well below that of many large economies. Accordingly, India accounts for only **0.69** per cent of global external debt, underscoring its relatively small contribution to global indebtedness.

Source: *Economic Survey 2025–26* (New Delhi: Ministry of Finance, GoI, January 2026), p. 72 and pp. 199–200.

FIXED CURRENCY REGIME

The fixed currency regime[4] is a method of regulating exchange rates of world currencies brought by the IMF. In this system, the exchange rate of a particular currency was fixed by the IMF keeping the currency in front of a basket of important world currencies (they were the UK£, US$, Japanese ¥, German Mark DM and French Franc FRF). Different economies were supposed to maintain that particular exchange rate in future. Exchange rates of currencies were modified by the IMF from time to time.

FLOATING CURRENCY REGIME

The floating currency regime[5] is a method of regulating exchange rates of world currencies based on the market mechanism (i.e., demand and supply). In the follow-up to the fixed currency system of exchange rate determination, it was the United Kingdom which blamed the system for its payment crisis of the late 1960s. Looking at the major loopholes in this system, the UK Government decided to switch over to the floating currency regime in 1973 - the same year the IMF allowed an option to its member countries to opt for either of the currency systems.

In the floating exchange rate system, a domestic currency is left free to float against a number of foreign currencies in its foreign exchange market and determine its own value. Such exchange rates are also called *market driven* or *based* exchange rates, which are regulated by factors such as the demand and supply of the domestic and the foreign currencies in the economy concerned.

MANAGED EXCHANGE RATES

A managed exchange rate system is a hybrid or mixture of the fixed and flexible exchange rate systems in which the Government of the economy attempts to affect the exchange rate *directly* by buying or selling foreign currencies or *indirectly*, through monetary policy[6] (i.e., by lowering or raising interest rates on foreign currency bank accounts, affecting foreign investment, etc.).

Today, most of the economies have shifted to this system of exchange rate determination. Almost all countries tend to intervene when the markets become *disorderly* or the *fundamentals* of economics are challenged by the exchange rate of the time. Some of the major examples of the managed exchange-rate system have been given below[7]:

1. Some countries allow to *free float* their currencies and allow the market forces to determine

[4] P. A. Samuelson and W. D. Nordhaus, *Economics* (New Delhi: Tata McGraw Hill, 2005), pp. 610-11.

[5] Ibid., pp. 611-15.

[6] Ibid., p. 615.

[7] The discussion is based primarily on Samuelson and Nordhaus, *Economics*, op. cit. pp. 613-15 and D. Salvatore, *International Economics* (New Jersey: John Wiley and Sons, 2004), pp. 717-22.

their exchange rate with rare Government intervention. This is the idea from which the *floating currency regime* basically emerged. The United States and the European Union are the major examples in this category.

2. Some economies have *managed with flexible* exchange rates, under which the governments buy or sell its currency to reduce day-to-day volatility of currency fluctuations and sometimes opt for systematic intervention for desired objectives. Canada and Japan fall in this category, besides many developing countries. India, too, falls under this category which follows the *dual currency regime* since the 1992-93 financial year.[8]
3. Some economies, particularly small ones, peg their currencies to a major currency or to a *basket* of currency in a fixed exchange rate - known as the *pegging of currencies.* At times, the peg is allowed to glide smoothly upward or downward - a system which is known as *gliding* or *crawling peg.* Some economies have a *hard fix* of a *currency board.* A *currency board* is working well in Hong Kong while the same failed in Argentina in 2002.

FOREIGN EXCHANGE MARKET

The market where different currencies can be bought and sold is called the foreign exchange market.[9] Out of the trades in different currencies, the exchange rate of the currency is determined by the economy.[10] This is an institutional framework for the exchange of one national currency for another.[11] This is particularly correct either in the case of a free float exchange (i.e., floating currency) regime or in a managed or hybrid exchange rate system. It is not allowed at all either in a ***fixed currency system*** or a ***hard fix*** (in a hard fix this happens once the currency to which the hard fix has been carried out itself starts fluctuating).

EXCHANGE RATE IN INDIA

Indian currency, the 'rupee', was historically linked with the British Pound Sterling till 1948 which was fixed as far back as 1928. Once the IMF was established, India shifted to the fixed currency system committed to maintain rupee's external value (i.e., exchange rate) in terms of gold or the US$ (dollar). In 1948, ₹3.30 was fixed equivalent to US$ 1.

In September 1975, India delinked the rupee from the British Pound, and the RBI started determining the rupee's exchange rate with respect to the exchange rate movements of the basket of world currencies (£, $, ¥, DM, Fr.). This was an arrangement between the fixed and the floating currency regimes.

In the 1992-93 financial year, India moved to the floating currency regime with its own method which is known as the 'dual exchange rate'.[12]

There are two exchange rates for rupee, one is the 'official rate' and the other is the 'market rate'. Here the point should be noted that it is the everyday changing market-based exchange rate of rupee which affects the official exchange rate and not the other way around. But the RBI may intervene in the forex market *via* the demand and supply of rupee or the foreign currencies. Another point which should be kept in mind is that none of the economies have till date followed an ideal free-floating exchange rate. They require some mechanism to intervene in the foreign exchange market because this is a highly speculative market.

MAJOR TERMS

Trade Balance The monetary difference of the total export and import of an economy in one financial year is called trade balance. It might be positive or negative, known to be either favourable or unfavourable, respectively, to the economy.

Trade Policy Broadly speaking, the economic policy which regulates the export-import activities of any economy is known as the trade policy. It is also called the foreign trade policy or the Exim Policy. This policy needs regular modifications depending upon the economic policies of the economies of the world or the trading partners.[13]

Depreciation This term is used to mean two different things. In the foreign exchange market, it is a situation when domestic currency loses its value in front of a foreign currency if it is market-driven. It means

[8] *LERMS, Union Budget 1992-93,* (New Delhi: Ministry of Finance, GoI, 1992).

[9] Stiglitz and Walsh, *Economics,* op. cit., p. 757.

[10] Samuelson and Nordhaus, *Economics,* p. 604

[11] D. Salvatore, *International Economics,* op. cit., p. 7.

[12] Ministry of Finance, ***LERMS.***

[13] D. Salvatore, *International Economics,* op. cit., pp. 235-36.

depreciation in a currency can only take place if the economy follows the floating exchange rate system.

In a domestic economy, depreciation means an asset losing its value due to either its use, wear and tear or other economic reasons. Depreciation here means *wear and tear*. This is also known as ***capital consumption***. Every economy has an official annual rate for different assets at which fixed assets are considered depreciating.

Devaluation In the foreign exchange market, when the exchange rate of a domestic currency is cut down by its government against any foreign currency, it is called devaluation. It means official depreciation is devaluation.

Revaluation A term used in a foreign exchange market which means a government increasing the exchange rate of its currency against any foreign currency. It is official appreciation.

Appreciation In the foreign exchange market, if a free-floating domestic currency increases its value against the value of a foreign currency, it is appreciation. In a domestic economy, if a fixed asset has seen an increase in its value, it is also known as appreciation. Appreciation rates for different assets are not fixed by any Government as they depend upon many factors which are unseen.

NEER & REER The nominal effective exchange rate (NEER) and real effective exchange rate (REER) are indices which are used as indicators of external competitiveness of a currency.

The *NEER* is the weighted average (i.e., weights being based on the average of India's bilateral trade) of bilateral nominal exchange rates of the home currency in terms of foreign currencies, with countries/regions represented by the 6/40 currencies during the preceding three years.

The *REER is* defined as a weighted average of nominal exchange rates adjusted for relative price differential (i.e., headline inflation) between the domestic and foreign countries. It relates to the idea of purchasing power parity (PPP).

EFF The Extended fund Facility (EFF) is a service provided by the IMF to its member countries which authorises them to raise any amount of foreign exchange from it to fulfil their BoP crisis, but on the conditions of structural reforms in the economy put by the body. It is the first agreement of its kind. India had signed this agreement with the IMF in the financial year 1981-82.

Hard Currency It is the international currency in which the highest faith is shown and is needed by every economy. The strongest currency of the world is one which has a high level of liquidity. Basically, the economy with the highest as well as highly diversified exports that are compulsive imports for other countries (as of high-level technology, defence products, life-saving medicines and petroleum products) will also create high demand for its currency in the world and become the hard currency. It is always scarce.

Until the Second World War, the best hard currency was the pound sterling (£) of the United Kingdom, but soon it was replaced by the US dollar. Some of the best hard currencies of the world today are the US dollar, Euro (€), Japanese yen (¥) and UK sterling pound (£). Meanwhile, by late 2015, the IMF allowed the SDR to be denominated in the Chinese 'yuan', paving the way for a new hard currency which was implemented in 2016.

Soft Currency A term used in the foreign exchange market which denotes the currency that is easily available in any economy in its forex market. For example, the rupee is a soft currency in the Indian forex market. It is basically the opposite term for the hard currency.

Hot Currency Hot currency is a term of the forex market and is a temporary name for any hard currency. Due to certain reasons, if a hard currency is exiting in an economy at a fast pace for the time, the *hard* currency is known to be *hot*. As in the case of the SE Asian crisis, the US dollar had become hot.

Heated Currency A term used in the forex market to denote the domestic currency which is under enough pressure (heat) of depreciation due to a hard currency's high tendency of exiting the economy (since it has become hot). It is also known as *currency under heat* or *under hammering*.

Cheap Currency A term first used by the economist J. M. Keynes (1930s). If a government starts repurchasing its bonds before their maturities (at full-maturity prices), the money which flows into the economy is known as the cheap currency, also called cheap money.

In the banking industry, it means a period of comparatively lower/softer interest rates regime.

Dear Currency This term was popularised by economists in the early 1930s to show the opposite of the cheap currency. When a government issues bonds, the money which flows from the public to the Government or the money in the economy in general is called dear currency, also called *dear money*.

In the banking industry, it means a period of comparatively higher/costlier interest rates regime.

LERMS

India announced the Liberalised Exchange Rate Mechanism System (LERMS) in the Union Budget 1992–93, and in March 1993 it was operationalised. India delinked its currency from the fixed currency system and moved into the era of floating exchange-rate system under it.

The Indian form of exchange rate is known as the 'dual exchange rate', one exchange rate of rupee is official, and the other is market-driven.[14] The market-driven exchange rate shows the actual tendencies of the foreign currency demand and supply in the economy *vis-à-vis* the domestic currency. It is the market-driven exchange rate which affects the official rate and not the other way round.

CURRENT ACCOUNT

A current account has two meanings - one is related to the banking sector and the other to the external sector:

1. In the banking industry, a business firm's bank account is known as current account. The account is in the name of a firm run by the authorised person or persons in which no interest is paid by the bank on the deposits. Every withdrawal from the account takes place by cheques with limitations on the number of deposits and withdrawals in a single day. The *overdraft* facility or the *cash-cum-credit* (c/c Account) facility to business firms is offered by the banks on this account only.
2. In the external sector, the current account refers to the account maintained by every Government of the world in which every kind of current transactions is shown - basically this account is maintained by the central banking body of the economy on behalf of the Government. Current transactions of an economy in foreign currency all over the world are export, import, interest payments, private remittances and transfers.

All transactions are shown as either inflow or outflow (credit or debit). At the end of the year, the current account might be positive or negative. The positive one is known as a surplus current account, and the negative one is known as a deficit current account. India had surplus current accounts for three consecutive years (2000-03) - for the first time in Indian economic history.

During 2024-25 (upto September), India had a current account deficit (CAD) of **1.2** per cent of GDP (US$ 75.3 billion) due to recent rise in in the merchandise trade deficit.

However, India had sufficient forex reserves to finance the CAD and intervene in the forex market to manage volatility in the Indian rupee. The tolerable level of the current account deficit was projected by RBI to be in the range of **2.00 to 2.50** per cent of the GDP(as per the *RBI Bulletin* of December 2024).

CAPITAL ACCOUNT

Every government in the world maintains a capital account, which shows the capital kind of transactions of the economy with outside economies. Every transaction in foreign currency (inflow or outflow) considered as capital is shown in this account - external lending and borrowing (concessional as well as commercial), foreign currency deposits of banks, external bonds issued by the Government of India, foreign direct investment (FDI), foreign portfolio investment (FPI). In case of the FPI, rupee is fully convertible, while in other cases it is partially convertible (barring special provisions).

There can be deficit or surplus in this account like the current account.

BALANCE OF PAYMENT

The outcome of the total transactions of an economy with the outside world in one year is known as the BoP of the economy.[15] Basically, it is the net outcome of the current and capital accounts of an economy. It might be favourable or unfavourable for the economy. However, negativity of the BoP does not mean it is unfavourable. A negative BoP is unfavourable for an economy if only the economy lacks the means to fill the gap of negativity.

[14] *LERMS, Union Budget 1992-93* (New Delhi: Ministry of Finance, GoI).

[15] Samuelson and Nordhaus, *Economics*, op. cit., p. 601.

The BoP of an economy is calculated on the principles of accountancy (***double-entry bookkeeping***)[16] and looks like the balance sheet of a company - every entry shown either as credit (inflow) or debit (outflow). If there is a positive outcome at the end of the year, the money is automatically transferred to the foreign exchange reserves of the economy. And if there is any negative outcome, the same foreign exchange is drawn from the country's forex reserves. If the forex reserves are not capable of fulfilling the negativity created by the BoP, it is known as a BoP crisis and the economy tries different means to solve the crisis in which going for forex help from the IMF is the last resort.

CONVERTIBILITY

An economy might allow its currency full or partial convertibility in the current and the capital accounts. If the domestic currency is allowed to convert into the foreign currency for all current account purposes, it is a case of full current account convertibility. Similarly, in cases of capital outflow, if the domestic currency is allowed to convert into the foreign currency, it is a case of full capital account convertibility (CAC). If the situation is of partial convertibility, then the portion allowed by the government can be converted into foreign currency for current and capital purposes. It should always be kept in mind that the issue of currency convertibility is concerned with foreign currency *outflow* only.

Convertibility in India

India's foreign exchange earning capacity was always poor and hence it had all possible provisions to check the foreign exchange outflow, be it for current purposes or capital purposes (remember the draconian FERA). But the process of economic reforms has changed the situation to unidentifiable levels.

Current Account

Current account is today fully convertible (operationalised on 19 August, 1994). It means that the full amount of the foreign exchange required by someone for current purposes will be made available to him at official exchange rate, and there could be an unprohibited outflow of foreign exchange (earlier it was partially convertible). India was obliged to do so as per Article VIII of the IMF which prohibits any exchange restrictions on current international transactions (keep in mind that India was under pre-conditions of the IMF since 1991).

Capital Account

After the recommendations of the S. S. Tarapore Committee (1997) on CAC, India has been moving in the direction of allowing full convertibility in this account, but with required precautions. India is still a country of partial convertibility (40:60) in the capital account, but inside this overall policy, enough reforms have been made and to certain levels of foreign exchange requirements, it is an economy allowing full CAC.

1. Indian corporates are allowed full convertibility in the automatic route up to US$ 500 million overseas ventures (investment by Ltd. companies in foreign countries allowed) per annum.
2. Indian corporates are allowed to prepay their ECBs *via* automatic route if the loan is above US$ 500 million per annum.
3. Individuals are allowed to invest in foreign assets, shares, etc. up to the level of US$ 2,50,000 per annum.
4. Unlimited amount of gold is allowed to be imported (this is equal to allowing full convertibility in capital account *via* current account route, but not feasible for everybody) which is not allowed now.

Meanwhile, RBI has been following the recommendations of the two committees (the *Tarapore Committees* of 1997 and 2006) set up on it, which had outlined certain fiscal preconditions/signposts before making rupee fully convertible in the capital account.

IMF Conditions on India

The BoP crisis of the early 1990s made India borrow from the IMF which agreed on some conditions. The medium-term loan to India was given for the restructuring of the economy on the following conditions:

1. Devaluation of rupee by 22 per cent (carried out in two consecutive fortnights – rupee fell from ₹21 to ₹27 against every US dollar).

[16] It means that each external transaction is recorded/entered twice - once as a credit and once as a debit of an equal amount. This is because every transaction has two sides - we sell something and we receive payment for it; similarly, we buy something and we have to pay for it (See Salvatore, *International Economics*, p. 432).

2. Drastic custom cut to a peak duty of 30 per cent from the erstwhile level of 130 per cent for all goods.
3. Excise duty to be increased by 20 per cent to neutralise the loss of revenue due to custom cut.
4. Government expenditure to be cut by 10 per cent per annum (the burden of salaries, pensions, subsidies, etc.).

The above-given conditions to which India was obliged were vehemently opposed by the Indian corporate sector, opposition in the Parliament and majority of Indians. But by the end of 1999–2000, when India saw the multiple benefits accruing out of the ongoing reforms, there was no ideological opposition to the idea. It should always be kept in mind that the nature of structural reforms India went through was guided and decided by these pre-conditions of the IMF.

This is how the direction of structural reforms of an economy is regulated by the IMF in the process of strengthening the BoP position of the crisis-driven economy. The purpose has been served in the Indian case. India has not only fulfilled these conditions but also moved ahead.

SPECIAL ECONOMIC ZONE

The special economic zone (SEZ) policy was announced by the Government in 2000 which was concretised through the SEZ Act, 2005. It mainly aims to develop 'export hubs' in the country to promote growth and development. As an idea it was not new - India had set up *Asia's first* 'export processing zone' (EPZ) in Kandla in 1965 itself. Later on, the idea obtained another encouragement through the 'export-oriented units' (EOUs). After the SEZ policy was formalised through an Act, the EOUs and EPZs are open to conversion to SEZ.

The SEZs can be set up by either the GoI, states or even private sector - in all three sectors of the economy - agriculture, industry and services. As per the Ministry of Commerce and Industry, the principal objectives behind creating SEZs in the country include:

1. generation of additional economic activity,
2. promotion of exports of goods and services,
3. promotion of investment from domestic and foreign sources,
4. creation of employment opportunities, and
5. development of infrastructure facilities.

Over the time, with the enforcement of a minimal alternate tax (MAT) and the adoption of a sunset clause for the removal of tax benefits, these zones began to lose their lustre. For the purposes of customs regulations, these zones are treated as foreign entities. Industry has repeatedly requested that the laws related to tax benefits should be maintained by the Government. Units in SEZs used to be exempt from paying income tax on export income for the first five years, 50 per cent for the next five years, and 50 per cent of the ploughed-back export earnings for another five years.

FOREIGN INVESTMENT

Though the importance of foreign investment in the economy was realised by the Government by the late 1980s, it was only liberalised after the country commenced the process of the economic reforms in 1991. In 1991 itself, India opened up to inflows of direct and indirect forms of foreign investments - more emphasis being on the former for being more durable and beneficial to the economy. Since then, much water has flown in the area, and today India is among the highest recipients of FDI in the world - in 2016-17 being the topmost recipient in the world (it is one of the aims of the 'Make in India' initiative).

By now, most of the sectors are open for 100 per cent FDI while all categories of the investors are allowed to invest in the security market of the country. Pushing in favour of enhanced inflows of foreign investment, related policy was further *liberalised* with the following changes:

1. The 'single brand retail trading' (SBRT) is now open for 100 per cent FDI under automatic route.
2. The 'construction' and 'real estate brokerage' are open to receive 100 per cent FDI under automatic route.
3. 'Aviation' sector is allowed to receive 49 per cent FDI under automatic route (it includes the public sector aviation company, Air India).
4. Foreign institutional investments (FIIs)/FPIs have been allowed in 'power distribution' over and above the FDI limit of 49 per cent under automatic route. Earlier, it used to be allowed but under the overall FDI limit.
5. The marketplace-based model of the 'e-Commerce' sector has been allowed to receive 100 per cent FDI under the automatic route.

But this ease came with a rider - sales of any vendor through them or its group companies limited to 25 per cent of the total sales of such vendor.

6. In the case of FDI in the 'pharma sector', the reference to Drugs and Cosmetics Act has been dropped - making things easier for the investors.
7. In the wake of the ***COVID-19 pandemic***, the Government gave an emphatic call for self-reliance (under the newly launched campaign, the *Atmanirbhar Bharat Abhiyan*) and raised the FDI limits in the defence sector to 74 per cent (from the existing 49 per cent) under automatic route. India already allows 100 per cent FDI in the sector on a case-by-case basis.
8. Upper limit of FDI was increased to 100 per cent (from 74 per cent) in the insurance sector[17], which was a long-awaited demand from the capital-starved industry.
9. As per the new FDI norms, now 'prior clearance' in India's companies will be required for investments from the countries with which India shares its land border. This norm applies on all existing and future FDIs in an Indian company. However, the indirect foreign investment (i.e., FPI) has been left unchanged. The move is aimed at checking 'opportunistic takeover' due to the *COVID-19 pandemic*, especially from China.

ECB LIBERALISED

With the changing dynamics of economy, India's needs for foreign loans have also gone for a change. Though the RBI has been quite careful about higher exposure to the external loans, its overall policy stance regarding it has been liberal. Following this stance, the *ECB* norms were further liberalised[18] by the RBI, which are as given below:

- All eligible borrowers to raise up to US$ 750 million per financial year under the automatic route (with sector-wise limits being abolished).
- The list of eligible borrowers enlarged - all entities eligible to receive FDI, port trusts, units in SEZs, SIDBI, Exim Bank and registered microfinance entities.
- Public sector oil marketing companies can borrow up to US$ 10 billion for working capital purposes with a minimum average maturity period of three years under the automatic route without mandatory hedging. This move is aimed at curbing volatility in the forex market arising out of dollar demand for crude oil purchases.

Foreign Currency Hedging

We can understand the 'hedging' of foreign currency risk related to the ECB in the following ways:

The firms/companies which own a liability in foreign currency (such as foreign loans they might have borrowed) are asked, at times, by the Government to 'reduce the risk' (hedge) involved due to such exposures – known as 'mandatory hedging'. Government might ask different proportion of foreign currency hedging (30 per cent, 50 per cent or even 100 per cent).

There are a few ways how the companies do it. One very popular way is signing a forward contract in the currency of need in advance – and this way the risk of exposure to foreign currency risk is neutralised.

- Manufacturing companies allowed up to US$ 50 million of ECB per year with the maturity of one year.
- In the case of ECB being raised from a foreign equity holder (and utilised for working capital, general corporate purposes or repayment of rupee loans), the maturity period will be five years.

In place of setting a sectoral cap, the RBI decided to set an overall prudential limit on the ECB at **6.5** per cent of the GDP. It was for the first time that the RBI put out such an open idea in the public domain - till then it was managed through its internal benchmark which was never be available in the public domain.

TRADE FACILITATION

With an aim to reduce trade barriers caused by inefficient and overly burdensome regulatory administrative procedures, the Trade Facilitation Agreement (TFA), negotiated at WTO, came into force in February 2017. A National Committee on Trade Facilitation (NCTF) was, accordingly, constituted in

[17] *Union Budget 2025-26* (New Delhi: Ministry of Finance, GoI, February 2025).

[18] Reserve Bank of India, Ministry of Finance, Government of India, New Delhi, March 2020.

August 2016 (with the Cabinet Secretary as the Chair). A National Trade Facilitation Action Plan (NTFAP) for 2017-2020 containing specific activities to further ease out the bottlenecks to trade was prepared.

For the period 2020 to 2023, a new NTFAP is under preparation, to take additional reforms to bolster trade facilitation efforts and transform the cross-border clearance eco-system through efficient, transparent, risk-based, coordinated, digital, seamless and technology-driven procedures. India has been making proactive strides in TFA implementation under the guidance of the NCTF. Many of the commitments (notified by the WTO), which were otherwise due by 2022, have already been implemented by 2021 which are as follows:

- Establishment of a Single Window (Article 10.4) and Risk Management for Clearance of Goods (Article 7.4), being the major ones. The transparency notifications covering information on import and export procedures, enquiry points, single windows, etc. were also carried out in April 2019.
- Further, various regulatory relaxation measures were extended for facilitating trade during COVID-19, which include 24 × 7 clearance; dedicated single window; condonation of delay in filing import declarations; waiver of late filing fees; and undertakings instead of bond being the major ones.

These initiatives reflect India's commitment towards facilitation of trade with an emphasis on transparency and openness. India has been at the forefront in undertaking initiatives aimed at maximizing predictability and automation in trade, reflecting in the consistent improvement on the *United Nation's Global Survey on Digital and Sustainable Trade.*

EXPORT PROMOTION SCHEMES

India officially acknowledges that in the interconnected global economy of today, efforts to streamline, speed up and coordinate trade procedures will enhance trade and help the country integrate itself with global production and supply chain. To lend continuity, the *Foreign Trade Policy, 2015-2020,* has already been extended by three years (i.e., up to March 2023). Other than 'trade facilitation', the Government has launched the following major schemes[19] to promote exports from the country:

RoDTEP (Remission of Duties and Taxes on Exported Products) The MEIS (Merchandise Exports from India Scheme) of 2015 was challenged by the United States in the WTO in early 2018 - with the final report of the WTO panel observing it a 'prohibited subsidy' - thus it needed to be withdrawn (though India put an appeal in the WTO regarding it). Meanwhile, in order to continue supporting the industry and to eliminate any uncertainty among the exporting community, the Government rolled out a new *WTO compliant scheme,* namely RoDTEP, for all export goods with effect from January 2021.

Under this scheme, duties and taxes levied at the central, state and local levels (such as electricity duties and VAT on fuel used for transportation) which are not getting exempted or refunded under any other existing mechanism will be refunded to exporters in their ledger account with Customs. The credits can be used to pay basic customs duty on imported goods or transferred to other importers - facilitating ease of transactions for exports.

PLI (Production-Linked Incentive) The scheme (announced in 2020-21) which applies to 13 eligible sectors (for more, see the chapter on *Industry and Infrastructure)* is expected to make Indian manufacturers globally competitive; attract investment in the areas of core competency and cutting-edge technology; ensure efficiencies; create economies of scale; establish backward linkages with MSMEs; enhance exports and make India an integral part of the *global supply chain.*

SEIS (Services Exports from India Scheme) Under this scheme, rewards (in the form of 'duty credit scrips') are given to the exporters of services on their net foreign exchange earnings (NFEE). The scrips (just like MEIS) are transferable and can be used to pay certain central duties and taxes. The service exporters are eligible for SEIS at the rate of 3 to 5 per cent of the NFEE.

EPCG (Export Promotion Capital Goods) Scheme This scheme allows exporters to import capital goods (except certain specified items under the scheme) for pre-production, production and post-production at *zero* customs duty. In return, the exporters are required to fulfil the export obligation to the tune of *six times* the import duties, taxes and cess saved amount on capital goods (to be fulfilled in six years).

[19] *Economic Survey* 2022-23 (New Delhi: Ministry of Finance, GoI, January 2023); *Economic Survey 2021-22* (New Delhi: Ministry of Finance, GoI); *Economic Survey 2020-21* (New Delhi: Ministry of Finance, GoI); *Economic Survey 2019-20* (New Delhi: Ministry of Finance, GoI).

AAS (Advance Authorisation Scheme) Advance Authorisation (AA) is issued to allow duty-free import of inputs (such as fuel, oil and catalyst), which are physically incorporated in export products.

DFIA (Duty Free Import Authorisation) This is issued on post export basis for products for which Standard Input-Output Norms (SION) have been notified. One of the objectives of the scheme is to facilitate transfer of the authorisation or the inputs imported as per SION, once export is completed. Provisions of DFIA Scheme are similar to AAS.

IES The Interest Equalisation Scheme (IES) was formulated to give benefit in the interest rates being charged by the banks to the exporters on their pre- and post-shipment rupee export credits. While extending the scheme, from 1 October 2021 onwards, subvention rates have also been reduced. Henceforth, reduced revised rates of 3 per cent (erstwhile 5 per cent) subvention to MSME manufacturing exporters and 2 per cent (erstwhile 3 per cent) apply to merchant and other manufacturer exporters.

EoU/EHTP/STP/BTP Scheme The objectives of these four schemes, i.e., EOU, Electronic Hardware Technology Park (EHTP), Software Technology Parks (STP) and Bio-Technology Parks (BTP), are to promote exports, enhance foreign exchange earnings, attract investment for export production and generate employment. The units (other than trading firms) undertaking to export their entire production of goods and services (except permissible sales in the DTA) may be set up under the schemes which are permitted to import inputs without payment of customs duty.

DES (Deemed Exports Scheme) Deemed Exports refer to those transactions in which the goods supplied do not leave the country and the payment for such supplies is received either in Indian rupees or in free foreign exchange. Under the scheme, exemption (or refund) of duties on manufactured products is given to ensure a *level playing field* to domestic manufacturers.

TMA (Transport and Marketing Assistance for Specified Agriculture Products Scheme) Launched in February 2019, it aims to mitigate the disadvantage of higher *cost of transportation* of export of specified agriculture products due to trans-shipment and to promote brand recognition for Indian agricultural products in specified overseas markets.

TIES (Trade Infrastructure for Export Scheme) The scheme has the objective to assist Central and State Government Agencies for the creation of appropriate *infrastructure* for the growth of exports from the States. The scheme provides financial assistance in the form of grant-in-aid to Central/State Government owned agencies for setting up or for upgradation of export infrastructure as per the guidelines of the scheme.

District as Export Hub The focus of this initiative is to make districts, active stakeholders in the promotion of exports - district export promotion committees (DEPCs) have been set up in each district. Products with export potential - including agricultural, geographical indication (GI) and toy clusters - have been identified in all 739 districts across the country. This scheme would help in diversifying the portfolio of export commodities.

CoO (Electronic Platform for Preferential Certificate of Origin) In view of the COVID-19 crisis, on-boarding of FTAs/preferential trade agreements (PTAs) was quickly done to allow electronic issuance to avoid physical movement.

Export Credit Guarantee The Export Credit Guarantee Corporation (ECGC) supports Indian exporters and banks by providing export credit insurance services. ECGC provides insurance cover on the export consignment to protect exporters from the consequences of the payment risks. It also provides Export Credit Insurance to Banks (ECIB) to protect the Banks from losses on account of export credit given to exporters due to the risks of insolvency and/or protracted default of the exporter borrower.

The ECGC launched a new scheme in July 2022, under which the insurance cover to banks providing pre-shipment and post-shipment finance has been enhanced to 90 per cent from an average coverage of 70 per cent for accounts with an export working capital limit of up to ₹20 crore to support small exporters.

Krishi Udan Scheme The scheme was launched in August 2020 on international and national routes to assist farmers in transporting agricultural products so that it improves their *value realisation. Krishi Udan 2.0* was launched in October 2021, enhancing the existing provisions, mainly focusing on transporting 'perishable food products' from the hilly areas, North-Eastern states, and tribal areas.

TRADE LOGISTICS

The ongoing COVID-19 pandemic has underscored the need for a *resilient logistics sector* that can respond to emergencies and supply chain disruptions. Despite the sector being plagued by some 'structural issues' such as highly fragmented ownership; few large players; lack of consolidation in operations; sub-optimal modal share with freight movement highly skewed towards the road sector; lack of an integrated approach by user sectors (multiple line ministries and agencies); absence of consistent policies and regulations; among others

The *National Logistics Policy* was rolled out with a vision to develop a modern, efficient and resilient logistics services sector that builds on dynamic processes, technology and professional manpower to seamlessly integrate multiple modes of transportation and inventory management to provide more reliable, cost-effective, greener, safer and equitable logistics solutions.

Some major ***Process Reforms*** carried out by the Government in recent times, which have contributed towards improving logistics efficiency, are as follows:

- Reduction in waiting time for inter-state border crossing due to GST;
- Revision in axle load norms for heavy vehicles leading to better carrying capacity;
- Introduction of paperless EXIM trade process through E-Sanchit; faceless assessment by 'Turant Customs' by Central Board of Indirect Taxes and Customs (CBIC);
- Installation of scanners at major ports; implementation of 'Port Community System *1X*' at all important ports;
- Radio Frequency Identification (RFID) tagging of all EXIM containers for track and trace; and
- Mandatory electronic toll collection system (i.e., FASTag) for reducing time loss at toll plaza.

Some major **Infrastructure initiatives**, at various stages of implementation, are as follows:

1. *Bharatmala Pariyojana* is a new umbrella programme for the highways sector that envisages building more than 80,000 km of roads, highways, greenfield expressways, bridges with an investment of around US$ 107 billion.
2. *Sagarmala* aims at Port Modernisation and New Port Development, Port Connectivity Enhancement, Port-linked Industrialisation, Coastal Community Development and extending impetus to Coastal Shipping. By now, 508 projects have been identified and 111 waterways have been declared 'National Waterways' for which work is underway in phases.
3. *Multi-Modal Logistics Parks* shall act as hubs for freight movement enabling freight aggregation, distribution and multi-modal transportation. They would provide modern mechanised warehousing space and value-added services such as customs clearance with bonded storage yards, warehousing management services, etc. The *Pradhan Mantri Gati Shakti National Master Plan (NMP)* is expected to play the role of catalyst in this regard.
4. *Dedicated Freight Corridors (DFCs)* aims at reduction in unit cost of transportation with higher speed of freight trains and better turnaround of wagons. Around 70 per cent of freight is expected to shift to DFC, freeing up capacity on the Indian Railways.
5. *Trade Infrastructure for Export Scheme (TIES)* aims to assist the creation of appropriate infrastructure for the growth of exports from the States.

Some **Digital and Technological initiatives** under development are as follows:

1. *Logistics Planning and Performance Monitoring Tool (LPPT)* will allow real-time monitoring of operational performance and asset utilisation of various logistics infrastructure such as ports, airports, various corridors comprising national and state highways, Inland Container Depots (ICDs), etc.
2. *India Logistics Platform (iLOG)* - Several IT-based solutions have been deployed by the Government over the years such as Indian Customs EDI Gateway (ICEGATE) and Single Window Interface for Trade (SWIFT) developed for trade facilitation; Port Community System (PCS) for cargo handling at seaports; Freight Operations Information System (FOIS) by Indian Railways and VAHAN (National Vehicle Registration System). However, each system owner has adopted a different approach, leaving critical gaps that require manual or offline processing at various stages.
3. *Component Systems* that would be latched with the iLOG with Aadhaar and Blockchain-based security protocols include truck visibility and positioning platform (integrated with e-way bill and Vahan); National e-registry of warehousing; digital trucking; logistics account number (LAN); digital green corridor; and digital port decongestion and container tracking and management system.

Today, the logistics sector employs over 12 million labour force in the country, involved mainly in land transportation, warehousing (storage and packaging), supply chain, courier and express services. To impart the right set of skills to this workforce, a curriculum on *logistics and supply chain* is being developed for classes 9 and 10 at the school level - to be introduced in Industrial Training Institutes (ITIs) and polytechnics under the PMKVY (Pradhan Mantri Kaushal Vikas Yojana), DDU-GKY (Deen Dayal Upadhyay Grameen Kaushalya Yojana) and state skill missions.

INDIA'S TRADE

Foreign trade has played an important role in making India's external sector resilient. Following a dip in 2019-20 amid the global downturn and the pandemic, overall exports rebounded strongly in 2021-22, reaching a record high in 2022-23. This momentum continued into 2023-24 and 2024-25. The trade scenario in the year 2025-26 (April-December), as per the *Economic Survey 2025-26*, has been as given below:

Merchandise Trade: *Exports* totalled US$ 437.7 billion (maintained similar levels to those observed in the previous year). Export composition was predominantly concentrated in petroleum products, telecom instruments, drug formulations, and biologicals, which collectively account for about 25 per cent of the total exports.

Imports totalled US$ 721.2 billion, increasing by 6.3 per cent (primarily driven by a rise in non-petroleum, non-gem, and jewellery items). Import composition continues to be dominated by crude petroleum, gold, and petroleum products, with these sectors accounting for over 33 per cent of total imports.

Services Trade: Services exports reached an all-time high of US$ 387.5 billion (registering a robust 13.6 per cent growth), while services imports totalled US$ 198.7 billion. As a result, the services trade surplus increased to US$ 188.8 billion, reaching ***the highest ever*** recorded. Effectively, the surplus in services trade covered around 66 per cent of the merchandise trade deficit.

Export Destinations

The USA remained the *top export destination* in the year, followed by UAE and the Netherlands (replacing China).

Import Sources

As regards imports, China, UAE, USA, Russia, and Saudi Arabia have a joint share of 40 per cent of the total imports of India.

CURRENT TRADE OPPORTUNITY

The dynamics of global trade has been through much change in recent times. Two factors have played a very vital role in this change, one being the rise of protectionism in the world and the Sino-US trade tensions. After the outbreak of the COVID-19 pandemic, several MNCs having their production bases in China were searching for alternative bases to continue their production. Thus, the current environment for international trade presents India an unprecedented opportunity to chart a China-like, labour-intensive, export trajectory and thereby create unparalleled job opportunities. To tap this opportunity, India should act[20] in the following direction:

- 'Assemble in India for the world' should be integrated into the 'Make in India'. By doing so, India can raise its export market share to about 3.5 per cent by 2025 and 6 per cent by 2030. Job creation out of this will be 4 crores by 2025 and 8 crores by 2030.
- The increased exports can contribute about 25 per cent for making India a $5 trillion economy by 2025.

The remarkable export performance of China in comparison to India is driven primarily by deliberate specialisation at large scale in labour-intensive sectors, especially 'network products' (products which are used in information technology for networking), where production occurs across Global Value Chains (GVCs) operated by the MNCs. China used this strategy to export primarily to affluent countries. In a similar way, India should focus on enabling *assembling operations* at the highest possible level in network products.

India's insecurity on the trade front related to regional and preferential trade agreements can be overcome by tapping this opportunity - by promoting the cause of manufacturing industries. By evaluating the impact of

[20] *Economic Survey 2019-20*, vol. 1 (New Delhi: Ministry of Finance, GoI), pp. 100-27.

India's trade agreements (for the period 1993-2018), we find that India's exports have increased by 13.4 per cent for manufactured products and 10.9 per cent for total merchandise while imports increased by 12.7 per cent for manufactured products and 8.6 per cent for total merchandise. This way, we find a clear gain of 0.7 per cent in trade balance surplus per year for manufactured products and 2.3 per cent per year for total merchandise.

INDIA AS PHARMACY OF THE WORLD

The ongoing COVID-19 pandemic presented both an opportunity and a challenge for India to emerge[21] as the pharmacy of the world - showing its vulnerabilities as well as its potential in this regard. The global pharmaceutical market is set to exceed US$ 1.5 trillion by 2023 - against this backdrop, the Indian pharma industry is currently valued at US$ 41 billion and is expected to grow to US$ 65 billion by 2024 and about US$ 120-130 billion by 2030. Certain encouraging facts related to pharma industry of the country are as given below:

- *3rd* largest in the world, in terms of volume (after China and Italy) and *14th* largest in terms of value.
- Share in global exports almost doubled to 2.6 per cent in 2019 from 1.6 per cent of 2010 - *11th* position (with top positions going to Germany, Switzerland and the United States).
- Emerged as a global hub for generic medicines (on top of being a raw material base and a skilled workforce).
- Has the largest number of US-FDA compliant pharma plants (more than 262 including APIs) outside of the United States.
- India's pharma sector has high value of TSC (trade specialisation coefficient), closer to 1, consistently from 2014-15 (the value of TSC lies between -1 and 1, wherein a higher TSC value denotes stronger export competitiveness of the country).

During 2020-21 (April-October), India had US$ 11.1 billion of pharma exports showing an impressive growth rate of 18.0 per cent - increasing in total exports to 7.3 per cent (from 5.1 per cent) - making it the third largest exported commodity. The commitment to supply COVID-19 vaccines to other countries has made India the epicentre for its manufacturing. According to data available from US-FDA, Indian pharma companies have garnered nearly **45** per cent of all new Abbreviated New Drug Application (ANDA) approvals during the first nine months of 2020-21 (which hints at export potential in the coming years). But before India emerges as the pharmacy of the world, certain *challenges* are also present, namely

1. Its excessive dependence on China for sourcing Active Pharmaceutical Ingredients (APIs) and Key Starting Materials (KSMs).
2. Disproportionate dependence on the United States for pharma exports.
3. Excessive dependence on manufacturing of the generic formulations.

The Government has adopted a few focused initiatives to pull through the challenges during 2020-21, namely the PLI (Production Linked Incentive) Scheme reported enhancing manufacturing capacities and exports besides for bulk drugs (which applies on Drug Intermediates, APIs and medical devices); and a scheme for promotion of parks for bulk drugs and medical devices. To emerge as the *pharmacy of the world*, the industry needs a broad-based development strategy led by the following components:

1. Broadening of market base together with product categories - for example, tapping the opportunities in newer product classes such as biosimilars, gene therapy and specialty drugs and increasing exports to large and traditionally underpenetrated markets (such as Japan, China, Africa, Indonesia, Russia/CIS countries, Brazil and Latin America).
2. Restructuring of the existing regulatory framework together with upgrading and building capacities at various National Institute of Pharmaceutical Education and Research (NIPERs).
3. Boosting of R&D expenditure to move up in the value chain from generics to Novel Chemical Entities (i.e., new complex pharmaceuticals).

BIPA AND BIT

Attracting adequate amounts of foreign investments was one of the major aims of the process of economic reforms which commenced in 1991. Accordingly, a Model BIT (Bilateral Investment Treaty) was crafted by the Government in 1993. Since then, India has signed 84 such treaties called the Bilateral Investment

[21] *Economic Survey 2020-21*, vol. 1 (New Delhi: Ministry of Finance, GoI), pp. 97-99, has quoted *Report of the High- Level Advisory Group*, 2019 (headed by S. S. Bhalla) of the Department of Commerce among other latest studies of recent times.

Promotion and Protection Agreements (BIPAs) with different countries - the first one with the United Kingdom in 1994 and the last with the UAE signed in 2018. They aim to increase foreign investments[22] for both inflows and outflows.

Objective These agreements aim to increase the comfort level and boost the confidence of investors by assuring a level playing field, a non-discriminatory treatment and an independent forum for dispute settlement.

New BIT In the wake of the changes which have occurred in India and around the world since the first Model BIT was announced, the Government finalised a new[23] *Model BIT in 2016* which is being used for 're-negotiation' of the existing BIPAs, CECAs (Comprehensive Economic Cooperation Agreements), CEPAs (Comprehensive Economic Partnership Agreements) and the FTAs (Free Trade Agreements). The essential features of the new model BIT are given below:

- An 'enterprise-based' definition of investment
- Non-discriminatory treatment through due process
- National treatment
- Protections against expropriation
- A refined Investor State Dispute Settlement (ISDS) provision under which investors to first exhaust local remedies before opting for international arbitration[24]
- The ISDS to award monetary compensation alone
- Excludes matters such as government procurement, taxation, subsidies, compulsory licenses and national security (to preserve regulatory authority of the Government)

[22] These agreements aim at only foreign direct investment (FDI) as since 1993-94 itself the rupee was fully convertible in the case of the foreign indirect investment (the Foreign Portfolio Investment-FPI).

[23] *India Brand Equity Foundation (IBEF)*, (New Delhi: Ministry of Commerce & Industry, GoI, March 2019).

[24] Normally, investment disputes arising between the host nation and the investor are resolved by the *ICSID (International Centre for Settlement of Investment Disputes)*, an agency of the World Bank group. But as India is not its member, 'a clause' in the BIPAs/BITs is dedicated to serve this purpose. However, these agreements crafted by India serve more purposes than the purpose served by the ICSID such as promoting investment, exploring possibilities of investments and allowing local resolution of the disputes among others.

Meanwhile, a re-negotiation process under the new Model BIT has faced resistance from some countries, though out of the 83 BITs, by now, 72 are already enforced while rest are under the process of re-negotiation.

RTAs BY INDIA

In general, multilateral trade agreements are the first-best solutions for deepening global trade and development as they are founded on the core principles of non-discrimination. Meanwhile, RTAs (Regional Trade Agreements) are efforts by nations aimed at deepening economic relations, usually with neighbouring countries, and tend to be *largely political* in nature. With the multilateral trade negotiations process under the WTO being a painfully slow one requiring broad-based consensus, RTAs have progressively assumed greater importance and a growing share in international trade.

While RTAs are broadly *compliant* with WTO mandates and remain broadly *supportive* of the WTO process, they remain ***second-best*** solutions that are discriminatory in nature against non-members and are inefficient as low-cost-producing non-members lose out to members. While bilateral RTAs have no equity considerations, megaregional trading groups may not necessarily be equitable if membership is diverse and small countries may lose out either way - if they are part of it, they may not have much say and if they are not, they may stand to lose.

India has always stood for an open, equitable, predictable, non-discriminatory and rule-based international trading system and views RTAs as building blocks in the overall objective of trade liberalisation as well as complementing the multilateral trading system under the WTO.

With the intention of expanding[25] exports market, India has been moving towards CECAs (Comprehensive Economic Cooperation Agreements) with trading blocs/partners, which cover FTA (free trade agreement) in goods, services, investment and identify areas of economic cooperation. In the case of the India-Association of Southeast Asian Nations (ASEAN), India- Korea, and India-Japan Agreements, this was also part of a *geopolitical strategy* that dovetailed well into *Look East Policy* of India.

[25] *Economic Survey 2022-23* (New Delhi: Ministry of Finance, GoI, January 2023), pp. 323-324.

By *February 2025*, India had concluded **13 FTAs** and **6 PTAs** (Preferential Trade Agreements). The most recent in the list are the India-UAE Comprehensive Economic Partnership Agreement (CEPA), which officially came into force in May 2022 and the India-Australia Economic Cooperation and Trade Agreement (Ind-Australia ECTA), which came into force on 29 December 2022.

Ongoing Negotiations India is presently engaged in FTA negotiations with some of its trading partners. Notable among these FTAs are - (i) India- UK FTA, (ii) India-Canada CEPA/Early Progress Trade Agreement (EPTA), and (iii) India-EU FTA.

Review of existing FTAs India has also initiated action to review some of the existing FTAs, namely–India-Singapore CECA, India- South Korea CEPA, and India-ASEAN Trade in Goods Agreement and initiated discussions on scoping for the CECA with Australia, as envisaged under Ind-Australia ECTA.

THE QUAD

The Quad[26] is the acronym used for the Quadrilateral Security Dialogue (QSD) which is also called the *Asian NATO*. This is an informal strategic forum of Australia, India, Japan and the United States - which has remained primarily involved in summits, exchange of information and military exercises between them - later on upscaling to ministerial and leadership level meetings.

Origin Its origin is traced back to the Indian Ocean Tsunami of 2004 when a temporary joint rescue operation was run by Australia, India, Japan and the United States (wherein the world recognised not only India's naval-military preparedness but also its significance in the Asia- Pacific region). However, the rescue mission ended after handing over charge to the UNO. Meanwhile, a new framework was birthed - the Quadrilateral, or Quad - with the Japanese PM (Shinzo Abe) voicing his long-standing idea of an 'arc of prosperity and freedom' that encompassed India, and brought it into a tighter maritime framework with Japan, the United States and Australia (which were already close military allies). The plan for a meeting of the Quad was strengthened when Prime Minister Manmohan Singh visited Tokyo in December 2006.

The evolving idea of Quad encountered growing concerns in China and soon we will see its dilution. Contrary to general perception, Australia wasn't the first to go slow on Quad, rather it was the United States, which felt that angering China would hamper its larger strategic efforts (move to sanction Iran in the UN Security Council and the six-nation talks on North Korea). Thus, experts believed the forum went through a period of hibernation with the formal withdrawal of Australia from it in 2008 (the phase between 2008 and 2015 is called *Quad 1.0*).

Situating Quad Experts have seen the diplomatic-military initiative of Quad as a response to the increased Chinese economic dominance, which of late started showing up in the form of *military dominance* of the world in general and the Asia-Pacific in particular (the border related skirmishes with India, South Korea, Japan and its incursions in the China Sea being the major examples of the latter).

Certain other attempts to bring about Chinese economic dominance of recent times have been through the TPP (Trans-Pacific Partnership) and its companion, the TTIP (Trans-Atlantic Trade and Investment Partnership) which fizzled out due to the reluctance of the United States to be part of it (under Donald Trump regime), which looked being revived under the administration of Joe Biden, and is in the process of transformation under the regime of Donald Trump in 2025.

Revival During 2017-19, we see a kind of revival (which is popularly called *Quad 2.0)* of the forum - main thrust coming from the United States (under Donald Trump, in the wake of his protectionist policies leading to a fierce Sino-US trade tension). Some recent instances of its revival can be seen in the following developments:

- The coming together of the *naval chiefs* of the four countries in India in 2018 (the Raisina Dialogue) is considered the *first indication* of the revival of the Quad's security structure.
- By late September 2019, the *first ministerial* (external affairs) level meeting took place in New York where collective efforts to advance a 'free, fair, open, prosperous and inclusive Indo-Pacific' was discussed.
- The *second ministerial* meeting was held in Tokyo in October 2020, though no joint statement was produced from the meeting.
- In February 2021, its *third ministerial* meeting was held (virtually) wherein the members agreed to

[26] Based on several official press releases by nations concerned and contemporary media reporting and analyses (*The Economist, The Guardian, The Wall Street Journal* being the main ones).

strongly oppose any attempts by China to alter the *status quo* in the Indo-Pacific region by force, and vowed to work with the ASEAN and Europe in this case.

- In November 2020, the world saw all four countries joining the *Malabar 2020* naval exercise in India (almost three years after Australia requested to join it). In the same month, a defence deal was agreed upon between Australia and Japan.
- By late January 2021, there was a National Security Advisor level talk (telephonic) between the United States and Japan wherein the latter did show its willingness to strengthen their bilateral alliance to achieve 'free and open' Indo-Pacific.
- By March 2021, the Quad members were working to develop a plan to distribute COVID-19 vaccines to countries in Asia as part of a broader strategy to counter China's influence.
- The *first meeting* (virtual) of the leaders of the four countries took place in March 2021 where a 'joint statement' was also released.
- Till ***March 2023***, the Quad Leaders had several meetings in which important developments in the Indo-Pacific were assessed along with the recent Ukraine crisis.

China has been busy cancelling out the importance of the forum with the claim that 'all the talk of a free and open Indo-Pacific is so much ocean spume (froth or foam)', as its foreign minister, Wang Yi, once put it. If such a claim of China seems off the mark, as per some experts, so too is the claim of an Asian NATO in the process of making!

DEGLOBALISATION AND INDIA

Global factors are yet to stabilise since the financial crisis hit the developed economies. Recovery among these economies is getting tough - even unconventional monetary policies have been tried (pursuing for negative interest rate regime). Meanwhile, several of these economies have signalled 'protectionist' rhetoric, the Brexit. The new Government in the United States has already taken various protectionist measures by now, and many more are soon to follow in the coming times.

Besides, in the past few years, the world has seen increased debate on the drawbacks of the globalisation process. Among experts as well as several nations, a general feeling seemed to be evolving against globalisation. The negotiations related to the WTO almost seem to be stalled. At the end of the tunnel, by late 2016, the world witnessed a rise in the 'protectionist sentiments' among important economies.

The two events mentioned above portray how the world (or at least the economies which matter most) has started to move slowly away from the much-celebrated idea of globalisation - ***de-globalisation*** taking over the world - shrinking scope for multilateral trade and economic interdependence. Again, this lack of willingness towards globalisation among different economies is not of the same degree nor universal to every economy - better yet, it seems selective.

India's prospects of export growth depend on its trading partners' carrying capacity of globalisation. Today, for India, three external developments are of significant consequence:

1. In the *short run*, global interest rates (as a result of the US elections and the implied change in its fiscal and monetary policy) will impact India's capital flows and exchange rates. Experts are already expecting higher fiscal stimulus and more dependence on unconventional monetary policy in coming times.
2. The *medium-term* political outlook for globalisation and in particular for the world's 'political carrying capacity for globalisation' may have changed in the wake of recent developments. A strong US dollar and declining competitiveness might incline many countries to follow protectionist policies. This will result in declining global trade hitting India hard.
3. Developments in the United States, especially the rise of the dollar, will have implications for China's currency and currency policy which will impact India and the world - if China is able to successfully re-balance its economy, the spillover effects will be positive; otherwise quite negative. China, with its underlying vulnerabilities, remains the country to watch for its potential to *unsettle* the global economy.

India's trade in goods and services both will be important in this case. India's services exports growth will test the world's 'globalisation carrying capacity' in services - depending on the restrictions in developed countries on two variables - *firstly*, the labour mobility; and *secondly*, outsourcing.

It is possible that the world's carrying capacity will actually be *much greater* for India's services than it was for Chinese goods. After all, China's export expansion over the past two decades was imbalanced in several ways:

- The country exported far more than it imported.
- It exported manufactured goods to advanced countries, displacing production there, but imported goods (raw materials) from developing countries.
- When it did import from advanced economies, it often imported services rather than goods (though capital goods is a major exception).

As a result, China's development created relatively a few export-oriented jobs in advanced countries, insufficient to compensate for the jobs lost in manufacturing - and where it did create jobs, these were in advanced services (such as finance), which were not possible for displaced manufacturing workers to obtain. In contrast, India's expansion may well prove much more balanced:

- India has tended to run a current account deficit, rather than a surplus.
- While its service exports might also displace workers in advanced countries, their skillset will make relocation to other service activities easier; indeed, they may well simply move on to complementary tasks, such as more advanced computer programming in the IT sector itself.
- On the other hand, since skilled labour in advanced economies will be exposed to Indian competition, their ability to mobilise political opinion might also be greater.[27]

Precisely speaking, the *political backlash* against globalisation in advanced countries, and China's difficulties in rebalancing its economy, could have major implications for India. And it will be advisable for India to keep close track of the changing global dynamics.

SETTLEMENT OF TRADE IN INR

By mid-2022, India took an initiative to promote trade in Indian rupee (INR). The initiative aims to support the increasing interest of the global trading community in INR as an international currency. The policy framework (as put in place by the RBI) involves invoicing (billing) of exports and imports in INR at market-determined exchange rates between the currencies of the trading partner countries, and settlement through special *Rupee Vostro* accounts opened with authorised dealer banks in India. This arrangement facilitates the trading needs of India in the following ways:

(a) Indian importers shall make payments in INR (which shall be credited into the Special Vostro account of the correspondent bank of the partner country), while

(b) Indian exporters shall be paid for the exports in INR from the balances in the designated Special Vostro account of the correspondent bank of the partner country.

Such an arrangement for settlement of international trade becomes relevant against the backdrop of aggressive hiking of policy rates (interest rate) by the US Fed Reserve in recent times and the consequent strengthening of US dollar to multi-decade high levels, resulting in weakening (depreciation) of currencies of various emerging market economies including INR. As per the *Economic Survey 2022-23*, this framework of trade settlement has the potential to bring in multiple *benefits* for the trading partners, especially for India, namely:

- To reduce the need for foreign exchange (especially, the US$) for settling trade deficits;
- To mitigate currency risk for Indian businesses;
- To reduce the need for holding forex reserves and dependence on foreign currency;
- To reduce vulnerability to external shocks; and
- To promote INR as an international currency.

One of the prerequisites for the emergence of an international currency is that the said currency needs to be increasingly used for trade settlement. In terms of foreign exchange market turnover (daily averages), as per the *BIS Triennial Central Bank Survey 2022*, the US dollar was the dominant currency (accounting for 88 per cent of the global forex turnover) while the INR accounted for 1.6 per cent. If the INR turnover rises to equal the share of non-US, non- Euro currencies in global forex turnover of 4 per cent, INR could be regarded as an international currency.

[27] Based on the discussion provided in the *Economic Survey 2016-17*, vol. 1 (New Delhi: Ministry of Finance, Government of India), pp. 6-9.

WAY FORWARD

India's external sector has performed well amidst unfavourable geopolitical conditions. To strengthen the external sector of India the *Economic Survey 2025–26* has provided[28] the following tips:

- Global trade dynamics have changed significantly in recent years, shifting from globalisation to rising trade protectionism, accompanied by increased uncertainty. This calls for a new strategic trade roadmap for India.
- To remain competitive and enhance its participation in global supply chains, India must continue reducing trade costs and improving facilitation to boost export competitiveness.
- Much remains to be done to enhance trade competitiveness. The good news is that doing so is entirely in our hands. On its part, the industry must continue to invest in quality.
- The state produces governance, and the private sector produces goods and services. If both these actors focus on quality and efficiency, then, despite the trade tensions and protectionism that are likely to come in the way of expanding global trade, India can increase its share in overseas markets and generate resources to sustain a higher level of capital formation. Then, it will be possible for us not just to dream of but actually realise higher economic growth rates on a sustained basis.

PREVIOUS YEARS' QUESTIONS

Prelims

1. Consider the following statements: (2024)

Statement-I: Recently, Venezuela has achieved a rapid recovery from its economic crisis succeeded in preventing its people from fleeing/emigrating to other countries.

Statement-II: Venezuela has the world's largest oil reserves.

Which one of the following is correct in respect of the above statements?

(a) Both Statement-I and Statement-II are correct and Statement-II explains Statement-I

(b) Both Statement-I and Statement-II are correct, but Statement-II does not explain Statement-I

(c) Statement-I is correct, but Statement-II is incorrect

(d) Statement-I is incorrect, but Statement-II is correct

Answers: 1. (d)

Explanation:

1. (d): Venezuela is still facing economic crisis and has seen rapid recovery in recent times (thus, Statement-I is incorrect) and citizens of the country are still fleeing abroad. But the country has the largest proven oil reserves of around 300 billion barrels (thus, Statement-II is correct).

[28] *Economy Survey 2025-26* (New Delhi: Ministry of Finance, GoI, January 2026), pp. 200-201.

SAMPLE OBJECTIVE QUESTIONS

1. Consider the following statements related to the external sector of the country:
   - **(i)** India's exchange rate regime is a 'stabilised arrangement' instead of floating.
   - **(ii)** India follows floating exchange rate system right since economic reforms commenced.
   - **(iii)** Rupee is fully convertible in capital account provided it is foreign investments in security market.

   How many of the above statements are correct?
   (a) Only one **(b)** Only two
   (c) All three **(d)** None of these

2. Consider the following statements related to the external debt of the country:
   - **(i)** Rupee's share of the debt is around one-third today.
   - **(ii)** Around 92 per cent of the debt is commercial and long-term in nature.
   - **(iii)** Debt service ratio is derived by dividing debt with the value of export receipts.

   How many of the above statements are correct?
   (a) Only one **(b)** Only two
   (c) All three **(d)** None of these

3. Consider the following statements related to the global position of the Indian rupee:
   - **(i)** It accounts for around 2 per cent of global forex turnover.
   - **(ii)** India started preparations to get the special drawing rights (SDRs) denominated in ₹ (Indian Rupee) by early 2010s.
   - **(iii)** The US dollar dominates global forex turnover with a share of around 92 per cent today.

   How many of the above statements are correct?
   (a) Only one **(b)** Only two
   (c) All three **(d)** None of these

4. Consider the following statements related to trade outcomes:
   - **(i)** Decline in rupee's nominal effective exchange rate results in lower exports from the country.
   - **(ii)** Inflation makes India's imports cheaper.
   - **(iii)** Rise in US dollar inflows into the country will necessarily hamper exports.

   How many of the above statements are correct?
   (a) Only one **(b)** Only two
   (c) All three **(d)** None of these

5. Consider the following statements related to the external sector of the country:
   - **(i)** Forex reserves vary as the Reserve Bank of India trades in gold.
   - **(ii)** Withdrawals from the reserve tranche depletes the forex reserves.
   - **(iii)** Higher special drawing rights (SDRs) quotas boost the forex reserves.

   How many of the above statements are correct?
   (a) Only one **(b)** Only two
   (c) All three **(d)** None of these

6. Consider the following statements related to the external sector of India:
   - **(i)** Forex reserves are taken into account in sovereign credit rating by rating agencies.
   - **(ii)** Debt cover ratio is the ratio of external debt and current account receipts.
   - **(iii)** Concessional external debts today account for around 8 per cent of the total debt.

   How many of the above statements are correct?
   (a) Only one **(b)** Only two
   (c) All three **(d)** None of these

7. Consider the following statements related to the exchange rate regime of the country:
   - **(i)** Throughout 2023 we saw the RBI intervening in the forex market of the country.
   - **(ii)** Excessive RBI intervention in forex market has made the USA and IMF term India as a currency manipulator.

(iii) India's dual exchange rate for rupee is officially recognised by the IMF as floating system.

How many of the above statements are correct?

(a) Only one **(b)** Only two
(c) All three **(d)** None of these

8. Which of the following external transactions belong to current account in the country? Select your answer by using the code given below:

(i) Inflows of portfolio investments
(ii) Import outflows of services
(iii) Inflows of the remittances
(iv) Interest payments of external debts
(v) Outflows of foreign aids
(vi) Outflows due to imports of educational services
(vii) Foreign direct investments in brownfield projects

Code:

(a) (i), (ii), (iv), (v), (vi)
(b) (ii), (iii), (iv), (v), (vi)
(c) (iii), (iv), (v), (vi), (vii)
(d) (i), (iii), (iv), (vi), (vii)

9. Consider the following statements related to currency convertibility in the country:

(i) Upto a certain level of the foreign direct investment the Indian rupee is fully convertible in foreign currencies.
(ii) Limited convertibility of Indian rupee in the capital account saves economy from external shocks.
(iii) Since the Indian rupee was made fully convertible in the current account the country has seen excessive rise in imports.

How many of the above statements are correct?

(a) Only one **(b)** Only two
(c) All three **(d)** None of these

10. Consider the following statements related to the external economy of the country:

(i) Local currency can depreciate if the country is following floating currency system.
(ii) Currency appreciation is not permitted by the IMF in those countries which follow fixed currency system.
(iii) India follows floating currency system since economic reforms commenced in the country.

How many of the above statements are correct?

(a) Only one **(b)** Only two
(c) All three **(d)** None of these

Answers: 1. (a) 2. (d) 3. (a) 4. (b) 5. (c) 6. (c) 7. (b) 8. (b) 9. (c) 10. (a)

SAMPLE SUBJECTIVE QUESTIONS

1. Critically examine India's balance of payment (BoP) management policy and give your suggestions to make the policy more resilient.

2. Briefly discuss about the recently signed PETA of India with EFTA. Why this agreement is considered a historic achievement?

3. Examine India's stand on her regional trade agreements (RTAs) and discuss about the recent initiatives taken by the Government in this regard.

4. 'Lack of full capital account convertibility of Indian Rupee has been hampering the country's foreign investment and trade prospects.' Critically examine.

5. Briefly discuss about the benefits and scope of trade settlement in the Indian Rupee. Give relevant illustrations.

SAMPLE MODEL ANSWER

1. **Briefly examine the benefits of settling trade in Indian currency (INR) and scope to internationalisation the INR.**

Ans. India took an initiative to promote trade in Indian rupee (INR) by mid-2022. The initiative aims to support the increasing interest of the global trading community in INR as an international currency. The policy framework (as put in place by the RBI) involves invoicing (billing) of exports and imports in INR at market-determined exchange rates between the currencies of the trading partner countries and settlement through special rupee vostro accounts.

The scope of such an arrangement for the settlement of international trade becomes relevant against the backdrop of aggressive hiking of policy rates (interest rates) by the US Federal Reserve in recent times and the consequent strengthening of the US dollar to multi-decade high levels, resulting in the weakening (depreciation) of currencies of various emerging market economies, including INR.

This framework of trade settlement, as per the Economic Survey 2022-23, has the potential to bring in multiple benefits for the trading partners, especially for India, such as:

- To reduce the need for foreign exchange (especially the US$) for settling trade deficits;
- To mitigate currency risk for Indian businesses;
- To reduce the need for holding forex reserves and dependence on foreign currency;
- To reduce vulnerability to external shocks; and
- To promote INR as an international currency.

This will help in internationalising the INR too, as it will get used more to settle foreign trade by other countries. As per the latest figure (Bank for International Settlement, March 2026), the INR accounted for around 1.51 per cent of the global forex turnover (while the US$ accounted for 89.2 per cent). If the INR turnover rises to equal the share of non-US, non-Euro currencies in global forex turnover of 4 per cent, the INR could be regarded as an international currency.

CHAPTER 17

International Economic Organisations and India

> If, as T. S. Eliot said, humankind cannot bear too much reality, recent events suggest that the world cannot bear too much globalisation either.*
>
> *Economic Survey 2016–17*, vol. 1 (New Delhi: Ministry of Finance, GoI), p. 7.

To watch the Author's videos on the significance of the Chapter, scan the QR Code given here

Exam Essentials...

- IMF Quota Formula

Note to the Reader...

This chapter should be read linking it to the preceding one (i.e., chapter 16) as external economy of a country will not be able to realise its potential till the international institutions/organisations are not favourable to its aspirations. Much water has flown since the IMF and World Bank started shaping the global economy– the rise and virtual fall of the WTO– and the lingering issues related to reforming the international multilateral development banks (MDBs), etc. All such aspects should be linked in a very dynamic way with the emerging challenges faced by India to have a contemporary hold on the subject matter.

In This Chapter...

INTERNATIONAL MONETARY SYSTEM

The international monetary system (IMS) refers to the customs, rules, instruments, facilities and organisations facilitating international (external) payments. Sometimes, the IMS is also referred to as an international monetary ***order*** or ***regime***[1]. The IMS can be classified according to the way in which exchange rates are determined (i.e., fixed currency regime, floating currency regime or managed exchange regime) and the form foreign reserves take (i.e., gold standard, a pure judiciary standard or a gold-exchange standard).

An IMS is considered good if it fulfils the following ***two objectives***[2] in an impartial manner:

1. maximises the flow of foreign trade and foreign investments and
2. leads to an ***equitable*** distribution of the gains from trade among the nations of the world.

The evaluation of an IMS is carried out in terms of *adjustment, liquidity* and *confidence* which it manages to wield.

Adjustment

Adjustment refers to the process by which the balance-of-payment (BoP) crises of the nations of the world (or the member nations) are corrected. A good IMS tries to minimise the cost of BoP and time for adjustment for the nations.

Liquidity

Liquidity refers to the amount of foreign currency reserves available to settle the BoP crises of the nations. A good IMS maintains as much foreign reserves to mitigate such crises of the nations without any inflationary pressures on the nations.

Confidence

Confidence refers to the faith the nations of the world should show that the adjustment mechanism of the IMS is working adequately and that foreign reserves will retain their absolute and relative values. This confidence is based on the transparent knowledge information about the IMS.

[1] D. Salvatore, *International Economics* (Hoboken, NJ: John Wiley & Sons, 2005), pp. 737–38; Samuelson and Nordhaus, *Economics* (New Delhi: Tata McGraw-Hill, 2005), pp. 609–12.

[2] D. Salvatore, *International Economics*, op. cit. p. 738.

BRETTON WOODS DEVELOPMENT

As the powerful nations of the world were hopeful of a new and more stable world order with the emergence of the UNO, they were also anxious for a more homogenous world financial order after the Second World War. The representatives of the United States, the United Kingdom and 42 other (total 44 countries) nations met at Bretton Woods, New Hampshire, USA, in July 1944 to decide a new IMS. The International Monetary Fund (IMF) and the World Bank [WB, with its first group-institution International Bank for Reconstruction and Development (IBRD)] were set up together - popularly called the ***Bretton Woods' twins***[3] - both having their headquarters in Washington DC, USA.

[3] For the new international monetary system, basically two plans were presented in the meeting - one by the US delegation led by *Harry D. White* (of the US Treasury) and the British delegation led by *John Maynard Keynes*. It was the US plan which was ultimately agreed upon.

J. M. Keynes had proposed a more impartial, practical and over-arching idea *via* his plan at Bretton Woods. His suggestions basically included three things:

(i) Proposal to set up an International Clearing Union (ICU), a central bank of all central banks, with its own currency (Keynes named this currency *'Bancor'*) - to mitigate the balance of payment crises of member nations.

This bank was supposed to penalise (no *such provision in the IMF*) the countries holding trade surpluses (with a global tax of one per cent per month) on the ground that such countries were keeping world demand low by under purchasing the products produced by other countries. The corpus collected *via* this tax was to be used to maintain an international buffer stock of primary goods (i.e., food articles) - to be used in the periods of food shortages among the member nations. (*In place, under the IMF provisions trade deficit countries are penalised.*)

(ii) For the reconstruction of war-devastated Europe, a *fund* was to be set up, on the basis of this plan for Relief and Reconstruction (in place of it the US-sponsored *Marshall Plan* took care of the needs of Europe).

(iii) There was a proposal of creating Commodity Buffer Stock to be operated by an International Trade Organisation (ITO). This stock of primary goods was to be used to stabilise their prices in the international market.

The operation of this ITO was making purchases when the world prices were low and selling when the prices became

INTERNATIONAL MONETARY FUND

The International Monetary Fund (IMF) was formed in 1944 and became operative on 27 December, 1945, with the main functions as exchange rate regulation, purchasing short-term foreign currency liabilities of the member nations from around the world, allotting special drawing rights (SDRs) to the member nations and the most important one as the bailor to the member economies in the situation of any BoP crisis.

The ***main functions***[4] of the IMF are given below:

1. to facilitate international monetary cooperation;
2. to promote exchange rate stability and orderly exchange arrangements;
3. to assist in the establishment of a multilateral system of payments and the elimination of foreign exchange restrictions and;
4. to assist member countries by temporarily providing financial resources to correct mal-adjustment in their BoP.

The Board of Governors of the IMF consists of one Governor and one Alternate Governor from each member country. For India, the finance minister is the *Ex-officio* Governor while the RBI Governor is the Alternate Governor on the Board.

The day-to-day management of the IMF is carried out by the Managing Director who is Chairman of the Board of Executive Directors. The Board of Executive Directors consists of 24 directors appointed/elected by member countries/group of countries is the executive body of the IMF. India is represented at the IMF by an Executive Director, who also represents three other countries in India's constituency, *viz.* Bangladesh, Sri Lanka and Bhutan.

high. The buffer stock operations, however, were to be helpful to the poor countries. Keynes was primarily interested in stabilising the input prices of the rich countries. (*Though the Charter of the ITO was drawn up and other formalities completed, it was never born because of US opposition.*) *For further reading, see* D. Salvatore, *International Economics,* pp. 742-3; B. Dasgupta, *Globalisation: India's Adjustment Experience* (New Delhi: Sage, 2005), p. 48.

[4] *Basic Facts About the United Nations* (New York, NY: United Nations, 2000), pp. 55-137.

India's Quota and Ranking

The IMF reviews members' quotas once every five years - last carried out in December 2010 - here, India consented for its quota increase. To support member nations tide over the economic constraints caused by the COVID-19 pandemic, IMF made an additional allocation of SDRs (Special Drawing Rights) on August 23, 2021. Under this, India was allocated SDR 12.57 billion (equivalent to around US$ 17.86 billion at the latest exchange rate). Thus, the total SDR holdings of India now stands at SDR 13.66 billion (equivalent to around **US$ 19.41 billion** at the latest exchange rate). India's current share in SDRs stands at 2.75 per cent. While 25 per cent of the quota is to be paid in ***cash*** (i.e., in 'Reserve' currency), the remaining 75 per cent can be paid in ***securities***.[5]

Once a member nation has signed the ***EFF*** (Extended Fund Facility) agreement with the IMF, borrowing[6] can be carried out by the member nation - India signed this agreement in the fiscal year 1981-82. ***India has been borrowing*** from the IMF due to critical BoP situations - once between 1981 and 1984 (SDR 3.9 billion) and next in 1991 (SDR 3.56 billion). India is now a *contributor* to the IMF as it has been participating in the Financial Transactions Plan (FTP)[7] of the IMF since September 2002 - at this time India was in a strong BoP situation and in a comfortable forex reserves position.

Current US/EU Financial Crises: Challenges Regarding International Payments

The recent financial crises of the United States and the EU nations have raised the questions of the challenges of international payments once again. At this crucial

[5] These securities are non-interest-bearing note purchase agreements issued by the RBI which can be encashed by the IMF anytime as per its requirement. They do not entail any cash outgo unless the IMF calls upon India to encash a portion of these notes. The 'Reserve' (paid in 'cash') asset portion of the quota is counted as a part of a country's 'Reserves'.

[6] Such facility from it is available once the member country has signed the agreement with the IMF called the Extended Fund Facility (EFF). Popularly, this is known as the '*Conditionalities of the IMF*' under which India started its Economic Reform Programme in 1991-92 once it borrowed from the IMF in the wake of the BoP crisis of 1990-91.

[7] FTP is the mechanism of the IMF through which it finances/repays its operations - member nations contribute money into it from their 'quota resources' on which they get 'interest'.

IMF Quota Formula

IMF quota (agreed in 2008) is broadly based on a member's "relative position in the world economy", which is decided[8] on the basis of the following variables with their assigned weights:

- Weighted average of GDP (50 per cent),
- Openness to the global economy (30 per cent),
- Economic variability (15 per cent), and
- International reserves (5 per cent).

For this purpose, GDP is measured through a blend of GDP based on market exchange rates (weight of 60 per cent) and on purchasing-power-parity (PPP) exchange rates (40 per cent). The formula also includes a 'compression factor' that reduces the dispersion in calculated quota shares across members.

juncture, the world seems tossing the idea of a reserved currency for all international payments - as if the famous Keynesian idea of such a currency (Bancor) is moving towards a kind of revival. The **Bancor** was a supranational currency that John Maynard Keynes and E. F. Schumacher[9] conceptualised in the period 1940-42, which the United Kingdom proposed to introduce after the Second World War. The proposed currency was to be used in international trade as a unit of account within a multilateral barter clearing system, the *International Clearing Union,* which would also have to be founded. The Bancor was to be backed by barter and its value expressed in weight of gold. However, this British proposal could not prevail against the interests of the United States, which at the Bretton Woods conference established the US Dollar as the world key currency. Milton Friedman[10], the famous US economist, insisted that Keynes' theories were incorrect who believed that, 'inflation was highly destructive and that only monetary policy could control it and that monetary policy is a heavyweight instrument and cannot be used for short-term economic management'.

[8] *International Monetary Fund,* Washington DC, March 2025.

[9] E. F. Schumacher, *Multilateral Clearing Economica, New Series,* vol. 10, no. 38 (May, 1943), pp. 150-65.

[10] M. Friedman, *The American Economic Review,* vol. 58, no. 1 (1968), pp. 1-17.

Since the outbreak of the financial crisis in 2008, ***Keynes's proposal*** was revived - in a speech delivered in March 2009 entitled *Reform the International Monetary System,* Zhou Xiaochuan, the Governor of the People's Bank of China, called Keynes's Bancor approach **farsighted** and proposed the adoption of IMF SDRs as a global reserve currency as a response to the financial crisis of 2007-08. He argued that a national currency was unsuitable as a global reserve currency because of the *Triffin dilemma*[11] - the difficulty faced by reserve currency issuers in trying to simultaneously achieve their domestic monetary policy goals and meet other countries' demand for reserve currency.[12] A similar analysis was articulated in the Report of the United Nation's *Experts on Reforms of the International Monetary and Financial System*[13] as well as in a recent IMF study.[14]

WORLD BANK

The World Bank (WB) Group today consists of ***five*** closely associated institutions propitiating the role of development in the member nations in different areas. A brief account is as follows.[15]

International Bank for Reconstruction and Development (IBRD)

The International Bank for Reconstruction and Development (IBRD) is the oldest of the WB institutions which started functioning (1945) in the area of reconstruction of the war-ravaged regions (Second World War) and later for the development of the middle-income and credit-worthy poorer economies of the world. Human development was the main focus of the developmental lending with a very low interest rate (1.55 per cent per annum) - the

[11] Z. Xiaochuan, "Reform the International Monetary System," *BIS Review 2009* (Basil, Switzerland: Bank of International Settlements, 28 November, 2011).

[12] Z. Xiaochuan, *Financial Times,* 12 December 2011.

[13] Recommendations by the Commission of Experts of the President of the General Assembly on reforms of the international monetary and financial system, UNO, 20 March 2009.

[14] *Reserve Accumulation and International Monetary Stability, IMF,* Washington DC, 13 April 2010.

[15] Based on *Basic Facts About the United Nations,* pp. 52-5; Publication Division, *India 2004* (New Delhi: Government of India, 2007); Publication Division, *India 2013* (New Delhi: Government of India, 2014).

areas of focus being agriculture, irrigation, urban development, healthcare, family welfare, dairy development and so on. It commenced lending for India in 1949.

After the process of reforms started in the WB in 2010, India was allotted additional shares in the IBRD (now holds 56,739 shares accounting to US$ 6,844.7 million). With this India emerged as the 7th largest shareholder (up from the 11th position) in IBRD with voting power of 2.91 per cent (up from 2.77 per cent).[16]

International Development Agency (IDA)

The International Development Agency (IDA), which is also known as the *soft window* of the WB, was set up in 1960 with the basic aim of developing infrastructural support among the member nations and long-term lending for the development of economic services. Its loans, known as ***credits***, are extended mainly to economies with less than $895 per capita income. The credits are for a period of 35-40 years, ***interest-free***, except for a small charge to cover administrative costs. Repayment begins after a 10-year grace period. In the beginning there was a human angle to its lending, but now there remain no hard and fast differences between the purposes for the IBRD and IDA lending.

Every year developing nations make enough diplomatic attempts to carve out maximum loan disbursal for themselves. India had been the ***biggest beneficiary*** of the IDA support. The total support (IBRD + IDA) for India had been $ 91.81 billion till date.[17] Since 2015, India did not avail any financial support from the IDA as it 'graduated' from the agency in the financial year 2014.[18]

International Finance Corporation (IFC)

The International Finance Corporation (IFC) was set up in 1956, which is also known as the *private arm* of the WB. It lends money to private sector companies of its member nations. The interest rate charged is commercial but comparatively low. There are many attractive features of IFC's lending. It finances and provides advice for private-public ventures and projects in partnership with private investors and, through its advisory work, helps governments of the member nations to create conditions that stimulate the flow of both domestic and foreign private savings and investment.

The IFC focuses on promoting economic development by encouraging the growth of productive enterprises and efficient capital markets in its member countries. It participates in an investment only when it can make a special contribution that complements the role of market investors [as a foreign financial investor (FFI)]. It also plays a catalytic role, stimulating and mobilising private investment in the developing world by demonstrating that investments there, too, can be profitable.

We have seen a great upsurge in the IFC investments in India which has undoubtedly strengthened the foreign investors' confidence in the Indian economy.

Multilateral Investment Guarantee Agency (MIGA)

The Multilateral Investment Guarantee Agency (MIGA), set up in 1988, encourages foreign investment in developing economies by offering insurance (guarantees) to foreign private investors against loss caused by *non-commercial (i.e., political) risks*, such as currency transfer, expropriation, war and civil disturbance. It also provides technical assistance to help countries disseminate information on investment opportunities.

International Centre for Settlement of Investment Disputes (ICSID)

The International Centre for Settlement of Investment Disputes (ICSID), set up in 1966, is an investment dispute settlement body whose decisions are binding on the parties. It was established under the 1966 *Convention on the Settlement of Investment Disputes between States and Nationals of Other States*. Though recourse to the centre is voluntary, once the parties have agreed to arbitration, they cannot withdraw their consent unilaterally. It settles the investment disputes arising between the investing foreign companies and the host countries where the investments have been made.

India is not its member (that is why the Enron issue was out of its preview). It is believed that being

---

[16] Publication Division, *India 2014* (New Delhi: Government of India, 2015), p. 322.

[17] Publication Division, *India 2013*, (New Delhi: Government of India) p. 415.

[18] International Development Agency, World Bank, Washington DC, USA, March 2019.

signatory to it encourages the foreign investment flows into an economy, but risks independent sovereign decisions, too.

ASIAN DEVELOPMENT BANK

Set up in 1966 with 31 founding members (India being one of them), by *March 2017* it has grown to encompass 67 members of which 48 are from the Asia-Pacific region and 19 from outside. It has its headquarters situated at Manila, Philippines.

The *purpose* of the Bank is to foster economic growth and co-operation in the region of Asia and the Far East and to contribute to economic development of the developing member countries, collectively and individually. The *major functions* of the Bank are listed below:

1. Promoting investment - public and private - and harmonious regional development with special regard to less developed member countries;
2. Co-ordinating development policies and plans (on request); promoting intraregional trade; providing technical assistance in financing, execution and project proposals;
3. Co-operating with the UNO and other international institutions - public and private - and undertaking other activities and provide other services advancing its purpose.

India's subscription to the Bank's capital stock is 6.331 per cent with a voting power of 5.363 per cent (as per the *ADB Annual Report, 2020*). India started borrowing from ADB's Ordinary Capital Resources (OCR) in 1986. The Bank's lending has been mainly in the energy, transport and communications, finance, industry and social infrastructure sectors.

The Bank has extended technical assistance to India in addition to loans from its OCR window. The technical assistance provided includes support for institutional strengthening, effective project implementation and policy reforms as well as project preparation.

India holds the position of Executive Director on the Board of Directors of the Bank - its constituency comprises India, Bangladesh, Bhutan, Lao PDR and Tajikistan. The Union Finance Minister is India's Governor on the Board of Governors of the Asian Development Bank (ADB) and Secretary, Department of Economic Affairs, is the Alternate Governor.

ORGANISATION FOR ECONOMIC CO-OPERATION AND DEVELOPMENT (OECD)

The roots[19] of the Organisation for Economic Co-operation and Development (OECD), Paris, go back to the rubble of Europe after the Second World War. Determined to avoid the mistakes of their predecessors in the wake of the First World War, European leaders realised that the best way to ensure lasting peace was to encourage co-operation and reconstruction, rather than punish the defeated.

The Organisation for European Economic Co-operation (OEEC) was established in 1947 to run the US-financed **Marshall Plan** for reconstruction of a continent ravaged by war. By making individual governments recognise the interdependence of their economies, it paved the way for a new era of cooperation that was to change the face of Europe. Encouraged by its success and the prospect of carrying its work forward on a global stage, Canada and the United States joined OEEC members in signing the new OECD Convention on 14 December, 1960. The OECD was officially born on September 30, 1961, when the Convention entered into force.

Other countries joined in, starting with Japan in 1964. Today, **38** OECD member countries worldwide regularly turn to one another to identify problems, discuss and analyse them, and promote policies to solve them. The track record is striking. The United States has seen its national wealth almost *triple* in the five decades since the OECD was created, calculated in terms of gross domestic product per head of population. Other OECD countries have seen similar, and in some cases even more spectacular progress.

There are many countries that a few decades ago were still only minor players on the world stage - China, India and Brazil have emerged as new economic giants. Most of the countries that formed part of the former Soviet bloc have either joined the OECD or adopted its standards and principles to achieve the common goals. Russia is negotiating to become a member of the OECD, and now the organisation has close relations with Brazil, China, India, Indonesia and South Africa through its 'enhanced engagement' programme. Together with them, the OECD brings around its table **40** countries that account for **80** per cent of

[19] Publication Division, *India 2012* (New Delhi: Government of India, 2013), p. 418.

world trade and investment, giving it a pivotal role in addressing the challenges facing the world economy.

India and the OECD India has 'enhanced engagement' (since 2007) with the body; however, 'accession' (membership) to it is distinct - though it has the potential in future leading to it. The accession process to it is complex and longer as it involves a series of examinations to assess a country's ability to meet its OECD standards in a wide range of policy areas. Meanwhile, India's relationship with the OECD has developed steadily since 1998 (when it joined its Steel Committee) - since 2007 being its 'Key Partner'. Since 2017, India has been participating as an *Associate* or *Participant* in 21 OECD bodies and adheres to 9 OECD legal instruments, making it an important contributor to several areas of importance - from corporate governance to fiscal matters to nuclear energy. Furthermore, India plays an active role in OECD's regional activities in Asia together with co-operation on various international fora.

WORLD TRADE ORGANIZATION (WTO)

The WTO came into being as a result of the evolution of the multilateral trading system starting with the establishment of the General Agreement on Tariffs and Trade (GATT) in 1947. The protracted Uruguay Round negotiations spanning the period 1986-94, which resulted in the establishment of the WTO, substantially extended the reach of multilateral rules and disciplines related to trade in goods, and introduced multilateral rules applicable to trade in agriculture (Agreement on Agriculture - AoA), trade in services (General Agreement on Trade in Services - GATS) as well as Trade Related Intellectual Property Rights (TRIPS). A separate understanding on WTO dispute settlement mechanism (DSM) and trade policy review mechanism (TPRM) was also agreed upon.

The WTO provides a rule-based, transparent and predictable multilateral trading system. The WTO rules envisage non-discrimination in the form of National Treatment and ***Most Favoured Nation (MFN)*** treatment to India's exports in the markets of other WTO members. National Treatment ensures that India's products, once imported into the territory of other WTO members, would not be discriminated *vis-à-vis* the domestic products in those countries. The MFN treatment principle ensures that members do not discriminate among various WTO members. If a member country believes that the due benefits are not accruing to it because of trade measures by another WTO member, which are violative of WTO rules and disciplines, it may file a dispute under the DSM of the WTO. There are also contingency provisions built into WTO rules, enabling member countries to take care of exigencies like BoP problems and situations like a surge in imports. In the case of unfair trade practices causing injury to the domestic producers, there are provisions to impose Anti-Dumping or Countervailing duties as provided for in the Anti-Dumping Agreement and the Subsidies and Countervailing Measures Agreement.

Membership The present membership[20] of the WTO is **166** (at its 13th Ministerial Conference in Abu Dhabi, two new members *Comoros* and *Timor Leste* were approved to become its 165th and 166th members). Besides its members, at present there are 23 observer governments. In addition to states, the European Union, and each EU country in its own right, is a member.

Ministerial Conferences Ministerial Conferences are the highest decision-making body of the WTO which is to meet at least every two years. These conferences bring all members together which are countries or separate customs territories. During these conferences, decisions on all matters can be taken. By now, **13** such conferences of the body have taken place - the last being *13th Ministerial Conference (MC13)* took place in Abu Dhabi, UAE (26-29 February 2024). Cameroon will host the **14th** Ministerial Conference (MC14) during 26-29 March 2026.

Previous Conferences *Geneva, Switzerland* (12-17 June, 2022); *Buenos Aires,* Argentina (10-13 December 2017); *Nairobi* (15-19 December 2015); *Bali* (3-6 December 2013); *Geneva* (15-17 December 2011); *Geneva* (30 November - 2 December 2009); *Hong Kong* (13-18 December 2005); *Cancun* (10-14 September 2003); *Doha* (9-13 November 2001); *Seattle* (30 November- 3 December 1999); *Geneva* (18-20 May 1998) and *Singapore* (9-13 December 1996).

Abu Dhabi Deal The 13th Ministerial Conference (MC13) of the WTO was held in Abu Dhabi, UAE

[20] As per the WTO website, February 2025.

between 26-29 February, 2024. A brief summary of the agreements[21] reached (popular as *the Abu Dhabi Package*) at the conference is being given below:

Agriculture No agreement was reached. India had sought a permanent solution on public stockholding (PSH), which refers to state policies on food procurement aimed at ensuring food security.

Two alternative solutions were envisaged in a draft agreement. One aimed to find a permanent solution to the issue while the other commits to intensify negotiations and extend to other developing countries the privileges only India currently enjoys under WTO rules (i.e., the 'peace clause' agreed at the 10th Ministerial Conference, Bali, 2013). The second solution was rejected by India as the country always wanted the first solution.

Fisheries No deal could be reached. Countries tried to agree to curb government subsidies that critics say encourage industrial fishing fleets to empty the world's oceans. A draft programme was agreed for future work beyond Abu Dhabi.

e-Commerce Countries agreed to extend a moratorium on placing tariffs on digital goods until the next ministerial conference. India and South Africa were opposed to the extension of a moratorium on e-commerce backed by the vast majority of countries which see it as vital to businesses to avoid tariffs on digital goods like film downloads.

Dispute Settlement Countries agreed to commit to continue negotiations in 2024 to try to resolve a crisis in its dispute settlement system which is non-operative since the USA vetoed it 4 years back. It means trade disputes to remain unresolved in void of the dispute settlement body (DSB).

BRICS BANK

Together with the process of globalisation, world regional forces have also been asserting their power through different short of alignments - the *Fortaleza Declaration* of heads of state (late July 2014) from Brazil, Russia, India, China and South Africa (the BRICS countries) is another such attempt - creation of a BRICS Bank, that is New Development Bank (NDB). Major highlights of the bank are given below:

1. The bank will have initial subscribed capital of \$50 billion - equally shared by the five nations.
2. The capital base is to be used for funding infrastructure and 'sustainable development' projects in the BRICS countries initially.
3. Other low- and middle-income countries will be able to receive funding as time progresses.
4. A *Contingent Reserve Arrangement* (CRA) of \$100 billion is to be also created to provide additional liquidity protection to member-nations during BoP problems.
5. The CRA is being funded 41 per cent by China, 18 per cent each from Brazil, India and Russia and 5 per cent from South Africa.
6. The CRA, according to the Declaration, is a framework for the provision of *currency swaps* in response to actual or potential short-term BoP (Balance of Payment) pressures.

More than the establishment of the NDB, the Fortaleza Declaration is remarkable for adoption of ***one-nation one-vote*** prescription for the proposed bank. The Bretton Woods institutions (the WB and the IMF) have structures that are not equitable.

As per the experts, *two factors* triggered the birth of the NDB:

1. BRICS have *emerged as a big economic power,* and solidified their ties in terms of commerce with the emerging market economies and developing countries (EMDCs) and they are a force to be reckoned with in the global economy.
2. Their *disenchantment* with the Bretton Woods institutions has been growing over the years.

Two statements of the *Fortaleza Declaration* make the situation clearer:

1. 'We are confronted with persistent political instability and conflict in various global hotspots and nonconventional emerging threats. On the other hand, international governance structures designed within a different power configuration show increasingly evident signs of losing legitimacy and effectiveness, as transitional and ad hoc arrangements become increasingly prevalent, often at the expense of multilateralism'.

[21] World Trade Organisation, *13th Ministerial Conference,* 26-29 February 2024, Abu Dhabi, UAE.

2. 'We believe the BRICS are an important force for incremental change and reform of current institutions towards more representative and equitable governance, capable of generating more inclusive global growth and fostering a stable, peaceful and prosperous world'.

The BRICS bank development comes at a time when reforms at the Bretton Woods institutions fail to fructify for one reason or the other and with the US and European nations still not reconciled to concede BRICS nations a greater voice in the governance structure of the Bretton Woods institutions.

Whether the BRICS-sponsored NDB will be a fitting alternative to the Bretton Woods twin depends on a host of factors. These major factors, among others, are its ability:

1. to put in place a conflict resolution mechanism,
2. to devise a robust credit appraisal mechanism, and
3. to put in place an effective supervisory regime.

The BRICS-sponsored development bank is not an isolated and unique initiative. Similar initiatives had sprung up in the past to blunt the might of Bretton Woods twin. The *Development Bank of Latin America* (created by *Andean* nations) in the 1960s, the Chiang Mai Initiative in the early 2000s (of 10 ASEAN nations plus China, South Korea and Japan) to establish a network of bilateral *currency swap pacts* in the wake of Asian currency crisis, and the establishment of the *Bank of South* by Latin American countries in 2009 were the result of escalating dissatisfaction with the US-dominated IMF and WB.

India and the NDB India is supposed to be the biggest beneficiary of the bank. This seems quite possible as certain priorities of India match well with the priorities and lending provisions of the bank such as the bank aims at prioritising environmentally sustainable projects (75 per cent of its funds dedicated to this cause alone) while India is working today on the world's biggest plan of promoting 'green energy' through multiple means. By ***February 2026***, India had availed a total fund of US$ 8.6 billion (inclusive of 'COVID-19 Emergency Program Loan' of US$1 billion) to promote projects across a variety of sectors such as renewable and green energy, transportation (roads and bridges), etc.

ASIAN INFRASTRUCTURE INVESTMENT BANK (AIIB)

The Asian Infrastructure Investment Bank (AIIB) was officially launched in 2014 by China with 21 Asian nations as the founding members. By *September 2024*, the bank had a total of 110 members (regional and non-regional) from across the world (including 14 prospective members). Still, the United States and Japan have not joined it, however, experts suggested them to support it, especially when the existing mechanism (the World Bank and Asian Development Bank) is not able to cater to the infrastructural needs of the continent.

The AIIB is aimed at providing finance to infrastructure projects in the Asia region, as a multilateral institution. It is planned to operate broadly in the same manner as existing multilateral development banks (MDBs) such as the WB and the ADB. While much of the debate is centred on whether the AIIB will complement or compete with existing organisations, it is intended to be more a commercial bank - with nations as shareholders, than a purely development aid institution. In the wake of the COVID-19 pandemic a proposal under consideration as per which the bank may also start financing social infrastructures. The AIIB will start with an authorised **capital base** of US$ 1 billion to be enhanced to **US$ 100 billion**.

Experts have termed it as a rival for the IMF, the WB and the ADB, which are regarded as dominated by developed countries like the United States.[22] The United Nations has addressed the launch of the AIIB as 'scaling up financing for sustainable development' and for the concern of Global Economic Governance.[23]

As per the experts and analysts, there are **several factors** which are behind such an initiative coming from China. The major ones are given below:

1. The Chinese Government has been frustrated with what it regards as the slow pace of reforms and governance, and wants greater input in global established institutions such as the IMF,

[22] *The Guardian*, 'Support for China-led development bank grows despite US opposition', UK edition, 13 March 2015.

[23] United Nations Financing for Development Office, 'Global Economic Governance', New York, 20 March 2015.

WB and ADB which, it claims, are dominated by American, European and Japanese interests.

2. The ADB, a Manila-based regional development bank designed to facilitate economic development in Asia, estimated in a report that developing Asian countries have an infrastructure demand of about US$ 8 trillion between 2010 and 2020 - $2.5 trillion for roads and railroads, $4.1 trillion for power plants and transmission, $1.1 trillion for telecommunications and $0.4 trillion for water and sanitation investments.[24]
3. Oxford Economics reported that by 2025, the region will constitute 60 per cent of global infrastructure investment, with China's share alone expected to increase from around 22 per cent to 36 per cent over the next decade.
4. Despite the significant economic growth enjoyed by countries such as China, India and South Korea in recent decades, many countries among the developing Asian regions are still mired in poverty, suffering from a profound lack of access to modern-day necessities such as sanitation, a reliable power grid and adequate transportation and communications networks.
5. It is believed that the new bank could allow Chinese capital to finance these projects and allow it a greater role to play in the economic development of the region commensurate with its growing economic and political clout.

Size of the AIIB Based on the lending capital ratios of the WB and European Development Bank, the AIIB could extend loans for infrastructure spending at around 100 per cent to 175 per cent of its subscribed capital. This would mean having outstanding loans of up to US$ 175 billion. With Public-Private Partnerships and increased subscriptions, considerably larger amounts could be leveraged for projects in the future.

An edge to China The Bank is supposed to give China an edge in the global economy in the following ways:

1. The AIIB will be a better way for China to deploy its massive foreign exchange reserves which are currently earning next to nothing in US Treasury bonds. China believes that the commercial financing of infrastructure differentiates the AIIB from the likes of the ADB which places a greater emphasis on poverty reduction.
2. The AIIB also supports China's strategic interests in its hugely ambitious 'Silk Road Economic Belt' policy.
3. By exporting technology, transferring development know-how and facilitating industrialisation using Chinese long-term finance to the under-developed economies, China will not only find a bigger market, promote prosperity of all nations along the 'Belt and Road', but also diversify its foreign asset portfolio.
4. It will make China emerge as a much bigger global power player which is supposed to be keen to challenge America's long-established strategy of institutionalising power in a rules-based order. The case of the AIIB shows that China now seeks to define this order for itself, with the battle for influence in Asia increasingly fought through rules and institutions.
5. The so-called 'rules-based order' was set up after the Second World War through policies such as the Bretton Woods agreement which established US-dominated organisations such as the WB and IMF in which China plays a minor role.

India and the AIIB India is one of the 21 founding members of the bank and is believed to benefit the most from it. India holds 8.6794 per cent of its shares (with a total investment of US$ 8.3673 billion) and avails a 7.614 per cent voting rights (with a total of 86,214 shares) in it. India's shareholding is the *second highest* after China which holds 30.8913 per cent shares.

India is presently the *largest* borrower (over one-third of the total loans forwarded) of the bank - for diverse projects it had borrowed a total of US$ 10.0 billion till ***February 2026*** with many more infra projects in the pipeline under consideration. Unlike most other MDBs set up by developed countries, the AIIB is the first major MDB where principal contributors are the borrowing members themselves.

[24] *The Economist*, 'An Asian Infrastructure Bank: Only Connect', 4 October 2013; B. N. Bhattacharya, *Estimating Demand for Infrastructure in Energy, Transport, Telecommunications, Water and Sanitation in Asia and the Pacific: 2010-2020* (London, UK: Asian Development Bank Institute, 9 September 2010).

REFORMING IMF AND WB

Demand for suitable reforms in the Bretton Woods institutions - IMF and WB - is long overdue. Majority of the experts believe that the disillusionment from the delay in reforming them led the emerging market economies to look into alternatives and the outcome was the creation of the two new international financial institutions, the AIIB and NDB. The biggest hurdle in the path of reforms, the United States, at last came in favour of reforms (by early 2017) after the G20 Summit on it had already commenced (London, 2016). The *major reforms proposed* in the IMF and WB are given below[25]:

Scan this QR Code to watch a author's video lecture that simplifies this topic

1. **Reforms in the IMF:** Proposal of a far-reaching reform of the IMF in order to restore its legitimacy and effectiveness so that it can help member nations fight immediate and future crises, touching the following areas:
   - **(i)** Increasing its resource base so that it is able to help out (bail out in the case of BoP situations) nations in times of crisis. G20 wishes to increase its resources from the current level of US$ 250 billion to US$ 750 billion. It should be remembered that just after the 'sub-prime crisis' of 2008, the WB had estimated the resource shortfall of up to US$ 700 billion in 2009 alone!
   - **(ii)** Merit-based selection of the head of the IMF, irrespective of nationality.
   - **(iii)** Eliminating the veto of the United States in key decisions.
   - **(iv)** Broadening the application of double majority voting as a way to increase the role of smaller members.
   - **(v)** Revising the rule of quota and vote distribution to reflect accurately and fairly the current and future economic weight of the members.
   - **(vi)** Transforming its Board of Directors from a bureaucratic body to a high-level policy decision-making forum of ministers.
2. **Reforms in the WB:** In the case of the WB, the following reforms have been proposed:
   - **(i)** Need of shareholders to replenish the capital base for 'soft' loans (while the IDA disburses interest-free, the IBRD disburses concessional loans to the eligible member nations and in recent years the WB has faced a resource crunch as several developed countries, especially the United States, proposed fund cuts).
   - **(ii)** Merit-based selection of the WB President - without regard to nationality.
   - **(iii)** Revamping of shareholdings and voting rights in the executive boards (to give a greater voice to emerging market economies and to borrowers).
   - **(iv)** Overhauling its operational modalities (so that it can react with less bureaucratic and time-consuming burdens to the legitimate needs of its borrowers).

It is believed that the successful launching and operation of the AIIB and NDB played an instrumental role in expediting the process of deliberations on reforming the IMF and WB. For reforms to take place, the United States and Europe will need to move away from their long-held positions towards these institutions which look a little difficult as nations have their own priorities to support the moves towards reforms.

[25] The write-up is based on multiple sources *(up to February 2026)* such as *The Economist, The Guardian, The Wall Street Journal*, several volumes of the *Economic Survey of India* and other media sources.

PREVIOUS YEARS' QUESTIONS

Prelims

1. Which one of the following launched the 'Nature Solutions Finance Hub for Asia and the Pacific'? (2025)
   (a) The Asian Development Bank (ADB)
   (b) The Asian Infrastructure Investment Bank (AIIB)
   (c) The New Development Bank (NDB)
   (d) The International Bank for Reconstruction and Development (IBRD)

2. Consider the following statements in respect of BIMSTEC: (2025)
   (i) It is a regional organisation consisting of seven member states till January 2025.
   (ii) It came into existence with the signing of the Dhaka Declaration, 1999.
   (iii) Bangladesh, India, Sri Lanka, Thailand and Nepal are founding member states of BIMSTEC.
   (iv) In BIMSTEC, the subsector of 'tourism' is being led by India.

   Which of the statements given above is/are correct?
   (a) (i) and (ii) (b) (ii) and (iii)
   (c) (i) and (iv) (d) (i) only

3. Consider the following statements with regard to BRICS" (2025)
   (i) The 16th BRICS summit was held under the chairmanship of Russia in Kazan.
   (ii) Indonesia has become a full member of BRICS.
   (iii) The theme of the 16th BRICS summit was strengthening multiculturalism for just global development and security.

   Which of the statements given above is/are correct?
   (a) (i) and (ii) (b) (ii) and (iii)
   (c) (i) and (iii) (d) (i) only

4. Consider the following statements in respect of the International Bank for Reconstruction and Development (IBRD): (2025)
   (i) It provides loans and guarantees to middle-income countries.
   (ii) It works single-handedly to help developing countries to reduce poverty.
   (iii) It was established to help Europe rebuild after World War II.

   Which of the statements given above are correct?
   (a) (i) and (ii) only (b) (ii) and (iii) only
   (c) (i) and (iii) only (d) (i), (ii) and (iii)

Answers: 1. (a) 2. (d) 3. (a) 4. (c)

Explanation

1. (a): The ADB unveiled this hub at COP28 with the goal of attracting significant investments in nature-based solutions projects across the Asia Pacific region.

2. (d): The Bay of Bengal Initiative for Multi-Sectoral Technical and Economic Cooperation (BIMSTEC) is a multilateral regional organisation established with the aim of accelerating shared growth and cooperation between littoral and adjacent countries in the Bay of Bengal region. It is a 7-member forum (thus, *Statement-I* is correct). BIMSTEC was originally formed as BIST-EC in June 1997, with Bangladesh, India, Sri Lanka and Thailand as the founding members, and its tourism sub-sector is led by Nepal and not India (thus, *Statements-II, III, and IV* are incorrect).

3. (a): The BRICS is a forum for cooperation among a group of leading emerging economies with Brazil, Russia, India, China, and South Africa as the original 5 members (today, it includes 5 additional countries–Egypt, Ethiopia, Indonesia, South Africa, and the United Arab Emirates). Its 16th Summit in Kazan, Russia, was chaired by Russia (thus, *Statements-I and II* are correct), which had "Strengthening Multilateralism for Just Global Development and Security" as its theme (thus, *Statement-III* is incorrect).

4. (c): Statements-I and III are correct, while Statement-II is incorrect (this is not the sole body helping developing countries to reduce poverty).

SAMPLE OBJECTIVE QUESTIONS

1. Consider the following statements related to India's interaction with the International Monetary Fund:
   (i) Lower SDRs quota of India has made its reserve tranche position lower than its current transactional requirements.
   (ii) India can withdraw its SDR quota in any of the hard currencies besides the Indian rupee.
   (iii) Borrowing from the reserve tranche is interest free for India.

   How many of the above statements are correct?
   (a) Only one (b) Only two
   (c) All three (d) None of these

2. Consider the following statements related to the global multilateral financial institutions:
   (i) The World Bank has enough corpus of fund to help infrastructural development in Asia.
   (ii) Bretton Woods institutions can raise more funds for development by revising the members' SDR quotas.
   (iii) India is the second highest stakeholder in the Asian Infrastructure Investment Bank floated by China.

   How many of the above statements are correct?
   (a) Only one (b) Only two
   (c) All three (d) None of these

3. Consider the following statements related to the recently concluded Abu Dhabi ministerial conference of the WTO:
   (i) Countries agreed to extend moratorium on tariff provisions for the digital items.
   (ii) The 'peace clause' of agricultural subsidies devised for India has been extended for all developing countries facing food security challenge.
   (iii) Curbing public fisheries subsidies could not be resolved.

   How many of the above statements are correct?
   (a) Only one (b) Only two
   (c) All three (d) None of these

4. Consider the following statements related to a good international monetary system:
   (i) It should be able to resolve and minimise the cost of balance of payment crises for the members.
   (ii) It should be adequately funded to infuse development funds to the members.
   (iii) It should be able to promote equitable distribution of gains from trade among the members.

   How many of the above statements are correct?
   (a) Only one (b) Only two
   (c) All three (d) None of these

5. Consider the following statements related to the formula used by the International Monetary Fund (IMF) to allot quotas to its members:
   (i) Members are allotted quota based on their 'relative strength' in the world economy.
   (ii) GDP carries 50 per cent weight in this formula.
   (iii) Forex reserves carry around 10 per cent eight in the formula.
   (iv) The formula was last revised in 2021.

   How many of the above statements are correct?
   (a) Only one (b) Only two
   (c) Only three (d) All four

6. Consider the following statements related to promotion and protection of foreign investments in the world:
   (i) The Multilateral Investment Guarantee Agency (MIGA) insures foreign investors against losses caused by all forms of risks.
   (ii) India has signed bilateral agreements to insure the losses of such investments caused by non-commercial risks.
   (iii) Bilateral Investment Promotion and Protection Agreements serve better purpose for India than the International Centre for Settlement of Investment Disputes (ICSID).
   (iv) India has opted out of the membership of the MIGA and ICSID.

How many of the above statements are correct?
(a) Only one **(b)** Only two
(c) Only three **(d)** All four

7. Consider the following statements related to the International Monetary Fund (IMF):
(i) The Fund can lend any amount of funds to members to address the balance of payment situation.
(ii) Borrowings from the Fund are possible only after a member has signed the extended fund facility (EFF) agreement with it.
(iii) India has been participating in the Financial Transaction Plan (FTP) of the Fund.

How many of the above statements are correct?
(a) Only one
(b) Only two
(c) All three
(d) None of these

8. Consider the following statements related to international economic organisations:
(i) The lending mandates of the New Development Bank (NDB) and World Bank are similar.
(ii) Mandate of the Asian Infrastructure Investment Bank (AIIB) is a mix of the mandates of both World Bank and International Monetary Fund (IMF).
(iii) The lending mandate of the AIIB extends beyond Asia.
(iv) The NDB does not lend to non-members.

How many of the above statements are correct?
(a) Only one
(b) Only two
(c) Only three
(d) All four

9. Consider the following suggestions which India has given to reform the International Monetary Fund (IMF):
(i) Enhancing the resource base of the Fund by increasing the quotas of the members.
(ii) Eliminating the US veto in its key decisions.
(iii) Revising the quota allotment formula in line with the current and future economic weight of the members.
(iv) Merit-based selection of the Head, irrespective of nationality.

How many of the above statements are correct?
(a) Only one
(b) Only two
(c) Only three
(d) All four

10. Consider the following statements related to India's interaction with UN economic organisations:
(i) India has been the biggest beneficiary of the International Development Association till it was eligible for borrowings.
(ii) India earns interest income by lending to the IMF (International Monetary Fund) from its unused SDRs (Special Drawing Rights).
(iii) India has been borrowing Indian rupee (INR) denominated concessional loans from the IMF.

How many of the above statements are correct?
(a) Only one **(b)** Only two
(c) All three **(d)** None of these

Answers: 1. (c) 2. (b) 3. (b) 4. (c) 5. (a) 6. (a) 7. (c) 8. (c) 9. (d) 10. (b)

SAMPLE SUBJECTIVE QUESTIONS

1. Briefly examine the position taken by India at the recently concluded Ministerial Conference of the WTO and its role at this global trade forum.

2. 'The current SDR quota formula of the IMF needs modification as per the changed global economic order.' Examine.

3. What are the major reforms proposed by the developing countries lingering in front of the International Monetary Fund and the World Bank? Explain.

4. Do you consider that the new multilateral financial institutions, New Development Bank and Asian Infrastructure Investment Bank, are symbols of a failing Bretton Wood arrangement? Comment.

5. Write a note on the benefits which accrues to India by being a member of the Organisation of Economic Cooperation and Development (OECD).

SAMPLE MODEL ANSWER

1. **India has been an ardent supporter of timely reforms in the multilateral development banks. What major points have been raised by India in this regard?**

Ans. India has been a long-time supporter of timely reforms in the multilateral development banks (MDBs), such as the International Monetary Fund and World Bank. The points raised by India majorly focus on their outdated governance, inefficient bureaucracy, and detrimental project impacts on the environment and national sovereignty, which may be summarised into the following ***four*** groups:

1. *Governance and representation*
   - The Global South is under-represented since the voting power is tied to financial contributions, giving wealthy nations disproportionate influence.
   - Decision-making is often swayed by the national interests of major shareholders.
   - Boards of Directors often share managerial roles with presidents, which creates a conflict of interest.
2. *Operational inefficiency*
   - Complexity of procedures causes undue delays in project approval and fund disbursement.
   - They often fail to account for the unique economic and social contexts of the borrowing countries.
   - Despite sovereign backing, they are often more risk-averse than private finance.
3. *Economic and sovereignty issues*
   - Loans can lead to unsustainable debt cycles when projects do not generate expected returns.
   - Loan conditions often mandate specific economic reforms (e.g., austerity), which undermines national sovereignty.
   - Recent shifts towards de-risking private investment have been criticised for 'socialising risk while privatising profits.'
4. *Environmental and social impact*
   - Large-scale infrastructure projects, such as coal-fired power plants or large dams, have historically led to deforestation and habitat destruction.
   - Funding has been linked to the forced resettlement of local populations and violations of indigenous rights.
   - While safeguards exist, they are often criticised for being too expensive for borrowers to implement (or for bypassing existing national legal frameworks).

CHAPTER 18

Tax Structure in India

> Through taxes, the Government in reality decides how to draw the required resources from the nation's households and businesses for public purposes - the money raised so is the 'vehicle' by which real resources are transferred from private goods to public goods.*
>
> *P. A. Samuelson and W. D. Nordhaus, *Economics* (New Delhi: McGraw Hill Education, 2020), pp. 405-434; J. E. Stiglitz and C. E. Walsh, *Economics* (New York: W. W. Norton, 2006), pp. 380-386.

To watch the Author's videos on the significance of the Chapter, scan the QR Code given here

Exam Essentials...

- Buoyancy and Elasticity of Tax
- Pigouvian Tax
- Tax Inversion vs Transfer Pricing

Note to the Reader...

Taxation is more than imposition of levies on incomes or productive activities. Its full picture is much broader which touches nuanced issues such as - how tax policies modify our economic behaviour, what are governments' expenditure priorities, and overall societal well-being, etc. Rather, tax is considered as the very 'backbone' of the fiscal capacity of the modern governments across the world.

This chapter should be read in tandem with the following Chapter 19 on the Public Finance. The ongoing debate on the legitimacy in state and taxation for enhancing tax compliance is equally important to understand the behavioural aspects of taxation in India.

In This Chapter...

TAX

Modern economists *define* tax as a mode of income redistribution.[1] There might be other ways also to look at it - the usual meaning of tax people think is that a tax is imposed by the Government to fulfil its important obligations on the expenditure front.[2] We may take an example to see how taxes redistribute income:

Suppose an economy has a flat rate of 30 per cent income tax. Just see the impact of this tax on the income disparity of two people A and B earning ₹50,000 and ₹80,000, respectively.

Individual	Nominal Income	Income Disparity before Tax	Income after Paying Tax	Income Disparity after Tax
A	₹50,000	₹30,000	₹35,000	₹21,000
B	₹80,000		₹56,000	

The table given above shows how the income disparity between two individuals A and B decreases from ₹30,000 to ₹21,000 after paying taxes - this is the *first level* when incomes of these individuals have been re-distributed.

Now the money the Government has received by tax collection, that is ₹39,000 (₹15,000 + ₹24,000), will be spent on different sectors - infrastructure, education, health and so on - which will provide services to one and all alike. Here income is redistributed at the *secondary level.* Consider a person who pays income tax, but does not take services of Government schools for his children's education, nor goes to the Government hospitals for medical services and compare him with a person who has no option other than the Government schools and the hospitals - the higher taxpayer getting no Government services and a lower taxpayer getting all the services. Here income looks re-distributed from the consumption side.

Incidence of Tax This is the point where a tax leaves its 'final' burden.[3] For example, when the GST is imposed in India on biscuit, the tax is actually paid out by the consumer who bears the final burden. Thus, the incidence of this tax is on the consumer.

Impact of Tax This is the point where a tax leaves its 'initial' burden.[4] For example, when the GST is imposed in India on biscuit, the producer bears its initial burden. Thus, the impact of tax is on the producer.

Direct Tax The tax which has both incidence and impact at the same point is the direct tax - the person who is hit, the same person bleeds.[5] For example, income tax, interest tax and so on.

Indirect Tax The tax which has incidence and impact at different points is the indirect tax - the person who is hit does not bleed[6], rather someone else bleeds. For example, GST, excise, custom duty, sales tax and so on are imposed on either the producers or the traders, but it is the general consumers who bear the burden of tax.

METHODS OF TAXATION

There are three methods of taxation prevalent in economies with their individual merits and demerits.

Progressive Taxation

Progressive taxation has increasing rates of tax for increasing value or volume on which the tax is being imposed.[7] Indian income tax is a typical example of it. The idea here is less tax on the people who earn less and higher tax on the people who earn more, classifying income earners into different slabs. This method is believed to discourage more earnings by the individual to support low growth and development unintentionally. Being poor is rewarded while richness is punished. Taxpayers also start evading tax by showing lower unreal income. But from different angles, this tax is pro-poor and taxes people according to their affordability/sustainability. This is the most popular taxation method in the world and a populist one, too.

Regressive Taxation

Regressive taxation is just opposite to the progressive method, having decreasing rates of tax for increasing

[1] P. A. Samuelson and W. D. Nordhaus, *Economics* (New Delhi: Tata McGraw Hill, 2005), p. 327.

[2] For further reference, J. E. Stiglitz and C. E. Walsh, *Economics* (New York: W.W. Norton & Company, 2006), pp. 378-79.

[3] Samuelson and Nordhaus, *Economics,* op. cit., pp. 75-77.

[4] Ibid.

[5] Ibid., p. 329.

[6] Ibid., p. 329.

[7] Samuelson and Nordhaus, *Economics,* 329; Stiglitz and Walsh, *Economics,* op. cit., p. 380.

value or volume on which the tax is being imposed.[8] There are not any permanent or specific sectors for such taxes. As a provision of promotion, some sectors might be imposed with regressive taxes. For example, to promote the growth and development of small-scale industries, India at one time had regressive excise duty on their productions - with increasing slabs of volume they produced, the burden of tax kept decreasing.

This method, while appreciated for rewarding the higher producers or income earners, is criticised for being more taxing on the poor and low producers. This is not a popular mode of taxation and not as per the spirit of modern democracies.

Proportional Taxation

In proportional taxation there is neither progression nor regression from the point of view of rate of taxes. Such taxes have fixed rates for every level of income or production; if they are neutral from the poor or rich point view or from the point of view of the levels of production.[9] Usually, this is not used by the economies as an independent method of taxation. Generally, this mode is used as a complementary method with either progressive or regressive taxation. If not converted into proportional taxes, every progressive tax will keep increasing and similarly every regressive tax will decrease to zero, resulting in completely futile tax methods. That is why every tax, be it progressive or regressive in nature, must be converted into proportional taxes after a certain level.

A GOOD TAX SYSTEM

What are the characteristics of a good tax system? There has always been a debate among economists and policymakers on the issue of design of the tax system. Taxation in developing economies has been even more debated as the trade-off assessment generates enough controversy. The main debatable issues in the design of a tax system are whether progressive or regressive taxation, direct tax or indirect tax collections should be higher, whether revenue deficit is better and so on. The controversies apart, there is a broad consensus on five ***principles***[10] of a good tax system among economists and policymakers. These are fairness, efficiency, administrative simplicity, flexibility and transparency.

Fairness

Though fairness (i.e., the first criterion of a good tax system) is not always easy to define, economists suggest the inclusion of two elements in the tax system to make it fair, namely ***horizontal equity*** and ***vertical equity***. When individuals in identical or similar situations pay identical or similar taxes, it is known as ***horizontal equity***. When 'better off' people pay more taxes, it is known as ***vertical equity***.

Efficiency

The efficiency of a tax system is its potential to affect or interfere with the efficiency of the economy. A good tax system raises revenue with the least cost on the taxpayers and least interference on the allocation of resources in the economy. The tax system affects the economic decisions of individuals and groups by either encouraging or discouraging them to save, spend, invest and so on. Taxes can improve efficiency of the economy - taxes on pollution or on smoking extend revenue to the Government and also serve broader social purposes. This is known as the ***double dividend*** of a tax.

Administrative Simplicity

Administrative simplicity is the third criterion which includes factors such as computation, filing and collection of the taxes that should be as simple as possible. Simplicity also checks tax evasion. Tax reform in India has simplification of tax as its major plank - also recommended by the Chelliah Committee.

Flexibility

A good tax system has the scope of desirable modifications in it if there is any such need.

Transparency

How much tax taxpayers are actually paying and what they are getting against it in the form of the public services should be ascertainable, that is, the transparency factor.

---

[8] Ibid.

[9] Samuelson and Nordhaus, *Economics,* op. cit., p. 329.

[10] Stiglitz and Walsh, *Economics,* op. cit., p. 382. A comprehensive analysis of good tax structure is also given in *Meade Committee Report,* Institute for Fiscal Studies (IFS), Washington DC, 1978.

Buoyancy and Elasticity of Tax

Tax buoyancy shows the relationship between tax revenue and GDP. It is the response of gross tax revenue to a change in the GDP. A tax is called buoyant when it grows with the growth in GDP (without increasing the tax rates). It depends on tax base, tax compliance, simplicity and rationality of tax system, etc.

Tax elasticity refers to changes in tax revenue in response to changes in tax rate. In practice, it shows the relationship between tax collection/ revenue and the changes made in the tax rates by the government—a tax rate increase/decrease may result in rise or fall in tax revenue. That is why such changes are done by governments after proper study of tax elasticity.

METHODS OF EXPENDITURE

Similar to the methods of taxation, the modes of government expenditure are also of three types - progressive, regressive and proportional.[11]

At first instance, it seems that as a country achieves better levels of development, sectoral and the item-wise expenditure of the economy must have decreasing trends. But practical experience shows that the level of expenditure needs enhancement every day, and the economy always needs more revenue to fulfil the rising expenditures. That is why for economies, the best form of government expenditure is progressive expenditure.

The best way of taxation and government expenditure is progressive, suiting each other beautifully. Most of the economies around the world follow progressive taxation with progressive expenditure.

VALUE-ADDED TAX

The value-added tax (VAT) is a method of tax collection as well as the name of a state-level tax (***at present***) in India. A tax collected at every stage of value addition, that is either by production or distribution, is VAT.[12] Its name itself suggests that this tax is collected on the value addition (i.e., production).

The production of goods or services is nothing but the stages of value additions where the production of goods is carried out by the industrialists or manufacturers. But these goods require value addition by different service providers/producers (the agents, the wholesalers and the retailers) before they reach the consumers. From production to the level of sale, there are many points where value is added in all goods. VAT method of tax collection is different from the non-VAT method in the sense that it is imposed and collected at different points of the value addition chain, that is ***multi-point tax collection***. That is why there is no chance of imposing tax upon tax which takes place in the non-VAT method - ***single-point tax*** collection. This is why VAT does not have a 'cascading effect' on the prices of goods and thus it does not increase inflation and is therefore highly suitable for an economy like India where, due to high level of poverty, a large number of people lack the market level purchasing capacity. It is a pro-poor tax system without being anti-rich because rich people do not suffer either.

Need of VAT in India

Over 160 nations in the world have implemented the VAT system of taxation regarding collecting their indirect taxes. There have been valid reasons why India should move towards the VAT method of tax collection. We may see some of the major reasons below[13]:

1. Due to single-point tax collection, the Indian indirect tax collection system was price-increasing (having a *cascading effect* on the price), which was highly detrimental to the poorer masses of society. The implementation of VAT will improve the purchasing capacity and thus the living standard of the poor people.[14]
2. India has a federal political system where alongside the Central Government, states have also been extended the power to impose and collect taxes. At the central level, there had been uniformity of taxes for the economy. But there was no 'uniformity' at the state-level taxes (i.e., state excise, sales tax, entertainment tax, etc.).

[11] Based on the discussion on Government Expenditure in Samuelson and Nordhaus, *Economics*.

[12] Ibid., p. 333.

[13] Derived from the points forwarded by the *GoI* and the *Empowered Group of State Ministers*.

[14] R. C. Chelliah, P. K. Aggarwal, M. C. Purohit and R. K. Rao, 'Introduction to Value Added Tax', in *Readings in Public Finance*, A. Bagchi, ed. (Oxford University Press, New Delhi, 2005), pp. 277-78.

This was detrimental to the development of a single market for the Indian economy as a whole. India basically had many markets, but no Indian market as such. To bring in uniformity at the state-level taxes, VAT was a necessary step in India.

3. With the process of economic reforms, India moved towards the market economy. And for this, firstly India needed to have a single market. Without uniformity at the state-level taxes (***uniform VAT***), this was not possible.
4. Indian federal design has resulted in economically weaker states and a stronger centre. As VAT increases the total tax collection (experience of the world suggests so), it was fit to be implemented at the state level.
5. India has been a country of high-level tax evasion. By implementing the VAT method of indirect tax collection, it becomes almost impossible to opt for large-scale tax evasion. To prove one's level of value addition, the purchase invoice/receipt is a must which ultimately makes it cross-check the level of production and sale in the economy.[15]
6. If some of the State-level taxes (which are many) are converted into State VAT, the complexity of taxation will also be minimised. And at the end, it is possible to merge some of the Centre's indirect taxes with it, that is arrival of the ***single VAT***.

Keeping this in mind, India started a tax reform *(Chelliah Committee* and *Kelkar Committee),* and a certain level of success has been achieved in this area.

1. In the year 1996, the Central Government started collecting its excise duty on the VAT method and the tax was given a new name, the CENVAT.
2. The next proposal was to merge the states' excise duty (imposed on intoxicants only) and their sales taxes into one tax - the State VAT or VAT. This could not take place due to states' lack of political will. Finally, only states' sales taxes could be modelled on value-added method and renamed as the VAT (introduced on April 1, 2005). Later on, all states proceeded with this reform (in 2008-09) with apprehensions of shortfalls in their tax collections, making the Centre to compensate them. In the beginning, a few states claimed for compensation in their revenue shortfall but by 2011-12, the VAT started generating higher tax collections in comparison to the erstwhile sales tax. Before the implementation of the GST (in which the VAT of states were merged into, except on petroleum and alcohol), the VAT collection was growing with a rate of 15 per cent per annum.
3. The GST (Goods and Services Tax) was finally implemented in 2017-18 (on July 1, 2017) merging 17 of the existing Central and State indirect taxes.

GOODS AND SERVICES TAX

After implementing the state VAT, the GoI wanted to opt for the proposed GST (Goods and Services Tax). This is aimed at integrating the indirect taxes of Centre and States into a *single national tax* - popularly known as the ***Single VAT*** of India. By creating a *single market* at the pan-India basis, it will help the business and industry in a big way. The tax has the potential to increase GDP up to 2 per cent (conservative estimates by some experts). All the benefits which the State VAT brought to the market and economy are the same in the case of the GST, too. The ***first proposal***[16] of the GST had suggested the following tax arrangements under it:

1. To be collected on the VAT method (will have all the same features of the VAT).
2. To be imposed at *pan-India* level with uniformity in tax - a *single rate* of indirect tax - replacing the multiple Central and State indirect taxes.
3. *Four* taxes of Centre (CENVAT; service tax; stamp duty and central sales tax) and *nine* taxes (excise duty, sales tax/vat; entry tax; lease tax; works contract tax; luxury tax; turnover tax; octroi and cess) of the States to be merged into the GST.
4. To have a single rate of 20 per cent (12 per cent to flow to Centre, and 8 per cent to the States).

Implementation Process

After studying the Kelkar Committee report, the Government in 2006 decided to introduce the new tax from the financial year 2010-11. The lack of consensus

[15] Ibid.

[16] *Vijay Kelkar Task Force on the FRBM Act 2003,* Ministry of Finance, *Economic Survey 2004-05* (New Delhi: Government of India, 2005), p. 40.

between the Centre and States delayed the process - to sort out the contentious issues, one after another, two independent *expert committees* submitted[17] their advice to the Government. Finally, the Constitution (101st Amendment) Bill, 2016, was cleared by the Parliament by early August 2016, paving the way for its implementation. By late September 2016, the GST Council (GSTC) was created by the Government. The Council has been entrusted with the power to make recommendations to the Union and the States on various issues - rates, floor rates, exemption, etc. - related to GST.

Finally, the new federal indirect tax, GST was enforced[18] by the Government on 1 July 2017. The major features of the tax are as given below:

1. To apply to all goods other than 'alcoholic liquor for human consumption' and 'five petroleum products', viz. petroleum crude, motor spirit (petrol), high speed diesel, natural gas and aviation turbine fuel.
2. A total of 8 central taxes subsumed under it [Central Excise Duty; Duties of Excise (Medicinal and Toilet Preparations); Additional Duties of Excise (Goods of Special Importance); Additional Duties of Excise (Textiles and Textile Products); Additional Duties of Customs (commonly known as Countervailing Duty, i.e. CVD); Special Additional Duty of Customs (SAD); Service Tax; and Central Surcharges and Cesses so far as they relate to supply of goods and services].
3. A total of 9 state taxes subsumed under it [State VAT; Central Sales Tax; Luxury Tax; Entry Tax (all forms); Entertainment and Amusement Tax (except when levied by the local bodies); Taxes on advertisements; Purchase Tax; Taxes on lotteries, betting and gambling; and State Surcharges and Cesses so far as they relate to supply of goods and services].
4. Concept of 'declared goods of special importance' dropped.
5. On inter-state transactions of goods and services, an 'Integrated GST' will be levied.
6. The threshold limit for exemption from levy of GST would be ₹20 lakhs for normal States and ₹10 lakhs for the Special Category States.
7. The threshold for availing the Composition scheme would be ₹50 lakhs - with the Service providers kept out of it.
8. States to receive compensation for five years for the loss of revenue due to the implementation of GST (for this the base year will be 2015-16 with growth rate of 14 per cent).
9. Minor changes in rules and regulations may be permitted with the approval of the Chairperson, if required (due to suggestions from the stakeholders or from the Law Department).
10. All exemptions/incentives on indirect taxes will rest withdrawn with obligation to pay GST. If any of them continues, it will be administered by way of a reimbursement mechanism.
11. Bands of rates (in per cent) of goods under GST shall be 5, 12, 18 and 28, and in addition there would be a category of exempt goods. Further, a cess would be levied on certain goods such as luxury cars, aerated drinks, pan masala and tobacco products, over and above the rate of 28 per cent (for payment of compensation to the States).
12. Keeping in mind the federal structure of India, there will be two components of GST - Central GST (CGST) and State GST (SGST) - both Centre and States levying GST across the value chain on every supply of goods and services. States will assess 90 per cent of the assessee with annual turnover below ₹1.5 crore while the remaining 10 per cent by the Centre. For taxpayers with over ₹1.5 core turnover, the split is 50:50 between the Centre and States.

GST Collections & Reforms As per the *Economic Survey 2025-26*, the GST has played a stabilising role by strengthening Government revenues, deepening formalisation, and reinforcing the Government's reform intent.[19] Gross GST revenue during **2025-26** (April-December) stood at **₹17.4 lakh crore**, recording a year-on-year growth of **6.7** per cent. The underlying strength of GST revenues is reflected in the steady expansion of the tax base, with registered taxpayers increasing from about 60 lakh in 2017 to over 1.5 crore

[17] First it was from the National Institute of Public Finance and Policy (NIPFP), followed by the Subramanian Committee, during 2016-17.

[18] *Ministry of Finance*, Government of India, New Delhi, July, 2017.

[19] *Economic Survey 2025-26* (New Delhi: Ministry of Finance, GoI, January 2026), pp. 43-47.

by 2025-26 (which indicates deeper formalisation of economic activity).

Looking ahead, the recent rationalisation of GST rates is expected to support demand by lowering tax incidence and improving price competitiveness. Since the lower rates are expected to stimulate higher consumption volumes and strengthen compliance, volume effects could offset the impact of rate reductions on revenues.

Inducing Voluntary Compliance To enhance voluntary compliance, the Government adopted several *behavioural initiatives* (based on taxpayers' behaviour) in recent times, incorporating factors such as deterrence; developing social and personal norms; reducing complexity and enhancing fairness and trust. Some of the major initiatives[20] in this direction are as summarised below:

1. **E-Way bill:** For the transportation of goods above a certain threshold of value, an electronic generation of bill (e-Way bill) is put in place. Through this, physical verification is possible which works as a deterrence against misreporting by the taxpayers.
2. **'PIN code to PIN code' distance mapping:** Mentioning origin and destination PIN codes in an e-Way bill is compulsory. This deters misuse of the bill for multiple trips and evasion of tax.
3. **Returns made public:** The return filing status of the taxpayer has been made available in the public domain (on the GST Portal). This enables the buyers to choose compliant taxpayers for conducting business. This helps the buyers to minimise business risk by increasing the probability of availing a timely 'input tax credit' (ITC). This measure uses *social* and *market* pressures to enhance compliance.
4. **Caution against mismatch in tax filing:** Making taxpayers informed about mismatch in their tax filing and 'induce' (i.e., encourage) them to correct it to avoid future litigation. This is done by cross-checking the tax filing forms (GSTR-2A and GSTR- 3B; and GSTR-1 and GSTR-3B).
5. **Repeat reminders:** Taxpayers are sent repeat reminders through SMS of due date of monthly filing and non-filing of return. This is aimed at inducing taxpayers to inculcate the habit of timely return filing.
6. **Free software:** In order to *ease* the compliance in the technology-driven GST regime, free software has been offered to taxpayers which takes care of services such as preparing invoices, GST returns, Income Tax returns, Balance Sheet and Profit and Loss statements. This eases compliance pressure on taxpayers, especially small businesses (which constituted more than 82 per cent of all GST taxpayers in March 2024).
7. **Questionnaire-based return filing:** To reduce complexity and simplify the return filing process, a questionnaire-based return filing system has been put in place. Based on the replies provided by the taxpayers in it, only relevant tables are visible to taxpayers on return dashboard. This is meant to *ease* compliance for taxpayers.
8. **Compliance rating put in public domain:** The GST Act provides for *public display* of compliance rating score of taxpayers based on record of compliance. This will work as a *deterrence* and induce punctual behaviour from taxpayers. Besides, public display of this information enhances transparency and improves trust of businesses in the tax administration, leading to evolution of a social norm of good compliance in the long run.
9. **Acknowledging contribution of compliant taxpayers:** A certificate is being issued to compliant taxpayers acknowledging their contribution in nation-building. This appreciation serves to motivate taxpayers to continue their compliant behaviour in the future as well.

GST-induced Formalisation The need for GST[21] has commenced a vigorous process of formalisation in the economy – as increasing number of 'non-formal' firms have been registering for the new tax. This will not only enhance the level of tax compliance in the country but have effect, in the medium to long term on income of people, tax collections (also direct taxes), social security of the employees and so on. Data made available in

[20] *Economic Survey 2019-20*, vol. 2 (New Delhi: Ministry of Finance, GoI), pp. 48-51.

[21] *Economic Survey 2025-26* (New Delhi: Ministry of Finance, GoI, January 2026), pp. 43-47; *Economic Survey 2022-2023* (New Delhi: Ministry of Finance, GoI) pp. 67, 370; *Economic Survey 2019-20*, vol. 2 (New Delhi: Ministry of Finance, GoI), pp. 285-87; and *Economic Survey 2017-18*, vol. 2 (New Delhi: Ministry of Finance, GoI), pp. 32-42.

Pigouvian Tax

Named After The British Economist Arthur C. Pigou (1877–1959), The Pigouvian Tax Is A Tax Imposed On Economic Transactions Which Create Negative Externalities (I.e., A Cost Which Is Borne By Those Who Were Not Part Of The Transaction). Carbon Tax, Fuel Cess, And All Environmental Taxes Are Its Examples Which Are Imposed As The Social Cost Of Such Private Transactions And Is Not Added In The Selling Prices Of Such Products.

the process of GST collections are already providing the experts and Governments a new understanding (through data mining) about the economy.

COMMODITIES TRANSACTION TAX

The *Union Budget 2013-14* introduced (basically, *reintroduced)* the Commodities Transaction Tax (CTT), however, only for ***non-agricultural*** commodity futures at the rate of **0.01** per cent (which is equivalent to the rate of equity futures on which a *Securities Transaction Tax, STT,* is imposed in India). Along with this, transactions in commodity derivatives have been declared to be made *non-speculative*, and hence for traders in the commodity derivative segment, any losses arising from such transactions can be set off against income from any other source (similar provisions are also applicable for the securities market transactions).

Like all financial transaction taxes, CTT ***aims*** at discouraging excessive speculation, which is detrimental to the market and to bring parity between securities market and commodities market such that there is no tax/regulatory arbitrage. *Futures contracts* are financial instruments and provide for price risk management and price discovery of the underlying asset commodity/currency/stocks/interest. It is, therefore, essential that the policy framework governing them is uniform across all the contracts irrespective of the underlying assets to minimise the chances of regulatory arbitrage. The proposal of CTT also appears to have stemmed from the general policy of the Government to widen the tax base.

CTT is a tax similar to STT, proposed to be levied in India, on transactions carried out on the domestic commodity derivatives exchanges. Globally, commodity derivatives are also considered as financial contracts. Hence, CTT can also be considered as a type of 'financial transaction tax'.

The concept of CTT was ***first*** introduced in the *Union Budget 2008-09*. The Government had then proposed to impose a CTT of 0.017 per cent (equivalent to the rate of equity futures at that point of time). However, it was withdrawn subsequently as the market was *nascent* then, and any imposition of transaction tax might have adversely affected the growth of organised commodities derivatives markets in India. This has helped Indian commodity exchanges to grow to global standards. [MCX is the world's ***No. 3*** commodity exchange; globally, MCX is ***No. 1*** in gold and silver, ***No. 2*** in natural gas and ***No. 3*** in crude oil.]

SECURITIES TRANSACTION TAX

The Securities Transaction Tax (STT) is a type of 'financial transaction tax' levied in India on transactions carried out on the domestic stock exchanges. The rates of STT are prescribed by the Central Government through its budget from time to time. In tax parlance, this is categorised as a ***direct tax***. The tax came into effect on *1 October, 2004*. In India, STT is collected for the Government of India by the stock exchanges. With charging of STT, long-term capital gains tax was made ***zero***, and short-term capital gains tax was reduced to 10 per cent (subsequently, changed to 15 per cent since 2008).

The STT framework was subsequently reviewed by the Central Government in the years 2005, 2006, 2008, 2012 and ***2013***. The STT rates were revised upwards in the years 2005 and 2006, while it was reduced for certain segments in 2012 and 2013. The STT provisions were altered in the year 2008 such that for professional traders (brokers), the STT came to be treated as an *expense* which can be deducted from the income instead of treating the same as an advance tax paid. The *Union Budget 2026-27* affected few changes in the STT rates, namely-the SST on 'futures' was raised to 0.05 per cent (from 0.02 per cent), and the STT on 'options premium' and 'exercise of options' were both raised to 0.15 per cent (from 0.1 per cent) and 0.125 per cent, respectively.

As on date, STT is not applicable in the case of *preference shares, government securities, bonds, debentures, currency derivatives, units of mutual fund other than equity-oriented mutual fund* and *gold exchange traded funds*, and in **such cases**, tax treatment of short-term and long-term gains shall be as per normal provisions of law.

Transactions of the shares of listed companies on the floor of the stock exchange or otherwise, mandated under the regulatory framework of SEBI, such as *takeover, buyback,* and *delisting offers,* also do not come under the STT framework. The *off-market* transactions of securities (which entails changes in ownership records at depositories) also do not attract STT.

CAPITAL GAINS TAX

Capital gains tax is a direct tax and applies on the sales of all 'assets' if a profit (gain) has been made by the owner of the asset - a tax on the 'gains' one gets by selling assets. The tax has been classified into two:

1. **Short-term Capital Gain (STCG):** It applies 'if the asset has been sold within 36 months of owning it'. In this case, the 'rate' of tax is similar to the normal income tax slab. But the period becomes '12 months' in cases of shares, mutual funds, units of the UTI and 'zero coupon bond' - in this case the 'rate' of tax is **15** per cent.
2. **Long-term Capital Gain (LTCG):** It applies 'if the asset has been sold after 36 months of owning it'. In this case, the 'rate' of tax is **20** per cent. In cases of shares, mutual funds, units of the UTI and 'zero coupon bond', there was 'exemption' (zero tax) though, where recently, an LTCG of 10 per cent (above ₹1 lakh of capital gains) was introduced[22] on them by the Government.

MINIMUM ALTERNATE TAX

The Minimum Alternate Tax (MAT) is a direct tax imposed on the 'zero tax' companies at the rate of 18.5 per cent on their book profit. This was first imposed in 1997-98.

Basically, income tax is paid as per the provisions of the Income Tax Act (IT Act), but companies calculate their profit (through profit and loss account) as per the provisions of the Companies Act. The IT Act allows several kinds of exemptions and other incentives from total income together with deductions on the gross income. Again, the rate of 'depreciation' under the Companies Act is higher than the IT Act. As a result of these exemptions, deductions and other incentives under IT Act together with higher depreciation under the Companies Act, companies show their taxable income either 'nil' or 'negative', and this way, the 'zero tax' companies emerge.

Practically, 'zero tax' companies might be having high 'book profit' and distributing huge dividends (under the Companies Act) to their shareholders, too, but by showing 'nil' or 'negative' taxable income (under the IT Act), they might not pay any income tax! To bring such companies under the income tax, *Section 115JB* was introduced in the IT Act in 1997-98 and MAT was imposed accordingly.

MAT is a way of making companies pay minimum amount of tax. It is applicable on all companies except those engaged in infrastructure and power sectors, free trade zones, charitable activities, venture and angel funds. Foreign companies with income sources in India also come under it. In 2015, the Government rationalised the MAT provisions for the FIIs (Foreign Financial Institutions) - now they do not need to pay MAT on their profits from capital gains on transactions in securities (which are liable to lower tax rate).

We may take an example - suppose a company has a 'book profit' of ₹10 lakh. And, after claiming the deductions, exemptions and depreciation, its 'gross taxable income' comes down to ₹6 lakh, its taxable income becoming ₹4 lakh. In this case, the applicable income tax would be ₹1.2 lakh (if rate of income tax is 30 per cent flat). But the company will pay a MAT of ₹1.85 lakh (at the rate of 18.5 per cent on its 'book profit' of '10 lakh). The company concerned needs to pay the tax which is higher - here, the tax to be paid will be ₹1.85 lakh.

At present, the tax is collected as an advance tax. The tax can be carried forward and set off (adjusted) against regular tax payable during the subsequent 10-year period (known as MAT credit). There has been a strong demand to abolish this tax in the country. In April 2017, the Government started phasing out the exemptions available to the companies on it from April 2017. In order that companies are able to use MAT credit, the carry forward period has been also increased to 15 years.

CORPORATE TAX REFORM

The joint stock companies (more popular as 'companies' and 'corporate' sector in India) pay a direct tax known as *corporate income tax* (CIT, popular

[22] *Union Budget 2018-19* introduced this tax (other than the Security Transaction Tax which these financial instruments already attract).

as 'corporate tax') on their annual profits. The existing rates used to be 30 per cent for the domestic and 35 per cent for the foreign companies, operating in the country. Following the ongoing process of corporate tax reforms, the Government, in September 2019, affected a major change in the CIT. The change[23] which was enforced from the fiscal year 2019-20 is briefly summarised below:

- For the existing companies (with gross turnover over ₹400 crores), the base corporate tax was cut from 30 to 22 per cent. Thus, the effective rate (i.e., inclusive of surcharge and cess) fell from 34.61 to 25.17 per cent. Companies can opt for the new tax rate by forgoing the deductions and exemptions availed by them. This will benefit 0.9 per cent of the companies (i.e., large ones) operating in the country (their number being 4,698).
- For the new manufacturing companies (with gross turnover below ₹400 crores), registered on or after 1 October 2019, the rate was cut from 25 to 15 per cent. In this case, the effective rate of tax fell down to 17.16 per cent. This will benefit 99.1 per cent companies (i.e., small and medium ones) of the country.
- This drastic move was aimed at three major objectives - firstly, boosting the production volume of the manufacturing sector which involves a large number of MSMEs (including the newly launched start-ups); secondly, attracting higher investments in manufacturing industries and thirdly, creating more job opportunities.
- The rate structure was left unchanged for the foreign companies.

Logic behind the reform In recent times, the corporate tax was cut by many countries across the world to attract investment and create jobs. India's move was an immediate response to rate cuts initiated by Asian developing countries, which compete with India in the global export markets. After the reform move, the corporate tax rate in India (for new manufacturing companies in particular) is lower than most ASEAN countries.

Countries	Tax Rate (%)
Timor	10
Singapore	17
Brunei	18.5
Vietnam	20
Thailand	20
Cambodia	20
Malaysia	24
Laos	24
Myanmar	25
Indonesia	25
Philippines	30

Source: Department of Revenue, Ministry of Finance, GoI, New Delhi, April 2020.

Other than attracting investment and enhanced job creation, the move is also expected to have a multiplier effect on the economy - increased income levels and higher tax collections in the medium to long term.

DIVIDEND DISTRIBUTION TAX

The ownership of joint stock companies (i.e., the Ltd. firms) rests in the hands of their shareholders. Thus, such companies pay a dividend (i.e., a part of profit) to their shareholders once they book operating profits. The dividend paid (distributed) by the companies to the shareholders used to attract a direct tax in India known as the dividend distribution tax (DDT). It means, before a dividend is to be paid to the shareholders, the DDT was to be paid to the tax department (that is known as payment of DDT in the 'hands of the companies'). The rate of tax *till March 2020* was 15 per cent.

Starting with the financial year ***2020-21***, the Government affected a major change[24] in regard to the DDT - now companies do not need to pay this tax anymore. The joint stock companies will transfer the dividend directly to the shareholders without deducting the tax. This way, the dividend earned by shareholders will be part of their personal income which will attract personal income tax (in place of dividend tax). It means, dividends will still attract the direct tax (i.e., individual income tax) in the hands of the recipients in place of the companies (which used to pay the DDT). But still, it will make a revenue loss to the Government as the tax will not apply with a flat rate of 15 per cent, but rather get paid as per the

[23] *Economic Survey 2019-20*, vol. 2 (New Delhi: Ministry of Finance, GoI), pp. 46-8.

[24] *Union Budget 2020-21* (New Delhi: Ministry of Finance, GoI).

income slabs of the recipients. The change is estimated to entail a revenue loss of ₹25,000 crores annually.

Experts and stakeholders used to argue that the DDT resulted in increasing the tax burden for investors who already pay an income tax (i.e., CIT) on their annual profits. This is used to pinch those investors who are liable to pay tax less than the rate of DDT if the dividend income is included in their personal income - as personal income tax has various slabs. Further, non-availability of credit of DDT to most of the foreign investors in their home country resulted in reduction of rate of return (ROR) on equity capital for them. The move is aimed at making the Indian equity market more attractive for investors - domestic as well as foreign. This move is supposed to provide a channel to the Indian population to be part of the formal process of wealth creation in the country besides routing investment in nation-building.

Tax Inversion vs Transfer Pricing

Tax Inversion This is a situation of tax structure. This takes place when a firm bases its headquarters in a low tax country while keeps its material operations in the high tax countries (generally their country of origin). This way, firms cut their tax payment liabilities. This is legal and is a method of tax avoidance. Multinational corporations (MNCs) keep doing this – several MNCs of the US-origin shifted their headquarters to the UK, during the 1970s and 1980s. The countries in the world which have very low tax regime for corporations have emerged as very attractive locations for the headquarters of big corporations. Bermuda, Virgin Islands, etc. are such countries (popularly known as the 'tax havens').

Transfer Pricing A term of international economics *via* which an MNC charges lesser prices for its exportable to its arm in another economy where tax rates are high, for increasing income. The East India Company did it heavily in pre-independent India.

Base Erosion and Profit Shifting

Base erosion and profit shifting (BEPS) is a kind of corporate tax planning under which the multinational companies (MNCs) 'shift' their profits from higher-tax countries to lower-tax countries 'eroding' the 'tax base' of the higher-tax countries. In practice, companies make profits in one country and shift them to other which has lower tax rates and take advantage of lower tax payments. This way, companies do not pay tax to the country where the profit is made.

As per the OECD (Organisation of Economic Cooperation and Development), developing countries (which heavily depend on corporate tax) have been losing conservatively 4–10 per cent of global corporate tax revenues (i.e., US$ 100–240 billion) annually since 2013. The ongoing joint OECD-G20 initiative of over 140 countries is presently collaborating to tackle this issue besides improving coherence in international tax rules, and ensure a more transparent tax environment. Meanwhile, the new withholding tax (i.e., equalisation levy) enforced by India in 2016 is supposed to tackle the BEPS issue to some extent at least in the digital sphere.

Tax Havens Tax havens are countries/territories/jurisdictions with attractive tax/financial rules for non-resident investors. They also provide secrecy/protection of investors' financial information and require minimal local presence. In a sense, they are paradise for those who want to escape high tax countries. The British Virgin Islands, Bermuda, Guam, Taiwan, and Jersey are some such countries in the world today. However, such locations have caused concerns of illegal tax avoidance and money laundering.

Equalisation Levy

India became the 'first' country in the world to impose a tax on online services offered by non-resident entities (which operate through subsidiaries with no permanent establishments in the country). Called equalisation levy, the direct tax was enforced in 2016 with the following features:

- Applies on online marketing, digital platforms selling goods/services, cloud computing, web designing, hosting and maintenance, and online download of software/applications.
- Imposed with 6 per cent rate on payments exceeding ₹1 lakh annually—the Indian clients purchasing/taking the services need to withhold this tax (**Withholding Tax**).
- The tax resolves the issue of base erosion and profit shifting (BEPS) by the multinational companies operating in digital economy, to some extent.

Contervailing Duty vs Anti-Dumping Duty

Countervailing duty (CVD) is imposed by the importing nation on imports if the exporting nation is found to offer export subsidies to their exports. This measure aims at balancing the price of imports with the domestic products. This duty is imposed in such a way that the imported item also remains competitive.

A similar duty, with the same aim, once imposed by the importing nation in the case the exporting country is found to export at *below fair market price* (it means the exporting nation is dumping the item in the importing nation) is known as 'anti-dumping' duty.

Both the duties are imposed after fulfilling the proper provisions of investigation conducted as per the specifications of the WTO.

LEGITIMACY AND TAXATION

Scan this QR Code to watch a author's video lecture that simplifies this topic

India commenced with a broad-based tax reforms programme in 1991 as an important part of the economic reforms process. Simplifying tax structure, cutting rate of taxes, enhancing tax compliance and broadening the tax base are the major contours of this reform programme. But even today, India has not fully translated its democratic vigour into commensurately strong fiscal capacity. The tax base of India is still not adequate. To build fiscal capacity, it is essential to create legitimacy in the state. In this regard the *Economic Survey 2015-16* presented a very timely and suitable piece of analysis (quoting 'exit from state', the famous terminology of Albert Hirschman). The document adds that to build fiscal capacity, the Government needs to put in place a better tax regime which is only possible once the Government is able to enhance its legitimacy among the citizens. The suggestions[25] forwarded by the Survey in this regard are briefly being given here.

1. The *spending priorities* of the Government must include essential services which are consumed by all citizens. For that matter, action needs to be taken on public infrastructure, law and order, less pollution and congestion, etc.
2. *Reducing corruption* must be a high priority. However, this will be fiendishly (clever and imaginative) difficult. This is needed not just because of its economic costs but also because it undermines the legitimacy of the state. The more citizens believe that public resources are not wasted, the greater they will be willing to pay taxes. Improving transparency through efficient auctioning of public assets will help create legitimacy and over time strengthen fiscal capacity.
3. *Subsidies to the well-off* need to be scaled back. At present,[26] it is estimated to be around ₹1 lakh crore. Phasing down these bounties and targeting subsidies for the poor is important in strengthening legitimacy.

   In the same way, the existing regime of tax exemptions redistributes income towards the richer private sector - it dilutes the legitimacy of the state in the eyes of the poor citizens. There is a need of putting in place a reasonable taxation provision for the 'better off' section in the country regardless of where they get their income from - industry, services, real estate or agriculture.
4. *Property taxation* needs to be developed. India lacks systematic data on property tax and whatever is present is very sparse. This proves the low attention the country has given to this issue. As property taxes are 'progressive', they are desirable. It makes more sense because evading this tax is difficult as they are imposed on immovable (non-mobile) assets. With the help of today's technologies, such properties can be easily identified.

Higher rates on properties (with values updated periodically) can be the foundation of local governments' finances. This can provide local public goods and strengthen democratic accountability and

25 *Economic Survey 2015-16* (New Delhi: Ministry of Finance, GoI), pp. 105-117. As per **Albert Hirschman,** when a state prioritises or over-emphasises redistribution without providing basic public goods, it risks the ***exit of middle class*** from the state (i.e., exit from the tax net).

26 *Economic Survey 2015-16*, vol. 1 (New Delhi: Ministry of Finance, GoI), pp. 105-117.

more effective decentralisation. Higher property tax rates would also put sand in the wheels of property speculation. *Smart cities* require smart public finance and for India's urban future, a sound property taxation regime will be vital.

One low-hanging fruit is to avoid raising the exemption threshold and allowing natural growth in income to increase the number of the taxpayers. The Survey has suggested a simple method for it - *inaction*. In 2016-17, the Government began this process - exemption limit for individual income tax has been left unchanged together with a programme to link corporate tax cut and phase out of the exemption regime existing for the companies.

EASE OF PAYING TAXES

India has given high attention to improving its rank in the Doing Business Report (discontinued since then and is in the process of being replaced by another similar report) the World Bank. It jumped up 79 positions (out of 190 countries) in the latest report improving from 142nd of 2014 to 63rd in 2019 *(Doing Business 2019)*. However, its rank still continues to trail on four parameters, one being Paying Taxes (rest of the three being Starting Business, Registering Property and Enforcing Contracts). A comparative picture[27] of *ease of paying taxes* in India and a few other countries (especially peers like China, Brazil and Indonesia) is summarised below:

- India's rank in ease of paying taxes has, however, improved from 156 in 2014 to 115 in 2019, but it has been much below expectations.
- India performs poorly in the case of a number of tax payments - while in India the number is 12 (from 59 of 2009), it is only 7 in China, 10 in Brazil and 26 in Indonesia.
- Hours taken per year in paying taxes are also comparatively higher in India - 250- 254 hours in India, while only 138 in China, 1501 in Brazil (quite higher) and 191 in Indonesia.
- In New Zealand, it takes only 140 hours per year in paying taxes. On this front, however, the situation has deteriorated in the country - time spent in paying taxes has doubled in the last decade (2009-19).
- India trails in the case of total tax payable (per cent of gross profits) in comparison to most of its peers as well - while it is 49.7 for India, it is 59.2 for China, 65.1 for Brazil and 30.1 for Indonesia.
- In the case of paying taxes, although Indonesia (26) has more than double the number of payments per year than India (10-12), its citizens spend far less time in paying them than India. Brazil seems to fare particularly poor in this segment.

These parameters provide a measure of the scope for improvement. To emerge an economy of US$ 5 trillion, India needs to channelise all of its resources and focus on improving the ease of paying taxes - businesses, industries together with individuals and companies feel at ease if it takes less time in paying taxes.

TAX ADMINISTRATION REFORMS

Making tax administration more transparent, efficient and taxpayer-friendly has been one of the major coordinates of India's tax reforms. A major step in this direction was taken by the Government in August 2020 with the launching of the platform 'Transparent Taxation - Honouring the Honest'. The platform[28] has the objective to impart greater efficiency, transparency and accountability, and to eliminate physical interface between taxpayers and tax officers and has *two key* features:

1. Usage of technology, data analytics and Artificial Intelligence and
2. Recognising taxpayers as partners in nation-building.

There are ***three pillars*** on which this platform is based, which are briefly discussed below:

A. Faceless Assessment

The existing *e-assessment* scheme was renamed in August 2020 as the Faceless Assessment scheme. The older scheme was based on the idea that automated random allocation of cases across income tax teams with dynamic jurisdiction and elimination of face-to-face contact between the income tax authorities and the taxpayer can lead to an efficient, non-discretionary, unbiased single window system of assessment. This was broadened in the new scheme by bringing 'all the pending assessment cases' across the country within its purview with declaring that any order passed outside the scheme shall be *invalid*.

[27] *Economic Survey 2019-20*, vol. 1 (New Delhi: Ministry of Finance, GoI), pp. 130-55.

[28] *Economic Survey 2020-21*, vol. 2 (New Delhi: Ministry of Finance, GoI), pp. 62-7.

A National Faceless Assessment Centre (NFAC), headed by Principal Chief Commissioner of Income Tax, has been set up under it, as the sole point of contact between the tax department and the taxpayer - with all notices or communications to and from the taxpayer, and internal communications related to assessment process routed through the centre. Regional Faceless Assessment Centres have also been put in place to facilitate and streamline the process.

B. Faceless Appeals

The Faceless Appeals scheme, 2020, has been set up to finalise all income tax appeals in a faceless manner under a faceless ecosystem with exception of appeals relating to serious frauds, major tax evasion, sensitive and search matters, international tax and black money.

The National Faceless Appeal Centre (NFApC) has been established as the apex body for conducting e-appeal proceedings in a centralised manner - with Regional Faceless Appeal Centres (RFACs) under it to facilitate the process. The NFApC will be the *only point* of contact between the taxpayer and the underlying Appeal Units; and Appeal Units and the NeAC/Assessing Officer. Under it all internal and external communications take place electronically, and the assessee or the Assessing Officer is not required to attend the proceedings personally or through an authorised representative.

C. Taxpayers' Charter

While regulating and enforcing tax laws, traditionally, the tax administration paid limited attention on the aspect of the tax services it was providing. However, in the last few decades, due to increased demand for better services to taxpayers, there has been worldwide recognition of the 'rights of the taxpayers' - accordingly, formal taxpayers' charters have been published or the expected behaviour from tax officials has been inserted in the 'mission statement' of the tax department. India's taxpayer's charter comprises *commitments* by the income tax department and *obligations* of the taxpayers, which are as given below:

1. Courteous, fair and reasonable treatment to taxpayers.
2. Treatment of taxpayers as honest unless the department has a reason to believe otherwise.
3. Fair and impartial appeal procedure and review mechanism.
4. Accurate and complete information for fulfilling tax compliance obligations.
5. Timely decisions in every income tax proceeding.
6. Collection of the correct amount of due tax.
7. Respect for taxpayer's privacy and ensuring no more intrusive than necessary enquiry, examination or enforcement action.
8. Maintaining confidentiality by not disclosing any taxpayer's information to the department unless authorised by law.
9. Ensuring accountability for the actions of the tax authorities.
10. Provision to allow a taxpayer to choose an authorised representative of his choice.
11. Provision for a mechanism to lodge a complaint and its prompt disposal.
12. Fair and impartial system to resolve tax issues in a time-bound manner.
13. Periodical publishing of the service standards and report.
14. Reduced cost of compliance as the department shall duly take into account the cost of compliance when administering tax legislation.

The Charter obliges the taxpayer:

(i) to honestly disclose full information and fulfil compliance obligations.
(ii) to be aware of compliance obligations and seek the help of the department if needed.
(iii) to keep accurate records.
(iv) to know the information and submissions made by an authorised representative.
(v) to make submissions in a timely manner.
(vi) to pay the amount due in a timely manner.

Need of Ombudsman

To ensure enforcement of taxpayers' rights or taxpayers' perspective, a dedicated institution is essential. This can be carried out by establishing an effective Ombudsman. Though it was established in 2011 (after being set up by the Government in 2003 itself), in the absence of law to support its functions and independence from the department, it proved *ineffective* and its decisions remaining *only advisory* in nature. It could settle complaints either through agreements between the complainant and the tax department through conciliation and mediation or by passing an award, with a token compensation for loss suffered by the complainant not exceeding ₹5,000. Thus, the institutions of the Ombudsman for direct and indirect taxes were, therefore, abolished in February 2019.

The present tax grievance redressal system consisting of grievance cells are the *Aaykar Sewa Kendras* (headed by tax officials) and the *e-nivaran* portal (a separate dedicated window for income tax grievance redressal).

Global experience (Australia, Canada, United Kingdom, Brazil, South Africa, Belgium and France) suggests an ombudsman system is necessary for ensuring protection of taxpayer's rights. To make the 'Honouring the Honest' platform more successful, India needs to put in place this institution with adequate teeth and independence from the tax department - to ensure trust between the taxpayers and tax authority.

FIFTEENTH FINANCE COMMISSION

The 15th Finance Commission (Chaired by Mr. N. K. Singh) submitted two reports. While the first report, consisting of recommendations for the financial year 2020-21, was tabled in Parliament in February 2020, the final report with recommendations for the 2021-26 period was tabled in Parliament on February 1, 2021. Its key recommendations[29] are given below.

Devolution criteria The criteria for distribution of central taxes among states for the 2021-26 period are the same as those for 2020-21. The Commission has used 2011 population data for determining the share of states during its entire award period. To reward efforts made by states in controlling their population, the Commission has used the Demographic Performance criterion. States with a lower fertility ratio will be scored higher on this criterion.

Grants-in-aid The Commission has recommended grants from the centre to states and local bodies worth ₹10.3 lakh crore for the 2021-26 period. These include the following:

1. revenue deficit grants to 17 states,
2. grants to urban and rural local bodies,
3. disaster management grants,
4. grants for eight sectors including health, education, and agriculture and
5. certain state-specific grants.

[29] Fifteenth Finance Commission (New Delhi: Ministry of Finance, GoI, February 2021).

Funding of defence and internal security A dedicated non-lapsable fund called the Modernisation Fund for Defence and Internal Security (MFDIS) will be constituted to primarily bridge the gap between budgetary requirements and allocation for capital outlay in defence and internal security. The fund will have an estimated corpus of ₹2,38,354 crores over five years (2021-26). Of this, ₹1,53,354 crores will be transferred from the Consolidated Fund of India. The rest of the amount will be generated from measures such as disinvestment of defence PSUs and monetisation of defence lands.

Fiscal Consolidation The Commission suggested that the Centre bring down fiscal deficit to 4 per cent of GDP by 2025-26. It recommended the fiscal deficit limit (as per cent of the GSDP, i.e., Gross State Domestic Product) for states to be:

1. 4 per cent in 2021-22,
2. 3.5 per cent in 2022-23 and
3. 3 per cent during 2023-26.

Extra annual borrowing worth 0.5 per cent of GSDP will be allowed to states during 2021-25 for undertaking power sector reforms.

The Commission observed that the recommended *path for fiscal deficit* for the Centre and states will result in a reduction of total liabilities of:

1. the Centre from 62.9 per cent of GDP in 2020-21 to 56.6 per cent in 2025-26 and
2. the states on aggregate from 33.1 per cent of GDP in 2020-21 to 32.5 per cent by 2025-26.

The Commission recommended forming a *high-powered inter-governmental group* to:

1. review the fiscal responsibility legislation [Fiscal Responsibility and Budget Management Act, 2003 (FRBM)] and
2. recommend a new fiscal responsibility framework and oversee its implementation.

OUTLOOK FOR THE FUTURE

Though the process of tax reforms has been slower (similar to the process of the economic reforms), especially in the case of indirect taxes, its positive outcomes have encouraged the country to opt for further reforms. Together with enhancing legitimacy in the state, there is a need to making taxpayers aware about the need of filing their tax returns. Certain suggestions[30] to improve the taxation system in current time are briefly summarised below:

- Structural reforms carried out recently in corporate tax are commendable, but slowly all of the deductions and exemptions enjoyed by the taxpayers should be withdrawn and reduction in the base rate should be attempted.
- The ease of filing GST should be enhanced on priority basis.
- The technical glitches related to the GST filing system should be corrected as soon as possible to lessen unnecessary harassment faced by the tax filers.
- Enhancing ease of paying taxes is an essential part of a good tax system. In this regard, India should take lessons from the peers such as China, Brazil and Indonesia other than New Zealand.
- Enhancing tax compliance is the need of the hour, especially in the case of the personal income tax. There is a need for a policy framework to be initiated to induce behavioural change in the taxpayers. The clamour for cutting personal income tax rates will not be practically possible for the Government (due to possible fall in revenue) till the base of this tax is not broadened for which encouraging non-taxpaying citizens to start paying tax will be required. This move will be further strengthened by withdrawing the existing deductions and exemptions enjoyed by the taxpayers.
- The presence of trust between taxpayers and the tax department is essential for encouraging voluntary compliance from the tax filers. For this to be carried out, the Government should put in place an effective and transparent tax administration - reduction of 'human interface' should be attempted at an increased pace.
- The presence of 'fear' and 'distrust' for the tax department in the minds of taxpayers dilutes tax filing, and they need to be corrected in medium to longer term.
- Litigations and involved delays cause enormous damage to the exchequer besides harassing the taxpayers and wasting the precious time of the appellate and various courts. All possible alternatives should be utilised to resolve them in speedier manner.
- The agile fiscal policy response adopted by Government (which encompassed a change in the mix of stimulus measures amidst an uncertain evolution of the pandemic situation) needs to continue given the increased levels of geoeconomic fragmentation and geopolitical uncertainties.

Looking ahead, ongoing reforms in taxation, including *GST 2.0* and personal income tax, are expected to enhance the efficiency of the tax system by simplifying structures, reducing compliance costs, and broadening the tax base. Wider use of *digital systems* in tax administration and public financial management is likely to strengthen compliance, improve expenditure disbursements, and enhance fiscal transparency. Together, these measures will enable progress along the medium-term debt path, thereby strengthening macroeconomic stability.[31]

---

[30] Based on the *Union Budget 2026-27* (New Delhi: Ministry of Finance, GoI, February 2026); *Union Budget 2025-26* (New Delhi: Ministry of Finance, GoI, February 2025); *Economic* Survey 2024-25 (New Delhi: Ministry of Finance, GoI, January 2025); *Economic Survey* 2023-24 (New Delhi: Ministry of Finance, GoI, January 2024); and other official sources.

[31] *Economic Survey 2025-26* (New Delhi: Ministry of Finance, GoI, January 2026), pp. 77-78; *Union Budget 2026-27* (New Delhi: Ministry of Finance, GoI, February 2026); *Union Budget 2025-26* (New Delhi: Ministry of Finance, GoI, February 2025); *Indian Economy: A Review* (New Delhi: Ministry of Finance, GoI, January 2024); and *Union Budget 2024-25* (New Delhi: Ministry of Finance, GoI, February 2024).

PREVIOUS YEARS' QUESTIONS

Prelims

1. With reference to the Government of India, consider the following information: (2025)

	Organisation	Some of its Functions	It Works Under
I	Directorate of Enforcement	Enforcement of the Fugitive Economic Offenders Act, 2018	Internal Security Division-I, Ministry of Home Affairs
II.	Directorate of Revenue Intelligence	Enforces the Provisions of the Customs Act, 1962	Department of Revenue, Ministry of Finance
III.	Directorate of General Systems and Data Management	Carrying out big data analytics to assist tax officers for better policy and nabbing tax evaders	Department of Revenue, Ministry of Finance

In how many of the above rows is the information correctly matched?

(a) Only (i) **(b)** Only (ii)
(c) All three **(d)** None

2. Which of the following statements with regard to recommendations of the 15th Finance Commission of India are correct? (2025)
   (i) It has recommended grants of ₹4,800 crores from the year 2022-23 to the year 2025-26 for incentivising states to enhance educational outcomes.
   (ii) 45% of the net proceeds of union taxes are to be shared with states.
   (iii) ₹45,000 crores are to be kept as a performance-based incentive for all states for carrying out agricultural reforms.
   (iv) It reintroduced tax effort criteria to reward fiscal performance.

   Select the correct answer using the code given below.

   (a) (i), (ii) and (iii) **(b)** (i), (ii) and (iv)
   (c) (i), (iii) and (iv) **(d)** (ii), (iii) and (iv)

Answers: 1. (a) 2. (c)

Explanation

1. (a): *Row I is incorrect* (The Directorate of Enforcement is a multi-disciplinary agency tasked with investigating money laundering and violations of foreign exchange laws which operates under the Department of Revenue, Ministry of Finance). *Row II is correct* (the Directorate of Revenue Intelligence is India's top agency for anti-smuggling intelligence, investigations, and operations, which comes under the Department of Revenue, Ministry of Finance, and operates as part of the Central Board of Indirect Taxes and Customs). *Row III is incorrect* (the Directorate General of Systems & Data Management functions under the CBIC and the Department of Revenue, Ministry of Finance).
2. (c): Except for Statement II, the rest are correct about the recommendations of the Commission.

Main

1. Explain the rationale behind the Goods and Services Tax (Compensation to States) Act of 2017. How has COVID-19 impacted the GST compensation fund and created new federal tensions? (2020).

SAMPLE OBJECTIVE QUESTIONS

1. Consider the following statements related to tax administration in the country:
   (i) A moratorium was put on India's equalisation levy at the recently concluded ministerial conference of the WTO.
   (ii) Equalisation levy checks the instances of base erosion and profit shifting (BEPS) by the multinational companies to some extent.
   (iii) General anti-avoidance rule (GAAR) of India aims to check tax avoidance by multinational companies.

   How many of the above statements are correct?
   (a) Only one (b) Only two
   (c) All three (d) None of these

2. Consider the following statements related to tax administration in the country:
   (i) Better tax administration leads to better tax buoyancy.
   (ii) Higher tax rates increase tax revenues till tax rates have reached their threshold levels.
   (iii) Base erosion and profit shifting (BEPS) undermine voluntary tax compliance.

   How many of the above statements are correct?
   (a) Only one (b) Only two
   (c) All three (d) None of these

3. Consider the following statements related to the relationship between taxation and government expenditures:
   (i) Government expenditures have increased progressively across the democracies.
   (ii) For progressive government expenditures, taxation also needs to be progressive.
   (iii) Progressive taxation with regressive expenditures is most preferred combination across the world.

   How many of the above are correct?
   (a) Only one (b) Only two
   (c) All three (d) None of these

4. Consider the following statements related to tax administration:
   (i) Taxpayers' charter sees tax department as the service provider.
   (ii) Instances of corruption make taxpayers 'exit from state' and evade taxes.
   (iii) Voluntary tax compliance is closely associated with the degree of legitimacy in state.

   How many of the above statements are correct?
   (a) Only one (b) Only two
   (c) All three (d) None of these

5. Consider the following statements related to India's regime of taxation:
   (i) India has always followed progressive method of taxation.
   (ii) For some sectors India follows regressive taxation too.
   (iii) Transfer payments should reflect governments fiscal capacity.

   How many of the above statements are correct?
   (a) Only one (b) Only two
   (c) All three (d) None of these

6. Consider the following taxes of the Central government:
   (i) Interest tax
   (ii) Dividend tax
   (iii) Luxury tax
   (iv) Gift tax
   (v) GST
   (vi) Cenvat

   How many of the above are actually taxes on income?
   (a) Only three (b) Only four
   (c) Only five (d) All six

7. Consider the following statements related to the reaction of taxpayers:
   (i) Hikes in the rates of indirect taxes are not liked by consumers.
   (ii) When the rates of indirect taxes are increased traders profit declines.

(iii) Higher rates of production taxes erodes the profitability of producers.

How many of the above statements are correct?

(a) Only one (b) Only two
(c) All three (d) None of these

8. Consider the following statements related to taxation:

(i) Base of tax broadens when there is a rise in inflation rate.

(ii) Local currency depreciates when governments' market borrowings rise.

(iii) Higher market borrowings by governments boost tax collections.

How many of the above statements are correct?

(a) Only one (b) Only two
(c) All three (d) None of these

9. Consider the following statements related to the act of taxation:

(i) Governments can take risk of cutting tax rates once the tax base has been broadened.

(ii) Lower rates of income tax incentivises taxpayers to work more.

(iii) Tax breaks increase tax expenditures.

How many of the above statements are correct?

(a) Only one (b) Only two
(c) All three (d) None of these

10. Consider the following statements related to taxation and redistribution by the governments:

(i) Redistribution without provisioning of basic public goods incentivises tax evasion.

(ii) Prioritising corruption free governance encourages tax compliance.

(iii) Legitimacy of State and tax compliance of taxpayers are directly connected.

How many of the above statements are correct?

(a) Only one (b) Only two
(c) All three (d) None of these

Answers: 1. (c) 2. (c) 3. (b) 4. (c) 5. (c) 6. (b) 7. (c) 8. (c) 9. (c) 10. (c)

SAMPLE SUBJECTIVE QUESTIONS

1. Why the implementation of the federal tax GST has been claimed to be historic in nature? Analyse with suitable examples.

2. Examine the recent policy initiatives undertaken by the government in recent times which have increased the process of formalisation in the country.

3. 'To build fiscal capacity, India needs to create legitimacy in state.' Examine.

4. Write a note on the recent tax administration reforms initiated by the government and their significance in enhancing tax compliance in the country.

5. 'For better tax buoyancy, the country needs to broaden the tax base, simplify tax administration and enhance voluntary compliance.' Examine by citing recent government initiatives in this regard.

SAMPLE MODEL ANSWER

1. **Do you think that the GST 2.0 initiated recently by the Government will promote inclusive growth in the country? Support your views with suitable views.**

Ans. The Government took an ambitious indirect tax reform initiative in September 2025 related to the goods and services tax (GST). Called the GST 2.0, the initiative is aimed at rationalisation of GST rates to:

(i) Simplify tax rates, and

(ii) Reducing the cost of living of the citizens.

The following changes were effected under it by the Government:

1. The previous four-slab structure (5 per cent, 12 per cent, 18 per cent, 28 per cent) was rationalised into only two, namely 5 per cent (merit) and 18 per cent (standard).
2. Rate reductions were also affected in the following ways:
   - Health and life insurance premiums were exempted from the GST.
   - Small cars and two-wheelers moved from the 28 per cent to the 18 per cent slab.
   - For items like ACs, TVs, and washing machines, the rates were reduced from 28 per cent to 18 per cent.
   - Many household goods (soap, toothpaste) and agricultural machinery moved to the 5 per cent slab.
   - A new 40 per cent GST rate was introduced for 'luxury' and 'sin' goods like tobacco, high-end cars, and online gaming.

GST 2.0, on the one hand, aims to ease the process of tax filing for business and industry; on the other, it touches the masses in the country through cutting the cost of living via reducing the GST rates on the essential items of daily use.

CHAPTER 19

Public Finance in India

The way modern governments manage all the money they receive – the public money – is the subject matter of public finance. The policy stance taken in this regard is declared annually by the governments *via* their fiscal policy, popularly known as the budget.*

*See Amaresh Bagchi (ed.), *Readings in Public Finance* (New Delhi: Oxford University Press, 2005); Paul A. Samuelson and William D. Nordhaus, *Economics* (New Delhi: McGraw Hill Education, 2020), pp. 405-411; Joseph E. Stiglitz and Carl E. Walsh, *Economics* (New York, NY: W. W. Norton, 2006), pp. 695-97.

To watch the Author's videos on the significance of the Chapter, scan the QR Code given here

Exam Essentials...

- Sovereign Bond
- Debt vs Deficit
- Zero-Based Budgeting
- Trilemmas
- Net Aid Donor

Note to the Reader...

This chapter deals with the process of government budgeting– which is the very core of economic management by modern governments across the world. The discussion on budget normally revolves around taxes, expenditures, government's borrowing plans, and its ultimate impact on the economic performance. But budgeting goes beyond economic indicators as it has a deep impact on our overall capacity to achieve anything in life– this aspect is normally missed by us– this is why official literatures like economic surveys, relevant reports of the NITI Aayog, RBI, ministries etc. are considered the part of the Indian economy. However, these are the essential literatures to understand the very political economy of the country. In simple words, budgeting has a direct link with one and all. Secondly, this chapter should be read in a close connection to the chapter on 'taxation' (i.e., the preceding chapter of the book).

In This Chapter...

INTRODUCTION

Public finance is a wide subject which includes all matters which are connected with public money, i.e., the money a government receives, spends, borrows, lends, raises or prints. Public finance, that is finances of the government, now termed *public economics*, not only discusses the issue of how much of the country's resources the government should acquire for its own use but also discusses the 'efficiency' with which the money should be used. Public finance is referenced in the ancient treatise ***Arthashastra***[1] of Kautilya which covers 'treasury, sources of revenue, accounts and audit' in a detailed manner. However, the subject has gathered much significance in the post-Second World War period once the governments' role in the economy started expanding[2] due to various reasons, namely the rise of the public sector, the delivery of public goods, law and order, defence, etc. By the Second World War, the importance of the government's role in the economy was urgently felt, and it was believed that all needs of the people cannot be met if the economy is left to the market (i.e., the private sector) in its entirety. For example, national defence, law enforcement and other major areas which must be cared for by the national government besides the supplies of ***affordable or free*** healthcare, education, social security measures, etc., could only be taken care of by the governments (***as they are not profit driven***). That is why there was an agreement among the experts and the policymakers to expand the government's role in the economy. This led to the ultimate rise of the public sector around the world.[3] Here we will be looking into the major concepts related to the area of public finance with special reference to India.

[1] L. N. Rangarajan (ed.), *The Arthashastra* (New Delhi: Penguin Books, 1992).

[2] The size of government expenditure for the developed economies stood at almost 10 per cent of their GDPs at the beginning of the twentieth century - which rose to 18 per cent only at the outbreak of the Second World War - went for a steep rise by 1980 to 40 per cent. The government expenditure was barely 9 per cent of the GDP in India at the time of independence, nearly doubled in the 1970s and reached 75 per cent in the 1980s - when questions were raised about their sustainability as revenue receipts failed to grow adequately resulting in rising budgetary deficits [see Amaresh Bagchi (ed.), *Readings in Public Finance* (New Delhi: Oxford University Press, 2005), pp. 1-4].

BUDGETING

Budget is an annual financial statement of a government's income (revenue) and expenditure; even[4] companies, organisations, etc. have such documents. The word 'budget' has its origin in the British parliamentary exercise of preparing such a statement way back in the mid-eighteenth century from the French word *bouget*, meaning a leather bag out of which the financial statement was brought out and presented in the Parliament. Today, this word is used to mean the annual statement in all economies around the world.

The Constitution of India has a provision (Article 112) for such a document called the Annual Financial Statement to be presented in the Parliament before the commencement of every new fiscal year - popular as the Union Budget. The same provision is applicable for the states, too.

Data in the Budget

The Union Budget has ***three sets***[5] of data for every sector or sub-sector of the economy concerned:

1. Actual data of the preceding year (here preceding year means one year before the year in which the budget is being presented). Suppose the budget presented is for the year 2025-26, the budget will provide the final/actual data for the year 2023-24. After the data we write either '**A**', meaning actual data/final data or write nothing (India writes nothing).
2. Provisional data of the current year (i.e., 2024-25) since the budget for 2025-26 is presented in

[3] It should be noted here that the world which had the form of the state economy (i.e., the Socialist countries at this time), majority of the economic activities were under government control. As the communist form of the state economy emerged by the late 1940s (i.e., People's Republic of China, 1949), it had 100 per cent state control over the economic activities.

[4] *Collins Dictionary of Economics*, op. cit.; *Oxford Dictionary of Business*, op. cit.

[5] Based on the budgetary documents of the Ministry of Finance, Government of India, New Delhi.

2024-25 itself, it provides Provisional Estimates for this year (shown as **PE** in brackets with the data).

3. Budgetary estimates for the following year (here the following year means one year after the year in which the budget is being presented or the year for which the budget is being presented, i.e., 2025-26). This is shown with the symbol '**BE**' in brackets with the data concerned.

One comes across certain other kinds of data too in day-to-day government economic literature, which are given below:

1. **Revised Estimate (RE):** RE is basically a current estimation of either the budgetary estimates (BEs) or the provisional estimates (PEs). It shows the contemporary situation and is an interim data.
2. **Quick Estimate (QE):** QE is a kind of RE which shows the latest situation and is useful in the process of opting for future projections for some sector or sub-sector. It is an interim data too.
3. **Advance Estimate (AE):** AE is a kind of QE but carried out ahead (in advance) of the final stage when data should have been collected. It also is an interim data.

Developmental and Non-developmental Expenditure

Total expenditure incurred by the government is classified into two segments - developmental and non-developmental. All expenditures of productive nature are developmental such as on the heads of new factories, dams, bridges, roads and railways - all *investments*.

The expenditures which are of consumptive kind and do not involve any production are non-developmental, i.e., paying salaries, pensions, interest payments, subsidies, defence expenses and so on.

This classification is not used in the Indian public finance management now (see *Plan* and *Non-Plan Expenditure*, in the next entry).[6]

Plan and Non-Plan Expenditure

Every expenditure incurred on the public exchequer is classified into two categories - the plan and the non-plan. All those expenditures which are carried out in India in the name of *planning* are the *plan expenditures* and the rest are *non-plan expenditures.* Basically, all asset creating and productive expenditures are planned and all consumptive, non-productive, non-asset building are non-plan expenditures and are developmental and non-developmental expenditures, respectively.

In the financial year 1987-88, there was a terminology change in Indian public finance literature when developmental and non-developmental expenditures were replaced by the new terms plan and non-plan expenditures, respectively. (It was suggested by the Sukhamoy Chakraborty Committee.)[7]

Meanwhile, a high-power panel headed by Dr. C. Rangarajan (Chairman, Prime Minister's Economic Advisory Council), in *September 2011* suggested redefining ***Plan*** and ***Non-Plan*** expenditures as ***Capital*** and ***Revenue*** expenditures, as the former set of terms 'blur the classification' - this will facilitate linking expenditure to *outcomes* and better public expenditure. Major suggestions of the panel are as follows:

1. *Plan* and *Non-Plan* distinction in the budget is neither able to provide a satisfactory classification of 'developmental' and 'non-developmental' dimensions of government expenditure nor an appropriate budgetary framework. It has therefore become 'dysfunctional'.
2. Suggests for *redefining the roles* of the Planning Commission (PC) and the Finance Ministry (FM). According to the panel the PC should be responsible for the formulation of the five-year plan, and the task of firming up the annual budgets should be entrusted to the FM.
3. The PC should dispense with the exercise of approving annual plans of States, and it could make a strategy or hold review meetings with the representatives of the States.
4. Public expenditures should be split into *capital* and *revenue* expenditures.
5. Public expenditure should have 'management approach' based on measurable 'outcomes', indicating that the responsibility should be assigned to the FM.

---

[6] *Union Budget 1987-88* (New Delhi: Ministry of Finance, GoI, 1987).

[7] *Review of the Working of the Monetary System,* headed by Sukhamoy Chakraborty, Reserve Bank of India, Government of India, New Delhi, 1985.

Analysis of the Situation While the need for looking beyond the budget is well accepted, there are many factors raising doubts on the 'efficacy' and 'relevance' of the five-year plans as the instrument. The division of expenditure between *Plan* and *Non-Plan* is artificial and creates problems, such as:

1. Plan expenditure tends to become priority especially when austerity and expenditure reduction has to be carried out periodically for fiscal consolidation. Non- Plan expenditure gets the ***cut*** even if it is vitally needed for economic development. An example is budget provision for the maintenance of assets such as hospitals, schools and irrigation dams already created under Plan, but whose maintenance is treated as non-Plan.
2. Review and implementation of schemes is another area of direct responsibility for the Ministry of Finance and the Ministry of Statistics and Programme Implementation. The Finance Minister himself had, in the budget speech for 2005-06, promised to ensure that programmes and schemes were not allowed to continue indefinitely from one plan period to another without an independent and in-depth evaluation. The PC, serving as the *focal point for Plan allocations*, dilutes the role of the FM in this case.
3. 'Output' and 'Outcome Budgeting' was introduced by the Central government in the Budget for 2005-06. Non-Plan expenditure remains out of its purview. This means, for example, the outcome of expenditure on running schools and hospitals will not be evaluated. This, again, is another fallout of the artificial division into Plan and Non-Plan.

This classification used to adversely affect the whole budget process, formulation and implementation. Looking at this anomaly, the government switched over from the 'plan' and 'non-plan' classification of expenditure to 'revenue' and 'capital' since the fiscal 2017-18 (as announced in the ***Union Budget 2017-18***).

Revenue

Every form of money generation in the nature of income, earnings is revenue for a firm or a government which does not increase the financial liabilities of the government, i.e., the tax incomes, non-tax incomes along with foreign grants.

Non-revenue

Every form of money generation which is not income or earnings for a firm or a government (i.e., money raised *via* borrowings) is considered a non-revenue source if it increases the financial liabilities.

Receipts

Every receiving or accrual of money to a government by revenue and non-revenue sources is a receipt. Their sum is called *total receipts*. It includes all incomes as well as non-income accruals of a government.

UNION BUDGET

As a practice, the annual financial statement (Article 112) of the Government of India (GoI) is called the Union Budget. Though the budgeting process in India traces its origin from the British tradition, today, most budgets in the world are technically similar in nature. The budget is broadly classified into two parts - *A. Revenue Budget and B. Capital Budget*, i.e., Revenue and Capital Receipts and Expenditures, respectively. A concise description of the items covered under both the budgets is given below:

A. Revenue Budget

The budget has two sets of descriptions, namely the *revenue receipts* and *revenue expenditures*, consisting of the following items:

1. **Revenue Receipts:** These consist of all revenue receiving (tax and non-tax) of the government, which are of two types:
   - **(i)** ***Tax Revenue Receipts:*** All revenues received *via* collections of the direct and indirect taxes are shown here (such as income tax, corporate tax, dividend tax, interest tax, expenditure tax, GST, central excise/CENVAT, custom duty, anti-dumping and countervailing duties, etc.)
   - **(ii)** ***Non-Tax Revenue Receipts:*** Here, we find all of the receiving of the government which accrue from sources other than taxes, which include:
     - **(a)** *Profits* and *dividends* which the government receives from its public sector undertakings (PSUs).
     - **(b)** *Interests* received by the government out of all loans forwarded by it, be it inside the country (i.e., internal

lending) or outside the country (i.e., external lending). It means this income might be in both domestic and foreign currencies.

(c) *Fiscal services* also generate incomes for the government, i.e., currency printing, stamp printing, coinage and medals minting, etc.

(d) *General services* also earn money for the government as the power distribution, irrigation, banking, insurance, community services, etc.

(e) *Fees, penalties* and *fines* received by the government.

(f) *Grants* which the governments receive - it is always external in the case of the central government and internal in the case of state governments.

2. **Revenue Expenditures:** All expenditures incurred by the government are either of *revenue kind* or *current kind* or *compulsive kind.* The basic identity of such expenditures is that they are of consumptive kind and do not involve the creation of productive assets. They are either used in running of a productive process or running a government. A broad category of things that fall under such expenditures in India are as follows:

   (i) *Interest* payment by the government on the internal and external loans

   (ii) *Salaries, Pension* and *Provident Fund (PF)* paid by the government-to-government employees

   (iii) *Subsidies* forwarded to all sectors by the government

   (iv) *Defence* expenditures by the government

   (v) *Postal Deficits* of the government

   (vi) *Law and order* expenditures (i.e., police and paramilitary)

   (vii) Expenditures *on social services* (include all social sector expenditures such as education, healthcare, social security, poverty alleviation, etc.) and *general services* (tax collection, etc.)

   (viii) *Grants* given by the government to Indian states and foreign countries

Revenue Deficit (RD) If the balance of total revenue receipts and total revenue expenditures turns out to be negative, it is known as revenue deficit, a new fiscal terminology used since the fiscal year 1997-98 in India.[8]

This shows that the government's *Revenue Budget* is running in losses and the government is earning less but spending more revenue - incurring a deficit. Revenue expenditures are of immediate nature (this has to be done), and since they are consumptive/ non-productive, they are considered as a kind of expenditure which sums up to a heinous crime in the area of fiscal policy. The governments fill the gap/ deficit with the money which could have been spent/ invested in productive areas.

A government might have its revenue expenditures less than its revenue receipts, i.e., having *(revenue surplus)* budget. Such fiscal policy is considered good where the government has been able to manage some money out of its revenue budget which could be spent for the creation of productive assets. Another thing that should be kept in mind is how the government has managed this surplus and whether the policies which made this happen are judicious enough or not. In the Second Plan, India emerged as a revenue-surplus state, but experts did not appreciate it as it had many bad impacts on the economy - higher tax rates culminated in tax evasion, corruption, creation of black money, etc.

RD may be shown in the quantitative form (as how much the gross/total deficit is in currency terms) or in percentage terms of the GDP for that particular year (shown as percentage of GDP). Usually, it is shown as a percentage of the GDP for domestic as well as international analyses. The *Union Budget 2026-27* has set a revenue deficit target of **1.5** per cent for the year 2026-27, which is the same as its Revised Estimate for 2025-26.

Effective Revenue Deficit Effective revenue deficit (ERD) is a new term introduced in the *Union Budget 2011-12.* Conventionally, RD is the difference between revenue receipts and revenue expenditures. Here, revenue expenditures include all the grants which the Union government extends to the State governments and the UTs - some of which ***create***

[8] Raja J. Chelliah, "The Meaning and Significance of the Fiscal Deficit," in Amaresh Bagchi (ed.), *Readings in Public Finance* (New Delhi: Oxford University Press, 2005), pp. 387-8. Also see *Union Budget 1997-98* (New Delhi: Ministry of Finance, GoI, 1997).

assets (though these assets are not owned by the GoI, but by the State governments and the UTs concerned). According to the FM *(Union Budget 2011-12)*, such revenue expenditures contribute to the growth in the economy and, therefore, *should not be treated as unproductive* in nature like other items in the revenue expenditures. And by this logic, a new methodology was introduced to capture the 'effective RD', which is the RD 'excluding' those revenue expenditures of the GoI which were carried out in the form of **GoCAs** (grants for creation of capital assets).

The GoCAs includes the GoI grants forwarded to the States and UTs for the implementation of the centrally sponsored programmes such as Pradhan Mantri Gram Sadak Yojana, Accelerated Irrigation Benefit Programme and Jawaharlal Nehru National Urban Renewal Mission. These expenses, though shown by the GoI in its Revenue Expenditures, are involved with *asset creation* and cannot be considered completely 'unproductive' like other items put in the basket of Revenue Expenditures - the reason why a new 'terminology' was created.

It is believed that the term was innovated by the government to *justify* the higher RDs of the period - by outlining that they were not 'typical' (i.e., consumptive kind) of being RD - as some of them were also used to create 'assets' (shown as the GoCAs). The government of the time has set a zero per cent effective RD by 2017-18, while RD will be still 1.5 per cent - which implied that by 2017-18, all of the RD would have been used for the creation of assets. Since 2014-15 onwards, the new government does not seem to be extending much significance to the concept, though the concept continues to exist - the *Union Budget 2026-27* has set an effective revenue deficit target of **0.3** per cent which is lower than its Revised Estimate of 0.6 per cent for 2025-26.

B. Capital Budget

The part of the budget which deals with the receipts and expenditures of the capital by the government is called capital budget. This shows the means by which the capital is managed and the areas where capital is spent.

1. **Capital Receipts:** All non-revenue receipts of a government are known as capital receipts. Such receipts are for investment purposes and supposed to be spent on plan development by a government. But the receipts might need a diversion to meet other needs to take care of the rising revenue expenditure of a government, as the case had been with India. The capital receipts in India include the following capital kinds of accruals to the government:
   - **(i)** ***Loan Recovery:*** This is one source of capital receipts. The money the government had lent out in the past in India (states, UTs, PSUs, etc.) and abroad comes back to the government when the borrowers repay them as capital receipts. The interests which come to the government on such loans are part of the revenue receipts.
   - **(ii)** ***Borrowings by the Government:*** These include all long-term loans raised by the government inside the country (i.e., internal borrowings) and outside the country (i.e., external borrowings). Internal borrowings might include the borrowings from the RBI, Indian banks, financial institutions and so on. Similarly, external borrowings might include the loans from the World Bank, the IMF, foreign banks, foreign governments, foreign financial institutions and so on.
   - **(iii)** ***Other Receipts by the Government:*** These include many long-term capital accruals to the government through the PF, Postal Deposits, various small saving schemes (SSSs) and the government bonds sold to the public (such as Indira Vikas Patra, Kisan Vikas Patra, Market Stabilisation Bond, etc.). Such receipts are nothing but a kind of loan on which the government needs to pay interests on their maturities. But they play a role in the capital raising process by the government.
2. **Capital Expenditure:** All the areas which receive capital from the government are part of the capital expenditure. It includes so many heads in India.
   - **(i)** ***Loan Disbursals by the Government:*** The loans forwarded by the government might be internal (i.e., to the states, UTs, PSUs, FIs, etc.) or external (i.e., to foreign countries, foreign banks, purchase of foreign bonds, loans to the IMF and WB, etc.).

(ii) ***Loan Repayments by the Government:*** Again, loan payments might be internal as well as external. This consists of only the *capital* part of the loan repayment as the element of interest on loans is shown as a part of the *revenue expenditure.*

(iii) ***Plan Expenditure of the Government:*** This consists of all the expenditures incurred by the government to finance the planned development of India as well as the Central government financial supports to the States for their plan requirements.

(iv) ***Capital Expenditures on Defence by the Government:*** This consists of all kinds of *capital* expenses to maintain the defence forces, the equipment purchased for them as well as the modernisation expenditures. It should be kept in mind that *defence* is a non-plan expenditure which has capital as well as revenue expenditures in its maintenance. The revenue part of the expenditure in the defence is counted in the revenue expenditures by the government.

(v) ***General Services:*** These also need huge capital expenditure by the government - the railways, postal department, water supply, education, rural extension, etc.

(vi) ***Other Liabilities of the Government:*** Basically, these include all the repayment liabilities of the government on the items of the Other Receipts. The level of liabilities depends on the fact as to how much such receipts were made by the governments in the past. The amount of payment liabilities in the year also depends on the fact as to which years in the past the governments had other receipts and for what duration of maturity periods. For example, the *PF liabilities* were not an item of such liabilities for almost the first three decades after Independence. But once the government employees started retiring, it kept increasing. Future India (especially the 1960s and 1970s) saw the expansion of the PSUs and excessive employment generation in them (devoid of the logic of labour requirement). We see the PF liabilities expanding extensively throughout the 1990 - the governments had been under pressure to manage this segment either by cutting interest on PF or at present trying to make it a matter of market economy. The same thing occurred with the element of *pension,* and we have been able to devise a market mechanism for it once pension reforms took place and with the arrival of a pension regulatory authority for the area.

Capital Deficit: There is no such term in public finance or in economics as such. But in practice, one usually hears the use of the term capital crunch, scarcity of capital in day-to-day economic news items. Basically, the government in the news is facing the problem of managing as much funds, money, capital as is required by it for public expenditure. Such expenditure might be of revenue kind or capital kind. Such difficulties have always been with the developing economies due to their high-level requirement of capital expenditures. Had there been a term to show this situation, it would naturally have been *Capital Deficit.*

Fiscal Deficit (FD): When balance of the government's total receipts (i.e., revenue + capital receipts) and total expenditures (i.e., revenue + capital expenditures) turns out to be negative, it shows the situation of FD, a concept being used since the fiscal year 1997-98 in India.[9]

Scan this QR Code to watch a author's video lecture that simplifies this topic

The situation of FD indicates that the government is spending beyond its means. To be more precise, we may say that the government is spending more than its income (though, in practice, all receipts of the government are not income. Basically, receipts are all forms of money accruing to the government, be it income or borrowings).

FD may be shown in the quantitative form (i.e., the total currency value of the deficit) or in the percentage form of the GDP for that particular year (percentage of GDP). In general, the percentage form is used for domestic or international (i.e., comparative economics) studies and analyses.

[9] Raja J. Chelliah, 'The Meaning and Significance of Public Deficit', op. cit.m p. 381 & p. 387. Also see *Union Budget 1997-98* (New Delhi: Ministry of Finance, GoI).

The FD of the governments (Centre and States) has been rising continuously due to diverse socio-economic reasons. The issue has been hotly debated during the period of economic reforms. After the fiscal responsibility law was enacted in 2003, we find a concerted effort (fiscal consolidation) from the government to contain it.

The *Union Budget 2026-27* has set a fiscal deficit target of **4.3** per cent of the GDP for the year (for 2025-26 the Revised Estimate of the deficit is 4.4 per cent, the same as the budgetary target).

Primary Deficit

The FD excluding the interest liabilities for a year is the primary deficit, a term India started using since the fiscal year 1997-98.[10] It shows the FD for the year in which the economy had not fulfilled any interest payments on the different loans and liabilities which it is obliged to - shown both in quantitative and percentage of GDP forms.

This new concept of deficit has not only helped governments to measure their dependence on loans but also led them to introspect into the pattern of expenditures and possible cuts in them. The *Union Budget 2026-27* has set a primary deficit target of **0.7** per cent of GDP for the year, which is lower than its revised estimate of 0.8 per cent for 2025-26.

Primary Surplus

Primary surplus is a situation in the budgeting process when the tax receipts of a government are higher than its total expenditures excluding interest payments. This concept is also being used in India since 1997-98 as an indicator to understand fiscal health in a better way.

The data related to it help the government in understanding the impact of interest payments on its revenues (income) together with prioritising the expenditures. It means that had the government not have the interest payment liabilities, it would have run into budgetary surplus. Rather, it also hints at the fiscal space available for a government to opt for revenue or capital expenditures. A variety of other information can be obtained by going into primary surplus data of a period such as situation of tax base, debt to GDP ratio, health of tax compliance, fiscal capacity of the government, tax expenditure, and sizes of revenue and capital expenditures.

Monetised Deficit

The part of the FD which is provided by the RBI to the government in a particular year is Monetised Deficit, a new term adopted since 1997-98 in India.[11] This is shown in both the forms - in quantitative and a percentage of the GDP for that particular financial year.

To finance its expenditures, the GoI depends on short and long-term borrowings. To borrow, the government issues short-term (Treasury Bills) and long-term (G-Secs) securities. These securities were to be subscribed (purchased) by the RBI on a compulsory basis. The value of investment made by the RBI in the year used to be the monetised deficit of the government. Once the fiscal responsibility law was enacted (in 2003), the situation has changed much.

Since 1997, the RBI stopped being the primary subscriber of the Treasury Bills (rather the RBI invests in them voluntarily) as an integral part of the ways and means advances (WMAs). Since 2013, an *ad hoc* '14-Day Intermediate Treasury Bills' has been put in place to meet the short-term needs of the government, which are not subscribed by the RBI. The compulsion for the RBI to subscribe the G-Secs was also dropped in 2007 (now the RBI just manages the borrowing programmes of the government). Thus, as the RBI no longer subscribes the primary issuance of either Treasury Bills or the G-Secs, technically speaking, monetised deficit looks *phased out*. But in practice, for the need of regulating monetary policy, the RBI keeps buying and selling all of the government securities (G-Secs, short- and long-term) - under the open market operations (OMOs). It means, on *de facto* basis, the RBI is not under any compulsion to invest in the G-Secs, in reality it needs to deal with them (thus in reality, monetised deficits have kept occurring since 2007). It all depends on FD - till budgets run in deficits, in reality, monetised deficits will be present.

The *Union Budget 2026-27* has set a record **market borrowing** target of ₹17.2 lakh crore ($187.6 billion) for the fiscal year 2026-27 (to finance the projected fiscal deficit of 4.3 per cent of the GDP in the year). This represents an approximate 17 per cent increase over

10 *Union Budget 1997-98*, (New Delhi: Ministry of Finance, GoI).

11 Raja J. Chelliah, op. cit., p. 389. Also see *Union Budget 1997-98*.

the ₹14.61 lakh crore borrowed in the 2025-26 fiscal year. Today, around 95 per cent of the government expenditures are financed through market borrowings which ultimately create a challenge for the RBI in chalking out the right monetary policy for the economy.

Deficit and Surplus Budget

When a budget proposes higher expenditures than the receipts, it is known as a *deficit budget*. Opposite to this, if the budget proposes lesser expenditures than the receipts, then it is called a *surplus budget*.[12]

In practice, governments the world over usually do not present a surplus budget as it symbolises the government's lower concerns towards development. But at times, as a political weapon, a government might come out with such a budget (e.g., the Uttaranchal Budget for 2006-07 was a surplus budget). How can a government propose for a surplus budget in a developing state when even developed countries still need development and are heading for deficit budgets? The Union Budget in India has never been presented as a surplus budget.

DEFICIT FINANCING

The act/process of financing/supporting a deficit budget by a government is deficit financing. In this process, the government knows well in advance that its total expenditures are going to turn out to be more than its total receipts and enacts/follows such financial policies so that it can sustain the burden of the deficits proposed by it.

First used in the area of public finance in the early 1930s in the United States,[13] today the term is being used by the corporate sector, too, and such a financial management of a firm might be followed by it as part of its business strategy. Again, a sick firm might need to follow a deficit financing route for many years to come as required by the firm to enable it to come out of the red (i.e., doing away with the losses).

Need of Deficit Financing

It was in the late 1920s that the idea and need of deficit financing was felt. It is when the government needs to spend more money than it is expected to earn or generate in a particular period, to opt for a desired level of growth and development. Had there been some means to opt for more expenditure with less income and receipts, socio-political goals could have been realised as per the aspirations of the public policy. And once the growth had taken place, the extra money spent above the income would have been reimbursed or repaid. This was a good public/ Government wish which was fulfilled by the evolution of the idea of deficit financing.

It was by the early 1930s that the United States first tried its hand at deficit financing soon to be followed by the whole Euro-American governments.[14] Through this route the developed world was able to come out of the menace of the Great Depression (1929).[15] The idea became popular around the world by the 1960s. India tried its hand at deficit financing in 1969, and since the 1970s, it became a routine phenomenon, till it became wild and illogical, demanding immediate redressal. The FDs in India did not only peak to unsustainable levels, but its composition was also not justified and not based on sound fundamentals of economics. Finally, India headed for a slow but confident process of fiscal reforms that is also known as the process of fiscal consolidation (to be discussed later).

---

[12] In the US economy if tax revenue falls short of government expenditures, the government has *a fiscal deficit*, and it means that the government needs to borrow in the capital market to cover the difference. Opposite to it, if the government runs a *fiscal surplus* (i.e., its tax revenues exceed its expenditure), then the government, like the household sector, will be a net saver and will represent a source of saving for the economy (see Stiglitz and Walsh, *Economics*, op. cit., p. 549).

[13] J. K. Galbraith, *A History of Economics* (London: Penguin Books, 1987), p. 226. *(The whole Chapter XVII on J. M. Keynes (pp. 221-36) is interesting to refer for the topic.)*

[14] For a detailed discussion on the topic, one may refer to Joseph. E. Stiglitz, *Economics of the Public Sector* (New York, NY: W. W. Norton, 2000).

[15] It should be noted here that although the governments had run deficits (i.e., budget deficit) even before the Keynesian idea of the deficit, the pre-Keynesian thinking was that in peacetime the budget should generally be *balanced* (i.e., neither deficit nor surplus), or even in surplus so that the government debt created by wartime deficits could be paid off. For further reference on the topic and its constraints, Stanley Fischer and William Easterly, *Economics of the government Budget Constraints*, World Bank Research Observer, 5, no. 2, July 1990, pp. 127-42; also reproduced in Amaresh Bagchi (ed.), *Readings in Public Finance*, op. cit. pp. 301-19.

Means of Deficit Financing

Once deficit financing became an established part of public finance around the world, the means of opting for it were also evolved by that time. These means are basically the ways in which the government may utilise the amount of money created as the deficit to sustain its budget for developmental or political needs. These means are given below in order of their suggested and tried preferences.

1. ***External Aids***[16] are the best money as a means to fulfil a government's deficit requirements even if it is coming with soft interest. If they are coming without interest, nothing could be better.

   When India went to borrow from the IMF in the wake of the financial crisis of 1990-91, the body advised India to keep its FD to the tune of 4.5 per cent of its GDP and noted it to be sustainable for the economy. What was the rationale behind these data? Basically, in those times with the foreign aids (soft loans either from the *WB* or from the *Aid India forum*) India was able to manage its budget to the tune of 4.5 per cent of its GDP. In 2002, when India's FD was around 6 per cent (5.7 per cent to be precise), the IMF validated it to be sustainable. There were two reasons - first, India was able to show a check on FD; and secondly, at the same time, the forex reserves of the country were suitably higher to neutralise the negative impacts of the higher FD than the suggested levels (4.5 per cent).

   External Grants are even better elements in this case (which comes free - neither interest nor any repayments), but it either did not come to India (since 1975, the year of the first Pokhran nuclear test) or India did not accept it (as happened post-Tsunami, arguing that grants/ aids come with a tag/condition attached to them). That is why this segment has not been discussed as a means to manage deficit.

2. ***External Borrowings***[17] are the next best way to manage FD with the condition that the external loans are comparatively cheaper and long term.

   Though external loans are considered an erosion in the nation's sovereign decision-making process, this has its own benefit and is considered better than the internal borrowings due to two reasons:

   (i) External borrowings bring in foreign currency/hard currency which provides an extra edge to the government spending as by this, the government may fulfil its developmental requirements inside the country as well as from outside the country.

   (ii) External borrowings are preferred to the internal borrowings due to 'crowding out effect'. If the government itself keeps borrowing from the banks of the country, from where will others borrow for investment purposes?

Sovereign Bond

The government proposed (in the *Union Budget 2019–20*) to raise part of its borrowings from the external markets. It means the government was in favour of issuing 'Sovereign Bond' – a proposal put forth for the *first time*. Such an initiative of the government might be based on the fact that the sovereign external debt of India is at quite comfortable level (5 per cent of the GDP).

The Government initiated it by issuing the three-year *Sovereign Green Bonds (SGrBs)* in 2023–24 through which ₹20,000 crore were raised from the external market. The fund will be utilised to finance green public infrastructure projects in the country aimed at meeting India's commitment to cut emission under the Paris Climate Agreement.

3. ***Internal Borrowings***[18] come as the third preferred route of FD management. But opting for it in a huge way hampers the investment prospects of the public and the corporate sector. It has the same impact on the expenditure pattern in the economy. Ultimately, the economy heads for a double negative impact - lower investment (leading to lower production, lower GDPs and lower per capita income, etc.) and lower demands (by the general public as

[16] Ibid.

[17] Ibid.

[18] Ibid.

well as by the corporate world) in the economy - the economy moves either for *stagnation* or a *slowdown* (one can see them happening in India repeatedly throughout the 1960s, 1970s, 1980s). The situation improved after the mid-1990s.

4. ***Printing Currency*** is the last resort for the government in managing its deficit.[19] But it has the biggest handicap that with it, the government cannot opt for the expenditures which are to be made in the foreign currency. Even if the government is satisfied on this front, printing fresh currencies does have other damaging effects on the economy:
   - **(i)** It increases inflation proportionally. (India regularly opted for it since the early 1970s and usually had to bear double digit inflations.)
   - **(ii)** It brings in regular pressure and obligation on the government for upward revision in wages and salaries of government employees - ultimately increasing the government expenditures necessitating further printing of currency and further inflation - a vicious cycle into which economies entangle themselves.

Now, it remains a matter of choice and availability of the above-given means, and which means a government adopts and in what proportion for fulfilling its deficit requirements.

Composition of Fiscal Deficit

The Keynesian idea of deficit financing, though he advocated it, had a catch to it also which was usually missed by Third World economies or intentionally overlooked by them. The catch is related to the question as to why an economy wants to opt for an FD. Thus, it becomes essential to opt for an analysis of the composition[20] of the FD of a government.

Out of the two broad expenditure obligations of a government - revenue expenditure and capital expenditure - the following combinations of expenditure composition are suggested:

1. An FD with a surplus revenue budget or a zero-revenue expenditure is the best composition of FD and the most suitable time for deficit financing.
2. The deficit requirements for lower revenue expenditures and higher capital expenditures are the next best situation for deficit financing, provided the RD is eliminated soon.
3. The last could be the situation when major part of deficit financing is to fulfil revenue expenditures and a minor part to opt for capital expenditures. The total money of the deficit might go to fulfil revenue expenditure, which could be the worst form.

Basically, there should be a judicious mix of plan and non-plan expenditure as well as revenue and capital expenditures in India. Lesser non-plan expenditures or higher plan-expenditures are better the reasons behind deficit financing in India (though India has a typical feature of capital expenditure which makes this combination of deficit financing not a suggested form - discussed further below).

Third World economies (including India) though opted for higher and higher FDs and deficit financing, and they either did not address or failed to address the composition of deficit favourable towards capital and non-revenue expenditures.

FISCAL POLICY

The real meaning, significance and impact of fiscal policy emerged in the wake of the Great Depression and the Second World War. Fiscal policy has been **defined** as 'the policy of the government with regard to the level of government purchases, the level of transfers, and the tax structure' - probably the best and the most acclaimed definition among experts.[21] Later, the impact of fiscal policy on macro-economy was beautifully analysed.[22] As the policy has a deep impact on the overall performance of the economy, fiscal policy is also **defined** as the policy which handles public expenditure and tax to direct and stimulate the level of economic

[19] L. N. Rangarajan, *The Arthashastra*, op. cit. pp. 259-62.

[20] J. Cullis and P. Jones, *Public Finance and Public Choice* (New York, NY: Oxford University Press, 1998).

[21] The acclaimed definition first came up in the widely used work *Macroeconomics* by Dornbusch and Fisher which is now available as R. S. Dornbusch, S. Fisher and Richard Startz, *Microeconomics* (New Delhi: Tata McGraw-Hill, 2002).

[22] John Hicks, the British Nobel Laureate, did show it, referring changes in taxes and government expenditure using the framework of the famous IS-LM model (Ibid).

activity (numerically denoted by the Gross Domestic Product).[23] It was J. M. Keynes, the ***first*** economist, who developed a theory linking fiscal policy and economic performance.[24]

Fiscal policy is also **defined** as 'changes in government expenditures and taxes that are designed to achieve macro-economic policy goals'[25] (such as growth, employment, investment, etc.). Therefore, we say that 'fiscal policy denotes the use of taxes and government expenditures'.[26]

How the taxes and the government expenditures influence the overall economy has been explained in brief here.[27] Let us first discuss the *taxes* and their impact on the economy:

1. Taxes have a direct bearing on people's income affecting their levels of disposable incomes, purchase of goods and services, consumption and ultimately their standard of living.
2. Taxes directly affect the savings of individuals, families and firms which affect investment in the economy - as investment affects the output (GDP) thereby influencing the per capita income.
3. Taxes affect the prices of goods and services as factor cost (production cost) is affected, thereby affecting incentives and behaviour of economic activities, etc.

Government Expenditures affect/influence the economy in two ways:

1. There are some expenditures on government purchases of goods and services, for example, construction of roads, railways, ports and purchasing foodgrains in the goods category and salary payments to government employees in the services category.
2. There are some expenditures due to the government's income support to the poor, unemployed and elderly (known as government ***transfer payments***).

[23] S. R. Maheshwari, *A Dictionary of Public Administration* (New Delhi: Orient Longman, 2002), p. 227.

[24] In his acclaimed work *The General Theory of Employment, Interest and Money*, 1936.

[25] Stiglitz and Walsh, *Economics*, op. cit, p. 729.

[26] Samuelson and Nordhaus, *Economics*, op. cit, p. 412.

[27] Based on the elaboration by Samuelson and Nordhaus, *Economics*, op. cit, pp. 412-13.

Deficit Financing in India

India was declared to be a planned economy right after Independence. As development responsibilities of the government were very high, there was a need of huge funds in rupee as well as in foreign currency forms. India faced continuous crises in managing the required fund to support its Five- Year Plans - neither foreign funds were provided nor internal resources mobilised in sufficient amount. (Due to lower tax collections, weaker banks that were privately owned, and negligible saving rate, etc.)[28]

By the late 1960s, the government headed for deficit financing, and from the 1970s onwards, India started opting for higher FDs and became more dependent on increased deficit financing with every new year. We may classify deficit financing in India into three phases.

The First Phase (1947–1970)

The first phase had no concept of deficit financing, and the deficits were shown as Budgetary Deficits. Major aspects of this phase were as follows:

1. Trying to borrow from inside and outside the economy but unable to meet the target.
2. In the 1950s, a serious attempt was made to increase tax collections and check revenue expenditures to be ultimately able to emerge as a surplus revenue budget economy. But huge cost was paid in the form of tax evasion, rise in corruption, stagnating standard of life and a neglected social sector.
3. Taking recourse to heavy borrowings from the RBI and finally nationalisation of banks so that their money could be used by the government to support the plans. This not only increased the interest burden of the governments but also ruptured the whole financial system in coming years - banks did not remain commercial entities and became part of the government's political statement.
4. Establishing giant PSUs with higher revenue expenditures (salaries) which increased the revenue expenditures of the future governments when the pensions and the PFs needed to be serviced.

[28] For a detailed data-based discussion, refer to Sudipto Mundle and M. Govinda Rao, "Issues in Fiscal Policy" in *The Indian Economy: Problems and Prospects*, Bimal Jalan (ed.) (New Delhi: Penguin Books, 2004), pp. 258-85.

5. Unable to opt for the required level of investment even after taking recourse to all the above-given means.

The Second Phase (1970–1991)

The second phase is considered the period of deficit financing, follow-up of unsound fundamentals of economics and finally culminating in severe financial crisis by the year 1990-91. Major highlights of this phase may be summed up as follows:

1. This phase saw the nationalisation policy and simultaneous revival of an increased emphasis on the expansion of the PSU (two points should be noted here specially - *first,* many of the South-East Asian economies have officially declared their acceptance of capitalism and privatisation. *Second,* China had declared that investments in the government-controlled companies are a loss of money at this time).
2. Upcoming PSUs increased the total expenditure of the government's revenue as well as capital.
3. Existing PSUs were taking their own due from the economy - the illogical employment creation excessively increased the burden of salaries, pensions and PF. Many of them had started accruing huge losses by this time. As the public sector does not have profit as its primary goal, there was a lack of profit and loss analysis. The PSUs had no connection between their need of labour force and the existing labour force. Ultimately, the responsibility of profit or loss did not remain the onus of the officers, thus making them centres of intentional losses and an institutionalised centre of corruption.
4. The governments have failed on both the fronts - checking population rise and mass employment generation - the burden of different *subsidies* kept increasing, making them unmanageable and highly illogical. Self-employment programmes could not pick up, or better said, it was politically suitable to opt for piece-meal wage employment programmes with different names.
5. Planned development remained highly centralised and devoid of any place for local aspirations - frustrations of the masses started showing up in the form of extremist and radical organisations raising their heads, creating a law-and-order problem and excessive expenditure on them. The outcome was a burdened police force and lagging judicial set-up.
6. The plan expenditures which governments were going for were through investments in the PSUs which were not committed to profit motive; deficit financing for the PSUs was not based on sound economics. Majority of the plan expenditures in a sense turned out to be non-economic, i.e., non-plan expenditure at the end.

As a result, it was tough to predict whether it was discrete to opt for huge FDs in India.[29]

The Third Phase (1991 onwards)

The third phase started with the initiation of the economic reforms process under the conditionalities put forth by the IMF (controlling FD was one among them). As the economy moved from government dominance to market dominance, there was a need for restructuring wherein public finance also required a touch of rationality.

In the wake of economic reforms, encouraging investment from the private sector was to be the government's priority. To enable the private sector to invest in the economy, they should be made available with enough funds. It means the government needed to drain the financial system less (i.e., reducing 'crowding out' of funds) so that the private sector receives the investible funds. For this to occur, the government adopted a variety of actions starting with the early 1990s, such as rationalising expenditures of the governments (Centre and State), raising its own tax and non-tax revenues, strengthening and expanding financial markets and so on (which will be discussed later).

INDIAN FISCAL SITUATION: A SUMMARY

In December 1985, the GoI presented a discussion paper in the Parliament titled 'Long-Term Fiscal Policy'. It was for the ***first time*** in the fiscal history of India that we see a long-term perspective on the fiscal issue from the government. This also included the policy of government expenditure. The paper was bold enough to recognise the deterioration in India's fiscal position and accepted it among the most important challenges of the 1980s - the paper laid down specific targets and policies to set things right. This paper was followed by a country-wide debate on the issue, and it was in

[29] This was the general feeling among experts, policymakers and the IMF alike.

1987 that the government came up with ***two*** bold steps in the direction:

1. a virtual freeze was announced on government expenditure, and
2. a ceiling on the budgetary deficit.

The above steps had a positive impact on the situation, but it was temporary as since mid- 1988, the situation again started deteriorating. The balance of payment (BoP) crisis at the end of 1990 was generated partly by the alarmingly high FD[30] as well as a high level of external borrowings. The IMF support to fight the crisis was present but with many macro-economic conditionalities, with checking the fiscal menace being a major one. With the process of economic reforms which started in 1991-92, the government also announced its commitment to reduce FD to 3-4 per cent (of GDP) by the mid-1990s (from the level of about 8 per cent during 1987-90). This step was among the many measures which the government started with the objective of stabilising the economy. We may take a look at India's fiscal situation up to 1990-91 in the following way:

1. The FDs of the Central government, after averaging below 4 per cent of the GDP till the 1970s, started climbing by being 5.77 per cent in 1980-81, 8.47 per cent in 1986-87 ending up at 7.85 per cent in 1990-91 after being above 7 per cent in the second half of the 1980s.[31]
2. The revenue (i.e., current) expenditure of the government (centre and states combined) increased from 11.8 per cent of GDP to 23 per cent between 1960 and 1990. The revenue receipts of the government also went up, on an average, from 14.6 per cent in 1971-75 to 20 per cent in 1986-90. But the gap between revenue receipts and expenditures remained negative - financed largely by domestic borrowings (as a result, the interest payments on domestic debt increased from 0.5 to 2.5 per cent of the GDP during 1975-90).[32] The RD kept increasing after 1979-80 and reached the highest level of 3.26 per cent of the GDP in 1990-91.[33]
3. The fiscal situation of the States was not good either. State governments which are primarily responsible for health, education and other social services had an aggregate revenue expenditure of 5 per cent of GDP on these accounts while their capital expenditure accounted for 2.5 per cent on social and other sectors.[34] The States' expenditure on the social sector decreased while their interest payments had increased during the 1980s.[35]

As per the experts, the debt situation in the States would have been even worse, except for the fact that the States, unlike the Centre, did not have independent powers to borrow either from the RBI or the market because of the statutory overdraft regulatory scheme.[36] Thus, their deficits have been self-limiting - whenever the States tried to cut down their deficits, the care of the social sector and capital expenditure suffered as well as development prospects in the States.

Now the question arises why the government has not been able to check the menace of FDs even though there has been a consensus to do so. ***There are several reasons***[37] which are as follows:

1. **Political Factor:** The political lobbies and sectional politics as well as the subsidies

[30] The proximate cause of the payment crisis in the mainstream perspective was faulty macro-economic policies, especially large fiscal deficits of the government during 1984-91, deficits that spilled over into the country's current account of the balance of payment. (See Mihir Rakshit, 'The Micro-economic Adjustment Programme: A Critique', *Economic and Political Weekly 26(34)* (August), quoted by Mihir Rakshit, '*Some Microeconomics of India's Reform Experience*', in *India's Emerging Economy: Performance and Prospects in the 1990s and Beyond* Kaushik Basu (ed.), (New Delhi: Oxford University Press, 2004), p. 84.

[31] S. D. Tendulkar and T. A. Bhavani, *Understanding Reforms* (New Delhi: Oxford University Press, 2007), p. 73.

[32] B. Jalan, *India's Economic Policy* (New Delhi: Penguin Books, 1992), p. 48.

[33] *Handbook of Statistics on the Economy 2002-03*, Reserve Bank of India, Table 221 (cited by Tendulkar and Bhavani, *Understanding Reforms*, p. 74).

[34] B. Jalan, *India's Economic Policy*, op. cit., p. 50

[35] Reserve Bank of India, *The Report of Tenth Finance Commission* (New Delhi, Government of India, 1994), as quoted in B. Jalan, *India's Economic Policy*, p. 50.

[36] This scheme has changed now. After the implementation of the suggestions of the *Twelfth Finance Commission*, states are now allowed to go for market borrowings to take care of their plan expenditures once they have passed and enacted their Fiscal Responsibility Acts (FRAs) in consonance with the FRBM Act, 2003.

[37] Based on the points raised by B. Jalan, op. cit., p. 49.

are supposed to be one big factor for rising government expenditure. We see this on a higher scale if there is a probable mid-term election or closer to a general election.

2. **Institutional Factor:** The administrative size combined with the processes of reporting, accounting, supervising and monitoring is receiving greater importance than the production and delivery of goods and services.[38]
3. **Ethical Factor:** This is a more powerful factor as it easily generates wide public support for the government expenditure. There are many heads of such expenditures such as subsidies (food, power, fertiliser, irrigation, etc.), poverty alleviation programmes, employment generation programmes, education, health and social services. The logic for such expenditures comes from the idea that the government should function as the protector of the poor and provider of jobs for them implying that such government expenditures benefit the poor.

It was in 2000 that the double menace of revenue and fiscal deficits received attention from the government at the Centre and some constitutional/statutory safeguards seemed necessary. Consequently, the Fiscal Responsibility and Budget Management Bill, 2000, was proposed in the Parliament.

Debt vs Deficit

Common people often confuse debt with deficit and take them as the same. As an example, debt is a provision which can keep flowing as demanded by the government while deficit is the actual debt which has been drawn. While government debt is a stock of liabilities, deficit is a flow of new debt.

Source: P. A. Samuelson and W. D. Nordhaus, *Economics* (New Delhi: McGraw Hill Education, 2020), p. 848.

FRBM Act, 2003

The fiscal policy of an economy has been considered as the building block for enabling the macro-environment by economists, policymakers and the IMF alike. It does not only provide stability and predictability to the policy regime but also ensures that national resources are allocated in terms of their defined priorities through the tax transfer mechanism.

[38] This factor seems to be getting a redress with the starting of *outcome* and *performance* budgeting from 2004-05 onwards.

Unproductive government expenditures, tax distortions and high deficits are considered to have constrained the Indian economy from realising its full growth potential. At the beginning of the fiscal reforms in 1991, the fiscal imbalance was identified as the ***root cause*** of the twin problems of inflation and the difficult BoP position.[39] Since then, the ***medium-term fiscal policy stance*** of the government has been on the following lines:[40]

1. Reducing the deficits (revenue and fiscal).
2. Prioritising expenditure and ensuring that these resulted in intended outcomes.
3. Augmenting resources by widening tax base and improving tax-compliance while maintaining moderate rates.

The fiscal consolidation which followed in 1991 failed to give the desired results as there was no defined mandate for it. Neither was there any statutory obligation to do so.[41] This is why the Fiscal Reforms and Budget Management Act (FRBMA) was enacted on 26 August, 2003, to provide the support of a strong institutional/statutory mechanism. Designed for the purpose of medium-term management of the FD, the FRBMA came into effect on 5 July, 2004.

The FRBM Bill, 2000, was passed by the Parliament with all political parties voting in favour and is considered a watershed in the area of fiscal reforms in the country. Main highlights of the FRBMA, 2003, are given below[42]:

- The GoI to take measures to reduce fiscal and revenue deficits so as to eliminate revenue deficits by 31 March 2008 (which was revised by the UPA government to March 31, 2009) and thereafter build up adequate revenue surplus.
- Rules to be made under the Act to specify annual targets for the reduction of FD and RD, contingent

[39] *Economic Survey 2006-07* (New Delhi: Ministry of Finance, Government of India, 2007), p. 18.

[40] Ibid.

[41] Ibid.

[42] *Economic Survey 2003-04* (New Delhi: Ministry of Finance, Government of India, 2004).

liabilities and total liabilities (RD to be cut by 0.5 per cent per annum and FD by 0.3 per cent per annum).

- The FD and RD may exceed the targets only on grounds such as national security, calamity or exceptional cases.
- The GoI not to borrow from the RBI except by the WMAs.
- The RBI not to subscribe to the primary issue of the GoI securities from 2006-07 (it means that the government bonds/papers will become market-based instruments to raise long-term funds by the government).
- Steps to be taken to ensure greater transparency in fiscal operations.
- Along with the Budget and Demands for Grants, the GoI to lay the following three statements before the Parliament in each financial year:
    - Fiscal Policy Strategy Statement (FPSS);
    - Medium-Term Fiscal Policy Statement (MTFPS); and
    - Macro-economic Framework Statement (MFS).
- The finance minister to make quarterly review of trends in receipts and expenditure in relation to the Budget and place the review before the Parliament.

Experience of the FRBM Together with the central compliance to the FRBM Act, we see the States also enforcing their fiscal responsibility acts (FRAs). Though these developments[43] brought in fiscal discipline[44] among the governments; however, follow-ups to the fiscal targets gave mixed results - barring a few years, in most of the years the targets were crossed by both of the governments. Based on this experience, the *Union Budget 2016-17* proposed to set up an expert committee to *review* the fiscal targets mandated under the FRBMA - as oftentimes, domestic or/and global environments[45] may make the government helpless in following the prescribed fiscal discipline without compromising the goals of development and economic stability. The committee (under the chairmanship of N. K. Singh) handed over its report by late 2017-18 advising certain flexibility in the fiscal regime with the following major advice:

- Debt should be the *anchor* of the fiscal policy (i.e., fiscal targets moving up or down depending on sustainable borrowings by the governments).
- Debt to GDP target of 60 per cent for General government (Centre + States) - 40 per cent in the case of Centre and 20 per cent for states - till 2020-21.
- A flexibility of 0.5 per cent in the FD target (i.e., the introduction of 'escape clause').

Accordingly, the FRBM Act was amended, and these new mandates were introduced in 2018-19. The flexibility made available through this amendment helped the Government to cover the extra expenditures incurred in the process of supporting the economy on account of the disruption caused by the *COVID-19 pandemic*.

The fiscal consolidation mandate is further slated for change in the near future as the *Fifteenth Finance Commission* has recommended to form a 'high-powered inter-governmental group' to:

1. review the fiscal responsibility legislation (FRBM Act), and
2. recommend a new fiscal responsibility framework and oversee its implementation.

FISCAL CONSOLIDATION IN INDIA

The average combined FDs (Fiscal deficits), of the Centre and States after 1975, had been above 10 per cent of the GDP till 2000-01. More than half of it had been due to huge RDs (Revenue Deficits). The governments were cautioned by the RBI, the PC as well as the IMF and the WB about the unsustainability of the FDs. It was at the behest of the IMF that India started the politically and socially painful process of fiscal reforms, a step towards fiscal consolidation.[46] A number of steps were taken by the government at the Centre in this direction, and there had been incessant attempts to also carry out the same in the states' public finances. Major

[43] *Economic Survey, 2013-14, 2014-15* and *2015-16*.

[44] The acceptance of the recommendations of the Thirteenth and Fourteenth Finance Commissions by the Government of India in this regard has been highly effective.

[45] We find similar views being forwarded by the *Economic Survey 2015-16*, vol. 1 & vol. 2 (New Delhi: Ministry of Finance, GoI, 2016).

[46] IMF imposed some macro-economic conditions on the economy while India borrowed from it for its BoP correction in 1990-91. One among the conditions was cutting down the government expenditure (i.e., salaries, pensions, interest and subsidies, etc.) by **10** per cent every year.

highlights in this direction can be summed up as given below:

1. Policy initiatives towards cutting RDs:
   (i) Cutting Down Revenue Expenditure:
   (a) Cutting down the burden of salaries, pensions and the PFs (down-sizing/ right-sizing of the government, out of every 3 vacancies 1 to be filled up, interest cut on the PF, pension reforms-PFRDA, etc.)
   (b) Cutting down the subsidies (Administered Price Mechanism in petroleum, fertilisers, sugar, drugs to be rationalised; it was carried out with mixed successes);
   (c) Interest burden to be cut down (by opting for lesser borrowings, pre-payment of external debts, debt swaps, promoting external lending, minimal dependence on costlier external borrowings, etc.)
   (d) Defence being one major item of the expenditure, bilateral negotiations initiated with China and Pakistan (the historical and psychological enemies against whom the Indian defence preparedness was directed to, as supposed) so that the defence force cut could be completed on the borders, etc.
   (e) Budgetary supports to the loss-making PSUs to be an exception than a rule
   (f) Expenditure reform started by the governments in different areas and departments
   (g) General Services to be motivated towards profit with subsidised services to the needy only (railways, power, water, etc.)
   (h) Postal deficits to be checked by involving the post offices in other areas of profit
   (i) Higher education declared as non-priority sector; fees of institutions of professional courses revised upward; etc.

   (ii) Increasing Revenue Receipts:
   (a) Tax reforms initiated (Cenvat, VAT, Service Tax, GST proposed, etc.)
   (b) The PSUs to be disinvested and even privatised (if a political consensus is reached which alludes today)
   (c) Surplus forex reserves to be used in external lending and purchasing foreign high-quality sovereign bonds, etc.
   (d) State governments allowed to opt for market borrowing for their plan expenditure, etc.
2. The borrowing programme of the government:
   (i) The WMA scheme commenced in 1997 under which the government commits to the RBI the amount of money it will pay as part of its market borrowing programme, to bring about transparency in public expenditure and to place political responsibility on the government.
   (ii) The RBI will not be the primary subscriber to G-Secs in the future – committed way back in 1997.
3. The fiscal responsibility on the governments:
   (i) The Fiscal Responsibility and Budget Management (FRBM) Act was passed in 2003 (voted by all political parties) which puts constitutional obligation on the government to commit many things as fiscal responsibility comes in the public finance – fixing annual targets to cut revenue and FDs as the government cannot borrow from the RBI except by the WMA, the government to bring in greater transparency in fiscal operations, along with the Budget the government to lay statements regarding fiscal policy strategy in the House, and Quarterly Review of trends of receipts and expenditures of the government.
   (ii) A mechanism (to include State governments under the umbrella of fiscal responsibility) was advised (now implemented, too) by the Twelfth Finance Commission which allowed the State governments to opt for market borrowing (without central permission) for their need of plan development provided they pass their FRAs and commit to the fiscal responsibility regarding cutting their revenue and FDs. By March 2016, all states and UTs had implemented their FRAs.

Zero-Based Budgeting

The idea of zero-based budgeting (ZBB) first came to privately owned organisations of the United States by the 1960s. This basically belonged to a long list of guidelines for managerial excellence and success, others being Management by Objectives (MBO), Matrix Management, Portfolio Management, etc., to name a few.[47] It was the US financial expert ***Peter Phyrr*** who first proposed this idea for government budgeting, and Jimmy Carter, the Governor of Georgia, USA, was the first elected[48] executive to introduce the ZBB to the public sector. When he presented the US Budget in 1979 *as the US President*, it was the first use of the ZBB for any nation state. Since then, many governments of the world have opted for such budgeting.

ZBB is the allocation of resources to agencies based on periodic re-evaluation by those agencies of the need for all the programmes for which they are responsible, justifying the continuance or termination of each programme in the agency budget proposal – in other words, an agency reassesses what it is doing from top to bottom from a hypothetical ***zero base.***[49]

There are three essential principles of the ZBB. Some experts view it in a different way. There are three essential questions which must be answered objectively before opting for any expenditure as per the techniques of the ZBB:

1. Should we spend?
2. How much should we spend?
3. Where should we spend?

There are *three* special features of this budgeting which distinguishes it from the traditional budgeting. These features, in brief, are as under the following:

1. The conventional aggregate approach is not applied in it, in which each department of the government prepares its own budget for many activities in the aggregate and composite form, making it difficult to scrutinise each and every activity. In place of it, every department needs to justify its existence and continuance in the budget document by using the mathematical technique of econometrics, i.e., cost–benefit analysis. In a nutshell, every activity of each department is 'X-rayed', and once the justification is validated, they are allocated the funds.
2. *Economy* in public expenditure is the *raison d'etre* (i.e., reason or explanation) of this budgeting. This is why the ZBB has provisions of close examination and scrutiny of each programme and public spending. Finally, the public spending is cut without affecting the current level of benefits of various public services accruing to the public.
3. *Prioritising* the competing needs is another special feature of the ZBB. Before allocating funds to the different needs of the economy, an order of priority is prepared with utmost objectivity. As the resources/funds are always scarce, in the process of prioritised allocation, the item/items at the bottom might not receive any funds.

Besides its benefits, there are certain ***limitations*** too before the ZBB which prohibit its assumed success, according to experts. These limitations have made it subject to criticism. The limitations are given below:

1. There are certain expenditures upon which the government/parliament does not have the power of scrutiny (as the 'charged Expenditure' in India).
2. There are certain public services which defy the cost–benefit analysis – defence, law and order, foreign relations, etc.
3. Scrutiny is a subjective matter and so this might become a prey to bias. Again, if the scrutinisers have a complete utilitarian view, many long-term objectives of budgeting and public policy might get marginalised.

---

[47] George R. Terry and Stephen G. Franklin, *Principles of Management* (New Delhi: AITBS, 2002), pp. 9-10.

[48] See Peter A. Phyrr, 'The Zero Base Approach to government Budgeting', *Public Administration Re-view*, 37 (Jan./Feb., 1977), p. 7; and Thomas P. Lauth, 'Zero-Base Budgeting in Georgia State government: Myth and Reality', *Public Administration Review*, 38 (Sept./Oct., 1978), pp. 420-30 cited in N. Henry, *Public Administration and Public Affairs* (New Delhi: Prentice-Hall, 2003), p. 217.

[49] N. Henry, *Public Administration and Public Affairs*, op. cit. p. 218.

4. It has scope for the emergence of the Ministry of Finance as the all-powerful institution dictating other ministries and departments.
5. Bureaucracy does not praise it as it evaluates their decisions and performances in a highly objective way.

Despite the above-given strong limitations, the ZBB has a sound logic and should be considered a long-term budgetary reform process. The basic idea of this form of budgeting is to optimise the benefits of expenditure in every area of activity and in this sense it is exceptional. To the extent the corporate world is concerned, this has been a very successful financial management tool.

In India, it is believed to have been in practice since 1997–99. We cannot say that India is a success in ZBB, but many of the profit-fetching PSUs have been able to use it successfully and optimise their profits.

In order to make a balance between fiscal consolidation and developmental needs, the fiscal legislative regime was changed by the government in 2018-19 by introducing debt-based fiscal targets with a scope to cross the FD target by 0.5 per cent. Meanwhile, the existing regime is again slated for change as the ***Fifteenth Finance Commission*** has recommended to form a 'high-powered inter-governmental group' to review the FRBM Act and recommend a new fiscal responsibility framework and oversee its implementation.

OUTPUT-OUTCOME FRAMEWORK

Economising expenditures and enhancing performance of expenditures have fascinated governments of the world, especially since the early 1960s, which resulted in the idea of ZBB. India also has its share of experiments in this direction. By 2019-20, the GoI developed the idea of the Output-Outcome Framework (OOF). The OOF is an important reform[50] towards outcome-based monitoring of developmental actions of the ministries and departments. This is a creative modification of a similar effort of the past (i.e., the 'Outcome and Performance Budgeting' initiated in 2005-06). The DMEO (Development Monitoring and Evaluation Office) at Niti Aayog has been working on it since 2017, which actively supports the government agencies in the process.

Under it, a framework of 'measurable indicators' has been put in place monitoring the objectives (i.e., 'Outcomes') of the Central Sector (CS) and Centrally Sponsored Schemes (CSSs) which account for around 40 per cent of the government's budget expenditures. This is a paradigm shift from measuring simply 'physical and financial' progress, to a 'governance model based' on outcomes. Actively tracking progress against defined targets, the framework provides two key benefits to improve governance:

1. Enhancing the development impact, and
2. Improving accountability and transparency.

Thus, the OOF 2019-20 lays the foundation of the journey towards a stronger portfolio of government development programmes. It enables performance-based 'budgetary allocations' and can also be used to drive budgetary and administrative convergence among existing schemes and programmes. With the cooperation of line ministries and implementing actors, a robust monitoring mechanism based on this framework can revolutionise the governance and implementation process.

CUT MOTION

In democratic political systems, there is a provision of Cut Motion in the House/Parliament (usually it is the opposition, but the floor might be crossed by members of the House belonging to the government due to presence of inner party politics). In the United States, the Budget provisions presented by the government must be passed by the Congress. Only then can they be enacted. Unlike this, in the British parliamentary system though the Budget of the government is voted by the House, usually this is considered a political document and passed unchanged. India has mixed provisions of voting on the Budget after discussion in both the Houses. There are different constitutional provisions by which the Parliament starts discussion to reduce the demands,

[50] As put forward by the *Union Budget 2019-20* (New Delhi: Ministry of Finance, GoI)

grants, etc. proposed by the government in the Budget:[51]

1. **Token Cut:** This motion intends to *reduce the demand by ₹100.* Such a motion is moved in order to express a specific grievance which is within the sphere of the responsibility of the GoI - the discussion remains confined to the particular grievance specified in the motion.
2. **Economy Cut:** This motion intends to *reduce the demand by a specified amount* representing the economy (in expenditure) that can be affected. Such specified amount may be either lump sum reduction in the demand or omission or reduction of an item in the demand - the discussion remains confined to the matter in which the economy can be affected.
3. **Disapproval of Policy Cut:** This motion intends to *reduce the demand to ₹1.* This represents *disapproval* of the policy underlying the demand - the discussion remains confined to the particular policy and is open to members to advocate an alternate policy.
4. **Guillotine** is the process in which the Speaker puts all the outstanding demands made by the Budget *directly to vote* in the House - ending further discussions (intended to cut short the discussion on the Budget). Through this, the Speaker may put the whole Budget to vote (i.e., allowing 'no discussion' on the Budget by the House). In recent years, this route was taken time and again by the GoI, to avoid an aggressive stance by the opposition.

Though this is a *short route* to get the Budget passed by the House (avoiding criticism by the opposition benches), it may turn out to be very dangerous - as the voting process may take the form of 'no confidence motion' and the government may be routed out of power. But, till date, *Guillotines* never resulted in routing a government out of power in India (as India follows the British model of parliamentary system).

Trilemmas

Putting the right kind of fiscal policy has always been the most challenging policy decision to be taken by the democratic governments around the world. There are some famous 'trilemmas' related to this aspect. Economics have by now many 'trilemmas' developed and articulated by economists from time to time, and the process still continues. Let us take a look at some highly popular and newsworthy ones:

1. The **'financial stability trilemma'**, put forward by Dirk Schoenmaker[52] (2008), explains the incompatibility within the Euro zone of:
   - (i) a stable financial system,
   - (ii) an integrated financial system, and
   - (iii) national financial stability policies.
2. By far the most high-profile current trilemma of the Eurozone (by Edward Chancellor[53]) was believed to be the seeming irreconcilability between its **three wishes**, namely:
   - (i) a single currency,
   - (ii) minimal fiscal contribution to bailouts, and
   - (iii) the ECB's commitment to low inflation.
3. Martin Wolf[54] spoke about the US Republican Party's **fiscal policy trilemma**:
   - (i) large budget deficits are ruinous,
   - (ii) a continued eagerness to cut taxes and
   - (iii) an utter lack of interest in spending cuts on a large enough scale.
4. Then we have the **Earth Trilemma** (EEE), which posits that for:
   - (i) economic development (E),
   - (ii) we need increased energy expenditure (E),
   - (iii) but this raises the environmental issue (E).
5. Above all these more recent trilemmas in economics, the prima donna of them all is Mundell's **'impossible trinity'**. This old

[51] Rules of Procedure and Conduct of Business in Lok Sabha, Parliament Secretariat, New Delhi.

[52] D. Schoenmaker, 'A New Financial Stability Framework for Europe', *The Financial Regulator*, vol. 13, no. 3, 2009.

[53] E. Chancellor, 'Germany's Eurozone Trilemma', *Financial Times*, 6 November 2011.

[54] M. Wolf, 'The Political Genius of Supply Side Economics', *Financial Times*, 2010.

trilemma asserts that a country cannot maintain, simultaneously, all three policy goals of:

(i) free capital flows,

(ii) a fixed exchange rate and

(iii) an independent monetary policy.

The impossible trinity has seen enough inflow since it was articulated almost five decades ago which has a strong theoretical foundation in the *Mundell–Fleming model* developed in the 1960s.

Dani Rodrik[55] argued that if a country wants more of globalisation, it must either give up some democracy or some national sovereignty. Niall Ferguson[56] highlighted the **trilemma** of a choice between commitment to globalisation, to social order and to a small state (meaning limited state intervention).

DIRECT BENEFIT TRANSFER

In 2015, the new government in Centre introduced the game-changing potential of technology-enabled Direct Benefits Transfers (DBTs), namely the *JAM (Jan Dhan-Aadhaar-Mobile) Number Trinity* solution. DBT was launched in 2013 to re-engineer the then existing delivery processes using modern Information and Communication Technology (ICT) to transfer benefits directly into the preferably Aadhaar-seeded bank accounts of accurately targeted beneficiaries.

In the span of the past decade, DBT has expanded[57] from a mere 24 schemes (as part of a pilot programme) in 43 districts in 2013 to over 300 Central schemes and greater than 2000 State schemes across India by December 2022. The *DBT paradigm* has helped the governments in:

- Accurate identification and targeting of beneficiaries;
- Greater inclusion and ease of availing services through online application;
- Transparency in fund transfers to beneficiaries;
- Curbing of leakages in the benefit delivery processes through the elimination of middlemen/ agents;
- Creating greater accountability on behalf of the Government;
- Facilitating reforms in Government processes through re-engineering;
- Increasing efficiency in scheme delivery processes; and
- Effectiveness of schemes through timely implementation.

As per the *Economic Survey 2025-26*, a saving of **₹3.48** lakh crore has accrued to the Government exchequer in the last decade through the DBT.

India's successful implementation of DBT has *won praise* from the International Monetary Fund and World Bank, among other international organisations, for efficiently providing support (subsidies, foodgrain, and cash benefits directly) to large masses at low-income levels (85 per cent of rural households and 69 per cent of urban households).

CHANGE IN FISCAL YEAR

To examine the 'desirability and feasibility' of having a new financial year,[58] the government did set up a high-level committee headed by the former Chief Economic Adviser Shankar Acharya in July 2016 with the following terms of reference:

1. To examine the genesis of the current financial year and the studies made in the past on the desirability of a new financial year;
2. To examine the suitability of the existing financial year from the point of view of estimation of receipts and expenditure of the governments; impact on agricultural crops, businesses,

[55] D. Rodrik, 'The Inescapable Trilemma of the World Economy', 27 June 2007, available at Erodrik.typepad.com/ dani_rodriks_weblog.

[56] N. Ferguson, 'Conservatism and the Crisis: A Transatlantic Trilemma', Centre for Policy Studies, Ruttenberg Lecture, 24 March 2009.

[57] *Economic Survey 2022-23* (New Delhi: Ministry of Finance, GoI, January 2023), pp. 212-213.

[58] This is not the first time India has looked at changing its fiscal year - in 1985, the L. K. Jha Committee had recommended moving to a January-December format. In March 2017, a Parliamentary Panel (Standing Committee on Finance, chaired by M. Veerappa Moily, Congress MP) also advocated to end with the decades-old tradition of April-March fiscal introduced by the Britishers - adopted in 1867 principally to align the Indian financial year with that of the British government. Prior to this change, the financial year in India used to be May-April.

taxation, statistics and data, budgetary process; and other relevant matters; and

3. To recommend a suitable financial year together with the changes needed in tax laws during a transitional period, changes in the coverage of the recommendations of the Finance Commission and the appropriate timing of change.

The Committee submitted its report (still not available in the public domain) by end of December 2016 and is under the consideration of the government. For shifting to a new financial year, there needs to be a consensus among the governments - the reason this proposal was floated by the PM in one of the meetings of the Governing Council of the NITI Aayog. The NITI Aayog proposed for the January-December fiscal year backed by an in-depth discussion paper (released by late 2016) - followed by a survey of *Deloitte* as per which 84 per cent of Indians being in its favour.

Aimed at aligning monsoon forecast (in other words, the agricultural prospects) with the budget and the fact that more than 156 countries and MNCs following the calendar year as the accounting period, the committee is supposed to opt in favour of the January-December fiscal (as the experts believe, taking clues from the comments of Shankar Acharya while he was interacting with the media after submitting the report). Majority of the experts believe that the fiscal year of a government should be closely aligned to its major economic activities as is followed by most of the nations in the world.[59]

In the case of such a change, the budget will have to be presented in November together with a reworked Parliament session along with changes in data collection and working of State governments. For the common man, the change will not have any big impact.

It is believed that opposition from the States and the expected disruption due to the implementation of the GST were the major reasons for putting the proposal on the back burner. Otherwise, from 2018-19 or 2019-20 India would have shifted to a new fiscal year.

[59] Different countries follow different financial years to serve their differing priorities - the United States follows October-September, Australia July-June (as the IMF and WB) while China January-December. Like India, Canada, the United Kingdom, New Zealand and Hong Kong follow the April-March period as their fiscal year.

PUBLIC DEBT

Public debt[60] is the total loans of the government of a country. Since this government is national, at times, this is also called 'national debt'. But in a broader sense, the concept of national debt also includes the non-Government debt.

Debts of the Governments While the Union GoI is mandated to borrow inside and outside the country the amount specified by the Parliament (Article 292), States are mandated (Article 293) to borrow only inside the country. Beginning the financial year 2005-06, States were also given access to external loans (on the recommendations of the Twelfth Finance Commission, 2005-10) for which sovereign guarantee is given by the Centre. While the 'general category' States receive external loans on a back-to-back basis (i.e., cost of interest and risk of exchange rate fluctuations borne by States), the 'special category' States receive loans from the Centre in the combination of 90 per cent loan and 10 per cent grant.

Public Debt of India The liabilities of the Centre have three segments, namely Internal Liabilities, External Liabilities and Public Account Liabilities. To the extent **Public Debt** of India is concerned, it includes only Internal and External Liabilities incurred by the Central government. The composition of the public debt is given below:

1. **Internal Segment** includes a variety of 'instruments' used by the Centre to mobilise resources inside the economy, namely:
   - **(i)** ***Dated Securities:*** Popularly known as G-Secs, they are primarily issued by the Centre as fixed coupon bonds of different maturities (short-, medium-and long term). They are today the single-most important source of deficit financing (more than 90 per cent) for the Centre.
   - **(ii)** ***Treasury Bills:*** T-Bills are zero coupon securities issued by the Centre at a discount and are redeemed at their face value at maturity. Issued for the short term (less than 365 days), today they have three tenures - 91, 182 and 364 days.
   - **(iii)** ***14-Day T-Bills:*** These 'non-transferable' T-Bills (introduced by the RBI in 2013 to

[60] Based on the documents of the Ministry of Finance and the Reserve Bank of India.

finance the Centre's WMAs as issuance of 'on-tap' treasury bills was phased out) are issued by the Centre to only States, foreign central banks and other specified bodies at an interest rate fixed at 3 per cent below the average yield of 91-day T-Bills in the preceding quarter.

(iv) ***Securities Issued to International Financial Institutions:*** Securities issued by the Centre as India's contributions to the international financial institutions such as the IMF, World Bank, Asian Development Bank (ADB), etc.

(v) ***Securities Issued Against 'Small Savings':*** The deposits under the small savings schemes (SSSs) are credited to the NSSF (National Small Savings Fund) from which withdrawals also keep taking place. The rest of the NSSF fund (net withdrawals) is invested in special G-Secs issued by the Centre.

2. **External segment** of the public debt includes the external liabilities created through external borrowings by the Centre for its own uses (excluding those taken by the States). This constitutes a variety of 'multilateral' and 'bilateral' loans from IMF, World Bank, ADB, Sovereign Funds, foreign governments, etc.

Adjusted Debt In 2010, the government articulated the concept of adjusted debt which indicates the debt amount after factoring in the impact of external debt (at current exchange rate of rupee) and netting out the Market Stabilisation Scheme (which was abolished in 2014) and NSSF (National Small Savings Scheme) liabilities not used for financing the deficit of the Central government. While analysing the General government Debt (consolidated debt for Central and State governments), 14-day T-bills investment by States and Central loans to State governments are also netted out to avoid double accounting.

Along with a quarterly report on public debt, an 'Annual Status Paper on government Debt' (since 2010-11) is also published by the government. The status paper aims to enhance transparency by providing a detailed account of debt operations during the year and an assessment of the health of the public debt based on internationally accepted debt performance indicators.

Net Aid Donor

India has been traditionally a net receiver of foreign aids. However, the position of the country has changed in recent decades backed by strong external vibrancy. The country has not only emerged as a net aid donor but has been refusing such aids too (India refused aid offers for Tsunami in 2004 and floods of Uttarakhand, Kashmir, and Kerala between 2014 and 2018).

India today provides monetary and non-monetary help to over 86 countries of the world today. India allocated a foreign aid of **₹5,685.56 crore** (US$ 680 million) for the year 2026–27, as per the *Union Budget 2026–27*. On the other hand, India has significantly reduced its reliance on foreign aid over the last decade (as per the latest official report, India received about US$ 2.37 billion in net official development assistance and foreign aid).

INDEPENDENT DEBT MANAGEMENT

Debt management has been in the news for some time now. However, the idea for a public debt management agency (PDMA) was proposed in the *Union Budget 2015-16*, but it was put on the back burner probably due to clear objections from the Reserve Bank of India (RBI). By ***March 2019***, the issue of having an independent debt management agency outside the preview of the RBI was again voiced by the policy think tank, the NITI Aayog, saying it was *an idea whose time has come*. There is strong logic in this:

- At present, the RBI manages the government debt, including market borrowings (the RBI has been reluctant to part with this function).
- There is a case of clear conflict of interest in this arrangement - on the one hand, the RBI decides the key interest rates (i.e., policy rates under monetary policy mechanism), while on the other, it also trades in government bonds (treasury bills, cash management bill and G-Secs).
- Lack of alignment between India's domestic bond market (which is controlled by the RBI's policy rates) and the external bond market/external commercial borrowings (which is linked to the global variables). India has seen a rise in its external commercial borrowings in past years primarily due to interest rates in the global market being much lower than

in India. This discrepancy looks awkward in today's times when the global financial market is converging.

- The size of fund which India needs for her infrastructural development depends much on the deepening of the bond market which is not possible due to the RBI having a hold on it which is linked to its monetary policy.

It is believed that once the debt management office is separated from the RBI, the government will be able to pay much more attention on the aspect of debt having an eye on the changing needs of fund over time. It will help the government to also cut the cost of fund. Such a step is still awaited from the Government (for more on this topic refer the title 'Reforming India's Public Debt Management' in the *Chapter 22*).

GENERAL GOVERNMENT FINANCES

Though States are also following their fiscal responsibility laws enacted by them, they also have been facing pressure on the fiscal front due to a variety of reasonable and populist reasons. Weaker fiscal position of the states ultimately drains the resources of the Centre and the overall fiscal situation of the economy gets deteriorated.

Thus, to get an overview of the fiscal position of the government as a whole, it is critical to analyse the General Government (i.e., Union plus states) finances. The General Government liabilities as a proportion of GDP increased steeply during 2020-21 on account of the additional borrowings made by the governments on account of the pandemic. As per the *Economic Survey 2025-26*, the fiscal position[61] of the General Government has been able to improve over the last three years and is expected to follow fiscal glide path in medium term:

- *Debt-to-GDP ratio* for 2025-26 is estimated to be **81.1** per cent (RE) in comparison to 84.5 per cent in 2024-25.
- *Gross Fiscal Deficit* for 2025-26 is estimated to be **7.8** per cent (RE) of the GDP (against 8.1 per cent in 2024-25).
- *Gross Revenue Deficit* for 2025-26 is estimated to be **2.4** per cent (RE) of the GDP (against 2.5 per cent in 2024-25).

[61] *Economic Survey 2025-26* (New Delhi: Ministry of Finance, GoI, January 2026), pp. 73-76.

Global Comparison A comparison of the change in General Government *debt-to-GDP ratio* from 2005 to 2021 across the countries highlights a *substantial increase* for most countries (in the case of Japan it increased from 174 per cent to 263 per cent; for USA, from 68 per cent to 128 per cent; for UK, from 39 per cent to 95 per cent; for France, from 67 per cent to 113 per cent; for China, from 26 to 72 per cent). However, for India, this *increase has been modest*, from 81 per cent of GDP in 2005 to around 84 per cent of GDP in 2021. For India, it has been possible on the back of resilient economic growth during the last 15 years, leading to a positive interest rate growth rate differential (IRGD) resulting in sustainable Government debt to GDP levels.

COVID-19 FISCAL STIMULUS

In order to facilitate a resilient recovery of the economy from the impact of the COVID-19 pandemic and the following lockdown, the GoI and RBI together announced a total stimulus[62] worth ₹29.87 lakh crore (i.e., 15 per cent of the GDP). Out of this, stimulus worth 9 per cent of GDP was provided by the government under the *Atma Nirbhar Bharat* package.

India's fiscal policy approach to the pandemic has been different from many other countries of the world (which launched one-time large stimulus to support demand) - India introduced fiscal stimulus in a phased manner. India's fiscal stimulus measures reflected flexibility of adapting to an evolving situation in order to enable resilient economic recovery in the following phases:

1. Special *economic and comprehensive package* announced in the initial phase was aimed to primarily provide a cushion to the vulnerable sections of the society and the small businesses - direct food transfers to the poor and vulnerable, livelihood programmes, guarantees and liquidity enhancing measures.
2. Measures to *stimulate consumer spending* were announced as steady unwinding of lockdown and restrictions started.

[62] *Union Budget 2022-23* (New Delhi: Ministry of Finance, GoI); *Economic Survey 2020-21*, vol. 2 (New Delhi: Ministry of Finance, GoI), pp. 58-62.

3. Measures under *Atma Nirbhar Bharat 3.0* was announced as economic recovery began, which was aimed at boosting investment through measures like Production Linked Incentives (PLIs), enhancing capital expenditure and steps to encourage investment in the infrastructure sector.

FISCAL OUTLOOK FOR 2025-26

India has seen deterioration in its fiscal position right since 2019-20, now well-footed on the path of recovery with even brighter future. In this case, the *Economic Survey 2025-26* has summarised the fiscal situation[63] in the following ways:

- The recent spikes seen in India's *debt* and *deficit* ratios have not only been due to higher spending necessitated by the pandemic-induced economic disruption but also due to the contraction in economic growth in the denominator (nominal GDP). In fiscal 2019-20, India's GDP growth slowed down due to the ongoing stress in the financial system - while the banking sector was undergoing repair and was recapitalising, the non-banking financial sector crisis renewed the uncertainties for the banking system. This kept credit growth muted, leading to slower GDP growth. The pandemic aggravated the situation in 2020-21, which caused the nominal GDP to contract, a *rare occurrence* in India.
- As India's economic recovery advances, amidst the continuing global uncertainties and risks, the *fiscal glide path* (committed and performed upon by the governments) illuminates the path for fiscal policy. That will ensure more significant fiscal space for policy action in uncertain times.
- In reality, *fiscal discipline translates into a fiscal stimulus* for all sections of the economy through lower interest rates. As governments make their fiscal situations sustainable and stick to that path, the risk premium embedded in their interest rates comes down, thus lowering the cost of capital for all sections of society (on their educational loans, housing loans, car loans and business loans) and putting more money in their hands.
- In the case[64] of the EMDEs (Emerging Market and Developing Economies), the *stimulus effect* of fiscal deficit (*via* diminishing risk-premium) is likely greater than it is for advanced economies. That is the reality, as financial markets do not treat advanced and emerging economies similarly on fiscal deficits. Therefore, the EMDEs reap greater rewards for fiscal prudence.
- The Union government needs to continue incentivising the states for reforms and higher capital spending to ensure a stronger General government. A growth strategy led by capital spending will ensure sustainable debt levels.
- Decreasing inflationary pressures augurs well for the economy. However, the governments need to be vigilant and agile in their response to it.
- Navigating global headwinds (geoeconomic fragmentation, geopolitical risks caused by the Russia-Ukraine conflict, tensions in the Middle East, etc.) will require strategic and prudential policy management and reinforcing the domestic fundamentals– there is a strong need for deregulation and reforms at the grassroots level to improve the overall competitiveness of the economy and to lift trend growth rates, supporting higher levels of economic activity.

[63] *Economic Survey 2025-26* (New Delhi: Ministry of Finance, GoI, January 2026), pp. 77-78.

[64] *Financial Sector and Economic Growth in India*, Margaux MacDonald and TengTeng Xu, IMF Working paper (WP/22/137), July 2022.

PREVIOUS YEARS' QUESTIONS

Prelims

1. Consider the following statements: (2025)
   (i) Capital receipts create a liability or cause a reduction in the assets of the Government.
   (ii) Borrowings and disinvestment are capital receipts.
   (iii) Interest received on loans creates a liability of the Government.

   Which of the statements give above are correct?
   (a) (i) and (ii) only **(b)** (ii) and (iii) only
   (c) (i) and (iii) only **(d)** (i), (ii) and (iii)

2. Suppose the revenue expenditure is ₹80,000 crores and the revenue receipts of the government are ₹60,000 crores. The government budget also shows borrowings of ₹10,000 crores and interest payments of ₹6,000 crores. which of the following statement are correct? (2025)
   (i) Revenue deficit is ₹20,000 crores.
   (ii) Fiscal deficit is ₹10,000 crores.
   (iii) Primary deficit is ₹4,000 crores.

   Select the correct answer using the code given below.
   (a) (i) and (ii) only **(b)** (ii) and (iii) only
   (c) (i) and (iii) only **(d)** (i), (ii) and (iii)

3. A country's fiscal deficit stands at ₹50,000 crores. It is receiving ₹10,000 crores through non-debt creating capital receipts. The country's interest liabilities are ₹1,500 crores. What is the gross primary deficit? (2025)
   (a) ₹48,500 crores **(b)** ₹51,500 crores
   (c) ₹58,500 crores **(d)** None of the above

4. With reference to Union Budget, consider the following statements: (2024)
   (i) The Union Finance Minister on behalf of the Prime Minister lays the annual Financial Statement before the Houses of Parliament.
   (ii) At the Union level, no demand for a grant can be except on the recommendation of the President of India.

   Which of the statement(s) given above is/are correct?
   (a) (i) only **(b)** (ii) only
   (c) Both (i) and (ii) **(d)** Neither (i) nor (ii)

5. Consider the following statements:

   Statement-I: If the United States of America (USA) were to default on its debt, holders of US Treasury Bonds will not be able to exercise their claims to receive payment.

   Statement-II: The USA Government debt is not backed by any hard assets, but only by the faith of the Government.

   Which one of the following is correct in respect of the above statements ?
   (a) Both Statement-I and Statement-II are correct and Statement-II explains Statement-I
   (b) Both Statement-I and Statement-II are correct, but Statement-II does not explain Statement-I
   (c) Statement-I is correct, but Statement-II is incorrect
   (d) Statement-I is incorrect, but Statement-II is correct

Answers: 1. (a) 2. (d) 3. (a) 4. (b) 5. (a)

Explanation:

1. (a): *Statement-I and II are correct* {capital receipts of the government create liability (if they have are loans) or reduce financial assets (such as the receipts of disinvestment)}. *Statement-III is incorrect* (interest received on loans is classified as a revenue receipt since it represents income and does not create any liability).

2. (d): All Statements are correct (Revenue Deficit = Revenue Expenditure - Revenue Receipts; Fiscal Deficit = Total Expenditure - Total Receipts (excluding borrowings; and Primary Deficit = Fiscal Deficit - Interest Payments).

3. (a): Gross Primary Deficit = Fiscal Deficit – Interest Payments

4. (b): The Annual Financial Statement (which is popularly known as the Union Budget) is presented by the Finance Minister on his/her behalf itself, and demand of a grant can be only made on the recommendation of the President of India.

5. (a): Both of the statements are correct- this is because the US Treasury Bonds are not backed by any underlying assets (i.e., collaterals) unlike corporate bonds. In case of India the Treasury Bills are backed by the Government of India and not by any underlying assets.

Main

1. Distinguish between Capital Budget and Revenue Budget. Explain the components of both these Budgets. (2021)

SAMPLE OBJECTIVE QUESTIONS

1. Consider the following statements related to government debt and deficit in the country:
   - **(i)** While debt is a stock of liabilities, deficit is a flow of new debt.
   - **(ii)** Like debt, deficit, too, has its internal and external elements.
   - **(iii)** At the end of a fiscal year, total debts are equal to the gross deficit of the economy.

   How many of the above statements are correct?
   (a) Only one **(b)** Only two
   (c) All three **(d)** None of these

2. Consider the following statements related to government budgeting in the country:
   - **(i)** Rise in primary deficit indicates government's increased dependence on market borrowings.
   - **(ii)** Decline in effective revenue deficits indicates decline in asset creation by states.
   - **(iii)** Rise in fiscal deficit necessarily results in crowding out of fund for the uses of the private sector.

   How many of the above statements are correct?
   (a) Only one **(b)** Only two
   (c) All three **(d)** None of these

3. Consider the following statements related to government budgeting in the country:
   - **(i)** In monetary policy communication, the communication is itself part of the policy.
   - **(ii)** Union Budget is not intended to pass a message to anyone, rather it is the substance of government's fiscal policy.
   - **(iii)** Union Budget has implications and inputs for all socio-economic stakeholders.

   How many of the above statements are **NOT** correct?
   (a) Only one **(b)** Only two
   (c) All three **(d)** None of these

4. Consider the following statements related to government budgeting in the country:
   - **(i)** Counter-cyclical fiscal stance of a government helps economy revive from slowdown.
   - **(ii)** Above-the-line public spendings are avoided by governments in election years.
   - **(iii)** Government collects more taxes due to fiscal drag but risks an economic slowdown.

   How many of the above statements are correct?
   (a) Only one **(b)** Only two
   (c) All three **(d)** None of these

5. Consider the following statements related to government budgeting in the country:
   - **(i)** Transfer payments are believed to encourage poverty trap.
   - **(ii)** The universal basic income is an idea whose time has come.

(iii) Leakage of public fund essentially increases with greater decentralisation of development.

How many of the above statements are correct?

(a) Only one (b) Only two
(c) All three (d) None of these

6. Consider the following statements related to the fiscal policy of the Government:
 (i) It aims to enhance social and economic well-being of all individuals and groups.
 (ii) Building fiscal capacity is the first requirement for its success.
 (iii) Fiscal capacity of governments is boosted by keeping direct tax rates at their minimum levels.

How many of the above statements are correct?

(a) Only one (b) Only two
(c) All three (d) None of these

7. Consider the following statements related to fiscal prudence of the governments in the country:
 (i) Fiscal behaviour of Centre has been more prudent than that of the states during reforms.
 (ii) Checking fiscal slippages in case of Centre is easier than that of the states.
 (iii) Offers of more freebies have hampered the fiscal position of states.

How many of the above statements are correct?

(a) Only one (b) Only two
(c) All three (d) None of these

8. Consider the following statements related to the process of government budgeting in the country:
 (i) Offering income support to farmers is fiscally better than the loan waivers.
 (ii) Farmers' investment support is fiscally better than income support.
 (iii) Offering unlimited amount of income support to farmers is not permitted by the World Trade Organisation.

How many of the above statements are correct?

(a) Only one (b) Only two
(c) All three (d) None of these

9. Consider the following statements related to government fiscal policy in the country:
 (i) Higher current account deficits induce inflationary pressures.
 (ii) Issuing sovereign bonds in a year increases primary deficit provided fiscal deficit remains intact over the year.
 (iii) Fixed fiscal deficit targets hamper socio-economic development in the country.

How many of the above statements are correct?

(a) Only one (b) Only two
(c) All three (d) None of these

10. Consider the following statements related to fiscal responsibility of the governments in the country:
 (i) The 15th Finance Commission advised for a federal fiscal responsibility law.
 (ii) Government incentivises states to cut their revenue and fiscal deficits by giving them more autonomy in market borrowings.
 (iii) Market borrowings by states leave better impact on the economy than that of central budgetary supports.
 (iv) Reducing extra-budgetary supports by governments brings more fiscal prudence.

How many of the above statements are correct?

(a) Only one (b) Only two
(c) All three (d) None of these

Answers: 1. (c) 2. (a) 3. (d) 4. (c) 5. (a) 6. (b) 7. (c) 8. (b) 9. (b) 10. (c)

SAMPLE SUBJECTIVE QUESTIONS

1. 'Mobilising resources for social priorities has emerged as the biggest fiscal challenge for the government in recent times.' Comment with the help of suitable examples.
2. Suggest measures to the Government for more prudent and transparent fiscal discipline in the economy. Cite relevant examples to support your views.
3. 'Independent public debt management is an idea whose time has come in the country.' Examine.
4. 'For attending the emerging fiscal responsibilities, Government needs to put in place a new fiscal responsibility framework.' Explain with the help of relevant examples.
5. Briefly examine the emerging fiscal challenges of the Government in light of the environmental issues.
6. What do you mean by reform with humane face? To what extent the Government in last decade has been able to carry forward this goal? Cite suitable illustrations to support your view.

SAMPLE MODEL ANSWER

1. **Write a critical note on the need of independent debt management in the country.**

Ans. The issue of independent debt management for the country has been a critical topic for discussion since it was first proposed by the Government in the Union Budget 2015-16. The proposal was to set up a public debt management agency (PDMA) out of the Reserve Bank of India (RBI), which currently manages the public debt. But it was put on the back burner probably due to clear objections coming from the central bank, as experts feel. By March 2019, the issue was again pushed by the policy think tank Niti Aayog (by saying that 'it was an idea whose time has come'). There looks to be strong logic in having an independent debt management body:

- At present, the RBI manages the government debt through the Public Debt Management Cell, including market borrowing (RBI has been reluctant to part with this function).
- There is a case of clear conflict of interest in this arrangement - on one hand, RBI decides the key interest rates (i.e., policy rates under the monetary policy mechanism), while, on the other hand, it trades in the government bonds (treasury bills, cash management bills, and G-Secs) also.
- Lack of alignment between India's domestic bond market (which is controlled by RBI's policy rates) and the external bond market/external commercial borrowings (which are linked to the global variables). India has seen a rise in its external commercial borrowings in past years primarily due to interest rates in the global market being much lower than in India - rather, India's financial market needs to converge with the global financial market.
- The size of the fund which India needs for her infrastructural development depends much on the deepening of the bond market, which is not possible due to the RBI having a hold on it, which is linked to its function of announcing the monetary policy.

It is believed that once the debt management office is separated from the RBI, debt and fund management will become more dynamic, which will help both public and private sectors. Such a piece of advice was first proposed by the Tarapore Committee, 1997 (set up on the capital account convertibility), and in recent times by the B. N. Srikrishna-chaired FSLRC (Financial Sector Legislative Reforms Commission Report, 2013).

CHAPTER 20

Sustainability and Climate Change: India and the World

> ... this is the only home we have and, as environmentalists are fond of saying, Mother Nature doesn't do bailouts ... so we better find a better way to grow.*
>
> * Thomas L. Friedman, *Hot, Flat, & Crowded* (London: Penguin Books, 2009), p. 23.

To watch the Author's videos on the significance of the Chapter, scan the QR Code given here

Exam Essentials...

- MISHTI
- COP30
- India and Green Development
- India and Climate Change
- LiFE
- Green Bonds

Note to the Reader...

Sustainability has emerged as the biggest challenge for economic management for the world today. However, the global efforts are said to be less than desired, and the danger of climate change is today shaping almost all developmental policies of the global governments. This chapter deals with the challenges and the dilemmas of growth and sustainability in a nuanced manner and aims to understand the options available at the disposal of India, together with her achievements in this regard.

In This Chapter...

INTRODUCTION

Improving living standards for mankind has been the single-minded goal of all nations and world bodies. After defining development in numerous ways for over two decades, there seems to be a consensus on 'human development'. While a large population on earth is still to receive the 'bare minimum' for development, humanity is at a crossroads where it is faced with the first of this kind challenge - the challenge of 'climate change'. The dilemma is that whatever we do for our development, there will be a repercussion on nature. An even bigger dilemma is in achieving a global consensus on how to check or restrict and finally reverse the process of climate change.

A survey of the global comparative opinion shows that people in India and indeed all countries have a marked and rising concern about sustainable development and climate change in recent years. However, the challenges are also formidable, especially in the context of finding the matching resources of the required magnitude given the economic conditions. Climate science has rightly taken up an important position in public debate. Even as the science of climate change grapples with uncertainties, the world is witnessing more extreme events. With rising extreme events and rising citizen demand, the world has little option but to listen to the voice of evolving science and respond adequately with strategies and policies rooted in the principles of multilateralism with equitable and fair burden sharing.[1]

Since 2010, the world has witnessed an increasing number of natural disasters and extreme weather conditions frequently making headlines in the news across the world. Policy-makers have been facing enormous pressure on availability of clean air, water and energy together with the problems of poverty and hunger, especially in the developing world.

The ***year 2015*** witnessed two landmark international events - the historic climate change agreement under the *UNFCCC in Paris* in December 2015 and the adoption of the *SDGs* (sustainable development goals) in September 2015. The Paris Agreement aims at keeping the rise in global temperatures well below 2°C, which will set the world towards a low-carbon, resilient and sustainable future, while the SDGs, which replace the MDGs (millennium development goals), set the development agenda for the next fifteen years.

[1] O. Morton, *Megachange: The World in 2050*, D. Franklin and J. Andrews, eds. (London: The Economist, 2012), pp. 92-110.

SUSTAINABLE DEVELOPMENT GOALS

The UN General Assembly in its 17th session in September 2015 announced a set of *17 SDGs* and 169 targets which will stimulate action over the next 15 years. This set of goals replaces the MDGs which were coming to an end in 2015 and will try to work in the areas which could not be completed earlier.

The SDGs were adopted after one of the largest consultation exercises in UN history. The goals were proposed in the United Nations Conference on Sustainable Development ***(Rio+20)*** in June 2012. The SDGs will be effective between 2016 and 2030.

The ***17 goals*** agreed upon under the SDGs are given below:

1. No Poverty
2. Zero Hunger
3. Good Health and Well-being
4. Quality Education
5. Gender Equality
6. Clean Water and Sanitation
7. Affordable and Clean Energy
8. Decent Work and Economic Growth
9. Industry, Innovation and Infrastructure
10. Reduced Inequality
11. Sustainable Cities and Communities
12. Responsible Consumption and Production
13. Climate Action
14. Life Below Water
15. Life on Land
16. Peace, Justice and Strong Institutions
17. Partnerships to Achieve the Goal

The 17 goals have a total of 169 targets and thus are very comprehensive in comparison to the MDGs. Countries need to evolve proper monitoring mechanism to track and achieve these targets under the set goals, a very challenging task. The major challenges faced by the countries in this regard will be in financing the implementation process, mustering participation from the stakeholders and evolving an administrative structure.

INDIA AND THE SDGS

India has taken several proactive steps at the national and sub-national levels to mainstream the SDGs into the policies, schemes and programmes of the Government. The major initiatives in this regard are given below:

- **SDG India Index:** The index was developed by the NITI Aayog to measure[2] the progress of states and union territories in the direction of achieving the goals and monitor their actions in this regard. There are 100 indicators[3] across the goals in which the states/UTs are given performance score (between 0 and 100) and are ranked accordingly. As per the *Economic Survey 2024-25* in India, state governments have been proactive and have laid out strategies and frameworks for achieving SDGs at district and block levels too. This multi-layered approach to SDG implementation is based on the Indian model of SDG Localisation comprising *four key pillars* (as per the *SDG India Index 2023-24*), namely– creating institutional ownership, fostering collaborative competition, enhancing capacities, and embracing a whole-of-society approach.[4]
- **SDGs Nexus:** As there exists a *nexus* between the SDGs targets and social indicators (such as education-electricity, health-energy, etc.), India has accordingly acquired a 'nexus approach' to the goals and started streamlining its social sector schemes and initiatives accordingly.
- **Voluntary National Review:** In *July 2020*, India presented its second VNR (Voluntary National Review) to the UNHLPF (United Nations High Level Political Forum) on Sustainable Development, which is the highest international platform for review and follow-up of the SDGs under the auspices of the UNESCO (United Nations Economic and Social Council). Besides highlighting India's achievements, the review presented the Indian model of *SDG localisation,* stakeholders' perspectives,[5] strategies of integrating businesses and the means of implementation.
- **Localisation:** Localisation of the SDGs is crucial for the realisation of the goals under the 2030 Agenda. In this regard, the *SDG India Index* and *Dashboard,* designed and developed by the NITI Aayog, is the principal tool through which not only the local bodies are being connected but their performance is also being measured and monitored.
- **COVID Response:** The pandemic threatened the very backbone of livelihood and sustainability. In this regard the governments initiated several measures starting with the arrangement of free food to agricultural- and MSME-related reforms which were directly or indirectly connected to the SDG goals.

MISHTI

India launched the Mangrove Initiative for Shoreline Habitats & Tangible Incomes (MISHTI) scheme for the development of "mangroves", covering around 450 square kilometres across 11 states and 2 union territories. The public-private partnership-based scheme is to run for the next five years, starting 2023–24.

PARIS AGREEMENT (COP 21)

The 21st Conference of Parties *(COP 21)* under the UNFCCC (United Nations Framework Convention on Climate Change) took place in Paris in December 2015. The Paris Agreement on post-2020 actions on climate change will succeed the *Kyoto Protocol.* Unlike the Kyoto Protocol, it provides a framework for all countries to take action against climate change. Placing emphasis on concepts such as climate justice and sustainable lifestyles, the Paris Agreement, for the ***first time***, brings together all nations for a common cause under the UNFCCC. One of the main focuses of the agreement is to hold the increase in the global average temperature to well below 2°C above preindustrial level and on driving efforts to limit it even further to 1.5°C.

The Agreement comprises 29 Articles and is supported by 139 decisions of the COP. It covers all the crucial areas identified as essential for a comprehensive and balanced agreement, including mitigation, adaptation,

[2] The salient features of the *SDG India Index Report, 2018* (which was developed by the NITI Aayog) have been discussed in detail in the *Economic Survey 2018-19,* vol. 2 (New Delhi: Ministry of Finance, GoI), pp. 105-08.

[3] *Economic Survey 2019-20,* vol. 2 (New Delhi: Ministry of Finance, GoI), pp. 168-72.

[4] *Economic Survey 2024-25* (New Delhi: Ministry of Finance, GoI, January 2025), pp. 352-53.

[5] India in this regard had consultations with over 1,000 CSOs (Civil Society Organisations), which was the cornerstone of the VNR Report preparation process. The consultations involved 14 groups and had the principle of *Leaving No One Behind* as its focus (which lies at the heart of SDGs), as per the *Economic Survey 2020-21,* vol. 2 (New Delhi: Ministry of Finance, GoI), pp. 205-07.

loss and damage, finance, technology development and transfer, capacity building and transparency of action and support.

A marked departure from the past is the Agreement's *bottom-up approach,* allowing each nation to submit its own national plan for reducing greenhouse gas (GHG) emissions, rather than trying to repeat a top-down approach advocated by the Kyoto Protocol, extending each country an emission reduction target. The ***salient features*** of the Agreement[6] are as follows:

1. It acknowledges the development imperatives of developing countries by recognising their right to development and their efforts to harmonise it with the environment, while protecting the interests of the most vulnerable.
2. It seeks to enhance the 'implementation of the Convention' while reflecting the principles of equity and CBDR-RC (Common but Differentiated Responsibilities and Respective Capabilities) in the light of different national circumstances.
3. Countries are required to communicate their climate action plans to the UNFCCC known as Nationally Determined Contributions (NDCs) every five years. Each party's successive NDC will represent a progression beyond the party's then current NDC, thereby steadily increasing global effort and ambition in the long term.
4. It is not mitigation-centric and includes other important elements such as adaptation, loss and damage, finance, technology development and transfer, capacity building and transparency of action and support.
5. Developed countries are urged to scale up their level of financial support with a complete road map towards achieving the goal of jointly providing US$ 100 billion by 2020. At the same time, a new collective quantified goal based on US$ 100 billion floor will be set before 2025.
6. It mandates that developed countries provide financial resources to developing countries. Other Parties may also contribute, but on a purely voluntary basis.
7. Developed countries are urged to take the lead in mobilisation of climate finance, while noting the significant role of public funds in the mobilisation of finance which should represent a progression beyond their previous effort.
8. It includes a robust transparency framework for both action and support.
9. Starting in 2023, a global stocktake covering all elements will take place every five years to assess the collective progress towards achieving the purpose of the Agreement and its long-term goals.
10. It establishes a compliance mechanism, overseen by a committee of experts that operates in a non-punitive way, and is facilitative in nature.

COP30

The COP30 was held in November 2025 in Belém, Brazil. A total of 29 decisions were taken at the conference which focus on moving from 'climate pledges to practical implementation.' The ***key outcomes***[7] of the summit are as given below:

- Focus on cooperation and narrowing the gap between commitments and delivery in energy, finance, and trade (called the 'Global Mutirao Agreement', which is named after the Brazilian tradition of *collective effort*).
- Parties reaffirmed the goal of mobilising *US$ 1.3 trillion* annually by 2035 for climate action in developing nations (Climate Finance).
- A major outcome was the political signal to *triple adaptation finance* by 2035 to help vulnerable countries cope with escalating climate impacts (Adaptation Finance).

Parties agreed on '59 voluntary indicators' to track progress in areas like food systems, water security, and infrastructure (Global Goal on Adaptation).

- A new platform was launched to coordinate technical support and capacity-building for workers

---

[6] *Economic Survey 2015-16,* vol. 2 (New Delhi: Ministry of Finance, GoI), pp. 179-81.

[7] *United Nations Framework Convention on Climate Change* (Bonn, Germany, November 2025).

and economies shifting away from fossil fuels (Just Transition Mechanism).

- The 'Tropical Forever Facility' was launched with a US$ 125 billion corpus to reward the conservation of tropical forests (on a 'payment-for-performance' model)— 20 per cent of payments are designated for Indigenous and local communities.
- The 'Health Action Plan' was launched, which includes 60 actions to strengthen global health systems against climate risks.
- 'Mission to 1.5°C' was launched to foster cooperation and monitor if national climate plans Nationally Determined Contributions (NDCs) align with the 1.5°C goal.
- Parties signed a declaration to combat climate change misinformation (for the *first time*) to promote 'information integrity' (against 'information pollution').

Few Unresolved Issues The summit ended with the following major unresolved issues:

- An explicit phase-out roadmap for fossil fuel was not included (due to opposition from major oil-producing nations). In response, a voluntary roadmap for fossil fuel transition and deforestation was decided to be developed outside the formal UN process.
- While over 122 parties submitted updated NDCs, current plans still put the world far short of the 1.5°C target (in place, the world is on a path towards 2.3°C–2.5°C of warming).
- The absence of the USA at the summit created a diplomatic vacuum which shifted the geopolitical dynamics during the negotiations.

COP31 is scheduled to take place from 9 to 20 November 2026—in an unprecedented "dual leadership" model, the summit will be physically hosted in Antalya (Turkey), while Australia will lead the formal negotiations.

GREEN FINANCE

In the past few years, the term 'green finance' has gained a lot of attention across the world. The idea was first mentioned in the UN document at the UN Conference on Sustainable Development (also known as *Rio+20*), 2012. Though it lacks a universal definition, green finance mostly refers to financial investments in projects and initiatives that encourage more sustainable economy.

There is no universal *definition* of green finance, though it mostly refers to financial investments flowing towards sustainable development projects and initiatives that encourage the development of a more sustainable economy[8]. By now, several working definitions have been set up - China's Green Credit Guidelines, the Climate Bonds Taxonomy of Green Bonds, the International Development Finance Club's (IDFC) approach to reporting on green investment, the World Bank/International Finance Corporation's (IFC) Sustainability Framework, and the UK Green Investment Bank Policies.

India and Green Development

Green finance is yet to pick up in India. Attaining the ambitious solar energy target, development of solar cities, setting up wind power projects, developing smart cities, providing infrastructure which is considered as a green activity and the sanitation drive under the *Clean India* or *Swachh Bharat Abhiyan* are all activities in need of green finance.

India created a corpus called the NCEF (National Clean Energy Fund) in 2010–11 out of the cess on coal produced/imported ('polluter pays' principle) for the purpose of financing and promoting clean energy initiatives and funding research in the area of clean energy. Some of the projects financed by this fund include innovative schemes as follows:

1. A green energy corridor for boosting the transmission sector,
2. Jawaharlal Nehru National Solar Mission's (JNNSM) installation of solar photovoltaic (SPV) lights and small capacity lights, installation of SPV water pumping systems, SPV power plants, grid-connected rooftop SPV power plants and
3. Pilot project to assess wind power potential.

[8] *Green Finance Study Group* - as quoted by the *Economic Survey 2015-16*, vol. 2 (New Delhi: Ministry of Finance, GoI), pp. 182-83.

By **February 2025**, most of the banks had issued *green bonds* in India. Proceeds from these bonds are mostly used for funding renewable energy projects such as solar, wind and biomass projects and other infrastructure sectors, with infrastructure and energy efficiency being considered as green in their entirety. By early 2016, the SEBI (Securities and Exchange Board of India) approved the guidelines for green bonds. India needs to take care of *certain issues*[9] involved with the mobilisation of green finance:

1. For a developing country like India, poverty alleviation and development are of vital importance and resources should not be diverted from meeting these development needs. Green finance should not be limited only to investment in renewable energy, as, for a country like India, coal-based power accounts for around 60 per cent of the installed capacity. Emphasis should be on *greening coal technology*.
2. Green bonds are perceived as new and attach higher risk and their tenure is also shorter. There is a need to reduce risks to make them investment grade.
3. There is also a need for an internationally agreed-upon definition of green financing as its absence could lead to over-accounting.
4. While environmental risk assessment is important, banks should not overestimate risks while providing green finance.
5. Green finance should also consider unsustainable patterns of *consumption* as a parameter in deciding finance, particularly conspicuous consumption and unsustainable lifestyles in developed countries.

CLIMATE FINANCE

The world is alive to the compulsion of combating climate change as unmitigated climate change risks pose irreversible costs. Complexity arises in the case of financing for addressing adaptation and mitigation of GHG emissions. Provision of finance is embedded in the convention and has also been mentioned in the *Paris Agreement* for addressing the adaptation and mitigation needs of developing countries. Tracking of climate finance is equally important. Lack of a clear **definition** of climate finance has led to controversies in recent estimates of climate finance.

The Paris Agreement mandates that transparent and consistent information on support provided and mobilised through public interventions for developing country Parties be provided by developed countries. However, it is silent on the definition of climate finance. While the question of what counts as climate finance would be decided at a later stage by the Standing Committee on Finance under the UNFCCC, it is important that it should highlight certain basic elements such as follows[10]:

1. Sources of funding, terms of funding and purpose of funding in addition to resources being committed/disbursed/new.
2. While defining climate finance, it is also important to define what cannot be counted towards climate finance.
3. Aid money meant for development purpose should not be counted as climate finance. With reference to funds provided for multiple purposes, only the share provided solely for climate change should be included under climate finance.
4. Systems should be in place to check for double counting or treatment of the ODA as climate finance.

There is an even greater gap in tracking adaptation finance and segregating it from development funds as a whole. As a result, very often, the entire amount allocated to a project is erroneously treated as adaptation finance. Any climate finance tracking exercise needs to carefully account for these problems.

GREEN CLIMATE FUND

The Green Climate Fund (GCF) is a global fund[11] created to support the efforts of developing countries to respond to the challenge of climate change, by helping them limit or reduce their GHG emissions and adapt to climate change. It seeks to promote a paradigm shift to low-emission and climate-resilient development, taking into account the needs of nations that are particularly vulnerable to climate change impacts.

It was set up by 194 countries who are parties to the UNFCCC in 2010. It aims to deliver equal amounts of funding to mitigation and adaptation. It has been given an important role in serving the agreement and supporting the goal of the *Paris Climate Agreement, 2015* by keeping climate change well below 2°C.

[9] Ibid.

[10] Ibid., pp. 185-86.

[11] Green Climate Fund (Incheon, South Korea, March 2019).

The fund was launched in 2014 with a pledge of US$ 10.3 billion (from both public and private sectors in the form of grants, loans, equity or guarantee) - the highest contribution was pledged by the United States (US$ 3 billion), followed by Japan (US$ 1.5 billion), the United Kingdom (US$ 1.2 billion), France (US$ 1.03 billion) and Germany (US$ 1.0 billion), while small amounts came from some developing nations and one city (Paris). Under the second replenishment (GCF-2) of December 2023, a record fund of $12.8 billion was pledged by 31 countries for the next four years.

In recent climate talks, the issue of targeting emissions to limit temperature rise by 1.5 to 2°C above pre-industrial level was intensely debated. However, climate finance (the real enabler in this direction) could not be resolved as desired.

GLOBAL ENVIRONMENT FACILITY

The Global Environment Facility (GEF) was established[12] on the eve of the 1992 *Rio Earth Summit* to help (mainly the developing countries) tackle earth's most pressing environmental problems. Both developed and developing countries are donors (40 in number) to the GEF. Its fund is replenished after every 4 years. At the last replenishment (GEF-8) in 2022, a fund of $5.25 billion was pledged by 29 donor countries (29 per cent higher than the last replenishment of 2019).

Today, it has become an international partnership of 186 countries, international institutions, civil society organisations and the private sector that addresses global environmental issues. By *March 2019*, the fund had provided over US$17.9 billion in grants and mobilised an additional US$ 93.2 billion in co-financing for more than 4500 projects in 170 countries.

INDCS

The INDCs are plans by governments communicated to the UNFCCC regarding the steps they will take to address climate change domestically. As per the *COP 19* decision (Warsaw 2013), all Parties were requested to prepare their INDCs, without prejudice to the legal nature of the contributions towards achieving the objectives of the convention and communicate well in advance of the COP 21.

[12] Global Environment Fund (Washington DC, USA, March 2020).

India's INDC India submitted its INDC to the UNFCCC in October 2015, which is quite exhaustive and covers elements such as adaptation, mitigation, finance, technology and capacity building. The 2015 NDC comprised 8 goals, 3 of which were quantitative targets to be achieved up to 2030. These 3 targets included– cumulative electric power installed capacity from non-fossil sources to reach 40 per cent; reduction in the emissions intensity of GDP by 33 to 35 per cent compared to 2005 levels; and creation of additional carbon sink of 2.5 to 3 billion tonnes of CO_2 equivalent through additional forest and tree cover.

The Paris Agreement (Article 4) provides that each Party shall communicate or update its NDC every 5 years. Accordingly, in ***August 2022***, India submitted the following[13] updates to its first NDC of 2015:

1. To put forward and further propagate a healthy and sustainable way of living based on traditions and values of conservation and moderation, including through a mass movement for *LIFE (Lifestyle for Environment)* as a key to combating climate change.

Scan this QR Code to watch a author's video lecture that simplifies this topic

2. To adopt a climate-friendly and cleaner path than the one followed hitherto by others at the corresponding level of economic development.
3. To reduce the Emissions Intensity of its GDP by 45 per cent by 2030, from the 2005 level.
4. To achieve about 50 per cent cumulative electric power installed capacity from non-fossil fuel-based energy resources by 2030, with the help of the transfer of technology and low-cost international finance, including from the Green Climate Fund (GCF).
5. To create an additional carbon sink of 2.5 to 3 billion tonnes of CO_2 equivalent through additional forest and tree cover by 2030.
6. To better adapt to climate change by enhancing investments in development programmes in sectors vulnerable to climate change, particularly agriculture, water resources, the

[13] *Economic Survey 2022-23* (New Delhi: Ministry of Finance, GoI, January 2023), pp. 222-223.

Himalayan region, coastal regions, and health and disaster management.

7. To mobilise domestic and new and additional funds from developed countries to implement the above mitigation and adaptation actions in view of the resource required and the resource gap.
8. To build capacities and create a domestic framework and international architecture for quick diffusion of cutting-edge climate technology in India and for joint collaborative R&D for such future technologies.

India's Climate Finance Expenditures India's expenditure related to adaptation increased from **3.7** per cent of GDP in 2015-16 to **5.6** per cent in 2021-22. Climate action, so far, has been financed through domestic resources, with the public sector playing a central role. On the other hand, the international flow of funds for climate actions is highly inadequate and has a mitigation bias.[14]

India and Climate Change

It India has been very sensitive to the issue of climate change and has been active in mitigating the crisis with the global community. The National Action Plan on Climate Change (NAPCC), launched in 2008, was India's first multidimensional step in this direction. The action plan has objectives of *adaptation and mitigation* through focused national missions. The missions also focus on key adaptation requirements and creation of scientific knowledge and preparedness. India decided to ***revise the NAPCC*** in line with its INDCs under the Paris Agreement to make it more comprehensive in terms of priority areas. The progress of implementation of the *eight national missions* is briefly explained[15] below:

1. The ***Perform, Achieve and Trade (PAT)*** scheme under National Mission for Enhanced Energy Efficiency (NMEEE) is designed on the concept of 'reduction' in energy consumption. By April 2019, 110 Designated Customers (DCs) were notified under it. The total energy consumption of these DCs comes out to be 15.244 million tons of Oil Equivalent (MTOE), and it is expected to receive a total energy savings of 0.5130 MTOE. By 2023, about 23 MTOE of energy savings is estimated under the scheme.
2. The ***National Solar Mission*** aims to increase the share of solar energy in the total energy mix. The target has been set at 100 GW *via* grid connected solar power projects, grid connected rooftop projects, and large and medium size land-based solar power projects. The total investment in setting up 100 GW will be around ₹6.5 lakh crores. A cumulative 33.5 GW of solar electric generation capacity was installed (by November 2022).
3. The ***National Water Mission*** focuses on monitoring of groundwater, aquifer mapping, capacity building, water quality monitoring and other baseline studies. There are 1071 assessment units categorised as over-exploited as per the assessment (last carried out in 2011) of the Central Ground Water Authority (CGWA). Directions have been issued for mandatory rainwater harvesting/ roof top rainwater harvesting for all target areas in the country. Rainwater harvesting has been made mandatory for drawing groundwater.
4. The ***National Mission for a Green India*** envisages a holistic view of greening and focuses on multiple ecosystem services along with carbon sequestration and emission reduction. The mission emphasises the landscape approach to treat large contiguous areas of both forest and non-forest, public and private lands with a key role of the local communities in planning, implementation and monitoring. Actions taken under it are afforestation activities (convergence with the MGNREGS also done), promoting alternate energy at household level, etc.
5. The ***National Mission on Sustainable Habitat*** is being implemented through three programmes: Atal Mission on Rejuvenation and Urban Transformation, Swachh Bharat Mission, and Smart Cities Mission. The actions under it consists of mandatory energy conservation for commercial buildings having load of 100 KW or above, mass rapid transit systems and six sub-sectors launched (solid waste management, water and sanitation, storm water drainage, urban planning, energy efficiency and urban transport).
6. The ***National Mission for Sustainable Agriculture*** aims at enhancing food security and protection

[14] *Economic Survey 2024-25* (New Delhi: Ministry of Finance, GoI, January 2025), pp. 222-273.

[15] *Economic survey 2020-21*, vol. 2 (New Delhi: Ministry of Finance, GoI), pp. 208-11.

of resources. Key targets include covering 3.5 lakh hectare of area under organic farming, 3.70 under precision irrigation, 4.0 lakh hectare under the system of rice intensification, 3.41 lakh hectare under diversification to less water consuming crops, 3.09 lakh hectare additional area under plantation in arable land and 7 bypass protein feed making. The mission has resulted in the formation of the network project NICRA (National Innovations on Climate Resilient Agriculture).

7. The ***National Mission for Sustaining the Himalayan Ecosystem*** aims to evolve suitable management and policy measures for sustaining and safeguarding the Himalayan ecosystem. The key achievements include setting up of a Centre of Glaciology at the Wadia Institute of Himalayan Geology, thematic task forces in 6 lead institutions, state climate change centres in 11 out of 12 Himalayan states, 40 training programmes under state climate change centres organised with 5500 people trained and formation of an Inter-University Consortium of 4 universities on Himalayan cryosphere and climate change.

8. The ***National Mission on Strategic Knowledge for Climate Change*** seeks to build a *knowledge system* that would inform and support national action for ecologically sustainable development. The key achievements include setting up of 11 centres of excellence and 10 state climate change centres, training programmes, 7 human capacity building and national knowledge network programmes in the areas of climate change science, adaptation and mitigation, and 8 global technology watch groups in the areas of renewable energy technology, advanced coal technology, enhanced energy efficiency, green forest, sustainable habitat, water, sustainable agriculture and manufacturing.

Climate Change Action Programme

The central sector scheme Climate Change Action Programme (CCAP) was launched in 2014 with the aim to build and support capacity at central and state levels, strengthening scientific and analytical capacity for climate change assessment, establishing appropriate institutional framework and implementing climate actions. Major actions[16] under the scheme are as follows:

- Energy audit studies have revealed an end-use saving potential to the extent of 40 per cent in the country - the Energy Conservation Building Code, 2018 has started setting minimum energy performance standards.
- Schemes such as UJALA for LED bulb distribution and replacing conventional streetlights by LED lights are being implemented.
- As part of the National Electric Mobility Mission Plan (NEMMP), 2020, Faster Adoption and Manufacturing of (Hybrid and) Electric Vehicles in India (FAME India) scheme was formulated in 2015 to promote manufacturing and sustainable growth of electric and hybrid vehicle technology.
- The National Bio-fuels Policy 2018 targets 20 per cent blending of ethanol in petrol and 5 per cent blending of biodiesel in diesel by 2030.

National Adaptation Fund on Climate Change (2015) supports concrete adaptation activities for the States/UTs that are particularly vulnerable to the adverse effects of climate change and are not covered under ongoing schemes. The scheme has been taken as a central sector scheme with the NABARD (with domestic and multilateral funds) as the national implementing entity.

Aligning Financial System with Sustainability

A sound financial system is required for cleaner forms of production. This is more so, as estimates point towards the requirement of trillions of dollars to achieve SDGs globally. Hence, the spotlight[17] is now on aligning the financial system with sustainable development with the following steps:

- The RBI (in 2007) sensitised banks to the various international initiatives and asked them to modify their lending plans in the light of such developments.
- The SEBI (in 2012) mandated the Annual Business Responsibility Reporting (ABRR), a reporting framework based on the National Voluntary Guidelines (NVGs) for listed companies with the purpose of pursuing sustainable management practices. The Indian Institute of Corporate Affairs

[16] *Economic Survey 2019-20*, vol. 2 (New Delhi: Ministry of Finance, GoI), p. 176.

[17] *Economic Survey 2020-21*, vol. 2 (New Delhi: Ministry of Finance, GoI), pp. 217-20.

(in 2011) developed the concept of NVG for adoption by the corporate sector.

- 'Climate bonds' remain focused on green bonds, which are specifically linked to climate-change mitigation, adaptation and resilience. India (US$ 10 billion) has the second largest emerging green bond market after China (US$ 110 billion), with a very high potential of growth. 'Green bonds' are being issued by financial, non-financial or public entities where the proceeds are used to finance 100 per cent green projects and assets. 'Social bonds' are yet another variant of the climate bonds popular in the country. Climate bonds are set to gain popularity in the coming years as issuers and investors both are inclined to adopt policies and strategies linked to SDGs.

Aimed to scale up the environmentally sustainable investments, India joined the *International Platform on Sustainable Finance (IPSF)* in October 2019. It aims to mobilise resources from the international financial market to help finance the transition to a green, low-carbon and climate resilient economy. Its twin objectives are:

1. Exchange and disseminate information to promote best practices in environmentally sustainable finance; and
2. Compare the different initiatives and identify barriers and opportunities to help scale up environmentally sustainable finance while respecting national and regional contexts.

INTERNATIONAL INITIATIVES OF INDIA

In order to mitigate the climate change risk and integrate the power of global community, India has taken some very vital initiatives on an international stage. These initiatives are discussed briefly below.

International Solar Alliance

The ISA is the *first* treaty-based inter-governmental organisation headquartered in India. With 120 signatory countries, the alliance creates a multi-stakeholder ecosystem where sovereign nations, multilateral organisations, industries, policymakers and innovators work together to promote the common and shared goal of meeting energy demands of a secure and sustainable world. It aims to pave the way for future solar generation, storage and technologies for member countries' needs by mobilising over US$ 1000 billion by 2030. The achievement of its objectives will also strengthen the climate action in member countries, helping them fulfil the commitments expressed in their INDCs. Some **major initiatives** under the alliance[18] are as given below:

- It has signed an MoU with the UNESCAP and enjoys a permanent observer status at the UN General Assembly with funding agreements with the World Bank, Asian Development Bank and European Development Bank.
- *World Solar Bank* and *One Sun One World One Grid Initiative* were initiated and aimed at global solar energy revolution. While the former would cater to the need for dedicated financing window (including low-cost fund) for solar energy projects, the latter aspires to develop an interconnected 'green grid'.
- Its solar rooftop programme has been noteworthy, with a demand of more than 9.5 GW aggregated from member countries. The ISA has diversified its programmatic focus on the health sector, cold storage chains for agriculture and vaccines and other innovative applications of solar energy.
- 'Coalition for Sustainable Climate Action' was launched in 2020, comprising global public and private corporates, to institutionalise its partnership with the corporate sector.
- In its member countries (with a grant of US$ 50,000), the ISA is assisting in setting up solar energy demonstration projects. Three such demonstration projects were inaugurated at the *5th Assembly of ISA* (17–20 October 2022).

Coalition for Disaster Resilient Infrastructure

In June 2024, India launched the Coalition for Disaster Resilient Infrastructure (CDRI) on the side-lines of the UN Secretary General's Climate Action Summit. This international partnership of national governments (39), UN agencies, multilateral development banks, the private sector and knowledge institutions aims to promote the *resilience* of new and existing infrastructure systems to climate and disaster risks. The coalition has the following[19] objectives:

[18] *Economic Survey 2022-2023* (New Delhi: Ministry of Finance, GoI), p.235; *Economic Survey 2020-21*, vol. 2 (New Delhi: Ministry of Finance, GoI), pp. 222–23; *Economic Survey 2019-20*, vol. 2 (New Delhi: Ministry of Finance, GoI), pp. 179–80.

[19] *Economic Survey 2020-21*, vol. 2 (New Delhi: Ministry of Finance, GoI), pp. 223–24.

➤ Enabling measurable reduction in infrastructure losses from disasters, including extreme climate events.

➤ Enabling universal access to basic services and prosperity as enshrined in the SDGs, working under the Sendai Framework for Disaster Risk Reduction and the Paris Climate Agreement.

➤ Conducting country-specific and global activities and providing member countries technical support and capacity development, with partnerships to facilitate and encourage investment in disaster-resilient infrastructure systems.

By *June 2024*, 40 countries, seven international organisations and two private sector organisations have joined as members of CDRI. Over a period, a network of organisations/stakeholders will be developed to advance disaster resilient infrastructure not only in India but in other partner countries as well.

LeadIT Group

The LeadIT Group (Leadership Group for Industry Transition) was launched by India and Sweden, with the support of the WEF (World Economic Forum) at the UN Climate Action Summit in New York in September 2019, as one of the nine action tracks identified by the UN Secretary-General to boost climate ambitions and actions to implement the Paris Agreement. In November 2021, the Joint Ministerial Statement released at the Leadership Summit called countries and companies to come out with roadmaps for *deep reductions in emissions across* all heavy industries and value chains in the coming decade.

During the *COP 27*, LeadIT members adopted a joint statement wherein members collectively agreed to:

(i) Promote value chain partnerships and material circularity;

(ii) Invest and cooperate on the planning and implementation of infrastructure to support energy and industry transitions;

(iii) Give multilateral development banks (MDBs) and multilateral climate funds mandates to de-risk investments in the transition of heavy industries in emerging and developing countries; and

(iv) Formulate roadmaps for heavy industry sectors that include regulatory frameworks, incentives, and long-term strategies, to facilitate transition finance and attract private investments.

LeadIT 2.0 was launched at the COP28 (Dubai) in December 2023 for the period 2024-26. India and Sweden also launched the 'Industry Transition Platform' to connect the governments, industries, technology providers, researchers and think tanks of the two countries.

LiFE

In November 2021, the PM of India proposed a 'One-Word Movement' in the context of climate – LiFE (Lifestyle for Environment) at the COP 26 in Glasgow. This *movement* calls for coming together with collective participation, to take lifestyle for environment forward as a campaign and as a 'mass movement' for environmentally conscious lifestyle in a manner that revolutionises many sectors and diverse areas such as fishing, agriculture, wellness, dietary choices, packaging, housing, hospitality, tourism, clothing, fashion, water management and energy.

INDIA'S FORESTS

Forests play a crucial role in adaptation and mitigation to climate change. They help to store more carbon (i.e., carbon sink) than any other terrestrial ecosystem (as per the *India State of Forest Report-2023*). India accounts for 2 per cent of the total global forest area in 2020 as per the Global Forest Resource Assessment-2020 of the FAO. The major features[20] of the forests in India are summarised below:

➤ The Forest and Tree cover of the country is 8,27,357 sq km (25.17 per cent of the geographical area of the country), consisting of 7,15,343 sq km (21.76 per cent) as forest cover and 1,12,014 sq km (3.41 per cent) as tree cover.

➤ As compared to the last biennial assessment of 2021, there is an increase of 1445 sq km in the forest and tree cover of the country (156 sq km forest cover and 1289 sq km tree cover).

➤ Area wise top three states having largest forest and *tree cover* are Madhya Pradesh (85,724 sq km) followed by Arunachal Pradesh (67,083 sq km) and Maharashtra (65,383 sq km).

[20] *India State of Forest Report 2023* (Dehradun: Forest Survey of India, Uttarakhand, December 2024).

- Area wise top three states having largest *forest cover* are Madhya Pradesh (77,073 sq km) followed by Arunachal Pradesh (65,882 sq km) and Chhattisgarh (55,812 sq km).
- In terms of percentage of forest cover with respect to total geographical area, Lakshadweep (91.33 percent) has the highest forest cover followed by Mizoram (85.34 percent) and Andaman & Nicobar Island (81.62 percent).
- 19 states/UTs have above 33 percent of the geographical area under forest cover. Out of these, eight states/UTs namely Mizoram, Lakshadweep, Andaman and Nicobar Island, Arunachal Pradesh, Nagaland, Meghalaya, Tripura, and Manipur have forest cover above 75 percent.
- The total mangrove cover is 4,992 sq km in the country.
- India is one of the ***17 megadiverse*** countries in the world. This is evident in the *Shannon–Weiner Index* for diversity, which is used for measuring species richness and abundance. The index also compares diversity of species among various habitats.
- The *carbon stock* in country's forest is estimated to be 7,285.5 million tonnes. There is an increase of 81.5 million tonnes in the carbon stock of country as compared to the last assessment of 2021.
- Regarding status on achievement of target under NDC (Nationally Determined Contributions) related to *carbon sequestration*, India's carbon stock has reached 30.43 billion tonnes of CO_2 equivalent; which indicates that as compared to the base year of 2005, India has already reached 2.29 billion tonnes of additional carbon sink as against the target of 2.5 to 3.0 billion tonnes by 2030.

India is among a few countries in the world where, despite ongoing developmental efforts, forest and tree cover are increasing considerably.

CLIMATE RISK INSURANCE

With looming climatic aberrations, the time[21] for introducing a climate risk insurance in the country has come - the country incurs losses to the tune of around US$ 10 billion annually due to extreme weather events, where about 80 per cent Indians remain uninsured. It is an important tool for providing security against loss of livelihoods and assets as a consequence of disasters.

This is of great significance especially for the farm community which mainly faces the risks of 'weather variability' and the 'uncertainty of crop yield' - the magnitude and intensity of the same being higher in India. As an overwhelming majority of farmers (contributing significantly to the economy and livelihood) depend on farming and have extremely limited means and resources to cope with the disastrous consequences of crop failure, it is high time for such an insurance.

Driven by agriculture and the process of development, natural (i.e., primary) forests are increasingly being converted into secondary forests inviting an increased risk of new[22] infectious diseases, which also needs to be included in the climate risk insurance.

Agriculture insurance in the country is very challenging because of a large number of small and scattered landholdings, varying climatic and soil conditions, lack of basic data and a variety of agricultural practices, making it *practically impossible* to implement the scheme on a wide scale. Further, there is widespread lack of knowledge about the nature and functions of crop insurance amongst the farmers, a majority of whom are illiterate and poor.

The *Weather Index Insurance* for agriculture introduced in 2003 did not find much success as it suffered from complex processes, moral hazard, adverse selection and low penetration of institutional credit.

Studies suggest moving towards *parametric insurance* that agrees to make payment on 'just the occurrence of a climate event' (data for which are easily accessible). Further, the use of climate information services could also be useful. The example of the Karnataka State Natural Disaster Monitoring Centre's *Varuna Mitra*, which has not only benefitted 3.5 lakh farmers through its weather advisories but also provides data to insurers at Panchayat scale to improve pay-outs to farmers, is a case in point.

[21] *Economic Survey 2020-21*, vol. 2 (New Delhi: Ministry of Finance, GoI), p. 221. It was the *Economic Survey 2016-17* which pitched for it in the country for the *first* time; the insurance industry has been deliberating on such possibilities since 2015.

[22] An example in this regard is the insurance bought by *Wimbledon* tennis tournament against a pandemic occurrence in 2003 following the SARS outbreak, thus receiving an insurance pay-out of US$ 142 million in 2020 which was utilised to pay the prize money and staff wages *(Insurance Journal 2020).*

Green Bonds

Green bonds raise funds as loans for investment in environmentally sustainable and climate-suitable projects. With growing focus on environmentally sustainable projects, these bonds have become widely accepted and popular over the last few years and help raise funds at lower cost in comparison to regular bonds. Major countries such as the UK, France, Germany, the USA, and China have already raised funds through it. As per IMF, during 2021, a total fund of around US$ 620 billion was raised across the world through green bonds. As per the data of SEBI, 15 Indian corporates issued green bonds of value ₹4,539 crore during 2017–22.

In keeping with the ambition to reduce the carbon intensity of the economy, the *Union Budget 2022–23* announced the issue of Sovereign Green Bonds (SGrBs). Accordingly, the RBI issued India's first SGrBs (of 5-year and 1-year maturity) in two tranches and raised a total of ₹16,000 crores (subscription was open for non-residents too). Over time, the SGrBs would provide a *pricing reference* for private sector entities for their domestic borrowings through environment, social, and governance (ESG) bonds.

WILDLIFE PROTECTION

India has a rich heritage of wildlife and a long history and tradition of conservation. The concern for wildlife is, indeed, the concern for the man himself. All forms of life - human, animal and plants are so closely interlinked that disturbance in one leads to an imbalance in others. Animals such as tigers, lions, and elephants are keystone and flagship species whose preservation benefits the entire ecosystems. As of August 2022, the state[23] of these animals in the country was as given below:

Tiger Reserves India was home to 55 *Tiger Reserves* (2 added in 2023) covering approximately 78,735.6 sq. km area in 18 States, with about 75 per cent of the wild tiger population at the global level. India achieved the goal of doubling the tiger numbers in 2018, four years before the targeted year 2022.

Asiatic Lions The population of *Asiatic Lions* has shown a steady increase, with a population of 674 individuals in 2020 to 356 by 2023 (105 died in 2021, 110 in 2022 and 103 in 2023).

Leopards India now (2020) has 13,874 (2022 survey) *leopards* compared to the previous estimate of 12,852 conducted in 2014.

Asiatic Elephants As per the latest census of 2017, India is home to 29,964 Asiatic elephants which is around 60 per cent of the Asiatic elephants which has worldwide population of 50-60 thousand.

Project Cheetah India began introduction of Cheetahs in the country under Project Cheetah, the world's first intercontinental large wild carnivore translocation project (cheetah was declared extinct from India in 1952). Under the scheme, 8 Namibian wild cheetahs were introduced in Kuno National Park, Madhya Pradesh.

The project is part of a long series of measures for ensuring sustainability and environmental protection. Cheetahs can help restore open forest and grassland ecosystems, conserve biodiversity and enhance the ecosystem services like water security, carbon sequestration, and soil moisture conservation, benefiting society. It will also lead to enhanced livelihood opportunities for the local community through eco-development and ecotourism activities. The Government has constituted a Task Force (for 2 years) for monitoring Cheetah introduction with the following tasks:

- Review, progress, and monitor the health status of Cheetah,
- Monitor hunting skills and adaptation of Cheetahs to the habitat of Kuno National Park.
- Monitor the release of Cheetah from Quarantine bomas to soft-release enclosures, grassland, and open forest areas.
- Open Cheetah habitat for eco-tourism and suggest regulations in this regard.
- Suggest and advise on developing tourism infrastructure in the fringe areas of Kuno National Park and other Protected Areas.

The *Wildlife (Protection) Act, 1972* was enacted by India to provide special legal protection to our wildlife

[23] *Economic Survey 2022-23* (New Delhi: Ministry of Finance, GoI, January 2023), pp. 238-239.

and the endangered species of fauna. This Act has been amended multiple times, the last being in *2022*, which has affected following changes:

- Rationalised the schedules to two (from 6),
- Removed the schedule for vermin species,
- Inserted a new schedule to increase number of species protected under Convention on International Trade in Endangered Species of Wild Fauna and Flora (CITES), and
- Empowers the government to regulate or prohibit the import, trade, possession, or proliferation of invasive alien species.

SINGLE-USE PLASTICS

India is committed to mitigating pollution caused by littered *single-use* plastics. However, per capita consumption of plastic in India is only 11 kg (much lower than the global average of 28 kg). To reduce pollution caused due to littered plastic waste in the country, the Government notified the Plastic Waste Management Amendment Rules, 2021, in August 2021 and in July 2022, a ***ban*** was imposed on the manufacture, import, stocking, distribution, sale of the single-use plastic. The measures will promote a *circular economy*, reduce the plastic footprint of plastic packaging, promote the development of new alternatives to plastic packaging and provide the next steps for moving towards sustainable plastic packaging by businesses. Under it, a number of initiatives[24] have been taken such as:

- Extended Producers Responsibility (EPR) has been fixed (with their defined targets) for all stakeholders such as producers, importers, and brand owners which includes;
- Mandatory reuse of rigid plastic packaging and recycling; centralised online portal to support the implementation of EPR;
- Provision for the sale and purchase of surplus EPR certificates;
- Levy of environmental compensation for non-fulfilment of EPR obligations; and provision for verification, audit, and monitoring.

This action of the Government aligns with the *5th United Nations Environment Assembly* (Nairobi, March 2022) which adopted a resolution "End plastic pollution: towards an international legally binding instrument."

BATTERY WASTE MANAGEMENT

The Government published the Battery Waste Management Rules, 2022, in August 2022 to ensure environmentally sound management of waste batteries with the aim to promote circular economy. The rules cover all types of batteries - electric vehicle batteries, portable batteries, automotive batteries, and industrial batteries - which replaced the existing Batteries (Management and Handling) Rules, 2001.

The rules' function based on the concept of Extended Producer Responsibility (EPR), where the producers (including importers) of batteries are responsible for the collection and recycling/refurbishment of waste batteries and the use of recovered materials from wastes into new batteries. The EPR mandates that all waste batteries be collected and sent for recycling/refurbishment, prohibiting disposal in landfills and incineration.

E-WASTE MANAGEMENT

The Government notified the E-Waste (Management) Rules, 2022, in November 2022. These rules replaced the E-waste (Management) Rules, 2016 and became effective from April 2023. These rules launched a new Extended Producer Responsibility (EPR) regime for e-waste recycling. The salient features of new rules[25] are as under:

- Applicable to every manufacturer, producer, refurbisher, dismantler, and recycler who must register (fully online) with CPCB.
- A total of 106 Electrical and Electronic Equipment (EEE) have been included under the EPR regime.
- Producers of notified EEE have been given annual recycling targets based on the generation from the previously sold EEE or based on sales of EEE.
- The recycled quantity will be computed based on end-products to avoid false claims.
- Provisions for environmental compensation and verification and audit have been introduced.
- Provision for generation and transaction of EPR Certificate has been introduced.

[24] *Economic Survey 2022-23* (New Delhi: Ministry of Finance, GoI, January 2023), pp. 239-240.

[25] *Economic Survey 2022-23* (New Delhi: Ministry of Finance, GoI, January 2023), pp. 241-242.

- Producers to ensure that their products do not contain *lead, mercury,* and *other hazardous* substances beyond the maximum prescribed concentration.
- Recognition and registration, skill development, monitoring, and ensuring the safety and health of workers involved in dismantling and recycling e-waste.

FUTURE OUTLOOK

India very well understands that action towards sustainability is an undeniable concern for humanity. India's National Agenda of development (evolved by the NITI Aayog) mirrors the SDGs and its policies ensuring the balance among *three pillars* of development - economic, social and environmental. India's future concerns together with performance commitments are given[26] below:

- India's efforts in mitigation have been ambitious. India has successfully established an installed electricity generation capacity of 213 GW from *non-fossil fuel sources,* which accounts for 46.8 per cent of the total capacity by November 2024– the goal is to reach 50 per cent by 2030.
- India is among a few countries in the world where, despite ongoing developmental efforts, forest and tree cover is increasing considerably. The forest and tree cover increased to 8.27 lakh square km which is 25.17 per cent of the geographical area of the country (as per the latest biennial *India State of Forest Report 2023*).
- Agriculture *crop residue burning* and construction and demolition (C&D) *waste* continues to be major concerns. Many countries are already using recycled C&D products in construction. The *Delhi PPP model* in C&D waste management can be a beacon for the other States and cities to replicate, enabling the Swachch Bharat Mission and supporting the SDGs.
- Scarce *financial resources* continue to be the biggest constraint despite the efforts of stakeholders from various walks of life. Developed countries should honour their financial obligations and promises under the multilateral environmental agreements. The world that benefited from carbon emissions (that made them developed) *must repay.*
- Development and *transfer of technology* at affordable costs is also crucial for developing countries.
- There needs to be a greater thrust on climate action following the announcement of India's target of becoming *Net Zero* by 2070 - climate finance and innovative strategies will remain critical to successful action towards this goal.
- More importantly, the global climate agenda will advance if advanced countries can set examples of policy and *behavioural changes* that work in their backyard and whose trade-offs are well recognised and accepted by their people. Then, it might be realistic to expect such policies and behavioural expectations of households to succeed in developing countries with suitable adaptation.

DEVELOPMENT WITH WISDOM[27]

Hardly anything makes economic sense unless its continuance for a long period of time can be projected without running into absurdities. Growth and development can occur to a 'limited objective', but it

[26] Based on the *Economic Survey 2025-26* (New Delhi: Ministry of Finance, GoI, January 2026), pp. 377-417; *Economic Survey 2024-2025* (New Delhi: Ministry of Finance, GoI, January 2025), pp. 298-300; *Economic Survey 2023-2024* (New Delhi: Ministry of Finance, GoI, January 2024), pp. 207-208; *Economic Survey 2022-2023* (New Delhi: Ministry of Finance, GoI, January 2023), pp. 216-242; *Economic Survey 2021-22* (New Delhi: Ministry of Finance, GoI), pp. 196-233; *Economic Survey 2020-21,* vol. 2 (New Delhi: Ministry of Finance, GoI), pp. 204-05 and *Economic Survey 2019-20,* vol. 2 (New Delhi: Ministry of Finance, GoI), p. 190.

[27] These virtuous opinions can be seen in a number of contemporary thinkers and writers since the 1970s:

E. F. Schumacher, *The Economics of Permanence' Resurgence,* 3(1), May/June 1970, reprinted in Robin Clarke, ed., *Notes for the Future: An Alternative History of the Past Decade.* (London: Thames and Hudson, 1975). Schumacher invoked Gandhi while advocating for the 'economics of permanence'.

J. Sachs, *Common Wealth: Economics for a Crowded Earth* (London: Penguin Books, 2009), pp. 29-35, pp. 55-155.

J. Sachs, *The End of Poverty* (London: Penguin Books, 2005), pp. 280-84.

T. Harford, *The Undercover Economist* (London: Abacus GB, 2006), pp. 90-104.

T. L. Friedman, *The World is Flat* (London: Penguin Books, 2006), pp. 383-85, pp. 495-504.

R. Guha, 'The Ecology of Affluence', in *The Ramachandra Guha Omnibus* (New Delhi: Oxford University Press, 2005), pp. 69-97.

cannot be stretched up to an 'unlimited extent'. How can the 'finite' earth support mankind's 'infinite' physical needs? Long before this was postulated by the 'Club of Rome' in 1972, the exact same thing was theorised by Gandhiji in the 1930s, 'Earth provides enough to satisfy every man's need, but not for every man's greed'. Mankind needs to introspect not only about its present needs but also the way those needs are being met.

Besides, we also need to 'differentiate' between our 'needs' and 'aspirations'. Our physical needs have a direct 'link' with the resources we have at our disposal to meet them. If mankind is to survive and prosper, we need to be aware of the repercussions of our activities on Mother Nature. Humanity needs to be wiser not only in selecting the tools for development but also in setting the goals of development.

PREVIOUS YEARS' QUESTIONS

Prelims

1. Consider the following statements: (2025)

Statement-I: At the 28th United Nations Climate Change Conference (COP28), India refrained from signing the 'Declaration on Climate and Health'.

Statement-II: The COP28 Declaration on Climate and Health is a binding declaration; and if signed, it becomes mandatory to decarbonise the health sector.

Statement-III: If India's health sector is decarbonised, the resilience of its health-care system may be compromised.

Which one of the following is correct in respect of the above statements?

(a) Both Statement-II and Statement-III are correct, and both of them explain Statement-I

(b) Both Statement-II and Statement-III are correct, but only one of them explains Statement-I

(c) Only one of Statements-II, and III is correct and that explains Statement-I

(d) Neither Statement-II nor Statement-III is correct

2. Consider the following statements: (2025)

Statement-I: Article 6 of the Paris Agreement on climate change is frequently discussed in the global discussions on sustainable development and climate change.

Statement-II: Article 6 of the Paris Agreement on climate change sets out the principles of carbon markets.

Statement-III: Article 6 of the Paris Agreement on climate change intends to promote inter-country non-market strategies to reach their climate targets.

Which one of the following is correct in respect of the above statements?

(a) Both Statement-II and Statement-III are correct, and both of them explain Statement-I

(b) Both Statement-II and Statement-III are correct, but only one of them explains Statement-I

(c) Only one of the Statements-II and III is correct, and that explains Statement-I

(d) Neither Statement-II nor Statement-III is correct

3. Consider the following statements: (2025)

Statement-I: Circular economy reduces the emissions of greenhouse gases.

Statement-II: Circular economy reduces the use of raw materials as inputs.

Statement-III: Circular economy reduces wastage in the production process.

Which one of the following is correct in respect of the above statements?

(a) Both Statement-II and Statement-III are correct, and both of them explain Statement-I

(b) Both Statement-I and Statement-II are correct, and Statement-I explains Statement-II

(c) Only one of the Statements-II, and III is correct and that explains Statement-I

(d) Neither Statement-II nor Statement-III is correct

4. Which organisation has enacted the Nature Restoration Law (NRL) to tackle climate change and biodiversity loss? (2025)
(a) The European Union
(b) The World Bank
(c) The Organization for Economic Cooperation and Development
(d) The Food and Agriculture Organization

5. Consider the following statements: (2025)

Statement-I: Of the two major ethanol producers in the world, i.e., Brazil and the United States of America, the former produces more ethanol than the latter.

Statement-II: Unlike in the United States of America, where corn is the principal feedstock, sugarcane is the principal feedstock for ethanol production in Brazil.

Which one of the following is correct in respect of the above statements?
(a) Both Statement-I and Statement-II are correct, and Statement-II explains Statements-I
(b) Both Statement-I and Statement-II are correct, but Statement-II does not explain Statement-I
(c) Statement-I is correct, but Statement-II is not correct
(d) Statement-I is not correct, but Statement-II is correct.

6. The World Bank warned that India could become one of the first places where wet-bulb temperatures routinely exceed 35°C. Which of the following statements best reflects(s) the implication of the above-said report? (2025)
(i) Peninsular India will most likely suffer from flooding, tropical cyclones and droughts.
(ii) The survival of animals, including humans, will be affected as shedding of their body heat through perspiration becomes difficult.

Select the correct answer using the code given below.
(a) (i) only (b) (ii) only
(c) Both (i) and (ii) (d) Neither (i) nor (ii)

7. Consider the following statements: (2024)

Statement-I: The European Parliament approved The Net-Zero Industry Act recently.

Statement-II: The European Union intends to achieve carbon neutrality by 2040 and therefore aims to develop all of its own clean technology by that time.

Which one of the following is correct in respect of the above statements?
(a) Both Statement-I and Statement-II are correct and Statement-II explains Statement-I
(b) Both Statement-I and Statement-II are correct, but Statement-II does not explain Statement-I
(c) Statement-I is correct, but Statement-II is incorrect
(d) Statement-I is incorrect, but Statement-II is correct

8. Consider the following materials: (2024)
(i) Agricultural residues
(ii) Corn grain
(iii) Wastewater treatment sludge
(iv) Wood mill waste

Which of the above can be used as feedstock for producing Sustainable Aviation Fuel?
(a) (i) and (ii) only (b) (iii) and (iv) only
(c) (i), (ii), (iii) and (iv) (d) (i), (iii) and (iv) only

Answers: 1. (c) 2. (a) 3. (a) 4. (a) 5. (d) 6. (c) 7. (c) 8. (c)

Explanation

1. (c): *Statement-I* is correct. *Statement-II* is incorrect (the COP28 Declaration on Climate and Health is a non-binding, voluntary political declaration that aims to galvanise support for action on climate change and health). *Statement-III* is correct (at COP28, India chose not to sign the "Declaration on Climate and Health"). This decision is primarily due to concerns about the practicality of reducing greenhouse gas emissions from cooling in the country's healthcare infrastructure (a point within the declaration).

2. (a): Statement-I is correct (Article 6 of the Agreement deals with the Nationally Determined Contributions). Statement-II is correct (Article 6 of the Agreement sets out the principles for carbon markets). Statement-III is correct (Article 6 of the Agreement facilitates both market-based and non-market-based international cooperation for countries to achieve their climate targets). Statements-II and III explain Statement-I.

3. (a): A circular economy aims to minimise waste (thus, Statement-III is correct) and reduce the need for new resources/inputs/raw materials (thus, Statement-II is correct) through the reuse and recycling of existing materials; this way, it reduces the emissions of greenhouse gases (thus, Statement-I is correct).

4. (a): The NRL is an environmental regulation enacted by the European Union (EU) which aims to halt and reverse the degradation of ecosystems across the EU, addressing both climate change and biodiversity loss.

5. (d): The USA is the largest producer of ethanol in the world (around 50 per cent of the global production, which it procures primarily from corn, while Brazil procures it from sugarcane (thus, *Statement-I* is incorrect while *Statement-II* is correct).

6. (c): Both of the statements are correct (such a warning came for India from the World Bank in 2022). The wet-bulb temperature is a measure that combines dry air temperature and humidity to indicate the lowest temperature to which air can be cooled by the evaporation of water. It is actually a measure of heat-stress conditions on humans. When the wet-bulb temperature reaches 35°C, it becomes extremely dangerous for humans and animals because sweat can no longer evaporate to cool the body.

7. (c): The concerned Act was passed by the European Union in April 2024 (thus, Statement-I is correct) but it aims to achieve carbon neutrality by 2025, not 2024 (thus, Statement-II is incorrect).

8. (c): All of the alternatives given in the question are used to produce sustainable aviation fuel. Since this involves an organic process, it is a 'sustainable' way of fuel production.

SAMPLE OBJECTIVE QUESTIONS

1. Consider the following statements related to the COP 28:
   (i) A global adaptation fund with fixed budget line was agreed by the parties.
   (ii) Parties agreed to phase out fossil fuels by 2050 with clear target of reduction.
   (iii) Countries agreed to not set up coal-fired power plants after 2030.

   How many of the above statements are correct?
   (a) Only one (b) Only two
   (c) All three (d) None of these

2. Consider the following statements related to India's forest during the decade of 2010-20:
   (i) Tree cover increased despite developmental works.
   (ii) Uttar Pradesh topped in littoral and swamp forests.
   (iii) Dense forest area decreased by about 20 per cent.

   How many of the above statements are correct?
   (a) Only one (b) Only two
   (c) All three (d) None of these

3. Consider the following statements related to Government's waste management and pollution control initiatives of recent times:
   (i) India's plastic use is around two-third of the global average.
   (ii) India's ban on single-use plastic is in line with the 2022 UN resolution on it.

(iii) E-waste recycling targets are linked to their annual sales.

How many of the above statements are correct?

(a) Only one **(b)** Only two
(c) All three **(d)** None of these

4. Consider the following statements related to the Paris Climate Agreement:

(i) It encourages countries to voluntarily try decoupling economy from greenhouse gas emission.
(ii) India has achieved the emission target 11 years ahead of the timeline of 2030.
(iii) Non-fossil fuel sources accounted for 40 per cent of India's installed electric capacity by 2023.

How many of the above statements are correct?

(a) Only one **(b)** Only two
(c) All three **(d)** None of these

5. Consider the following related to the sustainable development goals of the UNO:

(i) They were proposed at Rio+20.
(ii) The period to achieve these goals has been extended by five years at the COP 28 in 2023.
(iii) Enhancing global peace and building strong institutions are among its goals.

How many of the above statements are correct?

(a) Only one **(b)** Only two
(c) All three **(d)** None of these

6. Consider the following related to the Paris Climate Agreement:

(i) India submitted its first update on achievements on the front of her determined contributions (DCs) in 2023.
(ii) National Solar Mission of India has been globally appreciated.
(iii) Life for Environment (LiFE) was an Indian initiative agreed at COP 26 in Glasgow.

How many of the above statements are correct?

(a) Only one **(b)** Only two
(c) All three **(d)** None of these

7. Consider the following related to the Coalition for Disaster Resilient Infrastructure:

(i) It is an initiative by India in the direction of climate action.
(ii) Multilateral banks and private sector organisations are also its partners.
(iii) It was launched on the sidelines of the UN Secretary General's Climate Action Summit in 2019.

How many of the above statements are correct?

(a) Only one **(b)** Only two
(c) All three **(d)** None of these

8. Consider the following related to India's action against climate change, the PAT (Perform, Achieve and Trade):

(i) It is part of one of the missions of India's action plan on climate change.
(ii) This aims at reduction in energy consumption.
(iii) This is a scheme operating under enhanced energy efficiency (EEE).

How many of the above statements are correct?

(a) Only one **(b)** Only two
(c) All three **(d)** None of these

9. Consider the following related to the Green Climate Fund (GCF):

(i) It funds only the developing countries.
(ii) Cutting and reducing emissions of green house gases is one of its goals.
(iii) It aims to provide equal amounts funding to countries for mitigation and adaptation.
(iv) It gets its fund as grants, loans, equity, and guarantee from both public and private sources.

How many of the above statements are correct?

(a) Only one **(b)** Only two
(c) Only three **(d)** All four

10. Consider the following related to the UN sustainable development goals (SDGs):

(i) The United Nations High-Level Political Forum (HLPF) is the highest level international forum for review and follow-up of the SDGs.
(ii) The HLPF operates under the UNESCO (United Nations Economic and Social Council).

(iii) SDG India Index has been developed by the NITI Aayog with the active support of the HLPF.

How many of the above statements are correct?

(a) Only one **(b)** Only two

(c) All three **(d)** None of these

Answers: 1. (d) 2. (b) 3. (b) 4. (c) 5. (b) 6. (b) 7. (c) 8. (c) 9. (d) 10. (b)

SAMPLE SUBJECTIVE QUESTIONS

1. 'India has played a leading role in global action against climate change.' Examine.
2. 'Adaptation cannot be separated from mitigation in case of climate change and it needs an effective global framework.' Analyse in reference to the recently concluded COP 29.
3. Environmental and climate related issues are the major reasons due to which India needs to evolve a new budgetary responsibility framework.' Examine.
4. Briefly discuss about the recent efforts made by the Government in the direction of waste management in the country.
5. What is circular economy? Give your suggestions for its early adoption.

SAMPLE MODEL ANSWER

1. 'Decarbonisation is an engineering, financial and institutional task which involves unavoidable trade-offs.' Considering the statement briefly underline India's policy stand towards climate action.

Ans. Decarbonisation at scale is an engineering, financial, and institutional task, which involves unavoidable trade-offs–was first discovered by the advanced economies (Es). But this experience has not diminished the urgency of climate action; rather, it clarifies the conditions under which it can be sustained. For India, the lesson is to articulate a climate action pathway that protects growth, builds resilience, and preserves strategic flexibility.

India has grown sustainably, with per capita carbon emissions (2.9 tonnes) considerably lower than the global average (6.7 tonnes) in 2024, as per the Economic Survey 2025-26. India's climate action strategy has developed around the following ***three main pillars***:

1. *Adaptation* is at the forefront given the country's significant vulnerability to physical impacts of climate change (such as the loss of life and property, health concerns due to intensification of extreme weather events, concerns of water and food security, and slow-onset events like rising sea level, amongst others, as per the UNFCCC, 2023). India aims to realise this aim through public investments initiated by the central government, strategic planning at the state level, and community-driven programmes.

2. *Mitigation* action is being undertaken by phasing in renewables, improving energy efficiency and diversifying energy sources to green hydrogen and nuclear power. The approach is to prioritise energy security, affordability, and industrial competitiveness. However, this faces various challenges, such as limited access to advanced technologies, vulnerabilities in supply chains for critical minerals essential for clean energy, and constrained availability of reliable and affordable financial capital.
3. *Domestic resources* are playing the predominant role in climate action (as international climate finance and regulation both have become binding constraints). While global capital is abundant, it does not flow at scale to developing countries due to structural features of the international financial system and risk perceptions, resulting in a high cost of capital.

In recent years, India has made significant progress in enhancing its financial ecosystem through regulatory reforms–by introducing innovative instruments for sustainable finance such as thematic bonds (green, blue, yellow, transition, social, and sustainability) to support climate action. Environmental regulation is also transitioning from procedural, command and control approaches towards risk-based, technology-enabled, and outcome-oriented governance. There is a growing need to reform multilateral development finance, credit ratings, and the use of risk-sharing instruments, as per the *Economic Survey 2025-26*.

CHAPTER 21

Human Development in India

> The basic purpose of development is to enlarge people's choices. In principle, these choices can be infinite and can change over time. People often value achievements that do not show up at all, or not immediately, in income or growth figures - greater access to knowledge, better nutrition and health services, more secure livelihoods, security against crime and physical violence, satisfying leisure hours, political and cultural freedoms and sense of participation in community activities. The objective of development is to create an enabling environment for people to enjoy long, healthy and creative lives.*
>
> *Mahbub ul Haq (1934–98), *Founding Editor of the Human Development Report*, UNDP, 1990.

To watch the Author's videos on the significance of the Chapter, scan the QR Code given here

Exam Essentials...

- Household Consumption Expenditure Survey
- GIG Employment

Note to the Reader...

This chapter deals with the official area called the 'social sector', ultimately leading to the cause of human development in the country. This includes sub-sectors such as health (food and nutrition, water and sanitation, etc.), education (primary, secondary, and higher), social security/protection (livelihood, old age support, insurance, etc.)–all leading to the creation of 'human capital' in the country. The achievement in these sectors is today considered as the very core of development in a country across the world. Civil services aspirants should note that several questions are asked on these areas in the general studies (GS) of the preliminary exam (i.e., PT) besides in GS mains papers I, II and III (on a few occasions in GS Paper IV too).

In This Chapter...

INTRODUCTION

Economic growth remains the immediate focus of the world economies. But income enhancement can only bring the desired development in the country once it is supported by a conscious public policy aimed at it. Again, the presence of 'good governance' in the policy framework can hardly be missed. After the increased acceptance of welfare economics, the standard of life of the masses has emerged as the most popular tool to measure developmental achievements of the economies - the idea is much similar to the concept[1] of 'human development' articulated by the United Nations Development Programme (UNDP). In recent times, the world has started accepting the role of people's *attitudinal* and *behavioural* dimensions, too, in the gamut of development promotion.[2] Further, we see an increased and consensual acceptance among the nations on the issue of delivering 'happiness' and 'life satisfaction' to the citizens.[3] It means, over the last few decades the whole idea about the 'ultimate' aim of the economies has gone through a kind of metamorphosis. Making growth and development percolate to the *marginalised and disadvantaged sections* of society (i.e., the SCs, STs, OBCs, minorities and women) remains the official policy of 'inclusive growth' for India.[4]

The Government of India (GoI) has been conscious about the development of the social sector which includes areas such as health, education, shelter, social welfare and social security. Once the economy commenced the process of economic reforms, we see an increased attention to the strengthening of the social sector, enhancing the social infrastructure and situation.[5] But India is faced with a variety of interconnected and interdependent issues and challenges in areas such as inclusion, expansion, implementation, accountability, governance and decentralisation.[6]

Today, India is the youngest nation in the world in terms of size - while this 'youth bulge' provides India great opportunities, it also 'poses challenges'. These young people need to be healthy, suitably educated and appropriately skilled to contribute optimally to the economy.[7] The proportion of economically active population (15-59 years) in India increased from 57.7 per cent to 63.3 per cent during 1991-2024. If India has to reap the benefits of this *demographic dividend* in the years ahead, it is imperative that investments in social infrastructure are made in appropriate measure to achieve the desired educational and health outcomes.

India has to evolve a multi-pronged strategy with focus on bridging the gaps in access to social infrastructure through appropriate use of innovative technologies for enhancement of human potential for productive employment in various sectors and for improving the quality of life. Mobilising the civil society, media and other stakeholders of society in this regard will play a huge supportive role.

HUMAN DEVELOPMENT IN INDIA

For upward social mobility, human development is the key enabler. The disruptions caused by the COVID-19 pandemic (in 2020 and 2021) and Russia-Ukraine conflict (in 2022) have impacted the development trajectory of India and the world in a big way. These events took a heavy toll on the global human development, which declined for the *first time* in 32 years–over 90 per cent of the countries registered a reduction in their human development index (HDI). As per the latest *Human Development Report 2025* (titled *A Matter of Choice: People and Possibilities in the Age of AI*), the state of human development in India[8] has been as given below:

- India's rank has improved to 130th (from 134th in 2024) out of 193 countries.

[1] A. Sen, *Development as Freedom* (New Delhi: Oxford University Press, 2000), pp. 3-11.

[2] *World Development Report 2015: Mind, Society, and Behaviour* (Washington, DC: World Bank, 2015).

[3] *World Happiness Report-2012 and 2013*, sponsored by the UNO, New York, NY, 2013 and 2014.

[4] *Eleventh five-year plan (2007-12)* (New Delhi: Planning Commission, GoI).

[5] Increased allocations of fund as well as enhanced performance is reported by the *Economic Surveys of 1991-92 to 2014-15* (New Delhi: Ministry of Finance, GoI).

[6] A. Sen and J. Dreze, *An uncertain glory: India and its contradictions*, ed. A. Lane (London: Penguin Books, 2013), pp. vii-xiii.

[7] *Economic Survey 2014-15* (New Delhi: Ministry of Finance, GoI), pp. 131-46.

[8] *Human Development Report 2025* (New York: United Nations Development Programme, USA, 2025).

- The value of HDI increased to 0.685 (from 0.676 in 2023), keeping India in the Medium Human Development category but nearing the high threshold (equal to or higher than 0.700).
- Life expectancy reached a record high of **72 years** (from 67.7 years in 2024).
- Expected years of schooling rose to **13 years**, while mean years of schooling increased to **6.88 years**.
- Gross National Income (GNI) per capita jumped significantly to **$9,047 (PPP)**.
- *Comparison with Neighbours* (with their ranks given in brackets): China (75th), Sri Lanka (78th), and Bhutan (127th) rank higher than India, while Bangladesh (130th) is on par. Nepal (145th) and Pakistan (168th) rank lower.
- *Global Leaders:* Iceland ranked 1st globally, followed by Norway and Switzerland.
- *AI Leadership:* The report identifies India as a rising AI powerhouse, noting that 20 per cent of Indian AI researchers now remain in the country, up from nearly zero in 2019.

The report has outlined the following ***persistent challenges*** in the case of India:

Inequality: Deep-rooted income and gender disparities reduce India's overall HDI by **30.7** per cent, one of the highest such losses in the region.

Gender Gap: Female labour force participation remains a concern at **41.7** per cent , although recent measures like the 106th Constitutional Amendment (women's reservation in legislatures) are seen as positive steps.

Public Spending: Low public investment in health (3.8 per cent of the GDP) and education remains a hurdle to reaching 'High Human Development' status.

As per the UNDP, the Human Development Report 2026 will focus on the intersection of human development and planetary systems, introducing the *Nature Relationship Index (NRI)* to measure the people-nature connections with the aim to balance crisis narratives with transformational possibilities for environmental change.[9]

POVERTY ESTIMATES

Since India commenced the process of economic reforms, a major shift has taken place in the country's policy orientation towards poverty alleviation and employment generation - in place of *wage employment*, the focus has shifted to *self-employment* - so that 'gainful employment' could be created and poverty could be alleviated permanently.

The Planning Commission used to estimate poverty using data from the large sample surveys on household consumer expenditure carried out by the National Sample Survey Office (NSSO) *every five years*. It ***defines*** poverty line on the basis of monthly per capita consumption expenditure (MPCE). The methodology for estimation of poverty followed by the Planning Commission has been based on the recommendations made by experts in the field from time to time - the present estimates are based on the recommendations of the Expert Group headed by *Prof. Suresh D. Tendulkar* which submitted its report in December 2009.

As per this methodology, poverty estimates (NSSO, 68th Round, 2011-12) for the period 2004-05 to 2011-12 are as given below:

1. Total poverty declined from 37.2 to 21.9 per cent.
2. Rural poverty declined from 41.8 to 25.7 per cent.
3. Urban poverty declined from 25.7 to 13.7 per cent

Looking at the controversy and outrage on estimation of poverty (on the Rangarajan Committee of 2012 which submitted its report in 2014), the Government did set up a task force under Arvind Panagariya (the then Vice Chairman of NITI Aayog) in 2015 to develop a working definition of poverty. This task force concluded that the 'matter be considered in greater depth by the country's top experts on poverty before a final decision is made' and failed to reach a consensus on poverty line. It was in *February 2021* that the Government announced to set up a new expert committee to set a poverty line (planning minister said in response to a question in Rajya Sabha).

[9] The index measures inequality in achievement between women and men in *three* dimensions (i.e., reproductive health, empowerment, and the labour market). It shows the loss in potential human development due to inequality between female and male achievements in these dimensions. The value of GII ranges from 0, where women and men fare equally, to 1, where one gender fares as poorly as possible in all measured dimensions.

MULTIDIMENSIONAL POVERTY

Poverty is often defined by 'one-dimensional' measures - usually based on income, but no single indicator can capture the multiple dimensions of poverty. In place, the idea of multidimensional poverty encompasses the various deprivations experienced by poor people in their daily lives - such as poor health, lack of education, inadequate living standards, disempowerment, poor quality of work, the threat of violence and living in areas that are environmentally hazardous, among others. This measure of poverty can incorporate a range of indicators that capture the complexity of this phenomena in order to inform policies aimed at reducing poverty and deprivation in a country. Depending on the context of a country and the purpose of the measure, *different indicators can be chosen* to reflect the needs and priorities of a nation, as well as its constituent regions, districts, provinces, and so on.

It was in 2010 for the *first time* that such a measure, called the global multidimensional poverty index (GMPI,) was developed by the Oxford Poverty and Human Development Initiative (OPHI) and UNDP. The index is used by the UNDP it its Human Development Report too. The GMPI is computed by scoring each surveyed[10] household on *10 indicators/parameters* based on nutrition, child mortality, years of schooling, school attendance, cooking fuel, sanitation, drinking water, electricity, housing and household assets.

GMPI 2025 The latest GMPI 2025 (titled *Overlapping Hardships: Poverty and Climate Hazards*) was released in October 2025. Its key highlights are as given below:

Global Poverty: Out of 6.3 billion people across 109 countries, about 1.1 billion (18.3 per cent) live in acute multidimensional poverty.

Climate Nexus: For the ***first time***, the report maps climate hazards against poverty. Nearly 4 in 5 poor people live in regions exposed to at least one climate hazard, such as high heat, flood, or drought.

India's Progress: India's MPI value is recorded at 0.069, with the headcount ratio falling significantly to 16.4 per cent (based on 2019-2021 data) compared to 55.1 per cent in 2005-06.

[10] *NITI Aayog*, Press Note on Global Multidimensional Poverty Index and India, PIB, 7 September 2020.

Vulnerable Groups: Over half of those living in multidimensional poverty (approx. 584 million) are children.

India's NMPI In 2021, a National Multidimensional Poverty Index (NMPI) was introduced by the NITI Aayog – adding 2 new indicators (*maternal health* and *bank account*) to the original idea of the MPI evolved by the OPHI and UNDP which uses 10 indicators. The index is based on the national family health survey (NFHS) conducted under the aegis of the Ministry of Health and Family Welfare and International Institute for Population Science (IIPS).

NMPI 2023 The latest (titled *National Multidimensional Poverty: A Progress Review 2023*) was released by the NITI Aayog in January 2024. It captures the changes in multidimensional poverty in the country between the survey periods of NFHS-4 (2015-16) and NFHS-5 (2019-21) in the following ways:

- India has registered a significant decline in multidimensional poverty in India from **29.17** per cent in 2013-14 to **11.28** per cent in 2022-23 (i.e., a reduction of 17.89 percentage points)–a total of **24.82** crore individuals escaped multidimensional poverty.
- Uttar Pradesh registered the largest decline in the number of poor with 5.94 crore people escaping multidimensional poverty during the last nine years, followed by Bihar at 3.77 crore, Madhya Pradesh at 2.30 crore and Rajasthan at 1.87 crore.
- The pace of decline in poverty headcount ratio using exponential method was much faster between 2015-16 and 2019-21 (10.66 per cent annual rate of decline) compared to the period between 2005-06 and 2015-16 (7.69 per cent annual rate of decline).
- All 12 indicators of MPI have recorded significant improvement during the entire study period.

DEMOGRAPHICS

The population of India has gone through some major changes in the recent decades. These changes have not only restructured the contours of Indian demographics but have also brought new openings and challenges regarding it.

1. As per provisional results of *Census 2011*, the following facts regarding the Indian population

Household Consumption Expenditure Survey

A Household Consumption Expenditure Survey (HCES) of the National Statistics Office (NSO) is a statistical survey that collects data on the spending patterns of households by recording the goods and services they consume, providing insights into their standard of living and consumption patterns, and is often used to calculate economic indicators like Consumer Price Indices (CPI) and Gross Domestic Product (GDP). The highlights of the latest HCES 2023–24 have been summarised below:

- It has highlighted the 'narrowing urban-rural gap' in consumption expenditure with the average monthly per capita expenditure (MPCE) in rural and urban India in 2023–24 estimated at ₹4,122 and ₹6,996, respectively. Considering the imputed values of items received free of cost through various social welfare programmes, these estimates rise to ₹4,247 and ₹7,078, respectively, for rural and urban areas.
- The urban-rural gap in MPCE has declined to 71 per cent in 2022–23 from 84 per cent in 2011–12. It has further come down to 70 per cent in 2023–24, which confirms the sustained momentum of consumption growth in rural areas.
- Social sector initiatives have reduced inequality and increased consumption spending, as reflected in the survey.
- The ***Gini coefficient*** improved:
  - **(i)** for rural areas (declined to 0.237 in 2023–24 from 0.266 in 2022–23) and urban areas (declined to 0.284 in 2023–24 from 0.314 in 2022–23).
  - **(ii)** The bottom 5 per cent of the rural population, ranked by MPCE, has an average MPCE of ₹1,677, compared to ₹2,376 in urban areas.
  - **(iii)** The top 5 per cent have an average MPCEs of ₹10,137 in rural and ₹20,310 in urban areas.
  - **(iv)** The largest growth in average MPCE between 2022–23 and 2023–24 occurred among the bottom 5–10 per cent of the population in both rural and urban areas.
  - **(v)** The bottom 5 per cent of the rural population saw a 22 per cent increase, while the corresponding urban segment experienced 19 per cent growth in the MPCE.

dynamics are of high importance. The 2001-11 is the *first* decade in independent India wherein the population momentum, coupled with declining fertility, has dampened the pace of net additions to population. Thus, the net addition in this decade is less than that of the previous decade by 0.86 million. At present, a little more than *one out of every six* persons in the world is an Indian.

2. As per *Sample Registration System-2013* (SRS) data:

   (i) There has been a gradual decline in the share of population in the age group 0-14 from 41.2 to 38.1 per cent during 1971-81 and from 36.3 to 28.4 per cent during 1991 to 2013.

   (ii) On the other hand, the proportion of economically active population (15-59 years), or India's 'demographic dividend', has increased from 53.4 to 56.3 per cent during 1971-81 and from 57.7 to 63.3 per cent during 1991 to 2013.

   (iii) On account of better education, health facilities and increase in life expectancy, the percentage of *elderly* (60+) has gone up from 5.3 to 5.7 per cent and 6.0 to 8.3 per cent, respectively, in the same two periods.

   (iv) The growth rate of the *labour force* will continue to be higher than that of the population until 2021.

3. According to an *Indian Labour Report* (Time Lease, 2007):

   (i) 300 million youth will enter the labour force by 2025, and 25 per cent of the world's workers in the next three years will be Indians.

(ii) Population projections indicate that in 2020 the average age of India's population will be the lowest in the world - around 29 years compared to 37 years in China and the United States, 45 years in West Europe and 48 years in Japan.

(iii) Consequently, while the global economy is expected to witness a shortage of young population of around 56 million by 2020, India will be the only country with a youth surplus of 47 million *(Report on Education, Skill Development and Labour Force (2013-14) Volume III, Labour Bureau, 2014).*

As per the *Economic Survey 2014-15,* the main issue to address, then, is not just providing employment but increasing the employability of the labour force in India. To garner the 'demographic dividend', the Survey suggested the following ***policy initiatives*** in this regard:

1. A declining 0-14 population will impact both elementary (5-14 age group) and higher education (15-29 age group). Elementary education can be further subdivided into primary (5-9 age group) and middle/upper primary (10-14 age group). The focus should be on:
   - **(i)** Improving access to education considering the high dropout rates among senior students
   - **(ii)** Removing gender disparity especially in the higher age group and in rural areas
   - **(iii)** Improving quality of education, including pupil-teacher ratios and provision of amenities in schools, especially in view of the declining learning levels.
2. The *lag in demographic transition* between different states necessitate state-specific policies to optimally garner the benefits of the demographic dividend. Owing to substantial fertility decline in the south during the last two decades, the south is ahead in the demographic transition compared to the north, so the window is already wide open in the south compared to the north. India is better placed in this respect than most other countries. Thus, two sets of policy initiatives emerge for the states.
   - **(i)** The states which are already well into the demographic window should actively pursue policies for employment generation to the already bulging labour force.
   - **(ii)** The states just entering the window period have some time to plan and must pursue policies simultaneously in several areas such as education, health (including reproductive health), gender issues and employment generation from now on so that they can fully utilise the opportunity.

SOCIO-ECONOMIC AND CASTE CENSUS

The identification of the real beneficiaries is of paramount importance for the success of any targeted approach. In line with this approach, the *Dr. N. C. Saxena Committee* was constituted to advise on the 'methodology for a BPL census in rural areas'. Since June 2011, for the first time, a Socio-Economic and Caste Census (SECC) is being conducted through a comprehensive 'door-to-door' enumeration in both rural and urban India, and authentic information is being made available on the socio-economic condition and educational status of various castes and sections through the SECC.

The exercise was completed by *late 2016* and presently, the errors are in the process of rectification - the reason the report of the census has not been put in the public domain yet. Once the census is fully ready, its findings are expected to be used as guidelines in several areas such as identifying the level of poverty, target population for the disbursal of subsidies, selection for eligibility for educational scholarships, old age pension, reorienting the existing reservation policy, better implementation (by correct identification the beneficiaries) of the MGNREGA, National Food Security scheme and so on.

EDUCATION FOR ALL

To improve life quality and inclusiveness in general and to enjoy the benefits of the demographic dividend, quality education of all has been declared by the Government. Education and human capital development are among the foundational pillars of development and the *National Education Policy 2020* (NEP-2020) is built upon this principle.

Free and compulsory education starts in India at the age of 6 and ends at the age of 14 years under the ambit of the Right of Children to Free and Compulsory Education

(RTE) Act, 2009. The Act stipulates norms and standards for a recognised school imparting elementary education. The RTE norms provide for an all-weather building in elementary schools. The school building should, *inter alia,* consist of at least one classroom for every teacher and an office-cum-store-cum-Head teacher's room, barrier-free access, separate toilets for boys and girls, safe and adequate drinking water facility to all children and a playground. India's achievements in the direction, together with various policy actions of the Government, are summarised[11] below:

School Education in India has progressed with high pace and shows the following features today:

Schools & Teachers: India's school education system serves 24.8 crore students across 14.72 lakh schools with 98 lakh teachers. Government schools make up 69 per cent of the total, enrolling 50 per cent of students and employing 51 per cent of teachers, while private schools account for 22.5 per cent, enrolling 32.6 per cent of students and employing 38 per cent of teachers.

Enrolment: The NEP 2020 aims for a 100 per cent Gross Enrolment Ratio (GER) by 2030. The GER is near-universal at the primary (93 per cent) and the efforts are underway to bridge the gaps at the secondary (77.4 per cent) and higher secondary levels (56.2 per cent), driving the nation closer to its vision of 'inclusive and equitable education for all' (*Goal 4* of the SDGs).

School Dropout: School dropout rates have steadily declined in recent years, standing at 1.9 per cent for primary, 5.2 per cent for upper primary, and 14.1 per cent for secondary levels. However, challenges persist, with retention rates at 85.4 per cent for primary (class I to V), 78 per cent for elementary (classes I to VIII), 63.8 per cent for secondary (classes I to X), and 45.6 per cent for higher secondary (classes I to XII).

Programmes: The government has been striving to achieve the objectives of NEP 2020 through a range of programmes and schemes, including DIKSHA (Digital Infrastructure for Knowledge Sharing), STARS (Strengthening Teaching-Learning and Results for States), PARAKH (Performance Assessment, Review, and Analysis of Knowledge for Holistic Development), PM SHRI (Prime Minister's Schools for Rising India), ULLAS (Understanding of Lifelong Learning for All in Society), and PM POSHAN (Pradhan Mantri Poshan Shakti Nirman).

The pivotal role of early years in development is well-recognised by the Indian education system, as 85 per cent of brain development occurs before the age of six years. To strengthen the Early Childhood Care and Education (ECCE) landscape, the government launched the National Curriculum for ECCE, *Aadharshila,* and the National Framework for Early Childhood Stimulation, *Navchetana,* in April 2024:

(i) *Navchetana* focuses on the holistic development of children from birth to three years, offering 140 age-specific activities through a 36-month stimulation calendar. It emphasises the inclusion of differently-abled children, maternal mental health, and "*Garbh Sanskar*" (practices during pregnancy).

(ii) *Aadharshila,* blending Indian and international research, promotes play-based learning with over 130 activities for children aged three to six years that support child-led and educator-led learning. It aims to lay a strong foundation for lifelong learning, aligning with the National Curriculum Framework for Foundational Stage 2022 (NCF-FS) and improving the quality of ECCE through competency-based, user-friendly lesson plans. The *objective* is to improve the quality of ECCE delivered at the *Anganwadi* centre by prioritising competency-based lesson plans and activities presented in a simple and user-friendly manner.

Literacy & Numeracy: School education lays the foundation of a country's education system. The NEP 2020 stipulates that foundational literacy and numeracy (FLN) is critical for education and lifelong learning success. Towards this end, the Department of School Education and Literacy launched the National Mission, "National Initiative for Proficiency in Reading with Understanding and Numeracy (NIPUN Bharat)," in July 2021 to ensure that every child in the country necessarily attains FLN by the end of Grade 3, by 2026-27. It covers three years of FLN in preschool and Grades 1, 2 and 3. Towards this, the education system is deploying innovative pedagogies and teaching methods to ensure that every child achieves FLN.

[11] *Economic Survey 2024-25* (New Delhi: Ministry of Finance, GoI, January 2025), pp. 308-327.

Digital Divide: Digital literacy ensures that students remain competitive by mastering skills like analysing, synthesising, and communicating digital information. The *World Economic Forum (WEF)* identifies ICT skills as foundational for the 21st century. *UNESCO* defines digital literacy as- 'Includes competencies that are variously referred to as computer literacy, ICT literacy, information literacy and media literacy'. Digital literacy ranges from basic hardware and software use to advanced programming and network management.

Data from the 'Comprehensive Annual Modular Survey 2022-23' reveals a **rural-urban digital divide** in India with lower internet-searching capabilities in rural areas, especially among females. Sixty-three per cent of males and 55 per cent of females in rural areas can search the internet for information compared to 74 per cent males and 69 per cent of females in urban areas. The results highlight the need for focused efforts to close the digital gap.

The **NEP 2020** emphasises technology's role in improving education, removing barriers, and ensuring inclusivity for *Divyang* students. Schemes like DIKSHA, Study Webs of Active Learning for Young Aspiring Minds (SWAYAM), e-VIDYA, Pradhan Mantri Gramin Digital Saksharta Abhiyan (PMGDISHA) and e-content for *Divyang* are in place to achieve the objective of inclusive digital education. The government launched PM e-Vidya DTH Channel for Indian Sign Language, a significant step towards an 'inclusive and accessible' education system for hearing-impaired students in India. The ICT and Digital Initiatives component of *Samagra Shiksha* provides financial assistance to establish ICT labs and smart classrooms and covers government and aided schools having classes VI to XII across the country.

CwSN: Efforts have been made to boost Children with Special Needs (CwSN) enrolment at all levels, with notable increases observed in secondary and higher secondary enrolments. Although the COVID-19 pandemic caused a temporary decline, recovery efforts are ongoing to reintegrate out-of-school CwSN into formal education. According to the latest available data, 16.8 lakh CwSN are enrolled at the elementary level, 2.87 lakh at the secondary level, and 1.18 lakh are enrolled at the higher secondary level.

Social & Emotional Learning: The success of school education hinges not just on the student's academic achievements but also on enhancing their social and emotional learning (SEL). A good education enhances a child's mental and physical health, academic performance, and life skills.

In this context, ECCE (Early Childhood Care and Education) under NEP 2020 aims to achieve foundational literacy and socio-emotional development. The NEP 2020 states that 'The overall aim of ECCE will be to attain optimal outcomes in the domains of physical and motor development, cognitive development, socio-emotional-ethical development, cultural/artistic development, and the development of communication and early language, literacy, and numeracy.'

Higher Education

Indian higher education system is the laboratory of change for one of the largest young populations in the world, with more than 27 per cent of India's population in 15-29 years age bracket. The state of higher education has improved overtime, strengthened by development in infrastructure. Over the years, there has been a significant transformation in higher education ecosystem with the following features, as per the latest available official information:

- The number of Indian Institutes of Technology (IIT) increased from 16 in 2014 to 23 in 2023, Indian Institutes of Management (IIM) grew from 13 in 2014 to 20 in 2023, and medical colleges experienced remarkable growth, increasing from 387 in 2013-14 to 780 in 2024-25.
- Universities have also seen substantial expansion, rising from 723 in 2014 to 1,213 in 2024 (registering a growth of 59.6 per cent).
- Total Higher Education Institutions (HEIs) increased by 13.8 per cent from 51,534 in 2014-15 to 58,643 in 2022-23.

India's higher education system ranks *among the largest globally*, with 4.33 crore students enrolled in 2021-22, a 26.5 per cent increase from 3.42 crore in 2014-15. The Gross Enrolment Ratio (GER) for the 18-23 age group also increased from 23.7 per cent to 28.4 per cent during this same period (2014-15 to 2021-22). To achieve the government's goal of increasing GER to **50** per cent by 2035 in higher education, there is a need to double the educational network and infrastructure.

By **2040**, all higher education institutions (HEIs) are to become multidisciplinary institutions, as per the

New Education Policy 2020 which calls for making 'India a global knowledge superpower'. As per the *Economic Survey 2024-25*, the measures to achieve this aim include:

(i) greater opportunities for outstanding public education;
(ii) scholarships by private/philanthropic universities for disadvantaged and underprivileged students;
(iii) online education and Open Distance Learning (ODL); and
(iv) all infrastructure and learning materials accessible and available to learners with disabilities.

Recent Initiatives The major recent initiatives undertaken by the Government to improve the quality of learning and teaching in higher education, as per *Economic Survey 2022-23*, have been as given below:

- *'Pandit Madan Mohan Malaviya National Mission on Teachers and Teaching (PMMMNMTT)'* was launched which aims at building a strong professional cadre of teachers by setting performance standards and creating top-class institutional facilities for innovative teaching and professional development of teachers in higher education. It provides capacity building to all existing teachers (central, state and private teachers can take part in it as well as in induction training).
- *Higher Education Financing Agency (HEFA)* was established to provide sustainable financial model for higher education institutions, *Kendriya Vidyalayas, Navodaya Vidyalayas,* AIIMS and other educational institutions.
- *National Educational Alliance for Technology (NEAT)* was announced on *PPP mode* for using technology for better learning outcomes in higher education. The objective is to use 'artificial intelligence' to make learning more personalised and customised as per the requirements of the learner.
- *Education Quality Upgradation and Inclusion Programme (EQUIP)*, a 5-year vision plan (2019-24) put in place, *aimed* at ushering 'transformation' in India's higher education system by implementing strategic interventions.
- Some other schemes launched in 2019-20 were *SWAYAM 2.0* to offer 'online degree programmes' with enhanced features and facilities by top-ranking universities; *DEEKSHARAMBH,* a guide to student induction programme and *PARAMARSH* to mentor institutions seeking NAAC (National Assessment and Accreditation Council) accreditation. Under it, the *e-PGPathshala* has been offered as an Online Gateway of Post Graduate Courses.
- *Unnat Bharat Abhiyan (UBA)* has been launched to cater the rural local needs by leveraging higher education. The objective of the scheme is to engage reputed higher educational institutions (central and state, public and private) to understand and work in rural areas.
- *Scholarships* for weaker sections to access higher education has been launched such as Central Sector Scheme for College and University students and Special Scholarship Scheme for J&K.
- *Research & Development Cell (RDC),* to be established by the UGC in Higher Education Institutions (HEI), was launched in March 2022 with the mandate for promoting quality research that contributes meaningfully towards the goal of a *self-reliant* India, aligned with the provisions of NEP 2020. The RDC will aim at the creation of a conducive environment for enhanced research productivity; encouraging collaboration across industry, Government, community-based organisations, and agencies at the local, national, and international levels.
- *Guidelines for Pursuing Two Academic Programmes* simultaneously were issued by the UGC (April 2022), which allow the students keeping in view the objectives envisaged in NEP 2020. It provides for flexible curricular structures to enable creative combinations of disciplines for study, that would offer multiple entry and exit points, thus removing currently prevalent rigid boundaries, and create new possibilities for life-long learning through critical and interdisciplinary thinking. The Guidelines provide students to pursue two full-time academic programmes in physical mode or pursue two academic programmes, one in full-time physical mode and another in Open and Distance Learning (ODL)/Online mode; or up to two ODL/Online programmes simultaneously.
- *Central Scheme on Interest Subsidy (CSIS),* launched in 2009, provides full interest subsidy on education loan taken by students from economically weaker sections (EWS) having parental income less than ₹4.5 lakh per annum for professional study in India. The scheme provides Education loans without any collateral or third-party guarantee.

COVID-19 AND SCHOOLING

As schools are closed since March 2020 due to COVID-19, school education has been badly hampered in the country as per the ASER (Annual Status of Education Report, October 2021). The percentage of enrolled children from Government and private schools owning a smartphone increased enormously from 36.5 per cent in 2018 to 61.8 per cent in 2021 in rural India. If utilised well, the resultant reduction in the *digital divide* between rural and urban, gender, age and income groups is likely to reduce inequalities in educational outcomes. To enable this process, the Government has launched the following initiatives to make education accessible to children during this pandemic (as per the *Economic Survey 2021-22*):

PM eVIDYA Launched under the Atmanirbhar Bharat Abhiyan (May 2020), this initiative for school and higher education tried to unify all efforts related to digital/online/on-air education to enable multi-mode and equitable access to education for students and teachers. It includes four components as given below:

1. **One nation, One Digital Education Infrastructure:** All States/UTs have free access to a single digital infrastructure, i.e., *DIKSHA* under it. This artificial intelligence- based and highly scalable system can be accessed through a web portal and mobile application. Since lockdown till December 2020, it received over 800 crore hits.

   In April 2020, the *Vidya Daan* portal was launched on Diksha as a national content contribution programme to seek and allow contribution/donation of e-learning resources for school education by educational bodies, private bodies and individual experts.
2. **One Class, One TV Channel through Swayam Prabha TV Channel:** *Swayam Prabha* DTH channel was launched in October 2020 to support and reach those who do not have access to the internet.
3. **Extensive Use of Radio, Community Radio and Podcasts:** 12 Gyan Vani FM radio stations, over 300 community radio stations, *iRadio* and *Jio Saavn* mobile apps, etc. have been launched under it.
4. **For the Differently-Abled:** One dedicated DTH channel is being operated specifically for hearing impaired students in sign language, and for visually and hearing-impaired students, study material has been developed in Digitally Accessible Information System (DAISY) and in sign language.

SWAYAM This portal provides dedicated services to students of grades 9 to 12 on it - 1.5 crore students got enrolled in over 92 courses on it.

NROER The National Repository of Open Educational Resources (NROER) is an open storehouse of e-content - nearly 17,500 pieces of e-content are available for various school subjects in all grades.

PRAGYAT These guidelines on digital education were developed with a focus on online/blended/ digital education for students who are presently at home due to the closure of schools.

MANODARPAN This is an initiative for psychosocial support launched under the Atmanirbhar Bharat Abhiyan to strengthen and empower the human capital in the education sector.

NDEAR (National Digital Education Architecture) Launched in July 2021, the NDEAR is to be set up within the context of a 'Digital-First Mindset' where the digital infrastructure will not only support teaching and learning but also educational planning, administrative activities of the Centre and the States Union Territories in an inter-operable system.

Vidyanjali Launched in September 2021, the Vidyanjali web portal is aimed at connecting the Government and the Government-aided schools through a community/volunteer management program, which enables the community/volunteers to interact and connect directly with schools of their choice to share their knowledge and skills as well as contribute in the form of assets/material/equipment.

NATIONAL EDUCATION POLICY-2020

The National Education Policy-2020 was announced by the Government in July 2020 which replaced the 34-year-old National Policy on Education (NPE), 1986. The **major highlights** of the policy[12] are summarised below:

[12] *Economic Survey 2020-21*, vol. 2 (New Delhi: Ministry of Finance, GoI), p. 333; *Ministry of Human Resource Development* (New Delhi: GoI, 20 July 2020).

- Universalisation of education from preschool to secondary level with 100 per cent Gross Enrolment Ratio (GER) in school education by 2030.
- To bring 'out of school' (2 crores) children back into the mainstream through universalisation of access and expanding the open schooling system.
- The current 10 + 2 system to be replaced by a new 5 + 3 + 3 + 4 curricular structure corresponding to ages 3-8, 8-11, 11-14, and 14-18 years, respectively.
- Class 10 and 12 board examinations to be made easier to test core competencies rather than memorised facts.
- School governance is set to change, with a new standard framework based on online self-declaration in the public domain for both public and private schools.
- Emphasis on foundational literacy and numeracy, and no rigid separation between academic streams, extracurricular, vocational streams in schools.
- Vocational Education to start from Class 6 with Internships.
- Teaching up to at least Grade 5 to be in mother tongue/regional language, wherever possible. No language will be imposed on any student.
- Assessment reforms with *360-degree Holistic Progress Card,* tracking students' progress for achieving learning outcomes.
- A new and comprehensive National Curriculum Framework for school education, Early Childhood Care and Education, Teacher Education and Adult Education.
- By 2030, the minimum degree qualification for teaching will be a 4-year integrated BEd degree.
- The *National Research Foundation* will be created as an apex body for fostering a strong research culture and building research capacity across higher education.
- A new body, the *Higher Education Commission of India* (HECI), will be set up as a single overarching umbrella body for entire higher education, excluding medical and legal education with four independent verticals:
  - National Higher Education Regulatory Council (NHERC) for regulation.
  - General Education Council (GEC) for standard setting.
  - Higher Education Grants Council (HEGC) for funding.
  - National Accreditation Council (NAC) for accreditation.

Public and private higher education institutions will be governed by the same set of norms for regulation, accreditation and academic standards.

The new education policy has arisen after an unprecedented process of consultations and deliberations, which aims to usher the country into a new regime of education and skill required for future - India has hopes from it.

SKILL DEVELOPMENT

As per the ILO (2021), the future labour market situation of young persons is highly influenced by their initial experiences, including how quickly and how well they are able to access the labour market, and the skills and competencies acquired through education and training. General education improves knowledge of the people while *skill training* enhances their employability and equip them to tackle the requirements of the labour market. The Government has been extending extra emphasis on skilling the labour force as the country faces a major skill gap (outlined in detail by the *Economic Survey 2016-17*). In order to address the incremental manpower requirement and to empower youth with adequate skills, the MSDE (Ministry of Skill Development and Entrepreneurship) was created in 2014 and *Skill India Mission* was launched in 2015. The *New Education Policy 2020* also gives special emphasis to vocational education and skill development - integrating vocational education with general education has been identified as the key reform in the education system.

Skill India Mission The Mission[13] focuses on *skilling, re-skilling,* and *up-skilling* through short-term and long-term training programmes. Under the Mission, the government (through more than 20 Central Ministries/Departments) is implementing various skill development schemes across the country, major ones being - *Deen Dayal Upadhyaya Grameen Kaushalya Yojna* (DDUGKY), Rural Self Employment Training Institutes (RSETI), Deen Dayal Antyodaya Yojana-National Urban Livelihood Mission (DAY-NULM), *Pradhan Mantri Kaushal Vikas Yojana* (PMKVY), *Jan Shikshan Sansthan* (JSS), National Apprenticeship Promotion Scheme (NAPS) and Craftsmen Training Scheme (CTS).

[13] *Economic Survey 2022-23* (New Delhi: Ministry of Finance, GoI, January 2023), pp. 184-185.

STATUS OF EMPLOYMENT

Generating sufficient number of wage- and self-employment has been one of the prime aims in the Government in the direction of inclusive growth. As things have not been going as per the expectations in the job market, we saw increased debate on the issue of 'jobless growth' in recent past, which is believed to get worse due to lack of quality data regarding the status of employment and unemployment in the country. That is why the Government launched a new regular employment survey, namely the ***PLFS (Periodic Labour Force Survey)*** in 2017-18. As per the *Economic Survey 2025-26,* the latest information about the employment scenario in the country is as summarised below:

Employment Trends Employment trends can be studied from the *supply side* of labour through household surveys such as the PLFS conducted by the Ministry of Statistics and Programme Implementation (MoSPI), and the *demand side* of labour through enterprise or establishment surveys such as the Annual Survey of Industries (ASI) by MoSPI, Quarterly Employment Survey (QES) by Labour Bureau, etc. These enable a complete view of the labour market and the trends therein.

- The quarterly and monthly **PLFS (April 2025)** data[14] show a steady labour market with seasonal variations. It indicates that the first half of the financial year (FY) 2025-26 saw a declining unemployment rate (UR) in the current weekly status (CWS) with a stabilising labour force participation rate (LFPR), and substantial employment levels, signalling an improvement in employment conditions:
- A total of 56.2 crore people (aged 15 years and above) were employed during July-September 2025, reflecting the creation of 8.7 lakh new jobs compared to April-June 2025 in 2025-26.
- The PLFS data reveal a distinct and layered employment structure in India, marked by ***rural-urban*** differences. Rural employment is dominated by agricultural workers (57.7 per cent) and self-employment (62.8 per cent), with women workers showing relatively higher participation in them. In contrast, urban employment is primarily concentrated in the services sector (62.0 per cent), with regular wage or salaried jobs making up the largest share (49.8 per cent).
- These employment patterns have important ***gender*** dimensions. The proportion of women engaged in self-employment or contributing to household enterprises, especially in rural areas, is relatively high. Women's participation in regular wage jobs is 10.8 per cent during July-September 2025-26 in rural areas, coinciding with a major share of women working as 'own account workers/employers' (37.5 per cent) or 'helpers in household enterprises' (34.2 per cent). These patterns highlight a tendency among female workers towards independent work and entrepreneurship, which offers flexibility.
- The findings of the Time Use Survey (TUS) conducted by the Ministry of Statistics and Programme Implementation (MoSPI) highlight the ***dual burden*** that female workers face in terms of *caregiving* activities and unpaid work, which may explain their desirability or inclination towards flexible work models.
- India's vision for Viksit Bharat 2047 places women at the core of the national development agenda, with progress envisioned to be women-led. Estimates suggest that increasing participation to around 55 per cent by 2050 could be critical for maintaining a high annual GDP growth trajectory. While women's participation in paid work is rising slowly, the imbalance underscores the need for policies that promote shared domestic responsibilities and better care infrastructure.

Annual Survey of Industries The ASI (Annual Survey of Industries), conducted by MoSPI, is an important source of industrial statistics of the registered

[14] For a person to be categorised as employed as per *usual status* (i.e., principal status and subsidiary status written as 'ps+ss'), he/she must have pursued an economic activity for at least 30 days during the 365 days preceding the date of the survey. The *LFPR* (labour force participation rate) is the percentage of working-age population engaged in work or making tangible efforts to seek 'work' or being available for 'work' if it is available. 'Work' includes self-employment (subsistence agriculture and collection of firewood, poultry farming, etc., for self-consumption), regular wage/salaried employment, and casual labour. The *WPR* (worker population ratio) is defined as the percentage of employed persons in the total population. The *UR* (unemployment rate) is defined as the percentage of unemployed persons in the labour force. For a person to be categorised as employed as per *CWS* (current weekly status), he/she must have pursued an economic activity for at least 1 hour during the 7 days preceding the date of survey. Source: *Economic Survey 2022-23* (Ministry of Finance, GoI, January 2023), p. 158.

organised manufacturing sector of the economy. It covers all factories (those employing 10 or more workers using power and those employing 20 or more workers without using power). As per the latest *ASI 2022-23 (April-March),* the state of employment in industries did show the following trends:

- Manufacturing sector did show resilience, showing a more than 7 per cent increase in employment over the previous year. This translates into an addition of over 22 lakh jobs in 2022-23 over 2018-19 (pre-pandemic level), underscoring the sector's robust post-pandemic recovery. During the pandemic in 2020-21, the sector lost approximately 5 lakh jobs. The growth of the sector in 2022-23 indicates a strong rebound of the sector as economic conditions improved.
- A continued increase in the number of *large factories* (i.e., those employing more than 100 workers) has been seen–the number of such factories saw a robust growth of 7 per cent over the previous year. Notably, large factories now account for around 22 per cent of all operational factories, reflecting their growing presence and contribution to the industrial landscape.
- Small factories (employing fewer than 100 workers) also experienced a steady increase of 2 per cent.
- In terms of the *share of employment*, large factories continue to employ about 80 per cent of the total workers and 78 per cent of the TPE (Total Person Engaged) in the sector, whereas small factories, although larger in number, comprise a smaller share of employment in the sector.
- Seven industry groups in the sector contribute to around 54 per cent of the total employment which are– food products, textiles, basic metals, wearing apparel, motor vehicles, trailers and semi-trailers, machinery and equipment, and chemicals and chemical products.

Formal Employment Formalisation of the job market, as reflected in payroll data from the Employees' Provident Fund Organisation (EPFO), indicates that government initiatives are helping foster greater economic formalisation:

- EPFO membership stood at 32.7 crore as of March 2024, compared to 29.9 crore as of March 2023.
- Net additions to EPFO subscriptions have more than doubled, rising from 61 lakh in 2018-19 to 131 lakh in 2023-24.
- During the first eight months of 2024-25 (April to November 2024), cumulative net additions reached 95.6 lakh, marking a 3 per cent increase over the same period of the previous year (when it was 92.9 lakh).

eShram Portal The eShram portal was launched by the Ministry of Labour and Employment (MoLE) in 2021 to recognise unorganised workers. It helps register and support *unorganised workers* by providing them with a Universal Account Number (UAN) and for the creation of a comprehensive National Database of Unorganised Workers (NDUW). By December 2024, over 30.51 crore unorganised workers have registered on it.

Rural Wages As per data of Labour Bureau, in 2024-25 (April-September 2024), rural wages rose at above 4 per cent every month. On an average, the nominal wage rate in agriculture grew by 5.7 per cent for men and 7 per cent for women. In non-agricultural activities, nominal wage growth was slightly lower for men, at 5.5 per cent, but higher for women, at 7.9 per cent, during the same period.

When adjusted for inflation, the real wage rate in agriculture demonstrated modest growth, increasing by 0.6 per cent for men and 1.8 per cent for women. In non-agricultural activities, real wage growth was particularly noteworthy for women, reaching 2.6 per cent, compared to 0.4 per cent for men during the same period. These trends highlight a steady improvement in real wages for rural workers, with women experiencing a comparatively stronger increase.

GIG Employment

With the change in technology, evolution of new economic activities, innovation in organisation structures and evolving business models, the nature of work has also been changing. Digital platforms have emerged as enablers for employment creation with the power to easily discover job seekers and job providers – in the absence of middlemen. These *new forces* have created massive opportunities for the consumer and the service provider to interact through innovative ways. The new digital technology enables two-sided markets[15] which

[15] Two-sided market is one in which (i) two sets of agents interact through an intermediary or platform and (ii) the

has helped the e-commerce platforms (such as Amazon, Flipkart, Ola, Uber, Urban Clap, Zomato, Swiggy etc.) to emerge. The labour force works with them under the *flexi-staffing* model (in which India is today one of the world's largest markets). The economy which evolved in the process is known as the **gig economy**, and the workforce working in this segment is called *gig workers.* During the COVID-19–induced lockdown, we saw the increasing role of this economy.

- A significant growth occurred in the online retail business.
- Preference to 'work from home' resulted in cutting staff strength, engaging freelancers, outsourcing tasks (to reduce overhead costs) as well as hiring skilled services.
- With increasing demand in industries to hire project-specific consultants, logo/content designers, web designers, etc. for the white-collar workers, the delivery boys and taxi drivers engaged in platforms such as Uber/ Ola, Swiggy, Big Basket and Pizza Hut are now showing potential as well.

As a result, the gig economy has been popular among the workers in India. The benefit of the gig economy is that it allows *flexibility* in employer–employee relationship to both service seekers and service providers.

Job Contract The nature of *job contract* for a gig worker is different from the contract between an employer and an employee/worker in the following ways:

- Labour contract is usually shorter and more specific to the task or job assigned.
- Employment type might be either temporary or contractual and certainly not regular.
- Nature of payment against the work is more of piece rate, negotiable, may be as wage or partly as profit/reward than a fixed salary.
- Control over employees' work by the employer varies in degree, but in any case, is not full.
- Most of the time, workers are flexible to decide on when to work, where to work, etc.

As gig or platform workers were neither considered as *workers* nor *employees* (for more on this, see *Glossary*) under the definition of employee in the labour laws of India, they were not entitled to legal protections under labour laws. This is why they were devoid of their basic rights and social security protections. For the *first time,* these classes of workers were given the missing legal protection – they were defined as unorganised workers for providing them social security benefits (by the newly introduced *Code on Social Security, 2020*).[16]

LABOUR REFORMS

The multiplicity of labour laws and difficulty in complying with them has always been cited as an impediment to industrial development in India. This is why labour reforms have been made an active part of the ongoing economic reform process in the country. In a major initiative for *ensuring compliance* and promoting *ease of doing business,* the Government has initiated a number of labour reform measures. In the past few years, several new initiatives[17] have been taken by the GoI in this direction, which may be ***summed up briefly*** as given below:

1. The ***Apprentice Act 1961*** was amended in December 2014 to make it more responsive to industry and youth. The '*Apprentice Protsahan Yojana*' was also launched to support MSMEs in the manufacturing sector in engaging apprentices. The Government is also working affirmatively to bring a *single uniform law* for the MSME sector to ensure operational efficiency and improve productivity while ensuring job creation on a large scale.
2. A unified labour portal scheme called ***Shram Suvidha Portal*** has been launched for timely redress of grievances and for creating a conducive

decisions of each set of agents affect the outcomes of the other set of agents, typically through an externality (*Source:* M. Rysman, 'The Economics of Two-Sided Market', *Journal of Economic Perspectives* 23, no. 3 (2009), pp. 125-43).

[16] *Economic Survey 2020-21*, vol. 2 (New Delhi: Ministry of Finance, GoI), pp. 346-7.

[17] Ministry of Labour and Employment, GoI, New Delhi, March 2017 and *Economic Survey 2016-17*, vol. 1 (New Delhi: Ministry of Finance, GoI), p. 162.

environment for industrial development. Its main features are as follows:

(i) Unique Labour Identification Number (LIN) allotted to around 0.7 million units facilitating online registration.

(ii) Filing of self-certified, simplified single online return instead of 16 separate returns by industry.

(iii) Transparent labour inspection scheme *via* computerised system as per risk-based criteria and uploading of inspection reports within 72 hours by labour inspectors.

3. **Under Employees' State Insurance Corporation (ESIC) Project Panchdeep:** Digitisation of internal and external processes to ensure efficiency in operations, especially services to employers and insured persons.
4. **Under Employees Provident Fund (EPF):** Digitisation of a complete database of 56.4 million *(by March 2019)* EPF subscribers and allotment of universal account number (UAN) to each member, which facilitates portability of member accounts. UAN is being seeded with the bank account, Aadhaar card and other KYC details to promote financial inclusion. Direct access to EPF accounts will enable members to access and consolidate previous accounts.
5. **For Unorganised Workers:** The Rashtriya Swasthya Bima Yojana (RSBY) is a scheme under the Unorganised Workers' Social Security Act, 2008. It is a smart card-based cashless health insurance scheme, including maternity benefit, which provides a cover of ₹30,000 per family per annum on a family floater basis to below poverty line (BPL) families in the unorganised sector.
6. **National Council for Vocational Training Management Information System (NCVT-MIS)** portal has been developed for streamlining the functioning of Industrial Training Institutes (ITIs), Apprenticeship Schemes and assessment/certification of all NCVT training courses.
7. **National Career Services Portal:** The National Career Service (NCS) Portal was launched to provide a nationwide *online platform* for job seekers and employers for job matching in a dynamic, efficient and responsive manner.
8. **Payment of Bonus (Amendment) Act, 2015:** The Act passed in December 2015 has redefined the eligibility for bonus payment of the Payment of Bonus Act 1965 from ₹10,000 to ₹21,000 per month. This will not only enhance the bonus payment to the employees but also make more eligible to the same.

Recent Reforms The two years (2019 and 2020) were *landmark years* in the history[18] of labour reforms as the Government amalgamated, rationalised and simplified 29 existing central labour codes (i.e., laws) into 4 labour codes, namely:

1. Code on Wages, 2019
2. Industrial Relations Code, 2020
3. Occupational Safety, Health (OSH) and Working Conditions (WC) Code, 2020
4. Code on Social Security, 2020.

The move was aimed at bringing these laws in tune with the changing labour market trends and at the same time accommodating the minimum wage requirement and welfare needs of the unorganised sector workers, including the self-employed and *migrant* workers, within the framework of the legislation. The reforms were a long-drawn process spread over nearly a period of three decades.

HEALTH FOR ALL

The draft approach paper to the 12th Plan proposed the idea of 'universal health care' in 2012 for the first time. The funding situation did not seem conducive enough and that is why the Government did not think to launch it - falling growth rate in the wake of the western recession and many domestic factors. However, providing accessible, affordable and equitable quality health care, especially to the marginalised and vulnerable sections of the population, is one of the key objectives of the Government. There are innumerable challenges to the delivery of efficient health services in India, given the paucity of resources and the plethora of requirements in the health sector. Population health is also significantly influenced by social and environmental determinants such as age at marriage, nutrition, pollution, access to potable

[18] *Economic Survey 2021-22* (New Delhi: Ministry of Finance, GoI), pp. 375-76; *Economic Survey 2020-21*, vol. 2 (New Delhi: Ministry of Finance, GoI), p. 341.

water and hygienic sanitation facilities. However, the *National Health Policy 2017* clearly aims to go for 'universal healthcare' and mobilise the required fund (around 2.5 per cent of the GDP as was estimated by the 12th Plan) for the cause modelled on public-private partnership (PPP).

The Indian health sector has a *mix* of both public and private providers of health services. The private sector and the quality of care provided is variable, ranging from informal providers (quacks) to individually run nursing homes to large polyclinics and multiplex hospitals. The regulation for cost and quality of care is largely weak in most of the states. In the case of public sector, the health services are delivered through a network of health facilities including ASHA (a volunteer health worker) at the community level, Health Subcentres (HSCs), Primary Health Centres (PHCs), Community Health Centres (CHCs), District Hospitals, Government Medical College Hospitals and the state and central government assisted Employees' State Insurance (ESI) hospitals and dispensaries. Outreach and community level services are provided through coordination between ASHA, Anganwadi Workers (AWWs) and the Auxiliary Nurse Midwife (ANM) at the HSC.

> **Word Bank**
>
> **Disability Adjusted Life Years (DALYs)**
>
> DALYs express the premature death and disability attributable to a particular cause and are made up of two components: years of life lost (YLLs) and years of life lived with disability (YLDs). YLLs measure all the time people lose when they die prematurely, before attaining their ideal life expectancy. Ideal life expectancy is based on the highest life expectancy observed in the world for that person's age group. YLDs measure years of life lived with any short- or long-term condition that prevents a person from living in full health. They are calculated by multiplying an amount of time (expressed in years) by a disability weight (a number that quantifies the severity of a disability). Adding together YLLs and YLDs yields DALYs, a measure that portrays in one metric the total health loss a person experiences during their life.

Burden of Diseases

The report[19] ***India: Health of the Nation's States, 2017***, provides the first comprehensive set of findings for the distribution of diseases and risk factors across all States from 1990 to 2016. The concept of Disability Adjusted Life Years (DALYs) provides a framework for analysing the disease burden and risk factors. DALYs is the sum of years of potential life lost due to premature mortality and the years of productive life lost due to disability. One DALY represents the loss of the equivalent of one year of full health. Major findings of the report are given below.

- There has been significant improvement in the health status of the individual as LEB has increased by approximately 10 years during the period 1990–2015. The significance of DALYs as a critical health policy indicator is reflected by the inverse relationship between life expectancy and DALYs rates.
- The per person disease burden measured as DALYs rate dropped by 36 per cent from 1990 to 2016 in India, after adjusting for the changes in the population age structure during this period.
- Of the total disease burden in India measured as DALYs, 61 per cent was due to communicable, maternal, neonatal and nutritional diseases (CMNNDs) in 1990, which dropped to 33 per cent in 2016.
- There was a corresponding increase in the contribution of non-communicable diseases (NCDs) from 30 per cent of the total disease burden in 1990 to 55 per cent in 2016, and of injuries from 9 per cent to 12 per cent.
- In 2016, *malnutrition* still remained the most important risk factor (14.6 per cent) that results in disease burden in the country though the disease burden due to it has dropped in India substantially since 1990.
- Neonatal disorders and nutritional deficiencies as well as diarrhoea, lower respiratory infections

[19] The *India: Health of the Nation's States-2017* report is a collective effort of Indian Council of Medical Research (ICMR), PHFI and IHME, University of Washington (as per the *Economic Survey 2017-18*, vol. 2 (New Delhi: Ministry of Finance, GoI), pp. 176–83.

and other common infections are manifestation of maternal and child malnutrition.

- The contribution of *air pollution* to disease burden remained high in India between 1990 (11.1 per cent) and 2016 (9.8 per cent), with the levels of exposure remaining among the highest in the world. It causes burden through a mix of non-communicable and infectious diseases, mainly cardiovascular diseases, chronic respiratory diseases and lower respiratory infections.
- The *behavioural and metabolic risk factors* associated with the rising burden of NCDs have become quite prominent in India. In 2016, the dietary risks, which include diets low in fruit, vegetables and whole grains, but high in salt and fat, were India's third leading risk factor, followed closely by high blood pressure and high blood sugar (high fasting plasma glucose).
- Unsafe water, sanitation, and handwashing (WaSH), causing 5 per cent of health loss, was the *second leading* risk factor in 1990, but its ranking has dropped to seventh position in 2016.

Efficiency in the use of resources along with measures for preventive and curative health care is necessary to translate enhanced expenditure into improved health outcomes. In this context, the increase in use of antibiotics in developing countries like India where health care spending is low is a cause for concern.

Universal Health Care

The announcement of the *National Health Policy 2017* is a watershed step in the direction of assuring health to all - aimed at 'universal access[20] to good quality healthcare services. Subsequently, the Government launched '*Ayushman Bharat*' with two components:

1. Health and wellness centres to provide comprehensive primary health care and
2. *Pradhan Mantri Jan Arogya Yojana* (PMJAY) to provide health cover to 10.74 crore poor and vulnerable families up to ₹5 lakh per family per year for secondary and tertiary hospitalisation.

The focus of health care is on ***four*** important pillars, namely (i) preventive health care, (ii) providing affordable health care, (iii) building medical infrastructure and (iv) mission mode interventions. These are briefly discussed below:

1. **Preventive Health Care:** Major steps taken by the Government in this regard are as follows:
   - **(i)** To promote preventive health care, the AB-HWCs (Ayushman Bharat Health Wellness Centres) are being set up. These centres aim to deliver comprehensive primary healthcare services with focus on universal high-quality screening, prevention, control and management of common NCDs such as hypertension, diabetes and the three common cancers - oral cavity, breast and cervical cancer - while continuing to provide services for Reproductive, Maternal, Adolescent and Child health (RMNCH+A) and for communicable diseases (CDs).
   - **(ii)** Under *Mission Indradhanush*, 5.46 crore children and 1.32 crore pregnant women were vaccinated across the country till November 2024.
   - **(iii)** Apart from the above, recognising the need for addressing the social determinants of health, the Government has adopted a *multi-sectoral approach* and is increasingly synergising its efforts with other mission mode initiatives such as *Eat Right and Eat Safe, Fit India, Anaemia Mukt Bharat, Poshan Abhiyan* and *Swacch Bharat Abhiyan.*
   - **(iv)** Recognising the threat of 'nicotine addiction' among youth and children through gateway products such as *e-cigarettes*, the Government banned all commercial operations in e-cigarettes. Large pictorial warnings and quit line number on tobacco packs and the resulting increased call volumes from 20,000 to 2.50 lakh calls per month at the quit line services indicate that the Government's efforts to reduce tobacco use are starting to bear fruit.
2. **Healthcare Affordability:** Affordability is a major dimension of health care, especially in the case of India where a vast population lives below the poverty line. To make health care affordable, the Government has taken a number

[20] *Economic Survey 2019-20*, vol. 2 (New Delhi: Ministry of Finance, GoI), pp. 294-9.

of initiatives over a period of time as given below:

(i) As per the latest National Health Accounts (NHA) Estimates of 2020-21 and 2021-22, between 2014-15 and 2021-22, the share of *out of pocket expenditure* (OOPE) in the Total Health Expenditure (THE) declined from 62.6 per cent to 39.4 per cent. This reduction is a direct result of the government's efforts to increase public health spending, improve access to healthcare, and reduce financial hardship for individuals seeking medical care.

(ii) Free Drugs Service, Free Diagnostics Service, Free Laboratory Services, *Pradhan Mantri Bharatiya Jan Aushadhi Pariyojana* (PMBJP) and Pradhan Mantri National Dialysis Programme (PMNDP) are some important initiatives launched to address the high OoPE.

(iii) Primary health care accounts for 52.1 per cent of India's current public expenditure on health as per the National Health Estimates, 2016-17. The National Health Policy, 2017, recommended to spend at least two-thirds of Government health expenditure on primary health care.

(iv) Ayushman Bharat-Pradhan Mantri Jan Arogya Yojana (PM-JAY), the world's largest health insurance scheme, is a major step towards providing affordable health care to the identified poor. The scheme has been rolled out based on the deprivation and occupational criteria of the *Socio- Economic Caste Census* for rural and urban areas, respectively.

3. **Medical Infrastructure:** Lack of healthcare infrastructure has been a major hurdle at the forefront of the country. In recent times, the Government has taken several concerted efforts to improve it:

(i) The doctor-population ratio in India is **1.836** (population estimated to be around 1.40 billion) against the World Health Organization (WHO) recommendation of 1:1000. To address the shortage of doctors, the Government has embarked on an ambitious programme for upgradation of district hospitals into medical colleges. In the last 10 years, the Government has sanctioned 344 new medical colleges (the country had a total of 731 medical colleges by December 2024).

(ii) The norms for graduate and post-graduate seats in medical colleges have also been revised. The maximum intake capacity at MBBS level has been increased from 150 to 250 and the norms for setting up of medical colleges in terms of requirement of land, faculty, staff bed strength, etc. have also been rationalised.

(iii) The Government operates Centrally Sponsored Scheme establishment of New Medical Colleges attached with existing District/Referral Hospitals with fund sharing between Centre and States. As a result, the number of MBBS and PG seats have increased to 1,12,112 (from 51,348 in 2014) and 72,627 (from 31,185 in 2014), respectively by December 2024. These efforts would go a long way in addressing the shortage of doctors.

(iv) The *Pradhan Mantri Swasthya Suraksha Yojana* (PMSSY) was launched to augment the *tertiary healthcare* capacity in clinical care, medical education and research in underserved areas of the country, under which *AIIMS-like* institutions are built and Government Medical Colleges are upgraded by setting up 'Super Speciality' blocks.

(v) *National Medical Commission Act, 2019* was promulgated to enable constitution of 'National Medical Commission'. Reforms have also been brought about with the introduction of a common entrance test NEET-UG for admission to all MBBS courses including AIIMS and JIPMER.

4. **Mission Mode Interventions:** Mission mode interventions aim to deal with maternal health, child health and combat of communicable and NCDs, with the Government now focused on addressing this epidemiological transition from

CDs to NCDs. Major initiatives taken by the Government in this regard are as follows:

(i) Under *Ayushman Bharat* it marks a paradigm shift in the way health care is delivered. It targets universal health coverage with dual focus - *firstly*, by focusing on preventive, promotive and palliative care apart from ambulatory care; and *secondly*, by providing protection against catastrophic health expenditure for secondary and tertiary hospital care.

(ii) The new paradigm recognises and addresses the emerging challenges of NCDs due to changing epidemiology and also targets to sustain the efforts for RMNCH+A (Reproductive, Maternal, New-born Child plus Adolescent Health) and CDs through initiatives such as the Surakshit Matritva Aashwasan (SUMAN), Social Awareness and Action to Neutralise Pneumonia Successfully (SAANS) and TB Harega Desh Jeetega.

(iii) The AB-HWCs would follow a well-defined referral and return linkages to ensure continuum of care.

(iv) *Tele-consultation* to be used at all levels to improve 'referral advice' and undertake 'virtual consultation' including case management support by doctors and specialists.

WATER AND SANITATION

The WHO has repeatedly stressed the importance of clean water, sanitation and clean environment, as a prerequisite to achieving universal health. Showing high faith in the idea of the WHO, the Government has accorded high priority to provisioning of drinking water and sanitation together with clean air in the country. In order to prioritise the tasks, the Government launched a '10-Year Rural Sanitation Strategy' for the decade 2019-29 for rural areas. Similarly, the Universal Coverage of Water Supply has also been launched. Some highlights[21] in this regard are given below.

SBM-G Under SBM-G (Swachh Bharat Mission-Grameen), rural sanitation made an incredible leap in the target achievement from 39 per cent in 2014 to 100 per cent in till December 2021 (more than 10.86 crore toilets were built). Phase-II of the mission is being implemented during 2021-25, with the focus to sustain the ODF status of villages and covering all the villages with Solid and Liquid Waste Management (i.e., to convert the villages from ODF to ODF Plus). A total of 4,44,589 (out of 5,86,788) villages were declared ODF Plus by December 2024. Andaman & Nicobar Islands has declared all its villages as ODF plus model, thus becoming the first *Swachh, Sujal Pradesh*.

SBM-U Under the SBM-U (Swachh Bharat Mission-Urban), to further enhance sanitation, the *Union Budget 2021-22* announced to focus on complete faecal sludge management and wastewater treatment, source segregation of garbage, reduction in single-use plastics, reduction in air pollution by effectively managing waste from construction and demolition activities and bioremediation of all legacy dump sites. Termed the *SBM-U 2.0*, it is to be completed over a period of 5 years from 2021 to 2026.

Jal Jeevan Mission The mission accords the highest priority to improve the quality of life and enhance the ease of living of people, especially those living in rural areas, with the following objectives:

- To enable every rural household to get assured supply of potable water with a functional tap water connection (FTWC), at a service level of 55 litres per capita per day (lpcd) regularly on a long-term basis.
- To provide FTWC to every rural household in partnership with States.
- It is a decentralised, demand-driven and community-managed programme with the *Gram Panchayat* playing a key role in planning, implementation, management, operation and maintenance of water supply systems.
- It functions on the 'no one is left out' principle under which '*Har Ghar Jal Block*', '*Har Ghar Jal Panchayat*' and '*Har Ghar Jal Gaon*' sub-schemes are being run. In 2020-21, Goa became the first state in the country to have 100 per cent FTWC, i.e., differently abled, '*Har Ghar Jal Rajya*'.

By August 2024, out of 19.32 crore rural households in the country, more than 15.03 crore (77.83 per cent) households were reported to have tap water supply in their homes.

[21] *Economic Survey 2022-23* (New Delhi: Ministry of Finance, GoI, January 2023), p. 210.

Jal Jeevan Mission-Urban The *Union Budget 2021-22* announced the launching of this new drinking water supply mission for urban areas. The scheme aims at 'universal water supply' in all urban local bodies (4,378) with 2.86 crores household tap water connections as well as liquid waste management in 500 *AMRUT* cities.

HOUSING FOR ALL

'Housing for All' is the slogan of the Government for which the cut-off year was 2022. Two schemes, *Pradhan Mantri Awaas Yojana-Gramin* (PMAY-G) and *Pradhan Mantri Awaas Yojana-Urban* (PMAY-U), are being run to achieve the objective.

The recent NSO survey on 'Drinking Water, Sanitation, Hygiene and Housing Condition in India 2018' has given the following performance report[22] in this direction:

- About 76.7 per cent of the households in the rural and about 96.0 per cent in the urban areas had houses of pucca structure.
- More than four times increase in the number of houses were completed in a year under PMAY-G, from 11.95 lakh in 2014-15 to 47.33 lakh in 2018-19. In 2019-22, the cumulative target is 1.95 crore houses (5,27,878 houses were delivered by 17 January, 2020).
- Under PMAY-U, against assessed demand of 1.12 crore, 1.03 crore houses were sanctioned, 61 lakhs grounded for construction and 32 lakhs have been delivered as on 1 January, 2020. This scheme covers a range of social groups, comprising senior citizens, construction workers, domestic workers, artisans, differently abled (Divyang), transgender and leprosy patients. Women empowerment, by giving them ownership of the house, is slated to turn out to be a major push in the direction of inclusiveness.

SOCIAL SECTOR EXPENDITURE

The general government's (i.e., centre plus states) social sector expenditure (SSE), as per the *Economic Survey 2025-26,* has been keeping pace with the sector's growing importance which shows the following characteristics:

- The general government's social services expenditure (SSE) has shown a rising trend since FY17. The SSE as a percentage of total expenditure (TE) has increased from 23.3 per cent in 2020-21 to **26.6** per cent in 2025-26 (BE).
- During the five years from 2021-22 to 2025-26 (BE), the SSE grew at a compound annual growth rate (CAGR) of **12** per cent.

Word Bank

Social Services

Social services include education, sports, art and culture; medical and public health, family welfare; water supply and sanitation; housing; urban development; welfare of SCs, STs and OBCs, labour and labour welfare; social security and welfare, nutrition, relief on account of natural calamities etc.

- Expenditure on *education* (which includes education, sports, arts and culture) during the last five years from 2021-22 to 2025-26 (BE) has grown at a CAGR of **11** per cent to ₹9.8 lakh crore.
- Expenditure on *health* (which includes 'Medical and Public Health', 'Family Welfare' and 'Water and Sanitation') during the last five years from 2021-22 to 2025-26 (BE) grew at a CAGR of **8** per cent to ₹6.3 lakh crore.

POLICY SUGGESTIONS

Social infrastructure has positive externalities. It has a significant role in the economic development and welfare of a country. It is empirically proven and widely recognised that education and health impact the growth of an economy. Investing in *human capital* by way of education, skill development, training and provision of healthcare facilities enhances the productivity of the workforce and welfare of the population. In this regard, contemporary documents *suggest* the following actions[23] for the governments in the country:

Scan this QR Code to watch a author's video lecture that simplifies this topic

[22] *Economic Survey 2019-20*, vol. 2 (New Delhi: Ministry of Finance, GoI), pp. 298-99.

[23] Based on *Economic Survey 2025-26; Economic Survey 2024-25; Economic Survey 2023-24; and Economic Survey*

1. Action is needed in the direction of improving the quality of education - an important contributor to improvement in the quality of education would be an increase in the percentage of *qualified teachers.*
2. India needs to overcome the development challenges through innovative models of *delivery of services.* It has a critical role to play in India's march towards double-digit growth.
3. Without improvement in social infrastructure, development of a country is incomplete - expenditures on education, skill and health need to be enhanced.
4. Overhauling of the subsidy regime is needed at a faster pace. It will not only rationalise the subsidies but also bring in a variety of *other benefits* in the service delivery system - inclusion of the needy population; exclusion of the fake accounts; prevention of corruption and leakages; traceability; authentication of delivery; transparency and accountability. The idea of technology-enabled Direct Benefit Transfers (DBTs), namely the JAM (*Jan Dhan-Aadhaar*-Mobile) number trinity solution, introduced by the GoI in this regard is believed to be a game-changing move.
5. India needs to include the *behavioural dimensions* of the target population in its framework of policy-making to realise the desired results in the area of promoting the cause of social infrastructure. India has already included this aspect in its sanitation campaign (especially, in checking open defecation) - the same is also needed in other areas of importance.
6. There is a need for *integrating* the social sector initiatives of the Centre, states and local bodies. The new 'think tank' NITI Aayog can provide a suitable platform in this regard.
7. Strengthening of the *local bodies* (the PRIs) will not only boost the social sector but also have an effect of externality in the form of an aware, awakened and participative citizenry. Through them, India can garner the support of civil society and NGOs.
8. There is a need to orient the *private sector* (corporate world) towards this cause. Their inclusion in this area will not only bring in funds to this fund-scarce sector but also enable the country to use their expertise in the promotion of the social infrastructure.
9. Aimed to bridge the gap of information divide, the use of ICT needs to be encouraged at a mass scale.
10. Need of sensitising all stakeholders about the ensuing dangers of climate change and promoting sustainable behaviour for promoting and sustaining inclusive growth.
11. The *COVID-19* pandemic had shown the vulnerability of India's health sector. It is high time that expenditures on the sector were enhanced and a mission mode approach was applied to fight any such pandemic in future.
12. The disruption caused by the *COVID-19* pandemic has made the education sector to think away from the classroom or at least a dependable alternative of it.
13. Channelising women's economic potential through ecosystem services such as affordable market alternatives for care work, safe transportation and lodging, and long-term counselling support, can help capitalise the gender dividend for future economic and social development.

History suggests that when different aspects of human development like education, skill, employment, health, and rural development are dovetailed with technology, all-round revolutionary innovation resulting in technology-led growth and prosperity follows. Many volumes of the Economic Survey, especially after the COVID-19 pandemic, have invoked this vision and advised the Government to scale up its efforts in the above-cited areas.

2022-23 and several of its previous volumes besides the documents of the erstwhile *Planning Commission* and the new think tank *NITI Aayog.*

PREVIOUS YEARS' QUESTIONS

Prelims

1. Consider the following statements about 'PM Surya Ghar Muft Bijli Yojana': (2025)
   (i) It targets the installation of one crore solar rooftop panels in the residential sector.
   (ii) The Ministry of New and Renewable Energy aims to impart training on the installation, operation, maintenance and repair of solar rooftop systems at grassroots levels.
   (iii) It aims to create more than three lakhs of skilled manpower through fresh skilling and up-skilling under the scheme component of capacity building.

   Which of the statements given above are correct?
   (a) (i) and (ii) only **(b)** (i) and (iii) only
   (c) (ii) and (iii) only **(d)** (i), (ii) and (iii)

2. With reference to the *Pradhan Mantri Surakshit Matritva Abhiyan,* consider the following statements: (2024)
   (i) This scheme guarantees a minimum package of antenatal care services to women in their second and third trimesters of pregnancy and six months post-delivery health care service in any government health facility.
   (ii) Under this scheme, private sector health care providers of certain specialities can volunteer to provide services at nearby government health facilities.

   Which of the statement(s) given above is/are correct?
   (a) (i) only **(b)** (ii) only
   (c) Both (i) and (ii) **(d)** Neither (i) nor (ii)

3. With reference to the *Pradhan Mantri Shram Yogi Maan-Dhan (PM-SYM) Yojana,* consider the following statements: (2024)
   (i) The entry age group for enrolment in the scheme is 21 to 40 years.
   (ii) Age specific contribution shall be made by the beneficiary.
   (iii) Each subscriber under the scheme shall receive a minimum pension of ₹3,000 per month after attaining the age of 60 years.
   (iv) Family pension is applicable to the spouse and unmarried daughters.

   Which of the statement(s) given above is/are correct ?
   (a) (i), (iii) and (iv)
   (b) (ii) and (iii) only
   (c) (ii) only
   (d) (i), (ii) and (iv)

4. Consider the following statements regarding World Toilet Organization: (2024)
   (i) It is one of the agencies of the United Nations.
   (ii) World Toilet Summit, World Toilet Day and World Toilet College are initiatives of this organisation, to inspire action to tackle the global sanitation crisis.
   (iii) The main focus of its function is to grant funds to the least developed countries and developing countries to achieve the end of open defecation.

   Which of the statement(s) given above is/are correct?
   (a) (ii) only **(b)** (iii) only
   (c) (i) and (ii) **(d)** (ii) and (iii)

5. The total fertility rate in an economy is defined as: (2024)
   (i) the number of children born per 1000 people in the population in a year.
   (ii) the number of children born to a couple in their lifetime in a given population.
   (iii) the birth rate minus death rate.
   (iv) the average number of live births a woman would have by the end of her child-bearing age.

6. With reference to Corporate Social Responsibility (CSR) rules in India, consider the following statements: (2024)
   (i) CSR rules specify that expenditures that benefit the company directly or its employees will not be considered as CSR activities.
   (ii) CSR rules do not specify minimum spending on CSR activities.

Which of the statement(s) given above is/are correct?

(a) (i) only **(b)** (ii) only

(c) Both (i) and (ii) **(d)** Neither (i) nor (ii)

7. Consider the following statements: (UPSC 2023)

Statement-I: India's public sector health care system largely focuses on curative care with limited preventive, preventive and rehabilitative care.

Statement-II: Under India's decentralized approach to health care delivery, the States are primarily responsible for organizing health services.

Which one of the following is correct in respect of the above statements?

(a) Both Statement-I and Statement-II are correct, and Statement-II is the correct explanation for Statement-I

(b) Both Statement-I and Statement-II are correct, and Statement-II is not the correct explanation for Statement-I

(c) Statement-I is correct, but Statement-II is incorrect.

(d) Statement-I is incorrect, but Statement-II is correct

Answers: 1. (d) 2. (b) 3. (b) 4. (a) 5. (d) 6. (a) 7. (c)

Explanation

1. (d): All three statements are correct about the scheme PM Surya Ghar Muft Bijli Yojana.

2. (b): The mentioned Campaign/Abhiyan focuses on providing assured, comprehensive, and quality antenatal care to pregnant women, especially in their second and third trimesters– and aims to reduce maternal and infant mortality rates by ensuring timely medical check-ups and necessary interventions but it does not have any provision for 'six months post-delivery healthcare' (thus, Statement-I is incorrect). But under this Abhiyan certain specialists from the private sector healthcare providers can take part on voluntary basis, however, this is its non-primary feature (thus, Statement -II is correct).

3. (b): Statements-II and III are its correct features. But Statement-I (the entry age group for enrolment is 18 to 40 years, and not 21 to 40 years) and 4 (family pension is not applicable to the spouse and unmarried daughters) are incorrect about its features.

5. (d): Total fertility is defined as the number of average live births a women would have in her child-bearing age and is expressed as children per women.

6. (a): Statement-I is 'correct' as the CSR has the angle of philanthropy (actions towards welfare by a 'limited liability firm') as its benefit can not be enjoyed by either the company or its employees directly or indirectly. But Statement-II is 'incorrect' because as per the CSR guidelines, companies need to spend minimum 2 per cent of their annual profit for the cause.

7. (c): Public health care includes all of the aspects such as preventive, curative, and rehabilitative. Thus, statement-I is incorrect. States are primarily responsible for public health care as the subject belongs to State List. So, statement-II is correct.

Mains

1. Distinguish between 'care economy' and 'monetised economy'. How can care economy be brought into monetised economy through women empowerment? (2023)

2. Most of the unemployment in India is structural in nature. Examine the methodology adopted to compute unemployment in the country and suggest improvements. (2023)

3. What is the status of digitalisation in the Indian economy? Examine the problems faced in this regard and suggest improvements. (2023)

4. Examine the pattern and trend of public expenditure on Social Services in the post-reforms period in India. To what extent this has been in consonance with achieving the objective of inclusive growth? (2024)

5. Discuss the merits and demerits of the four Labour Codes' in the context of labour market reforms in India. What has been the progress so far in this regard? (2024)

SAMPLE OBJECTIVE QUESTIONS

1. Consider the following statements from the latest Human Development Report 2023-24:
   (i) India's gender inequality declined in the last decade and stands below the global average.
   (ii) Gender gap in labour force participation is around 48 per cent in India.
   (iii) India is ranked 108 out of 166 nations in the Gender Inequality Index.

   How many of the above statements are correct?
   (a) Only one
   (b) Only two
   (c) All three
   (d) None of these

2. Consider the following statements related to the gig economy in the country:
   (i) Gig economy provides employment flexibility to both employees and employers.
   (ii) Gig employees are categorised as unorganised workers.
   (iii) Gig employees do not get any social security benefits.

   How many of the above statements are correct?
   (a) Only one (b) Only two
   (c) All three (d) None of these

3. Consider the following statements related to unemployment allowance:
   (i) It may drag economy into poverty trap.
   (ii) If the allowance is higher than the after-tax earnings of the employed, it leads to unemployment trap.
   (iii) Poverty trap and unemployment trap reinforce each other.

   How many of the above statements are correct?
   (a) Only one (b) Only two
   (c) All three (d) None of these

4. Consider the following statements related to the Jal Jeevan Mission:
   (i) It has its rural and urban components.
   (ii) It aims to assure 100 litres of tap water per capita per day in rural areas.
   (iii) Goa emerged as the first state to have universal tap water connection.

   How many of the above statements are correct?
   (a) Only one (b) Only two
   (c) All three (d) None of these

5. Consider the following statements related to India:
   (i) In the Global Hunger Index 2023, India is ranked at 111 out of 125 countries of the world.
   (ii) India's rank in the Human Development Report 2023-24 has declined by two ranks.
   (iii) The adolescent birth rate of India has improved, as per the Gender Inequality Report 2023-24.

   How many of the above statements are correct?
   (a) Only one (b) Only two
   (c) All three (d) None of these

6. Consider the following statements related to population trap:
   (i) It occurs when the replacement level of fertility rate is achieved much before optimum economic growth.
   (ii) It happens when population growth rate of an economy overtakes its economic growth rate.
   (iii) It happens when an economy sees its fertility rate falling below replacement level.

   How many of the above statements are correct?
   (a) Only one (b) Only two
   (c) All three (d) None of these

7. Consider the following statements related to the latest Periodic Labour Force Survey (PLFS)-2022-23:
   (i) Unemployment rate for men in the country has declined over the previous year.
   (ii) This is an annual release of the National Sample Survey Organisation.
   (iii) The labour force participation rate (LFPR) in rural areas increased over the last year.

   How many of the above statements are correct?
   (a) Only one (b) Only two
   (c) All three (d) None of these

8. Consider the following statements about the Lakhpati Didi Scheme:
   (i) As a livelihood initiative, the scheme was launched by the Ministry of Labour and Employment in 2023-24.
   (ii) It aims to enable women earn above ₹1 lakh annually.
   (iii) The women beneficiaries should be members of a self-help group (SGH).

   How many of the above statements are correct?
   (a) Only one (b) Only two
   (c) All three (d) None of these

9. Consider the following statements related to fund allocations for the development of rural areas and social sector in the Interim Budget 2024-25:
   (i) It has increased over three times in case of the Vibrant Villages Programme.
   (ii) For PM-KISAN it remains as much it was in the preceding year.
   (iii) In case of the PM-POSHAN their was an increase of over 20 per cent.

   How many of the above statements are correct?
   (a) Only one (b) Only two
   (c) All three (d) None of these

10. Consider the following statements related to the Revised Estimates of Government expenditures for 2023-24:
   (i) Government expenditures on the centrally sponsored schemes (CSSs) were estimated to be more than double of its expenditures on the central sector schemes.
   (ii) The cost of interest payments was estimated to be higher than Government's establishment expenditures.
   (iii) Government's capital expenditures were estimated to be around three times higher than its grant-in-aid for creation of capital assets (GoCAs).

   How many of the above statements are correct?
   (a) Only one (b) Only two
   (c) All three (d) None of these

Answers: 1. (b) 2. (b) 3. (b) 4. (b) 5. (c) 6. (a) 7. (c) 8. (b) 9. (c) 10. (b)

SAMPLE SUBJECTIVE QUESTIONS

1. Briefly examine the need of labour reforms and recent steps taken by the government in this regard.
2. Analyse the significance of skilling and reskilling in the fast-changing workplaces in special reference to the Industry 4.0.
3. Briefly discuss the idea of universal healthcare and India's policy framework in this regard.
4. 'Universal Basic Income is an idea whose time has come.' Comment.
5. Briefly discuss about the scope of job creation and skill development under the New Education Policy 2020.
6. Write a note on the government's changing perception towards employment.
7. Briefly analyse Government's expenditure trends of the social sector.
8. Briefly discuss about India's efforts in the direction of fulfilling the minimum needs of the citizens.
9. Examine the gender dimension of employment in India and discuss the policy steps taken by the Government to address the issue.

SAMPLE MODEL ANSWER

1. Briefly discuss the dietary guidelines recently released by the Indian Council of Medical Research (ICMR) in the wake of increasing malnutrition, undernutrition, and obesity in the country.

Ans. The Dietary Guidelines of 2024 were jointly prepared by the ICMR and National Institute of Nutrition (NIN) and address India's evolving food environment. They tackle the *dual burden* of malnutrition-undernutrition and rising obesity while emphasising sustainable food choices, micronutrient sufficiency, and the prevention of diet-related non-communicable diseases (NCDs). Its key recommendations are as given below:

- Consuming a diverse range of foods,
- Increasing intake of vegetables and legumes, and
- Reducing consumption of salt, fat, and sugar.

The guidelines also promote

- Regular 'physical activity' and serve as a vital resource for public health policymakers, nutritionists, and the wider public.
- Dietary reforms should be treated as a public health priority and hold a prominent place in initiatives for the prevention of NCDs, alongside integration with AYUSH for effective management.
- The efforts to popularise locally grown food, traditional foods, and traditional cooking methods are reflected in the increasing number of social media influencers creating content around such knowledge and practices.
- The attractiveness and reach of 'social media' should be leveraged to disseminate the importance of nutrition in the prevention and management of NCDs.

The guidelines conclude that 'sustained awareness generation and education are possible only with a change in behavioural choices, and it can be enabled by embedding the messages in a culturally relevant manner.'

CHAPTER 22

Burning Socioeconomic Issues

> Indian Planners pursued growth as an end in itself, ignoring poverty reduction and other social objectives.*
>
> *J. Bhagwati and A. Panagariya, *India's Tryst with Destiny* (New Delhi: Collins Books, 2014), p. 9.

To watch the Author's videos on the significance of the Chapter, scan the QR Code given here

Exam Essentials...

- India as Currency Manipulator!

In This Chapter...

- Process Reforms in India
- Taxpayers' Services Enhance Trust in Tax System
- India's Self-Reliance vs. Multilateralism
- Resolving the Menace of Bad Loans
- Preparing Health Care for the Future
- Reforming India's Public Debt Management
- Monetisation of Public Assets - The Significance
- The Circularity of Economy
- Fulfilling the Minimum Needs of Citizens
- Regulating Crypto Ecosystem

PROCESS REFORMS IN INDIA

Introduction

Regulation has always remained among the most essential functions of the governments. Experiences and illustrations suggest that it is just not possible to have complete regulations in a world which is full of uncertainties, making it almost impossible to account for all possible outcomes. India has been a case of over-regulation, which makes regulations ineffective even after complying with the administrative process (as the *Economic Survey 2020-21* has concluded by quoting various comparative studies). For ease of living, India needs immediate reforms in the area.

NOTE: Many of the **burning issues** of high socio-economic importance have been covered in different chapters of the book at relevant places *aimed* at promoting their connectivity with a broader scheme of the subject matter and enhancing readers' ease of understanding. These issues (with the chapters given in brackets along with them) include ***Social stock exchange; Environmental, social and governance (ESG) investment (15); PLI Scheme, Semiconductor sector, Industry 4.0, Digital Infrastructure (10); Commercialising space sector (11); Consolidation of banks, Global monetary tightening & India, Central Banks Digital Currency (13); Trade facilitation, India as pharmacy of the world, The Quad, Settlement of Trade in INR (16); Abu Dhabi Package of WTO (17); Tax administration reforms, Taxpayers' charter, 15th Finance Commission (18); Climate risk insurance, COP 29, Green Bonds (20); and Human Development in India, National Education Policy-2020, Preparing Health Care for the Future, Gig Employment (21).***

Regulatory Framework of India

It is often believed that India's regulatory problems are due to the lack of regulatory standards and poor compliance to process. However, international comparisons show that India ranked better than its peers on these two parameters. Rather, the real issue seems to be 'effectiveness' of regulations caused by undue delays, rent seeking, complex regulations and quality of regulation (as per the 'World Rule of Law Index' of the World Justice Project, World Bank's Worldwide Governance Indicators and various studies of the World Bank).

We find unnecessary regulation in India. A study of *Quality Council of India* (conducted for the *Economic Survey 2020-21*) shows that voluntary closure of a company in the country with no dispute/litigation takes 1570 days (i.e., around 51 months) to complete - the comparative figures for Singapore, the United Kingdom and Germany are 12 months, 15 months and 12-24 months, respectively.

Causes and Remedies

The root cause of over-regulation has been the approach to account for every possible outcome. However, economic theory and real-life evidence show that in an 'uncertain and complex' world, it is just not possible to frame laws which can account for all possible outcomes. Therefore, the decision-making involves 'discretion', which is rather not considered good. Thus, laws are carefully framed to avoid discretionary powers given to officials, resulting in enacting more complex laws which make discretion even more non-transparent.

Evidences show that complex laws (i.e., over-regulation) make decisions more opaque, while the simpler laws enhance transparency. In practice, policy-makers in the country have given primacy to regulation *by default* over 'supervision' (aimed at avoiding discretion in decision-making, at all costs). Regulation attained this importance due to one more reason - unlike supervision, it can be easily measured. After all, regulations provide criteria (or checklists), making it easier for regulators to follow and reduce their accountability. In contrast, it is difficult to quantify the amount and quality of supervision. The optimal solution lies in:

1. Simple regulations combined with a transparent decision-making process.
2. Discretionary powers of decision-makers need to be balanced with improved transparency, stronger systems of *ex ante* accountability (such as bank boards) and *ex post* resolution mechanisms.

The new initiative of the Government, the *e-Marketplace* portal, is a very good example in this direction which has been successful in serving three goals - increasing price-related transparency in Government procurement, reducing procurement cost and easing decision-making by honest officials.

Recent Initiatives

At present, the administrative process reforms are being taken by the Government very seriously, and a few structural moves have already been taken:

1. **Labour Law:** Labour falls under the Concurrent List of the Constitution and, therefore, both Parliament and state legislatures can make laws regulating labour. There were over 100 state and 40 central laws regulating various aspects of labour such as the resolution of industrial disputes, working conditions, social security and wages, which make labour regulation very complex. To rectify this, the government merged the existing 29 central labour laws into 4 labour codes.
2. **Other Service Providers:** India's regulatory framework for OSPs (Other Service Providers) was, till recently, outdated and complex. For instance, the BPO (Business Process Outsourcing)

industry usually runs on global cloud-based systems, but India's regulations restricted its use and insisted on its localisation. Besides, there were cumbersome registration requirements and restrictions on 'Work from Home'.

The sector was liberalised by the Government initiating (November 2020) a few effective steps - no registration requirement for OSPs, BPO industry taken out of the ambit of OSP regulations, majority of requirements for 'Work from Home' and 'Work from Anywhere' abolished etc.

3. **Institutional Architecture:** Since independence, a plethora of autonomous bodies had proliferated, and there is a need to prune them consistently not just from a cost perspective but in order to maintain transparency, accountability and efficient supervision.

Taking effective steps in this regard (in 2020-21), the organisations such as the All India Handloom Board, All India Handicrafts Board, Cotton Advisory Board and Jute Advisory Board were *closed* by the Government, and the existing four film media units (Films Division, Directorate of Film Festivals, National Film Archives of India and Children's Film Society) merged into one body, the NFDC (National Film Development Corporation).

In this direction, a very effective move will be to enact a law aimed at 'transparency of rules' so that asymmetry of information can be abolished (as was proposed by the *Economic Survey 2016-17*). Due to frequent changes made in rules, citizens are forced to follow a long paper trail of circulars and notifications to know the current requirements. Once a law related to transparency of rules is enacted, it will simplify citizens' understanding of regulations by bringing transparency as all departments will need to mandatorily put all citizen-facing rules on their website, any rule not explicitly mentioned on the website will not be imposed by officials, all laws, rules and regulations will have to be always presented in an updated and unified form.

Conclusion

It means that the regulatory framework of India should be made simpler, which will lead to certain discretionary powers given to officials undoubtedly. But with the help of effective supervision, transparency and fixing accountabilities regulation can also improve the ease of living for citizens besides promoting the cause of 'minimum government and maximum governance'. The process reforms started by the Government need to be implemented in all possible areas.

India as Currency Manipulator!

Introduction

Exchange rates of world currencies have always been sensitive issues. Its criticality was enhanced even more once globalisation commenced. The issue of currency manipulation has been often reported in media more in the case of the United States, which did put several countries on the list of currency manipulators (including India) in the past four years.

Currency Manipulation

Under currency manipulation, a country influences its currency deliberately. Though the act is declared unfair by the UN economic institutions, economies do it to gain advantages of the following kinds:

1. **Trade Benefit:** Devaluation in currency boosts exports as domestic goods and services become cheaper for the buyers of foreign countries.
2. **Interest Benefit:** If the economy concerned is a net lender to foreign countries, it earns more interest on the overseas loans forwarded by it (in the case of being a net borrower, the economy loses more through interest payment, resulting in higher outflows of foreign exchange).
3. **Forex Flow Benefit:** Under-valuation of the domestic currency brings in enhanced flows of foreign currencies in the economy as interest rates tighten and investors get the chance to earn more by investing in the security market.

On Manipulators' List!

The United States in December 2020, included India (together with Taiwan, Thailand, China, Japan, Korea, Germany, Italy, Singapore and Malaysia) in its monitoring list of countries with potentially 'questionable foreign exchange policies' and 'currency manipulation' (a year after India was removed from the watchlist in May 2019). Once an economy meets *two* of the following *three criteria* (of the US Trade Facilitation and Trade

Enforcement Act of 2015), it is put on the monitoring list by the country:

1. A 'significant' trade surplus with the United States (at least $20 billion over a 12-month period). *(Over a 12-month period ending June 2020, India had a $22 billion trade surplus with the United States).*
2. A 'material' current account surplus equivalent to at least 2 per cent of the GDP (Gross Domestic Product) over a 12-month period. *(Over a 12-month period ending June 2020, India had a current account surplus but of only 0.9 per cent of its GDP).*
3. 'Persistent', one-sided intervention (when net purchases of foreign currency totalling at least 2 per cent of the country's GDP over a 12-month period are conducted repeatedly, in at least six out of 12 months). *[Over a 12-month period ending June 2020, net purchases of foreign exchange by the Reserve Bank of India (RBI) were of $64 billion, i.e., 2.4 per cent of India's GDP.]*

Data show India meeting two criteria. But the charge of currency manipulation against India does not sustain by some simple facts – the benefits it might get out of increased exports will get more than offset by the increased payment costs of its external debts!

India's Exchange Management

India switched from fixed to floating currency system in the year 1993-94. In the 'dual exchange rate' system of India, while one exchange rate is announced by the RBI every day, the other is determined by the market (i.e., the demand and supply of rupee and foreign currencies in India's foreign exchange market), which is recognised by the International Monetary Fund (IMF) as *free float* (i.e., floating currency system).

As India gave an emphatic call for *Make in India*, followed by *Atmanirbhar Bharat Abhiyan*, the Government looks to pushing in favour of boosting exports and attracting higher foreign investments. Like every other country, India also aspires to hold enough forex reserves to boost the confidence of foreign investors and expand essential imports of technology and capital goods. But there does not seem any manipulation in its exchange regime – no such hint has come from any of the international financial institutions (i.e., the IMF, World Bank or Bank for International Settlements).

Conclusion

In recent times, the United States has hardened its stance against all its trade partners who generated a sizeable trade surplus with it and shown protectionist tendencies, which has resulted in a kind of declared trade and currency war against its main trading partner, China. However, the United States has not been able to prove any claim of currency manipulation on either China or India. Finally, India was removed from the list of currency-manipulating countries by the USA in November 2022.

TAXPAYERS' SERVICES ENHANCE TRUST IN TAX SYSTEM

Introduction

Tax is defined by modem economics as a method of income redistribution serving the larger goal of welfare. But it took modern economies several more decades to change their traditional approach which gave 'limited attention to tax services' as regulator and enforcer of tax laws. It was by the late 1980s that the attention shifted towards the need of providing *better tax services* to taxpayers, with the Washington Consensus and deliberations for the World Trade Organization (WTO) playing the roles of facilitators in this regard.

The Need for Better Tax Services

On the increased demand for better services to the taxpayers, there has been a worldwide recognition of the 'rights' of the taxpayers - beginning with the United Kingdom (1986), several countries took initiatives towards this such as the United States (1988), New Zealand (2002) and Canada (2007), among others.

Besides recognising taxpayers' rights, the arrangement of an 'independent institution' like *Ombudsman* has proved very useful in many countries. The Ombudsman looks upon tax issues from the taxpayers' perspective besides ensuring that taxpayers understand their tax rights well and are treated fairly by the tax department.

As per the Organisation for Economic Co-operation and Development (OECD), the countries with an independent tax Ombudsman have performed *better* on the tax administration front through better *trust* between taxpayers and tax authorities, have exhibited a higher average tax to GDP ratio and lower time taken to file taxes. The Ombudsman functions in Australia, Canada, the United Kingdom, Brazil and South Africa, while *tax mediators* in Belgium and France function independent of the tax administration.

Case with India

Though late, the initiative towards this was also taken by India - in *2020-21* (which was proposed in the year's Union Budget) a formal 'taxpayers, charter' was notified and 'expected behaviour' from the tax officials were inserted in the 'mission statement' of the tax department. India's taxpayers' charter consists of '14 commitments' of the income tax department and '6 obligations' of the taxpayers.

As far as a tax Ombudsman is concerned, India's experience has not been good. After instituting Ombudsman for income tax (in 2003) and indirect taxes (in 2011), they were abolished in February 2019. The Ombudsman was appointed from among the serving officers responsible to investigate the grievances and complaints against the functioning of the tax authority. In the absence of an Act of law empowering its functions, the institution was *ineffective*, and its decisions were *only advisory* in nature. The Ombudsman could settle complaints either through agreements between the complainant and the tax department through conciliation and mediation or by passing an award, with a token compensation (not exceeding `5,000) for the loss suffered by the complainant.

Looking into the vital role which the Ombudsman plays in enhancing tax compliance and trust of taxpayers in the tax system, it is high time that India set up such an independent institution, with adequate teeth and independence.

Conclusion

Experts feel that there is a need to revitalise grievance redress system and incorporate a more holistic view of enhancing customer experience and protecting taxpayers' rights in the country. The Government has shown commitment to its pledge *Honouring the Honest* (of the Union Budget 2020-21) repeatedly till the latest *Union Budget 2026-27*.

INDIA'S SELF-RELIANCE VS. MULTILATERALISM

Introduction

During the COVID-19 pandemic, serious bottlenecks were faced by countries due to their dependence on the global supply chain - some also learnt hard lessons from it. Assessing the fault lines of the global supply chain, the Government of India thought to use the crisis as an opportunity and launched a long-term policy in the direction of self-reliance under the *Atmanirbhar Bharat Abhiyan* campaign. Such a call from India, which has been an ardent votary of globalisation and multilateralism, was interpreted by many as the rise of protectionism in India.

Self-Reliance vs. Multilateralism

Experts have seen India's recent push towards self-reliance antagonistic to its stand on multilateralism and globalisation. However, it was not for the first time that India gave such a call. Self-reliance has been among the *six major objectives* of planning in India since independence itself. But the timing of this call from India makes the world think this move in the colour of India's rising belief in 'protectionism'. This belief is emboldened by recent trade-related skirmishes of India with the United States and other countries where India has been blamed to be against the normal principles of multilateralism and for being protectionists. This makes global investors and governments feel as if India is reneging on its commitments to multilateralism and globalisation. However, this has not been the case. The world needs to interpret India's stance in the new and changing global perspectives.

The Changing Global Economic Order

Post-Cold War times have not been stable due to political as well as trade related reasons (in the case of trade, it has been due to the new body WTO). The state of global economic order received another element of *fluidity* by the Great Recession (of 2008) of the western developed economies which was further accelerated by the unprecedented rise of China as an economic power. It was further coloured by a global suspicion towards China in the aftermath of the *COVID-19* pandemic. Thus, the world has changed much since India gave its first call for self-reliance by the late 1940s. As another emerging global economic power, India needs to recalibrate its approach to multilateralism and carve out a favourable place for itself in the emerging global economic order. The world needs to read India's recent push in favour of self-reliance in the light of the following coordinates:

- The self-reliance campaign is India's attempt to mend its rising trade deficits with China.
- In the wake of *COVID-19 pandemic*, some major multinational companies are exploring the possibilities to relocate their production centres away from China - India is busy attracting them

with the help of her 'Make in India', 'Assemble in India' and 'self-reliance' push (as India is not against foreign investment, but rather supports it with one of the most competitive policy frameworks in the region). In a traditional sense, self-reliance means no foreign investment.

- Global economic order, which has been already fluid since the mid-1980s, is going through a process of new *churning* due to increasing Sino-US trade tensions and rising protectionism across the developed world - and India wishes to occupy a favourable place for herself in this emerging global economic order.
- Given the challenges of unemployment, demography and *surplus agricultural production*, India is unwilling to restructure its trade.
- India has been quite willing to play a more vibrant role on the international fora, and in recent years there has been increased activism from India towards it.
- India still remains very much committed to the cause of multilateralism - the reason it is considered among the staunchest votaries of globalisation in the WTO. India remains actively engaged in negotiating its free and preferential trade agreements.

Conclusion

Thus, India's recent emphasis on self-reliance is not antagonistic to either globalisation or multilateralism; rather, it is a way to protect her own socio-economic interests like other countries of the world. This time round, India's approach to self-reliance is smartly intertwined with domestic interests propelled by global funds (foreign investments) with the ultimate objective of situating herself favourably in the emerging global economic order.

RESOLVING THE MENACE OF BAD LOANS

Introduction

The rising size of bad loans (i.e., non-performing assets) of specially the public sector banks (PSBs) has hit the investment prospects in the country in a very big way. Being the main lenders to the infrastructure sector, the speed of infrastructure expansion was hit hard since 2012-13 onwards with the gross non-performing assets of banks reaching the peak of 11.2 per cent by 2017-18.

To solve the crisis of the high NPAs, the RBI had introduced multiple schemes over the last few years - flexible Refinancing of Infrastructure (5/25 scheme), Asset Reconstruction Companies (ARCs), Strategic Debt Restructuring (SDR), Asset Quality Review (AQR) and Sustainable Structuring of Stressed Assets (S4A).

As these measures could not be effective, the Government initiated two *new steps* in this regard - enforcement of the insolvency and bankruptcy law (IBC, 2016) and proposal to set a bad bank - for the resolution of the bad loan menace.

The Concept

Theoretically, bad banks work on a simple concept, that is banks' loans are classified into two categories, good and bad. The bad loans of the banks are bought or taken over by the bad bank, while the good loans are left with the bank itself. This way, bad loans do not contaminate the good assets of banks. As banks hit by the problem of bad loans become financially viable entities, they restart their lending process. While the concept of a bad bank is simple, the implementation can be quite complicated. A variety of organisational and financial options are there to design them. The RBI has signalled in favour of setting up such a bank, but it has also highlighted the concern of 'designing it properly'.

There are different models of creating a bad bank. India needs to opt for the model which suits its needs - a bad bank which can serve two purposes, firstly, putting away the loads of the NPAs from the balance sheet of banks (so that they can *technically* be fit to lend again) and secondly, infusing fresh capital into them (to make them *really* start lending). This model has been most used by the countries across the world - during the South-East Asian crisis (1996-97) as well as in the United States - when the Government of the countries did set up bad banks under their ownership. Such a move served both of the purposes. The advice (of the *Economic Survey 2016-17*) to set up a public sector rehabilitation agency (PARA) falls under this category.

Since 2017-18, the Government had been hinting at the idea of the bad bank, but the final decision to set it up was still awaited. Following the announcement made in the *Union Budget 2021-22,* the Government took initiative in this direction by setting up the NARCL (National Asset Reconstruction Company Ltd.) in September 2021 (51 per cent owned by the Government of India) to take over the bad assets of the banks. Along with it, the IDRCL (Infrastructure Debt Resolution Company Limited) has also been set up (51 per cent owned by the private sector) to *manage the assets* undertaken by it. The latter will work as a service and operational body by engaging market professionals and turnaround experts.

Conclusion

Majority of the experts believe that the experiment of the NARCL and IDRCL may be successful in making the banks come out of the menace of NPAs but at a high cost as the ARCs are supposed to ask for high discounts for the bad assets of banks as occurred in the case of the insolvency and bankruptcy law where high haircuts have been seen to leverage a bank out of the defaulted loans.

PREPARING HEALTH CARE FOR THE FUTURE

Introduction

The ongoing COVID-19 pandemic has emphasised the importance of the healthcare sectors and their inter-linkages with other key sectors of the economy, showcasing how a healthcare crisis can get transformed into an economic and social crisis. A line from Mahatma Gandhi - *it is health that is real wealth and not pieces of gold and silver* - seems to depict enough wisdom for the world in this regard.

Lessons from the Hard Times

The pandemic has put countries like India in a state of complete dilemma. While the wretchedness of the countries with one of the highest investments in health care was a cause of fear and scale of investments they need, the support system of their available health infrastructure also gave them some ray of hope. India has been no exception to this dilemma. Though India's health care has shown resiliency in these hard times, this should not be forgotten once the pandemic subsides.

The pandemic has helped showcase the role of technology-enabled platforms as an alternate distribution channel for remote delivery of healthcare services. These technology-enabled platforms offer a promising new avenue to address India's last-mile healthcare access and delivery challenges. These platforms, coupled with digitisation and the promise of artificial intelligence at scale, have led to a drastic uptake in the utilisation of *telemedicine* for primary care and mental health.

Telemedicine depends crucially on internet connectivity and health infrastructure. Therefore, both central and state governments need to invest in telemedicine on a mission mode to complement the government's digital health mission and thereby enable greater access to the masses. The National Health Mission (NHM) has played a critical role in mitigating inequity in healthcare access. Therefore, in conjunction with *Ayushman Bharat*, the emphasis on NHM should continue.

Outline for Future

A country like India needs to prioritise its policy focus and resource deployment very carefully not only to fight the current pandemic but also to prepare itself for the health crises of the future. In this regard, the following areas require attention:

- **Financial Impact:** From a financial perspective, India has one of the highest levels of OOPEs (out-of-pocket expenditures) in the world (65 per cent), which directly contributes to the high incidence of catastrophic expenditures and poverty. A negative correlation exists between the level of public expenditure on health and OOPE. Even a small increase in public expenditure on health can have high impact on OOPE - as per the estimates of the *Economic Survey 2020-21*, an increase from 1 per cent to 2.5-3 per cent of GDP (as envisaged in the National Health Policy-2017) can decrease the OOPE from 65 per cent to 30 per cent.
- **Information Asymmetry:** As a bulk of health care in India is provided by the private sector, it is critical for policymakers to mitigate information asymmetry in health care, which creates market failures and thereby renders unregulated private health care sub-optimal. The newly launched National Digital Health Mission can be utilised with the aid of artificial intelligence and machine learning algorithms to mitigate information asymmetry with respect to the patients. A standardised system for quality reporting on health care for hospitals, physicians and insurance companies can start with basic input indicators to be reported mandatorily by every healthcare stakeholder.

  Over time, this can evolve to cover *output* and *outcome* indicators such as infection rates and re-admission rates. A start has been made in this direction by the Niti Aayog through the Health Index at the state level.
- **Insurance Infrastructure:** With limited visibility into patients' medical records and no standardised treatment protocols, insurance

companies have a risk of 'adverse selection' at the time of policy issuance and a risk of 'moral hazard' at the time of claims. To safeguard against this risk, insurance companies ask for higher premiums and place restrictions on insurance coverage in the insurance policy. Addressing this information asymmetry can help lower premiums, enable the offering of better products and help increase the insurance penetration in the country.

- **Regulator:** Finally, a sectoral *regulator* to undertake regulation and supervision of the healthcare sector must be seriously considered. This is especially pertinent as regulation has grown in importance as a key lever for governments to affect the quantity, quality, safety and distribution of services in health systems.

Conclusion

Considering the significance of the healthcare system in striving to achieve the sustainable development goals of universal healthcare coverage, India needs to take steps not only to improve healthcare accessibility but also its affordability.

REFORMING INDIA'S PUBLIC DEBT MANAGEMENT

Introduction

Modern economies depend on loans in a big way for meeting various needs and responsibilities. In the post-war period, the Governments' dependence on loans has also increased many times on account of various reasons such as welfare measures, growth promotion, defence etc. One such category of loan is known as the public debt (which is also called the government debt), which, in the case of India, is all debts created by the Government of India - short term, long term, internal or external. Public debt leaves a deep impact on the economy. That is why experts and policymakers scrutinise the issues such as its size, interest rate, independence of the body managing it and so on.

The Case with India

The issue of public debt management has been debated by experts since the Union Budget 2015-16 first proposed to set up a public debt management agency implying that this responsibility will shift away from the RBI. The debate mainly revolves around the degree of independence such an agency will be given in this regard. It also touches upon the contentious issues related to the arrangement of it.

In 2019-20, the issue of having an independent debt management agency 'outside the preview' of the RBI was again voiced by the policy think tank, the NITI Aayog, which said that it was *an idea whose time has come.* Majority of the experts find strong logic in such a proposal which can be understood by going into *four major roles* which the RBI plays today:

1. At present, public debt is managed by the RBI.
2. Government's market borrowings are also managed by the RBI.
3. Announcing the monetary policy already remains among the chief functions of the RBI as the country's Central bank.
4. Under open market operations, the RBI trades in Government bonds (such as treasury bills, cash management bill and G-Secs).

Given the roles which the RBI plays today, we find a clear case of 'conflict of interest'. While on one hand it decides the key policy/interest rates (such as repo rate, reverse repo rate, term repo rate, standing deposit facility rate, marginal standing facility rate and bank rate) as a central bank, on the other hand it also trades in government bonds (interest rates of which are influenced by the policy rates set by the RBI itself). Such contradictions have created practical problems for India's financial market in particular and economic development in general, in the following ways:

Scan this QR Code to watch a author's video lecture that simplifies this topic

- We find a lack of alignment between India's domestic bond market (which depends on interest rates which are set by the RBI) and the external bond market/external commercial borrowings (which is linked to global variables).
- India has seen a rise in its external commercial borrowings in the past few years primarily due to interest rates in the global market being much lower than in India. This discrepancy looks awkward in today's times when the global financial market is converging.

The economic potential of India remains untapped due to a dearth of investible funds. That is why India started liberalising the rules of foreign investments. More so, the potential cannot be tapped till enough investment is not mobilised for the development of requisite infrastructure base. In this case, governments have always agreed with experts' opinion which favoured deepening of India's bond market. But practically, it does not seem possible till the RBI has a hold on it - which is directly linked to its other responsibility, the monetary policy. So, it looks kind of a vicious cycle - the RBI borrowing at the interest rates set by the RBI!

As policy rates leave an impact on every penny anybody mobilises right from individuals to corporates to governments, its ramifications and overall impact on the economy and its financial relations with global economy out there may be just imagined.

Conclusion

Majority of the experts believe that once the debt management office is separated from the RBI, the Government will be able to pay much more attention to the aspect of debt - by having an eye on the changing needs of fund over the time. It will help the Government to also cut the cost of fund. Though the RBI is believed to have shown reluctance to part with its role of Government debt manager, still such a step from the Government is expected anytime given the increased emphasis we see on self-reliance (under the *Atmanirbhar* campaign) and an aspiration to replace China as the global production hub - all of which depend on requisite availability of funds.

MONETISATION OF PUBLIC ASSETS – THE SIGNIFICANCE

Introduction

Public assets, in simple terms, are all the assets which are owned by the governments (centre, states and the local bodies) raised out of their capital expenditures. Some of them are the central public sector enterprises (CPSEs) and public sector enterprises (PSUs) owned[1] by the Central Government of India. Once the process of economic reforms commenced in the early 1990s, the Government has taken several steps to orient them towards efficiency and profit - one recent step being their monetisation.

[1] To understand the CPSEs and PSUs in detail, refer *Chapter 10* of the book.

Comprehensive Management

We find a paradigm shift in the Government's approach towards public assets in 2016 when the 'mandate' of the existing Department of Disinvestment (DoD) was changed from managing disinvestment to 'comprehensive management of the Governments investment in the public assets' (CMPA) with a subsequent change in its name to the Department of Investment and Public Asset Management (DIPAM). In brief, the CMPA involves the following four steps to be taken with respect to the CPSEs:

1. Achieving optimum return and accelerating growth.
2. Leveraging assets by capital and financial restructuring.
3. Improving investors' confidence through capital market exposure.
4. Rationalising the decision-making process for efficient management.

Asset Monetisation

One of the actions under the CMPA is 'monetising' these assets. Under it, the Government decided to hand over some of the existing national highways to private bidders (to earn revenues out of their operation) on a *toll-operate-transfer* (TOT) basis. Under the TOT model, stretches of national highway are to be bided out to private players. The private players (infrastructure developers, private equity and institutional investors like pension and wealth funds) operate, maintain and collect toll on the stretches of roads during the concession period (15-30 years).

The model has been designed to create an opportunity for the private sector to invest in *low-risk assets* and at the same time provide for efficient operations and maintenance of highways, which has broadly two benefits:

1. Plugging the leakages and enhancing transparency in the Government toll collection system, and
2. Helping the Government to securitise the assets and obtain fresh cash for creating new assets.

The TOT model has also been tried by other countries such as the United States, Puerto Rico and Malaysia, with varying degrees of success. In the case of India, certain hurdles have been faced as the country lacks a strong line of contactors with experience in such business pursuits. Bidders also show lack of interest as private road operators have not been able to generate profitable revenues from roads since 2010.

The Significance

The policy of monetising public assets is a very significant move by the Government which will leave a lasting impact on the ongoing process of economic reforms and accelerating the process of development in the country in many ways:

- **Providing a Level Playing Field:** The existence of many non-toll roads operated by the NHAI and states has been discouraging the private operators to invest in the road infrastructure. In this way, this move is an integral part of the 'factor market' reforms which were initiated under the second[2] generation of the economic reforms in 2000 which aimed at orienting economic activities towards market mechanism (by dismantling the regime of subsidies).
- **Boosting Economic Viability:** Roads have not been doing well on the front of toll collections due to several reasons for the last decade or so, and a large part of loans forwarded to the sector turned into non-performing assets of the PSBs. The move of monetising some of the roads will help these assets become economically viable.
- **Attracting Foreign Investment:** The road sector has not been able to attract foreign investment even after offering very liberal policy framework-lack of a 'business model' in the sector cited as a prominent reason for this. Such a business model is being expected from the TOT model.
- **Attempting to Operate Public Assets on Business Line:** Public assets never received attention from the Government as wealth builders or generators of income; however, some of the assets have been generating good revenues. In a recent policy shift, the Government has started seeing these assets as 'engines of growth' and 'sources of revenue' generation.
- **Strengthening Inclusive Growth:** This process will add wealth to the masses (through listing of these assets on stock exchanges) as well as generate fresh revenues which can be used for furthering the goal of inclusive growth.

Conclusion

Monetisation of public assets seems like the Government opting to conduct business, but this is not the case as neither every public asset can be run on a profit line nor can the Government afford relinquishing its role of promoting welfare. This should be a rebalancing act of the Government to optimise economic and social outcomes for the country.

[2] For more details on the *Generations of Economic Reforms* in the country, see Chapter 7.

THE CIRCULARITY OF ECONOMY

Introduction

The policy think tank of India, the *NITI Aayog*, proposed (2019-20) to adopt the idea of circular economy in the country by emphasising the need for sustainable development and resource circularity as the need of the hour. For the Aayog, it implies reusing waste back into the production cycle to produce new products and uses instead of wasting such materials with embedded resources.

As per the Aayog, by 2050, the world population would reach 9.7 billion of which 3 billion people would prosper to middle class consumption level. This would require 71 per cent more resources per capita, thereby raising total mineral and material demand from 50 billion tons in 2014 to 130 billion tons in 2050.

The Hypothesis

The idea of circular economy is originally based on 'steady-state economy' which is itself rooted in ecological economics. Steady-state economy suggests the use of materials and energy in such a way that they are held constant. Today, the idea of circular economy is applied by a diverse group of researchers and professionals emphasising different aspects of it. Therefore, it has several definitions which make it difficult to measure. However, most of its definitions focus on the 'use of resources' or 'system change'. The resource use view follows the *3-R approach* - Reduce (minimum use of raw materials); Reuse (maximum reuse of products and components); and Recycle (high-quality reuse of raw materials).

A circular economy tries to follow the example of an ecosystem. In it, there is nothing like *waste* because every residual item can be used to make a new product (but after eliminating the toxic substances), such as producers taking back their products after use and repairing them for a new useful life. This way, only recycling is not its part, rather assuring quality is also taken care of.

Vis-à-Vis the Traditional Approach

The idea of circularity is opposite to the 'linear' (or growth) economy. While the origins of the circular economy concept are to be found in 1960s environmentalism, it evolved under the influence of ecology and cybernetics which shaped the public environmental discourse of the period. The economy draws attention to the background of the present 'linear economy' in post-war policies that encouraged reconstruction and a social and economic democratisation across the West, including an expansion of 'mass-consumption'. The view of circularity emphasises the role of 1960s counterculture in generating a popular reaction against this expansionary growth-based agenda, and its influence in shaping subsequent environmentalism, including the 'metabolic' and ecological economic understanding of the environmental crisis.

Conclusion

To ensure that the material needs of humanity are supplied with, it is high time the world moved towards circularity of the economy. Several corporates have taken steps towards it, but they can be called just baby steps - an integrated effort, combining the forces of government and non-government entities, is required in this regard.

FULFILLING THE MINIMUM NEEDS OF CITIZENS

Introduction

Given the rampant poverty in the country, the governments have always been careful about provisioning of meeting the 'minimum needs' (i.e., the essential goods and services) of citizens. Today, the very ability of someone to access these needs (such as housing, water, sanitation, electricity and clean cooking fuel) is regarded as an important barometer of economic development in academic and policymaking circles.

Basic Needs Approach to Development

Some of the renowned economists of the world have tried to define development in terms of 'basic needs'. This approach to development places emphasis on the 'minimum' specified quantities of *necessities* such as food, clothing, shelter, water and sanitation that are necessary to prevent ill health and undernourishment (Paul Streeten, 1981; Louis Emmery, 2010) and defines poverty as a failure to achieve certain minimum *basic needs* or *capacities* (Amartya Sen, 1999). Taking inspiration from this approach, the Government developed a bare necessities index (BNI) in 2020-21 to measure the achievements in this regard (the index has been used by the *Economic Survey 2020-21).*

Progress in Provision of Minimum Needs

The BNI has prepared sourcing data from two NSO Rounds on the *drinking water, sanitation, hygiene* and *housing* condition in India - 69th (2012) and 76th (2018). Similarly, the data on the indicator 'household using *LPG for cooking*' for 2011-12 have been taken from the NSO Report on Energy Sources of Indian Households for Cooking and Lighting 2011-12. The index (comparing two different points, 2012 and 2018) presents the following picture regarding provisioning of the bare necessities (i.e., basic needs, minimum needs):

- Compared to 2012, access has improved across all states in the country in 2018 (the highest being in Kerala, Punjab, Haryana and Gujarat, and the lowest in Odisha, Jharkhand, West Bengal and Tripura).
- Improvements have been widespread for all five dimensions (water, housing, sanitation, micro-environment and other facilities).
- Inter-state disparities have declined in 2018 compared to 2012 across rural and urban areas, but they still exist.
- Improvement has been seen disproportionately more for the poorest households in comparison to the richest households across rural and urban areas. The improvement in equity is particularly noteworthy because while the rich can seek private alternatives, lobby for better services or if need be, move to areas where public goods are better provided for, the poor rarely have such choices.
- Improved access to these necessities has improved health and education.

As the needs of housing, water, sanitation, electricity and clean cooking fuel are jointly consumed by all the members of a household, these, thus, touch the life of every member in the household. As these are durable assets, they deliver services to the household over long periods of time.

Focused Efforts Improving access to these necessities has remained among the prime aims of the successive governments in the country. The ongoing schemes designed to deliver these necessities include the Swachh Bharat Mission (SBM), National Rural Drinking Water Programme (NRDWP), Pradhan Mantri Awaas Yojana (PMAY), Saubhagya and Ujjwala Yojana. As these schemes have been equipped with some *new features* (such as use of technology, real-time monitoring, geo-tagging of assets, social audit, embedded digital flow of information and direct benefit transfers wherever possible), a clear improvement has been seen in their efficiency, effectiveness and governance.

Deepening of the Idea The Government should target the population in need of these minimum needs across the country and prioritise them - in rural as well as urban areas. As civic amenities in urban areas are provided by the local self-governments, there is a need of convergence in implementation of schemes at centre-state and local levels. To assess the progress in enabling people access these necessities at local levels, a dedicated index can be developed at district level using suitable indicators and methodology.

Conclusion

Putting focus on the accessibility of minimum needs will not only improve the general well-being of the masses but also strengthen the broader goal of inclusive growth in the country. Experts believe that a focused approach and use of the networks of schemes will enable India to achieve the SDG goals of reducing poverty and improving access to drinking water, sanitation and housing by 2030.

REGULATING CRYPTO ECOSYSTEM

Introduction

Recent years have seen the rise of cryptocurrencies across the world. Investors reaping high profits out of them have also been reported in the contemporary media. Though financial regulators of most of the countries have shown their apprehensions and reservations about them, the recent collapse of the crypto exchange FTX and the ensuing sell-off in the crypto markets have placed a spotlight on the vulnerabilities in the crypto ecosystem. This way, an increasing need of regulating the crypto assets became a burning global issue.

Crypto assets (cryptocurrencies being the main newsmakers) are new forms of digital assets based on cryptographic techniques (i.e., blockchain technology). These assets are *self-referential* instruments and do not strictly pass the test of being a financial asset because they have no intrinsic cashflows attached to them. The crypto asset market has been very volatile, with its total valuation swinging from almost US$ 3 trillion in November 2021 to less than US$ 1 trillion in *January 2023* (as per the *Economic Survey 2022-23*).

Need of Regulation

The volatility of the crypto asset ecosystem has brought to the forefront several concerns related to their fragile backing and governance, and non-transparency. With related financial stability risks rising, the issue of crypto asset regulation has recently moved up the policy agenda of many nations. Their geographically pervasive nature necessitates a common approach of their regulation. International fora like *OECD* and *G20* are discussing a 'globally coordinated approach' to regulating crypto assets. In this context, right now, the global response to cryptos is evolving. A brief summary is presented below.

Regulatory Challenges

Monitoring and regulating cryptocurrencies have been tricky, and regulators across the globe find it challenging to keep track of the new and emerging issues in the fast-moving uncharted field.

- While crypto assets were apparently designed to 'disintermediate' traditional financial services, this has created new unregulated intermediating entities. Their promise of decentralisation has also yet to be realised in practice. New centralised intermediaries, such as crypto asset exchanges, wallet providers, and crypto conglomerates, require users to trust centralised entities. The increasing importance of these entities could force regulators to consider them as systemic financial market infrastructures (FMIs). Still, the fact that they are yet largely unregulated is a cause for concern globally.
- There are minimal global standards applicable to unbacked crypto assets, which do not currently mitigate all risks and vulnerabilities. Even as Standard-Setting Bodies (SSBs) have been making efforts to adjust and develop standards, these remain mainly focused on specific issues (financial integrity), sectors (payments, securities, and banking), products (global stablecoins), or entities designated as systemic by domestic authorities.
- There are regulatory gaps at each stage when crypto assets are issued, transferred, exchanged, or stored by non-bank entities.
- Crypto's cross-sector and cross-border nature limits the effectiveness of uncoordinated national approaches.
- The terminology used to describe the different activities, products, and stakeholders is not globally harmonised. The term "crypto asset" itself refers

Word Bank

Financial Market Infrastructure (FMI)[3]

As per BIS (Bank of International Settlements), Financial Market Infrastructure (FMI) is defined as a multilateral system among participating institutions, including the operator of the system, used for the purposes of clearing, settling, or recording payments, securities, derivatives, or other financial transactions.

to a broad spectrum of digital products that may need the attention of multiple domestic regulators based on their actual or intended use.

- There is a range of crypto actors - miners, validators, and protocol developers - that may not be easily covered by traditional financial regulation.

Global Efforts of Regulation

Countries of the world, along with their financial regulators, are presently busy evolving a proper framework to regulate crypto assets. Some of the efforts in this direction are being summarised below.

- The regulators in the *USA* have disqualified Bitcoin, Ether, and various other crypto assets as securities (in January 2023) which highlights their concerns.
- The *European Union's* digital finance strategy proposes onshoring, notification and licensing regimes for these assets.
- The *Japan* financial services agency (JFSA) introduced legislation in this regard in April 2017 itself by introducing actions like clients' asset segregation, operational risk and cyber security management, Know-Your-Customer, internal audits, and minimum capital requirements, etc. By June 2022, the country was aiming to establish a stable and efficient funds settlement system and to provide for the regulation of stablecoins.
- The *Swiss* Financial Market Supervisory Authority (FINMA) issued guidelines for initial coin offerings in February 2018 by introducing three categories of tokens - payment tokens, utility tokens, and asset tokens (with a clarification that tradable tokens at pre-financing and presale stage could be *treated as securities*).
- Following significant consumer research on the crypto asset market, the *UK* Treasury set out its roadmap for crypto asset regulation in April 2022, focusing on stablecoins and a proposal for a sandbox regime for blockchain-based FMIs. It proposed to bring crypto assets to the same high standards as for other financial promotions such as *stocks, shares, and insurance products*.
- The Monetary Authority of *Singapore* published guidelines to restrict the marketing of crypto assets in Singapore in January 2022, limiting crypto asset promotions to an entity's corporate website, official social media accounts, and mobile applications.

Conclusion

Though global efforts are being made, none of the policy provisions put in place by the national governments look foolproof. Given the diversity of challenges and concerns related to the crypto assets, it is getting too tough to devise a uniform and all-pervasive regulatory framework for these assets. Besides, going by the cross-border nature of these assets, a high degree of global cooperation and coordination is also required if global financial regulators wish to regulate these assets.

[3] *Economic Survey 2022-23* (New Delhi, Ministry of Finance, GoI, January 2023), p. 103.

PREVIOUS YEARS' QUESTIONS

Main

1. Explain how the Fiscal Health Index (FHI) can be used as a tool for assessing the fiscal performance of states in India. In what way would it encourage the states to adopt prudent and sustainable fiscal policies? (2025)

SAMPLE MODEL ANSWER

1. 'Cities of India are engines of growth, magnets of talents, and crucibles of innovation, the task is now to make urbanisation work better for citizens.'

Ans. Cities of India are engines of growth, magnets for talent, and crucibles of innovation; there is no doubt in it. At the same time, they are sites of *daily strain* clearly visible in long commutes, uneven services, and shared spaces often falling short of expectations. It means India's urban story is of an *unfinished promise*, as per the Economic Survey 2025-26.

In a real sense, cities are not merely habitats rather, they are a form of critical economic infrastructure. Density and proximity power productivity, deepen labour markets, and enable learning. Yet the same forces that create dynamism also generate congestion, environmental stress, and institutional complexity. India is already deeply urban in economic terms, with most of its national output generated in cities and in urban areas. The task now is to make urbanisation work better for citizens–in tangible and intangible ways. India's cities face myriads of challenges, such as:

- Persistent supply-side constraints in land, housing, and mobility.
- Restricted density, unclear titles, and limited land recycling constrain affordable housing.
- Transport systems remain overly reliant on private vehicles.
- Core services (such as sanitation, waste, and water services) have expanded markedly but must now evolve from expansion to reliability, circularity, and efficiency.

Beyond infrastructure, there is a need to improve the *intangible* foundations of urban life, such as civic norms, shared responsibility, and respect for public spaces.

The quality of urban life depends as much on collective behaviour as on budgets and physical infrastructure. In this regard, strengthening civic consciousness, alongside better institutions, is essential to create cities that feel not only efficient but also welcoming.

Economic Survey 2025-26

In This Section...

- State of the Economy
- Fiscal Developments: Anchoring Stability Through Credible Consolidation
- Monetary Management and Financial Intermediation: Refining the Regulatory Touch
- External Sector: Playing the Long Game
- Inflation: Tamed and Anchored
- Agriculture and Food Management
- Services: From Stability to New Frontiers
- Industry's Next Leap: Structural Transformation and Global Integration
- Investment and Infrastructure: Strengthening Connectivity, Capacity, and Competitiveness
- Environment and Climate Change: Building a Resilient, Competitive, and Development-Driven India
- Education and Health: What Works and What's Next
- Employment and Skill Development: Getting Skilling Right
- Rural Development and Social Progress: From Participation to Partnerships
- Evolution of the Ai Ecosystem in India: The Way Forward
- Urbanisation: Making India's Cities Work for Its Citizens
- From Import Substitution to Strategic Resilience and Strategic Indispensability

The ***Economic Survey 2025-26*** was tabled by the Union Minister for Finance and Corporate Affairs, Smt. Nirmala Sitharaman, in Parliament on 29th January 2026. The **highlights** of the Economic Survey are as follows:

STATE OF THE ECONOMY

1. The global environment remains fragile, with growth holding up better than expected but risks elevated amid intensifying geopolitical tensions, trade fragmentation, and financial vulnerabilities. The impact of these shocks may still surface with a lag.
2. Against this backdrop, India's performance stands out. The First Advance Estimates place FY26 real GDP growth at 7.4 per cent and GVA growth at 7.3 per cent, reaffirming India's status as the fastest-growing major economy for the fourth consecutive year.
3. Private Final Consumption Expenditure grew by 7.0 per cent in FY26, reaching 61.5 per cent of GDP, the highest since 2012 (FY23 also recorded a 61.5 per cent share). This growth is supported by low inflation, stable employment, and increasing real purchasing power. Strong agricultural performance has bolstered rural consumption, while improvements in urban consumption, aided by tax rationalisation, indicate broad-based demand momentum.
4. Investment activity strengthened in FY26, with Gross Fixed Capital Formation growing by 7.8 per cent and its share remaining steady at 30 per cent of GDP. This momentum was buoyed by sustained public capital expenditure and a revival in private investment activity, as evident from corporate announcements.
5. On the supply side, services remain the main driver of growth. In the first half of FY26, the Gross Value Added (GVA) for services increased

by 9.3 per cent, with an estimated 9.1 per cent growth for the entire fiscal year. This trend indicates a broad-based expansion across the sector.

FISCAL DEVELOPMENTS: ANCHORING STABILITY THROUGH CREDIBLE CONSOLIDATION

1. The government's prudent fiscal management has strengthened credibility and reinforced confidence in India's macroeconomic and fiscal framework. This led to three sovereign credit rating upgrades in 2025 - by Morningstar DBRS, S&P Global Ratings, and Rating and Investment Information (R&I), Inc.
2. The Centre's revenue receipts strengthened from an average of about 8.5 per cent of GDP in FY16-FY20 to 9.2 per cent of GDP in FY25 (PA). This improvement was driven by buoyant non-corporate tax collections, which rose from about 2.4 per cent of GDP pre-pandemic to around 3.3 per cent post-pandemic.
3. The direct tax base expanded steadily, with income tax returns filed increasing from 6.9 crore in FY22 to 9.2 crore in FY25. Higher return filings reflect improved compliance, greater use of technology in tax administration, and a growing number of individuals entering the tax net as their incomes rise.
4. Gross GST collections during April-December 2025 stood at ₹17.4 lakh crore, registering a year-on-year growth of 6.7 per cent. GST revenue growth is broadly aligned with prevailing nominal GDP growth conditions. In parallel, high-frequency indicators suggest robust transaction volumes, with cumulative e-way bill volumes during April-December 2025 growing by 21 per cent year-on-year.
5. The effective capital expenditure of the Central government rose from an average of 2.7 per cent of GDP in the pre-pandemic period to about 3.9 per cent post-pandemic and to a higher 4 per cent of GDP in FY25.
6. Through Special Assistance to States for Capital Investment (SASCI), the Centre has incentivised States to maintain capital spending at around 2.4 per cent of GDP in FY25.
7. The combined fiscal deficit of State governments stayed broadly stable at around 2.8 per cent of GDP in the post-pandemic period, like pre-pandemic levels, but has edged up in recent years to 3.2 per cent in FY25, reflecting emerging pressures on State finances.
8. India reduced its general government debt-to-GDP ratio by about 7.1 percentage points since 2020, even while maintaining high public investment.

MONETARY MANAGEMENT AND FINANCIAL INTERMEDIATION: REFINING THE REGULATORY TOUCH

Monetary Aspects

1. India's monetary and financial sectors have exhibited robust performance in FY26 (April-December 2025), underpinned by strategic policy actions and structural resilience across financial intermediation channels.

Banking Sector Performance

2. A significant improvement has been observed in the asset quality of scheduled commercial banks (SCBs), as evidenced by their GNPA ratio standing at 2.2 per cent in September 2025 and net NPA ratio at 0.5 per cent in September 2025, having reached a multi-decadal low level and record low level, respectively.
3. As of 31 December 2025, the year-on-year growth in outstanding credit by SCBs increased to 14.5 per cent compared to 11.2 per cent in December 2024.

Financial Inclusion

4. The Pradhan Mantri Jan Dhan Yojana (PMJDY), launched in 2014, has opened 55.02 crore accounts as of March 2025, with 36.63 crore in rural and semi-urban areas, establishing foundational savings and transaction infrastructure for previously unbanked populations.
5. The Stand-Up India Scheme offers bank loans ranging from ₹10 lakh to ₹1 crore to SC, ST, and women entrepreneurs for establishing greenfield enterprises.

6. The PM Street Vendor's AtmaNirbhar Nidhi (PM SVANidhi) scheme is providing collateral-free working capital loans to street vendors.
7. The Pradhan Mantri Mudra Yojana (PMMY) is financing micro and small enterprises in manufacturing, trading, services, and allied agricultural activities. By October 2025, the scheme had disbursed over ₹36.18 lakh crore across 55.45 crore loan accounts.

Other Aspects of the Financial Sector

8. During FY26 (till December 2025), 235 lakhs of demat accounts were added, pushing the total count beyond 21.6 crore. A key milestone was the crossing of the 12-crore mark for unique investors in September 2025, with nearly a fourth of them being women.
9. The mutual fund industry also expanded, with 5.9 crore unique investors as of the end of December 2025, of which 3.5 crore (as of November 2025) were from non-tier-I and tier-II cities, underscoring the diffusion of financial participation beyond traditional urban centres.
10. India's first international financial services centre at GIFT City is creating an enabling ecosystem to attract and channel global capital.

Outlook for the Sector

11. The systemic rise in regulatory quality has received international validation through the Financial Sector Assessment Program (FSAP) conducted jointly by the IMF and World Bank in 2025. Both reports noted an increasingly resilient, diversified, and inclusive financial system, with total financial sector assets at nearly 187 per cent of GDP in CY 2024 and capital markets expanding from 144 per cent of GDP in CY 2017 to 175 per cent in CY 2024. The assessments found that banks and NBFCs possess adequate capital buffers even under severe stress scenarios.

Main Points of the Survey

- First advance estimate projects real GDP growth and GVA growth for the financial year (FY) 2025–26 to be 7.4 per cent and 7.3 per cent, respectively.
- Potential growth for India is estimated at around 7 per cent, while real GDP growth for the financial year 2026–27 is projected at 6.8 per cent–7.2 per cent.
- Centre's revenue receipts rose to 9.2 per cent of GDP in the financial year 2024–25.
- Gross NPAs reach a multi-decadal low of 2.2 per cent in September 2025.
- 55.02 crore bank accounts opened as of March 2025 under PMJDY, with 36.63 crore in rural and semi-urban areas.
- Number of unique investors crosses the 12-crore mark in September 2025, with nearly 25 per cent being women.
- India's share of global merchandise exports nearly doubles from 1 per cent to 1.8 per cent between 2005 and 2024.
- Services exports touch an all-time high of US$ 387.6 billion in FY25, growing by 13.6 per cent.
- India remains the *world's largest recipient* of remittances, with inflows reaching US$ 135.4 billion in the financial year 2024–25.
- India's *foreign exchange reserves* increase to $ 701.4 billion as of 16th January 2026, providing cover for 11 months of imports and 94 per cent of external debt.
- Domestic inflation averaged 1.7 per cent for April–December, 2025.
- India's foodgrain production is estimated to have reached 3577.3 lakh metric tonnes (LMT) in agriculture year (AY) 2024–25, an increase of 254.3 LMT over the previous year.
- More than ₹4.09 lakh crore has been released to eligible farmers under PM-KISAN since its inception.
- Viksit Bharat-Gram-G is a comprehensive statutory overhaul of MGNREGS, aligning rural employment with the long-term vision of Viksit Bharat 2047.
- Manufacturing GVA grew by 7.72 per cent in the 1st quarter and 9.13 per cent in the 2nd quarter of the financial year 2025–26, reflecting structural recovery.
- Production-linked incentive (PLI) schemes across 14 sectors have attracted over ₹2.0 lakh crore

of actual investment, generating incremental production/sales exceeding ₹18.7 lakh crore and over 12.6 lakh jobs as of September 2025.

- India's semiconductor mission has advanced domestic capabilities, with 10 projects of about ₹1.60 lakh crore of investment.
- High-speed corridors increase nearly ten-fold, from 550 km (FY14) to 5,364 km (FY26, up to December 2025); 3,500 km of railway added in the financial year 2025–26.
- India is the world's *3rd largest* domestic aviation market, with the number of airports increasing from 74 in 2014 to 164 in 2025.
- Historic turnaround for *discoms;* recording a positive PAT of ₹2,701 crore in FY25 for the first time.
- India ranks *3rd globally* in overall renewable energy and installed solar capacity.
- India becomes the *fourth* nation to achieve autonomous satellite docking (SpaDeX) capability.
- Gross enrolment ratio (GER) stands at 90.9, 90.3, and 78.7 at the primary, upper primary, and secondary stages, respectively.
- India now has 23 IITs, 21 IIMs, and 20 AIIMs, alongside the establishment of 2 international IIT campuses in Zanzibar and Abu Dhabi.
- India accelerated maternal and child mortality reduction since 1990, outpacing global averages.
- As of January 2026, the *e-shram portal* has successfully registered over 31 crore unorganised workers, 54 per cent being women.
- Vacancies mobilised in the national career service portal exceeded 2.8 crore in FY25 and have already crossed 2.3 crore by September 2025.
- Multidimensional poverty index (MPI) as measured by Niti Ayog shows a decline from 55.3 per cent in 2005–06 to 11.28 per cent in 2022–23.
- The survey proposes disciplined *swadeshi* for strategic resilience: a calibrated three-tiered strategy that builds critical capabilities, reduces input costs, strengthens advanced manufacturing, and progresses from self-reliance to strategic indispensability.

EXTERNAL SECTOR: PLAYING THE LONG GAME

1. Between CY 2005 and CY 2024, India's share of global merchandise exports nearly doubled from 1 per cent to 1.8 per cent, while its share of global commercial services exports more than doubled from 2 per cent to 4.3 per cent.
2. According to UNCTAD's Trade and Development Report 2025, India ranked among the leading economies in trade partner diversification, ranking third in the Global South and recording a trade diversity score higher than all Global North economies.
3. India's total exports reached a record US$ 825.3 billion in FY25, registering a 6.1 per cent year-on-year growth, driven primarily by robust growth in services exports.
4. Non-petroleum exports reached a historic high of US$ 374.3 billion in FY25, while non-petroleum, non-gems and jewellery exports constituted nearly four-fifths of aggregate merchandise exports.
5. Services exports touched an all-time high of US$ 387.6 billion in FY25, growing by 13.6 per cent, reinforcing India's position as a global hub for technology and business services.
6. India's current account deficit remained moderate, supported by strong net inflows from services exports and remittances that offset the merchandise trade deficit. In Q2 FY26, India's CAD, at around 1.3 per cent of GDP, compared favourably with several other major economies.
7. India remained the world's largest recipient of remittances, with inflows reaching US$ 135.4 billion in FY25, supporting stability in the external account. The share of remittances from advanced economies increased, reflecting a growing contribution from skilled and professional workers.
8. India's foreign exchange reserves increased to US$ 701.4 billion as of 16 January 2026, providing import cover of about 11 months and covering over 94 per cent of external debt, thereby strengthening resilience against external volatility.

9. Amid a subdued global investment environment, India continued to attract substantial foreign direct investment, with gross FDI inflows reaching US$ 64.7 billion during April-November 2025.
10. India ranked fourth globally in greenfield investment announcements in 2024, with over 1,000 projects, and emerged as the largest destination for greenfield digital investments between 2020 and 2024.

INFLATION: TAMED AND ANCHORED

1. India recorded the lowest inflation rate since the beginning of the CPI series, with April-December 2025 average headline inflation coming in at 1.7 per cent. The moderation in retail inflation can primarily be attributed to the general disinflationary trend in food and fuel prices, which together account for 52.7 per cent of India's Consumer Price Index (CPI) basket.
2. Notably, among major Emerging Markets & Developing Economies (EMDEs), India has recorded one of the sharpest declines in headline inflation in 2025 over 2024, amounting to about 1.8 percentage points.

AGRICULTURE AND FOOD MANAGEMENT

1. Between FY15 and FY24, the livestock sector witnessed strong growth, with GVA rising by nearly 195 per cent. The fisheries sector has also performed well, with fish production increasing by more than 140 per cent during 2014-2024, compared to the increase from 2004-14.
2. With a good monsoon season, India's foodgrain production is estimated to have reached 3,577.3 lakh metric tonnes (LMT) in Agriculture Year (AY) 2024-25, an increase of 254.3 LMT over the previous year. This growth has been driven by higher output of rice, wheat, maize, and coarse cereals (Shree Anna).
3. Despite rising foodgrain output, horticulture, accounting for about 33 per cent of agricultural GVA, has emerged as a key driver of agricultural growth. In 2024-25, horticulture production reached 362.08 million tonnes (MT), surpassing the estimated foodgrain production of 357.73 MT.
4. To improve efficiency in agricultural marketing and infrastructure, the Government is implementing the Agriculture Marketing Infrastructure (AMI) sub-scheme under ISAM and the Agriculture Infrastructure Fund (AIF) to strengthen farm-gate facilities and encourage private sector participation. Price discovery has been enhanced through the e-NAM Scheme, which, as of 31 December 2025, has onboarded about 1.79 crore farmers, 2.72 crore traders, and 4,698 FPOs, covering 1,522 mandis across 23 States and 4 UTs.
5. Farmers' incomes are supported through assured MSP for mandated crops and PM-KISAN income transfers. In addition, the PM Kisan Maandhan Yojana (PMKMY) provides pension support, strengthening farmers' income security and social protection. Since its inception, under PM-KISAN, more than ₹4.09 lakh crore has been released to eligible farmers in 21 instalments. Under PMKMY, 24.92 lakh farmers are enrolled as of 31 December 2025.

SERVICES: FROM STABILITY TO NEW FRONTIERS

1. Services' share in GDP rose to 53.6 per cent in H1 FY26; services' share in GVA stood at the highest ever - 56.4 per cent - as per FAE of FY26, which shows the rising weight of modern, tradable, and digitally delivered services.
2. India is the world's seventh-largest exporter of services, with its share in global services trade more than doubling from 2 per cent in 2005 to 4.3 per cent in 2024.
3. The services sector continues to be the largest recipient of foreign direct investment inflows, accounting for an average of 80.2 per cent of total FDI during FY23-FY25, up from 77.7 per cent in the pre-pandemic period (FY16-FY20).

INDUSTRY'S NEXT LEAP: STRUCTURAL TRANSFORMATION AND GLOBAL INTEGRATION

1. Industrial activity strengthened in FY26, with Industry GVA growing 7.0 per cent (real terms) in H1, despite subdued and persistent global headwinds.

2. Manufacturing growth accelerated, with GVA expanding 7.72 per cent in Q1 and 9.13 per cent in Q2 FY26, reflecting structural recovery.
3. Production Linked Incentive (PLI) Schemes across 14 sectors have attracted over ₹2.0 lakh crore of actual investment, generating incremental production/sales exceeding ₹18.7 lakh crore and over 12.6 lakh jobs as of September 2025.
4. India's innovation performance has strengthened steadily, with its Global Innovation Index rank improving to 38th in 2025 from 66th in 2019.
5. The India Semiconductor Mission has advanced domestic capabilities, with 10 semiconductor manufacturing and packaging projects approved across 6 States, involving about ₹1.60 lakh crore of investment.

INVESTMENT AND INFRASTRUCTURE: STRENGTHENING CONNECTIVITY, CAPACITY, AND COMPETITIVENESS

1. The Government of India's capital expenditure has increased nearly 4.2 times, from ₹2.63 lakh crore in FY18 to ₹11.21 lakh crore in FY26 (BE), while effective capital expenditure in FY26 (BE) is ₹15.48 lakh crore, positioning infrastructure as a key growth driver.
2. National highway infrastructure expanded substantially, with the NH network growing by about 60 per cent from 91,287 km (FY14) to 1,46,572 km (FY26, up to December), and operational High-Speed Corridors increasing nearly ten-fold - from 550 km (FY14) to 5,364 km (FY26, up to December).
3. Railway infrastructure continued to expand, with the rail network reaching 69,439 route km as of March 2025, a targeted addition of 3,500 km in FY26, and 99.1 per cent electrification achieved by October 2025.
4. India has emerged as the world's third-largest domestic aviation market, with the number of airports increasing from 74 in 2014 to 164 in 2025.
5. The power sector recorded sustained capacity expansion, with installed capacity rising 11.6 per cent (year-on-year) to 509.74 GW as of November 2025, and the demand-supply gap declined from 4.2 per cent in FY14 to nil by November 2025.
6. Power sector reforms delivered a historic turnaround, with DISCOMs recording a positive Profit after Tax (PAT) of ₹2,701 crore in FY25 for the first time, alongside a reduction in AT&C losses from 22.62 per cent (FY14) to 15.04 per cent (FY25). Renewable energy constitutes around 49.83 per cent of total power generation capacity as of November 2025, with India ranking third globally in overall RE and installed solar capacity.
7. Teledensity reached 86.76 per cent, and 5G services are now available in 99.9 per cent of districts in the country.
8. Over 81 per cent of rural households have access to clean tap water under the Jal Jeevan Mission, as of October 2025.
9. Space infrastructure strengthened, with India becoming the fourth nation to achieve autonomous satellite docking (SpaDeX), alongside expanded indigenous missions and increased private-sector participation.

ENVIRONMENT AND CLIMATE CHANGE: BUILDING A RESILIENT, COMPETITIVE, AND DEVELOPMENT-DRIVEN INDIA

1. During 2025-26 (up to 31st December 2025), a total of 38.61 GW of renewable energy capacity has been installed in the country, which includes 30.16 GW of solar power, 4.47 GW of wind power, 0.03 GW of bio-power, and 3.24 GW of hydropower.

EDUCATION AND HEALTH: WHAT WORKS AND WHAT'S NEXT

1. India today operates one of the world's largest school systems, serving 24.69 crore students across 14.71 lakh schools, supported by over 1.01 crore teachers (UDISE+ 2024-25).
2. India has made notable gains in school enrolment by strengthening infrastructure and teacher capacity, with schemes like Poshan Shakti Nirman and Samagra Shiksha Abhiyan promoting access and equity. Gross Enrolment

Ratios (GER) are 90.9 at the primary stage (Grades I to V), 90.3 at the upper primary (Grades VI to VIII), 78.7 at the secondary stage (Grades IX and X), and 58.4 at the higher secondary stage (Grades XI and XII).

Higher Education

3. The number of higher education institutions (HEIs) has increased from 51,534 in 2014-15 to 70,018 as of June 2025, significantly improving access. This increase is marked by substantial growth in universities and colleges. The number of premier higher education institutions (HEIs) has expanded significantly between 2014-15 and 2024-25. It now stands at 23 IITs, 21 IIMs, and 20 AIIMS, alongside the establishment of 2 international IIT campuses in Zanzibar and Abu Dhabi.
4. Under the NEP, the higher education system has undergone several reforms.
   - **(a)** The National Credit Framework (NCrF), which aims to blend academic and skills-based learning, has been adopted by 170 universities.
   - **(b)** The Academic Bank of Credit covers 2,660 institutions, with over 4.6 crore IDs issued, including the generation of 2.2 crore Automated Permanent Academic Account Registry (APAAR) IDs with credits.
   - **(c)** 153 universities have introduced flexible entry-exit pathways and biannual admissions to achieve the NEP target of 50 per cent GER by 2035.

Health

5. Since 1990, India has reduced its maternal mortality rate (MMR) by 86 per cent, far exceeding the global average of 48 per cent. A 78 per cent decline in the under-five mortality rate (U5MR) was achieved, surpassing the global reduction of 61 per cent, and a 70 per cent decline in the neonatal mortality rate (NMR) compared to 54 per cent globally during 1990-2023.
6. The infant mortality rate (IMR) marked a drop of more than 37 per cent over the past decade, declining from 40 deaths per thousand live births in 2013 to 25 in 2023.

EMPLOYMENT AND SKILL DEVELOPMENT: GETTING SKILLING RIGHT

1. A total of 56.2 crore people (aged 15 years and above) were employed in Q2 FY26, reflecting the creation of around 8.7 lakh new jobs in Q2 compared to Q1 of FY26.
2. The Annual Survey of Industries (ASI), which covers the organised manufacturing sector, results for FY24 highlight the manufacturing sector's resilience, showing a 6 per cent year-on-year increase in employment over the previous year. This translates to an addition of over 10 lakh jobs in FY24 compared to FY23.
3. The Labour Codes have formally recognised gig and platform workers, expanding social security, welfare funds, and benefit portability.
4. As of January 2026, the e-Shram portal has successfully registered over 31 crore unorganised workers; women account for over 54 per cent of total registrants, substantially strengthening the reach of gender-focused welfare schemes.
5. The National Career Service (NCS) is a one-stop solution connecting job seekers, employers, and training providers with over 59 million registered job seekers and 5.3 million job providers across diverse sectors and mobilising approximately 80 million vacancies.

Skill Ecosystem

6. The National Scheme for Upgradation of ITIs proposes to upgrade 1,000 government ITIs, including 200 hub ITIs and 800 spoke ITIs, through smart classrooms, modern labs, digital content, and industry-aligned long- and short-term courses.

RURAL DEVELOPMENT AND SOCIAL PROGRESS: FROM PARTICIPATION TO PARTNERSHIPS

1. The World Bank has raised the poverty line from US$ 2.15 to US$ 3.00 a day, adjusted for the purchasing power of money to 2021 prices. According to the revised IPL, India's poverty rates in 2022-23 were 5.3 per cent for extreme

poverty and 23.9 per cent for lower-middle-income poverty.

2. The general government's social services expenditure (SSE) has shown a rising trend since FY22.
3. The SSE stands at 7.9 per cent of GDP in FY 2025-26 (BE) against 7.7 per cent in 2024-25 (RE) and 7 per cent in 2023-24.

Health of the Rural Economy

4. As of December 2025, the drone survey under SVAMITVA has been completed in 3.28 lakh villages, against a target of nearly 3.44 lakh villages notified for drone survey. 2.76 crore property cards have been prepared for nearly 1.82 lakh villages. Lead fertiliser companies distributed 1,094 drones to SHG Drone Didis in 2023-24 using their own resources, with 500 of these drones provided under the Namo Drone Didi Scheme.

EVOLUTION OF THE AI ECOSYSTEM IN INDIA: THE WAY FORWARD

Smaller, task-specific models deployed across sectors allow innovation to diffuse more evenly, reduce entry barriers for firms, and better fit the diversity of India's economic landscape. India's demand for AI is emerging from real-world problems rather than speculative frontier uses. Across healthcare, agriculture, urban management, education, disaster preparedness, and public administration, there is a growing appetite for AI systems that work on local hardware and operate in low-resource settings.

URBANISATION: MAKING INDIA'S CITIES WORK FOR ITS CITIZENS

The Namo Bharat Regional Rapid Transit System illustrates how high-speed regional connectivity can reshape urban and peri-urban labour markets. By sharply reducing travel times between cities and their surrounding regions, such systems expand access to jobs, support polycentric growth, and ease pressure on core metropolitan areas.

FROM IMPORT SUBSTITUTION TO STRATEGIC RESILIENCE AND STRATEGIC INDISPENSABILITY

1. 'Swadeshi' must be a disciplined strategy, as not all import substitution is either feasible or desirable; a disciplined approach to indigenisation is presented through a three-tiered framework that distinguishes critical vulnerabilities with high strategic urgency, economically feasible capabilities with strategic payoffs, and low strategic urgency or high-cost substitution.
2. A National Input Cost Reduction Strategy that treats competitiveness as infrastructure, recognising affordable and reliable inputs.
3. A progression from 'Swadeshi' to Strategic Resilience to Strategic Indispensability, in which intelligent import substitution invests in national strength and ultimately embeds India in global systems, so that the world moves from 'thinking about buying Indian' to 'buying Indian without thinking.'

Union Budget 2026–27

In This Section...

The *Union Budget 2026-27* was tabled in the parliament by the Union Minister for Finance and Corporate Affairs, Smt. Nirmala Sitharaman, on 1st February 2026. The **highlights** of the budget are as follows:

PART A

The first Budget prepared in Kartavya Bhawan is inspired by ***3 Kartavyas***:

- The First Kartavya is to accelerate and sustain economic growth by enhancing productivity and competitiveness and building resilience to volatile global dynamics.
- The Second Kartavya is to fulfil aspirations of people and build their capacity, making them strong partners in India's path to prosperity.
- The Third Kartavya, aligned with the vision of *Sabka Sath, Sabka Vikas,* is to ensure that every family, community, region, and sector has access to resources, amenities, and opportunities for meaningful participation.

BUDGET ESTIMATES

- The non-debt receipts and the total expenditure are estimated as ₹36.5 lakh crore and ₹53.5 lakh crore, respectively. The Centre's net tax receipts are estimated at ₹28.7 lakh crore.

- The gross market borrowings are estimated at ₹17.2 lakh crore, and the net market borrowings from dated securities are estimated at ₹11.7 lakh crore.
  - The Revised Estimates of the non-debt receipts are ₹34 lakh crore, of which the Centre's net tax receipts are ₹26.7 lakh crore.
  - The Revised Estimates of the total expenditure is ₹49.6 lakh crore, of which the capital expenditure is about ₹11 lakh crore.
- The fiscal deficit in BE 2026-27 is estimated to be 4.3 per cent of GDP.
- In RE 2025-26, the fiscal deficit has been estimated at par with BE of 2025-26 at 4.4 per cent of GDP.
- The debt-to-GDP ratio is estimated to be 55.6 per cent of GDP in BE 2026-27, compared to 56.1 per cent of GDP in RE 2025-26.

The First Kartavya is to Accelerate and Sustain Economic Growth and Proposes 6 Interventions

1. **Scaling up Manufacturing in 7 Strategic and Frontier Sectors**

   (i) Biopharma SHAKTI (Strategy for Healthcare Advancement through Knowledge, Technology, and Innovation) was announced, with an outlay of ₹10,000 crore over the next 5 years to develop India as a global biopharma manufacturing hub.

   (a) A biopharma-focused network is to be created with 3 new National Institutes of Pharmaceutical Education and Research (NIPER) and upgrading 7 existing ones.

   (b) A network of over 1,000 accredited India Clinical Trials sites is to be created.

   (ii) India Semiconductor Mission (ISM) 2.0 is to be launched to produce equipment and materials, design full-stack Indian IP, and fortify supply chains with a focus on industry-led research and training centres to develop technology and a skilled workforce.

   (iii) The Electronics Components Manufacturing Scheme outlay increased to ₹40,000 crore.

   (iv) Dedicated **Rare Earth Corridors** to be established, to support the mineral-rich States of Odisha, Kerala, Andhra Pradesh, and Tamil Nadu to promote mining, processing, research, and manufacturing.

   (v) The government is to launch a scheme to support States in **establishing 3 dedicated Chemical Parks** through a challenge route on a cluster-based plug-and-play model.

   (vi) Strengthening Capital Goods Capability

   (a) Hi-Tech Tool Rooms to be established by CPSEs at 2 locations as digitally enabled automated service bureaus that locally design, test, and manufacture high-precision components at scale and at lower cost.

   (b) A **Scheme for Enhancement of Construction and Infrastructure Equipment (CIE)** to be introduced to strengthen domestic manufacturing of high-value and technologically advanced CIE.

   (c) A **Scheme for Container Manufacturing** was announced to create a globally competitive container manufacturing ecosystem, with a budgetary allocation of over ₹10,000 crore over a 5-year period.

   (vii) Integrated Programme for the Textile Sector Announced

   (a) The National Fibre Scheme for self-reliance in natural fibres such as silk, wool and jute, man-made fibres, and new-age fibres.

   (b) Textile Expansion and Employment Scheme to modernise traditional clusters with capital support for machinery, technology upgradation and common testing and certification centres.

   - **Mega Textile Parks** to be set up in challenge mode with a focus on bringing value addition to technical textiles.
   - The **Mahatma Gandhi Gram Swaraj** initiative, to strengthen khadi, handloom, and handicrafts.

(c) Initiative to help in global market linkage and branding and will streamline and support training, skilling, quality of process and production.

2. **Rejuvenating Legacy Industrial Sectors**
   - **A Scheme to Revive 200 Legacy Industrial** clusters announced to improve their cost competitiveness and efficiency through infrastructure and technology upgradation.

3. **Creating 'Champion SMEs' and Supporting Microenterprises**
   - **A dedicated ₹10,000 Crore SME Growth Fund**, to be introduced, to create future Champions, incentivising enterprises based on select criteria.
   - The **Self-Reliant India Fund** is to be allocated with an additional ₹2,000 crore to continue support for microenterprises and maintain their access to risk capital.
   - The government to facilitate professional institutions such as ICAI, ICSI and ICMAI to design short-term, modular courses and practical tools to develop a cadre of 'Corporate Mitras', especially in Tier-II and Tier-III towns.

4. **Delivering a Powerful Push to Infrastructure**
   - **Public Capital Expenditure** to be increased to ₹12.2 lakh crore in FY 2026-27.
   - The government is to set up an **Infrastructure Risk Guarantee Fund** to strengthen the confidence of private developers regarding risks during the infrastructure development and construction phase.
   - The government is to accelerate the recycling of significant **real estate assets of CPSEs through the setting up of dedicated REITs.**
   - To promote **environmentally sustainable movement of cargo**, the following measures are proposed:

     (a) New **Dedicated Freight Corridors** to be established connecting Dankuni in the East to Surat in the West.

     (b) **20 new National Waterways** (NW) to be operationalised over the next 5 years, starting with NW-5 in Odisha to connect mineral-rich areas of Talcher and Angul and industrial centres like Kalinga Nagar to the Ports of Paradeep and Dhamra.
     - **Training Institutes** to be set up as Regional Centres of Excellence for the development of the required manpower.
     - Further, a **ship repair ecosystem** catering to inland waterways is to be set up at Varanasi and Patna.

     (c) A **Coastal Cargo Promotion Scheme to be Launched** for incentivising a modal shift from rail and road to increase the share of inland waterways and coastal shipping from 6 per cent to 12 per cent by 2047.
     - Incentives to be provided to **indigenise the manufacturing of seaplanes** and enhance last-mile and remote connectivity and promote tourism.

     (d) **Seaplane VGF Scheme** to be introduced to provide support for operations.

5. **Ensuring Long-term Energy Security and Stability**
   - An outlay of ₹20,000 crore over the next 5 years, announced for **Carbon Capture Utilisation and Storage (CCUS)** technologies.

6. **Developing City Economic Regions**
   - An allocation of ₹5,000 crore over 5 years, per city economic region (CER), was announced for implementing their plans through a challenge mode with a reform-cum-results-based financing mechanism.
   - Government to develop **Seven High-Speed Rail corridors between cities as 'growth connectors'** to promote environmentally sustainable passenger systems. These include:

     (i) Mumbai-Pune

     (ii) Pune-Hyderabad,

     (iii) Hyderabad-Bengaluru,

     (iv) Hyderabad-Chennai

     (v) Chennai-Bengaluru,

(vi) Delhi-Varanasi,

(vii) Varanasi-Siliguri.

- The government is to set up a '**High Level Committee on Banking for Viksit Bharat,**' to comprehensively review the sector and align it with India's next phase of growth while safeguarding financial stability, inclusion, and consumer protection.
- **The government is to restructure the Power Finance Corporation and Rural Electrification Corporation** to achieve scale and improve efficiency in the public sector NBFCs.
- A comprehensive review of the **Foreign Exchange Management (Non-debt Instruments) Rules** is proposed, to create a more contemporary, user-friendly framework for foreign investments, consistent with India's evolving economic priorities.

MUNICIPAL BONDS

- **An incentive of ₹100 crore for a single bond issuance of more than ₹1,000 crore** was announced to encourage the issuance of municipal bonds of higher value by large cities.

The Second Kartavya Is to Fulfil Aspirations and Build the Capacity of People

- The government is to set up a High-Powered **'Education to Employment and Enterprise'** Standing Committee to recommend measures that focus on the Services Sector as a core driver of Viksit Bharat.

CREATION OF PROFESSIONALS FOR VIKSIT BHARAT

- Existing institutions for Allied Health Professionals (AHPs) to be upgraded and new AHP Institutions to be established in private and Government sectors.
  (a) 100,000 Allied Health Professionals to be added over the next 5 years.
- **Five Regional Medical Hubs** to be established to promote India as a hub for medical tourism services.

AYUSH

- **3 New All India Institutes of Ayurveda** to be established.

ANIMAL HUSBANDRY

- Government to scale up availability of veterinary professionals by more than 20,000.
  (a) A loan-linked capital subsidy support scheme to be launched for the establishment of veterinary and para-vet colleges, veterinary hospitals, diagnostic laboratories, and breeding facilities in the private sector.

ORANGE ECONOMY

- The Indian Institute of Creative Technologies, Mumbai, will be provided support in setting up Visual Effects, Gaming and Comics (AVGC) Content Creator Labs in 15,000 secondary schools and 500 colleges.

EDUCATION

- **5 University Townships** to be created in the vicinity of major industrial and logistic corridors through the challenge route.
  (a) Through VGF/capital support, 1 girls' hostel to be established in every district.

TOURISM

- National Council for Hotel Management and Catering Technology **to be upgraded to National Institute of Hospitality.**
  (a) A pilot scheme for upskilling 10,000 guides in 20 tourist sites was announced through a standardised, high-quality 12-week training course in hybrid mode in collaboration with an IIM.
  (b) A **National Destination Digital Knowledge Grid** to be established to digitally document all places of significance - cultural, spiritual, and heritage.

HERITAGE AND CULTURE TOURISM

- 15 archaeological sites, including Lothal, Dholavira, Rakhigarhi, Adichanallur, Sarnath, Hastinapur, and Leh Palace, to be developed into vibrant, experiential cultural destinations.

SPORTS

- The **Khelo India Mission** to be launched to transform the sports sector over the next decade.

The Third Kartavya Is Aligned with the Vision of *Sabka Sath, Sabka Vikas* and Requires Targeted Efforts in the Following Four Areas:

1. **Increasing Farmer Incomes**
   - New initiatives to be undertaken for
     (a) Integrated development of 500 reservoirs and Amrit Sarovars.

HIGH-VALUE AGRICULTURE

- Government to support high-value crops such as:
  (a) Coconut, sandalwood, cocoa, and cashew in coastal areas.
  (b) **Coconut Promotion Scheme** to be launched to increase production and enhance productivity.

Bharat-VISTAAR (Virtually Integrated System to Access Agricultural Resources)

- The government to launch Bharat-VISTAAR, a multilingual AI tool to integrate the Agri Stack portals and the ICAR package on agricultural practices with AI systems.

2. **Empowering Divyangjan**
   - **Divyangjan Kaushal Yojana** for Divyangjans to offer task-oriented and process-driven roles in IT, AVGC sectors, and Hospitality and Food and Beverages sectors.
3. **Commitment to Mental Health and Trauma Care**
   - Government to set up NIMHANS-2 in North India.
     (a) The government to upgrade National Mental Health Institutes in Ranchi and Tezpur as Regional Apex Institutions.
4. **Focus on the Purvodaya States and the North-Eastern Region**
   - The government is to develop an integrated East Coast Industrial Corridor with a well-connected node at Durgapur, create 5 tourism destinations in the 5 Purvodaya States, and provide 4,000 e-buses.
     (a) A scheme to be launched for the development of Buddhist Circuits in Arunachal Pradesh, Sikkim, Assam, Manipur, Mizoram, and Tripura.

16TH FINANCE COMMISSION

- The government provided ₹1.4 lakh crore to the States for the FY 2026-27 as Finance Commission Grants as recommended by the 16th Finance Commission.

PART B

DIRECT TAXES

New Income Tax Act

- The New Income Tax Act, 2025, is to come into effect from April 2026.
- The simplified income tax rules and forms will be notified shortly. The forms were redesigned for easy compliance by ordinary citizens.

EASE OF LIVING

- Interest awarded by the Motor Accident Claims Tribunal to a natural person will be exempt from income tax, and any TDS on this account will be done away with.
- TCS Rationalisation.

- Reduce the TCS rate on sale of overseas tour programme package to 2 per cent (from the current 2 per cent -20 per cent).
- Reduce the TCS rate to 2 per cent (from the current 5 per cent) for LRS remittances for education and medical.
- Simplified TDS provisions for manpower supply will benefit labour-intensive businesses.
- Scheme for small taxpayers wherein a rule-based automated process for obtaining a lower or nil deduction certificate instead of filing an application with the assessor.
- Single-window filing with depositories for Form 15G or 15H for TDS on dividends, interests, etc.
- Extend time available for revising returns from 31st December to 31st March with payment of nominal fees
- The timeline for filing of tax returns to be staggered.
- TAN for property transactions involving NRIs will be replaced with the resident buyer's PAN-based challan.
- A one-time 6-month foreign asset disclosure scheme for small taxpayers to disclose their overseas income or assets.

RATIONALISING PENALTY AND PROSECUTION

- IT assessment and penalty proceedings are proposed to be integrated by way of common order for both.
- Taxpayers are allowed to update their returns even after reassessment proceedings have been initiated to reduce litigations, at an additional 10 per cent tax rate over and above the rate applicable for the relevant year.
- Penalty for misreporting of income is also eligible for immunity with payment of additional income tax.
- The prosecution framework under the Income Tax Act is to be rationalised.
- Non-production of books of account and documents, and the requirement of TDS payment, where payment is made in kind, to be decriminalised.
- Non-disclosure of non-immovable foreign assets with an aggregate value less than ₹20 lakh to be provided with immunity from prosecution with retrospective effect from 1st October 2024.

COOPERATIVES

- Extend the deduction already allowed to a primary cooperative society engaged in supplying milk, oilseeds, fruits, or vegetables raised or grown by its members to those supplying cattle feed and cotton seed also.
- Allow the inter-cooperative society dividend income as a deduction under the new tax regime to the extent it is further distributed to its members.
- Exemption for a period of 3 years allowed for dividend income received by a notified national cooperative federation on their investments made in companies up to 31st January 2026, for dividends further distributed to its member co-operatives.

SUPPORTING THE IT SECTOR AS INDIA'S GROWTH ENGINE

- Software development services, IT-enabled services, knowledge process outsourcing services, and contract R&D services relating to software development are to be clubbed under a single category of Information Technology Services with a common safe harbour margin of 15.5 per cent.
- The threshold for availing safe harbour for IT services to be enhanced from ₹300 crore to ₹2,000 crore.
- Safe harbour for IT services shall be approved by an automated rule-driven process and can be continued for a period of 5 years at a stretch.
- Unilateral Advanced Pricing Agreement (APA) process for IT services to be fast-tracked with the endeavour to conclude it within a period of 2 years, which can be extended by 6 months on the taxpayer's request.
- The facility of modified returns available to the entity entering APA is to be extended to its associated entities.

ATTRACTING GLOBAL BUSINESS AND INVESTMENT

- Any foreign company that provides cloud services to customers globally by using data centre services from India will be provided a tax holiday till 2047.
- A safe harbour of 15 per cent on cost to be provided if the company providing data centre services from India is a related entity.
- A safe harbour for non-residents for component warehousing in a bonded warehouse at a profit margin of 2 per cent of the invoice value. The resultant tax of about 0.7 per cent will be much lower than in competing jurisdictions.
- Exemption from income tax for 5 years to be provided to any non-resident who provides capital goods, equipment, or tooling to any toll manufacturer in a bonded zone.
- Exemption to global (non-India sourced) income of a non-resident expert, for a stay period of 5 years under notified schemes
- Exemption from Minimum Alternate Tax (MAT) for all non-residents who pay tax on a presumptive basis.

TAX ADMINISTRATION

- A joint committee of the Ministry of Corporate Affairs and the Central Board of Direct Taxes is to be constituted for incorporating the requirements of the Income Computation and Disclosure Standards (ICDS) in the Indian Accounting Standards (IndAS) itself. Separate accounting requirements based on ICDS will be done away with from the tax year 2027-28.
- Definition of accountant for the purposes of Safe Harbour Rules to be rationalised.

OTHER TAX PROPOSALS

- In the interest of minority shareholders, buybacks for all types of shareholders are to be taxed as capital gains. Promoters to pay an additional buyback tax, making the effective tax 22 per cent for corporate promoters and 30 per cent for non-corporate promoters.
- The TCS rate for sellers of specific goods, namely alcoholic liquor, scrap and minerals, will be rationalised to 2 per cent and that on *tendu* leaves will be reduced from 5 per cent to 2 per cent.
- STT on Futures to be raised to 0.05 per cent from the present 0.02 per cent. STT on options premium and exercise of options to be raised to 0.15 per cent from the present rate of 0.1 per cent and 0.125 per cent, respectively.
- To encourage companies to shift to the new regime, set-off of brought-forward MAT credit to be allowed to companies only in the new regime. Set-off using available MAT credit to be allowed to an extent of 1/4th of the tax liability in the new regime.
- MAT is proposed to be made the final tax. There will be no further credit accumulation from 1st April 2026. The rate of final tax is to be reduced to 14 per cent from the current MAT rate of 15 per cent. The brought-forward MAT credit of taxpayers accumulated till 31st March 2026 will continue to be available to them for set-off as above.

INDIRECT TAXES

Tariff Simplification

Marine, Leather, and Textile Products

- The limit for duty-free imports of specified inputs used for processing seafood products for export is to increase from the current 1 per cent to 3 per cent of the FOB value.
- The duty-free imports of specified inputs, which are currently available for exports of leather or synthetic footwear, are to be allowed.

ENERGY TRANSITION AND SECURITY

- The basic customs duty exemption given to capital goods used for manufacturing lithium-ion cells for batteries to be extended.
- The basic customs duty on the import of sodium antimonate for use in the manufacture of solar glass is to be exempted.

NUCLEAR POWER

- The existing basic customs duty exemption on imports of goods required for nuclear power projects to be extended till the year 2035.

CRITICAL MINERALS

- The basic customs duty on the import of capital goods required for the processing of critical minerals to be exempted.

BIOGAS-BLENDED CNG

- The entire value of biogas while calculating the Central Excise duty payable on biogas-blended CNG is to be excluded.

CIVIL AND DEFENCE AVIATION

- The basic customs duty on components and parts required for the manufacture of civilian, training, and other aircrafts to be exempted.
- The basic custom duty on raw materials imported for the manufacture of parts of aircraft to be used in maintenance, repair, or overhaul requirements by units in the defence sector to be exempted.

ELECTRONICS

- The basic customs duty on specified parts used in the manufacture of microwave ovens to be exempted.

SPECIAL ECONOMIC ZONE

- A special one-time measure to facilitate sales by eligible manufacturing units in SEZs to the Domestic Tariff Area (DTA) at concessional rates of duty is proposed. The quantity of such sales will be limited to a prescribed proportion of their exports.

EASE OF LIVING

- The tariff rate on all dutiable goods imported for personal use to be reduced from 20 per cent to 10 per cent.
- The basic customs duty on 17 drugs/medicines is to be exempted.
- Duty-free personal import of drugs/medicines and food for 7 more rare diseases.

CUSTOMS PROCESS SIMPLIFICATION

- Custom processes to have minimal intervention for smoother and faster movement of goods.

TRUST-BASED SYSTEMS

- Duty deferral period for Tier 2 and Tier 3 Authorised Economic Operators, known as AEOs, to be enhanced from 15 days to 30 days. The same is extended to the eligible manufacturer-importers.
- The validity period of advance ruling, binding on Customs, is to be extended from the present 3 years to 5 years.
- Government agencies will be encouraged to leverage AEO accreditation for preferential treatment in clearing their cargo.
- Filing of bill of entry by a trusted importer, and arrival of goods will automatically notify Customs for completing their clearance formalities (for import of goods not needing any compliance).
- The Customs warehousing framework to be transformed into a warehouse operator-centric system with self-declarations, electronic tracking, and risk-based audits.

EASE OF DOING BUSINESS

- Cargo clearance approvals from various government agencies to be seamlessly processed through a single and interconnected digital window by the end of the financial year.
- Processes involved in clearance of food, drugs, plants, animal and wildlife products, accounting for around 70 per cent of interdicted cargo, to be operationalised on this system by April 2026 itself.
- For goods not having any compliance requirement, clearance is to be done by Customs immediately after online registration is completed by the importer.

- Customs Integrated System (CIS) to be rolled out in 2 years as a single, integrated, and scalable platform for all the customs processes.
- Utilisation of non-intrusive scanning with advanced imaging and AI technology for risk assessment to be expanded in a phased manner with the objective to scan every container across all the major ports.

NEW EXPORT OPPORTUNITIES

- Fish caught by an Indian fishing vessel in the Exclusive Economic Zone (EEZ) or on the High Seas are to be made free of duty. Landing of such fish in a foreign port will be treated as export of goods.
- Complete removal of the current value cap of ₹10 lakh per consignment on courier exports-supports aspirations of India's small businesses, artisans, and start-ups to access global markets through e-commerce.

EASE OF LIVING

- Provisions governing baggage clearance to be revised during international travel. Revised rules to enhance duty-free allowances in line with the present-day travel realities.
- Honest taxpayers, willing to settle disputes, will be able to close cases by paying an additional amount in lieu of a penalty.

Glossary

> Concepts are the constituents of thoughts - consequently, they are crucial to such psychological processes as categorisation, inference, memory, learning, and decision-making.*
>
> * See Eric Margolis and Stephen Laurence, 'Concepts' in the *The Stanford Encyclopedia of Philosophy*, Edward N. Zalta, eds. [Stanford, USA: Metaphysics Research Lab, Centre for the Study of Language and Information (CSLI), 2012].

Abuse of Dominance A situation when a dominant firm/company (or a group of firms) is engaged in promoting its market position through 'anti-competitive' business practices, such as- predatory pricing, price squeezing, charging unreasonable prices, etc. Such practices hamper healthy competition in the economy and non-dominant firms face difficulties in their growth - they finally may shut down their operations. In recent times, it was in news globally - the US company *Microsoft* was facing litigation (under 'anti-trust' provision) for its Windows Operating System.

Though India used to regulate/restrict several such practices (under the MRTP Act, 1969), exact use of the term 'abuse of dominance' was not in practice. But the Competition Act, 2002 (which replaced the MRTP Act) has clear use of it - it defines such situation in clear terms.

Accounting Systems There are two prevailing systems of accounting followed by the governments - cash-based or accrual-based. In the *cash-based system,* income is counted when cash (or a cheque) is actually received, and expenses are counted when actually paid. On the other hand, in the *accrual-based system,* transactions are counted as they happen regardless of when the money is actually received or paid. Government of India is switching over from the cash-based system to accrual-based system (which is the popular practice across the world).

Accredited Investors Taking clues from other financial markets of the world the SEBI proposed to introduce a new category of investors' known also as 'qualified investors' or 'professional investors' in February 2021 - *accredited investors.* As per it, they are those who understand various financial products, risks and returns associated with them and thus, are able to take 'informed' investment decisions.

Accrual Accounting This is a method of accounting in which income/revenue or expenditures are shown when these transactions take place (and not when the payments are received against them). This follows the principle of matching as per which revenues and expenses should be recognised in the same period. Double-entry bookkeeping method is used in it.

The other method of accounting is 'cash accounting' or 'cash-based accounting' under which revenues and expenses are recognised when payments are received/made.

Acid Test Ratio It is a metric used to measure the ability of a firm (company) to pay back its short-term liabilities (i.e., loans). It is calculated by dividing the firm's most liquid assets (like cash) and short-term receivables (payments from sales) by its short-term liabilities.

This metric might be differentiated for the same firm due to differences in opinion of the financial analysts as how they classify various assets of the firm (for example, short-term assets like 'inventory' are not considered liquid assets by some since they may not be readily converted into cash).

Activity Rate The labour force of a country is known as the activity rate or *participation rate*. It is in per cent and always a proportion of the total population of the country – the economically active population. This rate varies from one country to another, depending upon several factors such as school leaving age, retirement age, popularity of higher education, social customs, opportunities, etc.

Agricultural Labourer A person who works on another person's land for *wages* in money or kind or share is regarded as an agricultural labourer. He or she has no risk in the cultivation, but merely works on another person's land for wages. An agricultural labourer has no right of lease or contract on land on which he/she works.

Algo Trading Algorithmic trading (Algo trading) refers to orders generated at superfast speed using advanced mathematical models that involve automated execution of trade. This faster way of trade is considered capable of bringing huge gains. The term came in news in India by 2022-23 (the NSE is facing charge from SEBI of allowing some traders preferential access to trading system through co-location facility of the exchange).

Alpine Convertible Bond An ACB (Alpine Convertible Bond) is a Foreign Currency Convertible Bond (FCCB) issued by an Indian company exclusively to the Swiss investors.

Amortisation Payment of a loan in installments by the borrower. It is usually done in an agreed period and every installment includes a part of the total loan plus the interest.

Angel Tax Angel tax is applicable (in India, by March 2019) on the unlisted companies that raise capital through sale of shares at a value above their fair market value. This excess capital is treated as 'income' and thus attracts income tax. This tax predominantly affects start-ups and the angel investments they attract.

Animal Spirit 'Confidence', considered as one of the essential ingredients of economic prosperity, was called by J. M. Keynes animal spirit. For Keynes, this is a 'naive optimism' by which an entrepreneur puts aside the fact of loss as a healthy man puts aside the expectation of death. But from where does this animal spirit come has been a mystery - can it be created artificially from outside or whether it is an innate thing some are born with, etc.

Antitrust A category of the government policy which deals with monopoly. Such laws intend to stop abuses of 'market power' by big companies and at times to prevent corporate mergers and acquisitions that would strengthen monopoly. The US has such laws and recently it was in news when Microsoft was its target.

Appreciation It shows increase in the value and is used in economics in the following two senses:

1. It is an increase in the price of an asset over time, such as price rises in land, factory building, houses, offices, etc. It is also known as *capital appreciation.*
2. It is an increase in the value of currency against any foreign currency or currencies. It is market-based if the economy follows the floating-currency exchange-rate system.

Arbitrage Earning profits out of the price differences of the same product in different markets at the same time. For example, buying and selling any product, financial securities (as bonds) or foreign currencies in different markets/economies. As globalisation is promoting liberalised cross border movement of goods and services around the world, arbitrage is prevalent today. To avoid arbitrage, the WTO member countries (i.e., the official countries in the process of globalisation) are under compulsion to chalk out homogenous economic policies and a level-playing field at the international level is emerging.

Asset Anything which has a 'money value' owned by an individual or a firm is an asset. It is of *three* types:

1. **Tangible Asset:** All physical assets such as land, machinery, building, consumer durables (refrigerator, car, TV, Radio, etc.), etc. *(the assets which are in the material form).*
2. **Intangible Assets:** All non-physical/immaterial assets such as brand names, goodwill, creditworthiness, knowledge, know-how, etc.
3. **Financial Assets:** All financially valid valuables other than tangibles and intangibles such as currencies, bank deposits, bonds, securities, shares, etc.

Assigned Revenue The term is used to refer to various tax/duty/cess/surcharge/levy, etc. proceeds which are (traditionally) collected by state government (on behalf of) local bodies (the PRIs), and subsequently adjusted with/assigned to the PRIs. The collection of such revenue is governed by relevant Acts of the local bodies.

Some examples of assigned revenue in India include entertainment tax, surcharge on stamp duty, local cess/surcharge on land revenue, lease amount of mines and minerals, sale proceeds of social forestry plantations, etc. State Finance Commissions recommend *devolution* of assigned revenue to local bodies on objective criteria, which may be specified by them in specific context.

AT1 Bonds These bonds are *unsecured* and *perpetual* in nature and are part of the Basel III norms decided by the Basel Committee on Bank Supervision (BCBS). It means that while bondholders earn interests on them, they cannot liquidate and get their money back neither do they ever mature. Issued under the Tier 1 capital of the banks, these bonds were in news recently in relation to the Yes Bank AT1 bond scam.

Autarky The idea of self-sufficiency and 'no' international trade by a country. None of the countries of the world has been able to produce all the goods and services required by its population at competitive prices; however, some tried to live it up at the cost of inefficiency and comparative poverty.

Back-to-back Loan A term of international banking, is an arrangement under which two firms (i.e., companies) in different economies (i.e., countries) borrow each other's currency and agree to repay (such loans) at a specified future date. Each company gets full amount of the loan on the repayment date in their domestic currency without any risk of losses due to exchange rate fluctuations. It has developed as a popular tool of minimising the exchange-rate exposure risk among the multi-national companies. This is also known as the *parallel loan*.

Bad Bank A bank created specially to buy the *bad debts* (called 'non-performing assets' in India) of the existing banks to clear such loans of the latter. This way, the banks with NPAs clear their 'balance sheet' and again start lending to the customers. The bad bank now tries to recover the bad debts it has bought through available legal means. Though such banks were set up in 20th century itself in the USA, it came in recent use once the US central banks' chief (Ben Bernanke) proposed the idea of using a government-run bad bank to clean up the 'sub-prime' loans of the private banks in the country (in wake of the sub-prime crisis of 2007).

It made news in India once the *Economic Survey 2016-17* suggested the Government of India to set up such a body - public sector asset rehabilitation agency (PARA) - to solve the 'twin balance sheet' (TBS) problem the country is faced with.

Bad Debt An accounting term to show the loans which are unlikely to be paid back by the borrower as the borrower has become insolvent/bankrupt. Banks might write off such bad debts against the profits of the trading as a business cost.

Balanced Budget The annual financial statement (i.e., the budget) of a government which has the total expenditures equal to the taxes and other receipts.

Most governments, in practice, run unbalanced budgets, i.e., deficit budgets or surplus budgets-either the expenditures being higher or lower than the taxes and the other receipts, respectively. It is done to regulate the economic activities.

Balance of Payments A balance sheet of an economy showing its total external transactions with the world-calculated on the principles of accounting.

Balloon Payment When the final payment of a debt is more than the previous payments, it is balloon payment.

Basing Point Price System A method of pricing in which a differential (i.e., varying) price is fixed for the same product for the customers of the different locations - nearer the customer, cheaper the product. This is done usually to neutralise the transportation cost of the bulky products such as cement, iron and steel, petroleum, etc.

Beer The bond equity earnings yield ratio (BEER) is a measure to compare the earnings on government bond (normally, 10-year G-Sec are taken as reference) and equities. BEER is calculated by dividing the yield (interest) of a government bond (10-year G-Sec) by the current earnings of a stock benchmark (such as the 50-share index Nifty).

Theoretically, if the reading is at 1, it means that both equity and bond markets are fairly valued. A reading greater than 1 would mean that the equity market is overvalued, while below 1 means that equity market is undervalued. BEER is the reverse of the PE (price-to-earnings) ratio (refer it in the *Glossary* itself).

Bellwether Stock A share which often reflects the state of the whole stock market. The technical analysts, associated with the stock market, usually keep a track-record of such shares and go on to forecast the future stock movements.

BFS For the purpose of supervision and surveillance of the Indian financial system, a Board for Financial Supervision (BFS) was set up by the RBI in November 1994. The board supervises commercial banks, non-banking financial companies (NBFCs), financial institutions, primary dealers, and the clearing corporation of India (CCI).

Biflation The simultaneous occurrence of inflation and deflation is termed biflation. This is considered a misnomer as prices cannot rise and fall simultaneously. Rather, it a neologism for a type of Cantillon effect.

When central banks change money supply in economy (by changing interest rate), it leaves a redistribution effect on the purchasing power of the people and disturbs the relative prices of goods and services. This is why some feel prices have gone up while some others feel prices have declined–leading to a misnomer which is called 'biflation'. This is known as Cantillon effect, which is named after the French economist, Richard Cantillon (1680–1734).

Bond An instrument of raising debt on which the bond-issuer pays a periodic interest (known as *'coupon'*). In theory, bonds could be issued by governments as well as private companies.

Bonds generally have a maturity period; however, some bonds might not have any definite maturity period (which are known as *'Perpetual Bonds'*).

Bracket Creep Increasing incomes due to inflation (via increased dearness allowances, individual income goes for an increase) pushes individuals into higher tax *brackets* and leaves them worse off (as their real income has not increased and their disposable income, i.e., income after tax payments, falls). This phenomenon is known as the bracket creep.

Brown Revolution Simply put, introducing the digital revolution in the farm sector is being called Brown Revolution - the term is believed to have been first used by the US farmer *Howarth Buffet* (brother of the billionaire global investor Warren Buffet).

Already introduced in USA and Europe, under it the tractor industry is expected to soon include combining tractor services for ploughing and sowing seeds to using sensors, cloud computing and artificial intelligence for precision farming. It is a kind of combining the forces of the fourth industrial revolution with the existing farm machines and tools.

Brownfield Location A derelict industrial area that has been demolished to accommodate new industries. This is opposite to the *greenfield location* where a new industry is set up in a new area.

Bubble The price rise of an asset unexplained by the fundamentals and still people interested in holding the assets. After the bursting of the bubble, assets cool down to their real prices.

Budget Line A line on the dual axis graph showing the alternate combinations of goods that can be purchased by a consumer with a given income at given prices.

Bullet Repayment It means a lump-sum payment for the *entire loan amount* at the time of maturity. Such arrangements may be put in place by the banking regulator (RBI in case of India) to fasten the process of recovery of the non-performing assets (NPAs) process of the banks. The distressed assets, in this way, come back to bank, may be with a lower profit element to them.

Bullion Precious metals such as gold, silver, and platinum that are traded in the form of *bars* and *coins* for investment purposes and are used for jewellery as base metals.

Business Cycle See Chapter 8, Section-B with the same heading.

Buyer's Market A short period of market situation in which there is excess supply of goods/services forcing price fall to the advantage of the buyers.

Camels An acronym derived from the terms capital adequacy (C), asset quality (A), management (M), earnings (E), liquidity (L) and systems for control (S). The acronym is used as a technique for evaluating and rating the operations and performance of banks all over the world.

Cantillon Effect See *Biflation*

Capital Capital is one of the three main factors of production (*labour* and *natural resources* are the other two), classified into *physical capital* (i.e., factories, machines, office, etc.) and *human capital* (i.e., training, skill, etc.). Different ways to look upon a company, listed on a stock exchange, are given below (from capital point of view):

1. **Authorised Capital:** This is the amount of share capital fixed in the Memorandum of Association (MoA) and the article of association of a company as required by the Companies Act. This is also known as the *Nominal* or *Registered Capital.*

   This is the limit (i.e., nominal value) upto which a company can issue shares. Companies often extend their authorised capital (via an amendment in the MoA) in advance of actual issue of new shares. This allows the timing of capital issue to be fixed in light of the company's need for new capital and the state of the capital market and allows share options to be exercised accordingly.
2. **Paid-up Capital:** The part of the authorised capital of a company that has actually been paid up by the shareholders. A difference may arise because all shares authorised may not have been issued or the issued shares have been only partly paid-up by then.
3. **Subscribed Capital:** The capital that has actually been paid by the shareholders (as they might have committed more than this to contribute). It means, the subscribed capital is the actually realised paid-up capital (paid-up capital is subscribed capital plus credit/due on the shareholders).
4. **Issued Capital:** The amount of the capital which has been sought by a company to be raised by the issue of shares (it should be kept in mind that this cannot exceed the authorised capital).
5. **Called-up Capital:** The amount of share capital the shareholders have been *called* to pay to date under the phased payment terms. It is usually equal to the 'paid-up capital' of the company except where some shareholders have failed to pay their due installments (known as *calls in arrears*).

Capital Adequacy Ratio A regulation on commercial banks, co-operative banks and the non-banking financial companies to maintain a certain amount of capital in relation to their assets (i.e., loans and investments) as a cushion (shock-absorber) against probable losses in their investments and loans.

A concept devised by the Bank for International Settlements (BIS), Basel, the provision was implemented in India in 1992 by the RBI (for a more detailed discussion, see Chapter 13 on 'Banking').

Capital Consumption The capital that is consumed by an economy or a firm in the production process. Also known as *depreciation.*

Capital-output Ratio A measure of how much additional capital is needed to produce each extra unit of the output. Put the other way round, it is the amount of extra output produced by each unit of added capital. The ratio indicates how efficient new investment contributes to the growth of an economy.

A capital-output ratio of 3:1 is better than the 4:1 as the former needs only three units extra capital to produce one extra output in comparison to the latter which needs four units for each extra unit output.

Carry Trade Borrowing funds at cheaper interest rate from one market and investing in another where interest rate is relatively higher is called carry trade. Such returns are made by arbitraging [see *Arbitrage* in Glossary itself] on the interest rate differentials seen across the countries. Therefore, we see increased foreign investments in India (in debt securities such as corporate bonds, government securities, etc.) from the countries whenever an interest rate cut is announced by their central banks.

Cash Cow A profitable business or firm (may belong to either public or private sector) which gives regular cash flow to the owner (this happens either due to regular demand of the popular goods produced by the firm or the compulsions of the consumer to buy the products). For example, the antiseptic lotion 'Dettol' is a cash cow for Reckitt and Colman in the private sector and LPG is a cash cow for the manufacturing and marketing government companies (provided there is no subsidy on LPG).

Caveat Emptor A Latin phrase which means *'let the buyer beware'*. Simply put, it means that the supplier has no legal obligation to inform buyers about any defects in his goods or services; the onus is on the buyer to himself determine the level of satisfaction out of the products.

Chinese Wall The segregation of the different activities of a financial institution (such as, jobbing, stockbroking, fund management, etc.) in order to protect clients' interest.

Circuit Limit A limit of regular fall in share indices of Stock Exchanges around the world after which the exchange a are closed for further trading. For example, circuit limit decided for the BSE (Bombay Stock Exchange) has been fixed at 10 per cent. The time there is a continuous fall in the BSE Sensex and it reaches 10 per cent, the exchange is closed to further trading.

Such a limit/provision prevents the share market from crashing down.

Circular Economy Several definitions of circular economy are used in scientific and professional literature because the concept is applied by a diverse group of researchers and professionals, emphasising different aspects of it. This makes it difficult to measure also. But most of its definitions focus on the 'use of raw materials' or 'system change'. Definitions that focus on resource use often follow the *3-R approach* - Reduce (minimum use of raw materials); Reuse (maximum reuse of products and components); and Recycle (high quality reuse of raw materials).

A circular economy tries to follow the example of an ecosystem. In it, there is nothing like waste because every residual item can be used to make a new product (but after eliminating the toxic substances) - such as producers taking back their products after use and repairing them for a new useful life. Thus, only recycling is not important in this system, rather assuring quality is also taken care of.

Classical Economics A school of thought in economics based on the ideas of Smith, Ricardo, Mill, etc. The school dominated the economic thinking of the world until about 1870, when the *'marginalist revolution'* took place.

Clean Coal Underground coal gasification and liquefaction, which converts coal into liquid and gaseous fuel alternatives, is a recognised 'clean coal' technology - handy in extraction of energy from coal seams which cannot be mined through conventional methods.

Collateral Any item/asset which accompanies/ subordinates/supplements a primary item is known as collateral. The term is used in banking industry while providing loans. This is also known as 'secondary/ subordinate security' - which borrowers/guarantors provide in the form of an asset (like land, building, etc.) while seeking a loan. The principal/primary security is usually the borrower's personal guaranty, or the cash flow of a business.

Except for highly creditworthy customers (who can get loans against their signatures), lenders always demand a collateral if the primary security is not considered to be reliable or sufficient enough to recover the loan in the case of a default - lenders have the legal right to seize the collateral.

Closed Shop The requirement that all employees of a given firm be members of a specified trade union. It is a method of restricting labour supply and maintaining high wages applied by a powerful trade union.

Collection Rate It is the ratio of customs earnings and imports' value of a country. This metric is used to understand the impact of special custom duties, countervailing duties and custom exemptions offered on imports by a country. Due to such exemptions offered by India on essential imports, we see the country's customs collections not increasing as much its imports increase, which makes collection rate lower or falling (if number of such exemptions increased due to some reason). For the year 2019, India's collection rate was 6.6 per cent (up from 5.5 per cent of 2014).

Collective Products A product which can only be supplied to a group. Many goods and services provided by the governments fall in this category, such as national defence, police administration, etc.

Committed Expenditure The expenditures of the governments from which they cannot deny (as they have already committed them to pay) are known as committed expenditure. The liabilities such as 'interest' (of the internal as well as external loans) and 'pension' (of the retired personnel of the governments) are examples of such expenditure.

Commodities Transaction Tax See Chapter 18, with the heading '*Tax Structure in India*'.

Commodity Money Products being used as the means of payment as in the traditional barter system. Such practices take place generally when the confidence in money has fallen down (as for example in the situations of high inflation and high depreciation).

Communitisation A method of privatising public service delivery without going for the tendering process. It is done by transferring powers including financial powers to the user community who will take up the job of revenue collection along with an effective and more practical governance of the service delivery. This model is bereft of profit motive and so, more transparent.

Service delivery in communitised elementary schools, health services and power tariff collection (which increased by 100 per cent) considerably improved since it was done (in 2002).

Comparative Advantage Comparative advantage refers to the ability of a company or an economy to produce something at a lower opportunity cost (i.e., by forfeiting potential benefit). By this, the company/economy gets the ability to sell its products cheaper than the prices offered by its competitors. It can be understood with the help of 'trade off' also - given two options (with their own set of advantages and disadvantages), the best option has the comparative advantage.

Articulated by James Mill, this concept was popularised by David Ricardo (his mentor was James Mill) by early 19th century. Among the key concepts of economic theory, this advocates the belief that 'all countries can mutually benefit from cooperation and voluntary trade.' Over the time, it became the foundational tenet of international trade. The concept gives the insight that trade will still occur even if one country has an 'absolute advantage' in all products. For example, China has the comparative advantage in global export market due to its 'lower wages' but China also keeps importing so many goods and services (where it has lower comparative advantage).

Consortium An *ad hoc* grouping of firms, governments, etc. brought together to undertake a particular project by pooling their resources and skills for major construction projects, loans, etc.

Conspicuous Consumption Consumption for the purpose of showing off ostentatiousness but not for the utility aspect - for example, the use of diamond-studded sandals, watches, pens, etc.

Contagion A situation or an effect of economic problems in one economy spreading to another, also known as the *domino effect*.

Contrarian A person following an investment strategy (specially in share market) just opposite to the general investors in a given period. For example, when a share is generally being sold by the investors, a contrarian keeps on buying them - the logic is that due to selling pressure, the price will fall below the intrinsic value of the share and there is a prospect of future profit out of the share.

Core Investment Companies (CICs) An NBFC carrying on the business of acquisition of shares and securities which satisfied the conditions: it holds not less than 90 per cent of its total assets in this form; its investments in the equity shares in group companies constitute not less than 60 per cent of its total assets; it does not trade in its investments in shares, debt or loans in group companies except through block sale for the purpose of dilution or disinvestment; and it does not carry on any other financial activity except investment in bank deposits, money market instruments, government securities, loans to and investments in group companies.

Correction A term usually used in stock market which shows a reversal of share prices in reaction to an excessive rise or fall in the past.

Countervailing Duty Countervailing duty (CVD) is imposed by the importing nation on imports if the exporting nation is found to offer export subsidies to their exports. This measure aims at balancing the price of imports with the domestic products. This duty is imposed in such a way that imported item also remains competitive. A similar duty, with the same aim, once imposed by the importing nation in case the exporting country is found to export at *below fair market price* (it means the exporting nation is dumping the item in the importing nation) is known as 'anti-dumping' duty.

Both the duties are imposed after fulfilling the proper provisions of investigation conducted as per the specifications of the WTO.

Creative Destruction The process by which an innovative entrepreneur takes risks and introduces new technologies to stimulate economic activity, replacing old technologies, is known as 'creative destruction'. As per *Schumpeter, Joseph A.* (1883-1950), creative destruction is the key to economic growth. But due to irregularity in such innovations, business cycle is followed by both collapse and crisis (J. A. Schumpeter, *Capitalism, Socialism and Democracy*, 1942).

Crony Capitalism An approach of doing business when the firms look after themselves by looking after their own people (i.e., families and friends). Used in a negative sense.

Cross Subsidy The process of giving subsidy to one sub-area and fulfilling it through the profits from the other sub-area. For example, in India kerosene oil is cross-subsidised against petrol and aviation fuel.

Crowdfunding This is a method of mobilising finance/fund. Crowd-funding refers to the collective effort of individuals who pool money - mostly through the Internet - to support start-ups. There are two basic forms of crowdfunding - 'community' crowdfunding and 'financial return' crowdfunding. The *former* includes donation-based concepts (donators get no financial returns in it) while in the *latter* contributors of funds get financial returns (from the project set up with the fund). In the financial model of crowdfunding, contributors might be given equity/share in the upcoming project.

Crowding-out Effect A concept of public finance which means an increase in the government expenditure which has an effect of reducing private the sector expenditure.

CSR The concept of corporate social responsibility (CSR) is fast gaining popularity among the corporate sector of the world. As per the experts, CSR is qualitatively different from the traditional concept of passive philanthropy by the corporate houses. Basically, CSR acknowledges the *debt* that the corporates owe to the community within which they operate. It defines the corporates' partnership with social action groups (i.e., the NGOs) in providing financial and other resources to support development plans, especially among disadvantaged communities. There is stress on long-term sustainability of business and environment and the distribution of well-being.

Decoupling Theory Decoupling theory holds that Asian economies, especially emerging ones, no longer depend on the United States economy for growth, leaving them *insulated* from a severe slowdown there, even recession - looked true for some time as Asian stocks rose while socks in the US fell. However, as fears of recession mounted in the US, stocks declined heavily. Looking this happen in late 2008, the decoupling theory regarding the Asian as well as the EU economies has now lost ground. But still, the emerging economies are able to have higher growth rates and exports in comparison to the US - that is why the theory is still debated by experts.

Deindustrialisation Sustained decrease in the share of the secondary sector (i.e., industry) in the total output (GDP) of an economy.

Demat Account It is a way of holding securities in an electronic or dematerialised form. Demat form of shares can be traded online. As such, the transactions are concluded much faster, which prevents theft, misuse, forging of original shares certificates or other documents, and allows an investor to buy or sell shares in any quantity. Demat accounts are offered by banks, and the dematerialised stock is held by the depository (National Securities Depository Ltd. [NSDL] or Central Securities Depository Ltd. [CSDL]).

Demerger The breaking-up of a company into more separate companies. Such companies are usually formed through mergers.

Derivatives The financial assets that 'derive' their value from other assets, such as shares, debentures, bonds, securities, etc. traded on the platforms of stock and commodity exchanges.

DIIs Domestic Investment Institutions (DIIs) are the financial institutions of Indian origin investing in India in different derivatives such as share, securities, corporate bounds, etc. They may be owned by governments or private entities in the form of mutual funds, pension funds, and insurance companies are the major examples in India.

Dirty Float A term of foreign exchange management when a country manipulates its exchange rate under the floating currency system to take leverage in its external transactions.

Discount House A financial institution specialising in buying and selling of short-term (i.e., less than one year) instruments of the money market. The SBI Discount and Finance House of India (SBI DFHI) is India's largest discount house.

Disgorgement Disgorgement is a common term in developed markets, though for most market participants in India it is a new thing. Disgorgement means repayment of illegal gains by wrongdoers. Funds that were received through illegal or unethical business transactions are 'disgorged', or paid back, with interest to those affected by the action. In the case of India, SEBI is responsible for this job unlike international practice of civil courts and market regulator both looking into it.

Disgorgement is a 'remedial' civil action, rather than a 'punitive' civil action. In the US, individuals or companies that violate Securities and Exchange Commission regulations are typically required to pay both civil money penalties and disgorgement. Civil money penalties are punitive, while disgorgement is about paying back profits made from those actions that violated securities regulations.

Interestingly, disgorgement payments are not only demanded of those who violate securities regulations. In the US, anyone profiting from illegal or unethical activities may be required to disgorge their profits. The money disgorged from the violating parties is used to create a 'Fair Fund' - fund for the benefit of investors who were harmed by the violation.

Dissaving The situation of higher current consumption over current disposable income by the households - the difference is met by withdrawals from the past savings (*i.e., decrease in saving*).

Domino Effect An economic situation in which one economic event causes a series of similar events to happen one after the other. For example, experts believe that the falling of share indices around the world in early-2008 was a domino effect of the sub-prime crisis faced by the US economy. A similar case is cited from the mid-1996 when all major stock markets crashed around the world due to the domino effect emanating from the South East Asian currency crisis.

Dow-Jones Index The US share price index which monitors and records the share price movements of all companies listed on the New York Stock Exchange (*with the exception of hightech companies which are listed on the Nasdaq stock exchange*). India has its equivalent in the BSE *Sensex*.

D-SIBs Since 2015, every year, the RBI releases a list of banks operating in the country as the Domestic Systemically Important Banks (D-SIBs). For foreign banks operating in India, there is a similar provision to declare them G-SIBs (Globally Systemically Important Banks). By April 2024, in India there were three banks in this category (SBI, ICICI Bank and HDFC Bank).

In simple words, this means that these banks are *too big to fail*. It has the implied meaning that failure of any of these banks would have a cascading effect on the whole financial system of India. Inclusion of banks in this list gives additional comfort to investors and depositors as they think that these banks will not be allowed to fail (immediately by the RBI and ultimately by the Government). This gives such banks an advantage to mobilise funds cheaper (through deposits) over their peers in the banking industry.

As per the norms, such banks need to set aside 'more capital' for their continued operation as part of the 'capital to risk-weighted assets ratio' (CRAR). Higher CRAR, which is more commonly used as the CAR (Capital Adequacy Ratio), provides banks the strength to tide over acute economic and financial stress. There are five 'buckets' created by the RBI into which the banks are put depending upon their Systemic Importance Scores (SISs). While the SBI (being in the 'third bucket') needs to set aside 0.60 per cent extra capital of its risk-weighted assets, ICICI and HDFC banks (being in the 'first bucket') need to set aside 0.20 per cent extra capital of their risk-weighted assets.

Dumping Exporting goods at a price lower than its price in the domestic market. To neutralise the effects of dumping, the importing country may impose a *surcharge* on such imports which is known as the *anti-dumping duty*.

Dutch Disease When an increase in one form of net exports drives up a country's exchange rate, it is called the Dutch Disease. Such instances make other exports non-competitive in the world market and impairs the ability of domestic products to compete with imports.

The term originated from the supposed effect of natural gas discoveries on the Netherland's economy.

EASE-Index EASE-Index (Enhanced Access & Service Excellence-Index) was published for the first time for the public sector banks (PSBs) in March 2019. Prepared by the *Boston Consulting Group*, the index measures the performance of the PSBs on 140 objective metrics across 6 themes, including customer responsiveness, credit off-take and digitalisation, among others.

EBITDA It stands for Earnings Before Interest, Taxes, Depreciation, and Amortisation (EBITA) and measures a company's profitability before deductions that are often considered irrelevant in the decision-making process. In other words, it's the net income of a company with certain expenses like amortisation, depreciation, taxes, and interest.

The investors and creditors often use this concept as a 'coverage ratio' to compare companies' net profits as - they might have high debts on them or large investments in fixed assets because this measurement excludes the accounting effects of non-operating expenses like interest and paper expenses like depreciation. Adding these expenses into their net income allows investors and lenders analyse and compare the real cash flows.

e-Business Using computers and the Internet to link both the *internal* operations (i.e., transactions and communications between the various departments/divisions of the business firm) and its *external* operations (i.e., all its dealings with the suppliers, customers, etc.).

e-Commerce Method of buying and selling goods and services over the Internet - a kind of direct marketing, i.e., without the help of any middle arrangement of sales.

Economies of Scale The long-run reduction in average/unit cost that occurs as the scale of the firm's output increases. The opposite situation is known as *diseconomies of scale*.

Economies of Scope The long-run reduction in average/unit cost that occurs as the scope (diversification) of the firm's activities increases.

Edgeworth Box A concept for the purpose of analysing the possible relationships between two individuals or countries. It is done using indifference curve.

The concept was developed by Francis Ysidro Edgeworth (1845-1926) who is also credited for analytical tools of *indifference curves* and *contract curves*.

Effective Revenue Deficit See Chapter 19, on *Public Finance in India*.

Elephants This term is used as a 'slang' in financial market for big companies with huge funds which they may use for diverse kinds of investments. Usually used for their huge investments in stock markets, they leave big impact on a country's security market. Professionally managed entities like mutual funds, pension funds, insurance companies and banks are some of its examples.

The concept can be understood by comparing it to the situation when an elephant enters the pool (i.e., buys stocks), the water level (stock price) increases, and once the elephant exits the pool (i.e., selling stocks), the water level (stock price) decreases. In this perspective, for individual investor the term mouse is used (as it leaves comparatively a very low impact on stock market).

Engel's Law The law which says that people generally spend a smaller part of their budget on food as their income rises. The idea was suggested by Ernst Engel, a Russian statistician in 1857.

Environmental Accounting The method of accounting which includes the ecological and environmental damages done by the economic activities in monetary terms. The *green GDP* of an economy is measured by the same method - experimented in Costa Rica, Mexico, Netherlands, Norway, and Papua New Guinea, among others. Indicative estimates suggest that conventionally measured GDP may exceed GDP adjusted for natural resources depletion and environmental degradation by a range between 1.5 per cent and 10 per cent.

Environmental Audit Assessment of the environmental impact of a firm/public body through its activities. This is done with an objective to reduce or eliminate the pollution aspect.

Environmental Taxes As against the Command and Control approach to managing environment, the Economic or Market Based Instruments (MBIs) approach sends economic signals to the polluters to modify their behaviour. The MBIs used for environmental taxes include pollution charges (emission/affluent and tax/pollution tax), marketable permits, deposit refund system, input taxes/product charges, differential tax rates, user administrative changes and subsidies for pollution abatement, which may be based on both price and quality. India has been already collecting taxes on *water* and *air* via the Water Act and the Air Act. Due to its experience, India is among the chief participants in devising the MBIs in the world.

Equity Share A security issued by a company to those who contributed capital in its formation shows ownership in the company. The other terms for it are 'stock' or 'common stock'.

Such shares might be issued via public issue, bonus shares, convertible debentures, etc. and may be traded on the stock exchanges.

Such shareholders have a claim on the earnings and assets of the company after all the claims have been paid for. Therefore, such shareholders are also known as the *residual owners*.

Escrow Account In simple terms, an 'escrow account' is held by a *third party account*. It is a separate bank account to hold money which belongs to others and where the money parked will be released only on the fulfilment of certain conditions of a contract. The term *escrow* is derived from the French word 'escrow' meaning a scrap of paper or roll of parchment, an indicator of the deed that was held by a third party till a transaction is completed. An escrow account is an *arrangement for safeguarding* the 'seller' against its 'buyer' from the payment risk for the goods or services sold by the former to the latter.

ESOPs Employee Stock Option Plans (ESOPs) is a provision under which a foreign company (i.e., MNC) offers shares to its employees overseas. Till February 2005 in the case of local firms, an MNC needed a permission from the RBI before allotting ESOPs, but since then, it does not need any permission provided the company has a minimum of 15 per cent holding in the Indian arm.

Expected Credit Loss Under the new Expected Credit Loss (ECL) norms (notified by the RBI in January 2023), banks are required to classify financial assets (loans and investments) into one of the three categories– Stage 1, Stage 2, and Stage 3– depending upon the assessed credit losses on them. This is to be reported by banks at the time of initial recognition as well as on each subsequent reporting date and make necessary provisions against them.

Exploding Arms A term associated with the mortgage business which became popular after the subprime crisis hit the US financial system in mid-2007. Exploding arms are mortgages with initial low, fixed interest rates which escalate to a high floating rate after a period of two to three years.

Externalities Factors that are not included in the gross income of the economy but have an effect on human welfare. They may be *positive* or *negative training* personnel is an example of the former while pollution falls in the latter.

FCCB Foreign Currency Convertible Bond (FCCB) is an unsecured instrument to raise long-term loan in foreign currency by an Indian company which converts into shares of the company on a predetermined rate. It is counted as the part of external debt. It is a safer route to raise foreign currency requirements of a company.

Federal Fund Rate The federal fund rate (also popular as *Fed Fund Rate* or *Fed Rate*) is the rate of interest banks charge each other on overnight loans in the USA. The rate is fixed by the US central bank Federal Reserve. This is equivalent to the *Repo rate* of India which is fixed by the RBI.

Fiduciary Issue Issuance of currency by the government not matched by gold securities, also known as *fiat money*.

Financial Closure Financial closure is defined as a stage when all the conditions of a financing agreement are fulfilled prior to the initial availability of funds. It is attained when all the tie-ups with banks or financial institutions for funds are made and all the conditions precedent to initial drawing of debt are satisfied.

Fire Sale Selling goods or assets at heavily discounted prices is called fire sale. Originally, it referred to the discount sale of goods that were damaged by fire, but over the time it generally means any sale where the seller is in financial distress - even 'clearance sales' offered by showrooms belong to it. In financial markets, we use this term when some stock or security is available well below its intrinsic value (as happens in the case of prolonged bear markets).

First Advance Estimates The Government of India introduced the First Advance Estimates (FAE) of GDP (gross domestic product) in 2016-17. This aims to serve as essential inputs to the Budget exercise. This is based on limited data and compiled using the Benchmark-Indicator Method (i.e., the estimates available for the previous year 2024-25 for the preparation of the Budget of 2025-26) and are extrapolated using relevant indicators reflecting the performance of sectors.

Fiscal Drag The restraining effect of the progressive taxation economies feel on their expansion - fall in the total demand in the economy due to people moving from lower to higher tax brackets and the government tax receipts go on increasing. To neutralise this negative impact, governments usually increase personal tax allowances.

Fiscal Neutrality A stance in policy making by governments when the net effect of taxation and public spending is neutral - neither encouraging nor discouraging the demand. For example, a *balanced budget* is the same attempt of fiscal policy when the total tax revenue equals the total public expenditure.

Fiscal Stance Fiscal stance is basically, the approach/orientation of a government's fiscal policy (i.e., expenditure patterns). The stance has been broadly classified into two categories in economics, namely *anti-cyclical* and *pro-cyclical* - based upon the expenditure behaviour of the government.

As per the established economic theory, when a government is spending during bad times (i.e., in times of slowdown/slackness, recession, etc.), the government is said to be following an *anti-cyclical* (i.e., counter-cyclical) fiscal stance. Opposite to it, when a government is spending more during good times (i.e., expansionary times when growth is comparatively higher), the government's fiscal stance is called to be *pro-cyclical*.

We find Indian Kings constructing palaces during famines and droughts to provide employment and improve the economic fortunes of the private sector (historical examples of anti-cyclical fiscal stance).

Fiscal Stimulus Economies across the world pick their fiscal policy stance (i.e., approach or orientation) as per their needs. One element of it is giving stimulus (with differing kinds of economic support) to the economy or sectors concerned. Broadly speaking, the nature of such stimulus/measures can be of two categories, namely - *'above-the-line'* and *'below-the-line'*.

Above-the-line measures include those for which full cost is reflected in the fiscal deficit, government debt, and increased borrowing needs in the short-term - which include additional spending (on health services, unemployment benefits etc.); capital grants and targeted transfers (for example, wage subsidies or direct transfers); or tax measures (for example, tax cuts or other relief) provided through standard budget channels.

Below-the-line measures involve the creation of assets, like equity injections, loans, asset purchase, etc. which may have little or no upfront impact on the fiscal deficit although they can later increase debt or reduce liquidity (as per the *IMF Fiscal Monitor*, April 2020).

Fisher Effect A concept developed by *Irving Fisher* (1867-1947) which shows the relationship between inflation and the interest rate, expressed by an equation popular as the *fisher equation*, i.e., the nominal interest rate on a loan is the sum of the real interest rate and the rate of inflation expected over the duration of the loan:

$$R = r + F$$

where R = nominal interest rate, r = real interest rate and F = rate of annual inflation.

The concept suggests a direct relationship between inflation and nominal interest rates - changes in inflation rates lead to matching changes in nominal interest rates.

The Fisher effect can be seen each time one goes to the bank; the interest rate an investor has on a savings account is really the nominal interest rate. For example, if the nominal interest rate on a savings account is 4 per cent and the expected rate of inflation is 3 per cent, then money in the savings account is really growing at 1 per cent. The smaller the real interest rate, the longer it will take for savings deposits to grow substantially when observed from a purchasing power perspective.

Flag of Convenience Shipping rights in oceans and seas are governed by international treaties. Flag of convenience is a grant of a shipping 'flag' by a member of these treaties to a non-member nation establishing the legality of shipping to the latter *(usually used for illegal activities).*

Forced Saving The enforced reduction of consumption in an economy. It may take place directly when the government increases taxes or indirectly as a consequence of higher inflation - a tool usually utilised by the developing countries to generate extra funds for investment. Also known as *involuntary saving.*

FoB This is the abbreviation of 'free-on-board' - when in the balance of payment accounting, only the basic prices of exports and imports of goods (including loading costs) are counted. It does not count the 'cost-insurance-freight' (CiF) charges incurred in transporting the goods from one country to another country.

Forward Contract A transaction contract of commodity on an agreed price which binds both the seller and the buyer to pay and deliver the commodity on a future date. The price agreed upon is known as *forward* rate.

One must not confuse this with the term 'future contract' as in it, the term of the contract cannot be decided by the mutual needs of the parties involved (which is possible in a 'forward contract').

Forward Trading A trading system in certain shares (as allowed by the SEBI in India) in which buyers and sellers are allowed to postpone/defer payment and delivery respectively after paying some charges. If the buyer wants deferment, it is known as *badla* (an Indian term for *contango*) and if the seller goes for deferment of delivery of shares, it is known as *undha badla* (in India, elsewhere it is known as *backwardation*).

Fractional Banking A system of banking in which banks maintain a minimum reserve asset ratio to maintain adequate liquidity to meet the customer's cash demands in its everyday business (*the SLR in India is such a provision,*).

Fragile Five The term was coined by Morgan Stanley in 2013, in reference to the five emerging market economies of Brazil, India, Indonesia, South Africa and Turkey. These economies were termed fragile (i.e., weak) by the financial credit rating firm on the simple logic - all were running sizeable current account deficits (CADs) which were being financed by inflows of foreign capital (i.e., foreign investments, more of indirect kind). As they were generally having fairly low foreign exchange (forex) reserves, they were *vulnerable* to the changing whims of international investors. Over the time this term was used by many other global financial institutions and banks to mean different economies of the time, but the meaning of it remaining the same.

When central banks of the developed economies (especially, the USA) did start tapering of interest rates, the currencies of these five economies tumbled as a result (as inflows of foreign capital fell down).

Free Goods The goods which are in abundance *(as air and water)* and are not considered as scarce economic goods. As such, goods have *zero supply price* and they will be used in large volumes resulting in rising environmental pollution (point should be noted that today air and water may not be considered as the typical free goods, at least the 'pure air' and 'pure water').

Free Trade The international trade among an agreed-upon group of countries without any barriers (such as tariffs, quotas, forex controls, etc.), promoted with the objective of securing international specialisation and an edge in their foreign trade.

Free Port A port that is designated as such is the one where imports are allowed without any duty, provided they are re-exported (i.e., *entrepot*). If the same is correct in the case of an area, it is known as the *free trade zone*.

Gallup Poll A method of survey in which a representative sampling of public opinion or public awareness concerning a certain subject/issue is done and, on this basis, a conclusion is drawn.

The credit of developing this research methodology goes to *George H. Gallup* (1901-84), a US journalist and statistician who in 1935 did set up the *American Institute of Public Opinion*. Through his efforts, the method developed in the period 1935-40. In the coming times, the poll technique was immensely used by business houses for their market research and the psephologists for election forecasting, around the world.

Game Theory The analysis of situations involving two or more interacting decision makers (that may be individuals, competing firms, countries, etc.) who have conflicting objectives. It is a technique which uses logical deduction to explore the consequences of various strategies that might be adopted by game players having competing interests.

Game theory is a branch of *Applied Mathematics* that studies strategic interactions between agents - where the agents try maximising their pay off. It gives *formal modelling approach* to social situations in which decision makers interact with other agents. The theory generalises maximisation approaches developed to analyse markets such as supply and demand model.

The field dates back from the 1944 classic *Theory of Games and Economic Behaviour* by John von Neumann and Oskar Morgenstern (Princeton University Press, N. Jersey, 1944 and 2004; 60th Anniversary Ed.). Neumann was a mathematician and Morgenstern an economist and this book was based on the former's prior research published in 1928 on the *Theory of Parlour Games* (in German).

The theory has found significant applications in many areas outside economics as usually construed, including formulations of nuclear strategies, ethics, political science, and evolutionary theory.

Giffen Goods The goods for which the demand increases as its price increases, rather than falls (opposite to the *general theory of demand*) - named after Robert Giffen (1837-1910). It applies to the large proportion of the goods belonging to the household budget (as flour, rice, pulses, salt, onion, potato, etc. in India) - an increase in their prices produces a large *negative income effect* completely overcoming the normal substitution effect with, people buying more of the goods.

Gig Economy A considerably new concept which came into being once the digital platform emerged. Inferring from the literature of the ILO and World Bank, this constitutes the economy of the digital world, which includes 'diverse category of platforms today, engaged in retailing, aggregating, contracting, freelancing, lending, facilitating payments, etc. (Amazon, Ola, Swiggy, Paytm, being a few examples). The economy made increased news globally during the COVID-19 induced lockdowns and restrictions on human movement when people were forced to work from home - making India emerge among the world's largest economies.

A largely unregulated segment, countries across the world have started formalising it regarding labour rights (with India formally classifying them with the unorganised labour force in 2020) of the employees engaged in it, tax provisions, data security and privacy etc.

Gini Coefficient An inequality indicator in an economy. The coefficient varies from 'zero' to 'one'. A 'zero' Gini coefficient indicates a situation of perfect equality (i.e., every household earning the same level of income) while a 'one' signifies a situation of absolute inequality (i.e., a single household earning the entire income in an economy).

Golden Handshake A payment (usually generous) made by a company to its employees for quitting the job prior to their service.

Golden Handcuff A royalty/bonus payment by a company to its staff (usually top ranking) to keep them with the company or to save them from poaching by other companies.

Golden Hello A large sum paid by a company to attract a new staff to its fold.

Golden Rule A fiscal policy stance which suggests that over the economic cycle, government should borrow only to 'invest' and not to finance the 'current expenditure'. The attempts towards 'balanced budgeting', 'zero-based budgeting' developed under the influence of this rule.

Goodhart's Law The idea of Goodhart which suggests that attempts by a central bank (as RBI in India) to regulate the level of lending by banks imposing certain controls can be circumvented by the banks searching the alternatives out of the regulatory preview.

Go-Go Fund The highly speculative mutual funds operating in the USA with the objective of earning high profits out of capital appreciation-adopt risky strategies for the purpose (investing in volatile unproven and small shares, etc.), also called the *performance funds*.

Grandfather Clause This is a clause normally found in a newly introduced law from which certain entity (individual, company, etc.) may be exempt from abiding - such actions of governments are called grandfathering. We may take an example - suppose a government ban owning a cat, a clause of the law may exempt (grandfather clause) those who already own a cat. Though this remains a controversial clause, we find it prevalent across the world [as per the *Farlex Financial Dictionary*, Farlex Inc., N. York, USA, 2012].

Greater Fool Theory A theory evolved by the technical analysts of stocks/shares according to which some even buy overvalued stocks with the conviction that they will find a *greater fool* who will buy them at even higher prices. This is also popular as *castle-in-the-air theory*.

Greenfield Investment An investment by a firm in a new manufacturing plant, workshop, office, etc.

Greenfield Location An area consisting of unused or agricultural land *(i.e., 'greenfield')* developed to set up new industrial plants.

Greenshoe Option A term associated with the security/share market. This is a clause in the underwriting agreement of an initial public offer (IPO) by a company which allows to sell additional shares (usually 15 per cent) to the public if the demand for shares exceeds the expectation and the share trades above its offering price. It gets its name from the *Green Shoe* company which was the first company to be allowed such an option (in the USA, early 20th century). This is also known as *'over-allotment provision'*.

The company availing this option uses the proceeds (i.e., from the greenshoe option) to prevent any decline in the market price of shares below the issue price in the post-listing period (in such cases, the aforesaid company uses the money to purchase its own shares from the market - as demand increases, the market price of its shares picks up).

Gresham's Law The economic idea that 'bad' money forces 'good' money out of circulation, named after Sir Thomas Gresham, an adviser to Queen Elizabeth I of England. This law does not apply to the economies where paper currencies are in circulation. The economies which circulate metallic coins (gold, silver, copper, etc.) of proportional intrinsic values face such situations when people start hoarding such coins.

Greenspan Put A financial market terminology named after the former chairman of the US central bank, Federal Reserve, to mean the helpful way he responded to big declines in the stock market by delivering a cut in interest rates.

Grey Market The 'unofficial' market of the newly issued shares before their formal listing and trading on the stock exchange.

Growth Recession An expression coined by economists to describe an economy that is growing at such a slow pace that more jobs are being lost than are being added. The lack of job creation makes it 'feel' as if the economy is in a recession, even though the economy is still advancing. Many economists believe that between 2002 and 2003, the United States' economy was in a growth recession.

In fact, at several points over the past 25 years the US economy is said to have experienced a growth recession. That is, in spite of gains in real GDP, job growth was either non-existent or was being destroyed at a faster rate than new jobs were being added.

Haircut The term is used in two senses. *Firstly*, it is used to show the difference between market value and collateral value of an asset. For example, when we go to borrow a loan to bank against gold as collateral what banks do is that they consider the collateral value of gold lower (₹25,0000) than its market value (₹35,000). *Secondly*, it is used to measure the 'spread' (i.e., margin) at which market makers (a type of share broker) trade a stock in the security market.

The term has been in news recently in India in the case of the insolvency proceedings of the banks' bad loans (NPAs). The assets of the borrowers (who borrowed from banks to invest in those assets) have been sold off at much lower prices than their investment values - it means assets have been sold off at hefty 'hair cuts'.

Hedge Funds Hedge funds are a class/type of investment companies/institutions (domestic or foreign in origin) which invest their funds in security market (in debts, shares, and derivatives) and keep shuffling their investment portfolios very actively/swiftly to 'minimise the risk of loss' (i.e., hedging) which their funds may be exposed to. This way, they are able to beat the average investment returns for their clients. However, they are considered risky investment choices for common investors. As they enter and exit the security market very swiftly, countries depending on their capital are considered vulnerable to the whims of such investors. As per a conservative estimate of the IMF, by early 2025, there were around 12 such global funds which were capable of investing over US$ 1800 billion at a time in the security markets of global economies!

Herfindahl Index This is a measure of the level of seller concentration in a market which takes into account the total number of firms and their relative share in the total market output. Also known as *Herfindahl-Hirschman Index*.

Hidden Price Rise A quantitative or qualitative decrease in a product without changing the price.

Hidden Tax Addition of an indirect tax into the price of goods or service without fully informing the consumer as, for example, the magnitude of the excise duty in tobacco and alcoholic products is so high that the taxes are added to the products directly.

Historic Cost The original cost of purchasing an asset such as land, machine, etc. which is shown in the balance sheet of a firm under this title with an adjustment for the replacement cost of the asset.

Hoarding An act of unproductive retention of *money* or *goods*.

Hog Cycles The cycles of over and under production of goods. This takes place due to time lag in the production process - this happens in the case of agricultural products specially.

Impossible Trinity See the topic *Trilemmas* in *Chapter 19*.

India's Sovereign Rating Presently, India is rated by six international credit rating agencies, namely Standard and Poor's (S&P), Moody's Investor Services, FITCH, Dominion Bond Rating Service (DBRS), the Japanese Credit Rating Agency (.), and the Rating and Investment Information Inc., Tokyo (R&I).

Indifference Curve A curve on the graph showing the alternative combinations of two products, each giving the same utility/satisfaction.

Induced Investment The part of investment (increase or decrease) which takes place due to a change in the level of national income.

Inferior Product The goods or service for which the income elasticity of demand is negative (i.e., as income rises, buyers go to purchase less of the product). For such products, a price cut results in lesser demands by the buyers.

Inflation For all types of inflation, see *chapter 8* of the book.

Insider Trading A stock market terminology which means transactions of shares by the persons having access to confidential information which are not yet public - such persons stand to gain financially out of this knowledge (the person might be an employee, director, etc. of the share issuing company or the merchant bank or the book runner to the issue, etc.). Such kind of trading in stocks is illegal all over the world.

Insolvency The situation when the liabilities of an individual or a firm to creditors exceed its assets - inability to pay the liabilities from the assets. Also known as *bankruptcy*.

Inventory The stocks of finished goods, goods under the production process and raw materials held by a firm.

Invisible Hand A term coined by Adam Smith (in his magnum opus *The Wealth of Nations, 1776*) to denote the way in which the market mechanism (i.e., the price system) coordinates the decisions of buyers and sellers without any outside conscious involvement. For him, this maximises individual welfare.

IPO An IPO or initial public offering refers to the issue of shares by the promoters of a company for the first time. The shares may be made available to the investors at face value of the share or with a premium as per the perceived market value of the share by the promoters. The IPO can be in the form of a fixed price portion or book building portion. Some companies offer only demat form of shares, others offer both demat and physical shares.

I-S Schedule Here 'I-S' stands for 'investment saving'. This graphic schedule displays the combinations of levels of national income and interest rate where the equilibrium condition for the real economy (investment = savings) holds.

Islamic Banking It is banking practiced as per the Islamic principle as prescribed in the *shariah* known as *Fiqh al-Muamalat* (Islamic rules on transaction). The Islamic law prohibits interest on both loans and deposits. Interest is also called *riba* in Islamic discourse. The argument against interest is that money is not goods and profit should be earned on goods and services only, not on control of money itself. But Islam does not deny that capital, as a factor of production, deserves to be rewarded. It, however, allows the owners of capital a share in a surplus which is *uncertain*.

It operates on the principle of sharing both profits and risks by the borrower as well as the lender. As such, the depositor cannot earn a fixed return in the form of interest as happens in conventional banking. But the banks are permitted to offer incentives such as variable prizes or bonuses in cash or kind on these deposits. The depositor, who in the conventional banking system is averse to risk, is a provider of capital here and equally shares the risks of the bank which lends his funds.

Investment finance is offered by these banks through *Musharka* where a bank participates as a joint venture partner in a project and shares the profits and losses. Investment finance is also offered through *Mudabha* where the banks contribute the finance and the client provides expertise, management, and labour, and the profits are shared in a prearranged proportion while the loss is borne by the bank.

Trade finance is also offered through a number of ways. One way is through *mare up,* where the bank buys an item for a client and the client agrees to repay the bank the amount along with an agreed profit later on. Banks also finance on lines similar to *leasing, hire purchase,* and *sell and buyback*. *Consumer lending* is without any interest, but the bank covers expenses by levying a service charge. Besides, these banks offer a host of fee-based products like money transfer, bill collections, and foreign exchange trading where the bank's own money is not involved.

Islamic banks have come into being since the early 1970s. There are nearly 30 Islamic banks all over the world within the conventional banking system. The whole banking system in Iran has moved over to the Islamic system since the early 1980s and even Pakistan is Islamising its banking system.

Many of the European and American Banks are now offering Islamic banking products not only in Muslim countries, but also in developed markets such as the United Kingdom. The concept is also catching up in countries like Malaysia and Dubai.

As per the Islamic experts, with growing indebtedness of many governments and with bulk of the borrowing going to servicing of the past debt and payment of huge interests, it could be an alternative to conventional banking as practiced in the rest of the world. Wherever it is practiced, *studies* have shown that the rate of return is often comparable and sometimes even higher than the interest rate offered by conventional banks to depositors.

India has no such full-fledged banks, though a few non-banking financial firms have been operating in Mumbai and Bangalore on Islamic principles. We find the traces of such financial operations by co-operatives even during pre-Independence era, too. In November 2017, the proposal of introducing such banking in the country was rejected by the RBI. It was in 2015-16 that an expert panel of the RBI (headed by Raghuram Rajan, the then RBI Governor) had stressed the need of thinking in the direction of introducing Islamic Banking in the country.

Isocost Line A line on the two-axis graph which shows the combination of factor inputs that can be purchased for the same money.

Isocost Curve A curve on the graph showing the varying combinations of factors of production (i.e., labour, capital etc.) that can be used to produce a given quantity of a product with a given technology.

J-curve Effect The tendency for a country's balance of payments deficit to initially deteriorate following a devaluation of its currency before moving into surplus.

Junk Bond An informal term denoting the financial securities issued by a company/bidder as a means of borrowing to finance a takeover bid. Such securities generally include high-risk, highinterest loans, that is why the term 'junk' is used. It is also known as *mezzanine debt*.

Kerb Dealings All the transactions taking place outside the stock exchanges.

Khilji Effect The rulers of the Delhi sultanate didn't understand formal macroeconomics. But they knew one lesson very clearly - it was important to "signal the government's intent to keep expectations in check". Alauddin Khilji personally inspected markets and it worked - checking prices from rising. Such an effect on market is popular in India as the 'Khilji Effect'.

India saw these time-tested lessons followed by the GoI in 2014-15 - Central Ministers publicly stated that matters are under control with sufficient quantity of 'onions' and 'potatoes'.

The Government brought these two commodities under the purview of the Essential Commodities Act, too. This did show the 'strong intent' of the government to control prices.

However, the routine statements claiming that 'prices will rise' often started the inflationary spiral (it was repeatedly done by the then Union Minister of Agriculture).

Kleptocracy A government which is corrupt and thieving - the politicians and bureaucrats in charge using the powers of the state to earn personal benefits/profits. Russia, after the disintegration, is considered to be a clear-cut example when Mafia-friendly government allotted valuable shares of the government companies when they were privatised.

Knightian Uncertainty In economics, Knightian uncertainty is a lack of quantifiable knowledge about some possible outcomes/results, as opposed to quantifiable risk. It is an acknowledgement of imperfect knowledge that makes future events essentially unpredictable. The phenomenon is named after the US economist *Frank Hyneman Knight (1885-1972),* an economist from the University of Chicago (he wrote about it in his seminal work *Risk, Uncertainty, and Profit, 1921*). He was one of the founders of the Chicago School and the Nobel laureates Milton Friedman, George Stigler and James M. Buchanan were all his students at Chicago.

The term was used by the Reserve Bank of India in its last monetary policy statement of the year 2021-2022 (February 2022) in reference to the 'uncertainty' related to the COVID-19, its new variants and their lethality.

Kondratieff Wave A business cycle of 50 years, named after the Russian economist Nikolai Kondratieff (wrote so in his book *The Long Waves in Economic Life,* 1925).

He argued that capitalism was a stable system (the business cycle of 50 years implied it) in contrast to the Marxist view that it was self-destructive and unstable - he died in one of Stalin's prisons.

Labour Force As per the newly introduced (in 2017-18) PLFS (Periodic Labour Force Survey) of India, labour force refers to those who are either engaged in any economic activities or are willing to pursue an economic activity in a reference period. It includes both (i) those who are in workforce; and (ii) those who are unemployed. Of these, *workforce* refers to the population who are actively engaged in any economic activities and producing goods and services in a reference period while *unemployed* refers to all those who are seeking and available for work but had not worked in a reference year due to lack of work. Hence, Labour force participation rate (LFPR) can be *defined* as the proportion of population in the labour force to the total population. Similarly, *worker population ratio* (WPR) can be defined as the proportion of employed persons to the total population.

LAF The abbreviated form of the Liquidity Adjustment Facility, is part of a financial policy provided to the banks by the RBI in India. The facility commenced in June 2000 under which the banks operating in India are allowed to park their funds with the RBI for short-term periods (i.e., less than one year which is usually from one day to seven days, in practice), known as the *Reverse Repo*. On such deposits to the RBI, the banks get an interest rate of 6 per cent per annum at present.

Laffer Curve A curve devised by the economist Arthur Laffer in 1974 which links average tax rates to total tax revenue. It suggests that higher tax rates initially increase revenue but after a point, further increases in tax rates cause revenue to fall (for instance by discouraging people from working). But it is tough to know whether an economy is on the Laffer curve, as higher taxation breeds evasion of taxes too.

Liar Loans A term associated with the financial world which created news after the US financial system was hit by the subprime crisis in mid-2007.

These are the loans wherein borrowers fraudulently mis-state their incomes often egged on by the lender or broker to the bank. Such frauds have been detected along the entire US mortgage financing chain by September 2007 - websites freely advertised that for a nominal fee, they could produce sufficient proof of income by generating bank statements, pay slips, income tax returns, and provide references. Lenders in turn *lied* about the real terms and conditions of the loans to borrowers and lied about the quality of loans sold to investors. The whole gamut of these deeds makes such mortgage loans the *'liar loans'*.

LIBOR The London Interbank Offered Rate (LIBOR) is the interest rate on dollar and other foreign currency deposits at which larger banks are prepared to borrow and lend these currencies in the Euro-currency market. The rate reflects market conditions for international funds and are widely used by the banks as a basis for determining the interest rates charged on the US dollar and foreign currency loans to the business customers.

Life-cycle Hypothesis An idea which states that current consumption is not dependent solely on current disposable income of the consumers but is related to their anticipated lifetime income. This hypothesis has its high applied value in the real-life economic management.

Life Insurance Some important terms:

- **Endowment Policy:** Insurance policies where a lump sum is payable either at the end of the policy term or if the insured dies during the policy tenure, are termed endowment policies.
- **Beneficiary:** A person or organisation legally entitled to receive benefits.
- **Term Life Insurance:** In most cases, term life insurance refers to a product that provides death benefit protection for a specified period of time, say for 30 years. Benefits are doled out under this scheme only if the insured dies during the term.
- **Whole Life Insurance:** It is a policy that provides insurance coverage for the entire life of the individual for a fixed premium throughout his life insurance, coupled with an investment component. Investments could be made in stocks or bonds that lead to accumulation of cash values. The augmented cash reserves are returned once one decides to surrender the policy.

  Universal life insurance was created to provide more flexibility than whole life insurance by allowing the policy owner to shift money between the insurance and saving components of the policy.
- **Variable Universal Life Insurance Policy:** A form of whole life insurance policy, this is a policy for those who weigh high risk threshold. It offers cash values that fluctuate based on the performance of the underlying mutual funds in the investment account. It is this investment of premiums in the equity market that carries with it an element of uncertainty.
- **Premium:** This is the amount that the policy holder pays to the insurance company for the benefits provided under an insurance policy. The frequency of premium payments is opted by the individual. Typical premium modes include monthly, quarterly, semiannual, and annual.
- **Annuity:** An agreement sold by a life insurance company that provides fixed or variable payments to the policy holder, either immediately or at a future date.
- **Group life insurance:** A life insurance policy issued to a group of people, usually through an employer.

- **Lapse:** Defaulting on premium payments leads to the termination of an insurance policy. A lapse notice is sent in writing to the policy holder when the policy has lapsed.
- **Lump Sum:** It refers to the proceeds of the policy that is paid to the beneficiary all at once rather than in installments. Typically, most life insurance policies make lump sum payment settlements.

Liquidation A process of 'winding up' a joint-stock company as a legal entity.

Liquid Asset The monetary asset that can be used directly as payment.

Liquidity The financial term is used in three different senses. At a very general level it means 'cash' (when banks face shortage of fund they say there is liquidity crunch). At another place, it shows an asset's quality to convert into 'cash' (in this sense it is used in the concept of SLR in the case of banks in India). And lastly, it also means the readiness (or speed) of money to be available for use (in this sense it is used in the case of stock of money i.e., M1, M2, M3 and M4).

Liquidity Coverage Ratio Liquidity coverage ratio (LCR) is a clause of *Basel III* norms (of the Basel based Bank for International Settlement) which aims at prudential regulation of the banking sector. Under it banks are supposed to maintain enough short-term liquidity (their needs of the next 30 days) so that they can survive acute financial stress if such situations arise in the economy.

Liquidity Preference A term denoting a preference among the people for holding money instead of investing it.

Liquidity Trap A situation when the interest rate is so low that people prefer to hold money rather than invest it.

In such situations investors do not go to increase investment even if the interest rates on loans are decreased. J. M. Keynes suggested for increased government expenditure or reduction in taxes to fight such a situation.

L-M Schedule Here 'L-M' stands for 'liquidity-money'. This is a schedule showing the combinations of levels of national income and interest rates where the equilibrium condition for the monetary economy, L = M, holds.

Local Area Bank Announced in the Union Budget 1996-97 to ensure a focussed savings and credit mobilisation by defining the clear boundary of operation, the Local Area Bank (LAB) operates to a narrow geographical area of three contiguous districts. The private sector is also allowed entry in the segment.

Locomotive Principle The idea that in a situation of worldwide *recession* (see Chapter 8 on Inflation and *Business Cycle*), increase in the total demand in one economy stimulates economic activities in the other economies *via* foreign trade.

Lorenz Curve A graph showing the degree of inequality in income and wealth in a given population or an economy. It is a rigorous way to measure income inequality. In this method (for example), personal incomes in an economy are arranged in increasing order; the cumulative share of total income is then plotted against the cumulative share of the population. The curve's slope is thus proportional to per capita income at each point of the population distribution. In the case of complete equality of income, the Lorenz curve will be a straight line and with greater curvature the inequality rises proportionally - the *Gini Coefficient* measures this inequality.

LoU Letter of Undertaking (LoU) is basically a kind of guarantee/promise given by the LoU-issuing bank/financial institution about the creditworthiness of a firm (corporate body).

By showing the LoU the drawee of the LoU can borrow from the eligible banks/financial institution inside India or abroad. In the case of a default in repaying the loan by the drawee (of the LoU), the bank/financial institution compensates the lending body. This term came in news in February, 2018 in a financial fraud with a public sector bank (Punjab National Bank).

Lump of Labour Fallacy The fallacy in economics that there is a 'fixed amount of work' to be done, i.e., a lump of labour - this may be shared in different ways to create fewer or more jobs in an economy. An economist, D. F. Schloss in 1891 called it the lump of labour fallacy because in reality, the amount of work to be done is not fixed.

Macro and Microeconomics In economics, two different ways of looking at the economy have been developed by economists i.e., macroeconomics and microeconomics.

Macroeconomics ('macro' in Greek language means 'large') looks at the behaviour of the economy *as a whole* such as the issues like inflation, rate of unemployment, economic growth, balance of trade, etc. It is the branch of economics which studies the economy in its *total* or *average* term.

Microeconomics (in Greek language 'micro' means 'small') looks on the behaviour of the *units,* i.e., the individual, the households, the firms, a *specific* industry, which together make up the economy.

Marginal Standing Facility (MSF) Operationalised on the lines of the existing Liquidity Adjustment Facility (LAF - Repo) in May 2011 under which all Scheduled Commercial Banks can avail overnight funds (against collaterals), up to one per cent of their Net Demand and Time Liabilities (NDTL). Though it operates like the 'repo' and serves similar purpose also for banks, it is a penal rate, the reason this rate is always set by the RBI a bit higher than the repo rate of the time. Banks are supposed to use this route once they have exhausted all other options to mobilise short-term fund.

Marginal Utility The increase in satisfaction/utility a consumer derives from the use/consumption of one *additional* unit of a product in a particular time period- it goes on decreasing, i.e., the *diminishing marginal utility.*

Market Capitalisation A term of security market which shows the market value of a company's share - calculated by multiplying the current price of its share to the total number of shares issued by the company.

Market Maker An intermediary (may be an individual or a firm) in the secondary market who buys and sells securities/shares simultaneously quoting two-way rates. For example, on the Over-the-Counter Stock Exchange of India (OTCEI) only 'market markers' are allowed to operate. The Discount and Finance House of India (SBI DFHI) is the chief market maker in the 'money market' of India. A market maker plays a very vital role by providing sustainability to liquidity in the secondary market.

Mark-to-market Loss The mark-to-market (MTM) loss is an entry used in accounting. It occurs when government securities held by banks are valued at the current market value. If a security was purchased at a certain price and the market price later fell, the holder would have an unrealised loss, and *marking* the security down to the new market price would result in MTM loss.

Marshall Plan A programme of international aid named after General George Marshall (a US Secretary of State) under which the USA contributed around 1 per cent of its GDP in total (between 1948-52) to western Europe to rebuild the economies ravaged in the Second World War.

Menu Cost The cost a firm bears in changing the prices of its product - it includes retraining the sales staff, reprinting of the new price list, labelling of goods, and informing the customers about the price change. Higher menu costs discourage the firms going for frequent price changes.

Mezzanine Financing Mezzanine financing is defined as a financial instrument which is a *mix* of 'debt and equity' finance. It is a debt capital that gives the lender the rights to convert to an ownership or equity interest in the company. It is listed as an asset on the company's balance sheet. As it is treated as equity in a company's balance sheet, it allows the company to access other traditional sources of finance.

In the hierarchy of creditors, mezzanine finance is subordinate to *senior debt* but ranks higher than *equity.* The return on mezzanine finance is higher in relation to debt finance but lower than equity finance. It is also available quickly to the borrower with *little* or *no collateral.* The concept of mezzanine financing is just catching up in India. Mezzanine financing is used mainly for small and medium enterprises, infrastructure and real estate. *ICICI Venture's Mezzanine Fund* was the first fund in India to focus on mezzanine finance opportunities.

MIBID The Mumbai Inter Bank Bid (MIBID) is the weighted average interest rate at which certain banks in Mumbai are ready to borrow from the call money market.

MIBOR The Mumbai Inter Bank Offer Rate (MIBOR) is the weighted average interest rate at which certain banks/institutions in Mumbai are ready to lend in the call money market.

Microcredit Smaller credit/loan to small and needy borrowers who are outside the reach of commercial banks, for the purpose of undertaking productive activities.

Misery Index An index of economic misery that is sum of the rates of inflation and unemployment for an economy - higher the value greater is the misery.

Modern Monetary Theory Quite popular today in the developed economies, the modern monetary theory states that national governments in place of targeting 'arbitrary' fiscal deficit should rather target 'full employment' by going for higher expenditures. The belief is based on the fact that a national government cannot go bankrupt as it has the legal power to print its currency. It means, without being concerned about its tax revenue, government should keep on spending to promote general well-being of the citizens.

Under such a monetary theory, money is made available by the central bank at cheaper cost (to boost demand in the economy) and governments increase their expenditures (by financing via increased internal borrowings). The central banks continue buying government debts (i.e., government securities) which is ultimately supplied with printing of fresh currency - this process can go on endlessly (as national governments have legal power to print as much currency as much they need!). Though the sustainability of such a monetary policy is being hotly debated across the world, we find governments getting more and more attracted to it. The only challenge this policy faces is the concern of a rise in the rate of inflation.

The idea of universal basic income is based on the world's increasing faith in the capability of the modern monetary theory. Now, even the governments in developing world are getting attracted to it - recently not only the Government of India but several states launched quasi-basic income schemes for farmers (either as income or investment support).

Monetary Neutrality This is an old controversial proposition as per which "change in stock of money affects only nominal variables (such as prices, wages, exchange rates, etc.) and not the real variables (such as GDP, consumption, employment, etc.) in an economy". This means that central banks are not able to influence real economy by increasing money supply because its effects will be neutralised by a proportional rise in prices and wages.

The term was 'introduced' by Friedrich Hayek (1899-1992). However, its origin is traced from the classical economist David Hume (1711-1776). While J. M. Keynes (1883-1946) outrightly rejected it, monetarists consider this to be correct but only in the long-run.

Money Illusion A phrase coined by J. M. Keynes to denote the misleading thinking among people that they are getting richer as a result of inflation when in reality the value of money decreases.

The phrase is used by some economists to argue that a small amount of inflation may not be a bad thing and could even be beneficial as it may help to 'grease the wheels' of the economy - a feeling of getting richer (let it be illusory itself!).

Most Favoured Nation As per the WTO agreements, member countries cannot *normally* discriminate between their trading partners. If any country grants one country a special favour such as a lower customs duty rate for one of their products, the same would need to be extended to all other WTO members. This principle is known as Most Favoured Nation (MFN) treatment.

MFN governs trade in *goods*. MFN is also a priority in the General Agreement on Trade in *Services* (GATS) and the Agreement on Trade-Related Aspects of *Intellectual Property* Rights (TRIPS). However, there are some *exceptions* under WTO regime which allow member countries to:

1. Set up a 'free trade agreement' that applies only to *goods* traded within the group (discriminating against goods from outside).
2. Give developing countries special access to their markets.
3. Raise barriers against products that are considered to be traded unfairly from specific countries.
4. To discriminate, in limited circumstances, in services.

But the agreements only permit these exceptions under strict conditions. In general, MFN means that every time a country lowers a trade barrier or opens up a market, it has to do so for the same goods or services for all its trading partners whether developed or developing.

Narrow Banking Short-term lending in risk-free asset is narrow banking. A suggestion for such banking was given by the committee on Financial System (CFS) in 1991 for the weak banks of India.

Nash Equilibrium A concept in game theory named after John Nash, a mathematician and Nobel prize winning economist, which occurs when each player is pursuing their best possible strategy in the full knowledge of the strategies of all the other players – once the equilibrium is reached, none of the players has any incentive to change their strategy.

Negotiated Dealing System The Negotiated Dealing System (NDS) is an electronic trading platform operated by the Reserve Bank of India to facilitate the issuing and exchange of government securities and other types of money market instruments. The goal of the NDS is to reduce inefficiencies stemming from telephone orders and manual paperwork while increasing transparency for all market participants.

Neo-classical Economics The school of economics based on the writings of Alfred Marshall (1842–1924) which replaced the classical economics by the 19th century, also known as the *'marginal revolution'*.

Net Income This is related to a limited liability firm/ company (i.e., Ltd.). It is derived by deducting the expenses of the company from its total revenue in a particular period (usually one year). If income tax and interest are not deducted, it is called *'operating profit'* (or 'loss', as the case may be). Net income is also called *earnings, net earnings* or *net profit*.

Net Stable Funding Ratio Net stable funding ratio (NSFR) is one of the clauses of the Basel III norms (of the Basel based Bank for International Settlement) aimed at prudential regulation of the banking sector. Banks are supposed to maintain sufficient long-term (upto one year) liquidity under it so that they could be sure of the stable source of fund in times of financial stress if such situations arise in the economy.

Net Worth Net worth for a company is its total assets minus total liabilities. This is an important determinant of the value of a company, considering it is composed primarily of all the money that has been invested since its inception, as well as the retained earnings for the duration of its operation. Net worth can be used to determine creditworthiness because it gives a snapshot of the company's investment history. This is also called *owner's equity, shareholders' equity,* or *net assets.*

In the case of an individual, net worth is the value of a person's assets, including cash, minus all liabilities – the amount by which the individual's assets exceed his liabilities is considered the net worth of that person.

Ninja A mortgage business terminology became a common word after the US subprime crisis of mid-2007, which is an acronym for the borrowers with no income, no job or assets.

Nominal Value The value of anything calculated at the current prices. It does not include the effect of inflation during the periods and gives a misleading idea of value.

Non-monetary Liabilities of RBI Non-monetary liabilities (NNML) of the RBI are liabilities which do not have any monetary impact. These comprise items such as the Reserve Bank's paid-up capital and reserves, contribution to National Funds (NIC-LTO Fund and NHC-LTO Fund), RBI employees' PF and superannuation funds, bills payable, compulsory deposits with the RBI, RBI's profit held temporarily under other deposits, amount held in state Governments Loan Accounts under other deposits, IMF quota subscription and other payments and other liabilities of RBI *less* net other assets of the RBI.

Similarly, NNML of banks includes items such as their capital, reserves, provisions, *etc*. NNML of the banking sector includes NNML of the Reserve Bank and that of other banks.

Non-workers The *Census of India* defines nonworkers as the persons who did not 'work at all' during the reference period. They constitute:

1. Students who did not participate in any economic activity paid or unpaid.
2. Household duties who were attending to daily household chores like cooking, cleaning utensils, looking after children, fetching water, etc. and

are not even helping in the unpaid work in the family farm or cultivation or mulching.

3. Dependent such as infants or very elderly people not included as *worker*.
4. Pensioners drawing pension post-retirement, not engaged in any economic activity.
5. Beggars, vagrants, prostitutes and persons having unidentified source of income and with unspecified sources of subsistence and not engaged in any economically productive work.
6. Others, which include all non-workers who may not come under the above categories such as rentiers, persons living on remittances, agricultural or nonagricultural royalty, convicts in jails or inmates of penal, mental or charitable institutions doing no paid or unpaid work and persons who are seeking/available for work.

[Also see the entry *'Worker'*]

Normal Goods The goods whose demand increases as the income of the people increases. It is just opposite of *inferior goods*.

Nostro Account A *nostro* (a Latin word for 'ours') account is an account that a foreign bank (which may be Rosbank in case of Russia) holds for a domestic bank (which may be SBI for India) in the foreign bank's currency (that is Ruble). Such accounts enable domestic banks to provide international banking services to their clients who have global banking needs.

Numeraire A monetary unit which is used as the basis for denominating international exchanges in a product and financial settlements on a common basis. For example, the US dollar being used as the numeraire of international oil trade, the Special Drawing Rights (SDRs) and the IMF transactions.

Nutri Cereals The existing 'coarse cereals' are now known as 'nutri cereals' (as per a GoI notification of April 20, 2018). The cereals put under this category are the millets - Sorghum (Jowar), Pearl Millet (Bajra), Finger Millet (Ragi/Mandua), Minor Millets/Foxtail Millet (Kangani/Kakun), Proso Millet (Cheena), Kodo Millet (Kodo), Barnyard Millet (Sawa/Sanwa/Jhangora), Little Millet (Kutki) and two Pseudo Millets (Black-wheat (Kuttu) and Amaranthus (Chaulai). Now, the new nomenclature will be used for production, consumption and trade purposes. The move is aimed at removing a lingering perception that these grains are inferior to rice and wheat, even as their health benefits are larger.

As per the ICMR (Indian Council of Medical Research), compared to rice Foxtail millet has 81 per cent more protein, little millet has 840 per cent higher fat, 350 percent higher fiber and 1,229 percent higher quantity of iron. The Council highlighted that recent research findings show millets contain 'anti-diabetic' properties and millet-based foods have low 'GI' (Glycaemic Index) and reduce the 'postprandial blood glucose' level and 'glycosylated haemoglobin'.

There has been demand in the country to declare these crops as 'Nutri Cereals' to boost their demand and allow farmers to get higher prices. Promotion of these cereals enhances sustainability in farming (as they need less water in comparison to rice and wheat) also. Besides, they have inbuilt mechanism to enhance farm income (crop loss will decline as they are climate resilient). The noted agriculture scientist *M. S. Swaminathan* had also suggested the name change in 2006 (National Commission on Farmers).

To popularise the consumption of these nutritious cereals, the government has already announced to include millets in the PDS (Public Distribution System) with the objective of improving nutritional security of the country.

NVS Non-Voting Shares (NVS) are the equity shares not having the right to vote at the general meetings of the company. But these shares get higher dividend than the shares having voting rights. A company in India may issue such shares maximum to the 25 per cent of the total issued share capital and such shares cannot get more than 20 per cent higher dividend than the shares with voting rights.

Okun's Law Based on the empirical research of *Arthur Okun* (1928-80), the law describes the relationship between unemployment and growth rate in an economy. According to it, if GDP grows at 3 per cent p.a., the unemployment rate would not change. In the case of faster growth rates, every extra above the 3 per cent will have a decrease in the unemployment rate by its half (i.e., a 4 per cent growth rate will decrease unemployment by 0.5 per cent - half of 1 which is the extra above 3 per cent). Similarly, a growth rate below 3 per cent will have the same but opposite impact on unemployment (i.e., increases it).

Though the law was perfectly correct for the period of the US economy Okun studied, it may not be valid today in either US or anywhere else. But in general, the law is still used by experts and policy makers as a rule of thumb to estimate the relationship between growth rate and job creation.

Open Market Operation An instrument/tool of monetary policy under which the sale/purchase of government Treasury Bills and bonds is done by the central bank (the RBI in the case of India) as a means of regulating money supply.

Operation Twist This is an act related to monetary policy responsibility of the central bank. Under it, the central bank purchases long-term government securities and sells short-term government securities - aimed at making long-term borrowing cheaper. The act aims at 'twisting' the prevailing interest rates (yields) on the short-and long-term securities in the financial system.

It was the central bank of USA (Federal Reserve Board) which took the *world's first* such step in 1961 (under the US President J.F. Kennedy). Since then, such actions have been taken by other central banks across the world as per their needs. After 2008 (the US sub-prime crisis), we find almost all recession-hit western economies trying this quite widely. It is believed to be named after the famous song 'Twist' of 1961 (of Ernest Evans who was popularly known as Chubby Checker).

The term made news in India when by late December 2019, the RBI announced a similar measure - *first* such step taken ever. Under it, the RBI announced to 'purchase' 10-year Government securities (G-Secs) of ₹10,000 crores (maturing 2029) and 'sell' short-term G-Secs (maturing 2020) of the similar amount. Soon after, interest rate on the long-term G-Secs (10-year) started moderating.

In the process of activating the desired kind of monetary policy, central banks keep studying the movement of interest rates on short- and long-term G-Secs - anchoring the interest rates to the current policy rate (i.e., repo rate in the case of India). Once the divergence in interest rates is against the objective of the monetary policy, central banks may go for 'operation twist'.

Opportunity Cost A measure of the economic cost of using scarce resources to produce particular goods or service in terms of the alternative thereby foregone, also known as the *economic cost*.

Over the Counter The financial papers/securities which can be bought or sold through a private dealer or bank rather than on a financial exchange. The term has its use in the non-financial world too-purchasing medicines from a medical store without the doctor's prescription is an over-the-counter deal in drugs.

Parallel Importing A type of arbitrage where an independent importer buys products of a particular supplier at low price in one country and resells it in direct competition with the supplier's distributors in another country where prices are higher.

It promotes free trade and competition by breaking down barriers to international trade and undermines price discrimination between markets covered by the suppliers.

Pareto Principle The maximisation of the economic welfare of the community. Named after the Italian economist Vilfredo Pareto (1843-1923), this points to a situation in which nobody can be made better off without making somebody else worse off.

By an efficient use of resources, an economy is able to do so, i.e., without making somebody else worse off, somebody might be made better off. In reality, change often produces losers as well as winners. Pareto optimality does not help judge whether this sort of change is economically good or bad.

Parkinson's Law A proposition by C. Northcote Parkinson which suggests that work expands according to the time available in which it is done.

PLFS In 2017-18, the Government of India launched a *new* regular employment-unemployment survey, namely, annual *PLFS (Periodic Labour Force Survey)* with certain changes in survey methodology, data collection mechanism and sampling design vis-à-vis the earlier quinquennial (once in every 5 years) EUSs (Employment and Unemployment Surveys) of NSO (National Statistics Office).

In the new survey, households are selected in both *rural* and *urban* areas by providing 75 per cent weightage to households where at least one member has secondary education (Class 10) or above. In the EUS, *affluence level* and earning from non-agricultural activities in rural areas and Monthly Per Capita

Consumption Expenditure (MPCE) of household in selected blocks in urban areas were used for stratification of households. Due to the changes in methodology and sampling design, labour market estimates based on PLFS are not strictly comparable with the results of earlier EUSs.

P/E Ratio Also called 'price multiple' or 'earnings multiple', the *price-to-earnings ratio* (P/E Ratio) measures the current share price to its per-share earnings (earning per share, i.e., EPS). It is used in the stock market by analysts to determine the relative value of a company's shares in one-to-one comparison. This ratio is derived by dividing the market value per share (numerator) with earnings per share (denominator). A high P/E ratio could mean that a company's stock is over-valued, or investors are expecting high earnings in future. In the case of loss-making companies, there is no P/E ratio (as there is no denominator).

Penny Stocks Very low-priced shares of small companies which have low market capitalisation. The term made news in mid-2006 when some of the 'penny stocks' did show a high rise in their trading prices in India at the BSE as well as the NSE.

Petroleum Pricing Petroleum products pricing in India follows a dynamic method which is based on the *Indian Crude Basket* (called *Indian Basket* also). Indian Basket is weighted average of the prices of *Oman & Dubai* (for sour grade) and *Brent* (sweet grade) crude oils. Actual price depends on the ratio in which sour and sweet grades of crude were used by the oil refineries in the previous financial year.

Crude oil with high amount of *sulphur* is termed 'sour' and with less sulphur is called the 'sweet' grade. The dynamic price is maintained by the Petroleum Planning and Analysis Cell (attached to the Ministry of Petroleum and Natural Gas), set up in 2002 by the Government as dismantling of the 'administered pricing mechanism' (APM) for petroleum began.

Phillips Curve A graphic curve depicting an empirical observation of the relationship between the level of unemployment and the rate of change of money wages and, by inference, the rate of change of prices.

It was in 1958 that an economist from New Zealand, A. W. H. Phillips (1914–75) proposed that there was a trade-off between inflation and unemployment-the lower the unemployment rate, the higher the inflation rate-governments simply need to choose the right balance between the two evils.

Piggyback Loan A term associated with mortgage business got popular in the wake of the US subprime crisis mid-2007. Piggyback loan is a second mortgage enabling a borrower to buy a house with little or no equity.

Pigou Effect Named after Arthur Cecil Pigou (1877-1959), a sort of wealth effect resulting from deflation/disinflation (i.e., price fall) - a fall in price level increases the real value of people's money, making them wealthier and inducing increased spending by them; higher demand creation leads to higher employment.

Ponzi Scheme It is an investing or deposit scheme (usually offered in India by the nonbanking financial companies such as Chit Funds) which offers *high returns with very low risks.* Such schemes are able to give high returns to their 'older investors' by mobilising funds from the 'newer investors' - creating a kind of pyramid of investors. The day they stop getting new investors, the existing investors stop getting returns and may lose their entire invested capital as the scheme collapses. This way, such schemes are a kind of financial scams. The Government has proposed to check such schemes from cheating innocent investors in the country.

Population Trap A situation of population growth rate greater than the achievable economic growth rate. This makes it difficult to alleviate poverty. Government is suggested to implement population control measures.

Positive Pay This concept (which was introduced by the RBI by early 2021) involves a process of 'reconfirming key details' of large-value cheques. The issuer of the cheque under it submits electronically, through channels like SMS, mobile app, internet banking and ATM, certain minimum details of that cheque (like date, name of the beneficiary, or payee and amount) to the drawee bank, details of which are cross-checked with the presented cheque by Cheque Truncation System (CTS). Any discrepancy is flagged by CTS to the drawee bank and presenting bank, who then take redressal measures.

Poverty Trap A situation where an unemployed getting unemployment allowance is not encouraged to seek work/employment because his/her after-tax earnings as employed is less than the benefits as unemployed, also known as the *unemployment trap.*

Predatory Pricing The pricing policy of a firm with the express purpose of harming rivals or exploiting the consumer. By price-cutting, firstly the rivals are ousted from the market and later the consumers are exploited as monopolistic suppliers by the firm.

Preference Shares The shares which bear a stated dividend and carry a priority over equity shares (in matters of dividend and assets), are also known as hybrid securities (since they have the qualities of equity shares as well as bond). Such shares in India cannot have a life over 10 years.

Price-earnings Ratio A concept used in the share market to equate various stocks - is a ratio found/calculated by dividing the market price of a share by the earning per share.

Primary and Secondary Market Primary market refers to buying of shares in an initial public offering (directly from the company issuing shares). The shares are bought by applying through a share application form. Secondary market refers to transactions where one investor buys shares from another investor at the prevailing market price or at an agreed price. The shares are bought and sold in the secondary market on the stock exchanges.

Primary Dealer Primary Dealer (PD) is an intermediary participating in the *primary* auctions of the government securities (i.e., G-See or the Gilt-edge securities or the Gilt) and the Treasury Bills (TBs) - through a PD, these instruments reach the secondary market.

Primary dealers are allowed participation in the call money market and notice money market. They get liquidity support from RBI via repos or refinance (against the G-Secs.).

Prisoner's Dilemma A popular example in *game theory* which concludes why co-operation is difficult to achieve even if it is mutually beneficial, ultimately making things worse for the parties involved. It is shown giving an example of two prisoners arrested for the same offence held in different cells. Each prisoner has two options, i.e., confess, or say nothing. In this situation, there are *three* possible outcomes:

1. One could confess and agree to testify against the other as a state witness, receiving a light sentence while his fellow prisoner receives a heavy sentence.
2. They can both say nothing and may turn out to be lucky getting light sentences or even be let off due to lack of firm evidence.
3. They may both confess and get lighter individual sentences than one would have received had he said nothing and the other had testified against him.

The second outcome looks the best for both the prisoners. However, the risk that the other might confess and turn state witness is likely to encourage both to confess, landing both with sentences that they might have avoided had they been able to co-operate by remaining silent.

In reality, firms behave like these prisoners, not setting prices as high as they could do if they only trusted the other firms not to undercut them. Ultimately, the firms are worse off, i.e., all firms suffer.

Provisioning Coverage Ratio This is a ratio of fund of banks' bad assets (i.e., the non-performing assets - NPAs) which banks need to maintain with themselves (out of their profits). Popularly called 'provisioning', this ratio is the percentage of bad assets of banks and is part of the prudential regulatory norms evolved by the Reserve Bank of India for the banks operating in the country. The PCR (provision coverage ratio) differs as per the classification a bank's NPAs (which are presently of three kinds, namely *sub-standard, doubtful,* and *loss assets,* as defined by the RBI).

For example, if the provisioning coverage ratio is 75 per cent for a particular category of NPAs, banks have to set aside funds equivalent to 75 per cent of its value out of their profits.

Purchase Tax A tax collected by states in India on goods. This is imposed on the *purchases* done by traders/manufacturers - basically collected by the seller and given to the states concerned. This is deducted once the traders/manufacturers pay value added tax (VAT) to the states - as VAT is paid on the differential value of the traded/manufactured goods. This tax is among the 9 state taxes merged into the indirect tax, the GST.

Purchasing Managers' Index The purchasing managers' index (PMI) is an indicator which gives an economic insight into a sector. Based on the surveys of businesses, the Manufacturing PMI and Services PMI are the most common ones. The headline PMI is a number from 0 to 100. A PMI above 50 represents an *expansion* when compared with the previous month, a PMI reading under 50 represents a contraction, and a reading at 50 indicates no change. The PMIs are prepared and published by the firm *IHS Markit* in India.

Q Theory As investment theory for firms proposed by the Nobel prize winning (1981) economist James Tobin (1918-2002). He theorised that firms would continue to invest as long as the value of their shares exceeded the replacement cost of their assets - the ratio of the market value of a firm to the net replacement cost of the firm's assets is known as *'Tobin Q'*. If Q is greater than 1, then it should expand the firm by investment as the profit it should expect to make from its assets (reflected by share price) exceeds the cost of the assets.

If Q is less than 1, the firm would be better off by selling its assets which are worth more than shareholders currently expect the firm to earn in profit by retaining them.

Random Walk When it is impossible to predict the next step. As per the Efficient Market Theory, the prices of financial assets (such as shares) follow a random walk-there is no way of knowing the next change in the price. The reason this theory provides is that in an efficient market, all the information that would allow an investor to predict the next price move is already *reflected in the current price.* Such belief has led some economists to conclude that investors cannot outperform the market consistently.

As opposed to this, some economists argue that asset prices are predictable and that markets are not efficient - they follow a *non-random walk* perspective.

Redlining The act of not lending to people in certain poor or troubled neighborhoods shown on the map with a 'red line'. Even if their creditworthiness has been judged based on other criteria, they are not considered as borrowers by the banks, simply because they live in that area.

Rent It has two different meanings in economics:

1. The first is layman, i.e., the income accruing from hiring land or other durable goods.
2. The second (also known as *economic rent*) is a measure of *market power,* i.e., the difference between what a factor of production is paid and how much it would need to be paid to remain in its current use.

For example, a cricket player may be paid ₹40,000 a week to play for his team when he would be willing to turn out for only ₹10,000, so his economic rent will be ₹30,000 a week.

Rent-seeking Spending time and money not on the production of real goods and services, but rather on trying to get the government to change the rules so as to make one's business more profitable.

It is like cutting a bigger slice of the cake rather than making the cake bigger, trying to make more money without producing more for customers. The term was coined by the economist Gordon Tullock.

Rent-seeking Behaviour The behaviour which improves the welfare of someone at the expense of someone else. A protection racket is the most extreme example of it, in which one group (i.e., the protected one) betters itself without creating welfare-enhancing output at all.

Replacement Cost The cost of replacing an asset (such as machinery, etc.). Opposite to *historic cost* (i.e., the original cost of acquiring an asset), replacement cost adjusts the effects of inflation.

Residual Risk What is left after one takes out all the other shared risk exposures to an asset, also known as *alpha* (a).

When one buys an asset, one is exposed to a number of risks, many of them not unique to the asset but reflect broader possibilities (such as the future behaviour of stock market, interest rate, inflation or even government policies, etc.). Exposure to this risk can be reduced by diversification.

Retail Banking A way of doing banking business where the banks emphasise the individual-based lending rather than corporate lending - also known as *high street banking.* Such banking focusses on consumer loans, personal loans, hire-purchase, etc., considered more cumbersome and riskier.

Retail Direct The Reserve Bank of India launched the scheme, Retail Direct, in 2021 which provides *one-stop solution* to facilitate investment in government securities by individual investors. Under it, individuals are allowed to open free of cost 'Retail Direct Gilt Account' directly with the RBI to trade in the primary and secondary markets of the government securities. This is aimed at deepening the government bond market and make common citizens earn fixed risk-free continuous income.

Reverse Takeover The term is used to mean two different kinds of takeovers:

1. Takeover of a public company by a private one, and
2. Takeover of a bigger company by a smaller one.

Residual Unemployment Unemployment of those who remained unemployed even in the times of full employment (as for example employing a severely handicapped person may far outweigh the productivity obtained from him).

Reverse Mortgage A scheme for senior citizens in India announced in the Union Budget 2007-08. Under this scheme, the senior citizens go to mortgage their house owned by them in reverse to a bank and the bank pays them the agreed money either in installments or lumpsum. Guidelines for reverse mortgage announced by the National Housing Bank (NHB) in May 2007 has a provision of maximum period of 15 years for such mortgage. Once the period of mortgage is complete, either the house should be vacated or the bank will sell the house at the market price and the loan of the bank will be settled. If the value of the house is more than the loan, the difference is paid to the senior citizens or their heirs. If the heir wants to possess the house, he/she needs to pay the loan.

Reverse Yield Gap An excess of returns on gilt-edged (government) securities above those on equities. This occurs during periods of high inflation because equities provide capital gains to compensate inflation while the gilt-edged securities do not.

Revealed Preference The notion that what one wants is revealed by what one does, not by what one says-actions speak louder than words.

Ricardian Equivalence An idea which (generated too much controversies) was originally suggested by David Ricardo (1772-1823) and more recently by Barro, that government deficits do not affect the overall level of demand in an economy.

This is because tax-payers know that any deficit has to be paid later, and so they increase their savings in anticipation of a higher tax bill in future; thus, government attempts to stimulate an economy by increasing public spending or cutting taxes, will be rendered impotent by private sector reaction.

The equivalence can be seen as part of a thread of economic thinking which holds that only decisions about real variables (e.g., consumption and production) matter, and that decisions about financing will, in a perfectly functioning market, never have an effect.

Risk Seeking An act whereby investors prefer an investment with an uncertain outcome to one with the same expected returns and certainty that it will deliver them - the act which cannot get enough risk.

Round Tripping Literally, round tripping means the ending of a journey (trip) at the place where it began from. In economics, it is related to external sector which comes under the regulatory control of the RBI in India (in the case of companies, SEBI also joins as regulator). Under it, the money (mostly black money) leaves a country of origin through various channels such as over-invoicing (showing higher prices of goods in bills), payments to shell (i.e., fake) companies located overseas, hawala route, etc. After remaining overseas for some time (known as the cooling period), the fund returns back to the country of origin (as white money) - completion of the trip. For return trips, normally, the legal instruments of foreign investment like Global Depository Receipts (GDRs) and Participatory Notes (PNs) are used.

In recent past companies like United Spirits, Unitech, Sterlite and Reliance ADAG were alleged to have indulged in stock price manipulation channelising funds through this route - using their shell companies, P-Notes and international investment banks.

Round-trip Trading Round-trip trading is an unethical trading of shares. Under it, the same trader or two traders sell and buy a share same day simply to push the trading volumes of the share upward. This is done to manipulate observers into believing that the share is in high demand (rather the company might not be running in profit). This increases the profit aspect of the company which gets reported through their balance sheet. The most infamous global case of it was the Enron power company of the USA (in India, the Satyam Computers was the first such reported case). This act is illegal across the world.

Rule of Thumb A rough-and-ready decision-making aid that provides an acceptably accurate approximate solution to a problem. Where refined decision-making processes are expensive (in terms of information gathering and processing them), such a method looks justified.

Rounding Error The error which comes up due to rounding off the figures in decimals, for example, considering 3.6 as 4 and 3.4 as 3. Such rounding off the data is never going to be mathematically correct.

Salary The payment made to employees of an organisation, firm, etc. for the use of labour as a factor of production. It differs from *wage* in the following two ways:

1. It is not paid on hourly basis (or for the actual number of hours worked by the employee) as wages are paid, and
2. It is usually paid on monthly basis whereas wages are paid on daily or weekly basis.

Satisfying Theory A theory which suggests that firms do not want only 'satisfactory' profits but maximum profits as well as other objectives such as sales increase, size increase, etc. might be having equal or greater importance than profits.

Say's Law Named after the French economist Jean Baptise Say (1767-1832), the law proposes that aggregate supply creates its own aggregate demand.

The logic of the law goes like this - the very act of production generates an income (in the form of wages, salaries, profits, etc.) exactly equal to the output which, if spent, is just sufficient to purchase the whole output produced. Ultimately, it gives an important clue, i.e., in order to reach full-employment level, all that is needed is to increase the aggregate supply.

The key assumption behind the law is that the economic system is 'supply-led' and that all income is spent. But in practice, some income 'leaks' into saving, taxation, etc., and there is no auto-guarantee that all income is 'injected' back as spending. Therefore, others suggest for a 'demand-led' idea of the economic system under which demand creation is attended vigorously.

Second-best Theory The idea was put forward by Richard Lipsey and Kelvin Lancaster (1924-99) in 1956 which suggests a way out of the situation when all the assumptions of an economic model are not met. As per the theory, the second-best situation is meeting as many of the assumptions as possible (but it might not give the optimum or the desired results).

Securities Transaction Tax See Chapter 18, *Tax Structure in India.*

Sequestration The process under which a third party *(the sequestrator)* holds a part of the disputed assets till the dispute is settled.

Shadow Banking When financial institutions create credit (forward loan) like a bank but are not under the banking regulatory framework of the country, they are supposed to be involved in shadow banking. Hedge funds are one such example. It also includes unregulated activities of regulated entities. Credit default swaps (CDSs) are the examples of it - regulated entities (like banks) provide loan protection in it to other lenders against default risks by the borrowers.

As such institutions do not accept traditional bank deposits, they easily escape the regulatory design of a country. Such acts are financially risky to the economy, as in it 'capital requirements' (of CRR, SLR, etc.) are bypassed by the institutions. Therefore, in cases of default, there remains no standby capital/ asset to counter it. After the 'subprime' crisis in USA (2007-08), shadow banking came under increasing scrutiny and regulation across the world. The NBFCs (non-banking financial companies) in India are an example of such banking.

Share Warrant Share or equity warrant is an instrument that empowers its holder to buy a particular stock/equity/share at a predetermined price within a stipulated time frame. However, to gain this right, the buyer of such warrants usually needs to make an upfront payment to the warrant's issuer. On exercise of such warrants, fresh shares are issued by the issuer company.

Sharpe Ratio The idea of William Forsyth Sharpe (Nobel Economist) which checks whether the rewards from an investment justify the risk. For this, Sharpe uses the past data of rewards and calculates it using standard deviation. Therefore, the ratio says nothing about the future performance of the investment.

Short Selling Selling shares without possessing them. After the prices fall to a certain extent, the short-seller covers his position by cheaper shares booking the difference in price as profits. It is also known as *bear operation.* Short-sellers, however, could get caught on the wrong foot if the market reverses the downtrend.

Shutdown Price That lower level of the prices for the product of a firm at which the firm decides to close *(shut)* down - as it has become impossible to recover even the short-run variable cost at the price. Many such instances we get in the Euro American economies during the period of the Great Depression (1929).

Skimming Price A pricing method of charging high profits - adopted by a firm when consumers are not price-sensitive and demand is price-inelastic.

Smurfing Smurfing (also called *structuring*) is a method in which small sizes of money is kept in several number of bank accounts to hide the real identity of the real owner. This has been a very commonly used method of money-laundering. During the reform period, as more prudential norms of banking regulation evolved, such acts declined in India. 'Smurfer' (or 'money mule') is a person who does this.

Social Costs The costs borne by the society at large resulting from the economic activities of the firms-pollution being a prominent example.

Solvency Margin The term made news in the 1970s concerning a life insurance company. The only requirement, till then, by a life insurance company was that the value of its assets should not be less than the value of its liabilities. The regulators in many countries felt that the value of assets should exceed the value of liabilities by a certain margin. This margin which came to be known as *'solvency margin'* became a useful device to force shareholders of a life insurance company either to keep in reserve a certain portion of the profit or to bring in additional capital if there is not sufficient profit to meet unforeseen contingencies. The European Union developed an empirical formula taking recourse to the past experience to determine the quantum of margin required. The IRDA has stipulated that the excess of assets (including capital) over liabilities should not be less than 150 per cent of the solvency margin arrived at by the EU formula.

Sovereign Bond The securities (backed by assets or/ and legal guarantee) issued (i.e., sold off) to borrow are known as bonds. Bonds are issued by both government and non-government agencies. When a national government issue it in overseas markets, it is known as Sovereign Bond. Buyers of the bond enjoy the profit element on bonds which is popularly known as 'bond yield'.

Today, the world has a highly developed bond market in which national governments issue such bonds to borrow in either foreign or their domestic currencies (in the case of India, the bonds by which rupee-denominated loans are borrowed from the overseas markets are known as 'masala bonds'). The term came in news when the Government of India proposed (in the *Union Budget 2019-20*) to finance a part of its expenditures by issuing such bond– the Sovereign Green Bonds issued by the Government in 2022 may be considered its cautious beginning.

Sovereign Risk The risk of a government defaulting on its debt or a loan guaranteed by it (all international loans by the private companies are basically guaranteed by the government of an economy).

Spot Price The price quoted for anything in a transaction where the payment and delivery is to be done now.

Spread A frequently used term of financial market which is the difference between two items, for example, the spread (i.e., the difference) an underwriter pays for an issue of bonds from a company and the price it charges from the public. Similarly, the returns on two different bonds if they are different; the difference is known as spread.

Standard Deviation It is a statistical technique to measure how far a variable moves over time away from its mean (average) value.

Standing Deposit Facility Scheme The Standing Deposit Facility Scheme (SDFS) is a new monetary tool given to the RBI (announced by the Union Budget 2018-19). Such a facility was proposed by the RBI in November 2015 itself. Such a tool was needed at the disposal of the RBI which it can use when the economy is flush with excess fund. This will allow 'uncollateralised deposit' of the liquidity in the economy if such a need arises. However, from 2022-23, it was declared as one of the policy rates for making monetary policy while the existing 'reverse repo rate' was made the 'fixed reverse repo rate' (for more details refer *Chapter 13*).

The need of such a tool was felt last time when the Government demonetised the high value currency notes of ₹500 and ₹1000 denominations in November 2016. As people were depositing the demonetised currencies in their bank accounts, the banking industry was flush with excessive fund (temporarily). To handle the situation, RBI increased banks, CRR (Cash Reserve Ratio) temporarily to syphon out the excess liquidity with the banks.

Stealth Tax A popular name given to an obscure tax increase for example, stamp duty, property tax, etc. They get implemented months later by the time they usually fade out from the public memory.

Sterilised Intervention This is an act of the central bank of India (RBI) related to its dual responsibilities, namely regulating monetary system through the right monetary policy and stabilising the exchange rate of rupee. Under sterilised intervention, the RBI intervenes in foreign exchange in a typically different way. Under it, to stabilise the exchange rate of rupee, RBI keeps buying foreign currencies while, it keeps selling government securities (to syphon out rupee pumped in the monetary system while purchasing foreign currencies). This way, the RBI aims to stabilise exchange rate while not allowing inflation to go out of bound (target). This process may be run in the reverse also (when foreign exchange is outflowing from the country).

Due to increased integration of the economy with the global economy, India has seen increase in external transactions (inflows and outflows of foreign currencies) also. As India has been following an active policy of attracting foreign investment (direct and indirect both), the exposure of economy to global economy has increased over time - getting very difficult for the RBI to fulfil its responsibility. Due to increased volatility in the global economy (caused by the Great Recession hitting the western economies), India started facing the volatile inflows and outflows of foreign exchange. Faced with the typical situation, the RBI commenced this act (suggested by the *Urjit Patel Committee* in 2014).

Stochastic Process It is a process that shows random behaviour. For example, *Brownian* motion, which is often used to describe changes in share prices by the experts in an efficient market (random walk), is such a process.

Sub-Prime Crisis The word 'sub-prime' refers to borrowers who do not have sound track record of repayment of loans *(it means such borrowers are not 'prime', thus they could be called 'less than prime' i.e., 'sub-prime')*. The 'sub-prime crisis', which has been echoing time and again recently, has its origin in the United States housing market by late 2007 - being considered as the major financial crisis of the new millennium.

Subsidy Bidding It is competitive bidding for subsidies, where companies bid against one another to serve an area at the lowest price - the lure is the subsidy and other benefits. This system is a way of administrating subsidies without leaving any room for some competitors or technologies gaining an edge over others. But competitive bidding has anticompetitive effects, since it gives a special advantage to one company. Regulators should adopt a consumer choice system, under which any subsidy for each high-cost customer it served. If the customer moved to a competing carrier, the subsidy would move, too.

Substitution Effect The replacement of one product for another resulting from a change in their relative prices.

Sukuk This is an Islamic financial certificate, similar to a *bond* (which is an instrument of raising loans) in the financial system, that complies with Islamic law the Sharia. As Sharia does not permit the issuance of normal interest-paying bonds, the issuer of a Sukuk essentially sells an investor group a certificate, and then uses the proceeds to purchase an asset that the investor group has direct partial ownership interest in. The issuer of Sukuk signs a contract with the investor group to buy back the Sukuk at future date (like maturity of a bond) at par value.

Sunk Costs The costs in commercial activities that have been incurred and cannot be reversed. The cost on advertisement, research and development, etc. are examples of such costs. Sunk costs are a big deterrent to new entrants in the commercial world as after the venture has failed, these costs cannot be recovered - there is no two-way process here.

Surety It is the guarantee of a debt of one party by another. A surety can be an organisation or person that assumes the responsibility of paying the debt in case the debtor defaults or is unable to make the payments. This is also known by its other name, *guarantor*.

Swap The act of exchanging one by another. It could be of many economic items:

- **Currency Swap:** The simultaneous buying and selling of foreign currencies could be *spot* or *forward/future* currency swaps. This is used by MNCs to minimise the risk of losses arising from exchange rate changes.

- **Debt Swap:** Exchanging one debt by another for a fresh term of repayment schedule at the same or usually lower interest rates.
- **Interest Rate Swap:** Exchanging one debt of a particular interest rate for another at lower interest rate.
- **Product Swap:** Exchanging one product for the other as wheat for milk (similar to barter).

SWIFT The Society for Worldwide Inter-bank Telecommunication (SWIFT) is a messaging network which connects banks and financial institutions across the world. International transactions of the banks and institutions are ultimately based on this network. The network was in news in India after the LoU (Letter of Undertaking) related banking fraud occurred with the Punjab National Bank in February 2018. Meanwhile, the RBI has enforced (February 2018) a new guideline under which all banks and financial institutions of India need to link their core banking system to the SWIFT to protect themselves from occurrence of any future financial fraud.

Swiss Formula Tariff cut formulae are either linear or non-linear. A Swiss formula is a nonlinear formula. In a linear formula, tariffs are reduced by the same percentage irrespective of how high the initial tariff is. As opposed to a linear formula, in a non-linear formula, tariff cuts are directly or inversely proportional to the initial tariff rate.

In the Swiss formula, tariff cuts are proportionally higher for tariffs which are initially higher. For instance, a country which has an initial tariff of 30 per cent on a product will have to undertake proportionally higher cuts than a country which has an initial tariff of 20 per cent on the same product.

Systemic Risk The risk of damage to the health of the whole financial system. In modern financial world, the collapse of one bank could bring down the whole financial system.

Takeover The process of one firm acquiring the other, also known as *acquisition*. As opposed to the merger which is an outcome of 'mutual agreement', takeovers are 'hostile' moves.

Takeovers may be classified into three broad categories:

1. *Horizontal takeovers* involve firms which are direct competitors in the same market;
2. *Vertical takeovers* involve the firms having supplier-customer relationship; and
3. *Conglomerate takeovers* involve the firms operating in unrelated markets but intend diversification.

Takeover Bid An attempt of acquiring the majority share in a firm by another firm. There are various *terms* to show the *'tactics'* applied in such bids either by the bidder or the bidded firms:

- **Black Knight:** The launch of an unwelcome takeover bid (as Mittal's for the Arcelor in recent past).
- **Golden Parachute:** A generous severance term written into the employment contracts of the directors (of a firm) which makes it expensive to sack them if the firm is taken over.
- **Green Mail:** A situation of takeover bid when the bought-up shares by a potential bidder is actually being bought by the directors of the firm itself.
- **Leveraged Bid:** A takeover bid being financed primarily by the loan.
- **Pac-man Defence:** A situation when the firm being bidded for takeover, bids for the bidder firm itself-also known as *reverse takeover bid.*
- **Poison Pill:** A tactic used by the firm being bidded of merging with some other firm in order to make itself less attractive (financially or structurally) to the potential bidder.
- **Porcupine:** Any agreements between the firm being bidded and its suppliers, creditors, etc., which are so complex that after the takeover, the bidder firm feels difficulties integrating it.
- **Shark Repellants:** The measures specially designed to discourage takeover bidders (e.g., altering the firm's articles of association to increase the proportion of shareholder votes needed to approve the bid above the usual 50 per cent level, etc.).
- **White Knight:** The intervention of a third firm in a takeover bid which either merges with or takes over the victim firm to rescue it from the unwelcome bidder.

Tax Expenditure Tax expenditure, which is also known as *revenue forgone*, is the difference between the official tax rate (which is imposed) and the effective tax rate (which is actually collected). This difference mainly occurs due to tax exemptions offered by the governments, basically to promote certain sectors in the absence of which they may not grow or even come up.

As such exemptions increase complexity and distort tax system, the Government has started withdrawing them in India since the past few years.

Tax Inversion This is a situation of tax structure. This takes place when a firm bases its headquarters in a low tax country while keeps its material operations in the high tax countries (generally their country of origin). This way, firms cut their tax payment liabilities. This is legal and is a method of tax avoidance. Multinational corporations (MNCs) keep doing this - several MNCs of the US-origin shifted their headquarters to the UK, during the 1970s and 1980s. The countries in the world which have very low tax regime for corporations have emerged as very attractive locations for the headquarters of big corporations. Bermuda, Virgin Islands, etc. are such countries (popularly known as the 'tax havens').

Taylor Rule A rule/concept aimed at establishing a relationship between the rate of inflation in an economy and in its aftermath the nominal interest rate announced by the Central Bank of the country. Proposed by J.B. Taylor (1948), this rule suggests that when there is an one percent increase in the inflation rate, the Central Bank increases nominal interest rate by more than one per cent. Though such a relationship between inflation rate and nominal interest rate of the Central Bank is difficult to establish, the concept has an academic importance.

Technological Unemployment Unemployment which results from the automation of the production activities *(i.e., machines replacing men).*

Terms of Trade This represents the ratio between the export prices and import prices of an economy. It is calculated by dividing the price of exports by price of imports and multiplying the result by 100. The terms of trade (TOT) index of an economy is defined by its trade balance (i.e., value of total exports minus value of total imports).

While the TOT values over 100 per cent show capital accumulation by the economy through trade, the values below 100 per cent show drain of capital from the economy through trade.

Third-party Insurance Motor third-party insurance or third-party insurance is a statutory requirement under the Motor Vehicle Act in India - also known as '*act only*' cover. A person purchasing a motor vehicle has to go for this compulsory insurance which benefits the third person (i.e., neither the vehicle owner nor the insurance company) - the person who becomes a victim of an accident by the vehicle. The amount of compensation is largely decided by the earning capacity of the accident victim.

Third Way An economic philosophy (better say rhetoric) which propagates it is neither capitalism nor socialism but a third (pragmatic) way.

The idea was popularised in the late 20th century by some political leaders having leftist leanings, including Bill Clinton and Tony Blair. Though it has been hard to pin down, it was earlier used to describe the economic model of Sweden.

Tight Money When money has become difficult to mobilise, the term is used to show the 'dear money' when the rates of interest run comparatively on the higher side.

Till Money The notes and coins the commercial banks keep to meet everyday cash requirements of their customers (this is counted as part of their CRR).

Tobin Tax A proposal of imposing small tax on all foreign exchange transactions with the objective to discourage destabilising speculation and volatility in the foreign exchange markets.

Proposed by the Nobel prize-winning economist James Tobin (1918-2002), the tax has never been implemented anywhere in the world so far.

Total Product This is the main/core product supported by many peripheral products/services, for example, a car, coming with loan facility, warranties, insurance, and after-sales service, etc.

Trade Creation The increase in international trade that results from the elimination or reduction of trade barriers (such as quota, customs, etc.).

Tragedy of the Commons This is a concept which raises the issue of 'over-exploitation' of resources which lack property rights (called 'commons' such properties are not owned privately but are open for free use by all). Grazing lands is a classic example which is carelessly over-used by common people. This can be checked by rationing and/or imposing tax, as per experts.

Rooted in the lectures (on population) of the British economist William Foster Llyod (1794-1852), the term was coined by the US ecologist Garrett Hardin (1915-2003) in 1968.

Transfer Payments The expenditure by the government for which it receives no goods or services. For example, the expenditures on tax collection, social sector, unemployment allowance, etc.

As such expenditures are not done against any products, they are not counted in the national income of the economy.

Transfer Earnings The return that an asset must earn to prevent its transfer to the next best alternative use. Any earning above the transfer earnings is known as its *'economic rent'*.

Transfer Price A term of international economics via which an MNC charges lesser prices for its exportable to its arm in another economy where tax rates are high, for increasing income. The East India Company did it heavily in pre-independent India.

Underwriting The process of acceptance by a financial institution of the financial risks of a transaction for a fee. For example, merchant banks underwrite new share issues, guaranteeing to buy up the shares not sold in a public offer (i.e., in the situations of under-subscription).

Unicorn A term of mythology is today used to mean a firm (company) which has valuation (as per the investors) of US$1 billion or more. Usually a *start-up*, such firms do not have an established performance record but as they look attractive due to diverse reasons (such as being a sunrise industry), accessing loans or investments is relatively easier for them. The term was *first* used by the venture capitalist Aileen Lee in 2013, as per whom, a firm with valuation over US$ 100 billion is 'super unicorn' (the companies such as Facebook, LinkedIn, etc.).

Unorganised Sector According to India's NCEUS (National Commission for Enterprises in Unorganised Sector) classification, the "unorganised sector' consists of all *unincorporated* private enterprises owned by individuals or households engaged in the sale and production of goods and services operated on a proprietary or partnership basis and with less than ten total workers". However, "*informal workers* consist of those working in the unorganised enterprises or households, excluding regular workers with social security benefits, and the workers in the formal sector without any employment benefits/social security provided by the employers".

Unsecured Loan The loan which is forwarded by banks only against the creditworthiness of the borrower is known as 'unsecured' loan. Such loans are also known as *signature loans* and *personal loans.* If the loan is supported by some form of collateral (of secondary security, such as land, building, etc.), then it is a 'secured' loan.

Basically, loans are provided by banks against two kinds of securities - the creditworthiness of the borrower (known as the 'primary security') and collateral (known as the 'secondary security').

Usual Status This is a term used in India's labour force surveys where the Usual Status gives an idea about average working condition of an individual for the entire reference year. It is further subdivided into two categories - one being *principal status (ps)* and other the *subsidiary status (ss).* While the principal status measures the activity in which an individual has spent relatively longer time of a reference year (major time criterion), the subsidiary status measures the activity status of an individual who has spent majority of days out of work force but have worked for a short period of time (more than 30 days).

Usury Charging an exorbitant rate of interest or even charging interest. Decried by many ancient philosophers and many religions, today most modern economies have some law regulating the upper limit of the interest rates and they consider interest as a reward to the lender for the lending risk.

VGF The Viability Gap Funding (VGF) is a fund assistance facility provided by the GoI to the private players in the infrastructure projects being developed under public private partnership (PPP). The fund is given by the GoI as one time 'grant' and it could be maximum 20 per cent of the project cost (in special cases, an additional 20 per cent might be approved by the states/ministries/authorities).

The facility, which was operationalised in September 2006, was aimed at attracting private investment towards this socio-economically desirable sector. Several infra projects were economically 'non-viable' which used to discourage private players away from such projects - this facility encourages them to take part.

Veblen Effect Named after the American economist Thorstein Bunde Veblen (1857-1929), this is a theory of consumption which suggests that consumers may have an 'upward-sloping demand curve' as opposed to a 'downward-sloping demand curve' because they practise conspicuous consumption (*a downward - sloping demand curve means that the quantity demanded varies inversely to the price i.e., demand falls with price rise*). The concept suggests that quantity demanded of a particular goods varies directly with a change in price (*i.e., as price increases, demand increases*).

Velocity of Circulation A measure of the average number of times each unit of money is used, to purchase the final goods and services produced in an economy in a year.

Venture Capital Fund Generally, a private equity capital which lends capital to the entrepreneurs who are innovative and cannot get the required fund from the conventional set-up of the lending mechanism.

In India, it was the Government of India which did set up the first such fund in 1998 - the IVCF (i.e., the IFCI Venture Capital Fund).

Vostro Account A *vostro* (a Latin word for 'yours') account is an account that a domestic bank (in case of India it may be SBI) holds for a foreign bank (which may be Rosbank in case of Russia) in the domestic bank's currency (that is Rupee). Such accounts enable domestic banks to provide international banking services to their clients who have global banking needs.

Walras' Law As per this law, 'the total value of goods demanded in an economy is always identically equal to the total value of goods supplied'. For this to happen, the economy should be in equilibrium. It also means that if there is an excess supply of certain things in one market, there must be excess demand for it in another market. Here 'another market' does not mean the market of another economy - it is taken as apple's market, grape's market (as 'separate' markets). This could be only correct in a barter economy (it does not work in an economy with currency as its mode of exchange). The idea was part of the 'general equilibrium theory' developed by the French mathematical *economist Marie-Esprit-Leon Walras* (1834-1910), after whom it is named.

Wasting Asset The natural resource which has a finite but indeterminate life span depending upon the rate of depletion (such as coal, oil, etc.).

Weightless Economy The situation of an economy when the output is increasingly produced from intellectual capital rather than physical materials - a shift in production from iron and steel, heavy machines, etc. to microprocessors, fibre optics and transistors, etc. This is the weightless economy, i.e., the *new economy* which arrived in the US (specially) by the end of the 20th century.

Welfare Economics The branch of economics which is concerned with the way economic activity ought to be organised so as to maximise economic welfare. The idea applies to the welfare of individuals as well as countries.

This is normative economics, i.e., it is based on value judgements. It is also called '*economics with a heart*'. This focuses on questions about *equity* as well as *efficiency*.

It employs value judgements about what *ought* to be produced, how production *should* be organised, the way income and wealth *ought* to be distributed, both in present times and in future. As different individuals in different communities have unique set of value judgements (guided by their attitudes, religion, philosophy, and politics), it has been difficult for the economists to reach a consensual idea upon which they could advise the governments in policy making, known as the *welfare criteria*. Economists and philosophers have been suggesting their brands of the *welfare criteria* since long-Vilfredo Pareto, Nicholas Kaldor, John Hicks, Scitovsky, Amartya Sen, as the few famous ones.

Wildcat Strike A strike called on by a group of employees without the support of their organised trade union.

Williamson Trade-off Model A model for evaluating the possible benefits and detriments of a proposed merger that could be used in the application of a discretionary competition policy. The model was developed by Oliver Williamson.

Winner's Curse The possibility that the winning bidder in an auction will pay too much for an asset since the highest bidder places a higher value on the asset than all other bidders.

Withholding Tax A tax imposed on the income on a foreign portfolio (investments). This tax is imposed to discourage foreign investments, to encourage domestic investment, and to raise money for the government.

Worker (Census Definition) The *first* definition of 'worker' by *Census* was given in 1872. Over time, the terms 'work' and 'worker' as defined by *Census of India* have undergone several amendments to suit the changing dimensions of work. 'Work' is defined as participation in any *economically productive activity* with or without compensation, wages or profit. Such participation may be physical and/or mental in nature. Work involves not only actual work but also includes:

1. Effective supervision and direction of work;
2. Part time help or unpaid work on farm, family enterprise or in any other economic activity; and
3. Cultivation or milk production even solely for domestic consumption.

Accordingly, as per Census of India, all persons engaged in 'work' defined as participation in any economically productive activity with or without compensation, wages or profit are workers. The reference period for determining a person as worker and non-worker is one year preceding the date of enumeration.

The Census *classifies* 'Workers' into two groups, namely, *Main Workers* (those workers who had worked for the major part of the reference period, i.e., 6 months or more) and *Marginal Workers* (those workers who had not worked for the major part of the reference period i.e., less than 6 months). The *Main* workers are classified based on Industrial category of workers into the following four categories: (i) Cultivators; (ii) Agricultural Labourers; (iii) Household Industry Workers; and (iv) Other Workers.

[See the entry *'Non-Worker'* too.]

Worker (NSO Definition) The NSO (National Statistics Office) data classifies the *workers* based on employment status into three categories - self-employed workers; regular wage/salaried employees; and casual labourers.

1. *Self-employed category* includes those who work for themselves and do not sell their labour power to anyone else in return for wage. This category of workers includes all those workers who operated their enterprises or are engaged in a profession or trade, either on own account, individually or with partners, or as home-based workers.
2. *Regular wage/salaried* employees are those who receive predetermined wages/salary on a regular basis. Such workers are better in qualitative terms than the rest as they receive pre-determined wages/salary with or without other benefits like social/job security.
3. *Casual worker* includes those who are hired for very short time period on daily or monthly basis.

The *own account workers* include those workers who operated their enterprises on their own account or with one or a few partners and ran their enterprise without hiring any labour during the reference period while *own account employers* are those own account workers who ran their enterprise by hiring labourers. However, *unpaid family labourers/helpers* included those who were engaged in their household enterprises, working full or part time and did not receive any regular salary or wages in return for the work performed during the reference period.

Worker Population Ratio The employment-to-population ratio is defined as the proportion of an economy's working-age population that is employed. As an indicator, the employment-to- population ratio provides information on the ability of an economy to create jobs. Worker population ratio (WPR) is defined as the number of persons employed per thousand persons [WPR = No. of employed persons × 1000/Total population]. Worker Population Ratio is an indicator used for analysing the employment situation in the country. This is also useful in knowing the proportion of population that is actively contributing to the production of goods and services in the economy.

Workfare Government programmes which make the receipt of unemployment-related benefits (as unemployment allowance) conditional upon participation in some local work scheme.

X-inefficiency A graphic representation of the 'gap' a firm shows in its actual and minimum costs of supplying its products. As per the traditional theory of supply, firms always operate on minimum attainable costs. As opposed to this, x-inefficiency suggests that firms typically operate at higher costs than their minimum attainable costs. This takes place due to many *inefficiencies* (such as organising the works, lack of co-ordination, lack of motivation, bureaucratic rigidities, etc.). Large corporates usually face this problem as they lack effective competition which could 'keep them on their toes'.

Yield Gap A method of comparing the performance of bonds and shares in an economy. It is defined as the average returns on shares minus the average returns on bonds.

Zero-coupon Bond A bond bearing zero coupon rate (i.e., no interest) sold at a price lower than its face value. Investors book profit when they sell it (at its face value). Such bonds are popularly used by the governments to raise long-term funds. In a situation of rate cut by the RBI, zero-coupon bonds gain value - it means, they sell at higher prices. When there is an increase in the rate, the opposite happens.

Zero-sum Game A situation in the *game theory* when the gains made by winners in an economic transaction are equal to the losses suffered by the losers. This is considered a special case in game theory. Most economic transactions are in some sense *positive-sum games*. But in popular discussion of economic issues, there are often examples of mistaken zero-sum mentality, such as profit comes at the expense of wages, 'higher productivity means fewer jobs', and 'imports mean fewer jobs here.'

Zero Tilling A relatively new farm production process, is a one-time operation in which a small drill places the seed and the fertiliser in a small furrow, saving the farmer a lot of time and other resources. At first utilised in Haryana in 1999-2000, by now it has spread to the other wheat growing states. The technique gives higher yield (by over 5 per cent) than the conventional wheat farming.

